Handbook of Research on Public Finance in Europe and the MENA Region

M. Mustafa Erdoğdu
Marmara University, Turkey

Bryan Christiansen
PryMarke, LLC, USA

A volume in the Advances in Public Policy and Administration (APPA) Book Series

BUSINESS SCIENCE Reference
An Imprint of IGI Global

Published in the United States of America by
Business Science Reference (an imprint of IGI Global)
701 E. Chocolate Avenue
Hershey PA, USA 17033
Tel: 717-533-8845
Fax: 717-533-8661
E-mail: cust@igi-global.com
Web site: http://www.igi-global.com

Library of Congress Cataloging-in-Publication Data

Names: Erdogdu, M. Mustafa, 1962- editor. | Christiansen, Bryan, 1960- editor.
Title: Handbook of research on public finance in Europe and the MENA region / M. Mustafa Erdogdu and Bryan Christiansen, editors.
Description: Hershey, PA : Business Science Reference, [2016] | Includes bibliographical references and index.
Identifiers: LCCN 2015051226| ISBN 9781522500537 (hardcover) | ISBN 9781522500544 (ebook)
Subjects: LCSH: Finance, Public--Europe. | Finance, Public--Middle East. | Finance, Public--Africa, North. | Fiscal policy--Europe. | Fiscal policy--Middle East. | Fiscal policy--Africa, North.
Classification: LCC HJ1000 .H359 2016 | DDC 336.4--dc23 LC record available at http://lccn.loc.gov/2015051226

This book is published in the IGI Global book series Advances in Public Policy and Administration (APPA) (ISSN: Pending; eISSN: Pending)

British Cataloguing in Publication Data
A Cataloguing in Publication record for this book is available from the British Library.

Advances in Public Policy and Administration (APPA) Book Series

ISSN: Pending
EISSN: Pending

MISSION

Proper management of the public sphere is necessary in order to maintain order in modern society. Research developments in the field of public policy and administration can assist in uncovering the latest tools, practices, and methodologies for governing societies around the world.

The **Advances in Public Policy and Administration (APPA) Book Series** aims to publish scholarly publications focused on topics pertaining to the governance of the public domain. APPA's focus on timely topics relating to government, public funding, politics, public safety, policy, and law enforcement is particularly relevant to academicians, government officials, and upper-level students seeking the most up-to-date research in their field.

COVERAGE

- Government
- Law enforcement
- Political Economy
- Politics
- Public Administration
- Public Funding
- Public Policy
- Resource allocation
- Urban Planning

IGI Global is currently accepting manuscripts for publication within this series. To submit a proposal for a volume in this series, please contact our Acquisition Editors at Acquisitions@igi-global.com or visit: http://www.igi-global.com/publish/.

The Advances in Public Policy and Administration (APPA) Book Series (ISSN Pending) is published by IGI Global, 701 E. Chocolate Avenue, Hershey, PA 17033-1240, USA, www.igi-global.com. This series is composed of titles available for purchase individually; each title is edited to be contextually exclusive from any other title within the series. For pricing and ordering information please visit http://www.igi-global.com/book-series/advances-public-policy-administration/97862. Postmaster: Send all address changes to above address.

Titles in this Series

For a list of additional titles in this series, please visit: www.igi-global.com

(R)evolutionizing Political Communication through Social Media
Tomaž Deželan (University of Ljubljana, Slovenia) and Igor Vobič (University of Ljubljana, Slovenia)
Information Science Reference • copyright 2016 • 333pp • H/C (ISBN: 9781466698796) • US $170.00 (our price)

Social, Economic, and Political Perspectives on Public Health Policy-Making
Rahmatollah Gholipour (University of Tehran, Iran) and Khadijeh Rouzbehani (University of Tehran, Iran)
Medical Information Science Reference • copyright 2016 • 329pp • H/C (ISBN: 9781466699441) • US $195.00 (our price)

Ethical Issues and Citizen Rights in the Era of Digital Government Surveillance
Robert A. Cropf (Saint Louis University, USA) and Timothy C. Bagwell (American Public University System, USA)
Information Science Reference • copyright 2016 • 303pp • H/C (ISBN: 9781466699052) • US $180.00 (our price)

Handbook of Research on Transitional Justice and Peace Building in Turbulent Regions
Fredy Cante (Universidad del Rosario, Colombia) and Hartmut Quehl (Felsberg Institute, Germany)
Information Science Reference • copyright 2016 • 559pp • H/C (ISBN: 9781466696754) • US $295.00 (our price)

Managing Big Data Integration in the Public Sector
Anil Aggarwal (University of Baltimore, USA)
Information Science Reference • copyright 2016 • 337pp • H/C (ISBN: 9781466696495) • US $205.00 (our price)

Management and Participation in the Public Sphere
Mika Markus Merviö (Kibi International University, Japan)
Information Science Reference • copyright 2015 • 399pp • H/C (ISBN: 9781466685536) • US $200.00 (our price)

Teaching Research Methods in Public Administration
Richard W. Schwester (City University of New York, USA)
Information Science Reference • copyright 2015 • 313pp • H/C (ISBN: 9781466681163) • US $185.00 (our price)

Emergency Management and Disaster Response Utilizing Public-Private Partnerships
Marvine Paula Hamner (LeaTech, LLC, USA) S. Shane Stovall (True North Emergency Management, USA) Doaa M. Taha (GMI, Ltd, USA) and Salah C. Brahimi (GMI, Ltd, USA)
Information Science Reference • copyright 2015 • 345pp • H/C (ISBN: 9781466681590) • US $200.00 (our price)

IGI GLOBAL
DISSEMINATOR OF KNOWLEDGE
www.igi-global.com

701 E. Chocolate Ave., Hershey, PA 17033
Order online at www.igi-global.com or call 717-533-8845 x100
To place a standing order for titles released in this series, contact: cust@igi-global.com
Mon-Fri 8:00 am - 5:00 pm (est) or fax 24 hours a day 717-533-8661

This handbook is dedicated to Zehra Naciye Erdoğdu, who is a plane tree that loved and nurtured one of the editors of this handbook and provided a shadow to rest under.

Editorial Advisory Board

Laura N. Harr, *Manchester University, UK*
Ebru Çağlayan Akay, *Marmara University, Turkey*
Jose J. Sempere-Monerris, *University of Valencia, Spain*
Federico Pablo-Martí, *University of Alcalá, Spain*
Fatma Nur Karaman Kabadurmuş, *Yaşar University, Turkey*
Özkan Zülfüoğlu, *Marmara University, Turkey*
Betül Gür, *İstanbul Commerce University, Turkey*
Güneş Yılmaz, *Trakya University, Turkey*
Sevda Mutlu Akar, *Balıkesir University, Turkey*
Nursel Aydıner Avşar, *Gediz University, Turkey*
Kemal Cebeci, *Marmara University, Turkey*
İ. Begüm Kösemen, *Marmara University, Turkey*
Yaşar Serhat Yaşgül, *Marmara University, Turkey*
Cengiz Bahçekapılı, *Marmara University, Turkey*
Mehmet Şişman, *Marmara University, Turkey*
H. Gülçin Beken, *Gümüşhane University, Turkey*
Coşkun Karaca, *Cumhuriyet University, Turkey*

List of Contributors

Table of Contents

Detailed Table of Contents

This chapter presents a historical and theoretical overview of the public finance in general and for developing countries in particular. The chapter highlights that modern governments need revenue and often a lot more revenue than they needed in the past, to provide the levels of assistance and public services that modern societies expect governments to provide. However, because of the various potential problems before raising the countries' tax levels with tax reforms, it is important that there must be a clear understanding of how that fiscal space will be used and how the additional tax burden will be distributed. It is emphasized that the necessary public institutions capable of enforcing the adopted policies competently and efficiently must exist. Otherwise, poor choices are likely to be made and the public investments undertaken tend to be not as productive as they had been expected.

Taxes and tax administration are important. Taxation is one of the main interfaces between state and society: how a tax system is administered may affect not only its yield, its incidence, and its efficiency but also the state itself. Taxation that is widely perceived to be unfair and administered capriciously and corruptly may not only bring the tax system into disrepute but weaken trust in government and even the legitimacy of the state. This paper discusses two important aspects of taxation – its 'transparency' and the increasingly important role of information technology (IT) in tax administration, as well as how these two topics relate to the broader issues just mentioned.

This chapter sets out the issues that should be considered in developing successful tax reform. Economic theory makes an essential contribution to the development of tax reform, incorporating issues of both economic efficiency and equity. However, other theoretical considerations demonstrate that successful tax design may be considerably more difficult than seems to be widely thought. In addition, there are matters of tax administration and compliance that have to be taken into account. The changing socio-economic environment within which tax systems have to operate as well, as the political process of tax reform, are also important. Finally, the chapter shows how to develop a systematic approach which can incorporate the many important issues that should be included in developing successful tax reform.

This chapter focuses on the concept and empirical estimation of tax effort around the world. It employs a cross-country study from a sample of 121, developing and developed countries during 1994-2012. Predicted tax revenue of a country is estimated empirically taking into account its specific economic, demographic, and institutional features and is considered as an approximation of its taxable capacity. Tax effort is then defined as the ratio between the share of the actual tax collection and the predicted tax revenue. The use of tax effort and actual tax revenue collection allows us to rank countries into four different groups. The results vary per country and region but, overall, tax revenue collection appears to be in line with its predicted value. This could reflect many efforts undertaken in the last decades to improve tax policy and tax administration. It also suggests that further improvements in domestic revenue mobilization may require other non-tax reforms aimed at removing economic, demographic and institutional constraints hindering tax revenue performance.

This chapter analyzes fiscal adjustments following economic shocks in the West African Monetary Union (WAEMU) countries. Using an unbalanced panel data, we examine empirically 81 developing countries including eight WAEMU countries over the 1980-2012 period. The paper compares the cyclicality of fiscal policy in WAEMU to other developing countries. While it focuses on the response of public investment to changes in GDP, we also examine responses of current public expenditure and fiscal balance. The paper finds that there is strong procyclicality in fiscal policy in WAEMU countries. Procyclicality is strongest in public investment and WAEMU countries are more procyclical in their fiscal policy compared to a group of countries that include European and Middle East and North African (MENA) countries.

Using ordinary least squares (OLS) with panel corrected standard errors for OECD panel data this chapter, in contrast to Compensation hypothesis, finds a negative relationship between openness and the rate of public sector growth. In addition, this inverse relationship is found to be the strongest when electoral systems are more competitive. The empirical results presented here also suggests that openness constrains government growth more when the governments are run by either left-leaning parties or by left-leaning coalitions. This result holds for most measures of government spending and is robust to the inclusion of a wide range of controls. Unlike the existing empirical literature, which focuses on the 'compensation effect' of openness on government growth, this study supports the 'competition effect' of openness drawn from the literature on local public finance.

The main objective of the chapter is to study the interaction between the level and composition of government expenditure and governance performance in Europe and in MENA countries. The perceived level of corruption provides a possible measure of governance performance. The idea is that more corruption entails greater than optimally volumes of public expenditure and an inefficient allocation of this. The study involves a descriptive and a simple econometric analysis. Results are enlightening and point out that total government expenditure appears to be positively correlated to poorer governance performance, and hence to more corruption, only when the volumes of public expenditure is already high.

The chapter examines tax structure and its relation to good governance and economic development in the MENA countries. First, it discusses how different tax systems and tax structures in the region compared with other countries. MENA region can be characterized with low level of tax-to-GDP ratio compared to other groups of countries. However, tax systems considerably diverge within the region. Most importantly, whether having hydrocarbon revenues meaningfully divides the region's countries with respect to tax composition, tax levels, tax ratios and tax regimes. Literature suggests that natural resource revenue is also an important determinant of governance and institutional development that have impact on economic development, while good governance, a more legitimate and responsive state is an essential factor for a more adequate level of tax effort. Therefore, the second section of the study examines the relationships between taxation and good governance with emphasis on the MENA region.

International tax competition has been significantly increased since 1980s as a result of liberalized financial and fiscal policies, while this leads sovereign nations faced budgetary deficit problems and public finance related considerations. This paper aims to analyze how Turkish tax system is affected by international tax competition, services submitted by tax havens and facilities used by multinationals. In 2006, a new Corporate Income Tax Law was introduced in Turkey. One of its purposes is to combat against harmful tax competition and therefore it covered defensive measures such as controlled foreign company (CFC), thin capitalization rule and transfer pricing regulation, to prevent companies from leaving their income abroad. This study aims to analyze effects of international tax competition in Turkey whether there are change in tax rates, tax structure, and tax revenue; and how the government respond it, as a beneficiary; or, a loser.

The objective of this chapter is to analyze empirically the potential dynamics of the relationship among the size of the shadow economy, fiscal burden and the official economy. The empirical analysis is based on the size estimates of the shadow economy in 17 developed and 11 transition economies of Europe for the period 1999-2013 and in 16 economies of Middle East and North Africa for the period 1999-2007. Direction of causal relations among shadow and official economies and the fiscal burden is investigated by exploiting the panel vector auto-regression approach and the associated impulse response analysis, which directly account for the potential endogeneity of the variables of interest. Findings mostly confirm the view that shadow and official economies are substitutes, and the dynamic effects of fiscal burden on the shadow economy are not as strong and clear as expected in the regions in question.

The aim of this chapter is to investigate shadow economy on an EU-27 and Turkey basis. For this purpose, firstly the definition, causes\ and consequences of shadow economy together with its relationship with tax evasion are discussed. In addition, the causes of shadow economy are examined for EU-27 during the period 2003-2012. It was done both statistically and empirically by employing scatter plot diagrams and the random effects model. While empirical findings confirm the effects of taxes, income level, trade and population on the shadow economy, statistical findings mention the effects of governance related indicators. Another main finding of this chapter is about Turkey. Accordingly, shadow economy in Turkey is observed to be higher than in the EU-27 and taking into consideration the comparative statistical findings about the causes of shadow economy, the main reasons of shadow economy in Turkey are thought to be governance related.

The volatility of the global economic market and the fierce competition in attracting foreign investments have determined European and MENA authorities to reconsider interactions with taxpayers. Thus, benefitting from international assistance, authorities have started implementing tax strategies and models like co-operative compliance, horizontal monitoring, whistleblowing. This empirical investigation is grounded on the "slippery slope" framework that attempts to solve the "riddle of tax compliance" via trust in and

this issue in Egypt. This chapter is focused on a review of the recent history of Egypt's public finances and a unique experiment that aims to better understand the potential for political institutions to affect tax compliance at a time when those institutions are under development.

Tunisia's tax system has undergone significant structural reforms over the last several decades. Even so, its structure exhibits some major flaws, shortcomings that spill over to and affect the performance of the overall Tunisian economy. Further, the tax system continues to underperform in some fundamental ways, ways that also affect the rest of the economy. Finally, the structure of the Tunisian tax system has some notable shortcomings. This paper discusses these issues. It presents details of the main taxes, it analyzes several main features of this tax system, and it suggests various specific tax reforms that can be introduced both in the short term and in the longer term.

The focus of this chapter is on the incidence of taxes in Jordan. All taxes must ultimately be paid by someone, and one of the most fundamental questions asked by economists is: "Who bears the final burden of a tax?" Taxes cause individuals and firms to change their behaviors, and the resulting changes in product and factor prices will affect the incidence and the distributional effects, of the tax. The answer to the question "Who bears the burden of the tax" requires us to estimate whether or not taxes are regressive; that is, do taxes as a share of income decrease or increase as income increases? This type of analysis is important for a country like Jordan, which is seeking to increase public revenue and encourage economic development. The analysis is also useful as a model for other countries in this important region.

This chapter first discusses the Turkish tax policy performance for the period of 2004-2013 in terms of equitable distribution of tax burdens. Then, it examines tax expenditures, which are believed to be one of the main sources of inequity in tax burden distribution, in terms of equity and fiscal transparency grounds. The chapter also estimates tax expenditure figures based on very limited data in Turkey. One of the main findings of the chapter is that because fiscal transparency and non-discrimination principles of taxation are violated in Turkey, there are considerable amount of hidden tax reliefs that are not counted as tax expenditures in the Turkish tax system.

Public utilities have been at the very centre of economic and social development of countries. Until the last decades, they were almost exclusively undertaken by public authorities. From the 1980s, they have been subject to liberalisation in many countries. Liberalisation of electricity means that the segments which are vertically integrated are unbundled and opened to private sector through privatisations. However, since the transmission and distribution segments are networks that exhibit severe natural monopoly characteristics, they should be either owned and operated by public bodies or regulated by independent regulatory authorities to protect consumer interest. In Turkey, the liberalisation process for the public utilities has begun in 1990s, but posed many problems at administrative and juridical stages. Lately, the legislative framework which is designed to be compatible with global standards has been completed. But at economic stage, we can easily observe the power of big companies and holdings outweigh the power of public authorities and counteract the public interest.

Chapter 20
Monetary and Fiscal Policy Interactions: An Empirical Evidence from Turkey 447
Asuman Oktayer, Yıldız Technical University, Turkey
Nagihan Oktayer, İstanbul University, Turkey

While the role of fiscal policy in price level determination was neglected by the conventional theory, a new point of view was adapted by the Fiscal Theory of the Price Level. In the context of the new theory, monetary and fiscal policy interactions were taken into account and the role of fiscal policy was underlined. This paper investigates the monetary and fiscal policy coordination in Turkey during the period 1989.1-2012.2 and sub-periods 1989.1-2001.1 and 2001.2-2012.2. In order to reveal if financial policies are monetary dominant or fiscal dominant in aforementioned periods, bounds testing procedure is applied by using quarterly data. While the empirical test results related to the entire period of 1989.1-2012.2 and sub-period of 1989.1-2001.1 indicate fiscal policy dominant regime, the findings regarding 2001.2-2012.2 imply monetary policy dominant regime in Turkey.

Chapter 21
Impacts of Global Financial Crisis and Changes in Monetary Policy of Central Banks: An Analysis of Central Bank of the Republic of Turkey (CBRT) and Bank of Israel (BOI) 474
İsmail Şiriner, Batman University, Turkey
Keremet Shaiymbetova, Kocaeli University, Turkey

The Great Financial Crisis (GFC) has hit developed and developing countries through a number of transmission channel. Some impacts are already disappearing while others are still to strike. In MENA region developing countries to experience the crisis were those with the most globally integrated financial sectors. Next came the impact on trade, as volumes and prices of commodities and manufactures collapsed across the globe. Successful economic policies pursued in the past do not promise these countries' immunity from the crisis. In fact, some MENA countries have already shown a limited capacity to learn from other countries' previous financial crises. Post-crisis spillovers and heightened capital flows have triggered a search for alternative monetary policy frameworks, especially for Turkey and Israel in MENA economies. This paper analyzes the review of the region's monetary regimes and policies, including: monetary policy expansion of the monetary policy framework in promoting financial stability alongside the primary price stability objective.

There have been important developments in the decentralization of the government structure in Turkey since the early 1980s. This paper examines the link between fiscal decentralization and local borrowing within Turkish provinces. It first discusses local government reforms throughout the history of the Turkish Republic with the focus on recent reform efforts and current local government structure. It then provides an empirical analysis of the effects of decentralization in Turkish provinces using cross-sectional and panel data approaches, and spatial econometrics. The dataset consists of 67 provinces from 1980 to 2000, and separately cross-sectional data on all 81 provinces for the year 2000. Using decentralization measures such as number of local governments per capita and ratio of own-source municipal revenue to total provincial tax revenue, and specific characteristics of the municipalities the analysis examines whether variations in local decentralization across these provinces and across time have had a significant impact municipal borrowing in those provinces.

This chapter uses the work-leisure choice model to compute equilibrium weekly hours worked for a number of Arab countries and compare them to the G7 countries. It shows that the labor supply curve is elastic in all Arab countries, and provide a new measure of labor productivity. This finding confirms previous research that workers respond to incentives, which has serious implications for tax and social security policies. The chapter also provides some policy simulations pertinent to the effects of taxation on welfare and poverty.

Foreword

In academia today, economists as a tribe care mostly about publishing journal articles, preferably in top journals based on international ranking lists that are worshipped religiously, with an academic death sentence for those who do not publish accordingly. This is an unhealthy development. It promotes the feeling that we no longer devote ourselves to science for the sake of science itself. In fact, we risk turning science into a kind of sport where one displays success or muscular prowess. Brain pulp is sacrificed and offered to these journals in order to secure profitable returns such as promotions, recognition, or awards. The problem is that journal articles only produce spare parts, and we need scholars to build machines with or without these spare parts, as we have always been a tool-making species. A good Handbook should aim to construct a machine such as a new motorcycle that is ready for us to ride so that we are well equipped for our odyssey into the future. I admire scholars like Mustafa Erdoğdu who take the time to organize such a Handbook, as well as those who contribute to it by writing chapters – in this case, 23 in total. To embark on a synthesis of facts and theories is a venture worth undertaking. The edifice of knowledge would have never grown to its present dimensions without such contributions. Obviously, a Handbook will also face the dilemma of incomplete knowledge in the present moment. This is okay as long as we openly acknowledge or introduce expressions of incertitude and provide an honest portrayal of partial knowledge. Nevertheless, a masterpiece of a Handbook can guide us in how we feel, think, and perceive, and can also work to prepare us for the future. Single contributions may be seen as performing disorderly motions, similar to atoms. However, we know that in the co-operation of a large number of atoms, statistical laws of orderly behaviour start operating and the same happens to a good Handbook. The quality of contributions may vary, as does a droplet that sinks depicting a Brownian movement. A Handbook is a large affair, similar to a production in which the orchestra and actors may have a different idea of speed, expression, and volume. But each Handbook has its particular average gravity in which all the pieces dance around an equilibrium pole directed by the editor in charge who, like a conductor, controls these different forces – aiming to create beauty and perfect harmony.

I see several familiar faces in this Handbook; scholars who have had a deep impact on my research and education. I was not only awed by their achievements but also motivated and mentally stimulated to contribute. I see dear friends and coauthors and others that I am eager to get to know or to read. I see scholars that have the gift of bringing magically alive the very topics that many others perceive as too boring to contemplate. But even those lost souls not able to be converted to the beauty of public finance will willingly admit that this topic lies at the heart of a civilized society. We still need to learn a lot and it is wonderful to see that the exploration of the MENA region has such a dominant role in this Handbook. An understanding of public finance requires an emphasis on the links between economic analysis and political issues, and several of the experts in this Handbook have carried out important work for national and international organizations. Whispering in the ears of princes is a challenging endeavour: it requires an innovative scholar on the frontline, ready to get dirty and to face the mine-fields. These scholars are well aware that knowledge must continually be renewed by ceaseless effort if it is not to be lost. With their knowledge they help to maintain and extend statues of sand that stand close to the shoreline, continuously threatened not only by the shifting sand but also by the ongoing rising tides that resemble political life cycles. Their brave hands of service must ever be at work in order that the statues continue to shine in the sun for us.

Enough, it is a foolish thing to make a long foreword. Let's read what these 23 contributions have to say!

Benno Torgler
Queensland University of Technology, Australia, & CREMA – Center for Research in Economics, Management and the Arts, Switzerland

Preface

The World economy has undergone considerable change since the late 1970s and economic integration has dramatically increased, generating interdependence of economic activities. The events of the last several decades that later came to be known as globalization have challenged the contemporary neo-classical synthesis in all branches of economics, especially in public finance. As capital has become much more mobile than labor and can flow to where taxes are the lowest, increased economic integration and the mobility of capital have made international considerations a central component of tax policy making around the world. National tax policy makers are increasingly involved in a game with one another that called as "international tax competition" in which sovereign countries aim to attract both portfolio and direct investment by lowering their tax rates on income earned by foreigners. Tax competition, tax evasion, and tax havens have become part of our lives.

Genschel *et al.* (2015) highlight that international tax competition "triggers a race-to-the-bottom, in which states undercut each other leading to no or at best, lower capital taxes than ever before. According to the baseline model, capital tax competition has one of two potential welfare effects. Either it decreases government revenue, which could be used for redistribution to the poor, or the tax burden is shifted to less mobile bases such as labor income. In any case, the overall welfare effect on income inequality is negative." Countries have responded international tax competition in two ways: "first, by shifting the tax burden from (mobile) capital to (less mobile) labor, and second, when increased taxation of labor has become politically and economically problematic, by reducing the social safety net" (Avi-Yonah, 2000, p. 1575). As Vito Tanzi explains in the introductory chapter, "[b]ecause of the growing globalization of economic activities and the increasing facility with which financial capital was able to move across countries … and to the pressures exercised by investors and their lobbyists, the laws were changed and income received by individuals from capital sources started to get preferential treatment. This made it possible for some individuals to receive very large incomes while paying very low taxes on them." The end result was that globalization has contributed to the growing unevenness of the income distribution now observed in many countries, both developed and developing.

Tax competition and taxation have broader implications for the fiscal responses of countries to globalization and their redistribution efforts. Given that tax competition affects countries differently[1], governments will choose diverse strategies to cope with these international pressures. Competition will more negatively affect income inequality in countries that predominantly redistribute via the tax system than in those that historically set up a welfare state by redistributing via social transfers (Troeger, 2013). Competition among countries has contributed to greater need for redistributive programs, but at the same time has reduced the scope for redistributive programs (Stiglitz, 2007).

Over the past decade, the world economy has seen overall economic growth weaken due to the worldwide financial crisis and associated reduction in economic activity. The global financial and Eurozone crises have awakened the world to the importance of the linkages between public financial and macrofiscal management. Improving our understanding that public financial management is crucial following the introduction of large stimulus packages to promote economic growth after the 2008-2009 financial and economic crises has become very important. Given that budget deficits have been increasing, many governments have been searching for possible ways of increasing tax revenues to finance public expenditures and narrow the budget deficit while minimizing distortions to economic activity. The challenge is to be prepared for the next generation of public financial management reforms. Effective tax systems are as essential for developing countries as they are for developed ones.

Taxation is imperative first and foremost because it determines the development status of countries by financing the system of public goods. Moreover, as Bayraktar, Moreno-Dodson, and Le put forward clearly in Chapter 8, "[t]axation is considered to be the least distortive way to finance public expenditures, when compared to money printing and borrowing, and, overtime, can be conducive to lower aid dependency and state building. However, many countries, developed and developing, experience a gap between their actual and potential levels of tax revenues, based on their economic, demographic and institutional architecture. Taxation reforms, both policy and administration, can contribute to close this gap, and must be designed and implemented according to the reality and feasibility in every country." Taxation ultimately is a function of politics, institutions, economics and technologies. The design of tax policy reforms must be constructed after comprehensive analysis of the country's taxable capacity, revenue performance, efficiency and equity considerations, as well as the political economy of tax reforms.

As an authoritative reference source, this publication assembled some of topmost scholars and experts with some of them a background in the World Bank and the International Monetary Fund (IMF) who can write clearly and accessibly. These authors cover a wide variety of public finance topics with great clarity and precision, illustrating them with a wealth of carefully-chosen examples and problems. Most of the chapter authors consider public finance from a comparative perspective and combine discussion of theory, empirical work, and policy objectives in compact form. The chapters are generally very balanced overview of market failures and government failures and thereby gain mature insight into desirable interactions between the market and the state.

The purpose of the volume is to provide an accessible introduction to the use of public finance and public policy to improve on market outcomes. It gives a balanced and insightful analysis of the scope and limits of what government can and should do. The chapters provide a rich, thought-provoking, and comprehensive overview of academic thinking about the role of government in the economy, emphasizing the role of political economy of institutional change in shaping how governments behave, and the resulting trade-offs between private and public provision. Some of the chapters would thus be of interest to researchers working in the relatively new area of institutional change and governance. There is an emphasis on the importance of the institutional context, drawing on examples from European, Middle Eastern and North African (MENA) countries. The authors use rigorous but accessible formalism. The mathematics has been kept to a minimum without sacrificing intellectual rigor. While the information presented is cutting edge, the approach makes the chapters accessible to not only academics but also government officials, development agencies, practitioners, and undergraduates whose only prior exposure to economics is at the introductory level.

This handbook is unique not only in its broad scope but also in its balance between theory and practice. It brings alive theory with relevant empirical evidence combining history and theoretical approaches with cutting-edge issues and debates. Authors write from the ground up to reflect current realities of public finance, enhancing the survey of traditional topics with an emphasis on empirical work. Some of the chapters offer useful insights into how policy makers should design taxes. Some others produce significant cross-fertilization and yield solutions to previously intractable problems. The volume covers topics such as different tax systems, fiscal transparency, shadow economy, attitudes toward tax evasion, tax compliance, international tax competition, tax reforms, public spending, tax expenditures, political economy aspects of budgeting, governance performance, privatization, distributional effects of fiscal policies, fiscal decentralization and local borrowing, the management of fiscal risks, monetary and fiscal policy interactions, effects of taxes and natural resource endowment on the supply of labor. The book provides numerous examples and case studies describing good practice in public financial management, and is highly relevant for use in both advanced and developing countries.

The introductory chapter *Public Finance in Developing Countries* is written by Vito Tanzi[2], who is the honorary president of the International Institute of Public Finance. His chapter presents a historical and theoretical overview of the public finance in general and for developing countries in particular. Tanzi indicates that modern governments need revenue and often a lot more revenue than they needed in the past, to provide the levels of assistance and public services that modern societies expect governments to provide. He warns, however, that because of the various potential problems before raising the countries' tax levels with tax reforms, it is important that there must be a clear understanding of how that fiscal space will be used and how the additional tax burden will be distributed. He adds that the necessary public institutions capable of enforcing the adopted policies competently and efficiently must exist. Otherwise, poor choices are likely to be made and the public investments undertaken tend to be not as productive as they had been expected.

In Chapter 2, Richard Bird focuses on core issues of taxes and taxation. His review offers a timely assessment of transparency and technology in taxation. Taxation that is widely perceived to be unfair and administered capriciously and corruptly may not only bring the tax system into disrepute but weaken trust in government and even the legitimacy of the state. This chapter first discusses some possible interpretations of 'transparency' in taxation and then briefly reviews the increasing role of IT in tax administration before concluding with some reflections about the interplay of transparency and technology in developing a 'smart' tax system. Bird emphasized that balancing the use of technology in taxation with the appropriate degree of public transparency about what is being done and why is an essential ingredient in the mix if how states collect and spend revenues is to be considered acceptably fair by a majority of the politically relevant population.

In Chapter 3, Simon James discusses the issues that should be considered in developing successful tax reforms. The purpose of the chapter is to examine the range of issues involved in the nature, context and process of tax reform. The author begins by introducing the context of European and MENA countries in general terms. Then, he examines economic criteria for assessing the merits of a particular tax or tax reform, primarily economic efficiency and equity and goes on to other theoretical contributions to the development of tax reform which are less frequently taken into account, namely optimal tax theory, the theory of the second best, and public choice theory. Later, the author raises significant issues regarding tax administration and compliance and examines the context of tax reform and the process of tax reform itself to establish a comprehensive and systematic approach to dealing with the entire range of relevant factors. James emphasizes that the tax system has to be designed to be sufficiently robust to accommodate continuing change in the socio-economic and political environment and to be sufficiently flexible to accommodate further adjustments as appropriate.

In Chapter 4, Nihal Bayraktar, Blanca Moreno-Dodson, and Tuan Minh Le focus on the concept and empirical estimation of tax effort around the world. The authors employ a cross-country study from a sample of 121 developing and developed countries during 1994-2012. Predicted tax revenue of a country is estimated empirically taking into account its specific economic, demographic, and institutional features and is considered as an approximation of its taxable capacity. Tax effort is then defined as the ratio between the share of the actual tax collection and the predicted tax revenue. The research indicates that taxable capacity and tax efforts present significant variations across countries, income groups and regions, as well as overtime. Overall, developing countries seem to have more limitations to expand the scope for tax revenues, which is heavily conditioned by their taxable capacity, in turn determined by lack of economic diversification, demographic challenges, and ineffective institutions. The analysis provides broad directions for tax policy reforms, especially in developing countries. The authors argue that further improvements in domestic revenue mobilization may require other non-tax reforms aimed at removing economic, demographic and institutional constraints hindering tax revenue performance.

In Chapter 5, Mehmet Serkan Tosun and Serdar Yılmaz analyze fiscal adjustments following economic shocks in the West African Monetary Union (WAEMU) countries. Using an unbalanced panel data, they examine empirically 81 developing countries including eight WAEMU countries during the period 1980-2012. They compare the cyclicality of fiscal policy in WAEMU to other countries including European and MENA countries. While they focus on the response of public investment to changes in Gross Domestic Product (GDP), they also examine responses of current public expenditure and fiscal balance. They find that there is strong procyclicality in fiscal policy in WAEMU countries. Procyclicality is strongest in public investment and WAEMU countries are more procyclical in their fiscal policy compared to a group of countries that include European and MENA countries. The findings of the chapter have important policy recommendations to offer to debt ridden European countries and MENA countries that are struggling to stimulate their stagnant economies.

The analysis in Chapter 6 offers an explanation to conflicting theories about the effects of openness on government growth. Using recent econometric techniques and panel data, Ali Rıza Özdemir demonstrates that there is a negative relationship between openness and the rate of public sector growth. The empirical results presented suggests that openness has a constraining effect on democratic governments that have a larger budget. It is also the case that openness constrains government growth more when the governments are run by either left-leaning parties or by left-leaning coalitions. This result holds for most measures of government spending and is robust to the inclusion of a wide range of controls. Unlike the existing empirical literature, which focuses on the 'compensation effect' of openness on government growth, this study supports the 'competition effect' of openness drawn from the literature on local public finance.

In Chapter 7, Lodovico Santoro and Salvatore Capasso examine public spending and governance performance from a comparative perspective. The study involves a descriptive and a simple econometric analysis. The main objective of the authors is to investigate if government expenditure are purposefully inflated and manipulated in order to increase rent-extraction and bribes. The analysis of the interplay between governance performance and corruption, on one side, and public expenditure, on the other focusing on European and MENA countries has delivered one interesting result: institutional and social factors such as the judicial system, the form of the government and the stability of the system all play an important role. This implies that corruption may be more or less detrimental, and correspondingly government may be more or less efficient, depending on the general economic and institutional context. Results are enlightening and point out that total government expenditure appears to be positively correlated to poorer governance performance, and hence to more corruption, only when the volumes of public expenditure is already high. A surprising finding of the chapter is that European countries rather than in MENA region are more associated with public expenditure and more inefficiency in the working of government.

In Chapter 8, Savaş Çevik examines tax structure and its relation to good governance and economic development in the MENA region. The author discusses first how different tax systems and tax structures in the region compared with other countries. He identifies that the problems in which the MENA countries suffer are substantially common to those of other developing countries such as the low level of income taxes, inefficiencies of tax administration, informal structure of economy and weak data to consider policy options. However, some of them are especially heavy in the region because of idiosyncratic features of the MENA countries. Second, the author deals with the role of taxation to build well-functioning institutions and qualified governance as well as a fiscal system that extract revenue to finance development and public services in the MENA region. He suggests that a legitimate tax system can help to establish a legitimate political interaction through the nation by establishing parties' effective participation in decision making process.

There is an undergoing debate about whether or not tax competition is detrimental to countries which export capital. In Chapter 9, Semih N. Öz considers this issue and analyzes how the Turkish tax system is affected by international tax competition, services submitted by tax havens[3] and facilities used by multinationals. The aim of the study is to discover whether there are change in tax rates, tax structure, and tax revenue; and how the government responds to it, as a beneficiary; or, a loser. The author first gives the general principles of international taxation that are related to residence and source principles. Then, he presents theories and an analytical framework for tax competition. Later, Öz evaluates the governments' response to international tax competition as a single country or as a part of international cooperation work and criticizes the OECD work on harmful tax competition. The author shows that Turkey has experienced a steady increase in tax revenue, while tax rates are declined. But, the distributional effect of this change it is not clear. Therefore, Öz suggests that additional work is needed to find out whether or not tax burden is shifted from high level income individuals to low level income individuals.

Knowledge about the size of the shadow economy is an important concern for fiscal policy makers in developing economies, particularly, in conducting effective revenue policies. The shadow economy is heavily related with tax evasion, and sometimes they are perceived as the same. In Chapter 10, Tarkan Çavuşoğlu and Debi Konukçu Önal analyze empirically the potential dynamics of the relationship among the size of the shadow economy, fiscal burden and the official economy. The empirical analysis is based on the size estimates of the shadow economy in 17 developed and 11 transition economies of Europe for the period 1999-2013, and in 16 MENA economies for the period 1999-2007. The direction of causal relations among shadow and official economies and the fiscal burden is investigated by exploiting the panel vector auto-regression approach and the associated impulse response analysis, which directly account for the potential endogeneity of the variables of interest. The findings mostly confirm the view that shadow and official economies are substitutes, and the dynamic effects of fiscal burden on the shadow economy are not as strong and clear as expected in the regions in question.

Chapter 11 by Hale Akbulut also investigates the shadow economy. But this time the aim is to investigate shadow economy on an EU-27 and Turkey basis. For this purpose, first the definition, causes and consequences of shadow economy together with its relationship with tax evasion are discussed. Second, the causes of shadow economy are examined for the EU-27 during the period 2003-2012. It was done both statistically and empirically by employing scatter plot diagrams and the random effects model. Both statistical and empirical findings confirm that there are a number of economic and governance related factors that cause shadow economy. Nevertheless, governance related indicators (such as: government effectiveness, accountability, rule of law and control of corruption) seem more effective statistically on the size of shadow economy as compared to economic indicators such as taxes and spending. Therefore, Akbulut suggests that governments have to improve particularly their governance indicators to achieve a decrease in shadow economy.

Delving into the primary topic of tax compliance from an economic-psychological perspective, Chapter 12 by Larissa Batrancea, Anca Nichita, Ioan Batrancea, and Erich Kirchler avail researchers, practitioners and laypersons the ability to grasp the importance of trust in authorities and power of authorities for raising compliance across Europe and the MENA region. Understanding the nature of tax compliance determinants is crucial to increase tax compliance and recent tax literature features new catalysts for compliance. The empirical investigation of this chapter is grounded on the "slippery slope framework" that attempts to solve the "riddle of tax compliance" via trust in and power of authorities. A two-step cluster analysis was run on the continuous proxies of trust in authorities and power of authorities, corresponding to 215 countries and territories worldwide, out of which 35 from Europe and 12 from the MENA region. The analyses yielded a four-cluster miscellanea of tax climates, i.e., trust high – power high (T+P+), trust low – power low (T-P-), trust high – power low (T+P-), trust low – power high (T-P+). As overall results, both European and MENA countries fall into three of the four clusters considered. While the majority of European countries are spread between two categories, almost all MENA countries register low levels of trust and power, these results suggesting the imperious need for stability and efficiency in every major area of these societies.

In Chapter 13, M. Mustafa Erdoğdu, Binhan E. Yılmaz, Murat Aydın, and İnci User engage with political economy of tax evasion and tax compliance issues focusing on deficiencies and problems within property taxation system in Turkey. First, the authors review political economy of taxation by elaborating social and political interactions between different groups in society. Then, they question if there are any political preferences, legal arrangements or cultural issues facilitating tax evasion and tax loss in Turkey. The authors identify the degenerating effects of frequent application of tax amnesties, having a lax tax reconciliation institution, and less than logical way tax information confidentiality principle is applied in Turkey. Later, they investigate peculiarities and specific difficulties of real estate sector in relation to taxation. Finally, to reduce tax loss in this sector they propose a comprehensive and original property tax reform based on a semi-public valuation system. The authors underlines that "*fighting with tax evasion and tax loss is not only important to raise revenues but probably more so to safeguard fairness*." They suggest that increased use of property taxes could not only help ease problems with taxes levied on mobile bases but also make the tax system fairer since the system becomes less distorting and less vulnerable to tax evasion.

In Chapter 14, Robert W. McGee and Serkan Benk summarize and analyze the latest World Values Survey data on attitudes toward tax evasion in Turkey. In addition to examining the overall viewpoints of the 1601-person sample, the authors examine ethical attitudes from the perspective of the following demographic variables: gender, age, marital status, education level, employment status, occupation, social class, income level, happiness, position on the political spectrum, sector of employment, and confidence in government. Comparisons with other studies are made to determine the similarities and differences between Turkish attitudes and the attitudes of people in other countries. According to findings, significant differences were related to employment status. Part-time workers, housewives and the self-employed were more opposed to tax evasion, whereas the retired and unemployed were least opposed. Those working in the private, nonprofit sector were somewhat more opposed (at the 10 percent level) to tax evasion, whereas those working for government were somewhat less opposed to tax evasion. The most important finding seems that "[t]he more confidence in government one had, the more opposed one was to tax evasion."

In Chapter 15, Sarah Mansour, Vjollca Sadiraj, and Sally Wallace focus on the future of public finances in Egypt, which is one of the most important countries in the Middle East. Like many countries, Egypt suffers from substantial tax non-compliance. It is well-known that tax compliance directly affects the ability to raise own source revenues and this ability is critical to the long term fiscal sustainability of a country. Non-compliance undermines the entire system of public finance in Egypt, yet there has been relatively little focus on addressing this issue in the country. According to authors, Egypt's public finances are in a state of transition as the country grapples with myriad state-building issues. The authors developed and implemented a unique public finance experiment in this chapter that aims to better understand the potential for political institutions to affect tax compliance when citizens and officials interact (in a lab setting) and citizens can recall officials. Their data suggest that recall elections give citizens' "voice" and they use it to express their distaste to government. They also find that when citizens see corruption (proxied in their experiment as an official choosing the greedy good), they reduce compliance.

In Chapter 16, James Alm explains Egypt's public finances which are in a state of transition as the country grapples with myriad state-building issues. The author indicates that Tunisia's tax system has undergone significant structural reforms over the last several decades. Even so, its structure exhibits some major flaws, shortcomings that spill over to and affect the performance of the overall Tunisian economy. Furthermore, the tax system continues to underperform in some fundamental ways that also affect the rest of the economy. There is also a widespread belief that the tax system is both unfair and distorting to individuals and firm, although precise quantitative assessments of these inequities and inefficiencies are seldom provided. Overall, it is clear that the current system is an outdated and an ad hoc system, designed for a world that no longer exists. James Alm first describes several main features of Tunisian tax system in some detail and then compares Tunisian tax practice to international practices and analyze some of the main effects of these taxes. Later, he presents some issues that need to be considered in any possible reform of the tax system and suggests various specific tax reforms that can be introduced both in the short term and in the longer term.

The goal of Chapter 17 is to provide a better understanding of the current distribution of taxes in Jordan and to estimate the effective rate of taxation on households. In this chapter, Sally Wallace and Andrey Timofeev focus on the incidence of taxes in Jordan and provide an analysis of the incidence of Jordan's main taxes: personal income, corporate income, real property and property transfer taxes, customs, general consumption tax, excises, and taxes on capital. The authors point out that all taxes must ultimately be paid by someone, and one of the most fundamental questions asked by economists is: "Who bears the final burden of a tax?" Equity is a real concern in Jordan, because while it is an upper- middle income country, more than 14 percent of the population is below the poverty line. An analysis of the incidence and distributional implications of the tax system in Jordan can provide useful information with respect to the equity of the system and provide input into tax reform discussions throughout the region.

In Chapter 18, Ömer Faruk Batırel discusses the Turkish tax policy performance for the period of 2004-2013 in terms of equitable distribution of tax burdens and examines tax expenditures in terms of equity and fiscal transparency grounds. Batırel first presents a brief history of the Turkish tax system and continues with an overview of the contemporary Turkish tax System. Then, the author evaluates the Turkish tax policy performance in terms of equitable distribution of tax burdens. Later, he estimates tax expenditure figures using very limited data because of unavailability. Under this serious constrain, both the policy performance and the tax expenditure analysis are made for the period of 2004-2013. It is claimed in the chapter that "*Turkey introduced very generous tax breaks that would never fit economic and social purposes*." It is indicated that the sharp increase of tax expenditures observed in recent years is mainly due to personal income tax reliefs since nearly two-thirds of the tax expenditures resulted from income taxes. One of the main findings of the chapter is that "because fiscal transparency and non-discrimination principles of taxation are violated in Turkey, there are considerable amount of hidden tax reliefs that are not counted as tax expenditures in the Turkish tax system."

Public utilities have been at the very center of economic and social development of countries. Until the last decades of the century, they were almost exclusively undertaken by public authorities. From the 1980s, they have been subject to liberalization in many countries. In Chapter 19, Mustafa Kahveci and Hülya Kirmanoğlu explore the structure and function of the electricity markets, the market failures they pose and the market reforms designed to correct them by national and international decision-makers from a political-economy point of view focusing on the Turkish case. Their research poses two questions: 'How compatible with the directives of the European Union is the market reform of the electricity sector in Turkey?' and 'who are the beneficiaries of the reform?' The authors explain that liberalization of electricity means the segments which are vertically integrated are unbundled and opened to private sector through privatizations. However, since the transmission and distribution segments are networks that exhibit severe natural monopoly characteristics, Kahveci and Kirmanoğlu suggest that they should be either owned and operated by public bodies or regulated by independent regulatory authorities to protect consumer interest. With this perspective the authors argue that liberalization in the energy sector does not serve to enhance the public interest, instead it promotes special interests. It follows that benefits reaped by special interest groups and costs borne by the people.

Due to the serious consequences in terms of economic growth and welfare, price stability is one of the most researched topics in economics. The conventional monetarist view that inflation is always a monetary phenomenon has a long tradition based on the quantity theory of money (QTM). The "unpleasant monetarist arithmetic" of Sargent-Wallace (1981), however, unveiled the fiscal roots of inflation and it became increasingly clear that the effectiveness of monetary policy in controlling inflation depends critically on its coordination with fiscal policy (Buti, 2003). Since Turkey has experienced both high inflation rates a very high public debt to GDP ratio but recently came close to solve these two problems, it present a good example for analysis. In Chapter 20, Asuman Oktayer and Nagihan Oktayer Işıklar empirically analyze the monetary and fiscal policy coordination in Turkey by applying autoregressive distributed lag (ARDL) cointegration procedure over the period January, 1989 to February, 2012 and the sub-periods of January, 1989 to January, 2001 and February, 2001 to February 2012. First, the Turkish economy is briefly discussed for the analyzed period in terms of fiscal balances. This is followed by the discussion of the empirical specifications of the chapter and then the empirical analysis and results are presented. While the empirical test results related to the entire period of January, 1989 to February, 2012 and sub-period of January, 1989 to January, 2001 indicate fiscal policy dominant regime, the findings regarding February, 2001 to February, 2012 imply monetary policy dominant regime in Turkey.

Starting with late 2007, the world economy was faced with the worst financial crisis since the Great Depression of the 1930s. This Global Financial Crisis or the Great Financial Crisis (GFC) has hit developed and developing countries through a number of transmission channel. Some impacts are already disappearing while others are still to strike. In Chapter 21, İsmail Şiriner and Keremet Shaiymbetova analyze MENA region developing countries' monetary regimes and policies, including: monetary policy expansion of the monetary policy framework in promoting financial stability alongside the primary price stability objective. The authors first analyze financialization of the world economy and then summarize the changes in monetary policy caused by GFC from inflation targeting to financial stability, from financial stability to macroprudential polices which is named generally as unconventional monetary policy measures. Şiriner and Shaiymbetova indicate that MENA region developing countries to experience the crisis were those with the most globally integrated financial sectors. The authors suggest that post-crisis spillovers and heightened capital flows have triggered a search for alternative monetary policy frameworks in the countries like Turkey and Israel. According to authors, an alternative to the current neoliberal monetary policy, macroprudential policy instruments can be used to create and sustain the stability in the economy and central banks must take into account not only inflation but also employment and growth.

There have been important developments in the decentralization of the government structure in Turkey since the early 1980s. In Chapter 22, Mehmet Serkan Tosun, Dilek Uz, and Serdar Yılmaz examine the link between fiscal decentralization and local borrowing within Turkish provinces. They first discuss local government reforms throughout the history of the Turkish Republic with the focus on recent reform efforts and current local government structure. Then, the authors provide an empirical analysis of the effects of decentralization in Turkish provinces using cross-sectional and panel data approaches, and spatial econometrics. The dataset consists of 67 provinces from 1980 to 2000, and separately cross-sectional data on all 81 provinces for the year 2000. Using decentralization measures such as number of local governments per capita and ratio of own-source municipal revenue to total provincial tax revenue, and specific characteristics of the municipalities the analysis examines whether variations in local decentralization across these provinces and across time have had a significant impact municipal borrowing in those provinces. According to the authors, there is a need for investment in local infrastructure for Turkey to meet EU standards of service delivery. They suggest that a good case can be made for permitting municipal governments to borrow as long as the "golden rule" of debt finance is followed: that they borrow only for financing capital (investment) expenditures such as those for infrastructure improvements, which provide a flow of benefits over time.

In Chapter 23, Weshah Razzak and Belkacem Laabas use the work-leisure choice model to compute equilibrium weekly hours worked for a number of Arab countries and compare them to the G7 countries. The purpose of the chapter is to measure hours worked, which allows the authors to compute the Frisch elasticity of labor supply, and labor productivity in a number of Arab countries for which no data have been published previously. Razzak and Laabas summarize first the main features of the Arab economies which have implications for the estimation of hours worked. Then, they present the model and calibrate the model for the G-7 countries and the Arab countries, estimate hours worked, compute the elasticity of labor supply, and labor productivity. Later, they engage with policy simulations, and present their findings. Their main contribution is to provide model-consistent estimates of hours worked. The authors show that the labor supply curve is elastic in all Arab countries, and provide a new measure of labor productivity. This finding confirms previous research that workers respond to incentives, which has serious implications for tax and social security policies. The authors also provide some policy simulations pertinent to the effects of taxation on welfare and poverty.

We believe these chapters will generate ideas for future research efforts as well as for the development of policies that will influence both global and national prosperity, not only in developing countries but also advance countries.

M. Mustafa Erdoğdu
Marmara University, Turkey

Bryan Christiansen
PryMarke, LLC, USA

REFERENCES

Avi-Yonah, R. S. (2000). Globalization, Tax Competition, and the Fiscal Crisis of the Welfare State. *Harvard Law Review*, *113*(7), 1575–1676. doi:10.2307/1342445

Benvenisti, E., & Nolte, G. (2004). Introduction: Challenges to the Welfare State in an Era of Globalization. In E. Benvenisti & G. Nolte (Eds.), *The Welfare State, Globalization, and International Law* (pp. vii–xxii). Berlin: Springer-Verlag. doi:10.1007/978-3-642-17008-9

Blossfeld, H.-P., Buchholz, S., Hofäcker, D., Bernardi, F., & Hofmeister, H. (2008). Converging Divergences? *International Sociology*, *23*(4), 561–595. doi:10.1177/0268580908090728

Buti, M. (2003). Interactions and Coordination between Monetary and Fiscal Policies in EMU: What Are the Issues? In M. Buti (Ed.), *Monetary and Fiscal Policies in EMU: Interactions and Coordination*. Cambridge: Cambridge University Press.

Dagan, T. (2004). The Cost of International Tax Cooperation. In E. Benvenisti & G. Nolte (Eds.), *The Welfare State, Globalization, and International Law* (pp. 49–78). Berlin: Springer-Verlag. doi:10.1007/978-3-642-17008-9_3

Genschel, P., Lierse, H., Schmidtke, H., Seelkopf, L., Traub, S., & Yang, H. (2015, March 5-7). Tax Competition and Inequality. *Paper prepared for the 14th Biennial Conference of the European Union Studies Association*, Boston.

Genschell, P. (2002). Globalization, Tax Competition, and the Welfare State. *Politics & Society*, *30*(2), 245–275. doi:10.1177/0032329202030002003

Plümper, T., & Troeger, V. E. (2012). Tax Competition and Income Inequality: Why Did the Welfare State Survive? *Department of Economics, University of Warwick. Working Paper Series, No: 83*, Coventry, UK.

Sargent, T. J., & Wallace, N. (1981). Some Unpleasant Monetarist Arithmetic. *Federal Reserve Bank of Minneapolis Quarterly Review*, *5*(3), 1–17.

Stiglitz, J. E. (2007). *Making Globalization Work*. New York: W.W. Norton & Company, Inc.

Troeger, V. (2013, February). Tax Competition and the Myth of the 'Race to the Bottom': Why Governments Still Tax Capital. *The CAGE-Chatham House Series*, No. 4. Retrieved from http://www2.warwick.ac.uk/fac/soc/economics/research/centres/cage/onlinepublications/briefing/0213bp_troeger1.pdf

ENDNOTES

1 Genschel et al. (2015) show that "the rich and the poor of the small country can achieve a higher net income when engaging in international tax competition. This explains why tax competition is politically robust even in a model where the rich have no power over the tax rate."

2 He was a former Professor and Chairman of the Economics Department, American University, Washington D.C. He also served as Head of the Tax Policy Division (1974-1981) and later as Director of the Fiscal Affairs Department (1981-2000) at the IMF. Vito Tanzi served as President of the International Institute of Public Finance (1990-94) and Undersecretary of State for Economy and Finance in the Italian Government (2001-2003). An economic effect (the Tanzi effect) named after him.

3 Tax havens are countries that impose little or no taxes or other forms of taxes. By offering sophisticated banking and communications facilities and stable political and business climate, they provide a wide range of tax avoidance advantages for enterprises (Öz, chapter nine in this handbook).

Chapter 1
Public Finance in Developing Countries:
An Introduction

Vito Tanzi
Honorary President of the International Institute of Public Finance, USA

ABSTRACT

After World War Two, when many countries became independent and the Bretton Woods institutions were created, economists and policymakers had statistical evidence of the enormous differences that existed, in the per capita incomes and in the standards of living, between rich and poor countries. Therefore, they became aware of the need for raising per capita incomes in the poor countries. Modern governments need revenue and often a lot more revenue than they needed in the past, in order to provide the levels of assistance and public services that modern societies expect governments to provide. It may seem to be desirable for governments to have more revenue to spend and leave the decisions, on how the extra revenue will be used, to a later time. However, this is not always the case.

INTRODUCTION

After World War Two, when many countries became independent and the Bretton Woods institutions were created, economists and policymakers had statistical evidence of the enormous differences that existed, in the per capita incomes and in the standards of living, between rich and poor countries. Therefore, they became aware of the need for raising per capita incomes in the poor countries. "Development economics", which had not existed before, was born as a special branch of economics and the search started for identifying *policies* that could make the economies of developing countries grow at fast paces, thus helping them to raise the standards of living of their populations. There was little controversy at that time that governments could play a major role in promoting economic growth. It was a time of great confidence in the ability of governments in solving economic problems. Public finance for developing countries became an important and special branch of "development economics" and of "public economics".

DOI: 10.4018/978-1-5225-0053-7.ch001

A factor that immediately attracted much attention was "capital accumulation". Economists attributed the existing differences in the per capita incomes among countries to differences in the amount of capital that they had; and differences in growth rates to differences in the rates at which capital was accumulated. Rich countries were rich because they had more capital and faster growing countries were countries that were accumulating more capital. In one of his writings, in 1930, Keynes had anticipated this view when he had written that "[the] modern age opened… with the accumulation of capital… [and that growth had been driven by] … the power of accumulation [of capital] by compound interest" (p. 361). Keynes' view was later incorporated in the growth models that became popular and that went under the name of Harrod and Domar models. These models made "capital output" and "marginal capital output ratios" important statistics. Governments were encouraged to direct their policies toward the creation of capital and foreign aid to poor countries was directed toward the goal of capital accumulation.

THE ROLE OF PUBLIC FINANCE IN THE EARLY YEARS

The attention paid to capital accumulation led immediately to the role that taxation could play in this accumulation. Taxation came to be recognized as a powerful instrument that governments could use to promote the needed capital accumulation that would make the countries' economies grow at faster rates. The popular economic theories at that time, especially those associated with the so-called Harrod and Domar models, pointed to the role that taxation could play.

Capital accumulation could be public or private. Net *public* investment would contribute directly to capital accumulation and, by providing infrastructure needed for private activities, could also provide a stimulus to private investment. Private investment could also be encouraged by other government policies. The broad strategy that was recommended was the following: (a) The level of taxation had to be increased, to make more resources available to the government. (b) Government *current* spending had to be kept low so that the budget could generate a surplus (before accounting for the spending for public investment). The public surplus so generated would be used to increase public investments in *physical* infrastructure and to finance *public* enterprises. This was the strategy generally recommended at that time (from the 1940s until the early 1970s). For a clear and prominent example, see the recommendations of the famous Musgrave Mission to Colombia, in the early 1970s. The larger was the surplus generated, the greater would be the capital accumulation and the expected positive impact on economic growth.

At that time *current* public spending was not considered productive and there was resistance to the growth of public debt. In any case, in the absence of a global financial market, which later would make it easier for governments to obtain foreign loans, public borrowing could not have provided many resources to governments. Borrowing from central banks, in the form of what came to be called "inflationary finance", was associated with the printing of money and with inflation. When used, that policy created inflation and, when inflation became high, because of time lags in the payment of taxes, it reduced real tax revenue, due to what came to be called the *Tanzi effect* (see Tanzi, 1977 and 1978).

Private investment would be encouraged by the creation of the publicly- financed, physical infrastructure but it could also be stimulated by generous and well -targeted tax incentives. The protection provided to domestic enterprise by high import duties and by other import restrictions were also assumed to encourage private domestic investment. There was much faith at that time in the impact that tax incentives and policies of import substitutions could have on private investment.

In summary, the development strategy recommended was: (a) to increase the level of taxation; (b) to keep the level of current public spending low; (c) to adopt effective tax incentives for investment; and (d) to restrict the import of finished products, especially products that could be produced (although at higher costs) by domestic enterprises, with some protection and subsidies.

This strategy placed a lot of weight on tax policy and on tax levels and the search for good tax structures, for effective tax incentives, and for high tax levels became intense. Econometric studies, that used relevant economic data from many countries, attempted to determine the *tax potential* that specific countries were assumed to have and to estimate the *tax gap* that was expected to exist between a country's *actual* tax level and the econometrically estimated, *potential* one. For an example of such studies (see Tanzi, 1987). The above strategy was accompanied by the creation of public enterprises, at a time when public ownership of some strategic sectors and various forms of economic planning were seen as desirable. Tax revenue was also needed to provide subsidies to the public enterprises and to compensate for the revenue losses due to use of tax incentives.

Countries were criticized by public finance experts and by the staff of international organizations for keeping their tax level below the estimated, potential one. The experts asserted that the move by a low-taxed country toward the higher, *potential* tax level would provide the *fiscal space* that would make it possible for the country to make the public investment that would promote more growth. This led to debates on: (a) how to raise the level of taxation; (b) what taxes would be preferable to use; and (c) what kind of infrastructure to build.

In the first couple of decades after World War Two, when the *value added tax* was not known --that tax was first introduced in France in the mid-1950s and was exported to other European countries later and to developing countries much later--, the *personal income tax* had been expected to play the leading role, in both providing revenue and in raising more revenue in a *fair* and *progressive* way, a way that would reflect the *ability to pay* of the taxpayers, in countries that often had highly uneven income distributions so that the taxable capacity was concentrated in the high percentiles.

The personal income tax had still the reputation, especially in the USA, of being the *fairest* of all taxes. It was considered the *ideal tax* to provide the needed fiscal space and to do it in a fair and efficient way. At that time potential disincentive effect of high marginal tax rates did not yet receive much attention. Domestic and foreign tax experts who provided advice to developing countries focused on this tax, especially when foreign trade taxes started to be criticized for the distortions in the allocation of resources that they created. Import duties had been the major "tax handle" of many governments in generating public revenue and in promoting industrialization through import substitution, as had been recommended by the influential Argentine economist Raul Prebisch. Some attention was also allocated to the possibility of using taxes on wealth and especially taxes on land ownership.

The tax reforms that were proposed in several countries, by experts who came mostly from advanced countries, especially in the 1950s and 1960s, focused on the personal income tax and, to a lesser extent, on the corporate income tax and the wealth taxes. Unfortunately the results, in generating tax revenue in a fair and progressive way, were not encouraging. The tax levels changed little. The tax reforms and the personal income tax failed to live up to the expectations and to deliver the hoped for fiscal space. In countries that were still largely agricultural, that had relatively few large establishments, and where informality was common and tax evasion easy, the personal income tax could not deliver the hoped for fiscal space.

The tax incentives for private enterprises made the tax systems complex and, in too many cases, led to "rent-seeking" and to acts of corruption. Furthermore, for various reasons, often having to do with poor choices of investment projects, lack of objective benefit-cost analysis, lack of appropriate "operation and maintenance" after the infrastructures had been built, or simply because of acts of corruption, wrong or inefficient projects were financed. As a consequence, the public investments undertaken were not as productive as they had been expected. The *marginal* capital output ratios turned out to be uncomfortably high in too many cases, raising questions about the basic model followed.

HUMAN CAPITAL AND PUBLIC INSTITUTIONS

In the 1960s economists interested in economic development started to question the implicit growth model that had given the dominant role to real investment in government policies. Several influential economists started arguing that some categories of *current* public spending (basic education, basic health and some others) could be as productive in generating growth as public investment. This was the time when "human capital" entered the economic policy debate and some attempts were made (by Barro and others) to provide estimates of human capital in different countries. Human capital would remain important in the economic literature in future years and spending on it would slowly crowd out spending for real public investment and also for essential public goods. With few exceptions (including China), most countries have spent less than they should have in financing infrastructure in recent decades.

Other economists, and especially Douglass North, started to call attention to the fact that policies are often just statements of intentions. They do not necessarily reflect the actual concrete actions. To become concrete policies must be carried and implemented by efficient institutions. The institutions can be seen as the necessary vehicles that transform intentions into concrete acts. If the institutions do not exist or are of poor quality, and are thus not capable of implementing and monitoring the policies, even policies that look good on paper or in intention may give disappointing results. Therefore, there was some shift in attention from policies (that is from the enacting of particular laws to promote some particular objective) to the *public institutions* and to the general *quality* of the institutions in the public sector (tax administrations, budget offices, justice systems, educational systems and so on).

Spending on public education came to be seen as essential not only for growth but also for promoting better income distributions, at a time when income distributions had attracted much attention. There was the realization that the tax systems were not contributing to reducing Gini coefficients. Unfortunately, even in this area there was some disappointment: while the higher spending on education was improving literacy, in many countries it did not seem to lead to the hoped for and desired impact on the income distribution or on the growth rates.

There was also awareness of the existence of what could be called *cross-institutional externalities*, externalities created when the poor performance of some essential institution, say justice, can have damaging effects on the performance of other institutions. For example, the performance of the tax administration can be reduced if tax evaders are not punished, because of the poor or slow functioning of the justice system.

Many countries continued to try to make the tax systems more productive, more efficient, easier to administer and more equitable. Over the years, several countries introduced reforms of tax systems, often with foreign assistance. There was some progress in some areas, as a consequence of the tax reforms, and less in others.

As to progress, the growing concern for neutrality and efficiency led to:

1. The progressive reduction in the importance of distortionary foreign trade taxes;
2. The growing reliance on more neutral, broad-based sales taxes and especially on the value-added tax, a tax which became popular in many countries, starting in the late 1970s and which acquired growing revenue importance in many countries over future years;
3. The elimination of many excises and nuisance taxes, including those on various luxury products, and the growing concentration on few excises, taxes that could be justified on grounds that the taxed products created negative externalities; or that could be justified by the "benefit received principle" of taxation, as for example gasoline taxes and excises on vehicles justified by the need to provide resources to build and maintain free public roads. The excise taxes now in use are mainly those on tobacco products, gasoline, cars, alcoholic beverages and, increasingly, soft drinks (because of the latter's sugar content, that leads to illnesses connected with obesity, and because of the environmental cost of the plastic bottles).

The above changes in tax structures made the tax systems more efficient. However, some of the changes (such as the elimination of excises on *luxury* products and on *non-essential* imports) may also have made the tax systems less progressive, while the personal income tax has continued to play a limited, or marginal, role.

The introductions and growing use of computers in recent decades has made it easier for tax administrations to store, retrieve, and crosscheck information on taxpayers. This has made them more efficient and has facilitated the introduction of other administrative reforms. For example, several tax administrations have been reorganized by *functions*, and no longer by *taxes*, as they were in the past. Tax administrations have been given also greater independence from political influences than in the past and some incentives have been provided, to make the tax administrations operate more efficiently.

GLOBALIZATION AND PUBLIC FINANCE

The tax administrations of many countries are now more efficient than they were in the past as indicated by their success with the use of value added taxes, taxes that are not easy to administer. However, following the example of the United States, in recent decades many developing countries abandoned the Haig-Simons principle of taxation, the principle that had required that *all* personal income be taxed in the same way, *regardless of sources*. That principle had allowed the different tax treatment of different l*evels* of income. Higher personal incomes, regardless of source, could be taxed at higher *marginal* tax rates, guaranteeing, at least in principle, that the personal income taxes and the tax system would be progressive.

Because of the growing globalization of economic activities and the increasing facility with which financial capital was able to move across countries, in recent years, starting in the late 1980s, and in reaction to the writing by some influential American economists (Lucas, Summers and others) and to the pressures exercised by investors and their lobbyists, the laws were changed and income received by individuals from capital sources started to get preferential treatment. This made it possible for some individuals to receive very large incomes while paying very low taxes on them. This trend spread to other countries, including developing countries.

Income from labor sources and from routine business activities continued to be taxed at higher, progressive rates. The net effect of these changes has been to make the statutory tax systems of many countries probably more efficient, at least in terms of the *global* allocation of resources, but not more efficient in terms of revenue generation, or more equitable in terms of the burden of taxation on individuals with different income levels.

Globalization is likely to have *reduced the fiscal space* to governments while it has made the tax systems less progressive. Therefore, globalization has contributed to the growing unevenness of the income distribution now observed in many countries, both developed and developing. By reducing the countries' fiscal space, globalization has also reduced the governments' ability to pursue redistributive policies that require additional public spending.

While the above developments have taken place in what could be described as the visible or transparent part of economic policies, there has been another development that may have contributed to make the tax systems less productive, in terms of resource generation, and less equitable. This is the growing tax evasion facilitated by and connected with the increasingly important globalization of economic activities. While in the past tax evasion was mainly an activity connected with *domestic* economic activities, in recent years it has become more and more an activity connected with *global* activities (see Tanzi, 2014).

Daily newspapers have been full of stories of enterprises or individuals who have managed to avoid or to evade large taxes, by taking advantage of ambiguities in the national tax laws, or by exploiting the opportunities offered to them by the existence of low tax countries, or tax havens. Corporations that operate globally have found increasingly easy and profitable to move their headquarters to low-tax jurisdictions, at times by buying foreign enterprises in countries to which they could shift part of their global income, in a process described as *inversion.* These developments have been attracting growing attention on the part of several advanced countries and on the part of the G20 and some proposals are under way to deal with these problems.

Globalization and the easier movement of financial capital, made possible by new communication technologies and by a financial market that has become global, and the possibility of shifting profits from high-tax jurisdictions to low-tax jurisdictions, have created major and growing difficulties for *national* tax authorities in both advanced and developing countries in a process that the author of this paper has called the creation of *fiscal termites.* S (see Tanzi, 2001). These describe opportunities that taxpayers who operate globally have had available to avoid, or evade, taxes. These *termites* have been slowly damaging the very foundation of the tax systems and making progressively more difficult for tax administrations to limit tax avoidance or tax evasion.

The developments described above have made it more difficult to increase fiscal space for those governments that would like to promote economic development with their policies, or to play a larger role in redistributing income.

PUBLIC SPENDING IN DEVELOPING COUNTRIES

While in the years after World War Two taxation had been at the center of the attention of public finance experts and policymakers, starting in the decades of the 1960s and 1970s the attention shifted towards the spending side of the budget. Within the spending side the attention changed from the exclusive financing of *physical* infrastructures toward financing *social* current spending, and especially spending for education, public health and selected other social programs, some of this spending aimed at helping those at the lower end of the income distribution. Economists and policymakers had come to believe that such social spending could be as productive in promoting growth as real public investment, and that that it would reduce absolute poverty. This was the time when "human capital" came to occupy the center stage of development economics.

At that time there was also the beginning of a conservative reaction that attempted to give a larger role to the private sector and to market forces and that in later years would lead to what came to be called the "Washington Consensus" associated with policies that would aim at reducing governmental intervention in economic decisions. The calls to rely on "public-private partnerships", to build needed physical infrastructures, was one aspect of this movement. Another was the privatization of public enterprises and, in some countries, also the privatization of pensions and educational systems.

Education, public health and public pensions and some other social programs can be much more expensive than real public investment and can require much higher tax revenue. The advanced countries that had introduced *welfare states* (that financed publicly education, health, pensions, family allowances and other social programs) after World War Two had had to raise tax levels to bring them, in several cases, above 40 percent of GDP and in addition had been forced to accumulate large public debts.

Most developing countries did not have the option of raising their tax levels to 40 percent of GDP, or even of coming close to that level, and their ability to borrow was more limited especially when the option of borrowing from central banks became limited because of the latter growing independence and the realization of the impact that borrowing had on inflation and on exchange rates.

There are a few important considerations that must be kept in mind when governments attempt to raise the tax level beyond a given level. These considerations are rather obvious but are often forgotten, or ignored. There are also considerations that lead to calls to rely more on private sector's alternatives to programs that require public spending.

The first consideration is that, when taxes are not raised progressively, but are raised in a broadly proportional way and with indirect taxes, as happens often in developing countries, households at the lower end of the income distribution (the poorer classes) often experience increases in tax burdens similar *proportionally* to the taxes that the richer households pay. When incomes are low, this tax increase can be very painful and can significantly reduce their standards of living. Thus, the tax increases make the poorer classes even poorer. Therefore, there must be a strong belief that the *use* of the tax revenue by the government will more than compensate the poorer classes for the higher taxes paid. The public spending must be more pro poor than the higher taxes and must consist of services that the poor value highly. This consideration becomes less important when the tax system is progressive so that the taxes can be collected mainly from taxpayers at the high end of the income distribution. The conclusion is that *the less progressive is the tax system, the less justification, ceteris paribus, there may be to attempt to increase the tax level.*

The second consideration is the one that focuses on the use by the government of the taxes collected. There is a minimum amount of taxes that is essential to any government, in any community, to allow it to finance and to carry out the *most essential functions* of the state (personal protection, defense of the country, provision of justice, essential infrastructure, basic administrative services, and so on) that a country as a community cannot do without. It is difficult to determine exactly what this essential level is, because it depends on various factors that differ from country to country, such as the need for defense spending, the efficiency in the use of the public resources, and so on. But this spending is not likely to require high tax levels and is not likely to exceed much ten percent of GDP.

Naturally, the tax level may be so low that, regardless of the best effort, a country's government may not be able to satisfy even the most basic, essential needs and to provide the most basic services to the citizens. There are still some developing countries today in which the governments face this situation. In those cases, there is no question that the tax level should be raised, almost regardless of the progressivity or lack of progressivity of the tax system and regardless of the way in which the additional, required, tax burden would be distributed.

The third consideration is that higher tax levels and tax rates *almost always* have some negative impact on the incentives of *some* individuals, families, or economic activities. There may be and there is controversy about the *empirical* importance of these disincentives, but *not on the fact that they exists.* Also, it must be kept in mind that the transfer of tax money, from the citizens to the government, by itself, is never a zero-sum game. There is *always* some leakage or some loss in the transfer, due to *administrative costs,* to the tax administration, to *compliance costs,* to the taxpayers, and to *welfare costs,* to the economy. In other words, the *net* revenue that the government receives *is always less than the total cost of collecting and paying the taxes.*

This takes us to a fourth consideration, the one that looks at the use that the government makes of the tax revenue. If the tax system is efficient in its structure; if the tax administration is efficient in its function; if the tax system is progressive, so that the taxes are collected mostly from individuals at the higher end of the income distribution; and if the government is capable of using efficiently and equitably the tax revenue, for activities that have high social and economic value, than the tax levels that the governments collects can be considered appropriate.

In the situation described in the above paragraph, low levels of taxation might be inefficient and tax reforms that reflect demands by governments for higher tax revenue can be justified and supported. There are countries that are close to the situation described above. However, this is a different argument from the one often made by some economists who maintain that only because a country's tax level is relatively low or lower than that of other countries a country must increase its tax level. There is always some need for a kind of implicit or explicit cost-benefit evaluation of the decision whether a country should or should not raise taxes. Tax reforms that aim at raising more taxes, rather than at making a tax system more efficient or more equitable, must be justified in terms of what they wish to achieve with the additional spending.

Tax resources can be used unproductively, because spending policies are deficient in various ways. Good intentions and good but vague pronouncements are not sufficient for determining whether tax levels should be raised. Unfortunately, in some countries problems associated with inefficient public spending acquire worrisome dimensions and the net benefit that the citizens receive from the policy of *taxing and spending more* can be low, or, in some cases, may even become negative.

It may be sufficient to mention inefficiency that exist in specific programs, inappropriate programs, investments in "white elephants", "rent seeking" by some groups connected with some public spending, such as unjustified subsidies, leakages of public money due to corruption by administrators or policymakers, salaries paid to ghost workers, and so on. Unfortunately these are not abstract possibilities but reflect situations that exist in some countries and that could be characterized as *termites of the state.* These *termites* are more common than it is often assumed. The sad truth is that there are still countries and especially developing ones where little, genuine benefits to the majority of citizens accompany the use of public resources collected from higher taxes.

It is often argued that, money spent for education, for public health, and for other forms of assistance, (such as subsidies for energy and for some products) directly or indirectly benefit the general population.

Affirmations of this nature must not be accepted at face value. They must always be subjected to scrutiny and must be evaluated because public spending that, at first sight, may seem to be clearly pro poor, may end up benefiting more the individuals who deliver the services (the providers), who often come from to the higher percentiles in the income distribution, than those who receive the services.

The above may happen when those who deliver the public services (administrators, teachers, nurses, doctors) appropriate in various ways (at time through limited or inefficient work performances) a significant part of the spending assumed to benefit only those who are legally the legitimate beneficiaries (see Tanzi, 1974, 2008 for examples). Studies that routinely assign the full benefits from the whole spending in these categories to those who should be the legitimate beneficiaries often end up exaggerating the benefits to them and the positive impact that they have on the income distribution.

When this spending is financed by proportional and not by progressive taxes, the *net* benefit from the public action, which includes taxing and spending, to the poorer income classes may be much reduced even though it is not completely eliminated. This consideration does not apply, or applies less, when pro poor programs are well targeted, are delivered efficiently, and are financed by efficient and progressive taxes.

CONCLUSION

Modern governments need revenue and often a lot more revenue than they needed in the past, in order to provide the levels of assistance and public services that modern societies expect governments to provide. This need for revenue has created a bias among many public finance experts for higher tax levels. Governments and especially those of developing countries are often encouraged to increase taxes and to spend the additional money for social services and especially for services that would benefit those at the lower end of the income distribution. The redistributive role of the state is now considered very important.

The highly uneven income distributions that characterize many countries and especially many developing countries have given more justification to these policies and to that role. Some experts have concluded that it does not matter how taxes are collected as long as the revenue collected is spent on social programs. Given this bias, it may not be considered politically correct to question the policies *of taxing more and spending more on social services*. Economists should not be against these policies, when the taxes can be raised efficiently and progressively and when, with a high degree of probability, the spending can be assumed to actually benefit those that it is intended to benefit, without making the beneficiaries of the programs permanently dependent on them. Unfortunately, there conditions may be less common than it is assumed or hoped.

Because of the various, potential problems mentioned above, it is important that, before additional "fiscal space" is created, by raising the countries' tax levels with tax reforms, there must be a clear understanding of how that fiscal space will be used and how the additional tax burden will be distributed. There must also exist the necessary public institutions capable of enforcing the adopted policies competently and efficiently.

At times it may be a mistake to rush toward increasing tax levels with tax reforms only because the tax level in a country seems low when compared with that of other countries. It may seem to be desirable for governments to have more revenue to spend and leave the decisions, on how the extra revenue will be used, to a later time. Unfortunately, in too many cases, the costs of the tax increase tend to be more certain than the benefits that would accompany the higher spending.

REFERENCES

Keynes, J. M. (1933). Economic Possibilities for our Grandchildren. In J. M. Keynes (Ed.), *Essays in Persuasion* (pp. 358–373). London: MacMillan and Co. Limited.

Tanzi, V. (1972, Summer). *Fiscal Reform in Colombia: The Report of the Musgrave Mission*. Inter-American Economic Affairs.

Tanzi, V. (1974). Redistributing Income through the Budget in Latin America. *Quarterly Review. Indexes - Banca Nazionale del Lavoro*, *27*(108), 65–87.

Tanzi, V. (1978). Inflation, Real Tax Revenue, and the Case for Inflationary Finance: Theory with an Application to Argentina. *IMF Staff Papers*, *25*(3), 417–451. doi:10.2307/3866679

Tanzi, V. (1987). Quantitative Characteristics of the Tax Systems of Developing Countries. In D. Newberry & N. H. Stern (Eds.), *The Theory of Taxation for Developing Countries* (pp. 205–241). New York: Oxford University Press for the World Bank.

Tanzi, V. (2008). The Role of the State and Public Finance in the Next Generation. *OECD Journal for Budgeting*, *8*(2), 1–27. doi:10.1787/budget-v8-art6-en

Tanzi, V. (2014). Globalization and Taxation: A Brief Historical Survey. *Rivista di Diritto Finanziario e Scienza delle Finanze*, *73*(1), 3–20.

Chapter 2
Transparency, Technology and Taxation

Richard Bird
University of Toronto, Canada

ABSTRACT

Taxes and tax administration are important. Taxation is one of the main interfaces between state and society: how a tax system is administered may affect not only its yield, its incidence, and its efficiency but also the state itself. Taxation that is widely perceived to be unfair and administered capriciously and corruptly may not only bring the tax system into disrepute but weaken trust in government and even the legitimacy of the state. This paper discusses two important aspects of taxation – its 'transparency' and the increasingly important role of information technology (IT) in tax administration, as well as how these two topics relate to the broader issues just mentioned.

INTRODUCTION

Taxes and tax administration are important. Taxation is one of the main interfaces between state and society: how a tax system is administered may affect not only its yield, its incidence, and its efficiency but also the state itself. Taxation that is widely perceived to be unfair and administered capriciously and corruptly may not only bring the tax system into disrepute but weaken trust in government and even the legitimacy of the state. One common complaint about taxation is that it is insufficiently 'transparent.'[1] One obvious way taxation may become more transparent is by exploiting the increasingly important role that information technology (IT) is playing in tax systems around the world.[2] Like increased transparency, however, increased use of technology in taxation may be a two-edged sword with respect to the broader role of taxation of society. This chapter first discusses some possible interpretations of 'transparency' in taxation and then briefly reviews the increasing role of IT in tax administration before concluding with some reflections about the interplay of transparency and technology in developing a 'smart' tax system.[3]

DOI: 10.4018/978-1-5225-0053-7.ch002

WHAT IS A TRANSPARENT TAX SYSTEM?

Transparency with respect to taxation may have many different meanings, ranging from the level of complexity of the language in the tax law to how the level, structure, administration and understanding of taxation may affect the building of a modern state. Five very different possible interpretations of this concept are noted in this section.

A Transparent System Is One That Is Simple

One common idea is that a system that is more transparent in the sense of being set out in simple, readily understandable language so anyone can understand it is inherently preferable to one expressed in the complex language more characteristic of tax laws and regulations. Many proposals for major tax reform have 'simplicity' as an objective. The idea is often that making taxation simpler and more transparent – for example, by reducing the number of taxes, the number of rates, the number of people who have to deal directly with the tax administration, or the length and complexity of the law – will improve public acceptance and understanding. In reality, however, few countries have achieved much in terms of simplifying either the language of tax law or the reality of the tax system. Taxation is complicated largely because the world is complicated. Unless people are willing to leave decisions about the taxes they pay entirely up to the discretion of officials – a condition seldom found in practice even in authoritarian regimes – complex and differentiated language is often necessary to cope adequately with the reality of the heterogeneity of the world and the taxpaying public

People do not like to pay taxes. They may try to dodge fiscal bullets in many ways. Some may have sufficient political influence to block or alter tax legislation before it is passed. Others – also usually at the upper end of the economic spectrum – may manage (with the aid of skilled advisers) to devise legal ways around the apparent intent of the law, for example, by carrying out many activities through offshore entities beyond the reach of domestic tax authorities. Still others may simply cheat – for example, by claiming improper deductions or under-reporting income or sales. Some may operate in the hidden or informal economy: such people are usually hard to catch and are sometimes little more than ghosts so far as the tax system is concerned. Others may be more like icebergs, with a small formal tax presence but most of their real economic activity hidden from fiscal sight. And finally, some may simply refuse to pay their taxes and try to dodge the consequences in a variety of ways through bribery and political influence up to and including fleeing the country.[4]

A delicate balance needs to be struck between restricting the ability of taxpayers to cheat and giving officials undue discretionary authority which can all too easily be abused to extort bribes or in other ways. Doing so is not easy anywhere, and the restraints established against abuse in either direction must constantly be monitored and adapted as necessary to deal with changing circumstances. The result is likely to be a complex (and changing) body of law and regulation that is all too likely not to be all that 'transparent' even to experts.[5]

A Transparent System Is One That Taxes Businesses, Not People

As mentioned earlier, one way to make taxation 'simpler' is to reduce direct interactions between people and the tax system. An obvious and often popular way to do so is to tax businesses more and people less. Many think that business and especially large companies (particularly large multinational companies) should pay much more in tax, perhaps because they think this means that they – the people – will pay less. However, the conflicting assertions often heard about who really pays corporate taxes are, given our present state of knowledge, generally based more on faith than evidence. Taxes imposed on business may be popular with those who no longer have to make explicit tax payments, but they are definitely less transparent to those (workers, consumers, shareholders) whose private incomes are ultimately going to be reduced as a result. Although the extent to which and the manner in which countries impose taxes on businesses rather than directly on personal income, consumption or wealth is determined more by history and specific contextual factors than by any consistent conceptual framework, basing taxes more on business than on people invariably makes taxation less rather than more transparent.

This point is even clearer with respect to the currently topical issue of the appropriate international division of the income (somehow defined) of multi-national corporations (OECD 2013c).[6] Satisfactory solutions to the knotty problem of how to measure and divide the international income pie are as difficult to find in theory as they are unlikely to be implemented in practice. In the end, international taxation may well be one of the "...many problems that people are unable to solve in the abstract, but are able to solve when placed in a real-world context."[7] In other words, the only feasible approach to improving outcomes may be to focus not so much on the precise solution to be reached as on the process by which any solution is likely to be reached – for example, by ensuring that the 'soft governance' institutional setting within which international discussions on such matters almost invariably take place is both sufficiently transparent and sufficiently inclusive for the results of the process to be broadly acceptable.

A Transparent System Is One That Is Salient and Visible

Does it matter if taxes are visible to voters or – in the language now often used in economics – 'salient' to consumers? It may make a big difference if someone is fully aware of a tax – or at least thinks he or she is. Taxation, like death, is an unpleasant reality. People understandably seldom like to be reminded of either. However, economists have long been in a minority when it comes to whether it matters or not if people "see" taxes. In the rational world in which economists spend much of their working day, it is hard to see much reason why it should matter. What matters in that world is what a tax does – to income, to prices, to consumption, to employment – not what people think it does. Objective reality rules. However, the real 'reality' of taxation is not quite so objective.

The evidence is, for example, that people make different and fewer purchases when a tax on sales is included in the posted price (as with value-added taxes in almost all countries) than when, as is common in the United States and Canada, it is added on at the cash register (Chetty, Looney, & Kroft 2007). Consumers may make more rational private spending decisions if they face the "full" (tax-included) price at the time when the decision is made (Chetty, 2009). However, the evidence also suggests that people are less likely to object to paying taxes or charges when they are paid invisibly – for example, where tolls are collected electronically (that is, invisibly) they are 20-40% higher than where they are collected manually (Finkelstein, 2008). Consequently, better private spending decisions may be 'purchased' at the hidden cost of greater (and perhaps, as John Stuart Mill suggested long ago,[8] less efficient) public expenditure than people would choose if the taxes they paid were more transparent, that is, separately quoted as in North America rather than 'hidden' in the posted price as in Europe (Bird, 2010).

Hidden taxes may result in a larger and less efficient public sector because people care less than they should about how much and how well government spends simply because they are not aware of how much they pay in taxes. Some may argue that people may be better off with a larger public sector even if they do not quite know how it is being financed. More plausibly, others may argue that it is easier to design and implement efficient taxes if governments do not face the difficult task not only of determining the incidence and effects of taxes but also having to explain such matters to the public in an understandable and persuasive fashion. Nonetheless, it is difficult to make a sustainable case for hiding the true size of the tax bill from the public in a democratic state.

Are people aware of the cost of government? Are they less willing to "buy" more public services when the tax price to them is, if not raised, then made more obvious? Is there some threshold of tax sensibility? Are hidden taxes undemocratic? Or are they instead, as some have suggested, not only necessary but desirable given the reality that "an important factor in the realities of the limits of taxation are the psychic costs of paying tax, costs which politicians will heed because they are clearly relevant to the prospects of re-election (Morag, 1985, p. 116)." Politicians may prefer to impose taxes with hidden (tax-inclusive) hands rather than being seen to put their all too visible hands in the pockets of taxpayers. Taxpayers may even prefer to have their fiscal feathers plucked invisibly.[9] But is ignorance bliss? As Shoup (1969, p. 37) notes: "those who view an informed electorate as a valuable community resource will favor tax consciousness, but those who believe the electorate mistakenly opts for too few public goods may extol tax anesthesia." While the importance attached to tax visibility is only beginning to be explored empirically, how one interprets the results of such studies is likely to depend on where one stands on the Shoup scale with respect to what might perhaps be called the 'wisdom of the people.[10]

A Transparent System Is One That Is Procedurally Fair and Accepted

Yet another approach to transparency focuses less on public understanding of the consequences of taxation than on the question of whether the tax system embodies clear and understood procedures that treat taxpayers respectfully. Frey and Feld (2002), for example, argue that systems that have such procedures and follow them strictly are more likely to be trustful of taxpayers and hence in turn more likely to have the trust of taxpayers, something that they argue – and even demonstrate empirically – tends to improve tax compliance – at least in Switzerland. How countries impose taxes can be an important determinant of how well they are, and can be, governed. In developing countries like those in the MENA region, for example, the first direct formal contact people, and particularly small businesses, have with the state is often through interaction with tax authorities. If this interaction results in negative relationships as a result of arbitrary or egregious administrative behavior resulting from administrative inefficiency and corruption, the result may be to weaken support for the state and even tend to increase cheating as a form of spite or reciprocity (Fox & Murray, 2014). A considerable amount of evidence both experimental and from surveys suggests that the extent and willingness with which people pay taxes is affected not only by the perceived compliance of their friends and neighbors but also by their own experiences with the tax system and their perception of the connection between what they pay to government and what they receive in exchange.[11]

A Transparent System Is One in Which People Know What They Are Paying For

The final approach to transparency considered here focuses on the last of these points, that is, not so much on the tax system itself as on its connection with government services. A benefit-related system – one in which what you pay is clearly connected with what you get – is arguably more transparent and hence likely to have a higher compliance rate (less evasion) and be less badly administered (less corruption and extortion) than the usual tax system. With the latter, money raised from general taxes, the incidence of which is often unclear, flows into the coffers of some government or other (in decentralized countries people may often not even know which one) and is then spent in ways that presumably benefit someone but may not be seen as a benefit by many taxpayers. Although as yet the evidence supporting this line of argument is largely anecdotal, if properly implemented the 'benefit' approach of establishing explicit linkages between taxes and expenditures may also achieve an important normative goal: indeed, under certain conditions, this approach, unlike any other, maximizes social welfare by equating the marginal social pain of taxation with the marginal social gain from public expenditure.[12]

The benefit approach may seem strange to those raised in the traditional world of public finance in which expenditures and taxes are generally treated as though each is immaculately conceived independent of the other. Nonetheless, this approach seems to embody the concept of tax transparency in the most meaningful sense. If taxes were fully transparent in this sense, each taxpayer knows more or less what he or she (and society more generally) is getting for each additional dollar of tax paid. This approach may thus be argued to be the relevant standard to which a really 'smart' tax system – defined as one that is as economically efficient as possible – should aspire. At the very least, the emphasis in this approach on the need to consider the linkage between the two sides of the budget in order to understand how 'transparently' tax systems operate provides a useful reference point.

However, three additional important elements need to be in place to make use of such a standard in practice. First, and simplest, spending must also be transparent. Secondly, and more complex, careful consideration must also be given to the extent to which it makes sense to explicitly link particular taxes and expenditures. And finally, and most importantly, such a system must also be politically acceptable and sustainable. Each of these points deserves at least a brief discussion.

Making Budgets Transparent

Much has been written recently about the virtues and mechanisms of budgetary transparency, public participation, and accountability (Khagram, de Renzio, & Fung, 2013). A striking example is Brazil, a country associated by many with both high levels of inequality and corruption which has nonetheless done much to make public budgeting more transparent initially at the municipal level and then more broadly through national laws on "fiscal responsibility" and budgetary transparency. While there remain serious challenges in this area, and the impact of transparency is much more evident at the local than at the national level, a recent study of Brazil's experience concludes that these reforms have increased both popular participation in budgeting and, more importantly, the extent to which fiscal decision making is publicly accountable in a meaningful way (Alves & Heller, 2013). Undoubtedly, other countries, developed and developing alike, could do much more along these lines than they now do.

Linking Taxes and Expenditures

An additional important issue is the extent to which particular taxes should be earmarked to particular expenditures. The basic principle is simple: when charges and taxes are imposed on those presumed to gain from the services funded, whether as individuals or as members of specific groups (drivers, area residents, etc.), those revenues should be earmarked to those expenditures and those expenditures—abstracting from issues arising from externalities—should be financed only from those revenues. Such earmarking must be clearly distinguished from the common practice of 'nominal' earmarking in which some levy is rationalized as financing an activity but has no marginal effect on the level of that activity.[13] Although there are well-known limitations to the extent to which extensive earmarking along these lines is consistent with sound budgetary practice, the introduction of more explicit budgetary links between taxes and the expenditures they are supposed to finance is important not only for reasons of efficiency – when there is indeed a strong benefit link – but also, more generally, to ensure that there is sufficiently broad political support for the implicit 'fiscal contract' between voters in their capacity as taxpayers and consumers of public services and officials and politicians to ensure that the system, and indeed, the state, is sustainable.[14] One important rationale for decentralizing the provision of public services to the lowest possible level of government – the principle of subsidiarity, as it is usually called in the context of the European Union – is precisely because doing so may, at least in principle, improve the transparency and accountability of governments at all levels to those they supposedly serve.

Taxation and State-Building

If transparency in taxation means better information about the relative costs and benefits of tax and expenditure decisions, resources should – given the existing distribution of private income – be better allocated and social welfare increased. If no one except the few lucky winners likes the existing distribution of income, the post-budget distribution may (unless government is controlled exclusively by the winners) be altered through taxes and especially expenditures (including transfers) until an acceptable balance of allocative efficiency and distributional acceptability are attained. Countries with fully transparent tax systems (in terms of knowledge of the costs and benefits of taxation) may of course alter not only the level but the structure of their tax (and expenditure) systems for the better, if they so choose. However, whether they choose to do so depends largely on such important but often complex and somewhat nebulous factors as social norms and political institutions.[15] We return briefly to this question later.

INFORMATION TECHNOLOGY AND TAXATION

Taxation is not really about collecting money. Fundamentally, good tax administration is about information: collecting the information governments need to be sure that people fulfill their legal obligations under the tax law in an efficient and effective way and making good use of that information without abusing privacy (Slemrod & Gillitzer, 2014). In this era of big data no modern tax administration can perform this task efficiently without making extensive use of modern information technology (IT) for a variety of purposes –to maintain taxpayer records, to facilitate (and minimize the cost of) tax compliance, to monitor tax collections, to carry out audits, to manage the administration itself, and, more broadly, to develop the information base necessary to ensure that each of these tasks is adequately dealt with.

In many countries, taxation has been one of the first government activities to introduce modern IT systems. Of course, not all experiences with tax IT have been successful (Bird & Zolt, 2008). The main problems have been less with the technology per se than with inadequate attention to the critical human and organizational aspects of introducing it into the tax system. However, many countries have been employing IT in tax administration in all sorts of different settings for some years. What the relevant IT is, what the preconditions for its successful adoption are, and what it can do once in place: none of this is a mystery.

Even the least developed countries need IT assistance these days not only to carry out the basic tasks mentioned above but also because some of their most important clients – multinational companies, banks, and large domestic firms – increasingly employ sophisticated computer systems which demand equal sophistication on the part of the revenue authorities. In addition to paying (or not paying) corporate taxes, such entities collect most other taxes in their role as government agents – payroll taxes and personal income taxes from employees and value-added taxes and excises from customers. The information provided by such companies is critical to enforcing taxes in general.

Experience suggests a number of lessons with respect to the successful application of information technology in tax administration:

- An appropriate strategy is needed to take into account the obstacles and the constraints arising from such organizational rigidities as civil service salary structure and procedural hurdles in acquiring the necessary expertise, hardware and software.
- Considerable organizational re-engineering - for example, consolidating return and payment forms, eliminating unnecessary and unused information required from taxpayers, and so on – is usually needed to gear the tax administration to a computerized environment.
- Whenever possible, equipment and software should be standardized and bought 'off the shelf' to facilitate operation, networking, and maintenance.
- The pace of change and the success of any modernization program depend ultimately on the training and skills of the people who are expected to use and operate the technology so appropriate incentives and accountability are needed at all levels of the administration.

At the extreme, countries may move largely to what may be called an automated (web-based IT driven) tax system like those in Denmark and Singapore, which provide extensively 'pre-filled' returns on line so that most taxpayers no longer need to file returns or to have any direct contact with the tax administration. There are clearly great gains from such systems both for taxpayers, by reducing compliance costs, and for tax administrations, by freeing substantial administrative resources to deal with more complex administrative problems such as auditing complex or questionable returns. The future of 'smart' tax administration lies in this direction. However, the move to what is called in Denmark 'no touch' taxation also gives rise to some potentially troubling questions from the broader perspective of the role of taxation in a democratic society.

Indeed, one reason tax transparency has become something that many countries need to think about more carefully is because modern information technology for the first time makes it possible to make everyone aware of (almost) everything, at least in principle.[16] *How well* revenue is raised — the effect of revenue-generation effort on equity, on the political fortunes of the government, and on the level of economic welfare — may in some ways be even more important than *how much* revenue is raised. Tax administration is a difficult task even at the best of times and in the best of places, and few countries satisfy these conditions. Even the best tax administration can easily be overloaded with impossible tasks or overburdened by the propensity of governments to alter tax legislation frequently, often with little thought of the administrative demands imposed by changes. Simple exhortations to do better are little help to resource-strapped administrators faced with difficult tasks. Indeed, experience around the world has shown that perhaps the single most important ingredient needed for effective tax administration is clear recognition at high political levels of the importance and complexity of the task and willingness both to provide the resources needed and to support good administrative practices — even if some political allies may be hurt as a result (Bird & Casanegra de Jantscher, 1992). Reluctance to support the efforts needed to collect taxes efficiently and effectively without fear or favor may be understandable in countries which are fragile politically like many in the MENA region and some in Europe. However, without sustained efforts along these lines no tax system, no matter how cleverly designed, will work as planned. Even the best tax design needs to be well administered if it is to work as intended.

Three separate compliance issues may be distinguished: the extent to which taxpayers comply with their legal tax obligations, the extent to which tax officials are able to detect and correct non-compliance, and the extent to which tax officials themselves comply with their obligations to collect only legal taxes in a legal way. All three may be more fully achieved when tax systems depend primarily on IT-based systems rather than on discretionary decisions by officials. Good IT systems not only facilitate compliance but also make it easier to control and monitor tax administration both externally – to control tax evasion – and internally – to control corruption and plain bad administration (although the latter may also require considerably more transparency than now exists in many countries).

Facilitating Compliance

The first task of any tax administration is to facilitate compliance: to make sure that those who should be taxed are taxed and that they comply with the rules. To do so:

1. Taxpayers must be found. If they are required to register, the registration process should be as easy as possible. Systems must be in place to identify those who do not register voluntarily. Tax authorities should adopt an appropriate unique taxpayer identification system to facilitate compliance and enforcement.
2. Tax liabilities must be established. This may be done administratively (as with most property taxes) or by some self-assessment procedure (as with most income taxes and VATs). Recently, as already mentioned, some countries have changed the game by increasingly 'pre-filling' tax returns with information obtained from reliable third-party sources.[17]
3. Taxes must be collected. In many countries, this is best done through the banking system. Experience suggests that it is seldom appropriate for tax administration officials to handle money directly.
4. Taxpayers must be serviced properly in the form of information, pamphlets, forms, advice agencies, payment facilities, telephone and electronic filing, and so on, to make taxpayer compliance with the system as easy as possible.

Enforcing Compliance

The approach to compliance just outlined essentially assumes that taxpayers should be treated like clients to be served rather than thieves to be caught. However, since some taxpayers are not honest, a second important task is to enforce compliance and reduce tax evasion. To do so, the administration needs to understand the extent and nature of the potential tax base in order to estimate the tax gap, preferably by sector and type. Without at least some idea of the number and type of individuals and firms not complying, no coherent enforcement strategy can be devised. Sometimes, the problem is that prospective taxpayers are swimming below the surface in the so-called informal economy. Sometimes, it is that many taxpayers who are in the system are substantially under-reporting. Without some knowledge of the unreported base, and its determinants, no administration can properly allocate its resources to improve tax collection and ensure everyone bears at least a roughly fair share of the tax burden.

Attempts to quantify the 'tax gap' – the amount of tax that should be legally collected but is not –are thus critical to good tax administration.[18] However, as experience with estimating the "VAT gap" in the European Union has shown (Barbone *et al.*, 2013), not only is it difficult to make such estimates even in developed countries, it can be equally difficult to make effective use of such estimates in assessing and improving tax systems and their operation. Nonetheless, work along these lines is an essential component of 'benchmarking' how well any tax system is functioning. Benchmarking can be thought of as a systematic process for identifying and measuring 'performance gaps' between how well a system functions and how well it should function if it did as well as some comparator, for example, similar systems in other countries. The idea is that by identifying such gaps one can first, identify problem areas, then next explore why these areas have problems, and finally, if all goes well, begin to understand how they gaps uncovered might perhaps be closed -- by changing laws, procedures, or people's behavior, as the case may be. Every step in this process, even if incomplete and partial, may encourage revenue administrations to collect and analyze data to help them do better what they are doing and policy-makers to consider broadening and simplifying tax structures so that the system can operate more effectively and efficiently.[19]

In addition to exploring the nature of the tax gap and extending the reach of the tax system into the informal economy to the extent feasible, close attention must also be paid to such simple but critical tasks as ensuring that those who are in the system file on time and pay the amounts due. Immediate follow-up of non-filers and those whose payments do not match their liabilities is important. Adequate interest charges must be imposed on late payments to ensure that non-payment of taxes does not become a cheap source of finance. An adequate penalty structure is needed to ensure that those who should register do so, that those who should file do so, and that those who under-report their tax bases are sufficiently penalized to increase the costs of evading tax.[20] And, of course, a smart tax administration must build up knowledge of its customer base in order to be able to assess the risk of evasion and audit questionable returns promptly and adequately.

Reducing Corruption

Good administration must keep not only taxpayers but also tax collectors honest. Even the best tax structure can be vitiated by capricious and corrupt tax administration. Developed countries took centuries to develop and implement systems to prevent dishonest tax officials from corrupt practices (Weber & Wildavsky, 1983). Tax officials must be adequately compensated so that they do not need to steal to live. Ideally, they should be professionally trained, promoted on the basis of merit, and judged by their adherence to the strictest standards of legality and morality. Temptation should be reduced by ensuring tax payments are made to banks not to tax offices and by reducing direct contacts between officials and taxpayers and reducing discretion (and increasing supervision) when they do have such contact.

IT may help not only to target taxpayer audits more productively but also to ensure that auditors operate within accepted parameters in assessing additional liabilities. IT may both permit a better assessment of tax potential and reveal how effectively and in what ways administrative actions affect the process of realizing that potential in the form of tax revenues.[21]

Countries need to think through carefully how transparent tax administration can or should be. As mentioned above, for example, should tax defaulters be publicly called to account – their deficiencies in compliance mercilessly revealed to the world? Should the same be done, perhaps with even more beating of the drums, for excessively energetic officials who devote some of their energies to filling their own pockets – or perhaps even when they stretch the law to fill state coffers? Will local mores and politics permit the former? Will civil service and union rules and social norms permit the latter? More and better information can certainly make the internal operation of a tax administration more transparent to top management, but should it also make it more transparent to the world?

A transparent tax system in the benefit sense discussed earlier, unpalatable as it may be to the many politicians and officials who think they know best how to manage other people's money, may improve the general democratic accountability of government. However, there are limits to how transparent any tax administration can be to the public at large and still do its job effectively. For obvious reasons, for instance, tax administrations do not customarily publish their audit plans. However, unless not only the rules under which audits are conducted but also the results of all audits are made public, how can the public know whether the rules are enforced properly?[22] However, provided the tax administration is willing and able to police staff activities and behavior, it is, so to speak, transparently clear that a good IT system permits a significant step forward in the ceaseless struggle of states to control the actions of their revenue agents.

This is not a trivial matter. Corruption in tax administration is a major problem in many countries. Everyone has their favorite stories, ranging from the official in one developing country some years ago with a salary of $100 a month who had two cars and a 5,000 hectare country estate to the small business in a MENA country recently that had to pay off sundry officials, many of them from various tax offices, every week or so in order to stay legally in business. While it is always difficult to assess the incidence of corruption in tax administration, a useful indicator may sometimes be the extent of competition for jobs in the tax office. In one developing country a few years ago, for example, reportedly over 100,000 people applied for about 50 jobs in the tax office. Tax officials were relatively well paid in that country and good jobs not that easy to find but it is difficult to avoid the inference that at least some among this army of applicants may have thought that certain extra-budgetary benefits were attached to the position.

Corruption in tax administration may take several forms. In many instances it is linked with evasion: taxpayer and tax official collude to defraud the state and split the gains in some negotiated way. In effect, this is bribery in which the bribe is paid not by the briber but by a third party (the public). In other instances, however, corruption may represent simple abuse of power, as when officials extort money from taxpayers on the threat of mistreatment – for instance, a huge reassessment – if they do not pay. Indeed, over-reporting by officials for such reasons may be considered an even more pernicious form of tax corruption than officials condoning under-reporting by taxpayers because it constitutes an even graver breach of the public trust.

Economists usually apply the same framework to the actions of tax officials as to those of taxpayers on the assumption that the extent to which officials deviate from good behavior is largely a function of the probability of such deviations being detected and the sanctions applied if it is (Hindricks, Keen, & Muthoo, 1999). Since IT provides managers with better information on the actions of officials it should increase the probability of detecting corruption in either of the forms mentioned above. Better internal flows of information in the tax administration can reduce corruption by reducing the net gains corrupt officials can expect to realize from their actions – provided of course that those in charge are not themselves corrupt.

This argument is right as far as it goes. But does it go far enough? As much work on the basic evasion model has shown, life is not so simple (Slemrod & Yitzhaki, 2002). Social norms, for example, clearly play an important role in determining how people – and even tax administrators are people– may react to increased expected losses from particular actions. In some circumstances, the results may even be perverse in the sense that increasing the probability of detection may, because of the accompanying growth in false positives, lead to so strong a negative feedback on the part of those unjustly expected that they may be led to behave differently in the belief that it is "better to be hung for a sheep than a lamb", as the old English saying has it. If Big Brother is watching me all the time and picking on me every time I make a (possible) slip, perhaps Big Brother is not worth my trust either, so I might as well cheat if I can. Managements that are not respectful of their personnel tend often not to be respected by them.[23]

This does not mean that using IT to control corruption in tax administration by monitoring the discretionary actions of officials more closely is a bad thing: it is clearly a good thing. However, as is true of with many good things – like chocolates, wine and making all taxpayer accounts fully transparent – one may have too much of it and induce perverse reactions. The point is not that corruption, like pollution or evasion, is something that can never be completely eliminated – although that too may be true. The point is rather that it may sometimes be best to let someone guilty escape in order to avoid the systemic consequences of falsely accusing (let alone convicting) innocent people. Just as some have emphasized that the service paradigm of treating taxpayers like clients rather than thieves may, in the long run, enhance the social norm of compliance (Alm & Martinez-Vazquez, 2003), so treating tax officials like fellow workers in a socially important common task – collecting taxes – may in some circumstances prove a more effective way to deal with corruption than placing cameras in the washrooms and monitoring keystrokes on individual computers. Improved IT, like improved transparency, can make a tax system work better in some ways, but it is not sufficient to produce the best tax system possible in the sense of being a good fit to the goals it is supposed to achieve and the environment in which it is supposed to achieve them.

Improved IT in tax administration can help deal with corruption. More transparency both within government and between government and citizens can strengthen the tax system as a pillar of a democratic state. But neither IT nor transparency (alone or together) can provide complete or definitive answers to all the problems that have bedeviled tax policy and tax administration since the beginning of recorded time. Still, if a government wants to clean up a tax or customs administration and keep it clean, a good, transparent IT system is definitely the way to go – so long as it does not go either too far ("all the way") or too fast ("full speed ahead)." Moderation in all things is a sound maxim whether dealing with basically good things like fiscal transparency and improving IT or bad things like corruption and evasion.

SMART TAXATION

The right mix of IT and transparency is critical to what might be called a 'smart' tax system. The key components of such a system are simple: a well-designed, relatively stable tax system with an appropriate administrative structure that fully utilizes the capacity of IT to assemble and utilize information, staffed with trained people, and properly managed as transparently as possible. Of course, it is much easier to say such things than to deliver them in any country. Countries exhibit a wide variety of tax compliance levels, reflecting not only the effectiveness of their tax administrations but also taxpayer attitudes toward taxation and government in general. Attitudes affect intentions and intentions affect behavior. Attitudes are formed in a social context by such factors as the perceived level of evasion, the perceived fairness of the tax structure, its complexity and stability, how it is administered, the value people attach to government activities, and the legitimacy of government. Government policies affecting any of these factors may influence taxpayer attitudes and hence the observed level of taxpayer compliance. Nonetheless, although countries and circumstances differ, a few basic concepts seem universally applicable.

First, it seldom makes sense to reform tax administration without simultaneously reforming tax structure to be both sensible and administrable. Considerable improvements can often be made in administration by small simplifications in tax policy. Reducing the number of income tax deductions, for instance, may permit countries to eliminate filing requirements for most wage earners. In addition to giving the administration simpler and more enforceable laws to administer it is equally important to simplify procedures for taxpayers, for example by eliminating demands for superfluous information in tax returns and consolidating return and payment forms.

Second, although it is important to identify and control taxpayers and to catch those who cheat few problems can be solved simply by calling in the tax police. Experience shows that there is much to be gained from viewing taxpayers as clients — perhaps not very willing clients, but still clients — rather than as would-be criminals. For example, *facilitating* compliance requires making taxation as transparent as possible to taxpayers by providing them with clear instructions, understandable forms, and assistance and information as necessary. *Monitoring* compliance requires the establishment and maintenance of taxpayer current accounts, management information systems that cover both ultimate taxpayers and third-party agents (such as banks) involved in the tax system, and appropriate and prompt procedures to detect and follow up on non-filers and delayed payments – all of which are much easier with good IT. *Improving* compliance requires a judicious mix of both these approaches as well as additional measures to deter non-compliance such as establishing a reasonable risk of detection and the effective application of penalties.

Third, since tax administration involves both tax officials and taxpayers, ideally both sides need to have something to gain if reforms are to be successful. The taxpayer service perspective emphasizes reducing taxpayer uncertainty by clarifying legal ambiguities, communicating clearly what the law is, ceasing to change it so often that no one quite knows what it is, and making it as simple and cheap as possible to comply as well as clear to all what they are paying and what they are paying for. Optimal enforcement strategy may include rewards (support) for compliers as well as penalties for non-compliers with the correct mix depending on such context-specific factors as the value attached to fairness (and its meaning), the degree of deference to authority (and the legitimacy attached to that authority), and the extent to which contributing to the finance of government activities is seen to be socially desirable (as opposed to privately desirable, as in the economic model of tax evasion, where penalties and probabilities of detecting evasion are seen as driving taxpayer compliance decisions).

Finally, although many in the political, economic, and administrative elite in most countries seem to think that the last thing any sane person should do is to give more power to 'the people' governments need revenues, taxes need to be paid, and everyone is better off if the costs of collecting those taxes are as low as possible. All states have to strike a balance between using the levers of force and persuasion to achieve a sustainable fiscal equilibrium. Even authoritarian states in which citizens have no real exit option can reduce tax costs by fostering loyalty and increasing the willingness to comply. Even the most open and liberal democracies need credible revenue enforcement mechanisms to prevent high levels of tax evasion. In all countries, citizens are more likely to pay taxes relatively willingly when they have some understanding of what is going on, feel that they are treated fairly in relation to others, and obtain something they value in return.

Undoubtedly, most people are – quite rationally – ignorant of most public policy issues. Few may be willing to put in the hard work needed to think such issues through rationally. Moreover, even with the best IT, bringing more people into the public policy process is likely to prove a slow process that may often be unduly influenced – even controlled – by those appealing more to passions than to reason. Indeed, the more the real issues facing tax policy designers and administrators are discussed publicly, the more likely are fundamental disagreements on norms to surface, thus increasing rather than reducing conflict. Moreover, policies that prove to be acceptable may not be those that favor growth, redistribution, or whatever other objective those who run things may have in mind. All this might be true. Still, even if the price of better accountability through more transparency is a less perfect tax system or a smaller public sector, anyone who thinks that people should as a rule have some say in deciding their own fates might think the price well worth paying. Similarly, even those most concerned with the importance of private control over private information may have to accept that the increasing use of IT in implementing taxation inevitably requires some degree of public access to some such information. A sustainable tax system requires striking the right balance in terms of the equilibrium of political forces. Balancing the use of technology in taxation with the appropriate degree of public transparency about what is being done and why is an essential ingredient in the mix if how states collect and spend revenues is to be considered acceptably fair by a majority of the politically relevant population.

REFERENCES

Alm, J., & Martinez-Vazquez, J. (2003). Institutions, Paradigms, and Tax Evasion in Developing and Transitional Countries. In J. Alm & J. Martinez-Vazquez (Eds.), *Public Finance in Developing and Transitional Countries* (pp. 146–178). Cheltenham, UK: Edward Elgar.

Alm, J., Martinez-Vazquez, J., & Torgler, B. (Eds.). (2010). *Developing Alternative Frameworks For Explaining Tax Compliance*. London: Routledge.

Alves, J., & Heller, P. (2013). Accountability from the Top Down? Brazil's Advances in Budget Accountability Despite a Lack of Popular Mobilization. In S. Khagram, P. de Renzio, & A. Fung (Eds.), *Open Budgets* (pp. 76–104). Washington: Brookings Institution.

Babcock, L., & Loewenstein, G. (1997). Explaining Bargaining Impasse: The Role of Self-Serving Biases. *The Journal of Economic Perspectives*, *11*(1), 109–126. doi:10.1257/jep.11.1.109

Barbone, L., Belkindas, M. V., Bettendorff, L., Bird, R., Bonch-Osmolovskiy, M., & Smart, M. (2013). Study to Quantify and Analyse the VAT Gap in the EU-27 Member States, *CASE Network Reports* No. 116/2013. Retrieved from http://ec.europa.eu/taxation_customs/resources/documents/common/publications/studies/vat-gap.pdf

Bentham, J. (1791). *Panopticon*. London: Printed for T. Payne.

Bird, R. (1982). Closing the Scissors, or the Real Public Sector Has Two Sides. *National Tax Journal*, *35*(4), 477–481.

Bird, R. (1994). *Where Do We Go From Here? Alternatives to the GST*. Toronto: KPMG Centre for Government.

Bird, R. (2005). Evaluating Public Expenditures: Does It Matter How They Are Financed? In A. Shah (Ed.), *Fiscal Management* (pp. 83–108). Washington, DC: World Bank.

Bird, R. (2010). Visibility and Accountability– Is Tax-inclusive Pricing a Good Thing? *Canadian Tax Journal*, *58*(1), 63–76.

Bird, R. (2013). Transparência e Tributaço: Algumas Reflexões Preliminares/Transparency and Taxation: Some Preliminary Reflections. In *Diniz de Santi, E. et al., Transparência fiscal e desenvolvimento: homenagem ao Professor Isaias Coelho* (pp. 171–198). Sao Paulo: Fiscosoft Editora Ltds.

Bird, R. (2014). *Global Taxes and International Taxation: Mirage and Reality*. Washington, DC: International Tax and Investment Center.

Bird, R., & Casanegra de Jantscher, M. (Eds.). (1992, September 15). *Improving Tax Administration in Developing Countries*. Washington: International Monetary Fund.

Bird, R., & Ebel, R. (Eds.). (2007). *Fiscal Fragmentation in Decentralized Countries: Subsidiarity, Solidarity, and Asymmetry*. Cheltenham, UK: Edward Elgar. doi:10.4337/9781781007617

Bird, R., & Jun, J. (2007). Earmarking in Theory and Korean Practice. In S. Phua (Ed.), Excise Taxation in Asia (pp, 49-86). Singapore: National University of Singapore.

Bird, R., Martinez-Vazquez, J., & Torgler, B. (2008). Tax Effort in Developing Countries and High Income Countries: The Impact of Corruption, Voice and Accountability. *Economic Analysis & Policy*, *38*(1), 55–71. doi:10.1016/S0313-5926(08)50006-3

Bird, R., & Slack, E. (2014, December). Local Taxation and Local Expenditure in Developing Countries: Strengthening the Wicksellian Connection. *Public Administration and Development*, *34*(5), 359–369. doi:10.1002/pad.1695

Bird, R., & Wallace, S. (2004). Is It Really So Hard To Tax the Hard-To-Tax? The Context and Role of Presumptive Taxes. In J.R. Alm, J. Martinez-Vazquez, & S. Wallace (Eds.), Taxing the Hard-To-Tax: Lessons from Theory and Practice (pp. 121-158). Amsterdam: North-Holland. doi:10.1016/S0573-8555(04)68806-7

Bird, R., & Zolt, E. (2008). Technology and Taxation in Developing Countries: From Hand to Mouse. *National Tax Journal*, *61*(4, Part 2), 791–821. doi:10.17310/ntj.2008.4S.02

Bird, R., & Zolt, E. (2014). Taxation and Inequality in the Americas: Changing the Fiscal Contract? In R. Bird & J. Martinez-Vazquez (Eds.), *Taxation and Development: The Weakest Link?* (pp. 193–237). Cheltenham, UK: Edward Elgar. doi:10.4337/9781783474332.00014

Bracco, E., Porcelli, F., & Redoano, M. (2013, February). Political competition, tax salience and accountability: Theory and some evidence from Italy. *CESifo Working Paper* No.4167.

Brautigam, D., Fjeldstad, O., & Moore, M. (Eds.). (2007). *Taxation and state-building in developing countries*. Cambridge: Cambridge University Press.

Brin, D. (1998). *The Transparent Society: Will Technology Force us to Choose between Privacy and Freedom?* New York, NY: Perseus Books.

Chetty, R. (2009, August). The Simple Economics of Salience and Taxation. *Working Paper 14246*, National Bureau of Economic Research, Cambridge, MA.

Chetty, R., Looney, A., & Kroft, K. (2007, August). Salience and Taxation: Theory and Evidence (Working Paper 13330). National Bureau of Economic Research, Cambridge, MA.

Cummings, R., Martinez-Vazquez, J., McKee, M., & Torgler, B. (2009). Tax Morale Affects Tax Compliance: Evidence from Surveys and an Artefactual Field Experiment. *Journal of Economic Behavior & Organization*, *70*(3), 447–457. doi:10.1016/j.jebo.2008.02.010

EY. (2014). Focus: transparency. Tax insights for business leaders. Retrieved from https://taxinsights.ey-vx.com/ey-ti-ed-1/pdf/ey-tax12-client-version-141127-(2).pdf

Finkelstein, A. (2009). EZtax: Tax Salience and Tax Rates. *The Quarterly Journal of Economics*, *124*(3), 969–1010. doi:10.1162/qjec.2009.124.3.969

Foucault, M. (1977). *Discipline and Punish*. London: Allen Lane.

Fox, W., & Murray, M. (2014). Taxing the Small: Fostering Tax Compliance among Small Enterprises in Developing Countries. In R. Bird & J. Martinez-Vazquez (Eds.), *Taxation and Development: the Weakest Link* (pp. 170–192). Cheltenham, UK: Edward Elgar. doi:10.4337/9781783474332.00013

Frey, B., & Feld, L. (2002, August). Deterrence and Morale in Taxation: An Empirical Analysis (Working Paper No. 760). *CESifo*.

Gemmell, N., & Hasseldine, J. (2012). The Tax Gap: A Methodological Review (Working Paper 09/2012). Victoria University, New Zealand.

Grinberg, I. (2013). Taxing Capital Income In Emerging Countries: Will FACTA Open The Door? *World Tax Journal,* October, 325-367.

Hindriks, J., Keen, M., & Muthoo, A. (1999). Corruption, Extortion, and Evasion. *Journal of Public Economics*, *74*(3), 395–430. doi:10.1016/S0047-2727(99)00030-4

House of Commons Treasury Committee. (2012). *Closing the Tax Gap: HMRC's Record at Ensuring Tax Compliance.* Twenty-ninth Report of Session 2010-12, March. London: The Stationery Office Limited.

Hutton, E., Thackray, M., & Wingender, P. (2014). *Uganda: Revenue Administration Gap Analysis Program – The Value-Added Tax Gap*. Washington, DC: International Monetary Fund.

Khagram, S., de Renzio, P., & Fung, A. (Eds.). (2013). *Open Budgets*. Washington: Brookings Institution.

Martinez-Vazquez, J., Vulovic, V., & Liu, Y. (2011). Direct versus Indirect Taxation: Trends, Theory, And Economic Significance. In E. Albi & J. Martinez-Vazquez (Eds.), *The Elgar Guide to Tax Systems* (pp. 37–92). Cheltenham, UK: Edward Elgar. doi:10.4337/9780857933898.00009

Mill, J. S. (1900). Principles of Political Economy (A. Haley, Ed.). (Vols. 1–2). New York: The Colonial Press. (Original work published 1848)

Mirrlees, J., Adam, S., Besley, T., Blundell, R., Bond, S., Chote, R., & Poterba, J. et al. (2011). *Tax by Design: The Mirrlees Review*. Oxford, UK: Oxford University Press.

Moore, M. (2008). How does Taxation Affect the Quality of Governance? *IDS working paper*. Brighton: IDS.

Moore, M. (2014). Revenue Reform and Statebuilding in Anglophone Africa. *World Development*, *60*(8), 99–112. doi:10.1016/j.worlddev.2014.03.020

Morag, A. (1965). *On Taxes and Inflation*. New York: Random House.

OECD. (2013a). *A Step Change in Tax Transparency. OECD report for the G8 summit*. June, Lough Erne, Enniskillen.

OECD. (2013b). Tax Administration. Paris.

OECD. (2013c). *Addressing Base Erosion and Profit Shifting*. Paris.

Rabushka, A. (2008). *Taxation in Colonial America*. Princeton, NJ: Princeton University Press.

Ribeiro, M. (2014). E-fisco: The Conflict between Revenue Collection Efficiency and the Fundamental Right to Privacy: The Experience of Brazil. *Tax Administration Review*, *37*, 70–86.

Sausgruber, R., & Tyran, J. (2008, October). Tax Salience, Voting, and Deliberation (Discussion Paper No. 08-31). Department of Economics, University of Copenhagen.

Schneider, F., & Enste, D. (2000). Shadow Economies: Size, Causes, and Consequences. *Journal of Economic Literature*, *38*(1), 77–114. doi:10.1257/jel.38.1.77

Shoup, C. (1969). *Public finance*. Chicago: Aldine Publishing.

Slemrod, J., & Gillitzer, C. (2014). *Tax systems*. Cambridge, MA: MIT Press. doi:10.7551/mitpress/9780262026727.001.0001

Slemrod, J., & Yitzhaki, S. (2002). Tax Avoidance, Evasion, and Administration. In A. Auerbach & M. Feldstein (Eds.), *Handbook of Public Economics* (Vol. 3). Elsevier Science.

Surrey, S. (1969). Complexity and the Internal Revenue Code: The Problem of the Management of Tax Detail. *Law and Contemporary Problems*, *34*(4), 673–710. doi:10.2307/1190905

Tanzi, V. (1970). International Tax Burdens: A Study of Tax Ratios in the OECD Countries. In *Taxation: A Radical Approach*. London: Institute for Economic Affairs.

Van Brederode, R. (Ed.). (2012). *Science, Technology and Taxation*. Kluwer Law International.

Vazquez-Caro, J., & Bird, R. (2011). Benchmarking Tax Administrations in Developing Countries: A Systemic Approach. *eJournal of Tax Research, 9*(1), 5-37.

Webber, C., & Wildavsky, A. (1983). *History of Taxation and Expenditure in the Western World*. New York: Simon and Schuster.

ENDNOTES

1 The lack of tax transparency has recently been highlighted especially with respect to international taxation (OECD 2013a; EY 2014). More generally, as recently stressed in the Mirrlees report in the UK, transparency is not only "an important part of a good tax system" but also "a virtue in itself" (Mirrlees *et al.*, 2011, pp. 34 and 123, respectively).

2 Some aspects of the relationship between taxation and technology are discussed in van Brederode (2012); information on the use of IT in tax administration in OECD countries may be found in OECD (2013b).

3 An earlier version of some of the ideas set out here may be found in Bird (2013).

4 An even more extreme reaction might be to create a new country: Rabushka (2008, p. 868), for example, goes so far as to conclude an exhaustive recent review of taxation in colonial America with the unequivocal statement that "The American Revolution....was a tax revolt, first and foremost." Some of the fiscal aspects of separatist movements are discussed further in Bird and Ebel (2007) while the various ways, short of fleeing the country, that people may be 'hard to tax' are covered in Bird and Wallace (2004).

5 While there are many good discussions of these issues in the literature, one of the best remains Surrey (1969). Of course, most countries make matters much worse by adding many largely unnecessary and often undesirable complications to the tax system, in effect often turning it into a quasi-spending system through tax incentives and the like but this important issue is not further discussed here.

6 The most important actions so far taken with respect to changing the current system focus on improving the transparency of international fiscal transactions by assessing the extent to which countries comply with international standards in terms of 'fiscal transparency' and, it is hoped, by implementing a proposed standard for the automatic international exchange of information (see http://www.oecd.org/tax/transparency/; accessed August 10, 2014). Some (Grinberg, 2013) are optimistic and think this process will lead to important changes in outcomes; others (Bird, 2014) are less optimistic.

7 Babcock and Lowenstein (1997, p. 122). The approach suggested in the text is developed further in Bird (2014).

8 "If all taxes were direct, taxation would be much more perceived than at present; and there would be a security which now there is not, for economy in the public expenditure (Mill [1848] 1900, p. 368)." Mill clearly understands 'direct' taxes to be those that are visible to people and indirect taxes to be those that are not. Unfortunately, much of the discussion of the direct-indirect tax mix in the literature (as recently ably summarized by Martinez-Vazquez, Vulovic and Liu, 2008) neither defines these terms in this way nor considers the potential importance and relevance of tax visibility: but see Tanzi (1970) and Bird (1982).

9 As Mill ([1848], 1900, p. 367) noted, "an Englishman dislikes, not so much the payment as the act of paying." Such attitudes seem to be invariant to time and place to at least some extent: Bird (1994, p. 13) reports a survey indicating that 75% of Canadians preferred to have the GST (Canada's VAT) included in the price and concluded that "Canadians may not agree on how much they like the government, the tax structure, or the GST, but they agree they cannot stand to be reminded of the GST every time they make a purchase."

10 For two interesting recent studies, see Sausgruber and Tyran (2008), who report experimental evidence from Denmark suggesting that how people vote is influenced by the salience of taxes but that deliberation and experience may reduce the initial bias, and Bracco, Porcelli and Redoano (2013), who report that municipal politicians in Italy are less likely to impose more salient taxes the stronger the political competition they face. There is much work still to be done in this area.

11 See, for example, Cummings *et al.* (2009) and Alm, Martinez-Vazquez and Torgler (2010) as well as the broader review of these issues from a governance perspective in Moore (2008, 2014). Another important aspect of how 'fair' people think taxes are in procedural terms relates to their perception of not only the fairness of the additional costs shifted to taxpayers by the move to the new tax technology discussed next but also the extent to which they accept as fair the increased ease with which the authorities can 'invade' their privacy. Although this issue is not discussed in detail here, an interesting recent evaluation of the situation in Brazil may be found in Ribiero (2014) and the general issue is discussed further in Bird and Zolt (2008).

12 For two quite different earlier explorations of this approach, see Bird (2005) and Bird and Slack (2014).

13 For a detailed discussion of the working and rationales of the different types of earmarking, see Bird and Jun (2007).

14 On this broader political interpretation of 'fiscal contracting', see Bird and Zolt (2014).

15 See Moore (2008, 2014), Brautigam, Fjeldstad and Moore (2007), Alm and Martinez-Vazquez (2003), and Bird, Martinez-Vazquez and Torgler (2008) for further discussion of some aspects of these big issues.

16 Ribiero (2014) labels this the 'Tax Panoptic' citing Michel Foucault (1977). Interestingly, Foucault himself drew this idea from Jeremy Bentham's (1791) famous model of an ideal prison (the Panopticon) in which the daily activities of all residents took place in spokes radiating from a central hub from which the authorities can observe them. The development and spread of IT has moved the real world in which many now live much closer to such a world – the 'transparent society' (Brin, 1998) that some fear (a prison?) but others may welcome. (See also note 11 above.)

17 As OECD (2013a) shows, most such countries are in Europe, although a few countries in other regions – though not as yet MENA – have also moved in this direction in recent years.

18 It should perhaps be mentioned that measuring specific tax gaps like the VAT gap in the EU (Barbone *et al.*, 2013) is a quite different exercise than measuring the 'hidden' or 'shadow' economy (Schneider and Enste 2000) although both are related exercises in estimating the potentially knowable unknown and both often make use of similar data. Gemmell and Hassledine (2012) suggest that, although the measurement errors of hidden economy estimates (and aggregate tax gap measures based on similar methods) are unknown, these errors may easily be so large as to swamp the apparent year-to-year changes in such estimates.

19 The uses and limitations of benchmarking tax administration are discussed in detail in Vazquez-Caro and Bird (2011).

20 An interesting question is whether those who are penalized for tax delinquency should be publicly identified. Some countries (e.g. Norway) have made much tax information, including penalties, public, although most do not, citing privacy concerns. The scanty empirical literature on the effects of public disclosure provides no clear evidence of its effect, positive or negative, on compliance (Slemrod & Gillitzer, 2014).

21 For example, by analyzing tax gaps not only from the 'top down' as is usually done but also from the 'bottom up' as seen, for example, in the sectoral approach of Hutton, Thackray and Wingender (2014).

22 For a recent interesting discussion – at times almost a 'dialogue of the deaf– between tax administrators and their critics about such issues, see the recent UK committee hearings on measuring the 'tax gap', as reported in House of Commons Treasury Committee (2012). A similar less public discussion has recently taken place in Canada with respect to audits focusing on whether the 'political' activities of certain charities exceed the strict limits set in the law. On the broader issue of the relation between IT transparency and social and legal concerns about privacy, see Bird and Zolt (2008).

23 See Frey and Feld (2002) – although they apply this argument to taxpayers, not tax officials.

Chapter 3
The Difficulties of Achieving Successful Tax Reform

Simon James
University of Exeter Business School, UK

ABSTRACT

This chapter sets out the issues that should be considered in developing successful tax reform. Economic theory makes an essential contribution to the development of tax reform, incorporating issues of both economic efficiency and equity. However, other theoretical considerations demonstrate that successful tax design may be considerably more difficult than seems to be widely thought. In addition, there are matters of tax administration and compliance that have to be taken into account. The changing socio-economic environment within which tax systems have to operate as well, as the political process of tax reform, are also important. Finally, the chapter shows how to develop a systematic approach which can incorporate the many important issues that should be included in developing successful tax reform.

INTRODUCTION

There is a constant stream of proposals for tax reform in Europe, the MENA Region and elsewhere. Some of the more comprehensive from around the world include the Mirrlees Review (Mirrlees, 2010, 2011) in the UK, the Final Report of the President's Advisory Panel for Federal Tax Reform (2005) in the USA and the Henry Review (2010) in Australia. However achieving successful tax reform is neither a simple nor an easy task. Bird and Oldman (1990) have suggested that the best approach to tax reform is one that takes:

into account taxation theory, empirical evidence, and political and administrative realities and blends them with a good dose of local knowledge and a sound appraisal of the current macroeconomic and international situation to produce a feasible set of proposals sufficiently attractive to be implemented and sufficiently robust to withstand changing times, within reason, and still produce beneficial results (Bird & Oldman, 1990, p. 3).

DOI: 10.4018/978-1-5225-0053-7.ch003

Successful tax reform can be a surprisingly complex process (Bird, 2004) even if there appears to be only a simple objective. The economic characteristics of an ideal tax system are well known and such a tax system might be summarised as being economically efficient and equitable. However, tax systems everywhere deviate from such ideal characteristics, often for very good reasons. To begin with, drawing on economic theory, it becomes clear that the theory of taxation does not necessarily imply that the process of tax design is a simple one. Indeed the literature on optimal taxation, the theory of the second best and public choice theory raise many issues that should be considered. For instance, the theory of second best offers the insight that the gains from a proposed reform depend on a much wider range of circumstances than are usually taken into account. Other areas that may not always get the attention they deserve are tax administration and tax compliance risks. Once a proposal has been developed, the process of successful implementation presents a new range of challenges. However, even that is not the end of the story. After a tax reform has been implemented, as Bird and Oldman (1990) suggest, the reform should be capable of withstanding changing times. The whole process of developing tax policy involves taking into account, not only of matters of immediate concern, but also a whole range of relevant factors in the wider context of tax reform. The aspects that should be considered include not just purely economic matters, but also political, social and technological issues. Furthermore, the situation is not a simple case of comparative statics – a comparison between presumed stable equilibria before and after the change, but a dynamic one in which different forces influence the progress of any reform in different ways over time.

It should also be pointed out that taxation is often much more than a powerful method of raising revenue. It is also a major instrument of government policy used to influence the distribution of income as well as discouraging some activities through additional taxation and encouraging others through tax concessions. Such tax concessions are known as 'tax expenditures', a term coined by Stanley S. Surrey in 1967 while Assistant Secretary for Tax Policy in the US Treasury Department. His description was that tax expenditures are those provisions:

containing special exemptions, exclusions, and other tax benefits [which] were really methods of providing governmental financial assistance. These special provisions were not part of the structure required for the income tax itself, but were instead government expenditures made through the tax system (Surrey, 1973, p. vii).

The use by governments of the tax system in a variety of different ways is also something that has to be taken into account in developing tax policy itself.

The purpose of this chapter is therefore to examine the range of issues involved in the nature, context and process of tax reform. It begins by introducing the context of European and MENA countries in general terms. The chapter then examines economic criteria for assessing the merits of a particular tax or tax reform, primarily economic efficiency and equity and goes on to other theoretical contributions to the development of tax reform which are less frequently taken into account, namely optimal tax theory, the theory of the second best, and public choice theory. The chapter then raises significant issues regarding tax administration and compliance. It examines the context of tax reform and the process of tax reform itself which is more complex than may be commonly thought. In order to establish a comprehensive approach to dealing with the entire range of relevant factors, a systematic approach to tax reform is presented. Finally some conclusions are drawn.

TAX REFORM IN EUROPE AND THE MENA REGION

Europe and the MENA Region contain a wide range of approaches to tax reform and circumstances in which they are applied. One of the key factors in Europe is the European Union (EU) though to some extent the tax policy of the EU is developed at the level of Member States rather than for the EU as a whole. In its communication regarding EU Tax Policy Strategy, the European Commission (2014) repeated its belief that Member States are free to choose the tax systems they prefer and there is no need for general harmonisation of European tax systems. Nevertheless, within that general position the main priority of EU tax policy is eliminating tax obstacles to cross-border economic activity and this requirement can clearly limit the ability of each Member State to develop its own tax system in isolation from those in the rest of the EU. Other priorities of EU tax policy are countering harmful tax competition and promoting greater cooperation between tax administrations in terms of control and countering fraud.

There is, of course, no equivalent of such general policies across all MENA countries though, as pointed out in the recommendations of the *MENA-OECD Investment Programme* (OECD, 2005) MENA countries have been reforming their tax systems to improve efficiency, encourage investment and stabilize revenue yield. In a later report, the OECD (2008, p. 245) concluded that MENA countries offer a wide range of fiscal and financial incentives to promote specific policies but that these posed challenges for policy makers in attempts to simplify tax systems as well as 'eliminate tax distortions, remove unnecessary administrative and compliance costs, increase transparency and improve government's capacity to generate revenue'. To achieve these aims successfully it is helpful to develop a systematic approach to tax reform which is the purpose of this chapter.

One issue that is sometimes raised is whether there are significant differences regarding taxation in 'developing countries' as compared to countries that may be considered more developed in economic terms. Of course, it should be pointed out that descriptions such as less developed or more developed countries have attracted criticism but, in any event, the basic principles of tax reform are widely applicable. Historically, economists have examined the effects of taxation on economic growth and, following the development of Keynesian economics, the role of taxation in promoting economic stability but both of these matters are of general interest. Also, the effects of taxation on economic efficiency and the distribution of income across households and regions are important regardless of a country's position regarding economic development. Both of these matters are of concern to the EU as well as MENA countries. There are some areas which may be of particular importance in some countries such as political and administrative constraints on tax reform and policies for increasing host-country returns from the exploitation of natural resources but again such the relevance of such matters is not confined to a particular group of countries. Finally, globalisation affects tax design in both European and MENA countries and, as with many other relevant factors, may be included in the process of developing tax reform presented below and the best place to start is by examining the criteria for assessing the advantages and disadvantages of a particular tax or tax reform.

CRITERIA FOR A GOOD TAX OR TAX REFORM

The main criteria involved in the design of a good tax system are efficiency, equity and some macroeconomic aspects. A useful way of examining these issues is using Musgrave's (1959) framework in his classic Public Finance text. Musgrave summarised the economic justification for the public sector in a three branch model consisting of the allocation branch, the distribution branch and the stabilisation branch and these deal respectively with the analysis of economic efficiency, the distribution of income and wealth and macroeconomic aspects. The design of a good tax or tax reform should draw on analysis from each of these three branches, together with some important issues of tax administration. They are summarised here and also discussed at greater length by James and Nobes (2014).

The Allocation Branch

The allocation branch is concerned with economic efficiency, essentially allocating resources so that output is maximised and consumers obtain the goods and services they value the most. In economic theory this is analysed in terms of Pareto efficiency - named after the Italian economist Vilfredo Pareto. A Pareto efficient output, sometimes known as a Pareto-optimal output, is where no further efficiency gains can be made that will make one individual better off without making someone else worse off. Inefficiency exists if resources could be re-allocated so that at least one person could be made better off without anyone else being made worse off. The implications for taxation depend on how efficiently particular markets are working. If markets are working efficiently, a good tax in terms of efficiency is one that does not distort choices so that decisions are made for economic reasons rather than tax reasons. If a tax does distort choices, it is said to impose an *excess burden* because, in addition to the tax paid, it becomes an obstacle to individuals consuming the combination of goods and services they value the most. Subject to a number of limitations and exceptions, in an efficient market it might be expected that taxes with a wider base are less likely to be distortionary than taxes with a narrower base.

Another conclusion is that taxes imposed on outputs that are inelastic in supply or demand, in other words the sales of which change relatively little when price changes, are also likely to be less distortionary than taxes on goods and services that are more price elastic in supply or demand. However, if a market economy is not working efficiently, it may be possible to use taxation to improve economic decisions. For example, the consumption of some products such as alcohol and tobacco might involve extra costs that consumers would not take fully into account, but which might be reflected by taxation. This possibility has led to a whole range of 'corrective' taxes being introduced in areas where markets are not considered to be working efficiently. Taxation is not only used to discourage the consumption of some goods but tax concessions may be used where the government wishes to encourage other things. One example is tax relief for saving in a pension scheme to encourage individuals to make provision for their old age.

An important aspect regarding efficiency are possible tax effects on the supply of factors of production, that is the willingness of individuals to work, save and invest and for firms to contribute to the economy in the most appropriate ways. The effects of taxation in these contexts are not always obvious. For instance, in terms of the supply of labour, economic theory suggests there may be a 'substitution effect' which may lead some individuals to substitute other activities or leisure for paid employment which is taxed. However, there may also be an 'income effect' which recognises that taxation reduces individuals' spending power and this may encourage them to work more because they are worse off. The substitution and income effects therefore may work in opposite directions and the final outcome is theoretically uncertain. This has led to a great deal of empirical research on the effects of taxation on the supply of factors of production and generated a number of implications for tax design.

The Distribution Branch

The distribution branch of public finance, as Musgrave (2008, p. 237) describes it, leaves 'the safe haven of Pareto optimality' and moves into the less tangible area of distributive justice. It is concerned with the redistribution of income and wealth towards that which society considers more equitable. What the distribution of income and wealth should actually be and what constitutes a fair tax are, of course, at least partly a matter of opinion. This is the aspect of tax policy that has provoked the most adverse responses in taxpayers – see, for example, James (2014). In terms of the revenue side of public finance, ideas regarding the fairness of taxation have frequently been based on concepts related to ability to pay and there has been much discussion in terms of the sacrifice of taxation and whether fair taxation should be related to equal absolute, equal proportional or equal marginal sacrifice. Another approach has been that taxes should be paid in line with the benefits gained from public expenditure but the nature of government expenditure is that it is often not directly traceable to individual recipients. The benefit approach is also inappropriate with respect to spending on welfare payments of various sorts - which makes up a very large part of modern government expenditure.

The distributional impact of taxes is also important. The study of the 'incidence of taxation' examines how the burden of taxes may be passed on to others through changes in prices and quantities. For example, taxes on goods and services may be formally levied on suppliers but they may be able to pass some of the burden on to their customers through higher prices. It was once thought that taxes such as income tax could not be passed on. However if, say, the supply of labour changes as a result of income tax, part of the burden might be then be passed on to consumers. Similarly if income taxes affect investment decisions then this may also determine how a tax affects other parts of the economy. Sometimes the incidence of taxation may have unexpected effects. For instance, a tax levied on 'luxury goods' in order to increase the tax paid by the rich might also have adverse effects on the employment prospects and incomes of poorer people involved in the production of such goods. More generally, a tax on one good might affect the demand for other goods and services and this could work through to affect the supply and demand of factors of production in different industries. There is also the phenomenon of 'tax capitalisation.' As the capital values of assets are influenced by the income from those assets, when a tax alters the net income from an asset, its capital value is likely to change as well. In considering the distributional aspects in developing tax reform, it is necessary also to consider the impact of a tax change on other parts of the economy.

The Stabilisation Branch

The stabilisation branch is concerned with the effects of taxes on macroeconomic variables which may be relevant to the design of particular taxes. Not all taxes are equally important in this regard and to be useful instruments of stabilisation policy they usually have to be imposed on a relevant variable such as consumption or income and to be sufficiently large to make a significant difference at the macroeconomic level.

Economic cycles have serious disadvantages – not only in economic downturns when, of course, unemployment (of capital as well as labour) may rise but also in boom times when inflation and other problems can emerge. So taxes may be used to try to achieve stable levels of employment and prices but such aims may be hard to achieve. This is because, of course, it is difficult to anticipate macroeconomic changes and the need for a stabilising response. Even after a government has decided it must take action, it may still take a significant amount of time to implement a tax change and then even more time for the economy to respond to that change. The result could be that the policy is not only ineffective but may actually increase rather than decrease economic fluctuations. Indeed Ben Slimane and Ben Tahar (2010, p. 50) found strong evidence that, instead of being counter-cyclical, fiscal policy is procyclical in MENA countries, with fiscal policy being expansionary in good rather than bad economic times. There is less evidence for this in European countries though there is still room for improvement. Golinelli and Momigliano (2009) surveyed the recent economic literature relating to the cyclical response of fiscal policies in the euro area. The results of their work are complex but it seemed that introducing budgetary rules limiting discretionary responses by governments might improve the stabilisation role of government and also achieve sounder public finances.

One feature of a tax system that might improve the effectiveness of stabilisation policy are automatic responses to changes in the level of economic activity. Thus when an economy moves into recession, the fall in national income should be partly offset by a fall in tax receipts. The most important example of such 'built-in flexibility' is that a progressive tax system will automatically cause tax receipts to change proportionately more than any original change in national income thus cushioning a recession and dampening a boom.

The Transition from Principles to Policy

The principles of efficiency and equity are major elements for successful tax design. However, there are other important theoretical dimensions which should also be considered if a proposed tax reform is to achieve a more comprehensive approach to the development of policy. Three of these dimensions are optimal taxation, the theory of the second best and the public choice approach and these are examined in turn.

Optimal Taxation

The work on optimal taxation attempts to combine the analysis of tax efficiency with questions of equity in taxation - which is not always a straightforward process. Heady (1993, p. 15) surveyed the optimal taxation literature specifically 'attempting to answer the question of whether, and to what extent, the literature on optimal taxation can provide guidance in the practical determination of tax policy'. It seems clear that the study of optimal taxation has not reached a stage where it can successfully incorporate the range of relevant factors indicated by Bird and Oldman (1990) above. Alm (1996) suggested that existing attempts to formulate an 'optimal tax system' were largely irrelevant to practical tax design because they failed to include many aspects involving fiscal and social institutions. Alm suggested that many of these could be incorporated in an optimal tax framework but acknowledged that it would never be possible to include all the 'incredible complexity' that must be considered in the design and reform of tax systems. In looking at gaps between optimal taxation and policy, Mankiw *et al.* (2009, p. 172) raised the possibility that 'the broader tradition in public finance includes...ideas that are often ignored in modern optimal tax theory'. The lesson from the optimal taxation literature seems to be that the development of successful tax reform is likely to require more than basic economic analysis.

Theory of Second Best

A related development is the theory of the second best. This presents a clear view of the complexity involved in moving from an ideal type of tax which meets the criteria of efficiency and equity as described above, through the range factors described by Bird and Oldman (1990), to a successful tax reform. The theory of the second best was established by Lipsey and Lancaster (1956, p. 12) who demonstrated that it 'is *not* true that a situation in which more, but not all, of the optimum conditions are fulfilled is necessarily, or is even likely to be, superior to a situation in which fewer are fulfilled'. Furthermore, if one of the Paretian conditions is unachievable then a second best optimum may be reached by departing from all the other optimum conditions. Moreover, there are no general conclusions about the direction or magnitude of the other changes that would be necessary to achieve a second best optimum. This may sound rather complex and counter-intuitive so a simple example may be helpful. Suppose a situation where two economic distortions are cancelling each other out, for example a market where there is only a single supplier (monopoly) selling to a single buyer (monopsony). The first best solution would be to remove both distortions but, if that were not possible and only one were removed, the price might move away from the optimum position. The theory of the second best indicates it might be better to have both distortions rather than only one. Lipsey and Lancaster (1956) actually use a tax illustration where a tax on one good distorts prices between that good and other goods. To achieve a second best optimum, a system of taxes on other goods and services would be needed, some of which would be less than and some more than the original tax and in some cases a subsidy might be needed. The lesson from 'second best' theory is that an 'obvious improvement' to taxation may not be so when the wider context is taken into account. Lipsey (1997, p. 362) made clear 'the cautionary warning from second best theory that any policy may have unexpected and undesirable consequences in apparently unrelated parts of the economy that need to be watched for and mitigated where necessary.'

The Public Choice Approach

Public choice has been described as the application of economic methodology to the study of politics. Mueller (2003) comprehensively examines the public choice approach and collective decision-making processes. The public choice literature covers topics such as the behaviour of bureaucracies, interest groups and political parties as well as electoral systems and different constitutional arrangements. Needless to say, this provides additional factors that might influence the success or otherwise of particular tax reforms. However, as Holcombe (1998, p. 359) concluded: despite 'the insights the public choice perspective offers, most analysis of tax policy does not take public choice considerations into account'. Clearly such important issues should be included in the development of tax policy.

TAX ADMINISTRATION AND TAX COMPLIANCE

In moving to more practical aspects, there are important issues involved in tax administration and compliance: the 'administrative realities' as described by Bird and Oldman (1990). Goode (1981, p. 249), points out that this area is properly dominated by insights from the theory and practice of management, together with legal and political considerations. Tradition and expediency may be significant factors as well. There may also be particular aspects that require attention, for example corruption in tax administration (Chandler & Wilde, 1992). However, Goode and others have examined economic aspects of tax administration, sometimes in terms of market-orientated solutions to problems and sometimes in terms of the administrative and compliance costs of taxes (see for example Sandford *et al.*, 1989). Nevertheless, equity and other matters have also been taken into account. In this context, as in others, simple reforms may be totally inadequate. Klepper and Nagin (1989, p. 239) suggest that a policy innovation designed, for example, to reduce one form of non-compliance might result in taxpayers transferring their non-compliance activities to take advantage of a now superior alternative opportunity. Simply assessing only the direct impact of that measure might be inadequate and misleading. More generally, a full evaluation of any aspect of compliance policy should take account of its effects on each of the relevant areas.

The literature on tax compliance is considerable – see for example, Andreoni *et al.* (1998), Fischer *et al.* (1992), Jackson and Milliron, (1986), James and Edwards (2010) and Richardson and Sawyer (2001). In the past, work on tax compliance has often been based on the effects of detection and penalties. This approach has to be followed with caution since an over-zealous policy of enforcing the law may produce undesirable and unnecessary side effects. For instance, at one stage the German tax system was reported by both Schmölders (1970) and Strümpel (1969) as being very rigid in its assessment procedures which led to an effective but expensive and confrontational system. The result 'of the relatively coercive tax-enforcement techniques is the high degree of alienation from the state…[which] negatively influences the willingness to co-operate' (Strümpel, 1969, p. 29). There may also be a reluctance to undertake legitimate commercial activities if there is a risk of heavy handed treatment from the tax authorities. The vast majority of the work on compliance has concentrated on taxpayers but the role of the tax authority is also important. Kirchler *et al.* (2006 and 2008) concluded that treating taxpayers reasonably and fairly, explaining rules and decisions and providing reliable information may not only improve how the tax system operates but may also lead to an increasing willingness on the part of taxpayers to comply with the spirit of the law.

More generally, as Posner (2000, p. 1782) suggested, some further explanation for tax compliance behaviour is required because penalties are usually modest for ordinary tax convictions and the chances of detection are low but most individuals still pay their taxes. In recent years tax compliance has increasingly been analysed more comprehensively and account taken of wider considerations. So, for instance, the OECD's (2004, p. 37) *Compliance Risk Management* cites the analysis of James *et al.,* (2001) which identifies the traditional approach to compliance based on penalties but also a behavioural approach which draws on a fuller understanding of individual behaviour with respect to taxation (see, for example, James, 2006). The European Commission's *Risk Management Guide for Tax Administrations* (2006, p. 6) states

Risk analysis also involves the why question: why is the taxpayer behaving in a particular fashion. This is important because it contributes to the assessment and the choice of the most efficient and effective form of treatment.

This approach has led to the development of more sophisticated compliance strategies so that the official response to problems of compliance may depend on the taxpayer's motivation and circumstances. Thus, for example, those who seem determined to evade taxation might be subject to the full force of the law, those who are less committed to tax evasion might be deterred by greater detection and those who are willing to comply but finding it difficult might be offered more and better assistance or the system may be changed to make it easier to comply. In this way action to enforce compliance can be tailored to be forceful where appropriate but supportive when that might achieve better results. An early pioneer in this approach was the Australian Tax Office but similar features may be seen elsewhere such as the UK where the penalty imposed on taxpayers' mistakes depends on whether the error was 'careless', 'deliberate' or deliberate and concealed' and whether the taxpayer was prompted or not in disclosing the error.

The OECD (2004, p. 8) views compliance risk management as a 'structured process for the systematic identification, assessment, ranking and treatment of tax compliance risks', This, of course, covers risks such as individuals not registering for tax, under-reporting incomes and claiming deductions to which they are not entitled. The OECD summarises how a revenue authority may develop a risk management strategy as follows:

- Identify risks
- Assess and prioritise risks
- Analyse compliance behaviour (causes, options for treatment)
- Determine treatment strategies
- Plan and implement stages.

As the OECD (2004, p. 8) makes clear, such an approach is consistent with management literature more generally and is developed further in section 7 below. The OECD (2009) also states that large businesses increasingly consider tax risk management to be a specific element of corporate governance.

The European Commission's *Risk Management Guide for Tax Administrations* (2006, p. 13) described risk management as 'taking deliberate action to improve the odds' of good outcomes and reducing the odds of bad outcomes. It is not a formula that will always produce the right result but is 'a way of working and thinking that will give better answers to better questions'. Risks consist of the characteristics of 'vulnerability, severity or significance and relative occurrence or frequency'. Finally Silvani and Baer (1997, p. 31) conclude that, while reform is not easy, fundamental reform to improve the effectiveness of tax administration is possible.

THE CONTEXT OF TAX REFORM

In the extract cited at the beginning of the paper, Bird and Oldman (1990) pointed out that reform also should take account of political and administrative realities together with 'a good dose of local knowledge and a sound appraisal of the current macroeconomic and international situation'. All this includes government policy more generally as well as the economic, social and political environment both nationally and, increasingly, internationally (James & Edwards, 2008). An analysis of the environment within which tax systems have to operate indicates trends towards greater complexity which are a major factor in the increasing complexity of tax systems and reforms (James, 1999). Economic variables range from increasing real incomes, which are often drawn from different sources, to an increasing variety of complex financial instruments. Social variables include rising levels of education, which may encourage taxpayers to take a greater and more effective interest in their tax affairs and demographic variables including changing family structure and increasing numbers of older people, who often have complicated financial affairs with a variety of investments and pension income. Political variables include those that result in the expansion of public expenditure in many countries which means taxes have to be ever more carefully designed to be acceptable to taxpayers as the tax burden rises. Technological factors have also presented further considerations in the design of tax reforms, in some ways making things easier, as with electronic filing, but in other ways, as with some of the implications of electronic commerce, adding further challenges. Globalisation has had an increasing impact on tax policy. It has been defined in various ways and Bhagwati suggested that:

[e]conomic globalisation constitutes integration of national economies into the international economy through trade, direct foreign investment (by corporations and multinationals) short-term capital flows, international flows of workers and humanity generally and flows of technology (2004, p. 3).

This, of course, has major implications for the design of national tax systems. As Sawyer observed:

With the increasing globalisation of business activity, mobility of capital (and to a lesser degree individuals), and the blurring of jurisdictional boundaries, the setting of domestic tax policy has taken on an increasingly international application. As a consequence of this international dimension, tax policy and practice cannot, or at least should not, be developed by a country in isolation of the international implications (2004, p. 8).

Taxation is inevitably affected by increasing economic interdependence and mobility together with the possibility of tax competition by countries attempt to attract resources through favourable tax arrangements (for example, see Hines and Summers, 2009 and Tanzi, 1996).

One possible constraint on tax reform in Europe is tax harmonisation. However, European tax harmonisation has not developed as rapidly as its early proponents hoped. The first significant step towards European tax harmonisation was included in the Messina resolution of 1955 and the Treaty of Rome of 1957 and involved the removal of customs duties between member states. Following that initiative, further moves were very cautious with provisions only for the harmonisation of legislation concerning turnover taxes, excise duties and other forms of indirect taxation to the extent that such harmonisation was necessary for the operation of the internal market. Since that time there have been many reports and reviews but not much progress - mainly because countries are often reluctant to lose control over their tax systems which form such an important instrument of their social and economic policies.

THE PROCESS OF TAX REFORM

The final part from the Bird and Oldman (1990) extract was that a reform should be 'sufficiently attractive to be implemented and sufficiently robust to withstand changing times'. One of the difficulties of applying economic theory to tax reform is that the latter is not an exercise in comparative statics – comparing two static positions, one before and one after the proposed change. In reality it is a dynamic process. The study of the progress of proposed tax reforms soon indicates that they will not only be influenced by different factors and interested parties in their development but, as soon as a definite proposal emerges, opposition may develop from those who feel they might be adversely affected. Furthermore inertia is often a factor in the process. As Rose and Karran (1987, p. 5) put it: 'If keeping out of trouble is a basic law of politics, then not making decisions about taxes is one way to avoid trouble – in the short run at least'. This means, of course, that tax reform is not a smooth process optimally designed to adapt to changing priorities, needs and other circumstances but a jerky process that is the outcome of a variety of forces proposing and opposing change. Nor is the final outcome of this process likely to be an optimal one. Biases may exist between those favouring and those opposing a change – the disadvantages of a reform may be seen easily by those who will suffer but the gains from change, even if they are potentially greater than the losses, may be less tangible and less likely to arouse public support. Sometimes the opposite might be true. The enthusiasm of those wanting to change things might overcome possibly greater disadvantages that are so diffuse there is no serious opposition. As Break and Pechman put it (1975, p. 13) 'the beauty of tax reform shines more brightly in the eyes of the reformers' than it does in the eyes of the public at large'.

One way of modelling the dynamic process of tax reform is to draw on the forcefield analysis from the work of Lewin (1951) and developed in this context by James and Edwards (2007). This approach allows the incorporation of the complex array of different factors and interests which may influence the development of tax systems and the nature of the political process itself, including the role of inertia. Forcefield analysis reflects the reality that at any time there will be all sorts of different pressures for change developing and a variety of developing forms of resistance to change as illustrated in Figure 1.

Figure 1 indicates that the tax system will be at some position – the status quo – which will almost certainly not be the optimal position. There will be pressures for change, possibly from a range of different interests. However, there may also be considerable resistance to change. Not only would change be likely to make some taxpayers worse off, but changing a tax system will involve both administrative, compliance and perhaps other economic costs. Individuals and businesses may have taken economic decisions in the light of existing tax rules and there may be difficulties in adapting to a new system. The outcome of the interaction through political and administrative process is uncertain but different groups are likely to press their cases with different levels of effort and effectiveness. Compromises may be reached but it is reasonable to assume that the outcome may not be the theoretical optimum. This approach also makes it clear that the whole process is a dynamic one. Both the pressures for change and the resistance to change will themselves be changing over time so reinforcing the point that any tax reform should be 'sufficiently robust to withstand changing times'.

Figure 1. A forcefield interpretation to the process of tax reform

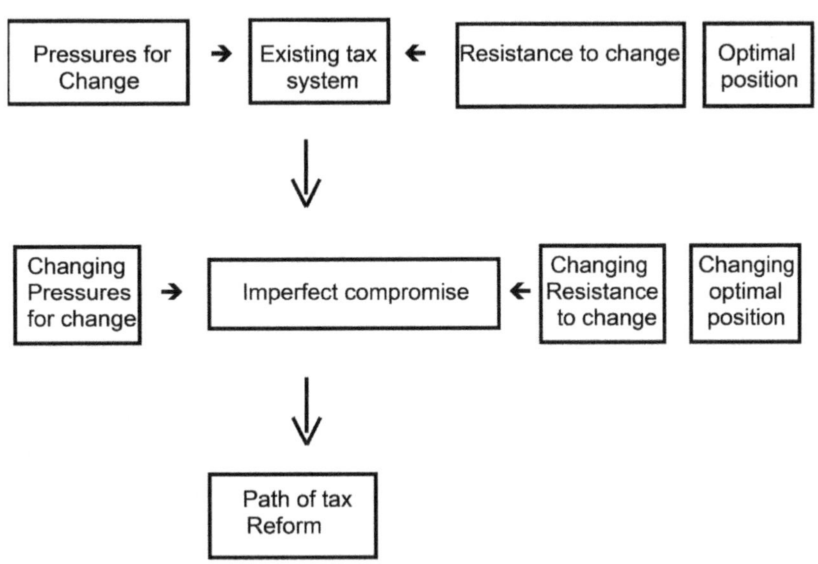

A SYSTEMATIC APPROACH TO TAX REFORM

Given there are considerable difficulties in achieving successful tax reform, the purpose of this section is to outline a systematic process for taking account of the wider range of factors relevant to developing proposed changes to the tax system. As mentioned above, the OECD (2004) has laid out a process for systematically identifying, assessing, ranking and treating of tax compliance risks. More generally the academic literature from the discipline of Management provides guidance on developing strategy which may be applied to tax reform. A key factor, which derives from the discussion so far, is the systematic analysis and understanding of the factors concerned, including not only the matters of immediate interest but also the wider environment in which the activity is being conducted. Furthermore, the process is dynamic. Mintzberg (2004, p. 55) argues that strategy is an interactive process and requires constant feedback from experience. It is not sufficient just to formulate proposals and assume their clear advantages will ensure they are successfully implemented. Once a tax change has been proposed, other forces are likely to come into play. Furthermore, the formulation and implementation of strategy go together (Grant, 2002, p. 25). A proposed tax reform should explicitly incorporate the process of implementation. Finally, it should be clear how the desired outcomes should be measured so that the reform can be refined and possibly reformulated if necessary in the light of experience.

There are certain distinct stages involved in a systematic approach to change. One possible ten stage process of developing tax reform is discussed by James and Edwards (2007) and may be summarised as follows:

1. Identify the aims of the reform.
2. Examine different methods of achieving these aims
3. Analyse in terms of the economic criteria.
4. Specify the administrative constraints.
5. Identify and assess different risks incorporating an analysis of the wider socio-economic context.
6. Analyse behaviour.
7. Establish the relationship(s) of the proposed change with other policies.
8. Develop strategies to achieve the aims of the reform.
9. Plan and implement strategies including intended outcomes.
10. Monitor and evaluate the performance of the strategies against the plan.

Such a systematic approach to tax reform may reduce the chances that important aspects might be given insufficient consideration or even overlooked altogether. Stage one is to identify explicitly the aims of the reform and how they might relate to the objectives of the tax system more generally. The main purpose of taxation is usually to raise revenue for public expenditure but there may also be other aims such as discouraging some activities or encouraging others as mentioned in section 2 above or policy objectives relating to income distribution. The aims of a particular reform may or may not be consistent with other such objectives. The next stage involves an examination of the different methods that might be used to achieve the aims of the reform. Taxation might be the best way but it may not. As Aaron and Galper (1985) argue, using taxation to support worthy causes may be unfair and inefficient in other respects. Although the tax system is often a tempting policy instrument, sometimes a non-tax method might be more appropriate.

The third stage, analysing the reform in the light of economic criteria, draws on the theory in section 2 above. Ideally a tax reform should lead to an improvement in both efficiency and equity. However, sometimes there is a trade-off so that a tax may be efficient but might be considered unfair because it is not related to individuals' circumstances. Alternatively it may take account of individual circumstances but this creates economic distortions and increases administrative and compliance costs. Furthermore, what is regarded as fair may vary from place to place and over time. It can be seen, therefore, that even applying economic criteria is not necessarily a straightforward process.

The next stage is to specify the administrative constraints, which may not be immediately apparent. There may be legal factors to take into account, including possible obligations under international agreements. There may be implications regarding the resources and staff skills available to the tax authority and it may have changing priorities in the use of scarce resources. The tax agency itself may require reform. It is sometimes true, as Devas *et al.* (2001, p. 211) stated, that 'reforms to tax administration are as important as tax policy changes for overall fiscal reform'. Although it is sometimes overlooked, the ability of the tax authority to deliver the proposed reform is an essential part of achieving change successfully.

Identifying and assessing risks forms stage five. As indicated above, the OECD and also other bodies have become aware of the usefulness of assessing risks. It should not be assumed that relevant variables will continue unchanged into the future. Indeed it is clear that the socio-economic-technological environment within which the tax system has to operate is constantly changing and any risks that these may pose should be built into the development of proposed reforms.

Stage six involves analysing behaviour. It was pointed out above that a long standing approach to examining taxpayers' compliance behaviour focuses on rates of detection and levels of penalties. However this has been increasingly supplemented by a more behavioural approach which also examines non-financial motives. Individuals do not always act only in their own immediate self-interest but are often influenced by a wide range of factors. Research in sociology and psychology has indicated that there are many important factors such as attitudes, social norms, social support and a certain background factors such as age, gender and culture. Psychology has developed a branch of 'fiscal psychology' (see, for example, Schmölders, 1959 and Lewis, 1982) which adds many specific insights to the way taxpayers are likely to behave in different circumstances. Allied with developments in behavioural economics with respect to taxpayers, the academic research contribution has moved towards a fuller understanding of behaviour in different circumstances (James, 2006).

Establishing the relationship(s) of the proposed change to other economic and social policies is the next step. The previous discussion in this paper has demonstrated how one change may have implications for other matters that may appear, at least initially, not to be affected. Further investigation might indicate that one or more existing policies may not be entirely compatible with the proposed reform – there may be trade-offs where some compromise should be reached between the advantages of the proposed reform and any disadvantages it may mean for other government objectives.

Step eight involves developing strategies to achieve the stated aims of the reform. As the process is complex, such strategies should be sufficiently comprehensive to deal with wider issues as well as flexible enough to deal with matters of particular concern. They should also, of course, pay particular attention to the issues of the highest priority as well as those where there is the highest chance of success.

The next stage is to plan and implement strategies including intended outcomes. The political context underlines the importance of gaining the support of stakeholders and this can be done in a number of ways such as involving them in the planning stages, consultation exercises and the provision of information and explanations about the intended strategy. Changes might be more acceptable if they are phased in over a period of time and the OECD (2006) has suggested it might be worth considering some compensation, possibly temporary, for those who are adversely affected. If some of the gains of the reform could be shared with any losers, it might make a significant difference to the possible opposition to the reform, as illustrated in Figure 1, and increase the chances of a more satisfactory outcome.

It is very advantageous that the plan includes intended outcomes and one or more methods for monitoring and evaluating progress. There are advantages if the relevant variables are quantifiable but not everything can be easily measured so provision should also be made for qualitative feedback. This should then complete the systematic development of the proposed reform and the final stage is assessment following implementation.

Step ten involves monitoring and evaluating the performance of the strategies against the plan but this, of course, is not always and easy task. Given the complexity of the whole process, a single indicator may well be insufficient to monitor the whole situation. As well as monitoring the continuing effects of the reform, this should be part of a wider monitoring of the changes with regard to the tax environment and practice, particularly taxpayer behaviour. As time passes different issues may well change in their importance with respect to the overall strategy and new ones may emerge. Finally, the results of the monitoring and evaluation of performance should be fed back into the continuous development of the most appropriate tax strategies.

Such a systematic approach would do much to improve the chances tax reforms being successfully developed and implemented. An example where this has often not been done is tax simplification. The case for tax simplification seems overwhelming when considered in isolation from other aspects of the tax system and the complex socio-economic environment in which taxes have to operate. The advantages of simplification may include savings in compliance and administrative costs, a reduction in uncertainty regarding the tax implications of economic decisions and an improvement in taxpayer compliance. However, attempts at simplifying modern tax systems have often not been very successful since they have not taken proper account of other important factors. There are very sound reasons why tax systems become complex in advanced economies and these must be considered if simplification is to be achieved (see, for example, James, *et al.*, forthcoming). A simplification policy that followed a systematic approach, as suggested in this chapter, would become part of general tax policy and appropriate trade-offs between simplicity and other goals could be made and so increase the chances of a successful outcome.

CONCLUSION

Bird and Oldman's (1990) succinct description of the best approach to tax reform covers many important issues. Although, at first sight, the economic theory of tax reform appears relatively straightforward, there are some difficult trade-offs between efficiency and equity. In addition, other theoretical considerations described above give an indication of how complex tax reform can be in practice. Tax administration and compliance are particular areas where a range of difficulties can arise that must be taken into account if tax changes are to be successful. Then there is the context within which such changes must take place – economic, social and technological factors may be significant – together with international considerations arising from globalisation and tax competition. Furthermore, successful tax reform is likely to be a dynamic process rather than a single one-off change. The tax system has to be designed to be sufficiently robust to accommodate continuing change in the socio-economic and political environment and to be sufficiently flexible to accommodate further adjustments as appropriate. Nevertheless, drawing on the available literature, it is possible to design a systematic process that can take account of the many issues involved in developing tax reform.

REFERENCES

Aaron, A. J., & Galper, H. (1985). *Assessing Tax Reform*. Washington, DC: Brookings Institution.

Alm, J. (1996). What is an "Optimal" Tax System? *National Tax Journal*, *49*(1), 117–133.

Andreoni, J., Erard, B., & Feinstein, J. (1998). Tax Compliance. *Journal of Economic Literature*, *36*(2), 818–860.

Ben Slimane, S., & Ben Tahar, M. (2010). Why is Fiscal Policy Procyclical in MENA Countries? *International Journal of Economics and Finance*, *2*(5), 44–53.

Bhagwati, J. (2004). *In Defense of Globilization*. Oxford: Oxford University Press.

Bird, R. M. (2004). Managing tax reform. *Bulletin for International Fiscal Documentation*, *58*(2), 42–55.

Bird, R. M., & Oldman, O. (1990). *Taxation in Developing Countries* (4th ed.). Baltimore: Johns Hopkins University Press.

Break, G. F., & Pechman, J. A. (1975). *Federal Tax Reform: The Impossible Dream?* Washington, DC: Brookings Institution.

Chander, P., & Wilde, L. (1992). Corruption in Tax Administration. *Journal of Public Economics*, *49*(3), 333–349. doi:10.1016/0047-2727(92)90072-N

. Compliance Risk Management: Managing and Improving Tax Compliance. (2004). *Centre for Tax Policy and Administration, OECD*, Paris. Retrieved from http://www.oecd.org/dataoecd/44/19/33818656.pdf

Devas, N., Delay, S., & Hubbard, M. (2001). Revenue Authorities: Are they the Right Vehicle for Improved Tax Administration? *Public Administration and Development*, *21*(3), 211–222. doi:10.1002/pad.174

Risk Management Guide for Tax Administrations. (2006). *European Commission*. Retrieved from http://ec.europa.eu/taxation_customs/resources/documents/taxation/tax_cooperation/gen_overview/risk_management_guide_for_tax_administrations_en.pdf

EU Tax Policy Strategy Communication. (2014, December 9). *European Commission*. Retrieved from http://ec.europa.eu/taxation_customs/taxation/gen_info/tax_policy/index_en.htm

Fischer, C., Wartick, M., & Mark, M. (1992). Detection Probability and Taxpayer Compliance: A Literature Review. *Journal of Accounting Literature*, *11*(1), 1–46.

Fundamental reform of personal income tax, Tax Policy Studies No. 13. (2006). *OECD*, Paris. Retrieved from http://browse.oecdbookshop.org/oecd/pdfs/product/2306081e.pdf

General Administrative Principles: Corporate Governance and Tax Risk Management, Forum on Tax Administration. (2009). *OECD*, Paris. Retrieved from http://www.oecd.org/dataoecd/37/19/43239887.pdf

Golinelli, R., & Momigliano, S. (2009). The Cyclical Reaction of Fiscal Policies in the Euro Area: The Role of Modelling Choices and Data Vintages. *Fiscal Studies*, *30*(1), 39–72. doi:10.1111/j.1475-5890.2009.00089.x

Goode, R. (1981). Some Economic Aspects of Tax Administration. *Staff Papers - International Monetary Fund. International Monetary Fund*, *28*(2), 249–274. doi:10.2307/3866931

Grant, R. M. (2002). *Contemporary Strategy Analysis: Concepts, Techniques, Applications* (4th ed.). Oxford: Blackwell.

Heady, C. (1993). Optimal Taxation As a Guide to Tax Policy: A Survey. *Fiscal Studies*, *14*(1), 15–41. doi:10.1111/j.1475-5890.1993.tb00341.x

Hines, J. R. Jr, & Summers, L. H. (2009). How Globalization Affects Tax Design. *Tax Policy and the Economy*, *23*(1), 123–158. doi:10.1086/597056

Holcombe, R. G. (1998). Tax Policy from a Choice Perspective. *National Tax Journal*, *51*(2), 359–371.

Jackson, B., & Milliron, V. C. (1986). Tax Compliance Research: Findings, Problems and Prospects. *Journal of Accounting Literature*, *5*(1), 125–165.

James, S. (1999). The Future International Tax Environment and European Tax Harmonisation: A Personal View. *European Accounting Review*, *8*(4), 731–747. doi:10.1080/096381899335781

James, S. (2006). Taxation and the Contribution of Behavioral Economics. In M. Altman (Ed.), *Foundations and Extensions of Behavioral Economics: A Handbook* (pp. 589–601). New York: M.E. Sharpe Publishers.

James, S. (2014). The Importance of Fairness in Tax Policy: Behavioral Economics and the UK Experience. *International Journal of Applied Behavioral Economics*, *3*(1), 1–12. doi:10.4018/ijabe.2014010101

James, S., & Edwards, A. (2007). A Strategic Approach to Personal Income Tax Reform. *Australian Tax Forum, 22*(2), 105-126.

James, S., & Edwards, A. (2008). Developing Tax Policy in a Complex and Changing World. *Economic Analysis and Policy*, *38*(1), 35–53. doi:10.1016/S0313-5926(08)50005-1

James, S., & Edwards, J. (2010). *An Annotated Bibliography of Tax Compliance and Tax Compliance Costs*, Economic and Social Research Council, Retrieved from http://www.esrc.ac.uk/my-esrc/grants/RES-000-23-1595/outputs/read/e026df04-3812-4aa1-96fe-10cd4b442e49

James, S., Hasseldine, J., Hite, P., & Toumi, M. (2001). Developing a Tax Compliance Strategy for Revenue Services. *Bulletin for International Fiscal Documentation*, *55*(4), 158–164.

James, S., & Nobes, C. (2014). *The economics of Taxation: Principles, Policy and Practice* (13th ed.). Birmingham: Fiscal Publications.

James, S., Sawyer, A., & Wallschutzky, I. (forthcoming). Tax Simplification: A Review of Initiatives in Australia, New Zealand and the United Kingdom, and the Influence of their Respective Tax Administrations. *eJournal of Tax Research.*

Kirchler, E., Hoelzl, E., & Wahl, I. (2008). Enforced versus Voluntary Tax Compliance: The "Slippery Slope" Framework. *Journal of Economic Psychology*, *29*(2), 210–225. doi:10.1016/j.joep.2007.05.004

Kirchler, E., Niemirowski, A., & Wearing, A. (2006). Shared subjective views, intent to cooperate and tax compliance: Similarities between Australian taxpayers and tax officers. *Journal of Economic Psychology*, *27*(4), 502–517. doi:10.1016/j.joep.2006.01.005

Klepper, S., & Nagin, D. (1989). Tax Compliance and Perceptions of the Risks of Detection and Criminal Prosecution. *Law & Society Review*, *23*(2), 209–240. doi:10.2307/3053715

Lewin, K. (1951). *Field Theory in Social Science*. New York: Harper.

Lewis, A. (1982). *The Psychology of Taxation*. Oxford: Blackwell.

Lipsey, R. G. (1997). Reflections on the General Theory of Second Best at its Golden Jubilee. *International Tax and Public Finance*, *14*(4), 349–364. doi:10.1007/s10797-007-9036-x

Lipsey, R. G., & Lancaster, K. (1956). The General Theory of the Second Best. *The Review of Economic Studies*, *24*(1), 11–32. doi:10.2307/2296233

Mankiw, N. G., Weinzierl, M., & Yagan, D. (2009). Optimal Taxation in Theory and Practice. *The Journal of Economic Perspectives*, *23*(4), 147–174. doi:10.1257/jep.23.4.147

Mintzberg, H. (2004). *Managers not MBAs: A Hard Look at the Soft Practice of Managing and Management Development, San Fransisco: Berret-Koehler*. Publishers.

Mirrlees, S. J. (Chair), (2010). Dimensions of Tax Design: The Mirrlees Review. Oxford: Oxford University Press.

Mirrlees, S. J. (Chair), (2011). Tax by Design: The Mirrlees Review. Oxford: Oxford University Press.

Mueller, D. C. (2003). The reason for collective choice – redistribution. *Public Choice III* (Ch. 3, 3rd ed.). Cambridge: Cambridge University Press.

Musgrave, R. A. (1959). *The Theory of Public Finance: A Study in Political Economy*. New York: McGraw-Hill.

Musgrave, R. A. (2008). Public Finance and the Three Branch Model. *Journal of Economics and Finance*, *32*(4), 334–339. doi:10.1007/s12197-008-9044-4

MENA-OECD Investment Programme: Recommendations on Frameworks to Support Development of National Tax Policy Reform Agendas. (2005). *OECD*. Retrieved from http://www.oecd.org/mena/investment/36086830.pdf

Posner, E. A. (2000). Law and Social Norms: The Case of Tax Compliance. *Virginia Law Review*, *86*(8), 1781–1819. doi:10.2307/1073829

Simple, fair and pro-growth: proposals to fix America's tax system. (2005). President's Advisory Panel for Federal Tax Reform. Retrieved from http://govinfo.library.unt.edu/taxreformpanel/final-report/

Review, H. (2010). Australia's Future Tax System: Final Report to the Treasurer, Part One Overview, Commonwealth of Australia, Canberra. Retrieved from http://www.taxreview.treasury.gov.au/content/downloads/final_report_part_1/00_AFTS_final_report_consolidated.pdf

Richardson, M., & Sawyer, A. (2001). A Taxonomy of Tax Compliance Literature: Further Findings, Problems and Prospects. *Australian Tax Forum, 16*(2), 137-320.

Rose, R., & Karran, T. (1987). *Taxation by Political Inertia*. London: Allen & Unwin.

Sandford, C. T., Godwin, M., & Hardwick, P. (1989). *Administrative and Compliance Costs of Taxation*. Bath: Fiscal Publications.

Sawyer, A. J. (2004). Is an International Tax Organisation an Appropriate Forum for Administering Binding Rulings and APAS? *eJournal of Tax Research, 2*(1), 8-70.

Schmölders, G. (1959). Fiscal Psychology: A New Branch of Public Finance. *National Tax Journal, 15*, 184–193.

Schmölders, G. (1970). Survey Research in Public Finance: A Behavioural Approach to Fiscal Theory. *Public Finance*, *25*, 300–306.

Silvani, C., & Baer, K. (1997). Designing a Tax Administration Reform: Experience and Guidelines. *IMF Working Paper*, Fiscal Affairs Department, WP/97/30. Washington DC: International Monetary Fund.

Strümpel, B. (1969). The Contribution of Survey Research to Public Finance. In A. T. Peacock (Ed.), *Quantitative Analysis in Public Finance* (pp. 13–32). New York: Praeger.

Surrey, S. S. (1973). *Pathways to Tax Reform*. Cambridge, MA: Harvard University Press. doi:10.4159/harvard.9780674436503

Tanzi, V. (1996). Globalization, Tax Competition and the Future of Tax Systems. *IMF Working* Paper No. 96/141. Retrieved from http://papers.ssrn.com/sol3/papers.cfm?abstract_id=883038

Tax Incentives for Investment: A Global Perspective Experiences in MENA and Non-MENA Countries. (2008). In *Making Reforms Succeed: Moving Forward with the MENA Investment Policy Agenda*OECD. Paris: OECD Publishing. Doi:10.1787/9789264052826-11-en

Chapter 4
Tax Revenues and Tax Efforts across the World

Nihal Bayraktar
Pennsylvania State University, USA

Tuan Minh Le
The World Bank, USA

Blanca Moreno-Dodson
The World Bank, USA

ABSTRACT

This chapter focuses on the concept and empirical estimation of tax effort around the world. It employs a cross-country study from a sample of 121, developing and developed countries during 1994-2012. Predicted tax revenue of a country is estimated empirically taking into account its specific economic, demographic, and institutional features and is considered as an approximation of its taxable capacity. Tax effort is then defined as the ratio between the share of the actual tax collection and the predicted tax revenue. The use of tax effort and actual tax revenue collection allows us to rank countries into four different groups. The results vary per country and region but, overall, tax revenue collection appears to be in line with its predicted value. This could reflect many efforts undertaken in the last decades to improve tax policy and tax administration. It also suggests that further improvements in domestic revenue mobilization may require other non-tax reforms aimed at removing economic, demographic and institutional constraints hindering tax revenue performance.

INTRODUCTION

The international development community is increasingly recognizing the centrality of effective taxation to development.[1] The G-20, multilateral institutions, and the donor community want to ensure that their assistance to developing countries to reinforce their tax systems is effective, coherent, and well harmonized (OECD, 2011), and that their own domestic resource mobilization increases over time.

DOI: 10.4018/978-1-5225-0053-7.ch004

On the one hand, tax revenues constitute a much better alternative, for financing public spending, than money printing and/or debt, and contribute to macroeconomic stability, therefore exerting a significant importance for private investment decisions and growth.[2] On the other hand, adequate tax revenue collections to meet the needs of society are associated with good governance, strengthened state-building and higher government accountability to its citizens. Finally, higher domestic tax revenues are conducive to lower the dependency from foreign aid.

Effective tax systems are as essential for developing countries as they are for developed ones. Most recently, given that budget deficits have been increasing in some countries, following the introduction of large stimulus packages to promote economic growth after the 2008-2009 financial and economic crises, and subsequent regional crises, many governments throughout the world have been searching for possible ways of increasing tax revenues to finance public expenditures and narrow the budget deficit while minimizing distortions to economic activity.

The first step to understanding tax revenue systems is to establish some commonly agreed upon performance measurements and benchmarks. In this regard this chapter deals with the concept and empirical estimation of countries' taxable capacity and tax effort, defines countries' tax effort typologies and draws some general policy implications for tax reforms.

Measuring tax revenue performance of countries is both theoretically and practically challenging.[3] The actual tax collection-to-gross domestic product (GDP) ratio is generally interpreted as a measure of tax effort and used as the basis for cross country comparison. This ratio is reasonable if one attempts to establish trends or to compare tax revenue performance across countries with similar economic structures and the same level of income per capita. However, when used to compare revenue mobilization performance across countries in different income groups and with different characteristics, the tax-to-GDP ratio could provide a "completely distorted" picture due to a range of diverse economic structures, institutional arrangements, and demographic trends affecting them. A number of tax economists have attempted to deal with this issue by applying an empirical approach to estimate the determinants of tax revenue collection and identify the impact of such variables on each country's taxable capacity. The development of a tax effort index, relating the actual tax revenues of a country to its estimated taxable capacity, provides us a useful measure which takes into account country specific fiscal, demographic, and institutional characteristics.

In this paper, the empirical methodology applied by Tanzi and Davoodi (1997), and Bird, Vazquez, and Torgler (2004) is extended. A cross-country analysis for a sample of 121, developing and developed countries during 1994-2012, and the two sub-periods of 1994-2003 and 2004-12 are undertaken. *Taxable capacity* refers to the predicted tax revenues that can be estimated with regression analyses, taking into account a country's specific economic, demographic, and institutional features. *Tax effort* is defined as the ratio between a country's actual tax collection and its taxable capacity. The concepts of taxable capacity and tax effort are also extended to measure total fiscal revenue capacity and fiscal revenue effort (including tax and non-tax fiscal revenues).

Estimating actual tax collection benchmarks and tax effort ratios allows us to rank countries into four different groups: (i) low tax collection, low tax effort; (ii) high tax collection, high tax effort; (iii) low tax collection, high tax effort; and (iv) high tax collection, low tax effort. This classification is based on the global average of tax revenue collection and a reference tax effort index of 1, corresponding to the case where the actual tax revenue collection is exactly the same as the predicted one.

The results show that while developed countries are in the high-tax collection group, the level of their tax efforts differs country by country, indicating that while some are collecting according to their predicted potential, others could still intensify their tax efforts. On the other hand, there is much more diversity in developing countries, with a high number of them showing tax revenue collection in line with their capacity (either low tax revenue collections and low tax efforts or high tax revenue collection and high tax effort), indicating that collected tax revenues reflect well their economic, demographic, economic, and institutional features.

The analysis provides comparison benchmarks for countries with various levels of tax revenue collection and tax effort. Countries should rely on different strategies for tax policy reforms, depending on their stage of development and their actual ratios levels of tax collection and effort. The analysis provides broad directions for tax policy reforms, especially in developing countries.

Section II provides an overview of the worldwide trends in tax revenue, using the tax-to-GDP ratios, across income-groups and geographic regions. Section III extends the existing literature to the empirical estimation of a country's predicted tax revenue (taxable capacity) and tax effort. This section also investigates the trends in taxable capacity and tax effort across regions. Based on the level of tax collection and the tax effort index, countries are classified into different groups. Some policy implications for fiscal policy reforms follow. Section IV concludes.

TRENDS IN TAXATION

Data

The simplest definition of tax revenue performance, which is commonly used in the literature, is the share of tax revenue in GDP. It does not give detailed information on tax collection relative to taxable capacity, but still provides us with a simple measure to determine trends across countries, income groups, and regions.

The dataset includes 121 developing and developed countries and covers the period of 1994-2012.[4] Countries are selected based on data availability. Tax havens and countries with tax revenues mainly associated with large natural resources are excluded in the study.[5] For the purpose of consistency, all series are extracted from World Bank's World Development Indicator (WDI) Database and/or from International Monetary Fund's Government Financial Statistics. Total and tax revenues are all estimated for the general government.[6] The average values of the tax collection for each country are reported in column (2), Appendix Table 10.[7]

Given that differences in income levels can be important factors in determining tax revenues of countries, tax rates are investigated across income groups and regions. Simple averages are calculated for each group. The data points for the years of 1994, 2006, 2006, and 2012 are reported in the following figures. The results confirm those presented in Bird (2007), Fox and Gurley (2005), and Le *et al.* (2008).

Income Classification and Taxation

A country's income per capita level is an important factor in determining its tax revenue collection. Higher-income countries can collect higher tax revenues, relative to developing countries, usually due to several factors such as higher ability and willingness of taxpayers, a more efficient tax administration and a smaller shadow economy.

When countries are classified based on the share of tax revenues in percent of GDP across income groups, it can be observed that differences across groups are sharp (see Figure 1).[8] The low-income group has the lowest tax-to-GDP ratio, but it has been significantly improving since 2000. This improvement is especially clear in most recent years. For this group of countries, the average share of taxes in GDP increased to 14.6 percent of GDP in 2012, from 11.8 percent in 2000 and 9.9 percent in 1994. Throughout the years, each income country group managed to increase their average tax-to-GDP ratio, but such increase is relatively higher in the low-income group. Even though there is still a lot of room for further improvements in this group, especially considering that raising enough public funds to finance development needs is always more challenging, recent developments are very promising.

The share of taxes as a percentage of GDP is almost 7 percentage points higher for the middle-income group when compared to the average share in the low-income group, and has been consistently rising since 1998, except for a slight drop in 2012; it was 17.2 percent in 1998, and 20.5 percent in 2012.

Not surprisingly, the highest tax share is found in the high-income group. The group includes both OECD and non-OECD countries. They collect almost 2-3 times higher tax revenues as a percentage of GDP than the low-income group and almost 10 percentage points higher tax revenues when compared to the middle-income group. However, following the global crisis of 2008-2009, tax collections in this group have decreased by a marginal amount of almost 2 percentage points between 2006 and 2012, a drop from 31.5 percent to 29.7 percent.

Geographical Regions and Taxation

Figure 2 presents the share of tax revenues as a percentage of GDP across regions.[9] It should be noted that high-income OECD countries are excluded as the focus of this paper is mainly on developing countries. They are grouped together and their tax shares are reported in the last part of the figure. The lowest tax rate belongs to the South Asia region (SAR); they collect 11.3 to 13 percent taxes as a share of GDP.[10] The East Asia and Pacific (EAP) region has the second lowest tax collection rate in the world with taxes

Figure 1. Tax revenue (in % of GDP) by income groups, 1994-2012
Source: The World Bank classification and WDI.

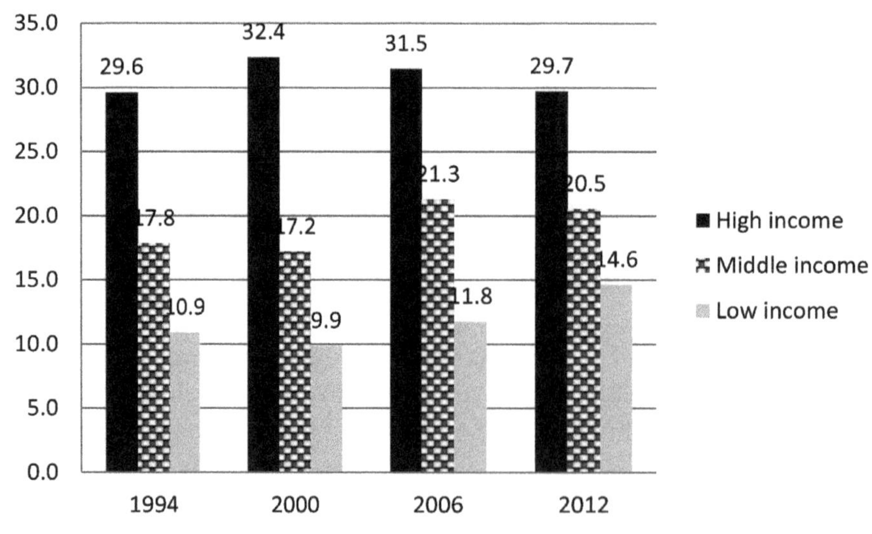

Figure 2. Tax revenues (as % of GDP) by regions, 1994-2012
Source: The World Bank classification and WDI.
Note: SSA is Sub-Saharan Africa, EAP is East Asia and Pacific, ECA is Eastern European and Central Asia, LAC is Latin America and Caribbean, MENA is Middle East and North Africa, SAR is South Asia. In these regions, high-income OECD countries excluded and all high-income OECD countries are reported in the last set of bars in the figure.

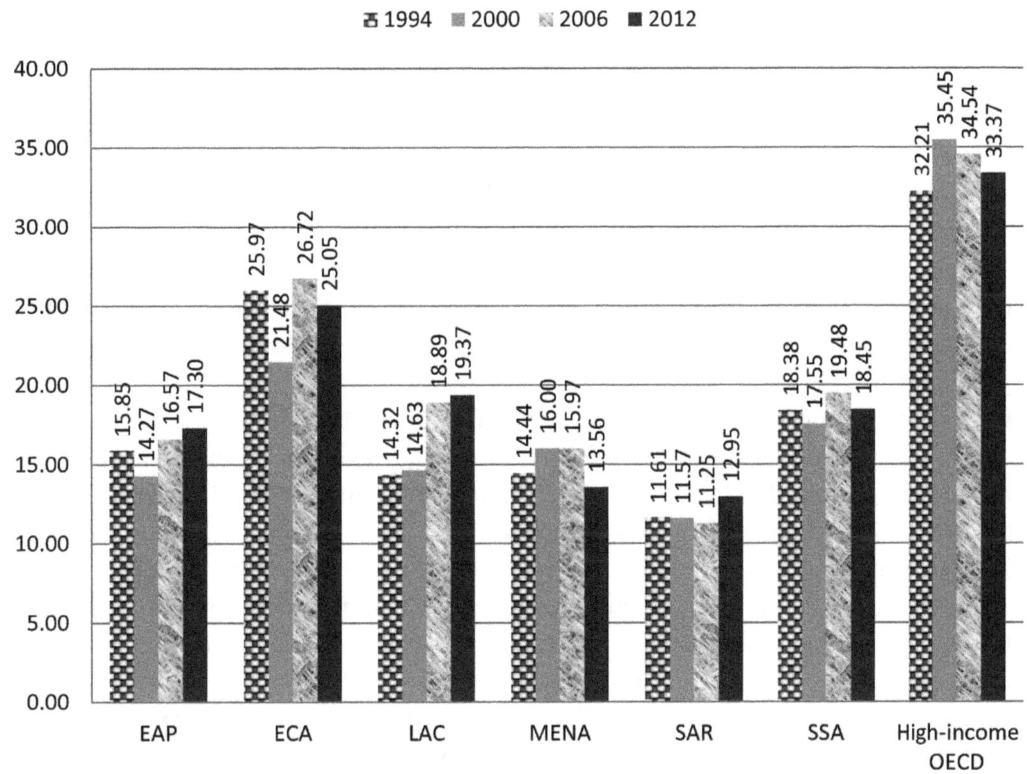

around 4 percentage points higher than the one observed for SAR. Latin America and Caribbean (LAC), Sub-Saharan Africa (SSA), and the Middle East and North Africa region (MENA) present similar tax collections, around 17 percent of GDP. The shares have been consistently rising in the LAC, but they fluctuate in SSA and MENA regions.

After a sharp drop in taxes as a percentage of GDP in the Eastern European and Central Asia (ECA) region in 1994, the share has been rising consistently from 21.5 percent in 2000 to 26.7 percent in 2006. After the economic crisis in 2008, it declined to 25 percent in 2012.

OECD high-income countries have the highest tax collection as a percentage of GDP, but they constitute the only group of countries which have seen a drop in tax revenues, on average, starting in 2000. It declined from 35.45 percent of GDP in 2000 to 34.54 percent in 2006 and to 33.37 percent in 2012.[11]

TAXABLE CAPACITY AND TAX EFFORT: EMPIRICAL EVIDENCE AND POLICY IMPLICATIONS

Definitions of Taxable Capacity and Tax Effort

Actual tax revenues as a share of GDP is one of the most commonly used measures of tax revenue performance for cross-country tax comparison. The biggest advantage of this measure is that it is easy to obtain and gives a quick overview of tax trends across countries. But, as indicated by Musgrave (1987)[12], this measure is more suitable for studies focusing on countries with similar economic structures and at the same level of income. The taxable capacity and/or the tax effort of countries can be more accurately measured if different country characteristics are taken into account.[13] In addition to its income per capita level, the taxable capacity of any country also depends on its economic structure (contributions to GDP by agriculture, industry and services), institutional arrangements, and demographic trends (Prest, 1979). Overall, it would not be accurate to determine the taxable capacity of countries only by examining their actual tax collection.

Cyan *et al.* (2012) compare three different methodologies available in the literature to compute the tax effort series of countries: traditional regression approach (the one used in this chapter); stochastic frontier analysis (Pitt & Lee, 1981; Battese, 1992; Battese & Coelli, 1992; Alfirman, 2003; Pessino & Fenochietto, 2010); and the ratio of total government revenue to its expenditures (Martinez-Vazquez & McNab, 2000; Mahdavi, 2008; Baicker & Skinner, 2011). Since the last methodology is constrained by limited data points due to incomplete public expenditure data for some countries, plus other fiscal policy considerations not necessarily captured in the government accounts, the comparison of the first two methodologies is more meaningful for the purpose of this study.

After comprehensive comparison analysis, Cyan *et al.* (2012) conclude that the results obtained from the first two methodologies produce highly-correlated, similar tax effort series. Therefore, the methodology used in this chapter can be considered as robust. It estimates the taxable capacity and the tax effort of countries through regression analysis using possible determinants of tax revenues as explanatory variables.[14] *Taxable capacity* is defined by the predicted tax-to-GDP ratio calculated using the estimated coefficients of the regression specification, taking into account the country specific characteristics.[15] *Tax effort* is the ratio between the share of actual collection to GDP and its taxable capacity. A "high tax effort" is defined as a tax effort index above 1, implying that the country effectively utilizes its tax base potential to generate tax revenues (Stotsky & WoldeMariam, 1997). A "low tax effort" is defined as a tax effort index below 1, indicating that the country is not fully using its potential to raise tax revenues.[16]

In addition to taxes, total fiscal revenues (adding revenues generated by other fiscal charges and fees) are also analyzed in a similar way. The same estimation techniques are used to calculate the capacity of countries in total fiscal revenue (tax plus non-tax revenue collections) generation, which is named as *fiscal revenue capacity,* and their effort in total fiscal revenue generation, named as *fiscal revenue effort*.

In this section, the estimation results are produced using a regression specification similar to the one used in Le *et al.* (2008). The fundamental difference is that the present exercise uses a broader data set consisting of general-government series (as opposed to only central government data), which captures better the ability of countries' tax revenue generation including subnational levels. Moreover, this study covers a much longer time period (instead of 1994-2003, it is now 1994-2012) and includes more countries (121 developing and developed countries instead of 104 countries). We also focus on sub-periods to understand how the tax effort of countries has changed overtime. The first sub-sample is 1994-2003 and the second one is 2004-12, in order to also capture the effects of the 2008-2009 global crises. Finally, this chapter also introduces some methodological refinements.

Empirical Specification, Variables, and Methodology

In the empirical specifications the tax (and fiscal) revenues to GDP ratio appears as a function of its possible determinants:[17]

$$TAX / GDP_{it} = \alpha_0 + \alpha_1.GDPPC_{it} + \alpha_2.DEMOG_{it} + \alpha_3.TRADE_{it} + \alpha_4.AGR_{it} + \alpha_5.GOVERNANCE\ QUALITY_{it} + regional\ dummies + time\ dummies + \varepsilon, \quad (1)$$

$$REV / GDP_{it} = \beta_0 + \beta_1.GDPPC_{it} + \beta_2.DEMOG_{it} + \beta_3.TRADE_{it} + \beta_4.AGR_{it} + \beta_5.GOVERNANCE\ QUALITY_{it} + regional\ dummies + time\ dummies + \varepsilon, \quad (2)$$

TAX/GDP is total tax revenues as a percentage of GDP;
REV/GDP is total fiscal revenues as a percentage of GDP;
GDPPC is constant GDP per capita (2000 US$);
DEMOG stands for a demographic variable; it is either the growth rate of population between 15-64 years old, or the age dependency rate;
TRADE measures trade openness (exports plus imports in percentage of GDP);
AGR is agriculture value added as a percentage of GDP;
GOVERNANCE QUALITY stands for bureaucracy quality index and/or corruption index; it is excluded in the basic specification.

We also include both regional and time dummies. The regions are defined in Table 13. The time dummies are annual.

World Bank's World Development Indicators Database, International Monetary Fund's Government Financial Statistics, and the International Country Risk Guide (ICRG) Database are the main data sources.[18]

As presented in Section II, higher-income countries tend to collect more taxes as a percentage of GDP. Thus, it is expected that *GDP per capita* will have a positive and significant impact on tax collection, as well as on fiscal revenue (Bahl, 1971; Fox & Gurley, 2005; Piancastelli, 2001).

Demographic characteristics of countries are captured by two variables: *age dependency* and *population growth*. As these two variables determine the share of productive population in a country, they are expected to affect its tax (and fiscal) collection capacity negatively. The tax base gets narrower with a higher age dependency ratio which indicates a lower percentage of productive (working age) population who pays more taxes, vis-à-vis the retired population. Regarding the expected negative effect of population growth on tax revenues, the main reason is that the tax system may not able to easily capture new taxpayers, especially in countries with weak tax administration capacity, (Bird, Martinez-Vazquez, & Torgler, 2004; Mkandawire, 2010). However, this effect may be expected to revert in the long run as more young people join the labor force.

Trade openness is one of the variables commonly considered as an important determinant of taxation (Rodrik, 1998; Piancastelli, 2001; Norregaard & Khan, 2007; Aizenman & JinJarak, 2009). The dynamic of international trade may have two opposite effects on tax revenues. On the one hand, higher trade openness is expected to lower taxes collected on imports and exports; thus, it may have a negative impact on tax and total fiscal revenue (Keen & Mansour, 2010). On the other hand, given that higher trade openness is associated with higher economic growth rates, open economies usually tend to grow faster; and as a result, more taxes can be collected (Allonso & Garcimartin, 2011). It is therefore expected that the second effect dominates over the first and trade openness has a positive impact on tax and total fiscal revenue.[19]

Given that it is relatively harder to tax the agricultural sector, it is expected that a higher share of *agriculture value added* to GDP, results in a lower ratio of collected taxes to GDP, due to a smaller tax base (Leuthold, 1991; Piancastelli, 2001; Jewell, Flanagan, & Cattell, 2005). Also, it has been shown that the demand for public goods and services is generally lower in a country with a higher share of agricultural production perhaps due to more people living in rural areas; as a result, the government may see a lower need to collect higher tax revenues (Tanzi, 1992). Thus, the expected sign of the agriculture value added ratio to GDP is negative.

Institutional and governance quality is considered as one of the most essential factors in determining tax revenue collections (Tanzi & Davoodi, 1997; Ghura, 1998; Abed & Gupta, 2002; Bird *et al.*, 2004, 2008; Gupta, 2007; Aizenman & JinJarak, 2012). Countries can collect higher tax revenues when the tax administration is more effective. In this regard, the *bureaucracy quality* and *corruption* index, which is a possible variable to measure institutional and governance quality, is expected to have a significant impact on tax revenues.[20] Lower index values indicate a more efficient bureaucracy and lower corruption. With this definition, we expect tax revenues to drop with increasing index values, meaning negative estimated coefficients of these variables.

A simple correlation matrix among all these variables indicates the expected signs (see Table 14 in Appendix). Tax revenue is positively correlated with GDP per capita and trade openness; and negatively correlated with age dependency ratio, population growth, agriculture value added, as well as the bureaucracy quality and/or corruption index, as defined above.[21] Given that the ratio of tax revenues as a share of GDP has been increasing recently, especially in the low-income and middle-income groups (see Figure 1), a higher correlation is expected. Average values of the variables for each country are reported in Table 10 in Appendix, while overall averages and other descriptive statistics are reported in Table 15 in Appendix.[22] Tax revenues are 23 percent of GDP on average, while total revenue represent 29 percent of GDP. The income level on average is $10,200 in constant 2005 dollars. The growth rate of the population is 1.7 percent. The economies of the countries in the sample can be considered as open since the share of trade – imports plus exports as a percent of GDP is 87 percent on average. The share of agricultural value added in GDP is low on average at 15.28 percent.

The regression methodology is an ordinary least square for panel datasets. One potential problem in using this methodology is the possible endogeneity and/or dual causality problem associated with institutional variables (bureaucracy index and corruption index in this chapter) and tax revenues. Higher tax revenues usually lead to improved governance, while improved governance can further increase tax revenues. We run the Hausman endogeneity tests to understand whether any statistically significant endogeneity problem is observed. Such a problem could lead to inconsistencies in estimated coefficients if a panel least squared technique was used for regression analyses. The null hypothesis of exogeneity is failed to reject, indicating an absence of a significant endogeneity problem.[23] We also run dual granger causality tests between the tax revenue ratio and the independent variables. The F-statistics of the test indicate that there is no causality from tax revenues to the independent variables, so we do not observe any dual causality in our sample. In the absence of any endogeneity or dual causality problems, the panel OLS method is used to estimate the coefficients of the regression specifications given in Equations (1) and (2).

Tax Capacity: Estimation Results

The estimation results for the specifications given in Equations (1) and (2) are presented in Tables 1, 2, 3 and 4 for tax revenues and total fiscal revenues, respectively. The tax capacity of countries is defined as the fitted values calculated using the estimated coefficients reported in Table 1, (Panel A) column (2).[24] The definition of the fiscal revenue capacity is similar (the predicted value of fiscal revenues, calculated using the estimated coefficients reported in Table 3 (Panel A) column (2)). For a robustness check, an alternative specification is also employed to estimate the tax capacity of countries. The results are reported in the last part of this section of the chapter.

Panel A presents the results obtained from the specifications with population growth as a proxy for the demographic characteristics of countries, while Panel B includes age-dependency ratios instead of population growth. The regressions capture the entire period of 1994-2012, as well as the two sub-periods of 1994-2003 and 2004-2012 to better understand the dynamics of the tax and total fiscal revenue capacity. In each panel, columns (1), (4) and (7) represent the regression on traditional tax determinants (includes only demographic and macroeconomic indicators). Columns (2), (3), (5), (6), (8), and (9) show the results when the institutional variables (corruption index or bureaucratic quality indicator) are added, one at a time, as possible determinants of taxes or fiscal revenue.

As reported in Tables 1 and 2, the estimated coefficients have the expected signs and, in general, they are mostly statistically significant. Real GDP per capita is the independent variable with the highest significance in determining the level of tax revenues. It should be noted, however, that in the regression specifications where institutional variables are included, the estimated coefficient of GDP per capita, as well as its significance, decline. Moreover, the institutional quality of countries appears to be more important in determining tax revenues for the period between 2004 and 2012. These findings could be interpreted as follows: when the institutional variables are included, together with per capita income, the later loses some of its significance, because the institutional quality variables already capture partially the effect of income.

These results could perhaps indicate that, with the recent improvements in tax policy and tax administration in developing countries and the on-going effort by high-income countries to rationalize their tax systems toward lower tax burden, particularly in direct income taxes, the income per capita level has become relatively less important than institutional quality in determining tax revenues. The higher economic significance of the estimated coefficients of the institutional variables supports this argument.

Agricultural value added as a percent of GDP is another highly significant determinant of tax revenues. The level of significance and the size of its estimated coefficients do not change with or without institutional variables in the regression specification.

The size of international trade in GDP is statistically significant but its impact on tax revenues is limited, perhaps due to the two opposite effects mentioned above, losses of tariff revenues versus positive GDP growth effects.

Table 1. Determinants of tax revenues and taxable capacity – Panel A: Population growth used as proxy for demographic characteristic (Regional dummies are included)

	Dependent Variable: Tax Revenue in % of GDP								
	1994-2012			1994-2003			2004-2012		
Constant	28.047 (42.764)***	27.489 (36.114)***	27.62 (35.019)***	26.268 (26.729)***	24.074 (21.695)***	23.621 (20.451)***	29.402 (33.592)***	31.515 (30.083)***	32.079 (30.345)***
GDP Per Capita (Constant)	2.24 (16.345)***	2.12 (13.377)***	2.16 (13.562)***	2.6 (12.454)***	2.17 (9.354)***	2.11 (8.877)***	2.02 (11.235)***	2.49 (11.257)***	2.52 (11.944)***
Population Growth	-1.269 (-6.979)***	-1.27 (-6.983)***	-1.265 (-6.954)***	-0.609 (-2.411)**	-0.701 (-2.79)***	-0.7 (-2.788)***	-1.971 (-7.458)***	-2.113 (-7.963)***	-2.145 (-8.116)***
Trade Openness (% of GDP)	0.012 (3.814)***	0.011 (3.508)***	0.011 (3.516)***	0.016 (3.258)***	0.013 (2.507)**	0.011 (2.11)**	0.007 (1.853)*	0.009 (2.266)**	0.01 (2.506)**
Agriculture Value Added (% of GDP)	-0.263 (-14.459)***	-0.261 (-14.317)***	-0.258 (-13.764)***	-0.268 (-11.138)***	-0.255 (-10.62)***	-0.235 (-9.412)***	-0.239 (-8.43)***	-0.238 (-8.468)***	-0.26 (-9.152)***
Corruption Index		-0.45 (-2.443)***			-0.33 (-4.124)***			-0.665 (-3.611)***	
Bureaucracy Index			-0.474 (-3.974)***			-0.353 (-4.255)***			-0.777 (-4.412)***
OBS	1709	1709	1709	877	877	877	832	832	832
Adjusted R2	0.64	0.64	0.64	0.66	0.67	0.67	0.63	0.64	0.64

Note: The estimation technique is panel OLS with regional and time dummies. t-statistics are reported in parenthesis. The estimated coefficients of GDP per capita are multiplied by 10,000. The dependent variable is the share of tax revenue in percentage of GDP. GDP per capita is in constant 2005 US$; population growth is the growth rate of population between 15 and 64 ages; trade openness is the sum of imports and exports in percentage of GDP; corruption index is recalculated such that lower values indicate lower corruption; bureaucracy index is recalculated such that lower values indicate higher bureaucracy quality. We also include both regional and time dummies. The regions are defined in Table 13. The time dummies are annual.

Table 2. Determinants of tax revenues and taxable capacity – Panel B: Age dependency used as proxy for demographic characteristic (Regional dummies are included)

	Dependent Variable: Tax Revenue in % of GDP								
	1994-2012			1994-2003			2004-2012		
Constant	30.51 (25.509)***	30.021 (24.655)***	29.994 (24.204)***	27.075 (15.494)***	25.317 (14.164)***	24.659 (13.47)***	33.327 (19.448)***	33.876 (19.469)***	34.189 (19.626)***
GDP Per Capita (Constant)	2.15 (15.651)***	1.98 (12.462)***	2.02 (12.686)***	2.56 (12.281)***	2.14 (9.19)***	2.08 (8.751)***	1.84 (10.142)***	2.06 (9.337)***	2.11 (10.021)***
Age Dependency Ratio	-0.067 (-4.107)***	-0.072 (-4.383)***	-0.07 (-4.256)***	-0.028 (-1.694)*	-0.037 (-1.749)*	-0.032 (-1.779)*	-0.097 (-4.063)***	-0.09 (-3.728)***	-0.087 (-3.622)***
Trade Openness (% of GDP)	0.016 (5.314)***	0.015 (4.89)***	0.015 (4.846)***	0.018 (3.624)***	0.015 (2.927)***	0.013 (2.553)**	0.015 (3.836)***	0.016 (4.035)***	0.017 (4.211)***
Agriculture Value Added (% of GDP)	-0.256 (-11.998)***	-0.249 (-11.541)***	-0.246 (-11.071)***	-0.262 (-8.923)***	-0.246 (-8.358)***	-0.23 (-7.627)***	-0.263 (-8.356)***	-0.271 (-8.535)***	-0.288 (-8.752)***
Corruption Index		-0.57 (-2.883)***			-0.418 (-3.999)***			-0.633 (-1.751)*	
Bureaucracy Index			-0.622 (-2.582)***			-0.434 (-4.074)***			-0.881 (-2.519)**
OBS	1709	1709	1709	877	877	877	832	832	832
Adjusted R2	0.64	0.64	0.64	0.66	0.67	0.67	0.62	0.62	0.62

Note: The estimation technique is panel OLS with regional and time dummies. t-statistics are reported in parenthesis. The estimated coefficients of GDP per capita are multiplied by 10,000. The dependent variable is the share of tax revenue in percentage of GDP. GDP per capita is in constant 2005 US$; population growth is the growth rate of population between 15 and 64 ages; trade openness is the sum of imports and exports in percentage of GDP; corruption index is recalculated such that lower values indicate lower corruption; bureaucracy index is recalculated such that lower values indicate higher bureaucracy quality. We also include both regional and time dummies. The regions are defined in Table 13. The time dummies are annual.

The age dependency ratio has the expected negative sign, and its estimated coefficients have higher significance for the sub period of 2004-2012, perhaps indicating significant increases in life expectancy worldwide. Similarly, the growth rate of population has a negative sign and it is statistically significant. In addition, its economic significance, when measured by the size of its estimated coefficients, increased in the second half of the time period, perhaps reflecting difficulties of young people to join the labor force whom therefore stay outside the tax base. It can be concluded that, in recent years, population growth and age dependency have become more important negative determinants of tax revenue collections.

Table 3 and 4 presents similar results for total fiscal revenues (tax and non-tax). All estimation results are as expected and statistically significant, except for trade openness and population growth rates for the period between 1994 and 2003, which then increase for the last sub-period, perhaps reflecting more recent trends in global trade and population growth affecting total fiscal revenues.

Similar to tax revenues, the economic significance of institutional variables in determining total fiscal revenue is high. In general, the results support the previous papers' findings, determining the factors affecting of tax and fiscal revenues (Tanzi & Davoodi, 1997; Bird & Gendron, 2007; Gupta, 2007; and Le, Moreno-Dodson, & Rojchaichaninthorn, 2008). Countries with higher income per capita levels, a lower population growth (and lower age dependency) rate, more trade openness, lower agriculture value added in GDP, and higher institutional quality tend to collect higher tax revenues and fiscal revenues as a whole.

Robustness Check for Regression Results

For the robustness check of the empirical results, we also run alternative specifications including three additional variables as determinants of tax revenue to GDP ratios. The size of a shadow economy can be another important variable in affecting negatively the tax revenue collections of any country because informal workers and economic activities remain outside the tax base. The shadow economy variable used in this chapter includes all market-based legal production of goods and services that are deliberately concealed from public authorities for any of the following reasons: (1) to avoid payment of income, value added, or other taxes, (2) to avoid payment of social security contributions, (3) to avoid having to meet certain legal labor market standards, such as minimum wages, maximum working hours, safety standards, etc., and (4) to avoid complying with certain administrative procedures, such as completing statistical questionnaires or other administrative forms (see Schneider *et al.*, 2010).

As the size of the shadow economy increases, governments are not be able to collect taxes effectively due to the fact that it gets harder to track profit, income, sales etc. (Bird *et al.*, 2004; Davoodi & Grigorian, 2007). The estimation results are reported in Table 5 Panel A. Since the data for the size of the shadow economy is limited, the total number of observations drops to 894 from 1709. But the signs and significance of coefficients are robust to the inclusion of this new variable. The size of the shadow economy is a statistically significant and a negative determinant of taxes.

Total consumption is also included as an alternative factor determining tax revenues. Higher consumption as a percentage of GDP has a positive effect on tax collection. Higher consumption improves tax revenues mainly through higher indirect taxes (Bird, 2008; Cardenas & Tuzemen, 2011). Thus, the sign is positive as expected and the other results are robust to the inclusion of this new variable.

The rents generated from natural resource rents[25] constitute another critical factor affecting tax and total fiscal revenues (Ndikumana & Abderrahim, 2010). In developing countries with natural resources,

Table 3. Determinants of fiscal revenue – Panel A: Population growth used as proxy for demographic characteristic (Regional dummies are included)

	Dependent Variable: Fiscal Revenue in % of GDP								
	1994-2012			1994-2003			2004-2012		
Constant	34.667 (47.904)***	34.157 (40.654)***	35.272 (40.531)***	31.143 (29.771)***	28.935 (24.465)***	29.404 (23.757)***	37.363 (37.318)***	39.255 (32.658)***	40.963 (34.028)***
GDP Per Capita (Constant)	2.51 (16.647)***	2.41 (13.761)***	2.62 (14.96)***	3.13 (14.066)***	2.7 (10.895)***	2.8 (11.022)***	2.14 (10.42)***	2.57 (10.102)***	2.82 (11.722)***
Population Growth	-0.97 (-4.838)***	-0.971 (-4.841)***	-0.976 (-4.865)***	-0.284 (-1.058)	-0.379 (-1.414)	-0.345 (-1.282)	-1.697 (-5.613)***	-1.824 (-5.991)***	-1.931 (-6.416)***
Trade Openness (% of GDP)	0.011 (3.352)***	0.011 (3.093)***	0.012 (3.543)***	0.006 (1.061)	0.002 (0.36)	0.002 (0.37)	0.014 (3.112)***	0.016 (3.426)***	0.018 (3.898)***
Agriculture Value Added (% of GDP)	-0.358 (-17.887)***	-0.356 (-17.746)***	-0.364 (-17.635)***	-0.34 (-13.288)***	-0.327 (-12.772)***	-0.318 (-11.885)***	-0.351 (-10.837)***	-0.35 (-10.864)***	-0.38 (-11.736)***
Corruption Index		-0.505 (-2.895)***			-0.432 (-3.891)***			-0.417 (-2.819)***	
Bureaucracy Index			-0.555 (-2.252)**			-0.298 (-2.607)***			-0.641 (-5.21)***
OBS	1709	1709	1709	877	877	877	832	832	832
Adjusted R2	0.63	0.63	0.63	0.66	0.67	0.67	0.60	0.60	0.61

Note: The estimation technique is panel OLS with regional and time dummies. t-statistics are reported in parenthesis. The estimated coefficients of GDP per capita are multiplied by 10,000. The dependent variable is the share of fiscal revenue in percentage of GDP. See Table 11 for the definitions of the variables. We also include both regional and time dummies. The regions are defined in Table 13. The time dummies are annual.

Table 4. Determinants of fiscal revenue – Panel B: Age dependency used as proxy for demographic characteristic (Regional dummies are included)

	Dependent Variable: Fiscal Revenue in % of GDP								
	1994-2012			1994-2003			2004-2012		
Constant	32.795 (24.907)***	32.506 (24.229)***	33.223 (24.347)***	29.287 (15.782)***	27.56 (14.504)***	27.728 (14.181)***	34.914 (17.884)***	35.629 (17.984)***	36.584 (18.57)***
GDP Per Capita (Constant)	2.41 (15.954)***	2.31 (13.199)***	2.51 (14.351)***	3.11 (14.002)***	2.69 (10.848)***	2.79 (10.98)***	1.9 (9.192)***	2.19 (8.703)***	2.43 (10.184)***
Age Dependency Ratio	-0.081 (-2.462)**	-0.085 (-2.283)**	-0.091 (-2.59)***	-0.022 (-1.876)*	-0.014 (-1.747)*	-0.019 (-1.767)*	-0.092 (-2.363)**	-0.091 (-2.685)***	-0.079 (-3.051)***
Trade Openness (% of GDP)	0.014 (4.219)***	0.014 (3.968)***	0.015 (4.378)***	0.007 (1.287)	0.003 (0.647)	0.003 (0.648)	0.019 (-4.235)***	0.02 (-4.466)***	0.022 (-4.931)***
Agriculture Value Added (% of GDP)	-0.398 (-17.022)***	-0.394 (-16.636)***	-0.407 (-16.665)***	-0.363 (-11.686)***	-0.347 (-11.126)***	-0.342 (-10.654)***	-0.442 (-12.353)***	-0.453 (-12.536)***	-0.491 (-13.204)***
Corruption Index		-0.51 (-3.118)***			-0.412 (-3.711)***			-0.603 (-2.001)**	
Bureaucracy Index			-0.702 (-3.193)***			-0.281 (-2.468)**			-0.844 (-4.312)***
OBS	1709	1709	1709	877	877	877	832	832	832
Adjusted R2	0.62	0.62	0.62	0.66	0.67	0.67	0.58	0.59	0.59

Note: The estimation technique is panel OLS with regional and time dummies. t-statistics are reported in parenthesis. The estimated coefficients of GDP per capita are multiplied by 10,000. The dependent variable is the share of fiscal revenue in percentage of GDP. See Table 11 for the definitions of the variables. We also include both regional and time dummies. The regions are defined in Table 13. The time dummies are annual.

such rents are an important source of non-tax fiscal revenues. In this case tax revenues could be lower because the government may not depend as much on taxes to raise fiscal revenue.

If this argument is true, we expect the impact of natural resources to be negative on tax revenues but positive on total fiscal revenues. In our regression, the sign of the share of natural resource rents in GDP is indeed negative, as it can be seen in Table 7 Panel C. Moreover this variable's economic and statistical significance is dominant. It is worth noting that resource rich countries have been already excluded in our dataset. It means that even for countries that are not resource rich, natural resource rents can still play a role in determining tax revenues. The rest of the variables still produce significant results. Overall, it can be seen that the results are robust to the alternative empirical specifications.

Tax Effort: Estimation Results

The predicted value of tax revenue collection (tax capacity) is the estimated value of tax revenues, calculated using the estimated coefficients given in column (2) in Table 1 (Panel A). The specification takes tax revenues as a function of GDP per capita, population growth, trade openness, agriculture value added (in percentage of GDP), corruption index, as well as regional and time dummies. Tax effort is the ratio of actual taxes to the tax capacity of the country, both as a percentage of GDP. Table 16 in Appendix shows the actual and predicted taxes (i.e. taxable capacity), as well as the tax effort for each country included in the study. The averages between 1994 and 2012 are reported in the first columns, while the averages for 1994 to 2003 and for 2004 to 2012 are presented in the following columns. The same exercise is repeated for total fiscal revenue in Table 17 in Appendix. The predicted value of total fiscal revenue is calculated, based on the second estimation results reported in Table 5 (Panel A).

Most countries' tax effort indexes are relatively stable over the two sub-periods 1994-2003 and 2004-2012. Exceptions are: Bulgaria, China, Congo, DRC, Costa Rica, El Salvador, Georgia, Macao (China), Nicaragua, Paraguay, and Thailand which all increased their tax efforts above 1 after 2003; on the contrary, Austria, Canada, Egypt, Malaysia, Pakistan, Philippines, Slovak Republic, and Sri Lanka all lowered their tax efforts below 1 after 2003. These results also show that several Latin American countries have managed to increase their tax efforts above 1 in recent years. Similar to tax predictions, average fiscal revenue predictions are reported for the period of 1994 to 2012, as well as for the two sub-samples in Table 17 in Appendix.

Figure 3 reports the average values of actual and predicted tax collection (tax capacity) as a percentage of GDP. Each dot in the figure indicates the position of a country, corresponding to their average tax revenues versus predicted tax revenues. The 45 degree line represents countries with the unitary tax effort. Along this line, tax collection exactly equals predicted tax capacity.

The predicted tax revenues are positively correlated with the actual collection, meaning that higher collection tends to be associated with higher tax capacity.[26] The countries above the 45° line are the ones with a relatively high tax effort (actual taxes are higher than predicted taxes). Their tax revenue collections are consistent with their predicted values given their macroeconomic, demographic and institutional indicators. On the other hand, countries located below the 45° line are collecting tax revenues below their tax capacity (low effort) and they have room to improve their tax collection effort.

Figure 4 presents the actual tax ratio and tax capacity on average across countries from 1994 to 2012. Between 1997 and 2004, corresponding to the period following the Asian financial crisis in 1997, taxable capacity ratios were above actual tax revenue collections, while between 2005 and 2008 actual tax collections were above taxable capacity ratios. With the financial crisis in 2008, actual tax collections

Table 5. Robustness check alternative determinants of tax revenues – Panel A: Size of shadow economy (in % of GDP) used instead of agriculture value added (Regional dummies are included)

	Dependent Variable: Tax Revenue in % of GDP								
	1994-2012			1994-2003			2004-2012		
Constant	30.405 (24.287)***	29.697 (20.18)***	28.637 (19.244)***	28.516 (16.541)***	25.289 (12.589)***	23.411 (11.543)***	31.733 (17.332)***	33.224 (15.263)***	33.245 (15.391)***
GDP Per Capita (Constant)	2.11 (10.17)***	2.01 (8.605)***	1.87 (7.943)***	2.41 (8.309)***	2.01 (6.342)***	1.75 (5.468)***	1.96 (6.556)***	2.19 (6.274)***	2.18 (6.347)***
Population Growth	-2.609 (-10.611)***	-2.572 (-10.322)***	-2.452 (-9.589)***	-2.005 (-6.038)***	-1.841 (-5.521)***	-1.607 (-4.77)***	-3.299 (-9.015)***	-3.382 (-9.103)***	-3.459 (-8.978)***
Trade Openness (% of GDP)	0.061 (1.817)**	0.051 (1.202)	0.043 (0.984)	0.028 (1.296)	0.036 (0.95)	0.033 (0.472)	0.023 (0.496)	0.044 (0.611)	0.023 (0.618)
Size of Shadow Economy (% of GDP)	-0.172 (-6.835)***	-0.169 (-6.699)***	-0.162 (-6.382)***	-0.177 (-5.437)***	-0.166 (-5.135)***	-0.148 (-4.58)***	-0.146 (-3.713)***	-0.152 (-3.844)***	-0.153 (-3.865)***
Corruption Index		-0.516 (-2.915)***			-0.506 (-3.056)***			-0.655 (-2.264)**	
Bureaucracy Index			-0.925 (-2.586)**			-0.708 (-4.545)***			-1.218 (-2.316)**
OBS	894	894	894	476	476	476	418	418	418
Adjusted R2	0.659	0.659	0.660	0.674	0.680	0.687	0.647	0.648	0.648

Note: The estimation technique is panel OLS with regional and time dummies. t-statistics are reported in parenthesis. The estimated coefficients of GDP per capita are multiplied by 10,000. As in Tables 1 and 2, the dependent variable in each panel is the share of tax revenue in percentage of GDP. See Table 11 for the definitions of the variables. We also include both regional and time dummies. The regions are defined in Table 13. The time dummies are annual.

Table 6. Robustness check alternative determinants of tax revenues – Panel B: Share total consumption in GDP is added (Regional dummies are included)

	Dependent Variable: Tax Revenue in % of GDP								
	1994-2012			**1994-2003**			**2004-2012**		
Constant	12.942 (9.621)***	10.285 (7.056)***	10.755 (7.326)***	8.431 (4.12)***	3.737 (1.763)*	2.881 (1.341)	16.627 (9.493)***	18.037 (8.961)***	19.259 (9.848)***
GDP Per Capita (Constant)	2.62 (19.558)***	2.28 (15.009)***	2.34 (15.294)***	3.06 (15.082)***	2.43 (11.076)***	2.32 (10.35)***	2.34 (13.21)***	2.51 (11.619)***	2.66 (12.863)***
Population Growth	-0.881 (-4.899)***	-0.862 (-4.821)***	-0.856 (-4.774)***	-0.279 (-1.142)	-0.413 (-1.723)*	-0.415 (-1.735)*	-1.541 (-5.765)***	-1.621 (-5.937)***	-1.688 (-6.237)***
Trade Openness (% of GDP)	0.011 (3.73)***	0.009 (2.856)***	0.009 (2.796)***	0.012 (2.514)**	0.006 (1.637)	0.003 (1.587)	0.009 (2.142)**	0.009 (2.279)**	0.01 (2.577)**
Agriculture Value Added (% of GDP)	-0.308 (-16.801)***	-0.302 (-16.505)***	-0.29 (-15.339)***	-0.311 (-12.865)***	-0.287 (-12.052)***	-0.254 (-10.232)***	-0.291 (-10.076)***	-0.29 (-10.03)***	-0.305 (-10.477)***
Total Consumption (% of GDP)	0.164 (12.23)***	0.173 (12.817)***	0.169 (12.594)***	0.192 (9.331)***	0.203 (10.066)***	0.203 (10.103)***	0.141 (8.109)***	0.135 (7.61)***	0.134 (7.64)***
Corruption Index		-0.361 (-4.582)***			-0.666 (-6.607)***			-0.187 (-2.419)**	
Bureaucracy Index			-0.575 (-3.65)***			-0.716 (-6.914)***			-0.324 (-2.968)***
OBS	1709	1709	1709	877	877	877	832	832	832
Adjusted R2	0.675	0.678	0.677	0.698	0.713	0.714	0.663	0.664	0.667

Note: The estimation technique is panel OLS with regional and time dummies. T-statistics are reported in parenthesis. The estimated coefficients of GDP per capita are multiplied by 10,000. As in Tables 1 and 2, the dependent variable in each panel is the share of tax revenue in percentage of GDP. See Table 11 for the definitions of the variables. We also include both regional and time dummies. The regions are defined in Table 13. The time dummies are annual.

Table 7. Robustness check alternative determinants of tax revenues – Panel C: Total natural resources rents in GDP is added (Regional dummies are included)

	Dependent Variable: Tax Revenue in % of GDP								
	1994-2012			1994-2003			2004-2012		
Constant	28.553 (43.6)***	27.808 (36.784)***	28.02 (35.672)***	26.697 (27.898)***	24.441 (22.667)***	24.149 (21.462)***	30.034 (33.669)***	31.696 (30)***	32.54 (30.395)***
GDP Per Capita (Constant)	2.1 (15.497)***	1.95 (12.419)***	2 (12.744)***	2.51 (12.342)***	2.07 (9.151)***	2.04 (8.819)***	1.86 (10.251)***	2.25 (9.975)***	2.34 (10.938)***
Population Growth	-1.088 (-5.953)***	-1.087 (-5.957)***	-1.081 (-5.917)***	-0.464 (-1.884)*	-0.558 (-2.279)**	-0.554 (-2.26)**	-1.78 (-6.47)***	-1.919 (-6.904)***	-1.985 (-7.173)***
Trade Openness (% of GDP)	0.012 (3.774)***	0.011 (3.38)***	0.011 (3.422)***	0.015 (3.004)***	0.011 (2.21)**	0.009 (1.88)*	0.008 (2.029)**	0.009 (2.331)**	0.01 (2.616)***
Natural Resources Rent (% of GDP)	-0.264 (-14.762)***	-0.261 (-14.589)***	-0.258 (-13.996)***	-0.252 (-10.748)***	-0.239 (-10.203)***	-0.221 (-9.073)***	-0.254 (-8.897)***	-0.251 (-8.841)***	-0.271 (-9.506)***
Corruption Index		-0.533 (-8.641)***			-0.573 (-7.36)***			-0.701 (-4.977)***	
Bureaucracy Index			-0.933 (-8.587)***			-0.969 (-7.175)***			-0.801 (-5.044)***
OBS	1664	1664	1664	877	877	877	787	787	787
Adjusted R2	0.665	0.676	0.665	0.687	0.693	0.693	0.663	0.666	0.670

Note: The estimation technique is panel OLS with regional and time dummies. t-statistics are reported in parenthesis. The estimated coefficients of GDP per capita are multiplied by 10,000. As in Tables 1 and 2, the dependent variable in each panel is the share of tax revenue in percentage of GDP. See Table 11 for the definitions of the variables. We also include both regional and time dummies. The regions are defined in Table 13. The time dummies are annual.

Figure 3. Actual tax collection and taxable capacity, averages over 1994-2009

Note: Predicted tax/GDP is taxable capacity, calculated based on the estimation results given in column (2) of the results in Table 1 (Panel A). Actual TAX/GDP is actual tax revenue in % of GDP. The line is the 45° line, which represents the points where the tax effort index is 1.

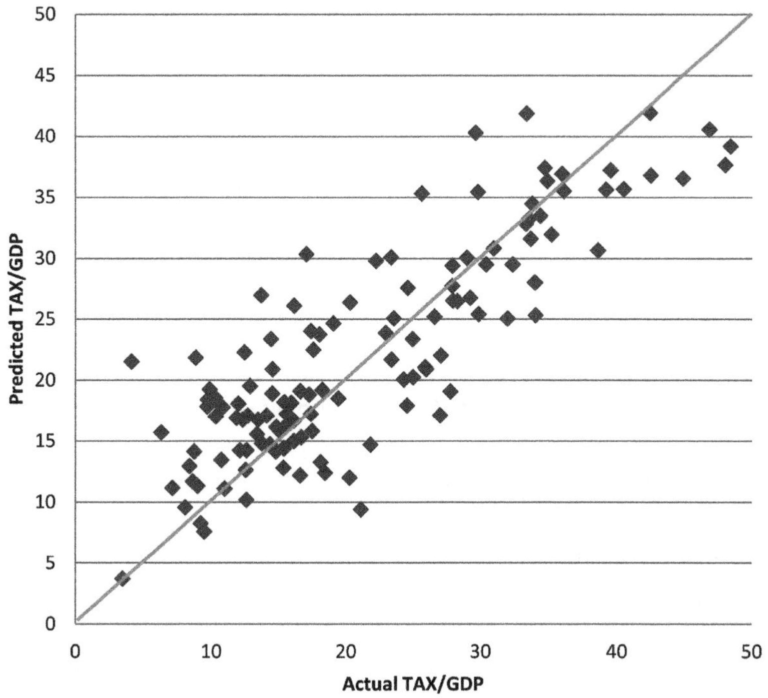

Figure 4. Average actual tax collection and taxable capacity over 1994-2009

Note: Predicted tax/GDP is taxable capacity, calculated based on the estimation results given in column (2) of the results in Table 1 (Panel A). Actual TAX/GDP is actual tax revenue in % of GDP.

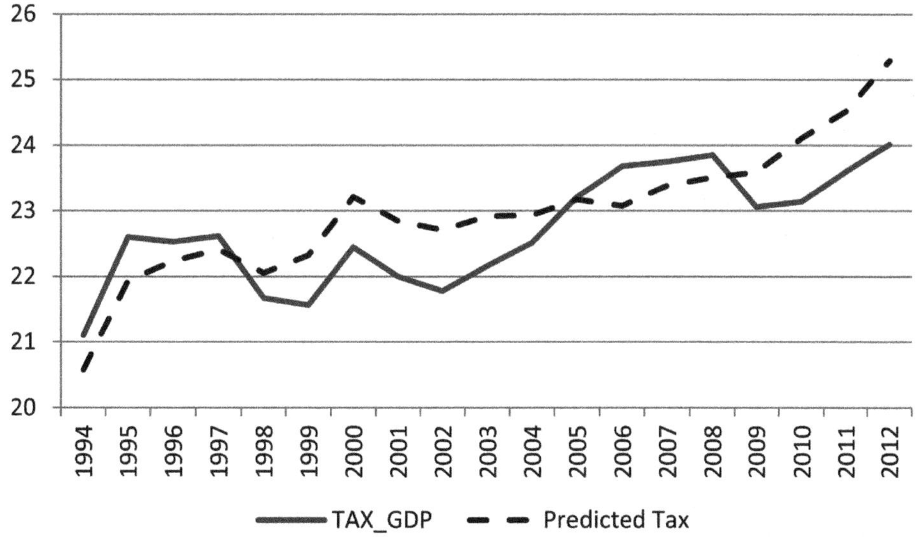

again fell below taxable capacity ratios. These results indicate that tax efforts tend to drop below 1 during crises periods.

The ranking of countries based on their tax effort is reported in Table 8. According to this ranking, Papua New Guinea has the highest tax effort (2.26), while Sudan has the lowest (only 0.401). Most developed countries are located around the value of 1. In the sub-Saharan Africa region, Seychelles (1.35), Namibia (1.2121) and Swaziland (1.232) have the highest tax effort indexes. In the MENA region, Morocco has the highest tax effort score (1.58). In Europe, Sweden, Hungary, and Denmark have the highest scores of approximately 1.25 each. In addition, Mongolia (1.69) and Vietnam (1.49) have the highest effort index in East Asia. It should be noted that France (1.23) and Brazil (1.46) also are on the top 20 list. China has increased its effort score significantly in recent years as shown in Table A7. It is now 0.80 on average. Japan and Hong Kong (China) are the two high-income countries with a low tax effort index with values of 0.56. Argentina's effort score is even lower, at only 0.515, and it is ranked second from the bottom.

Figure 5 presents a detailed analysis of countries, across 7 regions and overtime. It should be noted that high-income OECD countries are excluded in the regional data. These countries are reported in the last panel of the figure.

Since 1998, actual tax revenue collections in Sub-Saharan Africa have been increasing almost continuously, faster than their predicted values, and the tax effort index in the region has improved significantly.[27] It increased from 0.91 in 1998 to almost 1.07 in 2008, indicating the countries on average were collecting almost 15 percent higher actual tax revenues relative to their predicted values. It is not surprising that this period corresponds to higher growth rates in Sub-Saharan Africa. But, in any case, this result indicates that progress has been made in tax policy and administration beyond what was anticipated based on economic, institutional and demographic values.

In East Asia, the tax effort reached 1.26 in 2001 (indicating that actual taxes were higher than predicted taxes), but it declined quickly after this peak point and fell to 0.91 by 2005. After a jump in 2006, the index started to drop after the global financial crisis. Given that actual taxes are below predicted values, countries in this region could still deploy additional efforts to increase tax revenues.

In Eastern Europe and Central Asia, the gap between actual and predicted tax revenues was large, between 1996 and 2001, with actual values lower than predicted ones. Following this period, predicted taxes dropped with declining economic activity in the region and the tax effort index increased. At the same time, these countries started collecting almost 5 percentage points more tax revenues on average, reflecting their transition to market economies and important tax policy reform packages trying to extend the tax base to an emerging private sector, which also helped to close the gap between actual and predicted values for this group of countries. The highest effort index for the region was 0.98 in 2007. Similar to the other regions, the tax effort has declined after the global financial crisis in 2008.

Latin American countries clearly show a rising trend in the tax effort after 1998, although this trend has been reversed in most recent years following the global crisis. The tax effort index rose from 0.85 in 2000 to 1.16 in 2008, at which point the region reached its peak. This increasing tax effort is a result of higher actual tax revenues following tax reforms in the region. Throughout these years the ratio of actual taxes to GDP increased by almost 5 percentage points, from 15 percent to 20 percent. The more stable economic environment and steady growth rates were among the main factors behind these increased tax revenues (Fricke & Sussmuth, 2011).

The Middle Eastern and North Africa region had an initial drop in the tax effort index between 1994 and 2000, followed by an almost flat trend from 2001 to 2009 of around 0.95. The index dropped slightly

Table 8. Ranking of countries by tax effort index, averages 1994-2009

	Tax Effort		Tax Effort		Tax Effort		Tax Effort
Papua New Guinea	2.256	Netherlands	1.101	Cape Verde	0.963	Albania	0.760
Mongolia	1.694	Poland	1.097	Austria	0.961	Lithuania	0.747
Morocco	1.582	Belarus	1.094	Ghana	0.956	Dominican Rep.	0.745
Vietnam	1.492	Malaysia	1.091	Costa Rica	0.956	Ethiopia	0.741
Fiji	1.487	Macao (China)	1.079	Chile	0.952	El Salvador	0.737
Brazil	1.458	Benin	1.077	Romania	0.951	Switzerland	0.736
Tunisia	1.372	Bolivia	1.072	Myanmar	0.946	United States	0.727
Honduras	1.370	Australia	1.070	Botswana	0.941	Mauritius	0.725
Syrian Arab Rep.	1.363	Moldova	1.070	Philippines	0.931	Uganda	0.704
Seychelles	1.345	Togo	1.067	Iceland	0.929	Singapore	0.696
Israel	1.278	Croatia	1.066	Sri Lanka	0.921	Rwanda	0.666
Sweden	1.276	Germany	1.064	Zambia	0.919	Mexico	0.661
Hungary	1.262	South Africa	1.057	Peru	0.905	Bangladesh	0.650
Nepal	1.258	Macedonia	1.056	Jamaica	0.894	Congo, Dem. Rep.	0.640
Trinidad and Tobago	1.245	Jordan	1.053	Nicaragua	0.887	Yemen, Rep.	0.620
Lao PDR	1.244	India	1.049	Cote d'Ivoire	0.880	Georgia	0.619
Denmark	1.237	Slovak Rep.	1.032	Senegal	0.872	Guinea	0.611
Uruguay	1.237	Spain	1.027	Indonesia	0.863	Guatemala	0.609
Swaziland	1.232	Italy	1.018	Burkina Faso	0.853	Japan	0.563
France	1.231	Canada	1.015	Lebanon	0.849	Hong Kong (China)	0.560
Namibia	1.231	Norway	1.013	Bhutan	0.848	Tajikistan	0.556
Ukraine	1.216	Thailand	1.011	Ireland	0.843	Madagascar	0.546
Bosnia and Herz.	1.213	Portugal	1.010	Colombia	0.827	Cameroon	0.531
Zimbabwe	1.213	Bulgaria	1.008	China	0.807	Argentina	0.515
Burundi	1.204	Czech Rep.	1.006	Niger	0.801	Sudan	0.401
New Zealand	1.176	Paraguay	0.997	Luxembourg	0.797		
Finland	1.156	Pakistan	0.995	Sierra Leone	0.795		
Lesotho	1.150	Greece	0.981	Korea, Rep.	0.782		
Belgium	1.137	Mali	0.977	Latvia	0.777		
Cambodia	1.123	United Kingdom	0.976	Armenia	0.774		
Kenya	1.108	Egypt	0.968	Turkey	0.771		
Slovenia	1.103	Estonia	0.966	Kyrgyz Republic	0.770		

Note: See Table 16 in Appendix for details. Tax effort is the ratio of actual tax revenues in percentage of GDP to predicted tax revenues in percentage of GDP (taxable capacity). For Zimbabwe, the data is for the period of 1994-1997 and 2009-12.

Figure 5. Actual tax collection, taxable capacity and tax effort by regions, 1994-2012
Note: TAX_GDP is actual tax collection in % of GDP; predicted tax is the taxable capacity calculated based on the estimation results given in column (2) of the results in Table 1 (Panel A). Tax effort is the ratio of actual tax to taxable capacity. Regions are defined in Table 13.

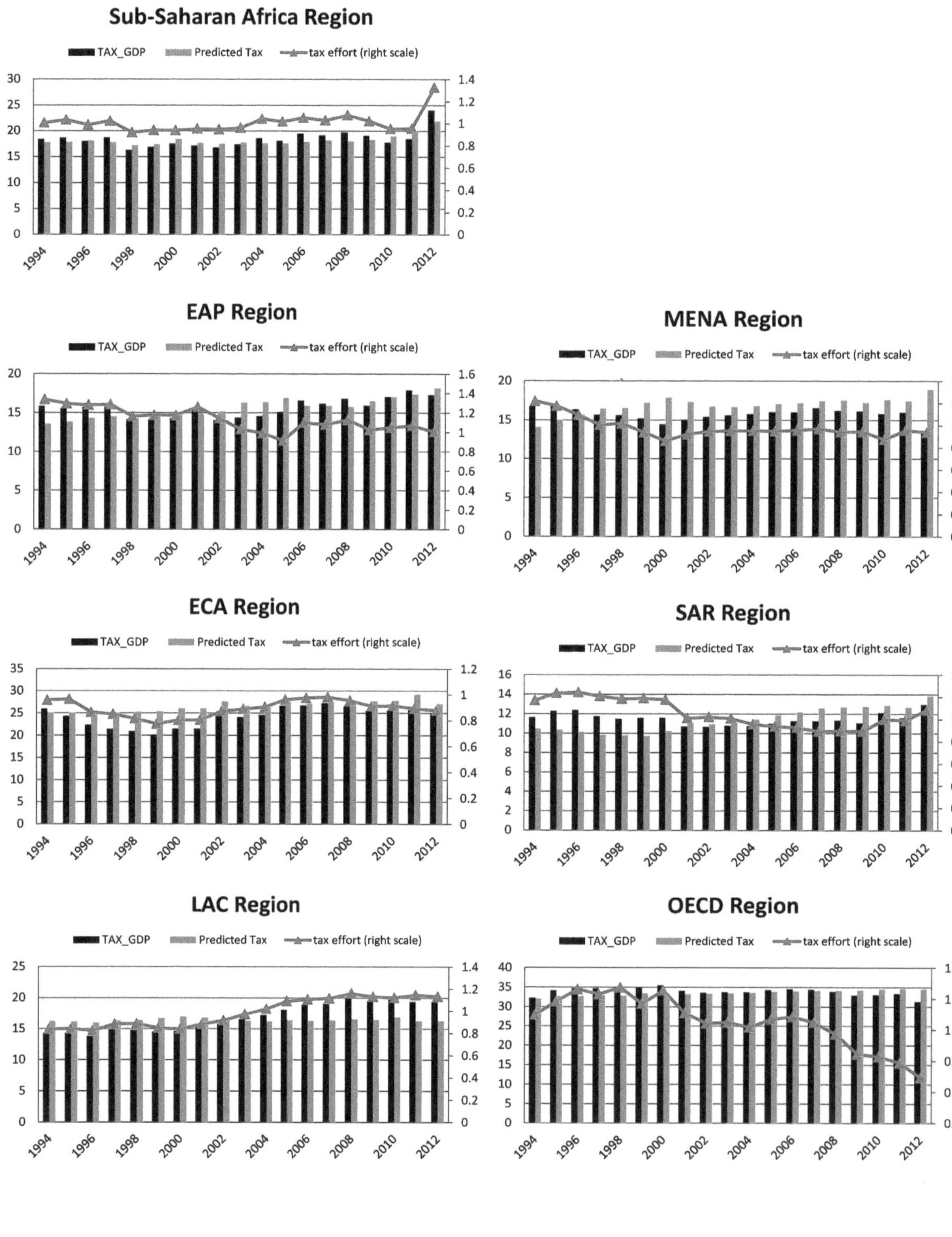

in 2010 but increased back to the 0.95 level in 2012. In this region, despite the fact that the actual tax ratio increased significantly between 2000 and 2008, the tax capacity of countries increased during the same period with improvements in macroeconomic and institutional conditions. As a result, the effort index remained almost constant between 2000 and 2008.

South Asia has the lowest actual and predicted tax revenues in the world. The rates are even lower than the ones observed in Sub-Saharan Africa, which is the poorest region in the world. After hitting the bottom in 2002 with actual tax revenues only at 10.7 percent of GDP, both actual and predicted taxes have increased significantly. Since the magnitude of increasing predicted taxes dominates the magnitude of increasing actual taxes, the tax effort index declined throughout the years from 1.24 in 1994 to 0.89 in 2009. In more recent years, however, larger actual tax revenues reflect higher tax effort indexes, which rose to 1.08 in 2012. Ongoing tax reforms in these countries are expected to continue improving their level of tax revenue collections.

When we focus on OECD high income countries, the tax effort has almost continuously declined after 2000 from 1.06 to 0.92 in 2012. This was mainly due to a drop in actual taxes and, at the same time, increasing predicted taxes. The drop in the effort index is more pronounced after 2006. Tax revenues fluctuate only slightly from year to year in these countries, which indicates that policy makers are more certain about the revenue they can raise in order to finance public expenditures.

When we focus on most recent years, the declining trend in both tax collection and the tax effort is clear and persistent. Due to the financial and economic crises of 2008-2009, economic activities declined significantly in almost every country. Overall, the expected effect on tax revenues has been negative, despite signs of recovery in some parts of the world. At the same time, many governments introduced stimulus packages including measures to lower tax rates, which put additional downward pressure on tax intake.

Country Classification Based on Tax Collection and Tax Effort

Countries are classified into different groups based on their tax efforts and actual tax collection. The value of 1 is used as the benchmark for the tax effort and 18.13 percent (median of the tax-to-GDP ratio in the sample) is used for actual tax revenues. A country is regarded as a low-collection country if its actual collection is lower than 18.13 percent, and regarded as a high-collection country if its collection is above that level. Similarly, countries with a tax effort index less than 1 are included in the low tax effort group, while those with a tax effort index more than 1 are placed into the high tax effort group.

Based on these definitions, the countries are ranked into four different categories: (i) low tax collection, low tax effort; (ii) high tax collection, high tax effort; (iii) low tax collection, high tax effort; and (iv) high tax collection, low tax effort. Table 9 gives the list of countries in each group.[28]

Group 1: Low Tax Revenue Collection and Low Tax Effort

The collection of taxes in this group of countries is low by international standards and also lies below their respective taxable capacity given their economic, social and institutional characteristics. These countries have significant potential for revenue enhancement. This group includes the highest number of developing countries from all geographic regions. They are mostly low-income countries and there is not a single developed country in the group. Most South Asian countries are found in this group.

Table 9. Classification of countries based on tax efforts and tax collection, 1994-2012

<table>
<tr><th colspan="2" rowspan="2"></th><th colspan="4">Tax Effort</th></tr>
<tr><th colspan="2">Low</th><th colspan="2">High</th></tr>
<tr><td rowspan="4">Tax Collection</td><td rowspan="2">Low</td><td>Developing Countries</td><td>Developed Countries</td><td>Developing Countries</td><td>Developed Countries</td></tr>
<tr><td>Albania; Argentina; Bangladesh; Bhutan; Burkina Faso; Cameroon; China; Colombia; Congo, Dem. Rep.; Costa Rica; Cote d'Ivoire; Dominican Rep.; Egypt, Arab Rep.; El Salvador; Ethiopia; Georgia; Ghana; Guatemala; Guinea; Hong Kong (China); Indonesia; Kyrgyz Republic; Lebanon; Madagascar; Mali; Mauritius; Mexico; Myanmar; Nicaragua; Niger; Pakistan; Paraguay; Peru; Philippines; Rwanda; Senegal; Sierra Leone; Singapore; Sri Lanka; Sudan; Tajikistan; Uganda; Yemen, Rep.; Zambia</td><td></td><td>Benin; Bolivia; Burundi; Cambodia; Honduras; India; Kenya; Lao PDR; Malaysia; Nepal; Syrian Arab Rep.; Thailand; Togo</td><td></td></tr>
<tr><td rowspan="2">High</td><td>Developing Countries</td><td>Developed Countries</td><td>Developing Countries</td><td>Developed Countries</td></tr>
<tr><td>Armenia; Botswana; Cape Verde; Jamaica; Latvia; Lithuania; Romania; Turkey</td><td>Austria; Chile; Estonia; Greece; Iceland; Ireland; Luxembourg; Switzerland; United Kingdom; United States; Japan; Korea, Rep.</td><td>Belarus; Bosnia and Herz.; Brazil; Bulgaria; Croatia; Fiji; Hungary; Jordan; Lesotho; Macao (China); Macedonia; Moldova; Mongolia; Morocco; Namibia; Papua New Guinea; Seychelles; South Africa; Swaziland; Trinidad and Tobago; Tunisia; Ukraine; Uruguay; Vietnam; Zimbabwe</td><td>Australia; Belgium; Canada; Czech Rep.; Denmark; Finland; France; Germany; Israel; Italy; Netherlands; New Zealand; Norway; Poland; Portugal; Slovak Rep.; Slovenia; Spain; Sweden</td></tr>
</table>

Note: Taxable capacity is calculated based on the estimation results given in column (2) of Table 1 (Panel A).

Some of these countries, such as Cameroon and Madagascar, depend heavily on aid to finance government spending. The majority of them have tax collection constraints associated with both tax administration and tax policy. For example, in Cameroon, Madagascar, and the Philippines, overly complex tax structures and multiple ad-hoc tax incentives restrict the already limited tax base, make tax avoidance and evasion easier, deepen the public perception of unfairness of taxes, and, as a result, create additional opportunities for tax corruption. In addition to the added complexity of their tax structures, the limited capacity of their tax revenue administration has caused chronic low tax revenue collections in some of these countries.

Group 2: High Revenue Collection and High Tax Effort

On the other extreme of the spectrum, given that the level of tax intake in this country group is already high by international standards and even above their respective taxable capacity, further increase in tax revenue collection does not need to be a policy objective per se in these countries.

Tax reforms should not focus necessarily on revenue-enhancing measures but rather on reducing tax-induced distortions to economic activity and promoting equity. For example, these countries could improve the business climate through further rationalizing their tax regimes and lowering compliance costs for small and medium size enterprises, as well as rebalancing the tax mix between direct and indirect taxation. In addition, any further improvements in the quality of governance (lower corruption and/or higher bureaucracy quality) could also lead to better taxation performance.

It is also worth noting that having high tax collection and high tax effort does not automatically mean that their tax structures or administrations should be considered as models for other countries to replicate. Many of these developing countries still have a highly complex and inefficient tax structure with widespread deductions, exemptions, and ineffective tax incentives.

Mainly, high and middle-income countries, including a significant number of developing countries like Brazil and South Africa[29], are included in this group. In addition to the Northern European countries, France, Germany, Italy, Portugal and Spain are also in this group.

Group 3: Low Tax Revenue Collection and High Tax Effort

Countries in this group seem to be caught in a 'trap' with relatively low levels of tax intake, despite their relatively high tax efforts in line with their economic, geographic and institutional architecture.

A sustained approach to break this trap would be to conduct important parallel reforms aimed at improving the underlying reasons behind their low taxable capacity, rather than focusing on tax policy and administration per se. Such reforms could focus, for example, on creating a favorable institutional, legal and regulatory environment to attract private investment, and diversifying growth sources. Most importantly, they should focus on reforms to improve the quality of governance. Demographic factors may be more difficult to change at least in the short run. Medium- to long-term reforms along these lines may expand the scope for raising additional tax revenue by broadening the tax base and enhancing the functioning of the tax administration.

This group has the fewest number of countries and they are all either low-income or middle income countries. There are no developed countries included. Interestingly, in this group of countries, especially for the low-income ones, the tax administration capacity is mostly weak and the tax regime is highly unstable. In addition, there are more advanced countries like India, Malaysia, and Thailand also included in this group.

Group 4: High Tax Revenue Collection and Low Tax Effort

Although countries in this group have already achieved relatively high tax revenue collections, they still have the potential to implement tax policy and administration reforms and reach a higher level of tax revenues, more consistent with their current economic, social and institutional realities. They still have untapped tax revenue potential, probably reflecting inadequate tax choices (types, rates and structure design) and/or a complex system of exemptions and loopholes that complicates the tax administration.

Almost every country in this group belongs to either the middle-income or high-income group. Most developing countries in this group are in the ECA region. Botswana is the only country from Africa. Developed countries include many large economies such as Chile, Japan, Korea, the United Kingdom, and the United States, which are still collecting below their tax revenue potential.

Robustness Check for Classification- Alternative Specification

The predicted tax rate is computed using the estimation results presented in column (2) of Table 1 – Panel A. This series is used to calculate the tax effort index and country classifications, presented in Table 5. In order to understand how the classification of countries may change when an alternative empirical specification is used to calculate the tax capacity and effort indexes, a robustness check is run using the estimated coefficients of column (3) specification in Table 3 – panel C. In this alternative specification, tax revenues are determined by GDP per capita, trade openness, population growth, bureaucracy quality, and regional and time dummies, to which we add natural resource rents. When the new classification (available upon request) and the initial one given in Table 5 are compared, we confirm the robustness of the results.[30]

CONCLUSION AND FUTURE RESEARCH

Taxation is considered to be the least distortive way to finance public expenditures, when compared to money printing and borrowing, and, overtime, can be conducive to lower aid dependency and state building. However, many countries, developed and developing, experience a gap between their actual and potential levels of tax revenues, based on their economic, demographic and institutional architecture. Taxation reforms, both policy and administration, can contribute to close this gap, and must be designed and implemented according to the reality and feasibility in every country.

Our research indicates that taxable capacity and tax efforts present significant variations across countries, income groups and regions, as well as overtime. Overall, developing countries seem to have more limitations to expand the scope for tax revenues, which is heavily conditioned by their taxable capacity, in turn determined by lack of economic diversification, demographic challenges, and ineffective institutions. The empirical results offer a glimpse at the emerging trends in revenue collection by different groups of countries and broad policy implications for their revenue reforms, the choice of tax mix, decision over streamlining fiscal incentive structures and administration procedures.

On the one extreme of the spectrum, countries with a low level of actual tax collection, by international standards, and also low tax effort, according to their characteristics, clearly have room to increase tax revenues in order to reach their taxable capacity while also contributing to fiscal stability and economic growth. Tax reforms aimed at increasing tax revenue collections would also bring these countries more in line with others with similar tax capacity, which are already collecting more.

On the other extreme of the spectrum, countries with both relatively high tax collection and relatively high tax effort need to sustain and consolidate their tax revenue performance, while exploring tax reforms that aimed at reducing distortions to economic activity and improving the equity of the tax system.

In the middle of the spectrum, countries with a relatively low level of tax collection but relatively high tax effort have little room to increase tax revenues without possibly creating additional distortions, unless they address the underlying reasons below their weak taxable capacity by conducting parallel, non-tax, reforms (economic, institutional, etc.) to expand their tax revenue potential. Inversely, countries with relatively high collections but relatively low tax effort have more room to improve tax policy and tax administration, in order to reach their full revenue potential.

It is worth noting that in recent years both the significance and the magnitude of the impact of institutional quality indexes on tax collection have increased strongly relative to the other factors. This finding indicates that countries with more effective and transparent governments (e.g., bureaucracy quality or corruption) can potentially raise tax collections without undue burden on the economy. It also suggests that in some countries, efforts to improve tax policy may be in vain unless underlying rigidities in the country's institutions are removed.

The results of this chapter need to be interpreted with care due to potential caveats in the modeling of tax capacity and effort, as well as in the comparison of the actual tax-to-GDP ratio across countries. This study can complement but not substitute detailed analysis of any individual country's tax system, which considers the country's fiscal policy and administration performance, taking into account also public expenditure needs and the overall level of development. There are some plausible venues for further research.

First, natural resource rich countries deserve special treatment due to the way the fiscal regimes are designed and administered, in order to effectively capture the differentiated impact of fiscal pressures and the inherent unpredictability and volatility of the underlying production and prices, compared to countries relying on traditional sources of revenues through consumption and non-resource income based taxes. Such special treatment could be done either empirically (by explicitly factoring the concept of resource dependency in regression specifications) or/and descriptive (in the context of country-specific country case studies) as necessary.

Second, the concept of tax capacity and tax effort could be usefully deepened in country specific tax system analysis. The divergence between tax capacity and tax effort, as aforementioned, suggests in broad policy sense whether a country could raise revenue up to its potential capacity. Such divergence can be unbundled into various types of tax gaps – reflected and measured in policy design, economic structure and the country's culture of paying taxes, and in tax evasion and avoidance – whereby specific revenue reform measures could well be targeted without imposing further burden on the country's investment environment or efficiency cost.

Finally, making fundamental changes in a tax system is always a challenge due to possible public resistance and political economy obstacles.[31] The blend of theory of taxation and the politics of it would be useful in country case studies. Taxation ultimately is a function of politics, institutions, economics and technologies. The design of tax policy reforms must be constructed after comprehensive analysis of the country's taxable capacity, revenue performance, efficiency and equity considerations, as well as the political economy of tax reforms.

REFERENCES

Abed, G. T., & Gupta, S. (2002). *Governance, Corruption, & Economic Performance*. Washington, DC: International Monetary Fund.

Ahmad, E., & Stern, N. (1986). *Taxation for Developing Countries. The Development Research Programme*. London School of Economics.

Aizenman, J., & Jinjarak, Y. (2009). Globalisation and Developing Countries – A Shrinking Tax Base? *The Journal of Development Studies*, *45*(5), 653–671. doi:10.1080/00220380802582338

Aizenman, J., & Jinjarak, Y. (2012, June). Income Inequality, Tax Base and Sovereign Spreads. *NBER Working Paper Series, No: 18176*. National Bureau of Economic Research. Retrieved from http://economics.ucsc.edu/research/downloads/Aiz_Jin_Gini_2012.pdf

Alfirman, L. (2003, November). Estimating Stochastic Frontier Tax Potential: Can Indonesian Local Governments Increase Tax Revenues under Decentralization? Discussion papers in economics / Center for Economic Analysis, Department of Economics, University of Colorado at Boulder, Colorado. *Working Paper No. 03-19*.

Alonso, J. A., & Garcimartín, C. (2011). Does Aid Hinder Tax Efforts? More Evidence. *CREDIT Research Paper. No: 11/04*.

Bahl, R. (1971). A Regression Approach to Tax Effort and Tax Ratio Analysis. *International Monetary Fund Staff Paper*, *18*(3), 570–612. doi:10.2307/3866315

Baicker, K., & Skinner, J. S. (2011, February). Health Care Spending Growth and the Future of U.S. Tax Rates. *NBER Working Paper No. 16772*.

Battese, G. E. (1992). Frontier Production Functions and Technical Efficiencies: A Survey of Empirical Applications in Agricultural Economics. *Agricultural Economics*, *7*(3-4), 185–208. doi:10.1016/0169-5150(92)90049-5

Battese, G. E., & Coelli, T. J. (1992). Frontier Production Functions, Technical Efficiency and Panel Data: With Application to Paddy Farmers in India. *Journal of Productivity Analysis*, *3*(1-2), 153–169. doi:10.1007/BF00158774

Bird, R. M. (2007). Tax Challenges Facing Developing Countries: A Perspective from Outside the Policy Arena. Working Paper.

Bird, R. M. (2008, March 12). Tax Challenges Facing Developing Countries. *Proceedings of Inaugural Lecture of the Annual Public Lecture Series of the National Institute of Public Finance and Policy*, New Delhi, India. University of Toronto, Institute for International Business Working Paper Series, IIB Paper No. 12.

Bird, R. M., & Gendron, P.-P. (2007). *The VAT in Developing and Transitional Countries*. Cambridge, UK: Cambridge University Press. doi:10.1017/CBO9780511619366

Bird, R. M., Martinez-Vazquez, J., & Torgler, B. (2004). Societal Institutions and Tax Efforts in Developing Countries (Working Paper 04-06). *Andrew Young School of Policy Studies*, Georgia State University, Georgia, Atlanta.

Bird, R. M., Martinez-Vazquez, J., & Torgler, B. (2006). Societal Institutions and Tax Efforts in Developing Countries (No: 04011). International Tax Program, University of Toronto..

Bird, R. M., Martinez-Vazquez, J., & Torgler, B. (2008). Tax Effort in Developing Countries and High Income Countries: The Impact of Corruption, Voice and Accountability. *Economic Analysis and Policy*, *38*(1), 55–71. doi:10.1016/S0313-5926(08)50006-3

Cardenas, M., & Tuzemen, D. (2011, December). Under-Investment in State Capacity: The Role of Inequality and Political Instability (Research Working Papers). The Federal Reserve Bank of Kansas City-Economic Research Department, No: RWP 11/07.

Chelliah, R. J., Baas, H. J., & Kelly, M. R. (1975). Tax Ratios and Tax Effort in Developing Countries. *IMF Staff Papers.*

Cyan, M., Martinez-Vazquez, J., & Vulovic, V. (2012, September). *Measuring Tax Effort: How much does the Estimation Approach Matter?* International Center for Public Policy, Andrew Young School of Policy Studies, Georgia State University.

Davoodi, H. R., & Grigorian, D. A. (2007, May). Tax Potential vs. Tax Effort: A Cross-Country Analysis of Armenia's Stubbornly Low Tax Collection. *IMF Working Paper No: WP/07/106.*

Dharmapala, D., & Hines, J. R., Jr. (2006, December). Which Countries Become Tax Havens? *NBER Working Paper No: 12802.*

Diamond, W. H., & Diamond, D. B. (2002). *Tax Havens of the World.* Newark, NJ: Matthew Bender Books.

Eissa, N., & Williamson Hoynes, H. (2008). Redistribution and Tax Expenditures: The Earned Income Tax Credit. *NBER Working Paper 14307.* Retrieved from http://www.nber.org/papers/w14307.pdf

Eltony, M. N. (2002). The Determinants of Tax Effort in Arab Countries. *Arab Planning Institute Working Paper Series No: 02-07.*

Fox, W. F., & Gurley, T. (2005). An Exploration of Tax Patterns around the World. *Tax Notes International: Special Reports, 37*(9), 793–807.

Fricke, H., & Sussmuth, B. (2011, January). Growth and Volatility of Tax Revenues in Latin America. *CESIFO Working Paper No: 3312.*

Ghura, D. (1998, September). Tax Revenue in Sub-Saharan Africa: Effects of Economic Policies and Corruption. *IMF Working Paper, No: WP/98/135.*

Global Monitoring Report 2005: Millennium Development Goals: From Consensus to Momentum. (2005World Bank. Washington, DC: World Bank.

Gonzalez-Paramo, J. M., & Moreno-Dodson, B. (2003). The Role of the State and Consequences of Alternative Forms of Public Expenditure Financing. *WBI Working Paper, Document No: 33052.*

Gupta, A. S. (2007, July). Determinants of Tax Revenue Efforts in Developing Countries. *IMF Working Paper, No: WP/07/184.*

Hines, J. R. Jr, & Rice, E. M. (1994). Fiscal Paradise: Foreign Tax Havens and American Business. *The Quarterly Journal of Economics, 109*(1), 149–182. doi:10.2307/2118431

Hines, J. R., Jr., & Summers, L. H. (2009, January). How Globalization Affects Tax Design. *NBER Working Paper 14664.*

ICRG. (2014). *International Country Risk Guide Index.* New York: The PRS Group.

Jewell, C., Flanagan, R., & Cattell, K. (2005). The Effects of the Informal Sector on Construction. In I.D. Tommelein (Ed.), *Construction Research Congress: Broadening Perspectives*. American Society of Civil Engineers.

Keen, M., & Mansour, M. (2010). Revenue Mobilisation in Sub-Saharan Africa: Challenges from Globalization I – Trade Reform. *Development Policy Review*, *28*(5), 553–571. doi:10.1111/j.1467-7679.2010.00498.x

Konrad, K. A., & Qari, S. (2012). The Last Refuge of a Scoundrel? Patriotism and Tax Compliance. *Economica*, *79*(315), 516–533. doi:10.1111/j.1468-0335.2011.00900.x

Le, T. M., Moreno-Dodson, B., & Rojchaichaninthorn, J. (2008, March). Expanding Taxable Capacity and Reaching Revenue Potential: Cross-Country Analysis. *World Bank Policy Research Working Paper. No: 4559*.

Leuthold, J. H. (1991). Tax Shares in developing countries: A panel study. *Journal of Development Economics*, *35*(1), 173–185. doi:10.1016/0304-3878(91)90072-4

Lotz, J. R., & Morss, E. R. (1967). Measuring "Tax Effort" in Developing Countries (Evaluation de l'effort fiscal dans les pays en voie de developpement) (Medicion del "esfuerzo tributario" de los paises en desarrollo). *Staff Papers - International Monetary Fund. International Monetary Fund*, *14*(3), 478–499. doi:10.2307/3866266

Lotz, J. R., & Morss, E. R. (1970). A Theory of Tax Level Determinants for Developing Countries. *Economic Development and Cultural Change*, *18*(3), 328–341. doi:10.1086/450436

Mahdavi, S. (2008). The Level and Composition of Tax Revenue in Developing Countries: Evidence from Unbalanced Panel Data. *International Review of Economics & Finance*, *17*(4), 607–617. doi:10.1016/j.iref.2008.01.001

Martinez-Vazquez, J., & McNab, R. (2000). Tax Reform in The Tax Reform Experiment in Transitional Countries. International Center for Public Policy Working Paper Series, at AYSPS, GSU paper, International Center for Public Policy, Andrew Young School of Policy Studies, Georgia State University.

Mkandawire, T. (2010). On Tax Efforts and Colonial Heritage in Africa. *The Journal of Development Studies*, *46*(10), 1647–1669. doi:10.1080/00220388.2010.500660

Morris, R., Rodrigues Braz, C., de Castro, F., Jonk, S., Kremer, J., Linehan, S.,... Tkacevs, O. (2009, November). Explaining Government Revenue Windfalls and Shortfalls an Analysis for Selected EU Countries. *ECB Working Paper No: 1114*.

Musgrave, R. (1987). Tax Reform in Developing Countries. In D. Newbery & N. Stern (Eds.), *The Theory of Taxation for Developing Countries* (pp. 242–263). Oxford: Oxford University Press.

Ndikumana, L., & Kaouther, A. (2010). Revenue Mobilization in African Countries: Does Natural Resource Endowment Matter? *African Development Review*, *22*(3), 351–365. doi:10.1111/j.1467-8268.2010.00250.x

Norregaard, J., & Khan, T. S. (2007, December 2007). Tax Policy: Recent Trends and Coming Challenges. *IMF Working Paper, No: WP/07/274*.

Pessino, C. & Fenochietto, R. (2012). Determining Countries' Tax Effort. *Hacienda Publica Española / Revista de Economía, 195*(4), 65-87.

Piancastelli, M. (2001, September 2001). Measuring the Tax Effort of Developed and Developing Countries: Cross Country Panel data Analysis – 1985/95. *Texto Para Discussao No: 818.*

Pitt, M. M., & Lee, L.-F. (1981). The Measurement and Sources of Technical Inefficiency in the Indonesian Weaving Industry. *Journal of Development Economics, 9*(1), 43–64. doi:10.1016/0304-3878(81)90004-3

Prest, A. R. (1979). The Taxable Capacity of a Country. In J. F. Toye (Ed.), *Taxation and Economic Development*. London, UK: Frank Cass.

Report of the International Conference on Financing for Development. (2002, March 18-22). *The United Nations*, Monterrey, Mexico. Retrieved from http://www.unmillenniumproject.org/documents/aconf198-11.pdf

Rodrik, D. (1998). Why Do More Open Economies Have Bigger Governments? *Journal of Political Economy, 106*(5), 997–1032. doi:10.1086/250038

Rutkowski, J. J., & Scarpetta, S. (2005). *Enhancing Job Opportunities*. Washington, DC: The World Bank Group. doi:10.1596/978-0-8213-6195-5

Sancak, C., Velloso, R., & Xing, J. (2010, March). Tax Revenue Response to the Business Cycle. *IMF Working Paper No: 10/71.*

Schneider, F., Buehn, A., & Montenegro, C. E. (2010, July). Shadow Economies All over the World: New Estimates for 162 Countries from 1999 to 2007. *World Bank Policy Research Working Paper No: 5356.*

Stotsky, J. G., & WoldeMariam, A. (1997, September). Tax effort in Sub-Saharan Africa. *IMF Working Paper No: WP/97/107.*

Tait, A. A., Grätz, W. L. M., & Eichengreen, B. J. (1979). International Comparisons of Taxation for Selected Developing Countries, 1972-76. *IMF Staff Papers, 26*(1), 123–156. doi:10.2307/3866567

Tanzi, V. (1987). Quantitative Characteristics of the Tax Systems of Developing Countries. In D. Newbery & N. Stern (Eds.), *The Theory of Taxation for Developing Countries* (pp. 205–241). New York: Oxford University Press.

Tanzi, V. (1992). Structural Factors and Tax Revenue in Developing Countries: A Decade of Evidence. In I. Goldin & L. A. Winters (Eds.), *Open Economies: Structural Adjustment and Agriculture* (pp. 267–281). Cambridge: Cambridge University Press. doi:10.1017/CBO9780511628559.023

Tanzi, V., & Davoodi, H. (1997). *Corruption, Public Investment, and Growth*. Washington, DC: IMF.

The Global Forum on Transparency and Exchange of Information for Tax Purposes. (2011, December 15). *Information Brief, OECD.*

Towards Global Tax Cooperation: Progress in Identifying and Eliminating Harmful Tax Practices. (2000OECD. Paris: OECD.

Monterrey Consensus. (2002). United Nations (Draft Outcome of the International Conference on Financing for Development, Doc. A/AC.257/L.13).

World Bank Doing Business Database. (2011).

World Development Indicators. (2014World Bank. Washington, DC: The World Bank Group.

World Development Report 1997: The State in Changing World. (1997World Bank. Washington, DC: The World Bank Group.

KEY TERMS AND DEFINITIONS

Fiscal Revenue: Total tax and nontax revenues of governments.

Tax Effort: The ratio of the actual tax collection to the predicted tax revenue (taxable capacity).

Taxable Capacity: The predicted tax revenue of a country and estimated empirically taking into account its specific economic, demographic, and institutional features and is considered as an approximation of its taxable capacity.

ENDNOTES

1. See World Development Report (1997), World Bank Global Monitoring Report (2005), The United Nations report on Financing for Development (2002), The UN Secretary-General's Report to the Preparatory Committee for Financing for Development (2002).
2. Gonzalez-Paramo and Moreno-Dodson (2003).
3. In the public finance literature the terms tax productivity and tax efficiency are also used to refer to revenue generation performance.
4. This chapter extends the initial analysis, reported in Le, Moreno-Dodson, and Rojchaichaninthorn (2008). In the new dataset, we have a higher number of countries and the time period has been extended from 2003 to 2012. The main difference is that general-government series are used instead of central-government series while constructing tax and total revenues of countries. Some results change significantly with broader revenue definitions.
5. Since their taxation policies are mainly outliers, the following natural resource-rich countries are excluded in the chapter: Algeria, Angola, Azerbaijan, Congo Republic, Ecuador, Equatorial Guinea, Iran, Iraq, Kazakhstan, Kuwait, Libya, Nigeria, Oman, Qatar, Russia, Saudi Arabia, United Arab Emirates, and Venezuela. The tax-haven countries have been determined based on the study by Dharmapala and Hines (2006). In their paper, Table 1 reports the list of tax havens, which are identified based on two alternative definitions: Hines and Rice (1994) and Diamond and Diamond (2002) definition and OECD (2000) definition. If any country is identified as a tax haven by using both definitions, we excluded this country.
6. When general-government data are not reported, central-government data are used; this was only an issue for a few countries. These countries are Bangladesh, Burkina Faso, Cambodia, Myanmar, Papua New Guinea, Sri Lanka, and Trinidad and Tobago. It should be noted that for these countries the difference between general government and central government tax revenues is expected to be negligible.

7 The detailed variable definitions are given in Table 11 in Appendix.

8 The income groups are defined based on the World Bank definition. Economies are divided according to 2012 GNI per capita, calculated using the World Bank Atlas method. The groups are: low income, $1,035 or less; lower middle income, $1,036 - $4,085; upper middle income, $4,086 - $12,615; and high income, $12,616 or more. The list of included countries is given in Table 12 in Appendix.

9 The countries in each region are listed in Table 13 in Appendix.

10 It should be noted that even though we use general-government data when calculating tax revenues, the tax ratio in SAR is still low.

11 Changes in EU countries' fiscal revenues are studied by Morris et al. (2009). They determine possible factors affecting taxes in the region. The listed factors are mostly non-macroeconomic variables.

12 Recent work by Le, Moreno-Dodson, and Rojchaichaninthorn (2008) leads to the same conclusion on the basis of cross-country analysis.

13 Improvements in revenue forecasting is important for governments to better evaluate fiscal balances and financing needs, especially during business cycles. In this regard, it is important to evaluate the response of revenue to output gap. Sancak, Velloso, and Xing (2010) find that as the output gap improves, the efficiency of taxes improves as well, where tax efficiency is defined as [tax revenue/ tax base]/standard tax rate.

14 See Lotz and Mross (1967 and 1970); Bahl (1971); Chelliah et al. (1975); Tait et al. (1979), Tanzi (1987); Stotsky and WoldeMariam (1997); Eltony (2002); Bird et al. (2004); Gupta (2007); Bird et al. (2008); Le, Moreno-Dodson, and Rojchaichaninthorn (2008).

15 It is worth noting that this methodology does not provide information on expected tax revenues of countries, but the series obtained give us information on their tax revenue potential, as pointed out by Cyan, Martinez-Vazquez, and Vulovic (2012).

16 It should be noted that cross-country tax effort calculations presented in the chapter cannot substitute for a comprehensive study of taxation, focusing on a particular country. There are potential problems related to this methodology such as the sensitivity of the calculation of the tax-effort index to the predicted results of a country's taxable capacity; systematic errors in measurement of independent variables; regression specifications can calculate the tax collection performance of a country in comparison with the average effort exercised by an average country in the selected sample, and this average may not be the actual tax collection performance. Given these potential problems, the results should be used to assess the feasibility of raising additional revenues, given the tax mix policy and collection effort attained at the average level, rather not the measure of actual performance (Ahmad & Stern, 1986; Chelliah, Baas, & Kelly, 1975; Le, et al., 2008).

17 See Tanzi and Davoodi (1997), Bird, *et al.* (2004), and Le *et al.* (2008) for details. Since tax revenue is in percent of GDP, it controls for fluctuations in the tax base, which can be approximated by GDP.

18 See Table 11 in Appendix for detailed definitions.

19 Financial pressures on governments increased with globalization due to a higher demand for government spending and costly tax collection (Hines & Summers, 2009). Being an open market economy can affect tax policies such that higher international involvement increases the economic distortions created by taxation, but at the same time can increase the level of taxes due to higher economic growth rates as it is observed in open economies.

20 The ICRG reports several indicators of institutional and governance quality. In the original database, the bureaucracy quality index and corruption index are reported as indexes numbers from 1 to 6. While "1" indicates the lowest bureaucracy quality or highest corruption, "6" corresponds to the highest bureaucracy quality or lowest corruption. In this chapter we re-index each of these measures such that lower numbers indicate a higher bureaucracy quality or lower corruption. Rescaling consists of defining a new range where -10 equates to least corrupt or best bureaucratic quality and -1 equates to most corrupt or worst bureaucratic quality.

21 Table Annex 1 in Le, Moreno-Dodson, and Rojchaichaninthorn (2008) also reports a similar correlation matrix (with a shorter time period and a smaller sample of countries). When we compare our correlation matrix with the one in Le, Moreno-Dodson, and Rojchaichaninthorn (2008), it can be seen that the correlation between tax revenues and GDP per capita is statistically stronger when data from recent years are included in the estimates.

22 The data set is not a balanced panel, but there are a large number of observations in the set. The total number of observations for tax revenue is 1884 for 121 countries.

23 Gupta (2007) and Bird *et al.* (2006) could not find any endogeneity problem in a regression specification similar to the one presented in this chapter. Bird et al. (2006) include ethnic fractionalization, language, and latitude as instrumental variables in the endogeneity test.

24 The tax capacity of countries, in addition to macroeconomic and demographic characteristics, and governance quality, can also depend on preferences of societies and their cultural and social characteristics, which were excluded in our regression specifications (Konrad & Qari, 2012). As a result the "tax capacity" term is measured approximately.

25 Total natural resources rents are the sum of oil rents, natural gas rents, coal rents (hard and soft), mineral rents, and forest rents. According to OECD Glossary of Statistical Terms, the economic rent of a natural resource "equals the value of capital services flows rendered by the natural resources, or their share in the gross operating surplus; its value is given by the value of extraction. Resource rent may be divided between depletion and return to natural capital." In extractive industries, the resource rent is defined as the portion of marginal revenue which is above and beyond marginal cost (Rent=Marginal revenue-Marginal cost).

26 Similar findings are reported in Chelliah *et al.* (1975) and Stosky and WoldeMariam (1997).

27 This fact has been also emphasized in Stotsky and WoldeMariam (1997) and Gupta (2007).

28 Le, Moreno-Dodson, and Rojchaichaninthorn (2008), report similar results for 1994-2003. However, the classification of countries is different in this chapter reflecting more data availability as well as new developments such as recent tax reforms and the 2008-2009 global crisis.

29 It should be noted that the data for Zimbabwe cover the periods of 1994-1997 and 2009-12.

30 Only 9 countries are classified differently. These countries are Bulgaria, Cambodia, the Czech Republic, Italy, Jordan, Mali, Portugal, the Slovak Republic and Thailand. As reported in Table 4, all of these countries' effort indices are very close to 1 and with the new specification, they move from the low-effort group to high-effort group or vice-versa. While Bulgaria, Cambodia, Czech Republic, Italy, Jordan, Portugal, Slovak republic and Thailand move from the high-effort to the low-effort group, Mali moves from the low-effort to the high-effort group.

31 As Bird (2008, p. 2) highlights, the design and implementation of tax policies are determined 'not only by ideas and vested interests but also by changing economic conditions, administrative constraints and technological possibilities, and especially, the political institutions with which these factors are at play'.

APPENDIX

Table 10. Variables by country, averages over 1994-2012

	Tax revenue in % of GDP	Fiscal revenue in % of GDP	GDP per capita	Age dependency ratio	Population growth	Trade openness	Agriculture value added (in % of GDP)	Bureaucracy Quality Index	Corruption index	Size of shadow economy (in % of GDP)	Natural resources rents (in % of GDP)	Final consumption (in % of GDP)
Albania	18.03	23.36	2396	55.65	0.13	65.90	27.81	-5.11	-4.89	34.31	2.18	99.15
Argentina	10.47	14.60	4445	58.93	1.34	33.30	7.93	-7.63	-5.26	25.30	6.28	77.58
Armenia	19.07	22.87	1539	52.64	-0.13	73.48	26.84	-3.21	-3.32	44.02	0.93	99.40
Australia	28.49	34.87	32223	49.04	1.35	40.05	3.14	-10.00	-8.63	13.96	5.30	74.76
Austria	35.68	37.95	35702	48.24	0.37	93.84	2.00	-10.00	-8.68	9.76	0.33	74.01
Bangladesh	8.39	10.55	410	66.01	2.41	38.26	22.18	-5.63	-4.68	35.29	3.75	83.43
Belarus	28.78	31.69	2913	45.39	0.00	129.97	12.03	-3.37	-4.63	46.41	2.68	75.39
Belgium	40.52	41.81	34338	52.06	0.46	147.94	1.17	-10.00	-7.74	21.92	0.02	75.37
Benin	16.11	19.40	522	90.71	3.45	52.42	33.53	-1.00	-1.00	49.79	2.50	88.36
Bhutan	8.36	19.92	1249	69.68	3.18	88.29	25.10	-1.00	-1.00	28.77	13.73	67.68
Bolivia	15.98	25.19	1029	75.36	2.37	60.94	14.74	-5.63	-5.42	66.07	16.75	84.11
Bosnia and Herzegovina	33.95	40.02	2456	45.60	-0.20	103.97	13.69	-1.00	-1.00	33.59	1.85	117.41
Botswana	23.12	39.70	5187	67.93	2.30	92.44	3.11	-6.00	-6.32	32.94	2.53	62.73
Brazil	28.98	33.75	4769	52.77	1.79	22.76	6.02	-6.37	-5.68	39.04	3.92	81.98
Bulgaria	28.10	34.26	3408	47.00	-0.71	115.52	10.84	-6.00	-6.00	35.30	2.07	85.06
Burkina Faso	12.13	13.50	381	97.06	3.15	37.30	36.11	-4.00	-5.16	40.53	4.84	91.36
Burundi	15.18	16.94	154	98.72	3.20	35.58	45.08	-1.00	-1.00	39.52	11.15	105.35
Cambodia	9.23	13.82	428	75.29	3.33	108.24	38.23	-1.00	-1.00	48.74	3.74	92.48
Cameroon	9.86	12.60	885	92.58	3.03	50.37	22.37	-4.95	-5.53	32.03	9.61	82.78
Canada	33.10	41.83	32857	45.65	1.09	71.77	2.28	-10.00	-9.26	15.71	4.88	76.87
Cape Verde	22.96	28.06	2166	79.36	2.78	82.42	9.42	-1.00	-1.00	35.42	0.18	80.58
Chile	18.30	22.20	7253	51.07	1.61	64.59	5.26	-7.74	-7.47	19.28	11.94	73.26
China	14.41	22.68	1691	43.64	1.36	50.97	14.03	-6.16	-4.89	12.69	5.81	54.42

continued on following page

Table 10. Continued

	Tax revenue in % of GDP	Fiscal revenue in % of GDP	GDP per capita	Age dependency ratio	Population growth	Trade openness	Agriculture value added (in % of GDP)	Bureaucracy Quality Index	Corruption index	Size of shadow economy (in % of GDP)	Natural resources rents (in % of GDP)	Final consumption (in % of GDP)
Colombia	14.11	22.72	3432	57.90	2.11	35.79	10.09	-6.32	-5.42	37.33	6.90	82.37
Congo, Dem. Rep.	7.60	17.41	144	95.81	2.85	78.39	48.84	-1.58	-2.89	47.31	21.42	90.52
Costa Rica	15.42	22.47	4523	54.58	2.77	90.03	9.55	-6.00	-6.63	25.74	0.56	82.33
Cote d'Ivoire	15.93	17.96	977	82.47	2.27	80.33	24.13	-6.05	-4.37	45.18	5.23	79.55
Croatia	33.76	36.42	9253	48.56	-0.53	85.92	6.16	-9.84	-8.26	32.14	1.50	82.10
Czech Republic	30.98	34.80	11820	43.05	0.25	119.43	3.39	-3.00	-5.32	18.37	0.63	71.63
Denmark	48.75	56.08	45182	50.83	0.19	87.58	2.16	-10.00	-10.00	17.74	1.96	75.48
Dominican Republic	12.89	14.42	3637	64.67	1.99	71.43	7.50	-4.37	-5.95	31.86	1.02	88.26
Egypt, Arab Rep.	15.54	25.95	1236	65.45	2.24	49.97	15.60	-6.00	-4.95	34.88	12.27	86.14
El Salvador	12.74	14.93	2681	73.07	1.29	67.14	11.86	-5.53	-5.84	45.11	0.62	100.31
Estonia	29.00	33.59	8896	49.38	-0.52	153.33	4.19	-5.58	-5.11	31.18	4.27	75.17
Ethiopia	8.95	11.74	165	96.28	3.20	39.14	49.02	-4.00	-5.00	38.64	8.87	89.88
Fiji	21.94	24.89	3421	57.74	1.30	121.56	15.74	-1.00	-1.00	32.42	1.98	85.72
Finland	43.44	51.80	34414	50.07	0.22	75.32	3.36	-10.00	-10.00	17.67	1.00	74.57
France	45.02	49.43	32461	53.88	0.46	51.90	2.70	-8.79	-7.47	15.02	0.09	80.63
Georgia	16.14	18.32	1331	50.44	-0.20	79.46	22.31	-1.00	-1.00	65.80	0.76	97.06
Germany	39.55	44.68	33406	48.97	-0.16	71.16	1.10	-10.00	-8.84	15.97	0.20	76.98
Ghana	16.14	18.15	503	78.46	2.87	84.30	36.29	-6.74	-4.95	40.66	6.17	91.23
Greece	33.78	40.29	19390	48.56	0.26	55.12	..	-8.00	-6.68	27.52	0.23	89.03
Guatemala	10.57	10.88	2132	90.33	2.79	57.28	13.01	-5.58	-5.42	50.47	2.16	93.97
Guinea	10.86	11.59	294	88.54	2.73	59.51	22.58	-5.63	-5.79	39.01	12.73	86.34

continued on following page

Table 10. Continued

	Tax revenue in % of GDP	Fiscal revenue in % of GDP	GDP per capita	Age dependency ratio	Population growth	Trade openness	Agriculture value added (in % of GDP)	Bureaucracy Quality Index	Corruption index	Size of shadow economy (in % of GDP)	Natural resources rents (in % of GDP)	Final consumption (in % of GDP)
Honduras	18.13	23.42	1351	80.94	2.93	114.60	15.96	-5.63	-4.95	48.32	2.77	86.47
Hong Kong SAR, China	12.46	20.01	25390	37.21	1.33	336.49	0.07	-8.21	-7.68	16.03	0.00	69.26
Hungary	38.64	45.06	9685	46.41	-0.11	134.17	5.38	-8.89	-7.11	24.41	0.90	76.75
Iceland	35.24	42.44	49071	52.20	1.22	81.44	8.67	-10.00	-9.74	15.58	0.00	80.51
India	14.85	17.39	715	60.30	2.08	35.19	21.48	-8.00	-5.26	22.18	5.02	72.84
Indonesia	13.21	17.13	1282	55.22	1.82	58.70	15.51	-6.26	-4.79	18.94	11.28	69.59
Ireland	30.16	33.04	46760	49.54	1.61	160.59	3.32	-10.00	-6.89	15.79	0.21	65.29
Israel	31.85	40.14	19293	61.49	2.27	73.57	..	-9.95	-6.74	22.01	0.18	82.16
Italy	36.14	37.98	29303	49.66	0.09	51.19	2.60	-7.63	-5.63	27.02	0.19	78.62
Jamaica	24.73	32.20	4179	64.29	1.07	94.04	6.87	-8.00	-4.89	34.77	2.20	90.70
Japan	17.06	40.76	34859	49.91	-0.46	24.36	1.39	-10.00	-6.95	10.96	0.03	75.26
Jordan	19.20	25.91	2254	70.46	3.32	123.25	3.13	-6.32	-6.53	18.51	1.08	99.74
Kenya	17.57	20.34	531	87.11	3.27	61.54	29.21	-6.37	-4.42	33.16	1.86	91.13
Korea, Rep.	17.87	21.73	16383	39.23	0.84	79.14	4.11	-8.21	-6.37	26.79	0.05	66.97
Kyrgyz Republic	14.51	18.32	464	62.95	1.88	104.59	33.71	-1.00	-1.00	40.42	4.43	97.62
Lao PDR	12.62	18.20	457	81.45	2.74	73.94	42.42	-1.00	-1.00	29.58	9.08	85.43
Latvia	23.37	28.35	5847	48.97	-1.14	99.87	4.87	-5.32	-4.11	29.21	2.09	83.17
Lebanon	15.43	20.05	5895	54.16	2.95	64.72	6.72	-5.63	-3.79	33.13	0.01	100.35
Lesotho	46.99	56.27	709	80.23	1.60	169.31	12.10	-1.00	-1.00	30.47	2.13	142.10
Lithuania	22.68	26.94	6667	48.31	-0.84	115.19	6.54	-5.32	-4.11	32.04	1.85	85.87
Luxembourg	34.34	40.07	73358	48.24	1.56	270.77	0.62	-10.00	-9.16	9.74	0.03	54.27
Macao SAR, China	23.38	26.59	24859	36.87	2.91	155.37	0.00	-1.00	-1.00	12.40	0.00	43.44

continued on following page

Table 10. Continued

	Tax revenue in % of GDP	Fiscal revenue in % of GDP	GDP per capita	Age dependency ratio	Population growth	Trade openness	Agriculture value added (in % of GDP)	Bureaucracy Quality Index	Corruption index	Size of shadow economy (in % of GDP)	Natural resources rents (in % of GDP)	Final consumption (in % of GDP)
Macedonia, FYR	27.97	31.35	2853	45.65	0.67	102.37	12.22	-1.00	-1.00	37.64	2.77	94.27
Madagascar	9.89	11.68	278	90.70	3.26	63.17	28.25	-4.00	-7.74	40.81	2.63	92.21
Malaysia	16.34	21.85	5323	55.78	2.79	191.12	10.31	-7.79	-6.00	30.92	12.03	57.39
Mali	14.36	16.12	421	98.56	2.99	64.63	41.47	-1.00	-5.26	40.69	6.00	89.27
Mauritius	17.27	21.16	4912	44.93	1.20	122.27	6.45	-1.00	-1.00	22.66	0.01	79.98
Mexico	12.66	14.52	7679	61.69	1.98	52.78	3.72	-7.63	-5.32	30.01	6.28	79.26
Moldova	24.97	28.90	770	46.54	0.43	125.76	21.92	-3.79	-3.42	44.45	0.24	104.09
Mongolia	20.54	27.00	977	56.33	2.20	113.84	25.38	-6.00	-5.95	17.60	20.60	75.01
Morocco	27.01	32.06	1899	59.51	2.06	67.38	16.35	-6.00	-5.95	34.93	1.40	78.35
Myanmar	3.21	6.05	..	52.66	1.77	1.40	57.16	-4.00	-3.58	50.33	..	88.15
Namibia	26.74	29.53	3435	76.19	2.53	96.68	10.39	-6.58	-5.63	30.29	1.00	84.36
Nepal	9.80	11.72	317	77.39	2.24	49.86	38.09	-1.00	-1.00	36.72	4.29	88.15
Netherlands	38.78	45.99	37766	47.83	0.30	130.94	2.55	-10.00	-9.42	13.18	1.49	73.04
New Zealand	29.91	36.75	25621	51.55	1.19	59.11	7.01	-10.00	-9.74	12.36	2.52	77.89
Nicaragua	11.90	15.23	1112	75.83	2.54	69.01	19.19	-4.00	-6.37	44.59	2.07	90.87
Niger	10.75	12.38	267	104.89	3.45	49.33	38.30	-4.21	-3.32	40.44	3.32	93.49
Norway	42.69	55.46	61620	53.09	0.90	71.59	1.97	-10.00	-9.16	18.72	14.64	65.73
Pakistan	10.81	14.34	657	77.21	2.95	33.43	24.55	-6.00	-4.68	35.71	4.65	86.40
Papua New Guinea	21.56	23.62	899	74.01	2.73	111.85	36.46	-6.37	-4.42	36.71	36.55	68.58
Paraguay	12.79	18.05	1570	71.02	2.66	98.93	18.86	-4.37	-3.89	38.83	2.51	75.67
Peru	15.76	19.04	2935	61.52	1.89	39.71	7.87	-5.63	-5.47	58.04	5.85	77.18
Philippines	13.57	15.25	1176	69.34	2.45	88.52	14.74	-7.42	-5.32	41.57	1.57	84.07

continued on following page

Table 10. Continued

	Tax revenue in % of GDP	Fiscal revenue in % of GDP	GDP per capita	Age dependency ratio	Population growth	Trade openness	Agriculture value added (in % of GDP)	Bureaucracy Quality Index	Corruption index	Size of shadow economy (in % of GDP)	Natural resources rents (in % of GDP)	Final consumption (in % of GDP)
Poland	32.35	38.63	7656	44.62	0.45	68.03	5.26	-8.16	-6.26	27.20	1.36	80.85
Portugal	33.53	39.63	17509	48.74	0.27	66.81	3.60	-8.00	-8.11	22.96	0.26	84.12
Romania	27.93	32.57	4296	45.15	-0.10	69.95	12.96	-4.00	-5.63	32.59	4.37	83.11
Rwanda	12.71	24.88	263	89.80	3.64	37.66	38.56	-1.00	-1.00	40.08	3.84	103.18
Senegal	16.61	18.51	730	91.53	3.03	66.85	17.52	-4.37	-5.42	43.74	1.86	91.92
Seychelles	33.58	41.68	11428	51.11	1.77	102.97	2.96	-1.00	-1.00	..	0.00	..
Sierra Leone	8.77	9.35	318	82.90	2.41	44.63	53.21	-1.21	-4.79	45.58	4.83	102.76
Singapore	14.28	22.69	26745	38.43	2.65	374.33	0.08	-9.84	-8.00	12.91	0.00	51.21
Slovak Republic	30.42	35.87	10891	42.90	0.61	146.15	4.68	-8.16	-5.95	18.13	0.43	76.38
Slovenia	34.86	37.45	16381	43.29	0.15	116.80	3.20	-6.16	-4.95	26.23	0.23	75.18
South Africa	26.93	33.66	5119	57.09	2.15	55.05	3.34	-6.63	-6.16	27.31	5.35	81.46
Spain	34.51	37.85	24155	46.48	0.86	55.31	3.88	-8.58	-7.79	22.49	0.08	77.09
Sri Lanka	14.52	16.42	1219	50.17	1.01	72.47	16.30	-6.00	-6.11	43.86	0.77	83.19
Sudan	6.29	7.58	647	86.32	2.94	30.93	35.49	-4.00	-3.26	34.10	11.83	81.30
Swaziland	25.90	27.60	2272	85.82	2.44	154.53	10.34	-1.00	-1.00	40.70	2.40	94.61
Sweden	48.02	55.62	38102	54.66	0.51	84.87	2.11	-10.00	-9.53	18.76	0.82	75.34
Switzerland	29.61	36.95	50944	47.70	0.73	83.57	..	-10.00	-8.58	8.54	0.04	70.85
Syrian Arab Republic	16.34	25.08	1510	75.60	3.54	70.00	24.87	-4.58	-6.00	19.06	24.51	77.39
Tajikistan	10.31	11.33	314	78.47	2.76	116.23	26.73	-1.00	-1.00	42.20	1.01	104.20
Thailand	17.39	20.36	2589	43.56	1.17	122.71	10.46	-6.53	-4.79	50.60	3.14	67.23
Togo	15.37	16.43	396	86.76	3.04	85.15	36.55	-1.58	-4.53	34.86	4.31	97.87
Trinidad and Tobago	26.15	29.87	10885	46.19	1.08	127.60	1.25	-7.37	-5.16	33.40	35.47	62.38

continued on following page

Table 10. Continued

	Tax revenue in % of GDP	Fiscal revenue in % of GDP	GDP per capita	Age dependency ratio	Population growth	Trade openness	Agriculture value added (in % of GDP)	Bureaucracy Quality Index	Corruption index	Size of shadow economy (in % of GDP)	Natural resources rents (in % of GDP)	Final consumption (in % of GDP)
Tunisia	24.59	28.35	3027	52.57	2.03	92.20	10.80	-6.00	-5.47	37.22	4.71	78.91
Turkey	20.32	34.64	6684	55.90	1.92	48.42	11.57	-6.37	-5.32	31.27	0.49	82.20
Uganda	11.88	18.15	309	106.78	3.37	40.71	31.72	-5.63	-5.11	42.31	6.46	90.96
Ukraine	33.99	40.69	1619	45.30	-0.36	101.01	12.14	-3.37	-3.84	49.72	6.73	78.74
United Kingdom	36.01	39.53	35246	52.72	0.52	57.25	1.04	-10.00	-8.42	12.50	1.62	84.65
United States	25.76	31.17	41384	50.25	1.09	25.05	1.25	-10.00	-8.21	8.63	1.19	81.93
Uruguay	24.81	27.21	5518	59.19	0.47	48.21	8.92	-5.79	-6.11	50.64	0.69	83.53
Vietnam	18.46	22.09	652	55.64	2.37	119.85	22.14	-5.95	-5.21	15.13	11.86	75.92
Yemen, Rep.	8.67	28.48	790	98.02	4.10	72.86	13.99	-4.42	-5.42	27.09	31.04	86.55
Zambia	17.32	18.22	632	95.98	2.64	71.71	20.87	-4.00	-5.95	47.12	12.29	83.70
Zimbabwe	24.59	27.39	546	84.27	1.48	87.21	18.33	-5.95	-2.95	61.81	6.14	97.32

Table 11. Variable definitions and sources

Variables	Description	Source
Tax revenue in % of GDP	Series is calculated using data series from GFS and WDI. In WDI the series that are used to calculate tax revenue including social security contribution is tax revenue (GC.TAX.TOTL. GD.ZS) and social contributions (GC.REV.SOCL.ZS) when available. Tax revenue refers to compulsory transfers to the general government for public purposes (when general data not available, we have used central government data). Certain compulsory transfers such as fines, penalties, and most social security contributions are excluded. Refunds and corrections of erroneously collected tax revenue are treated as negative revenue. Social contributions include social security contributions by employees, employers, and self-employed individuals, and other contributions whose source cannot be determined. They also include actual or imputed contributions to social insurance schemes operated by governments.	WDI (2014) and GFS (2014)
Fiscal revenue in % of GDP	Series: Revenue, excluding grants (% of GDP) (GC.REV.XGRT.GD.ZS).Revenue is cash receipts from taxes, social contributions, and other revenues such as fines, fees, rent, and income from property or sales. Grants are also considered as revenue but are excluded here.	WDI (2014) and GFS (2014)
GDP per capita		WDI (2014)
Age dependency ratio	Age dependency ratio (in %) is the ratio of dependents--people younger than 15 or older than 64--to the working-age population--those ages 15-64.	WDI (2014)
Population growth	Total population between the ages 15 to 64 is the number of people who could potentially be economically active.	WDI (2014)
Trade openness	Series: Trade (% of GDP) (NE.TRD.GNFS.ZS). Trade is the sum of exports and imports of goods and services measured as a share of gross domestic product.	WDI (2014)
Agriculture value added (in % of GDP)	Series: Agriculture, value added (% of GDP) (NV.AGR.TOTL.ZS). Cultivation of crops and livestock production. Value added is the net output of a sector after adding up all outputs and subtracting intermediate inputs. It is calculated without making deductions for depreciation of fabricated assets or depletion and degradation of natural resources. The origin of value added is determined by the International Standard Industrial Classification (ISIC), revision 3. Note: For VAB countries, gross value added at factor cost is used as the denominator.	WDI (2014)
Bureaucracy Quality Index	The institutional strength and quality of the bureaucracy is a shock absorber that tends to minimize revisions of policy when governments change. The original score ranges from 1 to 4. High points are given to countries where the bureaucracy has the strength and expertise to govern without drastic changes in policy or interruptions in government services. The score is recalculated to -10 to -1 where low points are countries with strength bureaucracy and high points are countries with weak bureaucracy.	ICRG (2014)
Corruption index	The assessment of corruption refers to the political system. Corruption index ranges from 1 to 6. High points are given to low corruption countries and low points are given to high corruption countries. The scores are recalculated to -10 to -1 where low points mean low corruption and high points mean high corruption.	ICRG (2014)
Size of shadow economy	The shadow economy includes all market-based legal production of goods and services that are deliberately concealed from public authorities for any of the following reasons: (1) to avoid payment of income, value added or other taxes, (2) to avoid payment of social security contributions, (3) to avoid having to meet certain legal labor market standards, such as minimum wages, maximum working hours, safety standards, etc., and (4) to avoid complying with certain administrative procedures, such as completing statistical questionnaires or other administrative forms.	Schneider, Buehn, Montenegro (2010)
Total consumption	Series: Final consumption expenditure, etc. (% of GDP) (NE.CON.TETC.ZS). Final consumption expenditure (formerly total consumption) is the sum of household final consumption expenditure (private consumption) and general government final consumption expenditure (general government consumption). This estimate includes any statistical discrepancy in the use of resources relative to the supply of resources.	WDI (2014)
Natural resources rents	Total natural resources rents are the sum of oil rents, natural gas rents, coal rents (hard and soft), mineral rents, and forest rents. The code of the series is NY.GDP.TOTL.RT.ZS	WDI (2014)

Table 12. Income groups

High-Income OECD	High-Income nonOECD	Middle-Income Countries		Low-Income Countries
Australia	Croatia	Albania	Lebanon	Bangladesh
Austria	Hong Kong SAR, China	Argentina	Lesotho	Benin
Belgium	Latvia	Armenia	Macedonia, FYR	Burkina Faso
Canada	Lithuania	Belarus	Malaysia	Burundi
Chile	Macao SAR, China	Bhutan	Mauritius	Cambodia
Czech Republic	Singapore	Bolivia	Mexico	Congo, Dem. Rep.
Denmark	Trinidad and Tobago	Bosnia and Herzegovina	Moldova	Ethiopia
Estonia	Uruguay	Botswana	Mongolia	Guinea
Finland		Brazil	Morocco	Kenya
France		Bulgaria	Namibia	Kyrgyz Republic
Germany		Cameroon	Nicaragua	Madagascar
Greece		Cape Verde	Pakistan	Mali
Iceland		China	Papua New Guinea	Myanmar
Ireland		Colombia	Paraguay	Nepal
Israel		Costa Rica	Peru	Niger
Italy		Cote d'Ivoire	Philippines	Rwanda
Japan		Dominican Republic	Romania	Sierra Leone
Korea, Rep.		Egypt, Arab Rep.	Senegal	Tajikistan
Luxembourg		El Salvador	Seychelles	Togo
Netherlands		Fiji	South Africa	Uganda
New Zealand		Georgia	Sri Lanka	Zimbabwe
Norway		Ghana	Sudan	
Poland		Guatemala	Swaziland	
Portugal		Honduras	Syrian Arab Republic	
Slovak Republic		Hungary	Thailand	
Slovenia		India	Tunisia	
Spain		Indonesia	Turkey	
Sweden		Jamaica	Ukraine	
Switzerland		Jordan	Vietnam	
United Kingdom		Lao PDR	Yemen, Rep.	
United States			Zambia	

Source: The World Bank classification.

Note: Economies are divided according to 2012 GNI per capita, calculated using the World Bank Atlas method. The groups are: low income, $1,035 or less; lower middle income, $1,036 - $4,085; upper middle income, $4,086 - $12,615; and high income,$12,616 or more.

Table 13. Regional classification

SSA		EAP	ECA		LAC	MENA	SAR
Benin	Swaziland	Australia	Albania	Luxembourg	Argentina	Egypt, Arab Rep.	Bangladesh
Botswana	Togo	Cambodia	Armenia	Macedonia, FYR	Bolivia	Israel	Bhutan
Burkina Faso	Uganda	China	Austria	Moldova	Brazil	Jordan	India
Burundi	Zambia	Fiji	Belarus	Netherlands	Chile	Lebanon	Nepal
Cameroon	Zimbabwe	Hong Kong SAR, China	Belgium	Norway	Colombia	Morocco	Pakistan
Cape Verde		Indonesia	Bosnia and Herzegovina	Poland	Costa Rica	Syrian Arab Republic	Sri Lanka
Congo, Dem. Rep.		Japan	Bulgaria	Portugal	Dominican Republic	Tunisia	
Cote d'Ivoire		Korea, Rep.	Croatia	Romania	El Salvador	Yemen, Rep.	
Ethiopia		Lao PDR	Czech Republic	Slovak Republic	Guatemala		
Ghana		Macao SAR, China	Denmark	Slovenia	Honduras		
Guinea		Malaysia	Estonia	Spain	Jamaica		
Kenya		Mongolia	Finland	Sweden	Mexico		
Lesotho		Myanmar	France	Switzerland	Nicaragua		
Madagascar		New Zealand	Georgia	Tajikistan	Paraguay		
Mali		Papua New Guinea	Germany	Turkey	Peru		
Mauritius		Philippines	Greece	Ukraine	Trinidad and Tobago		
Namibia		Singapore	Hungary	United Kingdom	Uruguay		
Niger		Thailand	Iceland				
Rwanda		Vietnam	Ireland				
Senegal			Italy				
Seychelles			Kyrgyz Republic				
Sierra Leone			Latvia				
South Africa			Lithuania				
Sudan							

Source: The World Bank classification.

Note: SSA is Sub-Saharan Africa, EAP is East Asia and Pacific, ECA is Eastern European and Central Asia, LAC is Latin America and Caribbean, MENA is Middle East and North Africa, SAR is South Asia.

Table 14. Correlation matrix, 1994-2012

	Fiscal revenue in % of GDP	Tax revenue in % of GDP	GDP per capita	Age dependency ratio	Population growth	Trade openness	Agriculture value added (in % of GDP)	Bureaucracy Quality Index	Corruption index	Size of shadow economy (in % of GDP)	Natural resources rents (in % of GDP)	Final consumption (in % of GDP)
Fiscal revenue in % of GDP	1.00											
	0.90	1.00										
GDP per capita	0.65	0.64	1.00									
Age dependency ratio	-0.46	-0.49	-0.25	1.00								
Population growth	-0.45	-0.55	-0.34	0.58	1.00							
Trade openness	0.16	0.14	0.21	-0.29	-0.06	1.00						
Agriculture value added (in % of GDP)	-0.61	-0.57	-0.34	0.36	0.43	-0.30	1.00					
Bureaucracy Quality Index	-0.46	-0.46	-0.45	-0.39	-0.28	0.05	-0.33	1.00				
Corruption index	-0.42	-0.40	-0.40	-0.22	-0.20	0.01	-0.40	0.83	1.00			
Size of shadow economy (in % of GDP)	-0.14	-0.06	-0.38	0.42	0.05	-0.27	0.38	-0.38	-0.31	1.00		
Natural resources rents (in % of GDP)	-0.08	-0.32	-0.20	0.21	0.27	-0.01	0.12	-0.14	-0.09	-0.28	1.00	
Final consumption (in % of GDP)	0.55	0.50	0.47	0.48	0.20	-0.22	0.42	-0.46	-0.46	0.39	0.15	1.00

Note: GDP per capita is in constant 2005 US$; population growth is the growth rate of population between 15 and 64 ages; trade openness is the sum of imports and exports in percentage of GDP; corruption index is recalculated such that lower values indicate lower corruption; bureaucracy index is recalculated such that lower values indicate higher bureaucracy quality. 125 countries are included and the number of observations is 1,900.

Table 15. Descriptive statistics, averages over 1994-2012

	Tax Revane in % of GDP	Fiscal Revenue in % of GDP	GDP Per Capita	Age Dependency Ratio	Population Growth	Trade Openness	Agriculture Value Added (in % of GDP)	Bureaucracy Quality Index	Corruption index	Size of Shadow Economy (in % of GDP)	Natural Resources Rents (in % of GDP)	Final Consumption (in % of GDP)
Mean	22.74	28.27	10211.41	62.94	1.68	87.11	15.28	-5.33	-5.78	31.95	6.13	82.19
Standard Deviation	11.14	12.09	15096.08	18.48	1.44	54.95	13.76	3.05	2.61	13.06	10.78	14.56
Minimum	1.63	3.00	118.64	24.68	-8.44	0.31	0.00	-10.00	-10.00	8.10	0.00	22.25
Maximum	63.48	73.32	87716.73	117.43	11.64	562.06	65.86	-1.00	-1.00	68.30	31.00	170.46
Count	1892	1884	2321	2375	2375	2326	2186	2375	2375	1098	2230	2278

Table 16. Actual taxation, taxable capacity (predicted tax) and tax effort by country

	1994-2012			1994-2003			2004-2012		
Country	Tax/GDP	Predicted Tax/GDP	Tax Effort	Tax/GDP	Predicted Tax/GDP	Tax Effort	Tax/GDP	Predicted Tax/GDP	Tax Effort
Albania	18.03	23.72	0.76	16.59	22.09	0.76	18.99	24.80	0.77
Argentina	10.47	18.59	0.57	9.80	18.69	0.53	17.20	17.57	0.98
Armenia	19.07	24.63	0.77	17.17	23.66	0.73	19.28	24.74	0.78
Australia	28.49	26.57	1.07	28.73	25.98	1.11	28.22	27.21	1.04
Austria	35.68	36.86	0.97	38.15	36.42	1.05	32.94	37.50	0.88
Bangladesh	8.39	12.90	0.65	7.79	11.64	0.67	8.62	13.38	0.64
Belarus	28.78	26.99	1.07	28.11	26.17	1.08	29.52	27.91	1.06
Belgium	40.52	36.05	1.12	41.20	36.01	1.14	39.66	36.10	1.10
Benin	16.11	14.96	..	15.34	13.71	1.12	16.37	15.43	..
Bhutan	8.36	9.13	0.98	8.27	8.83	1.02	8.52	9.62	0.91
Bolivia	15.98	14.19	1.13	15.11	14.15	1.07	18.14	14.29	1.27
Bosnia and Herzegovina	33.95	28.00	1.21	32.57	27.96	1.16	34.11	28.00	1.22
Botswana	23.12	24.96	0.92	17.08	22.18	0.77	25.71	26.15	0.98
Brazil	28.98	18.62	1.55	26.71	18.01	1.48	31.00	19.16	1.62
Bulgaria	28.10	28.13	1.00	26.69	27.45	0.97	30.45	29.26	1.04
Burkina Faso	12.13	14.21	0.85	10.70	13.98	0.77	12.48	14.27	0.88
Burundi	15.18	12.85	1.19	15.18	12.85	1.19	..	..	..
Cambodia	9.23	8.22	1.12	7.86	7.73	1.02	9.54	8.34	1.14
Cameroon	9.86	17.63	0.56	9.86	17.63	0.56	..	..	..
Canada	33.10	32.87	1.01	34.76	32.15	1.08	31.25	33.68	0.93
Cape Verde	22.96	22.30	1.03	..	..	..	22.96	22.30	1.03
Chile	18.30	19.25	0.95	17.46	18.58	0.94	19.23	19.99	0.96
China	14.41	16.55	0.86	11.42	15.55	0.73	18.14	17.79	1.02
Colombia	14.11	17.05	0.83	13.17	16.17	0.82	14.74	17.64	0.83
Congo, Dem. Rep.	7.60	10.63	0.73	4.61	10.77	0.44	11.87	10.43	1.14
Costa Rica	15.42	15.69	0.97	12.44	14.80	0.84	18.72	16.68	1.11
Cote d'Ivoire	15.93	18.13	0.88	16.49	17.60	0.95	15.31	19.18	0.80
Croatia	33.76	31.56	1.07	35.10	31.30	1.12	32.27	31.83	1.01
Czech Republic	30.98	30.82	1.01	30.57	30.51	1.00	31.43	31.26	1.01
Denmark	48.75	39.34	1.24	48.85	38.86	1.26	48.63	40.02	1.22
Dominican Republic	12.89	17.09	0.75	11.85	16.68	0.71	14.19	17.60	0.81
Egypt, Arab Rep.	15.54	16.53	0.94	16.38	16.07	1.02	14.60	17.04	0.86
El Salvador	12.74	16.74	0.76	10.40	16.95	0.61	15.33	16.51	0.93

continues on following page

Table 16. Continued

	1994-2012			1994-2003			2004-2012		
Country	**Tax/GDP**	**Predicted Tax/GDP**	**Tax Effort**	**Tax/GDP**	**Predicted Tax/GDP**	**Tax Effort**	**Tax/GDP**	**Predicted Tax/GDP**	**Tax Effort**
Estonia	29.00	30.79	0.94	28.75	30.12	0.95	29.26	31.46	0.93
Ethiopia	8.95	10.84	0.84	9.43	10.48	0.92	8.41	11.25	0.75
Fiji	21.94	14.68	1.50	21.63	13.63	1.59	22.24	15.72	1.41
Finland	43.44	36.97	1.18	44.95	35.99	1.25	41.76	38.05	1.10
France	45.02	36.41	1.24	45.11	35.89	1.26	44.92	36.99	1.21
Georgia	16.14	25.32	0.63	9.60	24.44	0.39	21.23	26.01	0.81
Germany	39.55	37.73	1.05	40.24	37.19	1.08	38.87	38.27	1.02
Ghana	16.14	14.53	1.15	17.72	13.12	1.35	15.55	15.06	1.07
Greece	33.78	34.43	0.98	33.75	33.94	0.99	33.82	34.93	0.97
Guatemala	10.57	15.74	0.69	9.81	17.16	0.59	11.42	14.16	0.81
Guinea	10.86	19.47	0.56	10.86	19.47	0.56	..	..	..
Honduras	18.13	13.23	1.37	17.20	13.45	1.28	18.23	13.20	1.38
Hong Kong SAR, China	12.46	23.18	0.54	9.85	23.21	0.42	13.11	23.17	0.57
Hungary	38.64	30.63	1.26	39.03	30.24	1.29	38.25	31.07	1.23
Iceland	35.24	37.58	0.94	33.49	36.04	0.93	37.18	39.31	0.95
India	14.85	12.86	1.16	13.87	11.97	1.16	15.95	13.85	1.15
Indonesia	13.21	15.57	0.86	13.98	14.67	0.96	12.44	16.48	0.76
Ireland	30.16	36.86	0.82	30.56	35.10	0.87	29.71	37.64	0.79
Israel	31.85	24.33	1.31	31.78	23.66	1.34	31.93	25.07	1.27
Italy	36.14	36.01	1.00	36.58	36.18	1.01	35.69	35.85	1.00
Jamaica	24.73	18.55	1.33	22.66	..	..	27.04	18.55	1.46
Japan	17.06	30.32	0.56	16.47	29.49	0.56	17.26	30.60	0.56
Jordan	19.20	18.00	1.08	19.14	17.76	1.09	19.27	18.27	1.06
Kenya	17.57	15.66	1.12	16.63	14.92	1.12	18.62	16.48	1.13
Korea, Rep.	17.87	22.91	0.78	16.80	22.15	0.76	19.05	23.77	0.80
Kyrgyz Republic	14.51	18.47	0.79	13.18	16.56	0.80	16.02	20.66	0.78
Lao PDR	12.62	8.42	1.50	..	..	..	12.62	8.42	1.50
Latvia	23.37	31.17	0.75	23.88	30.04	0.80	22.80	32.59	0.70
Lebanon	15.43	18.18	0.85	13.67	17.11	0.81	16.22	18.65	0.87
Lesotho	46.99	40.70	1.15	42.22	39.90	1.06	52.29	41.59	1.26
Lithuania	22.68	30.39	0.75	19.06	29.11	0.65	26.71	32.00	0.83
Luxembourg	34.34	42.02	0.82	33.03	41.40	0.80	35.81	42.71	0.84
Macao SAR, China	23.38	21.67	1.06	17.10	20.28	0.85	28.97	22.91	1.26
Macedonia, FYR	27.97	26.24	1.07	..	..	..	27.97	26.24	1.07

continues on following page

Table 16. Continued

	1994-2012			1994-2003			2004-2012		
Country	Tax/GDP	Predicted Tax/GDP	Tax Effort	Tax/GDP	Predicted Tax/GDP	Tax Effort	Tax/GDP	Predicted Tax/GDP	Tax Effort
Lithuania	25.55	29.14	0.88	23.57	29.39	0.80	26.05	29.06	0.90
Luxembourg	35.99	38.11	0.94	36.89	37.70	0.98	35.66	38.26	0.93
Macao SAR, China	20.72	..	..	16.56	..	..	23.84	..	..
Macedonia, FYR	29.67	..	..	..	..	..	29.67	..	..
Madagascar	9.89	17.18	0.58	9.07	16.48	0.55	10.71	17.88	0.62
Malaysia	16.34	15.19	1.08	17.40	14.53	1.20	15.17	15.93	0.95
Mali	14.36	14.53	1.01	13.47	13.47	1.00	14.87	15.14	1.02
Mauritius	17.27	24.09	0.72	16.27	23.28	0.70	18.38	24.98	0.73
Mexico	12.66	18.56	0.68	12.66	18.56	0.68	..	..	..
Moldova	24.97	23.34	1.07	21.89	21.59	1.02	28.05	25.08	1.12
Mongolia	20.54	11.79	1.72	16.86	10.50	1.60	26.66	13.93	1.92
Morocco	27.01	17.07	1.58	23.84	16.71	1.43	27.80	17.16	1.62
Myanmar	3.21	3.47	0.93	3.21	3.47	0.92	3.27	3.51	0.93
Namibia	26.74	21.87	1.23	27.83	21.13	1.33	25.37	22.81	1.11
Nepal	9.80	7.60	1.32	8.66	6.61	1.34	11.07	8.70	1.29
Netherlands	38.78	37.08	1.05	39.21	36.35	1.08	38.31	37.90	1.01
New Zealand	29.91	24.86	1.21	29.37	23.66	1.24	30.49	26.20	1.17
Nicaragua	11.90	12.95	0.92	10.28	12.71	0.81	13.69	13.21	1.04
Niger	10.75	13.73	0.81	..	..	..	10.75	13.73	0.81
Norway	42.69	42.14	1.01	42.72	41.51	1.03	42.66	42.84	1.00
Pakistan	10.81	10.90	1.00	11.98	10.44	1.15	9.50	11.41	0.83
Papua New Guinea	21.56	8.42	2.57	21.56	8.42	2.57	..	..	..
Paraguay	12.79	12.37	1.04	12.20	12.57	0.97	13.44	12.15	1.11
Peru	15.76	17.34	0.91	15.05	16.86	0.89	16.55	17.88	0.93
Philippines	13.57	14.65	0.94	14.30	13.89	1.04	12.75	15.50	0.82
Poland	32.35	30.61	1.06	30.83	30.13	1.02	32.85	30.77	1.07
Portugal	33.53	33.23	1.01	32.45	32.49	1.00	34.61	33.97	1.02
Romania	27.93	28.88	0.97	27.85	28.03	0.99	27.95	29.07	0.96
Rwanda	12.71	14.81	0.86	..	..	..	12.71	14.81	0.86
Senegal	16.61	19.06	0.87	15.25	18.96	0.80	18.66	19.22	0.97
Seychelles	33.58	25.72	1.31	34.11	25.24	1.36	32.98	26.33	1.25
Sierra Leone	8.77	10.68	0.85	8.83	11.60	0.80	8.69	9.52	0.92
Singapore	14.28	20.78	0.69	15.31	20.81	0.74	13.14	20.76	0.64
Slovak Republic	30.42	29.95	..	32.42	29.21	1.11	28.86	30.59	0.94

continues on following page

Table 16. Continued

Country	1994-2012			1994-2003			2004-2012		
	Tax/GDP	Predicted Tax/GDP	Tax Effort	Tax/GDP	Predicted Tax/GDP	Tax Effort	Tax/GDP	Predicted Tax/GDP	Tax Effort
Slovenia	34.86	32.13	1.09	35.05	31.48	1.11	34.63	32.94	1.05
South Africa	26.93	25.08	1.07	25.75	24.00	1.07	28.25	26.28	1.08
Spain	34.51	33.83	1.02	34.09	33.19	1.03	34.97	34.54	1.02
Sri Lanka	14.52	15.37	0.98	15.47	13.82	1.15	13.46	17.09	0.80
Sudan	6.29	12.56	0.50	6.29	12.56	0.50	..	..	..
Swaziland	25.90	21.03	1.23	21.50	20.43	1.06	28.35	21.40	1.32
Sweden	48.02	37.62	1.28	49.46	36.90	1.34	46.57	38.34	1.22
Switzerland	29.61	40.32	0.73	31.13	40.24	0.77	27.70	40.42	0.69
Syrian Arab Republic	16.34	12.16	1.36	17.37	11.83	1.48	14.61	12.71	1.15
Tajikistan	10.31	18.53	0.56	10.07	18.47	0.55	11.50	18.82	0.61
Thailand	17.39	17.21	1.01	16.07	17.10	0.94	18.72	17.31	1.08
Togo	15.37	14.01	1.10	..	..	..	15.37	14.01	1.10
Trinidad and Tobago	26.15	20.97	1.25	22.71	20.09	1.13	28.62	21.60	1.33
Tunisia	24.59	18.01	1.37	24.11	17.17	1.41	25.13	18.95	1.33
Turkey	20.32	27.62	0.74	..	..	..	20.32	27.62	0.74
Uganda	11.88	16.11	0.74	10.80	15.39	0.71	12.61	16.65	0.76
Ukraine	33.99	27.96	1.21	30.73	26.98	1.14	35.08	28.29	1.24
United Kingdom	36.01	37.39	0.96	35.45	36.81	0.96	36.57	37.97	0.96
United States	25.76	35.23	0.73	26.15	34.37	0.76	25.32	36.20	0.70
Uruguay	24.81	19.40	1.28	23.69	19.62	1.21	26.06	19.14	1.36
Vietnam	18.46	11.69	1.58	18.16	11.61	1.56	21.46	12.48	1.72
Yemen, Rep.	8.67	14.16	0.61	9.89	13.00	0.77	7.59	15.49	0.49
Zambia	17.32	18.83	0.92	17.81	19.09	0.93	16.69	18.50	0.90
Zimbabwe	24.59	19.24	1.29	23.57	19.47	1.21	25.60	19.01	1.37

Table 17. Actual fiscal revenue, revenue capacity (predicted revenue) and revenue effort by country

Country	1994-2012			1994-2003			2004-2012		
	Revenue/ GDP	Predicted Revenue/ GDP	Tax Effort	Revenue/ GDP	Predicted Revenue/ GDP	Tax Effort	Revenue/ GDP	Predicted Revenue/ GDP	Tax Effort
Albania	23.36	27.53	0.85	20.30	25.75	0.79	25.39	28.72	0.88
Argentina	14.60	22.57	0.65	14.25	22.69	0.63	18.14	21.35	0.85
Armenia	22.87	28.57	0.80	21.66	27.52	0.79	23.01	28.68	0.80
Australia	34.87	29.66	1.18	35.06	29.02	1.21	34.64	30.38	1.14

continues on following page

Table 17. Continued

Country	1994-2012			1994-2003			2004-2012		
	Revenue/ GDP	Predicted Revenue/ GDP	Tax Effort	Revenue/ GDP	Predicted Revenue/ GDP	Tax Effort	Revenue/ GDP	Predicted Revenue/ GDP	Tax Effort
Austria	37.95	40.39	0.94	38.51	39.90	0.97	37.32	40.94	0.91
Bangladesh	10.55	17.42	0.61	10.05	16.67	0.60	10.74	17.70	0.61
Belarus	31.69	30.14	1.05	29.66	29.41	1.01	33.95	30.94	1.10
Belgium	41.81	39.28	1.06	42.56	38.92	1.09	40.87	39.72	1.03
Benin	19.40	22.63	0.87	17.87	20.90	0.85	19.91	23.21	0.88
Bhutan	19.92	14.74	1.36	20.23	14.15	1.43	19.41	15.73	1.23
Bolivia	25.19	19.33	1.30	23.71	19.34	1.23	28.87	19.32	1.49
Bosnia and Herzegovina	40.02	30.75	1.30	37.14	30.48	1.22	40.34	30.78	1.31
Botswana	39.70	29.88	1.33	41.01	29.11	1.41	39.14	30.21	1.30
Brazil	33.75	22.93	1.47	31.29	22.82	1.37	35.93	23.03	1.56
Bulgaria	34.26	30.81	1.11	33.86	30.22	1.12	34.93	31.79	1.10
Burkina Faso	13.50	21.11	0.64	12.02	20.85	0.58	13.87	21.17	0.65
Burundi	16.94	17.43	0.98	16.94	17.43	0.98	..	..	..
Cambodia	13.82	13.22	1.05	12.79	13.20	0.97	14.05	13.22	1.07
Cameroon	12.60	24.26	0.52	12.60	24.26	0.52	..	..	..
Canada	41.83	36.47	1.15	43.44	35.81	1.21	40.03	37.21	1.08
Cape Verde	28.06	27.48	1.02	..	..	..	28.06	27.48	1.02
Chile	22.20	23.30	0.95	21.80	22.87	0.95	22.64	23.79	0.95
China	22.68	20.03	1.12	18.37	19.41	0.94	28.05	20.82	1.35
Colombia	22.72	21.74	1.04	19.41	21.11	0.93	24.94	22.15	1.12
Congo, Dem. Rep.	17.41	16.97	1.03	8.22	16.94	0.49	30.55	17.01	1.79
Costa Rica	22.47	21.08	1.07	20.99	20.82	1.01	24.12	21.36	1.13
Cote d'Ivoire	17.96	25.09	0.73	18.69	23.41	0.80	17.16	26.95	0.65
Croatia	36.42	34.26	1.06	36.96	33.88	1.09	35.83	34.63	1.03
Czech Republic	34.80	34.40	1.01	32.56	34.08	0.96	37.28	34.74	1.07
Denmark	56.08	42.56	1.32	56.28	42.09	1.34	55.87	43.09	1.30
Dominican Republic	14.42	21.60	0.67	13.45	21.34	0.63	15.64	21.93	0.71
Egypt, Arab Rep.	25.95	20.57	1.26	26.49	20.35	1.30	25.35	20.80	1.22
El Salvador	14.93	20.46	0.73	11.48	20.56	0.56	18.77	20.35	0.92
Estonia	33.59	33.18	1.01	32.68	32.37	1.01	34.50	33.98	1.02
Ethiopia	11.74	17.88	0.66	13.02	17.43	0.75	10.30	18.40	0.56

continues on following page

Table 17. Continued

Country	1994-2012 Revenue/ GDP	1994-2012 Predicted Revenue/ GDP	1994-2012 Tax Effort	1994-2003 Revenue/ GDP	1994-2003 Predicted Revenue/ GDP	1994-2003 Tax Effort	2004-2012 Revenue/ GDP	2004-2012 Predicted Revenue/ GDP	2004-2012 Tax Effort
Fiji	24.89	17.90	1.39	25.20	17.10	1.47	24.59	18.69	1.32
Finland	51.80	40.35	1.28	50.42	39.52	1.28	53.33	41.27	1.29
France	49.43	40.06	1.23	48.73	39.55	1.23	50.19	40.62	1.24
Georgia	18.32	28.80	0.62	10.87	27.21	0.40	24.11	30.03	0.80
Germany	44.68	40.56	1.10	45.34	40.31	1.12	44.03	40.81	1.08
Ghana	18.15	20.82	0.88	18.63	19.41	0.96	17.97	21.35	0.86
Greece	40.29	37.88	1.06	40.14	37.74	1.06	40.44	38.02	1.06
Guatemala	10.88	21.23	0.52	10.05	22.40	0.46	11.80	19.93	0.59
Guinea	11.59	24.68	0.47	11.59	24.68	0.47	..	..	..
Honduras	23.42	18.71	1.25	21.89	18.86	1.16	23.59	18.70	1.26
Hong Kong SAR, China	20.01	24.28	0.82	15.73	24.40	0.65	21.08	24.25	0.87
Hungary	45.06	33.74	1.34	44.36	33.40	1.33	45.77	34.08	1.34
Iceland	42.44	41.97	1.01	40.76	40.49	1.01	44.32	43.62	1.02
India	17.39	17.44	1.00	16.40	16.84	0.97	18.49	18.11	1.02
Indonesia	17.13	19.51	0.88	16.66	18.98	0.88	17.60	20.04	0.88
Ireland	33.04	41.10	0.80	33.64	40.03	0.84	32.37	41.57	0.78
Israel	40.14	27.96	1.44	42.43	27.79	1.53	37.60	28.14	1.34
Italy	37.98	39.18	0.97	38.60	39.09	0.99	37.36	39.26	0.95
Jamaica	32.20	21.58	1.49	31.96	..	..	32.23	21.58	1.49
Japan	40.76	30.87	1.32	30.34	30.55	0.99	44.23	30.97	1.43
Jordan	25.91	22.94	1.13	25.76	23.03	1.12	26.07	22.83	1.14
Kenya	20.34	22.44	0.91	19.85	22.20	0.89	20.89	22.71	0.92
Korea, Rep.	21.73	25.34	0.86	19.96	24.87	0.80	23.69	25.86	0.92
Kyrgyz Republic	18.32	23.93	0.76	15.75	22.31	0.71	21.25	25.77	0.82
Lao PDR	18.20	13.94	1.30	..	..	..	18.20	13.94	1.30
Latvia	28.35	33.16	0.86	27.38	32.34	0.85	29.43	34.07	0.86
Lebanon	20.05	23.18	0.86	17.78	23.11	0.77	21.06	23.21	0.91
Lesotho	56.27	24.62	2.28	51.84	23.77	2.19	61.20	25.56	2.39
Lithuania	26.94	32.71	0.82	24.81	31.65	0.78	29.32	33.88	0.87
Luxembourg	40.07	45.51	0.88	41.18	44.59	0.92	38.82	46.55	0.83
Macao SAR, China	26.59	25.95	1.01	20.73	24.18	0.86	31.80	27.52	1.15
Macedonia, FYR	31.35	29.89	1.05	..	..	..	31.35	29.89	1.05
Madagascar	11.68	24.10	0.49	11.24	23.31	0.48	12.11	24.89	0.49

continues on following page

Table 17. Continued

	1994-2012			1994-2003			2004-2012		
Country	Revenue/ GDP	Predicted Revenue/ GDP	Tax Effort	Revenue/ GDP	Predicted Revenue/ GDP	Tax Effort	Revenue/ GDP	Predicted Revenue/ GDP	Tax Effort
Malaysia	21.85	19.69	1.11	22.25	19.41	1.15	21.40	20.00	1.07
Mali	16.12	21.18	0.77	14.66	20.16	0.73	16.95	21.77	0.79
Mauritius	21.16	27.60	0.77	20.48	26.97	0.76	21.92	28.30	0.77
Mexico	14.52	23.45	0.62	14.52	23.45	0.62	..	..	..
Moldova	28.90	27.02	1.07	26.00	25.38	1.03	32.17	28.88	1.11
Mongolia	27.00	16.14	1.65	23.15	15.16	1.52	33.42	17.78	1.88
Morocco	32.06	20.55	1.56	29.60	20.38	1.45	32.68	20.59	1.59
Myanmar	6.05	..	..	6.01	..	..	6.47	..	..
Namibia	29.53	27.39	1.08	30.90	27.15	1.14	27.82	27.69	1.01
Nepal	11.72	12.27	0.95	10.49	11.61	0.90	13.08	13.00	1.01
Netherlands	45.99	40.24	1.14	46.26	39.78	1.16	45.69	40.75	1.12
New Zealand	36.75	27.85	1.31	32.69	26.81	1.22	41.26	29.02	1.42
Nicaragua	15.23	18.30	0.83	13.66	18.48	0.74	16.97	18.10	0.94
Niger	12.38	20.63	0.61	..	..	..	12.38	20.63	0.61
Norway	55.46	45.91	1.21	54.04	45.07	1.20	57.04	46.85	1.22
Pakistan	14.34	16.53	0.87	15.49	16.31	0.95	13.07	16.78	0.78
Papua New Guinea	23.62	13.64	1.74	23.62	13.64	1.74	..	..	..
Paraguay	18.05	17.59	1.03	17.00	18.05	0.94	19.22	17.07	1.12
Peru	19.04	21.82	0.87	18.27	21.71	0.84	19.90	21.94	0.91
Philippines	15.25	19.25	0.80	15.98	18.69	0.86	14.44	19.87	0.73
Poland	38.63	34.22	1.13	39.37	33.91	1.16	38.39	34.33	1.12
Portugal	39.63	36.81	1.08	38.12	36.48	1.04	41.14	37.15	1.11
Romania	32.57	32.08	1.02	31.89	31.02	1.03	32.72	32.31	1.01
Rwanda	24.88	21.28	1.17	..	..	..	24.88	21.28	1.17
Senegal	18.51	25.37	0.73	16.05	25.21	0.64	22.21	25.61	0.87
Seychelles	41.68	30.09	1.39	43.21	29.98	1.44	39.99	30.22	1.33
Sierra Leone	9.35	16.81	0.56	9.40	17.26	0.55	9.29	16.25	0.57
Singapore	22.69	24.02	0.95	26.23	23.65	1.11	18.75	24.42	0.77
Slovak Republic	35.87	33.78	1.06	37.98	33.20	1.14	34.22	34.23	1.00
Slovenia	37.45	35.25	1.06	37.23	34.67	1.07	37.73	35.97	1.05
South Africa	33.66	30.25	1.11	31.83	30.21	1.05	35.71	30.30	1.18
Spain	37.85	38.09	0.99	37.67	37.51	1.00	38.05	38.73	0.98
Sri Lanka	16.42	18.48	0.90	17.63	17.51	1.01	15.08	19.55	0.77

continues on following page

Table 17. Continued

	1994-2012			1994-2003			2004-2012		
Country	**Revenue/ GDP**	**Predicted Revenue/ GDP**	**Tax Effort**	**Revenue/ GDP**	**Predicted Revenue/ GDP**	**Tax Effort**	**Revenue/ GDP**	**Predicted Revenue/ GDP**	**Tax Effort**
Sudan	7.58	18.72	0.41	7.58	18.72	0.41	..	..	..
Swaziland	27.60	26.07	1.05	23.59	24.97	0.95	29.82	26.69	1.12
Sweden	55.62	41.20	1.35	57.57	40.50	1.42	53.67	41.89	1.28
Switzerland	36.95	43.94	0.84	38.85	43.68	0.89	34.57	44.26	0.78
Syrian Arab Republic	25.08	18.11	1.39	25.84	17.52	1.47	23.81	19.09	1.25
Tajikistan	11.33	25.09	0.45	10.90	24.84	0.44	13.45	26.38	0.51
Thailand	20.36	20.01	1.02	18.99	20.45	0.93	21.74	19.58	1.11
Togo	16.43	20.34	0.81	..	..	..	16.43	20.34	0.81
Trinidad and Tobago	29.87	23.76	1.27	26.44	23.70	1.12	32.32	23.81	1.38
Tunisia	28.35	21.57	1.32	28.02	21.28	1.32	28.72	21.89	1.31
Turkey	34.64	32.98	1.05	..	..	..	34.64	32.98	1.05
Uganda	18.15	23.70	0.77	19.87	22.27	0.89	17.01	24.65	0.70
Ukraine	40.69	30.68	1.32	36.95	29.41	1.26	41.94	31.11	1.35
United Kingdom	39.53	41.10	0.96	38.64	40.55	0.95	40.43	41.65	0.97
United States	31.17	38.85	0.80	32.36	38.29	0.85	29.84	39.48	0.76
Uruguay	27.21	22.15	1.23	26.13	22.38	1.17	28.42	21.89	1.30
Vietnam	22.09	16.53	1.34	21.79	16.48	1.32	25.07	17.08	1.47
Yemen, Rep.	28.48	21.00	1.36	26.36	19.63	1.33	30.37	22.22	1.39
Zambia	18.22	24.69	0.74	18.90	24.84	0.76	17.34	24.48	0.71
Zimbabwe	27.39	24.76	1.11	25.94	25.34	1.02	28.83	24.17	1.19

Chapter 5
Public Investment and Fiscal Sustainability in the West African Economic and Monetary Union (WAEMU):
Lessons for European and Middle Eastern and North African Countries

Mehmet Serkan Tosun
University of Nevada, USA

Serdar Yılmaz
World Bank, USA

ABSTRACT

In this chapter we analyze fiscal adjustments following economic shocks in the West African Monetary Union (WAEMU) countries. Using an unbalanced panel data, we examine empirically 81 developing countries including eight WAEMU countries over the 1980-2012 period. We compare the cyclicality of fiscal policy in WAEMU to other developing countries. While we focus on the response of public investment to changes in GDP, we also examine responses of current public expenditure and fiscal balance. We find that there is strong procyclicality in fiscal policy in WAEMU countries. Procyclicality is strongest in public investment and WAEMU countries are more procyclical in their fiscal policy compared to a group of countries that include European and Middle East and North African (MENA) countries.

INTRODUCTION

Low and volatile public investment levels are one of the reasons cited for slow growth in the West African Economic and Monetary Union (WAEMU) (Dessus & Varoudakis, 2013). WAEMU has been successful in taming the inflation and achieving macroeconomic stability. However, the WAEMU zone is prone to

DOI: 10.4018/978-1-5225-0053-7.ch005

economic shocks which are mitigated by reduction in public investments (Dessus & Varoudakis, 2013). The high exposure to shocks and the pro-cyclicality of fiscal policy are cited as the reasons for the low levels of infrastructure and other public investment in the Union.

Until recently, the cyclicality of fiscal policies in WAEMU zone has not attracted attention. The research on the WAEMU arrangements has focused on real-exchange-rate misalignment and the peg with the Euro (Devarajan, 1997; Amin, 2000; Gnansounou & Verdier-Chouchane, 2012) or optimum currency area (Couharde *et al.*, 2012). However recently there is greater research interest on the role of fiscal policies of the WAEMU in stimulating growth and countering the adverse effects of business cycles.

In this paper we analyze fiscal adjustments following economic shocks in the WAEMU zone to understand whether during the periods of fiscal contractions public investment has been used as shock absorber. Using an unbalanced panel data, we examine empirically 81 developing countries including eight WAEMU countries over the 1980-2012 period. We compare the cyclicality of fiscal policy in WAEMU to other countries including European and Middle Eastern and North African (MENA) countries. While we focus on the response of public investment to changes in GDP, we also examine responses of current public expenditure and fiscal balance. We also control for a number of economic, demographic and institutional factors that may explain changes in our fiscal policy variables. We find that there is strong procyclicality in fiscal policy in WAEMU countries. Procyclicality is strongest in public investment and WAEMU countries are more procyclical in their fiscal policy compared to other countries.

The findings of the paper have important policy recommendations to offer to debt ridden European countries and MENA countries that are struggling to stimulate their stagnant economies. For European countries, despite the need for fiscal flexibility to confront asymmetric impact of the economic crisis, the monetary union arrangements limit their ability to respond the economic shock.

The paper is structured as follows. The next section provides a review of literature on public investment and shocks. The following section provides a detailed description of the WAEMU, including the fiscal rules. This is followed by an empirical analysis on WAEMU countries and other developing countries. The final section provides a policy discussion and our concluding remarks.

FISCAL POLICY AND THE BUSINESS CYCLE

The link between business cycles, change in aggregate economic activity through contractions and expansions, and fiscal policy is an important public policy debate that has received increasing attention in recent years. Although, the conventional wisdom is that fiscal policy should be countercyclical,[1] a number of studies have presented evidence of procyclicality (Agenor *et al.*, 1999; Gavin *et al.*, 1996; Gavin & Perotti, 1997; Mpatswe *et al.*, 2011; Stein *et al.*, 1999; Talvi & Vegh, 1999).

Typically fiscal policies are pro-cyclical in many developing countries (Talvi & Vegh, 2005). The literature on cyclicality of fiscal policies suggests that access to international capital markets is an important factor. During bad times, countries lose access to international capital markets which makes pursuing counter-cyclical policies impossible (Aizenman *et al.*, 2000; Gavin & Perotti, 1997). In case of monetary unions, like WAEMU, strict fiscal rules, aimed at containing spillover effects if debt defaults in case of excessive borrowing, limit fiscal policy options to respond to shocks (De Grauwe, 2007). Political distortions, instability and other institutional characteristics and constraints are also noted as factors that could fuel procyclicality in developing countries (Talvi & Vegh, 2005; Alesina *et al.*, 2008; Frankel *et al.*, 2011).

In the context of Africa region, several studies documented the pro-cyclicality of fiscal policies. Thornton (2008), for example, argues that government consumption is highly pro-cyclical in Africa, particularly in those countries that are more reliant on foreign aid and that are less corrupt.[2] Similarly, Lledo *et al.* (2011) finds that government expenditures are more pro-cyclical in Africa than in other developing countries, albeit decline in pro-cyclicality over time. They suggest that lower external debt and concessional financing contribute to the diminishing cyclicality in the region.

Procyclicality of fiscal policy could be problematic for developing countries for a number of reasons. First, as we noted before, procyclicality means that developing countries wouldn't be able to counteract adverse effects of business cycles. That could negatively impact important public programs such as infrastructure projects and education, which in turn could impede economic development in those countries. This negative impact could even spillover to private investment. In a recent study on 39 low-income countries, Eden and Kraay (2014) showed evidence of crowding in of private investment from public investment. Their estimates show that "an extra dollar of government investment raises private investment by roughly two dollars, and output by 1.5 dollars." With procyclicality of public investment, this would imply that there could be an additional negative economic impact through decreases in both public and private investment during recessionary periods.

WEST AFRICAN ECONOMIC AND MONETARY UNION (WAEMU)

West African Economic and Monetary Union (WAEMU) is a customs and currency union organization of eight Western African countries: Benin, Burkina Faso, Cote d'Ivoire, Guinea-Bissau, Mali, Niger, Senegal and Togo. It was originally established as West African Monetary Union (WAMU) in 1962 to create a common monetary union among the member countries. In 1994, it was converted to West African Economic and Monetary Union (WAEMU) to promote economic integration among the countries that share the CFA franc as a common currency. The CFA franc is the currency issued by the Central Bank of West African States (*Banque Centrale des Etats de l'Afrique de l'Ouest*--BCEAO) and pegged to the Euro. Its convertibility is guaranteed by the French treasury.[3]

The organs of the WAEMU are the Commission, the Council and the Conference. The Commission operates under the auspices of the Council of Ministers and the WAEMU Conference. It administers the budget of the union and enforces the powers delegated by the Council of Ministers. The Council of Ministers sets the monetary and fiscal policy objectives of the Union. Member states are represented by two ministers, including the Minister of Finance, but each has only one vote. The Council meets at least twice a year and makes its decisions unanimously. The BCEAO organizes the Council of Ministers meetings and performs secretariat functions. The Governor of the BCEAO attends the Council meetings in an advisory capacity. The WAEMU Conference of Head of States is the supreme authority of the Union. It makes decisions on issues that could not be resolved by unanimous agreement of the Council of Ministers. It is the prerogative of the Conference to accept new members as well as withdraw or expulse current members. It meets at least once a year and makes its decisions unanimously.

The economic and monetary objectives of the WAEMU aim at promoting trade integration, greater economic competitiveness, harmonization of fiscal policies and macro-economic convergence. The policies for trade integration and economic competitiveness are pursued through the establishment of a customs union and progressive alignment of regulatory and legal environment for open markets. Member countries are encouraged to adopt the fiscal convergence pact rules to harmonize their fiscal policies and align their public financial management regulations. In addition, the convergence of macro-economic policies and indicators are promoted to achieve inflation targets and to eliminate possibilities for central bank financing.

WAEMU has been a qualified success; its member states are more fiscally disciplined than other their neighbors outside of the union (Couharde *et al.*, 2012). A major challenge for the WAEMU zone has been achieving stable economic growth rates.[4] Not only was the growth slow over the years, compared to other regions in Africa, it was also unstable. Figure 1 presents the volatility of average growth rate in WAEMU zone for a period of 1996 to 2012. For example, the average growth of 6.4 percent in 1996 dropped to 1 percent in two years and picking up to nearly 5 percent in 1999.

WAEMU Fiscal Rules

There has been a significant increase in fiscal rules in the developing world with balanced budget and debt rules the most prevalent form of fiscal rule.[5] WAEMU countries adopted those fiscal rules in 2000. The WAEMU treaty specifies four first order criteria for fiscal convergence: (i) fiscal balance[6] to GDP ratio should be zero or positive; (ii) overall debt to GDP ratio should be less than 70 percent[7]; (iii) no accumulation of arrears; (iv) annual inflation less than 3 percent. The first three rules are intended to achieve fiscal discipline and ensure fiscal space for investments without crowding out private sector investments. The last one ensures the consistency between fiscal and monetary policies to achieve price stability. Other criteria including limiting the wage bill to 35 percent of tax revenues and setting a 20 percent floor on the ratio of domestically financed investment to tax revenue strive to achieve the right balance between ensuring the fiscal space for investments and avoiding accumulation of debt and/or arrears.

Figure 1. WAEMU average GDP growth rate, constant prices 1996-2012
Source: Authors' calculation.

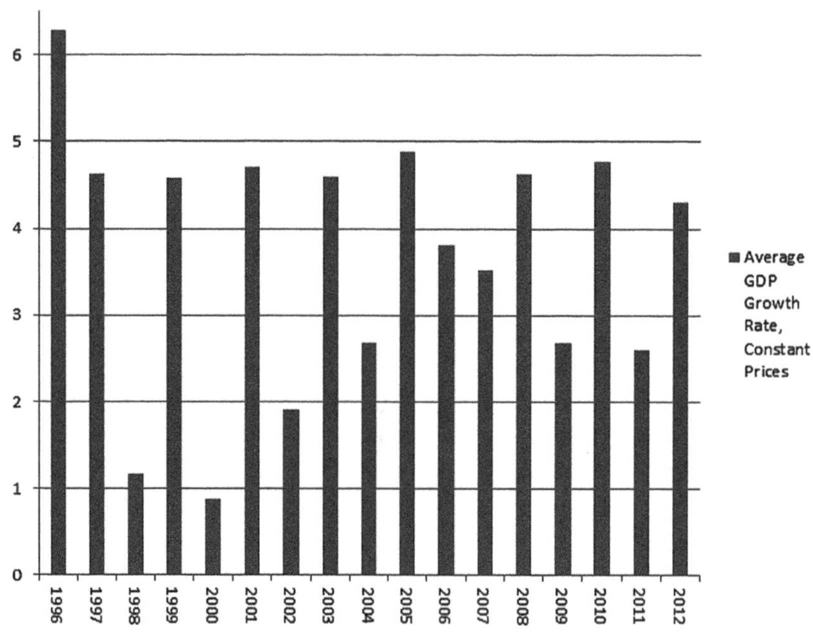

All together the design of these fiscal rules reflects the need for uniformity between the fiscal and monetary policies to improve the competitiveness of the regional economies. The WAEMU Commission, which prepares bi-annual progress reports and makes recommendations for correcting measure in case of non-compliance, is responsible for the monitoring of compliance by the member countries with the fiscal rules. In each of the member countries, the National Committees for Economic Policy (NCEP) are established to produce quarterly reports on the country's economic situation as well as to assist the commission with data gathering and monitoring performance towards the convergence criteria. In case of non-compliance, a member country is given 30 days to develop a strategy to address fiscal deficit. The Council of Ministers has the power granting the country access to WAEMU resources. If a member government fails to come up with a plan to address fiscal deficit in 30 days, the Commission has the power to recommend the Council the withdrawal of financial assistance, to issue of a statement to markets about the country's economic outlook and to recommend the BCEAO to review its support policy to the country.

Public investment and fiscal policy in WAEMU

The West African Economic and Monetary Union (WAEMU) plays a positive role on increasing the economic and financial interconnectivity among its member countries. Although this regional integration is a welcome development, the fiscal discipline requirements of the union might be producing sub-optimal outcomes in times of economic downturn. For example, fiscal discipline requirements might be forcing WAEMU countries to pursue procyclical fiscal policies. According to Dessus and Varoudakis (2013), public investment has been the primary vehicle of choice for pro-cyclical fiscal policy in the WAEMU.

The need for achieving fiscal discipline to ensure the stability of the monetary union is obvious. However, the design and implementation of fiscal rules require careful consideration as they need to leave scope for countercyclical policies while ensuring fiscal discipline. Like in every other monetary union, fiscal policy is the main tool to mitigate the impact of asymmetric shocks in the WAEMU zone. According to Ermal and Onder (2013) WAEMU's fiscal rules need further refinement to better reflect the economic characteristics of its member countries.

EMPIRICAL ANALYSIS AND RESULTS

We examine empirically how public investment responds to changes in the economy and the role of fiscal rules in that response. We first run regressions specifically for WAEMU countries for the period 1980-2012 and then run a second set of regressions where we compare WAEMU countries to other countries including European and Middle Eastern and North African countries. While our main dependent variable is *Public Investment*, we also use *Current Public Expenditure* and *Fiscal Balance* as alternative dependent variables for comparison. Our *Public Investment* variable is gross public fixed capital formation in real terms. We also use a number of other explanatory variables. One important variable is *Fiscal Rule* which is a dummy variable that indicates whether there is a clearly defined fiscal rule in the country. *Trade Openness*, traditionally defined as the ratio of the sum of exports and imports to GDP, captures vulnerability of economies to external shocks. Rodrik (1998) argues that more open countries have larger governments to stabilize the economy against external shocks. We use *Share of Urban Population* as a control for the level of urbanization and *Share of Population 65+* as a control for the demographic structure. Both urbanization and rising elderly population are expected to put strong upward pressure on public investment and overall public expenditures. Many studies also point to the importance of institutional factors in fiscal policy. We use *Quality of Governance* as the main institutional variable. *Quality of Governance* is the average of law and order, bureaucratic quality and corruption which are risk indicators from the International Country Risk Guide (ICRG) published by the PRS Group.[8] We expect that public investment would also be influenced by the overall I*nvestment Profile* of the country. Any risk associated with investment could potentially impact public investment as well through channels such as credit ratings.[9] Finally, we add two conflict variables that are also from the ICRG dataset. While *Improvement in Risk of External Conflict* controls for the risk of conflicts such as wars, cross-border conflicts and other foreign pressures, *Improvement in Risk of Internal Conflict* controls for the risk of conflicts such as civil war, terrorism, political violence and other civil disorders. We also include country and time fixed effects in all regressions and use robust standard errors.

We provide some summary descriptive statistics for our main regression variables in Table 1. We show the mean values for the full sample, as well as for the WAEMU countries and other countries. Share of public investment in GDP is significantly smaller in WAEMU countries. There is actually close to 2% difference between WAEMU and other countries. Another important difference is in the fiscal rules. Fiscal rules are more than three times more prevalent in the WAEMU than in other countries including European and MENA countries. Additionally, WAEMU countries have both a balanced budget rule and a debt rule. These together point to strong fiscal discipline in the WAEMU countries. In terms of other control variables, WAEMU countries are less open to trade, less urbanized, and also have younger populations, lower quality of governance, and poorer investment profiles than other developing countries. While they also have higher risk of external conflict than other countries, they have lower risk of internal conflicts.

Table 1. Summary statistics

	(1)		(2)		(3)	
Variables	**Number of Obs.**	**Full Sample**	**Number of Obs.**	**WAEMU Countries**	**Number of Obs.**	**Other Countries**
Share of Public Investment In GDP (%)	1,839	7.71 (8.36)	264	6.26 (3.53)	1,575	7.95 (8.90)
Fiscal Rule	1,851	0.153 (0.360)	264	0.394 (0.490)	1,587	0.113 (0.317)
Trade Openness (%)	973	71.69 (31.25)	121	61.99 (20.47)	852	73.07 (32.27)
Share of Urban Population (%)	1,036	42.90 (20.54)	136	38.53 (20.02)	900	43.56 (20.55)
Share of Population 65+ (%)	1,002	5.601 (4.434)	136	4.399 (4.367)	866	5.789 (4.418)
Quality of Governance	747	2.618 (0.879)	115	2.261 (0.702)	632	2.683 (0.893)
Investment Profile	746	7.597 (2.244)	115	7.548 (1.898)	631	7.605 (2.302)
Improvement in Risk of External Conflict	746	9.995 (1.370)	115	9.604 (1.158)	631	10.07 (1.394)
Improvement in Risk of Internal Conflict	746	8.823 (1.803)	115	8.887 (1.569)	631	8.811 (1.843)

Empirical Results

The regression results for the WAEMU sample are shown in Tables 2-4. Table 2 presents the results for *Public Investment* variable. Results in Table 2 show that gross public fixed capital formation (public investment) is highly procyclical in the WAEMU countries. We first start with the regression where change in public investment is regressed only on the change in GDP. We then add other control variables and see if cyclicality results change. In all other regressions in Table 2 we find that the restrictiveness of the fiscal rule is negatively associated with public investment in WAEMU countries, which is consistent with the fact that WAEMU countries have stronger fiscal discipline than other countries. We find, however, that this result is not statistically significant. Among the control variables added, the only significant results are for *Share of Urban Population* and *Share of Population 65+*. As expected, both urbanization and the demographic transition through rising elderly population are positively associated with public investment. We also find that as we add more control variables the magnitude and significance of the procyclicality variable—the change in GDP—remains the same which is an indication of the robustness of the finding.

Table 2. Public investment regressions for WAEMU countries

Variables	(1) Public Investment	(2) Public Investment	(3) Public Investment	(4) Public Investment	(5) Public Investment
Log of Real GDP	2.613*** (0.679)	2.613*** (0.679)	2.888*** (0.560)	2.884** (1.017)	2.930** (1.036)
Fiscal Rule		-0.105 (0.338)	-0.0926 (0.222)	-0.171 (0.269)	-0.0732 (0.300)
Quality of Governance				0.0763 (0.212)	0.102 (0.235)
Investment Profile				0.00715 (0.0162)	-0.00326 (0.0130)
Improvement in Risk of External Conflict				-0.0780 (0.0609)	-0.117 (0.0637)
Improvement in Risk of Internal Conflict				-0.0208 (0.0225)	-0.0155 (0.0213)
Trade Openness			0.00179 (0.00399)		0.00295 (0.00359)
Share of Urban Population			0.00379 (0.0272)		0.0430** (0.0149)
Share of Population 65+			0.0338 (0.0202)		0.187* (0.0787)
Constant	-0.237 (0.324)	-0.132* (0.0692)	-0.443 (0.781)	0.617 (0.671)	-1.698* (0.806)
Country fixed effects	Yes	Yes	Yes	Yes	Yes
Time fixed effects	Yes	Yes	Yes	Yes	Yes
Observations	256	256	121	115	100
R-squared	0.188	0.188	0.204	0.259	0.285
Number of countries	8	8	8	7	7

Robust standard errors in parentheses
*** $p<0.01$, ** $p<0.05$, * $p<0.1$

Table 3 presents the results for *Current Public Expenditure*. Results in Table 3 also show procyclicality but it is much less pronounced (smaller in magnitude and less robust) than the previous *Public Investment* model. Fiscal rule is again negatively associated with current public expenditure but it is again not statistically significant. None of the other control variables have statistically significant associations.

Table 4 presents the results for *Fiscal Balance* variable. Results in Table 4 also show procyclicality for fiscal balance. Given the results for public investment and current public expenditure, the results in Table 4 confirm that government revenues are also procyclical. Two of the control variables turn significant in the last two regressions. Both *Investment Profile* and *Trade Openness* are negatively associated with fiscal balance. Since fiscal balance is the difference between general government revenues and general government total expenditures, it is possible that improvement (deterioration) in investment profile also increases (decreases) general government expenditures more than revenues and lead to a decrease (increase) in fiscal balance. The result for trade openness is in line with Rodrik (1998) that more open countries have larger government expenditures to cope with external shocks. That would also lead to lower fiscal balance.

Table 3. Current public expenditure regressions for WAEMU countries

Variables	(1) Current Public Expenditure	(2) Current Public Expenditure	(3) Current Public Expenditure	(4) Current Public Expenditure	(5) Current Public Expenditure
Log of Real GDP	1.247** (0.489)	1.247** (0.489)	1.514** (0.594)	0.674 (0.385)	0.857* (0.382)
Fiscal Rule		-0.0694 (0.0471)	-0.0708 (0.0805)	-0.0556 (0.0468)	-0.128 (0.189)
Quality of Governance				-0.0854 (0.100)	-0.147 (0.152)
Investment Profile				-0.0123 (0.00842)	-0.00696 (0.0132)
Improvement in Risk of External Conflict				0.0341 (0.0199)	0.0346 (0.0270)
Improvement in Risk of Internal Conflict				0.0217 (0.0152)	0.0416 (0.0256)
Trade Openness			0.000981 (0.00144)		0.00128 (0.00153)
Share of Urban Population			0.00142 (0.0144)		-0.00634 (0.0174)
Share of Population 65+			0.0143 (0.00980)		0.00292 (0.0300)
Constant	0.0662*** (0.0124)	0.0662*** (0.0124)	-0.160 (0.509)	-0.178 (0.463)	-0.0897 (1.047)
Country fixed effects	Yes	Yes	Yes	Yes	Yes
Time fixed effects	Yes	Yes	Yes	Yes	Yes
Observations	140	140	99	96	81
R-squared	0.270	0.270	0.228	0.344	0.418
Number of countries	8	8	8	7	7

Robust standard errors in parentheses
*** $p<0.01$, ** $p<0.05$, * $p<0.1$

Table 4. Fiscal balance regressions for WAEMU countries

Variables	(1) Fiscal Balance	(2) Fiscal Balance	(3) Fiscal Balance	(4) Fiscal Balance	(5) Fiscal Balance
Log of Real GDP	0.0854 (0.0653)	0.0854 (0.0653)	0.200 (0.128)	0.359** (0.132)	0.439* (0.197)
Fiscal Rule		-0.00986 (0.0113)	0.0470 (0.0767)	0.00432 (0.0315)	0.171 (0.114)
Quality of Governance				0.00137 (0.0238)	0.0453 (0.0415)
Investment Profile				-0.0113*** (0.00256)	-0.0134** (0.00544)
Improvement in Risk of External Conflict				-0.00361 (0.00735)	5.50e-05 (0.0119)
Improvement in Risk of Internal Conflict				0.00435 (0.00637)	-0.00267 (0.00676)
Trade Openness			-0.00122 (0.000795)		-0.00161* (0.000733)
Share of Urban Population			-0.00273 (0.0144)		-0.00548 (0.0137)
Share of Population 65+			-0.0101 (0.0146)		-0.0180 (0.0213)
Constant	-0.0261*** (0.00495)	-0.0261*** (0.00495)	0.174 (0.587)	0.0406 (0.0909)	0.268 (0.506)
Country fixed effects	Yes	Yes	Yes	Yes	Yes
Time fixed effects	Yes	Yes	Yes	Yes	Yes
Observations	148	148	104	100	85
R-squared	0.318	0.318	0.360	0.388	0.443
Number of countries	8	8	8	7	7

Robust standard errors in parentheses
*** $p<0.01$, ** $p<0.05$, * $p<0.1$

In the second set of regressions for a broader set of developing countries, results for public investment in Table 5 are consistent with results from Table 2. We see high level of procyclicality in both WAEMU and other countries. Procyclicality is stronger, however, in WAEMU than in other countries. Among the control variables, the only significant variable is *Investment Profile* and that is only in the last regression in column (5). Favorable investment environment seems to have a positive association with public investment as well.

Current public expenditure shows similar results as well. Results in Table 6 show that procyclicality is visible mainly in WAEMU countries but not in other countries. *Share of Urban Population* is negative and statistically significant in regressions (3) and (5) which is not as expected. Fiscal Balance regressions in Table 7 show evidence of procyclicality again in WAEMU countries. There is also some evidence that fiscal rules are indeed having a positive impact on fiscal balance only in WAEMU countries. As in results in Table 4, both *Investment Profile* and *Trade Openness* have negative and statistically significant associations with fiscal balance. Among the other control variables we also now see a positive and significant association between improvement in the risk of internal conflict and fiscal balance which we didn't observe in previous regressions.

Table 5. Public investment regressions for all countries

Variables	(1) Public Investment	(2) Public Investment	(3) Public Investment	(4) Public Investment	(5) Public Investment
Log of Real GDP * WAEMU	2.375*** (0.566)	2.351*** (0.572)	2.802*** (0.563)	2.600*** (0.746)	2.684*** (0.724)
Log of Real GDP * 1-WAEMU	2.039*** (0.353)	2.047*** (0.356)	2.521*** (0.574)	2.345*** (0.636)	2.052*** (0.669)
Fiscal Rule * WAEMU		0.0198 (0.0333)	0.00502 (0.0449)	0.0259 (0.0493)	0.0137 (0.0592)
Fiscal Rule * 1- WAEMU		0.00850 (0.0246)	-0.0273 (0.0322)	-0.0356 (0.0399)	-0.0395 (0.0371)
Quality of Governance				0.00748 (0.0342)	0.00894 (0.0311)
Investment Profile				0.0138* (0.00692)	0.0169** (0.00762)
Improvement in Risk of External Conflict				-0.0126 (0.0114)	-0.0131 (0.0114)
Improvement in Risk of Internal Conflict				-0.00287 (0.00791)	-0.00839 (0.00766)
Trade Openness			-0.000794 (0.000755)		-0.000551 (0.00105)
Share of Urban Population			-0.00235 (0.00573)		-0.00204 (0.00525)
Share of Population 65+			-0.0151 (0.0164)		-0.0385 (0.0246)
Constant	-0.0544 (0.0725)	-0.0537 (0.0726)	0.168 (0.279)	-0.00628 (0.153)	0.358 (0.305)
Country fixed effects	Yes	Yes	Yes	Yes	Yes
Time fixed effects	Yes	Yes	Yes	Yes	Yes
Observations	1,754	1,754	930	736	674
R-squared	0.083	0.083	0.085	0.104	0.093
Number of countries	68	68	62	47	46

Robust standard errors in parentheses
*** p<0.01, ** p<0.05, * p<0.1

POLICY IMPLICATION FOR EUROPEAN AND MENA COUNTRIES

In the Eurozone,[10] fiscal rules are important tools to achieve fiscal discipline. However, monetary union rules limited the Eurozone countries fiscal flexibility to confront economic shocks (i.e. economic crisis). Like WAEMU countries, public investment is pro-cyclical in the Eurozone as well. Some flexibility in fiscal rules could help mitigate the pro-cyclicality of public expenditure, especially that of public investment. In addition, formal fiscal federalism arrangements would help cushioning of the impact of asymmetric shocks. Centralization of budget at the union level would allow transferring resources to countries hit by negative shocks from countries that are less affected. This would be equivalent to an interregional transfer within the union. Countries less affected by shocks would pay more tax to the central budget and finance transfers to those countries hit by negative shocks.

Table 6. Current public expenditure regressions for all countries

Variables	(1) Current Public Expenditure	(2) Current Public Expenditure	(3) Current Public Expenditure	(4) Current Public Expenditure	(5) Current Public Expenditure
Log of Real GDP * WAEMU	0.946* (0.480)	0.933* (0.495)	1.240*** (0.455)	0.881 (0.679)	1.422** (0.543)
Log of Real GDP * 1-WAEMU	0.727*** (0.192)	0.740*** (0.193)	0.0335 (0.302)	0.107 (0.279)	0.0245 (0.334)
Fiscal Rule * WAEMU		0.0212 (0.0220)	0.0217 (0.0206)	0.0149 (0.0218)	0.00673 (0.0256)
Fiscal Rule * 1- WAEMU		0.0432* (0.0222)	0.0364 (0.0286)	0.0437 (0.0276)	0.0351 (0.0296)
Quality of Governance				-0.00343 (0.0166)	-0.000706 (0.0172)
Investment Profile				0.00347 (0.00503)	0.00489 (0.00545)
Improvement in Risk of External Conflict				0.00283 (0.00650)	0.00213 (0.00627)
Improvement in Risk of Internal Conflict				0.00354 (0.00536)	0.00476 (0.00591)
Trade Openness			0.000487 (0.000443)		0.000482 (0.000684)
Share of Urban Population			-0.00876** (0.00372)		-0.00712* (0.00388)
Share of Population 65+			-0.0224 (0.0222)		-0.0118 (0.0145)
Constant	0.00824 (0.0937)	0.00503 (0.0933)	0.506** (0.206)	-0.00653 (0.0751)	0.255 (0.238)
Country fixed effects	Yes	Yes	Yes	Yes	Yes
Time fixed effects	Yes	Yes	Yes	Yes	Yes
Observations	1,192	1,192	781	658	596
R-squared	0.058	0.060	0.033	0.043	0.052
Number of countries	66	66	60	47	46

Robust standard errors in parentheses
*** p<0.01, ** p<0.05, * p<0.1

In the Eurozone, establishing a fiscal federal structure might be out of reach right now. In that context, pooling resources to finance locally important expenditure programs might be a good policy action. A Eurozone infrastructure fund would collect contributions from all member countries to finance counter-cyclical investments in countries affected by shocks. The main challenge to implement such a policy option is to avoid moral hazard. It will require a mechanisms to verify that shocks are exogenous rather than result of bad fiscal decisions. Otherwise such an investment fund will be a mechanism for awarding reckless fiscal decisions.

In the MENA region, governments are struggling to stimulate the economy following the Arab Spring. Under difficult circumstances, many countries have sought policy interventions to maximize the effectiveness of their efforts. In this context, public investment appears to be mildly counter-cyclical in

Table 7. Fiscal balance regressions for all countries

Variables	(1) Fiscal Balance	(2) Fiscal Balance	(3) Fiscal Balance	(4) Fiscal Balance	(5) Fiscal Balance
Log of Real GDP * WAEMU	0.0966 (0.0755)	0.0889 (0.0619)	0.194** (0.0805)	0.259*** (0.0649)	0.241*** (0.0721)
Log of Real GDP * 1-WAEMU	0.159*** (0.0543)	0.161*** (0.0548)	0.0331 (0.0732)	0.0444 (0.0978)	0.0390 (0.109)
Fiscal Rule * WAEMU		0.0109 (0.0134)	0.0180* (0.00982)	0.0170 (0.0103)	0.0244* (0.0126)
Fiscal Rule * 1- WAEMU		0.0216 (0.0199)	0.00327 (0.0104)	0.0133 (0.0113)	0.0138 (0.0111)
Quality of Governance				-0.0122 (0.0101)	-0.0116 (0.0111)
Investment Profile				-0.00584** (0.00227)	-0.00645** (0.00255)
Improvement in Risk of External Conflict				0.00133 (0.00337)	0.00226 (0.00323)
Improvement in Risk of Internal Conflict				0.00321*** (0.00108)	0.00316*** (0.00110)
Trade Openness			-6.82e-05 (0.000162)		-0.000435** (0.000188)
Share of Urban Population			-0.00216* (0.00111)		-0.00158 (0.00116)
Share of Population 65+			-0.00184 (0.00382)		0.00467 (0.00584)
Constant	-0.0589*** (0.0143)	-0.0592*** (0.0146)	0.0846 (0.0641)	-0.00343 (0.0514)	0.0759 (0.0858)
Country fixed effects	Yes	Yes	Yes	Yes	Yes
Time fixed effects	Yes	Yes	Yes	Yes	Yes
Observations	1,539	1,539	953	748	678
R-squared	0.092	0.098	0.082	0.086	0.095
Number of countries	80	80	70	52	51

Robust standard errors in parentheses
*** p<0.01, ** p<0.05, * p<0.1

the region, therefore, spending measures, particularly in public investment, have been favoured as they are deemed to have high multipliers. At the same time, those countries runs the risk of ending up with ineffective public investment projects.

CONCLUSION

In this paper, we examine empirically the cyclicality of fiscal policy in WAEMU countries and compare them to other countries including European and MENA countries. While we focus on the response of public investment to changes in GDP, we also examine responses of current public expenditure and fiscal balance. We also control for a number of economic, demographic and institutional factors that may explain changes in our fiscal policy variables. We find that there is strong procyclicality in fiscal policy in WAEMU countries. Procyclicality is strongest in public investment and WAEMU countries are more procyclical in their fiscal policy compared to other countries. While our empirical analysis confirms the procyclicality results found in previous studies on the behavior of public investment spending over the economic cycle, we control for other potentially important factors that could drive procyclicality. It is important to note our key fiscal policy variables show high degree of responsiveness (procyclicality) even after we control for fiscal rules, institutional quality, conflicts, and other economic and demographic factors. This result is consistent with public spending behavior observed in other studies across the sub-Saharan region more generally.[11] At the same time WAEMU countries are found to be more procyclical in public investment and other fiscal policy variables than other countries including the European and MENA countries.

WAEMU countries have strong fiscal discipline through fiscal rules (balanced budget and debt rule) that were adopted in 2000. As we discussed before, while it is important to have fiscal discipline to ensure macroeconomic stability, the design and implementation of fiscal rules should still be consistent with countercyclical policies. We didn't find strong evidence of any procyclical bias from fiscal rules, which is consistent with the arguments in Bova *et al.* (2013) that fiscal rules could improve on accountability and credibility and in turn make room for more countercyclical fiscal policy. Nevertheless, more flexibility in terms of countercyclicality could be introduced by moving to cyclically-adjusted balanced budget rules and including escape clauses in the fiscal rules.

REFERENCES

Agenor, P., McDermott, J., & Prasad, E. (1999). *Macroeconomic Fluctuations in Developing Countries: Some Stylized Facts*. International Monetary Fund WP/99/35.

Aizenman, J., Gavin, M., & Hausmann, R. (2000). Optimal Tax and Debt Policy with Endogenously Imperfect Creditworthiness. *The Journal of International Trade & Economic Development*, *9*(4), 367–395. doi:10.1080/096381900750056830

Alesina, A., Tabellini, G., & Campante, F. R. (2008). Why is Fiscal Policy Often Procyclical? *Journal of the European Economic Association*, *6*(5), 1006–1036. doi:10.1162/JEEA.2008.6.5.1006

Amin, A. A. (2000, August). Long Term Growth in the CFA Franc Zone Countries. *The United Nations University World Institute for Development Economics Research.*

Blanchard, O., & Fischer, S. (1989). *Lectures on Macroeconomics*. Cambridge, MA: The MIT Press.

Bova, E., Carcenac, N., & Guerguil, M. (2013). Fiscal Rules and the Procyclicality of Fiscal Policy in the Developing World. *IMF-World Bank Conference on Fiscal Policy, Equity and Long-Term Growth in Developing Countries Washington, DC, April 21-22.* Retrieved from http://www.imf.org/external/np/seminars/eng/2013/fiscalpolicy/pdf/fispols3.pdf

Courharde, C., Coulibaly, I., Guerreiro, D., & Mignon, V. (2012). Revising the Theory of Optimum Currency Areas: Is the CFA Franc Zone Sustainable? Centre d'Etudes Prospectives et d'Informations Internationales *Working Paper* No: 2012-13.

De Grauwe, P. (2007). *Economics of Monetary Union*. New York: Oxford University Press.

Dessus, S., & Varoudakis, A. (2013). Protecting Public Investment against Shocks in the WAEMU: Options for Fiscal Rules and Risk Sharing. *World Bank Policy Research Working Paper* No. 6562.

Devarajan, S. (1997). Real Exchange Rate Misalignment in the CFA. Zone. *Journal of African Economies*, *6*(1), 35–53. doi:10.1093/oxfordjournals.jae.a020922

Eden, M., & Kraay, A. (2014). "Crowding in" and the Returns to Government Investment in Low-Income Countries. World Bank Policy Research Working Paper 6781. Washington, DC: World Bank Group. Retrieved from http://documents.worldbank.org/curated/en/2014/02/19005742/crowding-returns-government-investment-low-income-countries

Frankel, J. A., Vegh, C. A., & Vuletin, G. (2011). On Graduation from Fiscal Procyclicality, *NBER Working Paper* 17619. Retrieved from: http://www.hks.harvard.edu/fs/jfrankel/GraduatnfromprocyclicalityV&V-Jul15.pdf

Gavin, M., Hausmann, R., Perotti, R., & Talvi, E. (1996). Managing Fiscal Policy in Latin America and the Caribbean: Volatility, Procyclicality and Limited Creditworthiness. *Inter-American Development Bank*, OCE Working Paper No. 326.

Gavin, M., & Perotti, R. (1997a). Fiscal policy in Latin America. *NBER Macroeconomics Annual*, *12*, 11–70. doi:10.1086/654320

Gavin, M., & Perotti, R. (1997b). Fiscal Policy and Private Savings in Latin America in Good Times and Bad. In R. Hausmann & H. Reisen (Eds.), *Promoting Savings in Latin America* (pp. 149–166). Paris: IDB/OECD.

Gnansounou, S., & Verdier-Chouchane, A. (2012). Mesalignement du taux de change effectif reel: Quand faudra-t-il de nouveau devalue le franc CFA? *African Development Bank Working Paper Series* No. 166, Tunis.

Hitaj, E., & Onder, Y. K. (2013). Fiscal Discipline in WAEMU: Rules, Institutions and Markets. *IMF Working Paper* WP/13/216.

Houssa, R. (2008). Monetary Union in West Africa and Asymmetric Shocks: A Dynamic Structural Factor Model Approach. *Journal of Development Economics*, *85*(1-2), 319–347. doi:10.1016/j.jdeveco.2006.05.003

Staff Report on Common Policies for Member Countries. (2012). *International Monetary Fund*. Retrieved from http://www.imf.org/external/pubs/ft/scr/2012/cr1259.pdf

Knack, S. (2001). Aid Dependence and the Quality of Governance. *Southern Economic Journal*, *68*(2), 310–329. doi:10.2307/1061596

Lledo, V. D., Yackovlev, I., & Gadenne, L. (2011). A Tale of Cyclicality, Aid Flows and Debt: Government Spending in Sub-Sharan Africa. *Journal of African Economies*, *20*(5), 823–849. doi:10.1093/jae/ejr022

Lucas, R. E. Jr, & Stokey, N. L. (1983). Optimal Fiscal and Monetary Policy in an Economy without Capital. *Journal of Monetary Economics*, *12*(1), 55–93. doi:10.1016/0304-3932(83)90049-1

Mauro, P. (1996). The Effects of Corruption on Growth, Investment and Government Expenditure. *IMF Working Paper* WP/96/98.

Mpatswe, G. K., Tapsoba, S. J.-A., & York, R. C. (2011). The Cyclicality of Fiscal Policies in the CEMAC Region. *IMF Working Paper* WP/11/205. Retrieved from https://www.imf.org/external/pubs/ft/wp/2011/wp11205.pdf

Stein, E., Talvi, E., & Gristani, A. (1999). Institutional Arrangements and Fiscal Performance: The Latin American Experience. In J. M. Poterba & J. von Hagen (Eds.), *Fiscal Institutions and Fiscal Performance* (pp. 103–134). Chicago, IL: University of Chicago Press.

Talvi, E., & Vegh, C. (2000). Tax base variability and procyclical fiscal policy. *NBER Working Paper* # 7499.

Tanzi, V. (1992). Structural Factors and Tax Revenue in Developing Countries: A Decade of Evidence. In I. Goldin & L. A. Winters (Eds.), *Open Economies: Structural Adjustment and Agriculture* (pp. 267–285). New York: Cambridge University Press. doi:10.1017/CBO9780511628559.023

Tanzi, V., & Davoodi, H. R. (2000). Corruption, Growth and Public Finances. *IMF Working Paper* WP/00/182.

Taylor, J. B., & Woodford, M. (Eds.), (1999). Handbook of Macroeconomics. Elsevier: Amsterdam.

Thornton, J. (2008). Explaining Procyclical Fiscal Policy in African Countries. *Journal of African Economies*, *17*(93), 451–464.

ENDNOTES

1 From a Keynesian perspective, there is a clear view that both public expenditure and public investment should move countercyclically. However, the typical assumption in neoclassical analysis of fiscal policy is that government spending is exogenously determined (Lucas & Stokey, 1983; Blanchard & Fischer 1989; Taylor & Woodford, 1999).

2 His findings suggest that government consumption is less pro-cyclical in countries with unequal income distribution and that are more democratic.

3 The CFA, initially pegged to the French franc, has been pegged to the euro at the parity of 655.96 CFA per euro since the launch of the European currency.

4 Research shows that WAEMU countries move at different speeds, which makes running a common monetary policy extremely difficult (Houssa, 2008).

5 Bova *et al.* (2013) show that the increase in fiscal rules was much more visible in the developing countries than in advanced economies.

6 The fiscal balance is defined as total revenues, excluding grants, minus total expenditures excluding donor financing.

7 Debt in the WAEMU countries is to a large extent on concessional terms.

8 This was recently used as a measure of governance quality by Knack (2001). These institutional variables, particularly corruption in government, were used in many other studies including Tanzi and Davoodi (2000), Mauro (1996) and Knack and Keefer (1995).

9 Subcomponents of *Investment Profile* are contract viability/expropriation, profits repatriation and payment delays. ICRG variable descriptions can be found at http://www.prsgroup.com/ICRG_methodology.aspx

10 The eurozone, also referred to as the euro area, is a monetary union of 19 European Union (EU) member countries that have adopted the euro as their common currency.

11 Mpatswe et al. (2011) found that public investment expenditures in the six CEMAC countries—Cameroon, Central African Republic, Chad, Congo, Equatorial Guinea, and Gabon—were strongly procyclical during the 1980–2008 period.

Chapter 6
The Effects of International Openness on the Public Sector Growth:
An Evidence from OECD Countries

Ali R. Özdemir
Gazi University, Turkey

ABSTRACT

Using Ordinary Least Squares (OLS) with panel corrected standard errors for OECD panel data this chapter, in contrast to Compensation hypothesis, finds a negative relationship between openness and the rate of public sector growth. In addition, this inverse relationship is found to be the strongest when electoral systems are more competitive. The empirical results presented here also suggests that openness constrains government growth more when the governments are run by either left-leaning parties or by left-leaning coalitions. This result holds for most measures of government spending and is robust to the inclusion of a wide range of controls. Unlike the existing empirical literature, which focuses on the 'compensation effect' of openness on government growth, this study supports the 'competition effect' of openness drawn from the literature on local public finance.

1. INTRODUCTION

Openness coming with globalization creates important changes on the structure of national economies as well as on many other things belong to the nations. One of the structural affect that it creates is related to size and scope of public sector in overall economy. While countries become more open in terms of increased volume of traded goods and services, and of increased mobility of capital, there has been a noticeable slow-down in the high rate of public sector growth in many of these countries in the most recent period. After all the criticisms about excessive rate of public sector growth in the earlier periods, this has been a positive development in government finance. Now, the question whether this seemingly inverse relationship between openness and government growth is a coincidence or real is still subject to an ongoing investigation.

DOI: 10.4018/978-1-5225-0053-7.ch006

In the investigation on the nature of the relationship between openness and the growth of government budget, the existing literature stresses around two alternative hypotheses. Under the first one, which is called "compensation hypothesis," the government budget grows faster when economies become more open in order to compensate for potential income and job losses due to increased external risks and macroeconomic instabilities. Under the second one "competition hypothesis" however, the government budget grows slower because competition for mobile factors of production between governments of open economies lowers the cost of the public sector provision of goods and services and adversely affects the ability of independent governments to exploit their citizens.

The existing empirical literature that seems to be supporting both of the hypotheses about the relationship between openness and the rate of public sector growth is still unsettled and far from convincing. For instance, some studies find significant positive relationship while some others suggest no or negative relationship. The reasons for these controversies in the results are multifold. First, the results that are produced in these studies using varies methods of econometrics. Some techniques are just simple correlations or regressions with no consideration of time series or cross section related problems, while some others do not control for multiple sources of influence. Second, especially in political science literature, what happens to wasteful size of government budget or revenue-expenditure package is not viewed that importantly. They do not disentangle the effect of interactive factors such as economic and institutional variables.

Using recent econometric techniques and panel data, this article demonstrates that there is a negative relationship between openness and the rate of public sector growth. The relationship is robust to the inclusion of other critical explanatory variables such as country size, relative price ratio, and political competition and ideology. The evidence presented here supports the notion that integration of world markets for goods and services will be held accountable for allocating resources efficiently and for suppressing the rate of growth of the public sector.

The investigation in this article proceeds as follows: Section two offers some theoretical explanations for why and how does openness influence the allocation of resources between public and private sectors. Section three reviews the empirical literature and raises some concerns about the empirical validity of the existing studies. Section four presents the regression results that are obtained based upon the empirical model discussed in section two. Section five contains additional regressions in order to test the robustness of the results and provide alternative explanations for the inverse effect of trade openness on government growth.

2. LITERATURE REVIEW

Reported in the literature are two distinctly opposing effects of openness on national government size. At one extreme, openness is associated with a higher rate of government growth due to its exposure to external risk and macroeconomic instabilities. At the other extreme, openness is associated with a slower rate of government growth through its effect on fiscal competition. Both explanations seem appealing. According to the "compensation hypothesis", government spending grows faster because of risk-reducing demands by citizens' fear of greater external risk. According to the "competition hypothesis" however, inter-jurisdictional tax competition for mobile factors of production in open economies helps to tame the Leviathan or lowers the public sector provision.[1]

Compensation Hypothesis

The primary reason why openness is positively associated with government growth is related to the "compensation hypothesis." This hypothesis accounts for the public sector expansion and is often characterized as a "responsive"[2] government explanation. As domestic economies are exposed to greater economic volatility caused both by international trade and financial openness, income and employment risks, faced by workers increase. Greater external risk produces more severe business cycles in open economies, resulting in layoffs and/or inflation. Lindbeck(1976) argued that the public sector grows faster in open economies because residents expect government to dampen the risk effects of the open economy on production, employment and consumption. One of the ways the government is expected to level peaks and valleys of business cycles is through use of spending and tax instruments.[3] Even there is inability to control aggregate demand, the government can maintain full employment by providing subsidies to firms in order to retain and retrain workers and by increasing public employment. Bates, Brock, and Tiefenthalen(1991) argued that public spending, which acts as a risk-reducing instrument, increases in highly open economies. This is the result of a greater political demand for expansionary spending policies such as income supplements and social insurance programs, which cushion and compensate workers for income and employment risks.[4] In addition, Epifani and Gancia (2009) argue that more open economies have increased government size because trade decreases the domestic cost of taxation.

Comparing public spending in 18 OECD countries, Cameron (1978) suggested that the degree of exposure of the economy to the international marketplace matters. Since open economies have higher rates of industrial concentration, which fosters labor unionization, a wider scope of collective bargaining, and the role of labor confederations, the demands for government transfers such as social security, pensions, unemployment insurance, and job training will increase. Garret (1995), using a similar set of countries, has shown that high levels of trade and capital mobility lead to greater spending in countries with strong left parties, and strong trade unions. He indicates that the assessment of the effects of openness on government growth only using trade and financial openness is oversimplified. This is demonstrated by the estimation of interactive effects of international economic integration and left-labor power on economic policies. The positive and significant effect of openness and partisan politics on various measures of public sector size has been confirmed by Swank's study (1998). However, Garret's results also indicate that when the left-leaning party and organized labor remain weak, openness constrains government growth.

Rodrik (1998) also argued that openness causes an increase in government growth because societies demand (and receive) an expanded government role as the result of accepting larger doses of external risk. Empirically, Rodrik shows that upon control of external risk, openness will not exert an independent effect on government consumption. Using the interaction variables of openness with external risk variables, such as *"price volatility"* and *"trade concentration"*, Rodrik has shown that the effect of openness on government consumption is strongest in countries with a greater concentration of exports in commodities with volatile world prices. Focusing on the linkage between international economic exposure and national labor market risks, the studies by Iversen and Cusack's(2000), Ram(2009) and Liberati(2007), however, suggest no significant positive effect of openness on government expansion as it is related to external risk. They argue that the expansionary effect of openness through importing external risk depends on greater volatility of the international markets as compared to domestic markets. Their OECD panel data study shows that the relationship between unemployment risk and welfare spending is connected to major shifts in domestic occupational labor market structure rather than external risk. Iversen and

Cusack(2000) argue that most of the risks being generated in modern industrial societies are the product of technologically induced structural transformations inside national labor markets. Their regression results, using a de-industrialization variable as measured by the share of service sector employment in total labor force, indicate that transformation in employment structure does not stem from openness but from changes in traditional sectors - the driving force behind the expansion of government spending.

Competition Hypothesis

An alternative factor that plays a critical role in relating openness to the governments' revenue-expenditure pattern is competition between governments. Some believe that the size of the public sector already exceeds the level demanded by citizens due to fiscal illusion and institutional features of representative democracies.[5] Under the "competition hypothesis"[6] in open economies, market-like competition among "Leviathan governments" is expected to constrain the wasteful fiscal choices made by non-benevolent policy-makers, and thus constrains the excessive rate of government growth.

Inter-jurisdictional tax competition produces a conceptual solution for the appropriate level of government revenue and expenditure (Tiebout, 1956). It is argued by Tiebout that if consumers or voters are fully mobile, and the number of independent jurisdictions is large, then the level of government revenues and expenditures could efficiently be set as residents sort based on tastes and preferences.[7] Oates (1972) shows that factor mobility, is one determinant of the level of public sector provision. The literature also indicates that the competition effect of openness is unavoidable, since a tax or spending choice of one independent government in an open economy setting affects the tax bases available to other governments. Public officials who are hurt from increasing tax rates on voters may engage in competition to capture a larger tax base at lower political cost. In addition, under the pressure of global competition,[8] politicians may change economic policies and institutional frameworks, which are factors of public sector production.

With fiscal competition between jurisdictions, the local public finance literature suggests a strong inverse effect of openness on the growth of the government budget.[9] Fiscal federalism models have long recognized openness as a potential way to decrease public good provision.[10] Public choice models also indicate that opening jurisdictions to factor mobility lowers the rate of government growth. Indeed, Brennan and Buchanan (1980) view competition, along with democratic systems as necessary for taming Leviathan tendencies, since government's budget, the part which goes to unproductive bureaucratic services, would be excessive in the absence of competition. Clearly, the underlying assumption of factor mobility imposes constraints on political authorities that would otherwise attempt to exploit the available resources of a country in a closed economy.

Edwards and Keen (1996), and Rauscher (1998) also theoretically examine the effect of factor mobility or openness on public budget. Considering a global marketplace where countries have some degree of democratic decision-making, government officials or politicians play a critical role in using society's resources efficiently or wastefully. Thus, the authors have postulated a more realistic government objective function in which authorities strive to achieve their own goals as well as the welfare of their citizens. The weight placed on each goal depends on many factors, including the effectiveness of the democratic process and openness. Regardless of whether tax competition is welfare improving or not, these studies suggest that an increase in the number of competing governments will reduce the rate of government growth.

Sinn (1992) extends the idea of inter-jurisdictional fiscal competition to the global marketplace using a 'club' model of government. He argues that openness provides a competitive global marketplace for these entrepreneurial governments using immobile factors of production such as economic policies and the institutional framework in order to compete for internationally mobile capital. This is especially true in countries that place more weight on free market mechanisms, property rights, and democratic political systems. Competition tends to produce many options for individuals and firms to increase their well-being, and to control government behavior more effectively in these countries. Politicians and other public officials attempt to extract rent from their principals, the voting public, by trying to raise tax revenues in excess of what would be needed to finance public good provision. Openness however, imposes two constraints on the Leviathan tendencies of such governments. First, governments have to be efficient enough to produce political support in the elections. Second, governments have to consider exit or non-entry of mobile factors of production so as not to jeopardize the prosperity of their voters.

Using a graphical analysis, Sinn(1992) shows that profits decrease upon openning a country to competition. Politicians have two tax policy options to attract more capital into an open country. One option is to shift the tax burden to immobile factors and reduce the tax rate on mobile capital. Another option is to reduce spending in order to reduce the tax rate on mobile factors. However, in the presence of tight electoral competition, a more successful strategy for government is to accept a decline in rents by lowering the tax on mobile factor while keeping the tax rate on immobile factor income unchanged. As a result, competition among governments for mobile factors tends to tame the Leviathan tendencies of governments and to lower the resource cost of public goods, thereby restraining excessive government growth.[11]

The Effects of Openness on Balance

Overall, past empirical research on globalization has produced mixed results about the consequences of greater integration of world economies. However, significant findings for the expansionary role of governments faced with global economic integration have been questioned by the more recent studies. Many of the past studies, which show highly significant positive effects of openness on government growth, suffer from numerous data and specification problems. Some of those studies test hypotheses either by correlating levels of expenditures and levels of openness at a single point in time, or by correlating the change in government size during a single political-economic era. Thus, they do not capture the dynamic effects of openness on government growth. The study by Cameron (1978), for example, shows a positive relationship between openness and public sector size using a cross-sectional data set with few control variables.

The empirical studies with reasonably accurate empirical procedures suggest that political competition does matter in current policymaking. Swank (1988) argued that a positive effect of openness on the rate of government growth is typically found in countries such as the Netherlands and the Scandinavian countries, which have "neo-corporatist" and "consensual" policymaking structures. In the absence of these institutional structures, however, countries are likely to respond to increased exposure to international markets with less government growth (Swank, 1988; p. 1135). Furthermore, Garret (1995) has argued that, with a high degree of integration, the expansionary effect of openness could be reversed. Rodrik (1999) and Liberati(2007) argue that the greater international economic integration forces countries to conduct their policies in a more competitive international market that can be described as global fiscal federalism.

Although the theoretical literature on the constraining effect of inter-jurisdictional tax competition can be extended to the global economy, until recently no existing empirical study investigates the effects at the global level; they look only at competition among sub-national units in the United States.[12] This is not surprising since both the movement of goods, services and factors was relatively limited before 1980s. It is time to investigate whether the negative effect of openness on government growth (through competition) dominates the positive effect of openness (through the compensatory insurance programs of government). Thereby, the investigation in this chapter is expected to answer the question of whether constraining effect of inter-jurisdictional competition on the growth of the state and local governments[13] can be applied to the growth national government at the global level.

3. THE EMPIRICAL MODEL

The basic model used in this study is:

$$g_{it}=\alpha_i+\beta x_{it}+\gamma z_{it}+\nu_i+\varepsilon_{it}\ i=1,\ldots,N;\ t=1,\ldots,T \tag{3.4.1}$$

where G is the vector of observations on the dependent variable.

Observations are indexed by both country (i) and year (t). N is the number of countries and T is the number of years. The vector α represents country specific effects. X is a vector of all control variables. Z is a vector of openness variables. The estimation procedure breaks the error term into two components: one (v_i) is assumed to be heteroscedastic across panels and contemporaneously correlated across panels. The other (ε_{it}) represents a standard error term, assumed to be independently and identically distributed (iid).

The model is estimated using ordinary least squares (OLS) with country specific fixed effects, namely the least squares dummy variable approach. Each country has a distinct set of institutions and data measuring conventions and procedures, which are likely to be correlated with some of the elements of X and Z. The OLS with fixed effects provides consistent estimates[14]. Beck and Katz's panels corrected standard errors procedure is used to correct for heteroscedasticity and to provide consistent standard errors and covariance estimates.

I have established a large panel database for democratic OECD countries. The data from 21 countries over a time-period of 38 years was used to estimate the model. The data set includes countries that are at advanced stages of democratic and economic development[15]. To construct this data set, I use the published statistics of IMF, World Bank, OECD, United Nations, and various other sources of data such as economic data handbooks and websites, as well as national data sources of different countries. Overall, this data set contains a comprehensive series of economic aggregates and provides a rich source of information about the socio-economic, institutional and political structure of OECD countries.

The use of panel data allows a researcher to address some of the problems that cannot be solved using cross-sectional or time series data alone. First, panel data account for country specific effects that come from their colonial history, financial institutions, religious affiliations and political regimes. Second, panel data provide more information, more variability, less collinearity among the variables, more degrees of freedom, and more efficiency. Third, panel data are better suited to study the speed of adjustments to economic policy changes and the impact of change in political regimes on fiscal outcomes. Last, the use of panel data avoids the problem of omitted variables(Hsiao 1986, Beck & Katz 1995, Baltagi 1995, Green 2000).

As dependent variable, the growth rate of per-capita real general government consumption expenditures (RPCGGCOG) and other aggregate spending measures are among the most common variables used in the literature and in this study. Especially, general government consumption expenditures measure fits the analysis better than other expenditures measures[16] due to presumption that the degree of openness, in terms of mobility of goods and services, is more related to government consumption than redistribution expenditures. Secondly, real government consumption measures are free of biases arising from cross-country differences in the relative price of government purchases.

As variable of interest or independent variable, OPEN, measured as (exports + imports) / GDP is used. Using this variable provides an opportunity to test how governments grow with respect to openness. Another independent variable, OPENG, that represents the growth rate of openness will be used to test how the rate of government growth changes as countries become more open. The results are expected to show whether openness is a constraining factor for OECD governments.

Among many factors, country size is distinguished in this research due to its interaction with openness in determining the rate of government growth. Two different measures of country size: land area, LAND, and population, SIZE, are used in most studies. Using land area, the study by Alesina and Wacziarg (1997) shows results consistent with the theoretical arguments that larger countries tend to have smaller governments after controlling for other variables. The result of the study by Ferris and West (1996b), using a population measure, is also consistent with this finding. However, a couple of studies by Joulfian and Marlow (1990 and 1991) usingpopulation measures cast doubt about the significance of this variable. One reason for this ambiguity is related to Musgrave's argument that an increase in population may signal a change in age distribution towards a younger population and, thus, more government spending.

Another aspect of openness arises with its power to increase the efficiency and lower the relative cost of public good provision through fiscal competition between countries. In fact, fiscal competition forces the governments of open economies to minimize waste in the utilization of tax revenues. By reducing waste in government, openness may reduce the effective price of the public good enough to induce residents to provide the public sector with more tax revenue than is available in the closed economy. In this case, government budget may be financed through an expanded tax base, even if the tax rates or tax burden per capita decline. This process of competition through openness lowers the effective tax price of public goods and services. The variable, RELIPI, is defined as the relative implicit price index of public goods and services to the GDP price index.

One of this chapter's interests is to show how the effect of openness on government growth varies based on the political structures of countries. For example, the influence of political institutions is related to the ideology of the party coalition in power. The variable, LEFTDUM, a left-leaning party dummy, represents ideology of the party or the coalition in the power. It is expected that the countries with more leftist governments will be constrained by openness more than countries with conservative governments. This expectation comes from the observation that governments with left ideologies are advocates of more government spending on various government programs. This will certainly lead to faster government growth when the left party or the coalition comes into power. However, this type of behavior is expected being constrained more heavily in the existence of openness.

A second significant political factor that affects the influence of openness on government growth is political competition. The variable, ENEP, the effective number of electoral parties, represents the degree of political competition. Competition between parties reduces the ability of government to exert monopoly power even further when economies become more open. Holcombe (1991) provides the following historical evidence for how factors producing competition in government help to explain changes

Table 1. Variables used in the regressions

Abbreviation	Description
RPCGGCOG	Growth of real per capita general government total consumption
RPCGTXPG	Growth of real per capita general government total expenditures
RPCPXPHG	Growth of real per capita total public expenditures
RPCGGDIG	Growth of real per capita general government current disbursements
RPCPRELG	Growth of real per capita general government current revenues
RPCPREHG	Growth of real per capita total public revenues
RPCGGCRG	Growth of real per capita total current government revenues
PCGDP_GR	Growth of real per capita GDP (in local currencies)
RELIPIG	The growth of relative implicit price index
UNEMPRG	Growth of rate of unemployment
OLDMIDSG	Growth of the ratio of elderly population to middle-age population (over 65 age/15-64 age)
FELABSHG	Growth of female labor force participation (=female labor force/total labor force)
LOCAL_DISL	Real per capita local government expenditures
POPDENSG	Population Density Growth
PUBXPDSHLL	Two years lagged value of total public expenditures share in GDP
TAXGDPLL	Two years lagged value of general government total tax revenue share in GDP
Eff_Parties	Effective number of electoral parties
OPEN	The ratio of sum of export plus import to GDP
OPENG	The growth of openness
OPEN* Eff_Parties	Represents the variable of OPEN in politically competitive systems
OPENG*Eff_Parties	Represents the growth of openness in politically competitive systems
LAND	Represents the size of the country in terms of land area
OPENLAND	Represents the variable openness when country size is controlled
SIZE	Represents the size of the country in terms of population
OPENSIZE	Represents the variable openness when country size is controlled
RELIPI	Represents the relative price index
OPEN*RELIPIG	Represents the variable openness interacted with growth of relative price index
OPEN*RELIPI	Represents the variable openness interacted with relative price index
OPEN*LEFTDUM	Represents the variable openness interacted with left party ideology
LEFTDUM	Represents the variable that takes 1 if the government if left party government

in the growth of governments. He links the decline in the power of governments during the 19th century to openness combined with individual freedom. He argues that the development of classical liberalism during this century coincided with the opening of international markets, and with advances in the technology of transportation. In a world of open economies, even in relatively poor countries, radio and television broadcasts can keep citizens informed about their countries and the rest of the world, and technologies such as telephone and fax make the world even smaller and enhance intergovernmental competition.

The voice of citizens would be more influential in this environment and would help to constrain budget increases in a given country. This effect of openness on government growth has become more evident with recent advancement of information technology.

In a more generalized estimation model of government, growth of real per capita GDP (PCGDP_GR), growth of relative price of public to private goods (RELIPIG) and growth of unemployment rate (UNEMPRG) as economic fundamentals, female labor force participation growth (FELABSHG), the ratio of older population to middle-aged population growth (OLDMIDSG), the share of urban population growth (URBPOPSG) as demographic characteristics and other control variables two years lagged variable of total public expenditure share (PUBXPDSHLL) and decentralization (LOCAL_DISL) are used (Hosley and Borcherding, 1977, Cameron 1978, Barro 1979, Atkinson and Stiglitz 1980, Peltzman 1980, Hicks and Swank, 1984, Borcherding 1985, Oates 1985 and 1989, Mueller 1987, Anderson and Tollison 1988 and 1991, Joulfian and Marlow 1990 and 1991, West 1991, Baumol 1993, Lindert, 1994 and 1996, Ferris and West 1996a and 1996b, and Persson and Tabellini 1998).

4. REGRESSION RESULTS

The results show that the traditional OLS estimation with panel corrected standard errors procedure can be used to obtain unbiased and consistent estimates. The results also show that the control variables[17], which are chosen in the light of related studies of the literature and used in all the regressions, are significant and have expected signs. Indeed, the analysis suggest that about 77 percent of the variation among OECD countries for the period 1960-1997 in the rate of government consumption growth can be accounted for by eight explanatory variables plus country and time dummies. In addition, all the regressions relate growth of government consumption to openness using country specific effects models indicated by Hausman test of model selection. Furthermore, various forms of time controls have been used to encounter time series related problems of data such as possible spurious correction, panel specific autocorrelation.

Table 2 displays benchmark results using control variables and interest variables of this chapter as well as country specific dummies and different forms of time specific dummies. All the control variables in each of six regressions contribute to the explanatory power at one percent significance level with their expected signs. Time controls take two different forms in the regressions of Table 2. The first three columns show the regression results using time specific dummies for each year while the last three columns show regression results using year, year-square and year-cubic time specific controls. Although estimations using time dummies for each year add more to over all explanatory power then the use of cubic time specification, none of the variables become insignificant due to the shift between two forms of time dummies. Nonetheless, any form of time control dummy itself contributes significant explanations in the variations of growth rates of government consumption.

The main interest variable of this chapter is openness defined as the degree of exposure of an economy to world economies in terms of trade ratio to GDP (OPEN). Table 2 shows that OPEN is significantly and inversely related to the rate of government growth. This result is shown with the coefficient of the variable in both column 2 and 5 as negative and statistically different from zero at the one percent significance level. In addition, the regression results in columns 3 and 6 show that any change in the rate of openness, OPENG is negatively related to the rate of government growth. The coefficient of this variable

Table 2. Benchmark regression results using opennes variables

		(1)	(2)	(3)	(4)	(5)	(6)
Control Variables	pcgdp-gr	0.324 (7.24)[19]	0.344 (7.53)	0.330 (7.38)	0.242 (5.79)	0.253 (5.60)	0.251 (5.98)
	relipig	0.620 (15.78)	0.629 (15.93)	0.610 (15.51)	0.564 (13.98)	0.569 (14.13)	0.555 (13.85)
	unemprg	0.007 (3.17)	0.007 (3.13)	0.007 (3.23)	0.007 (3.44)	0.007 (3.40)	0.007 (3.45)
	popdensg	53.07 (2.04)	65.67 (2.40)	50.13 (1.92)	95.51 (3.64)	102.5 (3.80)	92.18 (3.50)
	urbpopsg	0.382 (4.10)	0.388 (4.09)	0.384 (4.13)	0.356 (3.64)	0.362 (3.68)	0.363 (3.73)
	local-disl	-1.1e-06 (-2.46)	-1.1e-06 (-2.49)	-1.2e-06 (-2.40)	-1.3e-06 (-2.83)	-1.3e-06 (-2.85)	-1.2e-06 (-2.73)
	pubxpdshll	-12.47 (-5.92)	-12.47 (-5.83)	-12.30 (-5.76)	-15.05 (-7.04)	-14.84 (-6.84)	-14.77 (-6.80)
Interest Variables	Open		-0.031 (-2.88)			-0.022 (-2.10)	
	Openg			-0.03 (-1.58)			-0.036 (-2.02)
	Country Dummies	YES	YES	YES	YES	YES	YES
	Time Dummies	YES	YES	YES	NO	NO	NO
	Yearc				0.455 (2.72)	0.486 (2.97)	0.505 (3.04)
	Yearc2				-0.024 (-2.64)	-0.025 (-2.72)	-0.027 (-2.96)
	Yearc3				0.001 (2.32)	0.001 (2.34)	0.001 (2.64)
Nobs.		732	732	732	732	753	753
R2		0.768	0.771	0.769	0.721	0.722	0.723

Dependent Variable: Growth of real per-capita public sector consumption (RPCGGCOG)

is significant with the use cubic time controls, while it is not with the use year specific time controls. As a result, the regression result in Table 2 show that as the countries become more open or the rate of change in openness rises, the rate of government growth slows down.[18]

5. JOINT HYPOTHESIS TESTING AND CHECKS OF ROBUSTNESS

This section investigates the effect of openness on government growth using additional interest variables defined in section three for number of reasons. First, other factors could possibly affect the growth of government as they interact with openness. Factors such as country size, expenditure competition, ideology and political competition are given as examples in theliterature. An investigation of this sort will also help to improve the health of the relationship and will free it from possible statistical concern. In other words, inclusion of these additional explanatory variables in the regressions tests whether the coefficient on openness remains stable and statistically significant.

5.1. Country Size and Openness

Beside many factors, the measure of country size,[20] SIZE, are found as an effective factors in explaining the association between openness and government growth. In fact, small countries of northern Europe indicate a negative relation between country size and government growth. In contrast, countries, which are big in size such as the U.S., Germany, and Canada have smaller governments. The possible inverse relation can be supported by economies of scale and internalized externalities arguments. Note that the provision of most public goods and services is subject to significant indivisibilities. For instance, every country regardless of size needs one parliament. Then, to an extent, the relative cost of providing real government services should fall as a share of GDP with an increase in country size.

The results in column 2 of Table 3 shows that country size measured by population size has no significant effect on government growth. In addition, the inclusion of country size variable in the regressions does not interfere with the significant effect of openness. Furthermore,

the result in column 4 shows that the interaction coefficient of the variables land area and openness is negative and significant at 1% level. This result indicates that government growth of large countries is more constrained by openness. This is not because of country size but openness. Persson and Tabellini (1998) have shown a supportive result to this argument. Overall, the results show that country size alone is not a significant determinant of government growth. However, it becomes an important factor when it is interacted with openness.

Table 3. Sensitivity of regression results to the country size effects

	(1)	(2)	(3)	(4)
Control Variables	**Same control variables as Table 1 used here**			
OPEN	-0.031 (-2.88)		-0.031 (-2.84)	-0.030 (-2.75)
SIZE		-4.7e-06 (-0.80)	-2.8e-06 (-0.48)	1.5e-06 (0.26)
OPENSIZE				-8.4e-09 (-2.21)
Country Dummies	YES	YES	YES	YES
Time Dummies	YES	YES	YES	YES
Nobs	732	732	732	753
R2	0.771	0.768	0.771	0.772

Dependent Variable: Real per-capita public sector consumption growth (RPCGGCOG)

5.2. Openness and Effective Price of Public Good Provision

The effect of lower public goods prices through openness on government growth is shown to be a significant in this chapter. Column 4 in Table 4 shows that the estimates of coefficients on the growth of relative price implicit index (RELIPIG) and openness (OPEN) variables are both significant at 1% significance level. The estimation results in the same regression also show that the cross-product of the growth rate of relative price index and openness (OPENIPIG) is also negative and significant at the 1% significance level. These results indicate that as the public good provision become more expensive, government grows more rapidly. In addition, openness has even greater inverse impact on government growth for the countries, which have a growing relative price index of public goods. If the public goods in some countries become relatively more expensive than public goods in other countries, these countries will loose the tax base to other countries. Furthermore, openness is alone still a significant factor to constrain government growth even when the price effect of openness on government growth is controlled.

The regression analysis in Table 4 also includes different versions of the relative price ratio index and openness. The use of the relative price index (RELIPI) rather than the growth version of this variable (RELIPIG) in the regression in column 6 shows a similar result with the latter. In other words, the estimated coefficient of RELIPI is positive and statistically different from zero at the 1% significance level. The coefficient of the variable openness (OPEN) also included in the regression in column 6 is negative and significant at the 1% significance level. In addition, the coefficient of the cross-product variable (OPENIPI) included in the regression in column 7 is negative and significant at the 1% significance level. However, the coefficient of openness OPEN is not significant when the cross product of this variable and relative price index (OPENIPI) is included in this specification. These results show that

Table 4. Sensitivity of the regression results to the relative price effects

	(1)	(2)	(3)	(4)	(5)	(6)	(7)
Control Variables	**Same control variables as Table 1 used here**						
OPEN	-0.031 (-2.88)		-0.030 (-2.73)	-0.027 (-2.47)		0.032 (-3.05)	0.022 (0.86)
RELIPIG		0.620 (15.78)	0.629[21] (15.93)	0.820 (10.16)			
OPEN* RELIPIG				0.003 (-2.99)			
RELIPI					2.824 (2.35)	2.902 (2.43)	6.565 (3.34)
OPEN* RELIPI							-0.039 (-2.65)
Country Dummies	YES	YES	YES	YES	YES	YES	YES
Time Dummies	YES	YES	YES	YES	YES	YES	YES
Nobs.	732	732	732	732	732	732	732
R2	0.771	0.768	0.771	0.774	0.770	0.773	0.774

Dependent Variable: Real per capita public sector consumption growth (RPCGGCOG)

openness is a significant constraining effect of government growth, especially for the countries, which have a relatively high cost of public good provisions. The regression results in column 6 and 7 also show that the effect of openness on government growth is specific to countries which with high cost of public good provision or wasteful use of public funds.

5.3. Openness and Political Institutions

The results in this chapter show also that degree of the effect of openness on government growth may vary based on the political institutions of various countries. The empirical results in Table 5 show that ideology and political competition both are significant factors in determining government growth in open economies. The estimation result in column 1 shows that the coefficient of party or coalition dummy representing left ideology, LEFTDUM, is positive but not significant. This means that ideology of the governing party or parties does not matter much in terms of government growth. The estimation result in column 2 shows that the coefficient of the interaction term of openness with left party dummy, OPENLEFT, is negative and statistically significant at the 1 percent significance level. The coefficient of LEFTDUM is also negative and very significant in this specification. Furthermore, the coefficient of openness, OPEN, alone continues to be negative and significant in both of these specifications. These results show that the effect of openness on government growth is stronger if the governing parties of different countries are non-conservative.

The empirical results in Table 5 also show that in addition to the ideology, the effect of political competition could be strengthened to constrain the growth of government in economies that are increasingly becoming open. The specification in column 7 in fact stresses this point. The coefficient of the interaction term of political competition with the growth of openness, OPENGNEP, is negative and statistically significant at 1%. In this specification while political competition alone is significant, the growth of openness stands insignificant[22]. These results indicate that openness and political competition separately are two important factors to constrain government growth or to tame the Leviathan. In addition, the growth of openness strengthens the power of political competition to reduce the rate of government growth while the static level of openness does not matter much. This indicates how critical is the mobility of production factors in determining the spending and taxing policies of open economies.

6. CONCLUSION

The analysis in this chapter offers an explanation to conflicting theories about the effects of openness on government growth. Some associate government growth with the openness through its effect of creating an expansion of social insurance program. However, others associated it with openness through its effect on growth constraining inter-governmental fiscal competition. Unlike previous empirical studies such as Cameron (1978) and Rodrik (1998), the analysis in this chapter indicates that current slow-downs in the rate of government growth can be attributed to the degree of openness, among other factors. The empirical results using panel corrected standard errors procedure for OECD countries and the period 1960-97 leads to this conclusion. Overall, the analysis show that the variables used in this study explains on average three fourth of the variation in government growth. The benchmark results show that an increase of 10% in the ratio of trade to GDP causes on average 2% reduction in the rate of government growth.

Table 5. Sensitivity of the results to the ideology and political competition effects

	(1)	(2)	(3)	(4)	(5)	(6)	(7)
Control Variables	**Same control variables as Table 1 used here**						
LEFTDUM	0.132 (0.71)	1.108 (2.59)					
OPEN	-0.031 (-2.87)	-0.026 (-2.36)		-0.300 (-2.71)	-0.017 (-0.93)		
OPEN* LEFTDUM		-0.014 (-2.50)					
Eff_Parties			-0.236 (-2.00)	-0.202 (-1.72)	0.068 (0.24)	-0.248 (-2.12)	-0.193 (-1.66)
OPEN* Eff_Parties					-0.003 (-1.16)		
OPENG						-0.031 (-1.62)	0.061 (1.28)
OPENG* Eff_Parties							-0.027 (-2.48)
Country Dummies	YES	YES	YES	YES	YES	YES	YES
Time Dummies	YES	YES	YES	YES	YES	YES	YES
Nobs.	732	732	732	732	732	732	732
R2	0.771	0.772	0.769	0.771	0.771	0.770	0.772

Dependent Variable: Growth of real per capita public sector consumption (RPCGGCOG)

The analysis also shows the results are robust to exclusion and inclusion of many independent variables. The regression results with the inclusion of country size variables indicate that the constraining effect of openness in larger countries is greater than in smaller countries. This result seems counterintuitive to many researchers. However, since the government policy effectiveness in small economies is very limited, they keep social programs in place to prevent sudden changes in their residents' incomes. Therefore, they are more reluctant to reduce the role of government even if it could gain competitiveness in global market place.

The results, moreover, show that openness constrains the rate of government growth in countries which have a higher price of public good provision more effectively than in countries which have a lower price of public good provision. This means that public officials will have tighter budgets for public provided goods and services under the pressures of international competition. The empirical result that shows openness has a constraining affect on democratic governments that have a larger budget. Furthermore, openness becomes an effective force in constraining government growth for those countries that have competitive political systems and democracies.

This chapter suggests that more openness, less taxation and less distortion, and will in return result in more economic growth. In order for this claim to be true, there exists a need to examine the effect of openness on economic growth directly. This indeed is an essential project to pursue in the future in order to see efficiency implications of the constraining effect of openness on government growth. Is openness welfare enhancing constraint as public choice economist suggests, or is it welfare harming as traditional tax models presume?

REFERENCES

Alesina, A., & Wacziarg, R. (1997). Openness, Country Size and the Government. *Journal of Public Economics*.

Anderson, G. M., & Tollison, R. D. (1988). Legislative Monopoly and the Size of Government. *Southern Economic Journal*, *54*(3), 529–545. doi:10.2307/1058999

Anderson, G. M., & Tollison, R. D. (1991). Congressional Influence and Patterns of New Deal Spending 1933-1939. *The Journal of Law & Economics*, *34*(1), 161–175. doi:10.1086/467222

Atkinson, A., & Stiglitz, G. (1980). *Lectures on Public Economics*. London: McGraw-Hill.

Baltagi, B. (1995). *Econometric Analysis of Panel Data*. New York: John Wiley and Sons.

Barro, R. (1979). On the Determination of Public Debt. *Journal of Political Economy*, *87*(5, Part 1), 940–947. doi:10.1086/260807

Bates, R. H., Brock, P. L., & Tiefenthaler, J. (1991). Risk and Trade Regimes: Another Exploration. *International Organization*, *45*(Winter), 1–18. doi:10.1017/S0020818300001375

Baumol, W. J. (1993). Health Care, Education and the Cost Disease: A Looming Crisis for Public Choice. *Public Choice*, *77*(September), 17–28. doi:10.1007/BF01049216

Beck, N., & Katz, J. N. (1995). What to Do (and Not to Do) with Time –Series Cross-Section Data. *The American Political Science Review*, *89*(3), 634–647. doi:10.2307/2082979

Berry, D. W., & David, D. (1987). Explaining the Size of the Public Sector: Responsive and Excessive Government Interpretations. *The Journal of Politics*, *49*(2), 401–440. doi:10.2307/2131307

Borcherding, T. E. (1985). The Causes of Government Expenditure Growth: A Survey of the US Evidence. *Journal of Public Economics*, *28*(3), 359–382. doi:10.1016/0047-2727(85)90065-9

Brennan, G., & Buchanan, J. (1980). *The Power to Tax: Analytical Foundations of a Fiscal Constitution*. New York: Cambridge University Press.

Breton, A. (1987). Towards a Theory of Competitive Federalism. *European Journal of Political Economy*, *3*(1-2), 263–329. doi:10.1016/S0176-2680(87)80014-9

Breton, A. (1989). Growth of Competitive Governments. *The Canadian Journal of Economics. Revue Canadienne d'Economique*, *22*(4), 717–750. doi:10.2307/135496

Cameron, D. (1978). The Expansion of the Public Economy: A Comparative Analysis. *The American Political Science Review*, *72*(December), 1243–1261. doi:10.2307/1954537

Edwards, J., & Keen, M. (1996). Tax Competition and Leviathan. *European Economic Review*, *40*(1), 113–134. doi:10.1016/0014-2921(95)00057-7

Epifani, P., & Gancia, G. (2009). Openness, Government Size and the Terms of Trade. *The Review of Economic Studies*, *76*(2), 629–668. doi:10.1111/j.1467-937X.2009.00546.x

Ferris, S. J., & West, E. G. (1996a). The Cost Disease and Government Growth: Qualifications to Baumol. *Public Choice*, *89*(1-2), 35–52. doi:10.1007/BF00114277

Ferris, S. J., & West, E. G. (1996b). Testing Theories of Real Government Size: U.S. Experience, 1959-1989. *Southern Economic Journal*, *62*(3), 537–553. doi:10.2307/1060878

Garrett, G. (1995). Capital Mobility, Trade and Domestic Politics of Economic Policy. *International Organization*, *49*(04), 657–687. doi:10.1017/S0020818300028472

Green, W. H. (2000). Econometric Analysis. New York: Macmillan Publishing Company.

Hausman, J. (1978). Specification Test in Econometrics. *Econometrica*, *46*(6), 1251–1271. doi:10.2307/1913827

Hicks, A., & Swank, D. (1984). On the Political Economy of Welfare Expansion: A Comparative Analysis of 18 Advanced Capitalist Democracies, 1960-1971. *Comparative Political Studies*, *17*(1), 81–119. doi:10.1177/0010414084017001003

Holcombe, R. G. (1991). Constitutions as Constraints: A Case Study of Three American Constitutions. *Constitutional Political Economy*, *2*(2), 303–328. doi:10.1007/BF02393134

Holsey, C. M., & Borcherding, T. E. (1977). Why Does Government's Share of National Income Grow? An Assessment of the Recent Literature on the U.S. Experience. In *Budgets and Bureaucrats: The Sources of Government Growth*. Durham, NC: Duke University Press.

Hsiao, C. (1986). *Analysis of Panel Data*. New York: Cambridge University Press.

Iversen, T., & Cusack, T. R. (2000). The Causes of Welfare State Expansion. *World Politics*, *52*(April), 313–349. doi:10.1017/S0043887100016567

Joulfaian, D., & Marlow, M. L. (1990). Government Size and Decentralization: Evidence from Disaggregated Data. *Southern Economic Journal*, *56*(4), 1094–1102. doi:10.2307/1059894

Joulfaian, D., & Marlow, M. L. (1991). Public Sector Employment, Competition, and Government Size. *Public Finance*, *46*(2), 223–235.

Liberati, P. (2007). Trade Openness, Financial Openness and Government Size. *Journal of Public Policy*, *27*(02), 215–247. doi:10.1017/S0143814X07000670

Lindbeck, A. (1976). Stabilization Policy in Open Economics with Endogenous Politicans. *The American Economic Review*, *66*(2), 1–19.

Lindert, P. H. (1994). The Rise of Social Spending? *Explorations in Economic History*, *33*(1), 1–34. doi:10.1006/exeh.1996.0001

Lindert, P. H. (1996). What Limits Social Spending? *Explorations in Economic History*, *33*(1), 1–34. doi:10.1006/exeh.1996.0001

Mueller, D. C. (1987). The Growth of Government: A Public Choice Perspective. *International Monetary Fund Staff Chapters*, *34*(1), 115–149. doi:10.2307/3867026

Oates, W. (1972). *Fiscal Federalism*. New York: Harcourt, Brace and Jovanovich.

Oates, W. (1985). Searching for Leviathan: An Empirical Study. *The American Economic Review*, *75*, 748–757.

Oates, W. (1989). Searching for Leviathan: A Reply and Some Further Reflections. *The American Economic Review*, *79*, 578–583.

Özdemir, A. R. (2002). *Essays on the Determinants of the Level and Structure of Government Expenditures and Taxation.* (PhD Dissertation). University of Connecticut, Economics Department.

Peltzman, S. (1980). The Growth of Government. *The Journal of Law & Economics*, *23*(2), 209–288. doi:10.1086/466962

Persson, T., & Tabellini, G. (1992). The Politics of 1992: Fiscal Policy and European Integration. *The Review of Economic Studies*, *59*(4), 689–701. doi:10.2307/2297993

Persson, T., & Tabellini, G. (1998). The Size and Scope of Government: Comparative Politics with Rational Politicians. *European Economic Review*, *43*(4-6), 699–735. doi:10.1016/S0014-2921(98)00131-7

Ram, R. (2009). Openness, Country Size, and Government Size: Additional Evidence from a Large Cross-Country Panel. *Journal of Public Economics*, *93*(1-2), 213–218. doi:10.1016/j.jpubeco.2008.04.009

Rauscher, M. (1998). Leviathan and Competition Among Jurisdictions: The Case of Benefit Taxation. *Journal of Urban Economics*, *44*(1), 59–67. doi:10.1006/juec.1997.2060

Rodrik, D. (1998). Why Do More Open Economics Have Larger Governments? *Journal of Political Economy*, *106*(October), 997–1033. doi:10.1086/250038

Rodrik, D. (1999, Winter). How Far Will International Economic Integration Go?. *Journal of Economic Perspectives*.

Schneider, M. (1989). Inter-municipal Competition, Budget-Maximizing Bureaucrats, and the Level of Suburban Competition. *American Journal of Political Science*, *33*(3), 612–628. doi:10.2307/2111065

Schultze, L. C. (1992). Is There a Bias Toward Excess in U.S. Government Budgets or Deficits? *The Journal of Economic Perspectives*, *6*(2), 25–43. doi:10.1257/jep.6.2.25

Sinn, S. (1992). The Taming of Leviathan: Competition Among Governments. *Constitutional Political Economy*, *3*(2), 177–195. doi:10.1007/BF02393119

Swank, D. (1988). The Political Economy of Government Domestic Expenditure in the Affluent Democracies, 1960-1980. *American Journal of Political Science*, *32*(4), 1120–1150. doi:10.2307/2111203

Swank, D. (1998). Funding the Welfare State Revisited: Globalization and Taxation in Advanced Market Economies. *Political Studies*, *46*(4), 671–692. doi:10.1111/1467-9248.00161

Tiebout, C. (1956). A Pure Theory of Local Expenditure. *Journal of Political Economy*, *64*(5), 416–424. doi:10.1086/257839

West, E. G. (1991). Secular cost changes and the size of government: Towards a Generalized Theory. *Journal of Public Economics*, *45*(3), 363–381. doi:10.1016/0047-2727(91)90032-W

Wildasin, D. E. (1989). Inter-jurisdictional Capital Mobility: Fiscal Externality and a Corrective Subsidy. *Journal of Urban Economics*, *25*(2), 193–212. doi:10.1016/0094-1190(89)90034-X

Wilson, J. D. (1986). A Theory of Interregional Tax Competition. *Journal of Urban Economics*, *19*(3), 356–370. doi:10.1016/0094-1190(86)90045-8

Wilson, J. D. (1999). Theories of Tax Competition. *National Tax Journal*, *52*(2), 269–304.

Zax, S. J. (1989). Is There a Leviathan in Your Neighborhood? *The American Economic Review*, *79*(3), 560–567.

Zodrow, R. G., & Mieszkowski, P. (1986). Pigou, Tiebout, Property Taxation, and the Under-provision of Local Public Goods. *Journal of Urban Economics*, *19*(3), 356–370. doi:10.1016/0094-1190(86)90048-3

Zodrow, R. G., & Mieszkowski, P. (1989). Taxation and Tiebout Model: The Differential Effects of Head Taxes, Taxes on Land Rents, and Property Taxes. *Journal of Economic Literature*, *17*(September), 356–370.

ENDNOTES

1 Both traditional tax competition models and Leviathan models predict that independently functioning open economies will necessarily end up competing with each other for the mobile and scarce resources. However, whether fiscal competition as a behavioral response of public authorities to international tax differentials is a good thing or bad thing remains a question. The answer varies depending on efficiency and equity aspects of competition. With regard to equity, it is argued in the traditional tax literature that tax competition reduces equitable taxes on mobile factors, and reduces the tax system to one of mere benefit taxation (Sinn, 1992). Removal of more equitable taxes, mostly progressive income taxes, will reduce fairness among taxpayers. The prediction of public choice economists is consistent with the inequitable distribution effect of tax competition. They, however, argue that the move towards a more unfair tax structure due to international tax competition varies depending on the degree of political competition and the ideology of the incumbent party (Persson and Tabellini, 1992). In terms of the efficiency aspect, it is viewed as a bad thing in the traditional tax competition literature, but it is viewed as good thing in the public choice literature. This difference in efficiency views comes from underlying models of government and is not a direct issue of this chapter.

2 See Berry and Lowery (1987) for a detailed definition of the term "responsive" government.

3 Unemployment insurance and personal income tax represent some examples of these instruments and are called "built in stabilizers".

4 They also argue that countries which do not have the ability to make welfare payments and to provide insurance are more likely to impose trade barriers to be protected from external risks (Bates, Brock, Tiefenthaler, 1991).

5 According to Berry and Lowery (1987), this view is characterized as "excessive" government explanations. See their article for a detailed explanation of this view and see the study by Schultze (1992) for more explanations of excessive government growth.

6 This hypothesis is named as efficiency hypothesis in Garret (1995). See the chapter for a detailed description of this hypothesis.

7 It is apparent, in the purest form of Tiebout's model, that resource flows between jurisdictions obviate the need for political competition. See for instance, Özdemir (2002) for political competition arguments.

8 Breton (1987: 273) argues that competition in an open economy does not have to be ex-ante: *"Political competition is not something politicians choose or want... It is forced on people by the environment. One does not even have to be aware of that one is competing in order to be competitive."* Also, see another article by Breton (1989) for detailed discussion.

9 Although Tiebout (1956) argues that in an open economy setting, governments at various levels are most likely to engage in fiscal competition to match the public budget with voter's preferences, his article does not offer predictions about the growth rate of resources used by the public sector. A long subsequent literature, however, indicates that the openness, or exposure of a nation' economy to the international marketplace stimulates competition and constrains the rate of government growth.

10 See for example Oates (1972), Wildasin (1989), Zodrow and Miezowski (1986 and 1989), and Wilson(1986 and 1999).

11 In this sense, Sinn (1992) argues that competition among national governments for mobile resources can be considered as a subsititute for more direct attempts to curb the "power to tax" such as constitutional amendments. Brennan and Buchanan (1980) are first to raise this issue, but imperfactions in locational changes due to personal preferences cause them to dismiss this option. However, today many economists including Sinn (1992) believe that under reasonable conditions, competition comes with international openness could fully substitute for overt fiscal constraints.

12 See Zax (1989) and Oates (1985 and 1989) for instance.

13 See Zax (1989) and Schneider (1989) for instance.

14 Indeed, a Hausman test (1978) requires use of this estimation procedure. The test results also show no indication of autocorrelation in these estimations.

15 Only Turkey may represent some weaknesses in both of these measures.

16 I have run the regressions with other measure too.

17 These variables were selected after some experimentation to achieve the best overall fit for the regression but without for the significance of the coefficients on openness.

18 The estimations for the effect of openness on government growth focus only on government consumption. However, there are more expenditure and revenue measures used as dependent variable in this research. Central government expenditures, total public sector expenditures and total public sector revenue are among several of those measures. Re-estimation of the effect of openness using various measures of the dependent variable did not change the direction of the relationship. In fact, the estimated coefficients on openness are negative in all the regressions as before.[1] Therefore, the estimation results using most of the government growth measures support the relationship between openness and government growth found in Table 2. This is one evidence that the negative and significant relations between openness and government growth is not specific to any case, but openness has a statistically significant association with most types of government spending and revenue. Finally, the evidence using same measures from various data sources also shows that the relationship between openness and government growth apparently exists in various available data sets.

19 Values in parentheses represent t statistics.

20 Some studies use LAND, as an alternative measure of country size. Since LAND does not vary overtime, I do not use it here.

21 Relipig is taken out from control variables to avoid double counting.

22 The coefficient for the interaction term of openness with political competition turns out to be insignificant due to multi-collinearity due to inclusion of highly correlated two variables. This is true in the specification in column 5 of Table 5. Otherwise, the sign of the coefficient is in the expected to be in the opposite direction.

Chapter 7 Public Spending and Governance Performance: Evidence from Europe and the MENA Region

Lodovico Santoro
University of Naples, Italy

Salvatore Capasso
University of Naples, Italy

ABSTRACT

The main objective of the chapter is to study the interaction between the level and composition of government expenditure and governance performance in Europe and in MENA countries. The perceived level of corruption provides a possible measure of governance performance. The idea is that more corruption entails greater than optimally volumes of public expenditure and an inefficient allocation of this. The study involves a descriptive and a simple econometric analysis. Results are enlightening and point out that total government expenditure appears to be positively correlated to poorer governance performance, and hence to more corruption, only when the volumes of public expenditure is already high.

INTRODUCTION

Plenty of evidence has to these days confirmed the idea that government expenditure may provide public officials opportunities for rent-seeking or predator behavior. This implies that government expenditure may be purposefully inflated and manipulated in order to increase rent-extraction and bribes. In other words, corrupt bureaucrats and politicians may increase the volume of public expenditure beyond efficient levels just to extract resources for their own sake. With similar intent, public expenditure may be allocated towards that sectors which involve greater opportunities for corruption to occur. And this is the reason why one observes corruption affecting some public sectors, such as defense, or some kind of public expenditure, such as public investment, rather than others. The effects of this activity is that public expenditure may be inefficiently high and badly allocated among the different alternatives.

DOI: 10.4018/978-1-5225-0053-7.ch007

Yet measuring and quantifying inefficiency in public expenditure is extremely difficult. It is difficult both because one has to have clear what is the "social optimum" prior to determine the "sub-optimal" and inefficient provision of public goods and because public expenditure by its own nature is a multifaceted entity which is difficult to express in one measurable variable. For this reason, usually the efficiency of government's expenses and interventions are measured through various variables. For example, the World Bank provide six proxies for "governance performance" and implicitly for measuring government efficiency. Corruption is one on these. The idea is that more corruption is indeed an indicator of inefficiency in public expenditure. By following this route, we attempt to study the interconnection between public expenditure and government performance, measured through the perceived level of corruption, in the European countries and MENA countries. The results are enlightening. Total government expenditure appears to be positively correlated to poorer governance performance, and hence to more corruption, only when the volumes of public expenditure is already high. And indeed, in European countries rather than in MENA countries more public expenditure is associated to more inefficiency in the working of government. Moreover, the effect of government expenditure on governance performance also depend on which kind of expenditure one considers. Public expenditure in education, healthcare, welfare and public expenditure in defense all influence differently governance performance. This highlight the importance of other context factors affecting the interplay between corruption, government efficiency and public expenditure.

The chapter is structured as follows. In the second section, we review the related literature and provide some definitions and stylized facts. In the third section, we provide a descriptive analysis of public spending and governance performance in Europe and in the Middle East and North Africa (MENA). The forth section contains a simple econometric analysis of the interplay of these variables. The last section concludes.

RELATED LITERATURE

One of the main causes of corruption and, hence, a determinant of the quality of governance performance is the pervasive presence of the State in the economy. Government may contribute to the (private) economic activities through different channels and penetrate the market to a different degree. Since corruption entails the illicit actions of public officials who attempt to extract rent through the abuse of their public power, the higher is the level of involvement of the government in the economy, the larger is the set of potential rents on which corruption may feed. Of course, a high degree of government intervention in the economy is only a necessary but not a sufficient condition for corruption to occur. To this extent, other factors need to be in place. For example, as suggested by Mauro (1997), bureaucrats' degree of discretion, and hence their potential rent extraction, increases as it increases the opacity of the laws and of the regulation system. Along these lines, Clements *et al.* (1995) argue that government subsidies for industries multiply the opportunities for rent-seeking behaviors. Other factors which feed corruptive behavior are the provision of public goods and services above market prices (Tanzi, 1998), the level of public sector wage (Acemoglu & Verdier, 2000) and the nature of the system of tax collection (Blackburn, 2012).

Though it is reasonable to argue that the working of the system through which public funds are allocated influences corruption, it is also reasonable to conjecture that corruption, in turn, may influence public expenditure and finances. Indeed, to the extent that bureaucrats sets rules to allocates funds and decide upon the amount of expenditure, and these are the base to extract rents, it is plausible to assume that corrupt bureaucrats will determine public expenditure in order to facilitate bribing. This behavior evidently undermines government performance and delivers inefficient outcomes since social objectives are subordinated to other, private and subjective, objectives.

Thus, as Tanzi and Davoodi (1997) show, a government employing many corrupt public officials will allocate more public resources towards public investment rather than current public expenditure. The reason is that public investment, mostly in high technological infrastructure, may result in larger illegal profits for bureaucrats and a wider degree of discretion in managing these public resources. Yet, Tanzi and Davoodi are explicitly doubtful about the direction of causality. If, on the one hand, it is possible to presume that corruption is influenced by public investment, on the other hand only corrupt bureaucrats may finance – inefficiently – more public works than necessary in order to extract a rent. Importantly, the authors show that corruption, and a corresponding bad governance performance, leads to an increase in public investment and to a reduction of its productivity, and reduces current expenditure in favor of public investment.

As well as influencing the allocation of public expenditure among the two main categories of public spending (current and capital), corruption may also exert distorting effects on the allocation of funds among the subcategories and components of public expenditure. This also implies that corruption may affect the relative importance in governments' agenda of the various sectors of public intervention. In fact, as argued by Krueger (1974), it is actually the nature of public goods and services provided that determines the incentive for the bureaucrats to abuse their public power. For example, as suggested by Shleifer and Vishny (1993), given that corrupt public administrations tend to prefer larger public projects in order to obtain greater informal commissions, a greater than necessary amount of funds are channeled towards categories of public expenditure ensuring on average expensive tenders. This explains for example more corruption involved in the acquisition of high values goods, or goods whose value is difficult to quantify, such as high technology goods. In turn this also gives account of why in some public sectors, such as the defense sector, incentives to be corrupt are more severe. Indeed, the defense sector provides more opportunities for corruption to occur mostly because involved bureaucrats are senior public officials and firms are mainly oligopolistic supplier, and because of the generally high monetary values and secrecy of military purchases (Gupta, de Mello & Sharan, 2000).

For other components of government expenditure and other sectors the picture is less clear. As a matter of fact, the empirical analysis proposed by Mauro (1998) shows that while the relationship between corruption and public spending in education is definitely negative, the sign of this relationship is more uncertain in sectors such as health-care and welfare. Indeed in the health-care sector, rent-seeking opportunities and incentives for dishonest public officials appear to increase in correspondence of expensive supply tenders, for example investment in high technological medical equipment, and appear to decrease in correspondence of other health-care expenses. This determines opposite signs in the correlation between corruption and public expenditure for these kinds of goods and an overall uncertain relationship when one consider the health care sector as a whole. For example, data show that there is no connection between old-age pensions and corruptive practices, while they show a strong positive correlation between corruption and unemployment benefits and disability pensions.

Overall empirical investigations confirm that corruption may strongly influence the volume and the allocation of public resources. The literature goes further and interpret the results mainly in one direction: corruption greatly increases inefficiency and hence harms governance performance. Obviously a high level of public spending does not always implies high rate of corruption and low government performance. In fact, some countries display high volumes of government spending despite good measure of government performance, including low levels of corruption. Indeed, government performance is the results of the interplay of numerous factors whose interaction depends as well on the general institutional setting. It is for this reason that despite the expected forms of heterogeneity in governance performance between individual countries, one can identify a degree of homogeneity in some group of countries which are the result of the joint working of common institutional factors. The study of these common traits, and of the corresponding specular differences, allows to better understand government's functioning and to implement effective policy intervention to reduce anomalies and inefficiency. In the subsequent analysis we will scrutinize government performance of European and MENA countries. Those countries offer a very valuable setting to determine some interesting aspects of the nature of correlation between government spending and government performance.

PUBLIC SPENDING AND GOVERNANCE PERFORMANCE IN EUROPE AND IN THE MENA REGION

Data Description

Governance is a complex phenomenon which encompasses different processes all directed to the general activity of governing. In general governance includes the abilities of governments to implement efficient policies and to intervene effectively in the economy. This character of "generality" of governance entails an obvious difficulty in determining its measurement and quantification. This difficulty can be overcome through the use of different measures which however detect only specific aspects of governance. To this extent, the World Bank (WB) measures Governance trough six dimensions: Voice and Accountability, Political Stability and Absence of Violence, Government Effectiveness, Regulatory Quality, Rule of Law and Control of Corruption. Essentially, the World Bank's *Worldwide Governance Indicators (WGI)* dataset summarize the points of view on governance performance provided by enterprises, citizens and expert through surveys and cover 215 countries all over the world. As already argued, we focus on one specific indicator: control of corruption, to measure government effectiveness and to study the connection of this with public expenditure. The basic assumption, of course, is that corruption may be considered a strong determinant of government inefficiency. The WB' indicator *control of corruption* "reflects perceptions of the extent to which public power is exercised for private gain, including both petty and grand forms of corruption, as well as capture of the state by elites and private interests"[1]. The estimate of governance performance through this indicator ranges from -2.5 (weak) to 2.5 (strong). In order to make clearer its interpretation, we use a min max normalization so that 0 represents a weak performance, and correspondingly a high level of corruption, and 1 represents the best performance of the government, and correspondingly a low level of corruption.

Data on *Government Total Expenditure* are drawn from the *World Economic Outlook (WEO) Database* of the International Monetary Fund (IMF). Total expenditure data consists of total government expenses plus net acquisition of nonfinancial assets. For total government expenditure, we prefer to use the IMF data rather than the WB data because of the many missing data in the latter dataset. All variables are measured as a percentage of the Gross Domestic Product (GPD).

Data on the variables detecting functional government expenditures are instead drawn from the WB's dataset *World Development Indicators*. More specifically, in order to obtain a measure of public spending in *Defense*, we employ the Military expenditure data as a percentage of GDP in a given year. These data, are supplied by the Stockholm International Peace Research Institute (SIPRI) and are based on the NATO definition and include all current and capital expenditures on the armed forces[2].

Also data on total public spending in *Education* are drawn from the *World Development Indicators*. These are given by the total amount of government expenditure (current and capital) on education as a percentage of GDP. These data include public spending on public and private institutions for education, education administration expenses as well as transfers and subsidies for students, households and other private institutions.

From the same dataset we draw data on public expenditure on *Healthcare*. Public health spending consists of current and capital spending from both central and local government and includes funds accruing from donations and health insurance. The *World Development Indicators* does not contain data on welfare government expenditures as a share of GDP. Hence, in order to obtain variables which are comparable with the other government expenditure, we divide two other variables, *Social Contributions* and *Subsidies and other Transfers* by GDP. We employ these as a measure of welfare expenditure. The first variable, *Social contribution*, includes social security contributions by employees, employers, and self-employed individuals, and contributions by other subjects not determined. The second variable, *Subsidies and other Transfers*, includes subsidies, grants, and other forms of social benefits or non repayable transfers to firms, foreign governments and international organizations, as well as social security, social assistance benefits, and employer social benefits. Since these two variables are strongly correlated, in order to simplify matter and to save on space in the following analysis we will only use Social contribution. However we perform the analysis considering both and results do not change significantly. All data ranges from 2002 till 2012.

Descriptive Statistics

Governance performance depends on many factors. In addition to public spending and how this is functionally allocated, cultural and social traits, bureaucracy and political regimes are other important factors all of which contribute to determine governance performance to a different extent. This explains why countries with the same level and composition of public spending or economic conditions, but with different socio-political dimensions, may display very divergent levels of perceived governance performance. On the contrary, one may expect that countries with similar cultural and social traits and with close historical and political background may display similar levels of government performance despite differences in the level of public expenditure. And indeed, if we overall compare European countries on the one side, with countries in the MENA region some startling homogeneities within each group emerge.

A judgment of how well government works is often a matter of perception, more than the result of a precise measurement. As already argued, we will look at the degree of perceived corruption to infer how effectively and efficiently government works. Figure 1 and Figure 2 display data on the control of corruption as a measure of Governance Performance in Europe-28 and in Mena countries. Despite some variability within each group, Figure 1 and 2 show clear differences between the two areas with European countries exhibiting on average higher degree of performance (lower levels of corruption).

Let us now focus on each area in turn. Among the 28 member states of the European Union (EU), see Figure 1, Northern European countries display the highest levels of good governance performance. Considering the average over the time frame under scrutiny (2002-2012), the most highly skilled country is Denmark, with an index of Governance Performance close to one. Other Northern countries follow:

Figure 1. Control of corruption as a measure of governance performance in Europe-28 (average by country on 2002-2012 time span)
Source: Elaborations of authors on the Worldwide Governance Indicators (WGI) dataset - World Bank

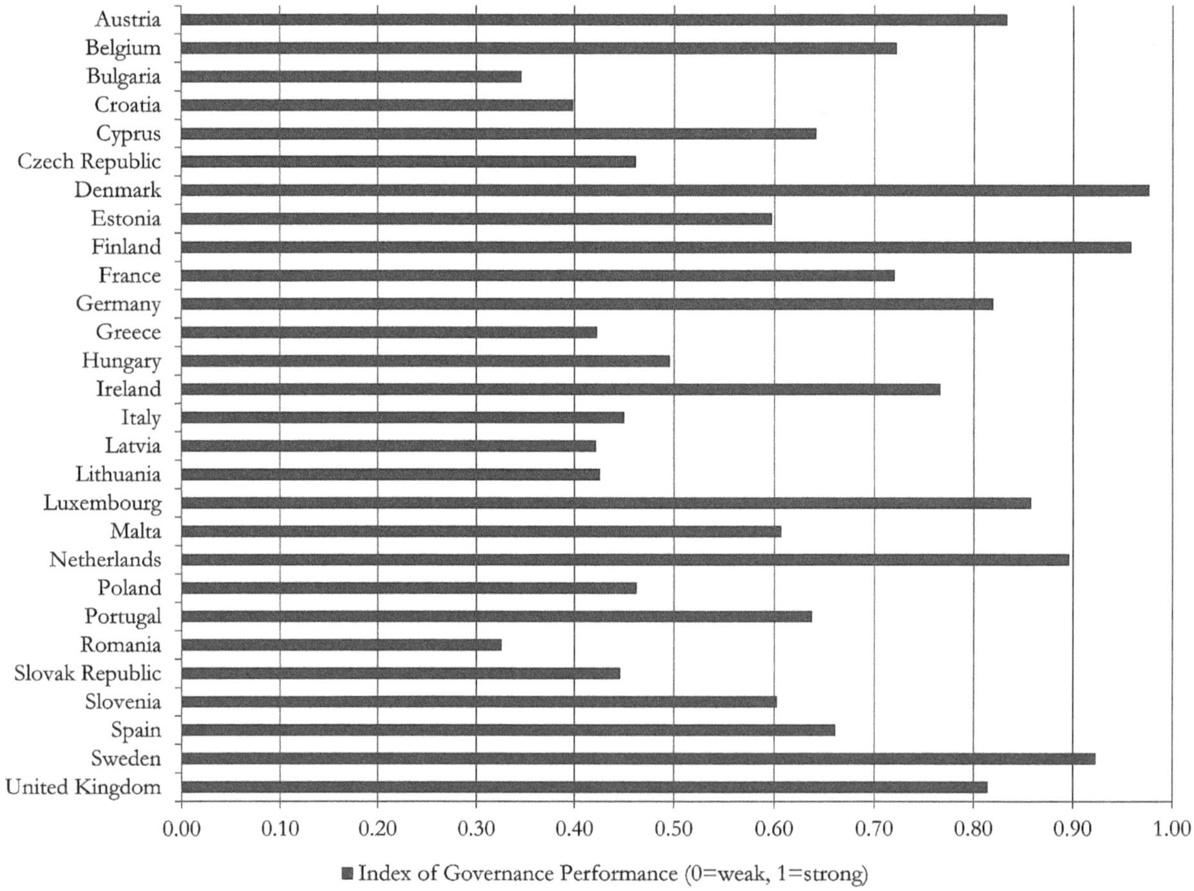

Finland with an index equal to 0.96, Sweden with an index equal to 0.92 and Netherlands with an index equal to 0.90. On the other hand, countries with a relatively lower degree of governance performance are the EU's latest member states, that is, in an increasing ranking of good governance performance, Romania, Bulgaria, Croatia, Latvia and Lithuania, although the latter two are north European countries. Hence, the data seems to show that the participation to the Euro-Area is correlated to an improvement in governance performance, and a decrease in perceived corruption. It may well be that the adoption of a single currency and the resulting political and economic constraints would lead to an improvement in the governance performance. All other European countries show an intermediate value of the index of good performance in the range 0.42 - 0.77. It's worth noticing that among these we find the so called PIGS countries: Portugal, Italy, Greece and Spain. It is useful to recall that PIGS is the acronym which identify the southern European countries with similar (bad) public finance conditions. Despite these countries are grouped under the condition of featuring the same bad governance, our measure of governance performance shows that there are relevant differences among them. Indeed, while Greece and Italy show the worst governance performance with an index, respectively, equal to 0.42 and 0.45, Portugal and Spain show an index relatively high (respectively equal to 0.64 and 0.66).

Figure 2. Control of corruption as a measure of governance performance in the MENA Region (average by country on 2002-2012 time span)
Source: Elaborations of Authors on the Worldwide Governance Indicators (WGI) dataset - World Bank

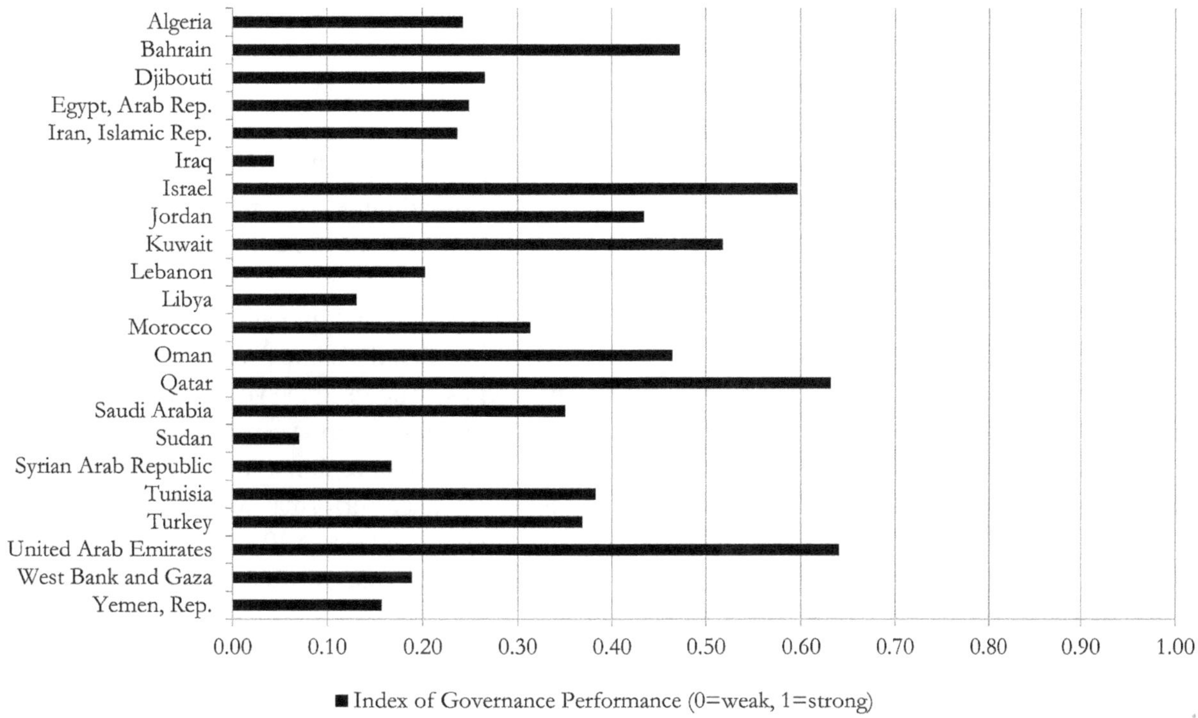

As already stressed, the MENA Region, as a whole, exhibits a higher level of perceived corruption and, therefore, a widely worse level of governance performance, compared with Europe. The reason of this gap is presumably to be found in the different political regimes, traditions and social systems in these countries. All the same, the MENA Region is far from being very homogeneous and shows significant differences among countries (see Figure 2). We believe that, in this case, the cause of such differences and of the lowest levels of governance performance can be identified in the presence of autocratic forms of government, poor protection of civil rights, a low freedom of press and in the general lack of democracy. As shown in Figure 2, the lowest indices of governance performance are found in Iraq (0.04), Sudan (0.07), Libya (0.13), Yemen (0.16), Syrian Arab Republic (0.17), West Bank and Gaza (0.19), Lebanon (0.20). Not by chance, most of these countries although formally they are presidential or semi-presidential or parliamentary republic, de facto experiences dictatorships, wars or, at least, a high level of political instability.

On the contrary, the most virtuous countries in the MENA Region are ruled by monarchical forms of government. In this subgroup, the best governance performance is observed for the members of the Organization of the Petroleum Exporting Countries (OPEC), that is Kuwait, Qatar, United Arab Emirates.

Up until now, we have drawn a general picture of the differences in the perceived governance performance indicator between Europe and MENA Region as whole and within these areas. Now, we attempt to analyze the interaction between governance performance and public expenditure. We will analyze the correlation between government efficiency and both total public spending and some of its basic functional components, such as Military, Education, Healthcare and Social Welfare measured by Social Contributions.

As already argued, the political-institutional form of a country affects the level of corruption as well as the level and the allocation of public spending. Indeed, the volume and the allocation of public expenditure are determined by political and institutional objectives. Yet political decisions, in turn, may be influenced by the objectives of individual bureaucrats in search of rent to extracts through corruption. Given the complexity of the connections between these variables, it is quite difficult to disentangle and isolate the impact of corruption on the level of public expenditure. We will attempt to do so by comparing per areas the amount of public spending with the corresponding level of perceived governance performance. With all the caveats, this comparison could provide at least some intuition of the impact of corruption on government efficiency.

Figure 3 depicts the comparative dynamics of total government expenditure and governance performance in Europe and the Mena Region. The picture clearly shows that the same divergence between the two areas we have observed in the governance performance indicator holds in the volumes of total public spending. In addition, the interaction between public spending and governance performance is quite similar for the two geopolitical areas. Both in Europe and in the Mena region a lower level of general public spending seems to be associated to relatively higher governance performance (lower corruption). This is particularly true for the years immediately following the financial crises 2009-2010. During these years, a jump in the public spending has been accompanied by a decrease in the level of governance performance and an increase in perceived corruption.

Figure 3. Control of corruption as a measure of governance performance (a) and general public spending (b) in Europe and in the MENA Region (average by year on the countries of each area)
Source: Elaborations of authors on the Worldwide Governance Indicators (WGI) dataset - World Bank (WB) (a) and World Economic Outlook (WEO) Database - International Monetary Fund (IMF) (b)

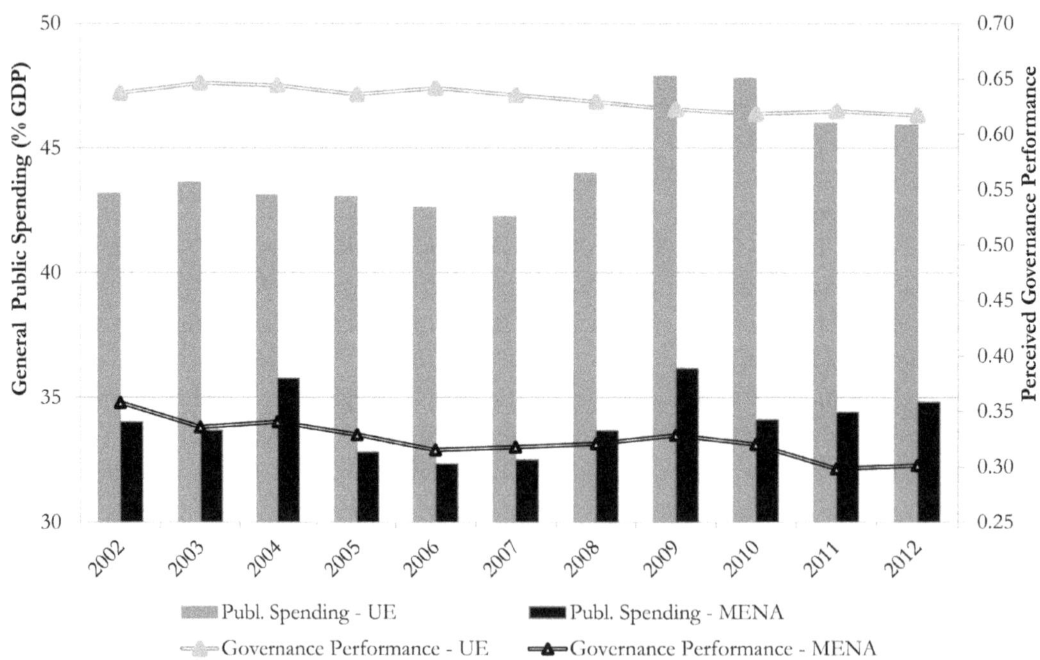

These results confirm the idea well established in the literature of a positive relationship between corruption and public spending. Corruption, by its own nature, feeds public expenditure and in turn, public expenditure embodies incentives for potentially corrupt bureaucrats. As argued, corrupt bureaucrats will attempt to divert public funds towards areas of public spending in which bribes can be more easily extracted. In this sense, corruption (or bad governance performance) reduces the efficiency and effectiveness of public resources and, therefore, it affects negatively economic growth.

Since corruption affects more public investment rather than current account expenditure, it is particularly harmful in the long run. As a matter of fact, one can argue that differences in the infrastructure gap among many countries is undoubtedly the result of a misallocation of public resources rather than the lack of these. In the last years, the economic crisis and the following austerity policies have led the policy makers to pay a greater attention to this gap, and its causes, especially in the European countries.

In order to develop anti-corruption policies, central and local governments need to better understand the allocation mechanisms of public resources and the corresponding incentives to corruption.

As explained in the previous section, the relationship of corruption with public expenditure is not uniform throughout the different functional components of public expenditure. Some components of the public sector display stronger incentives to corruption. This implies that in order to implement efficient anti-corruption policies, one has to determine in which spheres of Government's actions the level of bribing is more intense. This is the reason why we now analyze the interaction between the perceived governance performance and some basic functional components of public spending. Figures 4 and 5 draw, respectively, in Europe and the MENA region, the time-trend dynamics of four components of public spending and the perceived governance performance indicator. The data on governance performance in Figure 4 and 5 are the same as the ones in Figure 2 and 3. However a different scale in the former pictures allow us to draw some interesting features of the dynamics of government efficiency. While the governance performance in Europe (Figure 4) appears to be decreasing since the starting of the economic crisis in 2007, in MENA Region (Figure 5) it shows an increasing trend from 2006 up until 2009, when it starts to decrease. Moreover, in Europe the amount of public spending allocated to each of the four components of public spending is constant for the all the time span, whereas in MENA Region it is quite erratic. It is surprising to note that social contributions and healthcare public spending starts to increase after economic crisis, while following the crises public spending in education decreases.

By comparing the two figures, it is possible to identify a wide divergence between the two geopolitical areas as concerns the composition of government expenditure. The European governments (Figure 4) allocate much more public resources, in ascending order, to social contributions, healthcare, education rather than national defense (military spending). On the contrary, the governments of the MENA countries (Figure 5) spend much more on components such as military and education rather than on healthcare and social contributions. Starting from 2011 military expenditure in MENA Region starts absorbing even the greatest share of public resources. The increase in military expenditure in the area after the 2008 is the obvious effect of the spread of some civil insurrection[3] and of the intensification of the so called Israeli-Palestinian crisis.

Figure 4 and 5 also show a different degree of interaction between governance performance and components of public spending in Europe and in MENA region. While in Europe there seems to be no significant correlation between the various components of public spending and the perceived governance performance, in the MENA Region, instead, governance performance is positively related to public spending in education and, before 2007, to military spending.

Figure 4. Control of corruption as a measure of governance performance (a) and functional public spending (b) in Europe-28 (average by year on the European countries)
Source: Elaborations of authors on the Worldwide Governance Indicators (WGI) dataset - World Bank (WB) (a) and World Development Indicators (WDI) Database - World Bank (WB) (b)

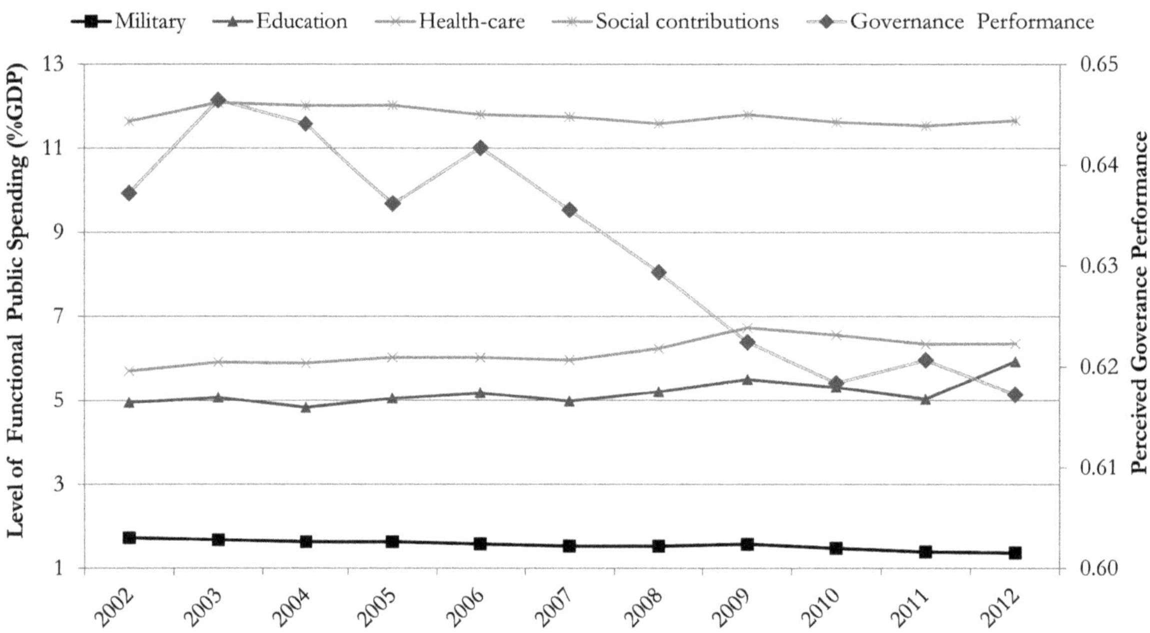

Figure 5. Control of corruption as a measure of governance performance (a) and functional public spending (b) in the MENA region (average by year on MENA countries)
Source: Elaborations of authors on the Worldwide Governance Indicators (WGI) dataset - World Bank (WB) (a) and World Development Indicators (WDI) Database - World Bank (WB) (b)

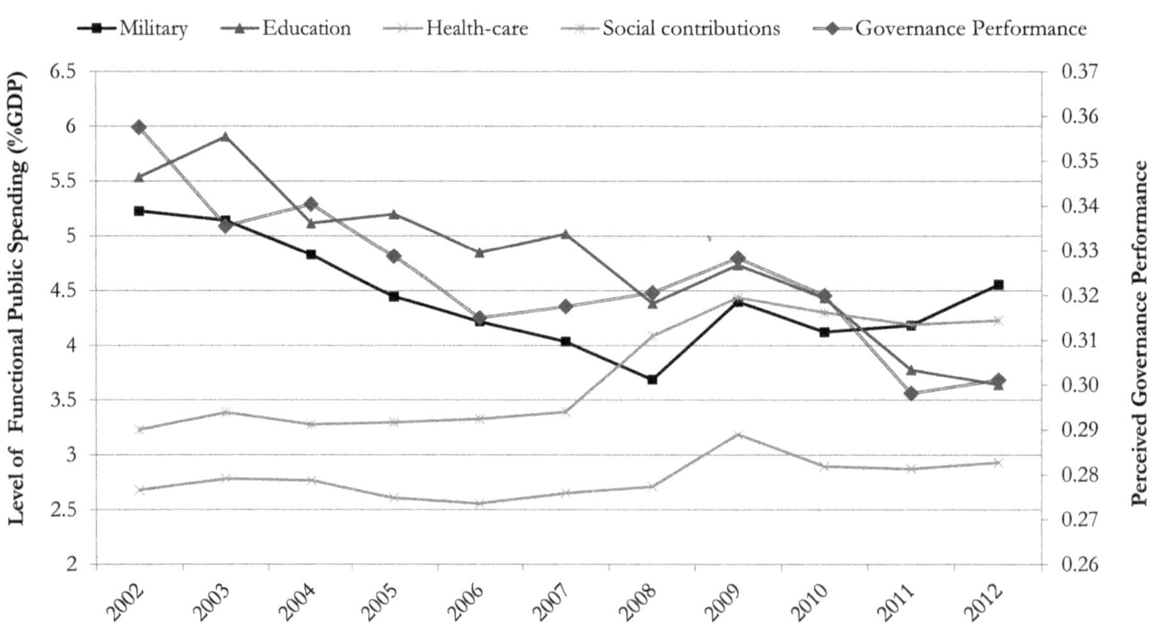

Even if we consider the average by country in each area, we find significant differences in the level and composition of public spending, in the perceived governance performance, as well as in the interaction between these two measures.

In the European area (Figure 6), the composition of functional public spending is similar for all countries, but with some exceptions. The highest public health-care spending is to be found in Austria, Denmark, France, Germany and Netherlands. It's interesting to note that in these countries we observe also the most remarkable indices of perceived governance performance. This can be explained by the solid trust of public opinion in the institutions of these countries as concerning some essential public services such as healthcare. Among all European countries, France, historically considered to be a State in favor of widespread welfare, has indeed the highest level of public spending in healthcare and in social contributions. This latter kind of government expenditure, quite high in Europe as a whole, receives a relatively smaller share of public funds in members which have only recently joint European Union (EU), that is Bulgaria and Romania.

The most remarkable military public spending – as a percentage of GDP – is observed in Greece (2.84), the United Kingdom (2.45), France (2.44), Bulgaria (2.21), Cyprus (2.04) and Portugal (2.0). Whereas, the countries which allocate less resources to national defense are Ireland (0.59), Luxembourg (0.60),

Figure 6. Control of corruption as a measure of governance performance (a) and functional public spending (b) in Europe-28 (average by country on 2002-2012 time span)
Source: Elaborations of authors on the Worldwide Governance Indicators (WGI) dataset - World Bank (WB) (a) and World Development Indicators (WDI) Database - World Bank (WB) (b)

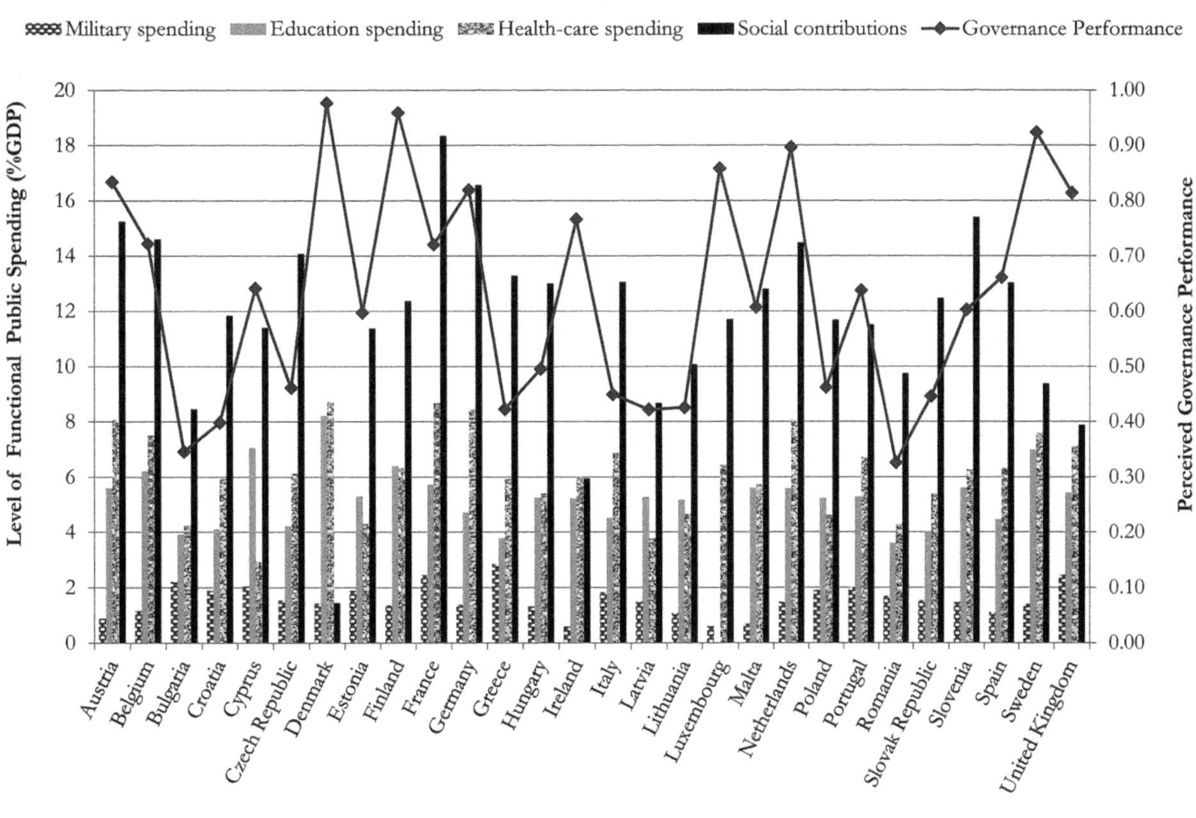

Malta (0.69), Austria (0.88), Lithuania (1.07). Generally, it does not emerge any significant relationship between this type of public spending and the perception of governance performance.

Education is a very important category of public spending since it can contribute to the human capital accumulation and, therefore, to economic growth. As Mauro (1998) points out, one of the main channels through which a low governance performance, and correspondingly a high level of perceived corruption, affects negatively economic growth is indeed the poor allocation of public resources towards education spending. In fact, public expenditures in education provide less opportunities to extract a rent compared to other sectors of government intervention. As it is for the public spending on healthcare, also expenditure in education appear to be positively related to governance performance. Depending on the percentage of public spending in education on GDP, we can classify European countries in three groups. In the first group, with a threshold in the ratio of spending in education on GDP above 6 percentage, we find the most virtuous countries. These are Denmark (8.21), Cyprus (7.05), Sweden (6.98), Finland (6.40), Belgium (6.21). The second, intermediate group, with a threshold above 5 percentage, contains almost half of the European countries: France (5.73), Slovenia (5.61), Malta (5.60), Austria (5.60), Netherlands (5.59), The United Kingdom (5.43), Estonia (5.30), Portugal (5.28), Latvia (5.28), Hungary (5.26), Poland (5.24), Ireland (5.23), Lithuania (5.18). In the last group we find countries that show the lowest level of public spending in education, below a threshold of 5 percentage of GDP. It's interesting to note that many countries that show a high, intermediate or low level of public spending in education, they show, respectively, a high, intermediate or low level of governance performance.

The picture widely changes if we consider the MENA Region (Figure 7). In this case we find a greater variability among countries both in governance performance and in the composition of public spending. As opposed to the European countries, these countries show clear different government priorities regarding the allocation of public resources in the various sectors of government intervention. In fact, in nearly every case, governments allocate a higher amount of resources in defense rather than in other sectors. Moreover, averaging on the entire time span 2002-2012, see Figure 8, some countries appear to spend in defense a greater amount of public resources than European countries spend in Education or Healthcare. This is the case of Oman, with a military public spending equal to 10.93 percent of GDP, Saudi Arabia (8.29), Israel (7.55), Djibouti (5.49), Jordan (5.28), Syrian Arab Republic (5.09) and Yemen (4.95). The relationship between these levels of military spending and the related governance performance indicators is puzzling. In only two of these countries – Israel and Oman –, a high level of military spending is associated to a high degree of perceived governance performance while this relationship remain negative in all other countries. A possible explanation could be found in a different public perception of the usefulness of military forces. The latter, in fact, depends on the specific geopolitical environment, and could be either seen as a safety and stability factor or as a wasteful component of public spending. In this last case, high perceived corruption could be explained by the fact that citizens would evaluate a high level of military spending as the politicians' expedient to increase their rent-extracting opportunities.

The highest levels of public spending on education, instead, is shown by the government of Djibouti (8.61 percent of GDP over the period considered). This is even higher that what European countries spend in education. The reason for this phenomenon is to be found in the relatively recent education reform which has occurred in this country. In August 2000, an education planning act has significantly improved the public educational system in Djibouti, making education compulsory up to a higher level and providing more resources for high schools and universities.

Figure 7. Control of corruption as a measure of governance performance (a) and functional public spending (b) in MENA region (average by country on 2002-2012 time span)
Source: Elaborations of authors on the Worldwide Governance Indicators (WGI) dataset - World Bank (WB) (a) and World Development Indicators (WDI) Database - World Bank (WB) (b)

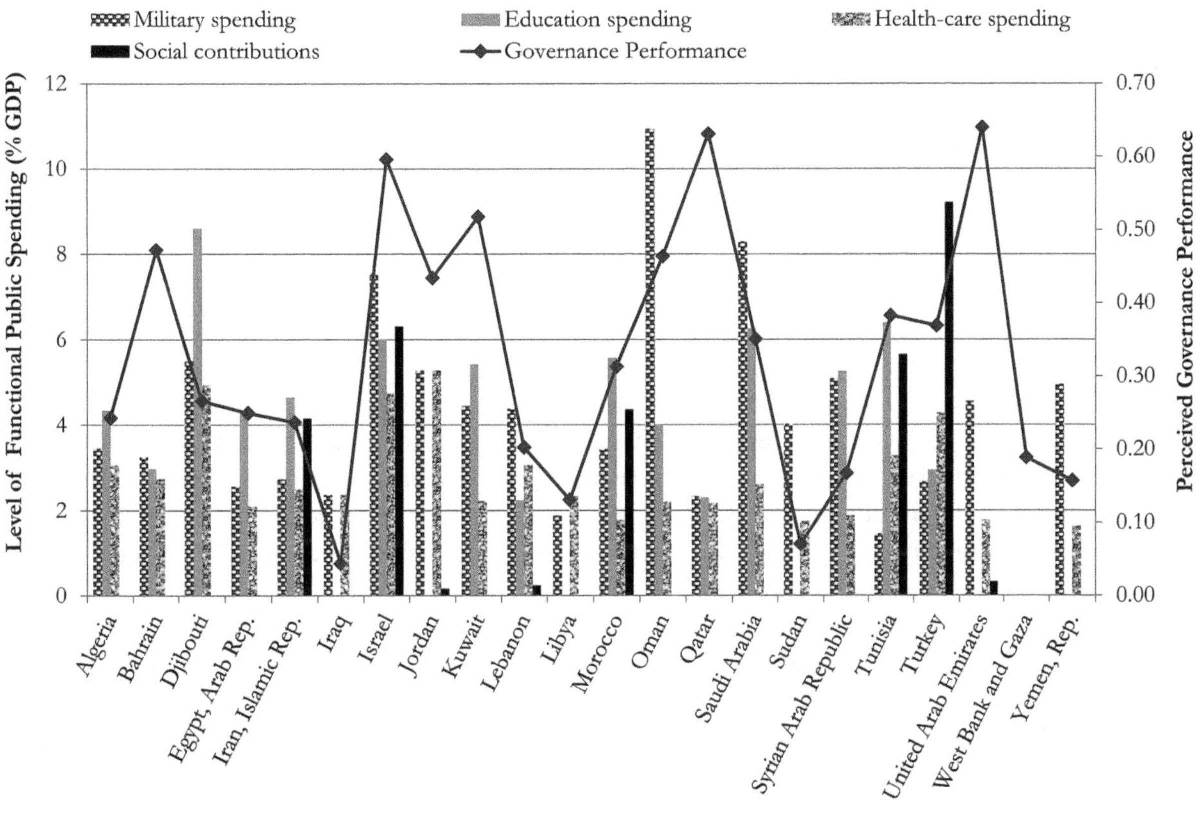

The relatively poor health services provided by the countries of the MENA Region is the reflex of the very low level of public spending in healthcare. In this sector only Jordan (5.27), Djibouti (4.92), Israel (4.72) and Turkey (4.26) spend more resources. With the exception of Israel, in these countries, unlike Europe, we don't find any relationship between the level of public spending on healthcare and the perception of governance performance.

Surprisingly, the highest level of public spending on social contribution is shown by Turkey (9.20 percent of GDP), whose social security system has experienced great changes starting from 2007. The other countries (for which data are available) show intermediate levels of spending on this component of public expenditure. This is the case of Israel (6.31), Tunisia (5.65), Morocco (4.35) and Iran (4.15). Only few countries, such as United Arab Emirates (0.32) and Jordan (0.16), display very poor levels of expenditure for social contribution.

The countries with the highest degree of perceived governance performance are the United Arab Emirates, Qatar, Israel and Kuwait. Among these countries only Israel shows a positive relationship between the social components of public spending (i.e. education, healthcare and social contributions) and governance efficiency. In the other three countries, the positive social opinion about the governance performance is likely due to the wealth coming from the petroleum industry.

On the contrary, the lowest level of perceived governance performance are found in Iraq (with a score equal to 0.04), Sudan (0.07), Libya (0.13), Yemen (0.16), Syrian Arab Republic (0.17) and West Bank and Gaza (0.19). At the same time, these countries also show a low level of public spending. In this case, one could argue that the low perception of governance performance mostly depends on the political environment, the frequency of wars or civil uprisings that characterize this group of countries.

A SIMPLE ECONOMETRIC ANALYSIS

In order to better analyze the nature of the relationship between governance performance and government expenditure, we regress in turn the index of governance performance on the measures of total government expenditure (as percentage of GDP) and on the measures of public spending by sector.

Of course, we are aware that this is a simple exercise and it is limited in that it does not consider other relevant determinant of governance performance. However, we also believe that despite the lack of many controls, this analysis can offer a valuable overall picture of the interaction between public spending and the perception index of governance performance, and the correspondent level of perceived corruption.

Our basic econometric specification is represented by an Ordinary Least Square (OLS) Fixed Effects (FE) Panel model, mostly unbalanced for the MENA countries. A fixed effects model allow us to control for omitted factors that differ between entities (i.e. the countries in our model) but not over time (i.e. the years in our model). The choice of a Fixed Effects rather than a Random Effects Panel model is confirmed by the Hausman test. According to this test, the coefficients of our fixed effects model are significantly efficient and consistent under the null hypothesis of not systematic difference in coefficients. Furthermore, in order to control for potential endogeneity in the regressors and to take care of problems of heteroskedasticity and autocorrelation, we employ an Instrumental Variable estimator for dynamic panel data models. Specifically, we use a "System - GMM" (Generalized Method of Moments) estimator, an approach developed by Blundell and Bond (1998) and formerly outlined in Arellano and Bover (1995). The "System - GMM" (S-GMM) treats the model as a system of equations in first-differences and in levels. The endogenous variables in the first-differences equation are instrumented with lagged values of their levels, while the endogenous variables in the level equations are instrumented with lags of their first differences. The advantage of using this estimation method is that it excludes serial correlation and heteroskedasticity of the errors. However, a greater difficulty in such estimation techniques consists in the choice of the number of lags of the endogenous and predetermined variables. We treat as endogenous both the governance performance indicator and the total and by sector government expenditure. In order to reduce the number of instruments, we use a temporal length of the lags to three years and we reduce the maximum length to two years. In an interesting introduction to the linear GMM (Generalized Method of Moments), provided by Roodman (2009) as a rule of thumb it is recommended to use a number of tools that does not exceed greatly the number of groups (i.e. the countries in our case). In order to check for the exogeneity of instruments we apply the Hansen (1982) *J*-test of overidentifying restrictions (1982). The null hypothesis of the Hansen *J*-test is that the instruments as a group are exogenous. In all specifications exogeneity of the instruments is confirmed by the Hansen *J*-test test for which we cannot reject the null hypothesis even at a 10% level of significance. Additionally, we use the Arellano and Bond (1991) test for serial correlation of the residuals up to the second order, AR(1) and AR(2), which can cause a bias to both the coefficients and to the estimated standard errors. Usually this test confirms only the absence of second order serial correlation, since the first differences induce serial correlation of the errors of the first order processed. In all specifications the AR test does not reject the null hypothesis of no autocorrelation of the errors of the second order.

In order to provide a general picture about the interaction between public spending and governance performance we firstly consider jointly the European and MENA countries (Table 1) and then perform the same regression separately by considering only the European countries (Table 2) and the MENA Region (Table 3). In this way, it is possible to identify the differences between the two areas about the effects of public spending, and its components, on the perceived governance performance indicator or, correspondently, on the perception of corruption in the public sector.

When one considers all countries (Europe-28 and MENA countries) (Table 1), the effect of general public spending on governance performance is not clear. Depending on the different estimator used, we find opposite results. By employing an OLS estimator, column (1), we find a negative coefficient of general public spending, which turns positive, column (2), by adopting the more robust System-GMM estimator[4]. The same unclear results emerge when one includes public expenditure in its components. As

Table 1. Regressions of perceived governance performance indicator on general and functional public spending in Europe-28 and in the MENA region

Dependent Variable: Governance Performance	(1) OLS-FE	(2) OLS-FE	(3) S-GMM	(4) S-GMM
General public spending	-0.000582 (0.000492)		0.00891 (0.00963)	
Military spending		0.0308*** (0.00675)		-0.0301 (0.0408)
Education spending		0.00251 (0.00642)		0.0726 (0.0555)
Health-care spending		-0.00914** (0.00400)		-0.0160 (0.0363)
Social contributions		-0.000966 (0.00206)		0.0236* (0.0138)
Constant	0.534*** (0.0199)	0.600*** (0.0380)	0.153 (0.395)	0.146 (0.233)
Observations	524	282	524	282
R-squared	0.003	0.116		
Number of countries	48	32	48	32
Hausman test (*p*-value)	0.000	0.000		
Number of instruments			7	16
Sargan-test (*p-value*)			0.000	0.000
Hansen *J*-test (*p*-value)			0.038	0.161
Lags of endogenous variables (used as instruments)			2_3	2_3
AR(1) test (*p*-value)			0.614	0.989
AR(2) test (*p*-value)			0.719	0.748

Notes: Regressions in columns (1) and (2) are based on Ordinary Least Square - Fixed Effects Panel Data Estimator; regressions in columns (3) and (4) are based on Blundell and Bond System-GMM estimator. Significant coefficients are indicated by *** (1% level), ** (5% level) and * (10% level); Robust standard errors in parentheses.

Table 2. Regressions of perceived governance performance indicator on general and functional public spending in Europe-28

Dependent Variable: Governance Performance	(1) OLS-FE	(2) OLS-FE	(3) S-GMM	(4) S-GMM
General public spending	-0.00144** (0.000644)		-0.00163 (0.00400)	
Military spending		0.0197* (0.0115)		-0.0256 (0.111)
Education spending		-0.00186 (0.00651)		0.0846 (0.0533)
Health-care spending		-0.00792* (0.00416)		0.0194 (0.0319)
Social contributions		0.000771 (0.00196)		0.0140 (0.0164)
Constant	0.696*** (0.0287)	0.668*** (0.0429)	0.704*** (0.185)	-0.105 (0.195)
Observations	308	238	308	238
R-squared	0.018	0.047		
Number of countries	28	27	28	27
Hausman test (*p*-value)	0.0001	0.0000		
Number of instruments			7	16
Sargan-test (*p-value*)			0.000	0.000
Hansen *J*-test (*p*-value)			0.307	0.088
Lags of endogenous variables (used as instruments)			2_3	2_3
AR(1) test (*p*-value)			0.230	0.872
AR(2) test (*p*-value)			0.016	0.194

Notes: Regressions in columns (1) and (2) are based on Ordinary Least Square - Fixed Effects Panel Data Estimator; regressions in columns (3) and (4) are based on Blundell and Bond System-GMM estimator. Significant coefficients are indicated by *** (1% level), ** (5% level) and * (10% level); Robust standard errors in parentheses.

it is for total spending, also the coefficient on military spending and social contributions change signs when instead of running an OLS one runs a System-GMM. This is not the case for public spending on education and expenditure in healthcare. While education appears to affect positively governance performance, healthcare expenditure has a negative impact (Column 2 and 4 of Table 1).

Though not robust, these results on education are in line with our previous descriptive analysis and with the idea present in the literature that a high level of public spending in education is often associated with low levels of administrative corruption and, thus, with a high level of perceived governance performance. In addition, one could argue that countries with a solid education system also show high rate of economic growth and greater accumulated wealth that, in turn, improves the social opinion about government's behavior on the one hand, and enable the citizens to better monitor and discourage public official from being corrupt, on the other hand. Public spending in healthcare, instead, has a negative impact on the perception of governance performance. According to Mauro (1998), in fact, public procurement of high technological medical equipment allows bureaucrats to extract more profitable bribes. The coefficient

Table 3. Regressions of perceived governance performance indicator on general and functional public spending in the MENA region

Dependent Variable: Governance Performance	(1) OLS-FE	(2) OLS-FE	(3) S-GMM	(4) S-GMM
General public spending	-5.32e-05 (0.000764)		0.00386* (0.00207)	
Military spending		0.0434*** (0.0135)		0.0363*** (0.00471)
Education spending		0.00700 (0.0236)		0.0628*** (0.0148)
Health-care spending		0.0120 (0.0135)		0.00306 (0.0127)
Social contributions		-0.0417*** (0.0133)		-0.00476 (0.00817)
Constant	0.341*** (0.0262)	0.238** (0.104)	0.208*** (0.0704)	-0.0997 (0.110)
Observations	216	44	216	44
R-squared	0.000	0.452		
Number of countries	20	5	20	5
Hausman test (*p*-value)	0.2940	0.0001		
Number of instruments			7	16
Sargan-test (*p-value*)			0.000	0.000
Hansen *J*-test (*p*-value)			0.422	1.000
Lags of endogenous variables (used as instruments)			2_3	2_3
AR(1) test (*p*-value)			0.131	0.998
AR(2) test (*p*-value)			0.897	0.763

Notes: Regressions in columns (1) and (2) are based on Ordinary Least Square - Fixed Effects Panel Data Estimator; regressions in columns (3) and (4) are based on Blundell and Bond System-GMM estimator. Significant coefficients are indicated by *** (1% level), ** (5% level) and * (10% level); Robust standard errors in parentheses.

of this type of public spending is negative and statistically significant at 5% level, column (2). By using a System-GMM, column (4), the coefficient remains negative, although it loses statistical significance.

When one includes in the regression only European countries the results are more clear (Table 2). Total public expenditure exerts a negative influence on the perceived governance performance, columns (1) and (2). This is in line with theory's prediction which indicates that corruption endogenously causes inefficient increase in public expenditure. The functional components of government expenditure seem to produce opposite effects on the governance perception index, depending on which estimation procedure one employs. However, the public spending on social contributions show a positive coefficient both in the OLS estimation and in the "System" - GMM estimation. This result is in line with the argument that a benevolent government which has built a solid social security system will be perceived capable and honest. Furthermore, social contribution is a sector of government intervention which offers to public officials less profitable opportunities for rent-extracting behavior compared with other sectors.

We finally regress governance performance on public spending by including only countries of the MENA Region (Table 3). In this case, the effect of general public spending on the perception index of governance performance is positive and significant when one runs the system-GMM (see column 3). This implies that an increase in government expenditure determines an increase in the perceived level of government efficiency. The explanation could be found in the relative lower level of public expenditure in these countries which entails that government services have not saturated the market, as it often occurs in richer countries (see the results on European countries) and there is space for an efficient increase in government expenditure.

Table 3 also includes the results of the regressions of governance performance on public spending in specific sectors. The effect of military spending on governance performance is positive and highly significant both under the OLS estimator, column (2), and the System-GMM estimator, column (4). As a matter of fact, a 1% increase of military expenses as a fraction of GDP leads to a significant increase in governance performance, 4.34% increase in the OLS estimate and 3.63% increase in the System-GMM estimate. Although military spending is recognized by the literature as a profitable opportunity for rent-extracting activities, in the MENA countries such component of public spending shows to be negatively related to corruption and, in turn, to be positively related to governance performance. This relationship could be explained by the particular institutional and political structure of the MENA Region. Most of these countries are ruled by dictatorships or by autocratic governments whose bureaucrats or politicians preserve their power exactly trough military presence in the country. Hence, military expenditure in these circumstances does not necessarily entails corruption, but rather could mean the reinforcing of the government. Moreover, since, as already argued, in these countries the level of government expenditure is relatively low, more government expenditure is interpreted as a necessity more than the channel through which feeding corruption. This could provide a valid explanation of the positive effect of both expenditure in education and in healthcare on the perceived government performance. The one and only sector of government intervention in which we find a negative relationship with governance performance is social welfare. This might be attributable to the lower per capita income level of most of these countries and to the fact that manipulating welfare expenses is, indeed, a channel through which local politicians and bureaucrats may increase their power and their consensus.

CONCLUSION

Measuring governance performance and its interaction with total and functional government expenditure is generally a complex and difficult task. Understanding the dynamics of corruption and public spending is even more difficult. The analysis of the interplay between governance performance and corruption, on one side, and public expenditure, on the other focusing on European and MENA countries has delivered one interesting result: institutional and social factors such as the judicial system, the form of the government and the stability of the system all play an important role. This implies that corruption may be more or less detrimental, and correspondingly government may be more or less efficient, depending on the general economic and institutional context. Hence, effective policies directed to enhance the efficiency of public expenditure cannot be designed without taking into account each country specific institutional framework.

REFERENCES

Acemoglu, D., & Verdier, T. (2000). The choice between market failure and corruption. *The American Economic Review*, *90*(1), 194–211. doi:10.1257/aer.90.1.194

Arellano, M., & Bond, S. (1991). Some tests of specification for panel data: Monte Carlo evidence and an application to employment equations. *The Review of Economic Studies*, *58*(2), 277–297. doi:10.2307/2297968

Arellano, M., & Bover, O. (1995). Another look at the instrumental variable estimation of error-components models. *Journal of Econometrics*, *68*(1), 29–51. doi:10.1016/0304-4076(94)01642-D

Blackburn, K. (2012). Corruption and Development: Explaining the Evidence. *The Manchester School*, *80*(4), 401–428. doi:10.1111/j.1467-9957.2012.02314.x

Blundell, R., & Bond, S. (1998). Initial conditions and moment restrictions in dynamic panel data models. *Journal of Econometrics*, *87*(1), 115–143. doi:10.1016/S0304-4076(98)00009-8

Clements, B., Hugounenq, R., & Schwartz, G. (1995). Government Subsidies: Concepts, International Trends and Reform Options. *International Monetary Fund (IMF) Working Paper 91.*

Gupta, S., de Mello, L., & Sharan, R. (2000). Corruption and military spending. *International Monetary Fund (IMF) Working Paper 23.*

Hansen, L. (1982). Large Sample Properties of Generalized Methods of Moments Estimators. *Econometrica*, *50*(4), 1029–1054. doi:10.2307/1912775

Krueger, A. O. (1974). The Political Economy of the Rent-Seeking Society. *The American Economic Review*, *64*(3), 291–303.

Mauro, P. (1997). Why Worry About Corruption ? *International Monetary Fund (IMF) Economic Issues* (6).

Mauro, P. (1998). Corruption and the composition of government expenditure. *Journal of Public Economics*, *69*(2), 263–279. doi:10.1016/S0047-2727(98)00025-5

Roodman, D. (2009). How to Do xtabond2: An Introduction to "Difference" and "System" GMM in Stata. *The Stata Journal*, *9*(1), 86–136.

Shleifer, A., & Vishny, R. W. (1993). Corruption. *The Quarterly Journal of Economics*, *108*(3), 599–617. doi:10.2307/2118402

Tanzi, V. (1998). Corruption around the World: Causes, Consequences, Scope, and Cures. *International Monetary Fund (IMF) Working Paper 63.*

Tanzi, V., & Davoodi, H. (1997). Corruption, Public Investment, and Growth. *International Monetary Fund (IMF) Working Paper 139.*

WGI - WB (World Governance Indicators - World Bank). (2014). Retrieved from http://info.worldbank.org/governance/wgi/index.aspx#home

World Development Indicators Data Bank. (2014). International Bank for Reconstruction and Development-International Development Association World Bank. Retrieved from http://data.worldbank.org/indicator/MS.MIL.XPND.GD.ZS

KEY TERMS AND DEFINITIONS

Bureaucrat (or Public Official): A person that performs an official role in the government, by carrying out any public legislative, administrative or judicial function.

Corruption: The abuse of public power in order to obtain a private benefit.

Public Consumption (or Current Public Spending): The amount of resources allocated by the government for the functioning of public services, such as the purchases in consumer goods, salaries, social transfers, and so forth.

Public Investment (or Capital Public Spending): The amount of government resources allocated for a productive aim, such as public infrastructures, hospitals, schools and council house.

Public Spending (or Public Expenditure): The total amount of public resources spent by the central government, local governments and state-owned companies. It is mainly shaped by public investment and current public spending.

Rent-Seeking: The set of lobbying activities in order to improve one's share of existing wealth without creating new wealth. For example the effort of someone to affect the enactment or the compliance of law in order to obtain a benefit.

Senior Public Official: The public official that performs a high public role in the government, such as chiefs of state, ministers or, at least, powerful politicians.

ENDNOTES

1 Data and methodology are available at http://info.worldbank.org/governance/wgi/index.aspx#home

2 For more details see http://data.worldbank.org/indicator/MS.MIL.XPND.GD.ZS

3 Here, we are referring to Libya, Syrian Arab Republic, Tunisia and Algeria. In these countries, oppressed by repressive and strongly corrupt governments, since the end of 2010 it was triggered a revolutionary wave of civil protests and revolts that have given rise to the so-called "Arab Spring"

4 Anyway, in such cases, it could be more reliable the "System" - GMM estimates, because they control for the potential endogeneity in the regressors and allow us to avoid serial correlation and heteroskedasticity of the errors.

Chapter 8
Tax Systems, Economic Development, and Good Governance:
A Comparative Analysis of the MENA Countries

Savaş Çevik
Selçuk University, Turkey

ABSTRACT

The chapter examines tax structure and its relation to good governance and economic development in the MENA countries. First, it discusses how different tax systems and tax structures in the region compared with other countries. MENA region can be characterized with low level of tax-to-GDP ratio compared to other groups of countries. However, tax systems considerably diverge within the region. Most importantly, whether having hydrocarbon revenues meaningfully divides the region's countries with respect to tax composition, tax levels, tax ratios and tax regimes. Literature suggests that natural resource revenue is also an important determinant of governance and institutional development that have impact on economic development, while good governance, a more legitimate and responsive state is an essential factor for a more adequate level of tax effort. Therefore, the second section of the study examines the relationships between taxation and good governance with emphasis on the MENA region.

INTRODUCTION

Despite diversification among them, tax systems of the MENA countries have some common features and challenges on account of the region's economic structure, political issues, and even cultural background. Moreover, globalization, international spillover of tax competition, and international experience of tax reforms put pressure on their tax system with regard to attract foreign direct investment (FDI), stimulate economic performance and development just as other developing countries. Given recent political turmoil and weak institutional capacity, taxation in the region may also function to build efficient institutions, good governance and a social contract between the governments and citizens.

DOI: 10.4018/978-1-5225-0053-7.ch008

The problems in which the MENA countries suffer are substantially common to those of other developing countries such as the low level of income taxes, inefficiencies of tax administration, informal structure of economy and weak data to consider policy options. However, some of them are especially heavy in the region because of idiosyncratic features of the MENA countries. With regard to tax structure, total tax as a share of Gross Domestic Product (GDP) is low compared to many developing regions as well as taxes on income and profits as a share of total taxes. Empirical literature suggests that the low level of total taxes and low share of income taxes are associated with corruption and weak governance which are the problems widespread throughout the region.

From this perspective, the chapter discusses tax systems of the MENA region in terms of building institutional capacity and good governance for development and thus, stimulating economic performance. The first section will discuss how different tax systems and tax structures in the region compared with other countries in terms of income and geographic classifications. Considering the international tendencies and experiences, tax rates and reforms are also discussed in this section. The last section will deal with the role of taxation to build well-functioning institutions and qualified governance as well as a fiscal system that extract revenue to finance development and public services.

TAX SYSTEMS AND TAX STRUCTURES IN THE MENA FROM COMPARATIVE PERSPECTIVE: HOW GOVERNMENTS IN THE MENA FINANCE THEMSELVES

The Structure of Government Revenue: An Overview

Since the MENA countries are diverse in terms of their tax systems for purpose of comparison, treating them as if they consist of a homogeneous category can lead misguidance in analysis of their tax systems. First of all, the region can be divided into two groups of revenue systems. Some of them which export oil/hydrocarbon heavily depend on revenue from ownership of the hydrocarbon resources (some countries such as Egypt that benefits revenue from the Suez Canal and several of the poorer Arab countries that receive substantial foreign aid could be considered in this category with regard to depending on non-tax revenues in government financing). While they tax the non-hydrocarbon sectors very lightly, subsidies are heavily used to keep prices low and to support citizens. Indeed, paternalistic subsidies such as food subsidies are common in the region. The second group of countries which imports oil/hydrocarbon uses taxation as the primary source of revenue. Their revenue systems are more comparable to those of the countries from out of the region. National tax systems of these countries may also exhibit different characteristics from Ottoman, French, or British inheritance.

Indeed, this classification as "resource-rich" and "resource-poor" countries points out some differences on economic and political structures of countries in the region, drivers of reforms, political relationships between governments and citizens, and policy options available to promote economic development. Although they differ among themselves as well, the MENA countries differ considerably from both OECD and non-OECD countries in the level of taxation and tax structure as well as their economic and social structure, poor governance and democracy, inefficient tax administration.

Compared to other groups of countries by region and income, some features of government revenue of the MENA region can be seen in Figure 1. First, generally the MENA region has low tax revenue as a percentage of GDP. This is the case especially for oil exporters of the MENA (Algeria, Bahrain, Iran, Iraq, Kuwait, Libya, Oman, Qatar, Saudi Arabia, United Arab Emirates and Yemen). Oil importer

Figure 1. The structure of general government revenue by region and income level (% of GDP, average 2005-2012)
Source: World Bank, World Development Indicators (WDI), Arab Monetary Fund (2011), International Monetary Fund (IMF), MENA Regional Outlook 2014
Note: EU=European Union; ECA=Europe-Central Asia; SSA=Sub-Saharan Africa; LAC=Latin America and Caribbean; EAP=East Asia Pacific

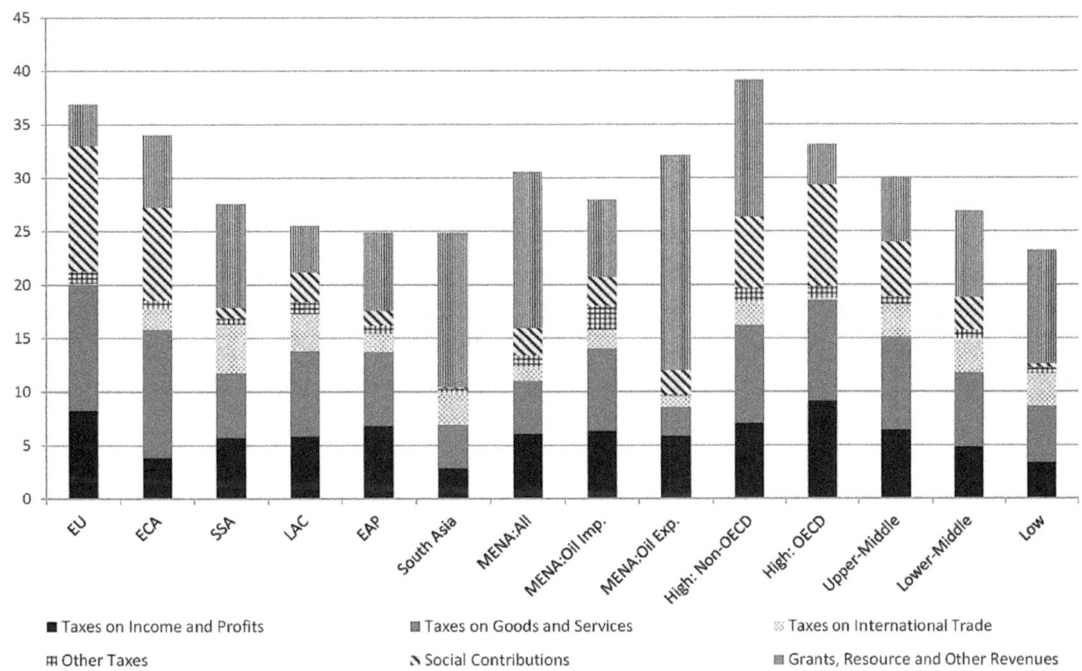

MENA countries (Egypt, Jordan, Lebanon, Morocco, Syria, and Tunisia) exhibit more or less similar revenue structure to other countries which are at the comparable income level, in terms of tax revenues as a share of GDP.

A second point is that the share of non-tax revenue (primarily hydrocarbon revenues and other public revenues) in total government revenue is quite high. The MENA countries that export oil are region that has the highest ratio of resource revenue as a percentage of GDP across all country groups. Accordingly they have the lowest tax burden among the groups, except of South Asia. In terms of non-tax revenues, oil importer MENA countries are comparable to other regions at similar income levels on contrary oil exporters MENA countries.

Considering tax composition, oil importer MENA countries rely on domestic taxes on goods and services compared to oil exporters of MENA region. Social security contributions that one of the most important revenue in EU and OECD are significantly low in all MENA countries relative to countries which at similar income levels. In contrast to the OECD and EU countries and in a similar manner to other developing countries, taxes on international trade in the countries of the MENA region relatively remain important. As can be seen, whether countries have natural resource (especially hydrocarbon revenue) appears to be one of important factors to consider government revenue and the level of taxes in the MENA region. It can be said that hydrocarbon economies who are large oil or gas producers rely mostly on resource revenues. In these countries, tax revenues, regardless of whether direct or indirect taxes, account for only a small share of government revenues.

A Closer Look at the MENA Countries' Tax Structure

When we look at the details of the MENA region countries from Figure 2, it can be seen that Kuwait, Libya, Iraq, Saudi Arabia, Oman, Qatar, UAE and Bahrain have less than five percent of tax revenues as a share of GDP, while it is negligibly low in Kuwait, Iraq, Saudi Arabia, UAE and Bahrain (1 to 2 percent). At the same time, oil-gas producing countries tend to have high levels of total government revenues, except of Iran and Bahrain.

Countries deprived of hydrocarbon resources (such as Jordan, Morocco, Tunisia, Lebanon, and to some degree Egypt and Syria) use largely tax revenues in public finance. In particular, the share of tax revenue in Jordan, Morocco and Tunisia is above 20% as a share of GDP, as tax-to-GDP ratios in Egypt and Lebanon are at about 15%. These countries use broad taxation as the main source of government financing. Morocco, Lebanon, Tunisia can be referred as relatively reforms in the tax structure and tax administration. However, there are some differences among them in tax structure. Direct taxes on incomes, profits and gains Morocco, Tunisia, Egypt, and Syria have a greater share of direct taxes on incomes, profits and gains compared to other oil importer MENA countries. Capability of collecting direct taxes in Morocco, Tunisia and Egypt is also related to relatively developed tax administration. Jordan and Lebanon stand out for their reliance on indirect taxes (Imam & Jacob, 2007).

Taxes in oil exporters of the MENA are mostly collected from limited sources as international trade, specific goods and corporate taxes on foreign firms. These countries do not have a tax system that is comprehensive and at line with international trends, while their main source is hydrocarbon revenue.

Figure 2. Government revenues as a share of GDP in the MENA countries (average 2005-2009)
Source: Arab Monetary Fund (2011); Crivell and Gupta (2014); IMF, World Economic Outllok; World Bank, World Development Indicators.

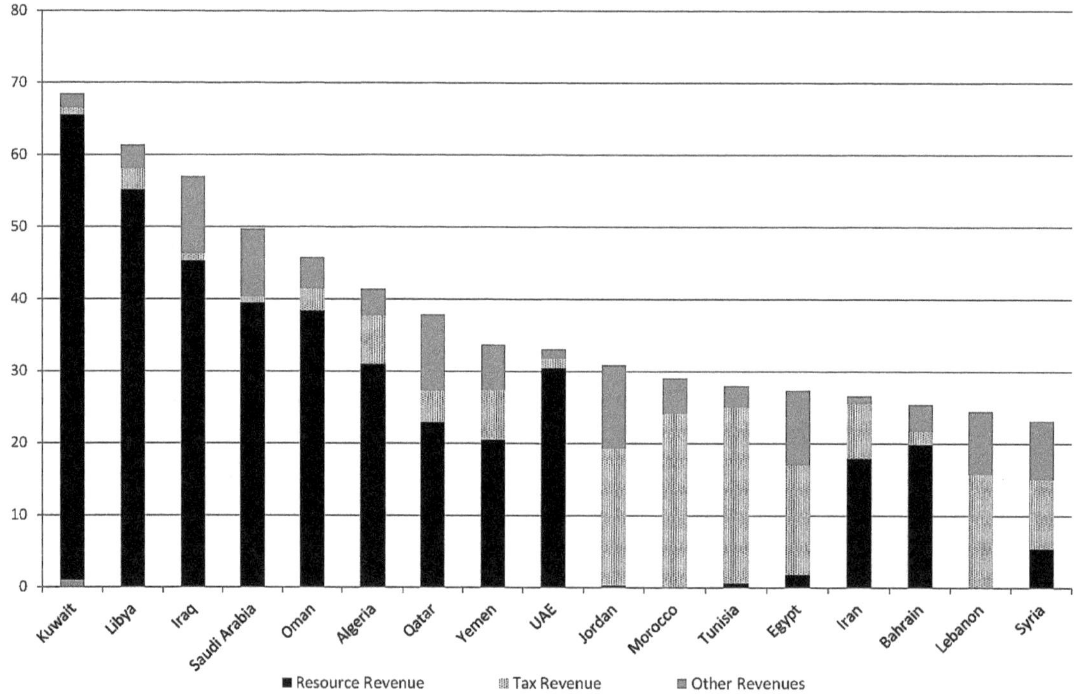

Because of the dependency on oil revenue, their total revenue is highly volatile due to oil price shocks. In general, there is a consensus that the oil-dependent countries must diversify their tax revenue sources for longer-run fiscal sustainability, since the hydrocarbon/oil revenues are exhaustible, volatile, uncertain and largely originate from external demand (Sturm et al., 2009).

Moreover, oil exporters of the MENA region are mostly small countries as those in gulf region. Small economies are heavily exposed to the global market behavior and have limited diversification opportunities because of their small domestic markets (World Bank, 2000). Hamdi and Sbia (2013) show that Bahrain is highly exposed to external shocks such as oil shocks and has failed to diversify its revenue structure despite of reform efforts. Taking into account their rulers have had little incentives to improve their tax system in current situation, tax reforms in these countries may be probable if oil run outs in the future.

Statutory Tax Rates and Tax Regimes in the MENA

Recently, in the resource-poor countries as Egypt, Tunisia, Morocco, and Lebanon, reforms have been introduced reforms to establish a modern tax system and tax administration, including enacting new taxes (e.g., VAT) and new tax laws (e.g., renew income tax act). The main objectives of these efforts have been to improve efficiency and to stabilize revenue yield by simplifying the tax system, removing tax obstacles to investment and growth, and modernizing the tax administration (James, 2015).

It is generally observed that resource-rich countries are particularly prone to have lower tax burden, especially through lower tax rates. This fact creates relatively simple tax systems and revenue administration that has simple tasks in these countries, at the same time. Figure 3 shows standard rates of value

Figure 3. Statutory tax rates by geographic region (2014)
Source: KPMG Tax Rates Database, www.kpmg.com

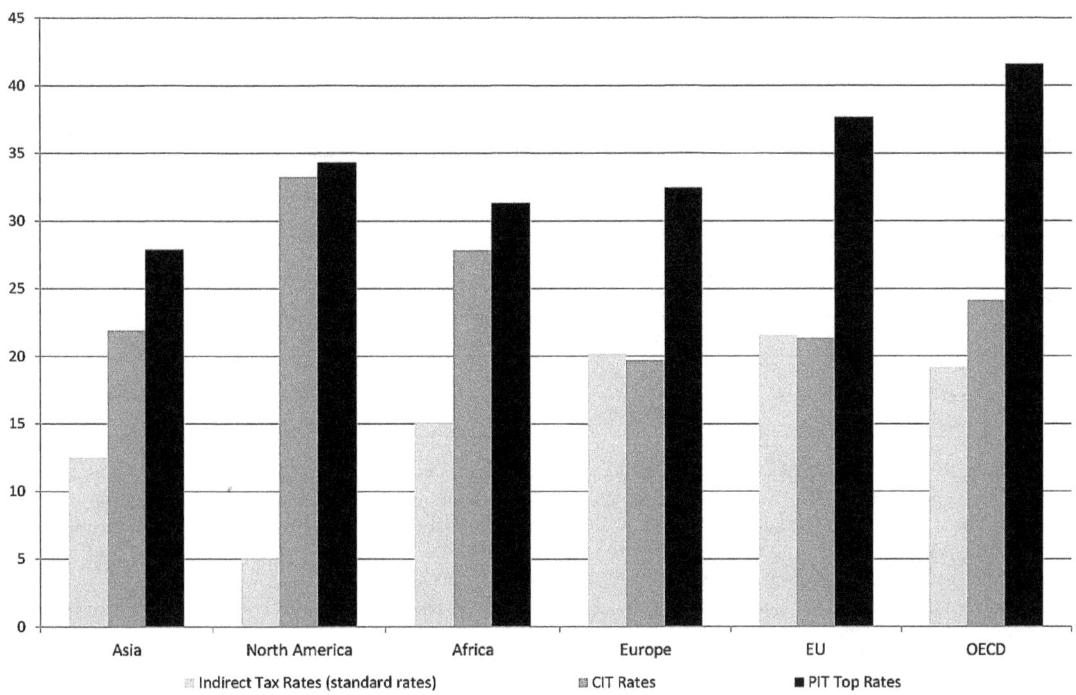

added tax (VAT) or general sale tax (GST), corporate income tax (CIT) rates and top rates of personal income tax (PIT) by geographic regions through the world for comparison purposes. European and the OECD countries generally have a high ratio of VAT and PIT.

Taking into account the effect of taxation on behaviors and economic growth, the overall trend for the last quarter of a century has been to reduce PIT rates, to simplify schedule and structure of PIT and to increase consumption tax. Tax competition to attract more investment and capital has resulted in reducing CIT rates. Statutory CIT rates have fallen by nine percentage points in the (weighted) OECD average since 1990.

Table 1 compares tax regimes and tax rates in the MENA countries. It can be said generally that tax regime and statutory rates between hydrocarbon economies and others are differentiated. Especially the Gulf Cooperation Council (GCC) countries (Saudi Arabia, Kuwait, United Arab Emirates, Bahrain, Qatar, and Oman) follow a different tax regime. Under GCC Unified Customs Regime, they impose a customs

Table 1. Statutory Tax Rates and Tax Regimes in the MENA

	CIT Rates	Indirect Tax Standard Rates (Tax Regime)	Top PIT Rates	Tax Treaty Network (***)
		Non-Resource Countries		
Egypt	25 (*)	10 (GST)	25	51
Jordan	14	16 (GST)	14	30
Lebanon	15	10 (VAT)	21	33
Morocco	30	20 (VAT)	38	37
Syria	22	NA (**)	22	20
Tunisia	25	18 (VAT)	35	48
Average	*21,83*			
		Resource-Rich Countries		
Algeria	19	17 (VAT)	35	20
Bahrain	NA (*)	NA	NA	39
Iraq	15 (*)	NA	15	a few
Kuwait	15	NA (**)	NA	40
Libya	20	NA	10	10
Oman	12 (*)	NA	NA	28
Qatar	10 (*)	NA (**)	NA	40
Saudi Arabia	20 (*)	NA (**)	NA	25
UAE	55 (*)	NA (**)	NA	60
Yemen	20 (*)	5 (GST)	15	a few
Average	*20,66*			

(*) These countries apply different rates for oil and gas companies. CIT rates for incomes of oil and gas companies are 46% at Bahrain; 40.55% at Egypt; 35% at Iraq; 55% at Oman; 35% at Qatar; 30% for natural gas sector and 85% for hydrocarbon and oil sector at Saudi Arabia; 55% at UAE; %35 at Yemen.

(**) No any indirect tax regime. However, introducing a VAT in the future is speculated.

(***) The number of tax treaties. The values indicate approximate numbers because the treaty numbers may vary by sources consider whether treaties in force or concluded.

NA = The tax does not applied.

Source: KPMG (2014), Deloitte (2014), CroweHorwath (2014)

duty rate of five percent on most imports into the country, while they have usually not VAT or GST. In most of the GCC countries, wholly owned GCC entities are exempt from corporate taxation. Again, these countries do not tax resident individuals under a PIT. Thus, in these countries, the CIT becomes a tool to tax foreign companies and investors and CIT rates in question are generally applicable to only foreign entities. Some of these countries impose some municipal taxes or religious taxes as zakat[1] as direct taxes on income.

According to Table 1, on average, corporate income tax rates tend to be higher in oil importer MENA countries than those on non-resource activities in resource-rich MENA countries. In particular Qatar and Oman are among countries that have the lowest CIT rates in the world. Many countries differentiate CIT tax rates to some extent by sectors (manufacturing, services, tourism, exporting, tobacco, agriculture, banking etc. or by profit levels (for instance, rates in Syria are progressive from 10% to 22%. In Oman, profits exceeding a certain amount of income are taxes. Before 2008, Kuwait used a progressive CIT rates ranged from 0 percent to 55 percent).

However, the most remarkable differentiation is seen in taxing of oil and gas profits in the oil exporter countries of the MENA region. Oil exporter countries apply different rates for oil and gas companies. CIT rates for profits of oil and gas companies are 46% at Bahrain; 40.55% at Egypt; 35% at Iraq; 55% at Oman; 35% at Qatar; 30% for natural gas sector and 85% for hydrocarbon and oil sector at Saudi Arabia; 55% at UAE[2]; %35 at Yemen. Resource-poor countries are expected to be responsive to competition for international investments and to revenue mobilization for public financing. Therefore, the rate reduction is more likely in these countries. Indeed, in the last few years, the CIT rate has decreased In Syria, Tunisia, and Egypt.

Generally, VAT/GST rates tend to be lower in resource-rich countries (Crivelli & Gupta, 2014, p. 94). However, most of oil exporters of MENA do not even a general indirect tax regime in the form of VAT or GST. Among these countries, only Algeria and Yemen applies a general sales tax or VAT. However, economic and fiscal pressures have revealed the debate towards the implementation of a VAT in some of these countries. Although it has not been officially announced, introducing a VAT in some GCC countries is speculated. While standard GST rates in Egypt, Lebanon, and Yemen are quite below the world average, standard VAT/GST rates in other oil-importer countries is close to the average of other groups of countries. Morocco and Tunisia in particular, tend to have higher VAT rate. Again, most of the GCC countries do not apply a personal income tax. Only Morocco, Tunisia, and Algeria have high top rates of PIT as European countries. In other MENA countries, PIT rates are below the world average.

TAXATION, INSTITUTIONS AND GOVERNANCE IN THE MENA REGION

As stated by Schumpeter a century ago, the fiscal history does indeed have an enormous influence of the history of nations. While the country's tax system reflects political interactions between the rulers and citizens (and among citizens), its political institutions, the distribution of power in the society, changes in fiscal methods/forms shapes societal and political relationships, possibly together with crises (Musgrave 1992). Margaret Levi (1988) emphasizes in her seminal study that "*the history of state revenue production is the history of the evolution of the state*". And she continues "*...changes in the relative bargaining power, transaction costs, and discount rates* [of rulers] *will lead to determinant modifications in revenue production policies.*"

While tax systems underwrite the capacity of states to carry out their goals, they can be considered as a reflection and one of the central areas of societal and political interactions beyond the raising revenue. Brautigam (2008) argued that taxation may play the central role in building and sustaining the power of states, and shaping their ties to society by establishing a social contract and stimulating institution building, therefore in the formation of democratic states. There are powerful linkages between taxation and state-building, state-sustaining, democratic relationships and accountable governance through the nation. The impact of tax system on development is not only related to extracting revenue to finance economic development but also building socio-political institutions to support development for long-run. Therefore, tax systems of countries in the MENA region should be considered with regard to these reflections as well.

It is widely recognized that the political relationships between governments and citizens, corruption, bad governance, unaccountable governments and lack of rule of law have been the problematic areas in many MENA countries (Farrag & Ezzat, 2015) in terms of establishing an effective social contract between the state and people. From this perspective, while problems of fiscal relationship between the government and citizens can be seen as one of reason of recent political turmoil, political challenges put forward the set of opportunities to improve institutions for economic and politic development through especially reforming fiscal system.

Good Governance and Taxation: An Overview

Although there is no consensus on the definition or measurement of governance, good governance as the political process of the effective provision of collective goods can be thought as having three main operational dimensions (Moore, 2007, p. 15): the *responsiveness* of states to citizens (an orientation to meeting citizens' needs), the *accountability* of states to citizens (the existence of institutionalized mechanisms as electoral democracy), the political and/or bureaucratic *capability* of states to determine policies and to deliver public services by considering citizens' demands and competing interests. Developing countries can be characterized low on all these dimensions and increasing governance is considered good for the nation (Moore, 2004). Indeed, the relationship between good governance and revenue system of the state is bidirectional.

While better governance helps participation of citizens in collective action of financing the state by increasing tax compliance, an effective and sustainable tax system can help improve the quality of governance and political institutions by producing a productive revenue bargaining system. The first argument can be questioned by examining the impact of political institutions on tax effort or the level of taxation. In many developing countries, tax effort and tax revenues as a share of GDP is considerably low. This fact can be explained not only by the low level of economic activity and tax bases but also by political institutions and political will according to Bird et al. (2008). As shown by Bird et al. (2008), a more legitimate and responsive state is likely an essential precondition for a more adequate level of tax effort, therefore countries can improve their tax performance through improving their governance structure and institutions such as enhancing voice or accountability and reducing corruption.

However, the tax system and fiscal relationship between the state (rulers) and taxpayers (citizens) can improve governance structure and institutions in the country. Considering the structure of government total revenue, depending on whether largely revenue in the form of broad taxation or non-tax revenue (mostly from either aid or natural resources) can be seen as an important factor that reflects the political process of revenue bargaining and state-citizen relationships. Depending on revenue in the form of taxation can be expected to stimulate good governance in a few ways (OECD, 2010; Moore, 2007; Moore 2013):

1. Governments which mainly depend on tax revenues have stronger incentives for promoting economic growth. Since the government becomes focused on obtaining revenue by taxing citizens, it is motivated to promote the prosperity of its citizens.
2. Since tax collection requires a functioning administration and bureaucratic apparatuses, its development may stimulate improvements in state capacity in general.
3. The experience of being taxed motivates citizens to be more responsive public policies, quality of public services, the value for money, the way the state uses tax revenue and corruption. Since taxation engages taxpayers in politics, governments which rely on tax revenues have incentives to improve government in order to ensure tax compliance. While citizens' reactions to taxation forces governments to explain their case for revenue, and to engage in bargaining of various kinds with taxpayers, revenue bargaining around taxation becomes a forum of healthy conflict between citizens and the state. Therefore, this process of revenue bargaining around taxation will tend to create more accountable governments. By taxing, the state is expected to be more responsive to citizens' demands and more capable.

A productive revenue bargaining might encourage taxpayers' complying, while it reduces the economic and political costs of taxation. Thus, taxing can become a forum of political interaction between state and citizen on revenue and policies by organizing conflicts and negotiations both among citizens and between rulers and citizens. Revenue bargaining with citizens over tax issues makes governments more accountable, while taxpayers mobilize to negotiate their demands on tax and public policies. Bargaining process is expected to result in efficient public policies and institutionalized process of assessment and collecting in tax administration, as both tax compliance and state capacity increases. Thus, the matter for developing countries is not only extracting more revenue to finance government spending through taxation but also establishing institutional framework that would produce more public benefit from public money (Tanzi, 2016).

Figure 4 shows that there are correlations between revenue mobilization and governments' effectiveness (R^2=0.58) and control of corruption (R^2=0.29). The efficiency of revenue mobilization, signals the institutional quality of revenue mobilizing at the country, given the country's stage of development, which is a clustered score of 16 criteria measured by World Bank Group International Development Association (IDA). Government effectiveness is intended to capture perceptions of the quality of public services, the quality of the civil service and the degree of its independence from political pressures, the quality of policy formulation and implementation, and the credibility of the government's commitment to such policies, while control of corruption is an indexed value to capture perceptions of the extent to which public power is exercised for private gain, including both petty and grand forms of corruption, and a high value of this variable indicates a good level of governance performance (Kaufmann et al., 2010). Thus, an efficient revenue mobilization is associated with more capable, effective and accountable governments.

Empirical evidence also supports this fact. Tanzi and Davoodi (1997) show that corruption reduces growth by lowering government revenue need to finance productive spending, while it reduces growth by increasing unproductive public spending and reducing the quality of infrastructure. Friedman et al.

Figure 4. Revenur mobilization, effectiveness, and corruption
Source: World Bank, World Governance Indicators; World Bank IDA, Country Policy and Institutional Assessment

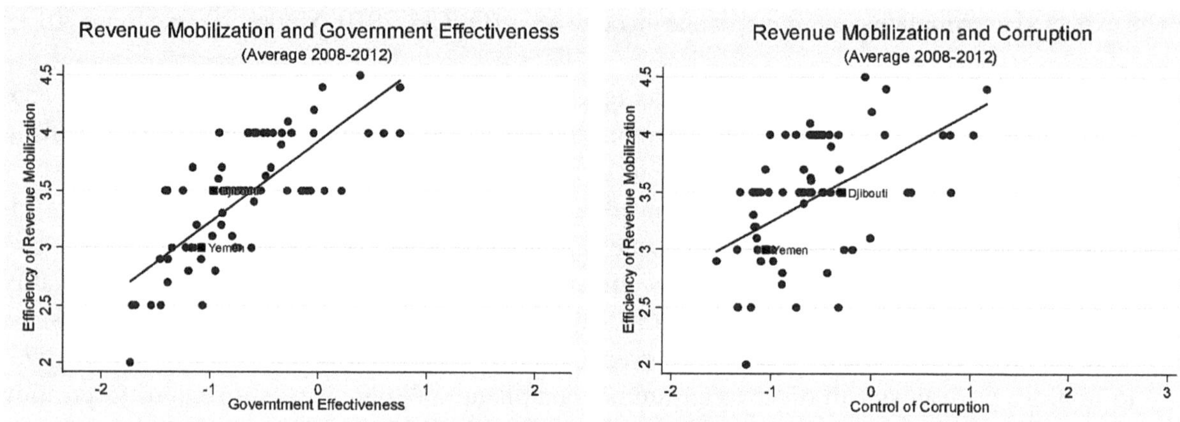

(2000) have found that corruption reduces tax revenues as a percent of both official and total GDP, while relatively uncorrupt governments can sustain high tax rates. Slemrod (2003) emphasizes and provides evidence that the perceptions of government performance and corruption affect an individual's willingness to evade taxes. It harms the governments' capabilities of revenue mobilization to raise funds through fostering to use tax evasion and tax avoidance schemes, and through rendering tax collection institutions less effective by colluding between taxpayers and collectors to reduce remissions (Kauffman, 2010; Ivayna et al., 2010). Corruption not only reduces the level of taxes but also distorts the composition of government revenue. Hwang (2002) shows that corruption inversely affects tax revenue as a share of GDP, while it is positively associated with the taxes on international trade. In MENA region, the low level of tax revenue and revenue composition which depends on resource revenue and other taxes than broader taxes such as income and consumption could be seen as related to poor governance performance of the region.

The relationship between governance and taxation in the MENA region has empirically studied relatively less. Imam and Jacobs (2007) find that corruption does not have a statistically significant impact on total tax revenues in the Middle East, while taxes requiring frequent interactions between tax authorities and individuals, namely trade taxes are most affected by corruption. Taxes on international trade and taxes on excise and specific services are negatively affected by corruption, direct taxes imposed on corporation and individuals are not much affected by corruption. Tosun (2006) finds that the quality of governance affects the tax structures in the MENA countries more than in other comparable non-OECD countries. However, according to his results, the quality of governance has a negative effect on only the payroll taxes and the property taxes, while the results for income and consumption taxes are not significant.

From the historical experience of Western Europe and later of North America, the development of 'fiscal state' and bargaining between governments and taxpayers has played a central role in state building and the emergence of parliamentary democratic governance. In fact, contemporary developing countries are products of a different fiscal and political environment, compared to Western Europe countries in the eighteenth and nineteenth centuries, despite some recent experiment on the fact that tax relationship has improved the growth and state capacity in some East Asian developmental states. Undoubtedly, tax regimes have become more complicated in all countries, while contemporary states tax more and spend a lot. On the other hand, historical Europe countries had heavily depended on revenues from their taxpayers relative to contemporary non-Europe countries which have opportunities for other revenue sources than their own taxpayers, like natural resource rents, foreign aids and foreign debts[3] (Moore, 2008, p. 334; Moore, 2007, p. 19).

However, it is the case that unresponsive governments to citizens' demands and weak tax systems coexist in many contemporary developing countries. An efficient tax system can be characterized as one that encourages economic growth, lessens extreme inequalities, provides enough funds of essential public services and promotes political accountability, builds the political legitimacy of the state. A small number of taxpayers, prevalence of non-tax revenue and complicated tax-benefit systems in most developing countries (resource-rich or not) lead to an invisible revenue-public services systems to citizens; reduce rulers' incentive to be responsive to citizen demands and results in the inefficient revenue bargaining and tax system.

Lack of dependence on citizens for revenue on account of generating revenue either from small number of taxpayers like a few multinational companies or from non-tax sources such as resource rents or foreign aids is seen as a major cause of bad governance and institutions. In this case, the state and rulers have no incentives to be responsive citizens' demands to negotiate with them, while citizens have no incentives to engage in politics and to monitor government policies including particularly tax policies.

As pointed out by Moore (2007), in the case of the lack of an efficient tax system and a productive revenue bargaining, taxpayers might be motivated to pass over collective action and instead to engage in individualized strategies to solve their problems, for example through bribery. Widespread bribery and corruption could partly be explained by revenue bargaining system in developing countries. As in some resource-rich MENA countries, if a few large transnational corporations provide a large proportion of the more potential tax bases, these taxpayers have strong incentives to negotiate individually with government, to influence both tax legislation and its practical application by the tax administration (Moore, 2007, p. 20). For instance, in UAE, actual tax rates on foreign companies (mostly banks and oil companies) are determined by individual concessions between the company and the respective emirate. In most developing countries including the MENA region, main direct formal contract of peoples and businesses with the stare is mostly through interaction with tax authorities. In the case of this interaction results in an experience of an arbitrary egregious administrative behavior, inefficient tax administration may be to weaken institutional quality between the people and the state (Bird, 2016).

Natural Resource Revenue and the Quality of Governance

As stated above, if the state has access to sources of revenue than broad taxation, it does not have incentive to bargain with citizen. A well-documented case for this argument is the "resource curse". States which earn large rents from oil, gas and mineral extracting sectors are not dependent on their citizens' revenue and thus, they have few incentives to promote broad economic development and to be responsive to citizens' demands. In such a case, an institutionalized and visible fiscal exchange and fiscal contract through revenue bargaining cannot be emerged[4]. Thus, natural resource wealth lead to reduce both the rulers' incentives to resource mobilization through taxing (supply side) (Moore, 1998; Moore, 2007) and the citizens' incentives for the public scrutiny of government by participating in public decision-making and consequently, domestic tax effort (demand side) (Collier, 2006).

Generally, statistical findings show a significant negative correlation between resource revenues (generally from hydrocarbons) and non-resource revenues (mainly taxes). Empirical findings from Bornhost et al. (2009), Ossowski and Gonzales (2012), Thomas and Treviño (2013) and Crivelli and Gupta (2014) confirm this fact with respect to the impact of natural resource revenues on non-resource domestic revenue for various group of countries. To findings of these studies, the presence of natural resource revenues is balanced the declining non-resource revenues. Any increase in resource revenue corresponds to a reduction in domestic (non-resource) revenues.

The left panel of Figure 5 that presents a data plot of resource revenues and tax revenues for 38 resource-rich countries confirms the negative correlation between the two variables as a share of GDP (R^2=0.41 for whole sample, R2=0.46 for the MENA). Right panel displays the relationship between 'fiscal dependency' on resource revenues (resource revenue as a share of total government revenue excluding grants) and natural resource rents (total natural resources rents as the difference between the price of a commodity and the average cost of producing it) (R^2=0.50).

Although natural resource was regarded as a contributing factor to be included in the production function to the country's economic growth (Rostow, 1960) prior to the 1980s, the literature was evolved in the fact that natural resource abundance could lead to poor economic performance in course of time. Sachs and Warner (1995, 1997) show that resource-rich countries grow more slowly than others and there is a clear negative relationship between natural resource and growth. In some cases as East Asian countries, the lack of natural resources has worked as motivating factor for creating developmental states, rapid economic growth and even making the people societally conscious on the nations' vulnerability. (Erdoğdu, 2015, p. 14; Erdoğdu, 2004, p. 274).

Beyond early studies that point out natural resource abundance's negative effect on manufacturing sector and productivity through the real exchange rate which is known the Dutch Disease (Corden & Neary, 1982; Krugman, 1987), a growing body of literature on poor economic performance in the resource rich countries emphasizes institutional and political features. Some studies concentrate on rent seeking behaviors of ruling elites (Davis & Tilton, 2005) or of entrepreneurs by departing from productive activities (Torvik, 2002). Findings support the importance of institutional structures and governance in the relationship between resource revenues (or rents) and economic performance. Sala-i-Martin and

Figure 5. Resource revenue, tax revenue, and natural resource rents
Source: Author's calculation from the data by Crivelli and Gupta (2014) and IMF, World Economic Outlook

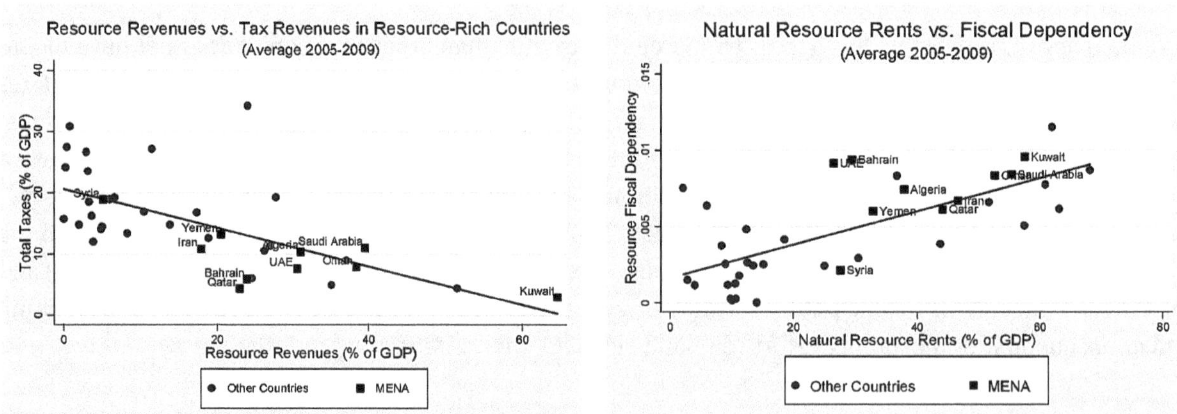

Subramanian (2003), Isham et al. (2003) and Robinson et al. (2006) argue that resource revenue erode institutional development and create dysfunctional governments and governance institutions by obstructing public pressures for institutional reforms and by making rulers avoid from accountability.

Mehlum et al. (2006) suggest that natural resource curse varies with the strength of institutions. Leite and Weidmann (1999) argue natural resource abundance creates opportunities for rent seeking and is an important factor that determines corruption level. Ades and Di Tella (1999) finds that countries where have higher rents tend to have higher corruption levels. Bhattacharyya and Hodler (2010) argue that the quality of political institutions also determines how natural resource revenues affect economic policy choices and corruption. Accordingly, higher natural resource revenues increase corruption by the political leaders if political institutions are weak, but not if political institutions are strong. Collier and Hoeffler (2009) show that weak accountability in resource-rich democracies leads to a reduction in growth.

Generally, a causal relationship may be anticipated toward illegitimacy and inefficiency of public authority (bad governance and bad governments) from dependency on rents (from natural resources or foreign aids) rather than taxes (Moore, 2008, p. 34). As seen in the Figure 6, increases in natural resource rents as a share of GDP are associated with the ruling's legitimacy (R^2=0.35) and bribery in relation with public officials (R^2=0.38). However, Kuwait, Oman, the UAE, and Qatar have higher legitimacy score despite their high level of natural resource rents. We see only four of MENA countries because of data availability in comparison with bribery to rents. It is clear that Yemen has a widespread bribery problem from viewpoint of enterprises surveyed.

Figure 7 presents relationships between government revenue and accountability supports the fact of negative correlation between non-tax revenue and accountability[5] (R^2=0.28) and of negative correlation between non-tax revenue and the level of democracy (R^2=0.47). However, the difference in accountability levels among the MENA countries is not clear, while some of oil exporter gulf countries such as Kuwait, Oman, UAE and Qatar have more or less same levels of voice and accountability score. But other resource-rich MENA countries have lower level of accountability than oil importer MENA. Kuwait, Oman, the UAE, and Qatar have better institutions on governance among resource-rich MENA countries, while governance levels are low in all MENA region compared to world average. On the other hand, the MENA countries except Lebanon exhibit autocratic tendencies, as oil exporter MENA countries have more autocratic administration than oil importers.

Figure 6. Natural resource rents, leticimacy, and bribery
Source: World Bank, World Development Indicators, Center for Systemic Peace, Enterprise Survey

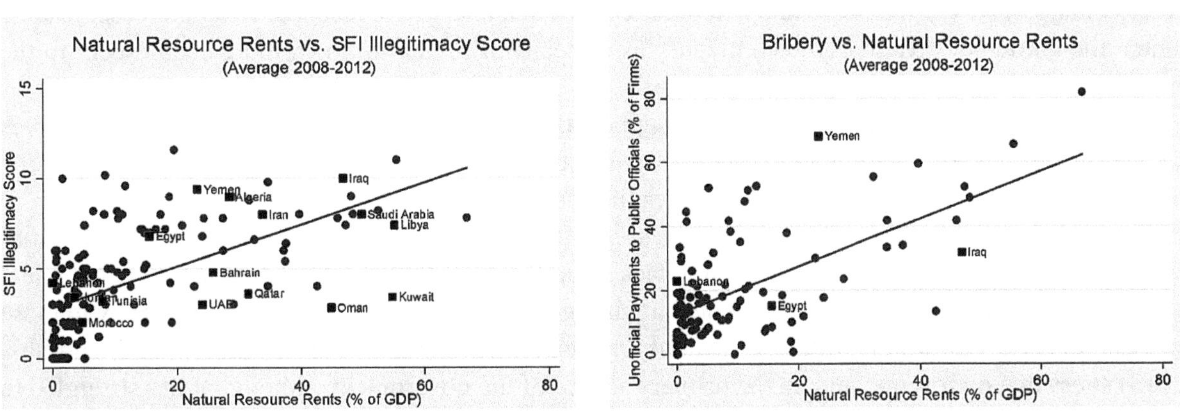

Figure 7. Non-tax revenure, accountability, and democracy
Source: World Bank, World Development Indicators; World Bank, Worldwide Governance Indicators; Center for Systemic Peace

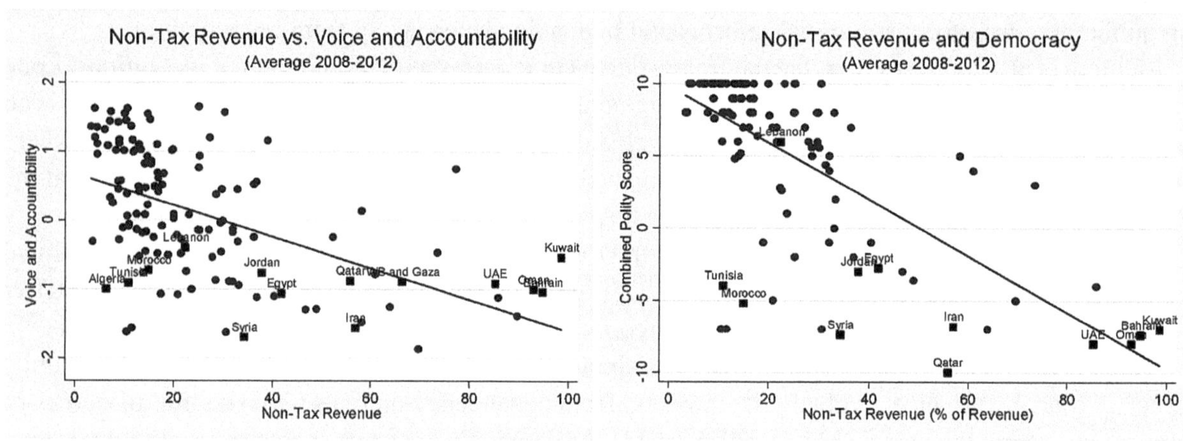

According to Collier and Hoeffler, (2005), public scrutiny is generally weaker in countries with high natural resource rents because of lower taxation, and patronage politics are thus more likely, as resource-rich countries have tended to be autocratic and also have tended to use their resource wealth badly[6]. Bhattacharyya and Hodler (2014) show that resource rents are negatively associated with financial development in countries with weak political institutions, but this negative effect decreases in absolute value as the quality of political institutions improves. They argue that this finding imply that the ruling elite has less incentive to foster contract enforcement while getting large natural resource rents, therefore, democratization could help to foster financial development in resource-rich countries. Crystal (1990), Ross (2001) and Herb (2005) argue that the alleviation of government accountability results from the greater availability of natural resource rents.

Governments may use their oil revenues to relieve social pressures that might otherwise lead to demands for greater accountability, while governments which derive sufficient revenues from the sale of oil, they are likely to tax their populations less heavily or not at all (Ross, 2001, p. 332). Ross (2009) shows evidence on the fact that oil revenue is strongly associated with a less favorable view of democracy amongst World Values Survey's respondents. More recently, from household survey data, McGuirk (2013) shows that increases in resource rents lower perceived tax enforcement, which itself is a significant predictor of the demand for accountability, as there are a negative relationship between a variety of aggregate tax measures and resource rents. When and where resource rents increase, leaders lighten the burden of taxation on the citizenry as a means of rendering them more acquiescent to the current regime's policies.

Some cases on Middle East countries also support these facts. For instance, Crystal (1990) observes that by oil discoveries, the governments of Kuwait and Qatar have become less accountable to the traditional merchant class. Brand (1992) argues that decreases in foreign aid in 1980s led to Jordan to have greater demand for political representation. In MENA case, contemporary paternalistic and non-systematic subsidy systems[7] contribute to the lack of accountability demand by making invisible fiscal connection and preventing efficient revenue bargaining. Furthermore, the resource dependency in these countries is persistent despite of efforts diversifying economic activities. For instance, Hamdi and Sbia (2013) stress that oil revenue remain the primary source of the government, although it has struggled to implement structural reforms to diversify economic activity since the late 1970s.

CONCLUSION

The MENA countries suffer from problems such as high level of youth unemployment, rapid demographic change caused by political turbulence and instability in the region, operating the rule of law, bloated public sector, and low levels of entrepreneurship, investment and FDI. These challenges that affect economic performance impose pressures to reform fiscal systems as well as public administration and economy policy in general. Tax policy should be designed to promote economic performance, to support economic development and to contribute solving these problems. International trends of tax reforms (by blueprints extracted from developed countries' experience) and international tax competition to attract FDI (such as lowering corporate tax rates) also imposes constraints on efforts about tax reforms in the region. Countries in the region need a "growth-friendly" tax system and tax administration as well as generating enough revenue for the provision of public services for economic and social development.

Improving the quality of governance through taxation is also important to promote economic growth and efficiency. Poor governance, common corruption and problematic political relationship are recognized as the most important obstacles to economic development in the region. Revenue systems which depend on revenue other than taxes (and those on consumption taxes and customs in tax systems) and benefit systems which consist of non-systematic, large subsidies and paternalistic fiscal policies could be considered as the main reasons causing the persistence of these problems. Modernizing tax systems and tax administration in the countries of the region would help to improve their governance, to create democracy and enhance the accountability of governments and to construct a fiscal contract between governments and citizens. A visible and transparent tax-benefit system (through taxes rather than non-tax revenue, and direct taxes rather than consumption taxes and customs) may also create public pressure to accountable governments and good governance, efficient public administrations.

Undoubtedly, the main objectives of taxation are to raise revenue and to promote economic performance of the country by increasing economic growth and ameliorating inequalities. Although improving the governance and institutions is not a main objective of tax reforms, a legitimate tax system can help to establish a legitimate political interaction through the nation. A legitimate tax system can be obtained by increasing tax policy's capability to reach foregoing main objectives and consequently by establishing parties' effective participation in decision making process, that is productive revenue bargaining.

ACKNOWLEDGMENT

The author is grateful to Professor M. Mustafa Erdogdu and two anonymous referees for valuable comments and suggestions; and Ernesto Crivelli and Sanjeev Gupta for invaluable data on resource revenue. All the remaining errors are, of course, the author's.

REFERENCES

Ades, A., & Di Tella, R. (1999). Rents, Competition, and Corruption. *The American Economic Review*, *89*(4), 98–993. doi:10.1257/aer.89.4.982

Arab Monetary Fund. (2011). *Economic Statistics Bulletin of Arab Countries*, 31. Retrieved from www.amf.org.ae

Bhattacharyya, S., & Hodler, R. (2010). Natural Resources, Democracy and Corruption. *European Economic Review*, *54*(4), 608–621. doi:10.1016/j.euroecorev.2009.10.004

Bhattacharyya, S., & Hodler, R. (2014). Do Natural Resource Revenues Hinder Financial Development? The Role of Political Institutions. *World Development*, *55*, 101–113. doi:10.1016/j.worlddev.2013.12.003

Bird, R. (2016). Transparency, Technology and Taxation. In M. M. Erdoğdu & B. Christiansen (Eds.), *Handbook of Research on Public Finance in Europe and the MENA Region*. Hershey, PA, USA: IGI Global.

Bird, R. M., Martinez-Vazques, J., & Torgler, B. (2008). Tax Effort in Developing Countries and High Income Countries: The Impact of Corruption, Voice and Accountability. *Economic Analysis and Policy*, *38*(1), 55–71. doi:10.1016/S0313-5926(08)50006-3

Bornhost, F., Gupta, S., & Thornton, J. (2009). Natural Resource Endowments and the Domestic Revenue Effort. *European Journal of Political Economy*, *25*(4), 439–446. doi:10.1016/j.ejpoleco.2009.01.003

Brand, L. A. (1992). Economic and Political Liberalization in a Rentier Economy: The Case of the Hashemite Kingdom of Jordan. In I. Harik & D. J. Sullivan (Eds.), *Privatization and Liberalization in the Middle East* (pp. 167–188). Bloomington, IN, USA: Indiana University Press.

Brautigam, D. A. (2008). Introduction: Taxation and State-Building in Developing Countries. In D. Brautigam, O. Fjeldstad, & M. Moore (Eds.), *Taxation and State-Building in Developing Countries* (pp. 1–33). Cambridge: Cambridge University Press. doi:10.1017/CBO9780511490897.001

Citizen-State Relations: Improving Governance through Tax Reforms. (2010). *OECD*. Retrieved from ww.oecd.org

Colgan, F. D. (2014). Oil, Domestic Politics, and International Conflict. *Energy Research & Social Science*, *1*, 198–205. doi:10.1016/j.erss.2014.03.005

Collier, P. (2006). Is Aid Oil? An Analysis of Whether Africa Can Absorb More Aid. *World Development*, *34*(9), 1482–1497. doi:10.1016/j.worlddev.2006.01.002

Collier, P., & Hoeffler, A. (2005). Democracy and Resource Rents (Working Paper GPRG-WPS-016). *Global Poverty Research Group*.

Collier, P., & Hoeffler, A. (2009). Testing the Neocon Agenda: Democracy in Resource-Rich Societies. *European Economic Review*, *53*(3), 293–308. doi:10.1016/j.euroecorev.2008.05.006

Corden, W. M., & Neary, J. P. (1982). Booming Sector and De-industrialisation in a Small Open Economy. *The Economic Journal*, *92*(368), 825–848. doi:10.2307/2232670

Crivelli, E., & Gupta, S. (2014). Resource Blessing, Revenue Curse? Domestic Revenue Effort in Resource-Rich Countries. *European Journal of Political Economy*, *35*, 88–101. doi:10.1016/j.ejpoleco.2014.04.001

CroweHorwath. (2014). *Europe, Middle East & Africa Tax Facts 2014*. Retrieved on January 15, 2015, from: www.crowehorwath.net

Crystal, J. (1990). *Oil and Politics in the Gulf: Rulers and Merchants in Kuwait and Qatar*. Cambridge: Cambridge University Press. doi:10.1017/CBO9780511558818

Davis, G. A., & Tilton, J. E. (2005). The Resource Curse. *Natural Resources Forum*, *29*(3), 233–242. doi:10.1111/j.1477-8947.2005.00133.x

Erdoğdu, M. M. (2004). South Korean State Capacity: From Development to Crisis Management. In K.S. Jomo (Ed.), After The Storm: Crises, Recovery and Sustaining Development in Four Asian Economies (pp. 260-302). Singapore: Singapore University Press.

Erdoğdu, M. M. (2015). Culture of Development and Developmental Capacity of States: The Korean Case. In B. Christiansen & J. Koeman (Eds.), Nationalism, Cultural Indoctrination, and Economic Prosperity in the Digital Age (pp. 1-51). Hershey, PA, USA: IGI Global. doi:10.4018/978-1-4666-7492-9.ch001

Farrag, F., & Ezzat, A. M. (2015). The Impact of Corruption on Economic Growth: A Comparative Analysis between Europe and MENA Countries. In M. M. Erdoğdu & B. Christiansen (Eds.), *Handbook of Research on Comparative Economic Development Perspectives on Europe and the MENA Region*. Hershey, PA, USA: IGI Global.

Friedman, E., Johnson, S., Kaufmann, D., & Zoido-Lobaton, P. (2000). Dodging the Grabbing Hand: The Determinants of Unofficial Activity in Countries. *Journal of Public Economics*, *76*(3), 459–493. doi:10.1016/S0047-2727(99)00093-6

Hamdi, H., & Sbia, R. (2013). Dynamic Relationships between Oil Revenues, Government Spending and Economic Growth in an Oil-dependent Economy. *Economic Modelling*, *35*, 118–125. doi:10.1016/j.econmod.2013.06.043

Hwang, J. (2002). A Note on the Relationship between Corruption and Government Revenue. *Journal of Economic Development*, *27*(2), 161–178.

Imam, P. A., & Jacobs, D. F. (2007). Effect of Corruption of Tax Revenues in the Middle East (IMF Working Paper WP/07/270). *International Monetary Fund*.

Isham, J., Pritchett, L., Woolcock, M., & Busby, G. (2003). The Varieties of the Resource Experience: How Natural Resource Export Structures Affect the Political Economy of Economic Growth (Working Paper 03-08). *Middlebury College Economics Discussion Papers*, Middlebury, Vermont.

Ivanyna, M., Mourmouras, A., & Rangazas, P. (2010). The Culture of Corruption, Tax Evasion, and Optimal Tax Policy (Working Paper 10/xx). *IMF Working Papers*.

James, S. (2016). The Difficulties of Achieving Successful Tax Reform. In M. M. Erdoğdu & B. Christiansen (Eds.), *Handbook of Research on Public Finance in Europe and the MENA Region*. Hershey, PA, USA: IGI Global.

Kaufman, D. (2010, April 19). Can corruption adversely affect public finance in industrialized countries? *Brookings Institution Opinions*.

Kaufmann, D., Kraay, A., & Matruzzi, M. (2010). The Worldwide Governance Indicators: methodology and analytical issues (Working Paper 5430). *World Bank Policy Research Working Papers*.

Corporate and Indirect Tax Rate Survey 2014. (2014). *KMPG*. Retrieved from www.kpmg.com

Krugman, P. (1987). The narrow moving band, the Dutch disease, and the competitive consequences of Mrs. Thatcher. *Journal of Development Economics*, *27*(1-2), 41–55. doi:10.1016/0304-3878(87)90005-8

Leite, C., & Weidmann, J. (1999). Does mother nature corrupt? natural resources, corruption, and economic growth (Working Paper WP/99/85). *International Monetary Fund*.

Levi, M. (1988). *Of Rule and Revenue*. Berkeley, CA: University of California Press.

McGuirk, E. F. (2013). The Illusory leader: Natural resources, taxation and accountability. *Public Choice*, *154*(3-4), 285–313. doi:10.1007/s11127-011-9820-0

Mehlum, H., Moene, K., & Torvik, R. (2006). Institutions and the resource curse. *The Economic Journal*, *116*(508), 1–20. doi:10.1111/j.1468-0297.2006.01045.x

Middle East Tax handbook 2014. (2014). *Deloitte*. Retrieved from www.deloitte.com

Moore, M. (1998). Death without taxes: democracy, state capacity and aid dependence in the fourth world. In M. Robinson & G. White (Eds.), *The democratic development state*. Oxford: Oxford University Press.

Moore, M. (2004). The development of political underdevelopment. In G. Harrison (Ed.), *Global encounters: IPE, development and global governance*. London: Palgrave Macmillan.

Moore, M. (2007). How does taxation affect the quality of governance (Working Paper 280). *IDS*, Brighton, UK.

Moore, M. (2008). Between coercion and contact: competing narratives on taxation and governance. In D. Brautigam, O. Fjeldstad, & M. Moore (Eds.), *Taxation and State-Building in Developing Countries* (pp. 34–63). Cambridge: Cambridge University Press. doi:10.1017/CBO9780511490897.002

Moore, M. (2013). Obstacles to increasing tax revenue in low income countries (Working Paper 15). *ICTD*.

Musgrave, R. A. (1992). Schumpeter's crisis of the tax state. *Journal of Evolutionary Economics*, *2*(2), 89–113. doi:10.1007/BF01193535

Ossowski, R., & Gonzales, A. (2012). Manna from heaven: the impact of nonrenewable resource revenues on other revenues of resource exporters in Latin America and the Caribbean (Working Paper 337). *Inter-American Development Bank*, Washington, DC.

Robinson, J. A., Torvik, R., & Verdier, T. (2006). Political foundations of the resource curse. *Journal of Development Economics*, *79*(2), 447–468. doi:10.1016/j.jdeveco.2006.01.008

Rostow, W. W. (1960). *The stages of economic growth*. Cambridge: Cambridge University Press.

Sachs, J. D., & Warner, A. M. (1995). Natural resource abundance and economic growth (Working Paper 5398). *NBER*.

Sachs, J. D., & Warner, A. M. 1997. Natural Resource Abundance and Economic Growth (Working Paper). *Center for International Development and Harvard Institute for International Development*, Harvard University.

Sala-i-Martin, X., & Subramanian, A. (2003). Addressing the natural resource curse: an illustration from Nigeria (Working Paper 9804). *NBER*.

Slemrod, J. (2003). Trust in public finance. In S. Crossen & H. W. Sinn (Eds.), *Public Finance and Public Policy in the New Century* (pp. 49–88). Cambridge: MIT Press.

Small states: meeting challenges in the global economy. (2000). *World Bank*, Washington, DC.

Sturm, M., Gurtner, F., & Alegre, J.-G. (2009). Fiscal policy challenges in oil-exporting countries a review of key issues (Working Paper 104). *European Central Bank Occasional Paper Series*.

Tanzi, V. (2016). Public Finance in Developing Countries: An Introduction. In M. M. Erdoğdu & B. Christiansen (Eds.), *Handbook of Research on Public Finance in Europe and the MENA Region*. Hershey, PA, USA: IGI Global.

Thomas, A., & Treviño, J. (2013). Resource dependence and fiscal effort in Sub-Saharan Africa (Working Paper 13/188). *International Monetary Fund*.

Torvik, R. (2002). Natural resources, rent seeking and welfare. *Journal of Development Economics*, *67*(2), 455–470. doi:10.1016/S0304-3878(01)00195-X

Tosun, M. S. (2006). Explaining the variation in tax structures in the MENA region (Working Paper 06-0018). *University of Nevada Economics Working Paper Series*.

ENDNOTES

1 Saudi Arabia levies zakat at 2.5 percent on Saudi and GCC nationals and companies owned by them. Libya levies jihad tax at 4 percent of profits.

2 The corporate tax rate applicable in the UAE is 0 percent (most activities) / 20 percent (foreign banking) / 55 percent (foreign oil companies). Although the tax rate applicable to oil companies is generally 55 percent of operating profits, the amount of tax actually paid by such companies is based on a rate agreed in individual concessions between the company and the respective emirate. This rate can range between 55 percent and 85 percent. Municipal taxes are also levied in some of the emirates in the UAE. In Dubai, a 10 percent municipal tax is charged on hotel revenues (usually passed on to the consumer as a service charge), a 10 percent municipality fee is levied on the rent from commercial property, and a 5 percent fee is levied on the rent of residential property. Abu Dhabi does not levy a municipality tax on rented premises, but landlords are required to pay certain annual license fees (which they may pass on to tenants).

3 Moore (2007) point outs that in historical European governments which depends on domestic sources as mainly taxes and domestic debts, the social contract with taxpayers had produced a revenue-raising system through parliamentary control. Thus, they could not avoid confronting and bargaining with their citizens as taxpayers or lenders. While contemporary governments enjoy some autonomy from their own citizens by borrowing heavily internationally, IMF that has an interest in a strong tax system to assure creditors can be repaid could be assumed to substitute the historic role of taxpayers in parliaments.

4 Indeed, the literature suggests other causal mechanisms than the implications of not having to tax. One complementary mechanism is that governments with large revenue from natural resources would buy off opposition and thus keep themselves in power (for a survey of this distinction, see Moore, 1997:21).

5 Non-tax revenue include grants other governments and international organizations, rents, interest, dividends, entrepreneurial incomes, fines, administrative fees and voluntary grants. The variable 'voice and accountability' is from Worldwide Governance Indıcators of World Bank and produced by Kaufmann et al. (2010).

6 However they argue findings on the adverse effect of democracy in resource rich countries. Accordingly, in the absence of resource rents democracies outperform autocracies, in the presence of large resource rents autocracies outperform democracies. Thus, they suggest that resource-rich democracies need a distinctive form of democracy, strong on checks and balances with perhaps less emphasis upon electoral competition.

7 One of the other common characteristics in the domestic political economy of oil rich countries is the use of subsidies, in particular of energy and subsidy systems are mostly unsuccessful in these countries (Colgan, 2014).

Chapter 9
International Tax Competition and Its Reflections in Turkey

Semih N. Öz
Ankara University Political Science Faculty, Turkey

ABSTRACT

International tax competition has been significantly increased since 1980s as a result of liberalized financial and fiscal policies, while this leads sovereign nations faced budgetary deficit problems and public finance related considerations. This paper aims to analyze how Turkish tax system is affected by international tax competition, services submitted by tax havens and facilities used by multinationals. In 2006, a new Corporate Income Tax Law was introduced in Turkey. One of its purposes is to combat against harmful tax competition and therefore it covered defensive measures such as controlled foreign company (CFC), thin capitalization rule and transfer pricing regulation, to prevent companies from leaving their income abroad. This study aims to analyze effects of international tax competition in Turkey whether there are change in tax rates, tax structure, and tax revenue; and how the government respond it, as a beneficiary; or, a loser.

INTRODUCTION

Recently the issue of international tax competition has risen to the fore of the fiscal and political policy debates. International flows of capital and goods and services around the world over the past decades have produced significant challenges for developed and developing countries. Using the facilities of some countries referred to as "tax havens", individuals hide their assets and firms reduce their profits from being taxed where they reside and use of public services. It is often argued that tax havens as a part of tax competition erode the tax base of high tax countries by providing opportunities to their tax payers.

In contrast to tax havens, high tax countries defined them as harmful tax competition. The gradual erosion of the tax base leads governments in high tax nations to take action against harmful tax competition. Governments may respond to international harmful tax competition in one of two ways: As a single country or as part of international collaboration. However, there is an important question related to harmful tax competition: How can a tax system be defined as harmful? The answer is very ambiguous; and, difficult to draw a borderline between tax competition and unfair tax competition.

DOI: 10.4018/978-1-5225-0053-7.ch009

There is an undergoing debate about whether or not tax competition is detrimental to countries which export capital. However, there are many examples of tax payers hide their income from tax authorities using facilities of tax havens (e.g., in 2008), such as 600 German and 50 American citizens who kept their money in Liechtenstein banks, usually in the form of foundations, to help them evade paying tax at home[1]. Governments can defend their fiscal sovereignty rights behind their national frontiers by making legislation and taking necessary precautions. However, the actions of a single country affected by harmful tax competition cannot be enough to solve their problems. Therefore, the second way is cooperating with other governments that are facing same problems to prevent tax evasion, which includes sharing information across borders.

This study aims to analyze effects of international tax competition in Turkey whether there are change in tax rates, tax structure, and tax revenue, and how the government responds to it as a beneficiary or as a loser. This study has five sections. The first part gives the general principles of international taxation that are related to residence and source principles. The second section gives theories and an analytical framework tax competition. The third section evaluates the governments' respond to international tax competition as a single country or as a part of international cooperation work. This part of the study included criticism of the Organization for Economic Co-operation and Development (OECD) work on harmful tax competition. The measures against harmful tax competition have been taken in Turkey is subject of the fourth section. The final section provides an evaluation of the overall study.

1. THE GENERAL PRINCIPLES OF INTERNATIONAL TAXATION

In general, within a taxation framework both personal and corporate income taxes can be levied by two alternative principles which include the *residence principle* and the *source principle*. Under the residence principle, tax payers are taxed uniformly on their worldwide income irrespective of the particular jurisdiction where their income earned. Under the source principle, however, individuals or companies are taxed in a particular jurisdiction where their income earned irrespective of where they reside. Residence- and source-based taxes generate distinct macro-economic implications by generating different effects on the required return on domestic investment and the after tax return on domestic saving (Bovenberg, 1992).

Under the *residence based taxation system*, taxpayers should pay their taxes since they benefit from public services where they reside[2]. Mostly physical presence in a state of 183 days of the year is enough for residence based taxation which is referred to as the 183 days rule. Compared to governments using residence based taxation, governments using source based system have diminished since countries have recognized that the failure to tax residents on income derived from foreign activities undermines the fairness of the tax system and provides residents with a tax incentive to invest abroad. However, a government cannot tax the worldwide income of its residents unless in practice it has the power to do so (UN, 2003b). Application of residence based taxation requires a stronger tax administration than that is in source based taxation system. In this case, governments need to know the activities of their residents in the foreign countries. That is why today governments give special concern to the exchange of information.

Within this context, the Turkish tax system is mainly based on the residence principle, while personal tax payers are required six months of residency in the country to pay tax for their worldwide income, corporate entities are taxed on their world-wide income, if their *legal head office* or the *place of effective management* is located in Turkey. A multinational operating in two countries in which the marginal tax rate on income is different would, *ceteris paribus*, prefer to shift income from the high-tax country to the low-tax country. Such shifting may be accomplished by settled prices of transactions between corporate affiliates or by jurisdictions' international financial policy (UN, 2003).

Investors should be neutral to taxes for their investment decisions considering the 'best' location from an economic perspective. However, there is conflict a between 'locational inefficiency' and 'market failures'; namely, investments may not be placed where the productivity of capital is high because of tax rates. On the other hand, taxation policy may be used to correct distortions or inefficiencies by using specific tax incentives. Determining whether a tax policy is correcting a market failure or is inefficient can be difficult (EU, 2004). Both *capital export neutrality* (CEN) and *capital import neutrality* (CIN) are main concepts which aim to ensure neutrality. Under CEN, investors receive the same tax treatment wherever they invest. CEN may be achieved by taxing residents on a worldwide basis and providing credit for taxes paid abroad. If CEN is imposed by all countries, it is believed this action would maximize world economic efficiency by removing tax consideration decisions on investments. Under CIN, all investors receive the same tax treatment, regardless of where they reside.

2. TAX COMPETITION

a. Definition of Tax Competition

Tax competition may be defined as the situation where independent jurisdictions compete non-cooperatively over the taxation of production factors to influence their location. However, modern literature over tax competition mostly concentrates on capital movements and its taxation. Governments compete with each other by lowering taxes for attracting foreign direct investments, portfolio investments, cross border shoppers, and skilled labor. The instrument of tax competition is mainly *tax rates*, but governments compete through tax bases, if the authorities use various facilities for determining tax base (i.e., deductions), tax treatment of losses, and depreciation rules (Talpos & Crasneac, 2010).

Tax competition may be classified into two groups in terms of public authorities involved that are *horizontal tax competition* and *vertical tax competition*. Horizontal tax competition is defined competition among governments at a single level (i.e. national sovereign governments or local governments). They are same level of government. *Vertical tax competition* is defined competition among different levels of same government (i.e., municipality/states and federal government). They share the same tax base and capital. While asymmetric tax competition occurs between almost equal size countries, asymmetric tax competition occurs if the competition is between countries that have different population size.

b. Tax Competition Theories

Tax competition is a highly debated topic not only in academic but also in policy circles (Gunessee, 2010). The extant literature on tax competition began with Tibeout's article titled, *A Pure Theory of Local Expenditures,* which analyses tax competition among local governments. Tiebout argued that the individuals' benefits less public service if they go to a low-tax jurisdiction. If citizens are faced with an offer that different types or levels of public goods and services, then each citizen will choose the community that best satisfies his or her own particular demands. *If consumers-voters are fully mobile, the appropriate local governments, whose revenue-expenditure patterns are set, adopted by consumer-voters* (Tiebout 1956).

Tiebout's analysis has both normative aspect, in arguing that provision of public goods at the local level is desirable and a positive aspect in predicting that people move in response to local taxes and goods (Pearce, 1992). In the Tiebout model, taxes are generally considered as the price that household pay for their local public goods (Oates, 2005). The assumption that the government can collect a non-distortionary "head tax" from each resident equal to the cost of providing her with her preferred level of public goods is also one of the questionable assumptions of Tiebout. The theoretical literature has located some problems with Tiebouts's argument, and many writers have clarified and extended Tibout's model (Kellman, 1997).

The analysis of tax competition among local governments has generated a large literature since the 1980s (Brueckner, 2010). A formal tax literature on tax competition rooted the model developed by Zodrow and Mieszkowski (1984) and Wilson (1986), of which their model are mostly known as the standard tax competition model. Since the 1980s, there has been much academic research on tax competition. In these models, terms of government interpreted as local, state, or provincial governments within a country, or countries within the world economy (Wilson, 1999). Zodrow and Mieszkowski's work related to analyses of Pigou's proposition that public services are undersupplied if financed by distorting taxes[3]. Some writers later studied about asymmetric tax competition, between countries that are different size.

Bucovetsky (1991) and Wilson (1991) extended the earliest models and indicated that the smaller jurisdiction would levy a lower tax rate, and would be better off, attracting more capital if there were only two jurisdictions differing in size of population. Habermacher and Kirchassner (2012) attempted to have a closer look at the consequences of asymmetric tax competition under different circumstances, and they found: *if size is the only (or at least the most important) difference between two communities between which there is tax competition, and if this difference is large enough, the smaller one will have lower taxes but possibly higher tax revenue per capita*[4]. Tiebout's theory focused on local governments, but with growing international flows of labor and capital, national governments are becoming more like local governments as they compete across national borders (Edward & Rugy, 2002).

Tax competition has effects on federalism in several ways. Goodsimith (1998) discussed the conceptual issue of regarding tax competition that arisen in the fiscal federalism literature: whether tax competition is good or bad and whether tax competition leads to lower or higher tax rates in equilibrium. The theoretical results can go either way, and empirical results can particularly for vertical tax competition, also find contrasting results (Goodsimith 1998)[5]. Tax competition theories suggest that there are at least two governments, they compete each other, and one side lost revenue. One may conclude that tax competition is harmful for the loser governments. However, we may question whether or not tax competition has desirable effects for governments. The answer of this question goes back to Brennan and Buchanan's (1980) model of government as Leviathan that needs to be timed (Talpos & Crasneac, 2010). Tax competition sets limits the growth of government (Mitchell, 2000) and provides politicians with incentive to improve government efficiency, and satisfaction for voters demands (Edward & Rugy, 2002)[6].

3. MEASURES AGAINST TAX COMPETITION

Governments may respond to international harmful tax competition in one of two ways: As a single country or as a part of international cooperation work.

a. Measures Behind the Frontiers

Governments can defend their fiscal sovereign rights behind their national frontiers by making legislation and taking necessary precautions. Since the actions of any single country cannot be adequate to combat harmful tax competition, they co-operate with other governments that are facing same problems to prevent tax evasion, which includes sharing information across borders.

International tax competition leads countries behind their national frontiers have implemented tax reforms that have broadened their tax bases and lowered tax rates. Increased international mobility has increased tax competition and put a downward pressure on tax rates (OECD, 2010b). Tax systems of many developing countries mostly are designed after World War II, in terms of post war economic conditions, trade protection, and capital and labor immobility when very different rates of direct and indirect tax were feasible—but this is no longer the case (Tanzi 1996). This was the case for developing as well as developed countries. Many OECD countries have lowered their personal and corporate income tax rates during the last decades. For instance, *statuary corporate income tax rates* have fallen globally from an average of 50 percent in the mid-1970s to 30 percent in the 2000s.

After the Tax Reform Act of 1986, the corporate income tax rate was lowered from 46% to 34% in the USA. Similar to corporate tax rates, personal tax rates show a clear downward trend (Loretz, 2008). On the contrary, rate reductions are compensated by additional base broadening measures. The way of broadening tax base is to limit tax expenditures that are provisions in the tax code that can be used by tax authorities to encourage certain activities or to support taxpayers in special circumstances. It is often argued that special tax reliefs are introduced in response to tax competition (OECD, 2010). However, broadening tax bases and lowering tax rates polices are center of tax equity and fairness debates.

Moreover, in order to combat tax havens many governments have introduced new regulations such as *CFC* or redefined their *transfer pricing* legislations. In addition, *dual income tax* has been a way of response of governments to international tax competition. It is accepted that the implementation of dual income tax systems which combine a progressive tax schedule for labor income and a lower flat tax rate on personal capital income and corporate income reflect a trade-off between *efficiency* and *equity* (OECD, 2010).

b. International Cooperation Against Tax Competition

As mentioned earlier, for governments under pressure of the tax competition an alternative possibility is collaborating with other governments facing same problems. In this context, as stated in Economic Communiqué of the G-7 Lyon Summit in 1996, the OECD established an international frame work to counter spread harmful tax competition and published its report *Harmful Tax Competition: An Emerging Global Issue* in 1998 (1998 Report). The Report focused on two issues: tax havens and preferential regimes in member countries. OECD forced tax havens to cooperate and member countries to curtail preferential regimes. 1998 Report mainly focused on globalization and its effect on taxation, such as financial and other service activities. The report described this effect as follows.

...globalization has had a positive effect on the development of tax systems. Globalization has, however, also had the negative effects of opening up new ways by which companies and individuals can minimize and avoid taxes and in which countries can exploit these new opportunities by developing tax policies aimed primarily at diverting financial and other geographically mobile capital.

Following publication of the Report, the OECD created a special forum called the *Forum on Harmful Tax Practices*. The Forum has focused on three areas of harmful tax practices in member countries (as preferential regimes); tax havens and involving non-OECD economies that is subject of *level playing field*. In the 1998 Report, the OECD established a framework to counter the spread of harmful tax practices with respect to geographically mobile activities. Following the Economic Communiqué of the G-7 Lyon Summit, like the OECD, in 1997 The EU Council agreed to a package of measures to tackle harmful tax competition in order to help to reduce distortions in the Single Market to prevent excessive losses of tax revenue and to develop tax structures.

The package included a *Code of Conduct* on business taxation, taxation of savings income and the issue of withholding taxes on cross-border interest, royalty payments between companies and; a commitment to roll back existing regimes and refrain from introducing any such measures in the future. The Code is not a legally binding instrument, but it clearly does have political force[7]. Since EU work concentrated on member countries' tax regimes, OECD work of tax competition will be discussed in the following sections.

i. Tax Haven Work

Tax havens[8] can be classified into two types. In one type, the country levies a very low tax rate on the income from manufacturing operations located in its jurisdiction. This type of tax havens may be defined as *production tax havens*. On the contrary, in the second type, the country offers a low tax on the income of corporations whose legal domicile is that country is defined as traditional tax havens (UN, 2003)[9]. Although there is no agreed-upon definition of tax havens (Jackson, 2010), the OECD identified key factors for tax havens in the 1998 Report as follows:

1. **No or Only Nominal Taxes:** No or only nominal taxation on the relevant income is the starting point to classify a jurisdiction as a tax haven.
2. **Lack of Effective Exchange of Information:** Tax havens typically have in place laws or administrative practices under which businesses and individuals can benefit from strict secrecy rules and other protections against scrutiny by tax authorities thereby preventing the effective exchange of information on taxpayers benefiting from the low tax jurisdiction.
3. **Lack of Transparency:** A lack of transparency in the operation of the legislative, legal or administrative provisions is another factor in identifying tax haven.
4. **No Substantial Activities:** The absence of a requirement that the activity be substantial is important since it would suggest that a jurisdiction may be attempting to attract investment or transactions that are purely tax driven.

In 2000, the OECD published the report, *Towards Global Cooperation: Progress in Identifying and Eliminating Harmful Tax Practices (*2000 Report), and listed 35 jurisdictions found to meet these tax haven criteria[10]. Six countries were omitted from the list since they had made advance commitment. The 1998 Report suggested that defensive measures would be more effective if applied by a wide number of countries. Some of the measures were for countries that do not have CFC or equivalent rules, to consider adopting such rules or to impose withholding taxes on certain payments to residents of uncooperative tax havens. Work of the OECD today continues as *Global Forum* on Transparency and Exchange of Information for Tax Purposes.

ii. Preferential Regime Work

The 1998 Report identifies four key criteria for the purpose of identifying and assessing harmful preferential tax regimes: *i*) no or low effective tax rates, *ii*) Ring fencing[11] of regimes, *iii*) lack of transparency[12]; and, *iv*) lack of effective exchange of information. In the 2000 Report, a list of 47 OECD member country regimes grouped under nine categories, which have been identified as potentially harmful. Forum assessed the regimes in the guideline of *Consolidated Application Note*. Then OECD published a progress report in 2006 (OECD, 2006c). Of those regimes, a total of 19 have been abolished, 14 have been amended to remove their potentially harmful features, 13 were found not to be harmful, and only one has been found to be harmful[13]. There were two regimes from Turkey in this work that included *Istanbul Off shore Banking Regime* and *Free Trade Zones* regimes.

c. Bank Secrecy

Bank secrecy was an important challenge of developed countries against tax havens. In 2000 OECD published a report, *Improving Access to Bank Information for Tax Purposes,* of which one of important results was to set out a standard access to bank information. Standards in the Report were summarized as follows: prohibition of anonymous accounts, require financial institutions to identify their customers, re-examine policies and practices that do not permit tax authorities to have access to bank information and take appropriate initiatives to achieve access for the verification of tax liabilities and other tax administration purposes, authorities to have access to bank information (OECD, 2000b). Three years after the publication of the Report, there has no longer been any OECD country that requires a domestic interest to obtain information for a treaty partner (OECD, 2003). These reports mean that the era of *bank secrecy* was over. Later, article 26 of OECD Model Tax Agreement related to exchange of information was modified accordingly.

d. Model Tax Agreement on Exchange of Information in Tax Matters

In 2001, the OECD changed its strategy to tax haven work and shifted the scope of its efforts to improving exchanges of tax information between member countries and tax havens. Today, one of the important outcomes of the OECD Harmful Project is the *Model Agreement on Exchange of Information on Tax Matters* which developed by a working group of Forum. The Model Agreement seeks to co-operation in tax matters through exchange of information by covering upon request for both civil and criminal tax matters.

e. Criticism of OECD Work

The OECD was formed in 1961 to achieve the highest sustainable economic growth and employment and a rising standard of living in Member countries, while maintaining financial stability, thus contributing to the development of the world economy. Since then, the OECD has become one of the world's most influential organizations. The OECD work about harmful tax competition was initiated in the late 1990s, but there remain controversial arguments about it. The work attracted several criticisms from some groups since there was not any empirical evidence of tax competition causing harm (Blumberg, 2001).

Some writers stated that the OECD not asking tax havens to stop being financial centers, but asking them to comply with international standards of disclosure, transparency and non-discrimination (Owens, 2000). However, some stated that the OECD's efforts were an attempt by large countries to dominate small countries (Blumberg, 2001). There was no evidence for a race to the bottom in capital taxation or a meltdown of total tax revenues (Genschel, 2001). Moreover, "Caribbean leaders have stated that tax competition is just another form of free trade in a globalized world" (Mitchell, 2000). From the early 1980s to the mid-1990s, governments of developed countries lowered statutory corporate and personal income rates and eliminated many allowances, exemptions credits, and reliefs (Swank & Steinmo, 2002). Some writers suggested that tax competition does not hurt big countries (Rixen, 2010). There has been little written in the extant literature on the underlying questions of why tax havens exist or why they persist in the face of overwhelming criticism (Rosenzweig, 2010). In the standard tax competition models of Zodrow and Mieszowski (1986) and Wilson (1986), a predicted race to the bottom for small open economies or a clear downward trend cannot yet be observed (Loretz, 2008).

The 1998 Report was accepted a challenge to many global jurisdiction that intentionally aided individuals and corporations in their attempt to minimize taxes paid to their home governments (Kudrle, 2008). Tax holidays related to the physical investment activities (i.e., manufacturing) were out of the scope of the OECD. Many of the tax havens have complained bitterly because of nature process and inadequate consultation and inadequate of treatment (Persuad, 2002). While governments lowering tax rates and broadening their tax base, they also shifted tax burden to consumption and labor and seem to compensate for corporate tax reductions by increasing value-added taxes (Loretz, 2008).

In the literature, two conflicting but complementary principles are generally used to justify taxes, the "*ability to pay*" principle, those who can pay more should pay more; and the "*benefit*" principle, those who benefit most should contribute most (Messere, 2000). Do tax competition change tax structure from "ability to pay" principle to "benefit" principle? Because ability to pay principle is more appropriate to progressive tax schedule, we may conclude that shift in tax burden to sales taxes means less equal taxation. In Latin America region many countries now have VAT and tax rates increased to double digits, exceeding 20 percent in some countries (Wibbles and Arce, 2003). On the other hand, there is a conflict between shift in tax revenue to sales tax and e-commerce taxation difficulties because e-commerce sales is another problematic area of governments' revenue collection[14].

4. TAX COMPETITION AND TURKEY

As a result of liberalization policies of the 1980s, Turkey faced several effects of international tax competition. As a member of the OECD, Turkey was part of OECD Harmful Tax Forum work and thus committed to eliminate any of her *preferential tax regime* found to be harmful. Other aspect of tax competition might be related to revenue loss. Turkey had to take counter measures to tackle harmful tax competition. Within this framework, Turkey reduced personal and corporate income tax rates, broadened its tax base, introduced a new Corporate Income Tax Law in 2006, covered measures such as CFC and transfer pricing practices, extended the scope of exchange of information of tax treaties and access to bank information, information sharing treaties, and reform of tax administration. The measures against harmful tax competition have been taken are given below in Turkey.

a. Reducing Tax Rates and Broadening Tax Base

As mentioned above, many developed countries have reduced their personal and corporate income rates since the 1980s, as a result of tax competition arguments. Political climate of supply side economists' arguments was another reason for decline in the tax rates. Moreover, some Nordic countries have introduced *dual income tax system* that has a feature a low rate on capital income. The main argument about tax rate reduction in the literature is that capital may leave countries with higher tax rates simply because they can get a better rate of return on their invested capital in countries with lower tax rates. However, tax rate is not the only determinant of investment.

Studies show that wage rates, quality of workforce, ability to access the markets, quality of infrastructure, political stability, and other factors are generally more important factors when deciding where to invest new capital (Steinmo, 2002). Moreover, how progressive a given rate schedule is depends on not only on the amount of basic tax relief but also width of respective brackets, and the rates applied to the income in each bracket (OECD 2000c).

In Turkey, personal income and corporate tax rates are declined and the tax bases are widened by eliminating deductions and exemptions. In 1980, the highest income tax rate bracket for individuals was 66%, whereas recently it has been reduced from 45% to 35%. In addition to the personal income tax rate, the corporate tax rate also declined from 30% to 20% in 2006. However, the nominal tax rates may be deceptive. Although the most basic measures of tax burdens are nominal or statutory tax rates, they may not be suitable for comparison.

Tax base definition may vary from countries to countries (OECD, 2000). For instance, the depreciation rate and method differences may also change effective corporate tax rates. Devereux, Griffith, and Klemm (2002) found that while statutory tax rate were falling, effective tax rates fell for profitable projects but remained fairly stable for low profit projects in EU and G-7 countries. Therefore, we may conclude that decline in statutory tax rate does not always mean decline in tax burden.

b. Tax Revenues

One of the major tax reforms which was aimed to adopting of a modern taxation system of Turkey was in the late 1940s. In conformity with a commission led by German[15] and Turkish tax experts a German based Personal Income Tax Law, Corporate Income Tax, and Fiscal Procedure Law were enacted by Parliament (Ates, 2012). Today, the Turkish tax system is mainly based on those to collect taxes. Tax revenue as percentage of Gross Domestic Product (GDP) between 1970 and 2012 in Turkey by comparison with OECD average is given *Table **1***. In this period, revenue excluding social security as percentage of GDP in Turkey increased two times while OECD average almost increased almost ten percent. In 2001 and 2003, tax to GDP ratio rose to its highest recorded level of 20.5 per cent; however, it remained below the OECD average. This means that Turkey's tax system still yields less revenue than that of many OECD countries[16].

One of the important achievements of Turkey in this period is the substantial increase in social security collected which rose from 1% to almost 7% of GDP. However, income tax revenue, corporate tax revenue, and taxes on goods and services between 1970 and 2012 in Turkey by comparison with OECD average is given *Table 2*. Turkey's tax structure shows a heavy reliance on indirect taxes. In 2012, taxes on goods and services consist of 45% total tax revenue. This rate is much higher than the OECD average. On contrary, in this period income tax revenue decreased from 25% to 16%. This shift from income tax

Table 1. Tax revenue as percentage of GDP

Years	Tax Revenue as Percentage of GDP		Tax Revenue (Excluding Social Security) as Percentage of GDP	
	Turkey	OECD Average	Turkey	OECD Average
1965	10,6	25,4	9,9	20,8
1970	9,3	27,4	8,7	22,1
1975	11,9	29,2	10,8	22,7
1980	13,3	30,8	11,5	23,7
1981	14,1	31,5	12,3	24,2
1982	13,7	31,9	11,8	24,5
1983	12,8	32,1	10,9	24,5
1984	10,7	32,3	8,8	24,6
1985	11,5	32,4	9,8	24,8
1986	13	33	11,3	25,3
1987	14	33,5	11,8	25,7
1988	13,2	33,5	11,2	25,7
1989	13,9	33,3	11,4	25,6
1990	14,9	32,9	12	25,3
1991	15,6	33,4	12,5	25,2
1992	16,7	33,6	13,3	25,2
1993	16,9	34,1	13,5	25,2
1994	16,5	34	13,9	25,3
1995	16,8	34,4	14,8	25,3
1996	18,9	34,8	15,9	25,8
1997	20,7	34,8	17,7	25,8
1998	21,1	34,8	18,1	25,9
1999	23,1	35,1	18,9	26,2
2000	24,2	35,2	19,6	26,3
2001	26,1	34,7	20,5	25,7
2002	24,6	34,4	19,7	25,4
2003	25,9	34,3	20,5	25,3
2004	24,1	34,3	18,3	25,4
2005	24,3	34,8	18,8	26
2006	24,5	35	19	26,2
2007	24,1	35	18,9	26,3
2008	24,2	34,5	18,2	25,6
2009	24,6	33,6	18,6	24,5
2010	26,2	33,8	19,7	24,6
2011	27,8	34,1	20,1	25
2012	27,7	..	20,1	..

Source: OECD, www.oecd.org

Table 2. Tax Revenues as Percentage of Total Taxation

Years	Income Tax Revenue		Corporate Tax revenue		Taxes on goods and services	
	Turkey	OECD Average	Turkey	OECD Average	Turkey	OECD Average
1965	24,8	26,2	4,8	8,8	54	38,4
1970	27	28	6,4	8,7	49,4	35,6
1975	32,9	29,8	5,1	7,6	41,3	32,8
1980	43,5	31,3	4,1	7,6	25,6	32,5
1981	40,7	31,2	8,8	7,6	24,9	32,5
1982	39,3	31	11,4	7,6	26,8	32,9
1983	39,2	30,5	9,6	7,2	29	33,7
1984	36,6	29,9	9,3	7,7	27,9	33,7
1985	27,5	29,7	9,5	7,9	36	33,7
1986	26,6	29,9	12	7,9	31,2	33,7
1987	24,9	29,5	10,7	7,8	32	34
1988	23,8	29,8	10,5	7,9	31,7	33,1
1989	26,4	28,9	9,6	8,2	28,2	32,4
1990	26,8	29,4	6,7	7,9	27,9	32,9
1991	28,7	27,7	6,1	8,1	29,3	32,7
1992	27,9	28,1	4,7	7,2	29,8	33
1993	27,1	27,5	4,9	7,4	31,8	33
1994	23,9	27,2	5,8	7,5	37,1	33,3
1995	21,6	25,9	6,7	8	37,6	33,8
1996	20,5	25,6	5,7	8	38,3	33,8
1997	21,7	25,6	5,7	8,5	37,1	33,6
1998	27,3	26,1	5,9	8,6	36,1	33,1
1999	23,8	25,6	7,6	8,7	35,9	33,4
2000	22,2	25,3	7,3	9,6	42	33
2001	22	25,8	6,8	8,9	40,1	32,7
2002	17,6	24,9	7,2	8,9	46,9	33,2
2003	15,7	24,5	8	8,9	49,4	33,4
2004	14,9	24,1	7,3	9,4	47,7	33,5
2005	14,7	23,9	7,1	10,1	49,3	33,2
2006	15,6	24	6	10,5	48,7	32,5
2007	17	24,6	6,8	10,6	47,7	32
2008	16,5	24,8	7,3	10	45,5	32,1
2009	16,4	24,7	7,7	8,4	45,7	32,5
2010	14	23,8	7,3	8,5	47,7	33,1
2011	13,5	24,1	7,5	8,7	45,2	32,9
2012	14,4	..	7,4	..	45	..

Source: OECD, www.oecd.org

revenue to indirect tax revenue is mainly subject of tax fairness and income distribution. As mentioned earlier, one of the output of tax competition is change in tax burden from direct taxes to indirect taxes.

The rapid increase in tax revenue relatively OECD countries' average over decades shows that Turkey may not been adversely affected by harmful tax competition, while income and corporate tax rates are substantially decreased. On the other hand, change in composition of tax structure, from direct tax to indirect tax, is subject of income distribution.

c. Regimes Reviewed Under OECD's Preferential Regime Work

As part of the preferential regime work of OECD, two regimes from Turkey were reviewed for the purpose of identifying those that constitute harmful tax practices: the Istanbul Offshore Banking Regime and the Free Trade Zones Regime. Despite never existing in practice (Oz, 2005), the OECD assessed Istanbul Banking Regime as potentially harmful. Since Member countries were required to remove the harmful features of any harmful preferential regimes within five years, the regime was abolished in 2001. On the contrary, the Free Trade Zones Regime of Turkey was determined not harmful. Today as a part of Global Forum Work initiated by OECD, Turkey's tax system is under peer review process from the point of transparency and exchange of information[17].

d. Tax Regulations Against Harmful Tax Competition

As part of the initiatives to harmful tax competition, new regulations have been introduced such as the CFC, transfer pricing legislations, withholding tax on payments related to residents of tax havens, and thin capitalization regulations in Turkey. Recently, the regulations introduced to protect tax base against harmful tax competition is given below in Turkey.

i. Controlled Foreign Company Regulations

The OECD has supported implementation of CFC regimes as a way of countering the profits to tax havens or low tax jurisdictions. The main purpose of CFC regimes is to avoid the tax bases erosion in the home state by way of the elimination of the deferral in the in the taxation of income earned or received by a CFC (Fontana, 2006). CFC practices first began in the USA in 1962, followed by France, Germany, New Zealand, and the United Kingdom. Beginning from the 1990s, a number of countries implementing CFC regimes increased significantly. In this context, CFC practices introduced to Turkish tax system by Article No.7 of Corporate Income Tax Law numbered 5520 in 1 January 2006.

The Residence principle is the basis of the CFC regime that covers practices on foreign subsidiaries having affairs with corporations residing in a country and taxation of those subsidiaries' income under specific circumstances. Governments regulate CFC regimes concerning either "*place of income earned*" or "*comparative tax approach*". When *place of income earned* is concerned, governments publish white or black lists. In the black list regime, if the subsidiary has relations with the countries that are in the black list, it is within the context of CFC regime. In contrast, if the subsidiary has relations with the countries published in the white list, it is out of the context of the CFC regime.

Therefore, some governments base their CFC regimes on a comparative tax approach. In this type of regime, legislation can be applied to any country where the amount of tax paid by CFC is less than the specified rate determined on the basis of a few criteria. They might be one of the following: i) the foreign statutory tax rate, ii) the foreign effective tax rate, iii) the foreign actual tax rate or the foreign actual tax paid by the CFC iv) the tax rate hypothetically payable at the residence country of the CFC (OZ, 2012).

In Turkey, the CFC regime is based on *comparative tax approach.* According to Article No.7 of Corporate Income Tax Law, corporations which are established in foreign countries and are directly or indirectly controlled by a full liable corporation which holds (separately or together) at least 50% of their capital, dividend or voting rights, will be deemed as CFC if all of the following cumulative criteria are fulfilled:

1. At least 25% or more of its gross income consists of "passive incomes" such as interest rate, dividend, license fee, security income, that are not sourced from commercial, agricultural or self-employment activities which require capital, organization and employment,
2. The foreign subsidiary should be subject to less than 10% effective tax burden over its corporate income of the commercial balance sheet profit,
3. Foreign subsidiary's annual gross income should exceeds 100,000[18] TL or foreign currency equal to this amount

The highest rate owned in any date within the related accounting period is taken as the control proportion. If the conditions mentioned are met, profit of a foreign subsidiary is included to full taxpayer corporation's income tax base beginning from the accounting period that contains the closure month of the foreign subsidiaries accounting period according to its share. If the income taxed in Turkey is redistributed by the foreign subsidiary later, the untaxed part of the profit is subject to corporate income tax.

In 2007, individual tax payers' incomes from CFCs are included in the Personal Income Tax Law. As a result of this amendment, whether these foreign subsidiaries distribute their income or not, when the conditions mentioned above in the Corporate Income Tax Law is met dividends are subject to income tax as capital gain[19].

ii. Transfer Pricing

Transfer pricing may be defined in a simple way as the amount charged by one segment of an organization for a product or service that it supplies to another segment of the same organization (UN, 2001). Another definition of transfer pricing is *the system of setting prices for transactions among subsidiaries of a multinational corporation, where the prices are not subject to market determination* (Pierce, 1992). The latter one includes taxation concerns. Paragraph 3 of the Preface of the 1979 OECD Report on Transfer Pricing and Multinational Enterprises explained that the term *transfer pricing* is neutral: the consideration of transfer pricing problems should not be confused with the consideration of problems of tax fraud or tax avoidance, even though transfer pricing policies may be used for such purposes (OECD, 1979).

However, it is very difficult to draw a line between tax fraud or tax avoidance and firm market or company pricing policies[20]. The 1979 Guideline of OECD was the first Report on transfer pricing issues. Later, other reports are published by addressing transfer pricing issues in the context of specific topics. OECD encouraged member countries to follow these Guidelines in their domestic transfer pricing practices. As part of initiatives to harmful tax competition, like CFC, transfer pricing rules were first introduced by Article No.13 of CIT Act numbered 5520 in 2007. The regulation is mainly based on OECD's work of Transfer Pricing Guidelines for Multinational Enterprises and Tax Administrations.

According to the Article, corporations shall be deemed to have distributed profits in a disguised manner through transfer pricing, if they are engaged in buying goods and services from persons or entities that are in the prices or amounts that are not in conformity with the arm's length prices or values. In this case, profits distributed in a disguised manner shall not be allowed as an expense recording in the calculation of corporate earnings.

In the determination of disguised capital, *the arm's length principle* is defined as the compliance of the prices and values applied in transactions concerning the purchase or sale of goods and services with the related parties, with the prices and values that would applied, had the parties to the said transactions were independent from each other, and not in the position of related parties. The methods for the determination of arm's length transfer prices are: *comparable uncontrolled price method*, *cost plus method* and *resale price method*.

If the mentioned methods cannot be used by the company for certain situations, the taxpayer may be allowed to adopt other methods. The Council of Ministers is authorized to issue procedural rules relating to transfer pricing and advance price agreements: Later, the *profit split method* and *transactional net margin method* were defined as two new methods for the determination of arm's length transfer prices. The profit distributed in a disguised manner through transfer pricing shall be reclassified as dividends distributed and necessary adjustments on taxes may be made for the party received the deemed dividends.

In order to make adjustments in this respect, the taxes assessed in the name of the company distributing dividends in a disguised manner must be finalized and paid. It may also be possible for companies to have unilateral, bilateral, or multilateral advance price agreements with Ministry of Finance. Few advance price arrangements were made by Ministry of Finance by part of transfer pricing regulation[21].

iii. Thin Capitalization Rule

To counteract negative consequences of debt finance tax collection, many countries have instituted thin capitalization rules that restrict the deductibility of interest above a certain debt level (Huizinga, 2014). In Turkey, thin capitalization rule has been introduced in its new form as part of Corporate Income Tax Law in 2006. When the ratio of borrowings from shareholders or related parties to the shareholders exceeds three times the shareholder's equity of the borrower company, the exceeding part, at any date of a certain accounting period, of the loans used by the company obtained directly or indirectly from shareholders or the persons related to shareholders shall be deemed as thin capitalization in the related accounting related period.

Except for the loans received from credit institutions that provide loans only to related companies, half of the loans received from related banks and similar institutions are to be taken into account during thin capitalization calculations. The scope of the term *related parties* consists of shareholders and the persons who are related with the shareholders that own 10% or more of the shares, voting rights or right to receive dividends of the company. Except for the foreign exchange differences, interest paid over an excess debt/equity ratio is considered as dividend distributed and will be subject to 15% dividend withholding tax.

Following these regulations and as part of reform of tax administration, a new division of "Thin Capitalization, Transfer Pricing and Cross-Border Transactions" has been set up at Tax Audit Board of Ministry of Finance in 2011.

iv. Withholding Tax on Payments Related to Residents of Tax Havens

Certain taxes may be collected through withholding by the payers in order to secure the collection of taxes. These include income tax on salaries of employees, lease payments to individual landlords, independent professional service fee payments to resident individuals, and royalty, license and service fee payments to nonresidents. On the other hand, some local withholding tax rates may be reduced based on the available bilateral tax treaty provisions.

As mentioned earlier, one of defensive measures suggestions of the OECD against the tax havens is to impose withholding taxes on certain payments to residents of uncooperative tax havens. According to Article 30/6 of the Corporate Income Tax Law, payments made to corporations (including branches of resident corporations) that are established or operational in countries which are regarded by the Council of Ministers to undermine fair tax competition due to tax and other practices, will be subject to withholding tax at the rate of 30% in Turkey irrespective of the fact that the payments in question are subject to tax or not, or the corporation receiving the payment is a taxpayer or not.

The Council of Ministers is authorized to determine the withholding tax rate for payments of goods and participation stock that are purchased on fair market value, for the leasing payments of the sea and air transportation vehicles and the payments that are mandatory to complete the work. However, the Council of Ministers has not yet published any list of countries related to residents of tax havens.

e. Information Exchange

Double taxation occurs when two states impose a comparable income tax with respect to the same item of income on the same taxable person[22]. If a government has levied direct taxes on incomes or property, there might be two reasons: (i) the person owning the property or receiving income was a resident; or (ii) because the income or property was located in the government's territory. The two bases for taxation raised the possibility of double taxation of foreign-source income or foreign-located property (UN, 2003a). Prevention of double taxation is a main concern of tax payers, governments, and international organizations since it decreases after tax income and cause economic distortions.

Double taxation occurs when a government imposes source based taxation, while the other imposes source based taxation. Starting with the League of Nations in the 1920s, there has been an ongoing effort to prevent double taxation. Presumably, after the Second World War, working on prevention of double taxation has been one of the main tasks of the OECD which issued its first convention model in 1963 with the Draft Double Taxation on Income and Capital. In 1977, the OECD update first major of its Draft with *the Model Convention and Commentaries* to reflect the experience of members with bilateral treaties, the new methods for tax evasion, and the development of new and more international business activities and relations.

However, tax treaties tend to allocate tax revenues more generously to residence countries then unilateral alternative does (Dagan, 2003), the United Nations (UN) developed a treaty model concerning interest of developing countries. In 1980, the UN introduced its first [23] model of tax agreement. However, the UN model and guidelines may not differ from the OECD Model (Piciotto, 1999). Experience has shown that unilateral measures may not be fully adequate to eliminate or alleviate the effects of double taxation[24]. Traditional tax havens are simply not covered by tax treaties because they do not typically impose an income tax (UN, 2003a). Article 26 of the both the OECD and UN Model Tax Conventions provide a basis for information exchange. In 2002, the OECD developed a new tax treaty Model that is solely based on exchange of information.

One of the main concerns of the OECD Harmful Tax Project has recently become the exchange of information between tax administrations. The Tax Information Exchange Agreement (TIEA), introduced by OECD in 2002, is a bilateral agreement that has been negotiated and signed between two countries to establish an official system for the exchange of information relating to taxes. The internationally agreed tax standard requires exchange of information on request in all tax matters for the administration and enforcement of domestic tax law without regard to a domestic tax interest requirement or bank secrecy for tax purposes.

Turkey has signed a total of 87 tax agreements, and only 16 of them covers Paragraphs 4 and 5 of Article 26 of the OECD Model convention which are related to internationally agreed tax standards. The list of the countries signed agreements contains Paragraphs 4 and 5 of OECD Model is given in Table 3. On the other hand, Turkey has signed tax information exchange agreements based on TIEA Model with five countries and only one with Jersey came into force in 2013. It may be concluded from data at Table 3 that Turkey does not pay attention to the exchange of information.

Table 3. List of Countries Signed agreement that meets the international standards

Jurisdiction	Type of EOI Arrangement	Date entered into Force
Australia	DTC	2009
Bahrain	DTC	2005
Brazil	DTC	2012
Canada	DTC	2011
Finland	DTC	2012
Germany	DTC	2012
Ireland	DTC	2010
Kosovo	DTC	not yet in force
Luxembourg	DTC	2005
Malaysia	DTC	1997
Malta	DTC	2013
Mexico	DTC	not yet in force
New Zealand	DTC	2011
Norway	DTC	2011
Switzerland	DTC	2012
Jersey	TIEA	2013
Bermuda	TIEA	not yet in force
Gibraltar	TIEA	not yet in force
Guernsey	TIEA	not yet in force
Isle of Man	TIEA	not yet in force

Source: OECD, www.oecd.org
(DTC: Double Taxation Convention; TIEA: Tax Information Exchange Agreement)

f. Tax Identification Numbers

The most straightforward and direct attempt to foster global legibility is the OECD's effort to standardize Taxpayer Identification Numbers (TIN). In many OECD countries, governments issue citizens with a number to ensure that they fulfill their tax obligations (i.e., a Social Security Number in the USA or a Tax File Number in Australia). Having a unique identifying number, every individual can be linked to a record of his or her tax compliance (Scharman, 2011). These unique numbers give government keep a track of economic transactions by requiring banks and other related organizations to report the information. In 1997, the OECD Council recommended to member countries *that Members should encourage non-resident recipients of income to disclose their residence country Tax Identification Number (TIN). Members should consider making this disclosure mandatory* (OECD, 1997). The OECD is now considering a unique international tax identification number.

Turkey began providing a unique tax ID number to tax payers in the 1980s. Later, the practice area of Tax ID number used was broadened. According to the Law Numbered 4358 dated April 2, 1998, real and legal persons shall submit their tax ID number for certain proceedings as determined by the Ministry of Finance. Within this context, banking transactions such as having an account in a bank, money transfers; or a property purchase would also require having a unique tax ID number. Later, a Citizen ID Number instead of a Tax ID Number was used in bank transactions. In the 2000s, having a unique ID number is also required for foreigners.

According to the Communique of Tax Identification Number dated August 26, 2006, foreigners must obtain a Tax ID Number in order to be eligible to work. Foreigners who are staying more than six months in Turkey are required to obtain Foreigner ID Number. For persons residing in Turkey longer than six months means the individual may be taxed according to the *residence principle*. Foreigners staying in Turkey more than six months are required to obtain a Foreigner ID number to access taxation, healthcare, education, and social security. Effective January 1, 2010, Turkey requires the use of an International Bank Account Number (IBAN) to identify beneficiaries on specific payments.

g. Change in Organization Structure of Revenue Administration

As mentioned earlier, application of the *residence based taxation* requires a strong tax administration. Since there are substantial resource costs expended by the tax collection agencies to minimize inappropriate income shifting, and substantial resources costs expended by the multinationals themselves to accomplish such shifting (UN, 2013), revenue administrations are changing their organizational structure. Global foreign direct investment rose by nine percent in 2013 to US$1.45 trillion, up from US$1.33 trillion in 2012 (UNCTAD, 2014). In Turkey, as in other OECD countries, there have been considerable changes in the organization structure of revenue administration over the last decade.

In the 2000s, instead of being a directorate under the Ministry of Finance, revenue administration turned to a unified semi-autonomous body. With Law No. 5345 adopted in 2005, the General Directorate of Revenue was abolished and the Presidency of Revenue Administration was established under the Ministry of Finance. Therefore, the tax policy function is shifted from General Directorate of Revenue to General Directorate of Revenue Policies as an administration entity under the Ministry of Finance[25].

A trend in administrations worldwide has been the establishment of special organizational arrangements for the revenue body's largest tax payers. Such special operations have focused tax administration efforts on relatively few taxpayers that account for a large percent of their total tax collection (IMF, 2002). Many of these large taxpayers have complex tax affairs that are part of them use facilities of tax haven countries submitted, characterized by the following factors:

1. Multiple operating entities that are widely dispersed geographically
2. Diverse business activities and/or involvement in transactions that raise complex law interpretation issues
3. Significant off-shore transactions, often with related parties
4. High volume of transactions in the course of day to day business activities
5. Use of complex financing arrangements
6. Use of professional tax advisers, part of whose brief is to minimize their exposure to taxation (OECD, 2004b).

Large tax payers are mostly multinational companies, some private groups, and publicly corporate companies (OECD, 2013b). Looking out for large tax payers by establishing such a unit and hiring skilled and expert staff, tax administrations attempt to save their national tax bases. In 2004, many OECD countries had a unit dedicated to large tax payers operation[26]. Today, almost all OECD countries have such a unit. Large Taxpayers Office under the Presidency of Revenue Administration was established by the Decree of 2006/10788 dated August 5, 2006. Criteria for identifying "large business" depends upon turnover, taxes paid, assets, employees, and industry involved.

5. CONCLUSION

This work centers on tax competition and its reflections in Turkey. As the world becomes more globalized and resources become more internationally mobile, the issue of tax competition is moving to the forefront of debates surrounding national tax systems. Tax havens are countries that impose little or no taxes or other forms of taxes. By offering sophisticated banking and communications facilities and stable political and business climate, they provide a wide range of tax avoidance advantages for enterprises. Rising tax competition has caused governments to adopt defensive measures to prevent tax payers from using lower tax rates abroad.

Governments may respond to international harmful tax competition in one of two ways: As a single country or as a member of international community. Governments defended their fiscal sovereign rights behind their national frontiers by making legislation and taking necessary precautions. Industrial nations have reduced their personal and corporate income tax rates since the 1980s. As a counteract measure to tax havens, countries have adopted foreign controlled companies legislation and transfer pricing rules. The second way is collaborating with other governments as facing same problems to prevent tax evasion: Following the G-7 Lyon Summit in 1996, the OECD initiated "harmful tax competition" project against the countries that are defined as tax havens. In 2000, the OECD listed a total of 35 jurisdictions found to meet the tax haven criteria. Today, the OECD work continues as Global Forum on Transparency and Exchange of Information for Tax Purposes. In 1997, the code of conduct for business taxation was set out in the conclusions of the EU Council of Economics and Finance Ministers to tackle harmful tax competition and to losses of tax revenue. It included a commitment to roll back existing regimes and refrain from introducing any such measures in the future.

As a result of liberalization policies of the 1980s, Turkey faced several effects of international tax competition. As a member of the OECD, Turkey participated actively in the OECD Harmful Tax Forum work and committed to eliminate any of her *preferential tax regime* found to be harmful. In this scope, following the analysis of Istanbul Offshore Banking Regime (IOBR) and Turkish Free Zones (TFZ), IOBR was abolished and TFZ not found as harmful. Other aspect of tax competition *might be* related to revenue loss. Turkey had to take counter measures to tackle harmful tax competition; therefore, Turkey reduced personal and corporate income tax rates, broadened its tax base, and introduced a new Corporate Income Tax Law in 2006 that covered measures such as controlled foreign company, transfer pricing practices, extended scope of exchange of information of tax treaties, access to bank information, information sharing treaties and reform of tax administration.

However, tax revenue as a percentage of GDP, excluding social security, rose from 8,7% in 1970 to 20,1% in 2012. In 1980, the highest income tax rate bracket for individuals was 66%, whereas recently has been reduced from 45% to 35%. In addition to personal income tax rates, corporate tax rates also declined from 30% to 20% in 2006. With these result we may ask the following question: Does tax competition hurt Turkey? The answer is still to be determined. Turkey has experienced a steady increase in tax revenue, while tax rates are declined. On the other hand, the question of whether or not tax burden is shifted from high level income individuals to low level income individuals has not been answered yet.

REFERENCES

Ates, L. (2012). Domestic Political Legitimacy of Tax Reform In Developing Countries: A Case Study of Turkey. *Wis. Int'l L.J., 30,* 706-760.

Baer, K., Benon, O. P., & Toro, R. J. (2002). *'Improving Large Taxpayers' Compliance: A Review of Country Experiences*. IMF Fiscal Affairs Department.

Blöchliger, H., & Vammalle, C. (2012). *Reforming Fiscal Federalism and Local Government Beyond The Zero-Sum Game*. Paris: OECD Fiscal Federalism Studies. doi:10.1787/9789264119970-en

Blouin, J., Huizinga, H., Laeven, L., & Nicodème, G. (2014). Thin Capitalization Rules and Multinational Firm Capital Structure. *IMF Working Paper* WP/14/12.

Blumberdg, M. (2001). The OECD's Report on Harmful Tax Competition Is 'Harmful Tax Competition Actually Harmful? Retrieved from http://www.globalphilanthropy.ca/images/uploads/Harmful_Tax_Competition_and_the_OECD.pdf

Bovenberg, R. (1992). Residence-and source-based taxation of capital income in an overlapping generations model. *Journal of Economics*, *56*(3), 267–295. doi:10.1007/BF01237183

Brennan, G., & Buchanan, J. (1980). *The Power to Tax: Analytical Foundations of a Fiscal Constitution*. New York: Cambridge University Press.

Browning, L. (2009, February 19). UBS Pressed for 52,000 Names in 2nd Inquiry. *New York Times*. Retrieved from http://www.dailymail.co.uk/news/article-2567957/Panel-faults-US-govt-offshore-tax-evasion.html#ixzz364AqblSg.

Brueckner, J. K. (2000). A Tiebout/ Tax-competition model. *Journal of Public Economics, 77*(2), 285–306. doi:10.1016/S0047-2727(99)00086-9

Bucovetsky, S. (1991). Asymmetric tax competition. *Journal of Urban Economics, 30*(2), 167–18. doi:10.1016/0094-1190(91)90034-5

Bucovetsky, S. (2009). An index of capital tax competition. *International Tax and Public Finance, 16*(6), 727–752. doi:10.1007/s10797-008-9093-9

Common Consolidated Corporate Tax Base Working Group. (2004, December 10). *EU*. Retrieved from http://ec.europa.eu/taxation_customs/taxation/company_tax/harmful_tax_practices/

Dagan, T. (2000). The Tax Treaties Myth. *New York University Journal of International Law & Politics. New York University. International Law Society, 32*(4), 939–996.

Devereux, M. P., Griffith, R., & Klemm, A. (2002). Corporate Income Tax Reforms and International Tax Competition. *Economic Policy, 35*, 451–495.

Edwards, C., & Rugy, V. (2002, April 12). International Tax Competition A 21st-Century Restrain on Government. *Policy Analysis, No: 431.*

Edwards, J., & Keen, M. (1996). Tax competition and Leviathan. *European Economic Review, 40*(1), 113–134. doi:10.1016/0014-2921(95)00057-7

Fitzgerald, V. (2010). International Tax Co-operation and Capital Mobility, International Tax Co-operation and Capital Mobility. *Oxford Development Studies, 30*(3), 251–266. doi:10.1080/1360081022000012680

Fontana, R. (2006, June). The Uncertain Future of CFC Regimes in the Member States of the European Union – Part 1. *European Taxation.*

Genschel, P. (2001, May). Globalization, Tax Competition, and the Welfare State. Max Planck Institute for the Study of Societies. *MPIfG Working Paper 01/1.*

Goodsmith, T. (1998, September). Tax Competition, Benefit Taxes, And Fiscal Federalism. *National Tax Journal, 51*(3), 579–586.

Gunessee, S. (2010, March). Strategic Tax Competition: An Experimental Study. *Public Finance Review, 38*(2), 217–243. doi:10.1177/1091142110367859

Habermacher, F., & Kirchassner, G. (2012, August 16–19). Asymmetric Tax Competition: Theoretical and Empirical Results. *Paper to be presented at the Annual Meeting of the International Institute of Public Finance*. Dresden. Retrieved from http://www.habermacher.net/attachments/bFile/Habermacher-Kirchgaessner_AsymmetricTaxCompetition_Draft_2012.pdf

Jackson, J.K. (2010). *OECD Initiative on Tax Havens CRS Report for Congress* R40114.

Jones, R., & Basu, S. (2010). Taxation of Electronic Commerce: A Developing Problem. *International Review of Law Computers & Technology, 16*(1), 35–51. doi:10.1080/13600860220136093

Kellman, K., Miller, J. H., & Scott, E.P. (1997, December). Political Institutions and Sorting in a Tiebout Model. *The American Review*, 1997, 977-922.

Kudrle, R. T. (2008). The OECD's Harmful Tax Competition Initiative and Tax Havens: From Bomshell to Domp Squib. Global Economy Journal, 8(1).

Loretz, S. (2008). Corporate taxation in the OECD in a wider context. *Oxford Review of Economic Policy*, *24*(4), 639–660. doi:10.1093/oxrep/grn035

Messere, K. (2000). 20th Century Taxes and Their Future (Bulletin). *International Bureau of Fiscal Documentation.*

Mitchell, D. J. (2000, September 18). An OECD Proposal To Eliminate Tax Competition Would Mean Higher Taxes And Less Privacy. *The Heritage Foundation, 1395.*

Morris, A., & Moberg, L. (2012). Cartelizing Taxes: Understanding the OECD's Campaign against "Harmful Tax Competition." *Colum. J. Tax L*, *1*, 1–64.

Oates, W. E. (2005). Toward A Second-Generation Theory of Fiscal Federalism. *International Tax and Public Finance*, *12*(4), 349–373. doi:10.1007/s10797-005-1619-9

OECD. (1964). *Turkey Economic Survey*. Paris.

OECD. (1979). *OECD Report on Transfer Pricing and Multinational Enterprises*. Paris.

OECD. (1997, May 22). Recommendation of the council on the use of tax identification numbers in an international context. (Adopted by the Council at its 894th session on 13 March 1997 [C/M(97)5/PROV]), C*(97)29/FINAL.*

OECD. (1998). *Harmful Tax Competition: An Emerging Global Issue*. Paris.

OECD. (2000a). Towards Global Tax Co-Operation: Progress in Identifying and Eliminating Harmful Tax Practices. Report To The 2000 Ministerial Council Meeting And Recommendations By The Committee on Fiscal Affairs, Paris.

OECD. (2000b). *Improving Access to Bank Information for Tax Purposes*. Paris.

OECD. (2000c). 2006 Update On Progress In Member Countries. Paris.

OECD. (2000d). Tax Burdens Alternative Measures OECD Tax Policy Studies (No. 2). Paris.

OECD. (2001). *Guidance in Applying the 1998 Report to Preferential Tax Regimes*. Paris.

OECD. (2001b). Paris: Taxation and Electronic Commerce – Implementing the Ottawa Taxation Framework Conditions.

OECD. (2003). *Improving Access to Bank Information for Tax Purposes the 2003 Progress Report*. Paris.

OECD. (2004). Electronic Commerce Facilitating cross-border tax collection.

OECD. (2004b). Tax Administration in OECD Countries: Comparative Information Series, Paris.

OECD. (2006a). *OECD' Project on Harmful Tax Practices: 2006 Update on Progress in Member Countries*. Paris.

OECD. (2006b). Fundamental Reform of Personal Income Tax. Tax Policy Studies No.13. Paris.

OECD. (2010). Choosing a Broad Base- Low Rate Approach to Taxation. Tax Policy Studies No.19. Paris.

OECD. (2013a). *Tax Transparency 2013 Report on Progress.* Paris.

OECD. (2013b).*Tax Administration 2013: Comparative Information on OECD and Other Advanced Emerging.* Paris.

Olsen, P. (2008, February 26). Tax Evaders, Beware The Liechten-sting. *Forbes.* Retrieved from http://www.forbes.com/2008/02/26/liechtenstein-tax-haven-markets-equity-cx_po_0226markets26.html

Owens, J. (2000, October 19). Towards world tax co-operation. *OECD Observer.* Retrieved from http://www.oecdobserver.org/news/printpage.php/aid/271/Towards_world_tax_co-operation.html

Öz, N. S. (2005). *Uluslararası Vergi Rekabeti ve Vergi Cennetleri.* Ankara: Maliye ve Hukuk Yayınları.

Öz, N. S. (2012). Controlled foreign company regime in Turkey and its valuation. *Intertax, 40*(11).

Persoud, B. (2002). The OECD Harmful Tax Competition Policy: A Major Issue for Small States, International Tax Competition: Globalisation and Fiscal Sovereignty. Commonwealth Secretariat.

Piciotto, S. (1999, November 4-5). The End Offshore? Regaining Public Control of Finance and Taxation in the Era of Globalization. *Paper for Conference on Governing the Public Domain beyond the Era of Washington Consensus? Redrawing the Line between the State and The Market*, Toronto.

Pierce, D. W. (1992). *The MIT Dictionary Of Modern Economics* (4th ed.). New York: Macmillan Press. doi:10.1007/978-1-349-22136-3

Pigou, A. C. (1947). *A Study in Public Finance* (3rd ed.). New York: Macmillan.

Rixen, T. (2010). From double tax avoidance to tax competition: Explaining the institutional trajectory of international tax governance. *Review of International Political Economy*, 2010, 197–227. doi:10.1080/09692290.2010.481921

Rosenweig, A.H. (2010). 52 *Wm. & Mary L. Rev. 923 2010-2011* (pp. 923- 996).

Sharman, J. C. (2012). Seeing Like the OECD on Tax. *New Political Economy, 17*(1), 17–33. doi:10.1080/13563467.2011.569022

Steinmo, S. (2002, September). Globalization And Taxatıon Challenges to the Swedish Welfare State. *Comparative Political Studies, 35*(7), 839–862. doi:10.1177/0010414002035007004

Swank, D., & Steinmo, S. (2002). The New Political Economy of Taxation in Advanced Capitalist Democracies. *American Journal of Political Science, 46*(3), 642–655. doi:10.2307/3088405

Talpoş, I., & Crâşneac, A. O. (2010)... *The Effects of Tax Competition, Theoretical and Applied Economics Volume XVII, No., 8*(549), 39–52.

Tanzi, V. (1996). Taxation in an Integrating World. Washington, DC: Brookings.

UN. (2001, September 10-14). Transfer Pricing, History C C State of the Art C Perspectives. *Ad Hoc Group of Experts on International Cooperation in Tax Matters Tenth meeting Geneva.*

UN. (2003a, December 15-19). The interaction of tax, trade and investment, Ad Hoc Group of Experts on International. Cooperation in Tax Matters Eleventh meeting Geneva

UN. (2003b). *Manual for the Negotiation of Bilateral Tax Treaties between Developed and Developing Countries*.

UNCTAD. (2014). *World Investment Report 2014*. United Nation Publication.

USA Department of Treasury (2000). The Deferral of Income Earned Through U.S. Controlled Foreign Corporations.

Wibless, E., & Arce, M. (2003, Winter). Globalization, Taxation, and Burden-Shifting in Latin America. *International Organization*, *57*(1), 111–136.

Wilson, J. D. (1986). A theory of interregional tax competition. *Journal of Urban Economics*, *19*(3), 296–315. doi:10.1016/0094-1190(86)90045-8

Wilson, J. D. (1999, June). Theories of Tax Competition. *National Tax Journal*, *52*(2), 269–304.

Zodrow, G. R., & Mieszkowski, P. (1984). Pigou, tax competition and the underprovision of local public goods. *Journal of Urban Economics*, *19*(3), 356–370. doi:10.1016/0094-1190(86)90048-3

KEY TERMS AND DEFINITION

Asymmetric Tax Competition: Tax competition between countries that are differed in population size.

Capital Export Neutrality: Under CEN investors, receive the same tax treatment wherever they invest.

Capital Import Neutrality: Under CIN all investors receive the same tax treatment, regardless of where they reside.

Controlled Foreign Company: Taxation of undistributed foreign subsidiary profits in the resident country, as if the profit is distributed.

Double Taxation: Occurs when two States impose a comparable income tax with respect to the same item of income on the same taxable person.

Horizontal Tax Competition: Competition among governments at a single level i.e. national sovereign governments or local governments.

Tax Competition: The situation where independent jurisdictions compete non-cooperatively over the taxation of production factors to influence their location.

Transfer Pricing: the amount charged by one segment of an organization for a product or service that it supplies to another segment of the same organization.

Vertical Tax Competition: Competition among different levels of same government, i.e. municipality/states and federal government.

ENDNOTES

1 In 2008 Liechtenstein was the one of last remaining jurisdictions listed by the OECD as uncooperative tax havens. The other uncooperative jurisdictions were the Principality of Monaco and Andorra.

2 As we'll see later, in case of race to the bottom situation, people pay price of public service they benefit.

3 For Pigou's work SEE (Pigou, A. 1947).

4 This result found for two Swiss cantons Zürich and Zug.

5 For instance the integration of Belgium into the European Union, made an international comparison on tax assignment in federal countries, and finally recommended giving some autonomy over the personal income tax (Blöchliger & Vammalle, 2012).

6 Discussion for results of international tax competition and coordination. SEE (Edwards& Keen 1996).

7 The Code of Conduct for business taxation was set out in the conclusions of the Council of Economics and Finance Ministers (ECOFIN) of 1 December 1997. SEE EU Code of Conduct.http://ec.europa.eu/ taxation_customs

8 The history of tax competition goes back to 1920s. "Tax competition has been an issue for governments for as long as they have taxed income. In 1934, Canadian mining millionaire Harry Oakes moved to the Bahamas to escape Canada's high tax rates, complaining that eighty-five percent of his income was being taxed away." (Morris & Moberg, 2012).

9 In this text, tax haven definition refer to this second type of tax haven unless otherwise stated.

10 OECD's 2000 Report includes the following jurisdictions as meeting tax haven criteria: Andorra, Anguilla, Antigua and Barbuda, Aruba, the Bahamas, Bahrain, Barbados, Belize, the British Virgin Islands, the Cook Islands, Dominica, Gibraltar, Grenada, Guernsey Sark Alderney, the Isle of Man, Jersey, Liberia, Liechtenstein, Maldives, the Marshall Islands, Monaco, Montserrat, Nauru, the Netherlands Antilles, Niue, Panama, Samoa, Seychelles, St. Lucia, St. Christopher & Nevis, St. Vincent & the Grenadines, Tonga, Turks & Caicos, the U.S. Virgin Islands, and Vanuatu.

11 If regimes are partly or fully insulated from the domestic markets of the country providing the regime, then it's defined "ring fencing". It may take a number of forms, including: 1) a regime may explicitly or implicitly exclude resident taxpayers from taking advantage of its benefits, 2) enterprises which benefit from the regime may be explicitly or implicitly prohibited from operating in the domestic market. (OECD 1998)

12 For instance the details of the regime or its application are not apparent; or, there is inadequate regulatory supervision or financial disclosure.

13 The only regime found harmful was the Luxembourg 1929 holding company regime. After the publication of 2006 Report, the Luxembourg 1929 holding company regime has been abolished by legislation enacted on 29 December 2006, with transitional rules for certain existing beneficiaries up to 31 December 2010.

14 E-commerce provides a different challenge to tax regimes. It leads to the gradual elimination of intermediaries, there might be discrepancies where foreign suppliers may be tax-exempted, whereas local suppliers would be required to charge sales taxes, direct orders from foreign suppliers will substantially increase the number of low-value shipments of physical goods to individual customers. (Jones & Basu, 2010). E-commerce may cause many taxation problems. "*For example, the tax*

administration in the country where the customer is located may encounter difficulties in ensuring that the right amount of tax is collected and remitted given that there may be no, or merely a limited, jurisdictional relationship between the administration and the supplier. Similarly, the supplier may encounter difficulties in determining the proper amount of tax and complying with the tax rules of the country where the customer is located." (OECD, 2004)

15 Tax reforms are like not ending story. For instance in the OECD's first economic survey about Turkey is stated that "in 1963 a reform needed to be taken as a first step and public revenue is planned to increase substantially" (OECD, 1964).

16 Tax to GDP ratios may not necessarily reflect differences in tax policies, across acer countries or in a country over time. Since tax loss may be permitted to carry forward and used to offset corporate tax liabilities will differ both over time. (OECD, 2002c).

17 The Global Forum is the continuation of a forum which was created in the early 2000s in the context of the OECD's work to address the risks to tax compliance posed by tax havens. The original members of the Global Forum consisted of OECD countries and jurisdictions that had agreed to implement transparency and exchange of information for tax purposes. (OECD, 2013a).

18 1 USD is equal to 2.1 TL in mid-August 2014.

19 Although OECD and EU recommended implementation of CFC regimes, as regarded compatible with tax treaties, national courts, national tax authorities and scholars have raised a number of criticisms and questions regarding OECD's approach. CFC regimes are also questioned in the context of EC law and fundamental freedoms. (Fontana, 2006).

20 Paragraph 3 of the Preface of the 1979 OECD Report on Transfer Pricing and Multinational Enterprises also mentioned that "multinational enterprises may adopt transfer pricing which are mot arm's length prices in order to minimize tax"

21 As a part of transfer pricing issue, it may be mentioned that consolidation of the accounts of group companies for tax purposes is not allowed in Turkey since each company is regarded as a separate taxpayer.

22 Beside occurrence of this type double taxation, there is also one more type of double taxation that is called economic double taxation. This refers to the taxation of two different tax payers with the same income. Prevention of this type double taxation is out of scope of this study.

23 The OECD Model Tax Conventions is based on residence taxation; while the United Nations Model Double Taxation Convention between Developed and Developing Countries is mostly based on source taxation. (Fitzgerald, 2010).

24 "This inadequacy stems from the diversity of tax systems, which, in turn, originates from differences among countries in legal and tax history, fiscal policy, revenue needs, and the level of compliance and enforcement. These differences are reflected in the approach that a country takes to the promotion of foreign investment, the characterization and computation of taxable income, and the various methods used for allocating income to domestic and foreign sources." (UN, 2003b). "Treaties provide certainty for investors and ease their bureaucratic hassle, and may collecting information and in establishing diplomatic relations between countries" (DAGAN, 2000).

25 General Directorate of Revenue Policies was established by the Article 12/A annexed to the Decree Law on Organization and Duties of Ministry of Finance No: 178 on 12/12/1983 by the Law No: 5452 on 01/02/2006.

26 The countries that have not such a unit was Belgium, Czech Republic, Germany, Iceland, Luxembourg, Portugal, Switzerland and Turkey. (OECD, 2004b).

Chapter 10
A Panel VAR Analysis of the Shadow Economy in Europe and MENA

Tarkan Çavuşoğlu
Hacettepe University, Turkey

Debi Konukçu Önal
Hacettepe University, Turkey

ABSTRACT

The objective of this chapter is to analyze empirically the potential dynamics of the relationship among the size of the shadow economy, fiscal burden and the official economy. The empirical analysis is based on the size estimates of the shadow economy in 17 developed and 11 transition economies of Europe for the period 1999-2013 and in 16 economies of Middle East and North Africa for the period 1999-2007. Direction of causal relations among shadow and official economies and the fiscal burden is investigated by exploiting the panel vector auto-regression approach and the associated impulse response analysis, which directly account for the potential endogeneity of the variables of interest. Findings mostly confirm the view that shadow and official economies are substitutes, and the dynamic effects of fiscal burden on the shadow economy are not as strong and clear as expected in the regions in question.

INTRODUCTION

Economic activities that are named as shadow, informal, hidden, unobserved, unrecorded, underground, black, or unofficial have always been on the agenda of policy makers for years in both developing and developed economies.[1] Estimating the size of economic activities incorrectly due to the presence of a large shadow economy may result in allocational inefficiencies in policy decisions, which put economies into the vicious circle of poor institutional quality. While poor quality of public administrations constitutes the basis for shadow economies to grow, large shadow economies, in return, erode public service quality by stimulating bribery to escape from taxation, detection and punishment, and by curbing the tax revenues that should finance public good provision and infrastructure investment. In this sense, econo-

DOI: 10.4018/978-1-5225-0053-7.ch010

mies in the Middle East and Africa, and the transition economies of Europe and Asia are of interest, as these economies are experiencing institutional transformation towards a universally accredited market mechanism with relatively large shares of shadow economies. In such immature economies, incomplete market structures together with weak institutional features discourage economic agents' compliance to legal requirements.

Therefore, the presence of large shadow economic activities is one of the crucial problems of developing economies which should be minimized not only for the sake of national good governance, but also to achieve international credibility in order to encourage inflows of foreign investment. Moreover, the size of a shadow economy should be minimized also because it hinders economic development as a source of economic uncertainty and as a type of social capital deficiency. The reason for the presence of larger shadow economies in developing areas compared to globally integrated advanced economies can be explained by regressive dynamics resulting from conformist aspects of societies and institutions rooted in cultural and moral values as well as in economic endowments.

The presence of shadow economies in most developing countries is characterized with inertia because of unwilling authorities and institutional incompetence, beside several economic reasons, such as, heavy fiscal burdens, high unemployment rates, high costs of doing business, etc. The close association of large shadow economies with low levels of economic development can be observed in the estimates of Buehn and Schneider (2012a), where the average Gross Domestic Product (GDP) share of the shadow economies in transition countries and in emerging and developing economies appear to be about twice that of those in the high-income OECD economies. That is, the average ratios of the shadow economy to official GDP lie between 8% and 29% in OECD countries, while they lie between 17% and 62% both in transition countries and in the Middle East and African countries.

Knowledge about the size of the shadow economy is an important concern for fiscal policy makers in developing economies, particularly, in conducting effective revenue policies. However, complications due to the interrelation between shadow activities and the sizes of the tax burden and the tax base generate controversies in policy decisions. The presence of overburdened taxpayers in an economy may be either the cause or the outcome of the shadow economy. Similarly, while the presence of the shadow economy may erode the tax base in an economy due to undeclared earnings, income earned from shadow activities may increase the tax base, if it is spent immediately in the official economy (Schneider & Enste, 2000, pp. 77-78). These ambiguities constitute a basis for the discussion of optimality in the size of the shadow economy and in the level of the tax burden.

Thus, in practice, while some policy makers are reluctant to fight against shadow activities, some are keen for reducing the size of the shadow economy. One problem in measuring the size of the shadow economy is the lack of a precise definition of the shadow activities. Activities that escape from the official estimates of the GDP can be categorized depending on whether they are legal or illegal. However, because illegal activities such as, drug dealing, prostitution, gambling, and smuggling cannot be detected and quantified, the size of the shadow economy can be measured through estimating the avoided amounts of payments and obligations to public authorities (Schneider & Williams, 2013).

In a joint publication of the OECD with the International Labour Office (ILO), the International Monetary Fund (IMF), and the International Statistical Committee of the Commonwealth of Independent States (CIS), the shadow economy, the so called the non-observed economy (NOE), is defined as activities that are under-ground, illegal, informal, missed because of deficiencies in the basic data collection program, or undertaken by households for their own final use (OECD, 2002, p. 37). The non-observed size of the shadow economy is estimated frequently by a latent-variable estimation approach in the relevant literature, called the multiple-indicators multiple-causes (MIMIC) procedure. It is found superior to the direct and indirect methods, which are based on surveys and samples in the former and on proxy indicators in the latter.

The MIMIC procedure is based on a set of structural equations employed for estimating the unobservable variable of the model, that is, the size of the shadow economy, through exploiting the possible causes of the leakages from the official economy. Schneider (2005) counts three main causes: (i) high burdens of taxes and social security contributions, which encourage informal supply and demand of both labor and output; (ii) intensive regulations, which restrict the freedom of choice in the official economy; (iii) low-quality public goods and services, which weaken taxpayers' trust in the state and deteriorate the tax morality. However, among these three causes, only the first can be quantified as a continuous variable in empirical analysis, while the other two are qualitative variables that need to be transformed into numbers that have arbitrarily determined discrete values.

The main motivation of this chapter is to analyze the interrelationship among the size of the shadow economy, fiscal burden, and the economic well-being that is measured by official GDP estimates. However, the empirical analysis of the issue is limited to the sample of developed and transition economies in Europe and to the sample of the economies in the Middle East and North Africa (MENA).[2] Comparison of the shadow economy dynamics based on these three samples may have implications for assessment of whether or not geographical differences, cultural divergences and disparate political histories are the driving forces behind differences in the size of the shadow activities in different regions.

The novel feature of this chapter is twofold. First, to our knowledge, this is the first attempt to investigate the direction of the causal relation among the size of the shadow economy, fiscal burden, and the size of the official economy in the literature. Second, the empirical analysis of the issue is carried out by a method that directly accounts for the potential endogeneity of the variables of interest, which is ignored in the literature of the shadow economy. Within this framework, our analysis aims at answering mainly the following research questions: (i) Is a large shadow economy an outcome of high fiscal burdens? (ii) Do fiscal burdens aggravate with the increase in the size of the shadow economy? (iii) Can shadow economy contribute to official GDP? (iv) Do economies with high official GDPs have small shadow economies?

In order to be able to answer these questions on an empirical basis, we employ the panel vector autoregression (panel-VAR) methodology which allows the dynamic analysis of the endogenous interactions among the size of the shadow economy, fiscal burden, and the official GDP. While fiscal burden and the per capita GDP are the two widely accepted determinants of the size of a shadow economy in the relevant literature, the issue of how shadow economy influences the fiscal burden and the GDP is an empirically vague part of the discussions in the shadow economy literature. Therefore, this study is a candidate for illustrating the shadow economy concern empirically based on a cross-regional comparison carried out with the data of a sample of European and MENA countries. The institutional aspects of the shadow economy, which are often proxied by qualitative discrete measures, are ignored in the empirical analyses as discrete variables are not convenient for use in time-series-based panel methods. The influence of qualitative factors are assumed to be reflected by the per capita real GDP levels in this study, as they are positively correlated with the quality of institutions in cross-country analyses.

The flow of the chapter is as follows. The next two parts of the study briefly present the theoretical background of the research questions and the recent empirical literature concerning the causes and outcomes of the shadow economy. A part that describes the empirical methodology and the data comes next and is followed by the part that presents the empirical findings and the implications of our estimations. The chapter is concluded with final remarks.

THEORETICAL AND EMPIRICAL LITERATURE

The seminal theory of Allingham and Sandmo (1972), which is one of the building blocks of the tax evasion literature, can analogously be exploited to explain the dynamics of the shadow economy as well (Schneider, 2014, p. 231). Based on a portfolio choice between the safe- and risky-asset, the theory demonstrates the behavior of a utility maximizing taxpayer who decides between reporting his actual income and underreporting it. The shadow economy, which Alm (2012, p. 58) defines as "… all market-based but unreported income from the production of legal goods and services" that would normally be taxed if they were reported, implies that shadow actors have exactly the same motivation as tax evaders. Both shadow economy activity and tax evasion behavior involve an income declaration decision under the uncertainty of investigation by authorities. This decision is made based on the maximization of the expected utility function of the representative agent, where the expected utility is determined by the probability of investigation, the tax burden, the penalty rate, and by the amounts of the actual- and undeclared-income.

Hence, within the framework of the Allingham-Sandmo tax evasion model, one can argue that the decision between staying and vanishing in the official economy depends on the degree of the legal deterrence, the level of the fiscal burden, and the type of the risk aversion, which determines the fraction of the actual income that is declared.[3] Recently, Sandmo (2012) discussed the need for extending the Allingham-Sandmo model to include variable labor supply and work in the shadow economy. His extensions imply that the substitution effect of an increase in the marginal tax rate encourages work in the shadow economy if the after-tax wage in the official labor market does not exceed the expected after-tax wage in the shadow labor market.

The works on shadow economy in the literature are mostly more empirical rather than theoretical.[4] One strand of this empirical literature particularly focuses on estimating the size of the shadow economy with alternative methods, which is ignored in this chapter for brevity. The other strand in which we are interested due to its coherence with the motivation of our chapter, focuses on the alternative causes and outcomes of the shadow economy. According to the percentage shares of the causes of the shadow economy, which are estimated by Feld & Schneider (2010, p. 120), about 35-38% of the size of the shadow economy is due to tax and social security contribution burdens, about 22-25% is due to low tax morale, about 10-12% is due to poor quality of state, and the rest is due to other minor factors. With evidence based on the data of over a hundred countries, Schneider (2005) and Schneider, Buehn, and Montenegro (2010) argue that it is the government actions, such as taxation and social security contributions, that underlie the presence of shadow activities. Similarly, Bovi & Dell'Anno (2010) find evidence on a proportional association between the level of tax burden and the shadow economy for 21 OECD countries.

Additionally, the two-sector dynamic and stochastic general equilibrium model estimates of Orsi, Raggi, and Turino (2014), along with the new method that they use in shadow economy estimations, explain the increasing size of the shadow economy in Italy by persistent increases in taxation. Works by Giles, Werkneh, and Johnson (2001) and, most recently, Vlachaki (2015), depart from the conventional approaches in the analysis of the relationship between shadow economy and tax burden through accounting for asymmetries. In the former, the effects of the upward and downward movements in the tax burden on the shadow economy in New Zealand are differentiated, but no statistically significant evidence of asymmetry is found. However, in the latter, the effect of the shadow economy on tax burden is of interest. In this respect, the regression estimates of the panel of 125 countries imply that, below a certain threshold, the shadow economy increases the indirect tax revenues to GDP ratio, whereas it decreases the tax revenue ratio above that threshold.

Many other studies in the literature argue that institutional deficiencies are much more important than tax burdens in stimulating the shadow activities. For example, Loayza (1996) argues that the shadow economy depends negatively on the quality of government institutions, beside its positive dependencies on the tax burden and labor-market restrictions. Friedman, Johnson, Kaufmann, and Zoido-Lobaton (2000) find no evidence to the influence of direct or indirect tax rates on the shadow economy with respect to the data sample of 69 countries. However, institutional influences, such as more bureaucracy, higher corruption, and a weak legal structure are found to be significantly associated with a larger shadow economy because economic agents find it optimal to hide their activities. As a result of hiding, first, the tax revenues, and then, the quality of public goods and services tend to fall, discouraging firms to remain in the official economy.

Similarly, estimations of Dreher, Meon, and Schneider (2014), based on a sample of 133 countries, imply that good institutions are related negatively with the shadow economy, without any effect of GDP per capita on the share of the shadow economy. However, recent studies that include an institutional perspective mostly investigate the relation of the shadow economy with corruption. In this context, Choi and Thum (2005) introduce a model of self–selection with heterogenous entrepreneurs, in which the presence of the shadow economy restricts the ability of the corrupt officials to introduce distortions to the economy for private interests. By adapting an explicit specification of institutional quality into this model, Dreher, Kotsogiannis, and McCorriston (2009) find negative effects of institutional quality on the shadow economy and corruption.

Thus, both studies confirm that the shadow economy and corruption are substitutes, while the shadow and official economies are complements. In contrast, estimations of Dreher and Schneider (2010) based on the data of 98 countries indicate complementarities between corruption and the shadow economy in low income countries, however, they indicate no significant relation when the perception-based corruption index is used instead of the structural model-based one. Considering the spatial aspects of a large sample of nations, Goel and Saunoris (2014) also find complementarity between corruption and the shadow economy.

Institutional influences to the shadow economy are treated also from other perspectives in the recent literature. For example, Torgler, Schneider, and Schaltegger (2010) and Teobaldelli (2011) touch upon the issue of fiscal decentralization as a type of institutional structure that serves to reduce the size of the shadow economy. The effect is explained by higher efficiency in taxation and public good provision owing to local autonomy compared to unitary states. Additionally, another new dimension is added to the shadow economy discussions by Lee (2013) and D'Hernoncourt and Meon (2012) by emphasizing the role of social capital in decreasing the size of shadow activities. Similarly, direct democracy (Teobaldelli & Schneider, 2013) and the quality of the legal framework (Dabla-Norris, Gradstein & Inchauste, 2008) are also argued to be among factors that are capable for reducing the incentives to operate in the shadow economy.

Finally, the need for access to the financial markets for production finance is argued to be another crucial factor discouraging activities in shadow economy (Bose, Capasso, & Wurm, 2012; Capasso & Jappelli, 2013; Feltenstein & Shamloo, 2013). In an economy with a developed financial intermediation system, economic agents that prefer to operate in the shadow economy are exposed to higher costs of finance and capital formation than those that operate in the official economy. Especially for capital and technology intensive sectors, the opportunity cost of hiding operations from authorities will be very high compared to their honest counterparts that have easy access to low cost credit opportunity owing to their past reputation in the banking sector.

The bidirectional interaction between shadow and official economies is among many other issues discussed in the shadow economy literature. In fact, one can simply argue that the institutional aspects mentioned above are associated positively with the level of economic welfare in a country. Therefore, economies with good institutional quality are expected to have higher per capita GDPs and, hence, lower sizes of shadow economy relative to institutionally immature economies. However, the relevant literature provides evidence on the relationship between shadow and official economies from two perspectives. One is based on the discussion of whether the shadow and official economies are complements or substitutes. The other is the direction of the causal relation. In this respect, Loayza's (1996) finding that any increase in the size of the shadow economy slows down the rate of per capita GDP growth in Latin America implies the rejection of the view of complementarity between the shadow and official economies in this region, pointing out a causal direction from shadow economy to official GDP growth.

This is also supported by Johnson, Kaufmann, and Shleifer (1997) for Eastern Europe and the former Soviet Union, with the negative effect of the output share of the shadow economy on the total output. The same study also emphasizes the importance of progress in institution-building to achieve lower shares of shadow activity. It is argued that the Eastern European countries have smaller shadow economies than the former Soviet Union countries, as the former are characterized with relatively fairer taxes, lighter regulations, higher tax revenues, and relatively better provision of public goods in the official economy compared to the latter.

In another study concerning the transition countries, by reversing the causal direction, Eilat & Zinnes (2002) provide empirical evidence on the opposite effects, however, of a change in official GDP on the size of the shadow economy. Alternating results are obtained in Schneider's (2005) estimations, which are based on the panel regressions of 104 countries. The shadow economy is found to increase annual GDP growth in industrialized countries, whereas it is found to reduce growth in developing low-income economies. La Porta & Shleifer (2008) state that GDP per capita is the most robust predictor of the size of the shadow economy. In this respect, the size of the shadow economy is argued to be high in poor countries because of the prevalence of labor intensive sectors, which provide subsistence income for laborers unable to be formally employed. However, in rich countries the size of the shadow economy is argued to be low owing to both capital intensive activities and high volume of transactions intermediated by financial institutions. More interestingly, Giles (1997) and Giles, Tedds, and Werkneh (2002) find evidence of a positive unidirectional causality from official to shadow economy, respectively, for New Zealand and Canada, which is unusual evidence in the literature, introducing a dilemma to the view of complementarity between the shadow and official economies.

Within the scope of the relevant literature, this chapter fills the gap of a direct causality analysis among the size of the shadow economy, fiscal burden, and the per capita GDP in the literature, based on a panel of countries representing the three economic regions of the world. In the next parts of the chapter, the methodology and the estimates of a trivariate panel-VAR analysis of the shadow economy dynamics are presented in the light of the literature reviewed above concerning the relationships among the variables of interest.

EMPIRICAL APPROACH AND DATA

The empirical investigation on the size of the shadow economy is carried out by exploiting the two recent panel-data estimation approaches, which deliberately take into account the concern of endogeneity in the determinants of the shadow economy (i.e., in the level of national income and the rate of fiscal burden). One is the Granger non-causality testing approach proceeded through a p-th order panel vector auto-regression (panel-VAR) estimations, which assumes the presence of heterogeneous unobserved individual effects in a system of equations for endogenous variables. Panel-VAR estimations make it possible to capture both the static and dynamic interdependencies among the variables without restriction on the links across units and allow for dynamic heterogeneities among cross-sectional units (Canova & Ciccarelli, 2013).

The other approach used in our empirical analyses is the panel two-step generalized method of moments (2S-GMM), in which the endogeneity bias is taken into account through the instrumental variable estimation in the single-equation framework. However, while the former approach has implications for a short-run economic analysis, the latter serves the estimation of the long-run relationship between the size of the shadow economy and its potential determinants. The p-th order panel-VAR model, which constitutes the basis for the Granger non-causality tests, can be shown by the following system of equations:

$$
\begin{aligned}
S_{it} &= \alpha_{1i} + \alpha_{11}T_t + \Sigma_{j=1}^{p}\beta_{1j}S_{i,t-j} + \Sigma_{j=1}^{p}\beta_{2j}F_{i,t-j} + \Sigma_{j=1}^{p}\beta_{3j}Y_{i,t-j} + \varepsilon_{S,it} \\
F_{it} &= \alpha_{2i} + \alpha_{21}T_t + \Sigma_{j=1}^{p}\phi_{1j}F_{i,t-j} + \Sigma_{j=1}^{p}\phi_{2j}S_{i,t-j} + \Sigma_{j=1}^{p}\phi_{3j}Y_{i,t-j} + \varepsilon_{F,it} \qquad (1) \\
Y_{it} &= \alpha_{3i} + \alpha_{31}T_t + \Sigma_{j=1}^{p}\delta_{1j}Y_{i,t-j} + \Sigma_{j=1}^{p}\delta_{2j}S_{i,t-j} + \Sigma_{j=1}^{p}\delta_{3j}F_{i,t-j} + \varepsilon_{Y,it}
\end{aligned}
$$

Endogenous variables of the system are, respectively, the size of the shadow economy, measured as a percentage of the official economy (S_{it}), the rate of fiscal burden (F_{it}) and the per capita Gross Domestic Product (GDP) in constant prices (Y_{it}). Each equation includes unobserved time-invariant country-specific fixed effects, denoted by α_i, and a deterministic time trend, denoted by T_t. Variables shown by $\varepsilon_{S,it}$, $\varepsilon_{F,it}$ and $\varepsilon_{Y,it}$ are the equation-specific disturbances. Due to the lagged dependent variables in the panel-VAR(p) equations, a correlation exists between the fixed effects and regressors, which should be eliminated to avoid the endogeneity bias problem in estimations. Therefore, the Helmert procedure along with the system GMM approach is used to provide consistent coefficient estimates in such dynamic panel specifications, as suggested by Alvarez and Arellano (2003) and Holtz-Eakin et al. (1988).[5]

Parameter estimates of the above panel-VAR(p) model are exploited for six pair wise Granger non-causality tests performed by the Wald statistics to illustrate whether or not knowing the history of a variable helps explain another variable. In this sense, any failure in rejecting the validity of the restrictions $\beta_{21} = \beta_{22} = \ldots = \beta_{2p} = 0$ and $\beta_{31} = \beta_{32} = \ldots = \beta_{3p} = 0$ in the first equation implies that neither the past rates of the fiscal burden nor the past levels of the per capita income are capable of predicting the current size of the shadow economy. Similarly, incapability of predicting the current levels of fiscal burden by exploiting the past information on the size of the shadow economy and on the levels of per capita income is implied respectively by the restrictions $\phi_{21} = \phi_{22} = \ldots = \phi_{2p} = 0$ and $\phi_{31} = \phi_{32} = \ldots = \phi_{3p} = 0$ in the second equation.

Finally, restrictions $\delta_{21} = \delta_{22} = \ldots = \delta_{2p} = 0$ and $\delta_{31} = \delta_{32} = \ldots = \delta_{3p} = 0$ in the third equation represent the absence of a Granger-type causality running from the size of the shadow economy and the fiscal burden towards the per capita income level. Hence, any rejection of one of these restrictions implies evidence in favor of Granger causality running from one variable to another. However, because this evidence will not be able to indicate the signs of the causal relationships, the impulse responses are utilized to reveal the signs. This helps tracing out the responsiveness of the dependent variables of the panel-VAR system to shocks to each of the variables, thereby, providing statistical evidence as to whether responses are positive, negative, or insignificant (Brooks, 2002, pp. 340-341). Moreover, a statistically significant reaction of one variable to an impulse in another variable implies that the latter is the causal for the former (Lutkepohl, 2007, p. 51). As stated by Hendry and Mizon (1998, p. 268), "... the presence or absence of Granger causality in the econometric model has a major effect on the estimated responses independently of its occurrence in the DGP."[6]

Following the analysis of the short-run dynamics based on panel-VAR estimations, the long-run shadow economy relationship is estimated by a fixed-effects panel regression,

$$S_{it} = \mu_i + \lambda T_t + \gamma_1 F_{it} + \gamma_2 Y_{it} + v_{it} \tag{2}$$

however, by the panel two-step GMM approach, with the assumption that regressors may not be exogenous, i.e., $E(F_{it}, v_{it}) \neq 0$ or $E(Y_{it}, v_{it}) \neq 0$. The validity of such an assumption may stem potentially from influences of the unofficial activities on fiscal burden and national income. In order to eliminate the resulting endogeneity bias in estimates, endogenous regressors are instrumented by their own lags in the GMM estimations.

The relevance of the instruments are examined with a battery of tests. An LM test of 'under-identification' is used to test the null hypotheses that the instruments are inadequate to identify the equation even for over-identification with the order condition. Moreover, the problem of weak-instruments is tested with a Wald test, to know if the estimators are subject to an unacceptably large bias due to 'weak identification'. Hence, the rejection of the null hypothesis implies the absence of a weak-instruments problem resulting from the insignificant correlation between the endogenous variables and the instruments. The computations of both under- and weak-identification test statistics are based on the reduced-rank tests of Kleibergen and Paap (2006).

The requirement that an instrumental variable must be orthogonal to the error process is another crucial aspect of the GMM estimation, which is diagnosed with a test of over-identification restrictions conducted by the Hansen's J statistic. This statistic implies instrumental validity with the failure in rejecting the null hypothesis and that instruments are uncorrelated with the errors. Alternatively, the orthogonality condition can be diagnosed by testing whether or not the specified endogenous regressor can actually be treated as exogenous. This 'endogenity test' is a GMM distance test, which is actually based on the comparison of the two J statistics computed by two separate estimations, one treating the specified regressor as endogenous and the other treating it as exogenous. Small values of the statistic correspond to a failure in rejecting the null hypothesis that the specified regressor may be treated as exogenous.[7] Overall, the results of these tests combine to indicate whether or not the setup in the two-step GMM procedure is relevant for estimating the shadow economy relationship consistently.

In estimations, the size of the shadow economy is proxied by figures computed by Buehn & Schneider (2012a) and Schneider (2013), who convert the index numbers estimated through the Multiple Indicators Multiple Causes (MIMIC) method into percentages of official GDP. On the other hand, figures used for quantifying the size of the fiscal burden are adopted from the Fiscal Freedom Index published by the Heritage Foundation. The index is computed on a 100-point basis by the following formula,

$$\text{Fiscal Freedom}_{ij} = 100 - \alpha(\text{Factor}_{ij})^2 \quad (3)$$

where Factor_{ij} represents one of the three (j=1, 2, 3) components used in computing the index number of the i-th country and α is a coefficient equal to 0.03 for controlling the variation among scores. The components of the fiscal freedom index are the top marginal tax rates on individual income, the top marginal tax rates on corporate income, and the total tax burden as a percentage of GDP. The arithmetic average of the fiscal freedom indices computed for each component constitutes i-th country's published score of fiscal freedom.

However, in order to directly use an indicator of burden instead of a freedom score in our estimations, we solve Equation (3) for Factor_i and obtain an average fiscal burden score lying between 0 and 100 likewise. Finally, in estimations, the size of the official economy is proxied by the US dollar value of the per capita gross domestic product in 2005 prices, of which the country figures are obtained from the World Development Indicators database of the World Bank.

EMPIRICAL FINDINGS

The main objective of our analysis is to investigate empirically whether the fiscal burden and the per capita income level are the causes or the outcomes of the size of the shadow economy in European and MENA economies. However, prior to econometric estimations, some descriptive statistics on the variables of interest may give a rough idea about the stance of the economies included in our sample. In this respect, Table 1 presents a summary of the statistics computed by using the data series of our panel-VAR estimations. Because of the lack of post-2007 estimates on the size of the shadow economy for MENA countries, we report the 1999-2007 averages of the series to be able to compare MENA with Europe.

According to average figures, the size of the shadow economy is slightly higher in transition Europe than MENA (28.2% and 25.6%, respectively). The lower average for MENA is because of the natural resource rich countries of the region (i.e., Bahrain, Saudi Arabia, Oman, etc.), which mostly rely on oil revenues rather than fiscal revenues. In transitional Europe, the small size shadow economies such as Slovakia and the Czech Republic have more or less the same shadow economy to official GDP ratios with the small size shadow economies of the MENA region. The higher average score of fiscal freedom as well as the higher average per capita income in MENA compared to transitional Europe (US$77.3 and US$10,498.9 in MENA and US$69.7 and US$8,822.4 in transitional Europe) are in accordance with their shadow economy sizes. The figures of developed Europe exhibit a particularity in the relationship between shadow economy and fiscal burden in comparison to the transition and MENA economies.

The particularity is the association of the small size of the shadow economy with low fiscal freedom, which implies a divergence from the conventional wisdom in cross-country comparisons. It may be explained by the dissimilar dynamics of the shadow economies in high- and low-income countries, which are mostly shaped by the quality of institutions and financial development in advanced economies. In order to perform a within-region analysis, the system of equations given in (1) is estimated separately for the 17 developed, 11 transitional European economies, and the 16 MENA economies.[8] This is expected to allow the analysis of the cross-country information to reveal the dynamics of each region in question.

The three endogenous variables of the panel-VAR system to be estimated are as follows: (i) the size of the shadow economy (as a percentage of the official GDP), (ii) the fiscal burden (an index number lying between 0 and 100 for low and high burdens, respectively, which is derived by solving the Fiscal

Table 1. Descriptive statistics

	Europe		MENA
	Developed	Transition	
	1999-2007	1999-2007	1999-2007
Size of the Shadow Economy (%)			
Mean	16.7	28.2	25.6
Std. dev.	5.3	5.5	7.4
Min.	8.2	16.8	16.5
Max.	29.5	37.6	38.7
Fiscal Freedom Index (0-100)			
Mean	51.4	69.7	77.3
Std. dev.	12.5	10.2	19.4
Min.	29.8	45.0	32.3
Max.	80.7	89.5	99.9
Per Capita GDP (USD - 2005 prices)			
Mean	40342.0	8822.4	10498.9
Std. dev.	14363.5	3958.5	12164.9
Min.	17819.7	2608.7	753.7
Max.	86127.2	20348.7	47081.2

Note: Due to the lack of comparable shadow economy estimates for MENA after 2007, the sample period of the statistics are restricted to the 1999-2007 period.

Freedom equation given in (3) for $Factor_{ij}$), (iii) the per capita GDP in constant 2005 prices (denominated in USD). These three variables, denoted respectively by S, F and Y, are exploited in natural logarithms throughout the estimations and found stationary with respect to the unit root test suggested by Levin, Lin& Chu (2002) for homogenous panels.[9] Table 2 presents the computed Wald statistics for testing the pair wise Granger non-causality hypotheses based on the estimations of the trivariate panel-VAR systems represented by (1).

However, a Granger non-causality test can imply only whether or not the current and past values of one variable are capable of forecasting the future values of another variable, but not the sign of the causal relations. Therefore, in Figure 1, the plots of the orthogonalized cumulative impulse responses of the panel-VAR shocks are presented to be able to identify the signs of the pair wise causal relations that are found statistically significant in the Granger non-causality tests. In Figure 1, the plots in the first two rows belong to developed and transition Europe, respectively, while those in the third row belong to MENA. According to the joint evidence in Table 2 and Figure 1, the null hypothesis that 'fiscal burden does not Granger cause income' is rejected at 5% significance level only for the developed and transition Europe, while the reverse non-causality hypothesis is not rejected (see the first row of Table 2).

However, impulse response analysis does not yield statistically significant information about the direction of the time paths of the responses of the shadow economy to the shocks in fiscal burden, as can be deduced from the error bands covering the zero-line at each time horizon in the impulse response plots (see the third column plots in the first and second rows of Figure 1). The only significant causal relation concerning the fiscal burden is observed for MENA, interestingly, running from income to fiscal burden

Table 2. Panel-VAR Granger non-causality test

Null Hypothesis	European Economies (1999-2012)		MENA Economies (1999-2007)
	Developed	**Transition**	
Fiscal burden (F) does not cause shadow economy (S)	11.45 (0.022)	9.848 (0.043)	0.031 (0.860)
Income (Y) does not cause shadow economy (S)	42.50 (0.000) (-)	17.81 (0.001) (-)	2.920 (0.087) (+)
Shadow economy (S) does not cause fiscal burden (F)	3.870 (0.424)	4.220 (0.377)	0.534 (0.465)
Income (Y) does not cause fiscal burden (F)	1.133 (0.889)	3.152 (0.533)	4.572 (0.032) (-)
Shadow economy (S) does not cause income (Y)	32.63 (0.000) (-)	11.92 (0.018) (-)	7.361 (0.007) (-)
Fiscal burden (F) does not cause income (Y)	4.188 (0.381)	3.211 (0.523)	0.285 (0.594)

Figures above are the computed Wald-test statistics followed by their probabilities of non-rejection in parentheses. Signs of the causal relationships estimated through orthogonalized impulse responses are denoted by (-) and (+). An intercept and a deterministic trend are included in each of the VAR equations. Robust standard errors are used in estimations. Respectively, VAR(4) and VAR(1) models are fitted for the European and the MENA economies.

Figure 1. Impulse response plots

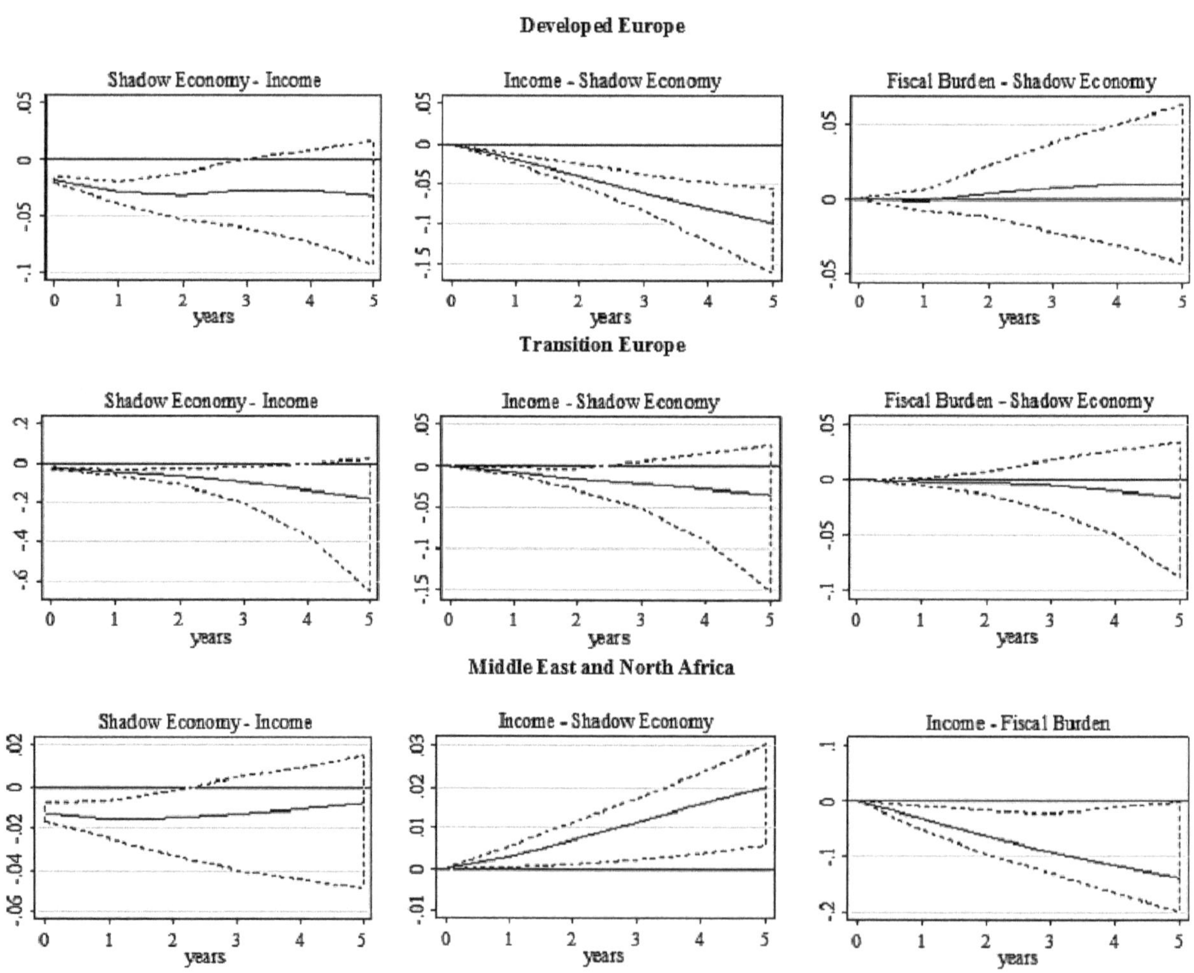

with a negative sign. This evidence is indicated by the rejection of the null hypothesis that 'income does not Granger cause fiscal burden' (see Table 1) together by the downward response of the fiscal burden to income shocks in the impulse response analysis (see the third column plot in the third row of Figure 1), where the error bands lie below the zero-line at most of the time horizons.

In fact, this finding is consistent with the past and prevailing economic dynamics in MENA peculiar to the region, because in most of the high-income MENA economies, fiscal burden is very low owing to their governments' budget relief with huge oil revenues. For example, with respect to the 1995-2014 averages of 156 countries, the null hypotheses that 'income does not Granger cause the shadow economy' and 'shadow economy does not Granger cause income' are both rejected at the conventional statistical significance levels for all three regions. In addition, impulse response plots indicate downward responses in case of shocks to shadow economy (see first column plots in each row of Figure 1) and shocks to income (see second column plots in the first two rows of Figure 1), with the exception of the MENA region, which exhibits upward response to shocks to income.

These findings imply that shadow and official economies are substitutes in Europe in both causal directions. However, in the MENA region, although the statistical evidence based on the Wald test for Granger non-causality is not strong enough, there seems to be an indication of a causal link from higher levels of income to larger shadow economy. This unusual result may be explained by the special features of the oil-rich countries, where labor market regulations and institutional quality are poor compared to their high levels of per capita income. In other words, economic welfare measured only by per capita GDP, disregarding the income distribution and the level of institutional development, may not be a good proxy in MENA for a composite determinant of the factors discouraging the shadow economy, while this proxy may work well for Western countries.

Overall, our Granger non-causality test results imply differences in the shadow economy dynamics between Europe and the MENA region, while similar evidence is obtained for both developed and transition Europe despite their economic and social disparities in the near past. In Europe, shadow and official economies seem to be substitutes, one discouraging the other. However, in MENA, although increases in the current and past sizes of shadow economy seem to be a good forecaster of the future declines in the per capita real GDP, this is not observed vice versa. In contrast, higher current and past levels of per capita real GDP appear to be a good forecaster of the future increases in the shadow economy. Since these results depend on cross-country information beside the time dimension owing to the use of panel data, one can interpret this evidence as a unique case due to the significant cross-country heterogeneities within MENA, where, even rich countries do not have institutional structures that discourage unrecorded activities.

The other interesting finding obtained for MENA that 'income inversely Granger causes fiscal burden', can similarly be interpreted with the cross-country perspective. This finding implies that per capita income levels of rich countries carry significant information for explaining the low levels of fiscal burden in MENA, while no such evidence exists for the European countries. It can be argued that the negative causal link from income to tax burden in MENA in empirical sense may be the reflection of the fact that natural resource rich countries rely less on fiscal revenues compared to relatively poor other MENA countries.

As the last step of the empirical investigations, a long-run static analysis is introduced by exploiting the two-step-GMM (2S-GMM) panel regression estimations, of which the estimation output is presented in Table 3 for each of the three regions in question.[10] These estimations take into account the potential endogeneity bias among the size of the shadow economy and its determinants. While estimates in the second column are instrumented by assuming the endogeneity of the income, those in the third are instrumented assuming the fiscal burden is endogenous.[11] For the 2S-GMM estimates in which the income variable is instrumented, instruments are found statistically valid in estimations for all three regions with respect to the results of the under- and weak-identification tests and found orthogonal to errors with respect to the Hansen's J test.

Table 3. Panel Two-step GMM Estimations

	LS	2S-GMM	2S-GMM
	European Developed Economies (1999-2012)		
Income (Y)	-0.2210** (0.0836)	-0.5950*** (0.0942)	-0.4376*** (0.0752)
Fiscal Burden (F)	0.0047 (0.0819)	0.0821 (0.0747)	0.0637 (0.0779)
Time Trend (T)	-0.0202*** (0.0014)	-0.0206*** (0.0010)	-0.0213*** (0.0009)
R-square	0.8514	0.8652	0.8693
Under-identification Test		$\chi^2(2) = 23.58$***	$\chi^2(2) = 13.42$***
Weak-identification Test		Wald-F = 77.01††††	Wald-F = 64.42††††
Hansen's J Test		$\chi^2(1) = 2.377$	$\chi^2(1) = 2.257$
Endogeneity Test		$\chi^2(1) = 11.19$***	$\chi^2(1) = 0.105$
Endogenous Variable		Income	Fiscal Burden
Instruments		2 lags	2 lags
# of Total Observations	238	204	204
# of Cross-section Units	17	17	17
	European Transition Economies (1999-2012)		
Income (Y)	-0.0757*** (0.0209)	-0.1675*** (0.0279)	-0.0913*** (0.0274)
Fiscal Burden (F)	0.0317 (0.0174)	-0.0009 (0.0126)	0.0461 (0.0248)
Time Trend (T)	-0.0100*** (0.0012)	-0.0095*** (0.0009)	-0.0099*** (0.0008)
R-square	0.9278	0.8919	0.9172
Under-identification Test		$\chi^2(4) = 25.66$***	$\chi^2(2) = 17.43$***
Weak-identification Test		Wald-F = 32.91††††	Wald-F = 21.25††††
Hansen's J Test		$\chi^2(1) = 4.344$	$\chi^2(1) = 0.219$
Endogeneity Test		$\chi^2(1) = 4.971$**	$\chi^2(1) = 1.654$
Endogenous Variable		Income	Fiscal Burden
Instruments		4 lags	2 lags
# of Total Observations	154	110	132
# of Cross-section Units	11	11	11
	MENA Economies (1999-2007)		
Income (Y)	-0.0294 (0.0994)	-0.0571 (0.0939)	-0.1199 (0.0809)
Fiscal Burden (F)	-0.0149 (0.0134)	-0.0325 (0.0172)	-0.0319 (0.0625)
Time Trend (T)	-0.0118*** (0.0027)	-0.0146*** (0.0029)	-0.0121*** (0.0019)
R-square	0.7324	0.7382	0.7115
Under-identification Test		$\chi^2(2) = 11.38$***	$\chi^2(2) = 6.415$

continues on following page

Table 3. Continued

	LS	2S-GMM	2S-GMM
Weak-identification Test		Wald-F = 28.96††††	Wald-F = 2.827
Hansen's J Test		$\chi^2(1) = 0.441$	$\chi^2(1) = 2.632$
Endogeneity Test		$\chi^2(1) = 4.691$**	$\chi^2(1) = 0.033$
Endogenous Variable		Income	Fiscal Burden
Instruments		2 lags	2 lags
# of Total Observations	144	112	112
# of Cross-section Units	16	16	16

Asterisks *** and ** denote the statistical significance of the estimated regression coefficients at 1% and 5% levels. Figures in parenthesis next to each regression coefficients are standard errors robust to heteroskedasticity. The detailed information for the test statistics can be found in the previous part of the chapter.

Additionally, the use of instruments to account for the endogeneity of the income variable as a regressor is found appropriate with respect to the endogeneity test results, where the hypothesis that income can be treated as exogenous is rejected significantly. On the other hand, endogeneity tests concerning the endogeneity of the other regressor (i.e., the fiscal burden), result in no evidence against the presumption that the fiscal burden can be treated as exogenous in the shadow economy regressions. However, the exogeneity assumption of the fiscal burden appears to be consistent only in estimations for Europe, not for MENA, as instruments fail to satisfy the identification and orthogonality conditions in the latter.

Thus, under these limitations, the coefficient estimates of the 2S-GMM panel regressions strongly imply that it is the per capita real GDP that affects the size of the shadow economy in the long-run, both in developed and transition Europe. The inverse relationship found between the income level and the size of the shadow economy shows that official and shadow economies are substitutes in Europe so that the former drives out the latter in the long-run. In contrast to what is widely accepted in the literature, fiscal burden does not seem to be the driving force of the shadow activities in Europe according to the panel regression estimates.

Thus, the finding that higher levels of per capita income are much more important than lower levels of fiscal burden in achieving smaller shadow economies in Europe may be the indication of the role of good institutional structures in discouraging shadow activities. Without loss of generality, it can be argued that a high per capita income level is both the source and the outcome of the presence of good-quality institutions in an economy.

The 2S-GMM panel regression estimates obtained for the MENA region do not result in any statistically significant effects of either the per capita income or the fiscal burden on the size of the shadow economy in the long-run. This ambiguity may be the result of the particularities of the MENA region. The shadow economy dynamics of this region differ from those in Europe in terms of the sources of the hidden activities. Loose labor market regulations encouraging informal wage employment and traditions driving out females from formal employment to self-employment (Charmes, 2012), and the political unrests, terror and money laundering (Warde, 2007) may be responsible for broadening the scope of the shadow economy in most of the MENA countries, unlike in Europe.

Moreover, institutional incapability, which limits MENA's integration to the world economy (Meon & Sekkat, 2004), may explain why neither per capita income level nor fiscal burden are found to be associated with the size of the shadow economy in the long-run analysis. In fact, although the level of per capita income is a good proxy for reflecting the level of institutional capabilities in general, it does not seem to fit the case of MENA, where most of the economies of the region have high per capita income levels owing to their natural resources, regardless of their institutional quality.

CONCLUSION

The shadow economy issue is analyzed for Europe and MENA with a cross-country perspective in this chapter. The four research questions set at the introduction to this chapter are attempted to be answered both through the analysis of short-run dynamics implied by the estimates of a dynamic system of endogenous variables and through the analysis of long-run dynamics modeled with a static fixed-effects regression that takes into account the potential endogeneity of the regressors.

Empirical investigations concerning the first two research questions show that fiscal burden in Europe and in MENA cannot be explained by the history of large size shadow economies. This implies that the presence of the shadow economy does not necessarily cause an increase in the prevailing burden of the taxpayers in these two regions. However, the joint evaluation of the Granger non-causality tests and the impulse responses implies the presence of an unclear but statistically significant causal relation running from past and current fiscal burdens to the future size of the shadow economy in both the developed and transition economies of Europe. That is, the direction and way fiscal burden influences the size of the shadow economy cannot be identified with the help of the impulse responses.

In fact, the static fixed-effects panel regression estimates show that these short-run influences already disappear in the long-run. Hence, contrary to the general presumption, fiscal burden does not appear to be influential on the size of the shadow economy, with respect to estimations based on the fiscal burden measure of the Heritage Foundation. Analyses with alternative measures may have opposite implications, however, which can be the subject of a future effort.

The strongest statistical evidence in empirical analyses is obtained for the third and fourth research questions, which concern the interaction between the sizes of the official and shadow economies. Empirical investigations of the short- and long-run shadow economy dynamics both imply that the shadow and official economies are substitutes in both developed and transition Europe. This implication is deduced by the Granger non-causality test results along with the time-path of the impulse responses, which provide strong statistical evidence on the presence of inverse bidirectional causal relations between the per capita GDP level and the size of the shadow economy in Europe. Although the inverse bidirectional relationships seem to be slightly weaker for transition economies than for developed ones, the similarity between the estimates may be interpreted as the convergence of the transition economies towards the advanced economies of Europe through engagements of the European Union.

These empirical findings show that per capita income growth in Europe is capable of reducing the size of the shadow economy, and the presence of the shadow economy plays a significant negative role on per capita income levels. On the other hand, although the presence of the shadow economy seems to be a detrimental factor for per capita income growth in MENA as in Europe, high per capita income levels are associated with large shadow economies in MENA. This controversy can be explained by the economic welfare resulting from natural resource revenues in many of the MENA countries. In other words, a high per capita income level represents high levels of financial, technological, and institutional development in the West, which discourages shadow activities due to high opportunity costs of engaging in informality in such a developed environment, whereas it represents an economic well-being which is not transformed into a universally credible economic and social environment in MENA.

Therefore, it can be argued that reducing the size of the shadow economy is not a priority for many of the high income MENA countries, as they rely on huge revenues from natural resources. This reasoning is supported also by the finding on Granger causality running from high income to low fiscal burden in the estimations for MENA. Again, this indicates the secondary role of fiscal revenues beside substantial revenue flows from natural resources in economic dynamics. Overall, these findings indicate the significant difference in the shadow economy dynamics between Europe and MENA. The transition economies of Europe, which are passing through an economic development process just like the economies of the MENA region, however, have shadow economy dynamics similar to those in developed Europe.

This is a manifestation of the need for good institutional and social capital structures in order to achieve lower size of shadow economies and higher compliance to legal obligations in developing economies. In order to achieve small size shadow economies in the MENA region, economic resources should be allocated to institutional transformation so that the MENA economies can be integrated to the world economy with universal standards. Otherwise, the prevailing inner economic and political dynamics will prevent the MENA economies from catching up the fast transition of the post-communist European economies.

The analysis in this chapter shows that the level of per capita income is much more important than the level of fiscal burden in explaining the size of the shadow economy in both developed and developing economies. However, per capita GDP is a broad measure, which encompasses the outcome of many income generating factors, such as good economic performances, sound legal and institutional structures, productive social and cultural relations, etc. Therefore, one limitation of the analysis is the inability of disaggregating the influence of these factors in estimations. Nevertheless, because the major part of the empirical analysis in this chapter rests on time-series based panel data approaches, which require the use of continuous variables in estimations, per capita GDP levels have to be used as a proxy for measuring the influence of the level of development in investigating the direction of the causal relations.

REFERENCES

Allingham, M. G., & Sandmo, A. (1972). Income tax evasion: A theoretical analysis. *Journal of Public Economics*, *1*(3-4), 323–338. doi:10.1016/0047-2727(72)90010-2

Alm, J. (2012). Measuring, explaining, and controlling tax evasion: Lessons from theory, experiments, and field studies. *International Tax and Public Finance*, *19*(1), 54–77. doi:10.1007/s10797-011-9171-2

Alvarez, J., & Arellano, M. (2003). The time-series and cross-section asymptotics of dynamic panel data estimators. *Econometrica*, *71*(4), 1121–1159. doi:10.1111/1468-0262.00441

Baum, C. F., Schaffer, M. E., & Stillman, S. (2003). Instrumental variables and GMM: Estimation and testing. *The Stata Journal*, *3*(1), 1–31.

Baum, C. F., Schaffer, M. E., & Stillman, S. (2007). Enhanced routines for instrumental variables/generalized method of moments estimation and testing. *The Stata Journal*, *7*(4), 465–506.

Bovi, M., & Dell'Anno, R. (2010). The changing nature of the OECD shadow economy. *Journal of Evolutionary Economics*, *20*(1), 19–48. doi:10.1007/s00191-009-0138-8

Brooks, C. (2002). *Introductory econometrics for finance*. Cambridge: Cambridge University Press.

Buehn, A., & Schneider, F. (2012a). Shadow economies around the world: Novel insights, accepted knowledge, and new estimates. *International Tax and Public Finance*, *19*(1), 139–171. doi:10.1007/s10797-011-9187-7

Canova, F., & Ciccarelli, M. (2013). Panel vector autoregressive models: A survey. In T. B. Fomby, L. Kilian, & A. Murphy (Eds.), *VAR models in macroeconomics – new developments and applications: Essays in honor of Christopher A. Sims, Advances in econometrics* (Vol. 32, pp. 205–246). London: Emerald Group Publishing Limited.

Charmes, J. (2012). The informal economy worldwide: Trends and characteristics. *Margin: The Journal of Applied Economic Research*, *6*(2), 103–132. doi: 10.1177/097380101200600202

Choi, J. P., & Thum, M. (2005). Corruption and the shadow economy. *International Economic Review*, *46*(3), 817–836. doi:10.1111/j.1468-2354.2005.00347.x

D'Hernoncourta, J., & Méon, P. G. (2012). The not so dark side of trust: Does trust increase the size of the shadow economy? *Journal of Economic Behavior & Organization*, *81*(1), 97–121. doi:10.1016/j.jebo.2011.09.010

Dabla-Norris, E., Gradstein, M., & Inchauste, G. (2008). What causes firms to hide output? The determinants of informality. *Journal of Development Economics*, *85*(1-2), 1–27. doi:10.1016/j.jdeveco.2006.05.007

Dreher, A., Kotsogiannis, C., & McCorriston, S. (2009). How do institutions affect corruption and the shadow economy? *International Tax and Public Finance*, *16*(9), 773–796. doi:10.1007/s10797-008-9089-5

Dreher, A., Méon, P. G., & Schneider, F. (2014). The devil is in the shadow. Do institutions affect income and productivity or only official income and official productivity? *Public Choice*, *158*(1-2), 121–141. doi:10.1007/s11127-012-9954-8

Dreher, A., & Schneider, F. (2010). Corruption and the shadow economy: An empirical analysis. *Public Choice*, *144*(1-2), 215–238. doi:10.1007/s11127-009-9513-0

Eilat, Y., & Zinnes, C. (2002). The shadow economy in transition countries: Friend or foe? A policy perspective. *World Development*, *30*(7), 1233–1254. doi:10.1016/S0305-750X(02)00036-0

Feld, L. P., & Schneider, F. (2010). Survey on the shadow economy and undeclared earnings in OECD countries. *German Economic Review*, *11*(2), 109–149. doi:10.1111/j.1468-0475.2010.00509.x

Feltenstein, A., & Shamloo, M. (2013). Tax reform, the informal economy, and bank financing of capital formation. *International Tax and Public Finance*, *20*(1), 1–28. doi:10.1007/s10797-012-9213-4

Friedman, E., Johnson, S., Kaufmann, D., & Zoido-Lobaton, P. (2000). Dodging the grabbing hand: The determinants of unofficial activity in 69 countries. *Journal of Public Economics*, *76*(3), 459–493. doi:10.1016/S0047-2727(99)00093-6

Gerxhani, K. (2004). The informal sector in developed and less developed countries: A literature survey. *Public Choice*, *120*(3-4), 267–300. doi:10.1023/B:PUCH.0000044287.88147.5e

Giles, D. E. A. (1997). Causality between the measured and underground economies in New Zealand. *Applied Economics Letters*, *4*(1), 63–67. doi:10.1080/758521835

Giles, D. E. A., Tedds, L. M., & Werkneh, G. (2002). The Canadian underground and measured economies: Granger causality results. *Applied Economics*, *34*(18), 2347–2352. doi:10.1080/00036840210148021

Giles, D. E. A., Werkneh, G. T., & Johnson, B. S. (2001). Asymmetric responses of the underground economy to tax changes: Evidence from New Zealand data. *The Economic Record*, *77*(237), 148–159. doi:10.1111/1475-4932.00010

Goel, R. K., & Saunoris, J. W. (2014). Global corruption and the shadow economy: Spatial aspects. *Public Choice*, *161*(1-2), 119–139. doi:10.1007/s11127-013-0135-1

Hendry, D. F., & Mizon, G. E. (1998). Exogeneity, causality, and co-breaking in economic policy analysis of a small econometric model of money in the UK. *Empirical Economics*, *23*(3), 267–294. doi:10.1007/BF01294408

Holtz-Eakin, D., Newey, W., & Rosen, H. S. (1988). Estimating vector autoregressions with panel data. *Econometrica*, *56*(6), 1371–1395. doi:10.2307/1913103

Johnson, S., Kaufmann, D., & Scleizer, A. (1997). The unofficial economy in transition. *Brookings Papers on Economic Activity*, *2*(2), 159–239. doi:10.2307/2534688

Kleibergen, F., & Paap, R. (2006). Generalized reduced rank tests using the singular value decomposition. *Journal of Econometrics*, *133*(1), 97–126. doi:10.1016/j.jeconom.2005.02.011

La Porta, R., & Scleifer, A. (2008). The unofficial economy and economic development. *Brookings Papers on Economic Activity*, *47*(1), 275–363.

Lee, D. (2013). How does social capital reduce the size of the shadow economy? *Global Economic Review: Perspectives on East Asian Economies and Industries*, *42*(3), 251–268. doi:10.1080/1226508X.2013.833846

Levin, A., Lin, C. F., & Chu, C. (2002). Unit root tests in panel data: Asymptotic and finite-sample properties. *Journal of Econometrics*, *108*(1), 1–24. doi:10.1016/S0304-4076(01)00098-7

Loayza, N. V. (1996). The economics of the informal sector: A simple model and some empirical evidence from Latin America. *Carnegie-Rochester Conference Series on Public Policy*, *45*, 129–162. doi:10.1016/S0167-2231(96)00021-8

Love, I., & Zicchino, L. (2006). Financial development and dynamic investment behavior: Evidence from panel VAR. *The Quarterly Review of Economics and Finance*, *46*(2), 190–210. doi:10.1016/j.qref.2005.11.007

Lutkepohl, H. (2007). *New introduction to multiple time series analysis*. Berlin: Springer-Verlag.

Meon, P.-G., & Sekkat, K. (2004). Does the quality of institutions limit the MENA's integration in the world economy? *World Economy*, *27*(9), 1475–1498. doi:10.1111/j.0378-5920.2004.00661.x

OECD. (2002). *Measuring the non-observed economy: A handbook*. Paris: OECD Publications Service.

Orsi, R., Raggi, D., & Turino, F. (2014). Size, trend, and policy implications of the underground economy. *Review of Economic Dynamics*, *17*(3), 417–436. doi:10.1016/j.red.2013.11.001

Sandmo, A. (2012). An evasive topic: Theorizing about the hidden economy. *International Tax and Public Finance*, *19*(1), 5–24. doi:10.1007/s10797-011-9185-9

Schaffer, M. E. (2010). xtivreg2: Stata module to perform extended IV/2SLS, GMM and AC/HAC, LIML and k-class regression for panel data models. Retrieved from http://ideas.repec.org/c/boc/bocode/s456501.html

Schneider, F. (2005). Shadow economies around the world: What do we really know? *European Journal of Political Economy*, *21*(3), 598–642. doi:10.1016/j.ejpoleco.2004.10.002

Schneider, F. (2013). *Size and development of the shadow economy of 31 European and 5 other OECD countries from 2003 to 2013: A further decline* [Unpublished manuscript]. Johannes Kepler University of Linz, Department of Economics. Retrieved from http://www.econ.jku.at/members/schneider/files/publications/2013/shadeceurope31_jan2013.pdf

Schneider, F. (2014). In the shadow of the state-the informal economy and informal economy labor force. *Law and Economics Review*, *5*(4), 227–248. doi: 10.2478/danb-2014-0013

Schneider, F., Buehn, A., & Montenegro, C. E. (2010). New estimates for the shadow economies all over the world. *International Economic Journal*, *24*(4), 443–461. doi:10.1080/10168737.2010.525974

Schneider, F., & Enste, D. H. (2000). Shadow economies: Size, causes, and consequences. *Journal of Economic Literature*, *38*(1), 77–114. doi:10.1257/jel.38.1.77

Schneider, F., & Williams, C. C. (2013). *The shadow economy*. London: Profile Books Ltd. doi:10.1017/CBO9781139542289

Teobaldelli, D. (2011). Federalism and the shadow economy. *Public Choice*, *146*(3-4), 269–289. doi:10.1007/s11127-009-9590-0

Torgler, B., Schneider, F., & Schaltegger, C. A. (2010). Local autonomy, tax morale, and the shadow economy. *Public Choice*, *144*(1-2), 293–321. doi:10.1007/s11127-009-9520-1

Vlachaki, M. (2015). The impact of the shadow economy on indirect tax revenues. *Economics and Politics*, *27*(2), 234–265. doi:10.1111/ecpo.12054

Warde, I. (2007). The war on terror, crime and the shadow economy in the MENA countries. *Mediterranean Politics*, *12*(2), 233–248. doi:10.1080/13629390701398033

ENDNOTES

1. Hereafter, economic activities that escape from official economy measurements are going to be called "shadow" throughout the manuscript for the sake of unity in expressions.

2 Transition economies are Bulgaria, Croatia, Czech Republic, Estonia, Hungary, Latvia, Lithuania, Poland, Romania, Slovak Republic, and Slovenia (11 economies). Advanced European economies are Austria, Belgium, Denmark, Finland, France, Germany, Greece, Ireland, Italy, Luxembourg, the Netherlands, Norway, Portugal, Spain, Sweden, Switzerland, and the United Kingdom (17 economies). MENA economies are Algeria, Bahrain, Egypt, Iran, Israel, Jordan, Kuwait, Lebanon, Libya, Morocco, Oman, Saudi Arabia, Syria, Tunisia, United Arab Emirates, and Yemen (16 economies).

3 Here, tax evasion means simply the taxpayer's deliberate act of underreporting his taxable income. Fiscal burden means discouragement due to high tax rates in narrow sense, and due to both high taxes and social security contributions in broad sense.

4 See Gerxhani (2004) for an extensive literature survey on shadow economy.

5 In all panel-VAR-based estimations, the routine coded by Love and Zicchino (2006) is used throughout the study.

6 DGP is the abbreviation for the data generation process.

7 The two-step GMM estimations and the diagnostics are carried out by routines coded by Baum et al. (2003, 2007).

8 Because of the lack of comparable shadow economy estimates for MENA after 2007, estimations are carried out with different sample periods for Europe and MENA. However, without loss of generality, it is assumed that inference based on the period 1999-2007 does not change considerably if the post-2007 data were available.

9 The Levin-Lin-Chu test statistics and the associated probability values computed respectively for the variables S, F and Y are as follows: For developed Europe, -3.957 (0.000), -1.989 (0.023), -5.046 (0.000); for transition Europe, -1.837 (0.033), -5.555 (0.000), -1.897 (0.0289), and for MENA, -5.391 (0.000), -5.678 (0.000), -8.323 (0.000). These statistics belong to estimations with demeaned data and a deterministic trend. The null hypothesis of unit root is rejected at 5% statistical significance level in all of the cases, implying the stationarity of the panel series.

10 Computations are carried out by the codes written by Schaffer (2010).

11 Endogenous variables are instrumented with their own lags. Lag lengths of the instruments are set to the earliest lag that exhibits a joint harmony in the results of the identification tests, endogeneity test and the Hansen's J test, indicating the validity of the selected instruments.

Chapter 11
Shadow Economy:
An Analysis for EU-27 and Turkey

Hale Akbulut
Hacettepe University, Turkey

ABSTRACT

The aim of this chapter is to investigate shadow economy on an EU-27 and Turkey basis. For this purpose, firstly the definition, causes\ and consequences of shadow economy together with its relationship with tax evasion are discussed. In addition, the causes of shadow economy are examined for EU-27 during the period 2003-2012. It was done both statistically and empirically by employing scatter plot diagrams and the random effects model. While empirical findings confirm the effects of taxes, income level, trade and population on the shadow economy, statistical findings mention the effects of governance related indicators. Another main finding of this chapter is about Turkey. Accordingly, shadow economy in Turkey is observed to be higher than in the EU-27 and taking into consideration the comparative statistical findings about the causes of shadow economy, the main reasons of shadow economy in Turkey are thought to be governance related.

INTRODUCTION

Today a large share of economic activities performs in the so-called "shadow economy" in both developed and developing countries. In addition to its large volume, the shadow economy is usually perceived as an economic problem as it has harmful effects on the economy such as distorting taxation justice and decreasing the efficiency of economic policies. These circumstances, together with some increasing economic problems such as budget deficit and unemployment, increased the concerns about shadow economy. However, the definition, structure and the causes of shadow economy are still not clear. This chapter investigates related deficiencies on an EU-27 and Turkey basis.

The chapter is built on three main aims. The first aim of the chapter is to clarify the definition and the structure of shadow economy. For that purpose, previous studies together with the work of the OECD (2002) are employed and the structure of shadow economy, its specific characteristics, its relationship with other non-observed economic activities, and tax evasion are investigated. The causes and consequences

DOI: 10.4018/978-1-5225-0053-7.ch011

of shadow economy are discussed and its measurement is given. The second aim of the chapter is to explore shadow economy and its causes in the EU-27. In line with these, both statistical and empirical relationships between shadow economy and various indicators are examined by using data from the period 2003-2012. The correlation between the shadow economy and some economic and governance related indicators are examined by employing scatter plots diagrams.

The last aim of the chapter is to explore the shadow economy in Turkey. The trend of the shadow economy in Turkey for the period 2003-2012 is given and a comparison with the EU-27 is made in order to have more rational inferences. The data of possible factors that cause shadow economy is compared with EU-27 averages. This chapter also presents a modest guide for policy makers as it relatively presents the effects of both economic and governance related indicators which would be beneficial while struggling with the shadow economy among the countries in question.

The chapter is organized as follows. It starts with the definition and some characteristics of the shadow economy and the impacts of shadow economy including both benefits and harms are also discussed. The causes and consequences of shadow economy are also given in that section. The following section investigates the measurement of the shadow economy and problems of data and measurement are given. In order to clarify the definition and structure of the shadow economy even further, its relationship with tax evasion is presented. The next section presents a detailed analysis of the shadow economy in the EU-27 and followed by an exploration of the structure of shadow economy in Turkey. The next section includes an empirical analysis which examines the relationship between shadow economy and its causes in the EU-27. Concluding remarks and views are provided in the last section.

BACKGROUND

Shadow Economy: Definition, Causes and Consequences

The shadow economy is one of the main problems of many countries in different forms and degrees. An important share of economic activities occurs in a shadow economy in both developed and developing countries. In addition, some economic problems such as the need for public finance, high unemployment rates, and budget deficit have increased the concerns about the shadow economy. However, a clear definition of shadow economy has not yet been formulated. Schneider and Enste (2000, p. 78) stated one commonly used definition of the shadow economy as "all economic activities that contribute to the officially calculated (or observed) gross national product but are currently unregistered." Choi and Thum (2002, p. 2) states that in simple term the shadow economy "constitutes activities that are not recorded in the government statistics."

Economists usually use different terms such as "shadow economy," "underground economy," "informal economy" or "hidden economy" without always clarifying what they mean. The OECD handbook for "Measuring the Non-Observed Economy" (2002, p.36) is a beneficial source that shed some light on the definition of shadow economy and its relationship with some other non-observed economic activities. The handbook states that "the groups of activities most likely to be non-observed are those that are underground, illegal, informal sector, or undertaken by households for their own final use." And "the deficiencies in the basic data collection program" are also admitted as being a part of non-observed economy.

Accordingly, non-observed economy consists of five main areas: (i) underground production; (ii) illegal production; (iii) informal sector production; (iv) household production for own final use; and (v) production missed due to deficiencies in data collection program[1].

The shadow economy takes part in a non-observed economy and is especially related to underground and informal economy and usually considers T4, T5, and T6 in Figure 1 which is solely the economic part of the non-observed economy (Garvanlieva, Andonov, & Nikolov, 2012, p.8).

The shadow economy is usually related to low income levels; however, it is not a set of survival activities performed by destitute people. Yet, in some situations the shadow economy has been intertwined with the formal economy. Individual workers may switch between the two sectors even during the same workday. Thus, the shadow economy is not an individual condition, but rather a process of income-generation characterized by one feature: it is unregulated by the institutions of the society, in a legal and social environment in which similar activities are regulated (Castells & Portes, 1989, p. 12).

We can define some special characteristics for shadow economy by benefiting from related literature. First, the shadow economic activity must create economic value. However, it is not a sufficient condition in order to qualify an economic activity as shadow economic activity because shadow economic activities are not included in national accounts (Danopoulos & Znidaric, 2007, p.70), and government fails to measure actual volume of production activities. Even if labor force shifts from shadow economy to formal sector, measure of Gross Domestic Product (GDP) growth rates will be misleading.

Because the increase in growth rate has been caused by decreasing shadow economy, and the real growth in total income has been considerably smaller than indicated by the GDP (Feige, 1979; Petersen, Thiessen, & Wohlleben, 2010, p. 425). Secondly, as shadow economic activities cannot be observed and reported to governmental organizations, they do not constitute a tax base for government. Thus, while shadow economic activities increase net real income of workers, they distort government revenues and increase tax burden on the official sector. Thirdly, shadow economic activities are irregular. There are no rules for shadow economic activities such as minimum wage standard or job security, and workers in the shadow economy cannot benefit from various opportunities such as retirement benefits and health insurance.

Another feature of the shadow economy concerns the characteristic of labor. Workers usually receive fewer benefits or less wage accompanied with worse working conditions and these characteristics can be subsumed under the general heading of "*down-graded labor*" (Castells & Portes, 1989, p. 26). And

Figure 1. Analytical framework
Source: OECD (2002, p. 43).

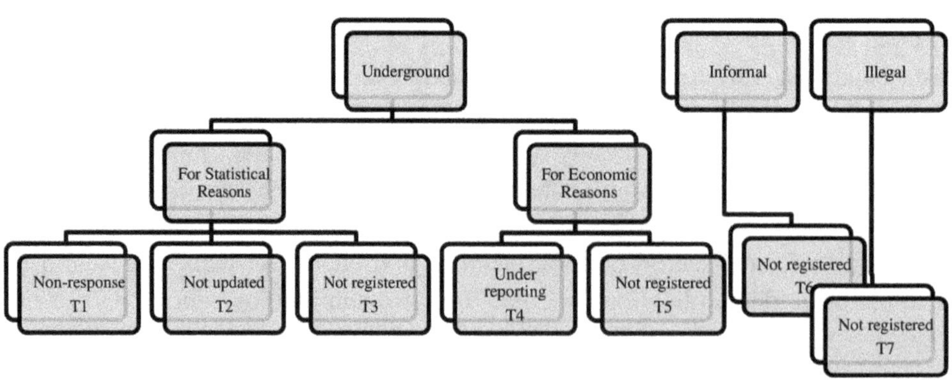

last, although the shadow economy is irregular and not included in national accounts, as Castells and Portes (1989, p. 26) suggested "it is an integral component of total national economies, rather than a marginal appendix to them." Thus, shadow economy and formal economy seems to have a systemic connection. The causes of shadow economy are not clearly defined, and there are different views about them. Schneider and Enste (2002) divided the economic causes of shadow economy into four groups: taxes, social security, transfer payments and regulations.

High tax rates are seen as one of the main causes of the shadow economy in a number of studies such as Schneider (1986, 2005, 2007), and that inference may be related to the inverse U shaped Laffer-Curve (Laffer, 1979, p. 75) which shows the relationship between tax rates and tax revenues. Accordingly, increasing tax rates will increase tax revenues; however, this is valid only up to a certain maximum tax rate level. Increasing tax rates beyond this level will result in tax evasion and avoidance and hence decrease in tax revenues. Gutmann (1981) modified the Laffer-Curve by including the shadow economy. For the economy consisting of the public sector, the official sector, and the shadow economy, he suggests that increasing tax rates beyond a certain level will result in a growing shadow economy. Indeed, as Petersen, Thiessen and Wohlleben (2010, p. 422) suggest, increasing burdens of direct and indirect taxes have created incentives to reduce labor supply and consumption in the official markets as governments often consider observable income and consumption as the major taxation base of the state.

Social security and transfer payments are seen as another main cause of the shadow economy as they break down the working incentives of people by guarantying a certain standard of living without any working obligation. In addition, Schneider and Enste (2002, p. 123) suggest that one of the incentives for transfer payment recipients to work illicitly is the increase in opportunity in finding a future regular job through contacts made during this occupation. The regulations especially aimed at labor markets create working disincentives for both employers and employees in the official sector, by increasing costs (Schneider, Buehn, & Montenegro, 2010, p. 445). Similarly, regulations about production such as license fees and registration requirements will increase production costs and tend people to work in shadow economy. Schneider (2012, p. 13) highlights that transition countries have higher levels of regulation and, hence, a higher shadow economy. Figure 2 gives an overview of the economic causes.

Besides tax and social security burdens, Dreher, Kotsogiannis, and McCorriston (2005, p. 2) suggest there is another school of thought that identifies institutional bureaucracy, regulatory discretion, corruption and weak legal system as the main causes of the shadow economy. Danopoulos and Znidaric (2007, p. 71) point to the fact that weak state institutions, official corruption, anemic or inconsistent law enforcement, and lack of political will on the part of the political system attract potential law breakers. There are a number of studies (Dreher, Kotsogiannis, & McCorriston, 2005; Torgler & Schneider, 2007a; Karlinger, 2009) which test the relationship between those factors and shadow economy empirically. Of those, Dreher, Kotsogiannis, and McCorriston (2005) and Torgler and Schneider (2007a) suggest that increase in institutional quality leads to a smaller shadow economy. Karlinger (2009) points to the effect of competition on shadow economy in countries having a different size of corruption.

Last, the volume of the shadow economy is affected by some macroeconomic variables such as inflation, unemployment, per capita income, and income equality. In addition, economic instability, uncertainty, and low standard of living increase tendency of people to work without records. Moreover, Castells, and Portes (1989, p. 28) point to the effects of international competition. Domestic production cannot compete with imports from countries which have low labor costs. This will inevitably tend domestic firms to either close down or to operate in the shadow economy.

Figure 2. Economic causes for the shadow economy
Source: Schneider and Enste (2002, p. 104).

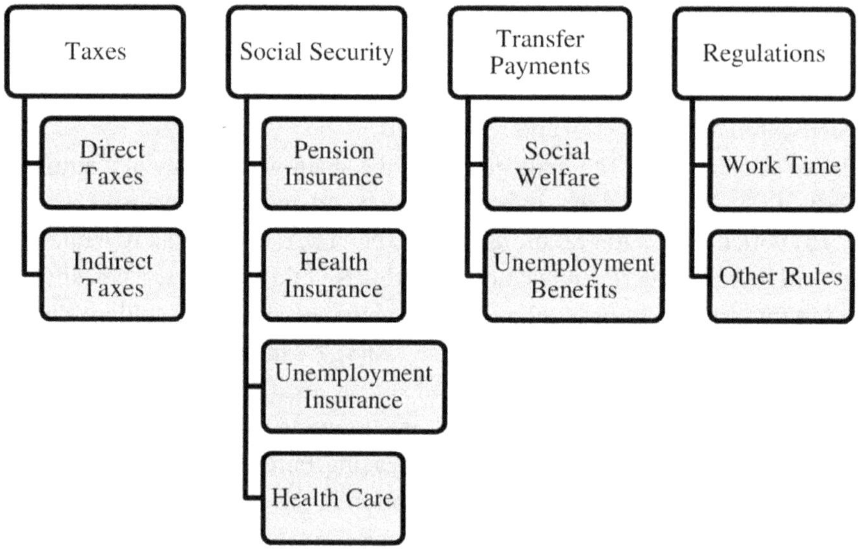

There are contradicting arguments about the effects of the shadow economy on overall economy and the basic arguments for and against it can be summarized as follows. The supporters of shadow economy argue that governments sometimes indulge in excessive and wasteful spending and also establish unnecessary and inefficient regulation in the economy. Shadow economy that arises from high tax rates makes governments to realize that there is a limit for how much they can spend (Spiro, 2005, p. 180). Another advantage of the shadow economy arises if there are many unnecessary and inefficient regulations. The shadow economy reduces the cost of bureaucracy and labor which in turn contribute to growth. As it decreased labor costs and creates new job opportunities, the shadow economy serves to decrease unemployment, thus forcing the official sector to reduce costs and improve quality due to competition.

However, the shadow economy contains some disadvantages. If tax revenues are decreased by tax evasion arising from high tax rates, governments may choose to increase tax rates in order to increase revenues. This policy will result in increasing tax burden on the formal sector and distort taxation justice. In addition, the shadow economy makes statistics less reliable and this may lead to incorrect economic policies. Danopoulos and Znidaric (2007, pp. 71-72) states the shadow economy renders government fiscal policy ineffective due to uncertainty about the actual amount of revenue. Last, as the shadow economy is easy to operate in small scaled firms, it is usually unproductive and less efficient.

How to Measure the Shadow Economy?

As mentioned in the previous section, the shadow economy is a critical issue and its incorrect measurement will distort the effectiveness of economic policies. As the size of shadow economy is still an unresolved issue, there are also difficulties in measuring it. Figure 3 gives the summary of all approaches including sub-categories.

Figure 3. A summary of approaches to estimate the size of shadow economy
Source: Frey and Pommerehne (1984), Schneider and Enste (2000), and Schneider and Enste (2002).

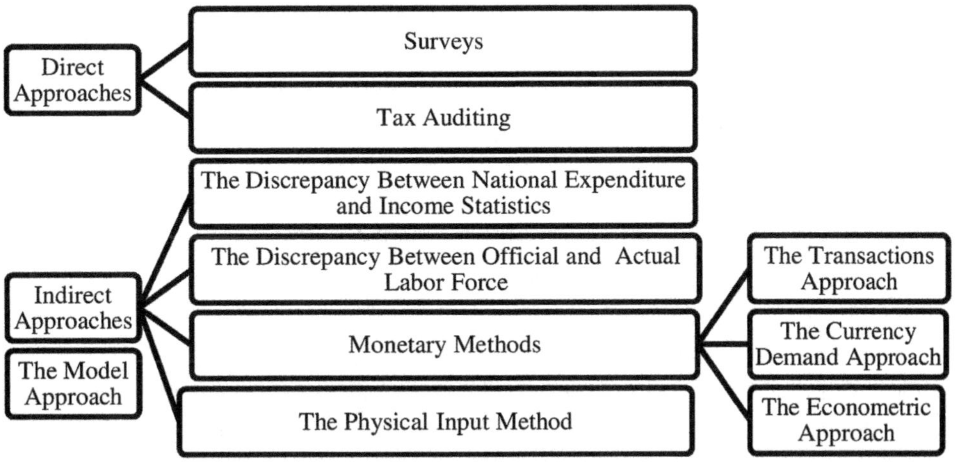

Direct approaches are microeconomic approaches which depend on either surveys or samples based on voluntary replies, or tax auditing and other compliance methods. Direct approaches provide detailed information on the structure of the shadow economy. The main disadvantage of this method is its dependency upon the individuals questioned. The individuals in the sample may not reflect the whole population and they may prefer to hide their behaviors. Moreover, even if individuals in the sample are honest, they may be uninformed about the shadow economy and the results are sensitive to their understanding. Some kind of household production may be mistaken as shadow economic activities (Petersen, Thiessen, & Wohlleben, 2010, p. 432).

The results of direct approaches are also sensitive to the feature of the survey. Isachsen and Strom (1989) found out that almost twice as many people admitted to operating in shadow activity by mail after being interviewed. Direct approach is also leads only to point estimates and is unable to provide estimates of the shadow economy over a longer period of time. Isaschsen, Knovland, and Strom (1982), Isaschsen and Strom (1985), Mogensen, Kvist, Kormendi and Pedersen (1995), and Feld and Larsen (2005, 2008, 2009) are examples of studies which employ sample surveys in order to measure shadow economy (Schneider & Enste, 2000, pp. 91-92; Schneider, 2014, p. 10).

Indirect approaches are macro-economic in nature which use different indicators in order to measure the shadow economy. Four indirect approaches are commonly used: the discrepancy between national expenditure and income statistics, the discrepancy between the official and actual labor force, monetary methods and physical input approach. The first approach is based on the presumption that the discrepancy between the expenditure and income reflects the shadow economy. However, Frey and Pommerehne (1984, p. 6) point to many other factors influencing the national accounts calculations. The discrepancy between expenditure and income may reflect omissions, errors and tax authorities' behavior. In that context, results are not completely reliable.

Measuring the shadow economy by the discrepancy between the official and actual labor force is based on the idea of a decline in labor force participation will reflect an increase in the shadow economy. However, Schneider and Enste (2002, p. 17) suggest that differences in the rate of participation may also have other causes and individuals may simultaneously work in both official sector and shadow economy.

Thus, the estimation results of this approach are not completely reliable. Monetary approach is based on the assumption that shadow economic activities are usually settled by paying cash. This assumption is reasonable as transactions paid in cash are easy to be hidden from fiscal administrations. Schneider and Enste (2002, p. 17) suggest that "if the demand for cash rises above the 'normal' relative or absolute value, one concludes that shadow economic activities are increasing." And, if the amount of currency used to make hidden transactions can be estimated, then it could be multiplied by the income-velocity of money in order to get a measure of the size of the shadow economy (Ahumada, Alvaredo, & Canavese, 2008, p. 97).

The size of shadow economy can be measured by monetary approach with three different methods: fixed ratio approach, transactions approach, and econometric approach. The first method assumes that the ratio between currency demand and money is fixed and the excess currency may reflect the size of shadow economy. This approach is first used by Cagan (1958) and it followed by Gutmann (1977) and Tanzi (1980). While Gutmann (1977) used statistical analysis, Tanzi (1980) estimated a currency demand function econometrically. The currency demand approach is employed by later studies (Tanzi, 1983; Bhattacharyya, 1990, 1999) and became the most commonly used methods. However, it has been criticized for the following reasons. Factors that cause shadow economic activity other than tax burden are ignored and, moreover, the assumption of equal velocity of money for both types of economies is suspicious. In addition, cash is not spent in the shadow sector only, but in the official sector. Therefore, the cash circulation in the shadow economy is much lower than in the official sector. However, shadow economic activities are usually paid immediately because of distrust, so money circulation in shadow sector may be faster than in the official sectors, too (Petersen, Thiessen & Wohlleben, 2010, p. 434).

The transactions approach was first developed by Feige (1979). This approach is based on an assumption that the relationship between the volume of transaction and money is constant over time. If this relationship holds, then the total stock of money gives an indication of total transactions in both the official and hidden economy. Relating total nominal Gross National Product (GNP) to total transactions, the hidden economy's GNP can be derived residually by subtracting officially measured GNP from total GNP (Frey & Pommerehne, 1984, p. 6).

The last monetary approach is the econometric approach. As there are a number of factors that affect currency demand other than shadow economy, recent studies have intensified effort to control these factors and ensure that the "extra" currency can really be attributed to the working of the underground economy (Frey & Pommerehne, 1984, p. 10). This approach is pioneered by Tanzi (1980) and Klovland (1980) and followed by some later studies (Tanzi, 1983; Isachsen, Klovland, & Strom, 1982; Langfeldt, 1982). It is assumed that shadow economic activities are paid for in cash and the velocity of money in both shadow and official sector are assumed to be equal. The main cause of shadow economy is assumed to be taxation and the discrepancy between currency demand with and without taxation is employed in order to measure shadow economy. However, this approach has been criticized for its unrealistic assumptions.

The last indirect measurement method which is the physical input method can be divided into two different methods. The first method is *Kaufmann-Kaliberda Method* and it is based on the assumption that electricity consumption is the single best physical indicator of overall economic activity (Kaufmann & Kaliberda, 1996). By employing electricity consumption they estimate a proxy for the overall economy and compare it with the official statistics. The difference between the growth of official GDP and the growth of electricity consumption is attributed to the growth of the shadow economy. However, it has also been criticized because all economic activities does not require electricity consumption. In addition, technical progress has been ignored and there may be considerable differences in the elasticity of electricity/GDP across countries or changes over time (Schneider & Enste, 2000, p. 96).

The second physical input method is the *Lacko Method.* In this method, it is assumed that a certain part of the shadow economy is associated with the household consumption of electricity. In order to measure the actual size of shadow economy, one should know how much GDP is produced by one unit of electricity in the shadow economy of each country. However, as it is not known, she takes the result of the known shadow economy and applies it to the other countries. This method again has been criticized because it only considers the shadow economy occurring in the household sector and as it employs a base value for shadow economy the results may not be reliable (Schneider & Enste, 2002, pp. 23-24).

The last approach in order to measure the shadow economy is the model approach. Direct and indirect approaches assume that only one indicator reflects the size of shadow economy, however the shadow economy is affected by various factors. The model firstly links the unobserved variables to observed indicators and the model approach considers the multiple causes that contribute to the growth of the hidden economy as well as its multiple effects (Karaboytcheva & Andrada, 2012, pp. 168). Secondly, the casual relationships among the unobserved variable (the shadow economy) are specified (Schneider & Enste, 2000, p. 98). In summary, there are various methods that can be used to measure the shadow economy and each of them has their own advantages and disadvantages.

MAIN FOCUS OF THE CHAPTER

Shadow Economy and Tax Evasion: Distinctions and Linkages

The shadow economy and tax evasion are related concerns, but the linkages and distinctions between them have to be clarified. We can start by mentioning different sectors in which productive activities take place. Human productive activities[2] are taking place in the household sector, the market sector, and the shadow economy. Figure 4 represents different types of economic sectors. The right rectangle (MKJL) represents the subsistence economy or household production. Household production is exemplified by Ironmonger (1999, p. 3) as the provision of meals, child care, clean clothes, accommodation, shopping, voluntary work and self education. The left rectangle (ABCD) represents the market sector or formal sector which consists of public and private sector and the rectangle (BLDM) which is between market production and household production represents the shadow economy.

In the System of National Accounts (SNA) literature, household production together with shadow economy is considered as informal sector (BDKJ). However, household production was almost neglected in theoretical and empirical economics (Petersen, Thiessen, & Wohlleben, 2010, p. 425).

As the income from the shadow economy and household sector is unobservable, only the market income remains as a base for taxation. However, people may earn a remarkable amount of income from these sectors, so they must also be considered. Due to difficulties in determining these income generating activities, tax burden usually falls on the formal sector. In that context, increasing tendency of tax evasion may lead people from the official sector to the shadow economy again. Therefore, the shadow economy and tax evasion are interpenetrating subjects. Nevertheless, the informal sector, which consists of the shadow economy and household production is not the only source of tax evasion and tax avoidance[3].

In Figure 4, one part of the market sector is legally withdrawn from the income tax base due to the existing tax allowances and exemptions (CDEF) while another part is illegally withdrawn from the income

Figure 4. Components of total income or wealth
Source: Petersen, Thiessen & Wohlleben (2010, p. 425).

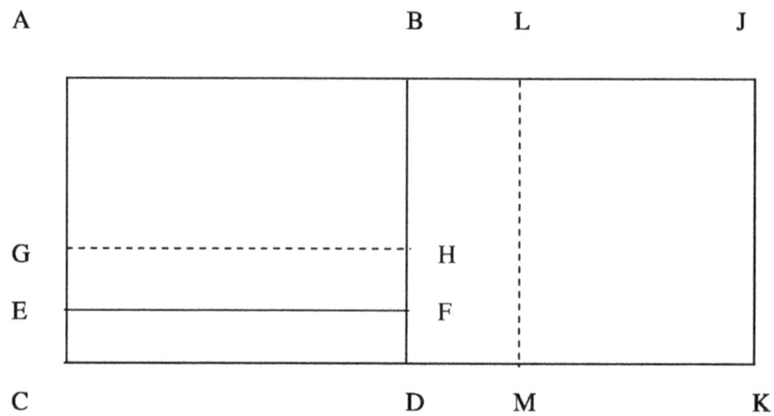

tax base (EFGH) in favor of tax evasion. This part (EFGH) is measured in the SNA, but not reported to the fiscal administration. The tax base here is hidden from tax authorities by underreporting incomes or overvaluing costs. A number of economic agents prefer this method in order to reduce production costs. Therefore, the size of tax distortion arising from formal economic activities is tidy.

However, many individuals engage in shadow economy depending on some reasons other than evading taxes. These reasons which have been discussed previously may include the intensity of regulations, distrust of public authority, dissatisfaction of public services and institutional quality, and avoiding international competition (Castells & Portes, 1989; Schneider & Enste, 2002; Dreher, Kotsogiannis, & McCorriston, 2005). In addition, Sam (2010, p. 168-172) suggests that while attempts to reduce shadow economy contribute to the government's revenue, measures to reduce tax evasion do not necessarily reduce tax evasion from the shadow economy. He also pays attention to the difference between taxable income and non-taxable income in the shadow economy. Accordingly, all economic activities are not taxable for example small enterprises are hardly taxed because their income is often below the tax threshold income level. In conclusion, tax evasion and shadow economy are intertwined; however, they do not reflect exactly same subjects.

The Shadow Economy and Causes in The EU-27

The shadow economy is sometimes perceived as the problem of developing countries; however, it is still a worthwhile issue for developed countries. On average across the EU-27, the shadow economy is as large as 18.4% of the economic activity in 2012 (Schneider, 2013). Figure 5 shows the size of shadow economies in 2012 and growth rates of shadow economy during the period 2003-2012 in the EU-27 countries.

As can be seen in Figure 5, Bulgaria (33.9%), Romania (30.7%), and Lithuania (30.1%) have the largest shares, while Austria (9.1%), Luxembourg (9.1%) and Netherlands (10.7%) have the smallest size of shadow economies. In general, the share of shadow economy increases from West Europe to East Europe. Overall, the EU-27 countries have negative growth rates for shadow economy, so size of shadow economies are decreased during 2003-2012 in all EU-27 countries. However, the size of shadow economy in EU-27 is 20.3% of the official economy on the average which can still be interpreted as a high percentage rating. As the structure and the size of shadow economies vary in different EU-27 countries,

Figure 5. Shadow economy (in % of official GDP (2003-2012 Averages)) and shadow economy growth (2003-2012) in EU-27
Source: Schneider (2013).

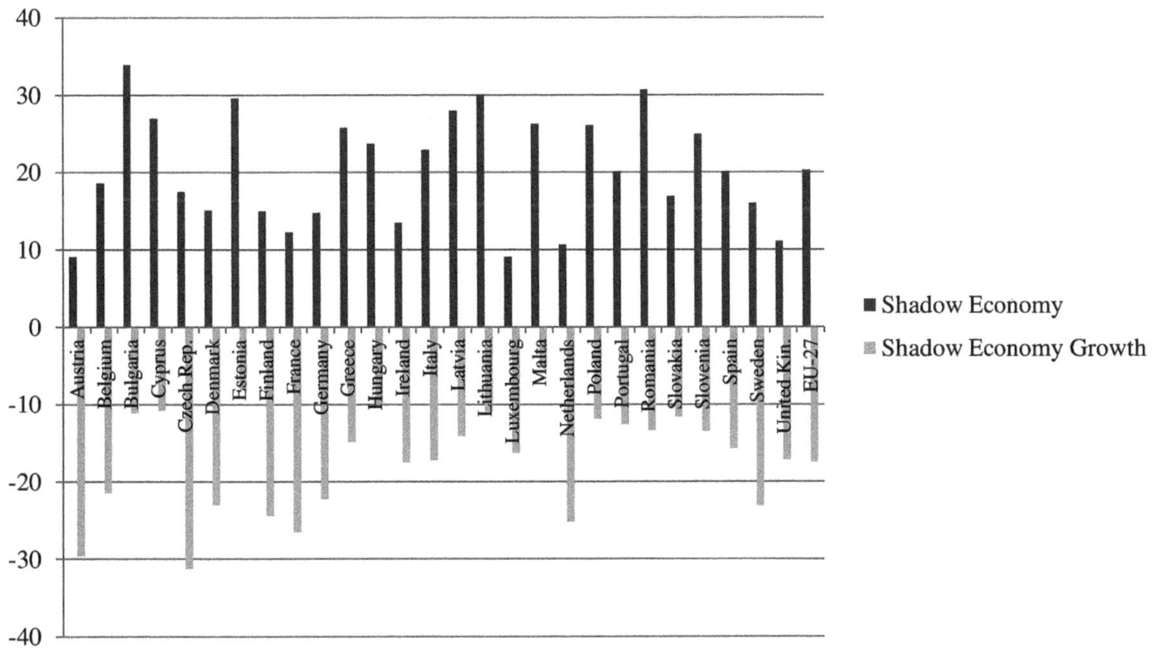

different policy measures have been used in order to reduce the size of shadow economy. These policy measures include improved detection, increased penalties, promoting benefits of formal work etc. and more detailed information about some specific measures can be found in Eurofound (2008, 2009), Jensen and Wohlbier (2012), Packard, Koettl, and Montenegro (2012) and Schneider and Williams (2013).

Different points such as government expenditures, tax burden, regulations, and institutional quality were listed as causes of shadow economy in the previous section. These factors are examined here to locate the main causes of the shadow economy in the EU-27, while scatter plots diagram is employed in order to observe the relationship between shadow economy and the other causes in question by using 2003-2012 data. As high tax burden is admitted as one of the main causes of the shadow economic activities, the correlation between top marginal tax rates and shadow economy is handled first. Although the relationship does not appear strong, a positive relationship is observed between top marginal tax rates and the size of shadow economy (Figure 6a). Therefore, countries with higher top marginal tax rates have larger size of shadow economies which is also consistent with our previous debates.

One of the other main causes of the shadow economy is huge government expenditures. It was mentioned above that the tendency to shadow economy may be caused by some kind of protest of people who think that government expenditures are excessive and wasteful. There seems no correlation between shadow economy and government spending (Figure 6b). Even so, Cyprus and Malta, both which have the highest government spending, face a high shadow economy. An interesting relationship is observed for agricultural shares (Figure 6c). Accordingly, an increase in the share of agriculture in GDP is positively related to shadow economy but only up to a certain level. Beyond this level of agricultural share, the size of shadow economy seems uncorrelated with the agricultural share.

Figure 6. Scatter plots of shadow economy and some selected indicators

Sources: Fraser Institute (EFW, 2013), Schneider (2013), Heritage Foundation (2014) and World Development Indicators (WB, 2014).

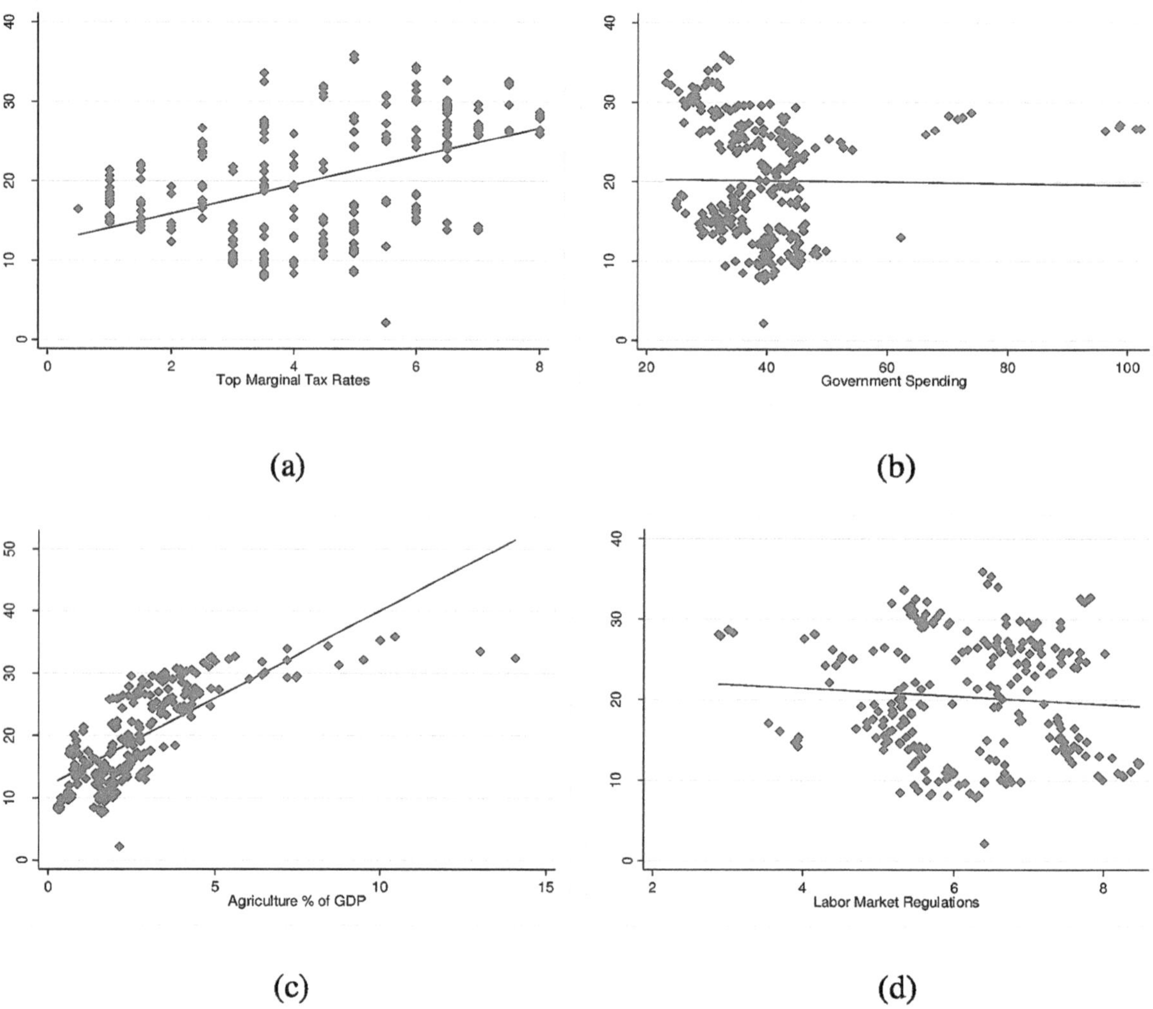

Additionally, it is worth mentioning that countries found in that region of the diagram which is denoted by largest agricultural share include Bulgaria and Romania, the two biggest shadow economies in the EU-27. Regulations especially related to labor markets are mentioned as important cause of shadow economy. The relationship between labor market regulations and shadow economy is observed to have weak correlation with the shadow economy (Figure 6d). Even Greece with lowest level of labor market regulations (4.34% for 2003-2012) still is one of the biggest shadow economies in Europe while the opposite is true for United Kingdom with highest level of labor market regulations (8.26% for 2003-2012).

Thus, labor market regulations are not a strong determinant of the shadow economy in the EU-27.

In addition to economic indicators such as taxes and expenses, the sectoral composition of the economy and regulations; indicators related to governance may be effectively based on the size of shadow economy. In that context, World Governance Indicators (WB, 2013) are employed here and the relationship between shadow economy and different governance indicators are observed. World Governance

Indicators[4] include six main topics: control of corruption, political stability and absence of violence/terrorism, regulatory quality, rule of law, voice and accountability and government effectiveness[5]. The relationship between control of corruption and shadow economy is observed as negative (Figure 7a) and this finding is consistent with the expectations.

In addition, Bulgaria and Romania which have large size of shadow economies, are the two countries that have lowest index rates for control of corruption on average (-0.1467 for Bulgaria, and -0.2192 for Romania). Similarly Austria, Luxembourg, and the Netherlands with small size of shadow economies have high index rates for control of corruption on average (1.8403 for Austria, 1.9529 for Luxembourg, and 2.1151 for the Netherlands).

All of other governance indicators again have a negative relationship with the size of shadow economy in EU-27 (Figure 7). However, the correlations of some indicators are not so strong. The index of political stability and absence of violence/terrorism has the weakest relationship with shadow economy. On the other hand, stronger relationships are observed for rule of law, voice and accountability and government effectiveness in the EU-27 countries.

In summary, control of corruption, regulatory quality, rule of law, voice and accountability and government effectiveness were observed to have stronger relationships with the size of shadow economies in the EU-27 compared to the political stability indicator. In addition, they seem also more effective when compared to economic indicators - top marginal tax rates, government spending and labor market regulations. These findings are important with respect to policy making and dealing with indicators which have stronger correlations with the shadow economy and they are recommended as a weapon which can be used to fight against shadow economy in the EU-27.

Some Notes on Shadow Economy in Turkey

Although Turkey managed to decrease the share of shadow economy to GDP especially after 2003, nevertheless it still maintains to be one of the main economic problems. Schneider (2013) estimated the share of shadow economy in 2012 (in % of GDP) as 27.2% which is higher than the EU-27 averages. Figure 8 shows the trend of the shadow economy in Turkey (in % of GDP) which is always higher than the EU-27 average. Although the shadow economy in Turkey is very large compared to the EU average, it is smaller than the EU-27's largest shadow economy – Bulgaria. Nevertheless, this does not mean that shadow economic activities in Turkey are low. Especially in recent years, several measures have been taken effect such as "KADIM - The Project of Struggling Against Informal Employment" by the Ministry of Labor and Social Security and "The Action Plan of Struggling Against Shadow Economy" by the Finance Ministry[6]. In addition to some other ministries, governmental and sometimes non-governmental organizations also help to serve combating shadow economy.

When we further make comparisons for tax evasion, a worse situation is observed in terms of Turkey. Figure 9 shows the trend of tax evasion (in % of GDP) in Turkey and the EU-27.

Although Turkey managed to decrease the share of tax evasion up to the global 2008 crisis, it started to increase again after that date depending on high inflation and decrease in the purchasing power of individuals. The difference between tax evasion shares of Turkey and Luxembourg which has lowest level of tax evasion share (as an average for the period of 2003-2012) seems worthwhile. In addition, average tax evasion in Turkey is higher than the EU-27 average and Romania which has highest level on average. The causes of the shadow economy in the EU-27 are examined by using scatter plots diagrams in the previous section, however as there is no large scale of data, this method is not preferred for

Figure 7. Scatter plots of shadow economy and world governance indicators in EU-27 for the period of 2003-2012
Source: World Governement Indicators (2013), WB (2014) and Schneider (2013).

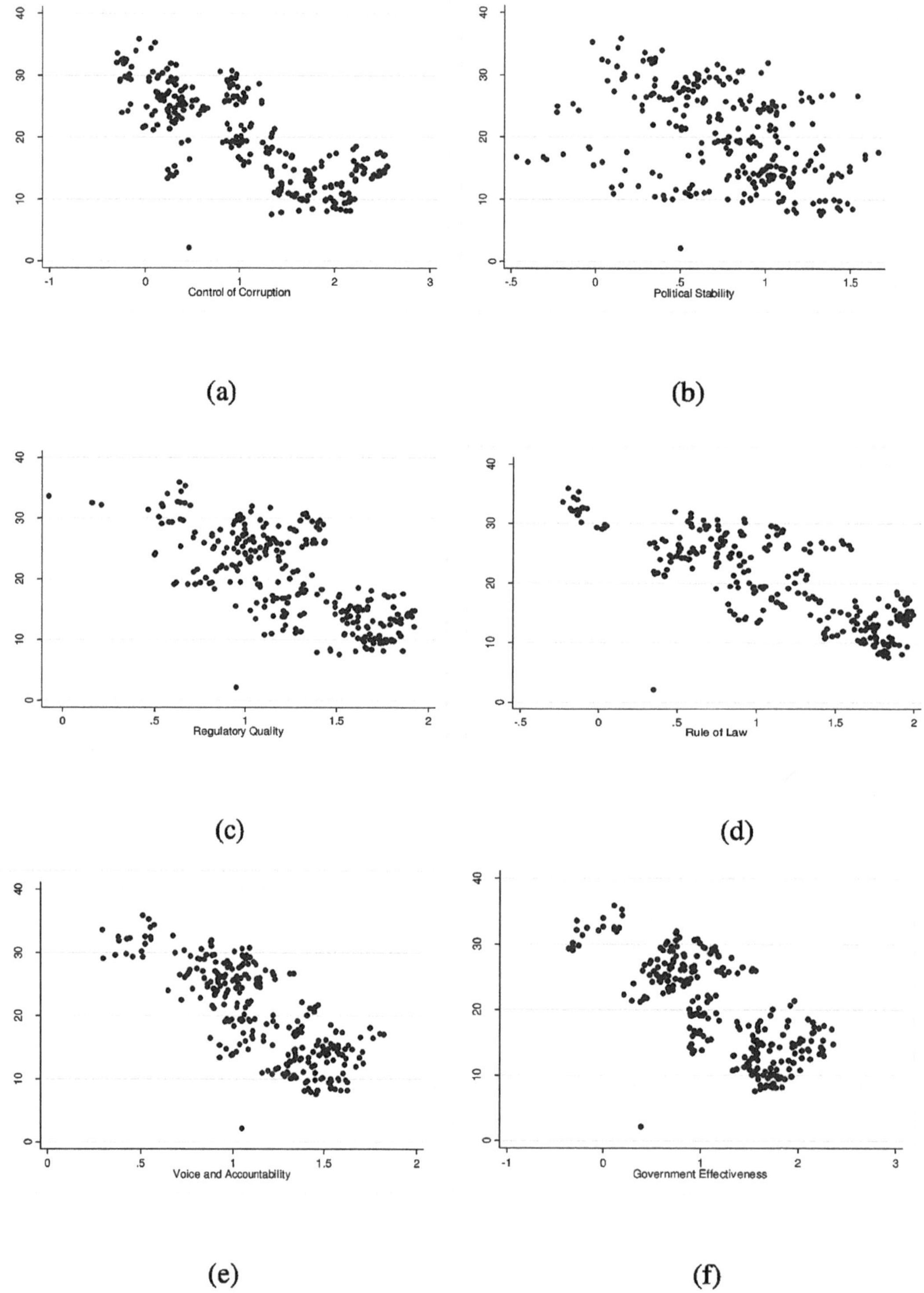

Figure 8. Shadow economy (in % of official GDP) in the EU-27 and Turkey
Source: Schneider (2013).

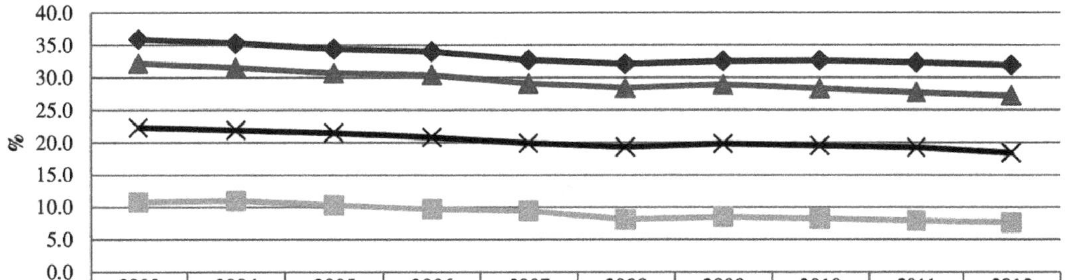

	2003	2004	2005	2006	2007	2008	2009	2010	2011	2012
Bulgaria	35.9	35.3	34.4	34.0	32.7	32.1	32.5	32.6	32.3	31.9
Austria	10.8	11.0	10.3	9.7	9.4	8.1	8.5	8.2	7.9	7.6
Turkey	32.2	31.5	30.7	30.4	29.1	28.4	28.9	28.3	27.7	27.2
EU-27	22.3	21.9	21.5	20.8	19.9	19.3	19.8	19.5	19.2	18.4

Figure 9. Tax evasion (in % of GDP) in selected EU countries and Turkey
Source: Schneider (2013).

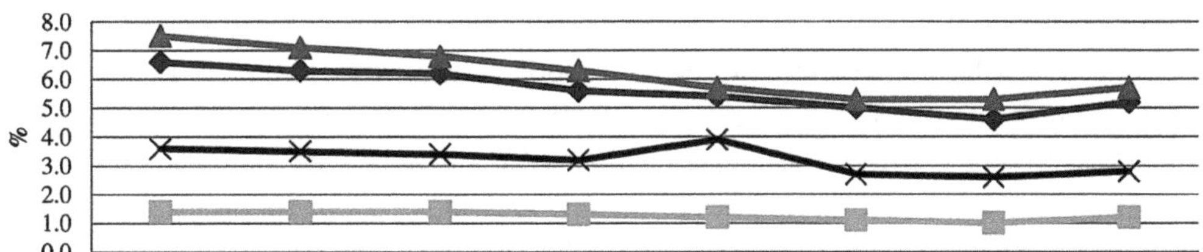

	2003	2004	2005	2006	2007	2008	2009	2010
Romania	6.6	6.3	6.2	5.6	5.4	5.0	4.6	5.2
Luxembourg	1.4	1.4	1.4	1.3	1.2	1.1	1.0	1.2
Turkey	7.5	7.1	6.8	6.3	5.7	5.3	5.3	5.7
EU-27	3.6	3.5	3.4	3.2	3.9	2.7	2.6	2.8

Turkey. The magnitudes and trend of possible causes are rather compared with EU-27 averages. Figure 10 shows top marginal tax rates for Turkey and the EU-27. While EU-27 countries have a top marginal tax rate of 4.44% on average, the rate is 6.88% in Turkey.

Additionally, rates are always higher than in the EU-27 within the period 2003-2012. However, it is worth noting that the situation differs when tax revenues as a share of GDP is employed. After a change in budget system in Turkey in 2006, tax revenues as a share of GDP become 19.77% (WB, 2014) on average (2003-2012). However, tax revenue share of the EU-27 is 26.65% on average, which is higher than in that of Turkey. One must also note that the composition of taxes have to be considered in order to talk about the effects on the shadow economy.

Indirect taxes may increase the size of shadow economy as they are more difficult to be retained and controlled. Furthermore, high indirect tax rates in some commodities such as cigarettes, alcohol and fuel oil may encourage smuggling thereby deepening the problem of shadow economy. In EU-27 the share of direct and indirect taxes are quite similar in recent years: the share of indirect taxes as a percentage of total tax burden is 34.5% and the share of direct taxes as a percentage of total tax burden is 33.2% in 2011 (EC, 2013, pp. 178-188). However, tax revenues in Turkey depend heavily on indirect taxes. While

Figure 10. Top marginal tax rates in Turkey and EU-27 during 2003-2012
Source: Fraser Institute (EFW, 2013).

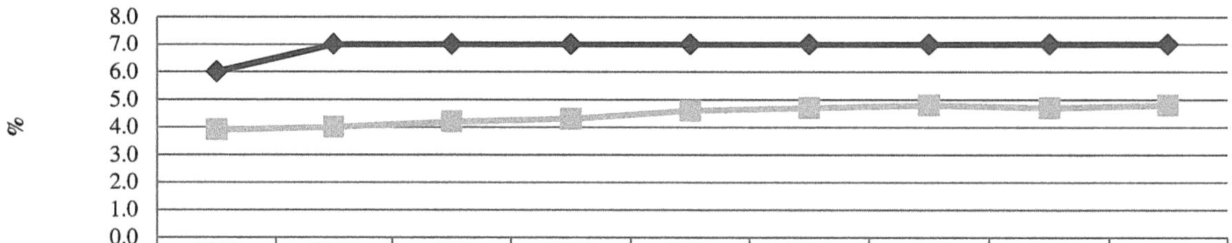

	2003	2004	2005	2006	2007	2008	2009	2010	2011
Turkey	6.0	7.0	7.0	7.0	7.0	7.0	7.0	7.0	7.0
EU-27	3.9	4.0	4.2	4.3	4.6	4.7	4.8	4.7	4.8

the share of direct taxes to tax revenues is 32.2%, the share of indirect taxes was 67.6% in 2011. Thus, in Turkey, the composition of taxation may be more explanatory for the shadow economy than its magnitude.

Figure 11 shows the trend of government spending as a share of GDP in Turkey and the EU-27. Figure 11 shows that rates in Turkey are lower than in the EU-27. Considering the weak relationship between government spending and the shadow economy in the EU, it may be suggested that the main cause of shadow economy in Turkey is not government spending.

A weak relationship was observed between labor market regulations and shadow economy in the EU-27. The index rates in Turkey are far below that of EU-27 averages for the period of 2003-2012 (Figure 12). Moreover, the average rate of Turkey which is 4.36% close to the rate of a country which has lowest rate in the EU-27: Greece 4.34%. Thus, the size of labor market regulations does not seem be an important cause of shadow economy in Turkey just as in the EU-27.

Factors related to governance seem quite important for Turkey. Figure 13 shows World Governance Indicators in Turkey and EU-27 as an average for the period of 2003-2012. As can be seen from the figure the quality of governance in Turkey is quite different from the EU-27.

All of these indicators have a lower index in Turkey. Even the signs of political stability and absence of violence/terrorism and voice and accountability indexes are negative on the average. The correlation between governance indicators and shadow economy was found to be stronger than economic causes for the EU-27. The effect of these factors may be more severe in Turkey, where a lower level of governance quality is operational. Thus, Turkey has to increase voice and accountability, control of corruption, regulatory quality, government effectiveness and political stability in order to struggle with the shadow economy.

Figure 11. Government spending (% of GDP) in Turkey and EU-27 during the period of 2003-2012
Source: WB (2014).

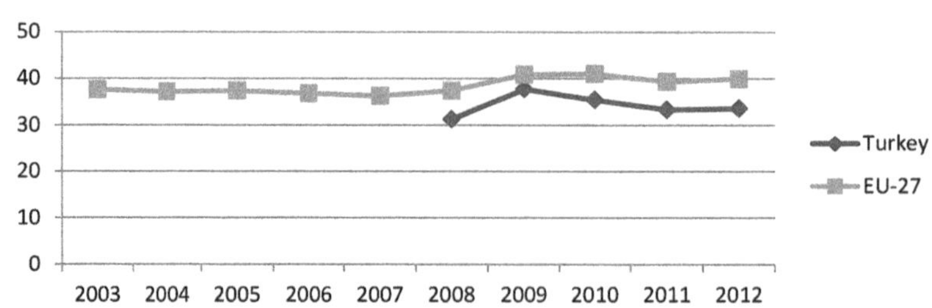

Figure 12. Labor market regulations in Turkey and EU-27 during the period of 2003-2012
Source: Fraser Institute (2013).

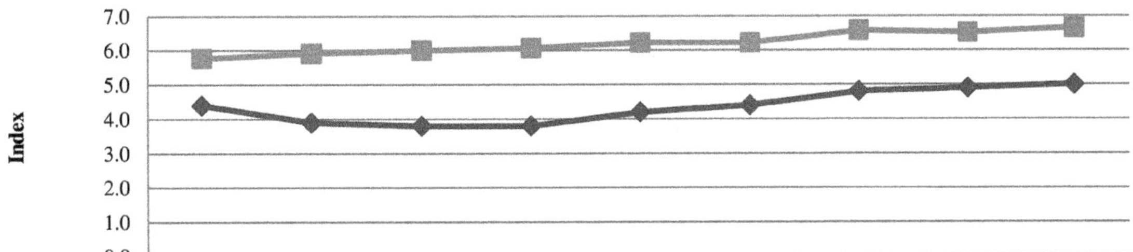

	2003	2004	2005	2006	2007	2008	2009	2010	2011
Turkey	4.4	3.9	3.8	3.8	4.2	4.4	4.8	4.9	5.0
EU-27	5.8	5.9	6.0	6.1	6.2	6.2	6.6	6.5	6.7

Figure 13. World governance indicators in Turkey and EU-27 as an average of the period 2003-2012
Source: World Governance Indicators (WB, 2013).

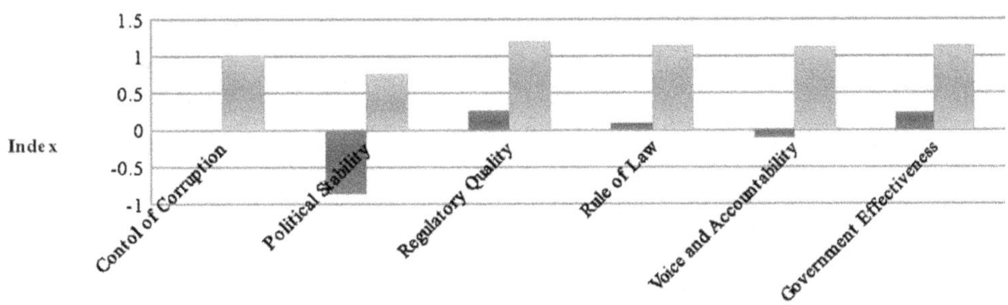

Last, the correlation between tax evasion and shadow economy is examined in the EU-27 (Figure 14a) and Turkey (Figure 14b) by using scatter plots diagram. As can be seen from the figure shadow economy and tax evasion are positively related and the correlation between them seems strong for both the EU-27 and Turkey.

Figure 14. Scatter plots of shadow economy and tax evasion in Turkey and EU-27 for the period of 2003-2010
Source: Schneider (2013).

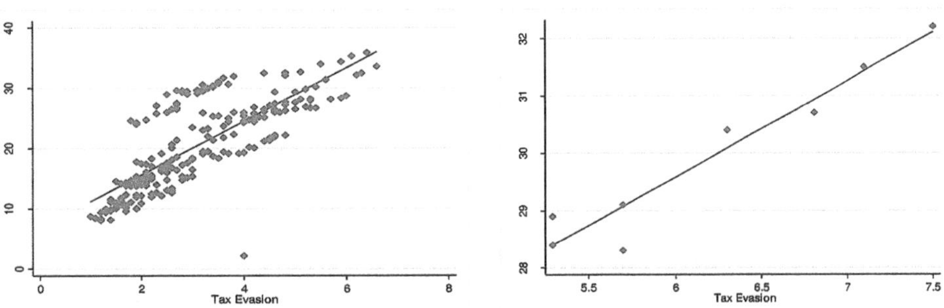

(a) (b)

An Empirical Analysis for EU-27

The causes of shadow economy are discussed in previous sections both theoretically and statistically. In this section, we tried to discover some empirical evidence about the determinants of shadow economy in EU-27. For this purpose, three different econometric models are employed and variables are determined in accordance with Torgler and Schneider (2007a, 2007b), Schneider (1997, 2005), and Schneider, Buehn and Montenegro (2010).

M1: $SHADOW_{it} = \beta_0 + \beta_1 TAXE_{it} + \beta_2 LOGGDPPC_{it} + \beta_3 LOGLABOR_{it} + \beta_4 AGR_{it} + \beta_5 LOGPOP_{it} + e_{it}$
M2: $SHADOW_{it} = \beta_0 + \beta_1 TAXE_{it} + \beta_2 LOGGDPPC_{it} + \beta_3 LOGLABOR_{it} + \beta_4 AGR_{it} + \beta_5 LOGPOP_{it} + \beta_6 TRADE_{it} + e_{it}$
M3: $SHADOW_{it} = \beta_0 + \beta_1 TAXE_{it} + \beta_2 LOGGDPPC_{it} + \beta_3 LOGLABOR_{it} + \beta_4 AGR_{it} + \beta_5 LOGPOP_{it} + \beta_6 TRADE_{it} + \beta_7 ECOFR_{it} + e_{it}$

where $SHADOW_{it}$ is the shadow economy as a percentage of official GDP, $TAXE_{it}$ is the tax evasion as a percentage of GDP, $LOGGDPPC_{it}$ is the log GDP per capita (constant 2005 US dollars), $LOGLABOR_{it}$ is the log of labor force participation rate as a percentage of total population within the age range of 15-64, AGR_{it} is the agriculture value added as a percentage of GDP, $LOGPOP_{it}$ is the log of total population, $TRADE_{it}$ is the trade as a percentage of GDP and $ECOFR_{it}$ is the index of economic freedom.

Data and Hypothetical Expectations about Coefficients of Variables

The data of GDPPC, LABOR, AGR, POP and TRADE is obtained from World Development Indicators 2014 database (WB, 2014). The data of SHADOW and TAXE is obtained from Schneider (2013). The data of ECOFR is obtained from the 2014 Index of Economic Freedom of Heritage Foundation. The index has four different components: rule of law, government size, regulatory efficiency and market openness[7].

The variable TAXE is expected to have an impact on shadow economy. The data is presented by Schneider (2013) accounts for indirect taxation and self employment. The increasing size of tax evasion may have a negative impact on people that work in the formal sector and may lead them into shadow economic activities. Moreover, statistical data and correlation diagrams have revealed a strong and positive relationship. Thus, the coefficient of TAXE is expected to be positive.

The per capita income level of countries is considered to have an impact on the size of the shadow economy. Low income levels tend people to search for new alternatives. Furthermore, since finding a job in the shadow economy is easier and people already suffer from having low incomes after high taxes, they often are inclined to engage in shadow economic activities. Thus, the coefficient of LOGGDPPC is expected to be positive.

The other factors that may be effective on the size of shadow economy are the demographical factors. As the population increases, it becomes more difficult to sustain a certain standard of living. Moreover, as Bahl (2003, p. 13) suggests, tax systems may lag behind in the ability to capture new taxpayers in some fast growing populations and this may increase the incentives to work in the shadow economy. Thus, the coefficient of LOGPOP is expected to be positive.

The sectoral composition of the economy may have an impact on shadow economy, because the agricultural sector which is often based on self-employed activities is more appropriate to hide the actual income and evade taxes. In addition, if we assume that more agricultural share in GDP means lower income levels, then it will lead to the increase of shadow economy, as well. Thus, the coefficient of LOGGDPPC is expected to be negative.

Torgler and Schneider (2007a, p. 19) indicate that individuals with an occupation have less leisure time at their disposal and, thus, time acts as a restriction to being active in the shadow economy (Schneider & Enste, 2002). Thus, the coefficient of LOGLABOR is expected to be negative. In models (2) and (3), the effect of trade on the size of shadow economy is measured. As hiding activities in trade is more difficult, the coefficient of TRADE is expected to be negative.

Last, in model (3) the effect of the economic freedom on the size of shadow economy is tested. The detail about the index of economic freedom has been supplied previously. Higher economic freedom represented by the variable ECOFR is expected to have a negative impact on the size of shadow economy.

EMPIRICAL RESULTS AND RECOMMENDATIONS

In this section panel data analysis is employed in order to test the relationship between shadow economy and various indicators in the EU-27 over the period 2003-2012. First, unit and/or time effects are tested using F and LR Tests in order to check the validity of the pooled regression which ignores the panel structure of the data and assumes that coefficient parameters are constant over time and for all units. The estimation results of the tests can be seen in Table 1.

In all three models, the F tests suggest that pooled regression is not appropriate as coefficient parameters differ according to time/unit effects. Similarly, LR tests suggest that there are unit effects in all models. Thus, the models have to be estimated with fixed effects or random effects model instead of pooled regression.

In the second step, the Hausman Test (1978) is employed in order to decide whether fixed effects or random effects model is suitable. The estimation results are given in Table 2. The test statistics indicate that random effects model is preferable in all of the models.

Table 1. The results of F and LR tests in order to test unit and/or time effects

Model 1		Test Value	d.f.	p-value	Result
LR TEST	Unit Effects	180.17	1	0.0000	Unit effects exist.
	Time Effects	0.00	1	1.0000	No time effects
F TEST	T/U Effects	21.20	F(26,180)	0.0000	Time and/or unit effects exist.
Model 2		**Test Value**	**d.f.**	**p-value**	**Result**
LR TEST	Unit Effects	177.83	1	0.0000	Unit effects exist.
	Time Effects	0.00	1	1.0000	No time effects
F TEST	T/U Effects	20.42	F(26,179)	0.0000	Time and/or unit effects exist.
Model 3		**Test Value**	**d.f.**	**p-value**	**Result**
LR TEST	Unit Effects	170.66	1	0.0000	Unit effects exist.
	Time Effects	0.00	1	1.0000	No time effects
F TEST	T/U Effects	19.36	F(26,179)	0.0000	Time and/or unit effects exist.

Note: Degrees of freedom in parenthesis.

Table 2. Hausman specification tests

	Model 1	Model 2	Model 3
$X^2(n)$	$X^2(5)$=6.01	$X^2(6)$=4.23	$X^2(7)$=4.96
p-value	0.3049	0.6452	0.6651
Result	REM is preferred.	REM is preferred.	REM is preferred.

Note: Degrees of freedom in parenthesis.

After determining which regression model to employ, the models were estimated with random effects model. Table 3 presents the estimation results.

As can be seen from Table 3, the coefficients of variables mostly meet expectations; however, the models have to be tested against econometrical problems. Based on this purpose, two common econometrical problems of panel data method - heteroscedasticity and autocorrelation - which may lead to efficiency problems are considered.

In order to test for heteroscedasticity, the test of Levene, Brown, and Forsythe is employed, as it is suitable for random effects regression. In addition, Bhargava, Franzini, and Narendranathan's Durbin-Watson and Baltagi-Wu's Locally Best Invariant (LBI) Tests were employed in order to test for autocorrelation. The related results are given in Table 4.

Table 3. Random effects estimation results

Dependent Variable: SHADOW Explanatory Variables	Model 1	Model 2	Model 3
TAXE	1.7640*** (4.74)	1.5767*** (4.08)	1.6186*** (4.08)
LOGGDPPC	-13.9593*** (-6.85)	-13.3609*** (-6.47)	-13.4894*** (-6.49)
LOGLABOR	-5.7740 (-0.97)	-7.1263 (-1.19)	-7.2383 (-1.21)
AGR	-0.1217 (-0.65)	-0.0705 (-0.7)	-0.0432 (-0.22)
LOGPOP	-0.8206** (-2.04)	-1.2734*** (-2.65)	-1.2263** (-2.51)
TRADE		-0.0171* (-1.72)	-0.0169* (-1.70)
ECOFR			0.0311 (0.50)
Wald Statistic Value	220.37***	224.09***	224.31***
Wald Probability	0.0000	0.0000	0.0000
R^2	0.8339	0.8400	0.8426
Number of Observations	212	212	212

Note: z-statistics in parenthesis. Significance Levels: *0.05<p<0.10, **0.01<p<0.05, ***p<0.01.

Table 4. Heteroscedasticity and autocorrelation tests

Tests	Model 1	Model 2	Model 3
W_0 Test	3.9943***	4.0573***	4.0690***
DW Test	2.0106	2.0101	2.0081
BW-LBI Test	2.1135	2.1120	2.1101

Note: Significance Levels: *0.05<p<0.10, **0.01<p<0.05, ***p<0.01.

Table 4. shows that there is a heteroscedasticity problem in all the three models, but there is no autocorrelation problem. Thus, we re-estimate the models of Huber, Eicker and White Estimator which gives robust variances in the case of heteroscedasticity. The robust estimation results are given in Table 5.

Table 5. shows that the coefficient of tax evasion has a positive sign and it is statistically significant at the 0.01 level in all the three models. Thus, in line with our expectations, higher tax evasion is associated with the larger size of the shadow economy. As tax evasion increases tax burden and the dissatisfaction of individuals in the formal economy increases, more people prefer to operate in the shadow economy. The coefficient of LOGGDPPC is always significant and with an expected negative relationship. This relationship indicates that lower level of income meaning a low standard of living will promote shadow economic activities.

On the contrary to our expectations, the coefficients of LOGPOP always have a negative sign. As the sample constitutes of developed countries, the result is not so surprising. Most of the countries in the

Table 5. Random effects model robust estimation results

Dependent Variable: SHADOW Explanatory Variables	Model 1	Model 2	Model 3
TAXE	1.7640*** (4.04)	1.5767*** (3.48)	1.6186*** (3.84)
LOGGDPPC	-13.9593*** (-6.55)	-13.3609*** (-6.33)	-13.4894*** (-6.04)
LOGLABOR	-5.7740 (-1.09)	-7.1263 (-1.34)	-7.2383 (-1.38)
AGR	-0.1217 (-0.96)	-0.0705 (-0.54)	-0.0432 (-0.26)
LOGPOP	-0.8206** (-1.44)	-1.2734*** (-2.04)	-1.2263** (-2.12)
TRADE		-0.0171* (-3.22)	-0.0169* (-3.17)
ECOFR			0.0311 (0.53)
Wald Statistic Value	1015.84***	979.20***	975.75***
Wald Probability	0.0000	0.0000	0.0000
R^2	0.8339	0.8400	0.8426
Number of Observations	212	212	212

Notes: z-statistics in parenthesis. Significance Levels: *0.05<p<0.10, **0.01<p<0.05, ***p<0.01.

sample have already high national income and therefore high population may not mean low per capita incomes. In addition, the result is consistent with the finding of Torgler and Schneider (2007b).

The coefficients of LOGLABOR and AGR variables are found to be statistically insignificant thus, having no impact on the size of shadow economy. Similarly, ECOFR which represents economic freedom in Model (3) has no effect on shadow economy. Last, the higher TRADE is associated with lower shadow economy in all the three models and this result is consistent with our expectations.

In summary, the results of the three models suggest that tax evasion has a positive effect on shadow economy in EU-27 countries over the period of 2003-2012. Other determinants of the size of the shadow economy are per capita GDP, population and trade. Economic freedom category seems to have no effect on the size of the shadow economy. However, some of its components may be effective on the size of shadow economy as our statistical findings in previous sections suggests.

FUTURE RESEARCH DIRECTIONS

The study tries to explore the determinants of shadow economy in the EU-27 and Turkey. As there are insufficient data, econometrical model cannot be estimated for Turkey. However, once the problem of data insufficiency is solved, econometrical analysis may be performed for Turkey. In addition, as the composition of taxation is quite different in Turkey as opposed to the EU-27, an econometrical model may be constituted considering different kinds of taxation such as taxes on income, taxes on wealth and taxes on consumption.

Statistical findings show that the quality of governance has a quite important effect on the size of shadow economy. The study employs economic freedom as an explanatory variable and not different components of governance are used in order to inhibit a decrease in degrees of freedom. However, having sufficient data, testing the effects of different governance related indicators may be worthwhile in future research.

CONCLUSION

The shadow economy is one of the main economic problems of both developed and developing countries. However, there are difficulties in defining the shadow economy and its structure. Economists sometimes use different terms in literature without explaining what they really mean. OECD (2002) has a clear distinction about shadow economy and other non-observed economic activities. Accordingly, the non-observed economy consist of underground production, illegal production, informal sector production, household production for own final use, production missed due to deficiencies in data collection program, and the shadow economy is involved in the informal and underground economy.

The shadow economy is heavily related with tax evasion, and sometimes they are perceived as similar. Nevertheless, distortion in tax revenues does not always take place in shadow economy. Some kind of tax evasion together with tax avoidance arises in the formal sector. However, statistical and empirical findings suggest they are closely related. The size of the shadow economy in EU-27 is nearly 20% of the official sector during the period 2003-2012, and can be perceived as high. Yet, the size of the shadow economy in Turkey is more than that of the EU-27. Failure to decrease the size of shadow economy necessitates the determination of causes of the shadow economy and their relative effectiveness.

As both statistical and empirical findings of this chapter suggest, there are a number of economic and governance related factors that cause shadow economy and their relative effectiveness varies. Governance related indicators statistically seem more effective on the size of shadow economy as compared to economic indicators such as taxes and spending. Governments have to relate with improving their indicators about governance in order to achieve a decrease in shadow economy. Government effectiveness, accountability, rule of law and control of corruption are critical indicators in particular. To sum up, policy makers have to discern main causes of shadow economy and consider them while struggling with shadow economy.

REFERENCES

Ahumada, H., Alvaredo, F., & Canavese, A. (2008). The Monetary Method to Measure the Underground Economy: The Forgotten Problem of the Initial Conditions. *Economics Letters*, *101*(2), 97–99. doi:10.1016/j.econlet.2008.06.001

Bahl, R. W. (2003, May 15-16). Reaching the Hardest to Tax: Consequences and Possibilities. *Paper presented at Hard to Tax: An International Perspective Conference*, Young School of Policy Studies, Georgia State University.

Bhattacharyya, D. K. (1990). An Econometric Method of Estimating the Underground Economy, United Kingdom (1960-1984): Estimates and Tests. *The Economic Journal*, *100*(402), 703–717. doi:10.2307/2233655

Bhattacharyya, D. K. (1999). On the Economic Rationale of Estimating the Hidden Economy. *The Economic Journal*, *109*(June), 348–359. doi:10.1111/1468-0297.00438

Cagan, P. (1958). The Demand for Currency Relative to the Total Money Supply. *Journal of Political Economy*, *66*(4), 303–338. doi:10.1086/258056

Castells, M., & Portes, A. (1989). World Underneath: The Origins, Dynamics, and Effects of the Informal Economy. In A. Portes, M. Castells, & L. A. Benton (Eds.), *The Informal Economy: Studies in Advanced and Less Developed Countries*. Maryland: The John Hopkins University Press.

Choi, J. P., & Thum, M. (2002). *Corruption and the Shadow Economy*. Center for Economic Studies and Ifo Institute for Economic Research.

Danopoulos, C. P., & Znidaric, B. (2007). Informal Economy, Tax Evasion, and Poverty in a Democratic Setting: Greece. *Mediterranean Quarterly*, *18*(2), 68–84. doi:10.1215/10474552-2007-006

Dreher, A., Kotsogiannis, C., & McCorriston, S. (2005). How Do Institutions Affect Corruption and the Shadow Economy. *Econ WPA Public Economic Series*, No. 0502012.

EC. (2013). *Taxation Trends in the European Union: Data for the EU Member States*, Iceland and Norway, Luxembourg: Eurostat. Retrieved from http://epp.eurostat.ec.europa.eu/cache/ ity_offpub/ks-du-13-001/en/ks-du-13-001-en.pdf

EFW. (2013). Economic Freedom of the World: 2013 Annual Report. Retrieved from www.freetheworld.com/2013/EFW2013-complete.pdf

Eurofound. (2008). Dublin: Tackling Undeclared Work in the European Union.

Eurofound (2009). *Measures to Combat Undeclared Work in 27 European Union Member States and Norway*. Dublin.

Feige, E. L. (1979, November-December). How big is the Irregular Economy? *The Challenge (Karachi), 22*(5), 5–13. doi:10.1080/05775132.1979.11470559

Feld, L. P., & Larsen, C. (2005). Black Activities in Germany in 2001 and 2004: A Comparison Based on Survey Data. *The Rockwool Foundation Research Unit*, No. 12.

Feld, L. P., & Larsen, C. (2008). "Black" Activities Low in Germany in 2006. *News from the Rockwool Foundation Research Unit.*

Feld, L. P., & Larsen, C. (2009). *Undeclared Work in Germany 2001-2007 – Impact of Deterrence, Tax Policy, and Social Norms: An Analysis Based on Survey Data*. Berlin: Springer.

Frey, B. S., & Pommerehne, W. (1984). The Hidden Economy: State and Prospect for Measurement. *Review of Income and Wealth, 30*(1), 1–23. doi:10.1111/j.1475-4991.1984.tb00474.x

Garvanlieva, V., Andonov, V., & Nikolov, M. (2012). Shadow Economy in Macedonia, *Center for Economic Analyses*, Skopje: Macedonia. Retrieved from http://www.cea.org.mk/%20documents/studii/cea%20shadow%20economy%20in%20macedonia%20final_4.pdf

Gutmann, P. H. (1977). The Subterranean Economy. *Financial Analysts Journal, 33*(6), 26–28. doi:10.2469/faj.v33.n6.26

Gutmann, P. M. (1981). Implications of the Subterranean Economy. In R. X. Bove and R. D. Klingenstein (Eds.), *Proceedings of the Wertheim's Underground Economy Conference*, (pp. 31-58). Wertheim.

Heritage Foundation. (2011). *2011 Index of Economic Freedom*. Retrieved from http://www.heritage.org/Index/ pdf/ 2011/Index2011_Full.pdf

Heritage Foundation. (2014). *2014 Index of Economic Freedom*. Retrieved from http://www.heritage.org/index/download

Ironmonger, D. (1999). *An Overview of Time Use Surveys*. Melbourne: Household Research Unit, Department of Economics, University of Melbourne.

Isachsen, A., & Strom, S. (1989). The Underground Economy in Norway with Special Emphasis on the Hidden Labor Market. In E. Feige (Ed.), *The Underground Economies: Tax Evasion and Information Distortion* (pp. 251–266). Cambridge: Cambridge University Press. doi:10.1017/CBO9780511571749.013

Isachsen, A. J., Klovland, J., & Strom, S. (1982). The Hidden Economy in Norway. In V. Tanzi (Ed.), The Underground Economy in the United States and Abroad (pp. 209–321). Lexington: Heath.

Isachsen, A. J., & Strom, S. (1985). The Size and Growth of the Hidden Economy in Norway. *Review of Income and Wealth, 31*(1), 21–38. doi:10.1111/j.1475-4991.1985.tb00496.x

Jensen, J., & Wohlbier, F. (2012). Improving Tax Governance in EU Member States: Criteria for Successful Policies, *European Economy Occasional Papers,* No.114.

KADIM Project. (2006). *The Republic of Turkey Ministry of Labor and Social Security: The Project of Struggling Against Informal Employment*. Ankara. Retrieved from http://www.kayitdisiekonomi.com/files/20061004-13-1.pdf

Karaboytcheva, M. K., & Andrada, L. R. (2012). The Impact of the Shadow Economy on the Country Risk Index. In M. Pickhardt & A. Prinz (Eds.), *Tax Evasion and the Shadow Economy* (6th ed., pp. 156–176). Cheltenham: Edward Elgar.

Karlinger, L. (2009). The Underground Economy in the Late 1990s: Evading Taxes, or Evading Competition? *World Development*, *37*(10), 1600–1611. doi:10.1016/j.worlddev.2009.03.001

Kaufmann, D., & Kaliberda, A. (1996). Integrating the Unofficial Economy into the Dynamics of Post-Socialist Economies: A Framework for Analysis and Evidence. In A. Bartlomiej (Ed.), *Economic Transition in Russia and the New States of Eurasia* (pp. 81–120). Armonk, New York: M. E. Sharpe.

Kaufmann D., Kraay, A., & Mastruzzi, M. (2010). The Worldwide Governance Indicators: Methodology and Analytical Issues. *Freedom House (2005-2009 eds.)*. Freedom of the Press.

Klovland, J. T. (1980). In Search of the Hidden Economy: Tax Evasion and the Demand for Currency in Norway and Sweden. Norwegian School of Economics and Business Administration, Mimeo.

Laffer, A. (1979). Statement Prepared for the Joint Economic Committee. In A. Laffer & J. Seymour (Eds.), *The Economics of the Tax Revolt: A Reader* (pp. 75–79). New York: Harcourt Brace Jovanovich.

Langfeldt, E. (1982, April). The Unobserved Economy in the Federal Republic of Germany: A Preliminary Assessment (Mimeo), University of Kiel.

Mogensen, G. V., Kvist, H. K., Kormendi, E., & Pedersen, S. (1995). *The Shadow Economy in Denmark 1994: Measurement and Results*. Copenhagen: Rockwool Foundation Research Unit.

OECD. (2002). *Measuring the Non-Observed Economy: A Handbook*. Retrieved from http://www.oecd.org/std/na/1963116.pdf

Packard, T., Koettl, J., & Montenegro, C. E. (2012). *From the Shadow: Integrating Europe's Informal Labor. The World Bank Report on Shadow Economy in the Central and Eastern Europe*. Washington, DC: The World Bank. doi:10.1596/978-0-8213-9549-3

Petersen, H. G., Thiessen, U., & Wohlleben, P. (2010). Shadow Economy, Tax Evasion, and Transfer Fraud- Definition, Measurement, and Data Problems. *International Economic Journal*, *24*(4), 421–441. doi:10.1080/10168737.2010.525973

Rosen, H. S., & Gayer, T. (2008). *Public Finance* (8th ed.). Singapore: McGraw-Hill. doi:10.1007/978-0-387-75870-1_22

Sam, C. Y. (2010). Exploring the Link between Tax Evasion and the Underground Economy. *Pakistan Economic and Social Review*, *48*(2), 167–182.

Schneider, F. (1986). Estimating the Size of the Danish Shadow Economy Using the Currency Demand Approach: An Attempt. *The Scandinavian Journal of Economics*, *88*(4), 643–668. doi:10.2307/3440435

Schneider, F. (1997). The Shadow Economies of Western Europe. *Journal of the Institute of Economic Affairs*, *17*(3), 42–48. doi:10.1111/1468-0270.00041

Schneider, F. (2005). Shadow Economies Around the World: What Do We Really Know? *European Journal of Political Economy*, *21*(3), 598–642. doi:10.1016/j.ejpoleco.2004.10.002

Schneider, F. (2007, July) Shadow Economies and Corruption All Over the World: New Estimates for 145 Countries. *Economics.*

Schneider, F. (2012). The Shadow Economy and Work in the Shadow: What Do We (Not) Know? *IZA Discussion Paper*, No. 6423.

Schneider, F. (2013). *Shadow Economy, Tax Evasion and Corruption in Portugal and in Other OECD Countries: What Can Be Done?* Retrieved from www.nipe.eeg.uminho.pt/Uploads/ShadPortugal_2013_Schneider.pdf

Schneider, F. (2014). The Shadow Economy and Shadow Labor Force: A Survey of Recent Developments. *Institute for the Study of Labor IZA Discussion Paper*, No. 8278.

Schneider, F., Buehn, A., & Montenegro, C. E. (2010). New Estimates for the Shadow Economies All Over the World. *International Economic Journal*, *24*(4), 443–461.

Schneider, F., & Enste, D. H. (2000, March). Shadow Economies: Size, Causes, and Consequences. *Journal of Economic Literature*, *38*(1), 77–114. doi:10.1257/jel.38.1.77

Schneider, F., & Enste, D. H. (2002). *The Shadow Economy: An International Survey*. Cambridge: Cambridge University Press.

Schneider, F., & Williams, C. C. (2013). *The Shadow Economy*. Institute of Economic Affairs. doi:10.1017/CBO9781139542289

Spiro, P. S. (2005). Tax Policy and the Underground Economy. In C. Bajada & F. Schneider (Eds.), *Size, Causes and Consequences of the Underground Economy* (pp. 179–201). Aldershot, UK: Ashgate Publishing.

Tanzi, V. (1980). The Underground Economy in the United States: Estimations and Implications. *Quarterly Review. Indexes - Banca Nazionale del Lavoro*, *135*(4), 427–453.

Tanzi, V. (1983). The Underground Economy in United States: Annual Estimates. 1930-1980. *Staff Papers-International Monetary Fund, 30*(2).

The Action Plan of Struggling Against Shadow Economy. (2011). *The Republic of Turkey Ministry of Finance,* Ankara. Retrieved from http://www.gib.gov.tr/index.php?id=1366

Torgler, B., & Schneider, F. (2007a). The Impact of Tax Morale and Institutional Quality on the Shadow Economy, *CESIFO Working Paper*, No. 1899.

Torgler, B., & Schneider, F. (2007b). Shadow Economy, Tax Morale, Governance and Institutional Quality: A Panel Analysis, *Department of Economics, Johannes Kepler University, Economic Working Paper Series*, No.1.

World Bank. (2013). *World Governance Indicators*. Retrieved from http://data.worldbank.org/data-catalog/world-governance-indicators

World Bank. (2014). *World Development Indicators*. Retrieved from http://data.worldbank.org/data-catalog/world-development-indicators

ADDITIONAL READING

Amaral, P., & Quintin, E. (2006). A Competitive Model of the Informal Sector. *Journal of Monetary Economics*, *53*(7), 1541–1553. doi:10.1016/j.jmoneco.2005.07.016

Cohn, G. (1998). The Ethics of Tax Evasion: A Jewish Perspective. *Journal of Accounting. Ethics and Public Policy*, *1*(3), 109–120.

Ruge, M. (2010). Determinants and Size of the Shadow Economy – A Structural Equation Model. *International Economic Journal*, *24*(4), 511–523. doi:10.1080/10168737.2010.525988

Tanzi, V. (1999). Uses and Abuses of Estimates of the Underground Economy. *The Economic Journal*, *109*(456), 338–247. doi:10.1111/1468-0297.00437

Thiessen, U. (2010). The Shadow Economy in International Comparison: Options for Economic Policy Derived from an OECD Panel Analysis. *International Economic Journal*, *24*(4), 481–509. doi:10.1080/10168737.2010.525986

Thomas, J. (1999). Quantifying the Black Economy: Measurement without Theory Yet Again? *The Economic Journal*, *109*(456), 381–389. doi:10.1111/1468-0297.00441

KEY TERMS AND DEFINITIONS

Corruption: An illegal and dishonest behavior displayed by public authority in order to get private gain.

Efficiency: Providing greatest amount of outputs with the lowest amount of inputs.

Formal Sector: Sector which generates income on which tax must be paid.

Governance: The action of governing.

Observable Consumption: Consumption that is recorded officially by government and constitutes a tax base of the state.

Observable Income: Income that is recorded officially by government and constitutes a tax base of the state.

Tax Evasion: Illegal behaviors displayed by individuals (both in formal and informal sector) in order to get rid of tax responsibilities.

ENDNOTES

1 For details see OECD (2002, pp. 37-41).

2 Ironmonger (1999, p.35) states that "Productive activities are those which result in the production of goods or the delivery of services, including goods and services that are not sold, and goods and services that are self-provided; includes preparation of meals, care of children and adults and time spent in educational activities."

3 According to Rosen and Gayer (2008) "Tax avoidance is altering behavior in order to reduce your legal tax liability, if contrast tax evasion is failing to pay legally due taxes" (pp. 370-372).

4 Estimate gives the country's score on the aggregate indicator, in units of a standard normal distribution, i.e. ranging from approximately -2.5 to 2.5 (WB, 2013).

5 For details see Kaufman, Kraay and Mastruzzi (2010).

6 More detailed information can be found in the web pages: http://www.kayitdisiekonomi.com/files/20061004-13-1.pdf and http://www.gib.gov.tr/index.php?id=1366.

7 For details see Appendix for 2011 Index of Economic Freedom (Heritage Foundation, 2011) found in http://www.heritage.org/Index/pdf/2011/Index2011_Full.pdf.

Chapter 12
Tax Compliance Behavior:
An Upshot of Trust in and Power of Authorities across Europe and MENA

Larissa Batrancea
Babes-Bolyai University, Romania

Ioan Batrancea
Babes-Bolyai University, Romania

Anca Nichita
Romanian Academy, Romania

Erich Kirchler
University of Vienna, Austria

ABSTRACT

The volatility of the global economic market and the fierce competition in attracting foreign investments have determined European and MENA authorities to reconsider interactions with taxpayers. Thus, benefitting from international assistance, authorities have started implementing tax strategies and models like co-operative compliance, horizontal monitoring, whistleblowing. This empirical investigation is grounded on the "slippery slope" framework that attempts to solve the "riddle of tax compliance" via trust in and power of authorities. The former is proxied by "Trust in national government" (Gallup World Poll), the latter by "Rule of law" (World Bank). The two-step cluster analysis run on 215 countries worldwide, including 35 from Europe, 12 from MENA, yielded four tax climates: trust and power high (T+P+), trust and power low (T-P-), trust high-power low (T+P-), trust low-power high (T-P+). While the majority of European countries are spread between T+P+ and T-P+, MENA countries generally belong to T-P-, demanding stability and efficiency in all major areas of the societies.

INTRODUCTION

Some of the first connections between Europe and the region referred nowadays as MENA have been established during the exploratory voyages undertaken by Marco Polo and Ibn Battuta. The former, born in 1254's Europe (Venice, Italy), had made the Far East known to the Europeans by virtue of the volume he signed and released in 1298 "Book of the Marvels of the World" or "Description of the World." The journeys depicted in the book had surged Europeans' desire of reaching the remote worlds. The latter, born in 1304's MENA (Tangier, Morocco), had made Europe known to inhabitants of Northern Africa, Arabia, Persia.

DOI: 10.4018/978-1-5225-0053-7.ch012

Centuries have elapsed since the explorers' itinerations, still the connections set through their intrepid efforts have not faded away. In this day and age, strategic economic, financial, political, social and cultural partnerships driven through enacted frameworks such as the Euro-Mediterranean Partnership (EUROMED) and the European Neighbourhood Policy (ENP) or challenging projects like "Desert Power 2050" endorsed by Desertec Industrial Initiative (Dii, 2012) strengthen the Europe-MENA ties, aiming at serving the interests of both regional partners. Within the aforementioned setting, the matter of tax compliance behavior heightens its prominence as fiscal obligations represent a main funding source for most partnerships. Delving into the primary topic of tax compliance from an economic-psychological perspective, the chapter will avail researchers, practitioners and laypeople to grasp the importance of trust in authorities and power of authorities for raising compliance across Europe and the MENA region.

How crucial is taxation for public goods and behavior regulation? What are the differences between traditional and present-day approaches to tax compliance? Which roles do Europe and MENA play within the global economy? What kind of theoretical paradigms and strategies do tax authorities employ for improving income disclosure across these regions? Where do tax compliance levels in Europe and MENA stand considering trust in authorities and power of authorities, the two chief dimensions of the "slippery slope" framework? These are some of the queries addressed by the present investigation.

The importance of taxes for modern societies has stirred the interest of laypeople, policy makers and scholars across disciplines, from traditional economics (Allingham & Sandmo, 1972; Yitzhaki, 1974) to vanguardist econophysics (Zaklan, Lima & Westerhoff, 2008; Zaklan, Westerhoff & Stauffer, 2009). For instance, drawing on the work of Schumpeter ([1918] 1954) regarding the question of fiscal sociology, i.e., the assessment of social phenomena underlying taxation and public finance (Campbell, 1993, p. 163), Martin, Mehrotra and Prasad (2009, pp. 3-4) contend that taxation reports are "pervasive, dynamic, and central to modernity." Namely, the academics provide a threefold rationale: taxation engages individuals in reciprocal relationships on which societies are built; it fosters a dynamic but frail interaction between authorities and taxpayers, in which both parties' interests may clash virtually any time; it secures fungible resources within a society.

In the same vein, stressing economic implications of taxation, Oliver Wendell Holmes, the US Supreme Court Justice, is credited with a simple yet terse assertion, viz., "I like to pay taxes. With them I buy civilization." Besides counting as leverage in supporting or hindering consumption, the main function of taxes resides in collecting state budget resources to finance public outlays. Therefore, within the boundaries of this sequential public goods game, the outcomes of all players (i.e., tax authorities and taxpayers) are intertwined. On one hand, authorities establish the level of wealth redistribution through tax codes and designate (in most countries) the system of basic needs to be publicly financed (e.g., education, healthcare, social care, infrastructure, national defense, etc.). On the other hand, taxpayers ultimately decide the level of budgetary resources at hand: law abiding citizens agree to fully disclose income as they understand the rights and obligations of the game; free loaders shirk taxpaying, thus decreasing public resources and imposing additional costs on society (e.g., insufficiently financed public goods, high monitoring expenditures, decreasing GDP, consistent informal sector). In the light of the game's dynamics, tax authorities are expected to encourage compliance behavior by understanding the manifold of variables influencing it, designing solid fiscal policies, efficiently using budgetary resources and securing the rule of law.

Traditional Economic and Law Approaches to Tax Compliance vs. Recent Psychological Developments

Tax compliance literature may represent a viable source for authorities interested in tailoring compliance-driven fiscal policies. Since the 1970s, after Allingham and Sandmo (1972), Srinivasan (1973) and Yitzhaki (1974) published their classical tax evasion models, a stream of pundits has focused on the economic determinants of tax compliance (i.e., audit probability, income, tax rates, fines). For instance, income levels have been examined in the attempt to find a relationship with tax evasion. As Pickhardt and Prinz (2014, p. 9) conclude in their extensive survey, although no unequivocal pattern has been identified in this respect, low and high income levels appear to be related to higher tax evasion compared to middle income levels (i.e., phenomenon dubbed as the "Cox Paradox").

The growing number of reported inconsistencies about the impact of economic variables has lead researchers to investigate (non)compliance motives beyond the dismal science (Levy, 2002). Interestingly, one of the catalysts for such investigations has been the attempt to elucidate the puzzle of tax compliance, i.e., why tax evasion levels are so low. As Alm and Torgler (2011, p. 635) define it, cheating should be theoretically more prevalent among taxpayers, considering the extremely low audit and penalty rates. Yet, taxpayers honor their fiscal obligations on a regular basis.

In recent years, scores of studies tackling legislative or psychological determinants of tax compliance have emerged (for a comprehensive review, see Kirchler, 2007; Pickhardt & Prinz, 2014).

The legal framework and the tax compliance phenomenon are conjoint, the former setting the boundaries within which the latter emerges. Moreover, as James and Alley (2002) convey, tax compliance implies abiding simultaneously by the *letter* (i.e., following prescriptions exactly as stipulated by the legislator) and the *spirit* of the law (i.e., paying the fair share, according to ones' overall income sources). Practice shows that achieving such desiderate is challenging, taking into account that the letter of the law *per se* often hinders tax compliance by engendering the "fiscal fog" phenomenon (James, 1998, p. 59). Regular taxpayers are puzzled by the convoluted nature of legal jargon, which in many countries requires an unusual high number of schooling years for proper understanding (Lewis, 1982). Besides impeding compliance among ordinary taxpayers, the legislators' ambiguous wording fuels noncompliance by cutting loopholes into the tax law and favoring taxpayers who can hire professional advisors to use such breaches (i.e., tax avoiders). Nevertheless, the solution for turning this negative aspect into an asset comes from praxeology theory (Von Mises, 1966). According to it, the possibility of breaking a norm denotes the need for refining it. Hence, tax authorities could design more efficient tax codes by analyzing the incidence and motives of tax noncompliance acts.

Reflecting upon the connection between law and taxes, Chinese philosopher Lao Tzu (Bahm, 1996, p. 53) opined that "the more laws are enacted and taxes assessed, the greater the number of lawbreakers and tax evaders." In this line of thought, another major hindrance for compliance originates from excessive regulation (Cussons, 2006; Owens & Hamilton, 2004), which in turn enhances the complexity level of tax laws, leaving room for creative interpretations of the *letter*. Notwithstanding this, tax literature acknowledges resources which authorities have right at hand for properly amending tax laws, including simplification (James & Wallschutzky, 1997, p. 448) and responsive regulation (Braithwaite, 2002; Braithwaite, 2007).

Based on the fact that tax compliance is a dynamic phenomenon, shaped not only by outward factors (i.e., legal framework) but also by inner resorts, numerous social scientists have turned to investigating psychological determinants of compliance decisions. Therefore, factors like attitudes, norms, motivational postures, tax morale, fairness concerns and education have been singled out as major compliance catalysts.

Psychological theories centered on reasoned action (Fishbein & Ajzen, 1975) and planned behavior (Ajzen, 1991) hold that behavioral predictions can be inferred via attitudes. Consequently, within the tax compliance setting, individuals who positively assess the attitude object (i.e., tax evasion) are assumed to comply less than individuals with negative assessments. Nevertheless, empirical investigations (Trivedi, Shehata, & Mestelman, 2005; Webley, Cole, & Eidjar, 2001) reporting significant yet weak influences of attitudes on self-reported behavior or no influence on actual behavior (Elffers, Weigel, & Hessing, 1987) suggest that the relationship between attitudes and compliance behavior is far from being straightforward.

As individual, social and cultural standards, norms leave a distinctive mark on tax compliance. On a personal level, norms co-occur with tax ethics and values, making compliance prevail among taxpayers with more developed tax ethics (Kirchler, Hoelzl, & Wahl, 2008, p. 218). In society, compliance is fostered when taxpayers associate honest income disclosure with the vast majority of the members within their reference group (Wenzel, 2005) and follow their behavior (Sigala, Burgoyne, & Webley, 1999). Nations that manage to enact tax laws incorporating proper norms register high levels of tax compliance (Torgler, 2005).

Moreover, tax compliance decisions are adjusted based on motivational postures, i.e., a comprehensive set of attitudes and beliefs evincing the social distance between tax authorities and taxpayers (Braithwaite, 2003). That is to say, compliance emerges among taxpayers who perceive themselves less distant relative to authorities and share "commitment" or "capitulation." Noncompliance is expected to arise in large social distance environments, where taxpayers experience "resistance," "disengagement" or "game playing."

Tax morale, i.e., the intrinsic motivation to pay fiscal obligations (Alm & Torgler, 2006) is properly mirrored through assessments of tax evasion morality (Schmölders, 1960). For the main, higher tax compliance is expected to be registered if tax evasion is deemed immoral by the majority of taxpayers.

Fairness concerns, be it distributive, procedural or retributive justice (Wenzel, 2003), arise in taxpayers' evaluations of overall tax systems (i.e., tax burden, interaction with tax authorities, audit frequency, level of sanctions, etc.). As a rule, the more fair tax systems are perceived, the more compliant citizens will be.

Education in general and tax knowledge in particular enables citizens to properly understand the importance of taxation and authorities' role in financing public goods systems through wealth redistribution. This understanding, in conjunction with other psychological variables, guides taxpayers on the road of compliance. Although tax literature seems to register mixed results concerning the relationship between education and compliance (as reported in Pickhardt & Prinz, 2014), most of the studies reveal a significant positive impact of tax knowledge acquired formally on citizens' attitudes and behavior (e.g., Fjeldstad & Heggstad, 2012; Groot & van den Brink, 2010; Mendel & Bevacqua, 2014; OECD, 2013c; Park & Hyun, 2003).

The Growing Importance of Europe and the MENA Region within the Framework of the World Economy

Year 2007 brought on the global economy stage the first signs of what Mandarin Chinese terms "*wēijī*" (i.e., "crisis"). For that matter, the two characters constituting the word are "*wēi*," which translates into "danger," and "*jī*" meaning "a beginning or turning point" in this case (Mair, 2009). Just like the "*jī*" characters expresses, 2007 is the turning point marking the growing importance of Europe within the world economy, for in the period 2007-2012 the European Union became the world's largest economy. While the podium is shared between the EU, US and China, the three economic giants yield more than half of the global GDP (Amadeo, 2014).

On the other side, as stated by the OPEC Secretary General (El-Badri, 2012), the strategic importance of the MENA region for the world economy stems from its geographic position and natural resources through which it meets global energy needs. For instance, eight OPEC members belonging to MENA hold 58% of global crude oil reserves and 43% of global gas reserves. Thus, it can be stated that natural advantages have also turned MENA countries into vital trading partners (Safadi, 2003) with other countries of the world in terms of fossil carbon resources.

As mentioned in the prologue, besides endorsing solid cultural connections, Europe and MENA share economic, political, social and human interests, benefiting each side upon achievement (Bertelsmann, 1999). Reliable witnesses to such ties stand: Union for Mediterranean (previously denominated "Barcelona Process"); bilateral initiatives like the European Neighbourhood Policy (European Commission, 2014), which granted about €12 billion financial support between 2007-2013, or Euro-Mediterranean Partnership (EUROMED), comprising *de jure* members like Algeria, Egypt, Israel, Jordan, Lebanon, Morocco, Syria, Tunisia, West Bank and Gaza.

The ultimate goal for such initiatives occasioned by the Barcelona Process is enhancing trust and cooperation between the two regions, taking into account the future inclusion of other MENA countries. In reference to the aforementioned mutual interests, a successful cooperation would translate into ensuring the following: regional economic market development; access to fossil carbon resources; free and safe trade; sustainable political stability and training of public administration; social justice; protection of human rights (Bertelsmann, 1999, p. 2).

Theoretical Developments on Tax Compliance and General Practices of Authorities to Improve Income Disclosure

Due to numerous spillover effects triggered by economic or political phenomena (monetary crisis in Europe, Arab Spring in the MENA region) and increasing underground economies, several governments facing staggering public deficits have begun redesigning fiscal policies. In this respect, tax compliance has become a primary topic on political agendas across Europe and the MENA region, many countries enacting double-tax treaties or joining OECD to damper harmful tax competition. In addition, various international bodies (OECD, World Bank, United Nations) have offered expert assistance to European and MENA countries in their quest of implementing efficient tax systems and mending compliance behavior.

Starting from empirical findings regarding tax behavior, different tax administrations around the world have recently begun to implement compliance models based on psychological determinants like trust (i.e., horizontal monitoring; whistleblower protection) or motivational postures (i.e., Australian Taxation Office Compliance Model). The defining characteristic for such compliance models is cooperation, reason for which they fully express the *co-operative compliance* approach (OECD, 2013a). As stated by the Organisation for Economic Co-operation and Development (OECD), the novel approach of "co-operative compliance" is derived from the concept of "enhanced relationship" - introduced in 2008 by the Forum and Tax Administration. Emphasizing the necessity to accurately comprehend and amend compliance behavior, the OECD approach aims to ensure correct income disclosure while cooperating with taxpayers. In the view of the "co-operative compliance" approach, trust and objective standards constitute the foundation of the relationship between tax authorities and taxpayers. Moreover, proper interaction with taxpayers is steered by a comprehensive set of pillars: 1) commercial awareness, i.e., understanding the characteristics of business transactions; 2) impartiality; 3) proportionality; 4) openness and responsiveness; 5) disclosure and transparency.

With respect to *horizontal monitoring*, the model was developed by the Netherlands Tax and Customs Administration (2012, p. 4) in the spirit of co-operative compliance, in order to serve both self-employed without any personnel and enterprises with employees. The novelty of the approach resides in the fact that tax authorities discard vertical supervisory processes (i.e., intense retrospective audits) in favor of horizontal cooperation (i.e., preliminary consultations). The interaction between taxpayers and tax authorities occurs via tax service providers, with whom tax authorities conclude covenants and which are responsible for correctly filing clients' tax returns. Compliance efficiency increases accordingly due to the involvement of the external professional party (i.e., tax service provider), therefore the supervisory burden enforced on honest taxpayers mitigates as they are no longer subject to regular audits. While compliance costs decrease, tax authorities can focus on higher-risk tax returns.

The core features of horizontal monitoring include: mutual trust, cooperation and understanding between parties; highlighting clear responsibilities of all entities; transparency and mutual knowledge regarding relevant taxation aspects, procedure and processes; reporting errors occurring unintentionally or in good faith; meta-monitoring. In the same vein, the benefits entailed by horizontal monitoring are manifold, including: fewer audits targeting honest taxpayers; red tape reduction; lower number of litigations; quicker solving of fiscal disputes. Aware of its numerous benefits, other European countries like Austria or Russia have implemented similar horizontal monitoring paths (OECD, 2013a, pp. 21-23).

In addition to other traditional supervisory techniques (e.g., employing professional staff, intense monitoring through auditing), tax authorities may resort to citizens' civic duty for spotting tax evaders by *whistleblowing*. According to Transparency International (2013, p. 19), the term, otherwise subject to translation intricacies, roughly denotes citizens' acts of voluntarily uncovering "wrongdoing that has occurred in their midst" (e.g., corruption, tax evasion) to the general public. That is, tax authorities examine information exposed by taxpayers to identify possible noncompliance acts; provided the information is credible and solid, suspected tax evaders are prosecuted, evaded tax liabilities are collected and informants are rewarded in accordance with the applicable law. Based on a legal framework enacted in the second half of the 19th century (Goel & Nelson, 2013; Internal Revenue Service, 2008, 2013), American tax authorities have been ensuring compliance also through the whistleblowing procedure, by establishing an IRS Whistleblower Office and awarding informants up to 30% of the collected proceeds (i.e., tax, penalty, interest).

Following the example set by the US Internal Revenue Service, EU members have also enacted whistleblowing laws, though in different degrees (Transparency International, 2013, p. 8). Thus, tax systems within only four countries (i.e., Luxemburg, Romania, Slovenia, United Kingdom) benefit from advanced whistleblowing legal frameworks. 16 countries exhibit partial frameworks (i.e., Austria, Belgium, Cyprus, Czech Republic, Denmark, Estonia, France, Germany, Hungary, Ireland, Italy, Latvia,

Malta, the Netherlands, Poland, Sweden), while the other 8 members enact very limited or no whistleblowing laws (viz., Bulgaria, Croatia, Finland, Greece, Lithuania, Portugal, Slovak Republic, Spain).

Chronologically, in 1998 United Kingdom became the first European country to pass a whistleblowing protection law (i.e., Public Interest Disclosure Act or PIDA). In 2004, it was followed by Romania, which became the first continental European country to protect whistleblowers from reprisals.

A particularly interesting aspect regarding whistleblowing has been noted by Transparency International (2013, pp. 19-20). Namely, the lack of a standard definition and the difficulty of translating the term distort taxpayers' perception concerning the phenomenon. This is the main reason for which "whistleblowing" is regarded either positive (i.e., Hungary, Romania, Slovak Republic), negative (i.e., Bulgaria, Czech Republic, Denmark, Estonia, Finland, Germany, Greece, Italy, Poland, Portugal), neutral (i.e., Latvia, Slovenia, Spanish, Sweden) or without any connotation (i.e., France, Lithuania, Malta, the Netherlands).

In what it concerns the countries from MENA region, the whistleblowing phenomenon is still in its infancy, as national authorities make efforts to align complex and rather dispersed tax systems (partially originating from British and French models) which facilitate noncompliance to international standards (Imam & Jacobs, 2007, p. 3). According to assessments quantified by the 2008 Global Integrity Index, the enforcement of laws sheltering informants in the region is "very weak" (Johnson & Martini, 2012). Clements (2013, p. 53) states that no clear legal pattern regarding the protection of whistleblowers can be identified, mainly because "Middle East culture historically has not included the concept of informing on someone." Transparency International experts (Johnson & Martini, 2012, p. 11) also report the absence of whistleblowing protecting mechanisms in the public sector and weak enforcement of some provisions in the private sector, which ultimately engender fear of retaliation among citizens. Thus, reforming the system through a holistic approach and increasing citizens' trust in the system are among the first steps needed to amend this shortcoming.

In the southern hemisphere, the co-operative compliance approach is embodied by the Australian Taxation Office Compliance Model (OECD, 2013a, p. 24). It successfully incorporates motivational postures as influencing income disclosure (Braithwaite, 2003), prescribes compliance strategies based on a Risk Differentiation Framework and citizens' attitudes towards the tax system. In other words, taxpayers willing and attempting to do the right things are assisted and counseled by authorities, while those disregarding tax regulations experience the full force of the law.

As members of various economic, political or social partnerships, several European and MENA countries have ratified double tax treaties at regional and interregional level, in the attempt of mitigating tax burden and eventually increasing tax compliance levels (PricewaterhouseCoopers, 2013). Moreover, during the last decade, the countries' efforts of amending income disclosure have been backed through assistance granted by international bodies like OECD (2009, 2013b), the United Nations or the World Bank. Therefore, both the OECD (1998) and the United Nations (2009) have been involved in decreasing noncompliance levels by focusing on tax havens, harmful tax competition and aggressive tax planning.

In order to strengthen tax systems through boosting investments, business integrity and public procurement policies, the OECD and the World Bank have been assisting MENA countries through long-term initiatives like the MENA Network of Public Procurement, MENA – OECD Business Integrity Network (OECD, 2014a) or MENA – OECD Investment Programme (OECD, 2014b).

Trust in Authorities and Power of Authorities, Main Dimensions of the "Slippery Slope" Framework

In social science literature, the concepts of trust and power are often approached in terms of their interconnectedness. Dasgupta (2000, p. 332) provides an interesting and thorough rationale by emphasizing the idea that trust is a "fragile commodity," which should be granted to another party based on credible promises and not mere words. Therefore, the credibility of a promise is the key element differentiating the act of "trusting someone" from "trusting someone blindly." Not to mention that credibility should be a prerequisite of the menace for sanctioning deviant behavior via enforcement mechanisms (i.e., power). According to Dasgupta, the fragility of trust resides in the following two aspects: 1) when an individual exhibits wavering trust towards the enforcement agency, he refuses to enter any agreement overseen by the respective agency; 2) an individual should trust an enforcement agency provided he trusts the fact that there are available mechanisms of removing the agency from power in case of agreement mismanagement.

In the field of tax compliance, trust in authorities and power of authorities are assessed with respect to their influence on taxpayers' behavior, which emerges during interactions with tax authorities. As the literature posits, these encounters vary between synergism and antagonism. Therefore, taxpayers' behavior may range from acting in accordance with the letter and spirit of the law to disregarding legal precepts (James & Alley, 2002). Noncompliance can be regarded as either tax avoidance or tax evasion, if the legislator explicitly disentangles the two concepts. When taxpayers diminish fiscal burdens with the help of legal professional assistance, they act within the boundaries of the law; yet making use of tax code loopholes contravenes the spirit of the law (Sandmo, 2003; Webley, 2004). When taxpayers shirk fiscal obligations through acts of omission or commission (Kirchler, 2007), they willingly express opposition towards the law's letter and spirit.

Trust in authorities and power of authorities are two main dimensions enclosed in the "slippery slope" framework, a theoretical attempt of explaining tax compliance via economic and psychological stances (Kirchler, Hoelzl & Wahl, 2008, p. 212). The former dimension captures the perceptions of taxpayers that authorities are benevolent and serve the common good. The latter dimension comprises the perceptions of taxpayers that authorities are capable to discover and sanction tax evaders. According to the "slippery slope" framework, boosting trust or power can engender tax compliance level. When trust in authorities increases, voluntary compliance prevails. On the account of heightening power, enforced compliance emerges. In addition to distinguishing between compliance types, the framework also draws attention on the impact authorities' approach towards taxpayers has on compliance (Kirchler *et al.*, 2008, p. 220): a "cops and robbers" approach fostered in antagonistic interactions crowds out voluntary compliance, while a "service and client" approach displayed within synergistic interactions boosts voluntary cooperation with authorities. The consistent influences of trust and power on tax compliance are documented in the literature by several research studies frequently run on self-employed and student samples (Kasper, Kogler & Kirchler, 2013; Kogler *et al.*, 2013; Kogler, Muehlbacher & Kirchler, 2013; Lisi, 2012; Lozza, Kastlunger, Tagliabue & Kirchler, 2013; Muehlbacher, Kirchler & Schwarzenberger, 2011; Wahl, Kastlunger & Kirchler, 2010).

Comparisons of Trust in and Power of Authorities Levels between Europe and MENA, in the Light of Underlying Tax Systems

The subsequent empirical section highlights the levels of trust in authorities and power of authorities registered by 35 European and 12 MENA countries.

In order to classify European and MENA states considering the grassroots dimensions *trust in authorities* and *power of authorities*, we followed the approach from Batrancea (2014b). Via a two-step cluster analysis run on 215 countries and territories, Batrancea (2014b) provides a four-cluster assortment of the worldwide tax climates, viz., trust high – power high (T+P+), trust low – power low (T-P-), trust high – power low (T+P-), trust low – power high (T-P+). As proxy for trust in authorities it was employed "Trust in national government" measured by Gallup World Poll and included in the Human Development Report 2013, while as proxy for power of authorities it was considered the 2012 "Rule of law" governance indicator determined by the World Bank, based on Kaufmann, Kraay and Mastruzzi (2010).

The variables "Trust in national government" and "Rule of law" are continuous, thus the Euclidean distance is computed within the process. A fundamental step in establishing the optimal number of clusters is checking the cluster quality based on the Silhouette measure of cohesion and separation. From Figure 1, one can see that its value is above.5, which ensures a good quality of the groups determined.

Figure 2 comprises a pie-chart depicting the group size in this four-cluster solution and a table displaying the size of the smallest and the largest cluster, as well as the ratio of the largest cluster to the smallest one. The value 2.65 of this ratio indicates a good data fit, considering that the literature recommends it should exceed 2.5 (Bacher, Wenzig & Vogler, 2004).

Figure 3 depicts an overall measure estimating the importance of the predictors, i.e., trust in and power of authorities. The fact that both predictors register values exceeding.8 denotes their substantial contribution in determining the four clusters. However, power of authorities has a slightly higher importance in this respect.

Figures 4-7 depict the assortment of tax climates yielded by the cluster analysis through box plots. PA denotes the power of authorities, while TA denotes the trust in authorities. In cluster 1, as trust in authorities exceeds the median value line in a negative direction and power of authorities exceeds the median value line in a positive direction, one can imply that T-P+ tax climate is representative for the countries belonging to this cluster. Following the same path of reasoning, countries pertaining to cluster 2 are defined by the tandem T-P-, cluster 3 has a T+P- tax climate, while cluster 4 can be labeled as T+P+.

The above analyses are useful tools for the core of this book chapter, as they offer the benefit of determining where do European and MENA countries stand in terms of trust in authorities and power of authorities.

Figure 1. Cluster quality

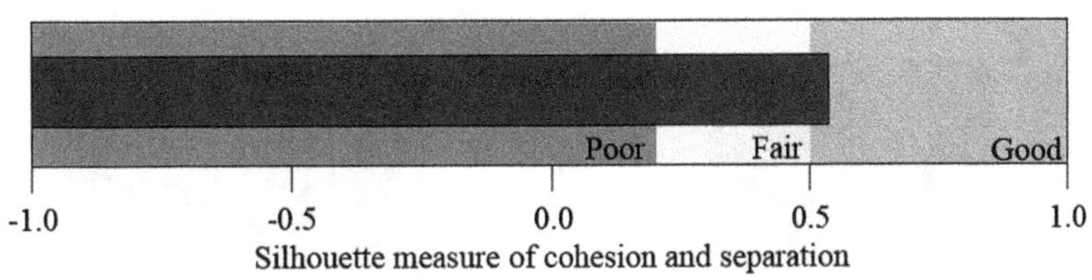

Figure 2. Clusters sizes

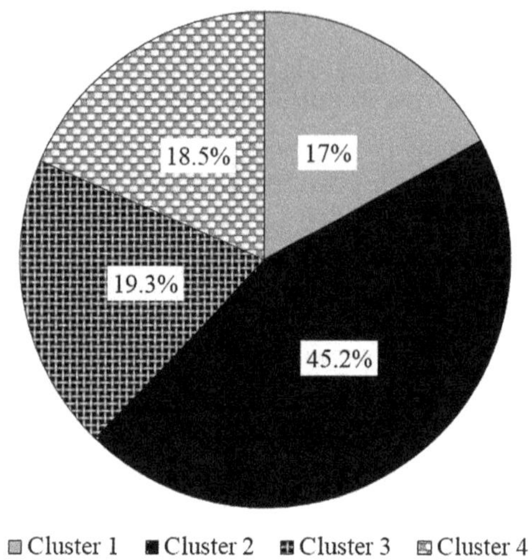

Size of smallest cluster	23 (17%)
Size of largest cluster	61 (45.2%)
Ratio of sizes: largest cluster to smallest cluster	2.65

Figure 3. Overall predictor importance

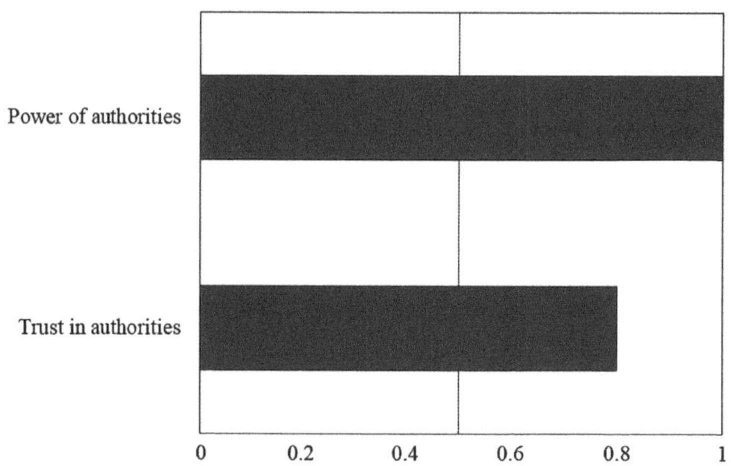

Figure 4. Cluster 1 (T-P+)

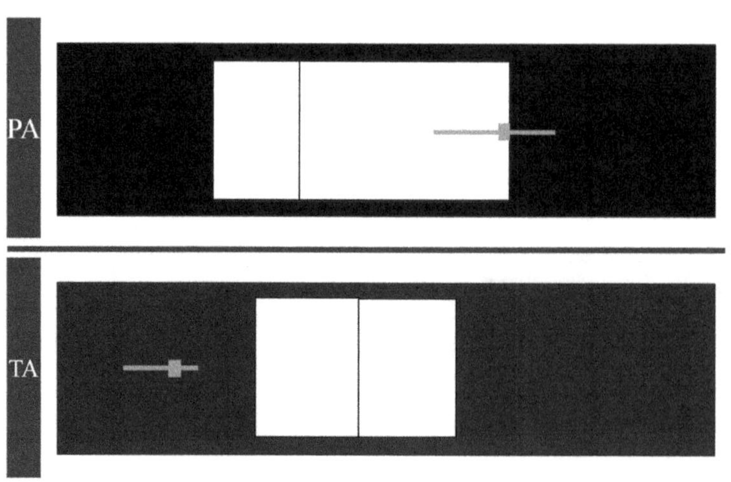

Figure 5. Cluster 2 (T-P-)

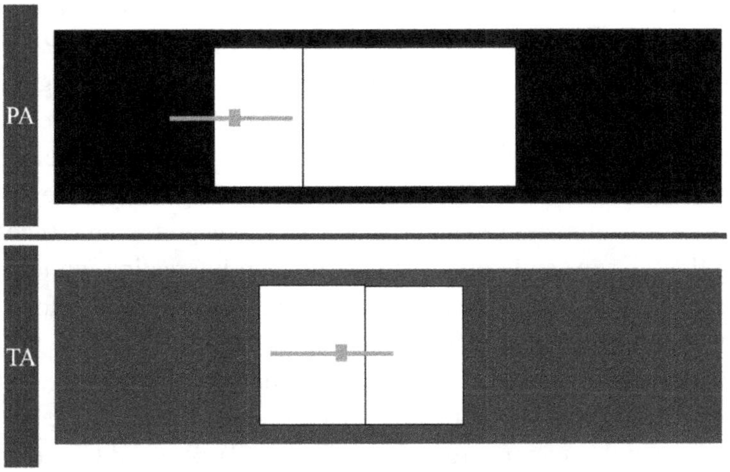

Figure 6. Cluster 3 (T+P-)

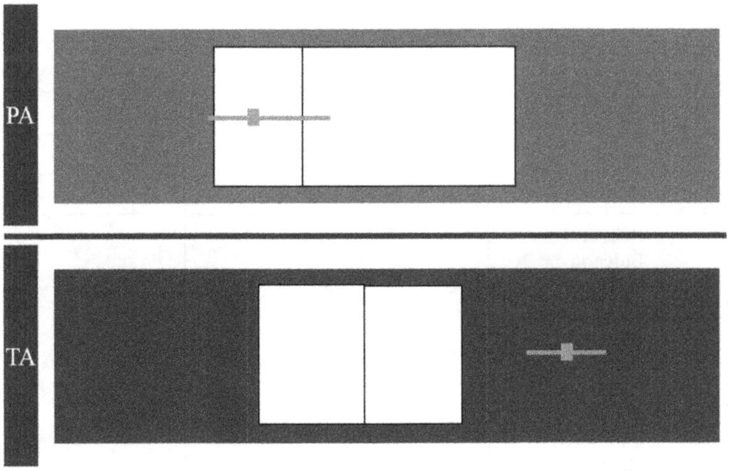

Figure 7. Cluster 4 (T+P+)

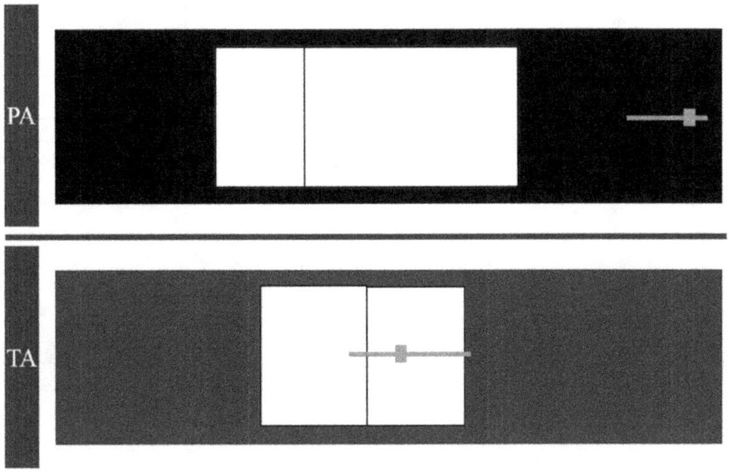

After operating the necessary analysis steps, Table 1 was designed to list the countries from Europe and MENA in each of the four clusters. A bird's eye view casted over the list reveals some interesting results in this direction: while the majority of MENA countries register a T-P- tax climate, the European countries are chiefly divided into two categories, viz., countries enjoying a high level of trust in and power of authorities and countries with a low level of trust, but a high level of power. Concerning the European cases, except for Estonia all countries in cluster 4 are highly developed and pertain to the Nordic, Continental or Anglo-Saxon tax climates. Notwithstanding a high or even highest level of tax burden (i.e., Nordic), these tax climates secure high quality public goods, an efficient social care system (most of the times) and a "service and client" approach when interacting with taxpayers (very often). Except for Belgium, France and Iceland, the European countries in cluster 1 belong either to the Eastern European and Baltic tax climates or to the Mediterranean tax climate. Although the high perceived level of power in these states could trigger a certain amount of enforced compliance, authorities are granted low levels of their taxpayers' trust which ultimately may impede a boost in the desired voluntary compliance levels. The outliers in this picture are Belarus, Russia, Turkey and Ukraine by classifying in the T-P- cluster, mainly due to the low "Rule of law" scores (i.e., see predictor importance).

Except for Israel, Qatar (T+P+) and Jordan (T+P-) which register a high trust especially due to the easiness of paying taxes (The World Bank Group & PricewaterhouseCoopers, 2013), there are significant

Table 1. The distribution of European and MENA countries across clusters

	CLUSTERS			
REGION	**(1) T-P+**	**(2) T-P-**	**(3) T+P-**	**(4) T+P+**
EUROPE	Belgium Bulgaria Cyprus Czech Republic France Greece Hungary Iceland Italy Latvia Lithuania Moldova Poland Portugal Romania Slovak Republic Slovenia Spain	Belarus Russia Turkey Ukraine		Austria Denmark Estonia Finland Germany Ireland Luxembourg Malta The Netherlands Norway Sweden Switzerland United Kingdom
MENA		Algeria Egypt Iran Iraq Lebanon Morocco Tunisia West Bank and Gaza Yemen	Jordan	Israel Qatar

differences between European and MENA countries concerning the "slippery slope" dimensions. These differences stem primarily from the nature of their underlying tax systems. While European states have established tax systems financing different social welfare state models (Cousins, 2005; Esping-Andersen, 1990; Hemerijck, 2013; Hemerijck *et al.*, 2013; Kettunen & Petersen, 2011), MENA countries range between two poles, with respect to taxation (Batrancea, 2014a). On one side, oil economies don't ground their development on fiscal obligations: excepting banks and oil/gas production companies which are subject to corporate rates of 35%-85%, regular companies pay lower rates (10-15%) and personal income is exempted from taxation. On the other side, non-oil economies regard taxes as important levers of financing public outlays, but face multiple drawbacks as a consequence of extremely narrow tax bases, nascent compliance systems and considerable underground economy. In the same vein, securing budget revenues through taxation in the MENA region is particularly challenging on the account of tax systems' intricacy and corruption (Imam & Jacobs, 2007, p. 3), which trigger low levels of trust in and power of authorities.

Nevertheless, these states can alter the aforementioned situation by using the characteristics of the underlying tax systems in their favor. Overall, MENA countries have among the least demanding taxation level (The World Bank Group & PricewaterhouseCoopers, 2013), granting tax incentives to attract substantial foreign direct investments. Moreover, given the ongoing Europe-MENA partnerships, sustained efforts of strengthening authorities' power to enforce the rule of law in the region could determine European foreign investors to reconsider their positions on MENA markets, impaired by political instability.

In addition, the perspective of diminishing hydrocarbon resources and the future need of introducing consumption taxes to balance budgets will ultimately determine MENA oil economies to ground state budgets on taxpayers' trust in their benevolence to ensure the common good and their power to maintain compliance.

CONCLUSION

Throughout this book chapter, the reader has witnessed the depiction of the role of taxation for modern society, the variety of traditional and current approaches to tax compliance, the relevance of Europe and MENA on the global economic stage, some of the paradigms and strategies applied by tax authorities for amending compliance, the distinction in terms of the "slippery slope" framework's dimensions between the two regions.

In many countries worldwide, taxation is imperative first and foremost because it determines their development status by financing the system of public goods. Secondly, taxes adjust individuals' propensity to consume, serving as policy leverage. Forasmuch public budgets depend on tax authorities' capacity to regulate and supervise wealth redistribution, but also on taxpayers' propensity to comply, there is no doubt about the interrelation of the two parties. With citizens gliding on a continuum between full income disclosure and full noncompliance, authorities are called to amend taxpayers' behavior.

The first key step in generating such result is understanding the nature of tax compliance determinants. Keeping in mind the complexity of human actions, tax literature acknowledges economic, legislative and psychological influences, among others. Because the magnitude of conventional economic factors is often reported as inconsistent, the following are singled out one by one among the determinants of tax compliance in various studies: language complexity, excessive regulation, attitudes, norms, motivational postures, tax morale or fairness concerns.

Just like tax literature features new catalysts for compliance, the globalization process underlines the rising importance of Europe and MENA for the interconnected versatile market. The first is counted among the world's largest economies, the second among the regions with the most valuable hydrocarbon resources.

The volatility of the global economic market and the fierce competition in attracting foreign investments have determined European and MENA authorities to reconsider interactions with taxpayers. As a result, benefitting from assistance granted by several international bodies (i.e., OECD, World Bank, UN), authorities have started implementing tax compliance strategies and models like co-operative compliance, horizontal monitoring, whistleblowing, all stemming from psychological determinants.

The empirical investigation concerning specific features of tax compliance behavior in countries from Europe and MENA is theoretically grounded on the "slippery slope" framework (Kirchler *et al.*, 2008). Developed through an interdisciplinary quest and integrating economic and psychological determinants of income disclosure, the aforementioned model attempts to solve the "riddle of tax compliance" (Bergman, 2009) via its two main dimensions, i.e., trust in authorities and power of authorities. In order to thoroughly serve the aims of this investigation, the former dimension is proxied by the "Trust in national government" variable (Gallup World Poll measurement), while the latter dimension is proxied by the "Rule of law" governance indicator (World Bank estimate).

With respect to the proposed methodological approach, a two-step cluster analysis was run on the continuous proxies of trust in authorities and power of authorities, corresponding to 215 countries and territories worldwide, out of which 35 from Europe and 12 from MENA. The analyses yielded a four-cluster miscellanea of tax climates, i.e., trust high – power high (T+P+), trust low – power low (T-P-), trust high – power low (T+P-), trust low – power high (T-P+). As overall results, both European and MENA countries fall into three of the four clusters considered. While the majority of European countries are spread between two categories, almost all MENA countries register low levels of trust and power, these results suggesting the imperious need for stability and efficiency in every major area of these societies.

The aforementioned set of strategies, paradigms, models aimed to boost compliance levels and strengthen cooperation between nowadays Europe and MENA represent the acme of what has been developing across centuries and had emerged from the journeys of Marco Polo and Ibn Batutta. The two explorers' trust in an ideal and their power of initiative, courage and determination had made them discover new worlds. Both Europe and MENA are tributary to their venturesome efforts, for the connections established between the regions had overcome centuries. Since time has been compliant with them, authorities from Europe and MENA have joined efforts to shape proper tax systems, conducive for voluntary tax compliance. Though challenging due to various economic, political or social shortcomings, the overall path is gradually heading towards promising results.

ACKNOWLEDGMENT

This work was supported by a grant of the Babes-Bolyai University through the Grants for Young Researchers Program, project no. GTC 34048/01.11.2013.

REFERENCES

Ajzen, I. (1991). The Theory of Planned Behavior. *Organizational Behavior and Human Decision Processes*, *50*(2), 179–211. doi:10.1016/0749-5978(91)90020-T

Allingham, M. G., & Sandmo, A. (1972). Income Tax Evasion: A Theoretical Analysis. *Journal of Public Economics*, *1*(3-4), 323–338. doi:10.1016/0047-2727(72)90010-2

Alm, J., & Torgler, B. (2006). Culture Differences and Tax Morale in the United States and in Europe. *Journal of Economic Psychology*, *27*(2), 224–246. doi:10.1016/j.joep.2005.09.002

Alm, J., & Torgler, B. (2011). Do Ethics Matter? Tax Compliance and Morality. *Journal of Business Ethics*, *101*(4), 635–651. doi:10.1007/s10551-011-0761-9

Amadeo, K. (2014). World's Largest Economy. Retrieved from http://useconomy.about.com/od/grossdomesticproduct/p/largest_economy.htm

Arab Reform Initiative. (2014). Arab Barometer. Retrieved http://arabbarometer.org

Bacher, J., Wenzig, K., & Vogler, M. (2004). SPSS Twostep Cluster - A First Evaluation. Universität Erlangen-Nürnberg, Wirtschafts- und Sozialwissenschaftliche Fakultät, Sozialwissenschaftliches Institut, Lehrstuhl für Soziologie, Arbeits- und Diskussionspapiere.

Bahm, A. J. (1996). *Tao Teh King by Lao Tzu. Interpreted as Nature and Intelligence*. Fremont: Jain Publishing Company.

Batrancea, L. (2014a). Taxpayers and Tax Authorities Interacting within the MENA Region: The Nexus between Trust, Power and Compliance. *The Annals of the University of Oradea. Economic Sciences*, *XXIII*(2), 241–250.

Batrancea, L. (2014b). *Depicting Worldwide Tax Compliance Behavior in a Four-Cluster Assortment Availing Trust in and Power of Authorities* (Working paper).

Bergman, M. (2009). *Tax Evasion and the Rule of Law in Latin America: The Political Culture of Cheating and Compliance in Argentina and Chile*. University Park, PA: The Pennsylvania State University Press.

Bertelsmann. (1999, December 7-9). Europe and the Middle East and North Africa: Steps towards Comprehensive Stability. *Discussion paper presented by the Bertelsmann Group on Policy Research, Center for Applied Policy Research (Munich) to the V. Kronberg Talks*.

Braithwaite, J. (2002). *Restorative Justice and Responsive Regulation*. Oxford: Oxford University Press.

Braithwaite, V. (2003). Dancing with Tax Authorities: Motivational Postures and Non-Compliant Actions. In V. Braithwaite (Ed.), *Taxing Democracy. Understanding Tax Avoidance and Tax Evasion* (pp. 15–39). Aldershot: Ashgate.

Braithwaite, V. (2007). Responsive Regulation and Taxation: Introduction. *Law & Policy*, *29*(1), 3–10. doi:10.1111/j.1467-9930.2007.00242.x

Campbell, J. L. (1993). The State and Fiscal Sociology. *Annual Review of Sociology*, *19*(1), 163–185. doi:10.1146/annurev.so.19.080193.001115

Clements, D. (2013). Blowing in the Wind? In Deloitte & Touche (Eds.), Middle East Point of View Summer 2013 (pp. 52-55).

Cousins, M. (2005). *European Welfare States: Comparative Perspectives*. London: Sage Publications.

Cussons, P. (2006). The Increasing Burden of Tax Administration and Compliance. In the World Bank Group & PricewaterhouseCoopers (Eds.), Paying Taxes: The Global Picture (pp. 16-17). Washington, DC.

Dasgupta, P. (2000). Economic Progress and the Idea of Social Capital. In P. Dasgupta & I. Serageldin (Eds.), *Social Capital: A Multifaceted Perspective* (pp. 325–424). Washington, DC: The World Bank.

Dii. (2012). *Desert Power 2050: Perspectives on a Sustainable Power System for EUMENA*. Desertec Industrial Initiative (Dii), Munich, Germany.

El-Badri, A. S. (2012, January 30-31). The MENA Region in the International Arena. *Keynote address of the OPEC Secretary General, to the Middle East & North Africa Energy 2012, Investing for the Future in Turbulent Times*, Chatham House, London, UK. Retrieved from http://www.opec.org/opec_web/en/2211.htm

Elffers, H., Weigel, R. H., & Hessing, D. J. (1987). The Consequences of Different Strategies for Measuring Tax Evasion Behavior. *Journal of Economic Psychology*, *8*(3), 311–337. doi:10.1016/0167-4870(87)90026-2

Esping-Andersen, G. (1990). *The Three Worlds of Welfare Capitalism*. Cambridge: Polity Press.

Euro-Mediterranean Partnership (EUROMED). (2014). European Union. Retrieved from http://eeas.europa.eu/euromed/index_en.htm

The EuroMed Partnership. (2014). EuroMed. Retrieved from http://www.enpi-info.eu/medportal/content/340/About%20the%20EuroMed%20Partnership

Feld, L. P., & Frey, B. S. (2002). Trust Breeds Trust: How Taxpayers Are Treated. *Economics of Governance*, *3*(2), 87–99. doi:10.1007/s101010100032

Fishbein, M., & Ajzen, I. (1975). *Belief, Attitude, Intention and Behavior: An Introduction to Theory and Research*. Reading, MA: Addison-Wesley.

Fjeldstad, O.-H., & Heggstad, K. K. (2012). *Building Taxpayer Culture in Mozambique, Tanzania and Zambia: Achievements, Challenges and Policy Recommendations. CMI Report R 2012:1. Chr*. Bergen: Michelsen Institute.

Goel, R. K., & Nelson, M. A. (2013). Effectiveness of Whistleblower Laws in Combating Corruption. *BOFIT – Institute for Economies in Transition, Bank of Finland, BOFIT Discussion Papers* 9.

Groot, W., & van den Brink, H. M. (2010). The Effects of Education on Crime. *Applied Economics*, *42*(3), 279–289. doi:10.1080/00036840701604412

Hemerijck, A. (2013). *Changing Welfare States*. Oxford: Oxford University Press.

Hemerijck, A., Dräbing, V., Vis, B., Nelson, M., & Soentken, M. (2013). European Welfare States in Motion. *NEUJOBS Working Paper*, No. D5.2.

Imam, P. A., & Jacobs, D. F. (2007). Effect of Corruption on Tax Revenues in the Middle East. *International Monetary Fund Working Paper* WP/07/270.

Whistleblower Office First Report to Congress. (2008). *Internal Revenue Service*. Retrieved from http://www.irs.gov/uac/Whistleblower-Office-Annual-Reports

IRS Whistleblower Office FY2013 Annual Report. (2013). *Internal Revenue Service*.

International Co-operation and Development. (2014). Retrieved from http://ec.europa.eu/europeaid/where/neighbourhood/overview/index_en.htm

James, S. (1998). *A Dictionary of Taxation*. Cheltenham: Edward Elgar.

James, S., & Alley, C. (2002). Tax Compliance, Self-Assessment and Tax Administration. *Journal of Finance and Management in Public Services*, *2*(2), 27–42.

James, S., & Wallschutzky, I. (1997). Tax Law Improvement in Australia and the UK: The Need for a Strategy for Simplification. *Fiscal Studies*, *18*(4), 445–460. doi:10.1111/j.1475-5890.1997.tb00273.x

Johnson, E., & Martini, M. (2012). *Corruption Trends in the Middle East and North Africa Region (2007-2011): U4 Expert Answer*. Transparency International.

Kasper, M., Kogler, C., & Kirchler, E. (2013). Tax Policy and the News: An Empirical Analysis of Taxpayers' Perceptions of Tax-Related Media Coverage and Its Impact on Tax Compliance. *WU International Taxation Research Paper Series*, No. 2013-07.

Kaufmann, D., Kraay, A., & Mastruzzi, M. (2010). The Worldwide Governance Indicators: Methodology and Analytical Issues. *World Bank Policy Research Working Paper*, No. 5430.

Kettunen, P., & Petersen, K. (Eds.). (2011). *Beyond Welfare State Models: Transnational Historical Perspectives on Social Policy*. Cheltenham: Edward Elgar. doi:10.4337/9781849809603

Kirchler, E. (2007). *The Economic Psychology of Tax Behaviour*. Cambridge: Cambridge University Press. doi:10.1017/CBO9780511628238

Kirchler, E., Hoelzl, E., & Wahl, I. (2008). Enforced versus Voluntary Tax Compliance: The "Slippery Slope" Framework. *Journal of Economic Psychology*, *29*(2), 210–225. doi:10.1016/j.joep.2007.05.004

Knowledge@Warton. (2012). *Europe's Financial Crisis and Its Impact on the Arab World*.

Kogler, C., Batrancea, L., Nichita, A., Pantya, J., Belianin, A., & Kirchler, E. (2013). Trust and Power as Determinants of Tax Compliance: Testing the Assumptions of the Slippery Slope Framework in Austria, Hungary, Romania and Russia. *Journal of Economic Psychology*, *34*(1), 169–180. doi:10.1016/j.joep.2012.09.010

Kogler, C., Muehlbacher, S., & Kirchler, E. (2013). Trust, Power, and Tax Compliance: Testing the 'Slippery Slope Framework' Among Self-Employed Taxpayers. *WU International Taxation Research Paper Series*, No. 2013-05.

Levy, D. M. (2002). *How the Dismal Science Got Its Name: Classical Economics and the Ur-Text of Racial Politics*. Ann Arbor: The Michigan University Press.

Lewis, A. (1982). *The Psychology of Taxation*. Oxford: Martin Robertson.

Lisi, G. (2012). Testing the Slippery Slope Framework. *Economic Bulletin*, *32*(2), 1369–1377.

Lozza, E., Kastlunger, B., Tagliabue, S., & Kirchler, E. (2013). The Relationship between Political Ideology and Attitudes toward Tax Compliance: The Case of Italian Taxpayers. *Journal of Social and Political Psychology*, *1*(1), 51–73. doi:10.5964/jspp.v1i1.108

Mair, V. H. (2009). *How a Misunderstanding about Chinese Characters Has Led Many Astray*. Retrieved from http://www.pinyin.info/chinese/crisis.html

Martin, I. W., Mehrotra, A. K., & Prasad, M. (2009). The Thunder of History: The Origins and Development of the New Fiscal Sociology. In I. W. Martin, A. K. Mehrotra, & M. Prasad (Eds.), *The New Fiscal Sociology: Taxation in Comparative and Historical Perspective* (pp. 1–28). New York: Cambridge University Press. doi:10.1017/CBO9780511627071.002

Mendel, J., & Bevacqua, J. (2014). *International Tax Administration: Building Bridges*. Sydney: CCH Australia.

Muehlbacher, S., Kirchler, E., & Schwarzenberger, H. (2011). Voluntary versus Enforced Tax Compliance: Empirical Evidence for the "Slippery Slope" Framework. *European Journal of Law and Economics*, *32*(1), 89–97. doi:10.1007/s10657-011-9236-9

Guide to Horizontal Monitoring within the SME Segment. (2012). Netherlands Tax and Customs Administration. Retrieved from http://download.belastingdienst.nl/belastingdienst/docs/guide_horiz_monit_dv4071z1pleng.pdf

OECD. (1998). *Harmful Tax Competition: An Emerging Global Issue*. Paris: OECD Publications.

OECD. (2009). *Experiences and Practices of Eight OECD Countries*. Forum on Tax Administration: Compliance Management of Large Business Task Group. Guidance Note. Retrieved from http://www.oecd.org/tax/administration/43241144.pdf

OECD. (2013a). *Co-Operative Compliance: A Framework – From Enhanced Relationship to Co-Operative Compliance*. OECD Publishing.

OECD. (2013b). *Together for Better Outcomes: Engaging and Involving SME Taxpayers and Stakeholders*. OECD Publishing.

OECD. (2013c). *Building Tax Culture, Compliance and Citizenship: A Global Source Book on Taxpayer Education*. OECD Publishing.

OECD. (2014a). *Practices to Strengthen Business Integrity in the MENA Region*. Retrieved from http://www.oecd.org/mena/investment/PracticesBusinessIntegrity.pdf

OECD. (2014b). *MENA-OECD Investment Programme: Fostering Investment, Growth and Employment in the Middle East and North Africa (MENA)*. OECD Publishing.

Owens, J., & Hamilton, S. (2004). Experience and Innovations in Other Countries. In H. J. Aaron & J. Slemrod (Eds.), *The Crisis in Tax Administration* (pp. 347–388). Washington, DC: Brookings Institution Press.

Park, C.-G., & Hyun, J. K. (2003). Examining the Determinants of Tax Compliance by Experimental Data: A Case of Korea. *Journal of Policy Modeling*, *25*(8), 673–684. doi:10.1016/S0161-8938(03)00075-9

Pickhardt, M., & Prinz, A. (2014). Behavioral Dynamics of Tax Evasion – A Survey. *Journal of Economic Psychology*, *40*(1), 1–19. doi:10.1016/j.joep.2013.08.006

PwC Middle East Tax and Legal Update. (2013, January). PricewaterhouseCoopers.

Regulation (EU) No. 232/2014 of the European Parliament and of the Council. (2014). *Official Journal of the European Union, L*, *77*, 27–43.

Safadi, R. (Ed.). (2003). *MENA Trade & Investment in the New Economy: The Fourth Mediterranean Development Forum MDF4*. Cairo: The American University in Cairo Press.

Sandmo, A. (2003). Three Decades of Tax Evasion: A Perspective on the Literature. Paper Presented at the Skatteforum (The Research Forum on Taxation), Rosendal, Norway.

Schmölders, G. (1960). *Das Irrationale in der öffentlichen Finanzwirtschaft*. Frankfurt am Main: Suhrkamp.

Schumpeter, J. A. [1918] (1954). The Crisis of the Tax State. In A. T. Peacock, W. F. Stolper, R. Turvey & E. Henderson (Eds.), International Economic Papers (pp. 5-38). New York: Macmillan.

Sigala, M., Burgoyne, C. B., & Webley, P. (1999). Tax Communication and Social Influence: Evidence from a British Sample. *Journal of Community & Applied Social Psychology*, *9*(3), 237–241. doi:10.1002/(SICI)1099-1298(199905/06)9:3<237::AID-CASP516>3.0.CO;2-7

Srinivasan, T. N. (1973). Tax Evasion: A Model. *Journal of Public Economics*, *2*(4), 339–346. doi:10.1016/0047-2727(73)90024-8

A Regional Alliance to Improve Public Procurement. (2014). The World Bank. Retrieved from http://www.worldbank.org/en/news/feature/2014/01/15/a-regional-alliance-to-improve-public-procurement

The World Bank Group, & PricewaterhouseCoopers (2013). *Paying Taxes 2014: The Global Picture: A Comparison of Tax Systems in 189 Economies Worldwide*. Retrieved from http://www.pwc.com/gx/en/paying-taxes/assets/pwc-paying-taxes-2014.pdf

Torgler, B. (2005). Tax Morale and Direct Democracy. *European Journal of Political Economy*, *21*(2), 525–531. doi:10.1016/j.ejpoleco.2004.08.002

Whistleblowing in Europe: Legal Protections for Whistleblowers in the EU. (2013). Transparency International. Retrieved from http://www.transparency.org/whatwedo/pub/whistleblowing_in_europe_legal_protections_for_whistleblowers_in_the_eu

Middle East and North African governments have high risks of defence-related corruption. (2013). Transparency International. Retrieved from http://www.transparency.org/news/pressrelease/20120206_middle_east_and_north_african_governments_have_high_risks_of_defen

Trivedi, V. U., Shehata, M., & Mestelman, S. (2005). Attitudes, Incentives, and Tax Compliance. *Canadian Tax Journal*, *53*(1), 29–61.

United Nations. (2009, October 19-23). Note by the Secretariat: Proposed Code of Conduct on Cooperation in Combating International Tax Evasion. *Committee of Experts on International Cooperation in Tax Matters, fifth session*, Geneva.

United Nations Development Programme. (2013). *Human Development Report 2013. The Rise of the South: Human Progress in a Diverse World. Explanatory Note on 2013 HDR Composite Indices.* Retrieved from http://hdr.undp.org/sites/default/files/Country-Profiles/IND.pdf

von Mises, L. (1966). *Human Action: A Treatise on Economics* (*3rd* Revised ed.). Washington, DC: Henry Regnery Company.

Wahl, I., Kastlunger, B., & Kirchler, E. (2010). Trust in Authorities and Power to Enforce Tax Compliance: An Empirical Analysis of the "Slippery Slope Framework." *Law & Policy*, *32*(4), 383–406. doi:10.1111/j.1467-9930.2010.00327.x

Webley, P. (2004). Tax Compliance by Businesses. In H. Sjögren & G. Skogh (Eds.), *New Perspectives on Economic Crime* (pp. 95–126). Cheltenham: Edward Elgar. doi:10.4337/9781843769835.00012

Webley, P., Cole, M., & Eidjar, O.-P. (2001). The Prediction of Self-Reported and Hypothetical Tax-Evasion: Evidence from England, France and Norway. *Journal of Economic Psychology*, *22*(2), 141–155. doi:10.1016/S0167-4870(01)00026-5

Wenzel, M. (2003). Tax Compliance and the Psychology of Justice: Mapping the Field. In V. Braithwaite (Ed.), *Taxing Democracy. Understanding Tax Avoidance and Tax Evasion* (pp. 41–69). Aldershot: Ashgate.

Wenzel, M. (2005). Motivation or Rationalisation? Causal Relations between Ethics, Norms and Tax Compliance. *Journal of Economic Psychology*, *26*(4), 491–508. doi:10.1016/j.joep.2004.03.003

Yitzhaki, S. (1974). A Note on Income Tax Evasion: A Theoretical Analysis. *Journal of Public Economics*, *3*(2), 201–202. doi:10.1016/0047-2727(74)90037-1

Zaklan, G., Lima, F. W. S., & Westerhoff, F. (2008). Controlling Tax Evasion Fluctuations. *Physica A. Statistical Mechanics and Its Applications*, *387*(23), 5857–5861. doi:10.1016/j.physa.2008.06.036

Zaklan, G., Westerhoff, F., & Stauffer, D. (2009). Analysing Tax Evasion Dynamics via the Ising Model. *Journal of Economic Interaction and Coordination*, *4*(1), 1–14. doi:10.1007/s11403-008-0043-5

Chapter 13
Political Economy of Tax Evasion and Tax Loss in the Real Estate Sector:
A Property Tax Reform Proposal for Turkey

M. Mustafa Erdoğdu
Marmara University, Turkey

Murat Aydın
Çanakkale Onsekiz Mart University, Turkey

Binhan E. Yılmaz
İstanbul University, Turkey

İnci User
Marmara University, Turkey

ABSTRACT

This chapter engages with political economy of tax evasion and tax compliance issues, particularly focusing on deficiencies and problems within property taxation system in Turkey. The chapter questions if there are any political preferences, legal arrangements or cultural issues facilitating tax evasion and tax loss in Turkey. It first identifies the degenerating effects of frequent application of tax amnesties, having a lax tax reconciliation institution, and less than logical way tax information confidentiality principle is applied in Turkey. Then, the chapter investigates peculiarities and specific difficulties of real estate sector in general in relation to taxation. Finally, a comprehensive property tax reform based on a semi-public valuation system is proposed to reduce tax loss in this sector.

INTRODUCTION

The most important weakness of the Turkish tax system is related to the large amount of unregistered economic activities and the high percentage of tax fraud among the registered tax payers. What follows is that tax revenue remains low with high economic and social costs. As will be elaborated later, tax constitutes a form of political interaction and it is important to understand how key actors can use the institutions and regulations in their own favor and how they be able to exert pressure over policy design and implementation.

DOI: 10.4018/978-1-5225-0053-7.ch013

Real estate sector, which is the focus of this chapter, is significantly different from other sectors in terms of the reasons why tax loss and evasion occur. First of all, why unregistered economic activities exist in this sector is not because it is difficult to get hold the tax subject since they have physical bodies that cannot be hidden or transferred to somewhere else. Thus, *the informality in this sector has come out as acquiescence of the current condition by the governments due to the political reasons.*

Probably because of the cultural legacy of the Ottoman Empire, the Turkish tax authorities have always exhibited a mild attitude towards real estate taxation in Turkey. As a result, real estate taxes have occupied almost a negligible share within the public revenue. Income generated from the real estate is taxed mainly in three ways in the Turkish tax system: 1) Taxing the rental income of immovable properties: 2) Taxing the real estate itself; and 3) Taxing the appreciation gains resulted in a transaction. According to Ministry of Finance (2015) figures, the revenue from property taxes was less than 1 percent of Gross Domestic Product (GDP) and only around 3.5% of total tax revenues in Turkey. This is much lower than the average in the OECD where property taxes amount to 2% of GDP and to around 5.5% of total tax revenues.

The chapter is structured as follows. The next section reviews political economy of taxation. It first provides a brief overview of the literature on tax evasion and tax compliance to reveal the motives behind tax noncompliance and then it engages with the political economy of tax related issues, such as power balance, voters' and politicians' perspectives. This section also questions if there are any political preferences and legal arrangements that facilitate tax evasion and tax loss in the real estate sector in Turkey. In answering this question, the section discusses the harmful effects of many tax amnesties enacted, having a lax tax reconciliation institution, and the exaggerated way tax information confidentiality principle is applied in Turkey. The third section investigates peculiarities and specific difficulties of the real estate sector in relation to taxation. The fourth section looks for possible solutions to tax evasion and tax loss problems in the real estate sector in Turkey and proposes a property tax reform based on a semi-public valuation system. The last section provides concluding remarks.

BACKGROUND: POLITICAL ECONOMY OF TAXATION

A Brief Literature Review: Tax Evasion and Tax Compliance

A deliberate omission of a statutory requirement to reduce or eliminate a tax liability is called *tax evasion*. Tax evasion is a pervasive and widespread phenomenon that entails important economic and social consequences. For instance, there can be massive revenue losses[1] with a reduction in spending on health, education, social security, infrastructure, and other needed public programs. Tax evasion also "creates major misallocations in resource use, alters the distribution of income in arbitrary, unpredictable, and unfair ways, and it may contribute to feelings of unjust treatment and disrespect for the law" (Alm, Bloomquist, & McKee, 2015, pp. 1170-1171). In short, "tax evasion represents a violation of fundamental social values leading to deleterious economic and political consequences" (Sossin, 1992b, p. 127). Increasing revenue through a reduction in tax evasion might ease the burden on economic agents who pay taxes and promote growth and equity by enhancing both allocative efficiency and incentives to invest and produce (Wadhawan & Gray, 1998).

Citizens' *tax compliance* is of utmost importance for a state to provide public goods and redistribute wealth. Tax compliance can be defined as the degree to which taxpayers comply with the tax law (James & Alley, 2002, p. 28). Most of the literature on tax compliance has relied on the seminal paper by Allingham & Sandmo (1972), which suggests that tax evasion is negatively associated with the probability of detection and the severity of punishment. Citizens are suspected of being reluctant to pay their share, under the assumption that, rather than voluntarily contributing to public goods, they are motivated to maximize their own benefit (Kirchler, Kogler, & Muehlbacher, 2014, p. 87). Tax evasion is supposed to decrease whenever the expected penalty increases. Even though this model, along with Yitzhaki (1974), has been the workhorse behind most academic research and its results have guided public policies, some of its implications do not square well with the real world evidence. A main point connected to the empirical and experimental findings is that these deterrence models predict far too little compliance and far too much tax evasion (for an overview, see Alm, 2012; Castro & Scartascini, 2013).

The contrast between the evidence and theory has provoked many to develop new theories. To explain the puzzle, two main strands of literature have developed by grounding the research in behavioral economics. One strand modifies the axioms of expected utility theory by adding risk and uncertainty to the models. The other incorporates additional costs of evading to the expected utility function by assuming that the decision-making process of the individual taxpayer is also affected by social interactions. Combining these two strands yields predictions more in line with the empirical evidence (Hashimzade, Myles, & Tran-Nam, 2012). There have been important contributions made in the last decade about tax compliance. For example, Feld and Frey (2007, p. 102) developed the concept of a *psychological tax contract* that goes beyond the traditional deterrence model and explained tax morale as a complicated interaction between taxpayers and the government.

Some recent work[2] conducted particularly with the involvement of psychologist Erick Kirchler revealed that normative factors play much more important roles than generally assumed for tax compliance. For instance, Hofmann, Hoelzl, & Kirchler (2008) show that "taxpayers' willingness to cooperate is not only influenced by audits and fines, but also by a number of internal variables" (p. 213). Çevik (2012) identifies internal variables as: interpersonal relations, social norms, social categories, culture and state-society-individual relations, social and psychological factors. Nerre (2008) defines national tax culture as "the entirety of all interacting formal and informal institutions connected with the national tax system and its practical execution, which are historically embedded within the country's culture, including the dependencies and ties caused by their ongoing interaction" (pp. 163-164).

As Traxler and Winter (2012) emphasizes, "people are governed by social norms: legal and social sanctions together contribute to compliance" (p. 395). There is empirical evidence supports the claim that the possibility of committing a fraud decreases when there is established social norms (Sour, 2003, p. 57). According to Bobek, Hageman, and Kelliher (2013), "[p]ersonal norms play a much stronger role than any other type of social norm" (p. 465). Traxler and Winter (2012) indicate that the strength of norm enforcing sanctions depends on the expected level of norm compliance. The more frequently deviations from a social norm are believed to occur, the less likely a norm violation is sanctioned (p. 395). Efficiency of tax administration was found to have a significant and positive moderating effect on the relationship between social norms and tax compliance (Çevik & Yeniçeri, 2013). A more legitimate and responsive state appears to be an essential precondition for a more adequate level of tax effort in developing countries (Bird, Martinez-Vazquez, & Torgler, 2004, p. 38).

We suggest that fairness perception of taxpayers is probably the most important determinant of tax compliance (see also James, 2014 in this respect). As social psychologists Tankard and Paluck (2015) indicate, "individuals' perceptions of norms guide their personal behavior" (p. 2). What follows is that, "perception can automatically influence behavior" (Ferguson & Bargh, 2004, p. 33). The two most important conditions that build up taxpayers' perception can be claimed as follows: 1) Fairness perception of the tax system by the citizens; and 2) The quality of public administration and public services. Fairness is a subjective issue and changes from one individual to another. Sheffrin (1993, p. 301) points out that public opinion about fairness of the tax system is fraught with difficulties. This is mainly because of the fact that public opinion is likely to be ill-formed and the effects of taxation are not well understood by the public. As Kirchler et al. (2012) suggest, fairness needs to be achieved on the distributive, procedural, and retributive levels. The trend in tax behavior research indicates a move from understanding taxpayers as selfish individuals trying to maximize their own gain to individuals with a sense of community who are ready to cooperate if all actors in the social system contribute to a climate of mutual trust. Batrancea et al. (2016) identify that fairness concerns arise in taxpayers' evaluations of overall tax systems and what is expected is the more fair tax systems are perceived, the more compliant citizens will be.

It should be clear that the quality of the public administration is crucial for ensuring high-quality public services and thus societal well-being. As Erdoğdu (2015) points out, "it is naïve to expect correct state action without administrative capacity. The existence of an extensive, internally coherent bureaucratic machinery is the first prerequisite for effective state action" (p. 22). Barone and Mocetti (2009) find that the attitude towards paying taxes is more positive when resources are spent more efficiently. They indicate that in the taxpayer's cost-benefit calculation public spending inefficiency is equivalent to a waste of resources and implies a less favorable ratio between the supply of public goods and the taxes used to finance them. Findings of a recent empirical study provides another support for this position. According to McGee and Benk (2016, chapter 14 in this handbook), "[t]he more confidence in government one had, the more opposed one was to tax evasion."

The trend in tax behavior research indicates a move from understanding taxpayers as selfish individuals trying to maximize their own gain to individuals with a sense of community who are ready to cooperate if all actors in the social system contribute to a climate of mutual trust. Batrancea *et al.* (2016) identify that fairness concerns arise in taxpayers' evaluations of overall tax systems and what is expected is the more fair tax systems are perceived, the more compliant citizens will be.

Political Economy of Evasion and Compliance

Taxation is one of the primary powers of any government over the citizens and corporate entities. Taxes are important as they finance various much needed public expenditures. As Shah (2013) succinctly puts it, "[w]e might not like the idea of paying taxes, but without it, democracies will struggle to function, and will be unable to provide public services." It is not controversial that tax is a social duty. Nevertheless, due to its nature, tax is a burden on taxpayers at least at the time of its collection.

Sossin (1992a) suggest that "[p]aying taxes is, like avoiding or evading them, a form of political interaction" (p. 179). Political opportunism, organized interests, and voters' demands play important roles in tax policymaking. Alt, Preston, and Sibieta (2009) identify that political economy research suggests three main conflicts of interest that tax policy resolves through institutional processes. "The first is a *class-interest view of politics*: citizens have different views about taxation based on their position in the income distribution. In a world in which citizens have different views about how taxes should be levied, political systems affect whose interests are represented and how. The second is between *organized and unorganized interests*: organized interests typically have advantages in securing favorable policy outcomes in return for electoral contributions that can be used to persuade voters. … The third conflict is that between *citizens and government*. Making economic activity taxable allows decision makers in governments to appropriate resources for their own objectives and to use them in ways that citizens may not like" (pp. 1208-1209).

O'Connor (1973) suggests that "[e]very important change in the balance of class and political forces is registered in the tax structure … Ruling classes normally attempt either to conceal or to justify or to rationalize tax exploitation ideologically" (pp. 202-203). Agenda setting and framing of policy choices may give politicians a central role in coordinating special interests (Ilzetzkiy, 2014, p. 32). Tax policy is a popular vehicle for targeting special interests in practice. One way to do this is favorably taxing influential groups. Groups that are bound to profit from preferential regimes naturally form a lobby to influence the design and implementation of such regimes, and to guarantee their permanence (Daude, Gutiérrez, & Melguizo, 2014, p. 10). Another way is to apply tax remission, which is particularly used in developing countries, as a way of vote rising for politicians. Governments tend to see financial remissions as political means of establishing social dialogue between them and their voters. It is brought into agenda just before elections or prior to important political decisions to gain supports (Yaraşır, 2013, p. 179). Interestingly, such political moves find also considerable support from opponent party members as well, since they would not like to be seen in the eyes of their voters as the ones who stop a favor (Savaşan, 2006, p. 57).

Key actors and elites is likely to use the institutions and regulations in their own favor. As Daude, Gutiérrez, and Melguizo (2014) clarify, "key characteristic of the elites is the ability of not only working around the institutional framework, but also working within the institutional framework to assure the 'right' decisions are taken" (p. 11). Groups that are bound to profit from preferential regimes naturally form a lobby to influence the design and implementation of such regimes, and to guarantee their permanence. Influence of certain groups enables them, through legal means, to customize the tax system, shifting the burden to others.

Brunori (2003) highlights the important point that political leaders "prefer to meet constituent service demands without incurring the risk of placing the burden of paying for those services on those constituents" (p. 38). One of the best examples for this can be observed the way in which property taxes applied all over the world. Bahl, Martinez-Vazquez, and Youngman (2010) highlight that the low rate of property tax collections are an issue in many OECD countries (see Table 1), and the property tax remains a weak revenue source in developing countries. This is because political pressure keeps property taxes down. Moreover, as Brown and Hepworth (2002) indicates, "[m]any countries have no provision for regular revaluations of the tax base or have postponed revaluations. In Austria, for example, the assessed value is only between 10 and 20 percent of the market value" (p. 40). Obviously, there is a successful political resistance to follow good assessment practices. This happens because "politics generally outweighs economics in this very visible tax and the losers from tax reform tend to be more vocal than the winners" (Slack, 2010, p. 13).

Compared to taxation an easy and politically almost costless source of revenue is borrowing. The reason is that borrowing does not create a pressure in the short term on the taxpayers, who are generally also the electors. Therefore, it is not surprising to see that politicians, who aim to come into power again in the following election, prefer borrowing rather than imposing a tax rise. As Buchanan (1987, p. 1045) explains the heart of the matter, future taxpayers shoulder the burden when government borrows to finance current spending.

Table 1. Estimates of tax revenues in OECD countries as % of GDP, 2013

	Total tax revenue	Income & profits	Social security	Payroll	Property	Goods & services	Other	EU Custom Duties
Austria (1)	42,5	12,5	14,6	2,9	0,7	11,5	0,2	0,1
Belgium	44,6	15,8	14,2	0,0	3,5	10,8	0,0	0,3
Canada	30,6	14,4	4,9	0,6	3,2	7,4	0,0	..
Chile	20,2	7,2	1,4	0,0	0,8	10,7	-0,0	..
Czech Republic	34,1	7,0	14,8	0,0	0,5	11,7	0,0	0,1
Denmark (1)	48,6	30,7	0,8	0,3	1,8	14,8	0,0	0,2
Estonia	31,8	7,2	11,1	0,0	0,3	13,0	0,0	0,2
Finland	44,0	15,3	12,7	0,0	1,3	14,6	0,0	0,1
France (1)	45,0	10,9	16,8	1,6	3,8	10,8	1,1	0,1
Germany (2)	36,7	11,4	14,0	0,0	0,9	10,2	0,0	0,2
Greece (1)	33,5	7,7	10,6	0,0	2,2	12,9	0,0	0,1
Hungary (3)	38,9	6,4	12,9	1,0	1,3	17,0	0,2	0,1
Iceland	35,5	16,4	3,6	0,4	2,5	12,1	0,5	..
Ireland	28,3	11,7	4,4	0,2	2,2	9,7	0,0	0,1
Israel	30,5	9,7	5,1	1,2	2,7	11,9	0,0	..
Italy	42,6	14,2	13,0	0,0	2,7	10,6	2,0	0,1
Japan (4)	..	9,5	..	0,0	2,7	5,3	0,1	..
South Korea	24,3	7,1	6,4	0,1	2,5	7,5	0,7	..
Luxembourg	39,3	13,9	11,3	0,0	2,9	11,2	0,1	0,0
Mexico (5)	..	6,0	3,1	..	..	..	..	..
Netherlands	..	..	..	..	..	..	..	..
New Zealand	32,1	17,8	0,0	0,0	2,0	12,4	0,0	..
Norway	40,8	18,6	9,7	0,0	1,2	11,3	0,0	..
Poland	..	..	..	..	..	..	..	..
Portugal	33,4	10,9	8,9	0,0	1,1	12,1	0,3	0,1
Slovak Republic	29,6	5,3	13,3	0,0	0,4	10,4	0,0	0,2
Slovenia	36,8	6,6	14,8	0,1	0,7	14,6	0,0	0,1
Spain (1)	32,6	9,6	11,3	0,0	2,1	9,1	0,3	0,1
Sweden	42,8	14,8	9,8	4,6	1,1	12,3	0,0	0,1
Switzerland	27,1	12,3	6,7	0,0	1,8	6,2	0,0	..
Turkey	29,3	5,9	8,0	0,0	1,4	13,5	0,5	..
United Kingdom	32,9	11,7	6,2	0,0	4,1	10,9	0,0	0,2
United States	25,4	12,1	6,2	0,0	2,8	4,3	0,0	..

Source: Revenue Statistics, OECD (2014).

… Not available

1. The total tax revenue has been reduced by the amount of any capital transfer that represents uncollected taxes. The capital transfer has been allocated between tax headings in proportion to the reported tax revenue, except for Austria where it has been allocated to the social security contributions heading.
2. From 1991 the figures relate to the united Germany.
3. The tax revenue figures are on a cash basis.
4. The tax revenue figures exclude revenue for Social Security funds, figures are not available.
5. Central government and Social security funds only.

It is important to recognize that "… taxation is often much more than a powerful method of raising revenue. It is also a major instrument of government policy used to influence the distribution of income as well as discouraging some activities through additional taxation and encouraging others through tax concessions" (James, 2016, chapter three in this handbook).

One other important issue needs to be mentioned is that "… globalization has contributed to the growing unevenness of the income distribution now observed in many countries, both developed and developing … [and it] has also reduced the governments' ability to pursue redistributive policies that require additional public spending" (Tanzi, 2016, chapter one in this handbook).

As these explanations imply, neither borrowing nor taxation decisions cannot be taken out the political contexts. It is also necessary to understand the political and economic forces which serve to make tax evasion possible, desirable, and even socially acceptable. The next section will examine some political and institutional obstacles that we think facilitate tax evasion and tax loss in Turkey.

Some Political and Institutional Obstacles to Combat Tax Evasion and Tax Loss in Turkey

Tax compliance is quite low and the shadow economy is large in Turkey. According to the results acquired from different studies, the size of the shadow economy in Turkey has been one of the highest in Europe. Turkey ranks the sixth among 31 European countries with the informality share of on average 26.5% during 1990-2013 period (Karaca, 2015). Turkey generates lower revenue than would be warranted by its level of development. This reflects not only the high degree of informality prevailing in labor, product and property markets, but also weaknesses in tax audits, tax litigation processes, and collection of tax debts. Local governments, despite having appropriate tax handles like property taxes do not exploit them adequately, reflecting deficiency of political will and institutional capacity.

Political factors and established institutions have played important roles in shaping the Turkish tax system. In contrast to the predictions in the literature, the high degree of income inequality has not led to high tax burden and more redistributive tax system, because the economic power of elites has contributed to various types of representation failures. Additionally, tax morale and voters' attitudes towards raising the tax burden have been adversely affected by perceptions of corruption and poor quality of public services, in a vicious circle leading to inadequate resources for improving such services. Tax reforms were numerous in Turkey. But, they had a tendency to occur during crisis periods and privileging rapid revenue mobilization over other objectives.

There are several interrelated problems that facilitate tax evasion and tax loss in Turkey. First, tax evasion and tax loss deterrence mechanism has a serious deficiency. According to the Turkish Tax Inspection Council (VDK, 2014, p. 39), the general inspection rate of taxpayers was 2.24% in 2014. This inspection rate is not very low. The main reason why the Turkish Tax system performs less than successful seems less related to the inspection rate, but more related to the enforcement mechanism. Our observation is that mainly because of political reasons, sometimes even if a tax fraud is detected, necessary action are not taken or the sanctions imposed are not deterrent enough. The reverse is also true. Sometimes, just because of political reasons over-inspection is carried out and extreme sanctions are imposed on certain taxpayers.[3] As both statistical and empirical findings of Akbulut's (2016) chapter in this handbook suggests, governance related factors such as government effectiveness, accountability, rule of law and level of corruption are more effective on the size of shadow economy as compared to economic indicators such as taxes and spending in Turkey.

We would argue that there are also three governmental practices which induce and facilitate tax evasion in Turkey. They are: frequent implementation of tax amnesties, having a 'lax' tax reconciliation institution, and exaggerated application of tax information confidentiality principle. These practices would have very negative long-term effects as we will be explained below.

Tax Amnesties

Frequent application of tax amnesties[4] is one of the most serious problems in relation to tax collection performance in Turkey. As Alm, Martinez-Vazquez, and Wallace (2009) point out, "tax amnesties are a controversial revenue-raising tool" (p. 235). Its advocates argue that tax amnesties raise revenue both in the short-term and long-term, by bringing former non-filers back into the tax system.[5] They often suggest that future tax revenues may increase if the amnesty is accompanied by more extensive taxpayer services, better education on taxpayer responsibilities, and stricter post-amnesty penalties for evaders and greater expenditures for enforcement. Its critics, on the other hand, claim that the immediate impact on revenues is almost always quite small. Some question whether tax amnesties really produce additional revenue given that they simply collect revenue that could have been raised by normal enforcement procedures anyway (Luitel & Sobel, 2007). They also question the long-term revenue impact of tax amnesties, especially because honest taxpayers might resent the special treatment of tax evaders. If the taxpayers resent the tax breaks given to evaders and if individuals come to believe that the amnesty is not simply a one-time opportunity, then they may reduce their current compliance in anticipation of another, future amnesty (Alm, Martinez-Vazquez, & Wallace, 2009, p. 235).

The historical record has so far demonstrated that "amnesty recoveries are seldom large enough to make any dramatic impact on state finances" (Mikesell & Ross, 2012, p. 557). The editor of a recently published book titled *Is Tax Amnesty a Good Tax Policy?: Evidence from State Tax Amnesty Programs in the United States,* Hari S. Luitel puts clearly that "the ability of a tax amnesty to generate even the short-term tax revenue was not supported by the evidence" (2014, p. 78). International experience shows that the costs of tax amnesty programs often exceed the programs' benefits and the overall level of tax compliance falls after an amnesty (Baer & Le Borgne, 2008, p. 2).

Luitel and Sobel (2007) find that when tax amnesties offered repeatedly, additional tax amnesties generate less short-term revenue than predecessors and tend to magnify revenue losses associated with disincentives for long-term tax compliance. Since amnesties imposes additional costs, Alm, Martinez-Vazquez, and Wallace (2009, p. 249) suggest that developing and transitional countries would be better off avoiding them.

Tax remission is used as a way of gaining support for important political decisions and / or vote rising for politicians in developing countries like Turkey. The number of tax remissions implemented in Turkey proves a good example for how frequent they are used for political purposes. In total, 32 tax remissions have been implemented since the foundation of the Turkish Republic in 1923. Turkey had one party administration until 1946. During that period, six tax remissions had been implemented. After multi-party period started in 1946, a total of 26 tax remissions have been implemented by 46 governments over a period of 68 years.

Tax remissions were implemented more frequently after the single party period and especially in the periods following the military coupes. Within the first three years of the 1960 military coup, five tax remissions and within the first three years of the 1980 military coup, three tax remissions were implemented. It is very clear that tax remission frequency was very high during the first three years of these two military coups, since on average every nine month a tax remission was implemented. Whereas on average every 43 months a tax remission was implemented in the remaining years, there are almost five times the difference between the first three years of military coup periods and the rest. We interpret this huge difference as tax remissions were used to buy support for the military coups.

In addition to the first three years of the two military coup periods, we identify two other distinct periods in which tax remission frequency is very high. The first one is 1988 – 1992 period and the second one is 2001 – 2003. During 1988 – 1992, four and during 2001 – 2003, three tax remissions were put into effect. In other words, during these two periods, on average every 12 months a tax remission was implemented. It is almost certain that the high frequency of tax remissions in the period 1988 – 1992 was related to the rapidly eroding share of the ruling Motherland Party votes.[6] On the other hand, the reason behind the high frequency of tax remissions during 2001 – 2003 seems somewhat different and most probably related to one of the most severe economic crisis that Turkey ever experienced.

During the four distinct periods of the Turkish Republic (1960 – 1963; 1980 – 1983; 1988 – 1992; and 2001 – 2003 periods) that lasted all together 13 years, 15 tax remissions were implemented. This means that on average every 10.4 months a tax remission was put into effect during these four periods. On the other hand, the number of tax remissions implemented during the remaining 79 years of the Republic has been 17, which means on average every 55.8 months one tax remission was put into effect. This simple data clearly illustrate that the Turkish governments have implemented tax remissions mainly because of political reasons.[7]

Tax Reconciliation (Tax Dispute Resolution)

Tax disputes between taxpayers and tax authorities are unavoidable. This is irrespective of the quality of the tax system. As Oats and Pemberton (2012, p. 57) claim, some degree of discretionary power is useful for all tax systems and discretionary power smoothens the process of revenue collection. However, too much discretion, potentially erodes trust and creates costly uncertainty which can have an adverse impact on tax morale at an aggregate level.

The most basic dispute resolution mechanism is going to court. Nevertheless, this does not mean that going to court is always the best way, considering the costs and risks it entails. It is for this reason that the Turkish law, like other continental civil law systems, provides for out-of-court administrative dispute resolution mechanisms. The institution of reconciliation is one of the most significant of such mechanisms (Gündüz, 2013). Tax reconciliation institution was brought into force in Turkey in 1963 (for an overview, see Yavaşlar, 2008). Within the scope of this institution tax authority and taxpayer reach a settlement by reducing the taxes and tax penalties assessed by the tax authority.

The reconciliation institution enables one of the two taxpayers who are equal in all aspects in front of the law to pay less tax. What is clearly unfair is that the other person is destitute of this opportunity. According to the official data (GİB, 2015, p. 88), taxpayers, who applied for reconciliation could disregard a total of 58.9% their tax liability and 98.9% fine liability for the tax year 2014. The same figures for the previous year were 87.0% and 99.0%, respectively. It is important to recognize that if something unjust occurs in the process of taxation, the most suitable place to solve this problem is a court that specializes on tax issues. As Öncel, Kumrulu, and Çağan (2008, p. 171) suggest, a real crime and punishment could only be forgiven by authorized bodies within the frame of constitutional principles.

Reconciliation institution has a potential to affect the public conscious in a very negative way. There are mainly two reasons for this. First, responsible tax payers, who comply with all the tax rules, are not paid back within the frame of total deductions that are accepted in these applications. Second, it is not taken into consideration whether the taxpayers who fulfill their tax liabilities will approve the privileges provided for those not fulfilling their tax liabilities. Indeed, these responsible taxpayers are not even considered as a part of this process and they are treated like a non-relevant audience. Third, the burden caused by those who do not fulfill their tax duties falls on responsible taxpayers and their tax burden becomes heavier. This is the natural consequence of decline in tax revenues. Obviously, this is neither fair nor sustainable.

The Veil of Tax Information Confidentiality

Tax information confidentiality is generally regarded as a fundamental human right. According to Blaufus, Bob, and Otto (2014), the majority of countries treat tax information confidentiality. However, there is wide variety in its scope. While a number of countries like Greece and New Zealand publicly list tax evaders to combat tax evasion, others like Finland, Iceland, Norway, and Sweden disclose all tax return information. Theoretically, there is reason to believe that a reduction in confidentiality or privacy of individual information could lead to more or less compliance. Two different effects are expected: first, a shame effect of increased tax compliance due to the anticipated shame of being declared as a tax evader; second, a contagion effect, arising when an individual observes non-compliance of other individuals and therefore reduces his/her own tax compliance.

There are a few studies which have tested the relationship between confidentiality and tax compliance using experimental methods. One such study is carried out in the USA by Laury and Wallace (2005) in a between-subjects design. Their findings suggest that a loss of confidentiality increases compliance. Findings of two other studies are consistent with Laury and Wallace's study. One of these studies conducted by Coricelli *et al.* (2010) a within-subjects design shows that tax publicity reduces both the number of evaders and the amount of tax evaded. The risk of being 'named and shamed' as an evader diminishes the probability that an individual will evade taxes by 8.2%. One other recent study carried out by Bø, Slemrod, and Thoresen (2014) in Norway in this vein attributes an approximately 3% increase in reported income to Internet public disclosure. Findings of another recent study performed by Blaufus, Bob, and Otto (2014) in Germany, on the other hand, suggest that the shame effect is not strong enough to override the contagion effect when both effects are present.

The experimental studies mentioned above are carried out in developed countries, where tax compliance is generally high. We have reasons to believe that in developing countries, where tax compliance is generally low, tax information confidentiality can function as an armor to protect tax evaders. It is fair to say that an important part of economic activity is masked in Turkey, thanks to the exaggerated implementation of tax information confidentiality principle. The Turkish Tax Law (TPL No. 5 and 6) declares that violation of tax confidentiality principle is a criminal offense punishable with imprisonment. Civil servants are not allowed to reveal the information obtained during taxation process to the third parties. They are obliged to keep this information as a secret even after quitting their jobs or after they retired.

The tax information confidentiality principle forms a legal excuse for the Turkish Revenue Administration to conceal tax data from public domain, as if they are strategic state secrets. They systematically reject to provide even some of the general tax data,[8] which does not indeed have a personal nature. This attitude not only harms democracy due to the nonfulfillment of the 'right to information' but also constitutes a hindrance to eliminating the unregistered economy in Turkey. As Gayer and Mourre (2012) show, "third-party information can dramatically lower the taxpayer's ability to misreport taxes" (p. 4).

PECULIARITIES AND SPECIFIC DIFFICULTIES OF REAL ESTATE TAXATION

Peculiarities and Politics of Real Estate Taxation

Property tax is widely regarded as an efficient and equitable means of raising revenue (see, Bird & Slack, 2006; Bahl, Martinez-Vazquez, & Youngman, 2010; Slack, 2010; World Bank, 2014). Taxes on land and buildings are generally argued to be more efficient than other types of taxes in that their impact on the allocation of resources in the economy is less adverse. This is because these taxes do not affect the decisions of economic agents to supply labor, to produce, invest and innovate to the same extent as some other taxes (Johansson *et al.*, 2008, p. 20). Moreover, recent empirical work on tax composition and growth indicates that a shift from income taxes to property taxes has a strong positive association with long-run economic growth (World Bank, 2014).

At least four characteristics of the property tax differentiate from other taxes: visibility, inelasticity, inherent arbitrariness, and, in at least some countries, the extent to which it reflects local autonomy. First, the property tax is a highly visible tax. Unlike the income tax, it is not largely withheld at source. Unlike the sales tax, it is not paid in small amounts with each daily purchase. Instead, the property tax generally has to be paid directly by taxpayers in periodic lump sum payments (Bird & Slack, 2006). As a result, taxpayers tend to be much more aware of the property taxes they pay and this would increase the resistance from tax payers (Slack, 2010).

It is well established that revaluation and the use of current market value in principle as the underpinning for the property tax base will improve the equitable distribution of the property tax between taxpayers (Dornfest, 2010). Owing to their attractive economic properties, increased use of real estate taxes could conceivably help ease problems with taxes levied on mobile bases. It could improve the allocation of capital and boost growth in the medium term, reinforcing efforts to consolidate public finances (Gayer & Igoseva, 2012, p. 19).

Although there are many reasons why governments should rely more on property taxes, such taxes are under-utilized in many countries. Tax revenue estimates of OECD countries for 2013 in Table 1 shows that property tax revenues rarely exceed three percent of GDP in any country and are often much less than that. The United Kingdom (UK) appears as the highest property tax revenue generating country among the OECD countries. Still, that amount of revenue stood only 4.1% of GDP in the United Kingdom. This figure was almost one-third of the revenue generated from income and profits. But obviously there are other countries in much worse situation. Among the OECD countries, Estonia is an extreme example in this respect. This country could generate just 0.3% of GDP and this was almost one-fourteenth of the amount the UK could collect from properties as a share of GDP for the same year.

Table 2 shows that there has been a significant decline of property taxes in OECD countries since 1965. While the average property tax share of total taxation in OECD countries was 7.9% in 1965, it declined to 5.3% within just 15 years, most probably as a result of neo-liberal resurgence. Since then, it seems that there is a stabilization of property tax share within total taxation. That figure stood as 5.5% for the OECD countries in 2012. An interesting and dramatic change can be observed from the table that the same figure was as high as 10.5% for Turkey in 1965 and declined to as low as 2.3% within 25 years, before it started to gradually improve later on and stood as 4.2% in 2012. This was almost one-third of the UK could collect tax from properties as the share of its total tax revenue for the same year. The data provided makes it clear that there is a wide variety between countries about how much tax they collect from properties and this may change dramatically from one period to another. What we can infer from this data is that *property taxation is clearly much more related to politics than technics.*

Obviously, there is much room for improvement in the practice of property taxation. However, as Brunori (2003, p. 7) indicates, the property tax is often regarded as the 'most hated' tax. According to Gayer and Igoseva (2012, p. 19), the main reason why real estate taxes are very unpopular, is that because people think it is unfair to tax something they already possess. This 'counter-economic' perception is an important factor to be taken into account. Sheffrin (2010) suggests that unpopularity of the property tax also stems from the potential for volatility and unpredictability of a tax that is based on market value. With market value assessment, there is the risk of potentially large annual swings in the distribution of the property tax burden in times when property values are rising rapidly and not uniformly (Haveman & Sexton, 2008). Johansson *et al.* (2008) suggest that "unpopularity of property taxation could be reduced if an up-to-date valuation system is applied and people with low incomes and illiquid assets would either pay low real estate taxes or would have a favorable tax treatment" (p. 45).

Specific Difficulties of Real Estate Taxation in Turkey

Clearly, accommodation is a basic human need and its taxation requires a sensitive political arithmetic. Accommodation is expected to have a political sensitivity in all countries. But, we think the history of the Turkish society has made this issue particularly sensitive for Turkey. As opposed to many countries which have experienced feudalism, land ownership in the Ottoman period had belonged to the state, not individuals. While taxes collected from the real estate had almost always been an important source of revenue for the state in Western countries, this was hardly the case in the Ottoman Empire. Thus, it should not be surprising that the Turkish people became very reluctant to pay real estate related taxes when the state started to collect such taxes later.

Most probably due to this legacy, the Turkish authorities have always been reluctant to collect real estate taxes. Even today, we can see the cases supporting this view. For example, 'the legal real estate values', which constitute a base for tax declarations, are determined by district appraisal committees (DACs) once for every four years. Unless the Cabinet of Ministers decide otherwise, the tax payable is increased half of the inflation rate in the mid years. The situation was even worse in the previous periods when the inflation used to be very high. Adjustments which should have been made frequently seem as to be delayed intentionally. Consequently, taxes collected from the real estate got eroded due to high inflation rates and became almost insignificant. To put it differently, *reluctance of the politicians' to collect real estate taxes has played a significant role in the high level of tax loss in this sector.*

As these explanations make it clear, the real estate sector is significantly different from other sectors in terms of the reasons causing tax loss and evasion. First, unregistered economic activities in this sector are not because of the difficulty of assessment, since these tax subjects have actually physical bodies that cannot be hidden or transferred to somewhere else. The informality in this sector has come out as acquiescence of the current condition by the governments due to political considerations. Huts made on state treasury lands and structures nonconforming to the zoning legislation are common in Turkey. In some cases, the state provides water and electricity infrastructures, and even title deeds for these

Table 2. Taxes on property (4000) as % of total taxation in OECD countries

	1965	1980	1990	2000	2007	2008	2009	2010	2011	2012
Australia	11,5	7,8	9,0	8,8	8,9	8,2	9,5	9,3	8,6	8,6
Austria (1)	4,0	2,9	2,7	1,3	1,4	1,3	1,3	1,3	1,2	1,3
Belgium	3,7	3,1	3,8	4,7	7,2	7,1	7,0	7,3	7,3	7,5
Canada	14,3	9,1	10,0	9,5	10,6	10,9	11,3	11,5	10,9	10,6
Chile	..	..	6,2	7,0	4,9	5,4	4,8	3,6	4,0	4,3
Czech Republic	..	..	..	1,4	1,2	1,1	1,1	1,3	1,5	1,5
Denmark (1)	8,0	5,8	4,2	3,2	3,8	4,1	4,0	4,0	4,1	3,8
Estonia	..	..	..	1,3	0,7	0,9	1,0	1,1	1,0	1,0
Finland	4,0	1,9	2,4	2,4	2,6	2,6	2,6	2,7	2,6	2,8
France (1)	4,3	4,8	6,3	6,9	7,9	7,6	8,0	8,5	8,4	8,5
Germany (2)	5,8	3,3	3,4	2,3	2,5	2,4	2,3	2,3	2,4	2,4
Greece (1)	9,7	4,6	4,6	6,1	5,3	5,5	4,8	3,3	5,5	5,6
Hungary	..	..	..	1,7	2,0	2,2	2,1	3,1	3,1	3,2
Iceland	4,0	6,3	8,4	7,9	6,1	6,1	6,5	7,0	6,7	7,1
Ireland	15,1	5,3	4,6	5,5	8,0	6,3	5,7	5,8	6,6	7,0
Israel	..	..	..	8,6	8,8	9,1	9,4	9,4	9,4	9,0
Italy	7,2	3,7	2,3	4,6	4,9	4,3	6,2	4,8	5,3	6,3
Japan	8,1	8,2	9,4	10,5	9,0	9,4	10,1	9,7	9,7	9,1
Korea	..	8,0	11,8	12,4	12,8	11,9	11,7	11,4	11,4	10,6
Luxembourg	6,2	5,7	8,3	10,6	9,7	7,5	6,7	7,1	7,0	7,1
Mexico	..	1,9	1,5	1,4	1,7	1,4	1,7	1,6	1,5	1,5
Netherlands	4,4	3,6	3,7	5,3	4,7	4,2	3,9	3,8	3,4	3,0
New Zealand	11,5	7,9	6,8	5,3	5,3	5,8	6,7	6,8	6,6	6,2
Norway	3,1	1,7	2,9	2,3	2,8	2,8	2,9	2,8	2,8	2,9
Poland	..	..	..	3,5	3,4	3,6	3,9	3,8	3,7	3,9
Portugal	5,0	1,4	2,7	3,7	4,2	3,8	3,7	3,7	3,5	3,9
Slovak Republic	..	..	..	1,8	1,4	1,3	1,5	1,5	1,4	1,6
Slovenia	..	..	..	1,7	1,6	1,5	1,6	1,7	1,6	1,8
Spain (1)	6,4	4,6	5,5	6,3	8,1	7,0	6,6	6,4	6,0	6,3
Sweden	1,8	0,9	3,5	3,4	2,4	2,3	2,4	2,4	2,4	2,4
Switzerland	9,9	8,3	8,4	9,0	7,9	7,4	7,4	7,4	7,0	6,6
Turkey	10,5	5,4	2,3	3,2	3,8	3,6	3,6	4,1	4,1	4,2
United Kingdom	14,5	12,0	8,2	11,6	12,6	11,7	12,2	12,1	11,6	11,9
United States	15,9	10,7	11,5	10,1	11,4	12,2	13,9	13,0	12,3	11,8
OECD Average	**7,9**	**5,3**	**5,7**	**5,5**	**5,6**	**5,4**	**5,5**	**5,5**	**5,4**	**5,5**

Source: Revenue Statistics, OECD (2014).

... Not available

1. The total tax revenue has been reduced by the amount of any capital transfer that represents uncollected taxes. The capital transfer has been allocated between tax headings in proportion to the reported tax revenue, except for Austria where it has been allocated to the social security contributions heading.

2. From 1991 the figures relate to the united Germany.

unlicensed structures. Since illegality in this sector is the result of *political preference*, it would not be realistic to expect necessary actions will be taken after tax inspectors detect wrongdoings.

The level of tax evasion and particularly tax loss is very high in the Turkish real estate sector. As many studies like Kırar (2008), Doğrul (2011), and Büyükduman (2014) revealed, there can be very big differences between the declared transaction value and real value of immovable properties. The share of personal income tax collected from immovable properties was as low as.04% in 2013 and their share was even lower in the central government tax revenue for the same year with just.009% (Ministry of Finance, 2015). The revenue from property taxes was less than 1 percent of GDP and only around 3.5% of total tax revenues in Turkey. This is much lower than the average in the OECD where property taxes amount to 2% of GDP and to around 5.5% of total tax revenues.

Public revenue generated from the real estate sector mainly comes from rental incomes in the Turkish case. Capital gains income tax collected from properties has been very low in Turkey for a quite long time. In 2010, the Turkish Revenue Administration compared the immovable property value declarations made by 1896 taxpayers with the market values. It was founded that undeclared tax base was 5.96 times more than declared tax base (Turkish Revenue Administration, 2011, p. 46).

In terms of tax and other similar obligations, the lowest level of tax loss and evasion in the real estate market is on title deed fees.[9] This is very much related to a recent change in tax law to oblige taxpayers to declare the real market value of the real estate in question during a transaction. The title deed fee collected from real estate sales was.019% of the aggregate tax revenue in 2013. On the other hand, even for the title deed fees, there are several estimations made that claim taxpayers are still paying much lower amounts than the actual market values. For example, according to a report prepared by the Association of Real Estate Developers and Investors in 2013, the title deed fee paid by taxpayers was only one third of the actual value and thus, the state's annual loss of revenue was around 5 million TL on average.

Value assessment difficulties of the real estate are the main reason for high level of tax loss. Though they may have similar features, the real estate values may vary significantly depending on their locations. Particularly difficult is to assess market value of the real estate which is not subject to sale. In such a case, what is in hand is not a real market price but a fictive value. The critical question begs an answered is that: "How will we tax something that has an unknown market value?" Current procedure is far from following a proper real estate valuation procedure. It is more like an appraisal[10] made with general considerations. Obviously, such appraisals are unlikely to reflect real market values. As Karasu and Karakaş (2012) point out, "[u]sually there is a huge difference between the taxable value and the current market value of the real estate."

In order to solve this problem what needs to be done is first to build a comprehensive real estate valuation system which will be able to come close reflecting market value of the real estate in question. As Bird and Slack (2006) claims, building a real estate valuation system and putting it into practice is not an easy task at all. Nevertheless, we argue that having such a system is crucially important to reduce tax losses in the real estate sector. Having such a working system would not only bring substantial benefits like increased tax revenues, but also serve for tax fairness. In any case, what is certain is that unless a proper real estate valuation system is developed, tax loss in the real estate system is bound to remain high. In the next section, we will introduce an original semi-public real estate valuation system, which we think has a big potential to change this situation radically.

A PROPERTY TAX REFORM PROPOSAL FOR TURKEY

Three main objectives of taxation can be identified as 1) to raise revenue; 2) to reduce inequalities; and 3) to promote economic performance. Çevik (2016, chapter seven in this handbook) makes the important point that "[a]lthough improving the governance and institutions is not a main objective of tax reforms, a legitimate tax system can help to establish a legitimate political interaction through the nation. A legitimate tax system can be obtained by increasing tax policy's capability to reach foregoing main objectives and consequently by establishing parties' effective participation in decision making process, that is productive revenue bargaining."

It is important to recognize that a compliance strategy based on detection and punishment may well be a reasonable starting point for tax administration but not a good ending point. Instead, what is needed is a multi-faceted administrative approach that emphasizes enforcement and also emphasizes such things as service and, especially, trust (Alm & Torgler, 2011).

What is generally overlooked or ignored is that fighting tax evasion and tax loss is not only important to raise revenue but probably more so to establish fairness. Surprisingly, many countries' laws do not regard tax evasion and tax fraud as disgraceful crimes. However, tax evasion is illegal and unfair confiscation of a value intending to meet social requirements. We think the most significant factor differentiating this act from theft, which is a disgraceful crime, is that, it requires a much severe penalty as it is a crime committed against the whole society. Therefore, we would argue that *to fight effectively with tax evasion the first thing to do is to define it as a disgraceful crime in the Turkish Criminal Code.*

As we have put forward earlier, taxation is mainly a political issue. However, if for a moment we consider taxation as a technical issue, we can see that there are two necessary conditions to prevent tax evasion. First, tax assessment should reflect the actual situation and second, there should be sufficient means to ensure tax collection. Unless these two conditions are satisfied simultaneously, tax loss and evasion are inevitable. Although prevention of tax evasion is critically depends on these two factors, it needs to be recognized that there are several other factors that influence tax compliance. Whether taxpayers will comply or resist their due taxes is closely related to the impact of all these factors on the taxpayers. Under the following subtitles, we will discuss the way in which governments will be able to make sure that economic activities are properly recorded and real estate tax bases reflect market values.

Ensuring Good Records of Tax Related Issues

Tax evasion in the real estate market in Turkey stems from the fact that a considerable amount of real estate sale and rental procedures are unrecorded. Therefore, it is not easy to trace tax generating activities and audit them. In a context where audits cannot be performed, tax evasion becomes easier. It is estimated that around 50-80% of the houses in Turkey and around 50% of the houses in Istanbul are unlicensed. While some of them are huts, some others are buildings, lacking condominium due to disobedience to rules. Not only to reduce tax loss and evasion but also to improve the quality and security of buildings, the state needs to be tough against unlicensed constructions. Within this framework, the state must both prevent illegal constructions and produce a permanent solution for the social problems leading to these unlicensed constructions.

It is fair to say that particularly in the last decade governments have institutionalized some practices that facilitated recording of tax related issues and those practices had quite positive effects on the reduction of tax evasion in Turkey. For example, requiring the use of citizenship number in purchase-sale activities made tax evasion much more difficult. Another practice was investing in digital infrastructure so that activity records could be accessed online by the relevant authorities.[11] Doing so saved time and it became easier to perform audits.[12] The third practice was bringing a requirement to debit rent payments above a certain amount into the bank accounts of the real estate owners. All these practices helped to reduce unrecorded economic activities and tax evasion in the real estate market.

We think there is at least one other practice which has a significant potential to reduce tax evasion in the real estate sector. It is to ban the use of cash in real estate purchase or sale activities and oblige that the payment could be transferred only via banks. For example, it can be required that for any financial activity costing more than 100 Turkish Lira (TL) payments are made by credit card or via bank transfer. For the people who do not obey this rule, severe penalties including imprisonment can be applied. As Gayer and Igoseva (2012) suggest, "legal sanctions against purchasers of undeclared work and the obligation to use electronic payment systems for purchases over a certain amount may deter tax fraud" (p. 10).

To increase the possibility that rental contracts will reflect market values, we propose establishing a new institution that we may call it as a *guiding authority for rents*. This *fast acting guiding authority* should have a sound knowledge about the current market values and for a rental contract to become legally bounding its approval should be required. The main job of such an authority can be identified as to record the related details of the tax generating activity and to guide the two sides so that the rental contracts will be close to reflect real market values. If this guiding authority is not convinced that the rent value agreed by the two sides do not reflect the current market value, it would issue its approval on the condition that the real estate will be revaluated. Under such circumstances, the tenant should agree to allow the valuation company to do its job in a reasonable time. In such a case, the landowner would be held responsible paying the valuation bill. If the company carried out the valuation process has its names in the state approved valuation companies list and the valuation difference is less than 15% of the declared amount, the state would pay the valuation amount to the land owner and declared amount would be accepted as the tax base. However, if the valuation difference would be more than 15% of the declared amount, the state would pay nothing. Moreover, this time only the exact valuation amount would be accepted for the tax base.

Preventing informal working of contractors and real estate agencies is another significant issue. Tax evasion and fraud problem in the real estate market can be eliminated by recording all the relevant parties on electronic data system and by making sanctions heavier for those who work unrecorded or make people work unrecorded. In this way, tax inspectors may control the whole system much easier. Thus, our suggestion is to employ sufficient number of well-paid qualified tax inspectors and *to make sure that tax inspectors would have been safeguarded against political and interest-based pressures*. It is also important that regular inspections are performed more frequently.

Establishment of a Semi-Public Valuation System

A feature of the real estate is that every one of them is unique and because of variety of reasons even the ones with very similar characteristics might have very different market values.[13] For example, a real estate might be invaluable just because of its specific geographical location. Hence, it would not be possible to reduce tax losses significantly without having an accurate real estate valuation system that takes into account all the important factors causing differences in market values. Moreover, if such market value would not be reflected on tax bases, what can be done to minimize tax losses would be quite limited.

In Turkey, 'real estate tax values' determined by district appraisal commissions (DACs) play a crucial role for taxpayers in their real estate related tax declarations. According to the Real Estate Tax Code no 1319 Article 29, real estate tax values 'assessed' (or more correctly *determined*) by DACs should be taken as the minimum declaration value. As stated by one of the director in the Revenue Administration during one of our interview, more than 90% of taxpayers make their tax declarations slightly above the real estate value determined by DACs. However, these values are generally much lower than actual market values. Sometimes a minimum declaration value can be as low as one seventh of the market value of the real estate in question. Our view is that *because DACs apply a flawed appraisal, which is far from a proper valuation, they are a part of the problem, rather than a part of the solution*. As mentioned previously, some political considerations take the priority in determining DAC figures and a valuation system reform is required to radically reduce tax losses in this sector.

A major tool to reduce tax loss can be either to develop a sound real estate valuation system for the public sector or to buy such a service from the private sector. In this way, the Revenue Administration would be able to cross-check the tax declarations made by taxpayers with the real estate valuations carried out by professionals. One of the practical issues with this tool is that such valuations would be very costly if valuation becomes a requirement for every real estate. Therefore, we suggest *a hybrid system* that will not cost much, but be rewarding. This system will not cost much to the treasury. Because most of the cost of valuation will be paid by the taxpayers, who made false tax base declarations. This system will be explained below.

The first prerequisite for a successful transformation in the right direction would be to stop employing DACs members with political considerations. Only the qualified people who would be successful in a merit-based central real estate valuation exam would be employed at this institution. The second thing would be to create a semi-public institution that will eventually replace DACs. This semi-public institution could be called as *Real Estate Valuation Council* (REVC), which will enable coordination among DACs. REVC would standardize valuation norms, determine the priorities in valuations and when it is needed to transfer valuation experts from one district to another. *It is crucial that this council be autonomous, have a transparent structure, and employment is based on merit and accountability.*

The council in question may create a valuation data base throughout Turkey and continuously improve the available data to ensure they always reflect the best available real estate value data. In order to reduce cost and work load, new valuations carried out particularly focus on districts experiencing significant changes that affects the real estate values. To speed up the database formation process, REVC can be given a privilege to benefit from the data of available valuation companies with a low fee. The Capital Markets Board (CMB) could be held responsible to ensure reliability of these data and prevention of any troubles in their transfer.

We also suggest that taxpayers are being obliged to submit their real estate tax declarations according to current market values similar to the current practice regarding the title deed fees. We think that other than politics the main reason why there has not been such a practice for the real estate tax is most probably related to the fact that there is no market transaction to take as a reference point for the tax base. The most rational solution to this problem seems as officially regarding the CMB approved real estate valuations as market values. However, as this value is indeed fictive, it is reasonable that the taxpayers are given a chance to take the tax base as 20% below this value. Declarations could be increased annually based on the Producer Price Index for the following five years. The new revaluation value obtained on the fifth year would be taken as the new tax base for the declaration in the sixth year.

Within this framework, the state can require a valuation for let us say flats or houses larger than 150 square meters and for workplaces larger than 70 square meters. In order to improve applicability of this suggestion, a total of 80% of the valuation fees might be deducted from the tax payable. Taxpayers in question can be excluded from inspection if they pay 20% more than the minimum real estate value determined by DACs. Otherwise, every year about 5% of the randomly selected real estate would face with two revaluations carried out by two different valuation companies again randomly selected by the REVC. If the tax declaration made by the taxpayer is not below 80% of the two valuation average, no fee is demanded from or no penalty is applied to the taxpayer. On the other hand, if the tax declaration made by the taxpayer is below 80% of the average of the two valuations, then both of the valuation costs and a tax penalty, not lower than five times of the tax loss, are collected from the taxpayer. Taxpayers are informed about the average value of the two revaluations made by these two different valuation companies and are required that they cannot declare their tax base as less than 10% of this value in the following year.

Before launching this practice, the state might invite CMB licensed valuation companies over a particular level of valuation capacity to give a sealed offer for a valuation fee on square meter basis to become one of the 30 companies[14] that their valuations will be officially accepted by the state. Valuation fee averages of 30 companies which make the highest reductions for their valuation fees is found out and a reduction of about 20-40% is calculated from this average. The first 30 or fewer companies which accept to apply this reduced fee[15] are given privilege for two years to become among the state approved companies, where their valuations could be deducted from tax payable by the taxpayers, who had these valuations performed.

Additionally, a cross-check and audit mechanism can be applied as an auto-control mechanism, which would ensure that valuations reflect market prices. The first thing to do for this can be to require valuation companies to provide a brief information (for example, valuation's approval date, names and registry numbers of the approved value, size of the valuated place in square meters, parcel and lot numbers) on their valuations within five working days. Following this declaration, a total of 5% of the valuations performed by valuation companies are randomly selected. In order to assess the validity of real estate valuations, two CMB approved valuation companies are again randomly selected. Average of the two valuations (the interval between the first and the second valuation must not be longer than two months) is taken and is compared to the previous valuation. If the previous valuation shows a deviation of more than 20% of the average of the last two valuations in question, a third valuation from another company is performed. If a deviation of more than 20% as the average of the three valuation in question is found, a penalty is charged to the company that carried out the previous valuation. The amount of such a penalty would be about ten times the cost of the three valuations. Experts who have put their signatures on such a flawed valuation document are given a warning. If the same situation repeats more than three times in the same year, relevant companies are given a warning. Licenses of the valuation experts, who have received three warnings within five years, and companies who have received three warnings in a year are invalidated.

Other Tax Reform Suggestions

It is important to ensure that both the buyer and the seller will pay their fair share of title deed fees. In the usual practice in Turkey, buyers are pressurized to pay title deed fee share of both parties. This increases the burden put on the back of one of the parties and reduces the possibility of honest declaration of the current market value of the real estate. In order to avoid such a result, payment of title deed fee can be made conditional on signing a statement that one undertakes any legal responsibility that might arise from a false declaration. In addition, a highly deterrent penalty may be imposed if the signature on the bill of the title deed fee is not belong to the person responsible to pay that title deed fee or that person's legal representative.

There are significant proportional differences among value added tax (VAT) rates implemented for the flats and houses in different sizes in Turkey and this encourages tax fraud. Therefore, it would be wise to minimize these differences. For examples, instead of the two rates for above and below 100 square meters, there might be four different VAT rates. One such rate would be set as up to 70 square meters, the other from 70 to 109 square meters, the next from 110 to 149 square meters, and the last for larger than 150 square meters. Reduction of big differences among VAT rates would mean elimination of a factor that encourages tax evasion and tax loss in the sector. Another policy that would reduce tax loss and evasion in the real estate sector would be to take the credit amount loaned from banks to purchase a real estate as a base in the assessment of the real estate's market value. For instance, it might be a condition that the value of a real estate cannot be declared below its credit value.

A very important issue requiring special attention is that real estate taxes are set and collected at the local level in Turkey. This poses challenges to intergovernmental fiscal frameworks. Our view is that currently there is a conflict of interest issue between the central government and local governments. On the one hand, the central government does not have much interest in a real estate tax increase, since that would hardly increase central government revenue. On the other hand, it is politically difficult for local governments to increase real estate taxes significantly because people would blame the local government for this rise and there might be political consequences for this policy change. But, if the central government would get a considerable share (one-third or half) from tax revenue and increasing real estate taxes becomes the state policy, this would very much ease the political pressure on local governments. It follows that it would be much easier to increase real estate taxes in this way.

Obviously, the process of obtaining valuations that are close to market value on a regular basis is not cheap. Moreover, as Slack (2010) warns, "no matter how economically desirable the long run outcome of property tax reform may be in terms of the equity and efficiency of the tax, its transitional effects may be sufficiently undesirable in political terms to kill it" (p. 13). In the same vein Nicodème (2012) stresses that "there are transition problems with any tax reform proposal as changes in the system will generate windfall gains and losses. Gradualism in reforms may be needed in this respect… the usual political economy problems are at stake with losers being often more vocal than winners. This is particularly the case because property taxes are very visible to taxpayers" (p. 28). Furthermore, where the losses are concentrated and the gains are dispersed, as is often the case with tax reform, negatively affected interests will be motivated to spend time and resources in political action that can result in permanent, institutionalized groups (for example, office towers, hotels, seniors, waterfront properties) in opposition to reform (Slack, 2010, p. 13).

Property taxes have important fiscal and non-fiscal effects. Therefore, the design of such a reform is critically important. According to Bird and Slack (2006), one must have modest expectations about a property tax reform and get some critical details right at the first place. This is because of the fact that the property tax is a highly visible and this visibility makes the tax difficult to sell politically. This is why Slack (2010) suggests that success of any tax reform, which is expected to result in major tax shifts among taxpayers, needs to "depend on the introduction of some form of phase-in mechanism.[16] Phase-ins are almost invariably politically necessary to cushion the impact of reform. Some form of relief is also needed for low-income taxpayers. Property tax credits (or circuit-breakers) that relate property taxes to income are best at designing relief to low-income taxpayers. For elderly taxpayers who have seen their property values increase but their incomes remain fixed, some form of tax deferral would be appropriate" (p. 13).

James (2016, chapter three in this handbook) makes the important point that "... successful tax reform is likely to be a dynamic process rather than a single one-off change. The tax system has to be designed to be sufficiently robust to accommodate continuing change in the socio-economic and political environment and to be sufficiently flexible to accommodate further adjustments as appropriate." Last but not least, the right mix of IT (information technology) and transparency is critical to what Bird (2016, chapter two in this handbook) calls as 'smart tax system'. Such a system requires "a well-designed, relatively stable tax system with an appropriate administrative structure that fully utilizes the capacity of IT to assemble and utilize information, staffed with trained people, and properly managed as transparently as possible."

CONCLUSION

This chapter examined tax evasion and tax compliance issues from a political economy perspective and investigated peculiarities and specific difficulties of real estate sector in general, and the Turkish case in particular. Consequently, a property tax reform based on a semi-public valuation system is proposed to reduce tax loss substantially in the real estate sector.

The chapter argued that one of the main reasons why collection of real estate related taxes are low in Turkey is related to the political preferences and institutional arrangements, which induce and facilitate tax evasion and tax loss. Such governmental practices that this chapter focused on are: frequent implementation of tax amnesties, having a 'lax' tax reconciliation institution, and exaggerated application of tax information confidentiality principle.

It is claimed that the coverage of tax information confidentiality principle in the Turkish Tax Law is extremely wide and its application by the tax officials is even wider. The confidentiality principle applied in the Turkish Tax Law forms a legal base to deny public access to almost any kind of information about taxes, as if they are strategic state secrets. This attitude not only masks a considerable part of unregistered economic activities but also can function as an armor to protect tax evaders. What is not acceptable here is that tax authorities remains indifferent to individuals suffering from injustice in taxation while they are very kind to protect the ones who resist fulfilling their citizenship duties.

The frequent application of tax amnesties in Turkey is another very serious problem. A total of 32 tax remissions have been implemented in Turkey since the foundation of the Republic in 1923. Tax amnesties were implemented more frequently after the single party period and especially in the periods following the military coupes. During the four short distinct periods of the Turkish Republic (1960 – 1963; 1980 – 1983; 1988 – 1992; and 2001 – 2003) that lasted all together 13 years, 15 tax amnesties were implemented. This means that, on average, every 10.4 months a tax amnesty was put into effect during this four periods. On the other hand, the number of tax amnesties implemented during the remaining 79 years of the Republic has been 17, meaning on average every 55.8 months one tax amnesty was enforced. This simple data clearly illustrate that the Turkish governments have implemented tax remissions mainly for political reasons. The reasons were either to buy support for the military coups or to increase votes.

Tax amnesties are a controversial revenue-raising tool. International experience provides evidence that the perceived benefits of tax amnesty programs are at best overstated and often the costs of tax amnesty programs exceed the programs' benefits. It is also important to recognize that the additional burden caused by those who did not pay their fair share of taxes is imposed on the other taxpayers. The historical record suggests that amnesty recoveries are seldom large enough to make any dramatic impact on the public revenue and the overall level of tax compliance falls after an amnesty. This seems as because honest taxpayers resent the special treatment of tax evaders, and many believe that the amnesty is not a one-time opportunity. Therefore, attempts to increase short-term revenue need to be carefully balanced against the long term erosion of voluntary compliance and trust. Hence, we see the abundance of tax amnesties as a hindrance to reduce tax evasion in Turkey.

Having a 'lax' tax reconciliation institution outside the judicial processes constitutes another problem. As a result of such an institution one of the two taxpayers, who are equal in all aspects in front of the law, pays less tax. On the other hand, the taxpayers who have paid their taxes in full do not receive any pay-backs over tax reduction rates. Since the other person is destitute of this opportunity, this leads to injustice. To make everything worse, the additional burden caused by the reductions are imposed on the honest taxpayers.

Applying tax amnesties outside the judicial processes and having a 'lax' tax reconciliation institution harms tax justice deeply because tax is perceived as a subject of bargaining. As suggested earlier, taxpayers need to feel that the tax system is being administered fairly and that tax liabilities are not arbitrarily determined. We would argue that leaving these problems unattended would have very negative effects on tax justice and voluntary tax compliance. Apart from those mentioned above, in cases people suspect that tax money is not spent in a way that will bring utmost social benefit or that the benefits are diverted to the politically favored people, it will become even more difficult for individuals to comply with taxes voluntarily.

What is generally overlooked or ignored is that fighting with tax evasion and tax loss is not only important to raise revenues but probably more so to safeguard fairness. Surprisingly, many countries' laws, including Turkey, do not regard tax evasion as a disgraceful crime. However, tax evasion is illegal and unfair confiscation of a value intending to meet social needs. We claim that the most significant factor differentiating this act from theft which is regarded as a disgraceful crime is that, it deserves a much severe penalty since it is a crime committed against the whole society. Therefore, we think that *the first thing to do for fighting effectively against tax evasion in Turkey is to define it as a disgraceful crime in the Turkish Criminal Code.*

Recently, there has been a significant shift in research emphasis from the analysis of enforcement to the incorporation of trust-building measures that encourage cooperation in tax compliance research. We argue that normative factors play much more significant roles than generally thought for tax compliance. What we would like to emphasize is that *government policies are crucial for trust-building*. If citizens of a country feel their taxation system as fair, regard their tax burden as reasonable and feel certain that what they pay will return them as a public service, there would not be much justifiable reason not to pay their taxes. Nevertheless, fulfillment of tax liabilities cannot be left to the mercy of taxpayers only. It is the responsibility of governments to apply sanctions for tax evaders to preserve the rights of other citizens who pay their taxes. When the government fails to perform this duty, honest citizens are victimized and next time it would not be reasonable to expect them to fulfill their tax duties in a responsible way as they did before.

The real estate sector upon which this chapter is focused differentiates significantly from other sectors regarding the factors causing tax evasion. The reason why tax related issues are unrecorded in this sector is not due to the difficulty of detecting tax subjects because they are physical bodies that are not possible to hide or transfer. Thus, *the informality in this sector is due to the politicians, who turn a blind eye to the current situation for political reasons.* Hut style houses constructed on treasury land and outlaw constructions are common examples that support this claim in Turkey. Therefore, it is not sensible to expect that after tax inspectors detect an informality, the problem will be solved. *Since the current problem is the result of political preference, solution will depend on the change of political preference in question.*

One of the main conclusions reached at this study is that the quality of public services is very important for tax compliance. Citizens must be able to see a significant improvement in the quality of services provided by government to be sure that the money they pay through taxes is used properly. It is also important to recognize that high corruption in the public sector discourages people to pay their taxes. Thus, fighting with corruption would, indeed, mean fighting with tax evasion and tax loss.

There is a government practice which assumes a large role in the current tax losses in the real estate sector related to the district appraisal commissions (DACs). 'The real estate tax values' are determined by DACs and these values tend to be significantly lower than market values. These unrealistic figures determine how the real estate tax declarations will be. When taxpayers make their real estate tax declarations according to these unrealistic figures, they do not face legal sanctions. However, the Ministry of Finance does not allow this to happen in relation to the title deed fee declarations and the result is that the revenue collected from this tax item is quite reasonable. This implies that the solution is very much related to the political will.

It needs to be recognized, however, that tax losses in this sector have another very important reason. That reason is the dramatic effect of locational differences on the real estate values. Even two pieces of real estate with very similar characteristics might have very different market values depending on their locations. Hence, *it would not be possible to eliminate tax loss and evasion without developing a method, which objectively takes into account all the important factors causing differences in the real estate values within the framework of demand conditions and ensure that these values are reflected on the real estate tax declarations.* A framework for such a method is proposed in the previous section of this chapter.

In conclusion, unless an integrated approach based on tax fairness is developed, procedural justice is adhered and respectful modes of communication between the Revenue Administration and taxpayers is established, tax evasion and particularly tax loss is expected to remain very high in Turkey in the foreseeable future. However, increased use of property taxes could help ease problems with taxes levied on mobile bases. Shifting the tax burden from financial intermediation more onto immovable property would make the tax system less distorting and less vulnerable to tax evasion. One of the crucial steps needs to be taken in this direction is to develop an objective a semi-public real estate valuation system that would reflect market values, which this chapter proposed in detail.

ACKNOWLEDGMENT

This chapter is based on a project titled, "Tax Loss Arising from Tax Avoidance and Evasion, as a Result of False Real Estate and Rent Value Declarations: The Case of Istanbul." It is gratefully acknowledged that this project is financed by Marmara University Scientific Research Projects Coordination Unit with the number: SOS-B-040310-0056. Earlier draft of this chapter benefited helpful comments and suggestions from Savaş Çevik, Larissa Batrancea, Erich Kirchler, Simon James, Tarkan Çavuşoğlu, Yücel Demirer, Bryan Christiansen, and anonymous reviewers. The chapter has also benefited the assistance of Sinan Ataer, Seda Şahin, Medine Akbaba, Bahadır Karatoy, and Serdar Günay for obtaining data.

REFERENCES

Akbulut, H. (2016). Shadow Economy and Tax Evasion: An Analysis for EU-27 and Turkey. In M. M. Erdoğdu & B. Christiansen (Eds.), *Handbook of Research on Public Finance Perspectives on Europe and the MENA Region*. Hershey, PA, USA: IGI Global.

Allingham, M. G., & Sandmo, A. (1972). Income Tax Evasion: A Theoretical Analysis. *Journal of Public Economics*, *1*(3-4), 323–338. doi:10.1016/0047-2727(72)90010-2

Alm, J. (2012). Measuring, Explaining, and Controlling Tax Evasion: Lessons from Theory, Experiments, and Field Studies. *International Tax and Public Finance*, *19*(1), 54–77. doi:10.1007/s10797-011-9171-2

Alm, J., Bloomquist, K. M., & McKee, M. (2015). On The External Validity of Laboratory Tax Compliance Experiments. *Economic Inquiry*, *53*(2), 1170–1186. doi:10.1111/ecin.12196

Alm, J., Kirchler, E., & Muehlbacher, S. (2012). Combining Psychology and Economics in the Analysis of Compliance: From Enforcement to Cooperation. *Economic Analysis & Policy*, *42*(2), 133–151. doi:10.1016/S0313-5926(12)50016-0

Alm, J., Martinez-Vazquez, J., & Wallace, S. (2009). Do Tax Amnesties Work? The Revenue Effects of Tax Amnesties during the Transition in the Russian Federation. *Economic Analysis & Policy*, *39*(2), 235–253. doi:10.1016/S0313-5926(09)50019-7

Alm, J., McKee, M., & Beck, W. (1990). Amazing Grace: Tax Amnesties and Compliance. *National Tax Journal*, *43*(1), 23–37.

Alm, J., & Torgler, B. (2011). Do ethics matter? Tax Compliance and Morality. *Journal of Business Ethics*, *101*(4), 635–651. doi:10.1007/s10551-011-0761-9

Alt, J., Preston, I., & Sibieta, L. (2009). The Political Economy of Tax Policy. In *Dimensions of Tax Design: The Mirrlees Review* (pp. 1204–1279). Oxford, UK: Oxford University Press.

Annual Report 2010. Presidency of Strategy Development Department. (2011Turkish Revenue Administration. Ankara: Ministry of Finance.

Baer, K., & Le Borgne, E. L. (2008). *Tax amnesties: Theory, Trends, and Some Alternatives*. Washington, D. C.: IMF.

Bahl, R., Martinez-Vazquez, J., & Youngman, J. M. (2010). Whither the Property Tax: New Perspectives on a Fiscal Mainstay. In *R. Bahl, J. Martinez-Vazquez, and J. M. Youngman (Eds.), Challenging the Conventional Wisdom of the Property Tax* (pp. 3–14). Cambridge, Mass., USA: Lincoln Institute of Land Policy.

Bahl, R., & Wallace, S. (2008, December). Reforming the Property Tax in Developing Countries: A New Approach. *International Studies Program Working Paper 08-19*. Retrieved from http://icepp.gsu.edu/files/2015/03/ispwp0819.pdf

Barone, G., & Mocetti, S. (2009). *Tax Morale and Public Spending Inefficiency* (Working Paper 732). Rome: Banca D'Italia.

Batrancea, L., Nichita, A., Batrancea, I., & Kirchler, E. (2016). Tax Compliance Behavior - An Upshot of Trust in and Power of Authorities across Europe and MENA. In M. M. Erdoğdu & B. Christiansen (Eds.), *Handbook of Research on Public Finance Perspectives on Europe and the MENA Region*. Hershey, PA, USA: IGI Global.

Bird, R. (2016). Transparency, Technology and Taxation. In M. M. Erdoğdu & B. Christiansen (Eds.), *Handbook of Research on Public Finance Perspectives on Europe and the MENA Region*. Hershey, PA, USA: IGI Global.

Bird, R., Martinez-Vazquez, J., & Torgler, B. (2004). Societal Institutions and Tax Effort in Developing Countries. *CREMA Working Paper* No. 2004 – 21.

Bird, R. M., & Slack, E. (2006). Taxing Land and Property in Emerging Economies: Raising Revenue... And More? In G. K. Ingram (Ed.), *Y.-H. Hong, Land Policies and Their Outcomes. Cambridge*. Mass.: Lincoln Institute of Land Policy.

Blaufus, K., Bob, J., & Otto, P. E. (2014). The Effect of Tax Privacy on Tax Compliance –An Experimental Investigation. *Arqus Discussion Paper*, No. 164.

Bø, E. E., Slemrod, J., & Thoresen, T. O. (2014). Taxes on the Internet: Deterrence Effects of Public Disclosure. *CESifo Working Paper: Public Finance*, No. 4107.

Bobek, D. D., Hageman, A. M., & Kelliher, C. F. (2013). Analyzing the Role of Social Norms in Tax Compliance Behavior. *Journal of Business Ethics*, *115*(3), 451–468. doi:10.1007/s10551-012-1390-7

Brunori, D. (2003). *Local Tax Policy: A Federalist Perspective*. Washington, DC: The Urban Institute Press.

Buchanan, J. M. (1987). Public Receipts of Public Debt. In J. Eatwell, M. Milgate, & P. Newman (Eds.), *The New Palgrave, A Dictionary of Economics* (Vol. 3). London: Macmillan.

Büyükduman, A. (2014). *Bir Kent Efsanesi Konut Balonu: Kent Ekonomisi Ne Diyor?* İstanbul: Scala.

Castro, L., & Scartascini, C. (2013). Tax Compliance and Enforcement in the Pampas: Evidence from a Field Experiment. *IDB Working Paper Series*. No. IDB-WP-472. Washington, D.C.: Inter-American Development Bank. Retrieved from http://publications.iadb.org/bitstream/handle/11319/4698/Tax%20Compliance%20and%20Enforcement%20in%20the%20Pampas%3a%20Evidence%20from%20a%20Field%20Experiment.pdf;jsessionid=69EE51DEDF52FCC1F16D467BC60841C9?sequence=1

Çetin, G. (2007). Vergi Aflarının Vergi Mükelleflerinin Tutum ve Davranışları Üzerindeki Etkisi. *Yönetim ve Ekonomi*, *14*(2), 171–187.

Çevik, S. (2012). Mükelleflerin Devlet ve Toplumla Etkileşimi, Bireysel Normlar ve Vergi Ahlakı, İlişkisi. *Maliye Dergisi*, *163*, 258–269.

Çevik, S. (2016). Tax Systems, Economic Development and Good Governance: A Comparative Analysis of the MENA Countries. In M. M. Erdoğdu & B. Christiansen (Eds.), *Handbook of Research on Public Finance Perspectives on Europe and the MENA Region*. Hershey, PA, USA: IGI Global.

Çevik, S., & Yeniçeri, H. (2013). The Relationship between Social Norms and Tax Compliance: The Moderating Role of the Effectiveness of the Tax Administration. *International Journal of Economic Sciences*, *2*(3), 166–180.

Coricelli, G., Joly, M., Montmarquette, C., & Villeval, M. C. (2010). Cheating, Emotions, and Rationality: An Experiment on tax evasion. *Experimental Economics*, *13*(2), 226–247. doi:10.1007/s10683-010-9237-5

Daude, C., Gutiérrez, H., & Melguizo, Á. (2014, January). 'Doctoring the ball': The Political Economy of Tax Incentives for Investment in the Dominican Republic, OECD Development Centre, *Working Paper*, No. 322. Retrieved from http://www.oecd.org/countries/dominicanrepublic/WP322AE.pdf

De Cesare, C. M. (1999). Challenges to Property Tax Administration in Porto Alegre, Brazil. *Land Lines*, September, *11*(5). Retrieved from http://www1.worldbank.org/publicsector/decentralization/June2003Seminar/ChallengesPropertyTaxAdmin.pdf

Doğrul, A. R. (2011). Gayrimenkul Alım Satımlarında Vergi Kayıp Kaçağı ve Bunun Önlenmesinde Bilgi Teknolojilerinin Rolü: Konya Örneği [Unpublished MA thesis]. Karamanoğlu Mehmetbey University Social Science Institute.

Dornfest, A. S. (2010). In Search of an Optimal Revaluation Policy: Benefits and Pitfalls. In R. Bahl, J. Martinez-Vazquez, & J. M. Youngman (Eds.), Challenging the Conventional Wisdom of the Property Tax (pp. 75-107). Cambridge, Mass.: Lincoln Institute of Land Policy.

Erdoğdu, M. M. (2015). Culture of Development and Developmental Capacity of States: The Korean Case. In B. Christiansen & J. Koeman (Eds.), *Nationalism, Cultural Indoctrination, and Economic Prosperity in the Digital Age* (pp. 1–51). Hershey, PA, USA: IGI Global. doi:10.4018/978-1-4666-7492-9.ch001

Fazio, R. H. (1990). Multiple Processes by Which Attitudes Guide Behavior: The Mode Model as An Integrative Framework. *Advances in Experimental Social Psychology*, *23*, 75–109. doi:10.1016/S0065-2601(08)60318-4

Feld, L. P., & Frey, B. S. (2007). Tax Compliance as the Result of Psychological Tax Contract: The Role of Incentives and Responsive Regulation. *Law & Policy*, *29*(1), 102–120. doi:10.1111/j.1467-9930.2007.00248.x

Ferguson, M. J., & Bargh, J. A. (2004). How Social Perception Can Automatically Influence Behavior. *Trends in Cognitive Sciences*, *8*(1), 33–39. doi:10.1016/j.tics.2003.11.004 PMID:14697401

Gayer, C., & Igoseva, R. (2012). Summary of the workshop. In C. Gayer & G. Mourre (Eds.), *Property Taxation and Enhanced Tax Administration in Challenging Times. Economic Papers 463, October* (pp. 11–19). Brussels: European Union.

Gayer, C., & Mourre, G. (2012). Property Taxation and Enhanced Tax Administration in Challenging Times. *European Economy Economic Papers 463*, October.

GİB. (2015). *Gelir İdaresi Başkanlığı 2014 Yılı Faaliyet Raporu*. Yayın No: 199, Gelir İdaresi Başkanlığı Strateji Geliştirme Daire Başkanlığı. Retrieved from http://www.gib.gov.tr/fileadmin/faaliyetraporlari/2014/2014_Faaliyet_Raporu.pdf

Gündüz, Z. (2013). Developments in Turkish Lax Legistlation, Disputes and Adjudication. *International Tax Review*, August 13. Retrieved from http://www.internationaltaxreview.com/Article/3242987/Developments-in-Turkish-tax-legislation-disputes-and-adjudication.html

Hacıköylü, C., & Heper, F. (2010). Emlak Vergisinde Matrah Tespitine İlişkin Sorunlar ve Çözüm Önerileri. *Maliye Dergisi*, *158*, 1–14.

Hashimzade, N., Myles, G.D. & Tran-Nam, B. (2012). Applications of Behavioural Economics to Tax Evasion. *Journal of Economic Surveys*. doi:10.1111/j.1467-6419.2012.00733.x

Haveman, M., & Sexton, T. A. (2008). *Property Tax Assessment Limits: Lessons from Thirty Years of Experience*. Cambridge, Mass.: Lincoln Institute of Land Policy.

Hofmann, E., Hoelzl, E., & Kirchler, E. (2008). Preconditions of Voluntary Tax Compliance: Knowledge and Evaluation of Taxation, Norms, Fairness, and Motivation to Cooperate. *Zeitschrift fur Psychologie mit Zeitschrift fur Angewandte Psychologie*, *216*(4), 209–217. doi:10.1027/0044-3409.216.4.209 PMID:22428111

Ilzetzkiy, E. (2014). A Positive Theory of Tax Reform, June. Retrieved from http://www.bus.umich.edu/ConferenceFiles/Tax-Systems/files/Ilzetzki--TaxReform.pdf

Isaac, D., & O'Leary, J. (2012). *Property Valuation Principles* (2nd ed.). London: Palgrave MacMillan.

James, S. (2014). The Importance of Fairness in Tax Policy: Behavioral Economics and the UK Experience. *International Journal of Applied Behavioral Economics*, *3*(1), 1–12. doi:10.4018/ijabe.2014010101

James, S. (2016). The Difficulties of Achieving Successful Tax Reform. In M. M. Erdoğdu & B. Christiansen (Eds.), *Handbook of Research on Public Finance Perspectives on Europe and the MENA Region*. Hershey, PA, USA: IGI Global.

James, S., & Alley, C. (2002). Tax Compliance, Self-Assessment and Tax Administration. *Journal of Finance and Management in Public Services*, *2*(2), 27–42.

Johansson, Å., Heady, C., Arnold, J., Brys, B., & Vartia, L. (2008). Tax and Economic Growth. *Economics Department Working Paper No. 620*, OECD. Retrieved from http://www.oecd.org/tax/tax-policy/41000592.pdf

Karaca, C. (2015). The Comparison of the Shadow Economy in Turkey and European Countries. In B. Christiansen & M. M. Erdoğdu (Eds.), *Comparative Economics and Regional Development in Turkey*. Hershey, PA, USA: IGI Global.

Karasu, M. A., & Karakaş, M. (2012). Belediyelerin Emlak Vergisindeki Gelir Kaybı: Şanlıurfa Belediyesi Örneği. *Maliye Dergisi*, *163*, 431–445.

Kırar, B. (2008). Taşınmazlarda Emlak Vergisine Esas Değer, Tapu Değeri ve Piyasa Değeri Arasındaki Farklılıkların İncelenmesi: Beşiktaş Örneği [Unpublished MA Thesis]. İstanbul Technical University Institute of Science and Engineering.

Kirchler, E. (2007). *The Economic Psychology of Tax Behaviour*. Cambridge: Cambridge University Press. doi:10.1017/CBO9780511628238

Kirchler, E., Hoelzl, E., & Wahl, I. (2008). Enforced versus Voluntary Tax Compliance: The "Slippery Slope Framework". *Journal of Economic Psychology*, *29*(2), 210–225. doi:10.1016/j.joep.2007.05.004

Kirchler, E., Kogler, C., & Muehlbacher, S. (2014). Cooperative Tax Compliance: From Deterrence to Deference. *Current Directions in Psychological Science*, *23*(2), 87–92. doi:10.1177/0963721413516975

Kirchler, E., Muehlbacher, S., Gangl, K., Hofmann, E., Kogler, C., Pollai, M., & Alm, J. (2012). Combining Psychology and Economics in the Analysis of Compliance: From Enforcement to Cooperation. *Tulane University Economics Working Paper* 1212.

Kirchler, E., Muehlbacher, S., Kastlunger, B., & Wahl, I. (2010). Why Pay Taxes? A Review of Tax Compliance Decisions. In J. Alm, J. Martinez-Vazquez, & B. Torgler (Eds.), *Developing Alternative Frameworks for Explaining Tax Compliance* (pp. 15–31). London: Routledge.

Laury, S., & Wallace, S. (2005). Confidentiality and Taxpayer Compliance. *National Tax Journal*, *58*(3), 427–438. doi:10.17310/ntj.2005.3.08

Leibfritz, W. (2009, June). Reducing Undeclared Work in Turkey - The Role of Tax Policy and Administration. *Background Paper prepared for the World Bank Country Economic Memorandum on Informality: Causes, Consequences, Policies*. Retrieved from http://siteresources.worldbank.org/TURKEYEXTN/Resources/361711-1277211666558/bpg_ReducingUndeclaredWork.pdf

Luitel, H. S. (2014). *Is Tax Amnesty a Good Tax Policy?: Evidence from State Tax Amnesty Programs in the United States*. London: Lexington Books.

Luitel, H. S., & Sobel, R. S. (2007). The Revenue Impact of Repeated Tax Amnesties. *Public Budgeting & Finance*, *27*(3), 19–38. doi:10.1111/j.1540-5850.2007.00881.x

Marcinkevičiūtė, L., & Petrauskienė, R. (2007). Performance Improvement of Public Administration Institutions: The Case of Lithuanian District Municipalities` Administrations. *Viešoji Politika Ir Administravimas*, *19*, 69–80.

McGee, R. W., & Benk, S. (2016). Attitudes toward Tax Evasion in Turkey: An Empirical Study using the Latest World Values Survey Data. In M. M. Erdoğdu & B. Christiansen (Eds.), *Handbook of Research on Public Finance Perspectives on Europe and the MENA Region*. Hershey, PA: IGI Global.

Mikesell, J. L. (2003). International Experiences with Administration of Local Taxes: A Review of Practices and Issues. Retrieved from http://citeseerx.ist.psu.edu/viewdoc/download?doi=10.1.1.199.304&rep=rep1&type=pdf

Mikesell, J. L., & Ross, J. M. (2012). Fast money? The contribution of state tax amnesties to public revenue systems. *National Tax Journal*, *65*(3), 529–562. doi:10.17310/ntj.2012.3.02

Public Accounts Bulletins. (2015). *Ministry of Finance, General Directorate of Public Accounts*, Ankara. Retrieved from https://portal.muhasebat.gov.tr/mgmportal/faces/khbDetail?birimDizini=General+Government&_afrLoop=1017212479336060&_afrWindowMode=0&_adf.ctrl-state=692ozugmw_4

Modugu, P. K., Eragbhe, E., & Izedonmi, F. (2012). Government Accountability and Voluntary Tax Compliance in Nigeria. *Research Journal of Finance and Accounting*, *3*(5), 69–77.

Nerre, B. (2008). Tax Culture: A Basic Concept for Tax Politics. *Economic Analysis and Policy*, *38*, 153–167.

Nicodème, G. (2012, October 26-28). Discussion: The Tax Treatment of Housing Gayer. In C. Gayer & G. Mourre (Eds.), Property Taxation and Enhanced Tax Administration in Challenging Times. European Economy Economic Papers 463.

Norregaard, J. (2013). Taxing Immovable Property: Revenue Potential and Implementation Challenges. *IMF Working Paper*, WP/13/129. Retrieved from http://www.imf.org/external/pubs/ft/wp/2013/wp13129.pdf

O'Connor, J. (1973). *The Fiscal Crisis of the State*. New York: St. Martin's Press.

Oats, L., & Pemberton, L. (2012 *, October*). Key Principles for Efficient Tax Administration and Main Reform Challenges. In C. Gayer & G. Mourre (Eds.), *Property Taxation and Enhanced Tax Administration in Challenging Times, Economic Papers 463* (pp. 51–61). Brussels: European Union.

Co-operative Compliance: A framework from Enhanced Relationship to Co-operative Compliance. Organization for Economic Co-operation and Development. (2013). OECD. Retrieved from http://www.oecd.org/ctp/administration/co-operativecompliance.htm

Revenue Statistics. Organization for Economic Co-operation and Development. (2014). OECD. Retrieved from http://www.oecd.org/ctp/tax-policy/revenue-statistics-tax-structures.htm

Official Gazette (2008). 5811 Sayılı Bazı Varlıkların Milli Ekonomiye Kazandırılması Hakkında Kanun, 22.11.2008 tarihli 27062 sayılı RG ve 5811 Sayılı Bazı Varlıkların Milli Ekonomiye Kazandırılması Hakkında Kanuna İlişkin Genel Tebliğ.

Official Gazette (2011). Maliye Bakanlığı, 5811 Sayılı Bazı Varlıkların Milli Ekonomiye Kazandırılması Hakkında Kanuna İlişkin Genel Tebliğ (seri no. 4), 07 Nisan 2011 Tarihli Resmi Gazete, Sayı: 27898.

Official Gazette (2013). 6486 sayılı Sosyal Sigortalar ve Genel Sağlık Sigortası Kanunu ile Bazı Kanunlarda Değişiklik Yapılmasına Dair Kanun ile 193 sayılı Gelir Vergisi Kanununa eklenen geçici 85'inci madde 29.05.2013 tarihli ve Sayı: 28661.

Öncel, M., Kumrulu, A., & Çağan, N. (2008). *Vergi Hukuku*. İstanbul: Turhan Kitabevi.

Ortega, D., Ronconi, L., & Sanguinetti, P. (2013). Reciprocity and Willingness to Pay Taxes: Evidence from a Survey Experiment in Latin America. *CIAS Working Paper 2*. Buenos Aires, Argentina: Centro de Investigación y Acción Social. Retrieved from http://www.fcias.org.ar/wp-content/uploads/2013/04/CIAS-Reciprocity_and_taxes_April-2013.pdf

Savaşan, F. (2006). Vergi Afları: Teori ve Türkiye Uygulamaları ("Vergi Barışı" Uygulama Sonuçları). *Afyon Kocatepe Üniversitesi İİBF Dergisi*, *8*(1), 41–65.

Schaltegger, C. A., & Torgler, B. (2007). Government Accountability and Fiscal Discipline: A Panel Analysis Using Swiss Data. *Journal of Public Economics*, *91*(1-2), 117–140. doi:10.1016/j.jpubeco.2006.07.003

Shah, A. (2013). Tax Avoidance and Tax Havens; Undermining Democracy. *Global Issues*, January. Retrieved from http://www.globalissues.org/print/article/54

Sheffrin, S. M. (1993). What Does the Public Believe about Tax Fairness? *National Tax Journal*, *46*(3), 301–308.

Sheffrin, S. M. (2010). Fairness and Market Value Property Taxation. In *R. Bahl, J. Martinez-Vazquez, & J. M. Youngmand (Eds.), Challenging the Conventional Wisdom on the Property Tax* (pp. 241–262). Cambridge, Mass.: Lincoln Institute of Land Policy.

Slack, E. (2010). The Property Tax … in Theory and Practice. *IMFG Working Paper 02*. Institute on Municipal Finance and Governance Munk School of Global Affairs University of Toronto. Retrieved from http://www.munkschool.utoronto.ca/imfg/uploads/72/property_tax_paperwithlogos.pdf

Sossin, L. (1992a). Squeezing Blood from Stones: The Income Tax Industry in Canada. *Journal of Law and Social Policy*, *8*, 178–203.

Sossin, L. (1992b). Welfare State Crime: The Politics of Tax Evasion in the 1980s. *Windsor Yearbook of Access to Justice*, *12*, 98–127.

Tankard, M. E., & Paluck, E. L. (2015). Norm Perception as a Vehicle for Social Change. Princeton University January, *Social Issues and Policy Review (in press)*. Retrieved from http://static1.squarespace.com/static/5186d08fe4b065e39b45b91e/t/550a18b8e4b0d34e8f584d3d/1426725048339/Tankard_Paluck_2015_SIPR.pdf

Tanzi, V. (2016). Public Finance in Developing Countries: An Introduction. In M. M. Erdoğdu & B. Christiansen (Eds.), *Handbook of Research on Public Finance Perspectives on Europe and the MENA Region*. Hershey, PA: IGI Global.

Torgler, B., & Schneider, F. (2007). The Impact of Tax Morale and Institutional Quality on the Shadow Economy. *IZA discussion paper* n. 2541. Retrieved from http://ftp.iza.org/dp2541.pdf

Traxler, C., & Winter, J. (2012). Survey Evidence on Conditional Norm Enforcement. *European Journal of Political Economy*, *28*(3), 390–398. doi:10.1016/j.ejpoleco.2012.03.001

VDK. (2014). *Vergi Denetim Kurulu Başkanlığı Faaliyet Raporu 2014*. Ankara: Vergi Denetim Kurulu Başkanlığı.

Velasquez, M., Andre, C., Shanks, T. S. J., & Meyer, M. J. (1990). Justice and Fairness. *Issues in Ethics*, 3(2). Retrieved from http://www.scu.edu/ethics/practicing/decision/justice.html

Verboon, P., & Goslinga, S. (2009). The role of fairness in tax compliance. *Netherlands Journal of Psychology*, *65*(4), 136–145. doi:10.1007/BF03080136

Wadhawan, S. C., & Gray, C. (1998). Enhancing Transparency in Tax Administration: A Survey. *EAGER Discussion Paper*, No. 5. Retrieved from http://pdf.usaid.gov/pdf_docs/pnadw512.pdf

World Bank. (2014, May 20). Turkey in Transition: Time for a Fiscal Policy Pivot? Report No. 85104-TR. *Turkey Public Finance Review*, Poverty Reduction and Economic Management Unit Europe and Central Asia Region. Retrieved from http://www.worldbank.org/content/dam/Worldbank/Feature%20Story/ECA/Turkey/turkey-pfr-report-21-may-2014.pdf

Yackley, A.J. (2009, September 8). UPDATE 3-Turkey Gov't Hits Media Group Dogan with Tax Fine. *Reuters*. Retrieved from http://uk.reuters.com/article/2009/09/08/turkey-dogan-idUKL815352620090908

Yaraşır, S. (2013). Vergi Afları ve Türkiye'deki Vergi Aflarının Değerlendirilmesi. *Vergi Dünyası*, *379*, 175–187.

Yavaşlar, F. B. (2008). Türk Vergi Hukuku'nda Uzlaşma. *Marmara Üniversitesi İ.İ.B.F. Dergisi*, *25*(2), 309–337.

Yitzhaki, S. (1974). A Note on Income Tax Evasion: A Theoretical Analysis. *Journal of Public Economics*, *3*(2), 201–202. doi:10.1016/0047-2727(74)90037-1

ENDNOTES

1 According to *Internal Revenue Service 2012* current estimates report cited in the Alm, Bloomquist, & McKee (2015, p. 1170), 'tax gap' (or difference between taxes owed and taxes paid) in the United States to be $450 billion annually.

2 See for instance: Kirchler (2007); Kirchler, Hoelzl, & Wahl (2008); Kirchler *et al.* (2010); Kirchler *et al.* (2012); and Kirchler, Kogler, & Muehlbacher (2014).

3 One such case was a record tax fine applied Turkey's biggest media group Doğan in 2009. According to Reuters, the group was fined $2.5 billion for unpaid taxes and the fine was equivalent to four-fifths of Doğan Yayın and parent Doğan Holding's combined market value of $3.1 billion lira. This act seemed as "keeping a lid on media criticism of Prime Minister Tayyip Erdoğan's administration" (*Reuters*, September 8, 2009).

4 Tax amnesties are government programs that typically allow a short period of time for tax evaders to voluntarily repay previously evaded taxes without being subject to penalties and prosecution that discovery of such tax evasion normally brings.

5 Alm, McKee & Beck (1990) show that amnesties may sometimes increase compliance and tax collection, especially if individuals perceive paying taxes is the social norm and amnesty is accompanied by heightened enforcement efforts.

6 While Motherland Party could get 45.14% of the votes in 1983 general elections, it could get only 36.31% of the votes in 1987 general elections and 21.80% of the votes in 1989 local elections.

7 It is interesting to note that a considerable number of tax remissions were implemented while Turgut Özal was on charge. Özal had become deputy prime minister just after the military coup in 1980 and then prime minister in 1983 when the democratic elections were conducted. Although he became President in 1989, Özal was de facto director of the economy until he passed away in 1993. During his term, eight tax remissions were implemented.

8 For a project about tax loss and evasion in the real estate sector, we needed data on the transactional value of the real estate purchased-sold or rented and data on the values declared by the taxpayers. We knew we could not access personal data due to 'tax confidentiality principle.' The surprising thing for us however was the fact that the Revenue Administration considered even global data on assessment values declared by the taxpayers and accrued amounts as subject to the confidentiality principle and it did not share this data with us. We met 20 public officers about this issue and 16 of them stated they did not possess those data and even if they had possessed it, they would not have

had the right to share them with the third persons. Some of these officers stated that the Ministry of Finance was particularly sensitive on the issue of the confidentiality principle of taxes.

9 For a study presenting the case empirically for Konya see Doğrul (2011), for a study presenting the case for Şanlıurfa see Karasu and Karakaş (2012). For a theoretical study presenting the factors giving ways to tax evasion see Hacıköylü and Heper (2010).

10 An appraisal is only a rough price estimate of a property by the knowledge of the local area and recent sale prices. Whereas a valuation is the process of determining the current worth of a property. A formal valuation can only be conducted by a qualified valuer who has undertaken prescribed education and training to ensure that all features and issues related to a particular property are taken into account.

11 As Tanzi (2016, chapter one in this handbook) indicates, the introductions and growing use of computers in recent decades has made it easier for tax administrations to store, retrieve, and cross-check information on taxpayers all over the World.

12 Before these two improvements, it was extremely difficult to check out if declarations of taxpayers reflected the truth or not. Moreover, these improvements reduced the possibility of false tax declarations.

13 See for instance, Isaac and O'Leary (2012).

14 We would argue that this is an important privilege. Workloads of the first 30 companies is expected to increase dramatically and the share of fixed expenses per each valuation would be expected to decline significantly. Another advantage of being a state approved company would be that, they may employ new valuation experts and other staff much easier and grow much faster.

15 First 30 companies of the tender can be given privilege in this issue.

16 See also James (2016, Ch. 3 of this handbook) in this respect.

Chapter 14
Attitudes toward Tax Evasion in Turkey: An Empirical Study

Robert W McGee
Fayetteville State University, USA

Serkan Benk
İnönü University, Turkey

ABSTRACT

This chapter summarizes and analyzes the latest World Values Survey data on attitudes toward tax evasion in Turkey. In addition to examining the overall viewpoints of the 1601-person sample, we examine ethical attitudes from the perspective of the following demographic variables: gender, age, marital status, education level, employment status, occupation, social class, income level, happiness, position on the political spectrum, sector of employment, and confidence in government. Comparisons with other studies will be made to determine the similarities and differences between Turkish attitudes and the attitudes of people in other countries.

INTRODUCTION

A number of studies on taxation have been done in the last few decades. Most such studies have taken a public finance perspective and have examined issues such as the optimum tax rate. Other studies have debated the best method of taxation. Some have debated the relative worth of a graduated income tax or a flat tax.

More recently, some scholars have focused on ethical aspects of tax evasion. Some studies have been theoretical, while others have been empirical. The present study reviews both the theoretical and empirical literature and presents the results of a study of the attitudes of Turkish taxpayers toward the ethics of tax evasion.

DOI: 10.4018/978-1-5225-0053-7.ch014

The present study uses the most recent (Wave 6) World Values Survey data, which was gathered by a team of social scientists in Turkey in 2011 and released in April, 2014. The question dealing with tax evasion was worded as follows: Please tell me for each of the following actions whether you think it can always be justified, never be justified, or something in between: Cheating on taxes if you have a chance. Participants selected a number from 1 to 10, where 1 = never justifiable and 10 = always justifiable. The sample size was 1601.

The present study found that, overall, there was strong opposition to tax evasion, with 86.6 percent stating that tax evasion was never justified. However, that also means that 13.4 percent thought tax evasion could be justified in certain circumstances. Only four of the 1601 individuals included in the sample believed that tax evasion could always be justified. Unfortunately, the individuals conducting the survey did not ask participants to explain the reasons for their views, so all we are able to determine are their views, not the reasons for their views. However, other studies of tax evasion have identified various reasons given over the centuries to justify tax evasion. Some of those studies are discussed in the literature review section.

The present study also examined several demographic variables in order to determine whether different subgroups had significantly different opinions on the tax evasion issue. An examination of the gender variable found that women were significantly more opposed to tax evasion. This finding confirms the findings in several other studies (McGee, 2012a). However, some studies have found that there is not a significant difference between male and female views on this issue, and a few studies have found that men were more strongly opposed to tax evasion (McGee, 2012a; Torgler, 2007).

In the employment status category, the group least opposed to tax evasion was the retired group, while the group most opposed was the part-time worker group. The sector of employment variable found a weak (10% level) correlation between sector and extent of opposition to tax evasion. Those who worked for nonprofit organizations were most opposed to tax evasion, while those who worked for government institutions were least opposed.

The relationship between the extent of confidence in government and view of tax evasion was linear. Those who placed a great deal of confidence in government were also most opposed to tax evasion, whereas those who placed no confidence at all in government were least opposed to tax evasion.

Some of the variables examined found no significant differences. The demographic variables having no significant differences included age, marital status, education level, occupation, social class, income level, level of happiness, and position on the left-right political spectrum.

LITERATURE REVIEW

Tax evasion has existed ever since the first government tried to extract taxes from the populace (Adams, 1982, 1993). Many older studies on the ethics of tax evasion have taken a religious perspective. The Christian Bible mentioned taxation in several places and seemingly indicated that there is at least some moral obligation to pay some taxes. Jesus supposedly said, "Render therefore unto Caesar the things which are Caesar's; and unto God the things that are God's." (Matthew 22, p. 21). His answer begs the question of what Caesar (the State) is entitled to. Saint Paul's statement does not shed much light on the question of government's entitlement to taxes either. "Render therefore to all their dues: tribute to whom tribute is due; custom to whom custom; fear to whom fear; honour to whom honour." (Romans 13, p. 7).

Basically, both of those statements say that we should pay our just debts. The unanswered question is, "When is there a duty to pay taxes?"

The most comprehensive theoretical study from the Christian (mostly Catholic) perspective was done by Martin Crowe (1944), a Catholic cleric who surveyed and summarized about 500 years of religious and philosophical literature, much of which was in Latin. Christian scholars of the past mostly believed that there is a duty to pay only just taxes, which again begs the question of what is just. Some, but not all early Catholic scholars believed that the duty to pay is less than absolute in some cases, the most frequent being in cases where the government is corrupt or wasteful or where there is an inability to pay.

Most of the more recent Christian literature on the subject has taken the position that the duty to pay taxes is less than absolute (Gronbacher, 1998; McGee, 1998, 2012a, 2012b; Schansberg, 1998). Pennock (1998) believed that tax evasion may be ethical in the case of an unjust war, and may even be a moral duty.

However, not all Christian literature takes the position that there is wiggle room when it comes to paying taxes. Two Mormon scholars who examined the literature of the Church of Jesus Christ of Latter-Day Saints found several places where tax evasion was condemned, but no cases that would indicate any wiggle room (Smith & Kimball, 1998). However, a survey of Mormon students found the rank and file opinion to be more flexible on this issue (McGee & Smith, 2012).

The literature of the Baha'i faith is only slightly less absolutist. Their literature states that tax evasion is always unethical except in cases where the government oppresses members of the Baha'i faith (DeMoville, 1998), which leads one to conclude that tax evasion in such cases would be unethical for Catholics, Methodists and Baptists but not Baha'is, a rather curious result.

At least two Jewish scholars have examined the Jewish religious literature. They found that Jewish scholars generally believe that tax evasion is almost never justified, although there is some justification for evasion in cases where the government is corrupt (Cohn, 1998, 2012; Tamari, 1998). A survey of Orthodox Jewish student opinion found that they believe there is some duty to pay taxes even to Hitler (McGee & Cohn, 2008). Their reasoning was based on four particular strains of thought in the Jewish literature. (1) One must never do anything to disparage another Jew, and if one Jew commits tax evasion, it makes all Jews look bad. (2) There is a duty to perform good works; evading taxes might result in going to prison; one may not do good works in prison. (3) The law is the law; one must obey all laws; if you don't like it, leave. (4) The law prohibits all lying.

All four of these positions are subject to criticism. Space does not permit a full examination of the flaws in these reasons. One may argue that there is, at times, a moral duty to evade taxes. Dietrich Bonhoeffer, the German theologian who was killed at the direct orders of Hitler, would probably take the position that there is a moral duty not to feed the evil regime of Hitler by paying taxes. One might also add that if doing the right thing (evading paying taxes to Hitler) means that others might be disparaged, the issue of disparagement is irrelevant. One might argue that a Jew who pays taxes to Hitler makes all other Jews look bad.

Paying taxes so that one may continue to do good works might also be attacked on philosophical grounds. Going to prison might make it possible to perform even more good works for more deserving people than would be possible if one stayed out of prison. If one took the Jewish side of this argument one step further, one might argue that there is a duty to obey tyrants, since doing so would allow us to stay out of prison, thus allowing us the opportunity to perform good works. Such an argument is untenable.

The argument that the law is the law is a position that Martin Luther King and Gandhi would disagree with. Bad laws need to be disobeyed. Some have argued that there is even a moral duty to do so.

One may also argue that lying is not always morally reprehensible. Aristotle addressed this issue more than 2,000 years ago, although Kant (1983) has disagreed with the Aristotelian position on this point. For example, if a Nazi asks if you are hiding a Jew in your basement, it is not unethical to say *no* when the correct answer is *yes*.

Several Muslim scholars have examined the issue of tax evasion through an ethical lens. Yusuf (1971) interpreted the Muslim literature to justify tax evasion in cases where the tax is on income or where the tax results in higher prices. Thus, there is no moral problem in evading sales, use or value added taxes, or tariffs. Ahmad (1995) took the same position as Yusuf, and cited Yusuf as one of his main sources.

However, Jalili (2012), another Muslim scholar, strongly disagreed with their views. According to Jalili, there is an absolute duty to pay taxes, but only in cases where the country follows Sharia law, since, in such cases, Allah is the tax collector. In cases where Sharia law is not being followed, the duty to pay may be less than absolute.

Some secular studies have also been done on the issue of tax evasion. Philosophy professors were found to be strongly against tax evasion (McGee, 2012c), as were, international business professors (McGee, 2006), U.S. accounting practitioners (Maranjyan & McGee, 2012) and Turkish tax practitioners (McGee, Benk, Yıldırım, & Kayıkçı, 2011), although the Turkish tax practitioners were not quite as strongly opposed to tax evasion as were the U.S. accounting practitioners.

A survey of German students found that tax evasion was less serious than accepting a bribe, buying stolen goods or claiming government benefits to which you are not entitled, and more serious than avoiding a fare on public transport (McGee, Benk, Ross, & Kılıçaslan, 2009). A similar survey of Mexican students found that tax evasion was less serious than buying stolen goods, prostitution or accepting a bribe, and more serious than avoiding a fare on public transport or claiming government benefits to which you are not entitled (McGee, Petrides, & Ross, 2012).

Several theoretical studies have been done on tax evasion in different countries. The reasons usually given for evading taxes are because it is easy to evade or because the government is corrupt and unworthy of receiving the tax funds (Torgler, 2003a, 2003b, 2010). Studies in this category include Armenia (McGee, 1999, 2000), Bulgaria (Pashev, 2008; Smatrakalev, 1998, 2012), Greece (Ballas & Tsoukas, 1998), Latin America (Alm & Martinez-Vazquez, 2010), and Russia (Alm, Martinez-Vazquez, & Torgler, 2006; Vaguine, 1998).

A few studies have been done of Turkish opinion. In a study of student opinion, Benk, McGee & Ross (2009) found that tax evasion was viewed as less serious than accepting a bribe, but more serious than buying stolen goods or claiming government benefits to which you are not entitled. However, paying cash for services to evade taxes was found to be far less serious than the other five crimes listed in the survey instrument.

A survey of 291 Turkish students that used a different survey instrument than the one used in the present study found that the extent of support for tax evasion depended on the facts and circumstances (McGee & Benk, 2011). Participants were given 18 different fact situations and were asked to indicate the extent of support for tax evasion using a Likert Scale of 1 to 7, where 1 indicated strong support and 7 indicated strong lack of support. The strongest reason to justify tax evasion was in cases where a significant portion of the money collected winds up in the pockets of corrupt politicians, their family or friends (Mean = 3.609). The second strongest reason to justify tax evasion was in cases where a large portion of the money collected is wasted (Mean = 3.766). In third place was the case where the taxpayer lived under an oppressive regime like Nazi Germany or Stalinist Russia (Mean = 3.855). Other strong reasons to evade taxes were in cases where the tax system is unfair (Mean = 3.945), where the government discriminates against the taxpayer because of religion, race or ethnic background (Mean = 3.951), to support a war the taxpayer considers to be unjust (Mean = 4.031), or where the government imprisons people for their political opinions (Mean = 4.035).

Support for tax evasion was weaker in cases where tax rates were too high (Mean = 4.238), where a large portion of the tax funds collected are spent on programs the taxpayer disapproves of (Mean = 4.471), or where the taxpayer cannot afford to pay (Mean = 4.638).

The weakest arguments to support tax evasion were in cases where a large portion of the money collected is spent on worthy projects (Mean = 6.338), where the money is spent on projects that benefit the taxpayer (Mean = 5.931), or where the money collected is spent wisely (Mean = 5.890).

THE PRESENT STUDY

Methodology

The present study uses the most recent (Wave 6) World Values Survey data, which was gathered by a team of social scientists in Turkey in 2011 and released in April, 2014. The Wave 6 data was collected in more than 50 countries and consisted of hundreds of questions, one of which dealt with attitudes toward tax evasion. The question was worded as follows: Please tell me for each of the following actions whether you think it can always be justified, never be justified, or something in between: Cheating on taxes if you have a chance. Participants selected a number from 1 to 10, where 1 = never justifiable and 10 = always justifiable. The findings are presented below.

Findings

Overall

Table 1 shows the overall results. A strong 86.6 percent believed that tax evasion is never justified. Of the remaining 13.4 percent, most thought it was almost never justified.

Gender

Table 2 shows the results by gender. Although both genders were firmly opposed to tax evasion, females were significantly more opposed to tax evasion than were men. This finding confirms the findings of some studies and contradicts the findings of other studies. A study of 82 countries found that women were significantly more opposed to tax evasion in 52 cases (63.4%), and somewhat more opposed in 24 cases (29.3%), while men were significantly more opposed in only 1 case (Taiwan), and were somewhat more opposed in 5 countries (6.1%) (McGee, 2012d). The Ross and McGee (2011) study of Switzerland found women to be significantly more opposed to tax evasion.

The McGee (2012d) study used the World Value Survey Wave 5 data, which was gathered between 2005-2009. The data in that study found that Turkish females were only slightly more opposed to tax evasion than were men; the differences in mean scores were statistically insignificant, which might lead one to conclude that Turkish women have become more opposed to tax evasion in the last few years. However, such is not the case. A comparison of the Wave 5 and Wave 6 mean scores found that both

Table 1. Overall results

Cheating on taxes is:	N	%
Never justifiable 1	1386	86.6
2	135	8.4
3	27	1.7
4	29	1.8
5	7	0.4
6	1	0.1
7	5	0.3
8	4	0.2
9	3	0.2
Always justifiable 10	4	0.2
Total	1601	
Mean	1.27	
Standard Deviation	0.942	

Table 2. Ranking by gender

(Cheating on taxes is: 1 = never justifiable; 10 = always justifiable)				
Rank	**Gender**	**Mean**	**Std. Dev.**	**n**
1	Male	1.32	1.114	779
2	Female	1.22	0.740	822
Significant Differences in Mean Scores				
Male v. Female		0.029		

men and women had become less opposed to tax evasion between Wave 5 and Wave 6. Female mean scores went from 1.14 in Wave 5 to 1.22 for Wave 6. Male mean scores went from 1.22 in Wave 5 to 1.32 in Wave 6.

The literature gives several reasons to explain why females are more opposed to tax evasion than men. In the Jewish culture, women are taught from an early age to respect authority (Cohn, 1998, 2012). In many other cultures women are also less rebellious, and thus have more respect for law and authority (McGee, 2012a; Torgler, 2007).

In the cases where there is not a significant difference between male and female view, one possible reason is because the culture in that particular country has achieved a high degree of gender equality, at least in terms of values and beliefs (McGee, 2012a; Torgler, 2007).

Age

Table 3 shows the mean scores by age, and also the ranking by age. The youngest group was most opposed to tax evasion, while the 30-39 year-old group was least opposed. This result is interesting, given the fact that most prior studies have found older people to be more opposed to tax evasion than younger people (McGee, 2012e). However, as can be seen in Table 4, the differences in mean scores between groups are not statistically significant, which means age is not a significant variable. Again, this finding runs contra to the findings in most other studies, which found that older people tend to be more opposed to tax evasion than younger people. The Ross and McGee (2011) study of Switzerland, which is representative of other studies (McGee, 2012a; Torgler, 2007), found older people to be more opposed to tax evasion than younger people. This finding conforms to more general studies that found the older a person gets, the more respect they have for law and authority (McGee, 2012a; Torgler, 2007).

Marital Status

Table 5 shows the results based on marital status. Widows were least opposed to tax evasion, whereas those living together or separated were most opposed to tax evasion. However, the sample sizes for these two groups were small. Table 6 shows that the differences in mean score were not significant.

This finding runs contra to the finding of an 82-country study, which found widows to be the group most opposed to tax evasion and divorced and single/never married people to be least opposed (McGee, 2012g). However, as Table 6 shows, the differences in mean scores are not significant.

The Ross and McGee (2011) study of Switzerland found the widowed group was most opposed to tax evasion, followed by the married and divorced groups. The single/never married group was least opposed to tax evasion. Similar results have been found in other studies, although the results are not uniform. Some studies have found that marital status is a significant variable while other studies have found no significant difference. If widows are more opposed to tax evasion than other groups, one explanation could be because widows tend to be older than average, and older people tend to have more respect for

Table 3. Ranking by age

(Cheating on taxes is: 1 = never justifiable; 10 = always justifiable)				
Rank	**Age**	**Mean**	**Std. Dev.**	**n**
1	30-39	1.33	0.986	434
2	50+	1.29	1.082	360
3	40-49	1.27	0.881	297
4	15-29	1.19	0.821	510
	Total	1.27	0.942	1601

Table 4. Age and attitudes toward tax evasion

ANOVA Analysis					
	Σ Squares	**Df**	**Mean Square**	**Fisher F-value**	**P value**
Between Groups	5.030	3	1.677	1.894	0.129
Within Groups	1414.085	1597	0.885		
Total	1419.116	1600			

Table 5. Marital status

(Cheating on taxes is: 1 = never justifiable; 10 = always justifiable)				
Rank	**Status**	**Mean**	**Std. Dev.**	**n**
1	Widowed	1.32	1.052	62
2	Single	1.27	1.027	433
2	Married	1.27	0.913	1041
3	Divorced	1.26	0.773	46
4	Separated	1.00	0.000	8
4	Living together as married	1.00	0.000	11
	Total	1.27	0.942	1601

Table 6. Marital status and attitudes toward tax evasion

ANOVA Analysis					
	Σ Squares	**Df**	**Mean Square**	**Fisher F-value**	**P value**
Between Groups	1.552	5	0.310	0.349	0.883
Within Groups	1417.563	1595	0.889		
Total	1419.116	1600			

law and authority than younger people. If single people are less opposed to tax evasion than some other groups, it could be because young people tend to be less averse to tax evasion and have less respect for the law than do older people (McGee, 2012a).

Education Level

Table 7 shows the education level demographic. Those with an incomplete primary education showed the least opposition to tax evasion, which those with an incomplete secondary education showed the most opposition to tax evasion. Those with university educations were about as opposed to tax evasion as were those with an incomplete primary school education. Thus, there appears to be no clearly defined linear relationship between the level of education and the attitude toward tax evasion. Table 8 shows that the differences in mean scores are not significant, which means that education level is not a significant variable. The Ross and McGee (2011) study of Switzerland found education level not to be a significant variable, either.

Other studies have found different results. Some studies found that the more highly educated a person is, the more opposed they are to tax evasion, while other studies found that the less educated persons were more strongly opposed to tax evasion than other groups (McGee, 2012a). The scholars who conducted these studies were unable to agree on the reason(s) why this relationship might exist, although possible explanations included culture, religion, age, relative respect for law and authority, and the income effect.

Table 7. Rankings by education level

(Cheating on taxes is: 1 = never justifiable; 10 = always justifiable)				
Rank	**Status**	**Mean**	**Std. Dev.**	**n**
1	Incomplete primary school	1.43	1.118	63
2	University - level education, with degree	1.39	1.265	236
3	Incomplete secondary school: university-preparatory type	1.29	0.944	45
4	Complete secondary school: technical/vocational type	1.26	0.878	136
5	Complete secondary school: university-preparatory type	1.25	0.768	467
6	Complete primary school	1.24	0.950	444
7	No formal education	1.21	0.768	91
8	Some university-level education, without degree	1.18	1.077	74
9	Incomplete secondary school: technical/ vocational type	1.04	0.208	45
	Total	1.27	0.942	1601

Table 8. Level of education and attitudes toward tax evasion

ANOVA Analysis					
	Σ Squares	**Df**	**Mean Square**	**Fisher F-value**	**P value**
Between Groups	8.472	8	1.059	1.195	0.298
Within Groups	1410.643	1592	0.886		
Total	1419.116	1600			

Employment Status

Table 9 shows the results based on employment status. Those in the "Other" category were least opposed to tax evasion. However, the sample size for that group was very small. The group ranked second was retired, followed by unemployed full-time, and students. The group most opposed was part-time workers. Table 10 shows that the differences between groups were significant.

The Ross and McGee (2011) study of Switzerland found housewives to be most opposed to tax evasion, followed by part-time and retired workers, students, the self-employed, full-time and unemployed individuals. Some other studies reached similar results, while the results of other studies differed (McGee, 2012a; Torgler, 2007). One reason given to explain why self-employed individuals might be less opposed to tax evasion than other groups was because they were better able to see the fruits of their labor taken from them than the groups who had taxes deducted directly from their pay checks (McGee, 2012a).

Table 9. Ranking by employment status

(Cheating on taxes is: 1 = never justifiable; 10 = always justifiable)				
Rank	**Status**	**Mean**	**Std. Dev.**	**n**
1	Other	2.43	3.359	7
2	Retired	1.41	1.360	174
3	Unemployed	1.36	1.146	77
4	Full time	1.30	0.993	429
5	Students	1.22	0.883	139
6	Self Employed	1.21	0.859	135
6	Housewife	1.21	0.693	540
7	Part time	1.16	0.526	100
	Total	1.7	0.942	1601

Table 10. Employment status and attitudes toward tax evasion

ANOVA Analysis					
	Σ Squares	**Df**	**Mean Square**	**Fisher F-value**	**P value**
Between Groups	17.501	7	2.500	2.841	0.006
Within Groups	1401.615	1593	0.880		
Total	1414.116	1600			
Significant Differences in Mean Scores					
		P value			
Other v. full time		0.034			
Other v. Part time		0.013			
Other v. Self employed		0.019			
Other v. Housewife		0.015			
Other v. Students		0.020			

Occupation

Table 11 shows the results for the occupation demographic. Foremen and supervisors were least opposed to tax evasion. Agricultural workers, members of the armed forces and security personnel were most opposed. Table 12 shows that the differences in mean scores are not significant. The other studies that have examined this variable found no consistent pattern (McGee, 2012a).

Social Class

The results for Social class are presented in Table 13. Those least opposed were the working class, followed by the upper class. Those least opposed were the lower class and the upper middle class. No clear pattern seemed to emerge when the various groups were ranked. However, as Table 14 shows, the difference in mean scores was insignificant.

Table 11. Ranking by occupation

(Cheating on taxes is: 1 = never justifiable; 10 = always justifiable)				
Rank	**Status**	**Mean**	**Std. Dev.**	**n**
1	Foreman and supervisor	1.70	0.422	10
2	Employer/manager of establishment with 10 or more employees	1.45	1.431	40
3	Non-manual-office worker: non-supervisory	1.43	1.345	152
4	Professional worker lawyer, accountant, teacher etc.	1.34	1.166	47
5	Semi-skilled manual worker	1.28	0.807	46
6	Skilled manual worker	1.26	1.106	323
7	Never had a job	1.22	0.738	673
7	Unskilled manual worker	1.22	0.599	97
7	Employer/manager of establishment with less than 10 employees	1.22	0.621	86
10	Farmer: has own farm	1.08	0.274	50
11	Member of armed forces, security personnel	1.00	0.000	6
11	Agricultural worker	1.00	0.000	4
	Total	1.26	0.920	1553

Table 12. Occupation and attitudes toward tax evasion

ANOVA Analysis					
	Σ Squares	**Df**	**Mean Square**	**Fisher F-value**	**P value**
Between Groups	12.165	12	1.014	1.199	0.278
Within Groups	1302.323	1540	0.846		
Total	1314.488	1552			

Table 13. Ranking by social class

(Cheating on taxes is: 1 = never justifiable; 10 = always justifiable)				
Rank	**Status**	**Mean**	**Std. Dev.**	**n**
1	Working class	1.32	0.994	390
2	Upper class	1.29	1.270	31
3	Lower middle class	1.26	0.909	692
4	Upper middle class	1.22	0.884	394
4	Lower class	1.22	0.619	68
	Total	1.26	0.922	1575

Table 14. Social class and attitudes toward tax evasion

ANOVA Analysis					
	Σ Squares	Df	Mean Square	Fisher F-value	P value
Between Groups	2.117	4	0.529	0.621	0.647
Within Groups	1337.060	1570	0.852		
Total	1339.177	1574			

The Ross and McGee (2011) study of Switzerland found no clear relationship between social class and view toward tax evasion. The lower class was the group most strongly opposed to tax evasion, but the upper class was almost as strongly opposed. The upper middle class was least opposed to tax evasion.

Other studies of this variable sometimes found significant differences between groups, but no distinct pattern could be found. In some studies, the upper class was most opposed to tax evasion, while in other studies the upper class was least opposed. Other studies found the lower or middle class to be either most opposed or least opposed. One explanation for the differences in viewpoints might have to do with the local culture, religion or income level (McGee, 2012a; Torgler, 2007).

Scale of Income

The data for the scale of income demographic are summarized in Table 15. The relationship between income level and attitude toward tax evasion seems to be curvilinear. Those most opposed to tax evasion are in the lower income group, while those least opposed are in the middle income group. However, as Table 16 shows, the differences in mean scores are not significant.

Table 15. Ranking by scale of income

(Cheating on taxes is: 1 = never justifiable; 10 = always justifiable)				
Rank	Status	Mean	Std. Dev.	n
1	Middle income	1.30	1.008	1073
2	High income	1.25	0.852	291
3	Low income	1.15	0.743	203
	Total	1.27	0.951	1567

Table 16. Scale of income and attitudes toward tax evasion

ANOVA Analysis					
	Σ Squares	Df	Mean Square	Fisher F-value	P value
Between Groups	4.0518	2	2.025	2.245	0.106
Within Groups	1411.223	1564	0.902		
Total	1415.274	1566			

A study of 82 countries found the relationship between income level and attitude toward tax evasion to be mixed (McGee, 2012h). In 13 countries, low-income people were significantly more averse to tax evasion than were medium-income people. In 23 countries, low-income people were somewhat more averse to tax evasion than were middle-income people, although the difference was not significant. In 10 countries there was no difference. In 5 countries, low-income people were significantly less averse to tax evasion than were middle-income people. In 15 countries, low-income people were less averse to tax evasion than were medium-income people, although the difference was not significant. In 21 countries, low-income people were significantly more averse to tax evasion than were high income people. In 24 countries, low-income people were more averse to tax evasion than high-income people, but the difference was not significant. In 10 countries, there was no difference. In 5 countries, low income people were significantly less averse to tax evasion than were high-income people. In 6 countries, low-income people were less averse to tax evasion than high-income people, but the difference was not significant.

The Ross and McGee (2011) study of Switzerland found no clear pattern between income level and attitude toward tax evasion. Those in the second highest income category were most opposed to tax evasion, while those in the next to lowest income category were almost equally opposed to tax evasion.

Other studies have reached different results. Some studies found that those in the higher income categories were less opposed to tax evasion, while other studies found that those in the lowest income groups were least opposed to tax evasion. A third group of studies found those in the middle income group were either more opposed or less opposed than those at either of the extremes (McGee, 2012a).

Happiness

The data on the relationship between happiness and attitude toward tax evasion is given in Table 17. The happiest two groups are also the two groups most opposed to tax evasion, whereas the two least happy groups are least opposed. However, as Table 18 shows, the differences in mean scores are not significant, meaning that happiness is not a significant variable.

The Ross and McGee (2011) study of Switzerland found those most opposed to tax evasion to be the happiest people and those least opposed to be the least happy groups. Other studies found differing results. One possible explanation might be that those who pay their taxes have more peace of mind than those who don't. Another explanation might be that those who don't pay their taxes are happier because they get to keep more of the fruits of their labor (McGee, 2012a).

Table 17. Ranking by happiness

(Cheating on taxes is: 1 = never justifiable; 10 = always justifiable)				
Rank	**Status**	**Mean**	**Std. Dev.**	**n**
1	Not very happy	1.32	1.136	184
2	Not at all happy	1.29	1.151	62
3	Rather happy	1.26	0.897	743
4	Very happy	1.24	0.869	605
	Total	1.26	0.927	1594

Table 18. Happiness and attitudes toward tax evasion

ANOVA Analysis					
	Σ Squares	Df	Mean Square	Fisher F-value	P value
Between Groups	0.875	3	0.292	0.339	0.797
Within Groups	1369.036	1590	0.861		
Total	1369.910	1593			

Left-Right Political Spectrum

Table 19 shows the relationship between position on the left-right political spectrum and attitude toward tax evasion. Those on the right tend to be most strongly opposed to tax evasion, while centrists tend to be least opposed. The relationship between variables thus is not linear. However, as Table 20 shows, the differences in mean scores are not significant, meaning that position on the left-right political spectrum is not a significant variable.

The Ross and McGee (2011) study of Switzerland found the differences in mean scores to be significant, but the relationship to be nonlinear. Although the far-left group was most opposed to tax evasion, the placement of the other groups in the ranking did not follow a discernible pattern. Other studies have found different results. Where the left (socialist) is more opposed to tax evasion, one explanation might be because of a sense of moral duty to pay. Where the right is more opposed to tax evasion, it might be because individuals in this group feel a stronger moral obligation for authority and the rule of law (McGee, 2012a).

Table 19. Ranking by left-right political spectrum

(Cheating on taxes is: 1 = never justifiable; 10 = always justifiable)				
Rank	**Status**	**Mean**	**Std. Dev.**	**n**
1	Center	1.29	1.002	739
2	Left	1.25	0.905	233
3	Right	1.22	0.849	478
	Total	1.26	0.939	1450

Table 20. Left-right political spectrum and attitudes toward tax evasion

ANOVA Analysis					
	Σ Squares	Df	Mean Square	Fisher F-value	P value
Between Groups	1.377	2	0.689	0.781	0.458
Within Groups	1275.603	1447	0.882		
Total	1276.980	1449			

Sector of Employment

Table 21 shows the data for the sector of employment variable. Those who worked for nonprofit organizations were most opposed to tax evasion, while those who worked for government institutions were least opposed. As Table 22 shows, the differences in mean scores was significant only at the 10 percent level.

The Ross and McGee (2011) study of Switzerland found that people employed by government were more opposed to tax evasion than were the other two groups, a finding that runs contra to that of the present study. Other studies that examined this variable had inconsistent results (McGee, 2012a).

Confidence in Government

Table 23 summarizes the data for the confidence in government variable. The relationship between the extent of confidence in government and view of tax evasion was linear. Those who placed a great deal of confidence in government were also most opposed to tax evasion, whereas those who placed no confidence at all in government were least opposed to tax evasion. Table 24 shows the differences in mean scores to be highly significant. The Ross and McGee (2011) study of Switzerland had the same findings. Some other studies of this variable found different relationships. In some cases the differences were insignificant (McGee, 2012a).

Table 21. Ranking by sector of employment

(Cheating on taxes is: 1 = never justifiable; 10 = always justifiable)				
Rank	**Status**	**Mean**	**Std. Dev.**	**n**
1	Government or public institution	1.44	1.283	187
2	Private business or industry	1.25	0.964	683
3	Private non-profit organization	1.00	0.000	8
4	Total	1.29	1.039	878

Table 22. Sector of employment and attitudes toward tax evasion

ANOVA Analysis					
	Σ Squares	**Df**	**Mean Square**	**Fisher F-value**	**P value**
Between Groups	5.867	2	2.933	2.730	0.066
Within Groups	940.230	875	1.075		
Total	946.097	877			

Table 23. Ranking confidence in government

(Cheating on taxes is: 1 = never justifiable; 10 = always justifiable)				
Rank	**Status**	**Mean**	**Std. Dev.**	**n**
1	None at all	1.41	1.343	256
2	Not very much	1.33	0.969	399
3	Quite a lot	1.23	0.819	537
4	A great deal	1.13	0.716	369
	Total	1.26	0.946	1561

Table 24. Confidence in government and attitudes toward tax evasion

ANOVA Analysis					
	Σ Squares	**Df**	**Mean Square**	**Fisher F-value**	**P value**
Between Groups	14.353	3	4.784	5.390	0.001
Within Groups	1381.959	1557	0.888		
Total	1396.313	1560			
Significant Differences in Mean Scores					
	P value				
A great deal v. None at all	0.001				

SUMMARY, CONCLUSION, AND RECOMMENDATIONS FOR FURTHER RESEARCH

The results showed that, overall, the vast majority of Turkish people were strongly opposed to tax evasion. This finding is similar to the findings in other studies. Most prior studies have found that most people are strongly opposed to tax evasion (McGee, 2012a). Of the 12 demographic variables tested in the present study, significant differences were found in four variables, whereas the differences in mean scores were insignificant in eight cases. Women were significantly more opposed to tax evasion than were men, although a comparison with the Wave 5 statistics found that both men and women are becoming less averse to tax evasion over time.

The employment status variable found significant differences. Part-time workers, housewives and the self-employed were more opposed to tax evasion, whereas the retired and unemployed were least opposed. Those working in the private, nonprofit sector were somewhat more opposed (at the 10 percent level) to tax evasion, whereas those working for government were somewhat less opposed to tax evasion. The more confidence in government one had, the more opposed one was to tax evasion. The mean scores for the other eight variables tested were not significantly different – age, marital status, education level, occupation, social class, income, degree of happiness and position on the left-right spectrum.

There is much room for further research. The data gatherers in the present study did not ask for the reasons behind the responses. Due to time constraints they could not, since they had to ask hundreds of questions. Future studies could attempt to determine the reasons behind the views. Examining the views of other sample populations could also prove fruitful. It is likely that the Turkish population has views on the issue that are similar to those in some other countries and different in other countries. The reasons for the differing opinions could be due to a variety of religious, cultural and other factors. Some studies have examined cultural factors (Alm & Torgler, 2006), but more needs to be done. One might also explore why the four significant demographic variables had significant differences in mean scores. One might also do longitudinal studies to see whether opinions in general have shifted over time. The reasons for any shifts might also be explored.

REFERENCES

Adams, C. (1982). *Fight, Flight and Fraud: The Story of Taxation*. Curacao: Euro-Dutch Publishers.

Adams, C. (1993). *For Good or Evil: The Impact of Taxes on the Course of Civilization*. London, New York, Lanham: Madison Books.

Ahmad, M. (1995). *Business Ethics in Islam*. Islamabad, Pakistan: The International Institute of Islamic Thought & The International Institute of Islamic Economics.

Alm, J., & Martinez-Vazquez, J. (2010). Tax Evasion, the Informal Sector, and Tax Morale in LAC Countries. In J. Alm, & Martinez-Vazquez & B. Torgler (Eds.), Developing Alternative Frameworks for Explaining Tax Compliance (pp. 260-291). London & New York: Routledge.

Alm, J., Martinez-Vazquez, J., & Torgler, B. (2006). Russian Attitudes toward Paying Taxes – Before, during and After the Transition. *International Journal of Social Economics*, *33*(12), 832–857. doi:10.1108/03068290610714670

Alm, J., & Torgler, B. (2006). Culture Differences and Tax Morale in the United States and in Europe. *Journal of Economic Psychology*, *27*(2), 224–246. doi:10.1016/j.joep.2005.09.002

Aristotle. (n. d.). *Nicomachean Ethics* (Translated by W. D. Ross). eBooks@Adelaide, The University of Adelaide. Retrieved from https://ebooks.adelaide.edu.au/a/aristotle/nicomachean/

Ballas, A. A., & Tsoukas, H. (1998). Consequences of Distrust: The Vicious Circle of Tax Evasion in Greece. In R. W. McGee (Ed.), The Ethics of Tax Evasion (pp. 284-304), Dumont, NJ: The Dumont Institute for Public Policy Research.

Benk, S., McGee, R. W., & Ross, A. M. (2009). An Empirical Study of Ethical Opinion in Turkey. *Journal of Accounting, Ethics &. Public Policy*, *10*(1), 83–99.

Cohn, G. (1998). The Jewish View on Paying Taxes. In R. W. McGee (Ed.), The Ethics of Tax Evasion (pp. 180-189). Dumont, NJ: The Dumont Institute for Public Policy Research.

Cohn, G. (2012). The Traditional Jewish View of Paying Taxes. In R. W. McGee (Ed.), *The Ethics of Tax Evasion: Perspectives in Theory and Practice* (pp. 149–158). New York: Springer. doi:10.1007/978-1-4614-1287-8_9

Crowe, M. T. (1944). The Moral Obligation of Paying Just Taxes. Washington, DC: The Catholic University of America Studies in Sacred Theology No. 84.

DeMoville, W. (1998). The Ethics of Tax Evasion: A Baha'i Perspective. In R. W. McGee (Ed.), The Ethics of Tax Evasion (pp. 230-240). Dumont, NJ: The Dumont Institute for Public Policy Research.

Gronbacher, G. M. A. (1998). Taxation: Catholic Social Thought and Classical Liberalism. In R. W. McGee (Ed.), The Ethics of Tax Evasion (pp. 158-167). Dumont, NJ: The Dumont Institute for Public Policy Research.

Jalili, A. R. (2012). The Ethics of Tax Evasion: An Islamic Perspective. In R. W. McGee (Ed.), *The Ethics of Tax Evasion: Perspectives in Theory and Practice* (pp. 167–199). New York: Springer. doi:10.1007/978-1-4614-1287-8_11

Kant, I. (1983). *Ethical Philosophy* (J. W. Ellington, Trans.). Indianapolis, Cambridge: Hackett Publishing Company.

McGee, R. W. (1999). Why People Evade Taxes in Armenia: A Look at an Ethical Issue Based on a Summary of Interviews. *Journal of Accounting, Ethics & Public Policy*, *2*(2), 408–416.

McGee, R. W. (2000). Taxation in the Republic of Armenia: An Overview and Discussion from the Perspectives of Law, Economics and Ethics. *ILSA Journal of International & Comparative Law*, *7*(1), 97–109.

McGee, R. W. (2006). A Survey of International Business Academics on the Ethics of Tax Evasion. *Journal of Accounting, Ethics & Public Policy*, *6*(3), 301–352.

McGee, R. W. (2012). Christian Views on the Ethics of Tax Evasion. The Ethics of Tax Evasion: Perspectives in Theory and Practice (pp. 201-210), New York: Springer.

McGee, R. W. (Ed.). (2012a). *The Ethics of Tax Evasion: Perspectives in Theory and Practice*. New York: Springer. doi:10.1007/978-1-4614-1287-8

McGee, R. W. (2012b). Christian Views on the Ethics of Tax Evasion. In R. W. McGee (Ed.), *The Ethics of Tax Evasion: Perspectives in Theory and Practice* (pp. 201–210). New York: Springer. doi:10.1007/978-1-4614-1287-8_12

McGee, R. W. (2012c). Attitudes on the Ethics of Tax Evasion: A Survey of Philosophy Professors. In R. W. McGee (Ed.), *The Ethics of Tax Evasion: Perspectives in Theory and Practice* (pp. 125–132). New York: Springer. doi:10.1007/978-1-4614-1287-8_7

McGee, R. W. (2012d). Gender and the Ethics of Tax Evasion: An Empirical Study of 82 Countries. In R. W. McGee (Ed.), *The Ethics of Tax Evasion: Perspectives in Theory and Practice* (pp. 415–439). New York: Springer. doi:10.1007/978-1-4614-1287-8_26

McGee, R. W. (2012e). Age and the Ethics of Tax Evasion. In R. W. McGee (Ed.), *The Ethics of Tax Evasion: Perspectives in Theory and Practice* (pp. 441–449). New York: Springer. doi:10.1007/978-1-4614-1287-8_27

McGee, R. W. (2012f). Education Level and the Ethics of Tax Evasion. In R. W. McGee (Ed.), *The Ethics of Tax Evasion: Perspectives in Theory and Practice* (pp. 451–457). New York: Springer. doi:10.1007/978-1-4614-1287-8_28

McGee, R. W. (2012g). Marital Status and the Ethics of Tax Evasion. In R. W. McGee (Ed.), *The Ethics of Tax Evasion: Perspectives in Theory and Practice* (pp. 475–484). New York: Springer. doi:10.1007/978-1-4614-1287-8_31

McGee, R. W. (2012h). Income Level and the Ethics of Tax Evasion. In R. W. McGee (Ed.), *The Ethics of Tax Evasion: Perspectives in Theory and Practice* (pp. 485–495). New York: Springer. doi:10.1007/978-1-4614-1287-8_32

McGee, R. W., & Benk, S.McGee. (2011). The Ethics of Tax Evasion: A Study of Turkish Opinion. *Journal of Balkan and Near Eastern Studies*, *13*(2), 249–262. doi:10.1080/19448953.2011.578869

McGee, R. W., Benk, S., Yıldırım, H., & Kayıkçı, M. (2011). The Ethics of Tax Evasion: A Study of Turkish Tax Practitioner Opinion. *European Journal of Soil Science*, *18*(3), 468–480.

McGee, R. W., & Gordon, M. Cohn. (2008). Jewish Perspectives on the Ethics of Tax Evasion. *Journal of Legal. Ethical and Regulatory Issues*, *11*(2), 1–32.

McGee, R. W., & Maranjyan, T. B. (2012). Attitudes toward Tax Evasion: An Empirical Study of Florida Accounting Practitioners. In R. W. McGee (Ed.), *The Ethics of Tax Evasion: Perspectives in Theory and Practice* (pp. 247–265). New York: Springer. doi:10.1007/978-1-4614-1287-8_15

McGee, R. W., Petrides, Y., & Ross, A. M. (2012). How Serious Is Tax Evasion: A Survey of Mexican Opinion. In R. W. McGee (Ed.), *The Ethics of Tax Evasion: Perspectives in Theory and Practice* (pp. 405–411). New York: Springer. doi:10.1007/978-1-4614-1287-8_25

McGee, R. W., & Smith, S. R. (2012). Ethics, Tax Evasion and Religion: A Survey of Opinion of Members of the Church of Jesus Christ of Latter-Day Saints. In R. W. McGee (Ed.), *The Ethics of Tax Evasion: Perspectives in Theory and Practice* (pp. 211–226). New York: Springer. doi:10.1007/978-1-4614-1287-8_13

Pashev, K. V. (2008). Monitoring of Tax Corruption in Transition Economies: Evidence from Bulgaria. In R. W. McGee (Ed.), *Taxation and Public Finance in Transition and Developing Economies* (pp. 321–362). New York: Springer. doi:10.1007/978-0-387-25712-9_18

Pennock, R. T. (1998). Death and Taxes: On the Justice of Conscientious War Tax Resistance. Journal of Accounting, Ethics & Public Policy, 1(1), 58-76. Reprinted in R. W. McGee (Ed.) (1998), The Ethics of Tax Evasion (pp. 124-142). Dumont, NJ: The Dumont Institute for Public Policy Research.

Ross, A. M., & McGee, R. W. (2011). Attitudes toward Tax Evasion: A Demographic Study of Switzerland. *Business Studies Journal*, *3*(2), 1–47.

Schansberg, D. E. (1998). The Ethics of Tax Evasion within Biblical Christianity: Are There Limits to "Rendering Unto Caesar"? Journal of Accounting, Ethics & Public Policy, 1(1), 77-90. Reprinted in R. W. McGee (Ed.) (1998), The Ethics of Tax Evasion (pp. 144-157). The Dumont Institute for Public Policy Research, Dumont, NJ.

Smatrakalev, G. (1998). Walking on the Edge: Bulgaria and the Transition to a Market Economy. In R. W. McGee (Ed.), *The Ethics of Tax Evasion* (pp. 316–329). Dumont, NJ: The Dumont Institute for Public Policy Research.

Smatrakalev, G. (2012). Is Tax Evasion Our National Sport? The Bulgarian Case. In R. W. McGee (Ed.), *The Ethics of Tax Evasion: Perspectives in Theory and Practice* (pp. 371–385). New York: Springer. doi:10.1007/978-1-4614-1287-8_23

Smith, S. R., & Kimball, K. C. (1998). Tax Evasion and Ethics: A Perspective from Members of the Church of Jesus Christ of Latter-Day Saints. In R. W. McGee (Ed.), The Ethics of Tax Evasion (pp. 220-229). Dumont, NJ: The Dumont Institute for Public Policy Research.

Tamari, M. (1998). Ethical Issues in Tax Evasion: A Jewish Perspective. In R. W. McGee (Ed.), The Ethics of Tax Evasion (pp. 168-178). Dumont, NJ: The Dumont Institute for Public Policy Research.

Torgler, B. (2003a). Tax Morale, Rule-Governed Behaviour and Trust. *Constitutional Political Economy*, *14*(2), 119–140. doi:10.1023/A:1023643622283

Torgler, B. (2003b). To Evade Taxes or Not to Evade: That Is the Question. *Journal of Socio-Economics*, *32*(3), 283–302. doi:10.1016/S1053-5357(03)00040-4

Torgler, B. (2007). *Tax Compliance and Tax Morale: A Theoretical and Empirical Analysis*. Cheltenham, UK: Edward Elgar. doi:10.4337/9781847207203

Torgler, B. (2010). Serious Tax noncompliance: Motivation and Guardianship. *Criminology & Public Policy*, *9*(3), 535–542. doi:10.1111/j.1745-9133.2010.00648.x

Vaguine, V. V. (1998). The "Shadow Economy" and Tax Evasion in Russia. In R. W. McGee (Ed.), *The Ethics of Tax Evasion* (pp. 306–314). Dumont, NJ: The Dumont Institute for Public Policy Research.

Yusuf, S. M. (1971). *Economic Justice in Islam*. Lahore: Sh. Muhammad Ashraf.

Chapter 15
The Future of Public Finances in Egypt

Sarah Mansour
Cairo University, Egypt

Vjollca Sadiraj
Georgia State University, USA

Sally Wallace
Georgia State University, USA

ABSTRACT

Egypt, a country of 82 million people with a GDP of $272 billion, is arguably one of the most important countries in the Middle East. At this stage of its transition, the structure and level of public finances are more critical than ever. Like many countries, Egypt suffers from substantial non-compliance, which undermines the entire system of public finance, yet there has been relatively little focus on addressing this issue in Egypt. This chapter is focused on a review of the recent history of Egypt's public finances and a unique experiment that aims to better understand the potential for political institutions to affect tax compliance at a time when those institutions are under development.

INTRODUCTION

Egypt, a country of 82 million people with a GDP of $272 billion, is the most populous and arguably one of the most influential countries in the Middle East. At this stage of its transition, the structure and level of its public finances are more critical than ever. Like many countries, Egypt suffers from substantial tax non-compliance, which undermines the entire system of public finance, yet there has been relatively little focus on addressing this issue in the country. This chapter is focused on a review of the recent history of Egypt's public finances and a unique laboratory experimental study that aims to shed some light on the determinants of tax compliance behavior at a time when political institutions are under development making existing field data obsolete.

DOI: 10.4018/978-1-5225-0053-7.ch015

The structure of public finances in Egypt is not unlike many countries—a combination of own-revenue sources including taxes, fees, and charges, and in addition, grants and loans. In general, the larger the share of own revenue sources in overall government revenue, the more sovereignty a country retains. Tax compliance directly affects the ability to raise own source revenues and this ability is critical to the long term fiscal sustainability of a country. Fiscal sustainability itself allows governments to engage in thoughtful long-term budgeting and planning which support the growth of nations.

The Arab Spring, which began in late 2010, called for new forms of representative governance in countries including Tunisia, Algeria, Yemen, Libya, and Egypt. Since 2011, Egypt witnessed the resignation of long-time ruler Mubarak, the election of President Morsi and the development of a new government. The ouster of Morsi in June 2013 continued the precarious political situation and increased concerns of the country's ability to serve the needs of its population. Partially as a result of this tumultuous period (and some would say years leading up to the Arab Spring), the government's budget is in a risky situation. In the financial statement of the Government of Egypt budget plan for the year 2014/15, tax revenues are estimated to reach 15.2 percent of GDP, a figure well below world averages of 35.6 percent in developed countries, 25.5 percent in emerging markets, and 22.8 percent in low-income countries (The Ministry of Finance, 2014) and the UN's estimate of 20 percent to reach the millennium development goals. Gross domestic budget sector debt has grown from 68 percent in March of 2011 to 80 percent in March 2013 yielding deficits of 10.7 percent of GDP which is far above the planned deficit of 7.6 percent. Outstanding public (domestic and external) debt is staggering at a rate of approximately 100 percent of GDP (The Ministry of Finance, 2013).

Since 2011, various leaders in the country have attempted to engage in a policy discussion regarding the country's public finances. The 2012/13 budget preparation circular in fact speaks to the social contract of government finances and the public. The two pillars referenced in the document call for transparency, accountability, and trust:

"Reconstruct trust and safety between citizens and government"

and

"Increase national income and economic growth…to assure a good life for citizens"[1] *(page 2 paraphrased)*

While tax compliance is a necessary component of strengthening and stabilizing Egypt's finances, there is very little research that can be called on to assist policy makers in the country. A series of reforms have been called for to spur lasting economic growth and development. Those reforms include structurally reforming the tax administration, strengthening of the judicial system, better protection of property rights, and more effective action against growing corruption—much of which is aimed at creating a more transparent and efficient government that is accountable to the population.

In this chapter, we take a novel look at factors affecting tax compliance in Egypt. We first provide a review of the country's fiscal structure and recent legislation focused on fiscal policy. We then turn to a discussion of determinants of tax compliance—one of the critical issues for solvency of government finance. In Egypt, there has been little study to date of the compliance issue. In addition, the political changes the country is experiencing (such as unprecedented political participation of citizens and the cherished initiated motion to withdraw confidence from the president[2]) render previous field data inadequate. Therefore, we designed a laboratory experiment on tax compliance to test several hypothesis based on the context of post-revolutionary Egypt.[3] One hypothesis builds on the idea that transparency bridges trust. So we test whether the ability of taxpayers to observe and hence evaluate the performance of public officials through decisions made on a public good would boost voluntary compliance. Secondly, we test the impact of allowing "citizens" to vote the incumbent government out of office on the tax compliance decision—an interaction akin to Egypt's recent elections and 'right to recall' recently enshrined in the new constitution that was approved in January 2014.

BACKGROUND AND CONTEXT

From the late 1990s and prior to the 2011 uprising, Egypt's economy had been growing at annual rates of between 3 and 7 percent (World Bank, 2014). The impact of the uprising and following political turmoil is evident in GDP growth numbers which fell to about 2 percent per year (The Ministry of Finance, 2012). Government revenues were likewise affected, although external support has been helpful to shore up own source revenues. Foreign direct investment completely contracted in 2011 and while showing signs of growth, in 2013, it is less than half the level of 2007. The Central government deficit hovers around 10.6 percent of GDP (2012)—double that of levels in the early and mid-2000s and high by international comparisons.[4]

Tax revenues represent about two-thirds of total government revenues but that distribution has been subject of wide variation in the mid-2010s (Figure 1). The Government's revised budget figures for 2012-13 report that "General resources" comprised 57 percent of total resources for the year (393.5 billion EGP). Financing sources (including borrowing) is estimated at 278.3 billion EGP for the same year. Expenditures sit at 585.8 billion EGP in the same year.

The statutory structure of Egypt's public finances is similar to that found in many countries. The system contains income, consumption, and property taxes, administered largely at the central government

Figure 1.

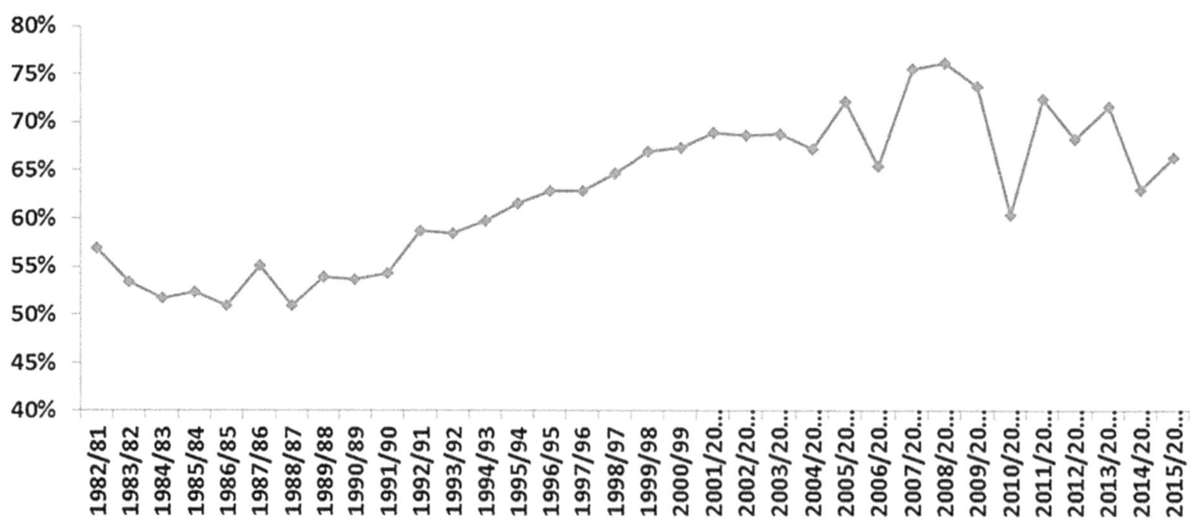

level.[5] Based on the 2014 Budget Report, in 2011/12 actual total revenue (including taxes and grants) were 303,622 million EGP and tax revenues were 68.3 percent of total revenue (207409.8 million EGP). The distribution of tax by major type of tax is as follows:

- **Taxes on Income:** 44.0%
- **Property Tax:** 6.3%
- **Sales Tax:** 40.8%
- **Customs:** 7.1%

Within the income tax category, the tax collected from corporations dwarf those on individuals. Corporate income taxes comprise 76 percent of taxes on income (69,550 million EGP in 2011/12) and 33.3 percent of total taxes collected whereas the income tax on "employed" generated 16,010 million EGP in 2011/12 (17.5 percent of taxes on income and 7.7 percent of total taxes). The share of corporate tax is similar to OECD countries while income tax on employed persons is somewhat lower than in OECD countries.

The structure of income taxation is progressive for persons and for companies. The schedule for the income tax on people is as follows (current rates as amended in 2013 and 2014):

Annual Taxable Income (EGP) Rate (%)

- **1 – 5,000:** 0
- **5,001-30,000:** 10
- **30,001-45,000:** 15
- **45,001-250,000:** 20
- **250,001 and Greater:** 25
- **Surcharge Income Greater than 1 Million (EGP):** 5

The schedule for company tax applies two rates:

Annual Taxable Income (EGP) Rate (%)

- **1-10,000,000:** 20
- **10,000,001 and greater:** 25

The income tax base for employed individuals, by law, is comprehensive and includes salaries, wages, and all fringe benefits. A deduction is allowed per taxpayer as are some social and private insurance contributions. As of 2014, dividends are taxed at a general rate of 10 percent. Interest is subject to a 20 percent withholding rate. Non-business capital gains are taxed at a general rate of 10 percent (listed securities) and regular tax rates for non-listed securities while capital gains of corporate bodies are generally taxed at 10 percent.

The heavy use of consumption taxes at the central level is not dissimilar to many countries that utilize a value added tax (VAT). OECD reports that among member states, consumption taxes account for about 33 percent of total tax revenue (OECD, 2015). Sales tax as reported in the Budget include a General Sales Tax (GST) on local and imported goods, excises (tobacco, cigarettes, oil and minor other goods), and limited sales tax on services. In 2011/12 total sales taxes amounted to 84,594 million EGP and 44 percent of those revenues came from the GST on local and imported commodities. An additional 31 percent came from excises and the remainder from miscellaneous sales taxes on goods and services.

The statutory consumption tax rates vary by commodity, with the basic rate being 10 percent but rates can run as high as 45 percent for some imported cars. Most consumable items are taxable although there is a turnover threshold below which merchants are exempt from sales tax (54,000 EGP for manufacturers and service providers and 150,000 EGP for wholesalers and retailers). Excise tax rates range from 40 to 50 percent for cigarettes to 100 percent for beer and wine. Excise tax rates vary widely among countries and Egypt's rates are not out of line with rates found in many countries.[6] Still, there have been calls for increased excise taxes to bolster overall revenue for the Government. President al-Sisi has advocated for increases in most important excises, and has suggested increasing the tax on all cigarettes to 50 percent and doubling the tax on beer. These excise tax proposals became law in July 2014.

The new Government of Egypt has identified tax policy as a priority and the figures above are a function of some changes in policy aimed at producing more revenue with a reasonable distribution of tax burden. The Egyptian Government has started making some changes to tax policy. A new income tax law was passed in 2012 with top income and corporate tax rates reaching 25 percent. With deficits of nearly 10 percent of GDP and rising public debt of 100 percent of GDP, structural reforms, particularly in tax administration are urgently needed. Egypt's economic freedom score is 54.8, making its economy the 125th freest in the 2013 Index. It is ranked 13th out of 15 countries in the Middle East/North Africa region, and its overall score is below the world and regional averages. It has been argued that total tax revenues should be higher by 2-3 percent of GDP (The Planning and Budgeting Committee, 2010).

In addition, the World Bank reports Egypt's tax to GDP ratio as 13.2 percent in 2012 (similar to the rate reported in the Government budget documents). Among OECD countries, the unweighted tax to GDP ratio is 33.7 percent in 2012 (OECD, 2015). The OECD may not be the appropriate comparison group, but regional peers of Egypt including Algeria and Morocco attain tax to GPD levels of 37.4 and 24.5 respectively. Countries with similar levels of GDP include Portugal (with taxes at 20.3 percent of GDP), Greece (22.4 percent), and Singapore (14 percent). There are cases of similarly sized countries (measured by GDP) that have lower tax to GDP ratios including the Philippines (12.9) and Pakistan (10.1).

Given these comparisons and the call for massive investments in infrastructure among other public goods, the tax to GDP ratio in Egypt could be considered too low to support the needs of its population. Since Egypt's tax rates and general structure of taxation are not widely out of line with international practices, the overall rate of taxation as a share of GDP suggests that there are significant leakages in the system. These leakages can come from tax evasion and avoidance, the existence of special tax privileges and exemptions, and myriad deductions and credits. As Egypt does not produce a tax expenditure budget, it is difficult to quantify the revenue lost to legal leakages of tax exemptions and deductions. We are also unable to find estimates of the level of tax evasion in Egypt but given the relatively low levels of collection to GDP, it is likely that tax evasion is an important contributor to the relatively low level of revenue.

Effective collection of sales, income, and customs taxes puts tax compliance high on the Government's agenda. However, there is almost no information regarding the actual behavior of taxpayers in Egypt. Economic theory can provide us with testable hypotheses regarding how taxpayers will respond via compliance to incentives in the tax system, but Egypt, being an example of a non-WEIRD[7] population, plus its unique context of post-revolutionary reform makes previous studies in other countries potentially off-base. Consequently, the external validity of previous empirical work becomes an empirical question. Throughout the revolution and subsequent government development, there has been a resounding call for accountability and transparency to build trust. Thus, an important step to understanding tax compliance in post-revolutionary Egypt is to identify taxpayer behavior that incorporates an element of interaction with government. By their nature field data are problematic for establishing causality and for isolating marginal effect of features of interest, such as transparency of institution and political participation. So we designed an experiment to offer some insights on tax compliance behavior in a controlled environment with a well-defined and transparent interaction between citizens and decision-makers.

TAX COMPLIANCE

Tax compliance is influenced by many factors including tax rates, penalty structures, and the probability of being caught. Compliance is also affected by the potential taxpayer's view of government. In cases where taxpayers receive poor services for taxes they pay due to mismanagement, corruption, or incompetence, taxpayers may be less inclined to participate in the tax system. Therefore corruption in general is expected to be an important part of compliance behavior.

Tax noncompliance is a significant problem in most societies, contributing to enormous losses to government revenues[8]. This loss of revenues not only threatens funds for the provision of crucial public goods and services, but it also contributes to social inequality and institutional mistrust (Wenzel, 2005). This serious phenomenon has encouraged researchers to investigate the factors behind it, leading to the mushrooming of the tax compliance literature following the leading theoretical work of Allingham and Sandmo (1972). Tax compliance behavior has been studied theoretically as well as empirically, using both field data and laboratory experiments, with the latter strongly increasing in the last 25 years.

The conventional economic theory for tax compliance stresses that the threat of detection and punishment is responsible for compliance. According to Allingham and Sandmo (1972), the problem of tax evasion is one of rational decision under uncertainty where the rational individual weighs the expected utility of the benefits from successful tax evasion with the uncertain prospect of detection and punishment. The individual pays taxes because he/she is afraid of getting caught. Assuming rational agents, this model predicts most individuals to evade taxes given the low levels of audit and penalty rates prevalent in most countries. Nevertheless, a higher degree of compliance than that predicted by the models of decision under risk is observed. So, although it has been established that detection and punishment affect compliance to a certain extent, the general agreement is that enforcement cannot explain all, or even most, of the tax compliance behavior (Graetz & Wilde, 1985; Elffers, 1991; Bosco & Mittone, 1997; Torgler, 2001). With low probability of detection and low penalties, it seems implausible that these economic factors can act by themselves as an effective deterrent to evasion, unless individuals' aversions to risk far exceed conventional assumptions[9]. Researchers have thus started to analyze factors other than detection and punishment that could answer the question "Why people pay taxes?"

Erard and Feinstein (1994b) advance the hypothesis of moral sentiments: 'One important reason why the conventional expected utility model of tax compliance over-predicts the prevalence and extent of tax evasion is that compliance behavior is assumed to be motivated solely by financial considerations, whereas in reality many taxpayers are influenced by a variety of other feelings, which we will call moral sentiments' (p. 74).

If moral sentiments play an important role in the tax compliance decision, then identification of factors that influence those moral sentiments the most becomes imperative. Gary Becker (1996) argues that values can no longer be treated as exogenous preferences so utility-maximizing approach need to augmented with accommodating often neglected aspects as habitual, social or political behavior, etc.

As Bowles (1998) stated: "If preferences are affected by the policies or institutional arrangements we study, we can neither accurately predict nor coherently evaluate the likely consequences of new policies or institutions without taking account of preference endogeneity" (p. 75).

Empirical validity of endogeneity of preferences and tax morale is at the heart of experimental studies conducted by Alm et al. (1993, 1999). They find that tax compliance is significantly higher (i) when taxpayers vote directly on the type of the public good than when the public good is imposed as well as (ii) when the vote is clear rather than close. In the same context, Lamberton *et al.* (2014) show that eliciting taxpayer preferences on government spending increases tax compliance. The main findings of these experimental studies are consistent with the findings of field data studies. [10] In their field studies, Pommerehne and Weck-Hannemann (1996) and Frey (1997) find that tax evasion at the Swiss cantonal level is lower in direct democratic cantons where referenda on budgetary issues are used as compared to purely parliamentary cantons. The hypothesis of the positive association between citizen participations and tax compliance, has been shown to be robust to variations in the tax, audit and fine rates (Alm *et al.*, 1999). This line of research has established that social or psychological tax contract between taxpayers and government, going beyond a pure fiscal exchange, emerges more easily if voters are actively participating in fiscal decision-making.

Surprisingly, however, tax compliance literature has rarely analyzed the effects of direct elections on tax compliance through its shaping of tax morale. Direct elections shape implicitly the evolutionary process of the tax law through taxpayers' possibility of direct participation in the election of government officials who in turn determine which public goods to provide with taxpayers' money, affecting this way the value of paying taxes. Such institutions help taxpayers better monitor and control the discretionary power of politicians. This reduces the principal agent problem between taxpayers and the government. As a consequence, tax revenues are spent more in accordance with the preferences of taxpayers, thus raising tax morale and tax compliance. This tool gives taxpayers a weapon against government officials if they were corrupt and act against their interests.

No empirical study– to the best knowledge of the author – has examined tax compliance behavior of citizens empowered with the right to recall a government official during his/her term in office. That is where this chapter comes to bridge a gap within the literature using tightly controlled environments and experimental methods.

We take up our experiment at the intersection of many of these existing arguments, including the effect of government corruption on tax morale. We seek to identify the impact of citizen's perception of corruption on taxpayer behavior (compliance) given a voting scheme that empowers taxpayers to vote the official out of the office. Given the lack of empirical data on this issue and the sensitivity of the question which renders any observational data highly unreliable, we turn to experimental methods to learn about the determinants of tax compliance. The hypothesis of the remaining part of this chapter is that tax compliance increases with individual perceptions of good governance (including a fair tax system, a government using tax revenues to provide valued goods and services, and a political system that is not corrupt). A recall scheme may "force" better governance and therefore encourage more tax compliance. We now turn to a discussion of the tax compliance/voting experiment.

TAX COMPLIANCE EXPERIMENT

Tax compliance behavior will be studied using data obtained via laboratory experiments in a unique setting, which is one in which the subjects (students) face the following political situation: the subjects are allowed to recall the official after observing his/her decision on which public good to fund with collected tax payments. A stylized interaction between the citizens and the official is simulated in the lab unfolding in time through 14 repetitions of five stages: (1) subjects earn lab dollars (eventually translated into Egyptian pounds), (2) make a tax declaration of that income, knowing parameters of tax rates, audit probabilities, and penalty structures, (3) find out if they were audited, and if so, the penalties reduce their net earnings, (4) the tax revenues are returned to the group as a public good's monetary benefits with the official making the decision on what kind of public good to fund, and finally, (5) citizens vote on whether to recall the official with the majority rule being used to aggregate votes. The two choices of public goods are a greedy good, which benefits the official to a greater extent than the citizens or a just good, which benefits the entire group (including the official) equally. We hypothesize that "corruption" (i.e., the official funding the greedy good) fuels tax evasion and recalls. Our approach is to utilize the comparative advantage of laboratory experiments which offers the potential to control for extraneous factors and to manipulate the variables of interest. Specifically, the main advantage of lab experiments is their ability to establish causal relationships through the control of confounding variables, and the random assignment of possible causal variables of interest. Replicability is another advantage of this methodology. Moreover, collecting a full array of data in interactive games, like ours, is an impossible enterprise outside the lab. And conducting our experiment at Cairo University, being a well reputed and safe place, enables us to address our sensitive research question at a tense time period then.

The basic experimental design is as follows. [11] Subjects are randomly matched into groups of five at the beginning of the experiment; groups remain fixed during the entire experiment whereas initial as well as recalled officials are randomly selected from each group of five. The reported income is taxable at the rate of 25% and the auditing rate is 20%. Taxes are paid on: (i) reported income if a subject is not audited but (ii) on the earned income in case of an audited subject, who in addition also pays a penalty on any undeclared income determined by a known penalty structure. Total taxes (but not penalties) paid by all subjects are tripled and used to fund one of the two feasible public goods as reported above. The marginal per capita return (mpcr) from the just-good, is 0.6 for each group member whereas in case of the greedy-good, the mpcr for each citizen and the official is 0.375 and 1.5, respectively.[12] Thus while the just-good is valued the same across group members, the greedy-good provides more benefit to the official at a cost of reduced benefit to the citizens--what we call a "corrupt" decision. The net of the round's earnings for each subject is then calculated (earned income minus taxes less penalties (if audited) plus the payoff from the public good chosen by the official and funded by tax revenues). The experiment consisted of 14 rounds. To investigate whether communication affects behavior (e.g., Blume & Sobel, 1995; Crawford & Sobel, 1982; Farrell & Gibbons, 1989) we allowed subjects after the tenth round (and only once) for a "cheap talk" chat via text messages within the group members.

After completion of the main experiment, subjects completed a post-experimental online questionnaire that included questions designed to get information about idiosyncratic individual characteristics such as views regarding the performance of political institutions, gender, religion, academic performance, propensity to trust, risk preferences etc.

The experiment was conducted in March 2013 and all 60 subjects who participated in the experiment were volunteers from undergraduate classes at Cairo University. Each subject participated only once and earned typically between \$26 and \$60.

IMPACT OF VOICE ON TAX COMPLIANCE IN EGYPT: EMPIRICAL RESULTS

The research question inserted in our experiment is the impact of "voice" in post-revolutionary Egypt on the tax compliance behavior of citizens (as a form of social contract along with the public good).

Our experimental design can accommodate two types of reactions to disappointment with the official's decisions. If the officials frequently choose the greedy-good (reducing the group member's net earnings), citizens can engage in retaliating behavior not only by voting the official out of power but also by reducing their tax compliance, thus reducing the pool of funds available for public good in the next round—effectively constraining the power of the official. However, the recall option also gives citizens a way to provide incentives to officials for making decisions that benefit the whole group without resorting to evading taxes.

Half of the subjects (30) served as group officials for 2 or 3 rounds, 5 (8%) subjects served for one full term (7 rounds) and no subject served for two full terms (14 rounds); Only 6 subjects (10%) never served as officials. The overall mean of tax compliance rate was 71%. Over the 14 rounds of the experiment, we find that citizens' compliance behavior decreases across rounds, however chatting (which is a kind of cheap talk that we allow via the computer after round 10) seems to have a positive effect on increasing compliance.

To examine the determinants of the tax compliance decision we have used a censored regression analysis (as compliance rate is bounded from 0 and 1) with clustering of data at the subject level (as each subject is making more than one decision); Results are shown in figure 2. The estimates for the model without demographics are reported in the first column whereas the ones with the demographics (as a robustness check) are reported in the second column. The dependent variable is a citizen's compliance rate, defined as the ratio between the claimed income and the earned one. We find that being audited in the previous round lowers compliance by 17 percent (pvalue=0.023), a behavior consistent with the gambler fallacy ("the tax administration got me in the last round, so they won't get me again"). Female students appear to comply less than male students (10 percent less, pvalue=0.087). Subjects who reported that they share secrets with others have higher compliance rates (14 percent, pvalue=0.063). We find little support either for positive reciprocity towards other citizens or herding behavior. Both predict the higher the compliance rate of others the higher own compliance. Our data show that the Total tax paid by others in the preceding round appear to have no significant effect on tax compliance behavior of citizens. However, the type of the public good being funded by the officials affect tax compliance negatively (-6.9 percent, one-sided pvalue=0.057) in that if the greedy-good is funded (the one benefitting the official), compliance falls. The strongest determinant of the tax compliance rate in a given round is the tax compliance rate in the previous round. Having a voice in the process, defined as concordance between the individual's vote and majority vote, has a significant positive impact on tax compliance (9.4 percent, pvalue=0.080).

Figure 2.

Compliance Rate Dependent Variable		
	(1)	(2)
VARIABLES	model	model
Income	0.008	0.015**
	(0.271)	(0.038)
Preceding Round Effects		
Audited (D)	-0.162**	-0.171**
	(0.034)	(0.023)
Penalty	0.038*	0.041*
	(0.097)	(0.090)
Tax paid by Others	0.003	0.001
	(0.754)	(0.869)
Good G was funded (D)	-0.078*	-0.069
	(0.084)	(0.114)
Compliance Rate	1.003***	0.949***
	(0.000)	(0.000)
Voice (D)	0.118**	0.094*
	(0.029)	(0.080)
Demographics		
Careful (D)		0.115
		(0.107)
Female (D)		-0.099*
		(0.087)
gpa=1 (D)		-0.116*
		(0.082)
Share secrets (D)		0.140*
		(0.063)
Trust Others (D)		0.078
		(0.304)
Others Evade Taxes (D)		-0.032
		(0.624)
Corruption big problem (D)		-0.004
		(0.938)
Constant	-0.138	-0.294
	(0.488)	(0.261)
Observations	538	538
ll	-350.3	-340.8
Robust pval in parentheses		
*** p<0.01, ** p<0.05, * p<0.1		

CONCLUSION

Egypt's public finances are in a state of transition as the country grapples with myriad state-building issues. The general structure of the tax system is similar to international norms, but there is a concern that non-compliance is costing the Government large amounts of lost revenues. One hypothesis is that the revenue loss is due to tax non-compliance, but little is known about the determinants of compliance in Egypt. Given that Egypt is developing its political system and citizens continue to demand a voice, we developed and implemented a unique public finance experiment to investigate tax compliance when citizens and officials interact (in a lab setting) and citizens can recall officials. Our data suggest that recall elections give citizens' "voice" and they use it to express their distaste to government. We also find that when citizens see corruption (proxied in our experiment as an official choosing the greedy good), they reduce compliance. This is consistent with rational models of tax compliance that establish the link between the high compliance and good level of public services. The external validity of the laboratory data cannot be ensured but the agreement between the signs of our estimates and the ones predicted by theoretical analysis suggest that our findings are expected to generalize well out of the lab.

This is the first tax compliance experiment we know of that has focused on the citizen-official interaction in Egypt. Future experiments will be done to directly test analyze other components of compliance, but this research has provided a meaningful start to a better understanding of the tax compliance issue in this important country.

REFERENCES

Allingham, M. G., & Sandmo, A. (1972). Income Tax Evasion: A Theoretical Analysis. *Journal of Public Economics*, *1*(3-4), 323–338. doi:10.1016/0047-2727(72)90010-2

Alm, J., McClelland, G. H., & Schulze, W. D. (1992). Why Do People Pay Taxes? *Journal of Public Economics*, *48*(1), 21–38. doi:10.1016/0047-2727(92)90040-M

Andreoni, J., Erard, B., & Feinstein, J. (1998). Tax Compliance. *Journal of Economic Literature*, *36*(2), 818–860.

Bai, C.-E., & Wei, S.-J. (2000, June). Quality of Bureaucracy and Open-Economy Macro Policies. *National Bureau of Economic Research Working Paper No. 7766.*

Becker, G. S. (1996). *Accounting for Tastes*. Cambridge: Harvard University Press.

Blume, A., & Sobel, J. (1995). Communication-Proof Equilibria in Cheap-Talk Games. *Journal of Economic Theory*, *65*(2), 359–382. doi:10.1006/jeth.1995.1013

Bosco, L., & Mittone, L. (1997). Tax Evasion and Moral Constraints: Some Experimental Evidence. *Kyklos*, *50*(3), 297–324. doi:10.1111/1467-6435.00018

Bowles, S. (1998). Endogenous Preferences: The Cultural Consequences of Markets and Other Economic Institutions. *Journal of Economic Literature*, *36*, 75–111.

Burki, S. J., & Perry, G. E. (1998). *Beyond the Washington Consensus: Institutions Matter*. Washington, DC: World Bank Publications. doi:10.1596/0-8213-4282-7

CAPMAS. (2013). *Annual Statistical Yearbook for the Arab Republic of Egypt*. Central Agency for Public Mobilisation and Statistics.

Crawford, V. P., & Sobel, J. (1982). Strategic Information Transmission. *Econometrica*, *50*(6), 1431–1451. doi:10.2307/1913390

Elffers, H. (1991). *Income Tax Evasion: Theory and Measurement*. Deventer: Kluwer.

Erard, B., & Feinstein, J. S. (1994). Honesty and Evasion in the Tax Compliance Game. *The Rand Journal of Economics*, *25*(1), 1–19. doi:10.2307/2555850

Farrell, J., & Gibbons, R. (1989). Cheap Talk with Two Audiences. *The American Economic Review*, *79*(5), 1214–1223.

Feld, L. P., & Tyran, J.-R. (2002). Tax Evasion and Voting: An Experimental Analysis. *Kyklos*, *55*(2), 197–221. doi:10.1111/1467-6435.00183

Graetz, M. J., & Wilde, L. L. (1985). The Economics of Tax Compliance: Fact and Fantasy. *National Tax Journal*, *38*, 355–363.

Kunicova, J., & Rose-Ackerman, S. (2005). Electoral Rules and Constitutional Structures as Constraints on Corruption. *British Journal of Political Science*, *35*(04), 573–606. doi:10.1017/S0007123405000311

Lederman, D., Loayza, N. V., & Soares, R. R. (2005). Accountability and Corruption: Political Institutions Matter. *Economics and Politics*, *17*(1), 1–35. doi:10.1111/j.1468-0343.2005.00145.x

Ledyard, J. O. (1995). Public goods: A Survey of Experimental Research. In J. H. Kagel & A. E. Roth (Eds.), *The Handbook of Experimental Economics* (pp. 111–194). Princeton: Princeton University Press.

Mauro, P. (1995). Corruption and Growth. *The Quarterly Journal of Economics*, *110*(3), 681–712. doi:10.2307/2946696

Financial Statement of State's General Budget for Fiscal Year 2012/2013. (2012). The Ministry of Finance.

The Financial Statement for the Government Budget Plan for the year 2014-2015. (2014). The Ministry of Finance.

Planning and Budgeting Committee Report on the Government Budget Bill for the year 2010/2011. (2010). The Planning and Budgeting Committee.

Torgler, B. (2001). Is Tax Evasion Never Justifiable? *Journal of Public Finance and Public Choice*, *19*, 143–168.

Wenzel, M. (2005). Motivation or Rationalisation? Causal Relations between Ethics, Norms and Tax Compliance. *Journal of Economic Psychology*, *26*(4), 491–508. doi:10.1016/j.joep.2004.03.003

ENDNOTES

1 For more details, go to http://www.mof.gov.eg/MOFGallerySource/English/PDF/Circular2013-2014.pdf

2 According to article 161, a two-thirds majority of parliament can initiate a motion to withdraw confidence from the president. Such a motion, however, has to be approved by the electorate in a public referendum. If rejected, the president remains in office and parliament is automatically dissolved.

3 The experiment was conducted in Cairo in 2013.

4 The World Bank Indicators series: http://data.worldbank.org/country

5 Local governments do have a property tax and agricultural tax with some discretion over rates but there is a mandated ceiling on those rates and little true revenue autonomy.

6 A very useful reference of comparative excise tax rates for EU countries is found in the European Commission report on excises: http://ec.europa.eu/taxation_customs/taxation/excise_duties/index_en.htm. This report demonstrates that there exists a very wide range of excise tax rates worldwide.

7 WEIRD stands for Western, Educated, Industrialized, Rich and Democratic.

8 Even in a country like the US, where levels of tax noncompliance are relatively low, the IRS (1997) estimated a revenue loss of around US$100 billion (see Andreoni, Erard, & Feinstein, 1998).

9 According to Feld and Tyran 2002, very high Arrow-Pratt measures of risk aversion (>30) must exist in order to account for the present compliance rate. Graetz and Wilde (1985) or Alm *et al.* (1992) report a range of between one and two for the U.S for different situations.

10 The field studies are limited as such data are confined to institutions and practices that have been in place lacking variability of the underlying parameters of interest.

11 Subjects are students from the University of Cairo. The instructions (in Arabic) were distributed in hardcopy to the subjects to ensure that subjects could refer to them at any time during the experiment for information on the audit rate, penalty structure, the value of the two public goods to officials and citizens and other details. Instructions are included in the Appendix. All subjects in our experiment knew that they faced the same tax rate as all other subjects.

12 See, for e.g., Ledyard (1995) for a definition of the marginal per capita return.

APPENDIX: SUBJECT INSTRUCTIONS FOR THE RECALL TREATMENT

Welcome and thank you for participating in today's experiment.

I. Introduction

This is an experiment in the economics of group decision making. Your earnings will be determined by your own decisions and the decisions of others as described in the following instructions. SO, IT IS IMPORTANT THAT YOU READ THESE INTRUCTIONS CAREFULLY.

This experiment is structured so that only you know your earnings. All of the money that you earn will be *paid to you privately in cash* immediately at the end of today's experiment. Various research agencies have provided the funds for the conduct of this research study.

If you have any questions, RAISE YOUR HAND and an experimenter will come up to you to answer questions in private. Please feel free to ask as many questions as you like.

Time

This experiment will last around two hours.

Scenario

In this experiment, you will be a member of a group of 5 individuals. You will be randomly assigned to a group and will remain in the same group for the entire experimental session.

Every group has an official who is selected randomly from among your group members by the computer at the beginning (before period 1) and in the middle (before period 8) of the experiment in the absence of a recall "election". Thus, a selected official remains the official of the group for seven periods unless the majority of members vote for a recall election. In case of a recall election, another official is selected randomly from among the eligible members of the group. A member of the group is eligible if he/she has not been a subject of a recall election during the last three elections. There are 14 decision periods in this experiment.

Anonymity

You will not know the rest of your group members, neither will they know you.

II. Monetary Payoff

You earn money in Experimental Pounds (EP) in each decision period. This amount will be displayed on your computer screen at the completion of the decision period. At the end of today's experiment, your total accumulated earnings in experimental pounds divided by the number of periods will be converted into Egyptian pounds at the below mentioned conversion rate. *The more experimental pounds you earn, the more Egyptian pounds you will be paid.*

1 Experimental Pound = 10 Egyptian Pounds

The following section explains how to earn money in each decision period.

III. Task and Decision Making Process

In this experiment, you will go through the below mentioned sequence of events in each of 14 decision periods.

Event I

All subjects are given a simple task to find the spelling mistakes in a piece of text on the computer. You will be given 2 minutes to conduct the task. You can make corrections to the text by using your mouse to place your cursor in the correct area and make the correction. Use the mouse to move you to other parts of the text. You will earn 2 Experimental Pounds for each mistake that you correct accurately. There are a total of 10 errors. This income will be displayed on your screen at the completion of the task.

Event II

Your earned income is what you earn in Event I. You will make the choice of how much of this earned income to report using the sliding scale on your screen. There is an income tax at 25% that you need to pay on the income you report. This tax rate is the same for all individuals belonging to the same group. As you move the slide to determine how much income you will report, you can see the consequences of your choice in terms of your net income if you are audited or not.

You can choose to report none of it, part of it or all of it. Consequently your reported tax liability is equal to:

25% Reported Income*

Event III

Once you choose the level of income you will report, a random audit will be performed. One subject out of five in the group will be chosen for audit so the likelihood of a subject being audited is 20%. If you are chosen for the random audit, your earned income will be disclosed to the official. If the audited individual's reported income in Event II is *less than* the earned income in Event I, then the individual pays, *in addition to the tax of* 25% of the *earned* income, a tax penalty that increases in the difference between the earned income and reported income as in the table that was handed out to you.

You pay a tax penalty only if you are audited and if your reported income is less than the earned income.

Event IV

Income taxes in this experiment will go into your group fund; they will be used to fund a *public project* that is valuable (in terms of experimental pounds) to you and your group members. Each experimental pound (EP) that goes in the public fund is tripled. Therefore,

Public fund = *3 * Income taxes collected from all the members in your group*

(Note: Tax penalty is not added to the public fund)

There are *two types* of public projects available in this experiment, Type C and Type G. The choice of which project is made available to you and your group is made by the official who is a member of your group.

The benefits of Type C good are shared equally among all 5 members of the group.

The benefits of Type G good accrue 50% to the official with the remainder split among the other four group members.

Earnings if Public Project of Type C is Funded

Public project earnings of:

- the official = Public fund / 5
- of each other member = Public fund / 5

Earnings if Public Project of Type G is Funded

Public project earnings of:

- the official = Public fund / 2
- of each other member = Public fund / 8

For example, if

Income taxes collected by the government in your group = 20 EP

*Public fund = 3*20 = 60 EP*

Earnings from public project of Type C:

When this project is chosen, then all the group members earn equal amount and the money in public fund is equally divided between all the group members.

Public project earnings = 60 /5 = 12 EP

Earnings from public project of Type G:

When this project is chosen, then the official will earn more than the rest of the group members: Half of the total amount of money in public fund is given to the official; the remaining half of the public fund is equally divided among all four remaining group members.

Public project earning of the official = 60/2 = 30 EP

Public project earnings of each other group members = 60/8 = 7.5 EP

Event V

Once the public good decision is made, you will see a screen that asks whether you would like a recall election or not. If the majority of the group chooses yes, then the computer will choose a new official.

The diagram in Figure 3 illustrates the sequence of events in every period.

Section IV below shows your total earnings or payoff in each decision period resulting from Events I to IV explained above.

IV. Earnings in Each Decision Period

Scenario I: If you are not audited

Total earnings = Earned Income – tax liability + public project earnings

(Note: As explained above, public project earnings depend on the type of public project provided to the group by the official)

Scenario II: If you are audited

Total earnings = Earned Income – tax liability – tax penalty + public project earnings

(Note: Tax penalty is equal to zero if your reported income is equal to your earned income)

(Also as explained above, public project earnings depend on the type of project provided to the group by the official)

Final earnings at the end of the experiment = (Total earnings in 14 rounds)/14

Figure 3.

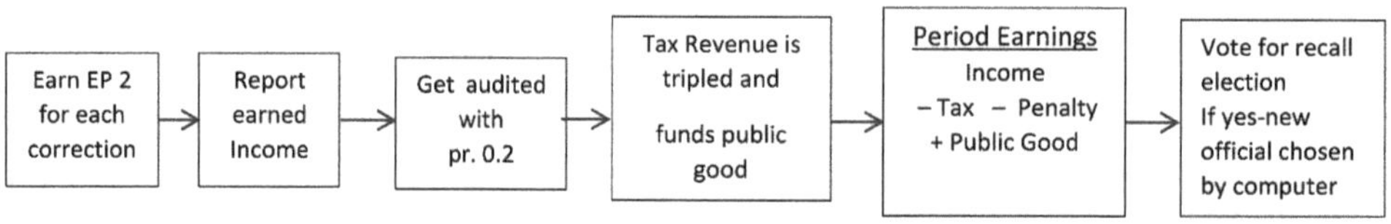

V. Questionnaire and Payment

At the end of today's experiment, you will complete a brief on-line questionnaire, receive payment of your earnings, and then the experiment is over. Information about your decisions will be kept without identifying information so no one can link you as an individual to the decisions that you make.

Chapter 16
Analyzing and Reforming Tunisia's Tax System

James Alm
Tulane University, USA

ABSTRACT

Tunisia's tax system has undergone significant structural reforms over the last several decades. Even so, its structure exhibits some major flaws, shortcomings that spill over to and affect the performance of the overall Tunisian economy. Further, the tax system continues to underperform in some fundamental ways, ways that also affect the rest of the economy. Finally, the structure of the Tunisian tax system has some notable shortcomings. This paper discusses these issues. It presents details of the main taxes, it analyzes several main features of this tax system, and it suggests various specific tax reforms that can be introduced both in the short term and in the longer term.

INTRODUCTION

Tunisia's tax system has undergone significant structural reforms over the last several decades. Even so, however, its structure exhibits some major flaws, shortcomings that spill over to and affect the performance of the overall Tunisian economy. Further, the tax system continues to underperform in some fundamental ways, ways that also affect the rest of the economy. Finally, the structure of the Tunisian tax system has some notable shortcomings. This chapter discusses these issues. It presents details of the main taxes, it analyzes several main features of this tax system, and it suggests various specific tax reforms that can be introduced both in the short term and in the longer term.

As demonstrated below, the flaws of the Tunisian tax system are many and significant. There are large amounts of tax evasion, with the size of the Tunisian underground economy estimated to be roughly 1/3 of official output. Reflective of this evasion, as well as of the extensive use of fiscal, financial, and other preferences, there is a narrow and shrinking tax base that is subject to especially high tax rates (especially on individuals). There are also significant limitations in tax administration. Contributing to the ineffective tax administration is a tax system that is excessively and unnecessarily complex. There is also a widespread belief that the tax system is both unfair and distorting to individuals and firm, although precise

DOI: 10.4018/978-1-5225-0053-7.ch016

quantitative assessments of these inequities and inefficiencies are seldom provided. Overall, it is clear that the current system is an outdated and an ad hoc system, designed for a world that no longer exists.

Given these problems, a comprehensive reform of the Tunisian tax system may well be justified, along the standard lines of broadening the bases of taxation and reducing the rates of taxation. However, comprehensive reform typically takes considerable time and effort. A more immediate strategy would be to enact several incremental reforms that would improve the operation of the Tunisian economy. Potential reform measures include expanding the base of indirect taxes, increasing value-added tax rates, reducing the widespread use of incentives, reducing personal income and/or Social Security contribution rates, reforming the simplified tax system, and improving tax administration. Indeed, the evidence in this paper suggests that tax rates on individuals could be reduced, maybe even substantially, without much fiscal impact. Reducing the overall tax burden on individuals, while shifting to a heavier focus on indirect taxes, is important for encouraging higher rates of formal sector job creation.

The next section describes the current Tunisian tax system in some detail. The following sections compare Tunisian tax practice to international practices and analyze some of the main effects of these taxes. The final section presents some issues that need to be considered in any possible reform of the tax system.

BACKGROUND: THE TAX SYSTEM IN TUNISIA

The Tunisian tax system can be divided into two major categories: direct taxes (including the corporate income tax, the personal income tax, and payroll taxes) and indirect taxes (e.g., the value added tax and consumption duties). The tax system includes the following taxes:

- Customs Taxes.
- Value Added Tax.
- Consumption Duties.
- Personal Income Tax.
- Corporate Income Tax.
- Registration Taxes and Stamp Duties.
- Various Taxes on Certain Products, Transportation, Insurance, Hotels, and the Like.

Even aside from the individual income tax, the government imposes a variety of taxes on the wages of workers. Some of these taxes are more properly viewed as "contributions" because individuals are entitled to benefits, the size of which varies with their contributions. Some may also be seen as a way to force people to save for old age or for insurance against health problems and occupational injury. Several have all the features of a tax, but nevertheless do not go into the general revenues of the government and instead are used to finance government and non-government provision of social insurance. In total, these various payroll taxes (or "Social Security contributions") constitute a significant additional burden on labor.

Since 1988, the Tunisian tax system has undergone a series of reforms as part of broader structural reforms in different economic sectors and financial companies. These reforms have affected all types of taxes. Overall, following broad principles of "best" international practices, tax rates have been reduced, tax bases have been broadened, incentives have been streamlined, and various administrative procedures have been implemented to ensure that taxpayers have more legal protections. The main reform procedures have included institution of a VAT (from 1 July 1988), establishment of a single tax on income and profits, redesign of registration and stamp taxes, rationalization of tax and financial incentives, revision of insurance sector taxation, reform of some local taxes, and promulgation of the Code of Tax Rights and Procedures. Collections from these various taxes and contributions are shown in Table 1 (in millions of TND), Table 2 (as a percent of taxes), in Table 3 (as a percent of GDP).

These tables indicate several main findings. First, the ratio of taxes plus Social Security contributions to GDP is fairly constant over time at roughly 25 percent of GDP. As discussed later, this ratio is comparable to other middle income countries. Second, the value added tax (VAT) is the most important single tax, accounting for nearly 1/3 of total taxes. Third and relatedly, indirect taxes are a more important source of revenues than direct taxes, as measured by total collections, percent of total Taxes, and percent of GDP. However, the relative importance of direct taxes (i.e., corporate income taxes, personal income taxes) has increased over time. Further, the relative importance of Social Security contributions has also increased over time. Both of these trends suggest a growing relative burden on labor. Each of the major taxes is considered next.

Personal Income Tax (PIT)

The personal income tax is due from any person who is a permanent resident of Tunisia. Nonresidents are also subject to the tax based on their Tunisian income. Taxable income is based on a "comprehensive income" concept, and includes in principle income from: salaries, wages, pensions and annuities; business profits; benefits of non-commercial professions; profits from farming and fishing; salaries, wages, pensions and annuities; property income; foreign source income if the individual has not paid income taxes in the country of source. Capital gains are taxed as ordinary income for residents, with some preferences for longer held properties; for example, the tax rate is 5 percent if the property is held longer than 10 years. The unit of taxation is the individual, and joint returns are not allowed.

There are various exemptions, exclusions, and deductions. The net income of individuals is determined after deduction of 10 percent for salaries and wages, 25 percent for pensions and annuities (which increases under some conditions to 80 percent for pensions and annuities from abroad under certain conditions, and 30 percent for property tax revenues and profits for non-commercial professions determined on a contract basis. Excluded forms of income include: salaries for foreign diplomatic and consular subject to reciprocity; payments for compensation for injury, dividends; interest from deposits and securities in foreign currency or convertible TND; interest of home savings accounts; interest from special savings accounts opened with the National Savings Bank of Tunisia (CENT) and banks and bonds revenue within certain limits. Deductions are allowed (within certain limits) for: premiums on life insurance contracts; deductions for marital status and dependents (e.g., married taxpayer, dependent children, dependent parents); a 500 TND additional deduction for employees earning the minimum wage; and income reinvested in the capital subscription of companies under the conditions laid down in legislation governing the tax benefits.

The tax rates imposed on the resulting based are progressive, starting at 15 percent for net income between 1500 and 5000 TND and rising to 35 percent on net income above 50,000 TND (see Table 4).

The personal income tax is paid mainly via source withholding tax on wages, fees, commissions, rents, movable capital, royalties, contracts, and amounts equal to or greater than 1000 TND paid by the state and public authorities or greater than 5000 TND paid by corporations and individuals under

Table 1. Composition of consolidated central government revenues for Tunisia (In millions of TND)

	2000	2001	2002	2003	2004	2005	2006	2007	2008	2009	2010
Taxes	5678.4	6221.5	6429.1	6630.8	7252.0	7904.2	8469.8	9508.1	11330.9	11763.7	12738.9
Taxes on income, profits, and capital gains	1596.8	1827.7	2024.3	2176.9	2385.2	2886.2	3106.7	3697.7	4560.9	4645.5	5047.4
Personal Income Tax	1021.8	1152.8	1213.6	1309.0	1436.8	1524.2	1716.8	1948.8	2145.3	2379.0	2614.4
Corporate Income Tax	575.0	674.9	810.7	867.9	948.4	1362.0	1389.9	1748.9	2415.6	2266.5	2433.0
Taxes on payroll and workforce	106.7	107.8	80.8	118.4	121.1	114.2	137.1	148.6	142.7	170.9	199.0
Taxes on property	121.3	134.0	138.9	135.6	148.7	169.6	206.7	216.8	237.4	264.1	280.3
Taxes on goods and services	2903.6	3157.1	3239.3	3359.8	3690.1	3836.8	4056.9	4373.2	5061.2	5377.3	5775.2
VAT	1929.7	2087.2	2103.2	2170.8	2426.7	2482.9	2652.8	2864.4	3480.9	3636.9	4031.3
Excises	790.6	865.5	914.2	954.2	1020.6	1050.5	1074.5	1149.7	1201.9	1260.8	1298.8
Taxes on international. trade and transactions	833.6	875.5	790.8	725.9	752.3	735.1	758.0	825.7	965.0	987.6	1142.6
Other taxes	116.4	119.4	155.0	114.2	154.6	162.3	204.4	246.1	363.7	318.3	294.4
Social Security contributions	1328.2	1445.2	1546.9	1780.8	1837.3	1925.1	2204.9	2446.2	2823.9	3431.5	3865.8

Note: "Social Security contributions" are not included in total "Taxes". Not all sub-items of "Taxes on goods and services" are listed.

Source: Government of Tunisia.

Table 2. Composition of consolidated central government revenues for Tunisia (As percent of total taxes)

	2000	2001	2002	2003	2004	2005	2006	2007	2008	2009	2010
Taxes	100	100	100	100	100	100	100	100	100	100	100
Taxes on income, profits, and capital gains	28.12	29.38	31.49	32.83	32.89	36.51	36.68	38.89	40.25	39.49	39.62
Personal Income Tax	17.99	18.53	18.88	19.74	19.81	19.28	20.27	20.50	18.93	20.22	20.52
Corporate Income Tax	10.13	10.85	12.61	13.09	13.08	17.23	16.41	18.39	21.32	19.27	19.10
Taxes on payroll and workforce	1.88	1.73	1.26	1.79	1.67	1.44	1.62	1.56	1.26	1.45	1.56
Taxes on property	2.14	2.15	2.16	2.05	2.05	2.15	2.44	2.28	2.10	2.25	2.20
Taxes on goods and services	51.13	50.74	50.38	50.67	50.88	48.54	47.90	45.99	44.67	45.71	45.34
VAT	33.98	33.55	32.71	32.74	33.46	31.41	31.32	30.13	30.72	30.92	31.65
Excises	13.92	13.91	14.22	14.39	14.07	13.29	12.69	12.09	10.61	10.72	10.20
Taxes on international. trade and transactions	14.68	14.07	12.30	10.95	10.37	9.30	8.95	8.68	8.52	8.40	8.97
Other taxes	2.05	1.92	2.41	1.72	2.13	2.05	2.41	2.59	3.21	2.71	2.31

Note: "Social Security contributions" are not included in total "Taxes". Not all sub-items of "Taxes on goods and services" are listed.
Source: Government of Tunisia.

Table 3. Composition of consolidated central government revenues for Tunisia (As percent of GDP)

	2000	2001	2002	2003	2004	2005	2006	2007	2008	2009	2010
Taxes	19.29	19.60	19.54	18.75	18.67	18.88	18.51	19.06	20.49	20.02	20.12
Taxes on income, profits, and capital gains	5.43	5.76	6.15	6.15	6.14	6.89	6.79	7.41	8.25	7.90	7.97
Personal Income Tax	3.47	3.63	3.69	3.70	3.70	3.64	3.75	3.91	3.88	4.05	4.13
Corporate Income Tax	1.95	2.13	2.46	2.45	2.44	3.25	3.04	3.51	4.37	3.86	3.84
Taxes on payroll and workforce	0.36	0.34	0.25	0.33	0.31	0.27	0.30	0.30	0.26	0.29	0.31
Taxes on property	0.41	0.42	0.42	0.38	0.38	0.41	0.45	0.43	0.43	0.45	0.44
Taxes on goods and services	9.86	9.94	9.85	9.50	9.50	9.16	8.87	8.77	9.15	9.15	9.12
VAT	6.56	6.57	6.39	6.14	6.25	5.93	5.80	5.74	6.29	6.19	6.37
Excises	2.69	2.73	2.78	2.70	2.63	2.51	2.35	2.31	2.17	2.15	2.05
Taxes on international. trade and transactions	2.83	2.76	2.40	2.05	1.94	1.76	1.66	1.66	1.75	1.68	1.80
Other taxes	0.40	0.38	0.47	0.32	0.40	0.39	0.45	0.49	0.66	0.54	0.46
Social Security contributions	4.51	4.55	4.70	5.03	4.73	4.60	4.82	4.90	5.11	5.84	6.10

Note: "Social Security contributions" are not included in total "Taxes". Not all sub-items of "Taxes on goods and services" are listed in the table.
Source: Government of Tunisia and World Development Indicators.

Table 4. Tax rates in personal income tax

Taxable Income (TND)	Tax Rate (Percent)
0-1500	0
1500-5000	15
5000-10,000	20
10,000-20,000	25
20,000-50,000	30
Over 50,000	35

the real Regime. It may also be paid via three installments each equal to 30 percent of the tax of the previous year payable during the 6th, 9th, and 12th months. The withholding and advance installments are deductible from the final tax.

Corporate Income Tax (CIT)

Like most corporate income taxes, the tax is imposed on the net income of companies, determined from accounting records in accordance with the law after deducting all expenses and professional charges, including: depreciation (on a straight line, declining balance, or accelerated basis); provisions for "bad" debts (under some conditions); inventory adjustments; donations and grants (up to a maximum of 2 percent of sales); and reinvested earnings (under some conditions). As with the personal income tax, capital gains are taxed as ordinary income. The tax is due from capital companies established in Tunisia, from cooperatives, from public non-administrative companies having a profit, and from foreign businesses not established in Tunisia because of their Tunisian source income. Losses may be carried forward for four years, and deferred depreciation may be carried forward indefinitely. The distribution of dividends is exempt from any tax.

The general tax rate in the corporate income tax is 30 percent. There is also a reduced rate of 10 percent that is applicable to small businesses, agriculture, handicrafts, and fishing, and there is a different (and higher) tax rate of 35 percent on firms in the financial, telecommunications, insurance, oil production, refining, transport, and distribution sectors.

The Ministry of Finance indicates that there were in total 103,772 companies in Tunisia at the end of 2012. Of these, 21,017 were joint-stock companies operating as offshore companies, 80,890 were joint-stock non-offshore companies, and 1859 were partnerships (27 offshore and 1832 non-offshore companies). The dominant sectors in terms of numbers of firms were services (27,476), industrial activities (22,638), non-commercial activities (19,228), wholesale trade activities (18,348), and retail trade activities (13,318).

Value Added Tax (VAT)

The value added tax (VAT) is imposed on the difference between revenues and purchased inputs (e.g., the "value added") in goods and services, merchandise imports, industrial and artisanal production, services, wholesale trade (other than food, drugs, and pharmaceuticals), retail trade when the overall annual turnover exceeds 100.000 TND (excluding food, medicines, pharmaceutical products, and products subject to the approval of administrative prices). Some professions are exempt, as are some products (e.g., books, newspapers, periodicals, milk, bread, couscous, vegetable oil) and some services (e.g., international air transport, maritime transport, bank interest receivable).

The tax base for imports is the customs value of the good, including all costs, duties and taxes other than VAT for taxable, as established by Decree No. 2003-477 of 3 March 2003. The base for other (internal) products is in the price of goods, works, or services, including all fees, charges, and taxes (excluding the VAT itself).

Tax rates vary by type of good: 6 percent for fertilizer, handicrafts, medical activities, canned food, and compound feed for cattle; 12 percent for computers, computer services, hospitality, food, equipment not produced locally, and 4 horsepower cars; and 18 percent as the general rate applicable to products and services not subject to another rate. Goods and services subject to these specific rates (e.g., 6 percent, 12 percent, 18 percent) and exempt goods and services are determined in specific tables. Exports are zero-rated.

The VAT is collected using the credit invoice method. The VAT paid on inputs is deductible (or credited) from the VAT collected on sales of the month. The credit is carried forward to the next month, or refundable under some conditions.

Consumption Duties

Consumption duties are applied to: wine, beer, alcohol and alcoholic beverages; tobacco; fuels; and personal vehicles. The taxes are imposed either as ad valorem rates (starting at 10 percent) or as specific taxes (e.g., on wine, beer, alcohol and alcoholic beverages, fuels).

Registration Fees

Various registration fees are imposed on such activities and transactions as the sale of property, the sale of business assets, gifts and inheritances, acts of companies, and legal judgments. These taxes are imposed either as ad valorem rates or as specific excises. For example, the sale of property is taxed at 5 percent of the value for the sale of property, sales of business assets are taxes at 2.5 percent of the value for sales of business assets, and gifts and inheritances are taxed at 2.5 percent for transfers between spouses, 5 percent between siblings, and 25 percent or 35 percent for other degrees of relationship. Specific taxes are 15 TND per action for the transfer of assets and securities under certain conditions, and 100 TND per action for company activities like incorporation.

Other Indirect Taxes

There are various miscellaneous indirect taxes such as: the professional training tax at the rate of 1 percent of gross payroll for manufacturing industries and the rate of 2 percent in other cases; the contribution to the fund to promote social housing at a rate of 1 percent of gross payroll; and a tax on insurance contracts at 5 percent of written premiums for insurance contracts for maritime and air transport and at 10 percent for other contracts.

Social Security Contributions

There are several payroll taxes that finance various types of social insurance for employees, including pensions and protection against risks like unemployment, disability, sickness and maternity. The applicable social security regimes differ according to the professional category. In the non-agricultural sector, there is a general regime, and a supplemental regime for self-employed; in agriculture, employees and the other operators are covered. The contribution rates vary by regimes, and the resulting benefits also vary by regime. For example, non-agricultural self-employed workers do not receive family benefits, and agricultural employees, self-employed workers in the non-agricultural sector, farmers and self-employed in agriculture, and public officials benefit from specific provisions.

Employers with employees are required to join the National Social Security Fund. Self-employed workers may join voluntarily, in order to ensure against the risks of labor accidents and occupational diseases. Public officials have a special regime. The Security Fund (CNSS) administers pensions, disability, survivor, death, unemployment, and family benefits through its regional offices in the capitals of governorates. Sickness, maternity, work accidents, and occupational diseases are managed by the National Fund of Health Insurance (CNAM).

The contribution rates are generally imposed on full wages of the worker (although the supplementary pension contributions are paid on the portion of salary that exceeds six times the minimum wage). Each program has a different employee and employer contribution rate. For example, the employer contribution to the old age, disability, and survivor scheme is 7.76 percent, and the employee contribution is 4.73 percent. The contribution rates for sickness and maternity are 5.08 percent and 3.16 percent. The mandatory contribution to the accidents and occupational diseases regime is borne only by the employer, and it varies between 0.4 percent and 4 percent by sector of activity; this contribution may be increased or reduced, depending on whether the employer breaches safety rules or makes extensive prevention efforts. Contributions are made to the CNSS on a quarterly basis. These rates are shown in Table 5.

In total, the combined employer and employee tax rate ranges from 26.15 to 29.75 percent. Participation in the supplementary pension adds another 9 percent to these contribution rates.

Fiscal, Financial, and Other Incentives

Passed as legislation in January 1994, the Investment Incentives Code governs both national and foreign investment. Three classes of incentives exist under the Investment Incentives Code: *financial* incentives that involve the direct transfer of funds (e.g., grants, loans) from the treasury; *fiscal* incentives like tax exemptions or credits whereby government revenue that is otherwise due is foregone; and the *giving of public lands* for nominal sums of money. These incentives are available to: "offshore" companies operating in export processing zones (EPZ); companies engaged in industrial, agricultural, tourism, and public works projects; companies that provide services; companies engaged in health, education, and environmental initiatives; and investments in underdeveloped regions. Small and medium sized enterprises are also accorded special status under the law. Commercial activities, financial services, mining operations, and energy activities are not eligible for any such incentives.

Tunisia's "offshore" investment framework operates as a traditional enterprise-specific EPZ regime. Offshore EPZ companies that export 70 percent of their finished goods or services are entitled to corporate income tax, VAT, customs duty, consumption taxes, turnover taxes, and foreign exchange control

Table 5. Contribution rates in social insurance programs

Type	Employer Contribution	Employee Contribution	Total
Old age, disability, and survivor	7.76%	4.73%	12.50%
Sickness and maternity	5.08%	3.16%	8.24%
Family benefits	2.21%	0.88%	3.10%
Accidents / Occupational diseases	0.4 – 4%	-	0.4 – 4%
Welfare workers - Special Fund of State	1.51%	0.38%	1.90%
Total	16.97 – 20.57%	9.18%	26.15 – 29.75%
Supplementary pension	6%	3%	9%

Note: The Supplementary pension is only for those companies that elect to join this regime.

exemptions. Nevertheless, the various employee-related taxes remain applicable, including the personal income tax and Social Security contributions, both for employee and employer contributions. Foreign nationals working for an offshore EPZ company are entitled to a preferential, fixed personal income-tax rate of 20 percent. Offshore EPZ companies enjoy the legal right to sell 30 percent of their finished goods or services in the local home market; however, such sales are subject to all applicable taxes, duties, and foreign exchange controls, including the 30 percent corporate income tax, the governing VAT, applicable customs duties, the 10 percent consumption tax, and the governing turnover tax.

Effective 1 January 2013, offshore EPZ companies will be subject to a 10 percent corporate income tax for their export sales. This legislative modification was required for Tunisia to comply with its international obligations arising under the WTO Subsidies Agreement. Nevertheless, the 20 percent differential between this forthcoming 10 percent income tax rate and the generally applicable 30 percent income tax rate constitutes an export subsidy that is per se prohibited by the WTO Subsidies Code. No available evidence appears to exist on the WTO website that demonstrates that the WTO Subsidies Committee has ever granted Tunisia an extension to maintain its offshore export subsidies.

There are also several "common" incentives, including tax relief on reinvested profits and income up to 35 percent of the income or profits subject to tax, customs duties exemptions for capital goods that have no locally made counterparts, and VAT exemptions on some capital goods imports (1999 Finance Act provisions).

More specific incentives are of several types. First, there are advantages to fully exporting companies. These incentives include, such as: full tax exemption on export-derived profits for the first 10 years and taxation at a low rate after for companies established before 2012; taxation at the rate of 10 percent for the first 10 years for the companies established in 2012; full exemption on reinvested profits and income; duty free profits for capital goods including merchandise transport vehicles, raw materials, semi-finished products, and services needed by the business; and the possibility of selling on the local market (i.e., 30 percent of turnover for industrial goods and agricultural products, along with payment of applicable duty and levies, increased to 50 percent for the year 2011).

Second, there are incentives for firms operating in zones designed for regional development. These incentives are similar to those for exporting companies, and include: full tax exemption on reinvested profits and income; deduction from the tax base for the personal or the corporate income tax of income or profits on investments in industry, tourism, handicrafts, or certain service activities (e.g., tax holidays); and assumption by the state of the employer's contribution to the Social Security system.

Third, there are incentives for agricultural development, including: full tax exemption on reinvested profits and income; full tax exemption for the 10 first years of operation; VAT suspension on imported capital goods that have no locally-made counterparts; state provision of infrastructure expenses to develop areas meant for fish farming and for cultivations using geothermal water; 7 percent bonus on investment value; 8 percent additional bonus on investment value granted for agricultural investments achieved in hard-climate regions (e.g., Gabes, Gafsa, Medenine, Kebili, Tataouine, Tozeur), which can go as high as 25 percent for areas around Gafsa that are in the process of converting from mining to other activities; and 25 percent additional bonus on investment value for fishing projects in the north coastline ports from Bizerte to Tabarka.

Fourth, there are specific incentives that relate to investments made by companies for environmental protection and waste processing (e.g., 50 percent tax reduction on reinvested income or profits, taxation of income and profits at a reduced 10 percent rate, 20 percent premium on the value of investments, and VAT suspension on specific capital goods).

Fifth, there are incentives for research development and technology promotion.

Sixth, there are specific incentives to support investment by education, training, cultural production, health and transport industries. These incentives include the deduction of reinvested profits up to 50 percent of net profits subject to corporate tax, a reduced tax rate of 10 percent on income and profits, and VAT suspension for imported capital goods having no similar locally-made counterparts.

Le Regime Forfaitaire

Like nearly all countries, Tunisia attempts to simplify the compliance burden on some specific types of taxpayers by the use of a simplified tax system, called *Le Regime Forfaitaire*. The use of this regime for some taxpayers is broadly consistent with the use of presumptive methods of income taxation for these taxpayers, in which the "desired" base for taxation is not itself measured but is instead inferred from some simple indicators that are more easily measured than the base itself. Presumptive methods are used for a variety of reasons: to reduce the compliance costs on taxpayers by making it easier for these taxpayers to compute their tax liabilities, to simplify tax administration by removing some taxpayers (usually those with small tax liabilities) from the tax rolls and by providing more obvious and more direct measures of tax liabilities, to improve tax equity by providing more objective indicators of tax assessment, to reduce corruption by eliminating official discretion in assessing tax liabilities, to encourage taxpayers to keep better accounts in order to provide documentation that may reduce their presumptive tax liabilities, and to improve incentive effects when, say, income above the presumptive level is not subject to taxation.

This simplified tax system in Tunisia has been in force since 1 January 2011. It is intended for individual-owned firms that meet certain criteria. For example, the individual cannot import, cannot manufacture alcohol-based products, and cannot own more than one vehicle whose load cannot exceed 3.5 tons. Most importantly, the annual turnover of the firm cannot exceed 100,000 TND (for firms that resell, process, and consume onsite) or 50,000 TND (for service activities). The tax rate is Tunisia is 2 percent for firms that resell/process/consume, and 2.5 percent for all other firms. The forfaitaire liability cannot be less than 50 TND for firms outside communal areas and less than 100 TND for other firms. Importantly, eligible firms do not have to pay other taxes. Recent information (2012) from the Ministry of Finance indicates that of 633,177 registered taxpayers, 408,369 are in *Le Regime Forfaitaire*.

Local Government Taxes

Local governments impose a variety of taxes and fees, including: a tax on commercial, industrial, or professional companies; a hotel tax; a property tax; a tax on undeveloped lands; market fees; and fees for electricity, street lighting, and maintenance. These taxes and fees in total generate little revenues.

ANALYSIS

Issues and Controversies: Some International Comparisons

Tunisia raises roughly one-quarter of GDP in taxes in 2010. A natural question to ask is whether Tunisia has an "adequate" *level* of revenue mobilization. This is no easy question to answer. There is also the question of whether the competitiveness of the Tunisian economy is weakened by overreliance on certain forms of taxation (e.g., income taxes) relative to other comparable countries; that is, the *structure* of taxation in Tunisia is a relevant consideration. The *tax rates* of the individual taxes are also essential factors. Each of these areas is discussed.

Level of Taxes

When the level of taxation (including Social Security contributions) in Tunisia (as a percent of GDP in 2010) is compared to a subset of relevant Middle East and North Africa (MENA) countries (e.g., Algeria, Bahrain, Djibouti, Egypt, Iran, Iraq, Israel, Jordan, Kuwait, Lebanon, Libya, Malta, Morocco, Oman, Qatar, Saudi Arabia, Syria, United Arab Emirates, West Bank and Gaza, Yemen), taxes relative to GDP are generally higher for Tunisia than for the median of other MENA countries. More generally, Table 6 shows the average level of taxes as a percent of GDP by country grouping for the last four decades. Tunisia's level of taxes is lower than industrialized countries but higher than developing countries, roughly half-way between the levels of taxes in these two groups.

A more traditional "tax effort" analysis gives similar conclusions. Using IMF data, it is possible to compare the tax ratio (Taxes plus Social Security contributions as a share of GDP) for 117 countries. These data show the ratio for Tunisia to be 23.5 percent of GDP in 2005, by comparison with an average for this sample of countries of 23.6 percent of GDP. This simple comparison suggests that Tunisia has an average level of taxation, although averages are misleading because countries may be different from one another in terms of their capacity to tax.

The use of ordinary least squares (OLS) regression analysis provides a more controlled examination of tax effort, in which a set of explanatory variables that reflect country differences in taxable capacity is used to predict taxes as a percent of GDP. These independent variables and the hypotheses about the ways in which they should effect tax revenue mobilization are:

- The level of per capita GDP should be positively related to the tax ratio because higher GDP suggests a greater capacity to tax.
- The degree to which the economy is open to trade is a determinant of the tax ratio. The greater a country's propensity to trade with other countries, the easier it is to raise revenues because the

Table 6. Tax revenues (Revenues as percent of GDP)

	Decade			
Country Group	**1970s**	**1980s**	**1990s**	**2000s**
Industrialized	30.1 (8.3)	33.7 (8.4)	35.5 (8.5)	33.4 (8.4)
Developing	16.2 (7.6)	17.3 (8.3)	17.0 (7.7)	17.0 (7.9)
Transition		47.7 (9.7)	29.6 (11.0)	29.1 (9.0)
Total	19.8 (9.9)	21.6 (11.3)	22.6 (11.5)	21.8 (10.4)

Notes: The numbers represent decade averages for the relevant country groupings, with standard deviations in parentheses.
Source: International Monetary Fund *Government Finance Statistics*, various issues.

(administrative) tax handles are in place; the government may also play a larger risk-reducing role in more open economies that are exposed to greater external risks. "Openness" is measured as the sum of imports and exports divided by GDP.

- The size of the agricultural sector relative to GDP should dampen taxable capacity and be negatively related to the level of the tax ratio. Countries with a larger agricultural share have fewer good (administrative) tax handles, and the agricultural sector itself can be politically hard to tax.
- Countries with smaller populations should raise a greater share of GDP in revenues than countries with larger populations because there are fixed costs of government that are independent of country size.
- The rate of population growth is also related to the level of revenue mobilization. Faster growing places tend to lag behind in the amount of revenue they raise per dollar of GDP, in part because of lags in moving the population into the tax base.

OLS regressions can be estimated with various combinations of these explanatory variables, with all variables measured in logarithms (see Box 1).

These results can be used to estimate an "expected" level of the tax ratio for Tunisia. For example, across the various specifications Tunisia "should" raise on average 25 percent of GDP in taxes. The

Box 1. Regression results for the determinants of tax revenue to GDP ratio

Some simple OLS regressions are reported in Box-Table I below. The dependent variable is the ratio of tax revenue to GDP; various explanatory variables are used in different specifications. The sample consists of 119 developed and developing countries for the period 2000 to 2009.

The explanatory variables are in general statistically significant and with the expected signs. The Tax/GDP ratio is significantly higher in countries where per capita GDP and openness are higher, and where the agricultural share of GDP and the population growth rate are lower. The regressions explain between 47 and 67 percent of the variation. The ratio of "predicted" Tax/GDP to "actual" Tax/GDP is used to generate the estimated "tax effort" of Tunisia.

Box-Table I: Regression results

	Specifications			
Variables	**(1)**	**(2)**	**(3)**	**(4)**
Constant	-0.65 (1.07)	2.97 (8.81)	1.21 (3.75)	3.23 (9.75)
Per Capita GDP	0.23 (12.11)		0.21 (6.19)	
Openness	0.31 (3.99)	0.27 (3.26)	0.22 (4.17)	0.32 (3.12)
Population Size	0.06 (1.61)			
Agricultural Share of GDP		-0.37 (7.81)		-0.26 (6.43)
Population Growth Rate			-0.19 (4.27)	-0.24 (8.41)
Adjusted R^2	0.59	0.47	0.67	0.65
Observations	119	119	119	119

Notes: Data are averages for the period 2000-2009. All variables are expressed in logarithms, except the population growth rate. t-statistics are shown in parentheses.

Source: Calculations by author

actual ratio of taxes to GDP in the 2000s was 24 percent. The ratio of the actual to the estimated is the "tax effort" coefficient. Thus Tunisia's tax effort coefficient is 0.96, which can be interpreted as showing that Tunisia ranks comparable to but slightly (or 4 percent) below the international average tax effort, although this difference is not highly significant.

Based on this international comparison, Tunisia appears to be an average-tax country, neither a high-tax nor a low-tax country. Some could point to this result as one of the competitive features of the Tunisian economy, and argue that taxes should be held at their present level. Others may see this as evidence that there is at least some room for additional taxes.

There are important reservations to this conclusion. These results show that overall collections in Tunisia are roughly at the international average. It may well be the case that liabilities are high, and that Tunisians who comply with the tax laws face tax burdens that are high by international standards; however, it is not possible to make such a comparison among the countries in the sample because data are not available. Estimates of the Tunisian "shadow economy" are presented later.

In this regard, an important attribute of a tax system is an ability to generate automatic growth in fiscal revenues over time. A common measure of this dynamic property is the ratio of the proportional change in tax revenues to the proportional change in GDP, known as "buoyancy". One way to measure buoyancy is with regression analysis. Using data from over the last decade to estimate the response of the natural logarithm of the revenue to the natural logarithm of GDP series, the resulting coefficient for GDP provides an estimate of the average buoyancy of the revenue series over the period. Over this period, tax revenue buoyancy has been roughly unity, or 1.02 for total tax revenues. Also, there are significant differences in performance among different sources of tax revenues. Personal and corporate income taxes, the VAT, and Social Security contributions have estimated buoyancies well in excess of 1, excises and international trade taxes had values much below 1. However, these estimates do not have significant precision.

Tax Structure

A different issue is whether Tunisia's tax *structure* (as opposed to the *level* of taxes) is similar to that of other countries. Table 7 presents International Monetary Fund *Government Finance Statistics* data for three tax groupings: income taxes, indirect taxes, and taxes on international trade. Table 7 demonstrates that the burden of income taxation is considerably higher in Tunisia than in other developing countries, and that the burden of indirect taxes sales taxes (including trade taxes) is lower in Tunisia than in other developing countries. These tax structure differences suggest that income taxes, particularly personal income taxes, are used more heavily in Tunisia than in many other comparable countries, supporting the observation made by many that Tunisia taxes labor very heavily.

Table 8 presents similar information, now broken down by specific countries and using International Monetary Fund *Government Finance Statistics* data for 2010, with taxes divided into four groups: income and payroll taxes, property taxes, indirect taxes, and taxes on international trade. The relative reliance on each of these groups is shown in Table 8, in a comparison of Tunisia with all countries for which data are available. Again, Tunisia has relatively heavier reliance on income and payroll taxes, and relatively less reliance on trade taxes, than the average country in this sample.

These comparisons do not control for country characteristics that might affect collections. By comparing actual personal income tax revenues (plus Social Security contributions) to estimated revenues, it is again possible to calculate indexes of tax effort by country, now by specific tax.

Table 7. Tax structure (Taxes as percent of total taxes)

		Decade			
		1970s	1980s	1990s	2000s
Income Tax	Industrialized	35.5 (15.1)	37.8 (13.7)	38.6 (10.9)	53.8 (8.1)
	Developing	29.6 (19.5)	28.6 (19.1)	27.6 (16.5)	28.3 (17.8)
	Transition	12.3 (14.4)	16.5 (13.8)	26.7 (9.6)	23.3 (6.5)
	Total	30.7 (18.8)	30.2 (18.5)	29.7 (15.4)	28.5 (16.4)
Indirect Taxes	Industrialized	27.2 (10.1)	29.4 (9.0)	30.5 (10.1)	19.8 (10.7)
	Developing	25.2 (14.3)	29.3 (17.3)	34.9 (17.7)	40.1 (17.8)
	Transition	10.5 (11.1)	21.8 (14.4)	37.9 (12.3)	42.1 (9.6)
	Total	25.3 (13.5)	28.9 (15.8)	34.2 (15.9)	39.0 (16.4)
Taxes on International Trade	Industrialized	4.6 (5.8)	2.8 (4.3)	1.0 (2.0)	1.0 (0.6)
	Developing	32.4 (18.4)	30.7 (20.2)	25.6 (18.9)	19.0 (18.0)
	Transition	7.7 (8.2)	5.2 (3.8)	7.6 (7.3)	5.4 (5.5)
	Total	25.2 (20.2)	23.8 (21.4)	18.2 (18.9)	14.1 (16.5)

Notes: The numbers represent decade averages for the relevant country groupings, with standard deviations in parentheses.
Source: International Monetary Fund *Government Finance Statistics*, various issues.

Table 8. Tunisia's tax structure in international perspective (Individual tax as percent of total taxes)

Country	Income and Payroll Taxes	Property Taxes	Indirect Taxes	Taxes on International Trade	Other Taxes
Argentina	26.3	8.4	35.0	3.8	0.1
Bahrain	36.3	3.8	16.1	43.8	0.0
Belarus	27.1	3.2	62.3	4.9	0.0
Bhutan	53.4	0.4	42.6	3.6	0.0
Bolivia	10.9	10.5	65.1	6.2	0.1
Bulgaria	31.6	1.5	61.2	3.8	1.8
Canada	57.0	11.7	27.3	0.8	0.0
Chile	22.8	4.1	61.3	7.6	4.2
Congo, Dem. Republic	12.6	0.0	23.8	24.7	38.8[a]
Congo, Republic	11.3	0.0	64.5	22.9	1.4
Costa Rica	22.4	0.5	68.7	8.4	0.0

continues on following page

Table 8. Continued

Country	Income and Payroll Taxes	Property Taxes	Indirect Taxes	Taxes on International Trade	Other Taxes
Cote d'Ivoire	29.1	1.7	23.3	45.4	0.5
Croatia	22.1	1.8	66.4	8.7	1.0
Czech Republic	40.1	2.4	53.9	3.1	0.4
Denmark	60.8	3.6	34.6	0.0	1.0
Dominican Republic	20.5	1.1	28.5	48.5	1.4
Estonia	39.2	2.2	58.4	0.2	0.0
Georgia	25.9	9.4	54.6	6.1	0.0
Hungary	36.1	2.6	55.6	4.0	1.7
India	37.3	0.1	37.3	25.1	0.2
Iran	53.0	2.5	19.9	23.3	1.3
Israel	53.2	7.7	37.3	0.9	0.7
Jamaica	41.9	0.6	40.5	8.9	8.1
Kazakhstan	52.7	6.0	36.3	4.1	0.7
Latvia	36.9	4.9	56.6	1.6	0.0
Lithuania	40.5	2.7	55.3	1.5	0.0
Macao, China	8.9	6.5	82.1	0.0	2.5
Madagascar	15.7	1.0	29.1	53.5	0.6
Maldives	4.6	0.0	29.7	64.4	1.3
Mauritius	14.6	5.8	46.2	33.4	0.1
Mexico	32.6	1.7	59.6	3.9	0.7
Moldova	17.5	6.1	68.9	7.5	0.1
Mongolia	28.4	0.1	56.2	10.1	1.3
Myanmar	34.5	0.0	58.2	7.2	0.0
Nepal	22.4	3.4	41.6	32.6	0.0
Nicaragua	17.1	-0.2	73.6	9.4	0.0
Pakistan	28.1	1.2	44.7	16.0	10.1[b]
Paraguay	17.9	0.0	59.4	18.2	4.4
Peru	26.8	0.0	67.0	12.4	3.2
Poland	35.5	5.2	55.9	3.5	0.0
Puerto Rico	66.8	0	22.0	0	11.2
Romania	34.5	2.7	54.8	6.2	1.1
Russian Federation	33.2	4.5	44.4	13.0	0.1
Seychelles	26.7	0.1	7.8	63.1	2.3
Singapore	50.2	6.5	31.2	2.5	9.6
Slovak Republic	35.9	2.8	54.3	7.0	0.0
Slovenia	36.3	2.5	57.6	3.6	0.0
South Africa	54.0	5.8	34.8	3.1	0.7

continues on following page

Table 8. Continued

Country	Income and Payroll Taxes	Property Taxes	Indirect Taxes	Taxes on International Trade	Other Taxes
Switzerland	58.1	12.3	28.6	1.1	0.0
Tajikistan	16.0	5.6	63.8	12.6	0.0
Thailand	32.2	2.3	53.1	11.9	0.5
Tunisia	36.5	2.1	48.5	9.3	2.0
Turkey	37.4	4.0	52.1	1.7	4.7
Ukraine	42.3	0.0	52.4	5.3	0.0
United States	66.4	13.2	19.5	1.0	0.0
Uruguay	26.2	9.3	57.1	4.7	3.1
Venezuela	42.5	5.5	39.7	11.4	0.9
Mean (unweighted)	**32.6**	**3.6**	**47.5**	**13.4**	**2.0**

Source: International Monetary Fund *Government Finance Statistics*, various issues.

As in the previous analysis, the first step in calculating income tax effort is to identify variables that measure the capacity of a country to raise income tax revenue. Per capita GDP is an overall measure of capacity, and countries with higher per capita GDP are expected to raise more income tax revenue. Population size is used as an independent variable to adjust for the size of a country, with the expectation that large countries are more prone to tax personal income. The openness of a country (measured as imports plus exports divided by GDP) could be expected to identify countries with more sophisticated administrations and therefore an ability to support an individual income tax. An OLS regression of the individual income tax as a percent of GDP on a sample of 35 countries (where all variables are entered in log form and where averages of the income tax to GDP ratio for countries are used for the period 2000-2010) gives estimated coefficients as hypothesized, with all three independent variables statistically significant.

These regression results are then used to estimate an expected or predicted level of personal income taxes plus Social Security contributions for Tunisia. A country of Tunisia's income, population, and openness would on average raise 6.8 percent of its GDP in personal income taxes and Social Security contributions. In fact, Tunisia raises on average 9.1 percent, or well above the predicted amount. Tunisia's tax effort index for these taxes (or the actual percent of personal income tax revenues plus Social Security contributions divided by the estimated percent) is 1.34, among the largest in our sample. These international comparisons suggest that there is not much room for increasing the effective tax rate for the income tax and indeed that there are arguments for reducing the burden of income taxation.

Similar comparisons can be made for the other major taxes. These comparisons indicate that Tunisia is a relatively heavy user of the corporate income tax and relatively light user of indirect taxes (assuming these including trade taxes).

Tax Rates

Tunisia's tax rates are generally above international levels. For the personal income tax, the dominant world-wide trend in the last 25 years is a significant decline in top marginal tax rates and overall marginal tax rates (Peter, Butrick, & Duncan, 2010). In a sample of 189 countries at all levels of income and in regions of the world, the GDP-weighted average top statutory PIT rate fell from a high of 62 percent in 1981 to 56 percent in 1986. During the ensuing eight year period (1986-1993), the PIT top rate fell by another 16 percentage points. It then increased by a modest 2 percentage points (1993-1996) before resuming its downward trend in 1996. Since then, the decline has continued, with average top statutory rates falling an additional 6.5 percentage points over the next 10 years. Overall, there has been a drop of 41 percent in the weighted top PIT rate, from a high of 62 percent in 1981 to a low of 36 percent in 2005. In addition, only 17 percent of unweighted top PIT rates were in excess of 40 percent in 2001-2005 compared to over 71 percent during the early 1980s. The proportion of countries with top PIT rates in excess of 60 percent declined from one-fourth in 1981 to less than 1 percent in 2005. Countries with lower top PIT rates (or 1 to 40 percent) became more widespread over time. The percentage of countries falling into this category increased from approximately 15 percent to over 73 percent between 1981 and 2005.

Overall in 2001-2005, 9.7 percent of the 189 countries had a top marginal tax rate of 0 percent, 15.8 percent had a top rate between 1 and 20 percent, 23.3 percent had a top rate between 21 and 30 percent, 34.0 percent had a top rate between 31 and 40 percent, 16.3 percent had a top rate between 41 and 60 percent, and 0.9 percent of the countries had a top rate above 61 percent. By this comparison, Tunisia's top personal income tax rate of 35 percent places it above (if not significantly above) the median of these 189 countries.

For the *corporate income tax* and the *VAT*, Tunisia's corporate income tax is 30 percent, while its standard VAT rate is 18 percent. Table 9 indicates that these rates are higher than many (if not all) of the selected countries. In this regard, the Ministry of Finance calculates that the weighted average customs-import-duty rate ranges between 10 percent and 15 percent for all taxed items. At least 123 countries world-wide now have some form of VAT, and no tax has ever spread so quickly and so widely. Other than the U.S., every country in the OECD now has a VAT, as do most countries in the Middle East and North Africa. The average standard rate in the OECD countries is now almost 18 percent, compared to 14 percent in the western hemisphere countries. In most countries, VAT rates have gone up over time.

Table 9. Statutory corporate and statutory VAT tax rates, selected countries

Country	Corporate Income Tax (percent)	VAT (percent)
Turkey	20.0	18.0
Malaysia	20.0, 28.0	10.0
Thailand	30.0	7.0
Korea	14.3, 27.5	10.0
Indonesia	10 to 30	10.0
Australia	30.0	10.0
India	33.7	12.5
Pakistan	35.0	15.0
Egypt	20.0	10.0
China	33.0	17.0
Sri Lanka	35.0	15.0
Bangladesh	40.0	15.0
Tunisia	30	18.0

Source: *Doing Business 2010.*

For *Social Security contributions*, Table 10 presents payroll tax rates for OECD countries and for Tunisia. Relative to these higher income countries, Tunisia's payroll tax rates are higher than 12 of these 21 countries. Relative to the generally lower income countries in Table 11, Tunisia's payroll tax rates are in general much higher.

Table 10. Tax rates from payroll taxes and social security contributions in OECD countries and Tunisia (In percent)

Country	Total Tax Rate (A) = (B)+(C)	Payroll Tax Rate (Other than SSC) (B)	Total Social Security Contribution (SSC) Rates (C) = (D)+(E)	Social Security Charges to Employers (D)	Social Security Charges to Employees (E)
Australia	Up to 7	Up to 7	0	0	0
Austria	29.15 - 29.3	7.5	21.65 - 21.8	21.65 - 21.8	NA
Belgium	32.89 - 48.66	0	32.89 - 48.66	32.89 - 48.66	NA
Canada	Rate varies	1 - 4.5	Rate Varies	Rate Varies	NA
Denmark	0	0	0	0	0
Finland	26.4 - 28.4	0	26.4 - 28.4	20.1 - 22.1	6.3
France	42.25 - 64.63	4.25 - 13.60	38 - 51.03	38 - 51.03	NA
Germany	40.8	0	40.8	20.4	20.4
Greece	43.86 - 54.36	0	43.86 - 54.36	27.96 - 34.96	15.90 -19.40
Ireland	18	0	18	12	6
Italy	36 – 42	0	36 - 42	32% - 36	4 - 6
Mexico	42.92 - 44.92	6 – 8	36.92	30.19	6.73
Netherlands	25.31	0	25.31	18.66	6.65
Norway	26.6	0	26.6	26.6	NA
Portugal	23.75	0	23.75	23.75	0
Spain	37.15 – 37.2	0	37.15 - 37.2	30.8	6.35 - 6.4
Sweden	81.34	48.52	32.82	32.82	0
Switzerland	13.1	0	13.1	6.55	6.55
Turkey	55.5 – 61	0	55.5 – 61	32.5 - 38	23
United Kingdom	0 - 23.6	0	0 - 23.6	0 - 11.8	0 - 11.8
United States	15.3	0	15.3	7.65	7.65
Tunisia	26.15 - 38.75	Up to 9	26.15 - 29.75	16.97 - 20.57	9.18

Notes: All contributions are computed as a percentage of the employee's salary.
Source: *International Bureau of Fiscal Documentation* (IBFD), various issues.

Table 11. Tax wedge in OECD countries, 2011

Country	Tax Wedge (percent of labor costs)
Belgium	55.5
Germany	49.8
Hungary	49.4
France	49.4
Austria	48.4
Italy	47.6
Sweden	42.8
Finland	42.7
Slovenia	42.6
Czech Republic	42.5
Estonia	40.1
Spain	39.9
Portugal	39.0
Slovak Republic	38.9
Denmark	38.4
The Netherlands	37.8
Turkey	37.7
Norway	37.5
Luxembourg	36.0
Poland	34.3
Iceland	34.0
United Kingdom	32.5
Canada	30.8
Japan	30.8
United States	29.5
Ireland	26.8
Australia	26.7
Switzerland	21.0
Korea	20.3
Israel	19.8
Mexico	16.2
New Zealand	15.9
Chile	7.0

Source: OECD (2012).

Problems: Some Partial and General Equilibrium Effects of Tunisia's Tax System

In this section we present some partial and general equilibrium analyses of Tunisia's tax system, in order to quantify many of the effects of this system of taxes. The partial equilibrium analysis emphasizes the calculation of effective tax rates for the taxation of corporate income and of labor income. The general equilibrium analysis emphasizes the overall impacts of the tax system, focusing specifically on personal income and payroll taxes. We start with a simple general equilibrium model, and then discuss later the effective tax rates.

A General Equilibrium Model of the Tunisian Economy

Consider a highly stylized economy in which there are three sectors: a sector in which labor and capital are subject to the full rates of payroll and income taxes; a sector that is for the most part legally exempt from taxation due either to explicit exemption from taxation, to the presence of extensive tax incentives (e.g., the offshore regime), or to the low effective rates of taxation under a simplified tax system; and a sector that is legally subject to full taxation but that illegally escapes all taxes because activities there are hard-to-tax (e.g., the shadow economy or an informal sector). If factors are mobile between these three sectors, then the imposition of payroll and income taxes in the taxed sector will cause labor and capital to respond by moving to the untaxed sectors. This movement will affect the wage of labor, the return to other factors of production, and the prices of consumer products. It will also influence the allocative effects of the taxes and the revenues that are collected.

To be more precise, let a stylized economy be divided into three sectors: a fully taxed sector that produces output (denoted X), a sector (Y) that is legally exempt from (most) taxation, and a sector (Z) that is legally subject to taxation but that illegally escapes taxation; for simplicity, assume that sector Y is legally exempt from all taxes. Demand for each output is a function of relative prices, and all agents (including government) are assumed for simplicity to have the same average and marginal propensity to consume each commodity (e.g., there is a single "representative" consumer). Each good is produced under competitive conditions with a production function that depends upon the amount of capital (K) and labor (L). Capital and labor are assumed to be fixed in supply to the entire economy; they are also assumed to be perfectly mobile among the three sectors. Because of perfect mobility, net factor returns must be equalized across sectors, where factor returns are assumed to be adjusted for the presence of any risk premia that may exist. Since capital and labor in sectors Y and Z are assumed to be untaxed due either to legal avoidance or illegal evasion, there are only two effective taxes: a tax on capital (T_K) and a tax on labor (T_L) in the taxed sector X; the only other tax that might be imposed is a tax on consumption of X, a tax that is equivalent to an equal-rate tax on capital and labor in X. As discussed above, the taxation of labor (and capital) in only some uses creates an incentive for resources to flow from the taxed sector (X) to the untaxed sectors (Y and Z).

The full set of equations is available upon request. These equations are calibrated with data that capture the main characteristics of the Tunisian economy, so that its numerical solution can then be used to examine the economic impacts of changes in tax rates. It is this computable general equilibrium model that forms the basis for much of the following analysis of the economic effects of the tax system.

Tax Base Erosion

It is widely suspected that the structure of taxes gives both an incentive and an opportunity for individuals to escape the payment of taxes. There are several avenues that are available. One avenue is to move from the formal sector to the untaxed informal sector of the Tunisian economy. Another avenue is outright evasion of the legally due tax liability; indeed, there is a widespread perception that compliance with the income and payroll taxes, especially by the self-employed, is very low. Still another, and legal, method of avoidance is for individuals to elect to be taxed under the simplified tax system or to take advantage of the incentive system.

Measuring the actual extent of this erosion via avoidance and evasion, and the associated revenue loss, is obviously quite difficult because there is little if any systematic information for Tunisia by which this notion can be tested. Tunisian government officials have suggested that the revenue loss due to evasion of the payroll programs themselves may be at least one-half of the actual collections from the programs, but this seems largely a guess, even if an informed one; officials make a similar estimate for the loss of personal income tax revenues.

The general equilibrium analysis suggests that taxes on the fully taxed formal sector (X) reduce the size of the formal sector by somewhere between 5 and 12 percent, depending mainly upon the elasticity of demand for formal sector output, with most of the resources moving into the legally exempt sector (Y). The resulting revenue loss also ranges from 5 to 12 percent.

These massive amounts of legal and illegal erosion compromise many dimensions of the fiscal system of Tunisia. Most obviously, base erosion leads to a loss in revenues, thereby affecting taxes that compliant taxpayers face and public services that citizens receive. Erosion creates misallocations in resource use when individuals and firms alter their behavior to evade or avoid their taxes and contributions. Its presence requires that government expend resources to deter noncompliance, to detect its magnitude, and to penalize its practitioners, even though these government enforcement activities seem infrequent and ineffective in Tunisia. Erosion alters the vertical and horizontal equity of taxation in unpredictable ways. Individuals with the same "true" level of income may pay very different amounts in taxes if some avoid/evade and others do not; individuals with different levels of "true" income may pay similar amounts of taxes even though their abilities to pay may differ greatly; and unless tax evaders are caught, evaders pay fewer taxes than honest taxpayers. Tax base erosion may contribute to feelings of unfair treatment and disrespect for the law, creating a self-generating cycle that feeds upon itself and leads to even more evasion. All of these results represent costs to the fiscal system of Tunisia.

Tax Incidence

In their entirety, the income and payroll taxes generate substantial revenues. Because these revenues must ultimately be paid by someone, they have a significant impact on the distribution of income; that is, who bears the burden of the taxes?

The general equilibrium model is used to examine the incidence of the taxes. Various numerical simulations of the model indicate that an increase in the tax rate on labor is shifted in part to capital (given that the taxed sector is assumed to be capital intensive) and in part to consumers of the taxed product (given that the labor tax increases the relative price of the taxed good). Even so, the main burden of any tax on labor (between 72 and 81 percent) is borne largely by labor in the form of a lower net-of-tax wage, which likely makes the overall burden of taxation regressive.

Allocative Effects

Taxes also affect the efficiency of resource use, or the "excess burden" of taxation. Measuring the excess burden requires knowledge of the responses of resources to the various taxes. This information can be generated from the general equilibrium model.

To illustrate, consider the tax on capital (K_X) in sector X, or T_K. In the absence of the tax, factor mobility will assure that the equilibrium price of capital will be the same in both sectors. In the presence of the tax, however, capital will move from sector X until the gross-of-tax price of capital in X exceeds the price of capital in Y and in Z by the amount of the tax. Capital thus moves from higher productivity uses in the formal sector to lower valued uses in the informal sector. The excess burden of this single tax on capital in sector X is measured by the usual welfare "triangle" of $(-1/2\ T_K \Delta K_X)$. When there are also taxes on labor in X (or L_X), the combined excess burden becomes $(-1/2 T_K \Delta K_X - 1/2 T_L \Delta L_X)$. Here, ΔK_X and ΔL_X represent the changes in factors that result from both taxes simultaneously. Estimation of the excess burden requires knowledge of these total factor responses. Assuming that the relevant derivatives are constant, the excess burden EB is measured by:

$$EB = -1/2\ T_K\ [(\partial K_X/\partial T_K)T_K + (\partial K_X/\partial T_L)T_L] - 1/2\ T_L\ [(\partial L_X/\partial T_K)T_K + (\partial L_X/\partial T_L)T_L],$$

where, for example, $\partial K_X/\partial T_K$ is the partial derivative of K_X with respect to T_K. These partial derivatives allow for all general equilibrium adjustments in production and in demand, and so may be viewed as "reduced form" coefficients that show the equilibrium responses of capital and labor in the taxed sector to changes in the taxes. As in the case of the incidence of the payroll taxes, the solution of the system of equations allows these partial derivatives to be calculated directly, as functions of the amounts and the shares of capital and labor in the three sectors, the taxes on the factors in the taxed sector, and the various elasticities of demand and of substitution.

In all cases, the existence of a hard-to-tax sector, in combination with a legally untaxed sector, generates a large excess burden, somewhere between 11 and 27 percent of taxes and between 3 and 7 percent of formal sectors output. These estimates are especially sensitive to the compensated elasticity of demand for the taxed good. They are also somewhat sensitive to the various elasticities of substitution in production. They do not depend significantly on the assumption regarding the magnitude of tax evasion. It should also be remembered that there are many other sources of inefficiencies as well.

Sectoral, Occupational, and Employment Effects

Closely related to the incidence and the allocative effects of the taxes are their sectoral, occupational, and employment effects. The assumption that it is mainly workers in the formal sector of the Tunisian economy who bear the burden of the taxes does not allow for any shifting of the burden of taxes via adjustments in wages and other prices. As noted earlier, the existence of sectors to which resources may move to avoid the taxes means that these taxes drive a wedge between the returns to factors of production in the different sectors. If labor is mobile, then labor will respond to an increased tax in the formal sector by moving between the sectors until the net-of-tax return across the three sectors is equalized. This movement will affect the wages of labor in the three sectors, raising wages in the formal sector as labor flows from this sector and reducing wages in other two sectors as labor moves into these sectors.

There will also be an impact on the returns to other factors and on product prices, as well as an impact on the overall unemployment rate.

Fully identifying these impacts requires a more detailed general equilibrium model of the economy than the one outlined earlier, one that allows for unemployment and that distinguishes labor types. However, there is some related work for other countries. For example, Alm and Lopez-Castano (2005) use a general equilibrium model of Colombia, in which the economy is divided into four sectors (farming, urban/informal, urban/unskilled, and urban/skilled) and which is calibrated with data from the 1999 social accounting matrix for Colombia. They find that the high rates of labor taxation lead to an overall increase in the number of unemployed workers, but also to an increase in employment in the informal sector. They also find that maintaining the level of expenditures of the programs financed by the taxes but changing the method of their finance to alternative revenues sources (e.g., deficit finance, company taxation) increases overall employment and formal sector employment.

Revenue Effects of Payroll Rate Reductions

A central issue in current discussions of Tunisia is the potential effect of payroll tax rate reductions on tax revenues. There are several ways of examining this issue. The simplest approach makes use of a basic accounting identity, in which tax revenues R are equal to the product of the tax rate t, the number of individuals subject to the payroll taxes $N(t)$, and the value of the associated wage base $W(t)$, so that $R = t \cdot N(t) \cdot W(t)$. Both $N(t)$ and $W(t)$ are assumed to be functions of (among other things) the tax rate, to reflect the likelihood that changes in the tax rate affect the payroll tax base. The proportional change in revenues is then simply $\Delta R/R = \Delta t/t + \Delta N/N + \Delta W/W$, so that the proportional change in revenues equals the sum of the proportional changes in the individual components. Recognizing that the number of individuals and the value of the wage base each depends upon the tax rate, the proportional change in revenues can also be written as $\Delta R/R = \Delta t/t\ (1 + \varepsilon_{N,t} + \varepsilon_{W,t})$, where $\varepsilon_{N,t}$ is the elasticity of the number of taxpayers with respect to the tax rate and $\varepsilon_{W,t}$ is the elasticity of the wage base with respect to the rate. Both elasticities will be negative in value because a reduction in tax rates will increase both N and W.

Now suppose that the payroll tax rates are reduced by, say, 50 percent. In the absence of any change in the tax base, payroll tax revenues would fall, also by 50 percent. However, conversations with numerous government officials suggest that both $N(t)$ and $W(t)$ will respond to the rate reductions. If each variable increased by, say, 25 percent (or an elasticity in each case of -1/2), then overall revenues would be unchanged by the rate reduction. If the elasticities are greater than -1/2 (in absolute value), then revenues would actually increase. More generally, if the sum of the absolute values of the two elasticities exceeds unity, then a rate reduction would increase tax revenues.

The relevant issue then becomes the magnitude of the elasticities. There is no information on these elasticities. However, evidence for other types of responses in other countries suggests that elasticities in excess of 1/2 (in absolute value) are extremely unlikely.

A slightly more complicated framework generates the same conclusion. Suppose that the equilibrium level of some tax base (e.g., the wages of workers subject to the labor taxes) depends upon the supply and the demand of this tax base. Then it is straightforward to show that the tax rate that maximizes the tax revenues collected from this tax base is $t_{Maximum}=(\varepsilon_S-\varepsilon_D)/(-\varepsilon_D\ (1+\varepsilon_S))$, where $t_{Maximum}$ is the revenue-maximizing tax rate, ε_S is the elasticity of supply of the tax base, and ε_D is the elasticity of demand, where both elasticities are assumed to be constant and where $\varepsilon_S \geq 0$ and $\varepsilon_D \leq 0$. Again, the crucial issue for the impact of any tax rate reduction is the magnitude of the elasticities. It is only when the elasticity of demand for the tax base exceeds -1 (in absolute value) that there is any chance that a reduction in tax rates will increase revenues.

The general equilibrium model discussed earlier also gives the same conclusion. For reasonable values of the various elasticities, values that approximate estimates derived from empirical work on these behavioral responses, it is never the case that a decrease in the tax rate on labor increases tax revenues. The typical result is that a reduction in the labor tax rate generates some increase in labor in the taxed sector, but that this increase in labor (and the corresponding increase in labor tax revenues) is not nearly sufficient to offset the loss in revenues from the rate reduction. Indeed, for plausible values of the parameters, a reduction of, say, 10 percent in the labor tax rate reduces tax revenues in most scenarios by 5 to 9 percent. It is only when the various elasticities (especially the elasticities of substitution between labor and capital in the various sectors and the elasticity of demand for sector *X*) are extraordinarily high – and in excess of most all elasticities estimated from empirical work – that revenue simulations give the result that a reduction in the labor tax rate increases labor tax revenues. Recall also that the stylized model assumes that labor (as well as capital) is perfectly mobile across the taxed sector, the legally untaxed sector, and the evasion sector. When factor mobility becomes less than perfect, the possibility that a reduction in the tax rate increases tax revenues becomes even less likely. The results from other general equilibrium analyses generate similar conclusions (Alm & Lopez-Castano, 2005).

The Tax Burden on Corporate Income and its Distorting Effects

The Tunisian system of incentives introduces a range of distortions in corporate behavior. However, measuring these distortions is quite difficult. In this section, several methods are used to suggest the magnitude of these efficiency losses.

One simple approach is to measure the average effective tax rate (*AETR*), calculated as total taxes actually paid as a fraction of gross corporate (accounting) income. If this measure differs across sectors and across asset types – as it likely does in Tunisia – then these differences give an indication of the ways in which the corporate income tax (together with all of its special provisions) creates incentives for resources to move between sectors and assets, thereby creating distortions in the allocation of resources.

Another approach is to calculate the marginal effective tax rate (*METR*) (Boadway, Bruce, and Mintz, 1984). *METRs* attempt to measure the impact of taxes on the marginal (or incremental) decision by economic agents to invest in capital. The *METR* is defined as the additional tax paid by a firm when it decides to invest in one more unit of capital. A positive *METR* indicates that investment is discouraged; a negative *METR* indicates that investment is subsidized even in the presence of the corporate income tax via such special provisions as accelerated depreciation, investment tax credits, tax holidays, and the like. *METRs* can be calculated by sector and also by asset types. Differences in *METRs* across sectors and across assets generate incentives for resources to reallocate due entirely to tax considerations, and therefore create efficiency losses.

The premise underlying *METR* calculations is that the gross rate of return on capital (net of economic depreciation) for a profit-maximizing firm must be equal to the financing cost of capital, adjusted for taxes. The size of this adjustment for taxes on a new investment is the marginal effective tax rate on capital; that is, the *METR* is the difference between the pre-tax rate of return on a marginal investment, or the gross rate of return on investment) and the required post-tax rate of return, expressed as a percentage of pre-tax rate of return.

More precisely, the marginal effective tax rate on a given type of capital investment is defined as the proportional difference between the gross-of-tax rate of return required by a firm r^G and the net-of-tax rate of return required by an investor r^N, where r^G is the difference between the marginal revenue product (or "user cost" of capital) and economic depreciation and the after-tax rate of return is the weighted average of the return to debt and equity held by the investor. Thus, the marginal effective tax rate is defined as:

$$METR = (r^G - r^N)/r^G.$$

For example, if the gross-of-tax rate of return to capital is 20 percent and the net-of-tax rate of return is 10 percent, then the *METR* on capital is 50 percent. Note that both methods may accurately capture the effective tax rates on those businesses that actually pay taxes. However, both methods are almost certain to overstate – perhaps quite significantly – the overall average effective tax rates on all businesses, including those that comply and those that do not comply. The widespread existence of tax evasion means that many businesses face an effective tax rate (marginal or average) of zero.

The detailed information needed to calculate these *AETRs* and *METRs* for more specific industry/ asset classifications is not yet available. Even so, it seems likely that these calculations would reveal greatly different rates of taxation by sector and by asset type, both of which contribute to the distorting effects of the Tunisian incentives system.

Box 2. A numerical example of calculating marginal effective tax rates

The calculation of a marginal effective tax rate (*METR*) for a hypothetical industry X in Tunisia and its assets is explained here using a numerical example. Assume that there are domestic investors (Tunisia) as well as foreign investors, where the foreign investors are assumed to be from the United States. Assume also that the following values hold for important tax parameters in hypothetical industry X, as given in Box-Table I:

Box-Table I: Tax parameters (In percent except last three rows)

Tax Parameter	Investor	
	U.S.	**Tunisia**
Statutory CIT Rate	34	30
Tax on Transfer of Property, Import Duty on Capital Goods	*	5
Capital Tax Rate	*	0
Tax Depreciation Rate-Building	*	10
Tax Depreciation Rate-Machinery	*	15
Property Tax Rate	*	5
Gross Receipt Tax Rate or Presumptive Tax	*	0.5
Sales Tax Rate	*	15
Present Tax Value of Accumulated Capital Cost Allowance for Building	*	0.093
Present Tax Value of Accumulated Capital Cost Allowance for Machinery	*	0.107
FIFO=1 and LIFO=0	0	1

where * denotes that this parameter is not used in the calculations. In most cases, the values in the table are those applicable for Tunisia. The present tax value of accumulated capital cost allowance for buildings and machinery has been calculated assuming a 50 percent allowance in the first year and declining depreciation from the next year. The same values of taxes (e.g., those levied in Tunisia) are assumed to apply to both the domestic and the foreign (U.S.) investor. Non-tax parameters are given in Box-Table II:

continues on following page

Box 2. Continued

Box-Table II: Non-tax parameters (In percent)

Non-Tax Parameter	U.S.	Tunisia
Expected Inflation Rate	2.40	4.57
Expected Real Interest Rate	3.1	6.0
Cost of Equity	6.89	6.89
Debt to Assets Ratio		
Debt Raised Abroad to Home Capital	40	40
Debt to Asset Ratio in Home Country	40	40
Rate of Economic Depreciation		
Building	*	2
Machinery	*	5

The ***first stage*** in the calculation of the *METR* for an industry is the computation of the real cost of financing. Using the formulae in Boadway, Bruce, and Mintz (1984), the real cost of financing for domestic and foreign investors, respectively, is calculated. These calculations give 2.3 percent and 3.6 percent, respectively.

The ***second stage*** is the computation of the net-of-tax rate of return. Again using the formulae in Boadway, Bruce, and Mintz (1984) for domestic and foreign investors, the net-of-tax rate of return on capital is calculated for each category of assets (building, machinery, inventory, and land). See Box-Table III.

Box-Table III: Rate of return on capital (In percent)

Rate of Return on Capital	U.S.	Tunisia
Net-of-tax Return	4.61	3.83
Gross-of-tax Return		
Building	6.60	4.73
Machinery	8.04	6.20
Inventory	6.24	6.93
Land	6.06	4.00

The ***third stage*** is the computation of the gross-of-tax rate of return on capital; these are calculated using Boadway, Bruce, and Mintz (1984), again applied separately for domestic and foreign investors. Given the assumed values above, the net-of-tax and gross-of-tax rates of return are in Box-Table III:

In the ***final stage*** of the calculation, the marginal effective tax rate for each type of asset using the two rates of return is calculated as: $METR = (r_g - r_n)/r_g$.

Based on the above assumptions and calculations, the results for industry X are in Box-Table IV. The total *METR* for industry X is the weighted average of the *METR* by asset type, where we assume that the value of each asset type in the industry is: building 30 percent; machinery 50 percent; inventory 10 percent; and land 10 percent.

Box-Table IV: METRs (In percent)

METR	U.S.	Tunisia
Building	30	19
Machinery	43	38
Inventory	26	44
Land	24	4
Industry X	**36**	**32**

The Tax Burden on Labor

There is little question that labor is taxed relatively heavily in Tunisia. As documented earlier, personal income tax rates (and, to a somewhat lesser extent personal income tax revenues) tend to be higher in Tunisia than in many other countries. Social Security contributions also increase significantly the burden on labor. In both cases, this burden is felt especially by labor in the formal sector of the economy.

An additional measure of the tax burden on labor is given by the "tax wedge", which is a measure of the difference between labor costs to the employer and the corresponding net take-home pay of the employee. The tax wedge is calculated by taking the sum of the personal income tax rate, the employee plus employer Social Security contributions rate (together with any payroll tax), minus any benefits to which contributions entitle the worker, and expressing this as a percentage of labor costs. The average tax wedge therefore identifies that part of total labor costs that are taken in tax and Social Security contributions net of cash benefits.

Table 11 presents recent (2011) estimates of the tax wedge for OECD countries, in descending order of the size of the tax wedge. Preliminary calculations for an average income, full-time worker in Tunisia indicate a relatively higher tax wedge, at 39.1 percent, in Tunisia.

SOLUTIONS AND RECOMMENDATIONS: EVALUATING TUNISIA'S TAX SYSTEM

Tax systems are designed to achieve multiple objectives. An obvious purpose is to raise the revenues necessary to finance government expenditures (sometimes termed "adequacy"), and also to ensure that the growth in revenues is adequate to meet expenditure requirements ("elasticity"). Another is to distribute the burden of taxation in a way that meets with a society's notions of fairness; such "equity" is typically defined in terms of "ability to pay", such that those with equal ability should pay equal taxes ("horizontal equity") and those with greater ability should pay greater taxes ("vertical equity"). Taxes can also be used to influence behavior of those who pay them; in choosing taxes, a common goal is to minimize the interference of taxes in the economic decisions of individuals and firms. Taxes should be simple, both to administer and to comply with because a complicated tax system wastes the resources of tax administrators and taxpayers. Consider now the performance of the Tunisia tax system in achieving these objectives.

There are Large Amounts of Tax Evasion

By all accounts, there are large amounts of income and consumption that escape taxation in Tunisia. Firm evidence on evasion is obviously difficult to find. Even so, estimates of the size of the "underground economy" (or all market-based goods and services, legal or illegal, that escape inclusion in official accounts) in Tunisia are also quite large. For example, Alm and Embaye (2013) estimate that the current size of the Tunisian underground economy is 32 percent, down from an estimated 45 percent in 1984 (see Table 12).

Table 12. Shadow economy estimates by income group, 1984-2006 (As percent of GDP)

Income Group	Observations	Mean	Standard Deviation	Minimum	Maximum
Low Income	621	38.2	10.3	20.5	85.8
Lower Middle Income	572	37.2	10.3	17.5	84.5
Upper Middle Income	395	33.4	7.2	21.3	68.2
High Income, Non-OECD	118	24.3	7.1	14.1	44.1
OECD	475	16.9	3.6	10.4	30.3
All Countries (Unweighted)	2181	31.7	12.0	10.4	85.8

Source: Alm and Embaye (2013).

There is a Narrow and Shrinking Tax Base

The goal of most tax reforms is to broaden the tax base, thereby allowing marginal tax rates to be reduced. However, the tax base in Tunisia has been narrowed in at least two important ways. One is legal and takes the form of exemptions or preferential treatment (e.g., "tax expenditures"), especially via the extensive system of incentives. To our knowledge, there is no systematic listing of the tax expenditures in the Tunisia tax system, which in itself is a problem. The second stems from administrative failures (especially enforcement problems) that allow the existence of enormous amounts of tax evasion.

One result of a small and falling tax base is that the government must emphasize collection of taxes from those "tax handles" that are more readily available. More visible taxpayers (such as labor in the formal sector) end up bearing increasing amounts of the tax burden.

There is Widespread Use of Fiscal, Financial, and Other Incentives

The use of incentives, especially in the corporate income tax, is widely acknowledged. A common argument is that, without these incentives, Tunisian firms simply cannot compete in the world economy. A counterargument is that incentives (and the resulting preferential tax treatments) have created a misallocation of investment that has led in turn to a loss in competitiveness. Also, there is little question that incentives are a significant fiscal drain on the budget, a cost that can be reflected in higher taxes on labor or in public investments that have been forgone.

Still, the crucial issue is: Why give these incentives? The main reason appears to be that many countries believe that they must have the incentives to compete with rival countries, especially when the country has little in the way of market size or resource endowment to attract foreign investors. Put differently, the introduction of a fiscal, financial, or other incentive type by one country leads to strategic responses by other, rival countries. A related reason is that the introduction of incentives also stems from the power of large domestic firms, who pressure the government to take measures that favor their enterprises. In both cases the result is the same: the incentives have little impact on investment because other countries have similar incentives, but the incentives have a large and negative impact on the tax collections of all countries and simply transfer revenues to large enterprises.

Even so, it is important to consider – and quantify – the benefits and costs of incentives. The possible benefits to a country that offers incentives may include increases in investment, gains from industrialization, the creation of jobs for persons who otherwise would be unemployed or employed at lower wages, the transfer of technology and training, and increases in revenues from taxes to which the incentives do not apply or from taxes payable after the initial reduction has ended. It is interesting that few countries have actually undertaken a rigorous analysis of these benefits. Overall, there is very little evidence that incentives are able to attract or to induce investment that would not have been undertaken anyway.

As for the costs, these include the loss of revenue, distortions in investment behavior leading to investments that are socially unproductive, administrative complications, political discord generated by favors to foreign-owned corporations, and discrimination against smaller firms that lack the resources and/or the influence to apply for the incentives.

The actual evaluation of benefits and costs has seldom been done. In one instance (Thirsk, 1991), the benefits in Jamaica were generally found to be positive but small, and smaller than their costs. In another instance, Indonesia eliminated all of its investment incentives as part of a comprehensive tax reform in the mid-1980s (Gillis, 1985), because there was much evidence that few if any incentives had the desired effects in attracting desired investments, that their administrative problems were enormous (especially for tax holidays), that they significantly distorted investment patterns, and that generated massive losses in tax revenues. On balance, these costs were deemed to be far in excess of the potential benefits. The conclusion in Indonesia was that the best policy for investment was deemed to be a reduced overall rate of taxation in the corporate income tax.

Indeed, there is now some evidence that the best way to encourage investment is simply to lower the tax rate in the corporate income tax, not to offer targeted incentives, since there is little evidence that incentives are more important to potential investors than such factors as political stability, potential market size, economic growth, or infrastructure There is also increasing evidence that the main effect of incentives is to shift income across jurisdictions (via such mechanisms as transfer pricing and financial policies) rather than to stimulate real activity in jurisdictions. In short, the main messages of this research are that incentives can stimulate investment, but that a country's overall economic characteristics are much more important than any incentives package both for the success or the failure of industries and as potential "drivers" of investment decisions by long-term investors (Hines, 2007). Moreover even if/when incentives stimulate some additional investment, they are not generally cost-effective. Again, this is not to deny that incentives can affect the movement of "capital", broadly defined. It is to question whether any such movement represents a transfer of "real" economic activity as opposed to simply a transfer of "paper" transactions that reduce a firm's tax liabilities without generating any real economic activity. It is also to question whether the benefit-cost ratio of any such incentive is greater than one. Overall, then, in the few instances in which detailed analyses have been performed, the benefits of incentives are less than their costs.

There are Significant Limitations in Tax Administration

A dominant theme in most assessments of the Tunisia tax system is the absence of effective tax administration. If taxes cannot be administered efficiently and equitably, then the goals of any tax reform will not be achieved. As noted by Surrey (1958), "...the concentration on tax policy on the choice of taxes may lead to insufficient consideration of the aspect of tax administration. In short, there may well be too much preoccupation with 'what to do' and too little attention to 'how to do it.'" Put differently, tax administration should be placed at the center, not the periphery, of tax reform efforts (Bird & Casanegra de Jantscher, 1992).

One indicator of administrative efficiency is the extent of tax evasion. As discussed earlier, there are apparently large amounts of evasion in Tunisia, with a wide range of negative effects. Evasion reduces the revenue and the elasticity of the tax system. It necessarily undermines the horizontal and vertical equity of the tax system, since equals are no longer taxed equally and the well-to-do are generally more successful in exploiting opportunities for evasion. The actual allocative effects of the tax system are likely to differ significantly from those implied by the statutes. In short, poor tax administration frustrates the achievement of all goals of taxation.

Other problems with the tax administration stem from the tax structure: the tax base has been narrowed by preferences, the system is overly complex, especially in its use of fiscal, financial, and other tax incentives, and over time the rate and base structures have become more and more complex, as discussed next. The structural and administrative problems are clearly related. Complexity in the rate and base structure makes administration more difficult and also reduces the compliance rate.

A vital issue in tax administration is the current absence of field audits. The effectiveness of any move toward self-assessment is likely to be compromised by the absence of audits. In the absence of an effective audit system, it is especially important to have in place a comprehensive system of withholding.

The Tax System is Excessively and Unnecessarily Complex

The limitations in tax administration are magnified by the overly complex tax system. Over time, the tax system has been adjusted to raise revenue, or to respond to requests for more favorable tax treatment, or to promote specific activities, or to redistribute income, or to protect the poor. Each of these changes likely complicates the tax system. Complexity in turn leads to higher administrative costs, more arbitrariness in administration, and an increasing erosion of confidence in the fairness and effectiveness of the tax system. Taxpayers are not inclined to pay a tax that they do not understand, that imposes high compliance costs, and that is administered by a tax administration that is viewed as arbitrary and ineffective.

There are numerous elements that complicate the tax system. Sometimes complication is a by-product of well-intentioned adjustments to the tax structure (e.g., the exemption of the purchases of items consumed by lower income individuals). Also, the corporate income tax in Tunisia, like that in most countries, is excessively complicated, especially given the heavy use of incentives. Still, there are areas where the system is needlessly complex. Clearly this is true for fiscal, financial, and other incentives. It may also be true for depreciation provisions.

All taxes impose compliance costs on taxpayers and administrative costs on government. Taxpayer compliance costs include time spent keeping receipts, logging appropriate books, and filing tax returns. Administrative costs include assessment, audit, and collection. Some taxes are less expensive to administer and to comply with than other taxes. This is due to such factors as the complexity of particular tax laws, the familiarity of taxpayers with various taxes, the process by which taxes are collected, and the status of data collection, enforcement, and monitoring for the various taxes. For example, taxes that are subject to source withholding are less costly to administer than taxes that require individual filing.

It is difficult to quantify the costs of administration and compliance across countries. However, there is some work that has calculated these costs, using a variety of methods. These studies demonstrate that there is substantial variation in the compliance and administrative costs across taxes and countries. Income taxes appear to be especially high in terms of administrative costs per dollar of revenue collected, with the more complicated the system the higher the cost. Broader-based taxes may be less costly to administer, but capital gains taxes are notoriously difficult to administer.

There are no data on compliance and administrative costs in Tunisia, so it is not possible to directly compute these costs. However, it seems likely that Tunisia's tax structure is a high-cost one. There is an inordinately high reliance on direct taxes, there is much less use of indirect taxes, the structure of the corporate income tax in Tunisia is very complex, and there is extensive use of incentives. All of these factors imply higher compliance and administrative costs than would be the case for a less complicated system and one that relies more on indirect taxes.

There are Horizontal and Vertical Inequities in Taxation, but these Inequities are not Quantified

There is little question that the practice of taxation in Tunisia introduces significant vertical and horizontal inequities. Unfortunately, little is known about the overall fairness of Tunisia's tax system; that is, who pays taxes in Tunisia, and how does the tax system affect the distribution of income? This lack of precise information has not stopped a general perception that Tunisia's tax system is regressive.

In a "fair" tax system, equally-situated individuals and companies will face the same tax obligations (i.e., "horizontal equity"). When this is not the case, some individuals will bear a heavier burden than others with comparable means. This weakens confidence in the system, and encourages taxpayers to look for avenues of nonpayment that will have negative consequences for revenues. It also may lead individuals and companies to make different economic choices in order to capture tax advantages, which in turn leads to economic inefficiencies. Indeed, there are many sources of horizontal inequities in the Tunisian tax system:

- Individuals who work in the formal sector of the Tunisia economy are subject to employer withholding on their wage income, while those who are self-employed or who work in the informal sector are less likely to pay the personal income tax. The result can be very different tax burdens, even for individuals with the same "true" income.
- Individuals differ in their opportunities for tax evasion, especially between the formal sector and the informal sector.
- Some individuals receive non-taxable benefits from their employer while others do not receive them or receive them at a lower rate. Again, the result can be very different tax burdens for households with equal income.
- Some consumers face very different effective indirect tax rates than others, given the uneven pattern of exemptions on the excises.
- The corporate income tax discriminates among firms, largely because of the existence of incentives and other tax preferences that are available to some firms, sectors, and asset types, and not to others.
- In addition to the formal provisions for tax relief, there seems to be discretionary relief on a case-by-case basis.

The horizontal inequity that may be the most contentious in Tunisia is that between workers subject to income tax withholding and workers in the self-employed sector. Again, this factor contributes to an especially heavy burden on formal sector labor.

Note that, if a tax system is "fair", individuals with greater ability to pay will pay greater amounts of taxes, as reflected in different effective tax rates by income class (i.e., "vertical equity"). However, these sources remain largely unexamined.

There are Large Efficiency Costs of Tunisian Taxes

As demonstrated by the general equilibrium calculations of excess burden discussed earlier, the system of taxes in Tunisia is introduces a wide range of distortions in individual and firm behavior, all of which generate significant efficiency costs. For example, the corporate income tax generates many distortions, perhaps more than any other tax in the system. Together with the extensive system of incentives, the corporate tax gives preferential treatment both to different types of investment and to different sectors, thereby leading firms to base their investment decisions mainly on tax considerations rather than on market forces. As discussed earlier, the use of tax incentives to increase investment and to generate growth is a questionable and unproven practice. The personal income tax also generates distortions: it discourages work effort, it reduces the return to savings, and it encourages individuals to move to the informal sector. The simplified tax system also leads to distortions. Unfortunately, there are no estimates of the overall efficiency cost of Tunisia taxes.

The Current System is an Outdated and an Ad Hoc System

Tunisian tax policy has, apparently and increasingly, become focused on accommodating the requests of specific individuals and of specific sectors of the economy. A move away from a transparent and rule-based approach to one with many preferential treatments has harmed the fairness of the system, has increased its distortions, and has increased the burden on taxpayers and tax administrators alike.

It is tempting to assume that favored tax treatments result from pressure from special interest groups. While some of this may go on, the Tunisia government is also likely – for good reasons – to reduce the tax on certain items of necessary consumption in order to help the poor or other target groups, or to reduce the tax on certain types of investments in order to encourage investments that the government considers worthwhile. Regardless of the motivation, however, these policies affect the fairness of the tax system, they lead others to clamor for favorable treatment, they make the system less transparent and more complex, and they lead to unintended and unforeseeable consequences. They also cause a revenue loss that must be made up by higher taxes on other sectors of the economy, and they may well generate corruption.

CONCLUSION: REFORMING TUNISIA'S TAX SYSTEM

There may well be a case for a comprehensive reform of the Tunisian tax system, along the standard lines of broadening the bases of taxation and reducing the rates of taxation. However, a comprehensive reform requires a major effort to study the entire system and to consider the major alternatives. This effort takes considerable time. In the meantime, there are several more incremental reforms that would improve the operation of the Tunisian economy. Potential reform measures include several specific recommendations.

Expand the Base of Indirect Taxes

The bases of indirect taxes have often been narrowed by deliberate policy choices. Broadening the bases will mean mainly two things. The first is fully extending taxes into the service sector. The second is simplifying and reducing existing exemptions and special treatment regimes after a thorough review of these exemptions. When outright elimination is not feasible, the exemptions may be phased out by not renewing them.

Increase VAT Tax Rates

The standard VAT tax rate (18 percent) is comparable (if slightly higher than) the standard rate in many countries. However, the preferential rates of 6 and 12 percent are quite low. These could be increased, even standardized, with little impact on competitiveness.

Reduce the Use of Fiscal, Financial, and Other Incentives

As discussed in detail earlier, these incentives reduce revenues, distort resource allocation, and introduce inequities, with little if any documented impact on intended activities. Their use should be significantly reduced.

Reduce Personal Income and/or Social Security Contribution Rates

There is abundant evidence that labor, especially in the formal sector, is heavily taxed. Reducing taxes on labor (with offsetting increases in indirect taxes) would have many positive economic effects.

Consider Reforms of *Le Regime Forfaitaire*

There are several specific reforms of the simplified tax system that should be considered, such as: ensuring that the tax burdens under the simplified tax system and under the regular tax system are comparable; reevaluating turnover thresholds, so as to ensure that only "small" taxpayers are eligible for the simplified system; adjusting the thresholds for inflation and other changing economic circumstances; and improving enforcement of the simplified tax system to ensure that individuals who participate are in fact eligible for participation and also to prevent purely artificial accounting schemes that allow participation.

Increase Enforcement Effort and Other Administrative Reforms

It is especially important to increase audit activities. World-wide experience also demonstrates that greater use of third-party information is an effective tool in compliance efforts. Finally, efforts to modernize tax administration have been shown to have a significant even if longer-term payoff.

REFERENCES

Alm, J., & Embaye, A. (2013). Using Dynamic Panel Methods to Estimate Shadow Economies around the World, 1990-2006. *Public Finance Review*, *41*(5), 510–543. doi:10.1177/1091142113482353

Alm, J., & Lopez-Castano, H. (2005). Payroll Taxes in Colombia. In R. Bird, J. Poterba, & J. Slemrod (Eds.), *Fiscal Reform in Colombia – Problems and Prospects* (pp. 191–223). Cambridge, MA: The MIT Press.

Alm, J., Martinez-Vazquez, J., & Wallace, S. (2004). *Taxing the Hard to Tax: Lessons from Theory and Practice*. Amsterdam, The Netherlands: Elsevier B.V.

Bird, R., & Casanegra de Jantscher, M. (Eds.). (1992). *Improving Tax Administration in Developing Countries*. Washington, D.C.: International Monetary Fund.

Boadway, R., Bruce, N., & Mintz, J. (1984). Taxation, Inflation, and the Effective Marginal Tax Rate in Canada. *Revue Canadienne d'Economique [The Canadian Journal of Economics]*, *27*(3), 286–299.

Doing Business, 2010 – Reforming through Difficult Times. (2010World Bank. Washington, D.C.: The World Bank and the International Finance Corporation.

Doing Business, 2012 – Doing Business in a More Transparent World. (2012World Bank. Washington, D.C.: The World Bank and the International Finance Corporation.

Gillis, M. (1985). Micro and Macroeconomics of Tax Reform in Indonesia. *Journal of Development Economics*, *19*(3), 221–254. doi:10.1016/0304-3878(85)90030-6

Hines, J. R. Jr. (2007). Corporate Taxation and International Competition. In A. J. Auerbach, J. R. Hines Jr, & J. Slemrod (Eds.), *Taxing Corporate Income in the 21st Century* (pp. 268–295). Cambridge, UK: Cambridge University Press. doi:10.1017/CBO9780511510823.020

Martinez-Vazquez, J., & McNab, R. (2000). The Tax Reform Experiment in Transitional Countries. *National Tax Journal*, *53*(2), 273–298. doi:10.17310/ntj.2000.2.06

OECD. (2012). *Taxing Wages, 2011*. Paris, France: Organisation for Economic Co-operation and Development Publishing.

Sabirianova Peter, K., Buttrick, S., & Duncan, D. (2010). Global reform of personal income taxation, 1981-2005: Evidence from 189 countries. *National Tax Journal*, *63*(3), 447–478. doi:10.17310/ntj.2010.3.03

Surrey, S. S. (1958). Tax Administration in Underdeveloped Countries. *University of Miami Law Review*, *12*(2), 158–188.

Thirsk, W. (1991). Jamaican Tax Incentives. In R. Bahl (Ed.), *The Jamaican Tax Reform* (pp. 701–725). Cambridge, MA: Lincoln Institute of Land Policy.

KEY TERMS AND DEFINITIONS

Computable General Equilibrium Model: A type of modeling in economics, which starts with a system of equations to represent an economy and then uses actual economic data to estimate how the economy reacts to changes in policies.

Horizontal Equity: A principle of fairness in taxation, which holds that individuals with the same ability to pay taxes should pay the same in taxes.

Marginal Effective Tax Rate: A measure of the impact of taxes on the marginal (or incremental) decision by economic agents to invest in capital, defined as the additional tax paid by a firm when it decides to invest in one more unit of capital.

Tax Effort: An index of how effectively a country uses its available tax instruments in collecting taxes, relative to what the country could be reasonably expected to collect from these tax instruments.

Tax Evasion: Intentional and illegal actions taken by agents by which they fail to pay their legally due tax liabilities.

Tax Incidence: The effects of a tax on the distribution of income.

Vertical Equity: A principle of fairness in taxation, which holds that individuals with greater ability to pay taxes should pay more in taxes.

Chapter 17
The Incidence of Taxes in Jordan

Sally Wallace
Georgia State University, USA

Andrey Timofeev
Georgia State University, USA

ABSTRACT

The focus of this chapter is on the incidence of taxes in Jordan. All taxes must ultimately be paid by someone, and one of the most fundamental questions asked by economists is: "Who bears the final burden of a tax?" Taxes cause individuals and firms to change their behaviors, and the resulting changes in product and factor prices will affect the incidence and the distributional effects, of the tax. The answer to the question "Who bears the burden of the tax" requires us to estimate whether or not taxes are regressive; that is, do taxes as a share of income decrease or increase as income increases? This type of analysis is important for a country like Jordan, which is seeking to increase public revenue and encourage economic development. The analysis is also useful as a model for other countries in this important region.

INTRODUCTION AND OVERVIEW

The focus of this chapter is on the incidence of taxes in Jordan. All taxes must ultimately be paid by someone, and one of the most fundamental questions asked by economists is: "Who bears the final burden of a tax?" Taxes cause individuals and firms to change their behaviors, and the resulting changes in product and factor prices will affect the incidence and the distributional effects, of the tax.[1] The answer to the question "Who bears the burden of the tax" requires us to estimate whether or not taxes are regressive; that is, do taxes as a share of income decrease or increase as income increases?

Understanding the incidence of taxes in Jordan is important from several perspectives. Over the past decade, Jordan has seen overall economic growth weaken due to the worldwide financial crisis and associated reduction in economic activity and increased pressure due to a renewed influx of refugees from countries including Syria, Iraq, and Egypt. The tax to GDP ratio has fallen from a high of 20.4 percent in

DOI: 10.4018/978-1-5225-0053-7.ch017

2006 to a current level of approximately 15 percent—on par with countries including Egypt and Lebanon (2011) and substantially lower than several middle income countries including Morocco, Turkey, Mexico. The OECD average tax to GDP ratio is 33.8 percent (Timofeev & Wallace, 2013). Increases in current account deficits in the face of the falling tax to GDP ratio have led to calls for Jordan to increase its tax to GDP ratio while maintaining a stable social environment and providing for economic growth.

An analysis of the incidence and distributional implications of the tax system in Jordan can provide useful information with respect to the equity of the system and provide input into tax reform discussions throughout the region. Why is equity a concern? While Jordan is an upper- middle income country, there is a significant portion of the resident population that falls below the poverty line. The Ministry of Planning, Department of Statistics reports that 14.4 percent of the population fell below the poverty line with 4400 JD per year in 2010 (UNDP, 2013). This represents a substantial portion of the population for whom taxes may represent an especially difficult burden.

The *poverty level* is one measure of income disparity in a country. Another equity-related concept is the *distribution of income* among population groups. A commonly accepted measure of distribution is the Gini coefficient, which measures the difference between complete equity in income distribution (each portion of the population holds the same level of income) and the actual distribution. A Gini of 0 measures perfect equality and a Gini of 1 measures complete inequality (all income concentrated in one person). The World Bank has published estimates of the Gini coefficient for a large number of countries for various years. A sample of those countries is reported in Table 1. These particular countries were chosen as they represent countries similar in relative geography, income, or economic base and are provided as illustrative comparisons. As seen there, the Gini coefficient in Jordan increased between 2008 and 2010 suggesting a less equal distribution of income. Coupled with the increase in poverty rates, it is important for the Government to consider the impacts of tax reform options on the distribution of tax burdens as they may acerbate tensions over income distribution in Jordan.

In this chapter, we address the following questions and issues in the context of Jordan:

- What is the concept of tax incidence and how is it measured?
- How does the current tax system treat low versus high income individuals?
- Are there imbalances in the distribution of taxes that create a perception of unfairness?
- What does the effect tax rate say about distortionary effects of the tax system on economic behavior?

Table 1. Gini Coefficients

Country		Year		
	2003/04	2008	2009	2010
Jordan	38.9	33.8	-	35.4
Georgia	40.4	41.3	41.7	42.1
Indonesia	-	34.1	35.6	38.1
Macedonia	39.0	44.2	43.2	43.6
Serbia	32.8	28.2	27.8	29.6
Turkey	43.4	39.0	38.7	40.0

Source*:* World Bank, World Development Indicators 2003, 2007, 2012

- Are some taxes more progressive and some more regressive?
- How does the distribution of tax burden in Jordan compare to that in other countries?

The goal of this chapter is to provide a better understanding of the current distribution of taxes in Jordan and to estimate the effective rate of taxation on households in Jordan. We estimate the incidence of all major taxes, and perform sensitivity analysis related to the incidence assumptions. This chapter will therefore provide a baseline for evaluating the equity of the system, comparisons to other countries, and provide possible changes to the tax system to increase or decrease the current progressivity of the system.

Methodology

Statutory incidence of taxation is the legal incidence—who by law is liable to pay tax. The economic incidence of taxes takes into consideration the ability of the tax to be shifted through the economy and can be very different from statutory incidence. In general, if a tax is imposed on a mobile factor or on a consumer good for which there are many substitutes, the tax will more easily be shifted to other components of the economy.

The economic study of tax incidence has yielded several principles which serve to inform practical analysis of taxes. The first principle is that only people (individuals) bear the tax burden. Those individuals may be residents of Jordan, or may be residents of other countries. Corporations are simply *legal entities made up of individuals*. By drawing a sharp distinction between individual and corporation, the principle points out a common fallacy that businesses have an independent ability to bear the tax burden. The corporate income tax is a popular focus of taxpayer ire. However, a corporate tax may be shifted in a variety of ways. The company bears the "statutory incidence" of the corporate income tax because its responsibility is to remit the tax payment to the government. However, the economic incidence will be borne by one or more of several possible candidates: the owners of the company who take in lower profits because of the tax, the consumers of the company's product (s) who face higher prices because of the tax, or the workers of the company who receive lower wages.

A second principle of tax incidence is that the incidence of a tax change depends on the change in real income. This may happen on the consumption side or income side. Therefore, the distribution of taxes depends on the consumption pattern of the individuals and on how income is distributed among Jordanians. Therefore both the sources and the uses of income must be analyzed in incidence analysis. There is a third principle underlying tax incidence analysis which is more theoretical in nature. This principle assumes that any tax changes are made in a revenue-neutral way so that the incidence of expenditure changes is not considered. This is referred to as "differential incidence" (Musgrave, 1952). This is an important assumption. Government expenditure is financed from tax revenue, non-tax revenues and borrowing from the public or private sectors.[2] Therefore, any change in tax revenues must be accompanied by a corresponding change in government expenditures, in government debt, in the money supply, or in another tax. In theory, it is important to consider what happens to the new revenue, or loss in revenue. For example, if there are additional revenues that come from a proportional tax and the additional revenues are spent on pro-poor expenditures, the net impact of the tax/expenditure change could be more equalizing in nature. In this analysis, we simply assume that there is no change in the distributional effects of government expenditures, and no distributional change due to the offsetting reduction in taxes or non-tax revenue.

That tax incidence does not depend on where the tax is imposed is a fourth important principle in incidence analysis. And, finally, incidence depends upon elasticity or responsiveness of buyers and sellers to changes in prices (the price elasticities of demand and supply). When a tax is imposed, individuals will adjust their behavior to reduce their tax liabilities. Those who are better able to adjust their behavior are better able to shift the burden to others and will bear less of the burden of the tax. For example, if consumers have a low response to gasoline prices, then consumers will bear more of the incidence of a tax on gasoline. Similarly, if workers are able to reduce their work effort or to shift their labor to untaxed sectors in response to an individual income tax or a payroll tax, then workers will bear less of the burden of an income or a payroll tax.

There are a number of steps in the methodology used to analyze the incidence and distribution of taxes. There are five main steps in the analysis:

- Determine the taxes to be analyzed.
- Identify appropriate data to measure household income and consumption, determine a measure of ability to pay.
- Appealing to the literature on tax incidence, make appropriate assumptions regarding the incidence of each tax.
- Once the incidence has been determined, allocate the tax to individuals based on their share of consumption or income (depending on the incidence assumption) or their share of factor income.
- Sort the population from lowest income to highest ability to pay (often proxied by income) to report how much tax is paid relative to income (by income groups) and also report the tax paid relative to income by each segment of the population, i.e., -- *the average effective tax rate* or the ratio of tax paid to income. If the average effective tax rate increases with income, the system is called "progressive" and if it falls as income rises, the tax is regressive.

At each step in the methodology, important decisions have to be made and many of those hinge on assumptions based on available data and existing literature. These assumptions become critically important in the incidence analysis. We perform some sensitivity tests on these assumptions to judge how large an impact they have.

The taxes that are analyzed in this report are: employee and self-employed income tax, corporate income tax, tax on capital (interest, dividends, rents), property tax, property transfer tax, excise taxes, customs duties, and general sales tax. We use 2011 as the base year for the analysis, and allocate a total of 3.3 billion JD in revenue, allocated as follows:

- Employee and self-employed tax: 148 million JD
- Corporate income tax (CIT): 523 million JD
- Property transfer tax: 171 million JD
- Property tax: 54 million JD
- Excise (SST): 779 million JD[3]
- Customs: 236 million JD
- General sales tax (GST): 1,600 million JD
- TOTAL: 3,511 million JD

The personal income tax is levied on salaried individuals (who largely pay tax through a withholding system) and individuals with self-employment and other income. The tax rates are 7 and 14 percent and there is a substantial basic deduction of 12,000 JD for individuals and 24,000 for families. This threshold is high relative to average monthly income and to the poverty line. As a result, a very small portion of the population is liable to pay the tax.

The corporate income tax is levied on profits of incorporated firms at a basic rate of 14 percent for general legal entities, 24 percent for the communications, insurance, and certain financial companies, and 30 percent for banks.

The real property tax base is the annual rental value of all residential, commercial, and industrial properties and vacant land (Bahl, 2010). The tax rate is 15 percent but it is a combination of a 10 percent municipal property tax, a 3 percent sewer fee, and a 2 percent education fee. Vacant land is taxed at a nominal rate of 2 percent. The property transfer tax is levied at a rate of 5 percent on the value of real property transferred.

Indirect taxes are the main source of tax revenues in Jordan. They include the General Sales Tax (GST), Special Sales Taxes (SST), and Import Duties. Together they accounted for about three quarters of the national tax revenues in 2011. Jordan uses the "credit-invoice" approach in its General Sales Tax (essentially a form of VAT) and Special Sales Taxes (essentially excises). GST is a broad-based sales tax with a standard rate of 16 percent, and reduced rates of 0, 4, 7 and 8 percent applied to selected items. Special Sales Tax is levied on certain selected goods and services according to ad valorem and specific rates.

The burden of the tax will be analyzed relative to the ability of the households to pay taxes. Ability to pay comes from a comprehensive definition of income and the assumption is the larger the income, the higher the ability to pay. To analyze the tax burden across households, we need to work with household level data—or what might be called micro data. Jordan's Household Expenditure and Income Survey (HEIS, 2010) provides detailed household level information on types of income (wages, capital, rental income, etc.) and detailed information on expenditures (tobacco, fuel, clothing, food, etc.). Survey data provided substantial detail, but can suffer from reporting biases—income is often underreported and expenditures may also be misreported. Based on discussions with the Department of Statistics and practices used in many other countries, this analysis relies on total household expenditures as a measure of ability to pay.

In fact, the actual distribution of income and expenditures by household reported in the HEIS is quite similar. Figure 1 shows the distribution of households by population decile (the lowest 10 percent of population in terms of household expenditures to the top 10 percent of the population). As seen there, income and expenditures are distributed very similarly among household deciles. Because our tax collections are for 2011, we inflate the 2010 expenditure base to 2011 levels using an expenditure inflation adjustment of 6.6 percent (based on macro data provided by USAID Fiscal Reform Project II staff). We made one additional adjustment to the 2011 data for the fuel subsidy that was instituted that year. The subsidy was made available to households with income less than 10,000 JD and was allocated as 70 JD per family member up to a total of six family members (420 JD limit). This subsidy adds to the households' ability to pay and to consume, so it is appropriate to scale up expenditures in this manner. Other government subsidies are included in total expenditures (as a proxy for income) by default since they were already available in 2010.

The next section of the report provides detail on the incidence and allocation methods for each major tax. These assumptions and methods are summarized in Table 2.

Figure 1. Distribution of Income and Expenditure by Expenditure Decile (2010)

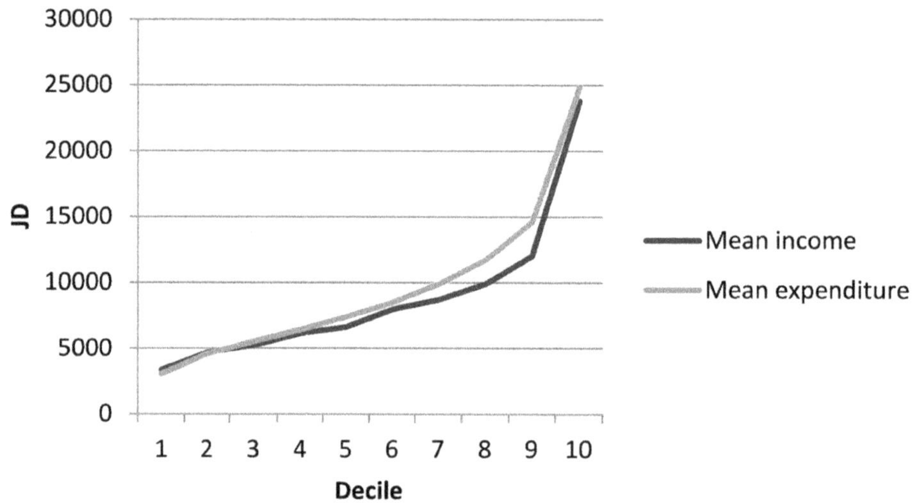

Table 2. Summary of Taxes Analyzed, Level of Revenue, Incidence Assumption, and Allocation Methods

Tax Source	Collection Attributed (2011)	Incidence Assumption	Allocation Method
Individual income tax	TOTAL: 74,000,000 Domestic:100% Foreign: 0%	100% Borne by labor in self-employed sector above threshold	Simulated 2009 law with HEIS data and then adjusted to total collection amount
Employee income tax (PAYE)	TOTAL: 74,000,000 Domestic: 98% Foreign: 2%	100% Borne by wage-earners (labor) above threshold	Simulated 2009 law for wage earners with HEIS data and then adjusted to total collection amount
Corporate income tax (partnerships and corporations)	TOTAL: 568,456,962 Domestic: 49% Foreign: 51%	50% Borne by labor (wage earners); 50% borne by capital ALTERNATIVE: 50% borne by consumer; 50% borne by capital NOTE: In all cases the portion borne by wages is assumed to remain domestic; portion borne by capital is assumed 51% foreign	Wages as reported in the HEIS, capital income from HEIS (sum of rental income q910, q912, q914, and income from interest, bonds, stocks q922)
Tax on interest, mutual funds	TOTAL: 3,273,111 Domestic: 100%	Allocated based on ownership of capital	Capital income from HEIS (sum of rental income q910, q912, q914 and income from interest, bonds, and stocks q922)
GST	TOTAL: 1,599,484,901 Domestic: 100% Foreign: 0%	100% Borne by consumers	Input and output taxes declared by vendors mapped to HEIS data on final consumption

Notes: Revenue data from ISTD and project staff. HEIS is used for distribution of tax revenue at the household level.

Incidence and Allocation Assumptions

Having identified appropriate data to measure households' ability to pay, next we make appropriate assumptions regarding the incidence of each tax *based on* the literature on tax incidence.

Incidence of taxes on labor: personal income (including salaried and self-employed workers). The incidence of taxes on wage income is a function of the labor supply elasticity—how much labor changes as wages change. The intuition is straightforward—if labor is mobile, then, as taxes on labor increase, individuals will seek to escape the tax by moving to sectors without the tax or otherwise reducing their work effort.

Based on relatively standard assumptions regarding this mobility and the incidence of taxes on labor, we assume that the income taxes fall 100 percent on labor. We allocate the income tax revenues across households based on the share of wage over the current 12,000/24,000 threshold held in each decile.

Incidence of the corporate income tax. The debate over the incidence of taxes is probably most contested in the case of corporate income taxes (Harris, 2009). The theoretical analysis done on the corporate income tax for developed countries in the 1960s and 1970s suggested that the tax could be borne by owners of capital (general financiers large and small), labor in the form of lower wages (which could be reduced to lower the firms' cost of business once a corporate income tax is imposed or increased), or consumers in the form of higher prices (Harberger 1962; McLure 1975; Hines 1999). Just like the incidence analysis of all other taxes, the true impact of the corporate income tax is affected by the type of market, competitiveness of output prices, mobility of capital and labor, wage constraints, price elasticity of demand for the output, and other factors.

Based on the literature (summarized in Harris, 2009; Felix, 2007), in our baseline distribution of tax burdens, we assume that 50 percent of the corporate income tax falls on capital and 50 percent on labor (wages). Of the 50 percent that falls on capital, we assume that 49 percent of that is on households in Jordan.[4] The HEIS provides detail on holdings of capital income (interest, dividends, property revenue) and wages, which allows us to allocate a portion of the corporate income tax revenue to capital and to labor income. We provide sensitivity analysis where we assume that 50 percent of tax is borne by capital and 50 percent is borne by consumers via general consumption.

Incidence of taxes on property transfer and property tax. Like the corporate income tax, there is some controversy regarding the incidence of these taxes. The "traditional view" of the property tax finds that capital owners bear no burden of the property tax on capital; the tax is borne by renters, consumers, and/or labor. In this case, the tax on land is borne by land owners since land cannot "escape" the tax. The "new view" treats the average tax as falling on capital and then the differentials around the average encourage capital to move among jurisdictions until the net of tax rates of return on capital are equal. The net rate of return to capital falls as a result but how much it falls depends on the effect on land and labor. Property taxes are more progressive under the new view than under the traditional view.

Finally, the benefits view of property tax incidence argues that the property tax is a benefits tax equal to the benefits received for the public services funded by the property tax. In this case, the tax is a user charge—and there is an inherent fairness to the tax based on the benefit principle (Hamilton 1975).

In this study, we apply alternative assumptions regarding the incidence of taxes on property based on the classical literature noted above. We assume first that 50 percent of the tax is borne by renters and 50 percent by owners of property and then we assume that 100 percent is borne by renters in the case of residential property. In the case of commercial property we use a set of alternative incidence assumptions including shifting of the tax to consumers.

Incidence of sales taxes. For indirect taxes, the tax burden of a particular group of households is commonly defined as a loss of their real incomes or in other words the reduction of the amount of consumption resulting from reduced purchasing power of their incomes.[5] In the indirect tax model, our approach is essentially a hybrid of simulation and tax allocation. Following the tax allocation approach, we start with actual taxes collected by businesses from their buyers and paid to their suppliers (or to Jordan Customs in the case of imported supplies). Then we percolate these output taxes net of input tax credits throughout the production chain in order to impute the tax element in the market price of final consumption,[6] which is the difference between the price actually paid by the final consumer and a counterfactual price that would be in place without taxes. Once we know the amount of tax in the market price of a consumer good, we apply these price changes to the actual household expenditures on specific commodities. Similar to the micro-simulation approach, we account for the tax burden in all household purchases, including the higher prices of purchases from informal vendors responding to tax increases in the formal sector through market arbitrage.

Following the conventional approach (as, for example, described in Sahn, and Stephen Younger, 2003), in this study the incidence of the sales taxes is assumed to be on the final consumer. Using data from HEIS allows us to relate the tax burden of the sales taxes to the size of a household budget. The Income and Sales Tax Department (ISTD) reports sales tax receipts by business activity code (ISIC) of the suppler. First, we aggregate the receipts into 81 industries in Jordan's input-output table, provided by the Department of Statistics under the Ministry of Planning. This allows us to calculate the "average actual rate" for each industry as the ratio of the total amount of net taxes paid in each industry divided by the total domestic sales for that industry. In addition, we estimate input taxes paid on imported inputs in each industry. This is calculated as a product of the average actual rate for a given imported input times the input-output coefficient from the I-O table for imported inputs.

However, with the exception of the part of output that is exported abroad at given world prices, the market prices of the final domestic consumption of goods and services are expected to include indirect taxes paid by businesses throughout the domestic production chain. Therefore, average actual rates for each industry are translated into effective rates on outputs (or percentage price changes caused by taxes). Similar to the approach in Rajemison *et al.* (2003), we use the Leontief inverse matrix for domestic production to compute the price changes resulting from the given net taxes imposed on various businesses throughout the production chain. Next we map output prices for these 81 industries into 33 main groups of commodities in the HEIS (16 groups of food commodities and 17 groups of non-food commodities). The impact of taxes on the market prices of products of respective industries is accounted in household budgets according to the relative share of household expenditures on those products. While the share of the "tax element" in household expenditures on a particular commodity group is estimated to be the same for all income levels, when applying this share to actual household expenditures, which vary across income deciles, we arrive at different amounts of the tax burden for different groups of households. This exercise is done for all 33 commodity groups. Finally, based on percentage price changes for each group of household expenditures, we compute the loss of real income (or purchasing power) for each decile of households.

Incidence of import duties. We use 2011 data on import duties paid as well as the value of imports declared by importers to Jordan Customs. For each industry, we calculate the "average actual rate" as the ratio of the total amount of import duty paid in that sector divided by the total imports for that sector.

Incidence analysis of import duties on final products relies on the similar set of assumptions as for the sales taxes but with a few adjustments. Because the burden of the sales taxes is analyzed separately, here we do not consider the additional tax burden arising from the inclusion of import duties in the taxable base for the sales taxes. Furthermore, for import duties on intermediate inputs, the incidence assumptions will differ between industries producing non-tradable outputs as opposed to products that have to compete with imports. For industries, producing non-tradable outputs

GST: Taxes on means of production are not allocated to final consumption due to lack of data on consumption of fixed capital by sector. Tax burden estimated only for private households but not for residents of collective living quarters (hotels, rooming houses and other lodging houses, institutions and camps). (e.g. personal services), we assume that import duties on inputs are fully passed forward to the final consumers.

However, for tradable products, the market price is determined by world markets and thus domestic producers will have to absorb import duty on their inputs. In addition to the change of real incomes of consumers (through market prices), customs duties also affect the income of the owners of factors of production in the tradable sector.[9] The impact of import duties on the aggregate factor income in the economy is derived by weighting percentage changes in sectoral value added with the shares of those sectors in the total income of factors of production. We allocate losses in factor income across households based on the share of wage and capital income in each decile.

The incidence assumptions and allocation methods used for all of the taxes are summarized in Table 2. In some cases, we list multiple incidence assumptions and will test those in our sensitivity analysis. The first assumption listed should be considered the "base case."

Findings

The level of direct tax paid by households varies from 171 JD per year in the first decile to 2,892 JD per year in the 10th decile (Figure 2). The distribution of the tax burden for direct taxes (personal, employee, corporate, property taxes and taxes on capital) is progressive (see Figure 3). The burden (tax divided by household budget) ranges from 4.9 percent (first decile) to 10.9 percent in the 10th decile. The progressivity is largely affected by the distribution of the personal and employee income tax. The large threshold eliminates most of the households from the income tax system. The assumption that the corporate income tax is shared by wages and capital means that some of the burden of corporate tax is found in all deciles—since there are households in each decile that report wage income.

Figure 2. Mean Direct Tax, JD 2011

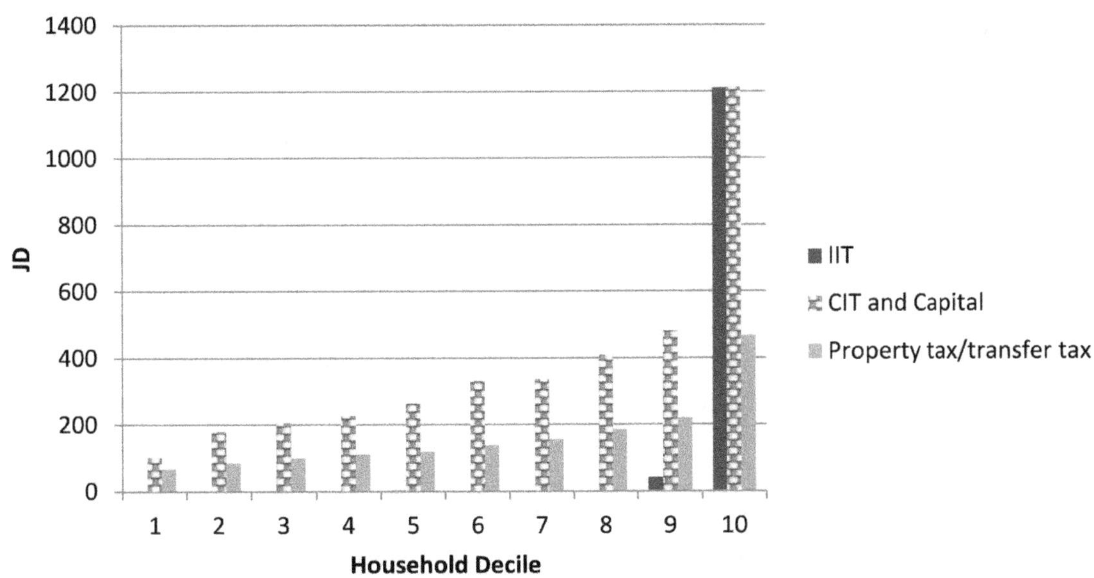

Figure 3. Direct Taxes as a Share of Household Expenditure, 2011

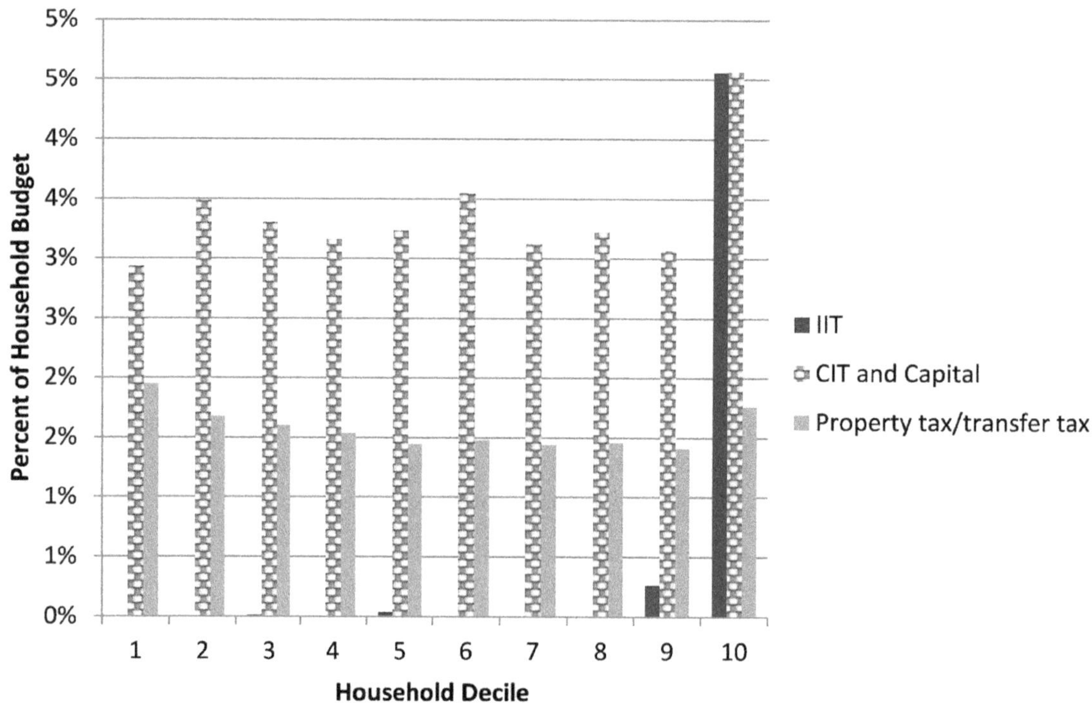

Under the aforementioned incidence assumption, the burden of the sales taxes is practically flat (Figure 4). It is only mildly progressive at the bottom, increasing from 8.22% for the first decile to 9.69% for the sixth decile, and then slightly regressive over deciles 7-10, dropping to 9.1% for the top decile. Thus all households essentially pay the same share of their budgets in sales taxes, with the middle class sacrificing a slightly higher share of their incomes than the poor or the rich.

A similar distributional pattern is found for the price increases caused by the import duties. This (gross) tax burden is increasing from 2.24% for the first decile to 2.55% for the fourth decile, and then mildly declining over deciles 5-9, and dropping to 1.90% for the top decile. However, higher prices of final consumption goods are not the only impact of import duties on household budgets. Given our assumption that the tax burden cannot be fully shifted forward in the domestic production of tradable goods, one has to take into account a change in returns to labor and capital in those sectors. We estimate that import duties have a positive impact on the aggregate level of factor incomes, off-setting more than half of the burden of price increases caused by the import duties. This is because higher output prices off-set higher input costs in three quarters of sectors producing tradable goods. However, because these gains are concentrated in relatively capital-intensive sectors, they off-set a significantly larger share of the purchasing power loss for the top-decile households than for households at other levels of income.

All in all, the gross combined burden of all indirect taxes (not account for the impact of import duties on factor incomes) is mildly progressive at the bottom, increasing from 10.45% for the first decile to 12.21% for the sixth decile, and then mildly regressive over deciles 7-9 before dropping to 11% for the top decile (Figure 5). This incidence is determined by interplay of the progressive burden of taxes on transport-related commodities, and to a lesser extent adult clothes and education, and the regressive burden of taxes on most other groups of commodities, especially tobacco. Even though the burden for

Figure 4. Sales Tax and Import Duty as a Share of Household Expenditures, 2011
Note: The offset refers to the impact of import duties on factor incomes

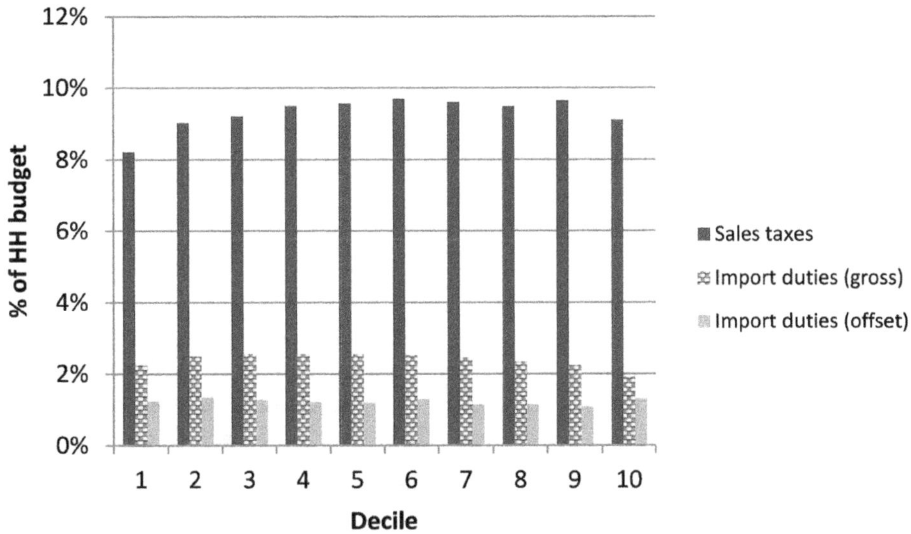

Figure 5. Indirect tax by item as a Percent of Household Expenditure, 2011
Note: These gross burdens do not account for the offsetting impact of import duties on factor incomes

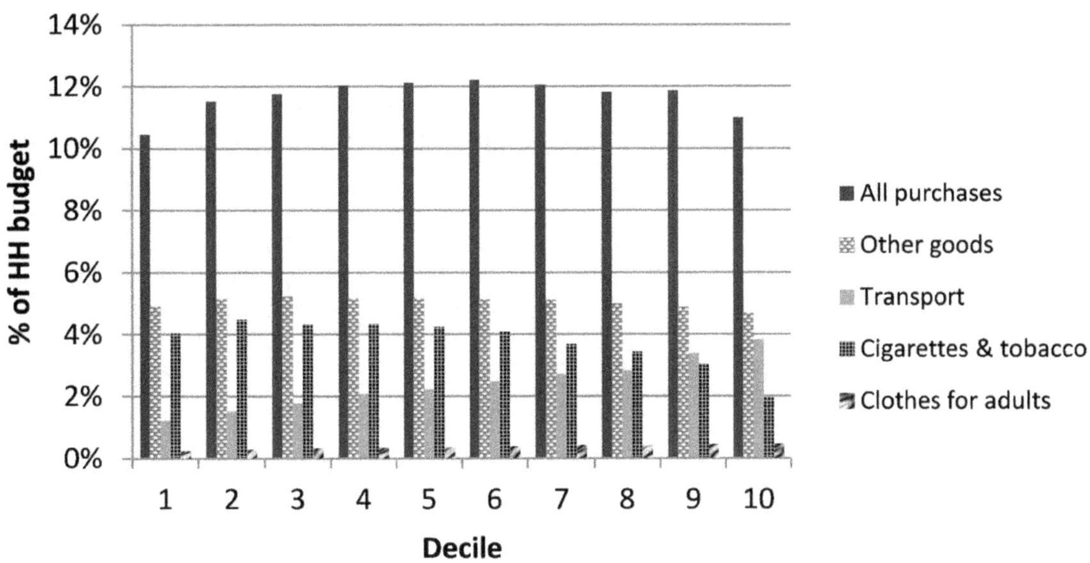

better-off household might be declining relative to their ability to pay, nevertheless it is increasing in absolute amounts. Thus the top decile pays eight times more in higher prices caused by indirect taxes than the bottom decile, roughly in line with differences in the size of household budgets

Finally, it has to be pointed out that the deviations from the proportional distribution of the tax burden for selected commodities are to a large extent due to the Special Sales Tax (see Figure 6). As one can see from the figure below, the burden of the SST on cars and motor fuels is sharply progressive.

Figure 6. Special Sales Tax Burden

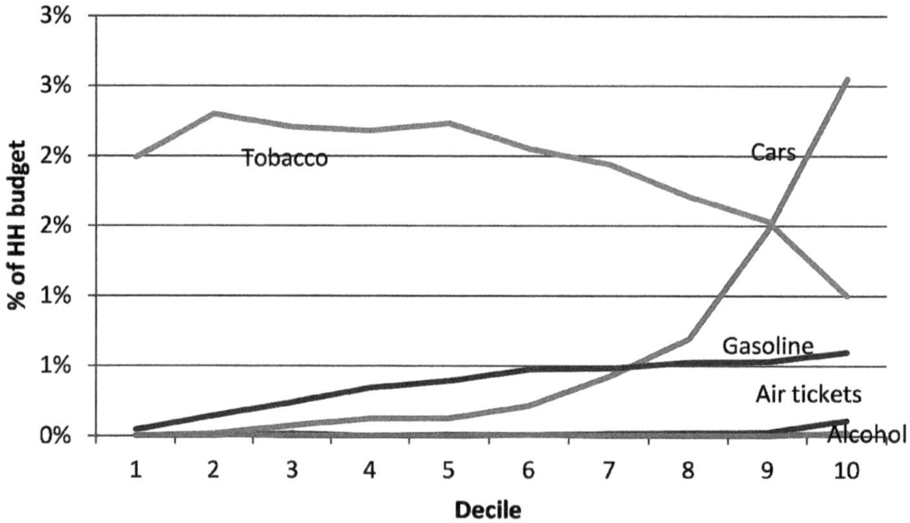

The entire burden story is summed up in Figure 7, which presents the tax burden of direct taxes, net burden of indirect taxes, and the combined tax burden as a share of household expenditures. The combined burden of the entire tax system is progressive and as noted earlier, this is driven by the very progressive distribution of the income tax and relatively flat distribution of consumption taxes.

The distributional implications are generally as expected with consumption taxes falling proportionally among the budget deciles and direct taxes progressively across the same deciles. Compared to other countries, the general distribution of Jordan's taxes is similar to that found in Pakistan, Jamaica, and

Figure 7. Direct plus indirect taxes as a share of household expenditure, 2011
Note: Direct taxes include: personal income (including employees and self-employed), corporate income tax, taxes on capital, property and property transfer tax; Indirect taxes include: GST, excises and the net impact of custom duties.

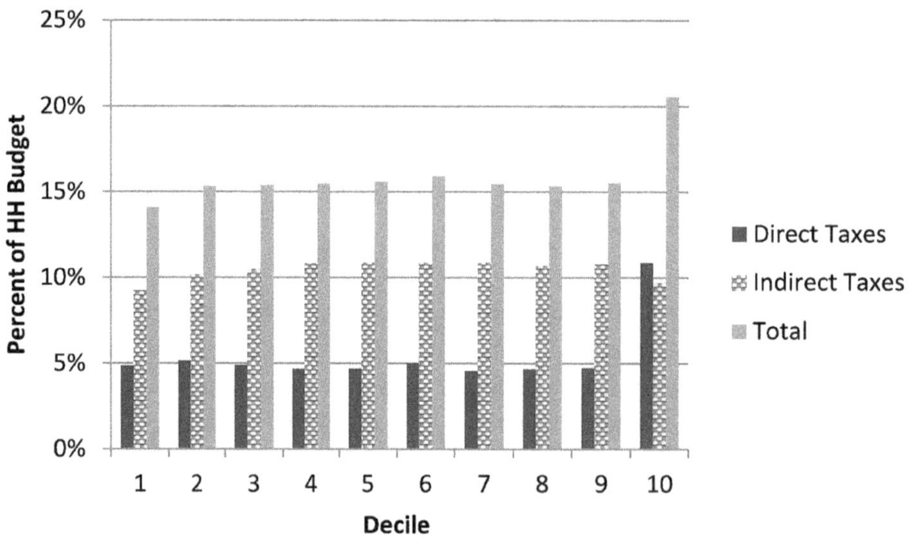

Chile. However, the level of indirect taxes as a share of the household budget in Jordan is larger than that found in those countries. For example, in Pakistan, the equivalent level effective tax rate for excise is approximately 9 percent (2007). In countries including Chile, South Africa, and Slovenia, among others, the system of direct taxes (notably the individual income tax) introduced progressivity in the overall burden of taxes. In these countries, the direct taxes play a larger role than in Jordan, so the resulting overall distribution of tax burden is progressive over a larger portion of the population. This is in contrast to the case of Jordan where the progressivity of direct taxes is almost exclusively found in the top two deciles.

The relatively proportional nature of consumption taxes in Jordan may reduce the potential for tax avoidance. In cases where the tax base is broad, it is not easy for individuals to find non-tax substitute goods. Therefore, from an efficiency stand-point, the distribution of the consumption tax is a positive attribute of the fiscal system. Regarding the direct taxes, the focus on upper income earners paying income tax may be problematic for just the opposite reason that the consumption tax distribution is positive. High income individuals often have several "levers" to pull to avoid taxes—they may be able to move money off-shore or into different forms of income that would be less taxable including investments abroad. So on efficiency grounds, the income tax case is weak.

From the perspective of equity, some might argue that a proportional consumption tax is unfair. How much equity is fair is a decision for Jordanians. Relative to many other countries with an income tax, the threshold of income tax in Jordan is quite high, which results in this steep progressivity of the tax burden. However, the expenditure side of the budget could be used to offset the consumption tax burden as in the case of the tax on fuels. Equity considerations should include an analysis of the expenditure side of the budget.

Sensitivity Analysis

As noted in this report, some incidence assumptions are more tenuous than others in the case of direct taxes. This is particularly true for the corporate income tax and the property and property transfer taxes. The first sensitivity analysis run was to substitute the 50 percent CIT on wages for 50 CIT on consumption (shifting the burden to final consumers). Because the distribution of consumption is quite similar to that of wages, there is virtually no change in the overall distribution of taxes using this assumption.

Similar sensitivity analyses were performed for the property taxes. In these cases, the burden first assumed to fall on owners of property. In the sensitivity analysis, the burden was shared between property owners and renters which will shift the burden of the tax down into the lower deciles. The net result is a property tax system that is markedly regressive—with a burden of 6.77 percent of household expenditures in the first decile compared to 4.8 percent in the base case. The level of property tax is not sufficient to offset the progressivity of the income tax and as a result the system of direct taxes remains progressive under these alternative assumptions but less so than in the baseline case.

There are other interesting demographics associated with the concept of tax burden including relative taxes borne by men versus women or in urban versus rural areas. The HEIS is comprised of 86.5 percent male head of households and 13.5 percent female (weighted, as reported in the survey). Regarding tax incidence, it would be interesting to know whether female headed households earn money or consume differently from male headed households. For example, if female headed households consume relatively less of their budget in tobacco, they would attract a lower amount of burden of taxes on tobacco (relative to their budget).

The comparisons among households by these demographics can be accomplished in several ways. First, we look at the relative number of female and male headed households in each decile, where the deciles are defined across the entire population. If household budgets were equally weighted across the distribution for both genders, we should see approximately 10 percent of female households in the first decile and the same for males. However, we see something quite different in the data. As shown in Table 3, female households are much more heavily concentrated in the lowest two deciles, while there are fewer female households (as a percent of all female households) in the top deciles. For males, we see a more even distribution across deciles except that the lowest decile is *less* concentrated in male households. Taxes that affect the low end of the income distribution could be expected to have a magnified impact on female households as a result.

Reported wages in female households are substantially lower than in male households. In the top decile, the average wage for women is half that for men (on average). This suggests that the burden of the personal income tax is largely irrelevant for female headed households. As noted earlier, taxes on tobacco are an important source of revenue, and over the income distribution create some regressivity to the system. Interestingly, among female households, tobacco consumption as a share of household budgets is on par or greater than that found in male households. This relative expenditure pattern suggests that the tobacco tax is *more* regressive when analyzed from a gender perspective than it is when the overall distribution is analyzed. Female households spend a smaller share of their budgets on transportation and communication in general, but there is also less progressivity to their consumption of these items—the top deciles do not spend more relative to their budget than the lower deciles. The fuel tax will therefore not be progressive as it is in the general population.

In general, women headed households spend the largest share of their budget on housing and household expenditures. The lowest decile for female headed household spends 27 percent of their budget on housing and household expenditures—the largest share being rent (or imputed rent), while for male households it is 22 percent. Direct taxes such as property tax will therefore add a relatively heavy burden on low-income female headed households relative to males.

Table 3. Percent of Gender-specific Households by Decile

Decile	% of Female Households	% of Male Households
1	23.9	7.8
2	11.5	9.8
3	9.7	10.1
4	9.2	10.1
5	7.4	10.4
6	6.8	10.5
7	7.8	10.3
8	6.9	10.5
9	9.2	10.1
10	7.6	10.4
Total	100	100

Overall, the implication of gender on tax burden is a mixed bag. Some direct taxes such as the income tax will impose less burden while property taxes will impose a higher burden on low income female households than male households at the same relative level of income/expenditures. Regarding consumption taxes, because the concentration of consumption varies across gender, we expect to see a slightly more regressive burden for tobacco taxes that is not outweighed by taxes on fuels for female households.

CONCLUSION

This study has provided an analysis of the incidence of Jordan's main taxes: personal income (employees and self-employed), corporate income, real property and property transfer taxes, customs, general consumption tax, excises, and taxes on capital (interest, dividends, rent). Using data from a variety of sources, total tax collections in 2011 were attributed to households in the HEIS based on household expenditures and reported income items under a set of assumptions regarding who bears the burden of the taxes. The major findings of the analysis are as follows:

- The total amount of tax paid per household ranges from a low of 493 JD in the first decile (lowest level of household budget) to a high of 5,469 JD in the top decile.
- The system of indirect taxes (customs, excise and general sales tax) is relatively proportional over all deciles—that is households pay roughly the same proportion of their income in these taxes (approximately 10.44 percent). There is mild progressivity to the burden of these taxes, with the share growing marginally from the first to the sixth decile, and then slightly regressive from the seventh through the tenth decile.
    - The rough proportionality of indirect taxes comes about from the broad base of these taxes. The burden of taxable goods consumed heavily by low income households as a share of their budget (tobacco for example) is offset in the total burden by goods consumed heavily by high income households relative to the size of their budget (vehicles and fuel for vehicles, for example)
- The system of direct taxes (personal and corporate income, property taxes and taxes on capital) are distributed in a progressive manner—households with larger budgets pay a larger percent of their household budget in direct taxes.
    - The current threshold of the personal income tax system is a principal driver in the progressivity of the direct tax system; most households are exempt from the personal income tax.
    - The burden of the corporate income tax is assumed to fall on capital and labor, which tempers the progressivity of the corporate income tax and results in some of the burden falling on households in the lower deciles.
- The overall distribution of tax burden in Jordan is not dissimilar to that found in many other countries, with the direct taxes providing progressivity to the system and the consumption system relatively proportional, with a small amount of regressivity from the middle to higher deciles. The main difference in Jordan, relative to other countries is the size of the indirect burden relative to the direct tax burden. While in developing countries indirect taxes typically outweigh direct taxes, in Jordan, there is a somewhat larger concentration of indirect taxes.
- Policy implications:

- The relatively proportional burden of the indirect taxes is due to a broad-mix of tax items. Retaining a broad tax base reduces the incentive for consumers to shift between taxable and non-taxable goods—retaining efficiency in the tax system.
- The personal income tax is almost exclusively concentrated in the highest decile where there is more ability for taxpayers to engage in avoidance activities. If the Government were to seek additional revenues from the personal income tax, there is some room in the distribution of taxes to lower the threshold and move some of the burden into the deciles below the 9th and 10th.
- The overall burden of tax in Jordan is somewhat low relative to peer middle income countries. There has also been a precipitous decline in tax revenue to GDP since the mid-2000s. If the Government sought to increase revenue through tax policy changes, small changes in the indirect tax rate could be revenue productive given their wide reach across the income distribution.
- Tax administration is a critical component of any change in tax policy. If Government were to make changes to the tax system, they should be as simple to administer and comply with as possible.
- Tax expenditures (revenue foregone due to exemptions, deductions, credits, etc.) not only reduce revenue, they provide additional avenues for tax avoidance and evasion (Heredia, 2014).
- The expenditure side of distribution should also be considered in an overall evaluation of the equity of the fiscal system in Jordan.[10] Price controls, subsidies, and other public expenditures could enhance or detract from the overall equity of the fiscal system.

In summary, Jordan's main taxes are distributed in a progressive manner due to the direct taxes in the system. The consumption taxes are relatively proportional, which increases the economic efficiency of the tax. There is "room" to reduce the income tax threshold and reduce tax expenditures (Heredia-Ortiz, 2014) in an effort to increase Jordan's tax to GDP ratio. The consumption tax level is robust, but there is some room to increase that relative to what is found in other countries. Small increases in the rate will have substantial impacts on revenue but very little impact on the relative fairness of the tax system.

REFERENCES

Alleyne, D., Alm, J., Bahl, R., & Wallace, S. (2004). *Tax Burden in Jamaica. International Study Program*. Atlanta, GA: Andrew Young School of Policy Studies, Georgia State University.

Atkinson, A. B. (2000). Increased Income Inequality in OECD Countries and the Redistributive Impact of the Government Budget. *UNU World Institute for Development Economics Research*, Working Paper No. 202.

Bird, R. M., & De Wulf, L. H. (1973). Taxation and Income Distribution in Latin America: A Critical Review of Empirical Studies. *International Monetary Fund Staff Papers*, *20*(3), 639–682. doi:10.2307/3866523

Bird, R. M., & Miller, B. D. (1991). The Incidence of Indirect Taxes on Low-Income Households in Jamaica. In R. Bahl (Ed.), *The Jamaican Tax Reform* (pp. 793–811). Cambridge, MA: Lincoln Institute of Land Policy.

Blejer, M. I., & Guerrero, I. (1990). The Impact of Macroeconomic Policies on Income Distribution: An Empirical Study of the Philippines. *The Review of Economics and Statistics*, *72*(3), 414–423. doi:10.2307/2109349

Caspersen, E., & Metcalf, G. (1994). Is A Value Added Tax Progressive? Annual Versus Lifetime Incidence Measures. *National Tax Journal*, *47*, 731–746.

Chen, D., Matovu, J. M., & Reinikka, R. (2001). A Quest for Revenue and Tax Incidence in Uganda. *IMF Working Paper /01/24*. Washington D.C.: IMF.

Devarajan, S., Fullerton, D., & Musgrave, R. A. (1980). Estimating the Distribution of Tax Burdens: A Comparison of Different Approaches. *Journal of Public Economics*, *13*(2), 155–182. doi:10.1016/0047-2727(80)90011-0

Felix, R. A. (2007). Passing the Burden: Corporate Tax Incidence in Open Economies. *Regional Research Working Paper RRWP 07-01*, Federal Reserve Bank of Kansas City.

Gemmell, N., & Morrissey, O. (2005). Distribution and Poverty Impacts of Tax Structure Reform in Developing Countries: How Little We Know. *Development Policy Review*, *23*(2), 131–144. doi:10.1111/j.1467-7679.2005.00279.x

Harberger, A. C. (1962). The Incidence of the Corporate Income Tax. *Journal of Political Economy*, *70*(3), 215–240. doi:10.1086/258636

Harris, B. H. (2009). Corporate Tax Incidence and Its Implication for Progressivity. Tax Policy Center, Urban Institute and Brookings Institution, Washington, D.C.

Heredia-Ortiz, E. (2014). *Evaluating Tax Expenditures in Jordan. Report prepared for Jordan Fiscal Reform II Project.* United Agency for International Development.

Hines, J. Jr. (1999). Three Sides of Harberger Triangles. *The Journal of Economic Perspectives*, *13*(2), 167–188. doi:10.1257/jep.13.2.167

Historical Effective Tax Rates 1979-2005. Publication 8885. (2007Congressional Budget Office. Washington, D.C: U.S. Government Printing Office.

Institute on Taxation and Economic Policy. (2003). *Who Pays? A Distributional Analysis of the Tax Systems in all 50 States*. Washington, D.C.: Institute on Taxation and Economic Policy.

Kiefer, D. W. (1984). Distributional Tax Progressivity Indexes. *National Tax Journal*, *37*, 497–513.

Killingsworth, M. (1983). *Labor Supply*. Cambridge, MA: Cambridge University Press. doi:10.1017/CBO9780511572104

MacKenzie, G. A. (1992). Estimating the Base of the Value-Added Tax in Developing Countries: The Problem of Exemption. *Public Finance*, *47*(2), 257–270.

Martinez-Vazquez, J. (1993). The Incidence of Tax Evasion: A Review of the Issues. *Andrew Young School of Policy Studies, Policy Research Program Archived Papers*. Atlanta, GA: Georgia State University.

Martinez-Vazquez, J. (2007). The Impact of Budgets on the Poor: Tax and Expenditure Benefit Incidence Analysis. In B. Moreno-Dodson & Q. Wodon (Eds.), *Public Finance for Poverty Reduction*. Washington, D.C.: The World Bank.

Rajemison, H., Haggblade, S., & Younger, S. D. (2003, September). Indirect Tax Incidence in Madagascar: Updated Estimates Using the Input-Output Table. *Cornell Food and Nutrition Policy Program Working Paper No. 147*.

Rochjadi, A., & Leuthold, J. H. (1994). The Effect of Taxation on Labor Supply in a Developing Country: Evidence from Cross-Sectional Data. *Economic Development and Cultural Change*, *42*(2), 333–350. doi:10.1086/452083

Sahn, D. E., & Younger, S. D. (2003). Estimating the Incidence of Indirect Taxes in Developing Countries. In F. Bourguignon & L. A. P. DaSilva (Eds.), *The Impact of Economic Policies on Poverty and Income Distribution Evaluation Techniques and Tools*. Washington, D.C.: The World Bank and Oxford Press.

Schneider, F. (2005). Shadow Economies of 145 Countries All Over the World: Estimation Results over the Period 1999 to 2003. Paper presented at the Annual Meeting of the European Public Choice Society, Durham, UK. Retrieved from http://www.businessenvironment.org/dyn/be/docs/48/Shadow%20 Economy%20in%20145%20countries%201999-2003.pdf

The World Bank. (2005). *World Development Report*. Washington, D.C.: The World Bank.

Timofeev, A., & Wallace, S. (2013, October 4). Tax Incidence Report: Jordan, Jordan Fiscal Reform II, DAI, Inc. /USAID Washington, D.C. Retrieved from http://frp2.org/English/Portals/0/PDFs/Technical%20Reports/Tax%20Incidence%20Report.pdf

UNDP. (2013, January 28). *Jordan Poverty Reduction Strategy – Final Report*. Retrieved from http://www.undp.org/content/dam/jordan/docs/Poverty/Jordanpovertyreductionstrategy.pdf

Wahid, U., & Wallace, S. (2008). The Incidence of Taxes in Pakistan: Primer and Estimates (International Studies Program Working Paper). *Andrew Young School of Policy Studies*, Georgia State University, Atlanta, GA.

Wallace, S. (2007). Tax Incidence. Encyclopedia of Social Sciences.

Wallace, S., Wang, D., & Xu, Y. (2006). On the Equivalence of an Ad Valorem Tax (International Studies Program Working Paper). *Andrew Young School of Policy Studies*, Georgia State University, Atlanta, GA.

Younger, S. D. (1996). Estimating Tax Incidence in Ghana: An Exercise Using Household Data. In D. E. Sahn (Ed.), *Economic Reform and the Poor in Africa*. Oxford: Clarendon Press.

Younger, S. D. (1999). The Relative Progressivity of Social Services in Ecuador. *Public Finance Review*, *27*(3), 310–352. doi:10.1177/109114219902700304

Younger, S. D., Sahn, D. E., Haggblade, S., & Dorosh, P. A. (1999). Tax Incidence in Madagascar: An Analysis Using Household Data. *The World Bank Economic Review*, *13*(2), 303–331. doi:10.1093/wber/13.2.303

ENDNOTES

1 Economic incidence actually estimates the change in welfare due to changes in prices, returns to capital, and returns to labor. In practical terms, it is typically operationalized by measuring changes in net income which can then be examined over the income distribution.

2 In 2004-05 the share of tax and non-tax revenue in total federal and provincial tax plus non-tax revenue was 73 and 26 percent respectively.

3 This includes JD 236 million of SST levied by Jordan Customs on imported cars in addition to the net tax liability of JD 520 million reported by ISTD, which does not include any SST on cars.

4 Based on data from the Jordan stock exchange, 51 percent of shares are owned by foreigners. We assume that this represents the distribution of corporate capital between domestic and foreign.

5 In theory, a broad-based value added tax should be equivalent to a tax on income after taxes less saving. Therefore, distributional effects of indirect taxes can be analyzed both by the use of income for consumption (the use method) and by sources of income (the sources method). Since in practice a VAT never applies to all commodities uniformly, the sources method becomes less reliable for analysis of either revenues or incidence. In the presence of exemptions of various commodities and businesses as well as subjecting some commodities to non-standard (e.g. zero) rates, the equivalence between sources and uses of income can break down completely. Furthermore, in addition to the VAT, in this study we also examine excises and customs duties, for which the relation to sources of income becomes moot.

6 For imported inputs, it is the sales taxes levied by the Customs on the duty-inclusive value of imports that are further percolated throughout the production chain.

7 Assumes that foreign companies/individuals face same basic market structure

8 Assumes that foreign companies/individuals face same basic market structure

9 Conceptually, the net burden of import taxes is a sum of three elements: 1) effect on the consumer prices; 2) effect on factor incomes; 3) offset to the burden of direct taxes due to the impact on factor incomes. Because direct taxes are smaller relative to indirect taxes, in our analysis of tax incidence we disregard the last element of the burden of import taxes.

10 Thus, taxation of cars and motor fuels, while being the main source of progressivity of indirect taxes at the upper tail of income distribution, is likely to be partially offset by government expenditures on roads, which disproportionally benefit car owners.

Chapter 18
The Distributional Effects of Tax Policy:
Tax Expenditures in Turkey

Ömer Faruk Batırel
Istanbul Commerce University, Turkey

ABSTRACT

This chapter first discusses the Turkish tax policy performance for the period of 2004-2013 in terms of equitable distribution of tax burdens. Then, it examines tax expenditures, which are believed to be one of the main sources of inequity in tax burden distribution, in terms of equity and fiscal transparency grounds. The chapter also estimates tax expenditure figures based on very limited data in Turkey. One of the main findings of the chapter is that because fiscal transparency and non-discrimination principles of taxation are violated in Turkey, there are considerable amount of hidden tax reliefs that are not counted as tax expenditures in the Turkish tax system.

When the rate of return on capital exceeds the rate of growth of output and income, as it did in the nineteenth century and seems quite likely to do again in the twenty-first, capitalism automatically generates arbitrary and unsustainable inequalities that radically undermine the meritocratic values on which democratic societies are based. (Piketty, 2014, p. 1)

INTRODUCTION

Since the late 1970s, there has been a general deterioration of income distribution in most countries around the world[1] (see Chu, Davoodi, & Gupta, 2000; Stiglitz, 2012; Piketty, 2014; Tanzi, 2016, Chapter 1 in this handbook). Even though the most recent data are not yet all available, as Martinez-Vazquez, Vulovic and Dodson (2012) suggest, "all indications are that inequality has increased as a consequence of the 2009 global crisis and the following recession" (p. 95). As a result, inequality became a heated topic after the global crisis[2] and the interest in income distribution, its changes and the underlying factors have

DOI: 10.4018/978-1-5225-0053-7.ch018

increased.[3] Widening income disparities that increasingly become visible have also heightened the interest in the role of fiscal policy as a redistributive instrument in the short run and in the long run, as well as in the progressivity (or the lack thereof) of tax and transfer policies (Chu, Davoodi, & Gupta, 2000).

Although the principal function of tax policy is to ensure the collection of sufficient tax revenues to financing public expenditures, it is indeed much more than that. "It is also a major instrument of government policy used to influence the distribution of income as well as discouraging some activities through additional taxation and encouraging others through tax concessions. Such tax concessions are known as 'tax expenditures'" (James, 2016, Chapter 3 in this handbook). Tax expenditures are a common channel for financing government policies outside the budgetary framework. Contingent liabilities are another common channel for such "hidden" spending that tends to arise from a government's explicit and implicit promises of financial support (Swift, Brixi, & Valenduc, 2004, p. 2). Tax expenditures are an important and possibly growing spending item in public budgets (Avram, 2014).

If used properly, tax expenditures can play an important role in implementing government policy priorities. For example, a number of well-regarded programs for the poor take the form of tax expenditures. Redistribution plays a central role in the tax and benefit system, and the trade-off between redistribution and efficiency is at the center of many debates about tax policy. Chu, Davoodi and (2000) claim that "[t]he major aim of tax policy as a redistributive instrument should be to raise the revenues needed to finance efficient pro-poor and other essential government expenditures and to avoid generating horizontal inequities."

Although operating on the tax side, tax expenditures resemble direct spending programs. They both have similar budgetary effects and provide selective benefits that alter the allocation of resources. Like spending programs, they may often be justified because of public policy benefits but should be regularly monitored and evaluated. Tax expenditures, however, do not regularly receive the same level of scrutiny as direct spending programs. Unless, tax expenditures are exposed to adequate scrutiny, they may invite fiscal opportunism. When scrutiny is lacking, as Ansu and Laursen (2004) suggest, "it is difficult, if not impossible, to evaluate the cost, efficiency, and equity impact of tax expenditures and the extent to which resources could be rationalized or better allocated to strengthen government finances and to support progress toward broader economic and social objectives" (p. xi). Therefore, it is important to discuss tax expenditures and ways of dealing with them. An analysis of tax expenditure can contribute to the tax policy debate and shed light on trade-offs with direct spending programs.

By lowering the final tax liability for some groups of taxpayers, tax expenditures effectively narrow the tax base. Due to extensive reliance on tax expenditures, developing countries face not only revenue losses higher than they had anticipated, but also the erosion of their tax bases. Interest in tax expenditures has recently resurfaced in the context of growing public deficits and a reluctance to increase tax rates for fear of hurting national competitiveness and discouraging economic activity (Avram, 2014). Reducing tax expenditures is a potentially powerful way to reduce budget deficits. However, tax expenditures may also provide important benefits. This tradeoff makes it important to identify the costs and benefits of major tax expenditures to determine which expenditures are most valuable (Chetty *et al.*, 2013).

With regards to income distribution and the role of fiscal and other economic policies, a number of questions arise: Is income distribution in Turkey becoming more unequal? What is the redistributive role of tax, transfer and other expenditure policies? Who bears the final burden of a tax? The limited availability of high-quality data for Turkey prevents a rigorous analysis of the questions above. Income distribution data for Turkey are expanding, but are still not adequate. Internationally comparable data on before-tax and after-tax household incomes are virtually nonexistent. The available data do not allow an assessment of the long-term evolution of income distribution. Nevertheless, a partial analysis of the incidence and distributional implications of the tax system in Turkey can be done and it may provide useful information with respect to the equity of the system and provide input into tax reform discussion in the country.

The organization of the chapter is as follows. The next section presents a brief history of the Turkish tax system and continues with an overview of the contemporary Turkish tax system. This part also identifies major government revenues. The subsequent section evaluates the Turkish tax policy performance in terms of equitable distribution of tax burdens. The following section is devoted to tax expenditures, which are believed to be one of the main sources of inequity in the distribution of tax burden. Here, tax expenditures are examined and the Turkish experience with tax expenditures is discussed on fiscal transparency rule and equity grounds. Also, tax expenditure figures are estimated using very limited data for Turkey. Both the policy performance measurement and the tax expenditure analysis are made for the period 2004-2013. The concluding section emphasizes the findings and their implication for society and the economy.

THE TURKISH TAX SYSTEM AND MAJOR GOVERNMENT REVENUES

Taxation is not just a means of financing government, it is also a major instrument of social and economic policy. According to Pechman (1987), it has three goals: "to transfer resources from the private to the public sector; to distribute the cost of government fairly by income classes (vertical equity) and among people in approximately the same economic circumstances (horizontal equity); and to promote economic growth, stability, and efficiency" (p. 5). Since tax constitutes a form of political interaction, the next section first briefly reviews history of the Turkish tax system.

A Brief History of the Turkish Tax System

Turkey has experienced three distinct phases in the field of taxation. These three phases can be identified as the Ottoman era, the Reformation era, and the Republican era. The Ottoman era started in the early 14th century and lasted nearly five and a half centuries. This era was characterized by a system of taxes and other fiscal liabilities with a religious basis. Ottoman rule had chosen to implement its fiscal functions through earmarked revenue sources. The major source of tax revenue was *ashar* (dime royal) levied on agricultural products, and the collection of these taxes was used to be made in kind. The remaining religious duties were *zakah* (net worth tax) of Muslims, *haraj*, annual tax payments made by defeated and captured countries under the glory rule of the empire, and *jizie* (cizye), a kind of military service tax paid by non-Muslims who were not obliged to join the army. A large sum of the so-called *örfi* taxes (customary taxes), which required approval from the head of the state and religious hierarchy, were the main source of the public revenue.

The Ottoman era ended with a whole-scale reorganization effort for the empire beginning in 1839. This reorganization heavily influenced by the European ideas and intended to effectuate a fundamental change of the empire from the old system based on theocratic principles to that of a modern state. The Reformation era represented a departure from the religious way of taxation towards a secularization of laws. During this period that lasted about 84 years, some taxes inherited from the Empire remained, but some western type of taxes were also adopted. Therefore, a hybrid tax system emerged. With the fall of the Ottoman Empire, the reformation era ended and the Turkish Republic was proclaimed in 1923. The Turkish Republic inherited a highly non-representative, non-communal, narrow-based, and low-numbered registered taxpayers, and it is still possible to detect the remains of that unique imperial fiscal system.

Since the proclamation of the Turkish Republic, Turkey has been struggling to establish a modern tax system. First, the young Turkish Republic introduced a secular unitary system of government. Second, all the religion-based laws, including the ones related to taxes, were abolished. Although this was a period of a shift towards a modern tax system, Turkey could manage to establish a 'proper' tax system only in the 1950s. The Turkish personal income taxation began with the progressively-rated unitary income tax system in 1950. This was mainly due to the world economic crisis and the conditions during World War II. Having several amendments since then, the Turkish tax system has recently gained a competitive advantage compared to some other countries.

A Brief Overview of the Contemporary Turkish Tax System

Turkey has a unitary tax system under which income derived from different sources is aggregated and tax due is computed on the total aggregate income. All Turkish taxes are imposed under laws drafted by or with the involvement of the Turkish Ministry of Finance and are promulgated by the Turkish Parliament. The Turkish tax system is based on self-assessment. Basic principles of the Turkish tax policy are: 1) Legality; 2) Non-discrimination; and 3) Ability-to-pay. Legality principle has been stated clearly in the Turkish Tax Law Art.73: "*No taxes, duties, and other fiscal liabilities shall be laid or abolished unless a related law enacted by the parliament*". Local governments and other public bodies have no implied or delegated taxing power. Those administrations and jurisdictions are only authorized to enforce tax laws passed by the single legislative body of the Republic. Nevertheless, amendment made to this strict limitation is slightly loosened later on. Executive power was granted the power of laying fiscal liabilities like custom duties and equivalent liabilities on imports for the sake of having favorable foreign trade account (Art.167).[4] Along with the articles that are the expression of legality principle, the principle of non-discrimination is also adopted in the tax law as a universal rule. An organic state approach is adopted and like the compulsory military service, taxes are regarded as a citizenship duty. Although the primary goal of taxation in Turkey is fiscal, the equity issue has not ignored. Indeed, ability-to-pay principle is put into constitution and defined as follows: Everyone is liable to pay taxes for meeting public expenditures in accordance with their respective ability.

Political factors and established institutions have played important roles in shaping the Turkish tax system. In contrast to the predictions in the literature, the high degree of income inequality has not led to high tax burden and more redistributive tax system, because the economic power of elites has contributed to various types of representation failures. Additionally, tax morale and voters' attitudes towards raising the tax burden have been adversely affected by perceptions of corruption and poor quality of public services, in a vicious circle leading to inadequate resources for improving such services. Tax reforms were numerous in Turkey. But, they had a tendency to occur during crisis periods and privileging rapid revenue mobilization over other objectives (Erdoğdu et. al., 2016, chapter 13 in this handbook).

As Ter–Minassian (2009) evaluates succinctly, "[w]hile the main tax instruments used in Turkey (VAT, excises, and income taxes) are the same as in most modern tax systems, their relative weights differ significantly from those in other OECD countries. The share of taxes on goods and services in total general government revenues is significantly higher in Turkey than in the rest of the OECD. The share of excises (the special consumption tax, SCT) is especially high (about 20 percent, compared with less than eight percent on average in the OECD). In contrast, the share of income taxes is nearly 15 percentage points lower than the OECD average, and social security contributions are also below the OECD average. The unusually heavy reliance on excise taxes reflects their relative ease of collection, compared with more complex taxes such as VAT and income taxes, and the fact that rates on some products (in particular petroleum products, alcoholic beverages and tobacco) are very high. In contrast, the revenue productivity of the VAT (defined as the ratio of VAT revenue as percent of GDP to the standard VAT rate) remains relatively low in Turkey (around 0.3, compared with an unweight average of over 0.4 for the OECD as a whole). This reflects: broader than average range of exemptions and preferential treatments, and coverage of the reduced rates, including under the unusually low one percent rate; and continuing weaknesses in the administration of the tax."

Brief Presentation of Turkish Tax System as of 2014

Central Government Taxes

Personal Income Tax

Turkish income tax defines taxable income as being comprised of commercial & industrial profits, agricultural gains, self - employed professional gains, wages & salaries, rents, interest & dividends and capital & occasional or windfall gains. Despite a temporary practice of uses of income approach, Turkey has adopted a narrow based but not comprehensive type sources of income approach. Taxpayer is the real person residing in Turkey. If a person has permanent residence in Turkey or has resided more than six months (183 days) in a year in Turkey, the individual is considered resident in Turkey.

Corporation Income Tax

In corporate taxation, the tax base is the gains earned by the corporations defined as taxpayers. Corporations are mainly capital companies like joint stock companies, limited companies, other shared companies, and cooperatives public economic corporations & enterprises and public utilities and business entities dependent to associations and foundations, investment funds and joint ventures. If legal or business centers in Turkey or a controlled non-resident corporation (50% or more shares of a non-resident corporation owned by Turkish resident corporation) resident taxpayer. If none of the centers exist in Turkey, corporations are treated as non-resident taxpayers. Public service, participation gains, investment fund gains, profits received from foreign country construction assembly technical and repair services, merger transfer, individual retirement accounts' gains are excluded from tax base. Turkish ship & boats' passenger and cargo gains,

Inheritance and Gift Tax

The transfer of property owned by Turkish citizens located in Turkey or outside the country to any person whether a Turkish national or foreigner without any market transaction is a taxable object. If any property located outside and owned by Turkish national is transferred to a foreign national having residence abroad excluded from tax. Tax base is the market value of the inherited, donated or gifted property. Debts are subtracted. In case of business property, the equity capital forms tax base.

Motor Vehicle Tax

Tax covers all land and aircrafts operated by engine (marine crafts excluded). Motor vehicles owned by public agencies, local governments and on reciprocity basis owned by foreign missions and personnel sent by international organizations and disabled persons having 90% degree of handicap or less than that level on condition that vehicle having special equipment to drive are excluded from

Value-Added Tax

Commercial, industrial, agricultural and self-employed professional activities consist of tax base of VAT. Second major category included in tax is imported goods and services. Additionally, communication, auction sales, natural gas & petroleum product distribution through pipe line system, and all kind of lotteries are defined as taxable activity. Exclusions are: exports, roaming services given to foreign customers, transit haulage, international passenger and cargo transportation on reciprocity basis, property services, financial services (banking and insurance transactions), deliveries in the free trade areas, data processing and software services within the technology development regions, gold, silver and valuable stones deliveries, some imported machinery and equipment for military health and educational purposes),

Excise Duties (Special Consumption Tax)

Banking and insurance tax, special communication tax, lottery games tax, customs tax (duty), stamp tax (duty).

Eleven Central Duty

Judicial, notary, tax judiciary, title deed & cadaster, consulate, passport, residence certificate, visa and ministry of foreign affairs approval, ship & harbor, license, franchise and diploma and traffic and outgoing passenger, ship health certificate tribute, ship registration duty and marine craft annual usage duty, central fund liability, resource usage supporting fund and one central valuable papers' liability, one education contribution share Turkish Air Force & National Aerospace Industry contribution share, personal identity information contribution share, social security health services contribution share.

Local (Municipal Taxes)

Seven local tax (property tax, announcement & advertisement tax, entertainment tax, communication tax, electricity & gas tax, fire insurance tax and environment cleanliness tax) and 12 local duty (occupation of public places, licensing to work at holidays, spring waters, brokerage, animal slaughtering, şcaling, building construction, registration and copying, reconstruction & city planning, opening a new business, examination & license and reporting, and health certificate) Local contribution to local infrastructures (road, water and sewage system).

THE TURKISH TAX POLICY PERFORMANCE

Tax policy is an integral part of fiscal policy. Valenduc (2004) identifies that "the main purpose of any tax system is to raise sufficient revenue to finance public outlays in an equitable way, with the lowest administrative and compliance costs" (p. 69). Although the principle aim of tax policy is to raise revenue, it has also been used to influence behavior towards desirable social and economic goals.

Bird (2007) makes the important point that "[t]ax policy decisions are not made in a vacuum. Nor are they made by a benevolent government. Instead, they reflect the outcome of a set of complex social and political interactions between different groups in society in an institutional context established by history and state administrative capacity" (p. 47). According to Alt, Preston, and Sibieta (2009), "[i]n a world in which citizens have different views about how taxes should be levied, political systems affect whose interests are represented and how" (pp. 1208-1209). Key actors and elites is likely to use the institutions and regulations in their own favor. As Daude, Gutiérrez, and Melguizo (2014) clarify, "key characteristic of the elites is the ability of not only working around the institutional framework, but also working within the institutional framework to assure the 'right' decisions are taken" (p. 11).

The major aim of tax policy as a redistributive instrument should be to raise the revenues needed to finance efficient pro-poor and other essential government expenditures and to avoid generating horizontal inequities. To this end, tax systems should have broad bases, limited exemptions and low rates. This view has formed a foundation for an agreement among many researchers and policymakers on the relative role of tax and expenditure policies in income redistribution (Chu, Davoodi, & Gupta, 2000)

The Turkish tax policy performance in terms of equitable distribution of tax burdens in this chapter is assessed using three types of ratios: the central government tax burden, the share of indirect vs. direct taxes, the contribution of wage earners to income tax revenue and the heaviness of specific legal transaction taxes.

The Dynamics of Tax Burden

Ter-Minassian (2009) asserts that "the appropriate level of the tax burden is very much country-specific and it is a reflection of the economic, institutional, and political conditions of each country." According to OECD Revenue Statistics (2014), Turkey has the eight lowest tax burden among 34 OECD countries with its 27.6% (compared with 27.9 in 2011) overall tax ratio in 2012. This ratio was only higher than Australia (27.3%), Ireland (27.3), Switzerland (26.9), South Korea (24.8%), United States (24.4), Chile (24.2%) and Mexico (19.6%). OECD average, on the other hand was 34.1% in 2013 compared with 33.7 in 2012 and 33.3 in 2011. Since the tax burden is relatively low in Turkey compared to many other countries, there should be scope for raising the tax burden over the medium term.

Turkey was not able to raise the total tax burden despite the considerable change observed in tax handles and the rise in per capita income during the period investigated. A benchmarking exercise of World Bank (2014) indicates that it is wise for Turkey to change its revenue composition to become more high-income in terms of property taxation, corporate taxation and its consumption taxation. A more recent study on property taxation in Turkey conducted by Erdoğdu et. al. (2016, chapter 13 in this handbook) reveals that there is a high level of tax loss and large room for a property tax increase in the real estate sector.

Figure 1 shows us the trend of central government tax revenues as a percentage of GDP and the ratio of tax revenues to public expenditures during 2004-2013.[5]

We see in the graph (Figure 1) that the ratio of tax revenues to public expenditures sharply declined just after global crisis in 2008. It recovered in the following two years but fell again 2012 and stabilized around 80% of the GDP afterwards. The tax take as a share of GDP has remained stable but there has been a dramatic shift in the composition of tax revenues. Given the importance of revenue growth for

Figure 1. Tax revenue ratios (2004-2013)
Source: MOF (different years); www.muhasebat.gov.tr: and www.gib.gov.tr

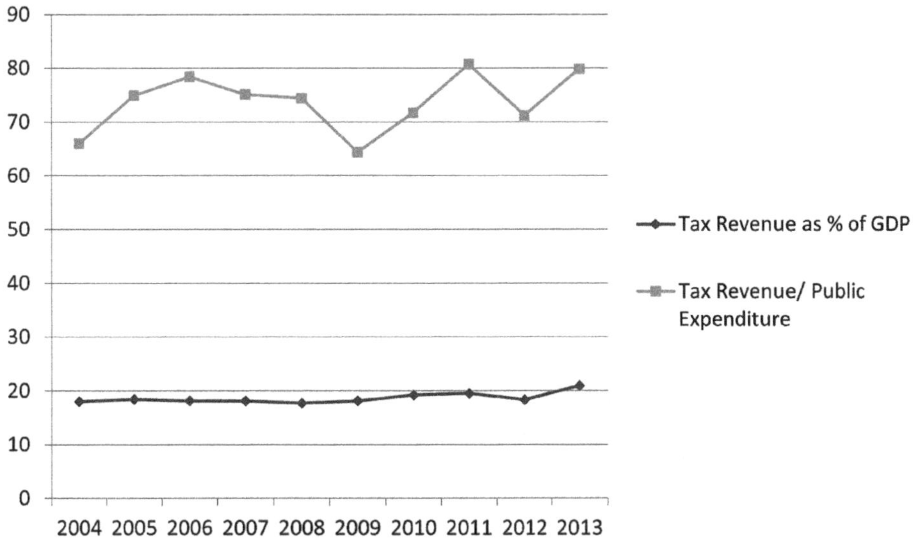

fiscal outcomes over the past decade, a closer look at the government revenue dynamics is warranted. Central government revenues in Turkey have averaged around 23% of GDP since 2000, with the variation largely being obtained to one percentage point of GDP over the period. The level of central government revenues is broadly in line with the other fast growing emerging markets, although it is low relative to OECD members. What is noteworthy is the change in the composition of tax revenues over this period. Revenues from the special consumption tax and taxes on international trade have grown significantly. Revenues from these two taxes increased by 13 percentage points of total central government revenues and now comprise about 40 percent of the total (World Bank, 2014).

The central government tax revenue as a percentage of GDP remained stable over time despite the fact that 76.338 million TL of GDP at constant prices by the end of 2003, reached 122.388 million TL of GDP in constant prices by the end of 2013. On the other hand, the tax to public expenditures ratio have increased from 60% to 80%.

This tendency reflects that the elasticity of tax revenue with respect to GDP growth rate is lower than unity or inelastic. In the course of the last decade, overall tax ratio could not have been raised but the tax to expenditure ratio increased, and a greater part of the public expenditures has started to be met by tax revenues.

The following section presents the worsening distributional inequity in tax burdens in the Turkish tax system. An indicator of inequitable tax burden distribution is first defined as a higher percentage of tax revenues being financed through indirect taxes; secondly as enlarging the percentage of personal income tax revenue that is withheld; and thirdly as the increased contribution of wage earners to income tax revenue. And last but not the least, the share of specific excise duties in sales taxation gets bigger and the importance of duties on legal transactions increases with a more unequal tax burden distribution.

Equity in Tax Burden Distribution

In recent decades, many developing countries have experienced an increase in income inequality in terms of both before-tax and after-tax measures. The opening up of low-income countries may have an adverse effect on the wages of unskilled workers in middle-income developing countries (Chu, Davoodi, & Gupta, 2000).

As Bird (2007) states, "[f]airness is a key issue in designing any tax regime. Indeed, from one perspective, taxes exist primarily to secure equity." The analysis of income distribution and the distributional implications of taxes and government spending is subject to many conceptual and practical difficulties. The difficulties are particularly severe for developing countries like Turkey. Income distribution data for Turkey are expanding, but are still not adequate. Internationally comparable data on before-tax and after-tax household incomes are virtually nonexistent.

With regards to income distribution and the role of fiscal and other economic policies, a number of questions arise: How does Turkey differ in income distribution both among developing countries and relative to industrial countries? Is income distribution in Turkey becoming more unequal? What is the redistributive role of tax, transfer and other expenditure policies? Unfortunately, the limited availability of high-quality data for Turkey prevents a rigorous analysis of these questions.

The poverty level is one measure of income disparity in a country. Another equity-related concept is the distribution of income among population groups. A commonly accepted measure of distribution is the Gini coefficient,[6] which measures the difference between complete equity in income distribution (each portion of the population holds the same level of income) and the actual distribution (Timofeev & Wallace, 2016, chapter 17 in this handbook).

The World Bank has published estimates of the Gini coefficient for a large number of countries for various years. A sample of those countries is reported in Table 1. These particular countries were chosen as they represent countries similar in relative geography, income, or economic base and are provided as illustrative comparisons.

As seen in Table 1, Turkey's Gini coefficient measuring income inequality fell from 43.4 in 2003 to 40.0 in 2011. Income distribution, however, is still among the OECD's most unequal in Turkey.

Clearly, there is at this point a need to better understand what role tax and spending policies have been playing *vis-à-vis* the changing trends in inequality. Does the degree of effective tax progressivity

Table 1. Gini coefficients

Country	Year			
	2003/04	2010	2011	2012
Argentina	-	44.5	43.6	-
Jordan	38.9	33.7	-	-
Georgia	40.4	42.1	41.6	41.4
Indonesia	-	35.6	38.1	-
Poland	-	33.2	32.8	-
Serbia	32.8	29.7	-	-
Turkey	43.4	38.8	40.0	-

Source: World Bank, World Development Indicators 2005, 2012, 2014.

play a role in improving income distribution? Does an increased share of revenues from VAT worsen income distribution? Are recent trends in expenditure policies offsetting or reinforcing the effects of changes of taxation? (Martinez-Vazquez, Vulovic, & Dodson, 2014, p. 96).

Earlier studies assume that three main sources of income bear the burden of taxes: capital income, labor income, and transfers. Transfers are found to be heavily concentrated at the lower end of income distribution, capital income is concentrated in both the upper and lower tiers (because of presence of retirees), and labor income is closest of the three series to being proportional to income. Thus, depending on whether a tax is allocated to capital income, labor income, transfers, or income in general, it can have either a progressive or regressive effect (Shah & Whalley, 1991, p. 166).

Taxation and public expenditure policies affect income distribution. Where the tax incidence falls depends (in the short run) on the price elasticity of demand (PED) and price elasticity of supply (PES). Tax incidence falls mostly upon the group that responds least to price (the group that has the most inelastic price-quantity curve). If the demand curve is inelastic relative to the supply curve the tax will be disproportionately borne by the buyer rather than the seller. If the demand curve is elastic relative to the supply curve, the tax will be born disproportionately by the seller. If PED = PES the tax burden is split equally between buyer and seller.

In their empirical analysis, Martinez-Vazquez, Vulovic, and Dodson (2014) find significant effects of both taxes and public spending on income distribution when they are considered jointly. These effects generally support the findings in individual country incidence analysis studies. The authors state that "[p]rogressive income taxes, when considered separately, have a positive impact on income distribution, contributing to decreasing inequality, and this effect is more pronounced the higher the degree of progressivity and the higher the share of GDP that is collected with the individual income tax. Corporate income taxes also have a positive effect on income distribution but this effect seems to be eroded away in economies that are very opened or globalized." They also find, in accordance with individual country incidence analysis studies, that "general consumption taxes, excise taxes and customs duties have a negative impact on income distribution, with some caveats depending on the specific type of tax being considered" (pp. 96-97).

Chu, Davoodi, and Gupta (2000) highlight the important point that the redistributive effects of these programs are not as large in developing countries as they are in industrial countries. According to them, "[t]he interaction between the progressivity of tax and transfer policies and income distribution is complicated by a set of factors that are unique to *developing* (and *transition*) *countries*, which, in general, have a number of weak fiscal features, such as a low tax-to-GDP ratio (reflecting poor governance, weak tax administration and widespread tax evasion), the predominance of indirect taxes and a limited menu of capital and wealth taxes, and a limited role for formal cash transfer and social protection policies. These features cast doubt on the ability of tax policy to redistribute income."

Nevertheless, according to Bird (2007), "[t]axes should kept be as low as possible on the poorest, who must consume to be productive. If people lack food to eat or lack basic clothing and shelter, or if they are not sufficiently healthy and educated to engage in productive work, they are unlikely to be economically productive. To some extent, equity (in the sense of not taxing the poor) and growth (in the sense of enhancing the productivity of the labor force) are thus fully compatible in poor countries. For instance, a good VAT in such a country might be one with a somewhat narrower base that excludes items that constitute a significant fraction of the consumption of poor people."

Turkey's taxation system in practice does hardly take into consideration horizontal or vertical equity. The distributional quality of Turkey will be discussed below in terms of the share of indirect taxes in total tax revenues.

Indirect Taxes vs Direct Taxes

Turkey's tax system is biased toward indirect taxes. The ratio of direct taxes to the national income in Turkey was about 19% in 2012, which was well below the OECD average of 34% (Karakas *et al.*, 2014, p. 9). On average, two thirds of the central government tax yield in Turkey comes from indirect taxes, and this share was as high as almost 70% by the year 2013. Indirect taxes consist of VAT, excise duties, special communication taxes[7], lottery games taxes[8], financial services taxes and legal transaction taxes. On the other hand, direct taxes are comprised of personal income tax, corporation income tax, motor vehicle tax and inheritance and gift tax.

Today, many income types in Turkey are taxed using the withholding technique, which does not require to make an annual declaration. The withholding rate is used as a final tax rate especially for capital income, namely interest. Since 1980s, the Turkish personal income tax has lost its equity nature and progressive incidence through the tax reliefs introduced and a high degree of scheduler way of taxation. It adversely affects rather than corrects income inequalities, and its incidence has become regressive over time.

Figure 2 depicts that indirect taxes constitute more than two-thirds of total tax revenues. It is well-known that the redistributive nature of VAT as an ad valorem tax is considerably restricted. Ter-Minassian (2009) indicates that "[w]hile the proportion of income that relatively well-off households spend on goods such as foodstuffs and medicines is smaller than the corresponding proportion of the income of the poorer households, a larger share of the VAT revenue foregone by applying a reduced rate to such goods is likely to benefit the better-off groups. A uniform (possibly somewhat lower) VAT rate would generate additional revenue that could be used for targeted income transfers to the less well-off households. A single-rate VAT also tends to be easier to administer" (p. 9).

Labor Contribution to Income Tax Yield

Turkey is characterized by above average inequality originating from the labor market. This reflects a very wide wage dispersion coupled with a low employment rate (OECD, 2012). Although the Turkish Personal income tax system is based on self-assessment, mostly labor income is subject to withholding and wage earners, who are paid by a single employer, are not obliged to submit an annual tax return. One of the main sources of distributional tax inequity in Turkey is that taxes are levied to a great extent by the withholding technique and are paid by laborers. Labor in the formal sector is highly taxed through both payroll taxes and high levels of indirect taxation on private consumption. Capital on the other hand is taxed at much lower effective rates (World Bank, 2014). This tendency led the personal income tax to become an employment tax.

In the Turkish tax system, mostly withholding rates are considered as the final rate in the sense that annual reporting is not necessary. Wages and salaries received from a single employer (by applying a tax rate schedule), all interest income, capital gains, copyright gains derived by selling & letting by their holders and their heirs (if not included in business income), and small farmers' gains only face withholding liability. On the other hand, commercial & industrial businessmen and self-employed pro-

Figure 2. Tax structure (2004-2013)
Source: MOF (different years); www.muhasebat.gov.tr: and www.gib.gov.tr

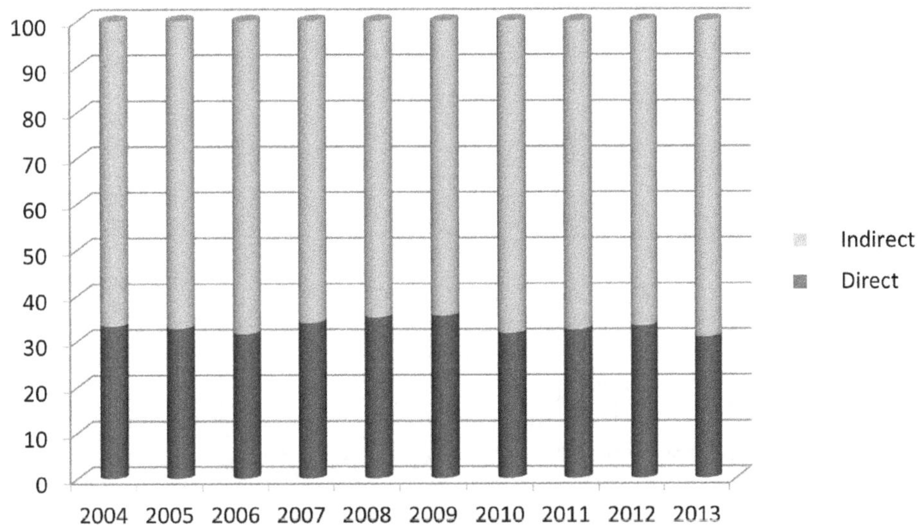

fessionals, big farmers, residential rent receivers are obliged to submit a tax return and pay their income tax according to a *tax schedule*.

Self- assessment is the only technique to ensure personal characteristics of income tax to be considered. Unless all taxpayers make an annual declaration, submit tax returns and notify personal characteristics, exemptions deductions adjustment of tax burden would not have been individualized at all. Personal characteristics such as physical condition (being disabled or not), marital status, age and dependency are only taken into consideration if the related information is submitted to the tax office annually. The Turkish personal income tax lost its personality by permitting almost all type of income withheld, and by releasing taxpayers from the duty to make annual declaration. Only small traders, self- employed professionals, title holders are required to submit annual tax returns. This practice leads to not being able to get the benefit of personal deductions. In Turkey, only a limited number of taxpayers are obliged to make self – assessment and personal exemption does not exist except for wage earners.

According to the 2012 income tax returns statistics, the number of taxpayers, who made annual declarations, is 1.854 647. Out of this figure, 87.4% of the total is small traders. Turkey is experiencing considerably low ratios of self-assessed income taxpayers to total population. The ratio is 2.4% in Turkey while it is close to 50% in the USA.

Figure 3 demonstrates that both the withholding share exceeded 90% of the income tax levied withholding and labor contributes more to income tax due to the wage earners, who are paid by a single employer and are not subject to self-assessment. Figure 4 shows that the laborers' (particularly minimum wage earners) share in total withheld income tax increased during the last decade.

The fact that revenue from social security contributions remains significantly below the OECD average, despite their relatively high rates, points to weaknesses in their administration, including fragmented audit and collection, and the impact of the moral hazard created by repeated amnesties" (Ter – Minassian, 2009, pp.4-5).

Reducing income taxes and increasing consumption taxes or indirect taxes is typically viewed as a way to bolster private saving rates. Given the high levels of indirect taxes, there is limited opportunity

Figure 3. Income tax structure (2004-2013)
Source: MOF (different years); www.muhasebat.gov.tr: and www.gib.gov.tr

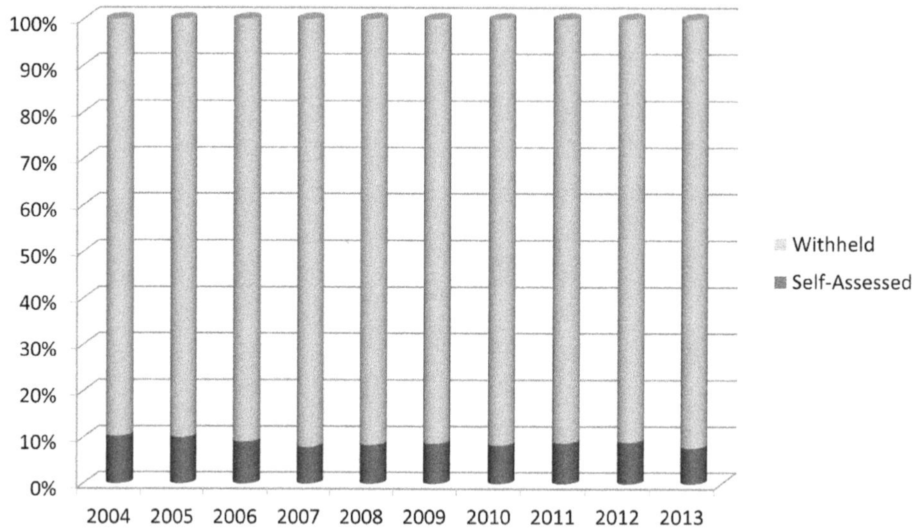

Figure 4. Labor contributions to income tax yield
Source: MOF (different years); www.muhasebat.gov.tr: and www.gib.gov.tr

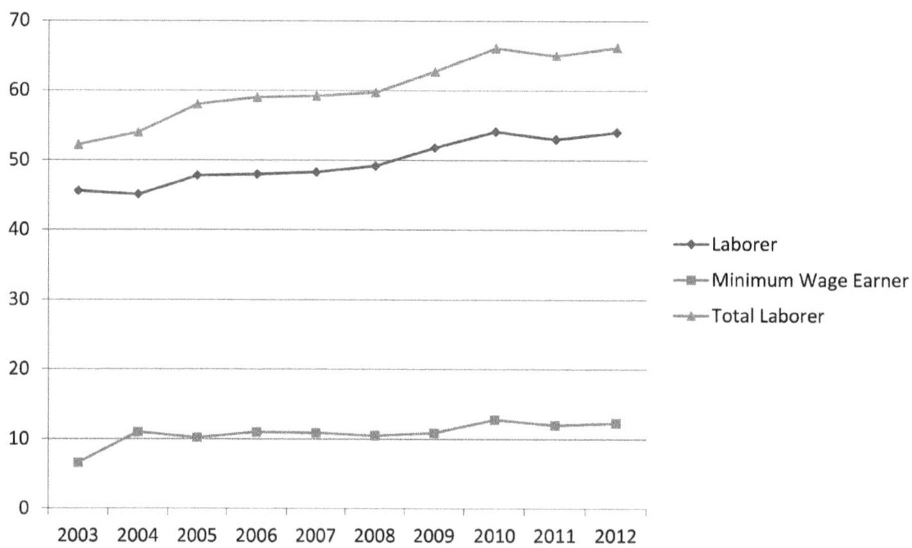

for this type of change in Turkey. Indeed, given the high levels of indirect taxation in the country there is reason to expect that the income effect of reducing indirect taxes (higher savings rate) may be greater than the substitution effect (more consumption), particularly at lower income levels and for those commodity groupings with high estimated expenditure elasticity.

A decrease in indirect taxes will make formal prices more attractive and increase formality. The increase in the level of private savings is due to the increase in disposable income when fewer taxes are collected. However, national savings might decline if the capital income tax offset is not enough to stem the fall in revenues from indirect tax revenues" (World Bank, 2014).

Another unfavorable tendency observed in terms of tax burden distribution is the rising share of excise duties. Turkish tax policy is not equitable or competitive. The taxation system creates a heavy burden both on wage-earners and on business. The share of taxes (without social security contributions) amounts to 29.3 percent of GDP. The OECD average is 27.5 percent, and among low-income countries, the ratio is just 17 percent. For wage earners, taxes and social security contributions total 42.7 percent of income, which represents the highest taxation rate among OECD countries. Another serious source of inequity is the level of indirect taxes (for example, a tax on consumption rather than income or assets) which are paid equally by the poor and the wealthy. This includes value-added tax and various consumption taxes. Indirect taxes constitute about 70 percent of Turkey's total tax revenue (the EU average is around 35 percent) (SGI, 2009).

VAT and Excise Duties Revenue

Contrary to the conventional wisdom and general world practice, yield obtained from excise duties is unusually high in Turkey. Indeed, excise duty yield is almost the same size of revenue obtained from VAT. Figure 5 depicts this deviation.

In Figure 5, it is easily noticed that the share of excise duties in total revenue is very close to that of VAT. This tax covers four commodity categories in Turkey. In the first category, petroleum products & derivatives and mineral oils including liquid petroleum gas, natural gas, and bio-fuel are listed. The second category covers first-hand motor vehicle sales. Tobacco products, alcoholic beverages and sparkling and cola water products are included in the third category, and the last group comprises some durable consumer goods, cosmetic products, electrical appliances and the so-called luxury items. Contrary to the EU practice, Turkey imposes excise duties on not only the classical socially-harmful goods (petroleum products, alcoholic beverages and tobacco products) but also it heavily taxes the automotive industry and other consumption goods. For the first hand motor vehicles, sales tax rates are differentiated as fol-

Figure 5. Relative shares of VAT and excise duties as % of total tax revenue
Source: MOF (different years); www.muhasebat.gov.tr: and www.gib.gov.tr

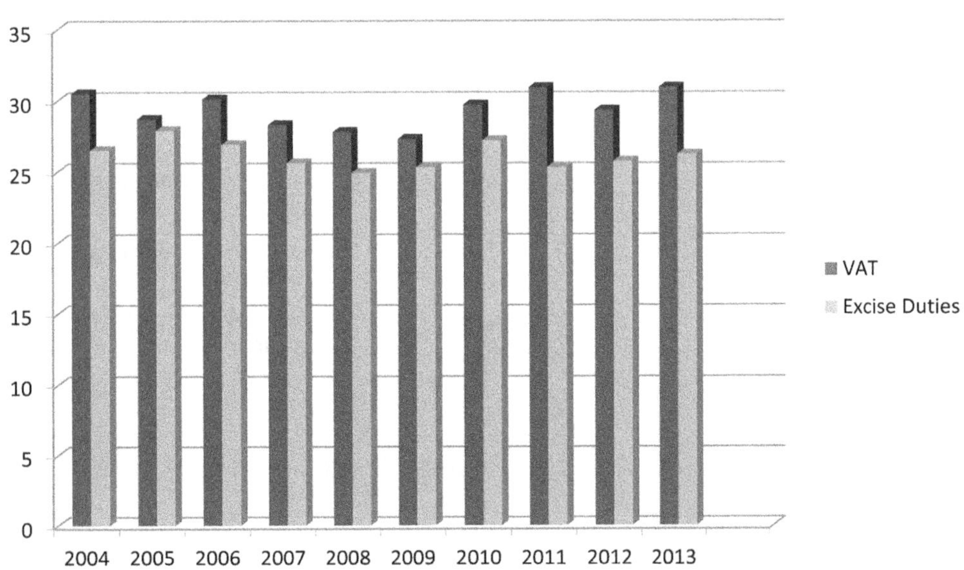

lows: 1% for buses, 4% for midi buses, 9% for mini buses, and the rates for cars for private use ranges according to the engine capacity (45% for cars equipped up to 1600 cubic centimeters engine, 90% for engines 1600-2000, and 145% for engines exceeding 2000 cm3, 0.5% for aircrafts and helicopters, 6.7-8% for marine vehicles, and 22-37% for motorcycles depending upon the engine capacity. Mostly imported cosmetic products, valuable stones, wireless systems and other electronic products face a rate of 20% and cellular phones 25%, respectively. Home appliances are subject to a 6.7% tax rate. Another indicator of inequitable distribution of tax burdens is the rising share of specific excise duties as a percentage of total tax revenue.

Share of Specific Excise Duties in Total Tax Take

Excise duties on petroleum products, alcoholic beverages and tobacco product as a source of central government tax revenue are supposed to be of a regressive nature, yielding a high percentage of revenue to the public budget. The tax base is defined specifically for socially harmful goods such as petroleum tobacco products and alcoholic beverages. The rates effective for 2014 are as follows: 25% for cola beverages, 63% for beer and 0% for other alcoholic beverages but also each liter minimum fixed amount (ranging between 0.74 – 118.18 TL) 65.25% for cigarette and 40% cigar & cigarillos minimum 0.1875 TL for each cigarette and cigar or for tobaccos per gram (0.049 TL).

It is observed that although the share of duties on petroleum products relatively decreased, the share of specific duties still comprise one-fifth of total tax revenue. Another source of inequity in the Turkish tax system is the heavy dependence on legal transaction taxes, which are mainly levied as a unit type.

Figure 6. Specific excises as % of tax revenues
Source: MOF (different years); www.muhasebat.gov.tr: and www.gib.gov.tr

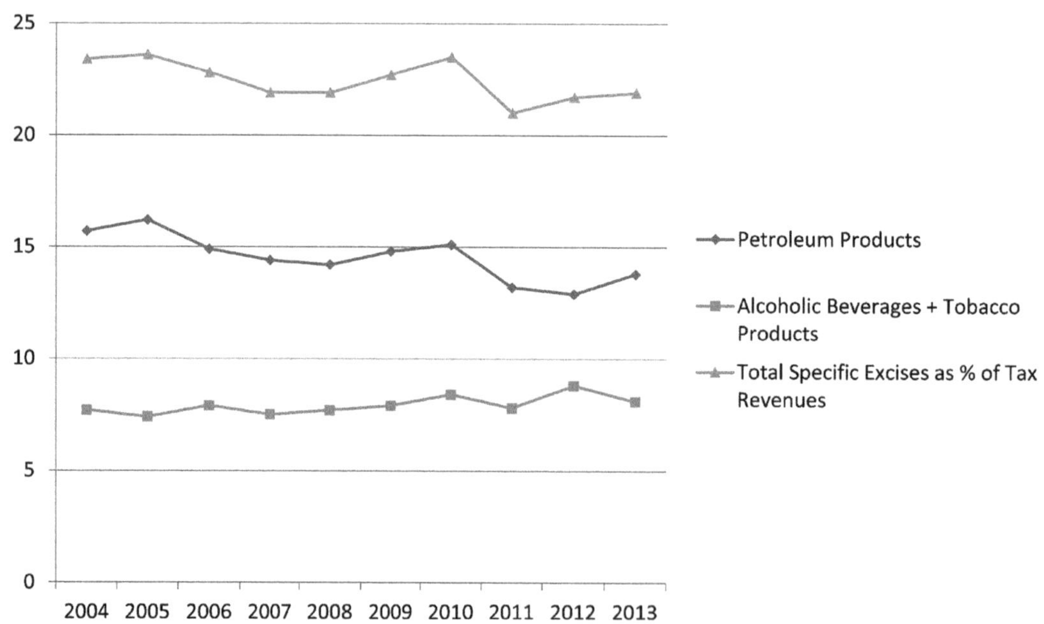

Legal Transaction Tax Share in Tax Revenue

Those liabilities are stamp duty, administrative duties and sale revenue of valuable papers and they are classified in budget revenues as asset sale revenues. In our opinion, the increase of this tax share is also an indicator of worsening tax burden distribution.

Let us briefly examine these three liabilities. Stamp tax (duty) imposes a heavy tax liability on taxable documents. These documents are used to prove or to ascertain a transaction signed by parties involved. Lots of documents are excluded from tax coverage for the sake of economic social and cultural reasons. Taxpayers of stamp duty are persons who signs the documents concerned. Tax base in some documents is the monetary value shown on the document and in other documents it is the nature of the document. If the document has more than one copy then the additional copy faces additional liability. If any document incorporates more than one transaction, each faces a different duty. Stamp duty rates are listed in and enclosed to the law (7.59 per thousand for payrolls, 1.89 per thousand for rent contracts and 9.48 per thousand for contracting outs, bids and 1.89 per thousand for other papers monetary value shown on). Lump sum taxes are adjusted by the revaluation coefficient. Payment is made either by stamping or in return for receipts.

Another liability on legal transactions is administrative duties mentioned above such as judicial, notary, passport, consulate, title - deed & cadaster, visa, license & diploma and traffic duties. The main characteristic of such duties is if the duty payment is made in advance, public service would not have been delivered at all. The burden of these liabilities is also relatively high. Some legal documents such as identity cards, passports, bank checks, driving permits and motor vehicle licenses are accepted as valuable papers and sold in return for a fee.

Figure 7 shows that legal transaction taxes, which are largely levied on the basis of unit type or per transaction, reached 7.5% of total tax revenues in 2013. The recent increase was 50% for stamp duty and 100% for administrative duties. With this level of yield, those liabilities started to contribute to public treasury as much as the size of Corporation Income Tax.

Financial Transaction Tax Share in the Public Budget

The taxes on banking and insurance transactions cover any kind of transaction made by banks, bankers, insurance companies, finance corporations except leasing of machinery and equipment and motor vehicles (subject to VAT). Internal money transfers of banks, life, export, transport insurance, credits given to small and medium businesses, pension funds are excluded from tax base. Taxpayers are banks, bankers and insurance companies. The tax base is the monetary payments for the transactions defined above and foreign exchange transactions (buying and selling) although the tax rate is set as 15% in law, it is reduced by executive power to 5% for regular transactions. There is also a sort of hidden credit liability called *Resource Utilization Support Fund.*[9] During the last decade, not only the share of the above-mentioned legal transaction taxes but also the relative contribution of financial transaction taxes to the public budget increased. It needs to be pointed out however that Financial Service Tax revenue dipped in 2008-2010 presumably because of the financial crisis.

The policy performance analysis for the period of 2004-2013 with respect to distribution of tax burden shows that Turkey depends heavily on goods and services taxes levied as a specific and regressive-type tax. Those include excise duties, and legal transaction and financial service taxes. On the other hand,

Figure 7. Legal transaction taxes as % of total tax revenue
Source: MOF (different years); www.muhasebat.gov.tr: and www.gib.gov.tr

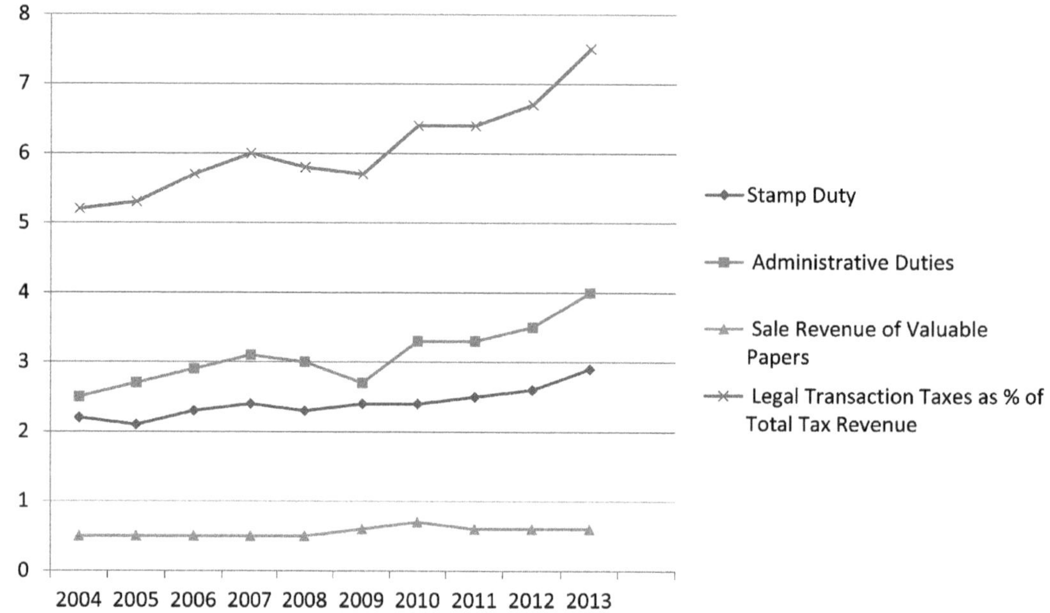

Figure 8. Financial service taxes as % of total tax revenue
Source: MOF (different years); www.muhasebat.gov.tr: and www.gib.gov.tr

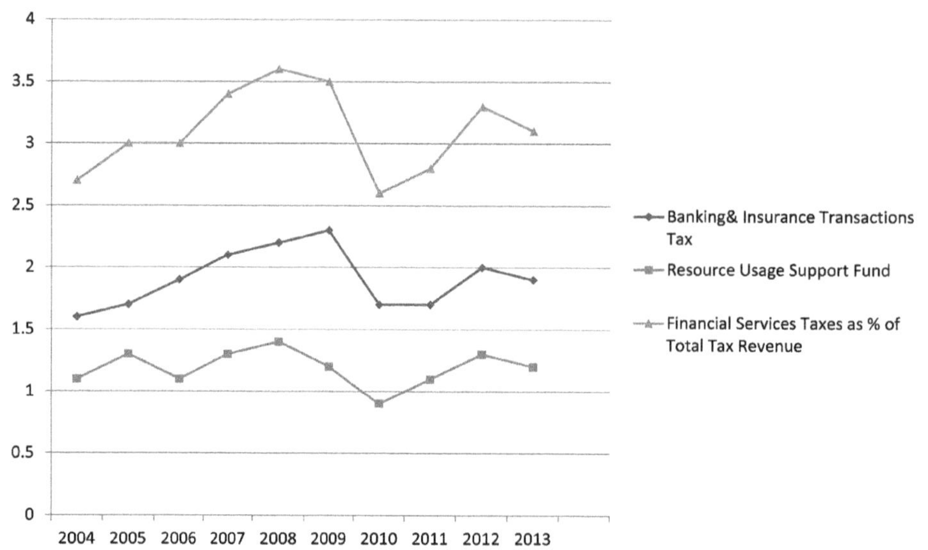

the performance of income taxes has worsened due to the informal economy, the low level of self- assessment and the excessive labor contribution to personal income tax yield.

According to the World Bank (2014), "the informal sector is shrinking and the room to raise rates further is limited. Indeed, it was the movement of labor into the formal sector that supported the rise in payroll tax revenues. General government revenues therefore benefited from declining informal employment as agricultural labor shedding gathered pace. The direct consequence of these trends is to make general government revenues more sensitive to cyclical changes in domestic demand. Another implication is that tax policy has shied away from the more difficult tax base of incomes taxes on both corporations and households. It is these two areas where tax policy must shift going forward as the pace of formal labor force employment growth slows." Figures 1 to 8, constructed based on data from Tables 1 and 2, significantly proved that the Turkish tax burden distribution gets worse off in terms of equity over time.

The next section looks at tax expenditures, which are regarded as disguised type of inequitable tax burden distribution, in Turkey. It is usually an ignored subject in tax policy studies and there are quite a few articles written on it.

TAX EXPENDITURES

In this section, we discuss another unfavorable aspect of the Turkish tax policy in terms of tax burden distribution by disclosing hidden tax reliefs named as tax expenditures. We will test the hypothesis that *tax expenditures, in real sense, favors certain groups of individuals, economic and social sectors.*

As far as the tax theory is concerned, tax burden distribution would worsen mostly by regressive-type taxes. Regressive taxes are taxes levied on a lump sum or unit (specific) basis. Lump sum income taxes and specific goods and services taxes are the main examples of inequitable taxes.

The measurement of tax performance comprises first the overall central government ratio. A low ratio means that, in the course of economic development and rising per capita income, the country is not able to increase the tax burden of the rich. Secondly, we consider the direct vs. indirect tax ratio, laborers' contribution to income tax revenue, and excise duties and legal transaction taxes as unit taxes and test whether they worsen the quality of equity in the tax burden distribution or not.

A Discussion of the Concept of Tax Expenditures

Governments frequently use the tax system to promote specific policies. This practice results in tax expenditures.[10] In broad terms, tax expenditures are concessions that fall outside a tax norm or benchmark to provide a benefit for a specific activity or class of taxpayer. The tax norm includes the rate structure, accounting conventions, deductibility of compulsory payments, provisions to facilitate tax administration, and international fiscal obligations (Swift, Brixi, & Valenduc, 2004, p. 3). Tax expenditures are similar to those direct spending programs that are available as entitlements to those who meet the statutory criteria established for the programs (US Joint Committee on Taxation, 2011, p. 2). Nevertheless, it is important to recognize that tax expenditures lower tax revenue and therefore hamper the revenue-raising function of the tax system. The consequence of introducing tax expenditures is that higher tax rates will have to be imposed on income, consumption, and any other tax base to finance a given level of public outlays (Valenduc, 2004, 71).

Tax expenditures are, in a general sense, the tax revenue foregone as a result of various tax reliefs. The benchmark is the standard tax system and any deviations and distortions from the standard type of exclusions, exemptions of any tax system will be referred as tax expenditures. But the difficulty arises from the question of what kind of reliefs would be labelled as a non-standard type and as a deviation from the standard path. Brown (2004, p. 46) highlights that there is an element of judgment involved in identifying which elements of the tax system are tax expenditures and which are structural features, given the diversity of tax arrangements. This fact makes international comparisons of tax expenditures difficult to interpret. According to the OECD, "the numbers of tax expenditures vary widely from country to country this could have much more to do with measurement details as well as broad questions in the definition of tax expenditures and of the benchmark tax, than with the issues in the actual tax laws and regulations of the various countries" (pp. 159-160).

The benchmark or standard tax system means uniformity and universality, which is practically not possible. Any deviation from this normative structure will lead to *negative tax expenditures*.[11] Negative tax expenditures occur when concessions impose a higher cost than benefit. In case of normative rate structure, the following characteristics of taxes are considered. Identification of the normative tax structure can best proceed by determining whether a given provision responds to one of the following questions: 1) Is the provision necessary to determine the base of the tax, normatively defined, in accordance with the fundamental nature of the tax? 2) Is the provision part of the generally applicable rate structure? 3) Is the provision necessary to define the taxable units liable for the tax? 4) Is the provision necessary to assure that the tax is determined within the time period selected for imposition of the tax? 5) Is the provision necessary to implement the tax in international transactions? 6) Is the provision necessary to administer the tax?

Although governments generally rely on direct spending to finance their policies, tax expenditures are a common channel for financing government policies outside the budgetary framework. Tax expenditures take many forms—from tax exemptions to tax credits—and are generally aimed at supporting targeted sectors, firms, or individuals. If used properly, tax expenditures can play an important role in implementing government policy priorities. For example, a number of well-regarded programs for the poor take the form of tax expenditures. In other cases tax expenditures may correct for a market failure by reducing the burden of complying with the tax system. Hence, as Marples (2015) stresses, "if the tax expenditure addresses a market failure or achieves a policy goal then a basis for retaining the tax expenditure exists." However, the assessment of tax expenditure policies and programs is often complicated by inadequate reporting and accounting practices, particularly in developing and transition countries. This lack of scrutiny is in stark contrast to the scrutiny generally applied to the spending side of government finances (Ansu & Laursen, 2004, p. xi). The use of tax expenditures does not provide the same assurances. Tax expenditures are seldom exposed to extensive analysis and scrutiny. Their true fiscal cost is hidden as revenue forgone.

Contingent liabilities are another common channel for such "hidden" spending that tends to arise from a government's explicit and implicit promises of financial support. Contingent liabilities are similar to tax expenditures in that they represent instruments of fiscal policy requiring no cash spending at the time of their issuance. Contingent liabilities show their fiscal costs only later, in the form of sudden claims on the government budget. As with tax expenditures, contingent liabilities have been known to provide politicians with an opportunity to implement various initiatives without submitting them to the level of competition applied to budgetary expenditures and without revealing their future possible fiscal costs. Contingent liabilities thus raise concerns about transparency and appropriate use similar to the concerns that tax expenditures raise (Swift, Brixi, & Valenduc, 2004, pp. 2-3).

According to Toder and Baneman (2012), taxpayers in all income groups benefit from tax expenditures, but on average, tax expenditures raise after-tax incomes more for upper-income taxpayers than for lower-income taxpayers. The authors point out that "[a]s a share of income, special rates for capital gains and dividends and itemized deductions provide the largest benefits for taxpayers in the top 1 percent of the income distribution, exemptions and exclusions benefit taxpayers in upper middle-income groups the most, and refundable credits provide the largest benefits to those in the bottom two quintiles of the distribution." Schuyler (2014) raises two other powerful drivers of progressivity as personal exemptions and the standard deduction. "They shelter from tax a much larger fraction of the incomes of lower- and middle-income people than the incomes of people with higher incomes. They are also in the baseline, which means the considerable progressivity they impart is similarly not reflected in the distribution of tax expenditures."

Avram (2014) finds that "with a few exceptions the impact of tax allowances and tax credits on inequality is small. Tax credits are generally more progressive than tax allowances. However, with the exception of refundable tax credits, the design of the allowances/credits appears to be less important than the characteristics of the population they are targeting and/or other features of the income tax system in determining the redistributive effect. Consequently, tax concessions appear ill-suited to target resources towards households in the bottom part of the income distribution."

The decision to introduce tax expenditures ideally should be based on an assessment of the costs and benefits of such a decision and on the merits of tax expenditures versus direct spending. Most developed countries have established tax reporting systems, which provide empirical information on their tax expenditures. Tax expenditure reporting[12] is used for fiscal transparency and for efficient resource allocation. Such tax reporting systems tend to be part of a country's overall fiscal system for strengthening government finance and contribute significantly to fiscal transparency. Even if most developed countries have implemented tax expenditure reporting, the gap between the level of scrutiny and transparency of tax expenditures compared with direct spending remains wide. Unless, however, tax expenditures are exposed to adequate scrutiny, they may invite fiscal opportunism (Swift, Brixi, & Valenduc, 2004, p. 2).

For a *normal income tax*, only personal exemptions for taxpayers and dependents and a general rate schedule are allowed. For the determination of business income, normal income tax law is assumed to require the general concept of matching income and expenses. Any of the other exclusions and deductions would be considered as tax expenditures from the viewpoint of income taxes. For example, exempted social security benefits, and even the taxation of capital gains on a realization basis are defended as tax expenditure items for the purpose of implementing normal income tax structure.

By its very nature, income tax is a personal tax. Therefore, any type of departures from its pure form will mean tax expenditure whether be it economic or social ones. In the case of corporation income tax as a capital tax, only the cost of capital would be allowed to be deducted depending on the political approach to the tax as being capital, economic profits or cash flow tax. For goods and services taxes like very familiar VAT, only public services and exports could be the exclusions provided that financial services are subject to another liability. Excise taxes also may be defined in normative way as covering goods and services that have a widespread negative externality. Although most of the tax expenditure data are related to personal income tax, the analysis would be applicable for any broad-based tax such as corporation income tax, property tax or wealth tax.

It is appropriate to evaluate tax expenditures with respect to cost, distributional consequences, alternative means of provision, and economic effects. Tax expenditure analysis can help both policymakers to evaluate the tradeoffs among potentially competing policy goals and the public to understand the actual size of government, the uses to which government resources are put, and the tax and economic policy consequences that follow from the implicit choices made (US Joint Committee on Taxation, 2011, p. 1). Also, an analysis of tax expenditure contributes to the tax policy debate and shed light on trade-offs with direct spending programs.

The arguments above lead us to examine tax expenditures in Turkey as a source of distributional tax inequity. It is claimed that Turkey introduced very generous tax breaks that would never fit economic and social purposes. First, the Turkish experience will be examined in terms of fiscal transparency rule and on equity grounds, and secondly, by using available data for the period of 2006-2013, we will try to estimate tax expenditure ratios.

Fiscal Transparency and Non-Discrimination Rule

Fiscal rules are often seen as devices to ensure fiscal discipline. They can be adopted to ensure a transparent, more predictable and even-handed approach to promoting fiscal responsibility. Nevertheless, as Ter-Minassian (2007) highlights, "fiscal rules are unlikely to be effective in countries where expenditure assignments are not clear … [and they] cannot secure fiscal discipline by themselves if the political will to adhere to them is lacking, or if the central government's commitment to a no bailout policy is not credible, thus leading to moral hazard."

A multi-stakeholder action network, the Global Initiative on Fiscal Transparency (GIFT), which aims to "advance and institutionalize global norms and significant, continuous improvements on fiscal transparency, engagement, and accountability in countries around the world" identifies 10 norms (see GIFT, 2012). Among them we will focus below fiscal transparency and non-discrimination rule.

Fiscal Transparency Rule

In Turkey, tax expenditures are defined as public revenue foregone as a result of tax exemptions, exclusions, deductions and similar tax reliefs. Fiscal transparency rule is essential for public awareness of what types of tax expenditures are in effect and what the magnitude of them costs to public budget. As Burton and Stewart (2011) highlight, "[g]ood governance and democratic principles suggest that direct spending ought be subject to a rigorous cost benefit analysis, carried out before the money is appropriated, which considers the merits of the policy and whether spending is the most appropriate government action…. Similar scrutiny of tax expenditures should be conducted... to analyze critically whether the tax expenditure is the best policy tool to achieve a particular objective" (p. 64). Moreover, GIFT (2012) states that "greater fiscal transparency, participation and accountability can play in facilitating more effective international cooperation in the pursuit of financial stability, poverty reduction, equitable economic growth, and stewardship of the environment and the global commons."

Turkish *Public Management and Budgetary Control Act* No.5018, the so-called fiscal framework of Turkish legislation, stipulates that every budget year, a list of tax expenditures and the resulting loss of revenue should be enclosed to the Central Government Budget Bill. This legal requirement seems to be complied with annual declaration and enclosure of tax expenditure list since 2006. It is claimed that the list enclosed to the Bill is incomplete in terms of covering the whole amount of reliefs. They are hidden and embedded in other laws. Nor the size of tax expenditures is accurately calculated. It is necessary to include all reliefs (exclusions, allowances, exemptions and deductions) introduced by any legislative source: tax laws, other laws and tax treaties. In addition, it is not sufficient to list the tax reliefs and make calculations by tax type. It is necessary to estimate every single tax relief item by item like it is the case in developed countries.

The current list prepared for 2014 and presented in Annex comprises 121 items. Most of them belong to Personal Income Tax (PIT) (59). The rest is distributed as 26 for Corporation Income Tax (CIT), and 11 for Excise Taxes. Other laws having tax expenditures are free trade areas, technology development regions, social security, R&D, electricity market, and petroleum products.

The most significant of those tax expenditures can be divided into seven different categories: (1) free trade zones; (2) investment incentives; (3) financial instruments; (4) regional employment incentives; (5) agricultural sector support; (6) social insurance and pension contributions; and (7) assistance to low-income and disadvantaged persons. These categories are not exhaustive and sometimes overlap.

As Glenday and Swift (2006) indicate, tax expenditures are primarily delivered through the PIT and CIT. Some of the major tax expenditures are granted with the aim of promoting: investment, employment, regional development, R&D, and trade incentives primarily delivered through the CIT. A range of tax expenditures aims to assist low-income individuals, in support of social policy. These are delivered primarily through the PIT and CIT and to a lesser extent through the VAT. Some major tax expenditures in this latter group include the deductibility of contributions to the social security system for pensions, disability, unemployment and health benefits as well as contributions to private pension and insurance company-based pension and health policies.

Compared to many industrial and emerging market countries, Turkey appears to make more extensive use of tax incentives, including in the form of tax holidays for investments in specific sectors (e.g., technological development) or regions (such as free trade zones, and so-called first priority regions). Ter–Minassian (2009, p. 8) suggests that the Turkish Finance Ministry should focus on reducing incentives under the CIT.

While the available empirical evidence on the effectiveness of tax incentives in promoting additional investment, job creation, and regional development is not conclusive, there is broad consensus in the literature that they are often less cost-effective than targeted public spending to address regional weaknesses (e.g., in infrastructure or labor force skills), and that tax holidays in particular are relatively inefficient in promoting sustained regional or sectorial development, as they favor investments with short gestation and payoff horizons. Moreover, with a rate of 20 percent, the Turkish CIT is already quite competitive in a global and European context. Therefore, according to Ter–Minassian (2009, p. 8) priority should be given to shortening the duration of existing incentive schemes (with respect of individual acquired rights), and firmly refraining from introducing new ones.

Before discussing the drawbacks of the Turkish tax expenditure practice, we introduce the fiscal transparency rule as a main principle of public budget. Turkey adopted the transparency rule in 2003, borrowing from the IMF public accounts regulation. This rule dictates that in the process of collection and usage of all public revenues, the public would be informed. For implementing this rule it is stated that "[t]he duties, authorities and responsibilities of all public servants should be clearly defined. The public budgetary process: preparation, parliamentary review and enactment, execution and audit ought to be publicly open and easily accessible. All tax reliefs and incentives are to be disclosed periodically. All public accounts should be kept in accordance with the standard public accounting system and generally accepted accounting and financial reporting principles." In the course of above-mentioned universal rule, the examination of tax expenditure list, like previous eight lists, discloses the following deficiencies.

Tax treaties made on the basis of OECD Model Tax Convention in Turkey have never been considered. Rate reductions for capital income foregone tax revenue and implicit tax expenditures embedded in tax treaties are never included in the list. Tax treaties are constitutionally law-enforced-type legal documents. In case of conflict arising among national tax laws and treaties, then the priority is given to the treaties by Constitution Art.90. Turkey first signed the tax treaty for avoiding double taxation with Austria on September 24, 1973 and lastly with Malta on January 31, 2013. Total number of treaties ratified since then amounted to 78.

Extensive exclusions and exemptions causing remarkable tax loss, which are incorporated in Stamp Duty and Administrative Duty Laws, have not been considered as tax expenditure. Revenue forgone by means of Council of Ministers' decrees to make rate changes of income, corporation income and value added taxes have been omitted. But, indeed, it should be the standard tax system procedure to consider deductions from taxable personal and corporate income as tax expenditures.

The followings cited in *Turkish Revenue Administration* web site as tax expenditure are never mentioned in the Tax Expenditure List (2014). Articles of laws passed to release some people and corporations from tax duty and considered as tax expenditure are presented in Box 1.

Most of the legislation cited above relates to the exemptions of wage incomes. The most prominent and comprehensive type of exclusions concerning profits and commercial activities are the Turkish ship and boats' passenger and cargo gains exclusion. According to this exclusion, all gains earned from operating ships, boats and yachts registered to the Turkish International Maritime Registration Office are totally excluded from Personal and Corporation Income Taxes and similar liabilities.

As identified, fiscal transparency rule in Turkey is violated in terms of universally accepted tax expenditure practice. Turkey used to give tax breaks and reliefs hidden and embedded in legislation other than tax laws as an impropriate practice. The Turkish tax expenditure practice is also against the equity and non-discrimination rule.

Equity and Non-Discrimination

According to this principle, while imposing taxes and similar liabilities, no discrimination could be made in terms of race, religion, language, gender, ethnicity or political philosophy of the people. Everyone is equal before the tax law. No individual group or profession could have any privilege, exclusion, concessions or relief unless other constitutional duties are concerned.[13] But *positive discrimination* may be made in favor of some members and segments of the society like women as a whole, elderly and disabled people, children and widows, orphans and martyrs and veterans. Everyone must pay taxes in proportion

Box 1.

Homeland Security Act No.3201 Art. Supp.21, Law for Damages Caused to Courthouses by Fire, Earthquake, Flood and Landslide No.4473 Art.46, Law of Exemption of State Forestry Administration from Certain Taxes Art.2, State Drama Law No.5441 Art.9, NATO Joint Infrastructure Program Law No.6095 Art.10, Welfare Payments in case of Disasters Affecting Public Life Act No.7269 Art.40,42,43,45, Army Solidarity Law No.205 Art.34, Export Encouragement Law No. 261 Art.1, Customs Duty Tariff Law No.474 art.2,3, State Personnel Act No.657 Related Payment Arts Shantytown Act No.775 Art.33, Maritime Labor Act. No.854, Art. 9, Turkish Military Personnel Law, Art. Supp. 17 and 18, State Opera and Ballet Act No.1309 Art.10, Labor Law No.4857 Art.8, Law for Financial Help to Farmers Having Damages from Natural Disasters No.2090 Art., Act of Salaries & Social Security of Village Elders Art.1, Board of Judges and Public Attorneys Act No.461 22, Law of Encouragement of Turkish Maritime Fleet and Docks No.2581 Art.1., Turkish International Ship Registration Law No.4490 Art.12, National Lottery Act No.320 Art.53, Law of Judges & Attorney Generals No.2802 Art.106,, Information Technologies and Communication Act No.2813Art. 5, Higher Education Personnel Act No.2914, art.12 and 14, Bosphorus Act No. Art.17, Encouragement of Saving and Acceleration of Public Investments Act No.2983 Art.14. Homeland Security Flight Allowances Act No. Art.6, Law of Financial Leasing No.3226 Art. 30. Tax Relief Act to Islamic Development Bank No.3259 Art.1., Allowances to the Veteran & Families Act No.3292 Art.2. Law of Allowances, Pensions & Travel Expenses of Members of Parliament No.3671, Art.1, Law of Public Investments & Services Made by Built, Operate and Transfer Model No.3996 No.12., Ministry of Foreign Affairs Act No.4009 Art.56. Privatization Act No. Art. 27., Competition Protection Act No.4054 Art. 37., Law of Telegram & Phone Act Supplements No.20 and Customs Law No.4458 Art.167.

to their respective income, wealth and consumption. If the individual had no ability-to pay, then the tax duty would not have emerged. So the ability-to-pay principle is a version of equity principle. Nationals and non-nationals without any discrimination would be taxpayers. As a constitutional rule, the equitable distribution of tax burden is the social objective of the tax policy.

It is alleged that the tax expenditure tool tends toward unfair results, both in the likelihood that undeserving groups of taxpayers obtain them, and in the operation of the tax expenditures once they have been enacted. According to the OECD (2010), "[s]elective and lucrative tax expenditures are most usually those that provide advantages for income from capital or for self-employment, rather than labor. Those who own wealth, including businesses, tend to be those with higher incomes. Upper-income taxpayers are more likely to take advantage of tax benefits for retirement saving and housing that are available in many countries. Once tax expenditures are in place, they are likely to benefit well-off taxpayers more than the rank and file. The well-to-do simply have more tax liability in the first instance, and so have more to gain from tax expenditures. To the extent that tax expenditures are complex and confront those who wish to claim the tax benefits with complex tasks, the most well to-do are most likely to have the financial and technical knowledge, or the hired assistance, to take advantage of those opportunities" (pp. 26-27).

In addition, under a progressive system, any tax expenditure that reduces taxable income or postpones the recognition of taxable income will benefit most those taxpayers who are in the highest tax-rate brackets. Those who are not taxable do not benefit at all from tax expenditures structured in that way. This effect has been labelled an 'upside-down subsidy', and has been considered a disadvantage of tax expenditures as a policy tool.

The Turkish Supreme Court ruled that "… non - discrimination rule refers that everybody having ability to-pay must be a taxpayer and paying taxes on their income, wealth and consumption without any discrimination."[14] In this respect, tax reliefs given particularly to capital income earners, property holders or certain businessmen are obviously against this universal principle. Now we try to estimate the Turkish tax expenditure ratios using very limited data available for Turkey.

Estimation of Tax Expenditure Ratios

Tax expenditure in a real sense is measured and estimated by the calculation of the difference of actual tax revenue and the revenue supposed to be collected with non-tax expenditure. It is claimed that estimation would be straightforward as computation of the cost of exemptions, deductions, exclusions and credits to the treasury. According to literature, the final revenue loss method is preferable. However, this method is unworkable – precisely because accounting for behavior is very difficult, and there is no single correct estimate. In practice, therefore, every country tends to use the initial revenue loss ("revenue forgone") method that have several important theoretical drawbacks.[15] While making estimations, the taxpayer's attitudes are assumed to remain unchanged.

An alternative way to measure tax expenditures is to express their values in terms of 'outlay equivalents'.[16] This method offers the opportunity of assessing the merits of alternative means of delivering the government benefit. Burton and Sadiq (2013) suggest that this method is "arguably the most accurate where the purpose of tax expenditure analysis is to determine the cost of the tax expenditure and whether it should be replaced with a direct spending program. Measuring the actual benefit in the hands of the beneficiaries, however, requires high quality data about the taxpayer" (p. 97). According to OECD (2010, p. 151), in practice only Sweden provides outlay equivalent measures, in their case as a supplement to their primary presentation, rather than as the primary presentation itself. Although the US once did the same as Sweden, it has discontinued the practice. Because of the high quality data problem we prefer to use revenue forgone method in this study.

A total tax expenditure estimate may usefully indicate, very roughly, what proportion tax expenditures comprise of government revenues or direct expenditures. However, Burton and Stewart (2011) right to warn that "this is only a rough estimate and used cautiously in debates about public policy" (p. 63). Tax expenditure data were published only after the 2006 fiscal year in Turkey. The data that appears in Figure 9 are estimates and final figures have not been compiled, yet. In addition, the 2006 and 2007 figures are incomplete in the sense that they do not include the reliefs set in other laws. Another setback is that estimation would not have been done on an item by item basis. In the Annex, Turkish tax expenditure items are listed. In the list, out of total 119 items, 56 articles are of personal income tax, 26 articles of corporation income tax, 16 articles of value-added tax and 21 articles of other existing laws. The probable loss of tax revenue is calculated for each tax type.

Based on this limited data, we observe that the total amount of tax expenditures in Turkey reached the level of 22.4 billion TL in 2013, equivalent to nearly US$10 billion at the time of writing. The sharp increase observed in recent years is due to personal income tax reliefs. Figure 10 shows that, in Turkey, nearly two-thirds of tax expenditures result from income taxes.

As observed in Figure 9, the share of tax expenditures embedded in other laws gradually increased and became around 10% of the total. This tendency is the result of government policy to prefer and introduce several income and corporation tax reliefs in other laws, which violates the fiscal transparency rule.[17]

According to Figure 11, the Turkish tax expenditure shares as a ratio of GDP, Central Government Revenue and tax revenue are considerably low, and they are 1.5%, 5.8%, and 6.9%, respectively. To put tax expenditures of Turkey into a perspective, Table 2 provides an international comparison of tax expenditures.

Figure 9. Tax expenditures estimates in Turkey
Source: MOF (different years); www.muhasebat.gov.tr: and www.gib.gov.tr

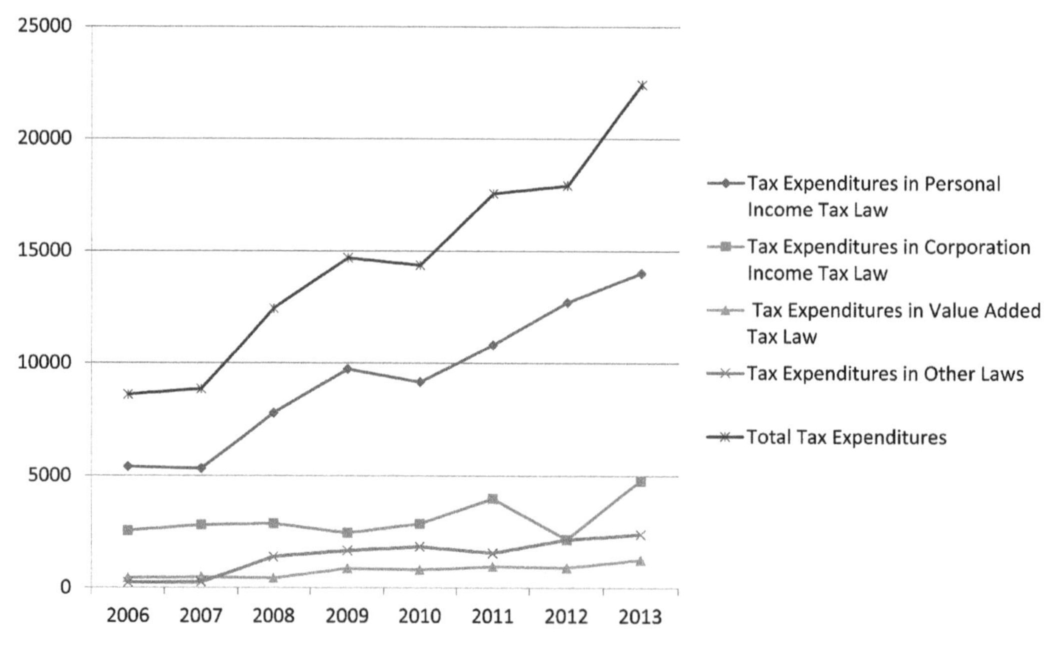

Figure 10. Tax expenditures structure in Turkey
Source: MOF (different years); www.muhasebat.gov.tr: and www.gib.gov.tr

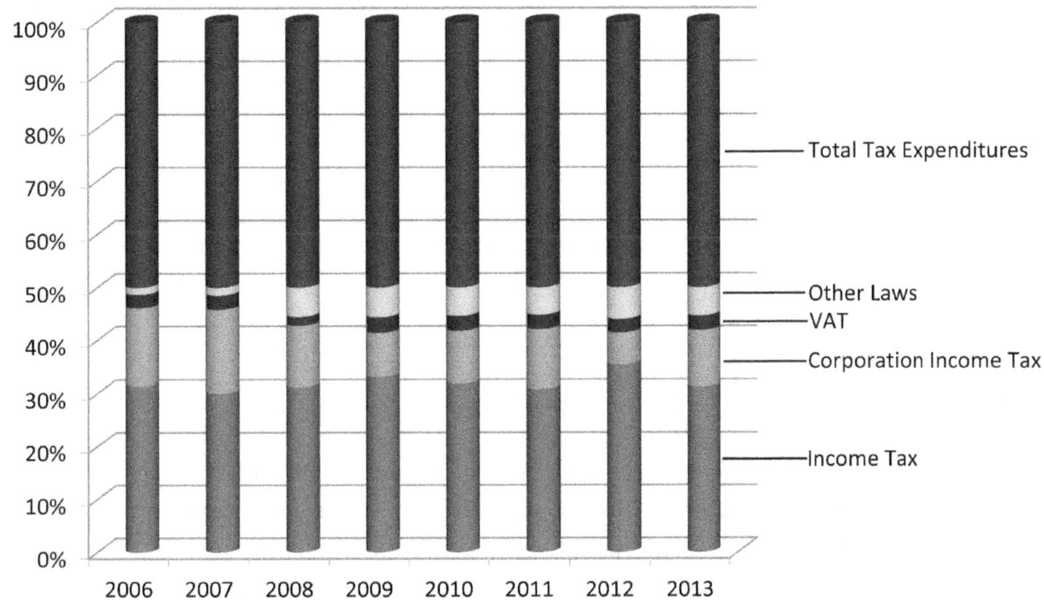

Figure 11. Tax expenditures ratios (2006-2013)
Source: MOF (different years); www.muhasebat.gov.tr: and www.gib.gov.tr

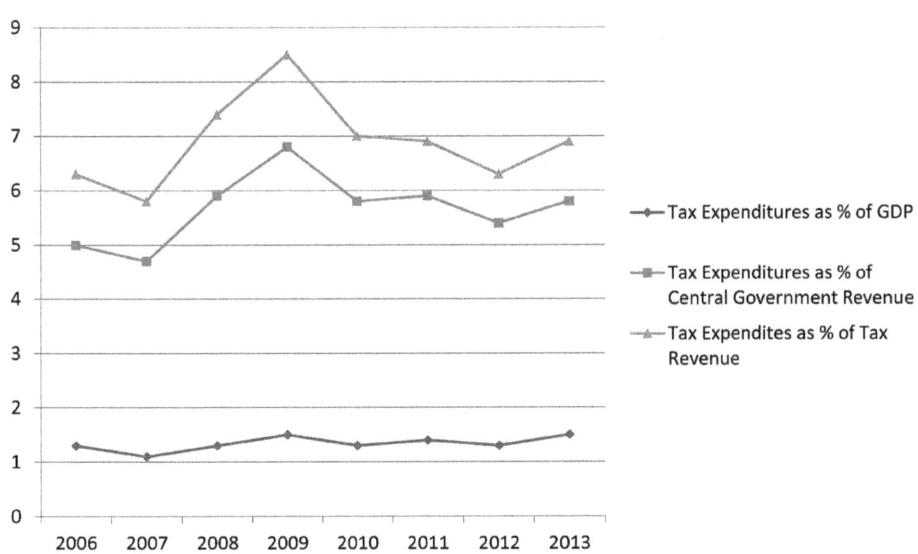

Numerical comparisons of tax expenditures across countries may attract attention, but they have profound limitations. As the OECD (2010) warns, "[s]ome useful conclusions may be drawn, but they should not over-reach the comparability of the data" (p. 148). It is important to keep in mind that clear challenges steam not only from the use of different benchmarks but also different coverage or completeness of tax expenditures even within one rather comparable benchmark.[18]

*Table 2. International comparison of tax expenditures (latest year available)**

	Canada (2004)	United Kingdom (2006)	United States (2008)	South Korea (2006)	Spain (2008)	Germany (2006)	Turkey (2013)	Netherlands (2006)
% of central government total tax and non-tax receipts	44.37	35.17	33.65	14.34	12.48	8.48	6.90	5.15
% of GDP	6.94	12.79	5.97	2.48	4.55	0.74	1.50	2.00

Source: MOF (2014) for Turkey and OECD (2010). *Tax Expenditures in OECD Countries*, pp. 225-225 for other countries.

* For every country except for Canada and Spain, fiscal years rather than calendar years are used. For the United Kingdom, fiscal year 2006-07 is used (from 6 April 2006 to 5 April 2007).

CONCLUDING REMARKS

Tax expenditures are a common channel for financing specific government policies outside the budgetary framework. If used properly, tax expenditures can play an important role in implementing government policy priorities. In other cases tax expenditures may correct a market failure by reducing the burden of complying with the tax system. Hence, their positive effects should not be underestimated. Nevertheless, the assessment of tax expenditure policies and programs is often complicated by inadequate reporting and accounting practices. Tax expenditures are seldom exposed to extensive analysis and scrutiny and their true fiscal cost is hidden as revenue forgone. Moreover, it appears that the redistributive effects of tax expenditures are minor in developing countries than advanced countries. Therefore, it is very important to apply effective tax expenditure management policies in a developing country like Turkey. Effective tax expenditure management policies would entail not only a double dividend for Turkey in terms of raising GDP per capita and reducing inequality but also improve transparency of its budget process and contributes to democratic oversight of taxing and spending.

The Turkish tax policy analysis for the period 2004-2013 from the tax burden distribution point of view led us to the following conclusions: The overall tax ratio could not keep pace with the growth of GDP, except for the year 2013. Turkey is not able to raise its tax revenue ratio due to the low level of income tax and property tax performance. It remained constant and at a comparatively low level with respect to OECD countries. The central government tax revenue ratio remained nearly constant, close to 20%. Worse still is, tax burden distribution became inequitable mainly because nearly two-thirds of total tax revenue come from indirect taxes, which exhibit a regressive character.

The rise of wage earners' contribution to income tax yielded 60% of it, the share of excise duties close to that of VAT, and the relative increase of specific legal transaction and financial services taxes. Indirect taxes, comprising nearly two-thirds of total tax revenue, largely results from the regressive nature of specific taxes. High income inequality is one of the results of high share of indirect taxation. It is claimed that *Turkey introduced very generous tax breaks that would never fit economic and social purposes*. In this study, another unfavorable aspect of the Turkish tax policy in terms of tax burden distribution has also been discussed through the disclosure of the so far hidden tax reliefs, named after tax expenditures. In terms of tax expenditures; fiscal transparency rule and non-discrimination principle of taxation are violated due to the implicit tax expenditures that are never included in the list. Moreover, extensive exclusions and exemptions, causing incorporation in Stamp Duty and Administrative Duty

Laws, have not been considered as tax expenditure. Revenue forgone by means of Council of Ministers' decrees to make rate changes of income, corporation income and value added taxes of even zero point has been omitted.

According to the results of tax expenditure estimation based on this limited data of a short-time horizon in Turkey, the total amount of tax expenditures reached the level of 22.4 billion TL in 2013, equivalent to nearly US$10 billion at the time if writing. The sharp increase observed in recent years is due to personal income tax reliefs, and nearly two-thirds of the tax expenditures resulted from income taxes. The ratios of Turkish tax expenditure to GDP, central government revenue and tax revenue look like considerably low compare to other countries, being 1.5, 5.8 and 6.9%, respectively. However, it is important to recognize that these figures are probably very conservative since this study could only disclose a limited number of hidden tax reliefs, which are outside the tax laws but have the similar effect. Moreover, these figures do not take into account tax concessions and exclusions related to defense related expenditures. Therefore, it would be hardly surprising to see that other researchers may come up with much higher figures, after they discover other hidden tax reliefs.

It needs to be acknowledged that unlike advanced countries, Turkey has not been able to use tax and transfer policies effectively to reduce income inequality. The government health care and primary and secondary education programs are not well targeted, but their incidence tends to be progressive. Although they seems as certain exclusions, deductions, exemptions and allowances, rate reductions and tax credits are given by law on the basis of economic and social reasons, indeed, they release some people, corporations and bodies from tax liability. What needs to be done is to favor a degree of progressivity without causing disincentive effects on work efforts to enrich redistributive policy instruments.

ACKNOWLEDGMENT

This chapter is highly benefited from the Turkish-medium paper "Türk Vergi Politikasının Performansı (2003-2013)" presented in the 12th Turkish Tax Congress, organized by the Marmara University Alumni Association (2014, April 11-12). The paper later published as an article titled "Vergi Harcamaları, Mali Saydamlık ve Anayasaya Uygunluk" by İstanbul Ticaret Üniversitesi Sosyal Bilimler Dergisi within Law Special Issue.

REFERENCES

Alt, J., Preston, I., & Sibieta, L. (2009). The Political Economy of Tax Policy. In *Dimensions of Tax Design: The Mirrlees Review* (pp. 1204–1279). Oxford, UK: Oxford University Press.

Ansu, Y., & Laursen, T. B. (2004). Preface. In H. P. Brixi, C. M. A. Valenduc, & Z. L. Swift (Eds.), *Tax Expenditures – Shedding Light on Government Spending through the Tax System: Lessons from Developed and Transition Economies* (pp. xi–xii). Washington, DC: The World Bank.

Batırel, Ö. F. (2013). Vergi Harcamaları, Mali Saydamlık İlkesi ve Anayasaya Uygunluk. *İstanbul Ticaret Üniversitesi Sosyal Bilimler Dergisi, 24*, 13-20.

Batırel, Ö. F. (2014). Türk Vergi Politikasının Performansı (2003-2013). *İstanbul Yüksek Ticaret ve Marmara Üniversitesi İİBF Mezunları Derneği, Türkiye XII.* Vergi Kongresi.

Bird, R. M. (2007, March 31). *Tax Challenges Facing Developing Countries: A Perspective from Outside the Policy Arena.* Retrieved May 27, 2015, from http://papers.ssrn.com/sol3/papers.cfm?abstract_id=1393991

Bird, R. M. (2016). Transparency, Technology and Taxation. In M. M. Erdoğdu & B. Christiansen (Eds.), Handbook of Research on Public Finance in Europe and the MENA Region. Hershey, PA: IGI Global.

Brixi, H. P. (2004). Managing Tax Expenditures: Policy Options. In H. P. Brixi, C. M. A. Valenduc, & Z. L. Swift (Eds.), *Tax Expenditures – Shedding Light on Government Spending through the Tax System: Lessons from Developed and Transition Economies* (pp. 227–233). Washington, DC: The World Bank.

Brown, C. (2004). Tax Expenditures in Australia. In H. P. Brixi, C. M. A. Valenduc, & Z. L. Swift (Eds.), *Tax Expenditures – Shedding Light on Government Spending through the Tax System: Lessons from Developed and Transition Economies* (pp. 45–68). Washington, DC: The World Bank.

Burton, M., & Sadiq, K. (2013). *Tax Expenditure Management: A Critical Assessment.* Cambridge, UK: Cambridge University Press. doi:10.1017/CBO9780511910142

Burton, M., & Stewart, M. (2011). *Promoting Budget Transparency through Tax Expenditure Management: A Report on Country Experience for Civil Society Advocates.* Melbourne Law School Legal Studies Research Paper 544. University of Melbourne. Retrieved July 30, 2015, from http://internationalbudget.org/wp-content/uploads/Promoting-Budget-Transparency-Through-Tax-Expenditure-Management.pdf

Chetty, R., Hendren, N., Kline, P., & Saez, E. (2013). *The Economic Impacts of Tax Expenditures: Evidence from Spatial Variation across the U.S.* Retrieved July 30, 2015, from http://obs.rc.fas.harvard.edu/chetty/tax_expenditure_soi_whitepaper.pdf

Chu, K.-Y., Davoodi, H., & Gupta, S. (2000). *Income Distribution and Tax, and Government Social Spending Policies in Developing Countries.* The United Nations University, WIDER Working Papers No. 214.

Daude, C., Gutiérrez, H., & Melguizo, Á. (2014). *'Doctoring the ball': The Political Economy of Tax Incentives for Investment in the Dominican Republi.*, OECD Development Centre, Working Paper, No. 322, January. Retrieved January 15, 2015, from http://www.oecd.org/countries/dominicanrepublic/WP322AE.pdf

Erdoğdu, M. M., Yılmaz, B. E., Aydın, M., & User, İ. (2016). Political Economy of Tax Evasion and Tax Loss in the Real Estate Sector: A Property Tax Reform Proposal for Turkey. In M. M. Erdoğdu & B. Christiansen (Eds.), Handbook of Research on Public Finance in Europe and the MENA Region. Hershey, PA: IGI Global.

GIFT. (2012). *The Global Initiative on Fiscal Transparency: High-Level Principles on Fiscal Transparency, Participation, and Accountability.* The Global Initiative on Fiscal Transparency DRAFT. Retrieved May 27, 2015, from http://www.fiscaltransparency.net/GIFT-High-Level-Principles-2012-08-ENG.pdf

Glenday, G., & Swift, Z. L. (2006, December). Establishing Tax Expenditure Accounts – Towards Better Fiscal Accountability and Transparency. In *Turkey Public Expenditure Review.* Washington, DC: World Bank.

James, S. (2016). The Difficulties of Achieving Successful Tax Reform. In M. M. Erdoğdu & B. Christiansen (Eds.), Handbook of Research on Public Finance in Europe and the MENA Region. Hershey, PA: IGI Global.

LeBlanc, P. (2014, July). Tax Expenditures: An OECD-Wide Perspective. In L. Bauger (Eds.), *The Use of Tax Expenditures in Times of Fiscal Consolidation* (pp. 17-18). European Commission Economic Papers 523. Retrieved May 27, 2015, from http://ec.europa.eu/economy_finance/publications/economic_paper/2014/pdf/ecp523_en.pdf

Marples, D. J. (2015, April 30). *Tax Expenditures: Overview and Analysis*. Congressional Research Service Report. Retrieved May 29, 2015, from http://fas.org/sgp/crs/misc/R44012.pdf

Martinez-Vazquez, J. Vulovic, V., & Dodson, B. M. (2012). The Impact of Tax and Expenditure Policies on Income Distribution: Evidence from a Large Panel of Countries. *Hacienda Pública Española, 200*(4), 95-130.

MOF. (2007, October). *Tax Expenditure Report*. General Directorate of the Revenue Policies, Ministry of Finance, No: B.07.0.GEP.10.10-2007.

MOF. (2015). *Public Accounts Bulletins*. General Directorate of Public Accounts, Ankara. Retrieved April 20, 2015, from https://portal.muhasebat.gov.tr/mgmportal/faces/khbDetail?birimDizini=General+Government&_afrLoop=1017212479336060&_afrWindowMode=0&_adf.ctrl-state=692ozugmw_4

OECD. (2010). *Tax Expenditures in OECD Countries*. Paris: OECD Publishing; doi:10.1787/9789264076907-en

OECD. (2012). *Income Inequality and Growth: The Role of Taxes and Transfers*. OECD Economics Department Policy Notes, No. 9. January. Retrieved May 29, 2015, from http://www.oecd.org/eco/public-finance/49417295.pdf

OECD. (2013). *Revenue Statistics 2013*. Paris: OECD Publishing; doi:10.1787/rev_stats-2013-en-fr

Oner, E. (2011). Tax Expenditures and the Situation in Turkey. *International Journal of Business and Social Science*, *2*(23), 165–170.

Pechman, J. A. (1987). *Federal Tax Policy* (5th ed.). Washington, DC: The Brookings Institution.

Piketty, T. (2014). *Capital in the Twenty-First Century* (A. Goldhammer, Trans.). Cambridge, UK: Harvard University Press. doi:10.4159/9780674369542

Schuyler, M. (2014, January 13). *Baked In the Cake: Why the Progressivity of the Income Tax Isn't Visible in the Distribution of Tax Expenditures*. Tax Foundation. Retrieved May 29, 2015, from http://taxfoundation.org/article/baked-cake-why-progressivity-income-tax-isn-t-visible-distribution-tax-expenditures

SGI. (2009). *Economy and Employment: Taxes Report, Sustainable Governance Indicators 2009: Bertelsmann Stiftung*. Retrieved September 9, 2014, from http://www.sgi-network.org/pdf/SGI09_EconomyAndEmployment_Taxes.pdf

Shah, A. (2001). *Whalley*. The Redistributive Impact of Taxation in Developing Countries.

Stiglitz, J. E. (2012). *The Price of Inequality: How Today's Divided Society Endangers Our Future*. New York: W. W. Norton & Company.

Surrey, S. S. (1973). *Pathways to Tax Reform: The Concept of Tax Expenditures*. Harvard University Press. doi:10.4159/harvard.9780674436503

Surrey, S. S. (1977). The Concept of Tax Reliefs Its Relation to Tax Policy and Budget Policy. In *Subsidies, Tax Reliefs and Prices, Proceedings of 33rd Congress of IIPF*. Academic Press.

Surrey, S. S., & Sunley, E. M., Jr. (1976). General Report. In Tax Incentives as an Instrument for Achievement of Governmental Goals (Vol. LXIa, pp. 15-63). Cahiers de Droit Fiscal International.

Swift, Z. L., Brixi, H. P., & Valenduc, C. (2004). Tax Expenditures: General Concept, Measurement, and Overview of Country Practices. In H. P. Brixi, C. M. A. Valenduc, & Z. L. Swift (Eds.), *Tax Expenditures – Shedding Light on Government Spending through the Tax System: Lessons from Developed and Transition Economies* (pp. 1–18). Washington, DC: The World Bank.

TARC. (2014, June). *The Definition, Measurement, and Evaluation of Tax Expenditures and Tax Reliefs*. Technical Paper Prepared for the National Audit Office, Tax Administration Research Centre. Retrieved July 30, 2015, from http://www.nao.org.uk/wp-content/uploads/2014/03/TARC-Tax-Expenditures-and-tax-reliefs-technical-paper.pdf

Ter-Minassian, T. (2007). Fiscal Rules for Subnational Governments: Can They Promote Fiscal Discipline? *OECD Journal on Budgeting*, *6*(3), 1-12. Retrieved May 27, 2015, from http://www.oecd.org/gov/budgeting/43469443.pdf

Ter-Minassian, T. (2009). *Challenges in Tax Reform for Turkey, in an International Perspective*. The Ministry of Finance-UNDP Seminar on Tax Policy Options on the Way to EU Accession, Ankara, Turkey.

Timofeev, A., & Wallace, S. (2016). The Incidence of Taxes in Jordan. In M. M. Erdoğdu & B. Christiansen (Eds.), Handbook of Research on Public Finance in Europe and the MENA Region. Hershey, PA: IGI Global.

Toder, E., & Baneman, D. (2012). *Distributional Effects of Individual Income Tax Expenditures: An Update. Urban-Brookings Tax Policy Center*. Paper presented at the National Tax Association Meetings, New Orleans, LA. Retrieved July 20, 2014, from http://www.taxpolicycenter.org/UploadedPDF/412495-Distribution-of-Tax-Expenditures.pdf

U.S. Joint Committee on Taxation. (2011, February 28). *Background Information on Tax Expenditure Analysis and Historical Survey of Tax Expenditure Estimates* (JCX-15-11). Retrieved August 13, 2014, from https://www.jct.gov/publications.html?func=startdown&id=3740

U.S. Joint Committee on Taxation. (2013, February 1). *Estimates of Federal Tax Expenditures for Fiscal Years 2012-2017*. Retrieved August 13, 2014, from https://www.jct.gov/publications.html?func=startdown&id=4503

US Joint Committee on Taxation. (2014, August 5). *Estimates of Federal Tax Expenditures for Fiscal Years 2014-2018*. Retrieved December 12, 2014, from https://www.jct.gov/publications.html?func=startdown&id=4663

Valenduc, C. (2004). From Tax Expenditure Reporting to Tax Policy Analysis: Some Experience from Belgium. In H. P. Brixi, C. M. A. Valenduc, & Z. L. Swift (Eds.), *Tax Expenditures – Shedding Light on Government Spending through the Tax System: Lessons from Developed and Transition Economies* (pp. 69–96). Washington, DC: The World Bank.

World Bank. (2014, May 20). Turkey in Transition: Time for a Fiscal Policy Pivot? Report No. 85104-TR. *Turkey Public Finance Review*. Retrieved November 11, 2014, from http://www.worldbank.org/content/dam/Worldbank/Feature%20Story/ECA/Turkey/turkey-pfr-report-21-may-2014.pdf

ENDNOTES

1 The charity Oxfam revealed that 85 billionaires own as much as the bottom half of the world's population.

2 A clear indication of this is that Thomas Piketty's 696 pages of book on inequality, *Capital in the Twenty-First Century*, was published in English translation in March 2014 and quickly became a best-seller. As of January 2015, the book had sold more than 1.5 million copies.

3 The popular Nobel Prize-winning economist Joseph Stiglitz drew on a lot of existing evidence of fast-rising inequality for a recent book, *the Price of Inequality*, published in 2012.

4 Other examples for delegation of taxing power of alteration are exemptions, exclusions, deductions credits and rates of taxes and similar liabilities within the upper and lower limits set by the related laws.

5 Secular tendency suggests that, in Turkey, central government tax revenues as a percentage of GDP were 13.0, 10.5, 12.9 14.8, 16.3, 14.3, 15.2 in 1930's, 1940's, 1950's, 1960's, 1970's, 1980's and 1990's, respectively.

6 Gini index measures the extent to which the distribution of income or consumption expenditure among individuals or households within an economy deviates from a perfectly equal distribution. A Lorenz curve plots the cumulative percentages of total income received against the cumulative number of recipients, starting with the poorest individual or household. The Gini index measures the area between the Lorenz curve and a hypothetical line of absolute equality, expressed as a percentage of the maximum area under the line. Thus a Gini index of 0 represents perfect equality, while an index of 100 implies perfect inequality (OECD, 2014).

7 Peculiar to Turkey, the tax covers all types of phone calls whether cellular or cable ones, phone cards, installation services and/or communication services, like transferring the locations and media, TV, and radio services. The taxpayers are the businesses involved in dealing with the cellular, satellite and cable phone services. Tax bases, like other excise duties, are included in the base of VAT, and the rates are 25% for cellular phone services, 5% for net services and 15% for others. For 2014, an initial lump-sum tax of 40 TL was determined for cellular phones as extra. Though it is named as the special communication tax, in fact, the tax is a general communication tax not a special one.

8 Lottery games, horse races and other type of lottery games or betting revenues are subject to lottery games tax in Turkey. The tax rates are 5% for sports games, 7% for tickets sold for horse races and 10% for other lotteries and betting.

9 *This hidden liability* imposed on consumer credits at 15% and credits borrowed by persons from abroad and import credits at % 6 foreign exchange and credits 3% (annual) if borrowing term 1-2 years 1% 2-3 years 0.5% more than 3 years 0%.

10 The pioneering articles on tax expenditures were written by great tax scholar Stanley S. Surrey. See Surrey 1973; Surrey & Sunley, 1976; Surrey, 1977.

11 US Joint Committee on Taxation (2011) defines negative tax expenditures as "[t]ax provisions that provide treatment less favorable than normal income tax law and are not related directly to progressivity … Special provisions of the law the principal purpose for which is to enforce *general tax rules*, or to prevent the violation *of other laws*, are not treated as negative tax expenditures even though they may increase the tax burden for certain taxpayers" (p. 2).

12 Tax expenditure reports consist of several main elements, such as descriptions of tax norms, tax bases, taxable units, tax rate schedules, tax period, and tax expenditure estimates, which may cover a 7-year period. Such reports also may state their purpose, legal requirements, rationale, assessment, and similar aspects (Swift, Brixi, & Valenduc, 2004, p. 6).

13 Turkish Constitution (TC) Art.10.

14 Turkish Supreme Court Ruling No. 2004/84. The court also made several reverse rulings and dismissed the cases sued against tax expenditure articles by justifying them on the basis of serving economic goals. See, Turkish Supreme Court Rulings 6.10.1986 1985/21, 1986/23 and 2002/39, 2004/125.

15 It is important to recognize that the revenue foregone method does not only fail to take into account behavioral changes on the parts of taxpayers but also fails to take into account interactions among different tax expenditures (OECD, 2010, p. 151).

16 The US Joint Committee on Taxation (2013) points out that "[a]n outlay equivalent is the dollar size of a direct spending program that would provide taxpayers with net benefits that would equal what they now receive from a tax expenditure" (p. 23).

17 For calculations made for the period of 2006-2010 by tax types see Oner (2011, p. 169).

18 LeBlanc (2014) clarifies this issue as "[s]ome typical examples include the treatment of owner-occupied housing and the question whether the non-taxation of imputed rents or the interest deductibility for mortgages are regarded as a tax expenditure and the issue of whether accelerated depreciation is recalled as a tax expenditure or not. Differences in public spending also influence the take up and potentially need for tax expenditures in a policy area (e.g. take-up of private pension incentives will in part depend on the layout and generosity of public pension systems). Furthermore, summing up single tax expenditures items will lead to an aggregation bias which will vary across countries" (pp. 17-18).

APPENDIX

Personal Income Tax

Art. 9: Small Artisans' Gains
Art 20: Tax Exemptions for Private Schools
Art 21: Exclusions of House-rent & Copyright Gains
Art 22: Exclusions of Capital Income
Art 23/1: Wages of Handicraft Carpets& Rug workers
Art.23/2: Wages of Workers in Small Farms
Art.23/3: Wages of Miners
Art 23/5: Wages of Village Administration
Art 23/6: House-Maid Wages
Art 23/7: Wages of Students & Inmates & Hospice' Workers
Art.23/8: Catering Benefits to Workers in Business Premises
Art.23/9: Dormitory Services to Workers
Art 23/10: Free Transportation Services of Workers
Art.23/12: Apprentice Wages
Art 23/13: Retirement Benefits Paid by Foreign Social Security Institutions
Art 23/14: Wages Paid by Non-resident Employers
Art 23/15: Wages of Two Sportsmen Employed by Large Businesses
Art 24/4: Fuel Benefits Paid to Workers& Government Employees
Art 25/3: All Kind of Bonus & Benefits & Welfare Payments Paid by Social Security Institutions
Art 25/4: Child Benefits Paid to Workers
Art 25/5: Benefits to the Workers for Marriage and Baby Birth
Art 25/6: Welfare Payments by Social Security
Art 25/7: Payments to Workers for Work Leave
Art 25/9: Welfare Payments Paid by Retirement Institutions
Art 25/10: All Compensations & Benefits Paid by Foreign Social Security Institutions
Art 29/1: All Bonuses & Prizes for Encouraging Science & Fine Arts
Art 29/2: Flight & Diving Payments & Per Diems
Art 29/3: All Prizes& Bonuses Paid to Amateur Sportsmen in Sport Games
Art 29/4: Referee Wages in All Kind of Sports Games
Art 30/1: Commercial Gains of Non-Residents through Fairs
Art 30/2: Self Employment Gains of Non-Residents through Fairs
Art 63/2: Premiums & Dues Paid to Social Security Institutions
Art 63/3: Private Insurance Premiums Paid for Wage-Earner & Dependents
Art 63/4: Employee Trade Union Dues
Art 80: Capital Gains Exclusion
Art 82: Occasional Gains Exclusion
Art 89/1: Private Insurance Premium Deductions from Taxable Income for Taxpayer and Dependents
Art 89/2: Private Education& Health Expenses of Taxpayer and Dependents Not Exceeding 10% of Taxable Income

Art 89/3: Deduction for Disabled Self-Employed& Small Traders
Art 89/4: Charity Payments to Central & Local Government, Tax-Exempt Foundations, Trusts and Associations Seeking Public Interest within the Limit of 10% Taxable Income
Art 89/5: Charity Payments for Public School, Dormitory & Health Center Building (fully deductible)
Art 89/6: the Cost of Food, Cleaning, Clothing and Fuel Materials Donated to Charity Institutions (fully deductible)
Art 89/7: All Donations Made for Cultural, Historical and Natural Heritage (fully deductible)
Art 89/8: Sport Sponsoring Expenditures (for amateur sport branches full, professional ones only 50%)
Art 89/9: 100% Research and Development Deduction
Art 89/10: All Cash & In Rem Donations for Natural Disasters
Art 89/11: All Cash Donations to Turkish Red Crescent and Green Crescent Associations
Art 89/12: Venture Capital Fund (Up to 10% Taxable Income)
Art 89/13: 50% of Service Income Delivered Abroad to the Non-Resident Individuals
Art Provisional 69: Investment Credit for 2010 Profits Only
Art Provisional 75: Wages of R-D Personnel till 12/31/2023
Art Provisional 76: Agricultural Products Warehousing Product Notes' Gains till 12/31/2014
Art Provisional 79: Donations & Charity Payments& Sponsoring Expenses to Agency of Eskişehir Capital of Turkish World Culture 2013 on Condition that to be Itemized & Deducted in Tax Returns
Art Provisional 80: Tax Credit for Wages of Workers Employed Investments in Depressed Regions as an Incentive until 12/31/2023
Art Prov. 82: Deduction of 75% of the capital gains earned by individual investors holding joint stock company stocks at least two years after purchasing from the market from taxable income expiry date: 12/31/2017
Art.Prov.83: All Kinds of Donations and Sponsoring Expenses Deductible from Taxable Income made for EXPO 2016 Antalya Agency
Art.Prov.85: Exemption of income earned from assets (money, gold and foreign currency) held abroad to the tax offices on condition that 2% income tax paid on them and transferred to Turkeys will be exempted.

Corporation Income Tax

Art. 4/1-b: Exemption of Public Health Centers
Art. 4/1-ç: Exemption of Public National and International Fairs & Exhibitions
Art 4/1-d: Non-profit Public Pre-schools Guest-houses & Military canteens serving to public officials only
Art. 4/1-ı : Local Public Utilities
Art.4/1-i: Public Utilities Run by Villages and Village Unions
Art 4/1-j: Joint-Stock Companies & Business Entities of Sports Clubs Run for Particularly for Sports Activity
Art 4/1-k: All Cooperatives but Consumption and Transportation
Art 4/1-l: Organizations of Credit Assurance Provided That Profits Not Distributed to Shareholders
Art 4/1-n: Infrastructure Corporations of Industrial Regions & Small Businesses
Art. 5/1-c: Corporate Profits Earned from Sale of Stocks Held Abroad
Art 5/1-e: 75% of Corporate Profits from Sale of Stocks & Realty Held At Least Two Years as Assets

Art. 5/1-f: 75% of Bond Revenue of Turkish Savings Deposit Board and Banks
Art 5/1-h: Profits of Construction, Repair & Assembly Works of Turkish Companies Operating Abroad Appeared in Financial Statements
Art 5/1-ı : Five Year Tax Holiday for Private Pre & Primary & Secondary School Businesses
Art 10/1-a: 100% Research and Development Deduction
Art 10/1-b: Sport Sponsoring Expenditures (for amateur sport branches full, professional ones only 50%)
Art 10/1-c: Charity Payments to Central & Local Government, Tax-Exempt Foundations, Trusts and Associations Seeking Public Interest within the Limit of 5% Taxable Income
Art 10/1-ç: Charity Payments for Public School, Dormitory & Health Center Building (fully deductible)
Art 10/1-d: All Donations Made for Cultural, Historical and Natural Heritage (fully deductible)
Art 10/1-e: All Cash & In Rem Donations for Natural Disasters
Art 10/1-f: All Cash Donations to Turkish Red Crescent and Green Crescent
Art 10/1-g: Venture Capital Fund (Up to 10% Taxable Income)
Art 10/1-ğ: 50% of Service Income Delivered Abroad to the Non-Resident Individuals
Art 32/a: Reduced Rated Corporation Income Tax for Certain Investments
Art. Prov.4: 75% Reduced Rated Corporation Income Tax for Textile& Clothing Industry Investments in Depressed Regions for Five Years
Art Prov.69: Investment Credit for 2010 Profits Only

Value Added Tax

Art 13/a-b: Exemption of Deliveries of Services to the Businesses Dealing with Hiring of Marine, Airway and Railway Vehicles
Art 13/c: Exemption of Delivery of Goods and Services to the Oil, Mining & Pipe Line Companies
Art 13/d: Exemption of Delivery of Machinery & Equipment to the Companies Holding Investment Incentive Certificate
Art 13/g: Exemption of Delivery of Motor Vehicles to the Prime Ministry
Art 17/1-b: Exemption of Educational and Cultural services Delivered by public Agencies, Chambers, Cooperatives and Foundations and Associations
Art 17/4-d: Exclusion of Renting of Non- Business Immovable Defined by Income Tax law Art 70
Art 17/4-g: Exclusion of Precious Metals & Papers and All Scraps of Metal, Plastics, Rubber & Glass
Art 17/4-k: Exclusion of Deliveries of Parcels & Buildings by Infrastructure Corporations of Industrial Regions & Small Businesses
Art 17/4-l: Exclusion of Deliveries of Asset Holding Companies Dealing with Factoring Services
Art 17/4-m: Exclusions of Delivery of Goods & Services to and from Turkish Savings Deposit Board
Art 17/4-r: Exclusion of Corporate & Bank Sales of Stocks & Realty Held At Least Two Years as Assets
Art 17/4-s: Exclusion of All Materials, Programs & Instruments Produced for the Disabled
Art 17/4-ş: Exclusion of Deliveries of Mortgage Residential Buildings to Site Housing Administration and Related Agencies
Art 17/4-y: Exclusion of Deliveries of Immovable Purchased from Tenants and Back-leased by Financial Leasing Companies
Art Prov. 29: Exclusion of Deliveries of Goods & Services for Implementing of Large Scale Projects

Art Prov. 32: Exclusion of Deliveries Related to City Underground, Subway, Tramway and Cable Lift Systems between Municipalities and Transportation Ministry until 12/31/2023

Excise Duties

Art 7/1-b: Exclusion of Mineral Oils to Oil Producing Companies
Art 7/1-c: Exclusion of Delivery of Mineral Oils to Public Administration in case of Natural Disasters Epidemics and Emergency Cases
Art 7/2: Exclusion of Sale of Motor Vehicles to the Disabled Every 5 Year Intervals
Art 7/3-a: Exclusion of Aircrafts Delivered to Turkish Air Institution
Art 7/3-b: Exemption of Delivery of Motor Vehicles to the Prime Ministry
Art 7/3-c: Exclusion of Heavy Trucks Used for Oil Producing Operations
Art 7/5: Exclusion of Delivery or Importation of Various Durable Consumption Goods to Public Administration Free of Charge
Art 7/6: Exclusion of Duty Free Articles
Art 8/2: Interest Reduction to Exporters for the Delay of Exportation Due to the Major Forces
Art Prov.5: Exclusion of Delivery of Some Mineral Oils to Electricity Generating Companies Until 12/ 31 /2019
Decree 2003/5868: Exclusion of Delivery of Fuels to Maritime Line Companies

Motor Vehicle Tax

Art 4: Exclusion of Motor Vehicles Registered to the Unions of Villages

Free Trade Zone Law

Art Prov. 3/A-B-C: Exemption of Tax Liabilities in Free Trade Zones

Technology Development Law

Art Prov.2: Tax Exemption of All Companies Operating Technology Development Regions until 12/ 31/ 2013

Social Security and Public Health Insurance Act

Art 88: Non-permission of Writing off the Unpaid Premiums in Determination of Income Tax Base

Research and Development Support Law

Art 3/1: Deduction of R&D Expenditures in Competitive & Innovative Projects Funded by Government
Art 3/2: Income Tax Incentive for the Private R&D Employees Working in Competitive & Innovative Projects Funded by Government

Electricity Market Law

Art 3/1: Exclusion of Profits of Merger & Transfer & Division of Companies Resulted from Privatization in Electricity Market

Art Prov.3/2: Value Added Tax Exemption for Deliveries in case of Privatization in Electricity Market

Green Crescent Law

Art 33: Full Deduction of Charity Payments made to Green Crescent from Income Tax Base by Taxpayers

Turkish Oil Act

ART 13: Duty Free Imported & Purchased Articles by Licensed Oil Purchasers

Chapter 19
Restructuring the Electricity Sector in Turkey:
Who are the Beneficiaries?

Hülya Kirmanoğlu
Istanbul University, Turkey

Mustafa Kahveci
Istanbul University, Turkey

ABSTRACT

Public utilities have been at the very centre of economic and social development of countries. Until the last decades, they were almost exclusively undertaken by public authorities. From the 1980s, they have been subject to liberalisation in many countries. Liberalisation of electricity means that the segments which are vertically integrated are unbundled and opened to private sector through privatisations. However, since the transmission and distribution segments are networks that exhibit severe natural monopoly characteristics, they should be either owned and operated by public bodies or regulated by independent regulatory authorities to protect consumer interest. In Turkey, the liberalisation process for the public utilities has begun in 1990s, but posed many problems at administrative and juridical stages. Lately, the legislative framework which is designed to be compatible with global standards has been completed. But at economic stage, we can easily observe the power of big companies and holdings outweigh the power of public authorities and counteract the public interest.

INTRODUCTION

Upgrading the energy sector has been one of the main concerns of industrialisation since its very beginnings. Oil, gas, and electricity are the main products of the energy sector and are consumed by residential and commercial buildings, as well as industry and the agriculture sector, with electricity accounting for 40% of all energy used. The electricity demand and supply increase as the economy grows, and this raises ecological, political, and geostrategic issues. Ecological problems due to high carbon emissions have been increasing on the global scene since classical non-renewable energy sources began being used

DOI: 10.4018/978-1-5225-0053-7.ch019

intensely due to growing populations living in cities. Current energy policies in many countries are being designed with renewable sources promoted to replace non-renewables.

Electricity is seen as an industry in which the competitive and network segments can be unbundled and subjected to liberalisation (corporatisation and privatisation). Historically they were public utilities which accounted for a significant part of fixed assets – they played an important role in the industrialisation process of western countries between the 18th century and the 1980s. From then onwards, they have been the targets of liberalisation in many countries. It first began in Britain and Latin American and other countries followed soon after.

In theory, the issue was handled as a technical and allocation-efficiency problem in the realm of neoliberal economics – in which the market is deemed as the ideal mechanism to improve efficiency by allocating scarce resources in a way to maximise social welfare, but political economy issues are ignored. The policy implications of these theories have been the electricity sector reforms aiming to restructure the sector through privatisation and regulation of the industry. In recent years there has been plenty of literature produced on the subject of electricity sector reforms, investigating the results of reforms in various countries and making comparisons across them (Newberry (2002); Jamasb, Newberry, Politt (2005); Jamasb (2006); Yi-Chong (2006); Politt (2007); Zhang, Parker, Kirkpatrick (2008); Karova (2011); Erdogdu (2014). Some studies handle the issue with a political and institutional perspective, and set models explaining performance of reforming attempts by economic, political and institutional factors (Chang & Berdiev (2011); Williams, Ghanadan (2006); Nagayama (2009); Henisz & Zellner (2006); Potrafke (2010)).

Again in theory, marginal cost pricing, which dominates automatically in competitive markets, would provide increases in efficiency. But in practice, there are problems resulting from market concentration – especially in utility sector markets, where the "market" is politically constituted. The electricity market is a typical example. It exhibits market failures from the very beginning of the acquisition of energy sources (production) to the end-user (consumers). In both theory and practice, the market is supported by regulation and government intervention in order to correct these failures.

However in practice it has appeared that, even in the countries where the regulation system is running well, there are several flaws which are hard to explain using the tools of neoclassical theory. Instead, the conceptualisation of political economy, where the state is not modelled as 'neutral' or 'benevolent dictator' as in neoclassical theory but rather as an agent of capitalistic interests, provides a more extensive basis for explaining the results coming out from the liberalisation process. As Harvey states, "When capital intervenes in struggles over the built environment, it usually does so through the agency of state power." (Harvey, 1985, p. 41). The 'built environment' in this statement implies infrastructural entities including electricity.

In this study, we aim to explore the structure and function of the electricity markets, the market failures they pose and the market reforms designed to correct them by national and international decision-makers from a political-economy point of view. Our research poses two questions: 'How compatible with the directives of the European Union (EU) is the market reform of the electricity sector in Turkey?' and 'who are the beneficiaries of the reform?'

The legislative process shaping energy policies in Turkey has been rather complicated over recent years. Is liberalising the electricity market from the government really being done for the sake of efficiency, thus for the public interest, or is it being done for the benefit of special interests? We argue that liberalisation in the energy sector does not serve to enhance the public interest, instead it promotes special interests.

In the first section, we draw a general picture of infrastructure industry in the neoliberal era where the new market players entered the scene and where the new functions of state are defined. In the second section we introduce the structure of electricity markets and the failures they cause. Third section is composed of legislative process including directives and regulations which have been shaping electricity markets in EU. In the fourth section, we introduce the size and composition of electricity sector in Turkey. In the fifth section, we reviewed the restructuring period in Turkey of electricity markets. And finally in the sixth section we assessed the consequences with regard to benefits reaped by special interest groups and costs borne by the people. [1]

THE BACKGROUND OF INFRASTRUCTURAL INVESTMENTS IN NEOLIBERAL ERA

Corporatisation and privatisation are two important but distinct concepts as the major aspects of liberalisation. The public enterprises can work within market principles, or privatised companies can work under government intervention. The former case poses some problems, because so long as the markets a public enterprise works in are not competitive, the prices set by the public enterprise may well be monopoly prices and do not maximise consumers' welfare. In this regard, there is not much difference between public and private enterprises. In Turkey, the experience shows that this situation pointed out a transition period for preparing the future privatisations as the politically appointed managers seek to solidify the financial position of the enterprises before privatisation.

The extant literature provides us no net conclusions concerning the effects of privatisations in utility industry on allocational and distributional grounds. The competitive markets are prerequisite of efficiency in both theory and practice. When there are imperfections in an industry as in electricity, the institutions built for monitoring the market are crucial. Otherwise, the market fails to achieve allocative efficiency, and cannot maintain the overall welfare. However, Stigler (1962), who is the prominent theoretician in regulation theory, stated no effect of regulation on electricity rates in his paper, concluding from his statistical analysis that electrical utilities did not need regulation because, in the absence of regulation, the market prices were not significantly above long run marginal cost and there were no pure monopoly profits which were above the competitive rate of return. But after more than 50 years, the nature of utility industry, especially in electricity sectors, has significantly changed.

In the globalisation era, large projects for infrastructure investments provide the opportunity for capital to circulate around the world as capital is searching for new profitable global investment opportunities. The international economic and financial organizations such as World Bank and International Monetary Fund designed new channels through which the capital circulates safely under the name of 'Post Washington Consensus'. Many of the infrastructure investments; energy, telecommunication and so forth, that the capitalist state made before, opened up to the private sector through financial and institutional facilities. The role of state has changed and decomposed between *supra* and *infra* levels. At international/regional levels, the authorities responsible for the "global governance", are seeking new institutional models, because "the regulatory environment in which capital moves around the world requires institutionalised management if it is not to dissolve into chaos."(Harvey, 2011, p. 201)

In this new order, new players appeared on the scene but the nation state, although it is losing slightly the dominant power, is still the "land of last resort". Public authorities cover a wide scope at economic (public monopolies), political (Government-Council of Ministers), administrative (Regulatory Authority) and legal (Council of State) stages. The executive branch of government should be balanced by autonomously operating public entities, but this norm is realised depending upon the level of democracy in the country. In general it is difficult to disunite the common interests of political class and its protected capitalist class; in developing countries, some features such as "lack of capacity in rural areas, high level of non-payment, technical or nontechnical energy losses in the transmission and distribution networks, institutional weaknesses and political interference" (Jamasb, Newbery, & Pollitt, 2005, p.2-3) intensify these difficulties. Again in developing countries, these special interests empowered by the state power reap greater benefits due to lack of labour and environmental standards. In developed countries where labour is relatively powerful and environmental constraints are strict, there is not much room for special interest groups to counteract public interest.

As the states are leaving their economic roles and functions to market forces in the global era, the regulation is considered to be crucial to watchdog the markets. In both developed and developing countries, a very significant part of the reforms that are on the agenda is to establish firm and autonomous regulatory institutions. Regulation is the new role of states, as monitoring the markets is getting crucial in a liberalised world order. Stiglitz (2010) is the prominent theorist who redefined this role of state in the globalised world where the competitiveness is the key element for both states and companies to perform well. Today, companies operating in the market, either public or private, are deemed as bounded by the market rules otherwise they would not survive. Market structure is important in adapting to these rules in the changing conditions of financial and technical environment. If the imperfect market conditions prevail in the sector, such as natural monopoly, then a system is to be organised to mimic the market conditions referred to as a 'regulatory system'.

"Regulation refers to the direct control by the government of an industry's structure, conduct and/or performance. It usually requires a freestanding regulatory body that, formally at least, operates independently of politicians but within a policy framework and regulatory system determined by the national government." (Bailey, 2002, p.357)

Depending upon how independent is the regulatory body from the government, and indeed how independent is the government from the strong corporate vested interests, the regulatory system serves to protect public interest. Before we investigate the political nature of reform process in Turkey, we need to further elaborate the structure of electricity markets.

THE STRUCTURE OF ELECTRICITY MARKETS AND MARKET FAILURES

In mainstream economic theory, markets maximise welfare under conditions of perfect competition by allocating resources to their best use through price mechanism. For an efficient operation of any product market, there needs to be a pricing mechanism that clears the excess quantity supplied or demanded for the related product. There are many obstacles in electricity sector that complicate or even prevent the market to operate "efficiently".

Some micro or macro based deficiencies of markets such as natural monopolies, public services, coordination problems, information failures, capital intensive and long lived assets and environmental externalities pose serious market failure problems in energy market. In addition to these, the large sunk investments and non-storable outputs in the electricity utility industry pose serious market failures and the requirements of technical, legal and economical rules and standards make electricity a difficult product to trade (MacGill et. al., 2006; Glanchan, 2013; Zhang, Parker, & Kirkpatrick, 2008).

The new role of governments to regulate the markets arises from these market failures in newly emerging utility markets. As electricity markets have four segments which are vertically integrated, some of these segments are subject to competition while some are not. The running of a vertically integrated business as well as ownership should be unbundled to achieve more competitive markets. The segments that compose the sector, namely generation, transmission, distribution and end-use/consumption have all their intrinsic characters with regard to competitively, pricing, capacity utilization, consumer protection and so forth.

An effective separation of segments is necessary in order to regulate the conditions of competition. "Unbundling requires the effective separation of activities of energy transmission from production and supply interests (EC^2, 2011)." Generation segment is most open to competition because some number of producers having varying capacities can meet the market demand efficiently, as opposed 'natural monopoly' which means a single firm satisfying the entire market demand in the most efficient way. In this case, depending upon the number of players in the market, the output capacity will grow and consumers' gain will increase; however, if the market is dominated by a few firms, effective regulation is important at this stage.

Even if this stage is competitive, since the output produced at this stage is transmitted to the consumers through the transmission segment which is monopoly and single buyer, there may be some complications in pricing mechanism that may not be beneficiary for the consumers. Transmission segment is the most imperfect segment in terms of competition because it exhibits natural monopoly characteristics since the optimal scale is very large and the average cost falls as an additional user is connected to the system along the optimal scale. In many countries, the capacity building and operating at this stage is organised by a public monopoly. A system operator is necessary for making the transactions and balancing the supply and demand from the distribution segment. Failure at one point in the network (e.g., failure of a generation plant) can have serious repercussions on the whole network if not managed properly. Therefore, there are strong externalities in terms of network security (Atiyas-Dutz, 2004).

The distribution segment shows regional monopoly characteristics and it will not be consumers' interest to liberalise the market without a well-designed regulatory system. The regulatory authority should set the retail prices at this last stage. The reasons why the electricity sector is being reformed may be grouped as pushing factors and pulling factors. The major pushing factor is the insufficiency of public budgets because of high debt and deficit problems to undertake big investment projects. The major pulling factor is the attractiveness of the sector for the private investors as regards the profits that are function of market (or regulation) prices.

In general, the success of reforms are assessed according to the following criteria (Jamasb et. al., 2005 p.11):

- Economic aspects of the reform: Corporatisation of state-owned utilities; unbundling of vertically-integrated utilities into generation, transmission, distribution and supply activities, and where necessary horizontal splitting; provision of third party access to networks; establishment of a competitive wholesale generation market, liberalisation of the retail supply market; privatisation of electricity assets
- Legal and administrative aspects of the reform: Enactment of an electricity reform law; regulatory reform, including adoption of incentive regulation for the natural monopoly network activities; establishment of an independent regulator; definition of rules concerning consumer protection, allocation of energy subsidies, and stranded costs.

All these features display the fact that the electricity sector needs high degree of pro-public government involvement. As capital circulates around the world in search for higher profits, supra-national bodies are needed to set the rules and standards in order to prevent the capital to exploit the society and nature as well. In this regard, European Union (EU) standards in the regional scale of Europe are worthy to consider.

EU DIRECTIVES ON ELECTRICITY MARKET

In the EU, the legal procedure for marketisation and liberalisation of electricity sector has begun in 1996 (Directive 96/92/EC) and continued with 2003 Package(EC, 1996,2003). The last package framing the legislative procedures to regulate electricity markets in EU is 2009 Package (EC, 2009). This package was proposed by the European Commission in 2007, and entered into force in 2009 after being adopted by the European Parliament and the Council of the European Union. It consists of two Directives and three Regulations for gas and electricity markets. Concerning electricity, the Directive (2009/72/EC) states the common rules for an internal market in EU. The regulation ((EC) No 714/2009) sets the conditions for access to the network for cross-border exchange of electricity (EC, 2009). Another regulation is on the establishment of the Agency for the Cooperation of Energy Regulators ACER ((EC) No 713/2009) for coordinating the national regulators (EC, 2009). The core elements of the Package (concerning electricity) include:

- **Creating a single market:** The main purpose of the Package is to create a single market of electricity for the countries in the EU. The single market is considered as a mean of price and quality standard (providing the best service with prices as low as possible) across Europe. As the Directive states: "In order to secure competition and the supply of electricity at the most competitive price, Member States and national regulatory authorities should facilitate cross- border access for new suppliers of electricity from different energy sources as well as for new providers of power generation."(Article 8) The Directive introduced the facilities for cross-border access under the name of open-access.
- **Open Access** means the "implementation of a system of third party access to the transmission and distribution systems based on published tariffs, applicable to all eligible customers" (Ertuna, 2010, p. 51). In Article 32 of the Directive, non-discrimination across users is emphasised: "Further measures should be taken in order to ensure transparent and non-discriminatory tariffs for access to networks. Those tariffs should be applicable to all system users on a non-discriminatory basis."
- **Unbundling:** The first step to separate competitive parts (production and retail sales) and networks (transmission and distribution) was taken in Directive 96/92/EC. However, the separation between activities was restricted in this Directive, and establishing national regulatory authorities was not compulsory. In the later Directives, common rules for the generation, transmission, distribution and supply of electricity were introduced. Separation of production/supply activities from transmission activities were designed in a way that interest based relations between vertically integrated companies be prevented.
- **Breaking up monopoly power:** The Directive set out rules for improving and integrating competitive electricity markets in the Community. As liberalisation entails "rules" to be effective in

failing markets as energy markets, the package is expected by its rules to push the competition and break up the power of energy monopolies.

- **Protecting consumers:** Consumers, either households or industrialists, are at the main target of reforms. As is stated in the Directive: "In order to develop competition in the internal market in electricity, large non-household customers should be able to choose their suppliers and enter into contracts with several suppliers to secure their electricity requirements. Such customers should be protected against exclusivity clauses the effect of which is to exclude competing or complementary offers. (Article 20):"

There are contrasting views on the efficiency and effectiveness of the Third Package (EurActiv, 2009): The Liberals are optimistic on the benefits of the free market hoping that the EU's newly liberalised energy market would "provide consumers with more choice and lower prices". According to bureaucrats, the Directive is beneficial for both consumers and business groups, but the consumer organisations question the status of unbundling. They argue that without full ownership unbundling it is not possible to advance competition in Europe's energy markets. Among the opponent groups, Greens point out the dangers of energy oligopolies and Socialists criticise the companies that abuse their dominant positions. They denounce "the almost gangster-like domination of the sector by energy oligopolies," and demand "granting extended powers to the national energy regulators". This latter demand shows us a greater confidence on national governments rather than the supra-national bodies to protect the most vulnerable consumers.

Before evaluating the consequences of electricity market reforms in Turkey, we will present a general overview of the electricity sector in Turkey.

THE SIZE AND COMPOSITION OF THE ELECTRICITY SECTOR IN TURKEY

In Turkey, the biggest increase in installed capacity had been realised prior to the 1990s before the reform attempts were begun. After the 1990s, the average growth in capacity per year was barely 10%. Total electricity capacity which was about 60 GW at the end of 2013 has increased to 66,6 GW as of the end of 2014.

In Turkey, the installed capacity in electricity is based on thermal, hydro and geothermal / wind resources. As it shown in Table 1, the thermal - based capacity had been in an increasing trend from 52.62% in 1994 to 65.55 in 2009. Afterwards with new subsidies to hydro, wind, and geothermal based power plants (Renewable Energy Law No: 6094, 2010) the share of these plants increased from 34.45% in 2009 to 38.6% to 2012, and as a result of this upward move thermal based power stations' share decreased from 65.55% in 2009 to 61.39% in 2012. Although the power plants using renewable sources such as geothermal and wind have a slight share in total capacity, they rose from 1.94% to 4.24% in three years.

As seen in Table 2, a total of 43.4% of the installed capacity is under public ownership and 56. 6% is under private ownership in 2012. Hydro based capacity is dominant in public sector (62.3% of all hydro based capacity is public), whereas thermal base is dominant in private sector (64.1% of all thermal capacity is private). As the share of the private sector increases in generating electricity, new subsidies are implemented by law to promote the private sector to use renewable sources. Table 1 shows that renewable sources based power plants are still small but have an increasing trend. Table 2 shows that all renewable source-based power plants are owned by the private sector.

Table 1. Electricity Installed Capacity by Resources 1969-2012 (GW)

Year	Thermal		Hydro		Geotherm.wind		Total		Increase
	GW	%	GW	%	GW	%	GW	%	%
1969	1.24	63.19	0.72	36.76			1.97	100	
1974	2.28	61.15	1.45	38.83			3.73	100	89%
1979	2.99	58.36	2.13	41.62			5.12	100	37%
1984	4.57	54.00	3.87	45.79	0.02	0.20	8.46	100	65%
1989	9.19	58.15	6.60	41.73	0.02	0.11	15.81	100	86%
1994	10.98	52.62	9.86	47.29	0.02	0.08	20.86	100	31%
1999	15.56	59.55	10.54	40.34	0.03	0.10	26.12	100	25%
2004	24.14	65.57	12.65	34.34	0.03	0.09	36.82	100	40%
2009	29.34	65.55	14.55	32.51	0.87	1.94	44.76	100	21%
2012	35.03	61.39	19.61	34.37	2.42	4.24	57.06	100	27%

Source: TEİAŞ Elektrik İstatistikleri (2012).
* Increase in total capacity by every five years

Table 2. The Distribution of Installed Capacity by Primary Energy Resources and the Electric Utilities in Turkey (2012) (Mw, %)

	Public		Private			
	MW	(%)	MW	(%)	TOTAL	%
THERMAL	12574.8	35.9	22452.5	64.1	35027.2	61.4
HYDRO	12216.7	62.3	7392.7	37.7	19609.4	34.4
GEOTHERMAL	0.0	0.0	162.2	100.0	162.2	0.3
WIND	0.0	0.0	2260.6	100,0	2260.6	4.0
TOTAL %	**43.4**		**56.6**		**57059.4**	**100.0**

Source: TEİAŞ Database (2012).

As of 2012, the major part of the capacity is thermal based. The thermal based power plants work with coal, gas or oil. Although nearly 100% of natural gas is imported in Turkey, the share of natural gas based power plants has been increasing. Share of the natural gas in the electricity production in Turkey is twice as more than the share of natural gas in the world electricity production and share of the coal is below the world in average (EMRA, 2010).This transformation causes two major problems, both import dependency of electricity generation and current account deficit increase. Turkey is seen as more dependent on the natural gas when compared with the other countries in the world.

In Table 3, the distribution of total capacity according to ownership status is shown. The increasing share of private sector in total built capacity from 1990 onwards is shown in this table. Private sector comprises auto-producers, production companies (IPPs and companies with BOT or BO contracts) and companies holding TOR rights[3]. The public share in total electricity generation diminished by half from 1990 when the liberalisation period began to the present time, whereas the private share has increased and is projected to surge in the near future.

Table 3. Electricity Generation by Ownership in Turkey 1990-2012 (%)

	EUAS	Affiliated partnerships Of EUAS	Concessionary Companies	Autoproducers	Companies holding TOR rights	Production companies*	Total
1990	90	-	2	7	-	-	100
2000	66	12	2	11	1	7	100
2005	53	6	-	10	2	28	100
2010	41	8	-	6	1	43	100

Source: Atiyas *et al.* (2012, p. 16).
* IPPs and companies with BOT or BO contracts

This trend can be predicted by observing the increasing share of private fixed investments in total fixed investments in energy sector. Following the similar trend in global markets, the public sector contribution has been decreasing as a result of liberalisation in the sector.

Table 4. shows that the share of gross fixed energy investment in total gross fixed investment increased from 4.96 in 2008 to 6.42 in 2013. In addition, the gross fixed energy investments made by private sector increased from 62.2% of total energy investments in 2008 to 80.0% of total energy investments in 2013. Whereas the gross fixed energy investment made by public sector decreased from 37.8% in 2008 to 20.0% in 2013. It is targeted to raise the installed capacity up to 110,000 MW in 2023 with new investments and power generation licenses (EÜAŞ, 2013). Among them, it is estimated that nuclear power stations will be put in operation and their share within the total power established will be 3.8% in 2021 (EPDK, 2012).

THE PATH TO LIBERALISE THE ELECTRICITY SECTOR IN TURKEY

The first electricity generating company in Turkey is a partnership formed by a foreign company (Ganz Electricity Company of Hungary) in 1914 in Istanbul. It was a thermal power plant having a capacity of 15 MW. When the Republic was established in 1923, the supply of electricity remained under the control of foreign companies until 1933, the year that all the electricity generating and distributing companies were nationalised. Between 1933 and 1946, the etatist policies were effective. After 1950, the conces-

Table 4. Gross Fixed Investments by Sectors (%)

Years	Energy Investments/ Total Investments (%)	Private Energy Investments / Total Energy Investments (%)	Public Energy Investments / Total Energy Investments (%)
2008	4.96	62.21	37.79
2009	7.72	70.63	29.37
2010	5.72	74.75	25.25
2011	4.35	75.63	24.37
2012	6.10	81.56	18.44
2013	6.42	80.00	20.00

Source: Ministry of Development (2014)

sion agreements with the private companies were used as a way to contribute the electricity production albeit their share remained quite low until the liberalisation period of the 1980s.

In 1970, the Turkish Electricity Company (TEK) was established as a public monopoly, covering all the stages from production to delivery. In harmony with the "import substitution policies" of this time period, TEK (as other public enterprises in critical industries, such as petrochemicals, telecommunications iron and steel) was implementing pricing policies to subsidise the private sector and the deficit resulted from these policies were being financed from central government budget. After a serious balance-of-payments crisis in the late 1970s, this inward oriented model was quitted and a new model, called "export promotion" or "outward oriented" was presented. In this model the public enterprises changed their role; instead of providing private sector with subsidised inputs, their assets and real estate properties were sold to some group of companies below their market value.

The ideological shift into "market economy" of the 1980s had its reflections on institutional restructuring of energy markets over the 1980s and later. The institutions needed to restructure the electricity sector began to rise after 1980's in accordance with the rise of liberalisation ideology. One of the main arguments for the transfer of state-owned industries to the private sector was the inefficiencies in the running of the state-industries. In the 1980s, all public bodies generating or distributing electricity at local level transferred their capacities to TEK. The installed capacity of Turkey was raised from 33 MW in 1923 to 6638.6 MW in 1982 (TEİAŞ, 2012). In 1984, the monopoly status of TEK was abolished and the sector was opened to the investments of private sector by either national or foreign investors that are subject to private law.

Until the end of the 1990s, some legal arrangements designed to institutionalise the process, and increased the share of private sector in electricity undertakings but the interventions of supreme courts in favour of public interest outlawed the process several times and consequently the share of private sector in total production stayed low. In 1993, TEK was separated into two segments as Turkish Generation and Transmission Company (TEAŞ) and Turkish Electricity Distribution Company (TEDAŞ). This was the first major corporatization in the electricity sector (Bagdadioglu & Odyakmaz, 2009, p.145). Public monopoly positions of these companies remained unchanged due to two main factors: firstly the strong opposition of trade unions and second, the refusal of (Transfer of Operating Rights) TOR model by Constitutional Court. Instead of TOR model, Built-Operate-Transfer (BOT) / Built-Operate (BO) models were replaced to eliminate the legal problems.

BOT/BO is a privatisation model according to which the private sector installs the capacity, operate for a certain period and consequently transfer the ownership to the public body. BOT law (n.3996) in 1994 and BO law (No. 4283) in 1997 were passed in order to make progress in the privatisation process. In the TOR model, operating rights are transferred to the private company whereas the ownership rights remain in the hands of public authority. The BOT/BO and TOR are different concession types with regard to competition implications; "BO and BOT contracts entailed take-or-pay clauses shielding these plants from any type of commercial risk including competition"(Atiyas *et. al.*, 2012, p. 17).

The constitution of legal base for liberalisation in utility sector through corporatisation and privatisation spread over nearly two decades in Turkey. The enactment of Competition Law and the Privatisation Law was in 1994 and the first Electricity Market Law (EML) No. 4628 was in 2001. The Electricity Market Regulation Administration (EMRA) was established as an independent authority by EML in 2001. With the enactment of Electricity Market Law in 2001, TEAŞ was further unbundled into three state-owned enterprises: **EÜAŞ** (Turkish Electricity Generation Joint Stock Company), TEİAŞ (Turkish Electricity Transmission Joint Stock Company) and TETAŞ (Turkish Electricity Trading Joint Stock Company).

EÜAŞ operates the state-owned power plants which are not transferred to private sector. EÜAŞ has been on the power generation part but the plants it owns are on the privatisation programme. TEİAŞ is a natural monopoly that owns and operates the transmission network throughout the country as well as building new capacity. TEİAŞ is also responsible "to set forth the principles and procedures regarding the activities related with real-time balancing and settlement of the active electricity demand and supply" (Electricity Market Balancing and Settlement Regulation, 2004). TETAŞ deals with wholesale activities as well as implementing previous BO, BOT, and TOR contracts.

After the 2001 economic crisis, the privatisations of public enterprises including the companies responsible for the generation and distribution of electricity were among the policy objectives stipulated by the IMF Stand-By Agreement to reduce the public debt. As stated in "Strategy Paper 2004", privatisation started in the distribution segment and 21 distribution regions were determined throughout Turkey. EML states that TEDAŞ can make a TOR contract with private distribution companies to privatise the distribution regions, while ownership right remaining in TEDAŞ: Privatisation of distribution regions took longer than planned in Strategy Paper 2004. It was anticipated that their privatisation was going to be completed in 2006, but it was the end of 2013 when the process was completed.

As to the privatisation of generation power plants, EUAŞ and its affiliated partnership still dominate in the sector, but in Economic Program for 2013-2015, it is stated that the tender announcements have been published in order to privatise one electricity generation company (Hamitabat Elektrik Üretim ve Ticaret A.Ş), and two thermal power plants (Kangal & Seyitömer) belonging to EÜAŞ. The Electricity Market Law No. 4628 was amended several times after 2001, and due to these amendments and new bylaws, the integrity of the law had been lost. Therefore, the Electricity Market Law No. 4628 is repealed and the Electricity Market Law No. 6446 is enacted in 2013.

The most significant changes made by the new law include (Electricity Law No 6446, 2013):

1. Further incentives are given for the use of renewable energy sources. First, the limit of unlicensed power generation is doubled and the Council of Ministers is allowed to increase this amount up to five times. Second, for the improvement of investment environment legal procedure is revised. Third, the guarantee of purchasing from unlicensed renewable source based electricity generator companies is enacted.
2. New measurements are taken to secure the electricity supply (e.g. the pre-licence system is introduced for the generator companies and the Energy Market Regulatory Authority (EPDK) is authorised to grant these pre-licences).
3. The generator companies' electricity production is limited by 20% of the total production in Turkey in order to minimise market concentration.
4. The generation companies are permitted to use self-produced electricity in their own facilities and final consumption points. And this consumption is not priced as final consumption tariff (which are decided by EMRA) in the case of transmission and distribution networks are not used.
5. The two major amendments to the types of licenses are as follows:
    a. -The auto-producer licence is abolished and the generation licence is granted to the companies that obtained auto producer licence before.
    b. -Wholesale and retail sale activities are combined under one licence type known as supply licences. Supply companies are permitted to perform import and export activities.

6. Organized Industrial Zones(OSB) are permitted to generate and distribute electricity after having obtained the generation and/or distribution licence. Aim of this amendment is to decrease the price of electricity which used in OSB.
7. A new entity, the Energy Markets Operation Joint Stock Company, is created to organise wholesale operations in electricity markets for reconciliation in financial transactions.

According to the 2013 EU Progress Report, "By the new Electricity Market Law that was enacted in March, 2013 with a view to creating more competition in the market and improving alignment with the EU Electricity Directive ('third package'), overall alignment with the internal energy market has further improved at a satisfactory level."

However, the following issues pose some problems: First is the cross subsidy in the national tariffs and government interventions to pricing mechanism. This mechanism refers to 'electricity price equalisation mechanism' declared by a communiqué published in March, 2013 to protect consumers from the price differences resulting from the cost differences across regions. The customers in the low- cost distribution regions subsidize customers in high cost regions (Bagdadioglu & Odyakmaz, 2009, p.150). Since there are differences between regions with regard to generation costs, the prices that consumers pay differ across the regions.

Second is the transfer from the EMRA to Ministry of monitoring position of the distribution companies counteract the EU directives. As stated in the 2013 EU Progress Report "The duties of the Energy Market Regulatory Authority (EMRA) in monitoring and supervising distribution companies are transferred to the Ministry, which is not in line with the acquis." The involvement of government in the markets directs us to analyse the political economy of liberalisations in the electricity sector.

POLITICAL ECONOMY OF ELECTRICITY MARKETS IN TURKEY

Although the reason as to why the electricity sector is liberalised relates to efficiency considerations, the results reveal the fact that while some groups of private sector benefit from the process, the large segments of society have borne the costs. The social losses generated by the liberalisation process of electricity production and distribution activities can be listed as follows:

The Dominance Of Large Companies

Table 5 shows the electricity distribution regions and the companies that are conceded the right to distribute electricity in those regions are shown, together with their share in total consumption and the number of generation plants they own.

When we examine the list, we see the dominance of big companies/holdings. They are somehow related to contractor companies. Enerjisa, which belongs to Sabancı Holding and comes 53rd in the ranking of 500 biggest companies in Turkey, has the ownership of 3 distinct contractor companies in three distribution regions in 2013. These three contractor companies that are taking part in the same holding control 25.5% of all electricity distributed to final consumers. In the same manner, another three contractor companies belonging to a consortium (Kolin-Limak-Cengiz Consortıum) controls another 22.3% of final consumption. This means that almost half of total electricity distributed to consumers in Turkey is

Table 5. Electricity Distribution Sector After the Privatization

Distribution Region	Consumption[4] (%)	Owner[5]	Electricity Generation facilities Of Owner Group[6]
DİCLE	3,4	Eksim Holding	
VANGÖLÜ	1,3	Türkerler Holding	10 HES[7] 1 RES[8] 1 JES[9]
ARAS	2,4	Çalık -Kiler Consortium	6 HES 2 RES 1 COAL
ÇORUH	3,2	AKSA Holding	13 HES 5 NATURALGAS 6 COAL 4 RES
FIRAT	2,2	AKSA Holding	13 HES 5 NATURALGAS 6 COAL 4 RES
ÇAMLIBEL	2,4	Kolin- Limak-Cengiz Consortıum	18 HES 7 NATURAL GAS 1 COAL 1 JES
TOROSLAR	8,5	ENERJİSA Group	13 HES 5 NATURALGAS 3 RES
MERAM	5	CENGİZ+ ALARKO	9 HES 9 NATURALGAS 1 COAL
BAŞKENT	10,1	ENERJİSA Group	13 HES 5 NATURALGAS 3 RES
AKDENİZ	4,8	Kolin- Limak-Cengiz Consortıum	18 HES 7 NATURALGAS 1 COAL 1 JES
GEDİZ	7,7	Elsan-Tümaş-Karaçay Consortıum	
ULUDAĞ	7,4	Kolin- Limak-Cengiz Consortıum	18 HES 7 NATURALGAS 1 COAL 1 JES
TRAKYA	2,5	AKSA Holding	13 HES 5 NATURALGAS 6 COAL 4 RES
AYEDAŞ	6,9	ENERJİSA Group	13 HES 5 NATURALGAS 3 RES
SAKARYA	4,3	Akkök-Akenerji –CEZ Consortıum	9 HES 1 RES
OSMANGAZİ	4,2	Polat Holding	8 RES
BOĞAZİÇİ	12,5	Kolin- Limak-Cengiz Consortıum	18 HES 7 NATURALGAS 1 COAL 1 JES
MENDERES	4,9	Bereket Holding	2 HES 3 RES
GÖKSU	1,6	AKEDAŞ	
YEŞİLIRMAK	4,8	Çalık Holding	2 HES 2 RES 1 COAL

Source: Data collected by authors

carried out by two big groups. Another issue that should be raised is that almost all the distributor companies have the possession of generation facilities such as hydro, wind or thermal generation facilities. Although this is not prohibited by the law, it is contradictory to unbundling principles.

The Costs Shifted on Consumers through Higher Prices

In mainstream theory, it is presumed that the electricity prices will be reduced in parallel with liberalisation of the electricity market and the consumers will buy much cheaper electricity. However, this hypothesis is not verified by the empirical data in Turkey. As is shown in Table 6 the prices of electricity began to increase after 2001 for both industry and household consumption and the price gap between the two groups has widened, meaning an income transfer from household to industry. This increase has accelerated since 2007.

The surge seen in electricity prices in 2007 reveals the fact that electricity is a political good as stated by Oğuz, Akkemik, and Göksel (2014). They asserted that the prices that had been slightly increased before the election year of 2007, were allowed to go up enormously afterwards. Another reason that lies behind this break could be linked to the privatisation program that aims to attract more investors to the sector by assuring high profit margins through higher prices.

Table 6. Energy Sector Employment in Total Employment

Years	Total (1000)	Electricity, Gas, Water, Sewerage system (1000)	Electricity, Gas, Water, Sewerage system (%)
2009	19873	118	0.59
2010	21162	150	0.71
2011	22461	181	0.81
2012	23475	227	0.97
2013	24433	218	0.89
2014	25194	196	0.78

Source: TURKSTAT Labour Force Statistics (2014).

Figure 1. Source: IEA Statistics, Electricity Information (2013)

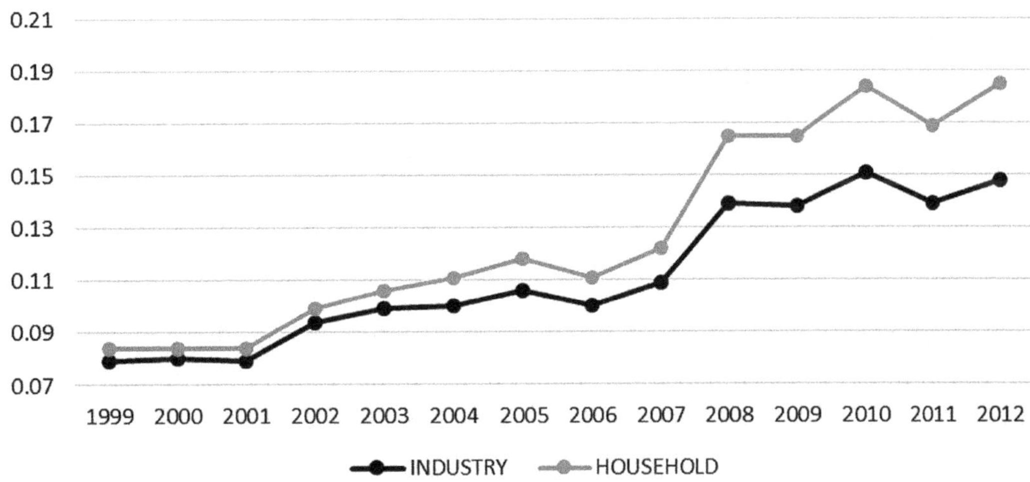

New Job and/or Higher Pay Oppurtunities

For the investments in any sector to be beneficiary for the labor force in a country, they must create new job oppurtunities and/or provide the existing labor force with higher wage income. As is shown in Table 6, no employment opportunity was seized by the labor class in Turkey. The share of energy sector (including water and system) employment in total employment is under 1%, even it slightly decreases over the last two years.

Environmental Impacts

In order to assess the damage that might be caused by the new facilities, the public authority (Ministry of Environment and Urbanisation) enforce the companies to obtain 'Environmental Impact Assessment' report. As this report is given by a Commission affiliated in the Ministry, and not an independent commission, some issues regarding the objectivity of the final conclusion are raised throughout the process. In Turkey, especially for hydroelectric power plants, there have been serious public protests against the investors with many of them ending up in the judicial process.

Another litigation issue that has been raising between the companies and the people living in the area is 'urgent expropriation'. In recent years, the enactment of the new law in 2013 facilitated the expropriations by authorising EMRA to adjudicate on whether the expropriation is pro or counter public interest. In pursuit of this amendment, rapid increase in the number of urgent expropriation decisions took place. While 250-urgent-expropriation decisions were made in 2013, this number increased to 165 in the first six months of 2014 and a total of 235 in the first nine months of the same year (Toker, 2014). Because of extensive usage of urgent expropriation decisions, a great number of cancellation verdicts were given by the courts, but the slow judicial process leads to irreversible damages.

CONCLUSION

In the last decades, the paradigm shift toward "more market and less government" has shown its impacts on utility sector. These reforms have created a new environment for private investments. New players have appeared on the scene searching for new opportunities to invest in areas where the state has left. Electricity is one of them. But as electricity markets pose serious market failures, the state is needed to involve in different ways. In Turkey, the market power of big companies causes high concentration levels at electricity generation/production stage that is potentially most open to competition. The public company which had been the monopoly before the unbundling and privatisation still has the biggest share in electricity production, but its assets have been on the privatisation program and are targeted to be transferred to the private sector where big companies are dominant.

The efficient market type is monopoly at transmission stage that is a network industry. The reasons why this should be public monopoly are various. Since increasing the transmission capacity is crucial for the generation stage to be efficient, the public sector has a primordial role. It also carries the role of balancing the supply and final demand, and the role of operating the whole system. As a result, a few big companies dominate in the sector causing both vertical integration and horizontal concentration. The labour and environmental problems that the society face and the rise in consumer prices exhibit the fact that the liberalisation process is not proceeding in accordance with social welfare maximisation principle of the efficiency theory.

REFERENCES

Atiyas, I., Çetin, T., & Gülen, G. (2012). *Reforming Emerging Energy Markets: Political Economy, Regulation and Competition in Turkey*. New York: Springer. doi:10.1007/978-1-4614-0290-9

Atiyas, İ., & Dutz, M. (2004). *Competition and Regulatory Reform in the Turkish Electricity Industry*. Istanbul: Sabancı University.

Bağdadioğlu, N., & Odyakmaz, N. (2009). Turkish Electricity Reform. *Utilities Policy*, *17*(1), 144–152. doi:10.1016/j.jup.2008.02.001

Bailey, S. J. (2002). *Public Sector Economics* (2nd ed.). New York: Palgrave.

Chang, C. P., & Berdiev, A. N. (2011). The Political Economy of Energy Regulation in OECD Countries. *Energy Economics*, *33*(5), 816–825. doi:10.1016/j.eneco.2011.06.001

Directive 2003/54/EC of the European Parliament and of the Council of 26 June 2003. (2003). *Official Journal of European Union* (L 176), 37-55. Retrieved from http://www.energy-community.org/pls/portal/docs/36275.PDF

Directive 2009/72/EC Of the European Parliament and of the Council of 13 July 2009. (2009). *Official Journal of European Union*, 2009, 15-35. Retrieved from http://eur-lex.europa.eu/LexUriServ/LexUriServ.do?uri=OJ:L:2009:211:0055:0093:EN:PDFfr

Directive 96/92/EC of the European Parliament and of the Council of 19 December 1996 Concerning Common Rules for the Internal Market in Electricity. (1996). *Official Journal of European Union* (L 027), 20-29. Retrieved from http://eur-lex.europa.eu/LexUriServ/LexUriServ.do?uri=CELEX:31996L0092:EN:HTML

Durakoğlu, S. M. (2011). Political Endowments and Electricity Market Regulation in Turkey: An Institutional Analysis. Badia Fiesolana: San Domenico (Fl).

Electricity Sector Reform and Privatization Strategy Paper. (2004, March 17). *High Planning Council*. Retrieved from http://www.oib.gov.tr/program/2004_program/2004_electricity_strategy_paper.htm

Electricity Market Report 2010. (2011). EMRA. Retrieved from http://www.emra.org.tr/documents/electricity/publishments/ElectricityMarketReport2010.pdf

Türkiye Elektrik Enerjisi 10 Yıllık Üretim Kapasite Projeksiyonu (2012 – 2021). (2012). EPDK. Retrieved from http://www.epdk.org.tr/documents/elektrik/rapor_yayin/Elk_Yayin_Uretim_Kapasite_Projeksiyonu_2012_2021.pdf

Erdoğdu, E. (2014). The Political Economy of Electricity Market Liberalization: A Cross-Country Approach. *The Energy Journal (Cambridge, Mass.)*, *35*(3), 91–128.

Ertuna, H. T. (2010). *Competition Law in the Electricity Market: Liberalization and its Consequences*. Retrieved from http://www.ankarabarosu.org.tr/siteler/AnkaraBarReview/tekmakale/2010-2/3.pdf

EÜAŞ. (2013). *Elektrik Üretim Sektör Raporu* 2013. Retrieved from http://www.enerji.gov.tr/File/?path=ROOT%2f1%2fDocuments%2fSekt%C3%B6r+Raporu%2fEUAS-Sektor_Raporu2013.pdf

EU Nears Energy Liberalisation Finishing Line. (2009). EurActiv. Retrieved from http://www.euractiv.com/energy/eu-nears-energy-liberalisation-f-news-221592

EC MEMO/11/125. (2011). European Commission. Retrieved from http://europa.eu/rapid/press-release_MEMO-11-125_en.htm?locale=en

European Commission, (2009). Regulation (EC) No. 714/2009 of the European Parliament and of the Council of 13 July 2009 on Conditions for Access to the Network for Cross-Border Exchanges in Electricity and Repealing Regulation (EC) No. 1228/2003. Official Journal of European Union, 2009, 55–93.

Glachant, J. M. (2013). *The Three Ages of Europe's Single Electricity Market*. Retrieved from http://www.energypost.eu/the-three-ages-of-europes-single-electricity-market/

Harvey, D. (1985). *Consciousness and the Urban Experience*. Oxford: Blackwell.

Harvey, D. (2011). *The Enigma of Capital and the Crises of Capitalism*. London: Profile Books.

Henisz, W., & Zelner, B. (2006). Interest Groups, Veto Points, and Electricity Infrastructure Deployment. *International Organization*, *60*(01), 263–286. doi:10.1017/S0020818306060085

Jamasb, T. (2006). Between the State and Market: Electricity Sector Reform in Developing Countries. *Utilities Policy*, *14*(1), 14–30. doi:10.1016/j.jup.2004.11.001

Jamasb, T., Newbery, D., & Pollitt, M. (2006). Core Indicators for Determinants and Performance of Electricity Sector in Developing Countries. *International Journal of Regulation and Governance*, *6*(1), 43–78.

Karova, R. (2011). Regional electricity markets in Europe: Focus on the Energy Community. *Utilities Policy*, *19*(2), 80–86. doi:10.1016/j.jup.2010.10.001

MacGill, I., Outhred, H., & Nolles, K. (2006). Some Design Lessons from Market-Based Greenhouse Regulation in the Restructured Australian Electricity Industry. *Energy Policy*, *34*(1), 11–25. doi:10.1016/j.enpol.2004.05.009

Gross Fixed Investments by Sectors, Basic Economic Indicators. (2014). Ministry of Development. Retrieved from http://www.kalkinma.gov.tr/Pages/TemelEkonomikGostergeler.aspx

Nagayama, H. (2009). Electric Power Sector Reform Liberalization Models and Electric Power Prices in Developing Countries: An Empirical Analysis Using International Panel Data. *Energy Economics*, *31*(3), 463–472. doi:10.1016/j.eneco.2008.12.004

Newbery, D. M. (2002). Problems of Liberalising the Electricity Industry. *European Economic Review*, *46*(4–5), 919–927. doi:10.1016/S0014-2921(01)00225-2

Electricity Market Balancing and Settlement Regulation. (2014). *Official Gazette*.

Oğuz, F., Akkemik, K. A., & Göksal, K. (2014). Can Law Impose Competition? A Critical Discussion and Evidence from the Turkish Electricity Generation Market. *Renewable & Sustainable Energy Reviews*, *30*, 381–387. doi:10.1016/j.rser.2013.10.024

Orta Vadeli Program 2013-2015. (2012). Retrieved from http://www.goc.gov.tr/files/files/orta-vadeli-program%20(2013-2015).pdf

Özülkü, H. (2006). Türkiye'de Elektriğin Tarihsel Gelişimine Özet Bakış (1900'den 2006'a Yılına Kadar), 10. *Enerji Kongresi Tebliği, Dünya Enerji Konseyi Türk Milli Komitesi*, 1-11. Retrieved from http://www.oocities.org/hasanozulku/melektriktarih.pdf

Pollitt, M. (2009). Evaluating the Evidence on Electricity Reform: Lessons for the South East Europe (SEE) market. *Journal of Regulatory Economics*, *33*(2), 159–172.

Potrafke, N. (2010). Does Government Ideology Influence Deregulation of Product Markets? Empirical Evidence from OECD countries. *Public Choice*, *143*(1-2), 135–155. doi:10.1007/s11127-009-9494-z

Regulation (EC) No 713/2009 of the European Parliament and of the Council of 13 July 2009 Establishing an Agency for the Cooperation of Energy Regulators. (2009). *Official Journal of European Union*, 2009, 1-14. Retrieved from http://eur-lex.europa.eu/LexUriServ/LexUriServ.do?uri=OJ:L:2009:211:0001:0014:EN:PDF

Türkiye Elektrik Dağıtım Sektörü Özelleştirmesi. (2010). Republic of Turkey Prime Ministry Privatization Administration. Retrieved from http://www.oib.gov.tr/2010/dosyalar/TEDAS%20Teaser%20T%C3%BCrk%C3%A7e%20v05-comments%20removed.pdf

Stigler, G. J., & Friedland, C. (1962). What Can Regulators Regulate? The Case of Electricity. *The Journal of Law & Economics*, *5*, 1–16. doi:10.1086/466579

Stiglitz, J. (2010). Government Failure vs. Market Failure: Principles of Regulation. In E. J. Balleisen & D. A. Moss (Eds.), Government and Markets, *Toward a New Theory of Regulation* (pp. 13-51). Cambridge: Cambridge University Press.

TEDAŞ. (2014). Dağıtım Şirketleri. Retrieved from http://www.tedas.gov.tr/Sirketler/Sayfalar/Anasayfa.aspx

TEİAŞ. (2012). *Elektrik İstatistikleri 2012*.

Toker, Ç. (2014) Torba Kamulaştırma Dönemi. *Cumhuriyet*. Retrieved from http://www.cumhuriyet.com.tr/koseyazisi/139637/Torba_Kamulastirma_Donemi.html

TURKSTAT. (2014). *Labour Force Statistics Database 2014*. Retrieved from http://tuikapp.tuik.gov.tr/medas/?kn=72&locale=tr

Williams, J. H., & Ghanadan, R. (2006). Electricity reform in developing and transition countries: A reappraisal. *Energy*, *31*(6–7), 815–844. doi:10.1016/j.energy.2005.02.008

Yi-Chong, X. (2006). The Myth of the Single Solution: Electricity Reforms. *World Bank Energy* (31), 802-814.

Zhang, Y., Parker, F., & Kirkpatrick, C. (2008). Electricity Sector Reform in Developing Countries: An Econometric Assessment of the Effects of Privatization, Competition and Regulation. *Journal of Regulatory Economics*, *33*(2), 159–178. doi:10.1007/s11149-007-9039-7

ENDNOTES

1 The price setting mechanism of electricity market will not be explored in detail in this study, for we focus on the political economic determinants rather than technical ones.

2 EC: European Commission

3 BO, BOT and TOR contracts will be explained in Section 5.

4 Republic of Turkey Prime Ministry Privatization Administration (2010)

5 TEDAŞ (2014) http://www.tedas.gov.tr/Sirketler/Sayfalar/Anasayfa.aspx

6 Home page of owner companies website

Chapter 20
Monetary and Fiscal Policy Interactions:
An Empirical Evidence from Turkey

Asuman Oktayer
Yıldız Technical University, Turkey

Nagihan Oktayer
İstanbul University, Turkey

ABSTRACT

While the role of fiscal policy in price level determination was neglected by the conventional theory, a new point of view was adapted by the Fiscal Theory of the Price Level. In the context of the new theory, monetary and fiscal policy interactions were taken into account and the role of fiscal policy was underlined. This paper investigates the monetary and fiscal policy coordination in Turkey during the period 1989.1-2012.2 and sub-periods 1989.1-2001.1 and 2001.2-2012.2. In order to reveal if financial policies are monetary dominant or fiscal dominant in aforementioned periods, bounds testing procedure is applied by using quarterly data. While the empirical test results related to the entire period of 1989.1-2012.2 and sub-period of 1989.1-2001.1 indicate fiscal policy dominant regime, the findings regarding 2001.2-2012.2 imply monetary policy dominant regime in Turkey.

INTRODUCTION

Due to the serious consequences in terms of economic growth and welfare, price stability is one of the most researched topics in economics. The determinants of price level and inflation have long been a central concern for economists in that sense. The conventional monetarist view has emphasized the importance of an independent central bank and has held that high inflation can only be ultimately triggered by high rates of money growth. The roots of this argument go to Milton Friedman's famous dictum that "*inflation is always and everywhere a monetary phenomenon*". The view that inflation is always a monetary phenomenon has a long tradition based on the quantity theory of money (QTM). In its simplest form, the QTM says that changes in money supply growth are followed by equal changes in the inflation rate.

DOI: 10.4018/978-1-5225-0053-7.ch020

In the context of traditional approach, monetary policy was accepted as one of the most important policies affecting the level of prices in the economy, they believed that controlling the supply of money was the route to low inflation. Hence, following that approach, an increasing number of countries have granted their central banks political independence and charged them with the task of the maintenance of price stability in the 1970s. However, this view was later on criticized seriously and came under attack.

Against this robust theoretical background, attention has increasingly been given to the role of fiscal policy in determining inflation since the 1980s. The "unpleasant monetarist arithmetic" of Sargent-Wallace (1981) unveiled the fiscal roots of inflation. The main result of the seminal paper by Sargent-Wallace is that persistent fiscal imbalances put pressure on the central bank to finance the government deficits, so the effectiveness of monetary policy in controlling inflation depends critically on its coordination with fiscal policy (Buti, 2003).

Following Sargent-Wallace, a considerable amount of literature has stressed that fiscal shocks affect price level, and specifications of fiscal policy matter for the consequences of monetary policy. The theory in which intertemporal budget constraint plays the key role is called "The Fiscal Theory of the Price Level (FTPL) or The New Theory of Price Determination". New view of price determination suggests that the statutory independence of the central bank may not be sufficient to achieve the goal. The central bank can only achieve price stability if it is supported by an appropriate fiscal policy. If required measures are not taken to assure an appropriate fiscal policy, the objective of price stability may not be obtained despite the independence of the Central Bank.

As a result, while the conventional view makes a clear definition of the actions and limitations of the monetary and fiscal policies, both Sargent and Wallace and advocates of the Fiscal Theory of the Price Level put forward that it is not possible to make such a strict distinction between the monetary and fiscal authorities as two different parts of the government and their relationship has important consequences on the price level. After these theoretical debates, an increasing attention has been given to the relationship and coordination between the monetary and fiscal policies in the extant literature.

In the context of the Fiscal Theory of Price Level, monetary and fiscal policy interactions were taken into account and the role of fiscal policy was underlined. The Turkish economy is an interesting case of study to bring out the importance of monetary and fiscal policy coordination. Examining how budget deficits were balanced will allow us to determine the dominant policy regime along the period of analysis.

Turkey has experienced high inflation rates, increasing public sector deficits, pressure of the government borrowing on thin financial markets over the decades after the liberalization. On the fiscal side, high financing requirement of the government with high real interest rates and a very sharp increase in the public debt to GDP ratio brought the debate of fiscal sustainability issues and deteriorated macroeconomic imbalances extensively.

In order to solve the problem, a permanent improvement in the revenue and expenditure balance of the public sector was needed. In this respect, the year 2001 constituted a cornerstone in the economic history of Turkey by the introduction of a new reform programme, "Transition to a Stronger Economy". The main aim of this program was to restrain inflation by restoring fiscal discipline, reducing the public debt, introducing social security reform and inflation targeting.

The goal of this chapter is to empirically analyse the monetary and fiscal policy coordination in Turkey by applying autoregressive distributed lag (ARDL) cointegration procedure over the period 1989.1-2012.2 and the sub-periods of 1989.1-2001.1 and 2001.2-2012.2. The remainder of the chapter is organized as follows. The following section addresses the theoretical background, specifications of the Fiscal Theory of Price Level and literature review. The Turkish economy is briefly discussed for the analysed period in terms of fiscal balances in section three. The following sections discuss the empirical specifications of the chapter and present the empirical analysis and results. Finally, the last section provides concluding remarks.

BACKGROUND

Monetary policy discussions in the 1960s, 1970s and early 1980s generally ignored the importance of fiscal policy. During the 1980s, the financial fragility associated with debt crisis showed the importance of the interaction between monetary and fiscal policies. The issue of fiscal and monetary policy coordination has attracted the attention of economists since the 1980s. The economic literature has long ago shown how the government inter-temporal budget constraint may affect monetary policy conditions and, in particular, price dynamics.

In their well-known paper, Sargent and Wallace (1981) put forward how difficult to operate a monetary policy under the circumstances where fiscal policy is unsustainable. They introduce the notion of a "monetary dominant" regime, where the monetary authority independently sets monetary policy and a "fiscal dominant" regime, where the fiscal authority independently sets its budget, announcing current and future deficits and, hence, determining the amount of revenues that must be raised through bond sales and seignorage. Sargent and Wallace state that, if the fiscal regime is dominant, sooner or later losing of its ability in controlling inflation is inevitable for monetary authority under the assumption that if the real rate of interest exceeds the growth rate of the economy.

Indeed, in such a situation, a decline in money growth today, designed to reduce inflation, will increase the debt to Gross Domestic Product (GDP) ratio, as bond finance replaces monetary finance, thus raising interest payments and deficits in the future. After all, deficit financing requires more money growth and this will result in a higher level of inflation. In other words, as Sargent and Wallace state, "tighter money now can mean higher inflation eventually".

A similar way of thinking lies behind the Fiscal Theory of the Price Level (FTPL) in explaining the determinants of price level. Inflation is a fiscal phenomenon and the price level is determined by the budgetary policies of the fiscal authority. However, this theory argues that monetization may not be the only channel through which fiscal policy becomes dominant and budget deficits cause inflation. The FTPL builds mainly on the contributions of Leeper (1991), Sims (1997), Woodford (1994, 1995, 1998 and 2001), Cochrane (1998, 2001, 2005), Canzoneri, Cumby and Diba (2001).

Proponents of FTPL suggest a different alternative approach in modelling the monetary and fiscal interactions. In the theory, it is stated that determining the nominal price level yields intertemporal government budget balance. Equilibrium is defined as the initial value of government debt equals to the present value of future primary surpluses, inclusive of seignorage. When monetary and fiscal interactions take this form, the price level is uniquely determined through the changes in the fiscal variables, but not the changes in the monetary base. Fiscal policy has direct effect on price stability rather than through the creation of money in this context[1].

Fiscal theory of price level links price determination to the government present value budget constraint. Governments inter-temporally balance their budgets by setting the current market value of the net liabilities equal to the discounted sum of expected future surpluses. In other words, inter-temporal budget constraint is satisfied when the current value of the net liabilities of the government is equal to the discounted present value of the future expected primary surpluses. If the constraint is satisfied without the change in either policy or the price level, the current fiscal policy is said to be sustainable.

If the government adjusts primary deficit to limit debt accumulation and central bank does not monetize debt, such a regime is called monetary dominant (MD) or Ricardian regime. On the other hand if the primary deficits are set independent of real liabilities, such regime is called fiscal dominant (FD) or non-Ricardian regime[2]. Under normal circumstances the economies are in one of two regimes. In an economy, experiencing Ricardian regime, the fiscal authority act prudently, government debt does not constitute an element of net wealth and monetary policy is free to target inflation. If the non-Ricardian regime is in effect, fiscal insolvency requires surprise inflation to deflate the nominal value of government debt, irrespective of the stance of monetary policy.

Advocates of FTPL take the government's inter-temporal budget constraint as an equilibrium condition. According to the theory, if the level of future budget surpluses is exogenously given, the price level is the only variable that can make the stock of nominal bonds consistent with the present value of those primary surpluses. As a result, it is the government's inter-temporal budget constraint that determines the price level. In the context of the theory, because the budget surplus is exogenous, the endogenous adjustment of the price level would be required in order to achieve fiscal solvency. Hence, fiscal policy becomes "active" with budget surpluses turning to be the nominal anchor, whereas monetary policy becomes "passive" in determining the price level (Bajo-Rubio, Díaz-Roldán, & Esteve, 2009).

In the seminal paper, Woodford (1995) proposes a non-Ricardian assumption and points out that allowing the price level fluctuation with unexpected shocks ease the government's budget constraint through taxing bondholders thereby reducing government's nominal liabilities. Present value of future surpluses equals to the government's outstanding nominal debt/price level. If real government debt were to grow explosively, no adjustments to fiscal and monetary policy would be made to keep it in line.

Carlstrom and Fuerest (2000) define weak and strong forms of FTPL. Both forms of the FTPL assume a dominant fiscal policy for price level determination. However, weak form of FTPL states that fiscal imbalances force monetary policy to increase money growth, which means money growth is dictated by the fiscal authority. In this form of the FTPL, inflation is still a monetary phenomenon. Strong form of FTPL, on the other hand, claims that even if money growth is unchanged, fiscal policy separately and independently affects the price level and the inflation rate.

Leeper (1991) explores the way in which government`s intertemporal budget constraint affects the conduct of monetary policy. Leeper focuses on the interaction of the rules characterizing the behaviour of the monetary and fiscal authorities. Leeper makes a distinction between "active" and "passive" policies. The passive or Ricardian policymaker is constrained by the requirement of the satisfaction of intertemporal budget constraint. A passive fiscal policy responds to higher debt levels with tax increases sufficient to balance the intertemporal budget. An active fiscal policy determines tax and spending levels without regard for any intertemporal budget considerations. An active monetary policy pursues its inflation target independent of any fiscal considerations. A passive monetary policy sets interest rates in such a way as to ensure intertemporal fiscal balance.

Following the theoretical developments, the FTPL has attracted much attention and empirical studies have been performed to find out the interactions between monetary and fiscal policy by economists for developed and developing countries. Bohn's (1998) study was one of the first to estimate this relationship for the United States. In his empirical study, he investigated the reaction of the primary surplus to an increase in the debt ratio and found significant evidence that the primary surplus was an increasing function of the debt-GDP ratio for 1916-1995 and various sub-periods. Another empirical study for the United States was performed by Canzoneri, Cumby and Diba (2001). The authors investigated the validity of Ricardian regime for the 1951-1995 period. Canzoneri, Cumby and Diba (2001) conclude that a positive shock in budget surpluses results in a decrease in current debt and an increase in future budget surpluses which is expected to be in accordance with Ricardian regimes. Their result shows that the FTPL is invalidated by the post-war data in the United States. It has to be mentioned that the econometric methodology of Canzoneri, Cumby, and Diba was applied by quite a few researchers afterwards.

Some researchers concentrated on the European Union and OECD countries. Debrun and Wyplosz (1999) and Mélitz (2000) estimated reaction functions respectively for the 12 European Union and 19 OECD countries in order to find out if the primary budget surplus responds positively to the level of government debt. They reached the results, which could not validate the FTPL hypothesis. Their findings show that, there is a statistically significant positive relation between public debt and the primary budget surplus, which makes it impossible to conclude that governments do not take into account their respective intertemporal budget constraints. Another study related to the issue was performed by Ballabriga and Martínez-Mongay (2002) for the European Union countries.

The authors focused on the behaviour of fiscal and monetary policy rules before the European Monetary Union (1979-1998). They concluded that the monetary dominant regime would have prevailed in Euro area countries throughout the years before the formation of Monetary Union. In another empirical study, Afonso (2005) examined the relationship between the primary budget surplus and government debt for the 15 European Union countries. He found evidence supporting the Ricardian regime hypothesis for the period 1970-2003. His results show that the governments of the member states have a tendency to use the primary budget surplus to reduce the debt to-GDP ratio throughout the sample period. Creel and Sterdyniak (2001) examined the issue with panel data and reaction functions for the United States, France and Germany for the period 1970-1999. They concluded that fiscal policy could be characterised by a Ricardian regime in Germany and the United States but by a non-Ricardian regime in the case of France.

Tanner and Ramos (2002) conducted an empirical study to evaluate if the policy regime can be characterized as fiscal or monetary dominant in Brazil for the period 1991-2000. The authors concluded that Brazil follow a monetary dominant regime only for the years 1995-1997. In the rest of the period, estimates suggest that the response of primary deficits to liabilities is statistically insignificant, as expected under fiscal dominant regime. Rocha and Silva (2004) also undertake a study in order to find an answer to the question, which argues that the fiscal theory of the price level could provide an explanation for the high inflation observed in Brazil during the end of the 1970s and beginning of the 1980s. Their conclusion is that the analysed data are consistent with a Ricardian regime. Zoli (2005) provided an analysis to find out the links between fiscal and monetary policy in emerging market countries. According to the results, only in the case of Argentina and Brazil does the evidence point clearly to a regime of fiscal dominance during the 1990s and early 2000s. The results are mixed for Colombia, Mexico, Thailand, and Poland.

Baldini and Ribeiro (2008) reported mixed findings in case of sub-Saharan African countries for the period 1980-2005. The results show that while some countries are characterized by fiscally dominant regime, others indicate monetary dominant regime. On the other hand, a number of countries are also characterized by lack of a clear monetary and fiscal policy regime. Nawaz et al. (2012) performed an empirical study to test the validity of FTPL in the five SAARC countries, which are Bhutan, India, Nepal, Pakistan and Sri Lanka for the period 1990-2009. Their finding indicates that FTPL is not valid in the selected SAARC countries.

Daly and Smida (2014) investigated whether the FTPL was able to deliver a reasonable explanation for the different performances of the price level in the different country of Euro Area from 1999 to 2013 and dealt with the problems of coordination between monetary and fiscal policies. They examined the causal relationship between output gap, public debt, budget deficit, interest rate and inflation rate. According to their results lack of coordination between the monetary and fiscal authorities result in inferior overall economic performance and weak policy stance in one policy area burdens the other area and is unsustainable in the long term.

Bianchi and Ilut (2014) studied post-World War II economic history for the USA. Their result is that the fiscal authority was the leading authority in the 1960s and the 1970s and when the fiscal authority is the leading authority, fiscal imbalances generate long lasting and persistent increases in inflation and the monetary authority loses its ability to control inflation. The authors argue that a disinflationary attempt of the monetary authority leads to more inflation if not supported by the fiscal authority.

Cevik, Dibooglu, and Kutan (2014) examined the interactions between fiscal and monetary policy for some former transition European economies over the period 1995-2010. Their results suggest that monetary and fiscal policy rules show switching characteristics between active and passive regimes, which mean all countries followed both active and passive monetary policies.

They conclude that although the policy mix and the interactions between monetary and fiscal policy point a diverse picture in their sample countries, the monetary policy seems to be passive in all countries after 2000 which consistent with the constraints imposed by European Union enlargement on monetary policy. As for Turkey, there are a number of empirical studies on the relationship between monetary and fiscal policy coordination. Using 1950-1987 annual data, Metin (1998) examined the relationship between the public sector deficit and inflation for Turkey and found a significant link from higher deficits to higher inflation.

Akçay *et al.* (2002) conducted a study over the 1970-2000 period to investigate the sustainability of fiscal stance and the long-run relationship between inflation and budget deficits in the Turkish economy. Empirical results imply an unsustainable fiscal outlook for this period but do not point to insolvency at this point in time. According to the authors, test results indicate to the necessity of a policy change towards fiscal austerity if insolvency is to be avoided in the medium to long term. Neyaptı (2003) empirically examined the relationship between budget deficits and inflation in a sample of 54 developed and less developed countries including Turkey. Her results show that budget deficits lead to inflation, especially, in case of the central bank is not independent and the financial market is not developed.

Cebi (2012) investigated fiscal and monetary policy interactions and their role in stabilisation of the economy for Turkey by using Bayesian estimation technique for the period of 2002–2009. His findings show that the monetary authority reacts to inflation in an active way. He also reaches significant fiscal policy feedbacks on debt for both spending and tax rules. According to the author, fiscal policy has contributed to the debt stabilisation but the results do not give any evidence on active stabilisation of output gap by fiscal means. Despite successful disinflationary attempts, the inflation in Turkey still has some degree of persistence.

AN OVERVIEW OF THE TURKISH ECONOMY

Over the decades, the Turkish economy has been characterized by high and persistent inflation, increasing public sector deficits, high level of interest rates, low growth rates, pressure of the government borrowing on thin financial markets and dollarization of the economy after the liberalization. On the fiscal side, high financing requirement of the government with high real interest rates and a very sharp increase in the public debt to GDP ratio brought the debate of fiscal sustainability issues and deteriorated macroeconomic imbalances extensively. Fiscal deficits were initially financed by the Central Bank resources, but domestic debt financing became the major source especially after the mid-1980s. Fiscal imbalances played a great role in dynamics of the Turkish economy.

The year 1980 was a turning point in the Turkish economy as in January of that year a new macroeconomic stabilization and liberalization program was introduced. Turkey shifted its economic policy from "import substituting industrialization" to "export-led growth strategy". As a part of this program, Turkey went through a gradual liberalization in its economy. Liberalization of the foreign trade regime, adoption of some export promoting incentives, implementation of some policies to attract foreign direct investments, removal of exchange rate controls and liberalization of capital accounts were some important components of the new program.

Because of incomplete financial and institutional infrastructure of the economy, the result of reforms was not compatible with expectations. In particular, the decision was made in 1989 to liberalize the capital accounts was highly untimely and premature. Since then, Turkey has been exposed to the instabilities, the accompanying problems, and, the risks of financial liberalization. High, volatile and persistent inflation[3] and high budget deficits worsened all the balances. Populist policies, government subsidies, the heavy burden of State Economic Enterprises led to the deterioration of the fiscal balances. The weak and fragile nature of the Turkish economy contributed to the rise of a series of crises over the years (Akyüz, 1990; Rodrik, 1990; Önder et.al., 1993; Öniş, 1998).

The early integration with the world economy made the Turkish economy more vulnerable and during the 1990s, economic crises began to affect the economy with increasing frequency. Amongst others, Turkey has experienced two major economic crises during the last two decades, one in 1994 and the second in 2001. While external factors played role to some extent, the main reasons for these crises were the unhealthy structure of the financial sector, with particular problems caused by the government banks and the development of an unsustainable domestic debt dynamic (Yeldan, 2001; Cizre-Sakallıoğllu & Yeldan, 2000, Özatay, 1996).

As can be seen from Figure 1, between 1990 and 2001, the ratio of domestic debt to GNP rose from 10.8% to 50.9%. On the other hand, in the same period, the public sector external debt to GNP ratio increased from 14.4% to 23.2%. Rate of increase in domestic debt was almost six times bigger than external debt, which means shifting external resources by domestic ones to close the financing gap. As the long-term external borrowing possibilities reached its limits, the government turned to the internal markets.

High public deficits and the lack of depth of domestic financial markets opened the way to sustained high real interest rates. The high and volatile inflation rate, which increased the risk premium, contributed to high real interest rates. Especially in the late 1990s, the government started to have difficulty in borrowing due to the increase in risk premium and expectations about the inability to roll over its debt. This led a further decrease in maturity and increase in interest rates.

Between 1992 and 1999, while the annual average real growth rate was less than 4%, the average real interest rate paid on domestic debt was 32%. Such a high level of real interest rates caused an increased level of public sector borrowing requirements. Finally, Turkey faced with a vicious circle of debt and interest payments. Besides the internal economic imbalances, the economic recession in Southeast Asia followed by the Russian crisis in 1998 and devastating earthquakes in August and November, 1999 pushed the country into an ever more difficult position.

In such an environment, Turkey encountered its second severe financial crisis in 2001. It was clear that in order to solve the problem, a permanent improvement in the revenue and expenditure balance of

Figure 1. Domestic, External and Total Government Debt
Data is retrieved from www.treasury.gov.tr, (15.07.2013).

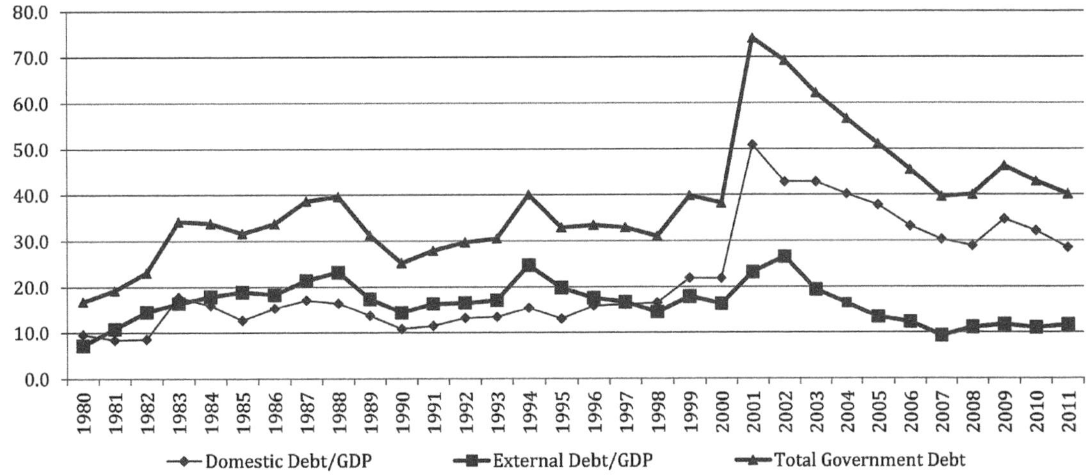

the public sector was needed. In this respect, an ambitious reform program *"Transition to a Stronger Economy"* was introduced in close cooperation with the IMF. Achieving fiscal discipline, reducing the public debt, strengthening the banking system, maintaining a floating exchange rate regime, improving the investment environment to attract larger amounts of foreign direct investment, introducing social security reform and inflation targeting were the major components of this economic program. In the implementation of the program, important steps were taken in structural reforms and in reducing the public deficit.

On the fiscal side, generating a primary surplus of 6.5% of GDP was targeted. Since the beginning of the program, the achievement of the targets was implemented rigorously and a considerable economic recovery began to be observed. As can be seen from Figure 2, central government primary surplus was maintained at 4.4% throughout the period from 2001 to 2008, which was 0.9% between 1990 and 1999. Simultaneously, the budget deficit recorded a high decrease; it was the equivalent of 12.4% of GDP in 2001, but decreased to 8.8% in 2003, 5.4% in 2004, 1.3% in 2005 and 0.6% in 2006. As a result of developments in public deficit and primary surplus, the central government's public debt fell from 74.1% of GDP in 2001 to 39.6% in 2007 (39.4% in 2011). The share of internal debt in total central government debt decreased from 50.9% in 2001 to 28.9% in 2008. Historically, low single-digit levels were reached in inflation. Inflation fell from 68.5% in 2001 to 7.7% in 2005.

Besides primary surplus, reduced public debt and inflation, reduced real interest rates, high economic growth and confidence in Turkish lira were some of the other impressive achievements of the program. In addition, the Law on the Turkish Central Bank has been amended in the context of the reform program, and the Central Bank gained its independence in conduct of monetary policy and mandated to focus on price stability. Direct financing by the central bank of the public debt issuance was prohibited as of November, 2001. It is not worth mentioning that, global economic crisis led to deterioration in the fiscal balances in Turkey in 2009, as was the case in many countries.

Figure 2. Total and Primary Government Surplus
Data is retrieved from www.treasury.gov.tr, (15.07.2013).

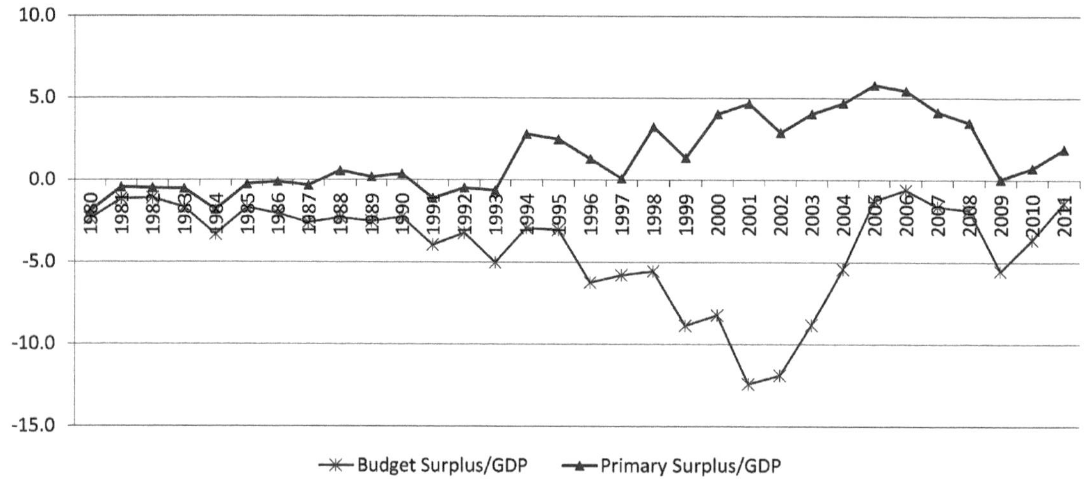

METHODOLOGICAL FRAMEWORK

In this study, in order to empirically distinguish between a Ricardian and a non-Ricardian regime in Turkey, the methodology suggested by Canzoneri et. al (2001) is based on by and large. To employ the methodology developed by Canzoneri et. al (2001), starting point is the government budget constraint in nominal terms. The government's budget constraint for period j can be written as,

$$B_j = \left(T_j - G_j\right) + \left(M_{j+1} - M_j\right) + B_{j+1} / \left(1 + i_j\right) \tag{1}$$

where M_j and B_j are the stock of base money and government debt at the beginning of period j, $(T_j–G_j)$ is the primary surplus during period j, and i_j is the interest rate for period j. The constraint above means that the government debt has to be paid off either by monetizing or by refinancing.

$$\frac{M_j + B_j}{P_j y_j} = \left[\frac{T_j - G_j}{P_j y_j} + \left(\frac{M_{j+1}}{P_j y_j}\right)\left(\frac{i_j}{1+i_j}\right)\right] + \left(\frac{y_{j+1} / y_j}{\left(1+i_j\right)\left(P_j / P_{j+1}\right)}\right)\left(\frac{M_{j+1} + B_{j+1}}{P_{j+1} y_{j+1}}\right) \tag{2}$$

Expressing the budget constraint in terms of M_j+B_j (total government liabilities), and making some algebraic manipulations Canzoneri et al. (2001) rewrite the budget constraint as above. The equation in where the discount factor is the ratio of real growth in GDP to the real interest rate, expresses that the ratio of total government liabilities to GDP has to be equal to the sum of primary surplus (including central bank transfers) to GDP ratio and discounted value of next period's liabilities to GDP ratio. By simplifying the notation, they show Equation (2) as follows:

$$w_j = s_j + \alpha_j w_{j+1} \tag{3}$$

where w_j is the total liabilities to GDP ratio, s_j is the surplus to GDP ratio and α_j is the discount factor. Iterating the equation above forward from the period t and taking expectations conditional on information available in period t, they get the present value constraint as:

$$w_j = s_j + E_t \sum_{j=t+1}^{+\infty} \left(\prod_{k=t}^{j-1} \alpha_k \right) s_j \Leftrightarrow \lim_{T \to +\infty} E_t \left(\prod_{k=t}^{T+t-1} \alpha_k \right) w_{t+T} = 0 \tag{4}$$

$\prod_{t}^{t-1} \alpha_k \equiv 1$. The FTPL treats (4) as an equilibrium condition which must be satisfied. There are two different ways to satisfy this condition. First, there may be an endogenous fiscal policy that makes the sequence $\{s_j\}$ satisfy, regardless of the values of initial liabilities to GDP ratio and the discount factors. Woodford (2001) calls this a Ricardian regime. Alternatively, if government does not adjust $\{s_j\}$, the surplus is just an exogenous process unrelated to debt. In order to satisfy (4), either the discount factor or the ratio of the liabilities to GDP must adjust which indicates a non-Ricardian regime.

Canzoneri et. al (2001) present many different fiscal policy rules that result in a Ricardian regime. Suppose that the sequence $\{s_j\}$ is expected to follow the rule:

$$s_j = c_j w_j + \varepsilon_j \tag{5}$$

where c_j is a time-varying response parameter, ε_j is a random variable which represents political factors and/or economic conditions. If the two conditions below (C1 and C2) are satisfied, then the fiscal policy rule will result in a Ricardian regime:

$$0 \leq c_j < 1, \qquad limsup\ c_j > c^* > 0 \tag{C1}$$

$$D_t \equiv 1 + \sum_{j=t+1}^{+\infty} \left(\prod_{k=t}^{j-1} \alpha_k \right) < +\infty \tag{C2}$$

Assuming c_j, α_j, ε_j are deterministic sequences, ε_j is bounded and C1 and C2 are satisfied, then the fiscal policy rule (5) will result in a Ricardian regime. Canzoneri et al. (2001) developed some implications of the theory above to discriminate between Ricardian or non-Ricardian regime. Consider the temporal relationship running from s_t to w_{t+1}. In case of an increase in s_t, the surplus pays off some of the debt and w_{t+1} falls in a Ricardian regime.

As for in a non-Ricardian regime there are three possibilities: first, if an innovation in s_t is not correlated with the surpluses and the discount factors, w_{t+1} should not be affected by the innovation in s_t. Second, if an innovation in s_t is positively correlated with future surpluses and the discount factors, w_{t+1} should rise. If w_{t+1} falls in case of an increase in s_t, then it's a Ricardian regime. Lastly, if innovations in s_t are negatively correlated with future surpluses and the discount factors, in this case w_{t+1} would fall in either of the regimes.

In order to test the existence of a long-run relationship between variables related to the Fiscal Theory of Price Level in Turkey, two versions of the FTPL stated in the previous section have been estimated by using the bounds testing procedure (autoregressive distributed lag –ARDL– cointegration procedure) developed by Pesaran et al. (2001) in a bivariate system as distinct from the methodology of Canzoneri et al. (2001). Before applying bounds testing procedure, stationarity of variables should be investigated.

Unit Root Tests

In the first stage, stationarity of the time series data is tested by applying unit root tests. Because the ARDL procedure assumes that all variables are either I(0) or I(1), it is important to perform the unit root test in order to ensure that no variable is integrated of order two or higher. If one of the variables in the model is found to be I(2), then the computed F-statistics produced by Pesaran et al. (2001) and Narayan (2005), can no longer be valid.

Among a number of alternative tests, we test for the unit roots of the variables using two different tests, namely the Augmented Dickey-Fuller test (hereafter ADF) (Dickey & Fuller, 1979), and the Zivot-Andrews test (hereafter ZA) developed by Zivot and Andrews (1992). The problem with the conventional unit root tests such as ADF is that it doesn't allow for the possibility of structural break. Assuming the time of the break as an exogenous phenomenon, Peron (1989) showed that the power to reject a unit root hypothesis decreases when the stationary alternative is true and the structural break is ignored.

Therefore, failure to find significant evidence of stationarity from the conventional unit root tests may reflect misspecification of the deterministic trend. Zivot and Andrews (1992) proposed a variation of Perron's (1989) original test in which they assume that the exact time of the break point is unknown. To investigate whether or not there is a structural break, the Zivot-Andrews unit root test is secondly performed in this study.

Bounds Testing Procedure

The approach has certain econometric advantages in comparison to other cointegration tests (Engle & Granger, 1987; Johansen, 1988; Johansen & Juselius, 1990). First of all, it is not important whether the series are I(0) or I(1). The test is applicable irrespective of whether the regressors in the model are purely I(0), purely I(1) or mutually cointegrated; however, it crashes if the series are I(2). Another advantage of the ARDL approach is that it relatively provides more robust results and super consistent estimates of the long-run coefficients in case of small samples. In a bivariate model, the Bounds testing procedure analyses a possible long-run relationship in the form of the unrestricted vector error correction model given below:

$$\Delta Y_t = c_0 + \sum_{j=1}^{n} \varphi_j \Delta Y_{t-j} + \sum_{j=1}^{m} \varpi_j \Delta X_{t-j} + \mu_1 Y_{t-1} + \mu_2 X_{t-1} + \varepsilon_t \tag{7}$$

where Y is the dependent and X is the independent variable, Δ is the first difference operator and ε_t is the error term.

To investigate the existence of a long-run relationship among the variables in the bounds cointegration procedure, the first step is to apply ordinary least squares (OLS) regression to Equation (7) by performing a Wald test (F statistics) for the joint significance of the coefficients of the lagged levels of the variables; H_0: $\mu_1=\mu_2=0$ implying no cointegration and H_1: $\mu_1\neq\mu_2\neq 0$ implying at least one cointegrating equation and thus a long-run relationship. Pesaran et al. (2001) present two sets of asymptotic critical values for testing cointegration for a given significance level. The set with lower value is computed assuming that the regressors are I(0) and the other set with upper value is computed assuming that the regressors are I(1).

If the computed F statistics exceeds the upper critical value, the null hypothesis of no cointegration can be rejected. If it falls below the lower critical value the null hypothesis cannot be rejected. Finally, if the F statistics value falls between the lower and upper critical values the result is inconclusive. If there exists a long-run relationship among the variables, the second step is to estimate the long-run model for Y_t by selecting the orders of ARDL (n, m) model in variables using the AIC (Akaike information criteria):

$$Y_t = c_0 + \sum_{j=1}^{n} \mu_1 Y_{t-j} + \sum_{j=0}^{m} \mu_2 X_{t-j} + \varepsilon_t \tag{8}$$

In the final step of the bounds testing procedure short-run dynamic parameters are obtained by estimating an error correction model (ECM) associated with the long-run estimates. In order to estimate the speed of adjustment of the dependent variable to independent variable(s), the lagged level variables in Equation (7) are replaced by ect_{t-1}:

$$\Delta Y_t = \gamma + \sum_{j=1}^{n} \varphi_j \Delta Y_{t-j} + \sum_{j=0}^{m} \varpi_j \Delta X_{t-j} + \lambda ect_{t-1} + \varepsilon_t \tag{9}$$

In Equation (9), φ_j and ϖ_j are the short-run dynamic coefficients of the model's convergence to equilibrium, λ is the speed of adjustment and *ect* is the error correction term derived from the long-run relationship. If the value of speed of adjustment is zero it means that there exist no long-run relationships, if it's between -1 and 0, there exists partial adjustment. A value smaller than "-1" indicates that the model overadjusts in the current period; finally, a positive value implies that the system moves away from equilibrium in the long-run.

DATA

In this study, in which we search for the validity of the FTPL in Turkey by performing a cointegration technique using quarterly data over the period 1989.1-2012.2, the definitions of the variables we use in the models are as follows: PBY is the ratio of non-interest primary balance to nominal GDP; PNDSY and TPLY are the shares of public net debt service and total public liabilities[4] in nominal GDP, respectively. We obtained data for non-interest primary balance and the components of monetary base[5] from electronic data dissemination system of the Central Bank of the Republic of Turkey, public net debt service from the Undersecreteriat Turkish Treasury and nominal GDP from the Ministry of Development of the Republic of Turkey. Simple calculations are made by ourselves.

Empirical Findings

In the empirical part of our study firstly, we test for the stationarity status of all variables under consideration to determine their order of integration by applying two alternative unit root tests over the periods 1989.1-2012.2, 1989.1-2001.1, and 2001.2-2012.2. This is to ensure that the variables are not I(2) stationary and so as to avoid spurious results. The results of the Augmented Dickey and Fuller Test are given in Table 1. As can be observed from the table, the results of the ADF unit root test suggest that the variables are each integrated of either order zero (I(0)) or order one (I(1)).

In Table 2, the results of the Zivot-Andrews unit root test, which is able to capture the impact of structural breaks, are reported. The Zivot-Andrews test with one structural break finds no additional evidence against the unit root null hypothesis relative to the unit root tests without a structural break. In other words, in models A, B and C the null hypotheses are not rejected for the variables. This result is consistent with the standard ADF test results.

Table 1. Unit root test results (Level and first difference)

Variables		Augmented Dickey and Fuller Test					
		Level			First Difference		
		Intercept	Intercept & Trend	None	Intercept	Intercept & Trend	None
PBY	1989.1-2012.2	-1.96 (3)	-1.93 (3)	-1.08 (3)	-12.99** (2)	-12.96** (2)	-13.08** (2)
PNDSY	1989.1-2012.2	-2.36 (4)	-2.26 (4)	-0.65 (4)	-3.31* (3)	-3.37 (3)	-3.33** (3)
TPLY	1989.1-2012.2	-2.46 (4)	-2.38 (4)	-0.59 (4)	-3.34* (3)	-3.36 (3)	-3.37** (3)
PBY	1989.1-2001.1	-4.49** (0)	-5.68** (0)	-3.58** (0)	-8.067** (2)	-8.061** (2)	-8.09** (2)
PNDSY	1989.1-2001.1	-2.05 (4)	-1.88 (4)	-0.14 (2)	-16.35** (1)	-2.86 (3)	-16.56** (1)
TPLY	1989.1-2001.1	-1.93 (4)	-1.97 (4)	0.09 (4)	-2.98* (3)	-2.99 (3)	-3.09** (3)
PBY	2001.2-2012.2	-0.88 (3)	-1.56 (3)	-0.95 (3)	-9.63** (2)	-9.50** (2)	-9.69** (2)
PNDSY	2001.2-2012.2	-1.77 (4)	-3.39 (9)	-2.67** (4)	-2.72 (9)	-3.33* (9)	-1.48 (3)
TPLY	2001.2-2012.2	-0.73 (2)	-3.10 (8)	-2.97** (2)	-2.94* (9)	-2.86 (9)	-1.92 (3)
Critical Values %1 %5		-3.54 -2.91	-4.12 -3.45	-2.59 -1.94	-3.54 -2.91	-4.12 -3.48	-2.59 -1.94

Note: Values in brackets are the lag lengths which are chosen by using SIC. *, ** denotes statistical significance at the 5% and 1% levels respectively. The null hypothesis under the ADF is that the variable contains a unit root.

Table 2. Zivot and Andrews test with one structural break

Variables		Model A		Model B		Model C	
		Break Date	Test Statistics	Break Date	Test Statistics	Break Date	Test Statistics
PBY	1989.1-2012.2	2000	-4.98 (1)	2008	-6.52 (1)	2008	-4.68 (1)
PNDSY		1993	-3.91 (3)	2008	-4.91 (3)	2008	-4.87 (3)
TPLY		1993	-3.91 (3)	2008	-5.29 (3)	2008	-5.05 (3)
PBY	1989.1-2001.1	1994	-0.87 (4)	1994	-0.87 (4)	1994	-0.87 (4)
PNDSY		1994	-2.56 (4)	1994	-2.56 (4)	1994	-2.56 (4)
TPLY		1994	-2.62 (4)	1994	-2.62 (4)	1994	-2.62 (4)
PBY	2001.2-2012.2	2005	-2.12 (3)	2005	-2.12 (3)	2005	-2.12 (3)
PNDSY		2005	-3.96 (3)	2005	-3.96 (3)	2005	-3.96 (3)
TPLY		2005	-2.99 (3)	2005	-2.99 (3)	2005	-2.99 (3)
Critical Values %1 %5		-5.34 -4.80		-4.93 -4.42		-5.57 -5.08	

Note: Model A allows for a change in intercept, Model B permits a change in trend and Model C permits a change both in intercept and slope. The values in brackets denote the number of included lags of difference automatically selected by AIC.

Bounds Tests for Cointegration

1989.1-2012.2

After having determined that the variables are not I(2) stationary, we conduct the ARDL cointegration procedure to examine whether the variables in question have common trends for the period 1989.1-2012.2. In the first step of the Bonds testing procedure, we test for the presence of a long-run relationship. F-statistics tests the joint null hypothesis that coefficients of the lagged level variables are zero indicating no long-run relationship between the variables. All estimated equations incorporate drift. A deterministic time trend was included whenever significant. An optimal dynamic structure was designated to make certain an absence of serial correlation in the estimated residuals on the basis of the Akaike Information model selection criteria (AIC).

Table 3 reports the results of the calculated F-statistics when non-interest primary balance is considered as a dependent variable in the regressions. The lag lengths are selected according to the results of Breusch-Godfrey test.

While the calculated F-statistics are less than the lower bounds for Model 1 and Model 2 at 1%, 5%, and 10% significance levels in the no trend case, they are higher than the upper bound level at 10% significance level for Model 1 in the case that includes trend. Thus the null hypothesis of no cointegration

Table 3. Bounds test results for cointegration (1989.1 – 2012.2)

Critical Value Bonds of the F Statistics: *Unrestricted Intercept and No Trend*						
k	90% level		95% level		99% level	
	I(0)	I(1)	I(0)	I(1)	I(0)	I(1)
1	5.69	6.43	6.80	7.63	8.97	10.12
Critical Value Bonds of the F Statistics: *Unrestricted Intercept and Unrestricted Trend*						
k	90% level		95% level		99% level	
	I(0)	I(1)	I(0)	I(1)	I(0)	I(1)
1	4.13	4.88	5.00	5.90	7.08	8.25
Calculated F Statistics F(Dependent Variable/ Independent Variable)						
		No trend			Trend	
Model 1	F(PBY / PNDSY):	0.98	(4 lags)	5.63*	(3 lags)	
Model 2	F(PBY / TPLY):	0.81	(4 lags)	2.74	(4 lags)	

The lag lengths are selected by using AIC. Critical values are extracted from Narayan (2005), Case III and case V. Taking account of the New Economic Program that was began to be implemented in 2001, a central dummy variable is used for structural break. For the reason that we use quarterly data, seasonal dummies are included in all our models in order to control for seasonality. * indicates the test statistic exceeds the 10% upper critical value, ** implies the value lies in the indeterminate region, *** denotes the test statistic drops below the lower critical value.

is rejected for Model 1, which contains an unrestricted constant and trend, indicating long-run relationships among the variables.

Once a long-run cointegration relationship is found between the variables, the second step is to estimate the long-run model for the dependent variable by selecting the orders of ARDL (n, m) model using AIC. The orders of ARDL specification are ARDL (2, 4) for Model 1. The result obtained by normalizing on the dependent variable in the model in long-run is reported in Table 4. The coefficient of PNDSY in Model 1 is 0.06, which mean that a one-unit increase in public net debt service/GDP (PNDSY) leads to a 0.06 unit growth in non-interest primary balance/GDP (PBY).

In the final step of ARDL cointegration procedure, the short-run dynamic parameters are obtained from Equation 9. The estimated short-run coefficients related to the period 1989.1-2012.2 are given in Table 5. The sign of the coefficient of the error correction term is found negative and statistically significant for the model in Table 5. The estimated coefficients of the short-run relationship in Table 5 indicate the presence of non-Ricardian fiscal policies in the period 1989.1-2012.2.

Table 4. Long-run elasticities (1989.1 – 2012.2)

	Dependent Var.	Coefficients	t-Statistics	
Model 1 (*Trend*) ARDL(2,4)	PBY			ect_{t-1} = PBY-0.060PNDSY + 0.096 - 0.001T (0.054) (0.001) (0.037)
Constant		-0.096	-2.069	
PNDSY		0.060	0.046	

The lag structure was specified on the basis of the AIC used during the OLS estimation of the bounds tests in choosing the short-run dynamics of the ARDL. The values in parentheses below the estimated coefficients are standard error terms.

Table 5. Short-run elasticities (1989.1 – 2012.2)

Model	Variable	Coefficient	Std. Error	t-Statistics	t-Prob.
Model 1: PBY / PNDSY *(Trend)* ARDL(4,3) PNDSY ⟶ PBY	C	-0.001	0.005	-0.207	0.836
	ΔPBY(-1)	**-0.175**	**0.188**	**-0.934**	**0.083**
	ΔPBY(-2)	-0.111	0.144	-0.769	0.444
	ΔPBY(-3)	**-0.235**	**0.116**	**-2.020**	**0.047**
	ΔPBY(-4)	**-0.282**	**0.103**	**-2.793**	**0.006**
	ΔPNDSY	**-0.040**	**0.018**	**-2.132**	**0.036**
	ΔPNDSY(-1)	**0.052**	**0.019**	**2.668**	**0.009**
	ΔPNDSY(-2)	**-0.043**	**0.020**	**-2.137**	**0.036**
	ΔPNDSY(-3)	**0.063**	**0.018**	**3.422**	**0.001**
	ecm(-1)	***-0.489***	***0.220***	***-2.216***	***0.029***

R-squared : R^2 =0.76

Diagnostic Tests

Autocorrelation : χ^2_{BG} =0.49 [0.77]

Heteroscedasticity : χ^2_{BP} =4.13 [0.60]

Functional form : χ^2_{RESET} =1.00 [0.15]

Normality : χ^2_{JB} =6.27 [0.23]

The estimation results written in bold letters are the statistically significant ones. The values in square brackets are probabilities.

To confirm the appropriateness of the ARDL model, a battery of diagnostic tests is conducted on the final model. The diagnostic tests, the results of which are reported in Table 5, are Breusch-Godfrey (Godfrey, 1978; Breusch, 1979) serial correlation LM test, Breush-Pagan (1979) heteroscedasticity test, Ramsey Regression Equation Specification Error Test (Ramsey, 1969) and Jarque-Bera (Bera & Jarque, 1980) normality test. The model passes all the relevant diagnostic tests. The diagnostic tests applied to the error correction model indicate that there is no evidence of serial correlation and heteroscedasticity. In addition, the Ramsey RESET test implies that the ARDL model is specified correctly and the Jarque-Bera normality test indicates that the residuals are normally distributed.

The results of the cointegration analyses between the variables in question indicate non-Ricardian fiscal policies for the period 1989.1-2012.2. Taking into consideration the new economic program aiming to strengthen the Turkish economy, which was announced in May 2001, we divide our whole research period into two sub-periods one of which is 1989.1-2001.1 and the other is 2001.2-2012.2. In order to make certain the presence of a structural break, we applied the Chow test.

The result of the Chow test shows that public net debt service/GDP (PNDSY) has different impacts on two different sub-periods of our population. After identifying that the two sub-periods should be modelled separately, we adopted the ARDL testing over the two periods one by one. We anticipate the estimation results of the two periods to be oppositely different as the government went to a policy shift in 2001. While the policy regime of the Turkish economy was fiscal dominant before 2001, it turned to monetary dominant by the new program, which began to be implemented in 2001.

1989.1-2001.1

The findings obtained by taking the lag lengths as "1" and "2" as indicated by the Breusch-Godfrey test results are reported in Table 6. The results given in Table 6 show that there are evidences of cointegration for the trend included cases of Model 1 and Model 2 in which the variable PBY is taken as dependent variable. This implies that both Model 1 and Model 2 with trend will be estimated with an error-correction term.

We next continued to get the long-run estimates via ARDL approach. When choosing the short-run dynamics of the ARDL error correction mechanism, the lag structure was designated on the basis of the AIC model selection criteria used during the OLS estimation of the bounds tests. The estimated long-run models for the dependent variable, PBY, are presented in Table 7. The selected orders of ARDL specifications determined by using the AIC are as ARDL (1, 4) for Model 1 and ARDL (1, 1) for Model 2. The signs of the coefficients of the long-run models in Table 7 point to non-Ricardian fiscal policies implemented in the period 1989.1-2001.1.

The coefficients belonging to the independent variables in error correction models in Table 7, show the effect size of them on the dependent variable. The coefficient of PNDSY is 0.057, which means a one-unit increase in public net debt service/GDP (PNDSY) causes a 0.057 unit rise in non-interest primary balance/GDP (PBY). As for the coefficient of total public liabilities/GDP (TPLY), which is 0.051, it implies that a one-unit growth in total public liabilities/GDP leads to a 0.051 unit increase in non-interest primary balance/GDP.

The short-run analysis results belonging to Model 1 and Model 2 covering the period 1989.1-2001.1 are given in Table 8. It is verified that the short-run dynamic impacts are sustained in the long-run by the sign of the error correction term to be found negative and significant for both models. The estimated coefficients of the error correction terms of Model 1 and Model 2 are -0.80 and -0.88, respectively, implying a fairly high speed of adjustment to equilibrium after a shock.

Table 6. Bounds test results for cointegration (1989.1-2001.1)

Critical Value Bonds of the F Statistics: ***Unrestricted Intercept and No Trend***						
k	90% level		95% level		99% level	
	I(0)	I(1)	I(0)	I(1)	I(0)	I(1)
1	4.19	4.94	5.22	6.07	7.56	8.68
Critical Value Bonds of the F Statistics: ***Unrestricted Intercept and Unrestricted Trend***						
k	90% level		95% level		99% level	
	I(0)	I(1)	I(0)	I(1)	I(0)	I(1)
1	5.78	6.54	6.98	7.86	9.89	10.96
Calculated F Statistics F(Dependent Variable/ Independent Variable)						
			No trend		*Trend*	
Model 1	F(PBY / PNDSY) :		1.63	(1 lag)	8.46**	(1 lag)
Model 2	F(PBY / TPLY) :		1.24	(1 lag)	6.62*	(2 lags)

The lag lengths are selected by using AIC. Critical values are extracted from Narayan (2005), Case III and case V. For the reason that we use quarterly data, seasonal dummies are included in all our models in order to control for seasonality. * indicates the test statistic exceeds the 10% upper critical value, ** implies the value lies in the indeterminate region, *** denotes the test statistic drops below the lower critical value.

Table 7. Long-run elasticities (1989.1-2001.1)

	Dependent Var.	Coefficients	t-Statistics	
Model 1 *(Trend)* ARDL(1,4)	PBY			ect_{t-1}= PBY-0.057PNDSY + 0.094 - 0.0013T (0.008) (-0.002) (-0.032)
Constant		-0.094	-2.543	
PNDSY		0.057	0.005	
Model 2 *(Trend)* ARDL(1,1)				ect_{t-1}= PBY-0.051TPLY + 0.101 - 0.0016T (-0.048) (0.034) (0.009)
Constant		-0.101	-1.941	
TPLY		0.051	0.074	

The lag structure was specified on the basis of the AIC used during the OLS estimation of the bounds tests in choosing the short-run dynamics of the ARDL. The values in parentheses below the estimated coefficients are standard error terms.

Table 8. Short-run elasticities (1989.1-2001.1)

Model	Variable	Coefficient	Std. Error	t-Statistics	t-Prob.
Model 1: PBY / PNDSY *(Trend)* ARDL(4,3)	C	0.0001	0.006	0.024	0.980
	ΔPBY(-1)	0.038	0.226	0.168	0.867
	ΔPBY(-2)	0.024	0.185	0.133	0.894
	ΔPBY(-3)	**-0.264**	**0.150**	**-1.753**	**0.089**
	ΔPBY(-4)	**-0.374**	**0.130**	**-2.876**	**0.007**
	ΔPNDSY	-0.010	0.024	-0.437	0.664
	ΔPNDSY(-1)	**0.092**	**0.024**	**3.806**	**0.000**
	ΔPNDSY(-2)	-0.045	0.029	-1.526	0.137
	ΔPNDSY(-3)	**0.051**	**0.026**	**1.942**	**0.061**
	ecm(-1)	***-0.803***	***0.271***	***-2.957***	***0.006***
Model 2: PBY / TPLY *(Trend)* ARDL(1,3)	C	0.001	0.006	0.240	0.811
	ΔPBY(-1)	0.051	0.186	0.275	0.784
	ΔTPLY	-0.022	0.026	-0.833	0.410
	ΔTPLY(-1)	**0.069**	**0.025**	**2.679**	**0.011**
	ΔTPLY(-2)	-0.036	0.028	-1.302	0.201
	ΔTPLY(-3)	**0.048**	**0.025**	**1.895**	**0.066**
	ecm(-1)	***-0.879***	***0.230***	***-3.822***	***0.000***

R-squared : R^2 =0.89

Diagnostic Tests

Autocorrelation : χ^2_{BG} =0.45 [0.76]

Heteroscedasticity : χ^2_{BP} =4.05 [0.55]

Functional form : χ^2_{RESET} =1.32 [0.28]

Normality : χ^2_{JB} =3.54 [0.20]

The estimation results written in bold letters are the statistically significant ones. The values in square brackets are probabilities.

Both in Model 1 and Model 2 containing trend, non-interest primary balance/GDP (PBY) responds positively to changes in public net debt service/GDP and total public liabilities/GDP respectively. The diagnostic test statistics of the specified ARDL models are displayed along with the empirical results of the short-run in Table 8. The equation for the underlying ARDL equation passes the diagnostic tests including serial correlation of the residuals, functional form misspecification, heteroscedastic disturbances and non-normal residuals.

Consequently, similar to the results of the cointegration analyses covering the whole period 1989.1-2012.2, we found that the fiscal policies implemented in Turkey between the periods 1989.1-2001.1 are also non-Ricardian as we expect. In addition to the positive relationship found between the variables PBY and PNDSY in the cointegration analyses performed for the whole period, a positive relationship between PBY and TPLY is found for the period 1989.1- 2001.1.

2001.2-2012.2

In Table 9, the computed F statistics of bound test developed by Pesaran, Shin and Smith (2001) are reported for all of the Models containing trend and no trend. The lag lengths are chosen as "6" and "7" by using Breusch-Godfrey test.

As can be observed from Table 9, even for 10% significance level, neither of the calculated F statistics, except for the F statistics of Model 1 containing trend, is higher than the upper bound level, which means the failure to reject the null hypothesis. In other words there exists a cointegrating relationship between the dependent and the independent variables just from public net debt service/GDP (PNDSY) to non-interest primary balance/GDP (PBY).

Table 9. Bounds test results for cointegration (2001.2 – 2012.2)

Critical Value Bonds of the F Statistics: ***Unrestricted Intercept and No Trend***						
K	90% level		95% level		99% level	
	I(0)	I(1)	I(0)	I(1)	I(0)	I(1)
1	4.23	5.00	5.26	6.16	7.62	8.82
Critical Value Bonds of the F Statistics: ***Unrestricted Intercept and Unrestricted Trend***						
K	90% level		95% level		99% level	
	I(0)	I(1)	I(0)	I(1)	I(0)	I(1)
1	5.91	6.63	7.13	7.98	10.15	11.23
Calculated F Statistics F(Dependent Variable/ Independent Variable)						
			No Trend		*Trend*	
Model 1	F(PBY / PNDSY) :		4.22	(7 lags)	10.14**	(7 lags)
Model 2	F(PBY / TPLY) :		1.55	(6 lags)	3.33	(6 lags)

The lag lengths are selected by using AIC. Critical values are extracted from Narayan (2005), Case III and case V. For the reason that we use quarterly data, seasonal dummies are included in all our models in order to control for seasonality. * indicates the test statistic exceeds the 10% upper critical value, ** implies the value lies in the indeterminate region, *** denotes the test statistic drops below the lower critical value.

The long-run model for the dependent variable estimated by selecting the orders of ARDL (n, m) model using AIC is reported in Table 10. The selected orders of ARDL model by using AIC is ARDL(10,9). The calculated coefficient of the independent variable in the long-run relationship in Table 10, indicates Ricardian financial policy implications between the periods 2001.2-2012.2 in Turkey. The coefficient of the ratio of public net debt service to GDP is negative and has a value of -0.044. This means a one-unit growth in public net debt service/GDP ratio results in a 0.044 decline in non-interest primary balance/ GDP ratio, which gives the impression of Ricardian policy implications.

The short-run dynamic parameters obtained from Equation 9 are given in Table 11. The diagnostic test results given in the same table imply that there is no evidence of serial correlation, non-normality, functional form misspecification and heteroscedasticity. The coefficient of the error correction term is found negative (and bigger than "1" in absolute term) and statistically significant. In other words the short-run dynamic impacts are sustained in the long-run. In the model, which aims to test whether the financial policies implemented in Turkey between the period 2001.2-2012.2 is Ricardian, it is observed that the signs of the dependent and independent variables are opposite to each other.

The signs of the coefficients of all lagged levels of ΔPBY are positive and except for the 6th. lagged value, all other lagged values of the coefficients of ΔPBY are found statistically significant. As for ΔPNDSY, except for the coefficients of the 1st., 4th. and 5th. lagged levels, all other lagged levels' co-efficients are statistically significant. In addition, the signs of all coefficients, which are statistically significant, are found negative. Therefore as we expect we can say that economic policies introduced in the post 2001 period is monetary dominant or Ricardian.

FUTURE RESEARCH DIRECTIONS

In 2008, the world experienced its worst financial and economic crisis since the Great Depression of the 1930s.The impacts of the global financial crisis on the Turkish economy was fairly limited. The prudent fiscal and monetary policy, healthy banking sector and strong international reserves, unlike many other emerging markets, prevented Turkey from the severe effects of the crisis. On the other hand, it was impossible to be totally not affected as being an open economy and being integrated with the global financial system. Several monetary and fiscal measures were introduced to lessen the impact of the crisis after 2008. Monetary and fiscal policy interactions issue should be investigated in the context of the measures to be taken to counter the crisis and their results in our future research.

Table 10. long-run elasticities (2001.2 – 2012.2)

	Dependent Var.	Coefficients	t-Statistics	
Model 1 (*Trend*) ARDL(10,9)	PBY			ect_{t-1}= PBY + 0.0439PNDSY - 0.242 + 0.002T (0.094) (0.046) (-0.004)
Constant		0.242	5.18	
PNDSY		-0.044	-4.656	

The lag structure was specified on the basis of the AIC used during the OLS estimation of the bounds tests in choosing the short-run dynamics of the ARDL. The values in parentheses below the estimated coefficients are standard error terms.

Table 11. Short-run elasticities (2001.2 – 2012.2)

Model	Variable	Coefficient	Std. Error	t-Statistics	t-Prob.
Model 1: PBY / PNDSY *(Trend)* ARDL(10,9)	**C**	**0.357**	**0.147**	**2.427**	**0.027**
	ΔPBY(-1)	**0.684**	**0.278**	**2.462**	**0.025**
	ΔPBY(-2)	**0.563**	**0.214**	**2.631**	**0.018**
	ΔPBY(-3)	**1.004**	**0.223**	**4.501**	**0.000**
	ΔPBY(-4)	**0.549**	**0.243**	**2.259**	**0.037**
	ΔPBY(-5)	**0.602**	**0.214**	**2.812**	**0.012**
	ΔPBY(-6)	0.177	0.165	1.070	0.299
	ΔPBY(-7)	**0.535**	**0.148**	**3.604**	**0.002**
	ΔPBY(-8)	**0.213**	**0.131**	**1.624**	**0.093**
	ΔPBY(-9)	**0.235**	**0.128**	**1.837**	**0.044**
	ΔPNDSY	**-0.105**	**0.029**	**-3.586**	**0.002**
	ΔPNDSY(-1)	-0.000	0.022	0.001	1.000
	ΔPNDSY(-2)	**-0.104**	**0.019**	**-5.498**	**0.000**
	ΔPNDSY(-3)	**-0.083**	**0.026**	**3.159**	**0.006**
	ΔPNDSY(-4)	-0.023	0.029	-0.782	0.445
	ΔPNDSY(-5)	0.030	0.026	1.156	0.263
	ΔPNDSY(-6)	**-0.046**	**0.019**	**-2.455**	**0.025**
	ΔPNDSY(-7)	**-0.049**	**0.018**	**-2.622**	**0.018**
	ΔPNDSY(-8)	**0.036**	**0.020**	**1.745**	**0.059**
	ecm(-1)	***-1.478***	***0.400***	***-3.692***	***0.002***
R-squared	: R^2 =0.85				
Diagnostic Tests					
Autocorrelation	: χ^2_{BG} =0.39 [0.69]				
Heteroscedasticity	: χ^2_{BP} =3.21 [0.37]				
Functional form	: χ^2_{RESET} =0.15 [0.88]				
Normality	: χ^2_{JB} =1.80 [0.45]				

The estimation results written in bold letters are the statistically significant ones. The values in square brackets are probabilities.

CONCLUSION

Achieving macroeconomic objectives requires a close degree of interaction between monetary and fiscal policies. Absence of coordination between the policies and related authorities results in a lower macroeconomic performance and is unsustainable in the long run both for the developed and developing countries. Imprudence in one of the policy area deteriorates the other area, which may lead to economic crises.

The newly experienced global economic crisis in 2008 has emphasized the importance of the coordination of monetary and fiscal policies once more. As being two complementary economic policies, fiscal policy is an important determinant of the efficiency of monetary policy. While a weak fiscal stance restricts the effectiveness of monetary policy, a strong fiscal stance increases the efficiency of monetary policy by deepening domestic financial markets, lowering interest rates and extending the maturities on domestic borrowing; therefore it contributes to confidence in the economy.

The Turkish economy is an outstanding case of study, in showing the positive effects of strengthening the fiscal policies over the economy. After the 2001 crisis, Turkey introduced a new economic program. Achieving fiscal discipline, reducing the public debt and strengthening the banking system were the major components of this economic program. Implementation of the new program was an important policy shift, which would have significant effects on the overall economy.

In this chapter, in order to reveal the effects of the policy shift, we empirically distinguish between a Ricardian (monetary dominant) and a non-Ricardian (fiscal dominant) regime in Turkey over the period 1989.1-2012.2 by using quarterly data. The cointegration test results containing the 1989.1-2012.2 period indicate a long-run relationship between primary balances/GDP and public net debt service/GDP. The results of the vector error correction model show that non-Ricardian policies were implemented throughout the period.

Having analysed the period of 1989.1-2012.2 and considering the new economic program aiming to strengthen the Turkish economy in May, 2001, we divide our whole research period into two sub-periods one of which is 1989.1-2001.1 and the other is 2001.2-2012.2 after making certain the presence of a structural break by performing Chow test. After identifying that the two sub-periods should be modelled separately, we adopted the cointegration and vector error correction model over the two periods one by one.

The cointegration test that we have performed between primary balances/GDP and public net debt service/GDP and primary balances/GDP and total public liabilities/GDP for our first sub-period of 1989.1-2001.1 indicates a cointegrating long-run relationship. The short-run results imply existence of fiscal policy dominant regime during the period 1989.1-2001.1 as expected. In 1980, Turkey embarked on a process of economic liberalization to catch up with developed countries. Removing price controls, subsidies and interest ceilings, liberalizing the foreign trade regime, relaxing capital controls, implementing some policies to attract foreign direct investments, and expanding the private sector were the main components of the new economic regime.

Because the liberalisation process of the 1980s was not adequately supported by strong macroeconomic policies and institutional reforms, expected returns of the new program could not be achieved. High, volatile and persistent inflation and high budget deficits worsened all the balances causing the monetary authority to lose its power to control price stability. As a result the economy suffered repeated crises during the 1990s.

In response to the crisis, the government introduced the new Economic Program, "Transition to a Stronger Economy", in 2001 in close cooperation with the IMF. Strict fiscal consolidation and achieving fiscal discipline, reducing the public debt, strengthening the banking system, making the central bank independent and introducing social security reform were the major components of this economic program. The central bank gained independence and authorized to focus on price stability. Direct financing of the public debt by the central bank was prohibited. On the fiscal side, generating a primary surplus of 6.5% of GDP was targeted in 2003 and beyond. With the embarkation of the new program, the achievement of the targets was implemented rigorously and a considerable economic recovery began to be observed such as sizeable primary surpluses and the decline in the stock of public debt.

Consequently, macroeconomic and structural policy shortcomings have been corrected by and large in the Turkish economy. The results of our econometric analysis related to the 2001.2-2012.2 period reflect the developments in the Turkish economy. In parallel with our expectations, the empirical evidence related to this second sub-period gives the impression of Ricardian regime.

In summary, our empirical results indicate that while the fiscal authority was the leading authority from 1989 to early 2001, by introduction of the new economic program, the monetary authority has become the leading one in Turkey. This paper shows that economic stability can partly be explained by a change in the balance of power between fiscal and monetary authorities. When the fiscal policies are the dominant policies, fiscal imbalances produce a continuing process of inflation and the monetary authority loses its power to control price stability and vice versa.

REFERENCES

Afonso, A. (2005). Ricardian Fiscal Regimes in the European Union. *European Central Bank, Working Paper Series*, No: 558.

Akçay, O. C., Alper, C. E., & Ozmucur, S. (2002). Budget Deficit, Inflation and Debt Sustainabilty: Evidence from Turkey, 1970-2000. In A. Kibritçioğlu, L. Rittenberg, & F. Selçuk (Eds.), *Inflation and Disinflation in Turkey* (pp. 77–96). London: Ashgate Publishing.

Aktaş, Z., Kaya, N., & Özlale, U. (2005). The Price Puzzle in Emerging Markets: Evidence from the Turkish Economy Using "Model Based" Risk Premium Derived from Domestic Fundamentals. *Central Bank of the Republic of Turkey, Economic Research Paper*, No: 05/02.

Akyüz, Y. (1990). Financial System and Policies in Turkey in the 1980s. In T. Arıcanlı & D. Rodrik (Eds.), *The Political Economy of Turkey* (pp. 98–131). London: Macmillan. doi:10.1007/978-1-349-11274-6_6

Bajo-Rubio, O., Díaz-Roldán, C., & Esteve, V. (2009). Deficit Sustainability and Inflation in EMU: An Analysis from the Fiscal Theory of the Price Level. *European Journal of Political Economy*, *25*(4), 525–539. doi:10.1016/j.ejpoleco.2009.04.001

Baldini, A., & Ribeiro, M. P. (2008). Fiscal and Monetary Anchors for Price Stability: Evidence from Sub-Saharan Africa. *IMF Working Paper,* WP/08/121.

Ballabriga, F., & Martínez-Mongay, C. (2002). Has EMU Shifted Policy? *European Commission, Directorate-General for Economic and Financial Affairs, Economics Papers*, No.166.

Bassetto, M. (2001). A Game-Theoretic View of the Fiscal Theory of the Price Level. *Federal Reserve Bank of Minneapolis, Working Paper 612*, March.

Bera, A. K., & Jarque, C. M. (1980). Efficient Tests for Normality, Homoscedasticity and Serial Independence of Regression Residuals. *Economics Letters*, *6*(3), 255–259. doi:10.1016/0165-1765(80)90024-5

Bianchi, F., & Ilut, C. (2014). Monetary/Fiscal Policy Mix and Agents' Beliefs. *NBER Working Paper,* 20194.

Bohn, H. (1998). The Behaviour of U.S. Public Debt and Deficits. *The Quarterly Journal of Economics*, *113*(3), 949–964. doi:10.1162/003355398555793

Breusch, T. S. (1979). Testing for Autocorrelation in Dynamic Linear Models. *Australian Economic Papers, 17*(31), 334–355. doi:10.1111/j.1467-8454.1978.tb00635.x

Breusch, T. S., & Pagan, A. R. (1979). A Simple Test for Heteroscedasticity and Random Coefficient Variation. *Econometrica, 47*(5), 1287–1294. doi:10.2307/1911963

Buiter, W. (1998, February). The Young Person's Guide to Neutrality, Price Level indeterminacy, Interest Rate Pegs and Fiscal Theories of the Price Level, *CEPR Discussion Paper* 1799.

Buiter, W. (1999). The Fallacy of the Fiscal Theory of the Price Level. *NBER Working Paper* 7302, August.

Buiter, W. (2001, July). The Fallacy of the Fiscal Theory of the Price Level Again. *Bank of England, Working Paper* 141.

Buti, M. (2003). Interactions and Coordination between Monetary and Fiscal Policies in EMU: What Are the Issues? In M. Buti (Ed.), *Monetary and Fiscal Policies in EMU: Interactions and Coordination*. Cambridge: Cambridge University Press.

Canzoneri, M. B., Cumby, R. E., & Diba, B. T. (2001). Is the Price Level Determined by the Needs of Fiscal Solvency? *The American Economic Review, 91*(5), 1221–1238. doi:10.1257/aer.91.5.1221

Carlstrom, C., & Fuerst, T. (2000). The Fiscal Theory of Price Level. *Federal Reserve Bank of Cleveland. Economic Review, Q-I, 36*(1), 22–32.

Çebi, C. (2012). The Interaction between Monetary and Fiscal Policies in Turkey: An Estimated New Keynesian DSGE Model. *Economic Modelling, 29*(4), 1258–1267. doi:10.1016/j.econmod.2012.04.014

Çevik, E. I., Dibooğlu, S., & Kutan, A. M. (2014). Monetary and Fiscal Policy Interactions: Evidence from Emerging European Economies. *Journal of Comparative Economics, 42*(4), 1079–1091. doi:10.1016/j.jce.2014.05.001

Cizre-Sakallıoğlu, U., & Yeldan, E. (2000). Politics, Society and Financial Liberalization: Turkey in the 1990s. *Development and Change, 31*(2), 481–508. doi:10.1111/1467-7660.00163

Cochrane, J. (1998). A Frictionless View of US Inflation. In B. Bernanke & J. Rotemberg (Eds.), NBER Macroeconomics Annual (pp. 323–384).

Cochrane, J. (2001). Long-Term Debt and Optimal Policy in the Fiscal Theory of the Price Level. *Econometrica, 69*(1), 69–116.

Cochrane, J. H. (2005). Money as Stock. *Journal of Monetary Economics, 52*(3), 501–528. doi:10.1016/j.jmoneco.2004.07.004

Creel, J., & Sterdyniak, H. (2001). La Théorie Budgetaire du Niveau Des Prix: Un Bilan Critique. *Revue d'Economie Politique, 111*(6), 909–940. doi:10.3917/redp.116.0909

Cushing, M. (1999). The Indeterminacy of Prices Under Interest Rate Pegging: The non-Ricardian Case. *Journal of Monetary Economics, 44*(1), 131–148. doi:10.1016/S0304-3932(99)00012-4

Daly, H., & Smida, M. (2014). Fiscal Theory of Price Level, *International Journal of Economics. Commerce and Management, 2*(11), 1–22.

Debrun, X., & Wyplosz, C. (1999). Onze Gouvernments et une Banque Centrale. *Revue d'Economie Politique*, *3*, 387–420.

Dickey, D. A., & Fuller, W. A. (1979). Distribution of the Estimators for Autoregressive Time Series with a Unit Root. *Journal of the American Statistical Association*, *74*(366), 427–431. doi:10.2307/2286348

Domaç, I. (2004). Explaining and Forecasting Inflation in Turkey, World Bank Policy Research (3287).

Engle, R. E., & Granger, C. W. J. (1987). Cointegration and Error-Correction: Representation, Estimation and Testing. *Econometrica*, *55*(2), 251–276. doi:10.2307/1913236

Godfrey, L. G. (1978). Testing Against General Autoregressive and Moving Average Error Models When the Regressors Include Lagged Dependent Variables. *Econometrica*, *46*(6), 1293–1302. doi:10.2307/1913829

Johansen, S. (1988). Statistical and Hypothesis Testing of Co-integration Vectors. *Journal of Economic Dynamics & Control*, *12*(2-3), 231–254. doi:10.1016/0165-1889(88)90041-3

Johansen, S., & Juselius, K. (1990). Maximum Likelihood Estimation and Inference on Cointegration-With Applications to the Demand for Money. *Oxford Bulletin of Economics and Statistics*, *52*(2), 169–210. doi:10.1111/j.1468-0084.1990.mp52002003.x

Leeper, E. (1991). Equilibria under 'Active' and 'Passive' Monetary Policies. *Journal of Monetary Economics*, *27*(1), 129–147. doi:10.1016/0304-3932(91)90007-B

McCallum, B. (1999a). *Issues in the Design of Monetary Policy Rules.* In J. Taylor & M. Woodford (Eds.). Handbook of Macroeconomics. London: North-Holland Pub. Co.

McCallum, B. (1999b, October). Theoretical Issues Pertaining to Monetary Unions. *NBER Working Paper* 7393.

McCallum, B. (2001). Indeterminacy, Bubbles, and the Fiscal Theory of Price Level Determination. *Journal of Monetary Economics*, *47*(1), 19–30. doi:10.1016/S0304-3932(00)00048-9

Mélitz, J. (2000). Some Cross-Country Evidence about Fiscal Policy Behaviour and Consequences for EMU, European Economy. *Reports and Studies*, *2*, 3–21.

Metin, K. (1998). The Relationship Between Inflation and Budget Deficit in Turkey. *Journal of Business & Economic Statistics*, *16*(4), 412–422.

Narayan, P. K. (2005). The Saving and Investment Nexus For China: Evidence from Cointegration Tests. *Applied Economics*, *37*(17), 1979–1990. doi:10.1080/00036840500278103

Nawaz, M., Iqbal, M., Ali, A., & Zaman, K. (2012). Fiscal Theory of Price Level: A Panel Data Analysis for Selected SAARC Countries. *Romanian Journal of Economic Forecasting*, *3*, 152–170.

Neyaptı, B. (2003). Budget Deficits and Inflation: The Roles of Central Bank Independence and Financial Market Development. *Contemporary Economic Policy*, *21*(4), 458–475. doi:10.1093/cep/byg025

Önder, İ., Türel, O., Somel, C., & Ekinci, N. (1993). *Türkiye'de Kamu Maliyesi, Finansal Yapı ve Politikalar*. İstanbul: Tarih Vakfı Yurt Yayınları.

Öniş, Z. (1998). Political Economy of Turkey in the 1980s, Anatomy of Unorthodox Liberalizm. In Z. Öniş (Ed.), *State and Market* (pp. 183–196). İstanbul: Boğaziçi University Press.

Özatay, F. (1996). The Lessons From the 1994 Crisis in Turkey: Public Debt (Mis)management and Confidence Crisis. *Yapı Kredi Economic Review*, *7*(1), 21–37.

Özatay, F. (1997). Sustainability of Fiscal Deficits, Monetary Policy and Inflation Stabilization: The Case of Turkey. *Journal of Policy Modeling*, *19*(6), 661–681. doi:10.1016/S0161-8938(97)00015-X

Özatay, F. (2007). Monetary policy challenges for Turkey in the European Union Accession Process. In E. Başçı, J. V. Hagen, & S. Togan (Eds.), *Macroeconomic Policies for EU Accession* (pp. 130–165). London: Edward Elgar Publishing. doi:10.4337/9781847205230.00014

Perron, P. (1989, November). The Great Crash, the Oil-Price Shock, and the Unit-Root Hypothesis. *Econometrica*, *57*(6), 1361–401.

Pesaran, M. H., Shin, Y., & Smith, R. J. (2001). Bounds Testing Approaches to the Analysis of Level Relationships. *Journal of Applied Econometrics*, *16*(3), 289–326. doi:10.1002/jae.616

Ramsey, J. B. (1969). Tests for Specification Errors in Classical Linear Least Squares Regression Analysis. *Journal of the Royal Statistical Society. Series B. Methodological*, *31*(2), 350–371.

Rocha, F., & Silva, E. (2004). Teoria fiscal do Nível de Preços: Um Teste Para a Economia Brasileira No Período 1966/2000. *Pesquisa e Planejamento Economico*, *34*(3), 419–435.

Rodrik, D. (1990). Premature Liberalization and Incomplete Stabilization: The Özal Decade in Turkey. *NBER Working Paper Series* No. 3300. Massachusetts: National Bureau of Economic Research.

Sargent, T. J., & Wallace, N. (1981). Some Unpleasant Monetarist Arithmetic. *Federal Reserve Bank of Minneapolis Quarterly Review*, *5*(3), 1–17.

Sims, C. (1997). *Fiscal Foundations of Price Stability in Open Economies, Mimeo.* Department of Economics, Princeton University.

Sims, C. A. (1994). A Simple Model for Study of the Determination of the Price Level and the Interaction of Monetary and Fiscal Policy. *Economic Theory*, *4*(3), 381–399. doi:10.1007/BF01215378

Tanner, E., & Ramos, A. (2002). Fiscal Sustainability and Monetary and Versus Fiscal Dominance: Evidence from Brazil, 1999-2000. *IMF Working Paper* WP/ 02/5.

Tekin-Koru, A., & Özmen, E. (2003). Budget Deficits, Money Growth and Inflation: The Turkish Evidence. *Applied Economics*, *35*(5), 591–596. doi:10.1080/0003684022000025440

Woodford, M. (1994). Monetary Policy and Price Level Determinacy in a Cash-In-Advance Economy. *Economic Theory*, *4*(3), 345–380. doi:10.1007/BF01215377

Woodford, M. (1995). Price Level Determinacy Without Control of a Monetary Aggregate. *Carnegie-Rochester Conference Series on Public Policy*, *43*(Dec), 1–46. doi:10.1016/0167-2231(95)90033-0

Woodford, M. (1998). Doing Without Money: Controlling Inflation in a Post-Monetary World. *Review of Economic Dynamics*, *1*(1), 173–219. doi:10.1006/redy.1997.0006

Woodford, M. (2001). Fiscal Requirement for Price Stability. *Journal of Money, Credit and Banking*, *33*(3), 669–728. doi:10.2307/2673890

Yeldan, E. (2001). *Küreselleşme Sürecinde Türkiye Ekonomisi: Bölüşüm, Birikim ve Büyüme*. İstanbul: Iletişim Yayınları.

Zivot, E., & Andrews, D. W. K. (1992). Further Evidence on the Great Crash, the Oil-Price Shock, and the Unit-Root Hypothesis. *Journal of Business & Economic Statistics*, *10*(3), 251–270.

Zoli, E. (2005, April). How Does Fiscal Policy Affect Monetary Policy in Emerging Market Countries? *Bank of International Settlements Working Papers*, No. 174.

KEY TERMS AND DEFINITIONS

Budget Constraint: The requirement that over the relevant horizon, the value of spending must equal the value of receipts.

Equilibrium: A situation of balance between various forces, such that there are no forces leading to change if the system is left undisturbed.

Fiscal Policy: Government's policy relating to levels of spending and taxation.

Monetary Policy: The central bank's decisions on the terms (usually short-term interest rates) at which it will lend Money and buy securities to the private financial sector.

Nominal Interest Rate: Interest rate paid/received without making allowance for fact that price of goods is changing.

Real Interest Rate: The cost of borrowing (or the return to saving) in real terms, i.e., after adjusting for inflation.

ENDNOTES

1 It has to be emphasized that, despite its popularity, there are some critical discussion of the Fiscal Theory of Price Level on theoretical grounds. Discussions and the underlying assumptions of these discussions can be found in the studies of McCallum (1999a, 1999b, 2001), Buiter (1998,1999, 2001), Cushing (1999) and Bassetto (2001).

2 Terminologically, Woodford employs "Ricardian" and "non-Ricardian" dichotomy of fiscal policy. Leeper and Sims use similar classification as "passive" and "active" fiscal policy.

3 Please see Özatay (1997, 2007), Tekin-Koru and Özmen (2003), Domaç (2004) and Aktaş, Kaya and Özkale (2005) for detailed information on inflation in Turkey.

4 We obtained total public liabilities by adding monetary base to public net debt service.

5 Monetary base is calculated as the sum of open market operations and reserve balances (deposits held by banks and other depository institutions in their accounts at the Central Bank of Republic of Turkey).

Chapter 21
Impacts of Global Financial Crisis and Changes in Monetary Policy of Central Banks:
An Analysis of Central Bank of the Republic of Turkey (CBRT) and Bank of Israel (BOI)

İsmail Şiriner
Batman University, Turkey

Keremet Shaiymbetova
Kocaeli University, Turkey

ABSTRACT

The Great Financial Crisis (GFC) has hit developed and developing countries through a number of transmission channel. Some impacts are already disappearing while others are still to strike. In MENA region developing countries to experience the crisis were those with the most globally integrated financial sectors. Next came the impact on trade, as volumes and prices of commodities and manufactures collapsed across the globe. Successful economic policies pursued in the past do not promise these countries' immunity from the crisis. In fact, some MENA countries have already shown a limited capacity to learn from other countries' previous financial crises. Post-crisis spillovers and heightened capital flows have triggered a search for alternative monetary policy frameworks, especially for Turkey and Israel in MENA economies. This paper analyzes the review of the region's monetary regimes and policies, including: monetary policy expansion of the monetary policy framework in promoting financial stability alongside the primary price stability objective.

DOI: 10.4018/978-1-5225-0053-7.ch021

INTRODUCTION

After the Great Moderation Process of the world economy, financial system and real economies face to unexampled crisis (Great Financial Crisis). The GFC has hit developed and developing countries through a number of transmission channels. Some impacts are already disappearing while others are still to strike. It has caused unique responses from central banks of most affected developing and advanced economies. Central banks and supervisions of the economies had to create new framework and unconventional instruments for monetary policy, which have headed to deviations in central banks' balance sheets, and to arrangements designed for leading expectations concerning long-term interest rates.

During and after GFC recent literature points out a huge number of studies, which examine batten down the hatches by central bank under the monetary policy in many economies as a part of GFC. The GFC has highlighted important shortcomings of the literature on monetary policy, and in particular, huge cavities in the forming of interconnection among the financial system and macroeconomic policies.

Even before the crisis, most central bankers understood that financial disruptions could be very damaging to the economy. This explains the extraordinary actions that central banks took during the crisis to shore up financial markets (Mishkin, 2011). Post-crisis period has brought emerging consensus that financial stability should be an objective of central banks. But, on the contrary opinion remains divided as to what extent it can be considered as an additional objective of monetary policy or completely separated. It is argued that the monetary policy horizon for achieving the inflation target could be lengthened to facilitate taking into account the financial stability concerns. IMF (2010) emphasized that in adopting such an approach, central banks need to lookout against the persistent deviations of inflation which may otherwise dilute policy accountability and create uncertainty of the long-term commitment to price stability.

The view that monetary policy should allow policymakers to lean against the building up of financial imbalances, even if short-term inflation expectations remain anchored, appears to be gaining ground. The balance of views within the central banking community has been shifting in this direction (Cagliarini, Kent & Stevens, 2010; Carney, 2009; Fischer, 2011; Shirakawa, 2009; Trichet, 2009; & Woodford, 2010). However Mishkin (2009, pp. 12-23) argued that the ineffectiveness of the monetary policy during financial crises is not only wrong, but it may also promote policy stagnancy in the face of a severe contractionary shock. To the contrary, monetary policy is more effective during financial crises because aggressive monetary policy easing can make adverse feedback loops less likely.

This paper highlights the main effects of GFC on the monetary policy and central banks behavior. We focus on monetary policy implementations by the Central Bank of the Republic of Turkey (CBRT) and Bank of Israel (BOI) that helped to temper the impact of the global financial crisis and as a result that mitigated the shocks to the economies of these countries. The paper is structured as follows: first the confront conditions of GFC and compulsory monetary policy development under financialization of the world economy is analyzed, then we summarize the changes in monetary policy caused by GFC from inflation targeting to financial stability, from financial stability to macroprudential polices which is named generally as unconventional monetary policy measures. A last study examines the main structure of "new" monetary policy and implementations of Monetary Policy by BOI and CBRT.

THE INITIAL CONDITIONS OF CRISIS: FINANCIALIZATION AND COMPULSORY FRAMEWORK FOR MONETARY POLICY

Financialization was one of three megatrends that swept the world in the last three decades, where the others are free markets and globalization. It is defined as the growing importance in daily financial activities, both at the national and international levels. The financialization dream was that financial innovation was creative, and that it supports economic development and contributes to global market efficiency. The outcome was a massive bubble, inflated by hidden leverage and a collapse requiring massive public sector bailout, from which the world has yet to totally unwind (Sheng, 2014). Epstein (2005, pp. 3) has described *financialization as the increasing role of financial motives, financial markets, financial actors and financial institutions in the operation of the domestic and international economies.*

The term used to summarize a broad set of the changes in the relation between the "*financial*" and "*real*" sector. The debate on financialization draws a range of different theoretical and methodological approaches and it is difficult to summarize[1]. The Cultural economists have highlighted the incompleteness and contradictions of the discursive strategies of financialization (Froud, Johal, Leaver & Williams, 2006, pp. 13), while macroeconomists have tried to identify the conditions for viable growth regimes; economic sociologists have argued that financial markets have to be constructed by specific actors with specific interest (MacKenzie & Millo, 2003), while post-Keynesian economists have highlighted the fragile nature of finance-led growth[2].

During financialization the importance of central banks increased and monetary policy stepped forward to struggle against inflation. High inflation in the advanced economies in the 1970s and in emerging economies in the 1980s and 1990s was instrumental in shaping modern thoughts about the practice of central banking (Figure 1). The tenets of the resulting framework are familiar and, to a large extent, uncontroversial (Eichengreen et. al., 2011)[3]:

First, there are no permanent tradeoffs between inflation and unemployment a sustained higher level of inflation does not lead to higher growth and a sustained lower level of unemployment. Second, high and volatile inflation depresses growth and distorts the allocation of resources. Third, inflation disproportionately harms the poorest segments of society, which lack instruments for protecting themselves from its disruptive effects. For all of these reasons, price stability was defined as a cornerstone of monetary policy

The actions needed to achieve price stability, such as the maintenance of high interest rates, can be politically unpopular, among other reasons because of slow growth. It follows that the pursuit of price stability can be made more credible and thus more effective by granting independence or at least operational autonomy to the central bank. Otherwise, central banks may be subject to political pressure to attach greater weight to other objectives, making it harder for them to contain inflationary expectations and deliver desirable outcomes (Eichengreen et. al., 2011).[4]

As was mentioned above financialization involves a shift in economic gravity from production and from the service sector to the financial sector. Similarly, financial assets are diverted away from the private sector to the public sector as deficits remain high and debt accumulates at a worrying rate. What should be seen is that what we are witnessing is a monetary-policy induced de-industrialization of the US economy. Knowing that all this is happening is one thing, but it is important to know what the fundamental cause behind this transformation is. There are many that would blame globalization

Figure 1. Inflation rate (average consumer prices)
Source: IMF[5] (here inflation rate compares the annual average consumer prices with the previous year's consumer prices.)

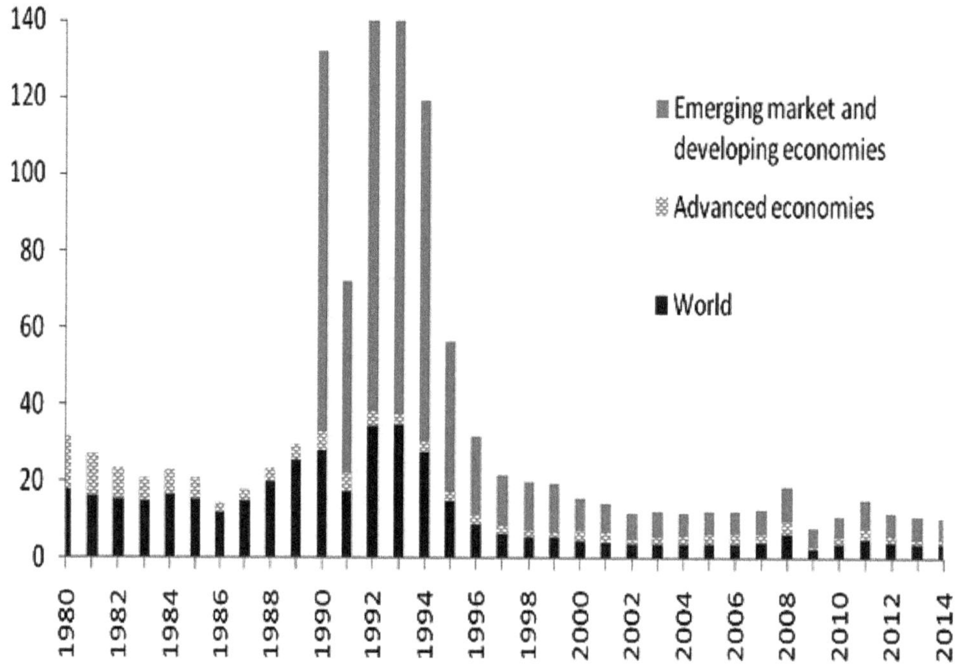

or economic liberalization and reply by suggesting that there must be more regulations or government interventions (Kriper, 2005, pp. 89).

What they overlook is that non-conventional monetary policies that have kept interest so low for so long and financial markets drive the process of financialization of the US economy awash with excess liquidity. In turn, these monetary policies are also the cause behind a sluggish and incomplete recovery from the Great Recession of 2007-2008. Whereas such artificially low interest rates were justified as a means to encourage business investments or home purchases, banks face weak incentives to offer credit to either firms or households. The reason is that it is more costly and risky to make loans to start-up businesses or households than to trade financial assets (Panitch, Leo, Albo, Greg, Gindin & Sam, 2010).

To issue new loans, banks must hire more loan managers to review applications, other staff to assess value of collateral and accountants to keep track of all this. And low interest rates also discourage saving by firms and households that are more likely to seek a "flutter" in placing surplus income in more risky and more remunerative financial assets, like bonds or stocks. As much as there have been fewer IPOs for new companies, most of the trading of shares is of companies that already exist (Orhangazi, 2008).

Before the introduction of "unconventional" monetary policy, financial assets served as contingent claims such that expanding the scope of financial markets and instruments would tend to increase overall efficiency. In turn, markets could do a better job pricing future outcomes to improve current allocation of resources relative to anticipated future needs and economic actors could seek portfolios with higher returns relative to risks (Foster, 2010).

With central bankers around the world following the lead of the FED, financial assets are busy chasing bubbles around the world with little left to spark a solid economic recovery and sustainable new job creation. There are those that think that increased concentrations of income, diversion of resources to the financial sector and a recovery require more regulations, more stimulus and perpetuation of current monetary policy. But all of these are symptoms of the same cause "unconventional" monetary policy (Stockhammer, 2010).

INFLATION TARGETING, EXCHANGE RATES AND ASSET PRICES

By the early 2000s, a growing number of central banks, in advanced countries and emerging markets alike, had converged on a policy framework; *flexible inflation targeting* that seemed capable of achieving these desiderata and delivering macroeconomic stability at the national and international levels. An inflation-targeting regime, in which the policy instrument is the interest rate, must operate within the context of a flexible exchange rate. This efficiently and unambiguously solves the well-known impossible trinity for financially open countries, and it allows the control of interest rates at a level consistent with the inflationary objective. Adding an exchange rate objective weakens the capacity to control the interest rate, affecting the ability to meet the inflation target (Walsh, 2009, pp. 199-201).

However, the exchange rate generally has effects on monetary policy, because persistent movements in it do affect inflation. In this case, the natural result is a leaning against the wind. When the exchange rate appreciates substantially, it prompts a decline in inflation in the medium term, which results in a reduction in the interest rate. This, in turn, induces pressures for depreciation. Nevertheless, these effects were not very significant because, in a floating regime, the pass-through coefficient from the exchange rate to inflation was limited (Kontonikas, Alexandros, & Ioannidis, 2005, pp. 1119).

In this orthodox view, monetary policy focuses on controlling inflation and works by managing expectations of future policy rates, which by the expectations theory of the yield curve determine the long-term interest rates that influence aggregate demand. Financial stability was attained by microprudential regulation of bank capital that counteracts the moral hazard generated by deposit insurance, together with periodic supervisory assessments and the necessary strictures meant to prevent excessive risk taking and malfeasance. Regardless of whether the microprudential regulator is situated in the central bank or a separate specialized regulatory agency, financial regulation is seen as a separate activity (Svensson, 2012).

Central bankers nowadays often observe that flexible inflation targeting was never as straightforward as this framework suggests and that issues of financial stability and spillovers were always on their minds. Still, it remains accurate to say that the basic theoretical framework sketched above did much to shape their thinking. Its clarity and simplicity enabled it to gain adherents in academia and financial markets as well as in central banks (Blinder, 2010, pp. 123-125).

An expansionary monetary policy undoubtedly can induce excessive increases in credit and asset prices. The ultimate role of monetary policy is to smooth the business cycle and control inflation. Therefore, very expansionary monetary policies, beyond what is needed to reach the inflation target, and could conceivably exacerbate an economic boom. Moreover, such a policy would have serious consequences for output once the monetary impulse is withdrawn. However, expansionary monetary policy by itself cannot explain the severity of the financial collapse and the recent global recession (Caballero, 2010, pp. 98-102).

FROM PRICE STABILITY TO FINANCIAL STABILITY

The central banks of the largest advanced economies have taken unprecedented policy actions and measures to combat the results of GFC, the deepest and most prolonged period of recession and financial instability since the 1930s.

The depth of the financial crisis has pointed out the need to reorganize the framework of financial stability and, above all, the objectives of financial regulation. One of the main factors of the crisis was inability of market actors to adequately assess systemic risk. As the result, the practical example is stated in situation where the bankruptcy of some financial institutions or even a group of institutions does not destroy intermediaries' services (Čihák, 2006, pp. 7). It may happen if financial intermediaries' services have close substitutes available for potential borrowers. But in this definition some important points are missing. For example asset bubbles. An explosion of asset bubbles during the recent crisis has shown that not all of them resulted in a breach of financial intermediaries. Asset bubbles can influence the financial stability only if key financial intermediaries use high debts to buy assets in the market that inflated the bubble, so they will be severely hit when the bubble bursts. In such a situation they may bump into balance constraints, the ability to significantly dislocate the intermediaries' service, and thereby adversely shape to the real economy. But not all asset-bubbles are a sign of the financial instability; only those that have an effect on the institutions involved in financial intermediation of real economy characterize it. Development of asset bubbles helps to demonstrate how the definition of financial instability is important to understand what tools are needed to counter it (Illing, 2001, pp. 3-5).

After the crisis, however, there is understood that the conventional approach to central banking needs to be rethought. Critics identified several related reasons[6]:

- The conventional approach is too narrowly focused, as it fails to account adequately for financial-sector risk.
- The conventional framework assumes limited or nonexistent cross-border spillovers of monetary policies. In fact spillovers are often of first-order importance. They can adversely influence monetary policy management, accentuate the volatility of real activity and increase financial-sector risk.
- If countries follow different monetary policy regimes (e.g., inflation targeting and exchange rate targeting)[7], the incompatibility of national monetary policies in the face of spillovers will strengthen.

Spillovers may be additionally accentuated if central banks follow unconventional monetary interventions (e.g. when interest rates are at their floor and constrained by the zero bound). As a consequence of weak domestic demand, as well as distressed banks unwilling to lend, the portfolio adjustments driven by unconventional policies may largely serve to increase of capital flows to countries with stronger growth prospects rather than boosting domestic credit as intended. High levels of government debt in developed countries and the slowing growth of traditional export markets for developing countries cause new sources of political pressure. The central banks will be under this pressure and it will be difficult to ignore it. The problem is that policy independence in theory may exceed policy independence in practice. In other words, the conventional framework fails to consider that national policies of one country can have powerful cross-border impacts to other country. The affected partner may not be able to adequately counteract these with exchange rate movements. In part this is caused by the fact that the existing system is not, in fact, one of fully flexible exchange rates (Carney, 2012).

In practice, some countries can effectively target exchange rates. For instance China's tight management of its currency's value relative to the US dollar is being a prominent case in point. This is the consequence of international transmission. It occurs even under flexible exchange rates, through both trade channels and capital flows. The consequences include the future re-emergence of global imbalances and the explosion of trade and capital controls when countries seek further insulation from cross-border spillovers (Stone et. al., 2009).

MONETARY POLICY AND FINANCIAL STABILITY[8]

Primarily central banks of emerging[9] and advanced economies gradually adopted and used combination of inflation targeting regimes and exchange rate flexibility. Efficiency of monetary policy was strongly believed to provide macroeconomic and financial stability. The near relation between inflation targeting and macroeconomic stability caused the confidence and belief that financial and macroeconomic stability can only and exclusively be attained by microprudential authority and regulation. Monetary policy would guard the inflation by functioning based on expectations of future interest rates. Also exchange rates would provide smoother balance of payments assays. The aim of microprudential policy regulation in the financial system including bank capital and banking supervision is to avoid disproportionate risk taking. But the volume has harmed reliance in this policy combination and independent financial authorization and regulation and synchronization of asset price booms and breakdowns that caused the recent the GFC (Canuto & Cavallari, 2013, pp.3). After the GFC convergence thinking started to change and found worldwide acceptance of coordination of monetary policy and macroprudential regulation as these are necessary for macroeconomic and financial stability. Also the confidence and faith in flexible exchange rate regimes, as adequate shock absorber, has been discredited.

After the GFC appeared two main lively debates among policymakers and scholars (Svensson, 2012); one of excited discussion was on the reasons of the GFC and how the risk of the prospective crises can be eliminated; and as a main result that loose monetary policy was underlying the crisis. The latter one dealt with future monetary policy after crisis; whether or not it should be revised according the consequences and lessons taken from recent crisis, and definition of relation between monetary policy and financial stability.

Experiencing the GFC start to highlight macroprudential approach which should not focus only on inflation, but it should also take into account the possible effects of capital inflows on credit, asset prices, risk-taking behavior and ultimately financial stability (Moreno, 2011, pp. 6). To understand the definition of financial stability and its interconnection between monetary and macroprudential policies it is required to discover consequences of linkages between monetary policy and macroprudential policy.

It is difficult to reach the precise definition of financial stability, as well as identify and even measure the financial stability. Actually, scholars usually rely on vague interpretation such as '*I'll know it when I see it*', that is not sufficient, especially for macroprudential policy authorities who try to create functioning delineation of the event to forecast and forestall the financial distortions and distress. The obvious approach to identify financial instability is to concentrate on the consequences of what happens within the global world and other major financial centers. As Deputy Governor of the Bank of England, Paul Tucker (2011), stayed: *financial stability prevails where the financial system is sufficiently resilient that worries about bad states of the world do not affect confidence in the ability of the system to deliver its core services to the rest of the economy. The key words are 'confidence' and 'resilience'*(Barwell, 2013). In other words, the financial stability mainly focuses on sustaining a stable delivery of daily financial key services which the all economy depends on such as payments services, credit supply etc.

As we restrictively defined or explained financial (in) stability, we will now focus on the financial stability and monetary policy interaction. For long period it has been understood that monetary policy can affect financial stability. The effects can potentially become adverse. The literature of the financial markets' imperfections knows several channels of the influence of monetary policy on financial stability. It can directly or indirectly control the tightness of loan limits and probability of default; the tracking the risky inducements of arbitrators; and positive/negative and pecuniary externalities such as asset prices and exchange rates that caused by changing price policy. Table 1 illustrates a number of channels from theoretical models and the effects of changes in the monetary policy stance on financial stability. Table 1 also sums up interconnected practical case (IMF, 2012).

While starting to consider and keeping thinking about the relationship between the monetary policy and financial stability, it is important and beneficial to distinguish short from long term (Alberola et al, 2011, pp.11-14). Economic theory and empirical cases provide a comprehensible conclusion that there is no trade-off between monetary stability and financial stability in the long term. While monetary policy strategy concentrated on low and stable inflation supports of financial stability. According to the empirical evidence monetary instability is one of the primary reasons that have historically led to financial instability. Therefore monetary stability is accepted as a compulsory but it is insufficient conditions for financial stability. The short-term relation between these two is even more complicated than as seen in the long-term. It is a crucial factor to cope with financial stability at the macro or systemic level where central banks also play a leading role.

*Table 1. Monetary Policy Effects on Financial Stability**

Sources of Financial Instability	Channel	Predicted Effect (↓ improves stability)		Selected Empirical Evidence		
		↓r	↑r			
Borrowing Constraints	Balance Sheet Channel	↑	↓	Sengupta (2010)	↑r	↓
				Jiménez and others (2009)	↑r	↓
				Gertler and Gilchrist (1994)	↑r	↓
				Asea and Blomberg (1998	↑r	↓
Risky Behavior of Financial Institutions	Risk-taking Channel	↓	↑	Jiménez and others (2009)	↓r	↓
				Ioannidou and others (2009)	↓r	↓
				Merrouche and Nier (2010)	↓r	X
	Risk-shifting Channel	↑	↓	Gan (2004)	↑r	↓
				Landier and others (2011)	↑r	↓
Externalities through Aggregate Prices	Asset price Channel	↓	↑	Altunbas and others (2012)	↓r	↓
				Del Negro and Otrok (2007)	↓r	↓
				IMF (2009)	↓r	X
	Exchange rate Channel	↑	↓	Hahm and others (2012)	↑r	↓
				Merrouche and Nier (2010)	↑r	↓
				Jonsson (2009)	↑r	↓

Source: IMF, 2012, pp. 7

↓r means a decrease of policy rates, ↑r means an increase of policy rates,"↓" means a decline of stability, "↑"an improvement of stability, and "X" no statistically significant effect.

Table 1. sum up how monetary policy effects on financial stability from different points of view.

Although many central banks were aware of serious destructive influence of financial disorders on the macro economy, central banks' instruments and models couldn't ensure necessary analytical proofs and information for prediction of the financial disorders as a major source of business cycle fluctuations. As a result, this logically caused a contradiction between monetary policy and financial stability. Monetary policy instruments focused on inflation and output gaps decrease. Afterwards prudential regulation and supervision prevented unwarranted risk which could promote financial instability (Hahm et al., 2012, pp. 4). Even though many central banks were kind to the dichotomy between those two policies, there were obvious sights that monetary policy could head towards financial stability concerns with pursuant respond to latent asset price bubble. As the asset prices are main factor in the monetary transmission channels, the intense debate concerned with question how should central banks react to potential asset price bubbles before the GFC[10].

This conflict in policies also causes reducing the credibility of central banks. What is clear in the context of financial stability is that monetary policy and macroprudential policies should be viewed as accompaniments, not replacements for preventing financial instability (Torre et al., 2012).

Modifications in the monetary policy approach can affect the tightness of borrowing constraints and the probability of default. Monetary expansionary relaxes collateral constraints, mitigating financial distortions both on the demand and supply side of credit. On the other hand, a decreasing of borrowing rates can adversely influence borrowers' quality. This can lead to higher default rates and hypothetically triggering a crisis. Changes in the monetary policy stance can influence the risk-seeking behavior of financial intermediaries by many channels. Two of the channels may move in reverse directions, as follows (IMF, 2012, pp. 7-8):

- *Risk taking.* Tighten monetary policy rates can encourage banks to wide their balance sheets and loosen monitoring and tracing borrowers. As result the other agents can also start seeking more risks in order to earn higher profits. These effects are possibly to be worse while monetary policy works to suit overlong expansions time. If monetary policy is anticipated to slowdown in the period of recessions to accommodate the financial system, it can motivate to associate further risks.
- *Risk shifting.* Increase in monetary policy rates can reduce intermediation margins, and push lenders, especially weakly capitalized intermediaries, to seek more risk. This channel may strengthen just prior a crisis, when intermediary force is high and competition limits the effect of policy rates to lending rates. As a result of rising in policy rates, the yield curve will straighten and this could require banks to seek risk in order to maintain profits.

To recapitulate, monetary policy, interacting with financial distortions, would have often ambiguous net effect on financial stability. This is caused by several channels working simultaneously. Their influence may differ according to the stage of financial cycle, financial structure and other characteristics of particular country.

GREAT FINANCIAL CRISIS AND CENTRAL BANKS

One crucial lesson that was not the first but forgotten one, enforced from this crisis is the linkage of financial cycle with economic cycle. As of 1990s, the world economy rapidly grew and it was named Great Moderation. In those years there were also crises but they were only bounded by developing countries and those economies accused by employing poor economic policies and weak institutional structure. Central Banks and economists developed macroeconomic models with very little role of financial frictions. Even if there were any frictions, it was assumed that markets would take care of themselves (Agrawal, 2010). Before the GFC, while supposing a contradiction between monetary and financial stability policies, there was almost common consent between / within most central banks and many researchers in theory and practice about followed policy framework for flexible inflation targeting by monetary authority such as central bank. Comparatively, there was minor consensus for tone reaction and responsibilities of the central banks to the asset-price bubbles. Inflation targeting as a main monetary policy framework is pursued by almost all central banks[11]. In the framework of inflation targeting regime, central banks involved a strong, credible liability to stabilize inflation mostly at clear numerical face in the long term, but at the same time in short term, it granted to follow stabilization of output in its natural levels for the central bank (Hahm et al., 2012).

Also it has to be mentioned that some factors that were barely interrelated with monetary policy like macroeconomic conditions caused the GFC such as (Svensson, 2012, pp. 38);

- Global imbalances resulting to low real interest rates and high asset prices;
- The Great Moderation period that contributed to a systematic risk underestimation and a significant growth of credit;
- Twisted inducements in financial markets followed by risen exorbitant levels of leverage, risk taking and a lack of due diligence;
- Regulatory and supervisory failures underestimating and disregarding the frailty of the financial sector;
- Outrageous information problems with extremely complex asset-backed securities and enormous hidden off-balance-sheet liabilities;
- Some of very specific circumstances, e.g. the U.S. support of homeownership for low-income inhabitant and related subprime mortgages contributing to the U.S. housing boom.

Beginning of 1990s, to encourage economic growth and welfare in advanced economies, (which caused the Great Moderation), monetary policy authorities have been orientated by the principle of stabilizing inflation forms under flexible exchange rate regimes. General consensus was that stable and lower inflation would diminish risk premium and support financial stability. As a result, several central banks have been given clear instructions for inflation targeting. At the end they have been extremely succeeded to catch this aim. Even though, this policy and guiding has not been sufficient to avoid the asset price busts (Prakash & Pau, 2012). As Hahm et al., (2012) mentioned, central banks mostly acknowledged on important role of financial frictions in business cycle instabilities and, the GFC relieve that the adverse impacts of financial disorders on whole economy and agents economic activity could be far worse than was anticipated for advanced economies. The GFC made it clear that financial resistances have distinguished and focus of macroeconomic policy analysis. Macro econometric models which are employed to estimate and forecast future policy analysis by central banks, herein after could not rule out financial frictions, as it was before GFC.

Another important point for central banks after GFC is that price and output stability cannot guarantee financial stability. Before the GFC, in academia and central banks, the general consensus was especially success of stable prices by inflation targeting strategy, and output stability, would ensure financial stability and contribute to that[12]. Once after achievement of price and output stabilities by monetary policy, as consequences of this policy, it will possibly stabilize asset prices and most probably avoid the asset price bubbles.

Without a doubt, as Great Moderation, central banker's achievement in stabilizing inflation and the reduced volatility of business cycle fluctuations, made especially monetary authorities self-satisfied and risk neutral from financial disorders. The mid-climate of economic environment leading up to GFC, however, certainly did not guard the economy from financial instability and disorders. Indeed, it may have promoted it. As a result, what are the implications of these lessons for basic policy strategy? (Hahm et al., 2012, pp. 11-14):

- **Flexible Inflation Targeting:** The first key point is that the lessons from the crisis do not invalidate the benefits of having a strong, credible commitment to stabilize inflation in the long run, which is the key rationale for adopting a flexible inflation-targeting framework.
- **The Lean vs. Clean Debate***:* In thinking about this debate, it is worth distinguishing between two different types of asset-price bubbles. Not all asset price bubbles are alike. Financial history and the GFC indicate that one type of bubble, which is the best referred to as a credit-driven bubble, can be highly dangerous. However, there is a second type of bubble that is far less dangerous, which can be referred to as an irrational exuberance bubble. This type of bubble is driven solely by overly optimistic expectations and poses much less risk to the financial system than credit- driven bubbles. However, the distinction between the two types of bubbles, one which (credit-driven) is much more costly than the other, suggests that the lean versus clean debate may have been miscast.

The accusation against monetary policy-makers is that they allowed an unsustainable growth of bank credit and asset prices to continue unchecked for far too long. Some conclude from this that the objectives of monetary policy should be altered to include financial as well as price stability. According to this view, rather than being focused purely on control of inflation, interest rates should also be used to dampen unsustainable credit expansion and asset price growth. Monetary policy should be used pro-actively to 'lean' against the credit cycle, instead of just being used to 'clean', i.e. to deal with a collapse of credit and asset prices after the event. On the other hand this implies that central banks step back from their current focus on price stability, lessening the inflation-targeting regimes adopted by central banks. The Governor of the Bank of England argues to the contrary, that monetary policy arrangements do not need to be changed. According to King (2009): *Inflation targeting is a necessary but not sufficient condition for stability in the economy as a whole. When a policy is necessary but not sufficient, the answer is not to abandon, but to augment it. Indeed, the overarching lesson of this crisis is that the authorities lacked sufficient policy instruments to take effective actions.* (Milne, 2009, pp. 609, 623-626)

Before the GFC, financial supervision and financial regulation was enough to achieve financial stability target for central banks, while price stability was a task to achieve by monetary policy. According to this approach, monetary policy made mainly contribution to financial stability by realizing suitable and optimal environment for macroeconomic stability. After the GFC, it has been observed that this approach is not sufficient to achieve the aims like financial stability by central banks and avoid assets bubbles. So that there is a developing broad consensus that monetary policy and financial stability should be more combined than before throughout policy agenda of the central banks. In addition employment started to be an essential problem and Keynesian economists argued that monetary policy that is focused on low inflation would not automatically prevent from unemployment as it was thought before. The GFC has shown that interest rate control was ineffective and economy needs other tools to achieve prosperity (Palley, 2015).

Macroprudential policy became a fundamental item in monetary policy settings after GFC. An optimal design of macroprudential policy could focus efficiently on the financial stability targets and, through its interaction with the monetary policy and microprudential policies could adapt better objectives and tools in the central banks' policy framework. The combination of a more articulated macroprudential framework in the policy toolbox of central banks contains two apparatuses: macroprudential tools and surveillance (Alberola et al., 2011). When central banks perform their target they still pursue the goal of preserving price stability and continue the evolution of real and financial sector. Therefore, a supplementary interrelation between monetary and macroprudential policies has been encouraged.

GFC affected all kinds of financial regulatory structures and almost in each country economy policy makers started re-evaluating and re-designing its structure. With this new shakeout, financial regulation has two joint themes (Agrawal, 2010); first, central banks become more responsible for heading the financial system. Second, countries start to set up a kind of central council that compose of all the financial regulators and can coordinate the overall policies. Usually the council is either being directed by Central Bank management or Finance Minister, subject to each country. After extended discussions between academics, central bankers and policy makers, with different country experience, central banks become as main ruler of macroprudential policies, because central banks have a competitive advantage and study macroeconomic and financial markets comprehensively[13].

However there is still no common answer from experience and debates, but in monetary economics proofs partly show that policy works finest when it is transparent, however there are circumstances when discretion is necessary[14] (Agrawal, 2010). As Blanchard et al. (2010, pp. 209) describe *The main challenge, here, is to find the right trade-off between a sophisticated system, fine-tuned to each marginal change in systemic risk, and an approach based on simple-to-communicate triggers and easy-to-implement rules.*

Monetary policy and regulation both offer plenty of cyclical tools. But the issue comes how to achieve coordination between the monetary and the regulatory authorities, or should the central bank be assigned for both policies. We can observe increasing trend of separation of the two authorities, but this can be challenged. Central banks are evident suitable candidates as macroprudential regulators. In some countries they already regulate the banks as they have ideal position for monitoring macroeconomic developments. The problems of coordination of actions of two separate agencies were fully displayed during the crisis, e.g. on the occasion of the bailout of Northern Rock. The other arguments for centralization of macroprudential responsibilities within the central bank are the potential implications of monetary policy decisions for leverage and risk. In the past there were two main reasons against giving both powers to the central bank. Firstly, concern arises about "softer" stance against inflation as the boosts in interest rate might have detrimental effect on bank balance sheets. The second argument stated that the central bank would have a very complex mandate and thus be less easily accountable. As both of the arguments have merit, it at least implies a need for increased transparency in case of giving responsibility for regulation to central bank. The alternative of separating monetary and regulatory authorities seems worse. (Blanchard et al., 2010, pp. 210).

CBRT VS. BOI AND MONETARY POLICY UNDER GREAT FINANCIAL CRISES[15]

The year 2001 is generally recognized as a main structural break point for Turkish economy. Before 2002 Turkish economy had a poor macroeconomic environment, an ineffective financial supervision framework that was divided between different institutions. Further it was dealing with sector specific problems in banking, such as the moral hazard issue due to savings deposit insurance schemes. All these taken together, headed to an important economic crisis under negative global sentiment. In the 1990s insufficient public banks were mainly dominating the banking sector, and Turkish banking sector as a whole had serious shortages, such as high risks in foreign currency, interest rates, and liquidity. The deficient in good governance principles, and unhealthy banks structure were crucial issues in Turkish banking sector. High inflation rates with 2 or 3 digits even in 1994, and high ratio of the budget deficit to GDP such as 11.9% in 2001, were common leaning and complicated the decision-making mechanisms of economic units. Also under these conditions, the country's unsustainable economic growth rates were low and volatile (average economic growth rate was 2.5% between 1990 and 2001). As a natural consequence of high interest rates in the Turkish economy, Turkish banks gave up their intermediation role like financing economic growth and real productive sectors already before the crisis (significant decreasing in the ratios of *total credits/total assets* and *total credits/deposits*, in turn, 47% and 84% in 1990 and 32.9% and 51% in 2000). In addition to decreasing of those ratios, the very high interest rate differences between Turkey and rest of the world also heartened Turkish banks to take advantages of borrowings from abroad and to finance public sector borrowing requirements with high interest rates in Turkish lira under exchange rate risk.

In June 1999, Banking Regulation and Supervision Agency (BRSA) was established as an independent institution authority and after February 2001 crisis, Kemal Derviş as an economy minister, entered into force the Program for Transition to a Strong Economy (PTSE)[16]. PTSE especially helped to diminish inflation rates (it was average 70% in 1990s and in 2004 reduced 1 digit level) and to reduce the indebtedness ratios such as budget deficit/GDP and debt stock/GDP to around Maastricht Criteria. Also economic growth rate began to be sustainable and notable improved till effects of GFC in 2009. In October 2005, a new Banking Law was approved and as a result of the new Banking Law internal and external coordination of monetary policy supervisions was enriched. Further remarkable steps were taken to meet the criteria by bank owners and management and for separating the responsibility areas of the BRSA and the SDIF. Also, new parameters and regulations were made for credits extended to group companies by banks. As a result of the restructuring program and the consolidation process, the number of banks in Turkey declined (from 79 banks in 2000 to 50 banks in 2008). Declining in the banks number resulted in stronger capital structure for banks such as capital adequacy ratio increased from 9% in 2000 to 30% in 2003 (Kenç et al., 2011). While in Israel economy rapid growth after last recession in 2003 occurred by expansionary global economic conditions, progress in the national security situation and growth-led economic policy. These were reflected in many positive developments, like a high level of economic activity, very low unemployment, a surplus in the current account of the balance of payments, a high rate of saving and a large cumulative decline in the ratio of public debt to GDP, a booming capital market, a high level of foreign direct investment, a decline in the economy's risk premium and a rise in its credit rating, high profits in the business sector, and an increase in the resilience of the banking system.

On the other side CBRT also became more independent with new regulations and those mentioned improvement in Turkish banking sector, and shifting understanding of the central banking after GFC period was the main reasons why the CBRT adopted an "off the beaten track" approach in monetary policy. However, not only changing the approach towards economic policies and central banking, but also the unconventional global economic environment was significant in persuading/encouraging the search for a new policy combination by the CBRT. After 2008, especially in developed countries like UK, EU, negative feedback between balance sheets of the public and banking system, and US continue to handicap economic recovery of the world economy. Traditional transmission mechanisms across advanced economies seemed to be weakened due to ongoing financial stability concerns. As a whole, these developments increased the requirement for trying alternative policy approaches and therefore encouraged the central banks to bend the limitations of the customary monetary policy outline (Kara, 2012).

In the post GFC period, under liquidity excess, Turkey came up against a new challenging environment, characterized by expanding current account deficits, strong short-term capital inflows, and swift credit expansion. Hereupon, CBRT adopted a new "policy mix" that put emphasis on financial stability goals, while other macroprudential policy measures were taken only with some delay (IMF, 2012). CBRT made macroprudential policy stride in return to the immediate impacts of the global financial crisis as well as to the expanding current account deficit in Turkey and to the financial risks related to the growing deficit, with a reinforced emphasis on financial stability since the last quarter of 2010. The macroprudential policies applied by the CBRT in response to the GFC in three phases: (Kenç et al., 2011, pp.6).

- Full liquidity support after Lehman Brothers' collapse (September 2008),
- The exit strategy (April 2010), and
- The new policy mix (late 2010).

The impacts of GFC in Turkey and Israel and their financial systems were solid. Various dynamics facilitated lessen these impacts, containing structure of its financial system and BOI's unconventional measures of GFC, the timing of the crisis, five years of rapid growth before GFC, and certain features of the economy. Besides to GFC Israel economy was less affected due to tight regulation, conservative mortgage market and absence of complex assets. Moreover the years prior to crisis all banks were obliged to meet Supervision of banks requirements that protected banks from worse scenarios of the crisis aftermath (Braude et. al., 2011).

However, in the last quarter of 2008 conditions started to change suddenly and intensely for Israel. This dramatically changes lead to the prices of shares and corporate bonds fell sharply and volatility increased significantly; risk spreads in the credit market (both the bank and non-bank markets) rose sharply, thus raising the price of credit in the economy in the financial markets.

Mostly it was result of general slowdown in the world economy caused by Great Recession. In addition Israel is the country that depends on foreign investment flow, which fell rapidly in the second half of 2008, and negatively affected profitability of the business. The gradual move from rapid growth to recession was followed by decline in GDP by 2-3 percent each quarter; especially it was obvious during the last quarter of 2008 and the first quarter of 2009.

In the first half of 2008, volatility augmented for, then in the second half of 2008 it reduced in value of Shekel in foreign exchange market. These changes in the value of the money were caused by intervention of BOI. Since then, Israel's export reduced the effects of GFC on Israel economy. However, between last quarter of 2008 and first quarter of 2009 economic growth rate was negative (2-3%) because of a significant deterioration in real economic activities.

In the same period after downsizing in 2009, Turkish economy began to experience very quick recovery on the back of powerful and solid domestic demand. Particularly rising capital inflows surcharged

Figure 2. Macroeconomic Indicators of Israel and the World
Source: Bank of Israel[17] (this figure includes a list of indicators for Israel that provides data from several countries)

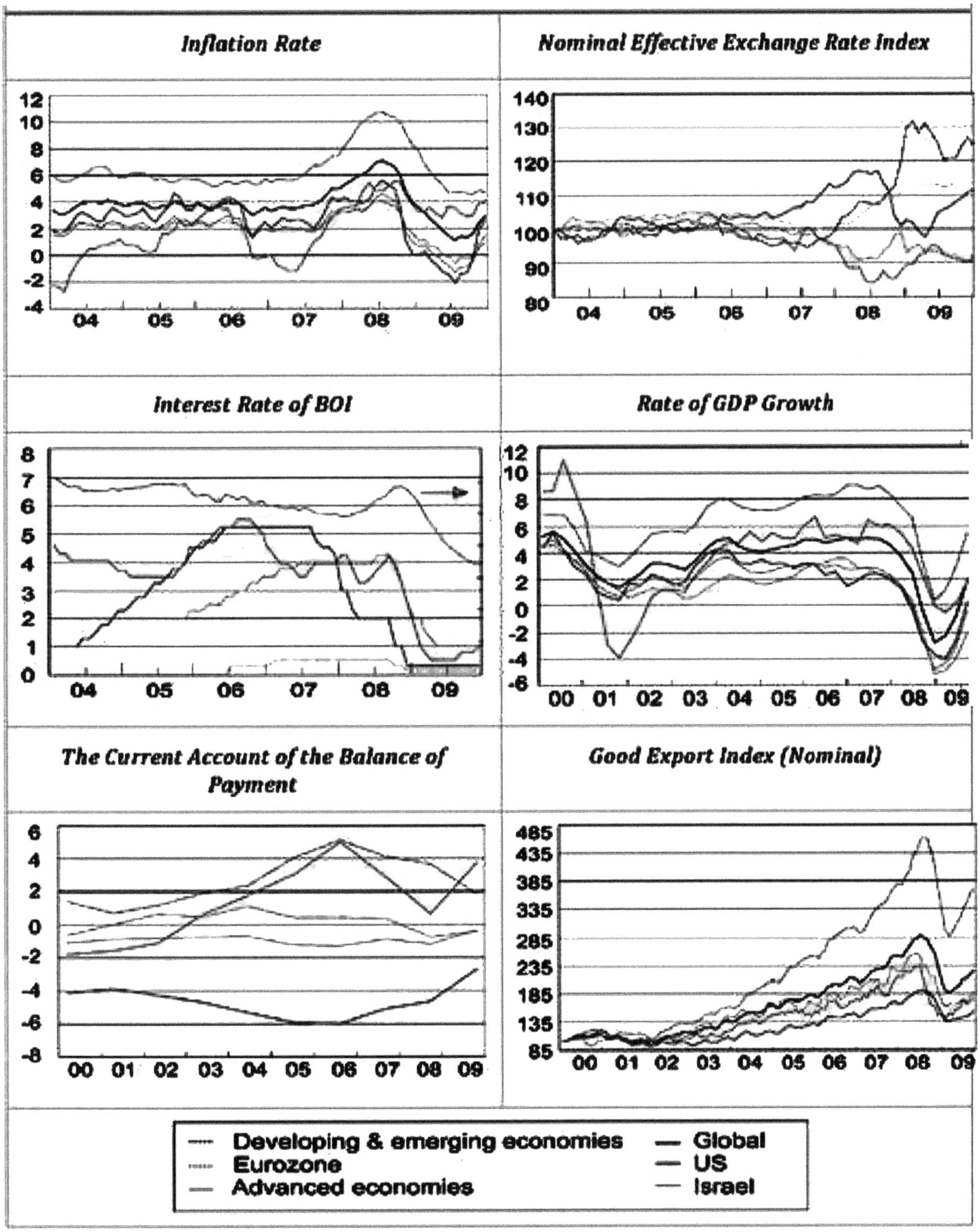

by historically low policy rates and quantitative easing policies across advanced economies supported domestic credit growth and led to an excessive appreciation in the Turkish lira. Domestic demand was increased by credit growth and in addition to that, strong position of Turkish Lira supported growing import volume. Thereupon, foreign trade and current account balance dispatched a remarkable worsening as is shown at Figure 3 and 4. This notable deterioration enlarged the fragility of the economy against unexpected changes in the world risk taking desire. Also, especially after 2010, as shown at Figure3, short-term capital flows and portfolio investments became main finance methods for current account deficit. But this is not a new development in Turkish economy. Because of volatility in capital flows was significant factor in macroeconomic stability of Turkey. The crucial role of capital flows in volatility and macroeconomic stability can be seen at Figure 5. In 1994, 2001 and 2008 crises was observed together with both sudden stop in capital flows and sharp falling of economic growth. Short-term capital flows and volatility in financing highlighted the requirement of increasing and encouraging the resistance of the economy against sudden changes in the global risk taking behavior. So therefore a new policy framework of CBRT with more flexible approach in monetary policy would be more useful (Kara, 2012, pp. 3-4).

Figure 3. Exports and Imports (Thousand USD)
Source: TUIK (According to the provisional data, produced with the cooperation of the Turkish Statistical Institute and the Ministry of Customs and Trade, in May 2013; exports were 13 316 Million Dollars with a 1.4% increase and imports were 23 209 Million Dollars with a 6.7% increase compared with May 2012. In May 2013 exports coverage imports was 57.4% while it was 60.4% in May 2012.)

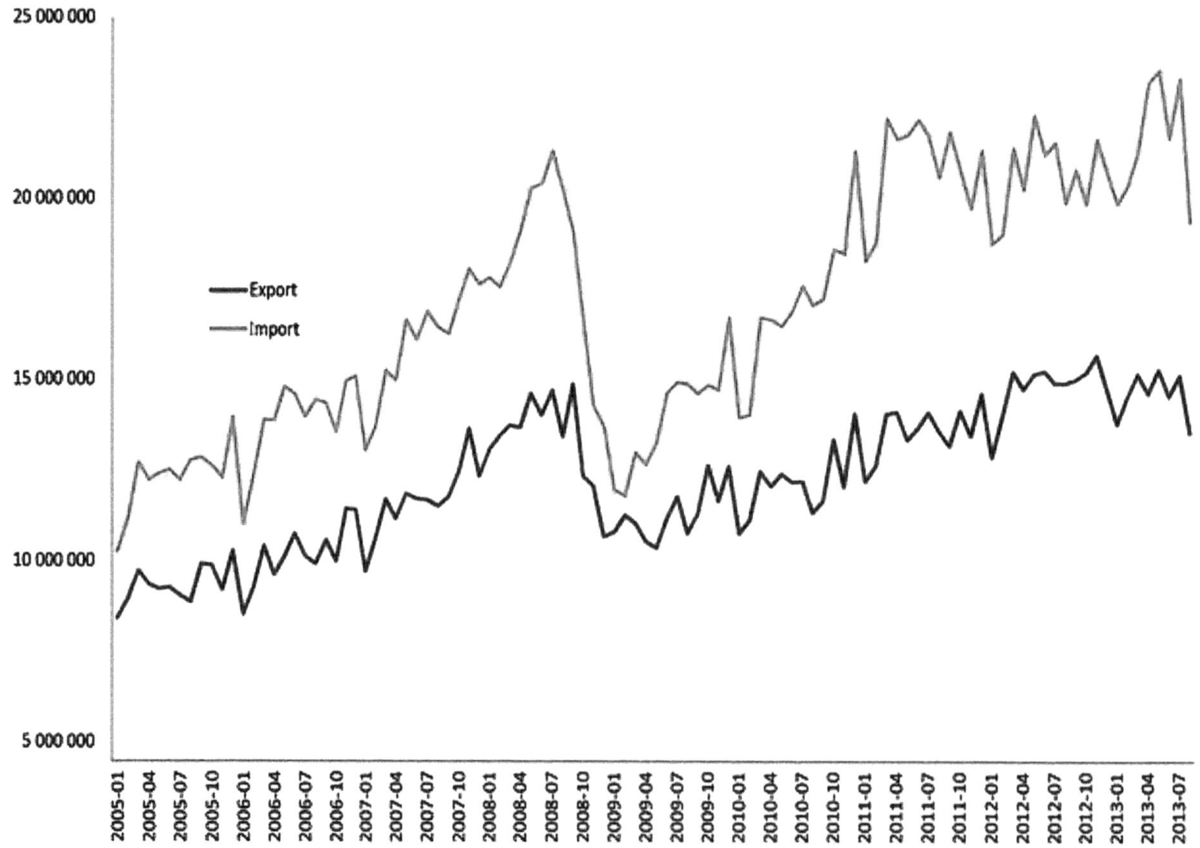

Coming across quickly increasing (particularly) short-term capital inflows in Turkey after the last quarter of 2010, CBRT employed a "new policy mix" that proposed to maintain macroeconomic and financial stability. Unremunerated required reserve ratios on all Turkish lira and FX liabilities of banks were increased to an average of 14% and 11.5% respectively (from their 5% and 9% troughs during the global crisis) by numerous phases, while higher interest rates were charged to shorter term bank liabilities. Moreover, interest rate corridor was extended considerably for easing enhanced volatility of short-term interest rates. CBRT's usage of the reserve requirements assisted both macroprudential and capital flow management purposes by aiming to moderate inflows and lengthen their duration (Lim et al., 2011).

In the mid of 2010, CBRT shifted to employ a new monetary policy framework. As a main part of this new policy, CBRT went to revision at inflation targeting and financial stability chosen as a second objective. As shown at Figure 6 and as Basci and Kara (2011) explains, main structure of new policy were settled so as to carrying out various aims. According to new policy framework, main focus is to create a structure for protecting and strengthening the resistance of the economy, when external balance, credit expansion and capital flows cause fragilities in the economy.

Figure 4. Main Sources of Current Account Deficit Finance (Billion USD)

Source: TUIK (Along with some other emerging market countries, Turkey experienced a credit boom in the period to mid-2011, accommodated by easy domestic policies and global monetary conditions, that led to large capital inflows and strong domestic demand, contributing to a sharp widening in the current account deficit and increase in short-term external debt)

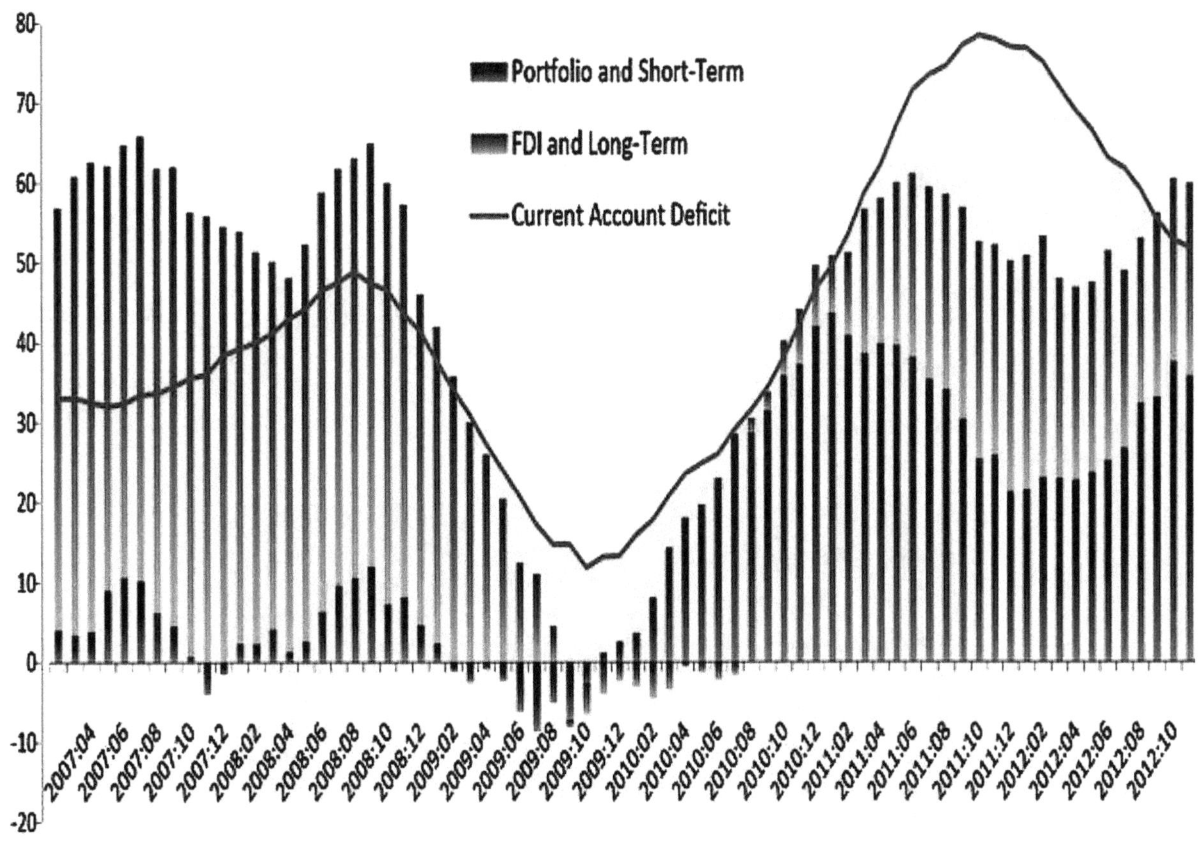

Figure 5. GDP Growth and Capital Flows (%)
Source: TUIK (Turkey has been exposed to large amounts of capital inflows like other emerging markets in 1990s and since the beginning of 2002 which are accompanied with a high growth performance. However, with recent crises in 2001 and 2008-2009, capital inflows exhibited sharp fall, followed by a substantial contraction in private investment and overall economic activity. The spillover from the global crisis in 2008-2009 increased the importance of analyzing the impact of external shocks, specifically capital inflow shocks, on Turkey's macroeconomic outcomes. External factors are likely to have a major role in Turkey's economic growth performance, particularly in the absence of strong domestic savings.)

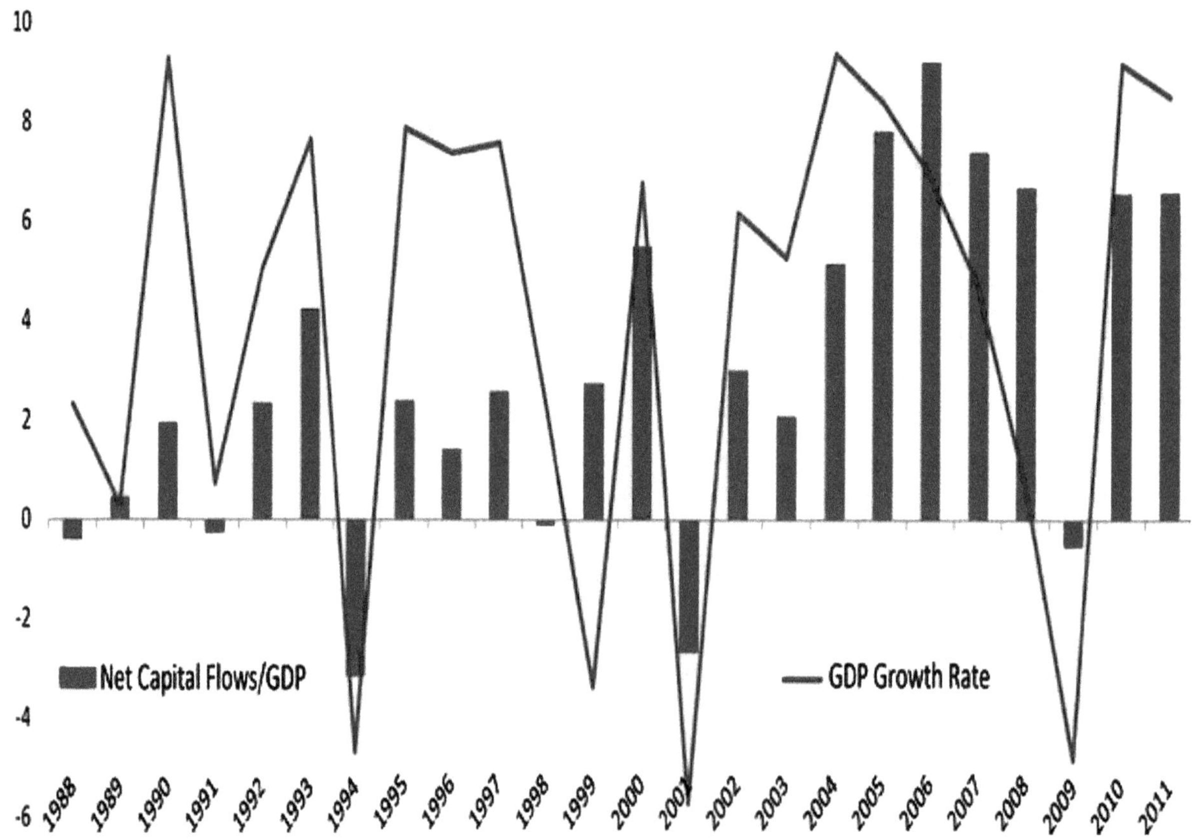

Figure 6. Policy Instruments and Objectives of CBRT
Source: Kara (2011, pp. 6)

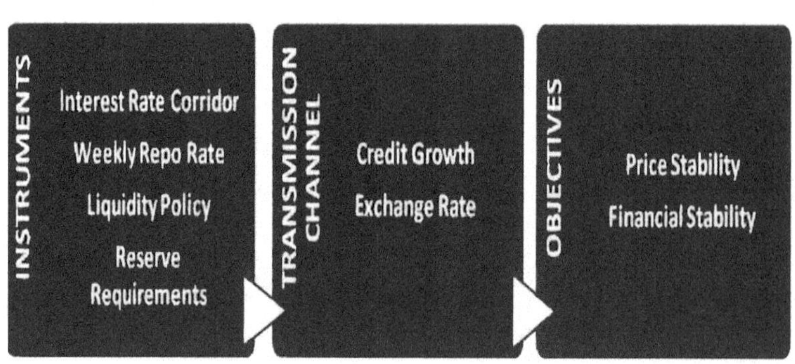

The main tools and the transmission mechanism utilized within the new policy framework can be summarized as at Figure 6. At the end of the diagram are policy tools: (i) interest rate corridor, one-week repo rate and liquidity management tools (ii) required reserves. In 2012 "reserve option mechanism" was adapted to this policy mix. Using these tools, the CBRT finally aims at affecting price stability and financial stability. The credit and exchange rate channels bridge the gap between the instruments and final objectives (Kara, 2012, pp. 5-6). In view of employed new policies, the main structure focused on easing the possible contrary impacts of capital flow volatility, aimed at soft landing and improving the external financing structure of account balance deficits. Interest rate corridor among overnight borrowing and lending rates, liquidity policies and required reserves became part of the new policy mix besides short-term policy rate.

For example the interest rate corridor and required reserves as transmission channels of the new policy instruments were not clear at the early stage. Credit and exchange rate is designated as intermediate variables and underlined by CBRT because of enhancing the communication of the transmission mechanism. Because these variables are openly visible and since the relevant data are publicized without delay, economic units can with no trouble pursued. This strategy, as a part of new policy, smoothed a more trustworthy and influential communication concerning the policy application for transmission mechanisms.

CBRT had loud and clear intention for addressing price and financial stability distresses as a whole by encouraging hiring less traditional tools. A basis strategy was policy-induced uncertainty in short-term market rates till mid of 2011. Initially, in order to prevent fast appreciation of the lira, the CBRT relied on the preannounced FX purchasing auctions, the volume of which was increased as capital flows strengthened. Seeing them as unsuccessful, the CBRT dropped sharply the overnight borrowing rate (6.5% to1.75%). CBRT used overnight borrowing and lending rates in the tool named "interest rate corridor" such as an indicating expedient.

At the same time, CBRT approached to the reserve requirements for controlling lending after short-term interest rates and liquidity management, because of according to the CBRT's estimations credit demand elasticity is low. Then, CBRT increased them, stopped rewarding them and in time began to set apart according their maturity since June 2010. Macroprudential tools were less used by BRSA comparatively to CBRT, so macroprudential policy led mainly under the guidance of the CBRT. However, in 2008 and 2009, BRSA has begun to use macroprudential tools for supporting stability of domestic financial market

Table 2. Intensity of use of Macroprudential Policy Instruments by CBRT

Caps on loan-to-value ratios	Caps on debt/ loan-to-income ratios	Caps on foreign currency lending	Ceiling on credit or credit growth	Limits on net open currency positions/ currency mismatch	Limits on maturity mismatch	Reserve requirements	Countercyclical capital requirement	Time-varying/ dynamic provisioning	Restrictions on profit distribution
3	0	6	0	4	0	0	0	0	3

Source: Lim et. al. (2011); IMF (2010)

Note: 0 represents no use of instruments, and 1 denotes the use of a single instrument. For each of the following attributes, i.e., multiple, targeted, time-varying, discretionary and used in coordination with other policies, the value of 1 is added. Most countries have used different kinds of macroprudential policies to contain the adverse effects of the volatile short-term capital flows. Table 2 shows that Turkey has also devised and used a number of new tools, such as the interest rate corridor and the Reserve Option Mechanism. These tools appear to have been effective in decreasing the sensitivity of portfolio flows in Turkey to global risk perception.

in return for GFC, like banks' dividend pay-outs were suddenly shortened to strengthen bank retentions and capital and banks were banned to loan to clients in foreign exchange. Also the key macroprudential measures were announced by the BRSA in June 2011. According to this approach, risk weights were raised for new consumer credits and increased general provisioning necessities for huge loans.

Especially due to reducing of credit growth by macroprudential policy, in late 2011, the monetary framework had to be considerably changed. When capital inflows weakened, the depreciation of Turkish Lira drove inflation 10.4% at the end of the year (target was 5%). In the light of these developments, The CBRT began public sales of foreign exchange and reduced the reserve requirements. As a result of current account deficit stood at 10% of GDP, the second highest in the world economy. When reserve requirements were reduced, it influenced credit growth through monetary and macroprudential ways. The similar situation was in Israel in 2008 until the end of the first quarter of 2009 with the peak of the GFC in Israel economy. During this period, uncertainty was significantly high in the financial markets regarded to short response times and extraordinary susceptibility to potentials and subjective discernments. However, monetary policy concentrated to provide financial stability and continued running of the financial markets. Policy had to balance the need for a quick and effective reaction with the desire to avoid steps with negative consequences in the long term.

In addition, due to GFC the policy implemented, wide set of tools were used both conventional and unconventional. A great deal of weight was put on monetary policy and its various tools and on the actions of the Bank Supervision Department and other regulatory authorities. Main important steps taken by monetary policy (Braude et. al., 2011, pp. 20); some of them can be described as aggressive monetary expansion, interest rate cuts and additional tools. Especially monetary policy played a central role against the GFC and its consequences. BOI started expansionary monetary policy. Interest rate was drastically reduced from 4.25 to 0.50 in 6 months. Secondly, BOI continued to buy foreign currency approximately in amount of $ 100 million per day. It assisted downgrading of exchange rate and so it

Table 3. CBRT's Experience of Macroprudential Instruments

Year	Background and Motivation	Action– Macroprudential Tools Used
2008-2009	The impact of the global financial crisis manifested itself in Turkey through a FX liquidity squeeze. Banks responded to the liquidity squeeze by reducing their FX loans and holdings of Eurobonds. Important motivations for the authorities to take action were to: Strengthen and preserve the financial position of banks Address the negative effect of the global financial crisis	**Caps on foreign currency lending:** moderation of FX lending by allowing non- FX earnings companies to obtain FX loans(2009) **FX liquidity**: change in FX liquidity ratio by allowing banks to temporarily classify FX loans as FX liquidity to help them meet FX liquidity adequacy ratios (2008) **Restriction of profit distribution**: introduction of restrictions on profit distribution (2008)
2009-2011	Turkey rebounded rapidly after the global financial crisis. The country saw a rapid increase in domestic demand, rapid credit growth, and increased foreign currency borrowing by banks. The motivations to take actions were to slow credit growth and improve credit quality.	**LTV**: introduction of caps on the LTV ratio for real estate loans(2010)

Source: Lim et. al. (2011) and Columba et. al. (2011, pp. 81-82)

Table 3 shows how CBRT uses macro prudential instruments in response to GFC. The 2007/8 crises underscored the need for countries to develop strong macroprudential policy framework. It should enable the authorities to identify the main sources of systemic risk and to develop a well-focused policy agenda to mitigate these risks. The framework needs to provide clarity as to which authorities are responsible for crisis prevention, ensure a high degree of accountability and willingness to act as well as mutually supportive policies among the relevant agencies while preserving the operational autonomy of established policy fields (IMF, 2011: Nier, Osiński, Jácome & Madrid, 2011).

reduced negative effect of GFC on export. Thirdly, BOI announced the statements regarding the stability of the banking system and the protection of depositors. They declared that Bank of Israel was organized to assist the banks with all the apparatuses available to it. As a last, BOI has taken actions by the Bank Supervision Department.

FUTURE RESEARCH DIRECTIONS AND CONCLUSION

Along with the Great Recession and policies undertaken the massive monetary policy stimulus was implemented to stabilize financial market and to avoid deflation. In this context, less negative outcomes contributed to moderate the effect of the crisis on the economy and on the financial system and to the relatively quick recovery especially in Israel and Turkey.

In the heat of financial crisis these two countries experienced relatively mild effect from it, together with the caution exercised in choosing the policy measures, also minimized the long-term costs of the policy response. In contrast to many developed countries, the public debt in Israel and Turkey grew only slightly during the crisis and the government was not forced to purchase "toxic" assets.

The stability of the banking system in Israel and Turkey were preserved all the way through the GFC and none of the banks went bankrupt. While 2008 and the beginning of 2009 were difficult periods for the banks in Israel, but not for Turkish banking system and banks. During this period in Israel and in 2009 in Turkish banks benefits dropped and in Israel their market values dropped sharply. In the last quarter of 2008, the uncertainties in the global financial markets had negative effects on the global liquidity flow and created an extraordinary demand especially for US dollar liquidity. This led to significant depreciation of the national currency as in other developing countries. Despite these developments in the exchange rate, slowdown in total demand and the decline in commodity and food prices inflation affected outlook positively, which let CBRT to act freely for monetary policy.

Aside from the pre-crisis factors which contributed to the resilience of the financial system in general and that of the banks in particular, several factors which were at work during the crisis itself contributed to the success of the Israel banking system at this time: the steps taken by the Supervisor of Banks as described above, an expansionary monetary policy, the provision of government guarantees for the raising of capital by the banks (even though they were not utilized) and the declarations of the Governor of the Bank of Israel and the Minister of Finance that the public's deposits were assured.

Central Banks (CBs) were considering developmental problems more in the past. And as main tool monetary policy has a critical role to play in growth. CBs have some monetary policy tools, which are direct instruments to affect the economic sectors of high priority. They were subsidizing interest rates, credit ceilings as a credit allocation techniques and controlling the capital movements. They had more than one aims instead of inflation targeting or financial stability, like employment and growth. Also they were financing government, managing exchange rates and supporting economics sectors of the economy. However, their roles were not limited on above.

Beginning of 1990s in developed countries and after GFC in developing countries as Turkey and Israel "modern" central banks under the neoliberal monetary regime have been keeping inflation at a very low level, reducing central bank support for government fiscal deficits, helping manage the country's integration into world trade and financial markets, reducing the influence of democratic, social and political forces on CB policy. Macroprudential policies are also part of this neoliberal approach of central banking's role.

Shortly this neoliberal approach to central banking / neoliberal monetary regime has some other futures, like central bank independence, focusing on inflation targeting/financial stability, using of indirect instruments of monetary policy like macroprudential tools. Policy practices of CBRT and BOI are main examples of this neoliberal monetary regime. After GFC, CBRT and BOI are enhanced as a neoliberal monetary regime's practices.

Also monetary policy conducted by independent CBs played an important role in reducing inflation rates. Only or mainly focusing on inflation as a monetary policy strategy means that the CB should not be concerned with other goals such as promoting full employment, supporting industrial policy or allocating credit to the sectors of high priority. Rational behind the inflation targeting stems from the old monetarist argument that in the long run, monetary policy can only affect inflation. However this theoretical tradition depends on invalid assumptions such as neutrality of money. As a whole neoliberal monetary regime and especially after GFC macroprudential policies were recommended by the IMF in the name of orthodoxy like a fully opened capital account, pure floating and market determined exchange rate and an inflation targeting policy.

After 1990s, developing countries began to accumulate reserves as a consequence of financial liberalization and globalization and the increase in developing country's reserves is related to changes not in real quantities (such as import or output) but in financial magnitudes. However accumulating reserves is also costly like the spread between the yield on liquid reserve assets and the external costs of funds. The sterilization policy caused an increase of interest rates, and alternative cost of not using this source on the creation of employment or education.

CBRT used to act as an agent of development before the mid 1980s. But in the 1990s, like most CBs, CBRT gave its priority to the macroeconomic stability - a combination of price stability and financial stability. To achieve the stability objective, CBRT started to use indirect instruments heavily, such as open market operations. In 2001, CBRT announced its independence after a change in its legislation. In the period of 2001-2006, CBRT adopted implicit inflation targeting strategy. In 2006, CBRT announced to adopt explicit inflation targeting.

As for Turkey several measures were taken to support the liquidity of the financial system and to ensure the efficient functioning of the credit markets by CBRT. Since the Central Bank can directly control national currency liquidity; it can support smooth functioning of financial and credit markets by providing the required liquidity. As for foreign exchange liquidity developments external conditions are more influential. For example, in a period when uncertainties surrounding the global economy were at high levels, the Central Bank adopted the strategy to use foreign exchange reserves to support the foreign exchange liquidity of the Turkish banking system. Within this framework, the Central Bank continued its activities as a financial intermediary in the foreign exchange deposit market; lending rates of this market were reduced and maturities were extended. Besides, during periods of ailing price movements, foreign exchange liquidity was injected via foreign exchange selling auctions. In 2014 CBRT increased the interest rates and moved toward normalization of economy. However, inflation rate was very close to double digits that were also result of economic and political instabilities in the world. In fact the economies of both countries are exposed to global price shocks that presented greater challenges to the conduct of monetary policy.

The high volatility of international food and energy prices during the last decade highlights the question of whether monetary policy should respond to external price shocks using the same rule it uses to respond to domestic price shocks. For instance, Israel adopted the headline inflation target range of 1-3% in 2003. Within a flexible inflation targeting framework, the monetary policy responds to both lagged and expected price changes in order to preserve price stability and financial stability while minimizing output/ gap volatility and maintaining interest rate stability. Due to the fact that an external price shock leads to a trade-off between inflation and output gap, a monetary policy that focuses on headline inflation may cause a deeper recession than a policy that responds to a measure of inflation that excludes external price shocks that are highly flexible - known as core inflation. As a result to provide a clear and holistic framework and prioritize the implementation of reforms, 25 comprehensive transformation programs were mapped out in parallel with the 10th Development Plan, a roadmap that lays out the medium-term perspectives and policies required to reach the 2023 targets. With the remaining program country authorities plan to make changes in monetary and macroprudential policies in prompting financial stability.

Developed and developing countries have to carefully consider Central Bank (CB) policies. In the past, many developed countries focused on development objectives and to reach them they used to use some monetary policy tools. Nowadays, most of developing countries aim to adopt a "new" monetary policy strategy namely "inflation targeting". This focuses only on the "price stability" or "financial stability". As consequences CB abandoned using the direct instruments and prefer the "market-based" operations such as indirect instruments as macroprudential tools. Unfortunately these new CB approaches also caused some problems especially in developing countries, for example rising current account deficits, unemployment, high debt ratios and unstable growth rates. These difficulties are often connected to the financial liberalization, which eliminates capital controls and exchange rate controls.

As an alternative of this neoliberal monetary policy CBs can start to deal the era of globalization and its negative effects on their economies. Macroprudential policy instruments can be used to create and sustain the stability in the economy but it mustn't change the main roles of CBs and their impact on the growth, employment and growth.

REFERENCES

Agrawal, A. (2010). Environment, community, government. In I. Feldman & M. Ticktin (Eds.), *In the Name of Humanity* (pp. 190–217). Durham, NC: Duke University Press. doi:10.1215/9780822393221-007

Alberola, E. (2011, December 15). Post-Crisis Monetary Policy Frameworks 2011: The Differences between Advanced and Emerging Economies.

Albo, G., Gindin, S., & Panitch, L. (2010). *In and Out of Crises: The Global Financial Meltdown and Left Alternatives*. Oakland, California: Spectre PM Press.

Arrighi, G. (1994). *The Long Twentieth Century: Money, Power, and the Origins of Our Times*. London: Verso.

Barwell, R. (2013). *Macroprudential Policy Taming the Wild Gyrations of Credit Flows, Debt Stocks and Asset Prices*. New YorkPalgrave Mackmillan.

Başçı, E., & Kara, H. (2011). Finansal İstikrar ve Para Politikası. *İktisat İşletme ve Finans, 26*(302), 9-25.

Benigno, G., Chen, H., Otrok, C., Rebucci, A., & Young, E. R. (2012). *Monetary and Macro-Prudential Policies: An Integrated Analysis*. Missouri University, No. 1208. Retrieved from http://economics.missouri.edu/working-papers/2012/WP1208_otrok.pdf

Bernanke, B. (2011, May). Implementing a Macroprudential Approach to Supervision and Regulation. *Speech Given at the 47th Annual Conference on Bank Structure and Competition*, Chicago. Retrieved from http://www.federalreserve.gov/newsevents/speech/bernanke20110505a.pdf

Bernanke, B., Gertler, M., & Gilchrist, S. (1999). The Financial Accelerator in a Quantitative Business Cycle Framework. In J. B. Taylor & M. Woodford (Eds.), Handbook of Macroeconomics Volume 1C (pp. 1341-1393). North-Holland, Amsterdam: Elsevier.

Bernanke, B. S., & Gertler, M. (2001). Should Central Banks Respond to Movements in Asset Prices? *The American Economic Review*, *91*(2), 253–257. doi:10.1257/aer.91.2.253

Blanchard, O., Dell'Ariccia, G., & Mauro, P. (2010). Rethinking macroeconomic policy. *Journal of Money, Credit and Banking*, *42*(1), 199–215. doi:10.1111/j.1538-4616.2010.00334.x

Blinder, A. S. (2010). How Central should the Central Bank Be? *The Journal of Economic Perspectives*, *48*(1), 123–133.

Borio, C. (2011, September). Central Banking Post-Crisis: What Compass for Uncharted Waters? *BIS Working Papers*, No. 353. Retrieved from http://www.bis.org/publ/work353.pdf

Braude, K., Erdman, Z., & Shemesh, M. (2011). *Israel and the Global Crisis. Jerusalem*: Bank of Israel.

Buiter, W. H. (2009). *Lessons from the Global Financial Crisis for Regulators and Supervisors*. London School of Economics.

Caballero, R. J. (2010). Macroeconomics after the Crisis: Time to Deal with the Pretense-of-Knowledge Syndrome. *The Journal of Economic Perspectives*, *24*(4), 85–102. doi:10.1257/jep.24.4.85

Cagliarini, A., Kent, C., & Stevens, G. (2010, February 9). Fifty years of Monetary Policy: What have we Learned? *Reserve Bank of Australia's 50th Anniversary Symposium*, Sydney.

Canuto, O., & Cavallari, M. (2013). Monetary Policy and Macroprudential Regulation: Whither Emerging Markets. *World Bank Policy Research Working Paper*, No.6310.

Carney, M. (2009, August 22). Some Considerations on Using Monetary Policy to Stabilize Economic Activity. *Remarks at the Symposium on Financial stability and macroeconomic policy sponsored by the Federal Reserve Bank of Kansas City*, Jackson Hole, Wyoming, USA.

Christiano, L., Ilut, C. L., Motto, R., & Rostagno, M. (2010). Monetary Policy and Stock Market Booms. *Economic Research Initiatives at Duke (ERID) Working Paper.* No. 69. Retrieved from http://ssrn.com/abstract=1684785

Christiano, L., Ilut, C. L., Motto, R., & Rostagno, M. (2010). Monetary Policy and Stock Market Booms. *National Bureau of Economic Research Working Paper No. 16402*.

Claessens, S., & Valencia, F. (2013, January 29). The Interaction Between Monetary and Macroprudential Policies. Retrieved from http://www.imf.org/external/np/pp/eng/2013/012913.pdf

Crowe, C., Dell'Ariccia, G., Igan, D., & Rabanal, P. (2011). *Policies for Macrofinancial Stability: Options to Deal with Real Estate Booms, Staff Discussion Note No. 11/02*. International Monetary Fund.

Epstein, J. L. (2005). School-Initiated Family and Community Partnerships. In T. Erb (Ed.), *This We Believe in Action: Implementing Successful Middle Level Schools* (pp. 77–96). Westerville, OH: National Middle School Association.

Fischer, S. (2011, February 11). Central Bank Lessons from the Global Crisis. *Proceedings of the 3rd P.R. Brahamananda Memorial Lecture*, Reserve Bank of India, Mumbai.

Foster, J. B. (2010). The Financialization of Accumulation. *Monthly Review (New York, N.Y.)*, *62*(5), 1–6. doi:10.14452/MR-062-05-2010-09_1

Froud, J., Johal, S., Leaver, A., & Williams, K. (2006). *Financialization & Strategy: Narrative and Numbers*. London, New York: Routledge.

Galati, G., & Moessner, R. (2011). Macroprudential Policy – A Literature Review. *BIS Working Papers No. 337*.

Goodhart, C. (2008). Lessons from the Crisis for Financial Regulation: What We Need and What We Do Not Need, http://www.rgemonitor.com/financemarkets-monitor

Goodhart, C. (2010, November). The Changing Role of Central Banks. *BIS Working Papers*, No. 326, Basel: BIS.

Hahm, J. H., Mishkin, F. S., Shin, H. S., & Shin, K. (2012). Macroprudential Policies in Open Emerging Economies. *National Bureau of Economic Research,* No.w17780.

Hein, E. (2011a). Redistribution, Global Imbalances and the Financial and Economic Crisis – The Case for a Keynesian New Deal. *International Journal of Labor Research*, *3*(1), 51–73.

Hein, E. (2011b) Financialisation, Re-distribution, and the Financial and Economic Crisis – A Kaleckian Perspective. In T. Niechoj, Ö. Onaran, E. Stockhammer, A. Truger, & van Treeck (Eds.), Stabilising an Unequal Economy? Public Debt, Financial Regulation, and Income Distribution (pp. 35-62). Marburg: Metropolis.

Illing, M., & Liu, Y. (2006). Measuring Financial Stress in a Developed Country: An Application to Canada. *Journal of Financial Stability*, *2*(3), 243–265. doi:10.1016/j.jfs.2006.06.002

Global Financial Stability Report. (2010, April). *IMF*. World Economic and Financial Surveys, Washington: International Monetary Fund.

The Interaction of Monetary and Macroprudential Policies-Background Paper. (2012, December). *IMF*. Washington: International Monetary Fund. Retrieved from http://www.imf.org/external/np/pp/eng/2013/012713.pdf

Kara, H. (2012). An Alternative Policy Tool to Cope with Capital Flow Volatility, OECD-EPC Meeting, Paris. Retrieved from http://www.tcmb.gov.tr/yeni/iletisimgm/H.Kara_EPC.pdf

Kenc, T., Turhan, M. I., & Yıldırım, O. (2011). The Experience with Macroprudential Policies of the Central Bank of the Republic of Turkey in Response to the Global Financial Crisis. *World Bank Policy Research Working Papers* No. WPS5834. Retrieved from http://www-wds.worldbank.org/external/default/WDSContentServer/IW3P/IB/2011/10/05/000158349_20111005142139/Rendered/PDF/WPS5834.pdf

King, M. (2008, June 10). Banking and the Bank of England. *Speech to the British Bankers Association*, London. Retrieved from www.bankofengland.co.uk

Kontonikas, A., & Ioannidis, C. (2005, December). Should Monetary Policy Respond to Asset Price Misalignments? *Economic Modelling*, *22*(6), 1105–1121. doi:10.1016/j.econmod.2005.07.004

Krippner, G. (2005). The Financialization of American Economy. *Socio-economic Review*, *3*(2), 173–208. doi:10.1093/SER/mwi008

Lechmanova, N. (2011, July 18). Macro-prudential regulation – Lessons from Asia. Special Report, Standard Chartered, London.

Lim, C., Columba, F., Costa, A., Kongsamut, P., Otani, A., Saiyid, M.,... Wu, X. (2011, October). Macroprudential Policy: What Instruments and How to Use Them? Lessons from Country Experiences. *IMF Working Paper No. 11/238*. Retrieved from http://www.imf.org/external/pubs/ft/wp/2011/wp11238.pdf

MacKenzie, D., & Millo, Y. (2003). Constructing a Market, Performing Theory: The Historical Sociology of a Financial Derivatives Exchange. *American Journal of Sociology*, *109*(1), 107–145. doi:10.1086/374404

Macroprudential Policy: An Organizing Framework. (2011IMF. Washington: International Monetary Fund.

Milne, A. (2009). Macroprudential policy: What can it achieve? *Oxford Review of Economic Policy*, *25*(4), 608–629. doi:10.1093/oxrep/grp036

Mishkin, F. S. (2009, May). Is Monetary Policy Effective during Financial Crises? *The American Economic Review*, *99*(2), 573–577. doi:10.1257/aer.99.2.573

Mishkin, F. S. (2011). Monetary Policy Strategy: Lessons from the Crisis. *NBER Working Paper 16755*, National Bureau of Economic Research, Cambridge, MA.

Moreno, R. (2011, January). Policymaking from a 'Macroprudential' Perspective in Emerging Market Economies. *BIS Working Paper* No. 336. Retrieved from: http://ssrn.com/abstract=1858690

Nier E. W., Osiński J., Jácome, J. I., & Madrid, P. (2011). Institutional Models for Macroprudential Policy, *IMF Staff Discussion Note 11/18*.

Orhangazi, Ö. (2008). Financialization and Capital Accumulation in the Non-Financial Corporate Sector: A Theoretical and Empirical Investigation of the US Economy: 1973-2004, *MPRA Paper No.7724*.

Palley, T. (2015). The Federal Reserve and Shared Prosperity: A Guide to the Policy Issues and Institutional Challenges. Real-World Economics Review no. 70, Washington DC.

Prakash, K., & Pau, R. (2012). Monetary and Macroprudential Policy Rules in a Model with House Price Booms. *The BE Journal of Macroeconomics*, *12*(1), 1–4.

Prates, D. M. (2012). How to Evaluate Financial Regulation in Brazil? *Paper prepared to the workshop "Growth with Financial Stability and New Developmentalism in Brazil"*, Sao Paulo: FGV-SP, March.

Roger, S., & Vlček, J. (2011). Macroeconomic Costs of Higher Bank Capital and Liquidity Requirements. *IMF Working Paper, WP/11/103*. Retrieved from http://www.imf.org/external/pubs/ft/wp/2011/wp11103.pdf

Shirakawa, M. (2009, June 26). Some Thoughts on Incentives at Micro- and Macro-level for Crisis Prevention. *Remarks at the Eighth Bank of International Settlements Annual Conference*, Basel, Switzerland. Retrieved from http://www.bis.org/review/r090703a.pdf

Şiriner, İ. (2013). *Political Economy of Macroprudential Policies: Case of the Central Bank of the Republic of Turkey*. Torino: IRES Publication.

Stockhammer, E. (2010). Neoliberalism, Income Distribution and the Causes of the Crisis. *Research on Money and Finance*, Discussion Paper no.19, June 2010

Stone, M. R., Roger, S., Nordstrom, A., Shimizu, S., Kisinbay, T., & Restrepo, J. (2009). The Role of the Exchange Rate in Inflation-Targeting Emerging Economies. *International Monetary Fund Occasional Paper No. 267.*

Svensson, L. E. O. (2012). The Relation between Monetary Policy and Financial Stability Policy. *International Journal of Central Banking*, *8*(Suppl. 1), 293–295.

The Interaction of Monetary and Macroprudential Policies: Executive Summary. (2013, January). *International Monetary Fund.* Retrieved from http://www.imf.org/external/np/pp/eng/2013/012913.pdf

Torre, A., Ize, A., & Schmukler, S. L. (2012). Financial Development in Latin America and the Caribbean: The Road Ahead. *World Bank Publications*. Retrieved from http://siteresources.worldbank.org/LACINSPANISHEXT/Resources/FLAGSHIP_eng.pdf

Tucker P. (2011, February 28). National Balance Sheets and Macro Policy: Lessons from the Past. *Speech by the Deputy Governor of the Bank of England at the Society of Business Economists' Annual Dinner*, London.

Wall, H. J. (2009). Journal Rankings in Economics: "Handle with Care, Federal Reserve Bank of St. Louis", April, Working Paper 2009-014A. Retrieved from. http://research.stlouisfed.org/wp/2009/2009-014.pdf

Walsh, C. E. (2009). Inflation Targeting: What Have We Learned. *International Finance*, *12*(2), 195–233. doi:10.1111/j.1468-2362.2009.01236.x

Woodford, M. (2010). Financial Intermediation and Macroeconomic Analysis. The Journal of Economic Perspectives, 24(4), 21–44. doi:10.1257/jep.24.4.21 doi:10.1257/jep.24.4.21

ADDITIONAL READING

Bank of Israel. (2013a). Annual Report, 2012. Jerusalem: Bank of Israel.

Bank of Israel. (2013b). The Government's proposed budget for 2013-14 from the perspective of the fiscal targets for the coming years, Bank of Israel press release, June. IMF country report No. 14/329 (2014). 2014 Article IV Consultation—Staff Report. Press Release; And Statement By The Executive Director For Turkey (December). Available at http://www.imf.org/external/pubs/ft/scr/2014/cr14329.pdf

KEY TERMS AND DEFINITIONS:

Asset Price Channel: Is the monetary transmission channel that is responsible for the distribution of the effects induced by monetary policy decisions made by the central bank of a country that affect the price of assets.

Balance Sheet Channel: This channel of monetary policy transmission refers to the role the financial position of private agents plays in the transmission mechanism of monetary policy. It arises because the shifts in policy affect not only market interest rates but also, the financial position of private economic agents because changes in interest rates affect bank balance sheets, cash follows and the net worth of companies and consumers. Higher interest rates result in reduced cash flow, reduced net worth, drop in loans, and decline in aggregate demand.

Exchange Rate Channel: The exchange Rate is one of the intermediate policy variables through which monetary policy is transmitted to the larger economy through its impact on the value of domestic currency, domestic inflation (the pass-through effect), the external sector, macroeconomic credibility, capital flows, and financial stability.

Interest Rate Corridor: Refers to the window between the repo rate and the reverse repo rate wherein the reverse repo rate acts as a floor and the repo as the ceiling. Ideally, rates in the overnight interbank call money market, where lending and borrowing is unsecured, should move within this corridor.

Kemal Derviş: When Derviş became Turkey's minister of economic affairs in March 2001, after a 22-year career at the World Bank, the country was facing its worst economic crisis in modern history and prospects for success were uncertain. Derviş used his independence from domestic vested interests and support of domestic reformers and civil society to push through a tough stabilization program with far-reaching structural changes and sweeping bank reforms that protected state banks from political use. Derviş also strengthened the independence of the central bank and pushed through deep structural reforms in agriculture, energy and the budget process. These reforms, and his reputation and top-level contacts in the U.S. and Europe, helped him to mobilize $20 billion in new loans from the International Monetary Fund and the World Bank. Rapid economic growth resumed in 2002 and inflation came down from an average of nearly 70 percent in the 1990s to 12 percent in 2003; interest rates fell and the exchange rate for the Turkish lira stabilized.

Liquidity Policy: Is designed to ensure that there are sufficient funds available to meet payments, transfers and withdrawals for bank' members

Macroprudential Policy: A method of economic analysis that evaluates the health, soundness and vulnerabilities of a financial system. Macroprudential analysis looks at the health of the underlying financial institutions in the system and performs stress tests and scenario analysis to help determine the system's sensitivity to economic shocks. Macroeconomic and market data are also reviewed to determine the health of the current system. The analysis also focuses on qualitative data related to financial institutions' frameworks and the regulatory environment to get an additional sense of the strength and vulnerabilities in the system.

Microprudential Policy- or **Microprudential Supervision:** Refers to firm-level oversight or financial regulation by regulators of financial institutions, "ensuring the balance sheets of individual institutions are robust to shocks"

Unconventional Monetary Policy: The widely used approach to evaluating the macroeconomic effects of unconventional monetary policy is the 'plug-in' approach, which uses estimates of the impact of unconventional policy measures on asset prices to plug them into standard macroeconomic models

ENDNOTES

1 One of the first prominent works to use the term financialization was Arrighi (1994) who identified long waves of economic development in global capitalism that involve hegemonic and geographic shifts. While the upswings of these long waves are characterized by increased manufacturing and trade activity, in the downturns a process of financialization occurs: the leading power had initially established a competitive advantage in terms of production, but it shifts towards financial activities as its growth model gets exhausted and other players catch up. In contrast to Arrighi most of the recent debates use the term more narrowly to refer to the period since the 1970s.

2 For contributions on the macroeconomics of financialization see Stockhammer (2005/06) and Hein (2011b), also see Ertürk et al., 2008, for a useful collection of seminal contributions and Stockhammer(2010) as a short survey

3 Available on: http://www.brookings.edu/~/media/research/files/reports/2011/9/ciepr%20central%20banking/rethinking%20central%20banking.pdf

4 Barry Eichengreen, et al (2011) available on http://www.brookings.edu/~/media/research/files/reports/2011/9/ciepr%20central%20banking/rethinking%20central%20banking.pdf

5 Annual Inflation Data available at: http://www.imf.org/external/pubs/ft/weo/2014/01/weodata/weorept.aspx?sy=1980&ey=2014&scsm=1&ssd=1&sort=country&ds=.&br=1&pr1.x=61&pr1.y=19&c=001%2C110%2C200&s=PCPIPCH&grp=1&a=1

6 Consolidated information from Christiano, Lawrence, Cosmin L. Ilut, Roberto Motto, & Massimo Rostagno, (2010)

7 Though the choice of regime itself may partly be a reaction to spillovers.

8 This part of study relies on Ismail Şiriner's Political Economy of Macroprudential Policies: Case of the Central Bank of the Republic of Turkey, IRES Publication, Torino: 2013.

9 In emerging markets, business cycle fluctuations and crises were for long time thought to be caused by financial imperfections. Typical for these periods of credit crunches or sudden stops are significant declines in consumption, output, relative prices, and asset prices. See for details; Beningno et al. (2013).

10 See for example Mishkin, F. 2011. "Monetary Policy Strategy: Lessons from the Crisis." NBER Working Paper 16755, National Bureau of Economic Research, Cambridge, MA.

11 When central bank had no aim for exchange rate peg, they would have ability to perform an independent monetary policy framework.

12 This point of view is supported with some research such as Bernanke et al. (1999) and Bernanke & Gertler (2001)

13 The central bank can implement a principal role to improve and establish coordination in macroprudential policy, so that it can bring various crucial advantages for success of monetary policy (Claessens & Valencia, 2013). Firstly, it can ensure that macroprudential policy draws on the central bank's expertise in financial and macroeconomic analyses, that data and analyses prepared for each policy field are also available to the other, and facilitate analyses of the side effects of each policy. Secondly, it can help shield the macroprudential policy function more from political influence than when it is assigned to a separate regulatory body. Another one, central bank is also subject of risks. It is formally responsible for both price and financial stability, and it could be tempted to use inflation to repair private balance sheets following a financial shock, which can possibly lead to a

loss of welfare. As a result of time consistency and other conflicts, a dual mandate can associate lower credibility and create reputational risks.

14 For example, as the crisis was forming up, some central bankers decreased the interest rates despite high inflation. This was criticized, as according to central banks rulebook these should be raised. But the policymakers experienced demand hit by the crises and lowering inflation. So they lowered policy rates. In case of macroprudential policies the same logic could be applied. Both rules and discretion are likely to be applied. As financial markets tend to overreact, macroprudential policies are not needed that much and discretion might matter more.

15 This part of study heavily relies on Ismail Şiriner's Political Economy of Macroprudential Policies: Case of the Central Bank of the Republic of Turkey, IRES Publication, Torino: 2013.

16 The Banking Sector Restructuring Program as part of the PTSE, included the following aims: 1. Operating and financial restructuring of public banks, 2. Resolving the status of banks transferred to the SDIF, 3. Private banks empowerment, 4. Supervisory and regulatory framework correction.

17 Consolidated data from http://www.boi.org.il/en/DataAndStatistics/Pages/Default.aspx

APPENDIX

Abbreviations

BOI- Bank of Israel
BRSA- Banking Regulation and Supervision Agency
CBRT – Central Bank of Republic of Turkey
CBs – Central Banks
EU- European Union
FED- Federal Reserve System or Central Bank of United States of America
FX – Foreign Exchange
GDP – Gross Domestic Product
GFC- Great Financial Crisis
IMF- International Monetary Fund
LTV – Loan to Value
MENA- Middle East and North Africa
PTSE- Program for Transition to a Strong Economy
TUIK- Turkish Statistical Institute (Türkiye İstatistik Kurumu)
UK – United Kingdom
US – United States

Chapter 22
Fiscal Decentralization and Local Borrowing in Turkish Provinces

Mehmet Serkan Tosun
University of Nevada, USA

Dilek Uz
University of California, USA

Serdar Yılmaz
World Bank, USA

ABSTRACT

There have been important developments in the decentralization of the government structure in Turkey since the early 1980s. This paper examines the link between fiscal decentralization and local borrowing within Turkish provinces. It first discusses local government reforms throughout the history of the Turkish Republic with the focus on recent reform efforts and current local government structure. It then provides an empirical analysis of the effects of decentralization in Turkish provinces using cross-sectional and panel data approaches, and spatial econometrics. The dataset consists of 67 provinces from 1980 to 2000, and separately cross-sectional data on all 81 provinces for the year 2000. Using decentralization measures such as number of local governments per capita and ratio of own-source municipal revenue to total provincial tax revenue, and specific characteristics of the municipalities the analysis examines whether variations in local decentralization across these provinces and across time have had a significant impact municipal borrowing in those provinces.

INTRODUCTION

In Turkey, the migration of rural households to cities in search of employment has started on a large scale in the 1950s. With the liberalization of the economy, development of an export sector based on manufacturing goods and increasing international trade, the urbanization has accelerated in the 1980s. The urbanization increased about three fold from 20 percent in 1950s to more than 60 percent in 2000.

DOI: 10.4018/978-1-5225-0053-7.ch022

Because of increasing demand for urban services due to high urbanization rates, the Government of Turkey has enacted Metropolitan Municipality Law in 1984 to establish metropolitan municipalities to better cope with these trends.

Metropolitan municipalities were established in major urban areas, both in megacities and mid-size secondary cities, to accommodate urban development patterns. Although they followed two different pathways, both patterns fueled demand for more infrastructure investments in metropolitan jurisdictions. In megacities like Istanbul, Ankara and Izmir with population more than 5 million, initial rural-to-urban migration gave way to intra-provincial urban-urban migration, which helped to establish sub-urban communities around megacity centers. Since, the initial infrastructure endowment of these sub-urban communities had been very low, initially there was a huge demand for basic infrastructure investments in these areas around mega cities. As the initial demand of establishing basic urban infrastructure (such as water, sewage, local roads) abates, the emerging need is in urban transport systems to link these sub-urban communities with city centers.

In secondary cities, rural-to-urban migration and industrial development still continue at an increased rate. The outcome of this high level urbanization is demand for infrastructure services to accommodate growth fueled with manufacturing employment in cities like Bursa, Eskişehir, İzmit, Kayseri and Gaziantep or service sector employment in cities like Antalya and Muğla.

The liberalization of the Turkish economy in the 1980s helped municipal governments (both metropolitan and district governments) to accommodate this demand for infrastructure investments with providing access to capital markets. Municipalities started to borrow for their infrastructure investment needs. In this paper, we examine the factors that led to the increase in local government borrowing. We first provide a review of the literature and arguments regarding fiscal decentralization and borrowing at the local level. This is followed by an overview of the local government structure and recent reform efforts. We then provide an empirical analysis of the effects of decentralization on local borrowing in Turkish provinces using cross-sectional and panel data approaches. We use cross-sectional data on all 81 provinces for the year 2000 and panel data that consist of 67 provinces over a period from 1980 to 2000. We examine if specific province characteristics and variations in the number of local government units or own-source revenue across these provinces and across time have had a significant impact on local borrowing.

FISCAL DECENTRALIZATION AND LOCAL BORROWING

The main theoretical arguments underlying the interest in decentralization are increasing efficiency, transparency and accountability in the government. While Stigler (1957) argued for bringing government closer to people, Musgrave (1959) argued that there should be difference between subnational governments to match diverse preferences of their residents. The decentralization theorem by Oates (1972) indicated that "each public service should be provided by the jurisdiction having control over the minimum geographic area that would internalize benefits and costs of such provision."

There has been worldwide interest in decentralization in recent decades. There have been attempts by both developed and developing countries to challenge central governments' policymaking power (World Bank, 1999). While the decentralization argument was made in response to various central government failures in developing countries, subnational governments also failed to provide adequate public services in most cases.[1]

Bird (2000) lists expenditure assignment, revenue assignment, intergovernmental transfers/grants, and subnational debt/borrowing as pillars of a decentralized system. The first step in the design of a decentralized system is expenditure assignment which is followed by the revenue assignment where local governments are expected to have some control over tax rates and tax bases. Intergovernmental transfer system is also an important part of a decentralized system, particularly in term of correcting fiscal imbalances within the country. Subnational borrowing is the last pillar of a decentralized system.

As Ebel and Yılmaz (2003) point out, local borrowing is important due to intergenerational equity, economic development and synchronization of expenditure and revenue flows. The benefit principle of taxation suggests that both current and future residents should contribute the cost of investment. For this purpose borrowing is an appropriate tool that offers means through which payments for capital projects can be spread over the life of the project so as to coincide more closely with the stream of future benefits (Oates, 1972). Borrowing is an appropriate tool for subnational governments in investing infrastructure projects to stimulate regional economy (Kolko, 2011). Borrowing also provides subnational governments to smooth out the mismatch and provide services without disruption (Kitchen, 2004).

At the same time there could be important moral hazard costs associated with local borrowing. It may be necessary to impose limitations on local government borrowing (Ter-Minassian & Craig, 1997).

LOCAL ADMINISTRATION SYSTEM, LAWS AND RECENT REFORM EFFORTS IN TURKEY

Turkey is a unitary country with a population of around 75 million people. The local government system in Turkey is based on a dual structure:[2] the appointed deconcentrated local governments, headed by governors, and decentralized local governments, elected by people (see Figure 1). Deconcentrated units are the representatives of the central government at the local level.[3] The whole territory of the country is divided into 81 territorial administrations, namely provinces. Provinces are also subdivided into districts (*ilçe*). Whereas decentralized local governments—organized as special provincial administrations (SPA), municipalities and villages—are elected by people. SPA is an intermediate-level local government unit operating at the provincial level covering both urban and rural areas. SPAs and provinces operate under the same geographical borders, thus the number of SPAs is also 81.

The second type of decentralized local government is a municipality. Municipalities provide municipal services only in urban areas within provincial boundaries. There are currently 1,396 municipalities, of which 30 are metropolitan municipalities, 51 are provincial municipalities, 519 are district municipalities within metropolitan municipality jurisdictions, 400 are district municipalities and 396 are township municipalities (see Table 1). Due to the high degree of urbanization, municipal population is concentrated in several large cities, leaving a large majority of municipalities with relatively small populations (see Table 1).

In Turkey, there is a two-tier municipal system in 30 large cities. Metropolitan municipalities were established in 16 cities in 1984, and 14 more cities in 2013. The objective was to reap the advantages of having large structures in the city management (metropolitan municipality) and benefits of participation and dynamism of small structures (district municipalities under a metropolitan municipality).

The third type of decentralized local government in Turkey is a village. Villages are small local authorities located in the rural areas. There are currently 18,323 villages.

Figure 1. Local administration structures in Turkey
Source: Yilmaz and Guner (2013).

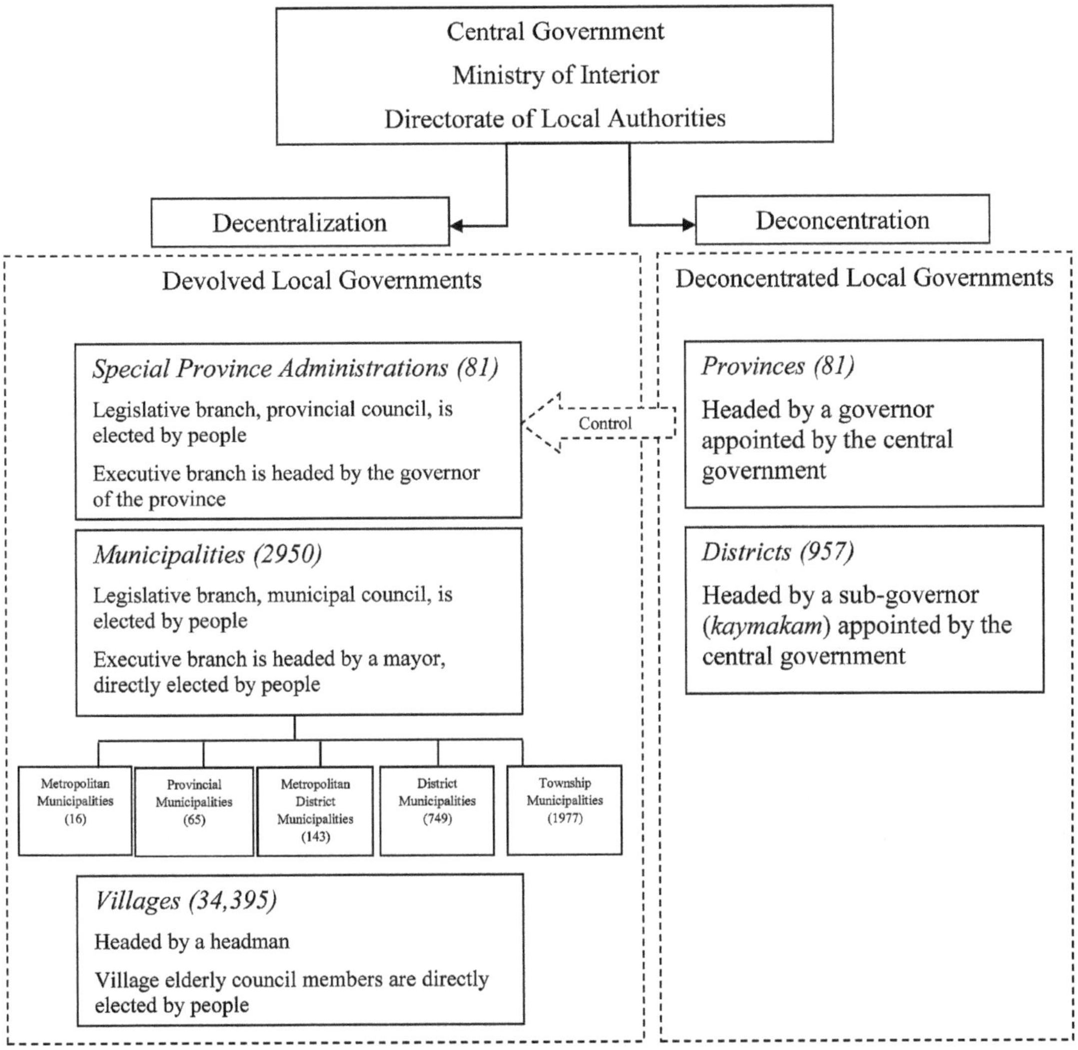

In Turkey liberalization efforts started in 1980s with the first civilian government after the military coup. A major reform during this period was the establishment of metropolitan municipal system in 1984 to manage large urban jurisdictions better. However, successive coalition governments failed to initiate other local government reforms in the 1990s; instead they opted for establishment of new municipalities for political purposes.[4]

After a long period of coalition governments, the current ruling party came to power with the promise to initiate public sector reforms including changes in the local government system. In 2004, a minimum population criterion of 750,000 was introduced in establishing a new metropolitan municipality.[5] In 1984 when metropolitan municipality concept was introduced, the establishment of a new metropolitan municipality was left to the discretion of the central government. This authority was abused by successive governments to award jurisdictions that voted for the ruling party at the center.

Table 1. Distribution of population across different types of municipalities

Population	Metropolitan	Provincial	Metropolitan District	District	Township	Total
0–2,000			1	39	37	77
2,001–5,000			11	196	323	470
5,001–10,000			37	98	34	169
10,001–25,000		1	112	81	2	196
25,001–100,000		23	190	43		256
100,001–500,000		27	148	3		178
500,001-1,000,000	10		20			30
1,000,001-2,000,000	13					13
2,000,001-3,000,000	4					4
3,000,000 +	3					3
Total	30	51	519	400	396	1,396

Source: Ministry of Interior, General Directorate of Local Authorities, General Activity Report for Local Authorities (2013, p. 12).

In 2005, the government reformed both Special Provincial Administrations (SPAs) and municipalities. SPAs were restructured along democratic principles.[6] Prior to 2005, the provincial governor (*vali*), appointed by the central government, was the head of provincial council and the executive arm of the SPA. The 2005 reforms separated these two posts and allowed council members to elect the head of provincial council.

In the municipal sector, reforms reflected service delivery realities over the past 75 years by formally devolving additional responsibilities to municipalities.[7] An important change is the increase in the population threshold to establish a new municipality to 5,000 from 2,000. The reason for this change is to reap the benefits of economies of scale in service delivery.[8]

In 2008, the government reduced the number of municipalities by changing the status of small municipalities that do not meet the minimum population criterion of 2,000 per village and by reorganizing municipalities within the borders of metropolitan municipalities.[9] As a result, the number of municipalities has been reduced from 3,225 to 2,950. This change, which came into effect before the 2009 elections, is intended to address issues of economies of scale and scope in service delivery.

In 2008 the government also changed the criteria for the allocation of intergovernmental transfer shares across special provincial administrations and municipalities to introduce equalization across regions.[10] Prior to this change, intergovernmental transfer system was based on population for both special provincial administrations and municipalities. The transfer formula for special provincial administrations is changed by reducing the weight for population to 50 percent and adding other criteria. For municipalities it reduced the weight for population to 80 percent and added a development index (20%) to the transfer formula.

There was a major policy change in 2012 that led to an increase in the number of metropolitan municipalities from 16 to 30 and reduced the number of municipalities dramatically from 2,950 to 1,396 (see Table 2). At the same time the extent of the metropolitan municipalities' jurisdiction was expanded to include the entire province.[11] The same law ended the SPAs in those provinces that have metropolitan municipalities. As Table 1 shows while the 2012 Law no. 6360 led to a dramatic decrease in the number of district and township municipalities, it led to a significant increase in the number of metropolitan district

Table 2. Number of municipalities by year

Year	Number	Year	Number
1923	421	1985	1703
1935	505	1988	1925
1945	583	1992	2270
1950	628	1993	2553
1955	809	1994	2715
1960	995	1997	2801
1965	1062	2000	3215
1970	1303	2008	3225
1975	1654	2010	2950
1980	1727	2014	1396

Source: Keles, (2000, p. 221); Ministry of Interior, General Directorate of Local Authorities, General Activity Report for Local Authorities (2013, p. 7).

municipalities. This is rather controversial as it is a significant reversal of the previous decentralization trend in Turkey. Akıllı and Akıllı (2014) show that one consequence of this law is a significant increase in the control of metropolitan municipalities from 30% of total geographic area of the country to 50% (Akıllı & Akıllı, 2014, p. 686).

FINANCES OF LOCAL ADMINISTRATIONS IN TURKEY

Despite the local reform efforts explained in the previous section, there is still a significant mismatch (or asymmetry) between expenditure responsibilities and revenue assignments in Turkish local governments. While decentralized government units such as municipalities have a number of assigned public expenditures particularly in utility service functions, local revenue assignments are very limited and ad hoc. In most cases, central government has strict control over tax rates, tax bases and creation of new local revenue instruments.

In the meantime, there has been an increase in both the domestic and foreign debt with a more noticeable increase in foreign debt. Recent trends in domestic and foreign debt of local administrations are shown in Table 3. Foreign financing of large projects such as subway construction seems to have played a role in the rise in foreign debt stock. Also, the short term debt has shown the largest increase compared to long term debt. Overall, total debt has reached about 2.8% of GDP in 2008. More than half of this debt has accrued to metropolitan municipalities. The rising indebtedness of municipalities is a serious problem for the local administrations as well as the central government.

In summation, there have been significant local administration reform efforts in Turkey since 1980s. On the other hand, despite extensive (and increasing) service delivery responsibilities of local administrations, and in particular municipalities, there is very limited local revenue autonomy. Another important issue is the rising indebtedness of Turkish municipalities in response to undertaking of major investment projects in recent years, which is the focus of our empirical analysis in the next section.

Table 3. Domestic and foreign debt stock of Turkish local administrations

Thousand TL	2006	2007	2008
Domestic Debt:	16,520,886	23,577,418	21,666,121
Short Term	5,140,894	7,384,146	8,375,623
Long Term	11,379,992	16,193,272	13,290,498
Foreign Debt:	2,298,433	3,602,482	4,797,097
Short Term	167,348	984,998	386,729
Long Term	2,131,085	2,617,484	4,410,368
Total Debt	18,819,319	27,179,900	26,463,218
Domestic Debt (% of GDP)	2.18	2.80	2.28
Foreign Debt (% of GDP)	0.30	0.43	0.50
Total Debt (% of GDP)	2.48	3.22	2.78

Source: From Tosun (2010) based on statistics from Turkish Ministry of Interior, General Directorate for Local Authorities. http://www.mahalli-idareler.gov.tr/Home/Dokumanlar/faaliyet_raporu.pdf

DATA, EMPIRICAL METHOD AND RESULTS

Data and Empirical Approach

We conduct our empirical analysis in two parts. First, we examine cross-sectional variation in decentralization across the current total of 81 Turkish provinces.[12] We picked 2000 as the year of analysis, which is the most recent data year before the 2001 financial crisis in Turkey. In these regressions, we regress the share of local of borrowing to total province revenue on a number of explanatory variables including the number of municipalities per capita as a decentralization (or fragmentation) measure, the ratio of municipal own-source revenue to total provincial tax revenues as a fiscal decentralization measure and other controls such as provincial GDP per capita, provincial development index, land area, share of urban population, and total number of vehicles.[13] We also use regional dummies to control for specific regional effects. Our main data source is the Turkish Statistical Institute (TÜİK). Provincial development index is provided by the Turkish State Planning Organization (DPT).

In the second part of the empirical analysis, we examine recent decentralization through changes in number of local governments per capita and by including observations from 1980 to 2000. However, we limit our analysis to the original 67 provinces to maintain data consistency throughout the entire period of study. We run a regression similar to the cross-sectional regression described above with the exception of share of urban population and provincial development index, which we excluded due to data limitations. On the other hand we use province and time fixed effects. The main data source for these variables is again TÜİK.[14]

Descriptive Statistics and Methodology

We run cross-sectional regressions for all 81 provinces using the spatial error model. In the spatial error model, spatial dependence is caused by the existence of spillover effects between units of observation (provinces) and the presence of a direct influence from activity (economic or other) in one province on neighboring provinces. Equation (1) features the spatial error model specification that uses maximum likelihood (ML) estimation.

$$Z = Decentralization\beta_1 + X\beta_2 + u \quad (1)$$

where $u = \lambda Wu + e$.

Z is the local borrowing ratio. The matrix **W** is an NxN row standardized spatial weight matrix (the rows sum to one). We model spatial relationships using first-order contiguity, which identifies contiguous provinces. The term **e** is an Nx1 vector of errors, and λ is a parameter to be estimated that shows the degree of spatial dependence among the error terms. *Decentralization* is an Nx1 vector representing specific decentralization variables (number of municipalities per capita and own-source revenue ratio) explained above. X is an nxm set of control variables (m is the number of controls) and where β_2 represents an mx1 vector of coefficients. Included in X are the land area, share of urban population, metrocity dummy, total vehicles per capita and region dummy variables for regions in the country.[15] Table 4 shows summary statistics for the cross-sectional regressions.

For the second part, we use panel data with 1,340 observations that include 67 provinces for the years 1980 through 2000. Table 2 shows that there have been significant changes in the number of municipalities over this period. With the exception of Bolu, Kars and Siirt, all of the original 67 provinces experienced increases in the number of municipalities.[16] In 25 provinces, number of municipalities doubled or more than doubled between 1980 and 2000. Complete summary statistics of variables used in the panel regressions are provided in Table 5. Two conventional approaches for estimating panel data are the fixed-effects and random-effects procedures. However, if the unobserved time-invariant individual effects (fixed effects) are correlated with other predictors in a regression, then the least squares estimator is "biased and inconsistent as a consequence of an omitted variable" (Greene, 2003, p. 285). Accordingly, the fixed-effects model has an advantage over random-effects estimation of removing the bias from the estimation caused by a possible correlation between explanatory variables and time-invariant province specific effects.

Results

Empirical results are provided in Tables 6 and 7. We start in Table 6 with the cross-sectional spatial regressions. We run separate regressions using ratio of total borrowing to total province revenue, ratio of domestic borrowing to total province revenue and the ratio of foreign borrowing to total province revenue as dependent variables. We also run two regressions for each of the dependent variables, one with GDP per capita and one with the provincial development index. Among the decentralization variables only the ratio of own-source revenue to total province tax revenue is consistently significant but only in the domestic borrowing regressions. In that case, the coefficient has a positive sign which means that provinces with greater own-source revenue generation engage in more domestic borrowing. This makes sense since we would expect places with greater fiscal decentralization to have better access to credit markets. Credit markets would also find it easier to lend to municipalities that can generate revenue on their own and hence have better prospect of paying back in the future. This is not seen, however, in the foreign borrowing regressions and the coefficients in the total borrowing regressions are positive but not statistically significant. This can also be explained with the fact that foreign borrowing is subject to very tight central government control. The Law on Public Finance and Debt Management (Law no.

Table 4. Summary statistics for cross-sectional spatial regressions

Variables	Obs.	Mean	Standard Deviation	Min.	Max.
Ratio of total borrowing to total province revenue	81	3.300	8.151	0	57.66
Ratio of domestic borrowing to total province revenue	81	1.552	3.851	0	32.35
Ratio of foreign borrowing to to total province revenue	81	1.748	7.418	0	57.16
GDP per capita	81	1.411e+06	842,235	315,761	4.331e+06
Development index	81	-2.44e-07	1.000	-1.440	4.808
Share of urban population	81	0.556	0.119	0.261	0.910
Land area (square km.)	81	9,673	6,581	850.5	40,814
Metro city dummy	81	0.185	0.391	0	1
Ratio of municipal own-source revenue to total province tax revenue	81	17.85	8.932	3.429	53.32
Number of municipalities per capita	81	6.31e-05	3.09e-05	7.39e-06	0.000149
Total motor vehicles per capita	81	0.0824	0.0479	0.0113	0.203
Region dummies:					
Mediterranean	81	0.0988	0.300	0	1
East Anatolia	81	0.185	0.391	0	1
Aegean	81	0.0988	0.300	0	1
Southeast Anatolia	81	0.0988	0.300	0	1
Black Sea	81	0.222	0.418	0	1
Marmara	81	0.136	0.345	0	1
Central Anatolia	81	0.1605	0.369	0	1

4749) stipulates that approval of the Treasury is required for external borrowing of all public agencies, including local governments. And it limits foreign borrowing only for infrastructure investments.

The other decentralization variable, number of municipalities per capita, is only significant in the regressions with the development index and only in the foreign borrowing and total borrowing regressions. In those two regressions where it is significant, the coefficient is negative which indicates that provinces with more municipalities per capita are less likely to engage in local borrowing. It is possible that provinces with more municipalities (that are more fragmented) have relatively small municipalities with lower large scale service responsibilities (such as infrastructure) and so are not as in need of revenue from borrowing as provinces with larger municipalities that serve a large populace. Among other municipality characteristics, being a metropolitan city is a consistently significant factor in total borrowing regressions. There are 16 provinces that have metropolitan municipalities, which engage in large scale infrastructure projects to better serve their residents. It makes sense that municipalities in those provinces engage in significantly greater overall borrowing. Another interesting finding is that provinces in the Mediterranean region tend to have greater overall local borrowing and greater foreign borrowing. The Mediterranean region has three provinces with metropolitan municipalities (Adana, Antalya and Mersin) and it has undertaken substantial tourism related infrastructure projects among others.

Table 5. Summary statistics for panel regressions

	Obs.	Mean	Std. Dev.	Min.	Max.
Log of ratio of total debt payments to total province expenditures	1204	1.5287	0.9036	-4.8547	3.4733
GDP per capita	1340	13.8335	0.5511	12.439	15.3654
Log of land area	1340	9.1905	0.5207	8.1047	10.8134
Years since metro city	1340	0.7627	2.5406	0	16
Ratio of own source revenue	1204	30.7828	21.4474	1.3913	99.0365
Log of Municipalities per capita	1340	-10.0298	0.5777	-12.8045	-8.7919
Log of Motor vehicles per capita	1340	-3.5536	0.7654	-6.3183	-1.6307
Mediterranean	1340	0.1045	0.306	0	1
East Anatolia	1340	0.1791	0.3836	0	1
Aegean	1340	0.1194	0.3244	0	1
Southeast Anatolia	1340	0.0896	0.2856	0	1
Black Sea	1340	0.209	0.4067	0	1
Marmara	1340	0.1493	0.3565	0	1
Central Anatolia	1340	0.1493	0.3565	0	1

Panel data regression results are reported in Table 7. We see that the decentralization results shown in the cross-sectional regression no longer hold when we add the time variation. The sign of the ratio of own-source revenue coefficients turn negative in most of the fixed effects regressions but they are not statistically significant with the exception of the fixed effects regression with only province fixed effects. On the other hand, the number of municipalities per capita now turns positive and significant in one OLS regression (with region dummies) and most of the fixed effects regressions. This is different from the cross-sectional regression results but it doesn't necessarily contradict those results. It is possible that the sign reversal is driven by the significant increase in the number of provinces and the number of municipalities over time. Hence the time variation may be dominating in this case. The sharp increase in local governments (that may correlate with high urbanization and infrastructure needs) may have required provinces to turn to more borrowing over time but provinces with large number of municipalities per capita (that may correlate with low urbanization and low infrastructure needs) may still borrow less than other provinces.

We get the same result with the metropolitan dummy in all the fixed effects regressions which show that provinces that have obtained the metropolitan municipality status after 1984 have clearly engaged in significantly greater local borrowing. Regressions with region dummies show that provinces in the Mediterranean region and Southeast Anatolia have done significantly greater local borrowing and the ones in East Anatolia have done significantly less compared to provinces in other regions. While GDP per capita is positive and significant in the OLS regressions, it turns negative in some of the fixed effects regressions. It is statistically insignificant in all fixed effects regressions. Similarly land area becomes insignificant in fixed effects regressions. Motor vehicles per capita has negative sign and is significant in almost all regressions. It looks like provinces with greater overall motor vehicles (cars, trucks, tractors, etc.) per capita and possibly less sophisticated urban transportation networks have less need for local borrowing.

Table 6. Cross-sectional spatial regressions

	(1)	(2)	(3)	(4)	(5)	(6)
Variables	**Ratio of Total Borrowing Rev.**	**Ratio of Total Borrowing Rev.**	**Ratio of Domestic Borrowing Rev.**	**Ratio of Domestic Borrowing Rev.**	**Ratio of Foreign Borrowing Rev.**	**Ratio of Foreign Borrowing Rev.**
GDP per capita	-1.443 (2.802)		-2.590* (1.339)		0.883 (2.554)	
Development index		-3.076* (1.759)		-1.209 (0.853)		-1.686 (1.674)
Share of urban population	-2.593 (5.112)	-0.771 (5.025)	-0.900 (2.420)	-0.723 (2.498)	-2.056 (4.751)	-0.214 (4.736)
Land area	-1.899 (1.448)	-2.371* (1.397)	-1.382** (0.674)	-1.301* (0.692)	-0.328 (1.364)	-0.834 (1.364)
Metro city dummy	5.032* (2.894)	6.175** (2.938)	1.521 (1.393)	1.875 (1.452)	3.538 (2.648)	4.249 (2.730)
Own-source rev. ratio	0.110 (0.118)	0.095 (0.113)	0.121** (0.051)	0.120** (0.052)	0.005 (0.110)	-0.001 (0.107)
Municipalities per capita	-2.850 (1.969)	-4.768** (2.163)	-0.438 (0.929)	-0.930 (1.080)	-2.662 (1.822)	-3.762* (2.071)
Motor vehicles per capita	0.387 (2.403)	1.450 (2.263)	1.054 (1.175)	0.555 (1.117)	-0.406 (2.204)	0.942 (2.116)
Mediterranean	10.409*** (2.922)	9.653*** (2.812)	-0.113 (1.285)	-0.240 (1.370)	10.022*** (2.855)	9.502*** (2.801)
East Anatolia	1.338 (3.478)	-0.199 (3.272)	1.297 (1.556)	1.787 (1.575)	-0.072 (3.199)	-1.604 (3.112)
Aegean	0.283 (2.943)	0.605 (2.757)	-1.448 (1.288)	-1.581 (1.354)	1.721 (2.852)	2.121 (2.754)
Southeast Anatolia	-3.313 (3.614)	-6.944* (4.008)	-1.425 (1.586)	-2.249 (1.913)	-1.988 (3.361)	-4.142 (3.815)
Black Sea	-2.396 (2.698)	-3.760 (2.666)	-1.817 (1.193)	-2.187* (1.295)	-0.576 (2.575)	-1.330 (2.615)
Marmara	0.387 (3.012)	1.197 (2.716)	-0.836 (1.314)	-1.360 (1.321)	1.173 (2.903)	2.303 (2.713)
Constant	8.682 (51.085)	-21.165 (23.184)	46.295* (23.924)	3.396 (11.978)	-37.820 (47.220)	-26.443 (22.376)
Observations	81	81	81	81	81	81

Standard errors in parentheses
*** p<0.01, ** p<0.05, * p<0.1

SUMMARY AND CONCLUSION

In this paper, we examined the link between decentralization and local borrowing within Turkish provinces. We first provided an overview of the local government structure and recent reform efforts. We then continued with an empirical analysis of the effects of decentralization on local borrowing in Turkish provinces using cross-sectional and panel data approaches. We used cross-sectional data on all 81 provinces for the year 2000 and panel data that consists of 67 provinces over a period from 1980 to 2000. We examined if specific province characteristics and variations in the number of local govern-

Table 7. Panel regressions

Variables	(1)	(2)	(3)	(4)	(5)	(6)	(7)
	OLS	**OLS**	**OLS**	**Fixed Effects**	**Fixed Effects**	**Fixed Effects AR1**	**Fixed Effects AR1**
GDP per capita	0.673*** (0.086)	0.529*** (0.102)	0.324*** (0.105)	0.082 (0.169)	0.076 (0.167)	-0.122 (0.147)	-0.1 (0.213)
Land area	0.029 (0.051)	0.016 (0.057)	-0.007 (0.055)	0.493** (0.201)	0.297 (0.196)	0.539*** (0.196)	0.307 (0.239)
Years since metrocity	0.029** (0.014)	0.037*** (0.013)	0.048*** (0.013)	0.070*** (0.013)	0.059*** (0.013)	0.055*** (0.018)	0.056*** (0.017)
Own-source rev. ratio	0.002 (0.001)	0.001 (0.001)	0.005* (0.003)	-0.002** (0.001)	0.004 (0.002)	-0.001 (0.001)	-0.001 (0.003)
Municipalities per capita	0.045 (0.049)	0.015 (0.054)	0.127** (0.055)	0.353** (0.138)	0.409*** (0.136)	0.274 (0.175)	0.311* (0.177)
Motor vehicles per capita	-0.283*** (0.068)	-0.353*** (0.068)	-0.007 (0.090)	-0.642*** (0.091)	-1.103*** (0.170)	-0.702*** (0.129)	-0.835*** (0.198)
Mediterranean		0.329*** (0.102)	0.323*** (0.098)				
East Anatolia		-0.559*** (0.108)	-0.288** (0.113)				
Aegean		-0.083 (0.100)	-0.152 (0.097)				
Southeast Anatolia		-0.008 (0.119)	0.279** (0.124)				
Black Sea		0.059 (0.096)	0.109 (0.094)				
Marmara		-0.078 (0.113)	-0.072 (0.109)				
Constant	-8.692*** (1.502)	-7.018*** (1.653)	-2.023 (1.808)	-3.989 (3.373)	0.267 (3.340)	-1.563*** (0.165)	-3.526** (1.512)
Province fixed effects	No	No	No	Yes	Yes	Yes	Yes
Year fixed effects	No	No	Yes	No	Yes	No	Yes
Observations	1,203	1,203	1,203	1,203	1,203	1,136	1,136
R-squared	0.077	0.136	0.213	0.448	0.503	0.134	0.1848

Standard errors in parentheses.
*** p<0.01, ** p<0.05, * p<0.1

ment units or own-source revenue across these provinces and across time have had a significant impact on local borrowing. Our findings from the cross-sectional analysis of 81 provinces show a positive link between the ratio of own-source revenue to total province tax revenue (fiscal decentralization) and local borrowing from domestic sources. This, however, has not been confirmed when we add the time variation in the panel data analysis. We find an association between the number of municipalities per capita and local borrowing which is also not found to be robust. There seems to be some evidence that as the number of provinces and municipalities expanded significantly since the 1980s province felt the need to borrow more to meet the rising demand for public services. On the other hand, being a province with a metropolitan municipality and being in the Mediterranean region seem to be positively (and robustly) associated with local borrowing.

A possible membership in the European Union in the future is likely to place heightened demand on the public administration system of Turkey. For Turkey to meet EU standards of service delivery there is a need for investment in local infrastructure. Therefore, a good case can be made for permitting municipal governments to borrow as long as the "golden rule" of debt finance is followed: that they borrow only for financing capital (investment) expenditures such as those for infrastructure improvements, which provide a flow of benefits over time. When this rule is followed, borrowing then not only becomes a viable alternative to other sources of financing, but, in fact, becomes a tool for the achievement of the goals of fiscal equity and efficiency.

REFERENCES

Akıllı, H., & Akıllı, H. S. (2014). Decentralization and Recentralization of Local Governments in Turkey. *Procedia: Social and Behavioral Sciences*, *140*, 682–686. doi:10.1016/j.sbspro.2014.04.493

Bird, R. M. (2000). Intergovernmental Fiscal Relations: Universal Principals, Local Applications. *International Studies Program Working Paper 00-2*, Andrew Young School of Policy Studies, Georgia State University, Atlanta.

Bird, R. M., & Fiszbein, A. (1999). Columbia: The Central Role of the Central Government in Fiscal Decentralization. In R. M. Bird & F. Vaillancourt (Eds.), *Fiscal Decentralization in Developing Countries* (pp. 172–205). Cambridge: Cambridge University Press. doi:10.1017/CBO9780511559815.007

Bird, R. M., & Smart, M. (2002). Intergovernmental Fiscal Transfers: International Lessons for developing Countries. *World Development*, *30*(6), 899–912. doi:10.1016/S0305-750X(02)00016-5

Bird, R. M., & Vaillancourt, F. (Eds.), (1999). *Fiscal Decentralization in Developing Countries*. Cambridge: Cambridge University Press. doi:10.1017/CBO9780511559815

Dillinger, W., & Webb, S. B. (1999). Fiscal Management in Federal Democracies: Argentina and Brazil. *World Bank Policy Research Working Paper No. 2121*.

Ebel, R., & Petersen, P. (2012). *Handbook on State and Local Finance*. Massachusetts: Oxford Press. doi:10.1093/oxfordhb/9780199765362.001.0001

Greene, W. H. (2003). *Econometric Analysis* (5th ed.). Upper Saddle River, New Jersey: Prentice Hall.

Keleş, R. (2000). *Yerinden Yönetim ve Siyaset*. Istanbul: Cem Yayınevi.

Kitchen, H. (2004, August 9-12). Financing Local Government Capital Investment. Trent University Economics Department Working Paper. Retrieved from https://www.trentu.ca/economics/WorkingPapers/Financing%20Capital%20Investment.pdf

Kolko, P. (2011). *Rethinking the State-Local Relationship: Local Economic Development*. San Francisco, CA: Public Policy Institute of California.

Musgrave, R. A. (1959). *The Theory of Public Finance*. New York: McGraw-Hill.

Oates, W. (1972). *Fiscal Federalism*. New York: Harcourt, Brace, Jovanovich.

Prud'homme, R. (1995). The Dangers of Decentralization. *The World Bank Research Observer*, *10*(2), 201–220. doi:10.1093/wbro/10.2.201

Rao, G. M. (1999). India: Intergovernmental Fiscal Relations in a Planned Economy. In R. M. Bird & F. Vaillancourt (Eds.), *Fiscal Decentralization in Developing Countries* (pp. 78–114). Cambridge: Cambridge University Press. doi:10.1017/CBO9780511559815.004

Rood, S. (2000). Decentralization, Democracy, and Development. In D. G. Timberman (Ed.), *The Philippines: New Directions in Domestic Policy and Foreign Relations* (pp. 11–135). New York: Asia Society.

Stigler, G. J. (1957). The Tenable Range of Functions of Local Government. In US Congress Joint Economic Committee (Ed.), Federal Expenditure Policy for Economic Growth and Stability (pp. 213-219). Washington, DC: Government Printing Office.

Tanzi, V. (2000, November 20-21). On Fiscal Federalism: Issues to Worry About. *Paper presented in the Conference of Fiscal Decentralization*, Washington, DC: IMF Headquarters.

Ter-Minassian, T., & Craig, J. (1997). Control of Subnational Government Borrowing. In T. Ter-Minassian (Ed.), *Fiscal Federalism in Theory and Practice* (pp. 156–172). Washington, DC: IMF.

Tosun, M. S. (2010). *Middle East and Western Asia. In United Cities and Local Governments (UCLG) Second Global Report on Decentralization and Local Democracy - Local Government Finance: The Challenges of the 21st Century* (pp. 233–253). Northampton, MA: Edward Elgar Publishing.

Tosun, M. S., & Yılmaz, S. (2010). Decentralization, Economic Development, and Growth in Turkish Provinces. *Emerging Markets Finance and Trade*, *46*(4), 23–44. doi:10.2753/REE1540-496X460405

World Development Report 1999/2000: Entering the 21st Century. (1999World Bank. New York: Oxford University Press.

ENDNOTES

1 See Rao (1999), Rood (2000), Bird and Fiszbein (1999), and Dillinger and Webb (1999) for studies on India, Philippines, Columbia and Brazil, respectively. Prud'homme (1995) and Tanzi (2000) also provided arguments for why decentralization may not work well. Bird and Vaillancourt (1999) indicated that it is not easy to design a decentralization policy that works.

2 The dual local government system of deconcentration and decentralization is very common in the Middle East and Francophone Africa. Compared with other public administration systems (i.e. Anglophone or Lusophone), local authorities in the French public administration system do not exercise much power on behalf of the State. Furthermore, they do not manage many delegated powers. Instead, local authorities have their own responsibilities; even though they are very closely controlled by the central government in carrying out those responsibilities.

3 SPAs are headed by an appointed governor. The deliberative branch of SPA is provincial council, which is headed by a president elected by the provincial council members amongst themselves. The head of the executive branch is governor, appointed by the central government as the head of the

province. The executive branch of SPAs is provincial executive board (*encümen*), which includes both elected and appointed members. Provincial council elects five of its members and governor appoints five of the department heads from his administration to serve in the executive board.

4 The number of municipalities increased from 1,727 in 1980 to 3,225 in 2000. The number provinces stayed stable from 1957 to 1989; however between 1989 and 2000, fourteen new provinces were established.

5 The 2004 Metropolitan Municipality Law no.5216 updated the Metropolitan Municipality Law of 1984.

6 The Parliament has enacted the 2005 Special Provincial Administration Law no.5302. Prior to this legislation the SPA system was regulated by an Ottoman Empire law dating back to 1913.

7 In 2005, the Parliament has also enacted a new municipality law—Municipality Law no. 5393. Prior to this legislation, municipal sector was regulated by the Municipality Law no.1580 of 1930.

8 However, this new increased threshold applies to establishment of new municipalities; it does not apply to existing municipalities that are above the minimum threshold of 2,000 (the minimum population criterion under the previous legislation).

9 The 2008 Law no. 5747.

10 The 2008 Law no. 5779.

11 The 2012 Law no. 6360.

12 From 1989 to 1999 fourteen new provinces are created by separation from other existing provinces.

13 Provincial development index is developed by the State Planning Organization. More about the index see Dinçer, Özaslan and Kavasoğlu (2003).

14 We use provincial GDP data of 2000 as the basis of analysis. However, TURKSTAT introduced a fourth revision to the GDP series and updated the base year to 1998 from 1987. Revised provincial GDP data do not exist yet. Since our analysis covers the period between 1980 and 2000 we believe that this change has a limited impact on the results.

15 Dummy for the Central Anatolian region is omitted to avoid perfect multicollinearity.

16 Tosun and Yılmaz (2010) examine the impact of decentralization through increases in the number of municipal governments in the 67 original provinces.

Chapter 23
Taxes, Natural Resource Endowment, and the Supply of Labor:
New Evidence

Weshah Razzak
Arab Planning Institute, Kuwait

Belkacem Laabas
Arab Planning Institute, Kuwait

ABSTRACT

We use the work-leisure choice model to compute equilibrium weekly hours worked for a number of Arab countries and compare them to the G7 countries. We show that the labor supply curve is elastic in all Arab countries, and provide a new measure of labor productivity. This finding confirms previous research that workers respond to incentives, which has serious implications for tax and social security policies. We also provide some policy simulations pertinent to the effects of taxation on welfare and poverty.

INTRODUCTION

The purpose of this chapter is to measure hours worked, which allows us to compute the Frisch elasticity of labor supply, and labor productivity in a number of Arab countries for which no data have been published previously. The Frisch elasticity captures the elasticity of hours worked to the wage rate, given a constant marginal utility of wealth. Labor productivity is Gross Domestic Product (GDP) per hours worked. We use the model to study the macroeconomic implications of some policy issues, such as the effect of taxes on welfare and poverty.

To measure weekly hours-worked, we calibrate a theoretical model; namely, the work-leisure choice model which Nickell (2003), Prescott (2004) and Shimer (2009) demonstrated its Goodness-of-Fit to G7 data.[1] We use this model because the data of the main predicting factors (such as consumption, income, the tax rate and the share of capital) are available for the Arab countries.

Our sample for the Arab countries includes two groups of countries: oil-producing and non-oil-producing nations. The former do not tax income and consumption. However, the average effective marginal

DOI: 10.4018/978-1-5225-0053-7.ch023

tax rate crucially determines the solution of the work-leisure choice model (i.e., the supply of labor). To contend with this problem, we introduce natural resource endowment in the production function of the oil-producing countries. The inclusion of natural resources in the model creates a wedge between real wages and the marginal product of labor similar to the *wedge* that taxes create. The increase in the share of natural resource reduces hours worked. It discourages work and reduces labor supply. This is because the wage rate in the oil-producing countries exceeds the equilibrium wage rate due to rent.

We make a number of contributions. First, we measure equilibrium hours worked for five Arab non-oil producers (Egypt, Jordan, Morocco, Syria, and Tunisia) and for seven oil-producers. These include Algeria and the Gulf Cooperation Council countries (GCC) which are Bahrain, Kuwait, Oman, Qatar, the United Arab Emirates (UAE) and the Kingdom of Saudi Arabia (KSA) for which the data on hours worked do not exist. Estimation of hours worked allows us to compute and analyze the Frisch elasticity of the labor supply, which has a major role in policy design. In addition, it allows us to measure productivity as GDP per hours worked in the Arab countries. Second, we are unaware of any published articles on the work-leisure model with a natural resource endowment.

We modify the model and show that such endowment works just like a tax on labor supply. Third, a theory is valid if it fits different data at different times and places. So far, the bulk of the evidence for the work-leisure model relies on data from developed countries (the G-7 and the OECD). We confirm the validity of the work-leisure, intertemporal-intratemporal substitution model using data from the Arab countries. We show that Arab countries' labor supply curves are just like the G-7 (also elastic), which has important policy implications.1F[2] People in non-oil-producing Arab countries work long hours, but their relative productivities are low; therefore, they are relatively poorer. People in oil-producing countries work much less, which is consistent with Noland and Pack (2007), among others, who show that fewer individuals are involved in the production and creation of wealth. Fourth, we solve the model stochastically and produce baseline projections of future labor supply for the Arab countries. Then we conduct policy scenarios. For the GCC oil-producing countries, we ask how much welfare will change if they embark on a policy to diversify their income (i.e., reduce the reliance on oil as the main source of income). We find very significant increases in the lifetime consumption equivalent, which is our measure of welfare. We also ask how much welfare will change because of the introduction of a permanent consumption tax.

Finally, we choose Morocco, a non-oil-producing country that has a high poverty rate, and ask how long it will take to eliminate poverty if the government reduces the effective marginal tax rate on households. We find that a small, permanent tax cut can reduce poverty by more than half in approximately 12 years.

Section 2 summarizes the main features of the Arab economies which have implications for the estimation of hours worked. We present the model in section 3. In section 4, we calibrate the model for the G-7 countries and the Arab countries, estimate hours worked, compute the elasticity of labor supply, and labor productivity. Section 5 includes policy simulations, and Section 6 is the conclusion.

A GENERAL DESCRIPTION OF THE ARAB ECONOMIES

The Arab countries are heterogeneous economies in which the economic growth rates exhibit high volatility and their productivity levels are low (Makdisi et al., 2006). Countries such as the Sudan,

Yemen, and Mauritania are classified as low-income poor countries, while other such as the GCC countries are classified as high-income due to oil exports. The remaining North African and Middle Eastern countries are considered to be middle-income countries. Low- and middle-income countries are mostly labor-abundant countries with high unemployment rates, especially among the youth and educated females. Labor income transfers from abroad (remittance) have a major role in financing final private expenditure, leading to a significant increase of the consumption ratio relative to GDP.

The GCC countries, on the other hand, are labor-scarce and their economies are dependent on expatriate labor, which creates a deep segmentation in labor markets. The GCC countries are also small open economies that do not impose direct income taxes because of their large natural resource endowments. Because of the rents extracted from the sale of the natural resources, the huge net operating surplus pushes the capital ratio to a high level that is significantly different from the average ratio observed in regular production functions. Almost all Arab countries are welfare states where the government provides health care, education, and unemployment benefits. The public sectors are relatively large, and in many countries, they are the main providers of job.

Productivity statistics are, therefore, very difficult to measure because the public sector's output is hard to measure. Arab economies have low female participation rates. However, in some GCC countries, the female participation ratio is high because of high wages in the public sector, and because the expatriate population is overwhelmingly active in the labor market. These structural economic features have significant impact on the average hours worked. In the GCC countries, hours are driven by the low tax rates, which tend to increase labor supply as is suggested by theory. However, large levels of rents tend to depress labor supply through inflating capital share and lowering the consumption ratio. These structural features of Arab economies seem to affect the labor supply.

Noland and Pack (2007) argue that Arab oil-producing countries are characterized by the generation of large oil rents and boom and bust cycles driven by the world price of their export. They show that the shares of rent in government revenues and in GDP are relatively high. These shares are between 70 to 85 percent of government revenues, and between 25 to 36 percent of GDP. They conclude: "fewer individuals are involved in the production of wealth, and the majority of them are involved in its distribution and consumption."

Finally, the quality of the data of the Arab countries is poor and do not conform to international standards. In the model which we present here, two variables play a major part in estimating hours worked: real GDP and real consumption. The National Income Accounts in the Arab countries are problematic in the sense that they do not use household expenditures surveys to measure consumption; rather it is computed as a residual from the national income identity. Real GDP is computed from the expenditures side, and it is not a chain measure.

THE MODEL

We begin with the model, which is found in Prescott (2004), to derive the labor supply.[3] A similar model is found in Nickell (2003) and Shimer (2009). The model's variables are lowercase. National Accounting Statistics are in uppercase. The utility function of a *stand in household* who faces a work-leisure decision is given by:

$$U = E\left\{\sum_{t=0}^{\infty} \beta^t [\log c_t + \alpha \log(100 - h_t)]\right\} \quad (1)$$

The utility function depends on the expected discounted sum of consumption c and leisure, where 100 is the number of hours available for individuals to work in a week and h is hours-worked in "market activities". The expectations operator E does not necessarily mean rational expectations, and $0<\beta<1$ is the discount factor and specifies the degree of patience.

A high value means more patience for consumption and leisure. The parameter α is >0 and denotes the value of the non-market productive time per household. It could be the relative value of the time spent working at home. Typically, it is the relative value of leisure. The production using this time is untaxed. The utility function includes one consumption good as in Christaino and Eichenbaum (1992).

The stock of capital evolves according to

$$k_{t+1} = (1-\delta)k_t + x_t, \quad (2)$$

where k is the stock of capital and x_t is gross investments. The depreciation rate is δ.

There is a *stand-in firm* with a Cobb-Douglas, constant returns to scale, technology of production:

$$y_t = A_t k_t^{\theta} h_t^{1-\theta} \geq c_t + x_t + g_t \quad (3)$$

where g is government expenditure.

Total factor productivity is *exogenous* and is given by A_t.[4] The parameter θ is the share of capital; $0<\theta<1$. For our purpose, we assume that technical progress is exogenous because it has no role in the inference being drawn.

The household's date t budget constraint is:

$$(1+\tau_c)c_t + (1+\tau_x)x_t = (1-\tau_h)w_t.h_t + (1-\tau_K)(r_t - \delta)k_t + \delta\, k_t + T_t \quad (4)$$

where w is the real wage, r is the real interest rate or rental capital, and T is transfer payment. The tax rates of consumption, investments, labor and capital are given by τ with the subscripts c, x, h, k, which denote consumption, investments, hours worked and capital, respectively.

We must emphasize the assumptions, as in Prescott (2004), that there is a government, which taxes consumption, investments, income from labor, etc., and the government budget constraint, which is unchanged in each period. All tax revenues, except those used to finance the pure public consumption good, are given back to the households either as transfer payments or in-kind. These transfers are lump sum, being independent of the household's income. Most of the public expenditures are substitutes for private consumption in the G-7 countries.

We see no reason for this not being the case in the Arab countries. Prescott (2004) states the substitution between public and private consumption is one-to-one, except for the military expenditures. The goods and services we are discussing here are typical: public education, health, etc. The assumption regarding the estimate of the pure public good g is twofold the military share of employment times GDP.[5]

Clearly, this is a very simple tax system than in reality. Introducing a more realistic accelerated depreciation and investment tax credits would affect the price of the investment good relative to the consumption good, but it would not alter the inference drawn from this model. This is a simple macroeconomic model rather than a public finance model.

There are many different ways to compute the tax rate.[6] Prescott (2004) derives the tax rate in the model theoretically. He derives an aggregate effective marginal tax rate on labor income using both the tax rate on consumption τ_c and on labor τ_h. It is the fraction of additional labor income that is taken in the form of taxes, holding investments fixed.[7]

$$\tau = \frac{\tau_h + \tau_C}{1 + \tau_C} \tag{5}$$

Following Prescott (2004), it is important to note that the National Income Account is adjusted to fit with economic theory, where households pay the taxes. The major adjustment is to treat "indirect taxes less subsidy" as "net taxes on final product". It means "net indirect tax" is not a cost component of GDP. Indirect taxes include value-added taxes, sales taxes, excise taxes, property taxes, etc., which are mostly levied on households.

Some indirect taxes such as diesel fuel taxes, property taxes on office buildings and sales taxes on equipments, etc. fall on all forms of products. It is assumed that two-thirds of the indirect taxes less subsidy fall directly on private consumption expenditures, and the remaining one-third is distributed evenly over private consumption and private investment.

Again, the National Accounting Statistics are in uppercase. The net indirect taxes on consumption are stated as follows:

$$IT_c = [2/3 + 1/3\frac{C}{C+I}]IT \tag{6}$$

where C is private consumption expenditures, I is private investment and IT is *net* indirect taxes. The model economy's consumption is $c=C+G-G_{mil}-IT_c$, where G is public consumption and G_{mil} is military spending. The model economy's output is given by $y=GDP-IT$.[8]

The consumption tax rate is:

$$\tau_c = \frac{IT_c}{C - IT_c} \tag{7}$$

Taxes on labor income are two: the income tax with a marginal tax rate, and a social security tax. The social security marginal tax rate, $\tau_{ss} = \frac{social\ security\ taxes}{(1-\theta)(GDP-IT)}$ where the denominator is labor income if labor is paid its marginal productivity.

The *average* income tax rate is:

$$\overline{\tau}_{inc} = \frac{Direct\,Taxes}{GDP - IT - Depreciation} \tag{8}$$

where direct taxes are paid by households and do not include corporate income taxes. Prescott's estimate of the marginal labor income tax $\tau_h = t_{ss} + 1.6\overline{\tau}_{inc}$ and the number 1.6 reflects the fact that the marginal income tax rates are higher than the average tax rates. This particular number (1.6) delivers a marginal income tax found in Feenberg and Coutts (1993) for the "U.S.". Their calculation of the marginal income tax is based on a representative sample of tax records.

They calculate by how much the tax revenue increases if every household labor income is increased by one percent. The total change in tax receipts divided by the total change in labor income is their estimate of the marginal income tax. This assumption may not fit the Arab countries. Therefore, we use sensitivity analysis and report the figures in Appendix 3. We recalibrated hours for values of 1.0, 1.6, 2.6, and 3.6. We prefer the central estimates because we believe the estimates are neither very low nor very high, and the tax rates in the Arab countries cannot be higher than 40 percent.

From the above we get the FOC, then the marginal rate of substitution equal to the price ratios:

$$\frac{\alpha/(1-h_t)}{1/c_t} = (1-\tau)w_t \tag{9}$$

And from the production function, the marginal product of labor is equal to the real wage rate:

$$w_t = (1-\theta)k_t^{\theta}h_t^{-\theta} = (1-\theta)y_t / h_t \tag{10}$$

The equilibrium labor supply is solved for from the two FOC above,

$$h_t = \frac{1-\theta}{(1-\theta) + \frac{c_t}{y_t}\frac{\alpha}{1-\tau_t}} \tag{11}$$

The ratio of consumption to GDP in Equation (11) captures the intertemporal substitution. The tax rate in Equation (11) captures the intratemporal substitution. If people expect the effective tax rate on labor income to be lower in the future, for example, they will increase their current consumption. It is important to note that our analysis of the labor supply abstracts from demographic factors, which are known to affects the supply of labor.

There is a voluminous literature of microeconomic analysis of the supply of labor, which is more difficult to incorporate into this simple macroeconomic model. Cole and Ohanian (1999, 2002), Chari, Kehoe and McGrattan (2003), and Fisher and Hornstei (2002) produced evidence of other factors that affect labor supply decisions. This paper focuses on the effect of a smaller number of variables to get a reasonable measure for hours worked in the Arab countries, which are unavailable. We also have insufficient demographic data to incorporate into our analysis.

Introducing Natural Resource Endowment Effect

For the GCC countries and Algeria, the theory predicts that a low tax rate τ increases hours worked. The GCC countries have a low tax rate. If we fit the model for the GCC, hours worked will be very high, greater than hours in the USA and Japan, which is nonsensical. To ameliorate this problem, we modify the production function by introducing a natural resource (oil and gas) endowment.

The production function becomes:

$$y_t = A_t N_t^{\omega} k_t^{\theta} h_t^{1-\omega-\theta} \tag{12}$$

where N_t could be the natural resource utilization rate, R_t. Stiglitz (1974) focuses on the ratio of resource utilization to the stock of natural resources, i.e., $\gamma=R/S$, while

Solow and Wan (1976) only use the flow.[9] The budget constraint in Equation (4) will include income per capita from natural resources on the RHS.

$$(1+\tau_c)c_t + (1+\tau_x)x_t = (1-\tau_h)w_t.h_t + (1-\tau_K)(r_t - \delta)k_t + \delta\, k_t + T_t + (P_t^o N_t / \hat{P}_t), \tag{13}$$

where P_t^o is the international price of the natural resource, N_t is the flow of natural resources, and $\hat{P}_t$ is population.

Solving the model the same way gives:

$$h_t^N = \frac{1-\omega-\theta}{(1-\omega-\theta) + \frac{c_t}{y_t}\frac{\alpha}{1-\tau_t}} \tag{14}$$

where the superscript N refers to natural resources. The share of hydrocarbon in output is ω. For $\omega > 0$, this formula predicts that h^N in Equation (14) is smaller than h in Equation (11). For $\omega = 1$, $h^N < 0$ and for $\omega = 0$, h^N is identical to h. For $h_t^N \geq 0$, ω^{max} must be equal to $1-\theta$.

2. Calibration

Developing countries in general and the Arab countries specifically do not report data on actual hours worked. Thus, we cannot measure the goodness of the fit of the model. To shed light on the performance of the model we will calibrate the model for the G-7 first because these countries report actual hours worked. We describe the G-7 data in the appendix 1 and the Arab countries data in appendix 2. Note that our data are measured in Purchasing Power Parity (PPP) terms. To calibrate the model for countries, $i=1,2,\ldots N$, we fix the share of capital θ to the *average* of its value over the sample.

The share of capital is measured from National Income Accounts, as gross operating surplus / GDP ratio. The ratio c_i/y_i is also the average over the sample. The value of the effective marginal tax rate τ_i also varies across countries. Since we compare our estimates of hours worked to those of the G-7 countries, we follow Prescott (2004) and choose the parameter α such that it maximizes the fit of the model (minimum error). However, for the Arab countries, we choose α arbitrarily because we do not have actual data. The results are reported in Table 1.The upper panel of Table 1 reports the calibration of the model's equilibrium hours worked for the G-7 countries for data from 2000 to 2008.

The model fits Canada, Italy, and Japan the best; slightly over-predicting in the case of Canada, and slightly under-predicting in the cases of Italy and Japan. On average, however, the fit is fine with an error of 0.06. The G-7's average of weekly hours worked per person is about 23.

The fit can be made tighter when we allow α to vary across countries. We do not report these results, but allowing α to vary across the G-7 countries shows that for Italy, the model has a value of α equal to the average of 1.78. Three countries including Canada, the United Kingdom (UK) and the USA have a value of α equal 1.6, which is below the G-7 average. The non-English speaking countries France, Germany, and Japan have a value of α higher than 2. These estimates of α indicate that the relative value of leisure is much higher in the non-English speaking G-7 countries.

Now we can turn to estimating hours worked for the Arab non-oil producing. Those are also labor-abundant countries. We have data from 1991 to 2006. We compute the effective marginal tax rate. Note that there are no time series data for the marginal tax rates for Arab countries. Since our results will depend on our assumptions about certain parameters in the model, we conduct a sensitivity analysis.

Table 1. Actual and Predicted Labor Supply for the G7 and Arab non-oil Producing Countries
$h=(1-\bar{\theta})/(1-\bar{\theta})+(c/y)(\bar{\alpha}/1-\tau)$

Estimates of the Labor Supply for the G7 (2000-2008)							
Country	**Actual *h***	**Predicted**	**Difference**	**α**	**θ**	**τ**	***c/y***
Canada	25.26	23.60	1.66	1.78	0.38	0.38	0.70
France	20.08	22.73	-2.65	1.78	0.38	0.37	0.75
Germany	19.33	21.88	-2.54	1.78	0.38	0.42	0.73
Italy	21.09	22.45	-1.36	1.78	0.38	0.40	0.72
Japan	26.98	28.40	-1.41	1.78	0.38	0.25	0.66
UK	24.05	21.30	2.75	1.78	0.38	0.38	0.80
US	26.06	23.71	2.35	1.78	0.38	0.30	0.79
Average G7	**23.26**	**23.20**	**0.06**	**1.78**	**0.38**	**0.35**	**0.73**
Estimates of the Labor Supply for the Arab Countries (1991-2006)							
Country	**Actual**	**Predicted**	**Frisch Elasticity**	**α**	**θ**	**τ**	***c/y***
Egypt	NA	18.47	4.4	1.78	0.48	0.24	0.98
Jordon	NA	21.03	3.8	1.78	0.48	0.28	0.79
Morocco	NA	16.68	5.0	1.78	0.48	0.39	0.89
Syria	NA	26.10	2.8	1.78	0.48	0.19	0.67
Tunisia	NA	17.11	4.8	1.78	0.48	0.35	0.92
Average	**NA**	**19.87**	**4.1**	**1.78**	**0.48**	**0.28**	**0.85**

1. Both $\bar{\alpha}$ and $\bar{\theta}$ are the average values across G7 countries. The individual values of α for G7 which minimizes the error are 1.6 (Canada), 2.2 (France), 2.1 (Germany), 1.7 (Italy), 2.1 (Japan), 1.6 (UK) and 1.6 (USA) respectively. Same average value of α is adopted for the Arab countries. Frisch elasticity is (100/*h*)–1

From the National Income Account for each country, we calculate the share of capital as gross operating surplus to GDP. The average value of θ is similar across Arab countries. Thus, we fix the share of capital, θ to the average, which is 0.48. Moreover, we try α of 1.78, which is the same as average G7 value.[10]

Note that we do not have data or estimates for α in other non-G-7 or OECD countries such as the Asian nations. We let c_i/y_i to differ across countries. We use the average of c_i/y_i over the sample. We do the same with the effective marginal tax rate. The lower panel of Table 1 reports the results of h_i for the non-oil-producing Arab countries.

These estimates seem sensible relative to the G-7. The average of the weekly hours worked per person is 19.87, which is lower than the G-7 average of 23.4. Beginning with the most obvious, the Syrians work much more than all other countries (26.1 hours) because they have the lowest tax rate among Arabs, and their *c/y* ratio is less than average of the G-7 countries. Egypt's estimate of hours worked is less than Jordan's despite the fact that the Jordon has a higher tax rate. This is because the consumption-output ratios are quite different. The Egyptians' *c/y* ratio is 0.98 while that of Jordan is 0.79. Egypt's *c/y* ratio significantly exceeds the G-7 average.

All Arab non-oil-producing countries have a high consumption to output ratio, far exceeding the developed countries in PPP terms. The North African nations, Tunisia and Morocco, work less than the Syrians and the Jordanians because they pay relatively higher taxes. Both Morocco and Tunisia have average weekly hours worked of approximately 17.

The results in Table 1 confirm the extant literature's findings that when people are taxed the same rate, they most probably supply the same amount of labor. Taxes affect labor supply decisions in the Arab countries. Our estimates of the Frisch elasticity in Table 1 suggest that the labor supply curves for the Arab countries are elastic, particularly in Egypt, Morocco, and Tunisia. These results are consistent with the extant literature.

Prescott (2004) argues that elastic labor supplies spares countries the trouble of facing the choice of either increasing taxes on the young, thereby reducing their welfare, or not honoring the promise made to the old to avoid making them worse off. One policy implication for large labor supply elasticity is that as the population ages, promises of payment to the current and future old people do not necessarily have to be financed by increasing taxes.

Our estimates of the labor supply can explain why the non-oil-producing Arab countries have low productivity. Table 2 reports the decomposition of income per working age population relative to the average G-7. We decompose GDP per working age population into GDP per hour and hours per working age population (i.e., labor productivity multiplied by labor utilization). The Arab non-oil producing countries do not seem to have problems with labor utilization. They work long hours, but their relative productivity level is significantly lower than the G-7. The Arabs work relatively long hours, produce relatively less output per hour, and they are poorer than the G-7 countries. These results are sensible and hardly surprising. This model predicts that any increase in the tax rate in the Arab non-oil-producing countries will make them even poorer.

Now we turn to the oil-producing Arab countries. They also have labor shortages. The majority of the labor force is imported. These countries include the GCC countries plus Algeria. We have data from 1991 to 2003. The GCC's effective marginal tax rate is relatively very low, about 5 per cent. It represents social security tax. The GCC countries do not have income and consumption taxes. Algeria differs from the GCC in taxation. Algeria's effective marginal tax rate is 34 per cent.

We estimate hours-worked over two samples. The first sample is during the periods when the price of oil was low; hence, oil revenues to GDP were low. The second sample is when the price of oil was

Table 2. Productivity Decomposition of Arab Non-Oil Producing Countries Relative to Average G7 – Sample 1991 to 2006 Hours are based on a value of $\alpha = 1.78$

Country	GDP per Person	GDP per Hour	Hours per Person
Egypt	15.80	21.48	73.55
Jordan	12.73	15.17	83.89
Morocco	15.90	23.97	66.32
Syria	6.21	5.94	104.6
Tunisia	22.06	32.43	68.03
G7	100.00	100.00	100.00

high; hence, the revenues to GDP were high. The share of hydrocarbon in GDP ω is from each country's budgets.

It is the ratio of oil and gas revenues to GDP, $p^o q^o / (p^o q^o + p^{no} q^{no})$, where the superscript *o* denotes hydrocarbon (oil and gas), hence p^o is the price of the hydrocarbons and q^o is the quantity. The superscript *no* denotes the non-hydrocarbon revenue.

Results of the estimates of hours worked for the GCC and Algeria are shown in Table 3. For sensitivity analysis, we use values of α 1.3, 1.5, and 2.0. The average predicted equilibrium weekly hours worked in the GCC is between a high of approximately 20 hours and a low of 13, during the sample when oil revenues as a share of GDP were low. This is a sensible range compared with previous estimates of the G-7, and Arab non-oil-producing countries. This average is lower than the average of the non-oil-producing Arab countries.

Algerians work slightly longer hours than the average GCC, but less than Bahrain. Bahrain, Oman, and the UAE predicted weekly hours worked exceed the average GCC. They also work longer hours than the average Arab countries do. Bahrain and Oman in particular implement active labor market policies to reduce unemployment and to encourage their citizens to work. Kuwait, Qatar, and Saudi Arabia work relatively fewer hours than all other Arab countries.

Hours worked plummet in the second sample over the period of high hydrocarbon revenues. The average of hours worked falls between 5 and 7 hours. For Algeria, it falls between 5 and 7 hours. Among the GCC, Oman's hours-worked decline is the largest, between 8 and 12 hours. On average, GCC's hours worked could decline to nearly eight hours a week due to higher hydrocarbon revenues. This says a lot about the extent of the rent in these economies and reflects the manifestation of the oil curse in the labor market. In the leisure – work model, leisure is a normal good. As income increases, the income effect induces workers to buy more leisure, hence less work.

TWO POLICY SIMULATION EXPERIMENTS

Diversification, Consumption Tax, and Welfare in GCC

We provide a baseline, stochastic projection for hours worked until 2050. We choose 2050 arbitrarily to indicate the long run. Then, we simulate policy scenarios. The first policy scenario is about the welfare effect of taxes. The GCC countries have been discussing ways to diversify their income source, away

Table 3. Labor Supply with Natural Resource Endowment for Oil Producing Countries $h^N = (1-\theta-\omega)/[1-\theta-\omega + (c/y)(\alpha/1-\tau)]$

	Low Hydrocarbon Revenue Period 1991-1999						High Hydrocarbon Revenue Period 2002-2003						Difference in Hours
	h^N	Frisch Elasticity	τ	c/y	θ	ω	h^N	Frisch Elasticity	τ	c/y	θ	ω	
Algeria	20.4	3.9	0.34	0.73	0.47	0.19	13.2	6.6	0.38	0.61	0.55	0.27	-12.6
Bahrain	25.8	2.9	0.05	0.73	0.49	0.19	18.8	4.3	0.05	0.72	0.53	0.26	-7.0
Kuwait	12.8	6.8	0.05	0.81	0.49	0.36	7.2	12.8	0.05	0.71	0.53	0.40	-5.6
Oman	21.7	3.6	0.05	0.83	0.49	0.22	9.8	9.2	0.05	0.73	0.53	0.37	-11.9
Qatar	15.4	5.5	0.05	0.78	0.49	0.33	13.1	6.6	0.05	0.42	0.53	0.39	-2.30
KSA	16.9	4.9	0.05	0.74	0.49	0.32	7.9	11.7	0.05	0.65	0.53	0.40	-9.0
UAE	26.0	2.8	0.05	0.63	0.49	0.23	19.6	4.1	0.05	0.65	0.53	0.27	-6.4
Average	**19.8**	**4.43**	**0.05**	**0.75**	**0.49**	**0.29**	**12.72**	**8.14**	**0.05**	**0.65**	**0.53**	**0.35**	**-7.83**
(α=1.29)													
Algeria	16.5	5.0	0.34	0.73	0.47	0.19	10.6	8.5	0.38	0.61	0.55	0.27	-5.9
Bahrain	21.2	3.7	0.05	0.73	0.49	0.19	15.2	5.6	0.05	0.72	0.53	0.26	-6.0
Kuwait	10.2	8.8	0.05	0.81	0.49	0.36	5.7	16.5	0.05	0.71	0.53	0.40	-4.5
Oman	17.6	4.7	0.05	0.83	0.49	0.22	7.7	11.9	0.05	0.73	0.53	0.37	-9.9
Qatar	12.4	7.1	0.05	0.78	0.49	0.33	10.5	8.6	0.05	0.42	0.53	0.39	-1.9
KSA	13.6	6.4	0.05	0.74	0.49	0.32	6.2	15.2	0.05	0.65	0.53	0.40	-7.4
UAE	21.4	3.7	0.05	0.63	0.49	0.33	15.9	5.3	0.05	0.65	0.53	0.27	-5.5
Average	**16.07**	**5.72**	**0.05**	**0.75**	**0.49**	**0.29**	**10.19**	**10.51**	**0.05**	**0.65**	**0.53**	**0.35**	**-5.0**
(α=1.55)													
Algeria	13.3	6.5	0.34	0.73	0.47	0.19	8.40	10.9	0.38	0.61	0.55	0.27	-4.9
Bahrain	17.2	4.8	0.05	0.73	0.49	0.19	12.20	7.2	0.05	0.72	0.53	0.26	-5.0
Kuwait	8.1	11.4	0.05	0.81	0.49	0.36	4.50	21.4	0.05	0.71	0.53	0.40	-3.6
Oman	14.2	6.0	0.05	0.83	0.49	0.22	6.10	15.4	0.05	0.73	0.53	0.37	-8.1
Qatar	9.9	9.1	0.05	0.78	0.49	0.33	8.30	11.1	0.05	0.42	0.53	0.39	-1.6
KSA	10.9	8.2	0.05	0.74	0.49	0.32	4.90	19.5	0.05	0.65	0.53	0.40	-6.0
UAE	17.4	4.7	0.05	0.63	0.49	0.23	12.8	6.8	0.05	0.65	0.53	0.27	-4.4
Average	**12.96**	**7.38**	**0.05**	**0.75**	**0.49**	**0.29**	**8.11**	**13.56**	**0.05**	**0.65**	**0.53**	**0.35**	**-4.8**
(α=2)													

θ is the share of capital. τ is the effective marginal tax rate; *c/y* is consumption to GDP ratio; h^N is equilibrium hours-worked predicted by the model; and ω is the share of hydrocarbon revenues in GDP. Frisch elasticity is $(100/h)-1$.

from oil, for some time. Here, we assume that the GCC governments pursue policies to diversify the sources of income (i.e., relies less on oil). We study the effect of a reduction in the share of oil in GDP.

We examine the effect of a permanent reduction in the share of hydrocarbon in GDP, ω, by an amount equal to 0.25 standard deviations. We assume that the GCC countries have successfully managed to diversify their economies away from hydrocarbon by the year 2020, leading to a permanent reduction in the share of oil and gas in GDP from the year 2021 to 2050 (the end of our simulation). The share of oil and gas revenues, as we stated earlier, is $\omega = p^o q^o / (p^o q^o + p^{no} q^{no})$.

Diversification is taken to mean a reduction in the value of ω coming through an increase in $p^{no}q^{no}$ (the non-hydrocarbon output), leading to a higher share of labor in the production function and a lower share of natural resources. The increase in labor supply increases output and consumption. We measure the welfare effect of the policy by the *lifetime consumption equivalent,* which is the change in real consumption required to make the households indifferent to the policy.

We solve the model numerically over the period 2004 to 2050 using stochastic simulation with 10000 iterations.[11] We set the parameters α=2 and θ=0.51, which are the average values for the GCC over the sample 1991-2003. We assume that the parameter ω evolves as a random walk over the forecasting period; the error term has a mean of zero and a standard deviation equal to the sample value.

To simplify the solution of the model further, we appeal to the stochastic implications of the lifecycle-permanent income theory of consumption, and assume that the conditional expectations of the future marginal utility of consumption follow a random walk (Hall, 1978). Working age population grows at historical trend. We assume that the starting value of the capital stock is twice as large as real GDP in 1960. We fix the depreciation rate at 0.05. The value of the exogenous technical change *A* in the production function is the constant term; we calibrate it such that the value of output in 2004 is not far away from 2003 in order to ensure we have a sensible projection.

The baseline level of consumption is increasing in all GCC countries, but leveling off in the far future. The consumption to output ratio projection depends on the projected level of output from the production function. In the baseline solution, Bahrain's ratio has a negative trend suggesting that output is projected to increase by more than consumption. This ratio rises in Kuwait, Oman, and Saudi Arabia. The most significant positive trend is in Saudi Arabia. The ratio is constant in the UAE.

There has been much discussion about introducing consumption tax in the GCC. Thus, our second policy simulation studies the effects of introducing a 5 percent permanent value added tax (VAT). A consumption tax τ_c in the GCC on welfare, translates to a 9.5% increase in the tax rate τ (Equation 5). We re-solve the model again under this assumption.

The results of the two policy simulations are reported in Table 4, which has 14 columns with the countries listed in the first column. We report the averages of the share of hydrocarbon in GDP ω; the standard deviation of ω; and the consumption to GDP ratio over the sample from 1991 to 2003. In the second panel, columns 5, 6, and 7 report the average projected hours worked, the value of the share of hydrocarbon, and the consumption – output ratio, *c/y*, respectively. In the third panel (columns 8, 9, 10, and 11), we report the results of the first policy, policy I.

In column 11, we quantify the policy of a $0.25\sigma_\omega$ reduction in US dollars. In addition, in the last three columns we report the results of the second policy. Note the jump in the labor supply under policy I. The reduction in the hydrocarbon revenues is very small because we intended to show the welfare impact of a small change in policy. The reduction is 0.1 on average, which is about US$1.4 billion. This reduction in hydrocarbon revenues is matched by an equal reduction in government spending to keep the budget

Table 4. Taxes, Natural Resources and Labor Supply Projections for GCC Average values

Country	Average Sample Data (1991-2003)			Base Run (2004-2050)			Policy I (2020 – 2050)				Policy II (2004 – 2050)		
	ω	σ_ω	c/y	h^N	ω	c/y	h^N	ω	0.25 σ_ω in million USD	τ	h^N	ω	τ
Bahrain	0.22	0.04	72.5	16.4	0.25	71.0	17.1	0.24	153.3	0.05	15.7	0.25	0.095
Kuwait	0.38	0.07	83.7	11.4	0.35	64.3	12.5	0.33	1017.2	0.05	10.9	0.35	0.095
Oman	0.26	0.07	79.5	7.4	0.39	73.3	8.8	0.37	839.8	0.05	7.0	0.39	0.095
Qatar	0.37	0.07	65.7	13.4	0.36	39.2	14.8	0.35	351.7	0.05	12.8	0.36	0.095
KSA	0.32	0.04	70.7	16.2	0.29	60.4	17.0	0.28	3812.9	0.05	15.6	0.29	0.095
UAE	0.30	0.07	63.5	18.7	0.23	66.1	19.9	0.21	2187.5	0.05	18.0	0.23	0.095
GCC	**0.31**	**0.06**	**72.6**	**13.9**	**0.31**	**62.38**	**15.0**	**0.30**	**1393.7**	**0.05**	**13.6**	**0.31**	**0.095**

h_t^N is hours-worked (Equation 10).
ω is the share of oil and gas (gas is converted into oil using the standard scale of 6.6).
σ_ω is the standard deviation of the natural resource revenues in GDP.
c/y is the consumption to GDP ratio.
τ is the tax rate.
Consumption and ω follow a random walk process over the simulation horizon from 2004 to 2050.
Policy I is the diversification policy, where the GCC manages to diversify by 2020, and reduce the share of hydrocarbon by 0.25 σ_ω.
Policy II is the tax rate increases policy, where a 5% permanent increase in VAT (9.5 percent in the tax rate in Equation 5).

constraint unchanged. We assume that the government can reshuffle the budget in any way it chooses such that it remains fixed.8F[12]

Table 5 reports the lifetime consumption equivalent of the two policies. Clearly, the welfare improvement, resulting from the diversification policy and measured in lifetime consumption equivalent, is positive and sizable. In the case of Oman, it is 14 per cent, followed by Qatar (10.8 per cent), and Kuwait (9.3 percent). The Kingdom of Saudi Arabia (KSA) gains relatively less from diversification because it is already the most diversified economy in the GCC. The share of manufacturing and agriculture in GDP are reasonably high. The World Bank Development Statistics reports Saudi Arabia's agriculture, manufacturing and services value added in the total GDP in 2008 to be 2.3, 8, and 27.2 percent, respectively.

Table 5. Lifetime Consumption Equivalent

Country	Policy I	Policy II
Bahrain	3.87	- 4.79
Kuwait	9.29	- 4.80
Oman	13.99	- 3.77
Qatar	10.88	- 4.78
KSA	4.21	- 4.81
UAE	5.07	- 4.82

- Policy I is the diversification policy, where the share of hydrocarbon in GDP falls by 0.25 standard deviation from 2021 to 2050.
- Policy II is an introduction of a 5 percent permanent increase in VAT, which amounts to a 9.5 percent increase in the tax rate.

Bahrain is the smallest oil-producer as its main source of income is not oil. Its welfare improvement from the diversification policy is equal to that of Saudi Arabia. In the UAE, the welfare improvement measured by lifetime consumption equivalent is 5 per cent, the third lowest. The share of agriculture, manufacturing and services value added in 2006 reported by the World Bank Development Statistics are 2, 12.25, and 39.11 percent, respectively. Qatar, Kuwait and Oman benefit the most from diversification. Qatar and Kuwait rely heavily on hydrocarbon revenues.[13]An introduction of a permanent 5 per cent VAT reduces welfare by around 4.6 per cent in terms of lifetime consumption equivalent. The positive change in the labor supply, resulting from the diversification policy, is greater in magnitude than the negative change resulting from the tax policy. One can only imagine a sizable welfare effect of a policy change larger than 0.25 standard deviations in hydrocarbon share in the economy. The point is clear: diversify and benefit.

Tax Policy, Labor Supply and Poverty Reduction

Here, we discuss the policy simulation pertinent to poverty reduction in the Arab countries. The question is about the efficacy of tax policy in reducing poverty. We ask whether a decrease in the tax rate, which increases the supply of hours, productivity and GDP, reduces poverty. And, if so, by how much and how long does it take?

We choose Morocco as a case study for poverty for two reasons. Morocco's poverty level is high (a total of 21 per cent of the population), and we have some data on income distribution. The poverty data are based on the World Bank data found in POVNET for 2007 and the base year for real expenditures in 2005. For this reason, we use data for real consumption and output from the Penn Table 6, which has data up to 2007 for Morocco and the base year is 2005.

We solve the model over the period 1991-2006, and simulate the model stochastically with 10,000 iterations over the period 2008 to 2040. In the baseline solution, τ the effective marginal tax rate is equal to 0.39. We set α to 1.78, which is the average we used earlier, and the share of capital θ equal to 0.55, which is also the average over the sample.

Here, too, we guess that the capital stock's starting value is twice the size of real GDP in 1960. We assume the depreciation rate 0.05. Consumption is a random walk, with a standard normal error term of a zero mean and standard deviation equal to that of the sample average from 1991-2007. The value of the exogenous technical change A in the production function is the constant term, and calibrated such that the value of output in 2008 is not far from the value in 2007 in order to ensure we have a sensible projection. The policy reduces the tax rate to 0.30 permanently. The simulated values of real consumption are used to compute poverty headcount. There are three parameters in the poverty function: mean real consumption expenditures, Gini coefficient and the poverty line. We fix the poverty line at US$72 US per household, per month, in PPP terms. The Gini coefficient is fixed.

The only parameter that changes is mean real consumption expenditure, which is updated over the simulation period. We report the results in Table 6. Figure 1 plots the poverty reduction dynamics. Clearly, a tax reduction policy reduces poverty. As income level rises, and growth rate of real consumption rises, poverty declines by more than half in 2020 (i.e., in 12 years). Everything else remains unchanged; poverty could be eliminated by 2050. One can clearly advocate more tax reduction than the one we assumed, and cut poverty even faster and by more.

Table 6. Morocco's Poverty Reduction Policy Simulation

	Hours		GDP Per Capita		∂y/dτ	Income Multiplier	Δc_t^s	Poverty %
2007	Baseline	Policy	Baseline	Policy				21.59 [i]
2008	15.99	17.97	5682.52	6014.69	-1.27	5.85	2.26	20.48
2010	15.96	17.94	5905.58	6280.19	-1.15	6.34	2.58	18.27
2015	15.97	17.95	6487.00	6967.58	-0.94	7.41	1.69	14.72
2020	15.92	17.90	7076.94	7662.59	-0.81	8.28	1.20	10.50
2025	15.93	17.91	7703.77	8395.41	-0.72	8.98	2.68	7.57
2030	15.92	17.90	8356.12	9154.61	-0.66	9.56	1.51	5.61
2035	15.93	17.91	9042.68	9949.86	-0.62	10.03	1.74	4.01
2040	15.94	17.92	9767.29	10785.58	-0.58	10.43	1.37	2.92
2045	15.93	17.91	10527.96	11659.88	-0.56	10.75	1.31	2.11
2050	15.92	17.90	11328.41	12577.27	-0.53	11.02	1.46	1.54

i Actual data

-Data are in PPP 2005 base year. Real PPP GDP.

- **∂y/dτ** is the tax multiplier, where an increase in the tax rate reduces income.

- $(y^s - y^b / y^b)100$ is the GDP multiplier, where the superscript s *d*enotes simulation solution value and *b* denotes the baseline simulation value.

- Δc_t^s is the consumption growth after policy.

Figure 1.

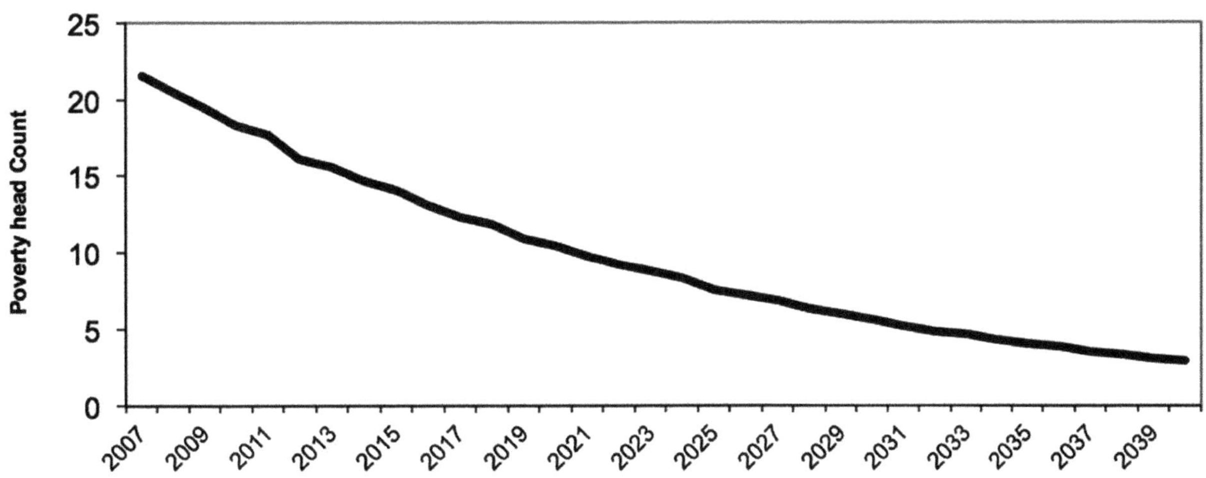

CONCLUSION

The absence of data on hours worked makes policymaking very difficult. Our main contribution is to provide model-consistent estimates of hours worked, the Frisch elasticity of labor supply and labor productivity for the Arab countries, and compare them with the G-7 countries. We use the work-leisure model of the labor supply, which has been tested extensively in the literature. This chapter uses data from Arab countries to confirm the predictions of the model and add more supporting evidence to existing ones. We found that supply of labor of a number of Arab countries is just as elastic as labor supply in the G-7 countries, and labor productivity is relatively lower than the G-7 countries.

There are two types of Arab countries: non-oil-producing countries such as Egypt, Jordan, Morocco, Syria, and Tunisia and major oil-producing countries such as the Gulf Cooperation Council (GCC) members. Algeria is a major gas producer. Although the model explains the data of the first group of Arab countries well, where results are comparable to the G-7, the second group of Arab countries (the GCC) is more interesting because there are no taxes in these countries. Without taxes, the model's performance and predictions are of limited value.

To ameliorate this deficiency, we introduce natural resource endowment effect in the work-leisure model. We define effective capital as the product of physical capital and natural resource capital. We found that natural resource endowment acts like a tax (i.e., reduce labor supply).

Oil rich GCC countries rely heavily on their natural resources as income. The government budget swells during periods of high oil and gas prices, which beget rents. The opposite occurs when hydrocarbon revenues decline and the budgets shrink. People work longer hours to compensate for the loss in rent, and smooth out consumption. We show that the data support such a theory over periods of actual high and low hydrocarbon revenues. The supply of labor could decline by up to seven hours a week per person during periods of high oil revenues.

In terms of the estimated Frisch elasticity, the Arab countries labor supplies are found to be very elastic, more so in the oil-producing countries. An elastic labor supply could imply less interventionist government policies. In addition, as populations' age, transfer payments to current and future old generations need not be financed by increasing tax rates. It can open doors to social security policies that encourage savings (Prescott, 2004). Elastic labor supplies are also good for demand policies that aim at increasing employment and hours.

We simulate the model for scenarios under a minimum number of additional assumptions. We demonstrate that a reduction in the effective marginal tax rate in the Arab countries can reduce poverty substantially, cut it in half in about 12 years in the case of Morocco. High taxes, even a five percent increase in the value-added tax (VAT), in the oil-rich countries would reduce welfare in terms of the lifetime consumption equivalent. But, most importantly, the model suggests that welfare significantly increases as oil revenues decline in oil-producing countries. To change the natural resource curse to a blessing, it is recommended that the GCC countries diversify their income away from oil while they can. Our results indicate that a permanent reduction of hydrocarbon by the year 2020 could increase labor supply, real GDP and consumption, leading to a significant welfare improvement.

ACKNOWLEDGMENT

This chapter is written when the author was an adviser at the Arab Planning Institute. The views in this paper belong to the authors and they do not represent the Arab Planning Institute or the country members. We would like to thank two anonymous referees, Mustafa Bentour, Rached Thamri, Riadh Ben Jelili, Ahmed Al Kawaz, Francisco N De Simone, Robert Shimer, Iris Claus, Christi Smith, Mathias Stifler, and the participants of the 13th ICMAIF 2011 conference at the University of Crete – Greece for valuable comments

REFERENCES

Akhand, H., & Liu, H. (2002). Marginal Income Tax rates in the United States: A Non-Parametric Approach. *Journal of Monetary Economics*, *49*(2), 383–404. doi:10.1016/S0304-3932(01)00105-2

Alogoskoufis, G. S. (1987). On Intertemporal Substitution and Aggregate Labor Supply. *Journal of Political Economy*, *95*(5), 938–960. doi:10.1086/261497

Altonji, J. G. (1982). The Intertemporal Substitution Model of Labor Market Fluctuations: An Empirical Analysis. *The Review of Economic Studies*, *49*(5), 783–824. doi:10.2307/2297189

Auerbach, A., & Kotlikoff, L. J. (1987). *Dynamic Fiscal Policy*. Cambridge: Cambridge University Press.

Barro, R. J. (1979). On The Determination Public Debt. *Journal of Political Economy*, *87*(5, Part 1), 940–971. doi:10.1086/260807

Barro, R. J., & Sahasakul, C. (1983). Measuring the Average Marginal Tax Rate from the Individual Income Tax. *The Journal of Business*, *56*(4), 419–452. doi:10.1086/296211

Barro, R. J., & Sahasakul, C. (1986). Average Marginal Tax Rates from Social Security and the Individual Income Tax. *The Journal of Business, 59*(4, Part 1), 555-566.

Baxter, M., & King, R. (1993, June). Fiscal Policy in General Equilibrium. *The American Economic Review*, *83*, 315–334.

Boldrin, M., Christiano, L. J., & Fisher, J. D. M. (2001, March). Habit Persistence, Asset Returns, and the Business Cycle. *The American Economic Review*, *91*(1), 149–166. doi:10.1257/aer.91.1.149

Card, D. (1991). Intertemporal Labor Supply: An Assessment. *NBER*, Working Paper No. 3602. Cambridge, MA.

Christiano, L. J., & Eichenbaum, M. (1992, June). Current Real Business Cycle Theories and Aggregate Labor Market Fluctuations. *The American Economic Review*, *82*, 430–450.

Cole, H. L., & Ohanian, L. E. (1999). The Great Depression in the United States from a Neoclassical Perspective. *Federal Reserve Bank of Minneapolis Quarterly Review*, *23*(Winter), 2–24.

Cole, H. L., & Ohanian, L. E. (2002, January). The Great UK Depression: A Puzzle and a Possible Resolution. *Review of Economic Dynamics*, *5*(1), 19–44. doi:10.1006/redy.2001.0140

Cooley, T. (Ed.). (1995). *Frontiers of Business Cycle Research*. Princeton: Princeton University Press.

Development Challenges for the Arab Region: A Human Development Approach. (2009). United Nations.

Dutkowsky, D. H., & Dunsky, R. M. (1996). Intertemporal Substitution, Money, and Aggregate Labor Supply. *Journal of Money, Credit and Banking*, *28*(2), 216–232. doi:10.2307/2078024

Feenburg, D. R., & Coutts, E. (1993). An Introduction to the TAXSIM Model. *Journal of Policy Analysis and Management*, *12*(1), 189–194. doi:10.2307/3325474

Hall, R. E. (1978). Stochastic Implications of the Lifecycle – Permanent Income Hypothesis. *Journal of Political Economy*, *86*(6), 971–987. doi:10.1086/260724

Hall, R. E. (1980). Labor Supply and Aggregate Fluctuations. *Carnegie-Rochester Conference Series*, *12*, 7–33. doi:10.1016/0167-2231(80)90019-6

Hanson, G. D. (1985, November). Indivisible Labor and the Business Cycle. *Journal of Monetary Economics*, *16*(3), 309–327. doi:10.1016/0304-3932(85)90039-X

Heckman, J. J. (1993). What has been Learned about Labor Supply in the Past Twenty Years. *American Economic Review*, 83(2), 116-121.

Heston, A., Summers, R., & Aten, B. (2006). *Penn World Table Version 6.3. Center for International Comparisons of Production, Income and Prices*. University of Pennsylvania.

Kehoe, T. J., & Prescott, E. C. (2002, January). Great Depressions of the 20th Century. *Review of Economic Dynamics*, *5*(1), 1–18. doi:10.1006/redy.2001.0151

Kydland, F. E., & Prescott, E. C. (1982, November). Time to Build and Aggregate Fluctuations. *Econometrica*, *50*(6), 1345–1370. doi:10.2307/1913386

Lucas, R. Jr. (1972). Expectations and the Neutrality of Money. *Journal of Economic Theory*, *4*(2), 103–124. doi:10.1016/0022-0531(72)90142-1

Lucas, R. Jr, & Rapping, L. A. (1969, September-October). Real Wages, Employment and Inflation. *Journal of Political Economy*, *77*(5), 721–754. doi:10.1086/259559

Makdisi, S., Fattah, Z., & Limam, I. (2006). Determinants of Growth in the MENA Countries. In J. B. Nugent & M. H. Pesaran (Eds.), *Explaining Growth in the Middle East, Contributions to Economic Analysis* (Vol. 278, pp. 31–60). Amsterdam: Elsevier. doi:10.1016/S0573-8555(06)78002-6

Mankiw, N. G., Rotemberg, J. J., & Summers, L. H. (1985). Intertemporal Substitution in Macro Economics. *The Quarterly Journal of Economics*, *100*(1), 225–251. doi:10.2307/1885743

McGrattan, E. R., & Prescott, E. C. (2003, August). Taxes, Regulations, and the Value of US Corporations: A General Equilibrium Analysis. *Research Department Staff Report 309, Federal Reserve Bank of Minneapolis*.

McGrattan, E. R., & Prescott, E. C. (2003, May). Average Debt and Equity Returns: Puzzling? *The American Economic Review*, *93*(2), 392–397. doi:10.1257/000282803321947407

Nickell, S. (2003, December). Employment and Taxes, *CESIFO* Working Paper No.1109.

Noland, M., & Pack, H. (2007). *The Arab Economies in a Changing World*. Washington, DC: Peterson Institute for International Economics.

Olovsson, C. (2009). Why Do Europeans Work So Little. *International Economic Review*, *50*(1), 39–61. doi:10.1111/j.1468-2354.2008.00523.x

Prescott, E. C. (2004). Why Do Americans Work So Much More Than Europeans? *Federal Reserve Bank of Minneapolis Quarterly Review*, *28*(1), 2–3.

Ragan, K. S. (2006). *Taxes, Transfers, and Time Use: Fiscal Policy in a Household Production Model* [PhD Thesis]. University of Chicago.

Rogerson, R. (2007). Taxation and Market Work: Is Scandinavia an Outlier? *Economic Theory*, *32*(1), 59–85. doi:10.1007/s00199-006-0164-9

Seater, J. J. (1982). Marginal Federal Personal and Cooperate Income Tax rates in the U.S., 1909 – 1975. *Journal of Monetary Economics*, *10*(3), 361–381. doi:10.1016/0304-3932(82)90033-2

Shimer, R. (2009, January). Convergence in Macroeconomics: The Labor Wedge. *American Economic Journal. Macroeconomics*, *1*(1), 280–297. doi:10.1257/mac.1.1.280

Solow, R., & Wan, F. Y. (1976). Extraction Costs in the Theory of Exhaustible Resources. *The Bell Journal of Economics*, *7*(2), 359–370. doi:10.2307/3003261

Stephenson, E. F. (1998). Average marginal tax Rates Revisited. *Journal of Monetary Economics*, *41*(2), 389–409. doi:10.1016/S0304-3932(97)00081-0

Stiglitz, J. (1974). Growth with Exhaustible Natural Resources: Efficient and Optimal Growth Paths. *The Review of Economic Studies*, *41*, 123–137. doi:10.2307/2296377

ENDNOTES

1 Prescott (2004) provides evidence that – everything else being constant – significant differences in international hours worked almost disappear when tax rates are similar. Scandinavians pay relatively higher taxes; Ragan (2006) and Rogerson (2007) argued that Scandinavian governments subsidize market inputs into home production and provide more transfers (e.g. subsidized daycare) to households that supply more labor. Olovsson (2009) uses home production data to account for the differences in hours worked between Scandinavians and others.

2 Lucas and Rapping (1969), Hall (1980), Andrew and Nickell (1982), Alogoskoufis (1987a, 1987b), Dutkowsky and Dunsky (1996), Nickell (2003), Prescott (2004), and Shimer (2009) among many

others have provided evidence that support the model. Card (1991) cited a number of surveys at the micro level, which seem to suggest that the intertemporal substitution proposition offers little explanation to labor supply decisions. Heckman (1993) cited more supportive evidence. The literature is voluminous, but most cited work evidence against the intertemporal substitution model are Altonji (1982) and Mankiw, Rotemberg and Summers (1985).

3 Prescott cites a number of papers as the basis of this theory: business cycle literature of Cooley (1995) and Cooley and Ohanian (1999); in the depression literature, he cites Kehoe and Prescott (2002); in public finance, Christaino and Eichenbaum (1992), and Baxter and King (1993); and in the stock market literature McGrattan and Prescott (2003) and Boldrin, Christian and Fisher (2001). The labor supply is consistent with Lucas and Rapping (1969), Lucas (1972), Kydland and Prescott (1982), Hansen (1985) and Auerbach and Kotlikoff (1987).

4 It is hard to model the evolution of technical progress A_{it} in the Arab countries because of the lack of data. The stock of R&D and patents registered in the US are very low. Saudi Arabia, Egypt, Syria, Jordan, Kuwait and the UAE combined registered 367 patents in the US during the period from 1980 to 2000. Compare that to Korea, which registered 6328 patents. In addition, human capital stock and its quality are poor; see Development Challenges for the Arab Region: A Human Development Approach, UN (2009).

5 Prescott (2004) uses one consumption good following Christiano and Eichenbaum (1992). Rogerson (2003) finds that one consumption good is not a good assumption for explaining the aggregate labor supply in Scandinavian countries, because Scandinavians spend more time working at home than others due to high income tax.

6 There is a literature on the methods of estimating average marginal income tax rates in the US, where differences seem significant. Differences in the computation of income tax rates could affect the tax rate τ in model. For more on the debate, see Barro (1979), Seater (1982), Barro and Sahasakul (1983, 1986), Stephenson (1998), and Akhand and Liu (2002).

7 Setting up the Langrange multiplier and taking the derivates with respect to c and h, we get:

$$\partial L/\partial c = (1/c) - \lambda(1+\tau_c) = 0 \Rightarrow \lambda = \frac{1}{c(1-\tau_c)};$$

$$\partial L/\partial h = a/(100-h) - \lambda(1+\tau_h)w = 0 \Rightarrow \lambda = \frac{\alpha}{(1-\tau_h)(100-h)}\frac{1}{w}$$

$$\frac{\frac{\alpha}{100-h}}{\frac{1}{c}} = \left(\frac{1-\tau_h}{1+\tau_c}\right)w = \left(1-\frac{\tau_h+\tau_c}{1+\tau_c}\right)w = (1-\tau)w$$

8 In the Arab countries, public consumption is large, and so is the subsidy. In some Arab countries, only the *total* amount of subsidy is reported, which is the sum of production and consumption goods subsidy. Because of the large fuel subsidy, for example, the indirect tax rate is smaller than otherwise.

9 In any case, it is immaterial for our case whether we have h or E in the production function because the share parameter $0<\beta<1$ is what enters in the equilibrium solution of the hours worked.

10 One could easily allow these parameters to change across countries, but we fix them because we are comparing hours in the Arab countries to the G7 hours, which are the yardstick for the fit of the model.

11 When solving, an approximated Jacobian is used when linearizing the model. Then the approximation is updated each iteration by comparing the residuals, which result from the new trial value of the endogenous variables with the residuals of the linear equation. The method is not significantly different from Newton, but it runs faster. The innovations to stochastic equations are generated by drawing a set of random numbers from a standard normal distribution each period. These draws are scaled to match the variance-covariance system by multiplying the vector by its standard deviation because the covariance matrix is diagonal.

12 The Penn Table 6 data are only available to the year 2003 for the GCC countries.

13 The Kuwaiti data are available from the same source for 2003 only. The shares are 0.46, 2.27 and 48.5 percent, respectively. We do not have similar data for Qatar or Bahrain.

APPENDIX

Table 7. Data appendix

Average 2000-2008	Canada	France	Germany	Italy	Japan	UK	USA
General government final consumption expenditure, %GDP	19.24	23.31	18.70	19.62	17.86	20.54	15.58
Consumption of fixed capital, % GDP	13.01	13.00	14.89	15.28	20.62	11.26	11.85
Household final consumption expenditure, % GDP	55.84	56.46	58.47	59.04	57.08	64.88	70.03
Working Age Population to Total Population	0.69	0.63	0.67	0.67	0.66	0.66	0.67
Employment to Age working population	0.72	0.65	0.67	0.58	0.75	0.71	0.72
Taxes individuals, % GDP	12.23	7.64	8.91	10.72	5.19	10.48	10.38
Social Security Contributions, Employees % GDP	2.01	4.02	6.11	2.30	4.28	2.64	3.00
Taxes on goods and services, % GDP	8.42	11.00	10.35	11.01	5.22	10.97	4.73
Military Expenditure, % GDP	1.20	2.46	1.38	1.92	0.97	2.46	3.76
τ_c	0.16	0.22	0.20	0.20	0.09	0.19	0.07
τ_{ss}	0.04	0.07	0.11	0.05	0.07	0.04	0.05
Capital Share	0.38	0.35	0.38	0.46	0.35	0.34	0.37
τ_{inc}	0.16	0.10	0.12	0.15	0.07	0.13	0.12
τ_h	0.28	0.23	0.30	0.28	0.18	0.26	0.25
τ	0.38	0.37	0.42	0.40	0.25	0.38	0.30
c/y	0.70	0.75	0.73	0.72	0.66	0.80	0.79
GDP Per Person, GDP Less IT in PPP 2005 divided By Population aged 15-64	42510.72	38698.09	37867.03	35733.27	40045.97	39364.55	57049.32

Source:OECD

Table 8.

Country	Actual Weekly Worked Hours	Capital Share	Consumption Output Ratio, PWT 6.2 (1991-2003/04)	Investment Ratio, PWT 6.2 (1991/03/04)	Population (Millions)	Labor force (Millions)	Employment (Millions)	Population Aged 15-64% Total Population	Employment to Population Aged 15-64
Algeria		0.51	0.69	12.67	29.79	10.46	8.01	60.14	0.44
Bahrain		0.35	0.73	9.89	0.63	0.29	0.27	68.50	0.64
Egypt		0.45	0.96	5.41	64.91	19.24	17.35	58.89	0.45
Kuwait		0.57	0.84	10.67	2.05	1.08	1.09	70.99	0.74
Jordan		0.36	0.77	14.39	4.60	1.23	1.21	68.35	0.38
Morocco		0.56	0.90	11.52	27.76	9.56	8.55	60.67	0.51
Oman		0.53	0.80	9.30	2.29	0.82	0.76	59.81	0.55
Qatar		0.50	0.66	18.70	0.61	0.34	0.33	73.49	0.72
KSA		0.51	0.71	9.96	20.06	6.64	6.34	58.67	0.54
Syria		0.33	0.73	7.79	16.06	4.73	5.09	55.11	0.57
Tunisia		0.24	0.92	13.35	9.33	3.09	2.71	62.78	0.46
UAE		0.61	0.63	23.12	3.04	1.75	1.72	73.98	0.75
Source	ILO	UN	WDI-PWT	PWT	WDI	WDI	ILO	WDI	ILO
(average 1991-2006)									

ILO is the International Labor Organization
BP is British Petroleum
PWT is Penn World Table 6.3
WDI is World Bank
IFS is International Financial Stats, the IMF

Table 9.

Country	Employment to total population Ratio	Oil and Gas Reserves, Billions Barrels of Equivalent Oil	GDP Per Capita PPP PWT 6.2 (1991/03/04)	τ_c	τ_{ss}	τ_{inc}	$\tau_{inc}+\tau_{ss}$	τ	ω Share of Hydrocarbon Revenues
Algeria	0.27	38.0	4826.0	0.18	0.05	0.10	0.21	0.33	0.23
Bahrain	0.44	0.8	15562.4	0.00	0.04	0.01	0.05	0.05	0.22
Egypt	0.27		3955.0	0.09	0.05	0.08	0.17	0.24	
Kuwait	0.53	107.7	21698.5	0.00	0.04	0.00	0.04	0.04	0.32
Jordan	0.26		3835.6	0.16	0.04	0.08	0.16	0.28	
Morocco	0.31		3630.0	0.19	0.10	0.11	0.28	0.39	
Oman	0.33	9.7	13127.0	0.00	0.04	0.01	0.05	0.05	0.20
Qatar	0.53	113.6	23284.6	0.00	0.03	0.00	0.03	0.03	0.35
KSA	0.31	302.4	14086.7	0.00	0.06	0.00	0.04	0.04	0.25
Syria	0.31		1799.0	0.00	0.00	0.12	0.20	0.19	
Tunisia	0.29		6296.2	0.22	0.05	0.08	0.16	0.31	
UAE	0.56	137.8	24455.5	0.00	0.04	0.00	0.02	0.01	0.26
Source	ILO	BP	PWT	WDI, IFS	SS	WDI, IFS	Computed	Computed	WDI, IFS

ILO is the International Labor Organization
BP is British Petroleum
PWT is Penn World Table 6.3
WDI is World Bank
IFS is International Financial Stats, the IMF

Table 10. Sensitivity Analysis of the Effective Marginal Tax Rate Calculations

	Lower Bound Estimate		Central Estimate		Upper Bound Estimate			
Country	τ_1	***h***	τ_2	***h***	τ_3	***h***	τ_4	***h***
Algeria	0.28	17.8	0.33	16.8	0.41	15.1	0.50	13.1
Egypt	0.20	21.5	0.24	20.6	0.31	19.1	0.38	17.5
Jordan	0.24	24.4	0.28	23.4	0.34	21.9	0.41	20.0
Morocco	0.34	19.9	0.39	18.6	0.49	16.1	0.58	13.7
Syria	0.12	30.6	0.19	28.8	0.32	25.4	0.44	21.9
Tunisia	0.30	20.3	0.35	19.2	0.43	17.2	0.51	15.1
Average	**0.24**	**22.4**	**0.28**	**21.3**	**0.44**	**19.1**	**0.45**	**16.8**

τ_1 corresponds to a tax rate with $\tau_h = t_{ss} + 1\overline{\tau}_{inc}$

τ_2 corresponds to a tax rate with $\tau_h = t_{ss} + 1.6\overline{\tau}_{inc}$

τ_3 corresponds to a tax rate with $\tau_h = t_{ss} + 2.6\overline{\tau}_{inc}$

τ_4 corresponds to a tax rate with $\tau_h = t_{ss} + 3.6\overline{\tau}_{inc}$

See definitions of the social security tax and tax on income in the appendix τ_{ss} τ_{inc}

$h = (1-\theta)/[(1-\theta) + (c/y)*(\alpha/1-\tau)]$ are hours-worked using predicting factors $\theta=0.48$;

Average Arab countries c/y and $\alpha=1.55$

Compilation of References

. Compliance Risk Management: Managing and Improving Tax Compliance. (2004). *Centre for Tax Policy and Administration, OECD*, Paris. Retrieved from http://www.oecd.org/dataoecd/44/19/33818656.pdf

A Regional Alliance to Improve Public Procurement. (2014). The World Bank. Retrieved from http://www.worldbank.org/en/news/feature/2014/01/15/a-regional-alliance-to-improve-public-procurement

Aaron, A. J., & Galper, H. (1985). *Assessing Tax Reform*. Washington, DC: Brookings Institution.

Abed, G. T., & Gupta, S. (2002). *Governance, Corruption, & Economic Performance*. Washington, DC: International Monetary Fund.

Acemoglu, D., & Verdier, T. (2000). The choice between market failure and corruption. *The American Economic Review*, *90*(1), 194–211. doi:10.1257/aer.90.1.194

Adams, C. (1982). *Fight, Flight and Fraud: The Story of Taxation*. Curacao: Euro-Dutch Publishers.

Adams, C. (1993). *For Good or Evil: The Impact of Taxes on the Course of Civilization*. London, New York, Lanham: Madison Books.

Ades, A., & Di Tella, R. (1999). Rents, Competition, and Corruption. *The American Economic Review*, *89*(4), 98–993. doi:10.1257/aer.89.4.982

Afonso, A. (2005). Ricardian Fiscal Regimes in the European Union. *European Central Bank, Working Paper Series*, No: 558.

Agenor, P., McDermott, J., & Prasad, E. (1999). *Macroeconomic Fluctuations in Developing Countries: Some Stylized Facts*. International Monetary Fund WP/99/35.

Agrawal, A. (2010). Environment, community, government. In I. Feldman & M. Ticktin (Eds.), *In the Name of Humanity* (pp. 190–217). Durham, NC: Duke University Press. doi:10.1215/9780822393221-007

Ahmad, E., & Stern, N. (1986). *Taxation for Developing Countries. The Development Research Programme*. London School of Economics.

Ahmad, M. (1995). *Business Ethics in Islam*. Islamabad, Pakistan: The International Institute of Islamic Thought & The International Institute of Islamic Economics.

Ahumada, H., Alvaredo, F., & Canavese, A. (2008). The Monetary Method to Measure the Underground Economy: The Forgotten Problem of the Initial Conditions. *Economics Letters*, *101*(2), 97–99. doi:10.1016/j.econlet.2008.06.001

Aizenman, J., & Jinjarak, Y. (2012, June). Income Inequality, Tax Base and Sovereign Spreads. *NBER Working Paper Series, No: 18176*. National Bureau of Economic Research. Retrieved from http://economics.ucsc.edu/research/downloads/Aiz_Jin_Gini_2012.pdf

Aizenman, J., Gavin, M., & Hausmann, R. (2000). Optimal Tax and Debt Policy with Endogenously Imperfect Creditworthiness. *The Journal of International Trade & Economic Development*, *9*(4), 367–395. doi:10.1080/096381900750056830

Aizenman, J., & Jinjarak, Y. (2009). Globalisation and Developing Countries – A Shrinking Tax Base? *The Journal of Development Studies*, *45*(5), 653–671. doi:10.1080/00220380802582338

Ajzen, I. (1991). The Theory of Planned Behavior. *Organizational Behavior and Human Decision Processes*, *50*(2), 179–211. doi:10.1016/0749-5978(91)90020-T

Akbulut, H. (2016). Shadow Economy and Tax Evasion: An Analysis for EU-27 and Turkey. In M. M. Erdoğdu & B. Christiansen (Eds.), *Handbook of Research on Public Finance Perspectives on Europe and the MENA Region*. Hershey, PA, USA: IGI Global.

Akçay, O. C., Alper, C. E., & Ozmucur, S. (2002). Budget Deficit, Inflation and Debt Sustainabilty: Evidence from Turkey, 1970-2000. In A. Kibritçioğlu, L. Rittenberg, & F. Selçuk (Eds.), *Inflation and Disinflation in Turkey* (pp. 77–96). London: Ashgate Publishing.

Akhand, H., & Liu, H. (2002). Marginal Income Tax rates in the United States: A Non-Parametric Approach. *Journal of Monetary Economics*, *49*(2), 383–404. doi:10.1016/S0304-3932(01)00105-2

Akıllı, H., & Akıllı, H. S. (2014). Decentralization and Recentralization of Local Governments in Turkey. *Procedia: Social and Behavioral Sciences*, *140*, 682–686. doi:10.1016/j.sbspro.2014.04.493

Aktaş, Z., Kaya, N., & Özlale, U. (2005). The Price Puzzle in Emerging Markets: Evidence from the Turkish Economy Using "Model Based" Risk Premium Derived from Domestic Fundamentals. *Central Bank of the Republic of Turkey, Economic Research Paper*, No: 05/02.

Akyüz, Y. (1990). Financial System and Policies in Turkey in the 1980s. In T. Arıcanlı & D. Rodrik (Eds.), *The Political Economy of Turkey* (pp. 98–131). London: Macmillan. doi:10.1007/978-1-349-11274-6_6

Alberola, E. (2011, December 15). Post-Crisis Monetary Policy Frameworks 2011: The Differences between Advanced and Emerging Economies.

Albo, G., Gindin, S., & Panitch, L. (2010). *In and Out of Crises: The Global Financial Meltdown and Left Alternatives*. Oakland, California: Spectre PM Press.

Alesina, A., & Wacziarg, R. (1997). Openness, Country Size and the Government. *Journal of Public Economics*.

Alesina, A., Tabellini, G., & Campante, F. R. (2008). Why is Fiscal Policy Often Procyclical? *Journal of the European Economic Association*, *6*(5), 1006–1036. doi:10.1162/JEEA.2008.6.5.1006

Alfirman, L. (2003, November). Estimating Stochastic Frontier Tax Potential: Can Indonesian Local Governments Increase Tax Revenues under Decentralization? Discussion papers in economics / Center for Economic Analysis, Department of Economics, University of Colorado at Boulder, Colorado. *Working Paper No. 03-19*.

Alleyne, D., Alm, J., Bahl, R., & Wallace, S. (2004). *Tax Burden in Jamaica. International Study Program*. Atlanta, GA: Andrew Young School of Policy Studies, Georgia State University.

Allingham, M. G., & Sandmo, A. (1972). Income tax evasion: A theoretical analysis. *Journal of Public Economics*, *1*(3-4), 323–338. doi:10.1016/0047-2727(72)90010-2

Alm, J., & Martinez-Vazquez, J. (2010). Tax Evasion, the Informal Sector, and Tax Morale in LAC Countries. In J. Alm, & Martinez-Vazquez & B. Torgler (Eds.), Developing Alternative Frameworks for Explaining Tax Compliance (pp. 260-291). London & New York: Routledge.

Alm, J. (1996). What is an "Optimal" Tax System? *National Tax Journal*, *49*(1), 117–133.

Alm, J. (2012). Measuring, explaining, and controlling tax evasion: Lessons from theory, experiments, and field studies. *International Tax and Public Finance*, *19*(1), 54–77. doi:10.1007/s10797-011-9171-2

Alm, J., Bloomquist, K. M., & McKee, M. (2015). On The External Validity of Laboratory Tax Compliance Experiments. *Economic Inquiry*, *53*(2), 1170–1186. doi:10.1111/ecin.12196

Alm, J., & Embaye, A. (2013). Using Dynamic Panel Methods to Estimate Shadow Economies around the World, 1990-2006. *Public Finance Review*, *41*(5), 510–543. doi:10.1177/1091142113482353

Alm, J., Kirchler, E., & Muehlbacher, S. (2012). Combining Psychology and Economics in the Analysis of Compliance: From Enforcement to Cooperation. *Economic Analysis & Policy*, *42*(2), 133–151. doi:10.1016/S0313-5926(12)50016-0

Alm, J., & Lopez-Castano, H. (2005). Payroll Taxes in Colombia. In R. Bird, J. Poterba, & J. Slemrod (Eds.), *Fiscal Reform in Colombia – Problems and Prospects* (pp. 191–223). Cambridge, MA: The MIT Press.

Alm, J., & Martinez-Vazquez, J. (2003). Institutions, Paradigms, and Tax Evasion in Developing and Transitional Countries. In J. Alm & J. Martinez-Vazquez (Eds.), *Public Finance in Developing and Transitional Countries* (pp. 146–178). Cheltenham, UK: Edward Elgar.

Alm, J., Martinez-Vazquez, J., & Torgler, B. (2006). Russian Attitudes toward Paying Taxes – Before, during and After the Transition. *International Journal of Social Economics*, *33*(12), 832–857. doi:10.1108/03068290610714670

Alm, J., Martinez-Vazquez, J., & Torgler, B. (Eds.). (2010). *Developing Alternative Frameworks For Explaining Tax Compliance*. London: Routledge.

Alm, J., Martinez-Vazquez, J., & Wallace, S. (2004). *Taxing the Hard to Tax: Lessons from Theory and Practice*. Amsterdam, The Netherlands: Elsevier B.V.

Alm, J., Martinez-Vazquez, J., & Wallace, S. (2009). Do Tax Amnesties Work? The Revenue Effects of Tax Amnesties during the Transition in the Russian Federation. *Economic Analysis & Policy*, *39*(2), 235–253. doi:10.1016/S0313-5926(09)50019-7

Alm, J., McClelland, G. H., & Schulze, W. D. (1992). Why Do People Pay Taxes? *Journal of Public Economics*, *48*(1), 21–38. doi:10.1016/0047-2727(92)90040-M

Alm, J., McKee, M., & Beck, W. (1990). Amazing Grace: Tax Amnesties and Compliance. *National Tax Journal*, *43*(1), 23–37.

Alm, J., & Torgler, B. (2006). Culture Differences and Tax Morale in the United States and in Europe. *Journal of Economic Psychology*, *27*(2), 224–246. doi:10.1016/j.joep.2005.09.002

Alm, J., & Torgler, B. (2011). Do Ethics Matter? Tax Compliance and Morality. *Journal of Business Ethics*, *101*(4), 635–651. doi:10.1007/s10551-011-0761-9

Alogoskoufis, G. S. (1987). On Intertemporal Substitution and Aggregate Labor Supply. *Journal of Political Economy*, *95*(5), 938–960. doi:10.1086/261497

Alonso, J. A., & Garcimartín, C. (2011). Does Aid Hinder Tax Efforts? More Evidence. *CREDIT Research Paper. No: 11/04*.

Alt, J., Preston, I., & Sibieta, L. (2009). The Political Economy of Tax Policy. In *Dimensions of Tax Design: The Mirrlees Review* (pp. 1204–1279). Oxford, UK: Oxford University Press.

Altonji, J. G. (1982). The Intertemporal Substitution Model of Labor Market Fluctuations: An Empirical Analysis. *The Review of Economic Studies*, *49*(5), 783–824. doi:10.2307/2297189

Alvarez, J., & Arellano, M. (2003). The time-series and cross-section asymptotics of dynamic panel data estimators. *Econometrica*, *71*(4), 1121–1159. doi:10.1111/1468-0262.00441

Alves, J., & Heller, P. (2013). Accountability from the Top Down? Brazil's Advances in Budget Accountability Despite a Lack of Popular Mobilization. In S. Khagram, P. de Renzio, & A. Fung (Eds.), *Open Budgets* (pp. 76–104). Washington: Brookings Institution.

Amadeo, K. (2014). World's Largest Economy. Retrieved from http://useconomy.about.com/od/grossdomesticproduct/p/largest_economy.htm

Amin, A. A. (2000, August). Long Term Growth in the CFA Franc Zone Countries.*The United Nations University World Institute for Development Economics Research.*

Anderson, G. M., & Tollison, R. D. (1988). Legislative Monopoly and the Size of Government. *Southern Economic Journal*, *54*(3), 529–545. doi:10.2307/1058999

Anderson, G. M., & Tollison, R. D. (1991). Congressional Influence and Patterns of New Deal Spending 1933-1939. *The Journal of Law & Economics*, *34*(1), 161–175. doi:10.1086/467222

Andreoni, J., Erard, B., & Feinstein, J. (1998). Tax Compliance. *Journal of Economic Literature*, *36*(2), 818–860.

Annual Report 2010. Presidency of Strategy Development Department. (2011Turkish Revenue Administration. Ankara: Ministry of Finance.

Ansu, Y., & Laursen, T. B. (2004). Preface. In H. P. Brixi, C. M. A. Valenduc, & Z. L. Swift (Eds.), *Tax Expenditures – Shedding Light on Government Spending through the Tax System: Lessons from Developed and Transition Economies* (pp. xi–xii). Washington, DC: The World Bank.

Arab Monetary Fund. (2011). *Economic Statistics Bulletin of Arab Countries*, 31. Retrieved from www.amf.org.ae

Arab Reform Initiative. (2014). Arab Barometer. Retrieved http://arabbarometer.org

Arellano, M., & Bond, S. (1991). Some tests of specification for panel data: Monte Carlo evidence and an application to employment equations. *The Review of Economic Studies*, *58*(2), 277–297. doi:10.2307/2297968

Arellano, M., & Bover, O. (1995). Another look at the instrumental variable estimation of error-components models. *Journal of Econometrics*, *68*(1), 29–51. doi:10.1016/0304-4076(94)01642-D

Aristotle. (n. d.). *Nicomachean Ethics* (Translated by W. D. Ross). eBooks@Adelaide, The University of Adelaide. Retrieved from https://ebooks.adelaide.edu.au/a/aristotle/nicomachean/

Arrighi, G. (1994). *The Long Twentieth Century: Money, Power, and the Origins of Our Times.* London: Verso.

Ates, L. (2012). Domestic Political Legitimacy of Tax Reform In Developing Countries: A Case Study of Turkey. *Wis. Int'l L.J.*, *30,* 706-760.

Atiyas, I., Çetin, T., & Gülen, G. (2012). *Reforming Emerging Energy Markets: Political Economy, Regulation and Competition in Turkey.* New York: Springer. doi:10.1007/978-1-4614-0290-9

Atiyas, İ., & Dutz, M. (2004). *Competition and Regulatory Reform in the Turkish Electricity Industry*. Istanbul: Sabancı University.

Atkinson, A. B. (2000). Increased Income Inequality in OECD Countries and the Redistributive Impact of the Government Budget. *UNU World Institute for Development Economics Research*, Working Paper No. 202.

Atkinson, A., & Stiglitz, G. (1980). *Lectures on Public Economics*. London: McGraw-Hill.

Auerbach, A., & Kotlikoff, L. J. (1987). *Dynamic Fiscal Policy*. Cambridge: Cambridge University Press.

Babcock, L., & Loewenstein, G. (1997). Explaining Bargaining Impasse: The Role of Self-Serving Biases. *The Journal of Economic Perspectives*, *11*(1), 109–126. doi:10.1257/jep.11.1.109

Bacher, J., Wenzig, K., & Vogler, M. (2004). SPSS Twostep Cluster - A First Evaluation. Universität Erlangen-Nürnberg, Wirtschafts- und Sozialwissenschaftliche Fakultät, Sozialwissenschaftliches Institut, Lehrstuhl für Soziologie, Arbeits- und Diskussionspapiere.

Baer, K., Benon, O. P., & Toro, R. J. (2002). *'Improving Large Taxpayers' Compliance: A Review of Country Experiences*. IMF Fiscal Affairs Department.

Baer, K., & Le Borgne, E. L. (2008). *Tax amnesties: Theory, Trends, and Some Alternatives*. Washington, D. C.: IMF.

Bağdadioğlu, N., & Odyakmaz, N. (2009). Turkish Electricity Reform. *Utilities Policy*, *17*(1), 144–152. doi:10.1016/j.jup.2008.02.001

Bahl, R. W. (2003, May 15-16). Reaching the Hardest to Tax: Consequences and Possibilities. *Paper presented at Hard to Tax:An International Perspective Conference*, Young School of Policy Studies, Georgia State University.

Bahl, R., & Wallace, S. (2008, December). Reforming the Property Tax in Developing Countries: A New Approach. *International Studies Program Working Paper 08-19*. Retrieved from http://icepp.gsu.edu/files/2015/03/ispwp0819.pdf

Bahl, R. (1971). A Regression Approach to Tax Effort and Tax Ratio Analysis. *International Monetary Fund Staff Paper*, *18*(3), 570–612. doi:10.2307/3866315

Bahl, R., Martinez-Vazquez, J., & Youngman, J. M. (2010). Whither the Property Tax: New Perspectives on a Fiscal Mainstay. In *R. Bahl, J. Martinez-Vazquez, and J. M. Youngman (Eds.), Challenging the Conventional Wisdom of the Property Tax* (pp. 3–14). Cambridge, Mass., USA: Lincoln Institute of Land Policy.

Bahm, A. J. (1996). *Tao Teh King by Lao Tzu. Interpreted as Nature and Intelligence*. Fremont: Jain Publishing Company.

Bai, C.-E., & Wei, S.-J. (2000, June). Quality of Bureaucracy and Open-Economy Macro Policies. *National Bureau of Economic Research Working Paper No. 7766*.

Baicker, K., & Skinner, J. S. (2011, February). Health Care Spending Growth and the Future of U.S. Tax Rates. *NBER Working Paper No. 16772*.

Bailey, S. J. (2002). *Public Sector Economics* (2nd ed.). New York: Palgrave.

Bajo-Rubio, O., Díaz-Roldán, C., & Esteve, V. (2009). Deficit Sustainability and Inflation in EMU: An Analysis from the Fiscal Theory of the Price Level. *European Journal of Political Economy*, *25*(4), 525–539. doi:10.1016/j.ejpoleco.2009.04.001

Baldini, A., & Ribeiro, M. P. (2008). Fiscal and Monetary Anchors for Price Stability: Evidence from Sub-Saharan Africa. *IMF Working Paper,* WP/08/121.

Ballabriga, F., & Martínez-Mongay, C. (2002). Has EMU Shifted Policy? *European Commission, Directorate-General for Economic and Financial Affairs, Economics Papers*, No.166.

Ballas, A. A., & Tsoukas, H. (1998). Consequences of Distrust: The Vicious Circle of Tax Evasion in Greece. In R. W. McGee (Ed.), The Ethics of Tax Evasion (pp. 284-304), Dumont, NJ: The Dumont Institute for Public Policy Research.

Baltagi, B. (1995). *Econometric Analysis of Panel Data*. New York: John Wiley and Sons.

Barbone, L., Belkindas, M. V., Bettendorff, L., Bird, R., Bonch-Osmolovskiy, M., & Smart, M. (2013). Study to Quantify and Analyse the VAT Gap in the EU-27 Member States, *CASE Network Reports* No. 116/2013. Retrieved from http://ec.europa.eu/taxation_customs/resources/documents/common/publications/studies/vat-gap.pdf

Barone, G., & Mocetti, S. (2009). *Tax Morale and Public Spending Inefficiency* (Working Paper 732). Rome: Banca D'Italia.

Barro, R. J., & Sahasakul, C. (1986). Average Marginal Tax Rates from Social Security and the Individual Income Tax. *The Journal of Business, 59*(4, Part 1), 555-566.

Barro, R. (1979). On the Determination of Public Debt. *Journal of Political Economy, 87*(5, Part 1), 940–947. doi:10.1086/260807

Barro, R. J., & Sahasakul, C. (1983). Measuring the Average Marginal Tax Rate from the Individual Income Tax. *The Journal of Business*, *56*(4), 419–452. doi:10.1086/296211

Barwell, R. (2013). *Macroprudential Policy Taming the Wild Gyrations of Credit Flows, Debt Stocks and Asset Prices*. New YorkPalgrave Mackmillan.

Başçı, E., & Kara, H. (2011). Finansal İstikrar ve Para Politikası. *İktisat İşletme ve Finans, 26*(302), 9-25.

Bassetto, M. (2001). A Game-Theoretic View of the Fiscal Theory of the Price Level. *Federal Reserve Bank of Minneapolis, Working Paper 612*, March.

Bates, R. H., Brock, P. L., & Tiefenthaler, J. (1991). Risk and Trade Regimes: Another Exploration. *International Organization*, *45*(Winter), 1–18. doi:10.1017/S0020818300001375

Batırel, Ö. F. (2013). Vergi Harcamaları, Mali Saydamlık İlkesi ve Anayasaya Uygunluk. *İstanbul Ticaret Üniversitesi Sosyal Bilimler Dergisi, 24*, 13-20.

Batırel, Ö. F. (2014). Türk Vergi Politikasının Performansı (2003-2013). *İstanbul Yüksek Ticaret ve Marmara Üniversitesi İİBF Mezunları Derneği, Türkiye XII.* Vergi Kongresi.

Batrancea, L. (2014b). *Depicting Worldwide Tax Compliance Behavior in a Four-Cluster Assortment Availing Trust in and Power of Authorities* (Working paper).

Batrancea, L. (2014a). Taxpayers and Tax Authorities Interacting within the MENA Region: The Nexus between Trust, Power and Compliance. *The Annals of the University of Oradea. Economic Sciences*, *XXIII*(2), 241–250.

Batrancea, L., Nichita, A., Batrancea, I., & Kirchler, E. (2016). Tax Compliance Behavior - An Upshot of Trust in and Power of Authorities across Europe and MENA. In M. M. Erdoğdu & B. Christiansen (Eds.), *Handbook of Research on Public Finance Perspectives on Europe and the MENA Region*. Hershey, PA, USA: IGI Global.

Battese, G. E. (1992). Frontier Production Functions and Technical Efficiencies: A Survey of Empirical Applications in Agricultural Economics. *Agricultural Economics*, *7*(3-4), 185–208. doi:10.1016/0169-5150(92)90049-5

Battese, G. E., & Coelli, T. J. (1992). Frontier Production Functions, Technical Efficiency and Panel Data: With Application to Paddy Farmers in India. *Journal of Productivity Analysis*, *3*(1-2), 153–169. doi:10.1007/BF00158774

Baum, C. F., Schaffer, M. E., & Stillman, S. (2003). Instrumental variables and GMM: Estimation and testing. *The Stata Journal*, *3*(1), 1–31.

Baum, C. F., Schaffer, M. E., & Stillman, S. (2007). Enhanced routines for instrumental variables/generalized method of moments estimation and testing. *The Stata Journal*, *7*(4), 465–506.

Baumol, W. J. (1993). Health Care, Education and the Cost Disease: A Looming Crisis for Public Choice. *Public Choice*, *77*(September), 17–28. doi:10.1007/BF01049216

Baxter, M., & King, R. (1993, June). Fiscal Policy in General Equilibrium. *The American Economic Review*, *83*, 315–334.

Becker, G. S. (1996). *Accounting for Tastes*. Cambridge: Harvard University Press.

Beck, N., & Katz, J. N. (1995). What to Do (and Not to Do) with Time –Series Cross-Section Data. *The American Political Science Review*, *89*(3), 634–647. doi:10.2307/2082979

Ben Slimane, S., & Ben Tahar, M. (2010). Why is Fiscal Policy Procyclical in MENA Countries? *International Journal of Economics and Finance*, *2*(5), 44–53.

Benigno, G., Chen, H., Otrok, C., Rebucci, A., & Young, E. R. (2012). *Monetary and Macro-Prudential Policies: An Integrated Analysis*. Missouri University, No. 1208. Retrieved from http://economics.missouri.edu/working-papers/2012/WP1208_otrok.pdf

Benk, S., McGee, R. W., & Ross, A. M. (2009). An Empirical Study of Ethical Opinion in Turkey. *Journal of Accounting, Ethics &. Public Policy*, *10*(1), 83–99.

Bentham, J. (1791). *Panopticon*. London: Printed for T. Payne.

Bera, A. K., & Jarque, C. M. (1980). Efficient Tests for Normality, Homoscedasticity and Serial Independence of Regression Residuals. *Economics Letters*, *6*(3), 255–259. doi:10.1016/0165-1765(80)90024-5

Bergman, M. (2009). *Tax Evasion and the Rule of Law in Latin America: The Political Culture of Cheating and Compliance in Argentina and Chile*. University Park, PA: The Pennsylvania State University Press.

Bernanke, B. (2011, May). Implementing a Macroprudential Approach to Supervision and Regulation. *Speech Given at the 47th Annual Conference on Bank Structure and Competition*, Chicago. Retrieved from http://www.federalreserve.gov/newsevents/speech/bernanke20110505a.pdf

Bernanke, B., Gertler, M., & Gilchrist, S. (1999). The Financial Accelerator in a Quantitative Business Cycle Framework. In J. B. Taylor & M. Woodford (Eds.), Handbook of Macroeconomics Volume 1C (pp. 1341-1393). North-Holland, Amsterdam: Elsevier.

Bernanke, B. S., & Gertler, M. (2001). Should Central Banks Respond to Movements in Asset Prices? *The American Economic Review*, *91*(2), 253–257. doi:10.1257/aer.91.2.253

Berry, D. W., & David, D. (1987). Explaining the Size of the Public Sector: Responsive and Excessive Government Interpretations. *The Journal of Politics*, *49*(2), 401–440. doi:10.2307/2131307

Bertelsmann. (1999, December 7-9). Europe and the Middle East and North Africa: Steps towards Comprehensive Stability. *Discussion paper presented by the Bertelsmann Group on Policy Research, Center for Applied Policy Research (Munich) to the V. Kronberg Talks.*

Bhagwati, J. (2004). *In Defense of Globilization*. Oxford: Oxford University Press.

Bhattacharyya, D. K. (1990). An Econometric Method of Estimating the Underground Economy, United Kingdom (1960-1984): Estimates and Tests. *The Economic Journal*, *100*(402), 703–717. doi:10.2307/2233655

Bhattacharyya, D. K. (1999). On the Economic Rationale of Estimating the Hidden Economy. *The Economic Journal*, *109*(June), 348–359. doi:10.1111/1468-0297.00438

Bhattacharyya, S., & Hodler, R. (2010). Natural Resources, Democracy and Corruption. *European Economic Review*, *54*(4), 608–621. doi:10.1016/j.euroecorev.2009.10.004

Bhattacharyya, S., & Hodler, R. (2014). Do Natural Resource Revenues Hinder Financial Development? The Role of Political Institutions. *World Development*, *55*, 101–113. doi:10.1016/j.worlddev.2013.12.003

Bianchi, F., & Ilut, C. (2014). Monetary/Fiscal Policy Mix and Agents' Beliefs. *NBER Working Paper,* 20194.

Bird, R. M. (2000). Intergovernmental Fiscal Relations: Universal Principals, Local Applications. *International Studies Program Working Paper 00-2*, Andrew Young School of Policy Studies, Georgia State University, Atlanta.

Bird, R. M. (2007). Tax Challenges Facing Developing Countries: A Perspective from Outside the Policy Arena. Working Paper.

Bird, R. M. (2007, March 31). *Tax Challenges Facing Developing Countries: A Perspective from Outside the Policy Arena*. Retrieved May 27, 2015, from http://papers.ssrn.com/sol3/papers.cfm?abstract_id=1393991

Bird, R. M. (2008, March 12). Tax Challenges Facing Developing Countries. *Proceedings of Inaugural Lecture of the Annual Public Lecture Series of the National Institute of Public Finance and Policy*, New Delhi, India. University of Toronto, Institute for International Business Working Paper Series, IIB Paper No. 12.

Bird, R. M. (2016). Transparency, Technology and Taxation. In M. M. Erdoğdu & B. Christiansen (Eds.), Handbook of Research on Public Finance in Europe and the MENA Region. Hershey, PA: IGI Global.

Bird, R. M., Martinez-Vazquez, J., & Torgler, B. (2004). Societal Institutions and Tax Efforts in Developing Countries (Working Paper 04-06). *Andrew Young School of Policy Studies*, Georgia State University, Georgia, Atlanta.

Bird, R. M., Martinez-Vazquez, J., & Torgler, B. (2006). Societal Institutions and Tax Efforts in Developing Countries (No: 04011). International Tax Program, University of Toronto. .

Bird, R., & Jun, J. (2007). Earmarking in Theory and Korean Practice. In S. Phua (Ed.), Excise Taxation in Asia (pp, 49-86). Singapore: National University of Singapore.

Bird, R., & Wallace, S. (2004). Is It Really So Hard To Tax the Hard-To-Tax? The Context and Role of Presumptive Taxes. In J.R. Alm, J. Martinez-Vazquez, & S. Wallace (Eds.), Taxing the Hard-To-Tax: Lessons from Theory and Practice (pp. 121-158). Amsterdam: North-Holland. doi:10.1016/S0573-8555(04)68806-7

Bird, R., Martinez-Vazquez, J., & Torgler, B. (2004). Societal Institutions and Tax Effort in Developing Countries. *CREMA Working Paper* No. 2004 – 21.

Bird, R. (1982). Closing the Scissors, or the Real Public Sector Has Two Sides. *National Tax Journal*, *35*(4), 477–481.

Bird, R. (1994). *Where Do We Go From Here? Alternatives to the GST*. Toronto: KPMG Centre for Government.

Bird, R. (2005). Evaluating Public Expenditures: Does It Matter How They Are Financed? In A. Shah (Ed.), *Fiscal Management* (pp. 83–108). Washington, DC: World Bank.

Bird, R. (2010). Visibility and Accountability-- Is Tax-inclusive Pricing a Good Thing? *Canadian Tax Journal*, *58*(1), 63–76.

Bird, R. (2013). Transparência e Tributaço: Algumas Reflexões Preliminares/Transparency and Taxation: Some Preliminary Reflections. In *Diniz de Santi, E. et al., Transparência fiscal e desenvolvimento: homenagem ao Professor Isaias Coelho* (pp. 171–198). Sao Paulo: Fiscosoft Editora Ltds.

Bird, R. (2014). *Global Taxes and International Taxation: Mirage and Reality*. Washington, DC: International Tax and Investment Center.

Bird, R. (2015). Transparency, Technology and Taxation. In M. M. Erdoğdu & B. Christiansen (Eds.), *Handbook of Research on Public Finance in Europe and the MENA Region*. Hershey, PA, USA: IGI Global.

Bird, R. (2016). Transparency, Technology and Taxation. In M. M. Erdoğdu & B. Christiansen (Eds.), *Handbook of Research on Public Finance Perspectives on Europe and the MENA Region*. Hershey, PA, USA: IGI Global.

Bird, R. M. (2004). Managing tax reform. *Bulletin for International Fiscal Documentation*, *58*(2), 42–55.

Bird, R. M., & De Wulf, L. H. (1973). Taxation and Income Distribution in Latin America: A Critical Review of Empirical Studies. *International Monetary Fund Staff Papers*, *20*(3), 639–682. doi:10.2307/3866523

Bird, R. M., & Fiszbein, A. (1999). Columbia: The Central Role of the Central Government in Fiscal Decentralization. In R. M. Bird & F. Vaillancourt (Eds.), *Fiscal Decentralization in Developing Countries* (pp. 172–205). Cambridge: Cambridge University Press. doi:10.1017/CBO9780511559815.007

Bird, R. M., & Gendron, P.-P. (2007). *The VAT in Developing and Transitional Countries*. Cambridge, UK: Cambridge University Press. doi:10.1017/CBO9780511619366

Bird, R. M., & Miller, B. D. (1991). The Incidence of Indirect Taxes on Low-Income Households in Jamaica. In R. Bahl (Ed.), *The Jamaican Tax Reform* (pp. 793–811). Cambridge, MA: Lincoln Institute of Land Policy.

Bird, R. M., & Oldman, O. (1990). *Taxation in Developing Countries* (4th ed.). Baltimore: Johns Hopkins University Press.

Bird, R. M., & Slack, E. (2006). Taxing Land and Property in Emerging Economies: Raising Revenue ... And More? In G. K. Ingram (Ed.), *Y.-H. Hong, Land Policies and Their Outcomes. Cambridge*. Mass.: Lincoln Institute of Land Policy.

Bird, R. M., & Smart, M. (2002). Intergovernmental Fiscal Transfers: International Lessons for developing Countries. *World Development*, *30*(6), 899–912. doi:10.1016/S0305-750X(02)00016-5

Bird, R. M., & Vaillancourt, F. (Eds.), (1999). *Fiscal Decentralization in Developing Countries*. Cambridge: Cambridge University Press. doi:10.1017/CBO9780511559815

Bird, R., & Casanegra de Jantscher, M. (Eds.). (1992, September15). *Improving Tax Administration in Developing Countries*. Washington: International Monetary Fund.

Bird, R., & Ebel, R. (Eds.). (2007). *Fiscal Fragmentation in Decentralized Countries: Subsidiarity, Solidarity, and Asymmetry*. Cheltenham, UK: Edward Elgar. doi:10.4337/9781781007617

Bird, R., Martinez-Vazquez, J., & Torgler, B. (2008). Tax Effort in Developing Countries and High Income Countries: The Impact of Corruption, Voice and Accountability. *Economic Analysis & Policy*, *38*(1), 55–71. doi:10.1016/S0313-5926(08)50006-3

Bird, R., & Slack, E. (2014, December). Local Taxation and Local Expenditure in Developing Countries: Strengthening the Wicksellian Connection. *Public Administration and Development*, *34*(5), 359–369. doi:10.1002/pad.1695

Bird, R., & Zolt, E. (2008). Technology and Taxation in Developing Countries: From Hand to Mouse. *National Tax Journal*, *61*(4, Part 2), 791–821. doi:10.17310/ntj.2008.4S.02

Bird, R., & Zolt, E. (2014). Taxation and Inequality in the Americas: Changing the Fiscal Contract? In R. Bird & J. Martinez-Vazquez (Eds.), *Taxation and Development: The Weakest Link?* (pp. 193–237). Cheltenham, UK: Edward Elgar. doi:10.4337/9781783474332.00014

Blackburn, K. (2012). Corruption and Development: Explaining the Evidence. *The Manchester School*, *80*(4), 401–428. doi:10.1111/j.1467-9957.2012.02314.x

Blanchard, O., Dell'Ariccia, G., & Mauro, P. (2010). Rethinking macroeconomic policy. *Journal of Money, Credit and Banking*, *42*(1), 199–215. doi:10.1111/j.1538-4616.2010.00334.x

Blanchard, O., & Fischer, S. (1989). *Lectures on Macroeconomics*. Cambridge, MA: The MIT Press.

Blaufus, K., Bob, J., & Otto, P. E. (2014). The Effect of Tax Privacy on Tax Compliance –An Experimental Investigation. *Arqus Discussion Paper*, No. 164.

Blejer, M. I., & Guerrero, I. (1990). The Impact of Macroeconomic Policies on Income Distribution: An Empirical Study of the Philippines. *The Review of Economics and Statistics*, *72*(3), 414–423. doi:10.2307/2109349

Blinder, A. S. (2010). How Central should the Central Bank Be? *The Journal of Economic Perspectives*, *48*(1), 123–133.

Blöchliger, H., & Vammalle, C. (2012). *Reforming Fiscal Federalism and Local Government Beyond The Zero-Sum Game*. Paris: OECD Fiscal Federalism Studies. doi:10.1787/9789264119970-en

Blouin, J., Huizinga, H., Laeven, L., & Nicodème, G. (2014). Thin Capitalization Rules and Multinational Firm Capital Structure. *IMF Working Paper* WP/14/12.

Blumberdg, M. (2001). The OECD's Report on Harmful Tax Competition Is 'Harmful Tax Competition Actually Harmful? Retrieved from http://www.globalphilanthropy.ca/images/uploads/Harmful_Tax_Competition_and_the_OECD.pdf

Blume, A., & Sobel, J. (1995). Communication-Proof Equilibria in Cheap-Talk Games. *Journal of Economic Theory*, *65*(2), 359–382. doi:10.1006/jeth.1995.1013

Blundell, R., & Bond, S. (1998). Initial conditions and moment restrictions in dynamic panel data models. *Journal of Econometrics*, *87*(1), 115–143. doi:10.1016/S0304-4076(98)00009-8

Bø, E. E., Slemrod, J., & Thoresen, T. O. (2014). Taxes on the Internet: Deterrence Effects of Public Disclosure. *CESifo Working Paper: Public Finance*, No. 4107.

Boadway, R., Bruce, N., & Mintz, J. (1984). Taxation, Inflation, and the Effective Marginal Tax Rate in Canada. *Revue Canadienne d'Economique [The Canadian Journal of Economics]*, *27*(3), 286–299.

Bobek, D. D., Hageman, A. M., & Kelliher, C. F. (2013). Analyzing the Role of Social Norms in Tax Compliance Behavior. *Journal of Business Ethics*, *115*(3), 451–468. doi:10.1007/s10551-012-1390-7

Bohn, H. (1998). The Behaviour of U.S. Public Debt and Deficits. *The Quarterly Journal of Economics*, *113*(3), 949–964. doi:10.1162/003355398555793

Boldrin, M., Christiano, L. J., & Fisher, J. D. M. (2001, March). Habit Persistence, Asset Returns, and the Business Cycle. *The American Economic Review*, *91*(1), 149–166. doi:10.1257/aer.91.1.149

Borcherding, T. E. (1985). The Causes of Government Expenditure Growth: A Survey of the US Evidence. *Journal of Public Economics*, *28*(3), 359–382. doi:10.1016/0047-2727(85)90065-9

Borio, C. (2011, September). Central Banking Post-Crisis: What Compass for Uncharted Waters? *BIS Working Papers*, No. 353. Retrieved from http://www.bis.org/publ/work353.pdf

Bornhost, F., Gupta, S., & Thornton, J. (2009). Natural Resource Endowments and the Domestic Revenue Effort. *European Journal of Political Economy*, *25*(4), 439–446. doi:10.1016/j.ejpoleco.2009.01.003

Bosco, L., & Mittone, L. (1997). Tax Evasion and Moral Constraints: Some Experimental Evidence. *Kyklos*, *50*(3), 297–324. doi:10.1111/1467-6435.00018

Bova, E., Carcenac, N., & Guerguil, M. (2013). Fiscal Rules and the Procyclicality of Fiscal Policy in the Developing World. *IMF-World Bank Conference on Fiscal Policy, Equity and Long-Term Growth in Developing Countries Washington, DC, April 21-22*. Retrieved from http://www.imf.org/external/np/seminars/eng/2013/fiscalpolicy/pdf/fispols3.pdf

Bovenberg, R. (1992). Residence-and source-based taxation of capital income in an overlapping generations model. *Journal of Economics*, *56*(3), 267–295. doi:10.1007/BF01237183

Bovi, M., & Dell'Anno, R. (2010). The changing nature of the OECD shadow economy. *Journal of Evolutionary Economics*, *20*(1), 19–48. doi:10.1007/s00191-009-0138-8

Bowles, S. (1998). Endogenous Preferences: The Cultural Consequences of Markets and Other Economic Institutions. *Journal of Economic Literature*, *36*, 75–111.

Bracco, E., Porcelli, F., & Redoano, M. (2013, February). Political competition, tax salience and accountability: Theory and some evidence from Italy. *CESifo Working Paper* No.4167.

Braithwaite, J. (2002). *Restorative Justice and Responsive Regulation*. Oxford: Oxford University Press.

Braithwaite, V. (2003). Dancing with Tax Authorities: Motivational Postures and Non-Compliant Actions. In V. Braithwaite (Ed.), *Taxing Democracy. Understanding Tax Avoidance and Tax Evasion* (pp. 15–39). Aldershot: Ashgate.

Braithwaite, V. (2007). Responsive Regulation and Taxation: Introduction. *Law & Policy*, *29*(1), 3–10. doi:10.1111/j.1467-9930.2007.00242.x

Brand, L. A. (1992). Economic and Political Liberalization in a Rentier Economy: The Case of the Hashemite Kingdom of Jordan. In I. Harik & D. J. Sullivan (Eds.), *Privatization and Liberalization in the Middle East* (pp. 167–188). Bloomington, IN, USA: Indiana University Press.

Braude, K., Erdman, Z., & Shemesh, M. (2011). *Israel and the Global Crisis. Jerusalem*: Bank of Israel.

Brautigam, D. A. (2008). Introduction: Taxation and State-Building in Developing Countries. In D. Brautigam, O. Fjeldstad, & M. Moore (Eds.), *Taxation and State-Building in Developing Countries* (pp. 1–33). Cambridge: Cambridge University Press. doi:10.1017/CBO9780511490897.001

Brautigam, D., Fjeldstad, O., & Moore, M. (Eds.). (2007). *Taxation and state-building in developing countries*. Cambridge: Cambridge University Press.

Break, G. F., & Pechman, J. A. (1975). *Federal Tax Reform: The Impossible Dream?* Washington, DC: Brookings Institution.

Brennan, G., & Buchanan, J. (1980). *The Power to Tax: Analytical Foundations of a Fiscal Constitution*. New York: Cambridge University Press.

Breton, A. (1987). Towards a Theory of Competitive Federalism. *European Journal of Political Economy*, *3*(1-2), 263–329. doi:10.1016/S0176-2680(87)80014-9

Breton, A. (1989). Growth of Competitive Governments. *The Canadian Journal of Economics. Revue Canadienne d'Economique*, *22*(4), 717–750. doi:10.2307/135496

Breusch, T. S. (1979). Testing for Autocorrelation in Dynamic Linear Models. *Australian Economic Papers*, *17*(31), 334–355. doi:10.1111/j.1467-8454.1978.tb00635.x

Breusch, T. S., & Pagan, A. R. (1979). A Simple Test for Heteroscedasticity and Random Coefficient Variation. *Econometrica*, *47*(5), 1287–1294. doi:10.2307/1911963

Brin, D. (1998). *The Transparent Society: Will Technology Force us to Choose between Privacy and Freedom?* New York, NY: Perseus Books.

Brixi, H. P. (2004). Managing Tax Expenditures: Policy Options. In H. P. Brixi, C. M. A. Valenduc, & Z. L. Swift (Eds.), *Tax Expenditures – Shedding Light on Government Spending through the Tax System: Lessons from Developed and Transition Economies* (pp. 227–233). Washington, DC: The World Bank.

Brooks, C. (2002). *Introductory econometrics for finance*. Cambridge: Cambridge University Press.

Brown, C. (2004). Tax Expenditures in Australia. In H. P. Brixi, C. M. A. Valenduc, & Z. L. Swift (Eds.), *Tax Expenditures – Shedding Light on Government Spending through the Tax System: Lessons from Developed and Transition Economies* (pp. 45–68). Washington, DC: The World Bank.

Browning, L. (2009, February 19). UBS Pressed for 52,000 Names in 2nd Inquiry. *New York Times*. Retrieved from http://www.dailymail.co.uk/news/article-2567957/Panel-faults-US-govt-offshore-tax-evasion.html#ixzz364AqblSg.

Brueckner, J. K. (2000). A Tiebout/ Tax-competition model. *Journal of Public Economics*, *77*(2), 285–306. doi:10.1016/S0047-2727(99)00086-9

Brunori, D. (2003). *Local Tax Policy: A Federalist Perspective*. Washington, DC: The Urban Institute Press.

Buchanan, J. M. (1987). Public Receipts of Public Debt. In J. Eatwell, M. Milgate, & P. Newman (Eds.), *The New Palgrave, A Dictionary of Economics* (Vol. 3). London: Macmillan.

Bucovetsky, S. (1991). Asymmetric tax competition. *Journal of Urban Economics*, *30*(2), 167–18. doi:10.1016/0094-1190(91)90034-5

Bucovetsky, S. (2009). An index of capital tax competition. *International Tax and Public Finance*, *16*(6), 727–752. doi:10.1007/s10797-008-9093-9

Buehn, A., & Schneider, F. (2012a). Shadow economies around the world: Novel insights, accepted knowledge, and new estimates. *International Tax and Public Finance*, *19*(1), 139–171. doi:10.1007/s10797-011-9187-7

Buiter, W. (1998, February). The Young Person's Guide to Neutrality, Price Level indeterminacy, Interest Rate Pegs and Fiscal Theories of the Price Level, *CEPR Discussion Paper* 1799.

Buiter, W. (1999). The Fallacy of the Fiscal Theory of the Price Level. *NBER Working Paper* 7302, August.

Buiter, W. (2001, July). The Fallacy of the Fiscal Theory of the Price Level Again. *Bank of England, Working Paper* 141.

Buiter, W. H. (2009). *Lessons from the Global Financial Crisis for Regulators and Supervisors*. London School of Economics.

Burki, S. J., & Perry, G. E. (1998). *Beyond the Washington Consensus: Institutions Matter*. Washington, DC: World Bank Publications. doi:10.1596/0-8213-4282-7

Burton, M., & Stewart, M. (2011). *Promoting Budget Transparency through Tax Expenditure Management: A Report on Country Experience f or Civil Society Advocates*. Melbourne Law School Legal Studies Research Paper 544. University of Melbourne. Retrieved July 30, 2015, from http://internationalbudget.org/wp-content/uploads/Promoting-Budget-Transparency-Through-Tax-Expenditure-Management.pdf

Burton, M., & Sadiq, K. (2013). *Tax Expenditure Management: A Critical Assessment*. Cambridge, UK: Cambridge University Press. doi:10.1017/CBO9780511910142

Buti, M. (2003). Interactions and Coordination between Monetary and Fiscal Policies in EMU: What Are the Issues? In M. Buti (Ed.), *Monetary and Fiscal Policies in EMU: Interactions and Coordination*. Cambridge: Cambridge University Press.

Büyükduman, A. (2014). *Bir Kent Efsanesi Konut Balonu: Kent Ekonomisi Ne Diyor?* İstanbul: Scala.

Caballero, R. J. (2010). Macroeconomics after the Crisis: Time to Deal with the Pretense-of-Knowledge Syndrome. *The Journal of Economic Perspectives*, *24*(4), 85–102. doi:10.1257/jep.24.4.85

Cagan, P. (1958). The Demand for Currency Relative to the Total Money Supply. *Journal of Political Economy*, *66*(4), 303–338. doi:10.1086/258056

Cagliarini, A., Kent, C., & Stevens, G. (2010, February 9). Fifty years of Monetary Policy: What have we Learned? *Reserve Bank of Australia's 50th Anniversary Symposium*, Sydney.

Cameron, D. (1978). The Expansion of the Public Economy: A Comparative Analysis. *The American Political Science Review*, *72*(December), 1243–1261. doi:10.2307/1954537

Campbell, J. L. (1993). The State and Fiscal Sociology. *Annual Review of Sociology*, *19*(1), 163–185. doi:10.1146/annurev.so.19.080193.001115

Canova, F., & Ciccarelli, M. (2013). Panel vector autoregressive models: A survey. In T. B. Fomby, L. Kilian, & A. Murphy (Eds.), *VAR models in macroeconomics – new developments and applications: Essays in honor of Christopher A. Sims, Advances in econometrics* (Vol. 32, pp. 205–246). London: Emerald Group Publishing Limited.

Canuto, O., & Cavallari, M. (2013). Monetary Policy and Macroprudential Regulation: Whither Emerging Markets. *World Bank Policy Research Working Paper*, No.6310.

Canzoneri, M. B., Cumby, R. E., & Diba, B. T. (2001). Is the Price Level Determined by the Needs of Fiscal Solvency? *The American Economic Review*, *91*(5), 1221–1238. doi:10.1257/aer.91.5.1221

CAPMAS. (2013). *Annual Statistical Yearbook for the Arab Republic of Egypt*. Central Agency for Public Mobilisation and Statistics.

Card, D. (1991). Intertemporal Labor Supply: An Assessment. *NBER*, Working Paper No. 3602. Cambridge, MA.

Cardenas, M., & Tuzemen, D. (2011, December). Under-Investment in State Capacity: The Role of Inequality and Political Instability (Research Working Papers). The Federal Reserve Bank of Kansas City-Economic Research Department, No: RWP 11/07.

Carlstrom, C., & Fuerst, T. (2000). The Fiscal Theory of Price Level. *Federal Reserve Bank of Cleveland. Economic Review, Q-I*, *36*(1), 22–32.

Carney, M. (2009, August 22). Some Considerations on Using Monetary Policy to Stabilize Economic Activity. *Remarks at the Symposium on Financial stability and macroeconomic policy sponsored by the Federal Reserve Bank of Kansas City*, Jackson Hole, Wyoming, USA.

Caspersen, E., & Metcalf, G. (1994). Is A Value Added Tax Progressive? Annual Versus Lifetime Incidence Measures. *National Tax Journal*, *47*, 731–746.

Castells, M., & Portes, A. (1989). World Underneath: The Origins, Dynamics, and Effects of the Informal Economy. In A. Portes, M. Castells, & L. A. Benton (Eds.), *The Informal Economy: Studies in Advanced and Less Developed Countries*. Maryland: The John Hopkins University Press.

Castro, L., & Scartascini, C. (2013). Tax Compliance and Enforcement in the Pampas: Evidence from a Field Experiment. *IDB Working Paper Series*. No. IDB-WP-472. Washington, D.C.: Inter-American Development Bank. Retrieved from http://publications.iadb.org/bitstream/handle/11319/4698/Tax%20Compliance%20and%20Enforcement%20in%20the%20Pampas%3a%20Evidence%20from%20a%20Field%20Experiment.pdf;jsessionid=69EE51DEDF52FCC1F16D467BC60841C9?sequence=1

Çebi, C. (2012). The Interaction between Monetary and Fiscal Policies in Turkey: An Estimated New Keynesian DSGE Model. *Economic Modelling*, *29*(4), 1258–1267. doi:10.1016/j.econmod.2012.04.014

Çetin, G. (2007). Vergi Aflarının Vergi Mükelleflerinin Tutum ve Davranışları Üzerindeki Etkisi. *Yönetim ve Ekonomi*, *14*(2), 171–187.

Çevik, E. I., Dibooğlu, S., & Kutan, A. M. (2014). Monetary and Fiscal Policy Interactions: Evidence from Emerging European Economies. *Journal of Comparative Economics*, *42*(4), 1079–1091. doi:10.1016/j.jce.2014.05.001

Çevik, S. (2012). Mükelleflerin Devlet ve Toplumla Etkileşimi, Bireysel Normlar ve Vergi Ahlakı, İlişkisi. *Maliye Dergisi*, *163*, 258–269.

Çevik, S. (2016). Tax Systems, Economic Development and Good Governance: A Comparative Analysis of the MENA Countries. In M. M. Erdoğdu & B. Christiansen (Eds.), *Handbook of Research on Public Finance Perspectives on Europe and the MENA Region*. Hershey, PA, USA: IGI Global.

Çevik, S., & Yeniçeri, H. (2013). The Relationship between Social Norms and Tax Compliance: The Moderating Role of the Effectiveness of the Tax Administration. *International Journal of Economic Sciences*, *2*(3), 166–180.

Chander, P., & Wilde, L. (1992). Corruption in Tax Administration. *Journal of Public Economics*, *49*(3), 333–349. doi:10.1016/0047-2727(92)90072-N

Chang, C. P., & Berdiev, A. N. (2011). The Political Economy of Energy Regulation in OECD Countries. *Energy Economics*, *33*(5), 816–825. doi:10.1016/j.eneco.2011.06.001

Charmes, J. (2012). The informal economy worldwide: Trends and characteristics. *Margin: The Journal of Applied Economic Research*, *6*(2), 103–132. doi: 10.1177/097380101200600202

Chelliah, R. J., Baas, H. J., & Kelly, M. R. (1975). Tax Ratios and Tax Effort in Developing Countries. *IMF Staff Papers*.

Chen, D., Matovu, J. M., & Reinikka, R. (2001). A Quest for Revenue and Tax Incidence in Uganda. *IMF Working Paper /01/24*. Washington D.C.: IMF.

Chetty, R. (2009, August). The Simple Economics of Salience and Taxation. *Working Paper 14246*, National Bureau of Economic Research, Cambridge, MA.

Chetty, R., Hendren, N., Kline, P., & Saez, E. (2013). *The Economic Impacts of Tax Expenditures: Evidence from Spatial Variation across the U.S.* Retrieved July 30, 2015, from http://obs.rc.fas.harvard.edu/chetty/tax_expenditure_soi_whitepaper.pdf

Chetty, R., Looney, A., & Kroft, K. (2007, August). Salience and Taxation: Theory and Evidence (Working Paper 13330). National Bureau of Economic Research, Cambridge, MA.

Choi, J. P., & Thum, M. (2002). *Corruption and the Shadow Economy*. Center for Economic Studies and Ifo Institute for Economic Research.

Choi, J. P., & Thum, M. (2005). Corruption and the shadow economy. *International Economic Review*, *46*(3), 817–836. doi:10.1111/j.1468-2354.2005.00347.x

Christiano, L., Ilut, C. L., Motto, R., & Rostagno, M. (2010). Monetary Policy and Stock Market Booms. *Economic Research Initiatives at Duke (ERID) Working Paper.* No. 69. Retrieved from http://ssrn.com/abstract=1684785

Christiano, L., Ilut, C. L., Motto, R., & Rostagno, M. (2010). Monetary Policy and Stock Market Booms. *National Bureau of Economic Research Working Paper No. 16402*.

Christiano, L. J., & Eichenbaum, M. (1992, June). Current Real Business Cycle Theories and Aggregate Labor Market Fluctuations. *The American Economic Review*, *82*, 430–450.

Chu, K.-Y., Davoodi, H., & Gupta, S. (2000). *Income Distribution and Tax, and Government Social Spending Policies in Developing Countries.* The United Nations University, WIDER Working Papers No. 214.

Citizen-State Relations: Improving Governance through Tax Reforms. (2010). *OECD*. Retrieved from ww.oecd.org

Cizre-Sakallıoğlu, U., & Yeldan, E. (2000). Politics, Society and Financial Liberalization: Turkey in the 1990s. *Development and Change*, *31*(2), 481–508. doi:10.1111/1467-7660.00163

Claessens, S., & Valencia, F. (2013, January 29). The Interaction Between Monetary and Macroprudential Policies. Retrieved from http://www.imf.org/external/np/pp/eng/2013/012913.pdf

Clements, B., Hugounenq, R., & Schwartz, G. (1995). Government Subsidies: Concepts, International Trends and Reform Options. *International Monetary Fund (IMF) Working Paper 91*.

Clements, D. (2013). Blowing in the Wind? In Deloitte & Touche (Eds.), Middle East Point of View Summer 2013 (pp. 52-55).

Cochrane, J. (1998). A Frictionless View of US Inflation. In B. Bernanke & J. Rotemberg (Eds.), NBER Macroeconomics Annual (pp. 323–384).

Cochrane, J. (2001). Long-Term Debt and Optimal Policy in the Fiscal Theory of the Price Level. *Econometrica*, *69*(1), 69–116.

Cochrane, J. H. (2005). Money as Stock. *Journal of Monetary Economics*, *52*(3), 501–528. doi:10.1016/j.jmoneco.2004.07.004

Cohn, G. (1998). The Jewish View on Paying Taxes. In R. W. McGee (Ed.), The Ethics of Tax Evasion (pp. 180-189). Dumont, NJ: The Dumont Institute for Public Policy Research.

Cohn, G. (2012). The Traditional Jewish View of Paying Taxes. In R. W. McGee (Ed.), *The Ethics of Tax Evasion: Perspectives in Theory and Practice* (pp. 149–158). New York: Springer. doi:10.1007/978-1-4614-1287-8_9

Cole, H. L., & Ohanian, L. E. (1999). The Great Depression in the United States from a Neoclassical Perspective. *Federal Reserve Bank of Minneapolis Quarterly Review*, *23*(Winter), 2–24.

Cole, H. L., & Ohanian, L. E. (2002, January). The Great UK Depression: A Puzzle and a Possible Resolution. *Review of Economic Dynamics*, *5*(1), 19–44. doi:10.1006/redy.2001.0140

Colgan, F. D. (2014). Oil, Domestic Politics, and International Conflict. *Energy Research & Social Science*, *1*, 198–205. doi:10.1016/j.erss.2014.03.005

Collier, P., & Hoeffler, A. (2005). Democracy and Resource Rents (Working Paper GPRG-WPS-016). *Global Poverty Research Group*.

Collier, P. (2006). Is Aid Oil? An Analysis of Whether Africa Can Absorb More Aid. *World Development*, *34*(9), 1482–1497. doi:10.1016/j.worlddev.2006.01.002

Collier, P., & Hoeffler, A. (2009). Testing the Neocon Agenda: Democracy in Resource-Rich Societies. *European Economic Review*, *53*(3), 293–308. doi:10.1016/j.euroecorev.2008.05.006

Common Consolidated Corporate Tax Base Working Group. (2004, December 10). *EU*. Retrieved from http://ec.europa.eu/taxation_customs/taxation/company_tax/harmful_tax_practices/

Cooley, T. (Ed.). (1995). *Frontiers of Business Cycle Research*. Princeton: Princeton University Press.

Co-operative Compliance: A framework from Enhanced Relationship to Co-operative Compliance. Organization for Economic Co-operation and Development. (2013). OECD. Retrieved from http://www.oecd.org/ctp/administration/co-operativecompliance.htm

Corden, W. M., & Neary, J. P. (1982). Booming Sector and De-industrialisation in a Small Open Economy. *The Economic Journal*, *92*(368), 825–848. doi:10.2307/2232670

Coricelli, G., Joly, M., Montmarquette, C., & Villeval, M. C. (2010). Cheating, Emotions, and Rationality: An Experiment on tax evasion. *Experimental Economics*, *13*(2), 226–247. doi:10.1007/s10683-010-9237-5

Corporate and Indirect Tax Rate Survey 2014. (2014). *KMPG*. Retrieved from www.kpmg.com

Courharde, C., Coulibaly, I., Guerreiro, D., & Mignon, V. (2012). Revising the Theory of Optimum Currency Areas: Is the CFA Franc Zone Sustainable? Centre d'Etudes Prospectives et d'Informations Internationales *Working Paper* No: 2012-13.

Cousins, M. (2005). *European Welfare States: Comparative Perspectives*. London: Sage Publications.

Crawford, V. P., & Sobel, J. (1982). Strategic Information Transmission. *Econometrica*, *50*(6), 1431–1451. doi:10.2307/1913390

Creel, J., & Sterdyniak, H. (2001). La Théorie Budgetaire du Niveau Des Prix: Un Bilan Critique. *Revue d'Economie Politique*, *111*(6), 909–940. doi:10.3917/redp.116.0909

Crivelli, E., & Gupta, S. (2014). Resource Blessing, Revenue Curse? Domestic Revenue Effort in Resource-Rich Countries. *European Journal of Political Economy*, *35*, 88–101. doi:10.1016/j.ejpoleco.2014.04.001

Crowe, M. T. (1944). The Moral Obligation of Paying Just Taxes. Washington, DC: The Catholic University of America Studies in Sacred Theology No. 84.

Crowe, C., Dell'Ariccia, G., Igan, D., & Rabanal, P. (2011). *Policies for Macrofinancial Stability: Options to Deal with Real Estate Booms, Staff Discussion Note No. 11/02*. International Monetary Fund.

CroweHorwath. (2014). *Europe, Middle East & Africa Tax Facts 2014*. Retrieved on January 15, 2015, from: www.crowehorwath.net

Crystal, J. (1990). *Oil and Politics in the Gulf: Rulers and Merchants in Kuwait and Qatar*. Cambridge: Cambridge University Press. doi:10.1017/CBO9780511558818

Cummings, R., Martinez-Vazquez, J., McKee, M., & Torgler, B. (2009). Tax Morale Affects Tax Compliance: Evidence from Surveys and an Artefactual Field Experiment. *Journal of Economic Behavior & Organization*, *70*(3), 447–457. doi:10.1016/j.jebo.2008.02.010

Cushing, M. (1999). The Indeterminacy of Prices Under Interest Rate Pegging: The non-Ricardian Case. *Journal of Monetary Economics*, *44*(1), 131–148. doi:10.1016/S0304-3932(99)00012-4

Cussons, P. (2006). The Increasing Burden of Tax Administration and Compliance. In the World Bank Group & PricewaterhouseCoopers (Eds.), Paying Taxes: The Global Picture (pp. 16-17). Washington, DC.

Cyan, M., Martinez-Vazquez, J., & Vulovic, V. (2012, September). *Measuring Tax Effort: How much does the Estimation Approach Matter?* International Center for Public Policy, Andrew Young School of Policy Studies, Georgia State University.

D'Hernoncourta, J., & Méon, P. G. (2012). The not so dark side of trust: Does trust increase the size of the shadow economy? *Journal of Economic Behavior & Organization*, *81*(1), 97–121. doi:10.1016/j.jebo.2011.09.010

Dabla-Norris, E., Gradstein, M., & Inchauste, G. (2008). What causes firms to hide output? The determinants of informality. *Journal of Development Economics*, *85*(1-2), 1–27. doi:10.1016/j.jdeveco.2006.05.007

Dagan, T. (2000). The Tax Treaties Myth. *New York University Journal of International Law & Politics. New York University. International Law Society*, *32*(4), 939–996.

Daly, H., & Smida, M. (2014). Fiscal Theory of Price Level, *International Journal of Economics. Commerce and Management*, *2*(11), 1–22.

Danopoulos, C. P., & Znidaric, B. (2007). Informal Economy, Tax Evasion, and Poverty in a Democratic Setting: Greece. *Mediterranean Quarterly*, *18*(2), 68–84. doi:10.1215/10474552-2007-006

Dasgupta, P. (2000). Economic Progress and the Idea of Social Capital. In P. Dasgupta & I. Serageldin (Eds.), *Social Capital: A Multifaceted Perspective* (pp. 325–424). Washington, DC: The World Bank.

Daude, C., Gutiérrez, H., & Melguizo, Á. (2014). *'Doctoring the ball': The Political Economy of Tax Incentives for Investment in the Dominican Republi.*, OECD Development Centre, Working Paper, No. 322, January. Retrieved January 15, 2015, from http://www.oecd.org/countries/dominicanrepublic/WP322AE.pdf

Daude, C., Gutiérrez, H., & Melguizo, Á. (2014, January). 'Doctoring the ball': The Political Economy of Tax Incentives for Investment in the Dominican Republic, OECD Development Centre, *Working Paper*, No. 322. Retrieved from http://www.oecd.org/countries/dominicanrepublic/WP322AE.pdf

Davis, G. A., & Tilton, J. E. (2005). The Resource Curse. *Natural Resources Forum*, *29*(3), 233–242. doi:10.1111/j.1477-8947.2005.00133.x

Davoodi, H. R., & Grigorian, D. A. (2007, May). Tax Potential vs. Tax Effort: A Cross-Country Analysis of Armenia's Stubbornly Low Tax Collection. *IMF Working Paper No: WP/07/106.*

De Cesare, C. M. (1999). Challenges to Property Tax Administration in Porto Alegre, Brazil. *Land Lines*, September, *11*(5). Retrieved from http://www1.worldbank.org/publicsector/decentralization/June2003Seminar/ChallengesPropertyTaxAdmin.pdf

De Grauwe, P. (2007). *Economics of Monetary Union*. New York: Oxford University Press.

Debrun, X., & Wyplosz, C. (1999). Onze Gouvernments et une Banque Centrale. *Revue d'Economie Politique*, *3*, 387–420.

DeMoville, W. (1998). The Ethics of Tax Evasion: A Baha'i Perspective. In R. W. McGee (Ed.), The Ethics of Tax Evasion (pp. 230-240). Dumont, NJ: The Dumont Institute for Public Policy Research.

Dessus, S., & Varoudakis, A. (2013). Protecting Public Investment against Shocks in the WAEMU: Options for Fiscal Rules and Risk Sharing. *World Bank Policy Research Working Paper* No. 6562.

Devarajan, S. (1997). Real Exchange Rate Misalignment in the CFA. Zone. *Journal of African Economies*, *6*(1), 35–53. doi:10.1093/oxfordjournals.jae.a020922

Devarajan, S., Fullerton, D., & Musgrave, R. A. (1980). Estimating the Distribution of Tax Burdens: A Comparison of Different Approaches. *Journal of Public Economics*, *13*(2), 155–182. doi:10.1016/0047-2727(80)90011-0

Devas, N., Delay, S., & Hubbard, M. (2001). Revenue Authorities: Are they the Right Vehicle for Improved Tax Administration? *Public Administration and Development*, *21*(3), 211–222. doi:10.1002/pad.174

Development Challenges for the Arab Region: A Human Development Approach. (2009). United Nations.

Devereux, M. P., Griffith, R., & Klemm, A. (2002). Corporate Income Tax Reforms and International Tax Competition. *Economic Policy*, *35*, 451–495.

Dharmapala, D., & Hines, J. R., Jr. (2006, December). Which Countries Become Tax Havens? *NBER Working Paper No: 12802.*

Diamond, W. H., & Diamond, D. B. (2002). *Tax Havens of the World.* Newark, NJ: Matthew Bender Books.

Dickey, D. A., & Fuller, W. A. (1979). Distribution of the Estimators for Autoregressive Time Series with a Unit Root. *Journal of the American Statistical Association*, *74*(366), 427–431. doi:10.2307/2286348

Dii. (2012). *Desert Power 2050: Perspectives on a Sustainable Power System for EUMENA.* Desertec Industrial Initiative (Dii), Munich, Germany.

Dillinger, W., & Webb, S. B. (1999). Fiscal Management in Federal Democracies: Argentina and Brazil. *World Bank Policy Research Working Paper No. 2121.*

Directive 2003/54/EC of the European Parliament and of the Council of 26 June 2003. (2003). *Official Journal of European Union* (L 176), 37-55. Retrieved from http://www.energy-community.org/pls/portal/docs/36275.PDF

Directive 2009/72/EC Of the European Parliament and of the Council of 13 July 2009. (2009). *Official Journal of European Union*, 2009, 15-35. Retrieved from http://eur-lex.europa.eu/LexUriServ/LexUriServ.do?uri=OJ:L:2009:211:0055:0093:EN:PDFfr

Directive 96/92/EC of the European Parliament and of the Council of 19 December 1996 Concerning Common Rules for the Internal Market in Electricity. (1996). *Official Journal of European Union* (L 027), 20-29. Retrieved from http://eur-lex.europa.eu/LexUriServ/LexUriServ.do?uri=CELEX:31996L0092:EN:HTML

Doğrul, A. R. (2011). Gayrimenkul Alım Satımlarında Vergi Kayıp Kaçağı ve Bunun Önlenmesinde Bilgi Teknolojilerinin Rolü: Konya Örneği [Unpublished MA thesis]. Karamanoğlu Mehmetbey University Social Science Institute.

Doing Business, 2010 – Reforming through Difficult Times. (2010World Bank. Washington, D.C.: The World Bank and the International Finance Corporation.

Doing Business, 2012 – Doing Business in a More Transparent World. (2012World Bank. Washington, D.C.: The World Bank and the International Finance Corporation.

Domaç, I. (2004). Explaining and Forecasting Inflation in Turkey, World Bank Policy Research (3287).

Dornfest, A. S. (2010). In Search of an Optimal Revaluation Policy: Benefits and Pitfalls. In R. Bahl, J. Martinez-Vazquez, & J. M. Youngman (Eds.), Challenging the Conventional Wisdom of the Property Tax (pp. 75-107). Cambridge, Mass.: Lincoln Institute of Land Policy.

Dreher, A., Kotsogiannis, C., & McCorriston, S. (2005). How Do Institutions Affect Corruption and the Shadow Economy. *Econ WPA Public Economic Series*, No. 0502012.

Dreher, A., Kotsogiannis, C., & McCorriston, S. (2009). How do institutions affect corruption and the shadow economy? *International Tax and Public Finance*, *16*(9), 773–796. doi:10.1007/s10797-008-9089-5

Dreher, A., Méon, P. G., & Schneider, F. (2014). The devil is in the shadow. Do institutions affect income and productivity or only official income and official productivity? *Public Choice*, *158*(1-2), 121–141. doi:10.1007/s11127-012-9954-8

Dreher, A., & Schneider, F. (2010). Corruption and the shadow economy: An empirical analysis. *Public Choice*, *144*(1-2), 215–238. doi:10.1007/s11127-009-9513-0

Durakoğlu, S. M. (2011). Political Endowments and Electricity Market Regulation in Turkey: An Institutional Analysis. Badia Fiesolana: San Domenico (Fl).

Dutkowsky, D. H., & Dunsky, R. M. (1996). Intertemporal Substitution, Money, and Aggregate Labor Supply. *Journal of Money, Credit and Banking*, *28*(2), 216–232. doi:10.2307/2078024

Ebel, R., & Petersen, P. (2012). *Handbook on State and Local Finance*. Massachusetts: Oxford Press. doi:10.1093/oxfordhb/9780199765362.001.0001

EC MEMO/11/125. (2011). European Commission. Retrieved from http://europa.eu/rapid/press-release_MEMO-11-125_en.htm?locale=en

EC. (2013). *Taxation Trends in the European Union: Data for the EU Member States*, Iceland and Norway, Luxembourg: Eurostat. Retrieved from http://epp.eurostat.ec.europa.eu/cache/ ity_offpub/ks-du-13-001/en/ks-du-13-001-en.pdf

Eden, M., & Kraay, A. (2014). "Crowding in" and the Returns to Government Investment in Low-Income Countries. World Bank Policy Research Working Paper 6781. Washington, DC: World Bank Group. Retrieved from http://documents.worldbank.org/curated/en/2014/02/19005742/crowding-returns-government-investment-low-income-countries

Edwards, C., & Rugy, V. (2002, April 12). International Tax Competition A 21st-Century Restrain on Government. *Policy Analysis, No: 431.*

Edwards, J., & Keen, M. (1996). Tax Competition and Leviathan. *European Economic Review*, *40*(1), 113–134. doi:10.1016/0014-2921(95)00057-7

EFW. (2013). Economic Freedom of the World: 2013 Annual Report. Retrieved from www.freetheworld.com/2013/EFW2013-complete.pdf

Eilat, Y., & Zinnes, C. (2002). The shadow economy in transition countries: Friend or foe? A policy perspective. *World Development*, *30*(7), 1233–1254. doi:10.1016/S0305-750X(02)00036-0

Eissa, N., & Williamson Hoynes, H. (2008). Redistribution and Tax Expenditures: The Earned Income Tax Credit. *NBER Working Paper 14307*. Retrieved from http://www.nber.org/papers/w14307.pdf

El-Badri, A. S. (2012, January 30-31). The MENA Region in the International Arena. *Keynote address of the OPEC Secretary General, to the Middle East & North Africa Energy 2012, Investing for the Future in Turbulent Times*, Chatham House, London, UK. Retrieved from http://www.opec.org/opec_web/en/2211.htm

Electricity Market Balancing and Settlement Regulation. (2014). *Official Gazette*.

Electricity Market Report 2010. (2011). EMRA. Retrieved from http://www.emra.org.tr/documents/electricity/publishments/ElectricityMarketReport2010.pdf

Electricity Sector Reform and Privatization Strategy Paper. (2004, March 17). *High Planning Council*. Retrieved from http://www.oib.gov.tr/program/2004_program/2004_electricity_strategy_paper.htm

Elffers, H. (1991). *Income Tax Evasion: Theory and Measurement*. Deventer: Kluwer.

Elffers, H., Weigel, R. H., & Hessing, D. J. (1987). The Consequences of Different Strategies for Measuring Tax Evasion Behavior. *Journal of Economic Psychology*, *8*(3), 311–337. doi:10.1016/0167-4870(87)90026-2

Eltony, M. N. (2002). The Determinants of Tax Effort in Arab Countries. *Arab Planning Institute Working Paper Series No: 02-07*.

Engle, R. E., & Granger, C. W. J. (1987). Cointegration and Error-Correction: Representation, Estimation and Testing. *Econometrica*, *55*(2), 251–276. doi:10.2307/1913236

Epifani, P., & Gancia, G. (2009). Openness, Government Size and the Terms of Trade. *The Review of Economic Studies*, *76*(2), 629–668. doi:10.1111/j.1467-937X.2009.00546.x

Epstein, J. L. (2005). School-Initiated Family and Community Partnerships. In T. Erb (Ed.), *This We Believe in Action: Implementing Successful Middle Level Schools* (pp. 77–96). Westerville, OH: National Middle School Association.

Erard, B., & Feinstein, J. S. (1994). Honesty and Evasion in the Tax Compliance Game. *The Rand Journal of Economics*, *25*(1), 1–19. doi:10.2307/2555850

Erdoğdu, M. M. (2004). South Korean State Capacity: From Development to Crisis Management. In K.S. Jomo (Ed.), After The Storm: Crises, Recovery and Sustaining Development in Four Asian Economies (pp. 260-302). Singapore: Singapore University Press.

Erdoğdu, M. M. (2015). Culture of Development and Developmental Capacity of States: The Korean Case. In B. Christiansen & J. Koeman (Eds.), Nationalism, Cultural Indoctrination, and Economic Prosperity in the Digital Age (pp. 1-51). Hershey, PA, USA: IGI Global. doi:10.4018/978-1-4666-7492-9.ch001

Erdoğdu, M. M., Yılmaz, B. E., Aydın, M., & User, İ. (2016). Political Economy of Tax Evasion and Tax Loss in the Real Estate Sector: A Property Tax Reform Proposal for Turkey. In M. M. Erdoğdu & B. Christiansen (Eds.), Handbook of Research on Public Finance in Europe and the MENA Region. Hershey, PA: IGI Global.

Erdoğdu, E. (2014). The Political Economy of Electricity Market Liberalization: A Cross-Country Approach. *The Energy Journal (Cambridge, Mass.)*, *35*(3), 91–128.

Ertuna, H. T. (2010). *Competition Law in the Electricity Market: Liberalization and its Consequences*. Retrieved from http://www.ankarabarosu.org.tr/siteler/AnkaraBarReview/tekmakale/2010-2/3.pdf

Esping-Andersen, G. (1990). *The Three Worlds of Welfare Capitalism*. Cambridge: Polity Press.

EU Nears Energy Liberalisation Finishing Line. (2009). EurActiv. Retrieved from http://www.euractiv.com/energy/eu-nears-energy-liberalisation-f-news-221592

EU Tax Policy Strategy Communication. (2014, December 9). *European Commission*. Retrieved from http://ec.europa.eu/taxation_customs/taxation/gen_info/tax_policy/index_en.htm

EÜAŞ. (2013). *Elektrik Üretim Sektör Raporu* 2013. Retrieved from http://www.enerji.gov.tr/File/?path=ROOT%2f1%2fDocuments%2fSekt%C3%B6r+Raporu%2fEUAS-Sektor_Raporu2013.pdf

Eurofound (2009). *Measures to Combat Undeclared Work in 27 European Union Member States and Norway*. Dublin.

Eurofound. (2008). Dublin: Tackling Undeclared Work in the European Union.

Euro-Mediterranean Partnership (EUROMED). (2014). European Union. Retrieved from http://eeas.europa.eu/euromed/index_en.htm

European Commission, (2009). Regulation (EC) No. 714/2009 of the European Parliament and of the Council of 13 July 2009 on Conditions for Access to the Network for Cross-Border Exchanges in Electricity and Repealing Regulation (EC) No. 1228/2003. Official Journal of European Union, 2009, 55–93.

EY. (2014). Focus: transparency. Tax insights for business leaders. Retrieved from https://taxinsights.ey-vx.com/ey-ti-ed-1/pdf/ey-tax12-client-version-141127-(2).pdf

Farrag, F., & Ezzat, A. M. (2015). The Impact of Corruption on Economic Growth: A Comparative Analysis between Europe and MENA Countries. In M. M. Erdoğdu & B. Christiansen (Eds.), *Handbook of Research on Comparative Economic Development Perspectives on Europe and the MENA Region*. Hershey, PA, USA: IGI Global.

Farrell, J., & Gibbons, R. (1989). Cheap Talk with Two Audiences. *The American Economic Review*, *79*(5), 1214–1223.

Fazio, R. H. (1990). Multiple Processes by Which Attitudes Guide Behavior: The Mode Model as An Integrative Framework. *Advances in Experimental Social Psychology*, *23*, 75–109. doi:10.1016/S0065-2601(08)60318-4

Feenburg, D. R., & Coutts, E. (1993). An Introduction to the TAXSIM Model. *Journal of Policy Analysis and Management*, *12*(1), 189–194. doi:10.2307/3325474

Feige, E. L. (1979, November-December). How big is the Irregular Economy? *The Challenge (Karachi)*, *22*(5), 5–13. doi:10.1080/05775132.1979.11470559

Feld, L. P., & Larsen, C. (2005). Black Activities in Germany in 2001 and 2004: A Comparison Based on Survey Data. *The Rockwool Foundation Research Unit*, No. 12.

Feld, L. P., & Larsen, C. (2008). "Black" Activities Low in Germany in 2006. *News from the Rockwool Foundation Research Unit*.

Feld, L. P., & Frey, B. S. (2002). Trust Breeds Trust: How Taxpayers Are Treated. *Economics of Governance*, *3*(2), 87–99. doi:10.1007/s101010100032

Feld, L. P., & Frey, B. S. (2007). Tax Compliance as the Result of Psychological Tax Contract: The Role of Incentives and Responsive Regulation. *Law & Policy*, *29*(1), 102–120. doi:10.1111/j.1467-9930.2007.00248.x

Feld, L. P., & Larsen, C. (2009). *Undeclared Work in Germany 2001-2007 – Impact of Deterrence, Tax Policy, and Social Norms: An Analysis Based on Survey Data*. Berlin: Springer.

Feld, L. P., & Schneider, F. (2010). Survey on the shadow economy and undeclared earnings in OECD countries. *German Economic Review*, *11*(2), 109–149. doi:10.1111/j.1468-0475.2010.00509.x

Feld, L. P., & Tyran, J.-R. (2002). Tax Evasion and Voting: An Experimental Analysis. *Kyklos*, *55*(2), 197–221. doi:10.1111/1467-6435.00183

Felix, R. A. (2007). Passing the Burden: Corporate Tax Incidence in Open Economies. *Regional Research Working Paper RRWP 07-01*, Federal Reserve Bank of Kansas City.

Feltenstein, A., & Shamloo, M. (2013). Tax reform, the informal economy, and bank financing of capital formation. *International Tax and Public Finance*, *20*(1), 1–28. doi:10.1007/s10797-012-9213-4

Ferguson, M. J., & Bargh, J. A. (2004). How Social Perception Can Automatically Influence Behavior. *Trends in Cognitive Sciences*, *8*(1), 33–39. doi:10.1016/j.tics.2003.11.004 PMID:14697401

Ferris, S. J., & West, E. G. (1996a). The Cost Disease and Government Growth: Qualifications to Baumol. *Public Choice*, *89*(1-2), 35–52. doi:10.1007/BF00114277

Ferris, S. J., & West, E. G. (1996b). Testing Theories of Real Government Size: U.S. Experience, 1959-1989. *Southern Economic Journal*, *62*(3), 537–553. doi:10.2307/1060878

Financial Statement of State's General Budget for Fiscal Year 2012/2013. (2012). The Ministry of Finance.

Finkelstein, A. (2009). EZtax: Tax Salience and Tax Rates. *The Quarterly Journal of Economics*, *124*(3), 969–1010. doi:10.1162/qjec.2009.124.3.969

Fischer, S. (2011, February 11). Central Bank Lessons from the Global Crisis. *Proceedings of the 3rd P.R. Brahamananda Memorial Lecture*, Reserve Bank of India, Mumbai.

Fischer, C., Wartick, M., & Mark, M. (1992). Detection Probability and Taxpayer Compliance: A Literature Review. *Journal of Accounting Literature*, *11*(1), 1–46.

Fishbein, M., & Ajzen, I. (1975). *Belief, Attitude, Intention and Behavior: An Introduction to Theory and Research*. Reading, MA: Addison-Wesley.

Fitzgerald, V. (2010). International Tax Co-operation and Capital Mobility, International Tax Co-operation and Capital Mobility. *Oxford Development Studies*, *30*(3), 251–266. doi:10.1080/1360081022000012680

Fjeldstad, O.-H., & Heggstad, K. K. (2012). *Building Taxpayer Culture in Mozambique, Tanzania and Zambia: Achievements, Challenges and Policy Recommendations. CMI Report R 2012:1. Chr.* Bergen: Michelsen Institute.

Fontana, R. (2006, June). The Uncertain Future of CFC Regimes in the Member States of the European Union – Part 1. *European Taxation*.

Foster, J. B. (2010). The Financialization of Accumulation. *Monthly Review (New York, N.Y.)*, *62*(5), 1–6. doi:10.14452/MR-062-05-2010-09_1

Foucault, M. (1977). *Discipline and Punish*. London: Allen Lane.

Fox, W. F., & Gurley, T. (2005). An Exploration of Tax Patterns around the World. *Tax Notes International: Special Reports*, *37*(9), 793–807.

Fox, W., & Murray, M. (2014). Taxing the Small: Fostering Tax Compliance among Small Enterprises in Developing Countries. In R. Bird & J. Martinez-Vazquez (Eds.), *Taxation and Development: the Weakest Link* (pp. 170–192). Cheltenham, UK: Edward Elgar. doi:10.4337/9781783474332.00013

Frankel, J. A., Vegh, C. A., & Vuletin, G. (2011). On Graduation from Fiscal Procyclicality, *NBER Working Paper* 17619. Retrieved from: http://www.hks.harvard.edu/fs/jfrankel/GraduatnfromprocyclicalityV&V-Jul15.pdf

Frey, B., & Feld, L. (2002, August). Deterrence and Morale in Taxation: An Empirical Analysis (Working Paper No. 760). *CESifo*.

Frey, B. S., & Pommerehne, W. (1984). The Hidden Economy: State and Prospect for Measurement. *Review of Income and Wealth*, *30*(1), 1–23. doi:10.1111/j.1475-4991.1984.tb00474.x

Fricke, H., & Sussmuth, B. (2011, January). Growth and Volatility of Tax Revenues in Latin America. *CESIFO Working Paper No: 3312*.

Friedman, E., Johnson, S., Kaufmann, D., & Zoido-Lobaton, P. (2000). Dodging the Grabbing Hand: The Determinants of Unofficial Activity in Countries. *Journal of Public Economics*, *76*(3), 459–493. doi:10.1016/S0047-2727(99)00093-6

Froud, J., Johal, S., Leaver, A., & Williams, K. (2006). *Financialization & Strategy: Narrative and Numbers*. London, New York: Routledge.

Fundamental reform of personal income tax, Tax Policy Studies No. 13. (2006). *OECD*, Paris. Retrieved from http://browse.oecdbookshop.org/oecd/pdfs/product/2306081e.pdf

Galati, G., & Moessner, R. (2011). Macroprudential Policy – A Literature Review. *BIS Working Papers No. 337*.

Garrett, G. (1995). Capital Mobility, Trade and Domestic Politics of Economic Policy. *International Organization*, *49*(04), 657–687. doi:10.1017/S0020818300028472

Garvanlieva, V., Andonov, V., & Nikolov, M. (2012). Shadow Economy in Macedonia, *Center for Economic Analyses*, Skopje: Macedonia. Retrieved from http://www.cea.org.mk/%20documents/studii/cea%20shadow%20economy%20in%20macedonia%20final_4.pdf

Gavin, M., Hausmann, R., Perotti, R., & Talvi, E. (1996). Managing Fiscal Policy in Latin America and the Caribbean: Volatility, Procyclicality and Limited Creditworthiness. *Inter-American Development Bank*, OCE Working Paper No. 326.

Gavin, M., & Perotti, R. (1997a). Fiscal policy in Latin America. *NBER Macroeconomics Annual*, *12*, 11–70. doi:10.1086/654320

Gavin, M., & Perotti, R. (1997b). Fiscal Policy and Private Savings in Latin America in Good Times and Bad. In R. Hausmann & H. Reisen (Eds.), *Promoting Savings in Latin America* (pp. 149–166). Paris: IDB/OECD.

Gayer, C., & Mourre, G. (2012). Property Taxation and Enhanced Tax Administration in Challenging Times. *European Economy Economic Papers 463*, October.

Gayer, C., & Igoseva, R. (2012). Summary of the workshop. In C. Gayer & G. Mourre (Eds.), *Property Taxation and Enhanced Tax Administration in Challenging Times. Economic Papers 463, October* (pp. 11–19). Brussels: European Union.

Gemmell, N., & Hasseldine, J. (2012). The Tax Gap: A Methodological Review (Working Paper 09/2012). Victoria University, New Zealand.

Gemmell, N., & Morrissey, O. (2005). Distribution and Poverty Impacts of Tax Structure Reform in Developing Countries: How Little We Know. *Development Policy Review*, *23*(2), 131–144. doi:10.1111/j.1467-7679.2005.00279.x

General Administrative Principles: Corporate Governance and Tax Risk Management, Forum on Tax Administration. (2009). *OECD*, Paris. Retrieved from http://www.oecd.org/dataoecd/37/19/43239887.pdf

Genschel, P. (2001, May). Globalization, Tax Competition, and the Welfare State. Max Planck Institute for the Study of Societies. *MPIfG Working Paper 01/1*.

Gerxhani, K. (2004). The informal sector in developed and less developed countries: A literature survey. *Public Choice*, *120*(3-4), 267–300. doi:10.1023/B:PUCH.0000044287.88147.5e

Ghura, D. (1998, September). Tax Revenue in Sub-Saharan Africa: Effects of Economic Policies and Corruption. *IMF Working Paper, No: WP/98/135*.

GİB. (2015). *Gelir İdaresi Başkanlığı 2014 Yılı Faaliyet Raporu*. Yayın No: 199, Gelir İdaresi Başkanlığı Strateji Geliştirme Daire Başkanlığı. Retrieved from http://www.gib.gov.tr/fileadmin/faaliyetraporlari/2014/2014_Faaliyet_Raporu.pdf

GIFT. (2012). *The Global Initiative on Fiscal Transparency: High-Level Principles on Fiscal Transparency, Participation, and Accountability*. The Global Initiative on Fiscal Transparency DRAFT. Retrieved May 27, 2015, from http://www.fiscaltransparency.net/GIFT-High-Level-Principles-2012-08-ENG.pdf

Giles, D. E. A. (1997). Causality between the measured and underground economies in New Zealand. *Applied Economics Letters*, *4*(1), 63–67. doi:10.1080/758521835

Giles, D. E. A., Tedds, L. M., & Werkneh, G. (2002). The Canadian underground and measured economies: Granger causality results. *Applied Economics*, *34*(18), 2347–2352. doi:10.1080/00036840210148021

Giles, D. E. A., Werkneh, G. T., & Johnson, B. S. (2001). Asymmetric responses of the underground economy to tax changes: Evidence from New Zealand data. *The Economic Record*, *77*(237), 148–159. doi:10.1111/1475-4932.00010

Gillis, M. (1985). Micro and Macroeconomics of Tax Reform in Indonesia. *Journal of Development Economics*, *19*(3), 221–254. doi:10.1016/0304-3878(85)90030-6

Glachant, J. M. (2013). *The Three Ages of Europe's Single Electricity Market*. Retrieved from http://www.energypost.eu/the-three-ages-of-europes-single-electricity-market/

Glenday, G., & Swift, Z. L. (2006, December). Establishing Tax Expenditure Accounts – Towards Better Fiscal Accountability and Transparency. In *Turkey Public Expenditure Review*. Washington, DC: World Bank.

Global Financial Stability Report. (2010, April). *IMF*. World Economic and Financial Surveys, Washington: International Monetary Fund.

Global Monitoring Report 2005: Millennium Development Goals: From Consensus to Momentum. (2005World Bank. Washington, DC: World Bank.

Gnansounou, S., & Verdier-Chouchane, A. (2012). Mesalignement du taux de change effectif reel: Quand faudra-t-il de nouveau devalue le franc CFA? *African Development Bank Working Paper Series* No. 166, Tunis.

Godfrey, L. G. (1978). Testing Against General Autoregressive and Moving Average Error Models When the Regressors Include Lagged Dependent Variables. *Econometrica*, *46*(6), 1293–1302. doi:10.2307/1913829

Goel, R. K., & Nelson, M. A. (2013). Effectiveness of Whistleblower Laws in Combating Corruption. *BOFIT – Institute for Economies in Transition, Bank of Finland, BOFIT Discussion Papers* 9.

Goel, R. K., & Saunoris, J. W. (2014). Global corruption and the shadow economy: Spatial aspects. *Public Choice*, *161*(1-2), 119–139. doi:10.1007/s11127-013-0135-1

Golinelli, R., & Momigliano, S. (2009). The Cyclical Reaction of Fiscal Policies in the Euro Area: The Role of Modelling Choices and Data Vintages. *Fiscal Studies*, *30*(1), 39–72. doi:10.1111/j.1475-5890.2009.00089.x

Gonzalez-Paramo, J. M., & Moreno-Dodson, B. (2003). The Role of the State and Consequences of Alternative Forms of Public Expenditure Financing. *WBI Working Paper, Document No: 33052*.

Goode, R. (1981). Some Economic Aspects of Tax Administration. *Staff Papers - International Monetary Fund. International Monetary Fund*, *28*(2), 249–274. doi:10.2307/3866931

Goodhart, C. (2008). Lessons from the Crisis for Financial Regulation: What We Need and What We Do Not Need, http://www.rgemonitor.com/financemarkets-monitor

Goodhart, C. (2010, November). The Changing Role of Central Banks. *BIS Working Papers*, No. 326, Basel: BIS.

Goodsmith, T. (1998, September). Tax Competition, Benefit Taxes, And Fiscal Federalism. *National Tax Journal*, *51*(3), 579–586.

Graetz, M. J., & Wilde, L. L. (1985). The Economics of Tax Compliance: Fact and Fantasy. *National Tax Journal*, *38*, 355–363.

Grant, R. M. (2002). *Contemporary Strategy Analysis: Concepts, Techniques, Applications* (4th ed.). Oxford: Blackwell.

Green, W. H. (2000). Econometric Analysis. New York: Macmillan Publishing Company.

Greene, W. H. (2003). *Econometric Analysis* (5th ed.). Upper Saddle River, New Jersey: Prentice Hall.

Grinberg, I. (2013). Taxing Capital Income In Emerging Countries: Will FACTA Open The Door? *World Tax Journal,* October, 325-367.

Gronbacher, G. M. A. (1998). Taxation: Catholic Social Thought and Classical Liberalism. In R. W. McGee (Ed.), The Ethics of Tax Evasion (pp. 158-167). Dumont, NJ: The Dumont Institute for Public Policy Research.

Groot, W., & van den Brink, H. M. (2010). The Effects of Education on Crime. *Applied Economics*, *42*(3), 279–289. doi:10.1080/00036840701604412

Gross Fixed Investments by Sectors, Basic Economic Indicators. (2014). Ministry of Development. Retrieved from http://www.kalkinma.gov.tr/Pages/TemelEkonomikGostergeler.aspx

Guide to Horizontal Monitoring within the SME Segment. (2012). Netherlands Tax and Customs Administration. Retrieved from http://download.belastingdienst.nl/belastingdienst/docs/guide_horiz_monit_dv4071z1pleng.pdf

Gündüz, Z. (2013). Developments in Turkish Lax Legistlation, Disputes and Adjudication. *International Tax Review*, August 13. Retrieved from http://www.internationaltaxreview.com/Article/3242987/Developments-in-Turkish-tax-legislation-disputes-and-adjudication.html

Gunessee, S. (2010, March). Strategic Tax Competition: An Experimental Study. *Public Finance Review*, *38*(2), 217–243. doi:10.1177/1091142110367859

Gupta, A. S. (2007, July). Determinants of Tax Revenue Efforts in Developing Countries. *IMF Working Paper, No: WP/07/184*.

Gupta, S., de Mello, L., & Sharan, R. (2000). Corruption and military spending. *International Monetary Fund (IMF) Working Paper 23.*

Gutmann, P. M. (1981). Implications of the Subterranean Economy. In R. X. Bove and R. D. Klingenstein (Eds.), *Proceedings of theWertheim's Underground Economy Conference*, (pp. 31-58). Wertheim.

Gutmann, P. H. (1977). The Subterranean Economy. *Financial Analysts Journal*, *33*(6), 26–28. doi:10.2469/faj.v33.n6.26

Habermacher, F., & Kirchassner, G. (2012, August 16–19). Asymmetric Tax Competition: Theoretical and Empirical Results. *Paper to be presented at the Annual Meeting of the International Institute of Public Finance*. Dresden. Retrieved from http://www.habermacher.net/attachments/bFile/Habermacher-Kirchgaessner_AsymmetricTaxCompetition_Draft_2012.pdf

Hacıköylü, C., & Heper, F. (2010). Emlak Vergisinde Matrah Tespitine İlişkin Sorunlar ve Çözüm Önerileri. *Maliye Dergisi*, *158*, 1–14.

Hahm, J. H., Mishkin, F. S., Shin, H. S., & Shin, K. (2012). Macroprudential Policies in Open Emerging Economies. *National Bureau of Economic Research,* No.w17780.

Hall, R. E. (1978). Stochastic Implications of the Lifecycle – Permanent Income Hypothesis. *Journal of Political Economy*, *86*(6), 971–987. doi:10.1086/260724

Hall, R. E. (1980). Labor Supply and Aggregate Fluctuations. *Carnegie-Rochester Conference Series*, *12*, 7–33. doi:10.1016/0167-2231(80)90019-6

Hamdi, H., & Sbia, R. (2013). Dynamic Relationships between Oil Revenues, Government Spending and Economic Growth in an Oil-dependent Economy. *Economic Modelling*, *35*, 118–125. doi:10.1016/j.econmod.2013.06.043

Hansen, L. (1982). Large Sample Properties of Generalized Methods of Moments Estimators. *Econometrica*, *50*(4), 1029–1054. doi:10.2307/1912775

Hanson, G. D. (1985, November). Indivisible Labor and the Business Cycle. *Journal of Monetary Economics*, *16*(3), 309–327. doi:10.1016/0304-3932(85)90039-X

Harberger, A. C. (1962). The Incidence of the Corporate Income Tax. *Journal of Political Economy*, *70*(3), 215–240. doi:10.1086/258636

Harris, B. H. (2009). Corporate Tax Incidence and Its Implication for Progressivity. Tax Policy Center, Urban Institute and Brookings Institution, Washington, D.C.

Harvey, D. (1985). *Consciousness and the Urban Experience*. Oxford: Blackwell.

Harvey, D. (2011). *The Enigma of Capital and the Crises of Capitalism*. London: Profile Books.

Hashimzade, N., Myles, G.D. & Tran-Nam, B. (2012). Applications of Behavioural Economics to Tax Evasion. *Journal of Economic Surveys*. doi:10.1111/j.1467-6419.2012.00733.x

Hausman, J. (1978). Specification Test in Econometrics. *Econometrica*, *46*(6), 1251–1271. doi:10.2307/1913827

Haveman, M., & Sexton, T. A. (2008). *Property Tax Assessment Limits: Lessons from Thirty Years of Experience*. Cambridge, Mass.: Lincoln Institute of Land Policy.

Heady, C. (1993). Optimal Taxation As a Guide to Tax Policy: A Survey. *Fiscal Studies*, *14*(1), 15–41. doi:10.1111/j.1475-5890.1993.tb00341.x

Heckman, J. J. (1993). What has been Learned about Labor Supply in the Past Twenty Years. *American Economic Review*, 83(2), 116-121.

Hein, E. (2011b) Financialisation, Re-distribution, and the Financial and Economic Crisis – A Kaleckian Perspective. In T. Niechoj, Ö. Onaran, E. Stockhammer, A. Truger, & van Treeck (Eds.), Stabilising an Unequal Economy? Public Debt, Financial Regulation, and Income Distribution (pp. 35-62). Marburg: Metropolis.

Hein, E. (2011a). Redistribution, Global Imbalances and the Financial and Economic Crisis – The Case for a Keynesian New Deal. *International Journal of Labor Research*, *3*(1), 51–73.

Hemerijck, A., Dräbing, V., Vis, B., Nelson, M., & Soentken, M. (2013). European Welfare States in Motion. *NEUJOBS Working Paper*, No. D5.2.

Hemerijck, A. (2013). *Changing Welfare States*. Oxford: Oxford University Press.

Hendry, D. F., & Mizon, G. E. (1998). Exogeneity, causality, and co-breaking in economic policy analysis of a small econometric model of money in the UK. *Empirical Economics*, *23*(3), 267–294. doi:10.1007/BF01294408

Henisz, W., & Zelner, B. (2006). Interest Groups, Veto Points, and Electricity Infrastructure Deployment. *International Organization*, *60*(01), 263–286. doi:10.1017/S0020818306060085

Heredia-Ortiz, E. (2014). *Evaluating Tax Expenditures in Jordan. Report prepared for Jordan Fiscal Reform II Project*. United Agency for International Development.

Heritage Foundation. (2011). *2011 Index of Economic Freedom*. Retrieved from http://www.heritage.org/Index/ pdf/2011/Index2011_Full.pdf

Heritage Foundation. (2014). *2014 Index of Economic Freedom*. Retrieved from http://www.heritage.org/index/download

Heston, A., Summers, R., & Aten, B. (2006). *Penn World Table Version 6.3. Center for International Comparisons of Production, Income and Prices*. University of Pennsylvania.

Hicks, A., & Swank, D. (1984). On the Political Economy of Welfare Expansion: A Comparative Analysis of 18 Advanced Capitalist Democracies, 1960-1971. *Comparative Political Studies*, *17*(1), 81–119. doi:10.1177/0010414084017001003

Hindriks, J., Keen, M., & Muthoo, A. (1999). Corruption, Extortion, and Evasion. *Journal of Public Economics*, *74*(3), 395–430. doi:10.1016/S0047-2727(99)00030-4

Hines, J. R., Jr., & Summers, L. H. (2009, January). How Globalization Affects Tax Design. *NBER Working Paper 14664*.

Hines, J. R. Jr. (2007). Corporate Taxation and International Competition. In A. J. Auerbach, J. R. Hines Jr, & J. Slemrod (Eds.), *Taxing Corporate Income in the 21st Century* (pp. 268–295). Cambridge, UK: Cambridge University Press. doi:10.1017/CBO9780511510823.020

Hines, J. R. Jr, & Rice, E. M. (1994). Fiscal Paradise: Foreign Tax Havens and American Business. *The Quarterly Journal of Economics*, *109*(1), 149–182. doi:10.2307/2118431

Hines, J. R. Jr, & Summers, L. H. (2009). How Globalization Affects Tax Design. *Tax Policy and the Economy*, *23*(1), 123–158. doi:10.1086/597056

Hines, J. Jr. (1999). Three Sides of Harberger Triangles. *The Journal of Economic Perspectives*, *13*(2), 167–188. doi:10.1257/jep.13.2.167

Historical Effective Tax Rates 1979-2005. Publication 8885. (2007Congressional Budget Office. Washington, D.C: U.S. Government Printing Office.

Hitaj, E., & Onder, Y. K. (2013). Fiscal Discipline in WAEMU: Rules, Institutions and Markets. *IMF Working Paper* WP/13/216.

Hofmann, E., Hoelzl, E., & Kirchler, E. (2008). Preconditions of Voluntary Tax Compliance: Knowledge and Evaluation of Taxation, Norms, Fairness, and Motivation to Cooperate. *Zeitschrift fur Psychologie mit Zeitschrift fur Angewandte Psychologie*, *216*(4), 209–217. doi:10.1027/0044-3409.216.4.209 PMID:22428111

Holcombe, R. G. (1991). Constitutions as Constraints: A Case Study of Three American Constitutions. *Constitutional Political Economy*, *2*(2), 303–328. doi:10.1007/BF02393134

Holcombe, R. G. (1998). Tax Policy from a Choice Perspective. *National Tax Journal*, *51*(2), 359–371.

Holsey, C. M., & Borcherding, T. E. (1977). Why Does Government's Share of National Income Grow? An Assessment of the Recent Literature on the U.S. Experience. In *Budgets and Bureaucrats: The Sources of Government Growth*. Durham, NC: Duke University Press.

Holtz-Eakin, D., Newey, W., & Rosen, H. S. (1988). Estimating vector autoregressions with panel data. *Econometrica*, *56*(6), 1371–1395. doi:10.2307/1913103

House of Commons Treasury Committee. (2012). *Closing the Tax Gap: HMRC's Record at Ensuring Tax Compliance.* Twenty-ninth Report of Session 2010-12, March. London: The Stationery Office Limited.

Houssa, R. (2008). Monetary Union in West Africa and Asymmetric Shocks: A Dynamic Structural Factor Model Approach. *Journal of Development Economics*, *85*(1-2), 319–347. doi:10.1016/j.jdeveco.2006.05.003

Hsiao, C. (1986). *Analysis of Panel Data*. New York: Cambridge University Press.

Hutton, E., Thackray, M., & Wingender, P. (2014). *Uganda: Revenue Administration Gap Analysis Program – The Value-Added Tax Gap*. Washington, DC: International Monetary Fund.

Hwang, J. (2002). A Note on the Relationship between Corruption and Government Revenue. *Journal of Economic Development*, *27*(2), 161–178.

ICRG. (2014). *International Country Risk Guide Index*. New York: The PRS Group.

Illing, M., & Liu, Y. (2006). Measuring Financial Stress in a Developed Country: An Application to Canada. *Journal of Financial Stability*, *2*(3), 243–265. doi:10.1016/j.jfs.2006.06.002

Ilzetzkiy, E. (2014). A Positive Theory of Tax Reform, June. Retrieved from http://www.bus.umich.edu/ConferenceFiles/Tax-Systems/files/Ilzetzki--TaxReform.pdf

Imam, P. A., & Jacobs, D. F. (2007). Effect of Corruption of Tax Revenues in the Middle East (IMF Working Paper WP/07/270). *International Monetary Fund.*

Imam, P. A., & Jacobs, D. F. (2007). Effect of Corruption on Tax Revenues in the Middle East. *International Monetary Fund Working Paper* WP/07/270.

Institute on Taxation and Economic Policy. (2003). *Who Pays? A Distributional Analysis of the Tax Systems in all 50 States*. Washington, D.C.: Institute on Taxation and Economic Policy.

International Co-operation and Development. (2014). Retrieved from http://ec.europa.eu/europeaid/where/neighbourhood/overview/index_en.htm

Ironmonger, D. (1999). *An Overview of Time Use Surveys*. Melbourne: Household Research Unit, Department of Economics, University of Melbourne.

IRS Whistleblower Office FY2013 Annual Report. (2013). *Internal Revenue Service.*

Isaac, D., & O'Leary, J. (2012). *Property Valuation Principles* (2nd ed.). London: Palgrave MacMillan.

Isachsen, A. J., Klovland, J., & Strom, S. (1982). The Hidden Economy in Norway. In V. Tanzi (Ed.), The Underground Economy in the United States and Abroad (pp. 209–321). Lexington: Heath.

Isachsen, A. J., & Strom, S. (1985). The Size and Growth of the Hidden Economy in Norway. *Review of Income and Wealth*, *31*(1), 21–38. doi:10.1111/j.1475-4991.1985.tb00496.x

Isachsen, A., & Strom, S. (1989). The Underground Economy in Norway with Special Emphasis on the Hidden Labor Market. In E. Feige (Ed.), *The Underground Economies: Tax Evasion and Information Distortion* (pp. 251–266). Cambridge: Cambridge University Press. doi:10.1017/CBO9780511571749.013

Isham, J., Pritchett, L., Woolcock, M., & Busby, G. (2003). The Varieties of the Resource Experience: How Natural Resource Export Structures Affect the Political Economy of Economic Growth (Working Paper 03-08). *Middlebury College Economics Discussion Papers*, Middlebury, Vermont.

Ivanyna, M., Mourmouras, A., & Rangazas, P. (2010). The Culture of Corruption, Tax Evasion, and Optimal Tax Policy (Working Paper 10/xx). *IMF Working Papers*.

Iversen, T., & Cusack, T. R. (2000). The Causes of Welfare State Expansion. *World Politics*, *52*(April), 313–349. doi:10.1017/S0043887100016567

Jackson, J.K. (2010). *OECD Initiative on Tax Havens CRS Report for Congress* R40114.

Jackson, B., & Milliron, V. C. (1986). Tax Compliance Research: Findings, Problems and Prospects. *Journal of Accounting Literature*, *5*(1), 125–165.

Jalili, A. R. (2012). The Ethics of Tax Evasion: An Islamic Perspective. In R. W. McGee (Ed.), *The Ethics of Tax Evasion: Perspectives in Theory and Practice* (pp. 167–199). New York: Springer. doi:10.1007/978-1-4614-1287-8_11

Jamasb, T. (2006). Between the State and Market: Electricity Sector Reform in Developing Countries. *Utilities Policy*, *14*(1), 14–30. doi:10.1016/j.jup.2004.11.001

Jamasb, T., Newbery, D., & Pollitt, M. (2006). Core Indicators for Determinants and Performance of Electricity Sector in Developing Countries. *International Journal of Regulation and Governance*, *6*(1), 43–78.

James, S. (2016). The Difficulties of Achieving Successful Tax Reform. In M. M. Erdoğdu & B. Christiansen (Eds.), Handbook of Research on Public Finance in Europe and the MENA Region. Hershey, PA: IGI Global.

James, S., & Edwards, A. (2007). A Strategic Approach to Personal Income Tax Reform. *Australian Tax Forum, 22*(2), 105-126.

James, S., & Edwards, J. (2010). *An Annotated Bibliography of Tax Compliance and Tax Compliance Costs*, Economic and Social Research Council, Retrieved from http://www.esrc.ac.uk/my-esrc/grants/RES-000-23-1595/outputs/read/e026df04-3812-4aa1-96fe-10cd4b442e49

James, S., Sawyer, A., & Wallschutzky, I. (forthcoming). Tax Simplification: A Review of Initiatives in Australia, New Zealand and the United Kingdom, and the Influence of their Respective Tax Administrations. *eJournal of Tax Research.*

James, S. (1998). *A Dictionary of Taxation*. Cheltenham: Edward Elgar.

James, S. (1999). The Future International Tax Environment and European Tax Harmonisation: A Personal View. *European Accounting Review*, *8*(4), 731–747. doi:10.1080/096381899335781

James, S. (2006). Taxation and the Contribution of Behavioral Economics. In M. Altman (Ed.), *Foundations and Extensions of Behavioral Economics: A Handbook* (pp. 589–601). New York: M.E. Sharpe Publishers.

James, S. (2014). The Importance of Fairness in Tax Policy: Behavioral Economics and the UK Experience. *International Journal of Applied Behavioral Economics*, *3*(1), 1–12. doi:10.4018/ijabe.2014010101

James, S. (2015). The Difficulties of Achieving Successful Tax Reform. In M. M. Erdoğdu & B. Christiansen (Eds.), *Handbook of Research on Public Finance in Europe and the MENA Region*. Hershey, PA, USA: IGI Global.

James, S. (2016). The Difficulties of Achieving Successful Tax Reform. In M. M. Erdoğdu & B. Christiansen (Eds.), *Handbook of Research on Public Finance Perspectives on Europe and the MENA Region*. Hershey, PA, USA: IGI Global.

James, S., & Alley, C. (2002). Tax Compliance, Self-Assessment and Tax Administration. *Journal of Finance and Management in Public Services*, *2*(2), 27–42.

James, S., & Edwards, A. (2008). Developing Tax Policy in a Complex and Changing World. *Economic Analysis and Policy*, *38*(1), 35–53. doi:10.1016/S0313-5926(08)50005-1

James, S., Hasseldine, J., Hite, P., & Toumi, M. (2001). Developing a Tax Compliance Strategy for Revenue Services. *Bulletin for International Fiscal Documentation*, *55*(4), 158–164.

James, S., & Nobes, C. (2014). *The economics of Taxation: Principles, Policy and Practice* (13th ed.). Birmingham: Fiscal Publications.

James, S., & Wallschutzky, I. (1997). Tax Law Improvement in Australia and the UK: The Need for a Strategy for Simplification. *Fiscal Studies*, *18*(4), 445–460. doi:10.1111/j.1475-5890.1997.tb00273.x

Jensen, J., & Wohlbier, F. (2012). Improving Tax Governance in EU Member States: Criteria for Successful Policies, *European Economy Occasional Papers,* No.114.

Jewell, C., Flanagan, R., & Cattell, K. (2005). The Effects of the Informal Sector on Construction. In I.D. Tommelein (Ed.), *Construction Research Congress: Broadening Perspectives*. American Society of Civil Engineers.

Johansen, S. (1988). Statistical and Hypothesis Testing of Co-integration Vectors. *Journal of Economic Dynamics & Control*, *12*(2-3), 231–254. doi:10.1016/0165-1889(88)90041-3

Johansen, S., & Juselius, K. (1990). Maximum Likelihood Estimation and Inference on Cointegration-With Applications to the Demand for Money. *Oxford Bulletin of Economics and Statistics*, *52*(2), 169–210. doi:10.1111/j.1468-0084.1990.mp52002003.x

Johansson, Å., Heady, C., Arnold, J., Brys, B., & Vartia, L. (2008). Tax and Economic Growth. *Economics Department Working Paper No. 620*, OECD. Retrieved from http://www.oecd.org/tax/tax-policy/41000592.pdf

Johnson, E., & Martini, M. (2012). *Corruption Trends in the Middle East and North Africa Region (2007-2011): U4 Expert Answer*. Transparency International.

Johnson, S., Kaufmann, D., & Scleizer, A. (1997). The unofficial economy in transition. *Brookings Papers on Economic Activity*, *2*(2), 159–239. doi:10.2307/2534688

Jones, R., & Basu, S. (2010). Taxation of Electronic Commerce: A Developing Problem. *International Review of Law Computers & Technology*, *16*(1), 35–51. doi:10.1080/13600860220136093

Joulfaian, D., & Marlow, M. L. (1990). Government Size and Decentralization: Evidence from Disaggregated Data. *Southern Economic Journal*, *56*(4), 1094–1102. doi:10.2307/1059894

Joulfaian, D., & Marlow, M. L. (1991). Public Sector Employment, Competition, and Government Size. *Public Finance*, *46*(2), 223–235.

KADIM Project. (2006). *The Republic of Turkey Ministry of Labor and Social Security: The Project of Struggling Against Informal Employment*. Ankara. Retrieved from http://www.kayitdisiekonomi.com/files/20061004-13-1.pdf

Kant, I. (1983). *Ethical Philosophy* (J. W. Ellington, Trans.). Indianapolis, Cambridge: Hackett Publishing Company.

Kara, H. (2012). An Alternative Policy Tool to Cope with Capital Flow Volatility, OECD-EPC Meeting, Paris. Retrieved from http://www.tcmb.gov.tr/yeni/iletisimgm/H.Kara_EPC.pdf

Karaboytcheva, M. K., & Andrada, L. R. (2012). The Impact of the Shadow Economy on the Country Risk Index. In M. Pickhardt & A. Prinz (Eds.), *Tax Evasion and the Shadow Economy* (6th ed., pp. 156–176). Cheltenham: Edward Elgar.

Karaca, C. (2015). The Comparison of the Shadow Economy in Turkey and European Countries. In B. Christiansen & M. M. Erdoğdu (Eds.), *Comparative Economics and Regional Development in Turkey*. Hershey, PA, USA: IGI Global.

Karasu, M. A., & Karakaş, M. (2012). Belediyelerin Emlak Vergisindeki Gelir Kaybı: Şanlıurfa Belediyesi Örneği. *Maliye Dergisi*, *163*, 431–445.

Karlinger, L. (2009). The Underground Economy in the Late 1990s: Evading Taxes, or Evading Competition? *World Development*, *37*(10), 1600–1611. doi:10.1016/j.worlddev.2009.03.001

Karova, R. (2011). Regional electricity markets in Europe: Focus on the Energy Community. *Utilities Policy*, *19*(2), 80–86. doi:10.1016/j.jup.2010.10.001

Kasper, M., Kogler, C., & Kirchler, E. (2013). Tax Policy and the News: An Empirical Analysis of Taxpayers' Perceptions of Tax-Related Media Coverage and Its Impact on Tax Compliance. *WU International Taxation Research Paper Series*, No. 2013-07.

Kaufman, D. (2010, April 19). Can corruption adversely affect public finance in industrialized countries? *Brookings Institution Opinions*.

Kaufmann D., Kraay, A., & Mastruzzi, M. (2010). The Worldwide Governance Indicators: Methodology and Analytical Issues. *Freedom House (2005-2009 eds.)*. Freedom of the Press.

Kaufmann, D., Kraay, A., & Mastruzzi, M. (2010). The Worldwide Governance Indicators: Methodology and Analytical Issues. *World Bank Policy Research Working Paper*, No. 5430.

Kaufmann, D., Kraay, A., & Matruzzi, M. (2010). The Worldwide Governance Indicators: methodology and analytical issues (Working Paper 5430). *World Bank Policy Research Working Papers*.

Kaufmann, D., & Kaliberda, A. (1996). Integrating the Unofficial Economy into the Dynamics of Post-Socialist Economies: A Framework for Analysis and Evidence. In A. Bartlomiej (Ed.), *Economic Transition in Russia and the New States of Eurasia* (pp. 81–120). Armonk, New York: M. E. Sharpe.

Keen, M., & Mansour, M. (2010). Revenue Mobilisation in Sub-Saharan Africa: Challenges from Globalization I – Trade Reform. *Development Policy Review*, *28*(5), 553–571. doi:10.1111/j.1467-7679.2010.00498.x

Kehoe, T. J., & Prescott, E. C. (2002, January). Great Depressions of the 20th Century. *Review of Economic Dynamics*, *5*(1), 1–18. doi:10.1006/redy.2001.0151

Keleş, R. (2000). *Yerinden Yönetim ve Siyaset*. Istanbul: Cem Yayınevi.

Kellman, K., Miller, J. H., & Scott, E.P. (1997, December). Political Institutions and Sorting in a Tiebout Model. *The American Review*, 1997, 977-922.

Kenc, T., Turhan, M. I., & Yıldırım, O. (2011). The Experience with Macroprudential Policies of the Central Bank of the Republic of Turkey in Response to the Global Financial Crisis. *World Bank Policy Research Working Papers* No. WPS5834. Retrieved from http://www-wds.worldbank.org/external/default/WDSContentServer/IW3P/IB/2011/10/05/000158349_20111005142139/Rendered/PDF/WPS5834.pdf

Kettunen, P., & Petersen, K. (Eds.). (2011). *Beyond Welfare State Models: Transnational Historical Perspectives on Social Policy*. Cheltenham: Edward Elgar. doi:10.4337/9781849809603

Keynes, J. M. (1933). Economic Possibilities for our Grandchildren. In J. M. Keynes (Ed.), *Essays in Persuasion* (pp. 358–373). London: MacMillan and Co. Limited.

Khagram, S., de Renzio, P., & Fung, A. (Eds.). (2013). *Open Budgets*. Washington: Brookings Institution.

Kiefer, D. W. (1984). Distributional Tax Progressivity Indexes. *National Tax Journal*, *37*, 497–513.

Killingsworth, M. (1983). *Labor Supply*. Cambridge, MA: Cambridge University Press. doi:10.1017/CBO9780511572104

King, M. (2008, June 10). Banking and the Bank of England. *Speech to the British Bankers Association*, London. Retrieved from www.bankofengland.co.uk

Kırar, B. (2008). Taşınmazlarda Emlak Vergisine Esas Değer, Tapu Değeri ve Piyasa Değeri Arasındaki Farklılıkların İncelenmesi: Beşiktaş Örneği [Unpublished MA Thesis]. İstanbul Technical University Institute of Science and Engineering.

Kirchler, E., Muehlbacher, S., Gangl, K., Hofmann, E., Kogler, C., Pollai, M., & Alm, J. (2012). Combining Psychology and Economics in the Analysis of Compliance: From Enforcement to Cooperation. *Tulane University Economics Working Paper* 1212.

Kirchler, E. (2007). *The Economic Psychology of Tax Behaviour*. Cambridge: Cambridge University Press. doi:10.1017/CBO9780511628238

Kirchler, E., Hoelzl, E., & Wahl, I. (2008). Enforced versus Voluntary Tax Compliance: The "Slippery Slope" Framework. *Journal of Economic Psychology*, *29*(2), 210–225. doi:10.1016/j.joep.2007.05.004

Kirchler, E., Kogler, C., & Muehlbacher, S. (2014). Cooperative Tax Compliance: From Deterrence to Deference. *Current Directions in Psychological Science*, *23*(2), 87–92. doi:10.1177/0963721413516975

Kirchler, E., Muehlbacher, S., Kastlunger, B., & Wahl, I. (2010). Why Pay Taxes? A Review of Tax Compliance Decisions. In J. Alm, J. Martinez-Vazquez, & B. Torgler (Eds.), *Developing Alternative Frameworks for Explaining Tax Compliance* (pp. 15–31). London: Routledge.

Kirchler, E., Niemirowski, A., & Wearing, A. (2006). Shared subjective views, intent to cooperate and tax compliance: Similarities between Australian taxpayers and tax officers. *Journal of Economic Psychology*, *27*(4), 502–517. doi:10.1016/j.joep.2006.01.005

Kitchen, H. (2004, August 9-12). Financing Local Government Capital Investment. Trent University Economics Department Working Paper. Retrieved from https://www.trentu.ca/economics/WorkingPapers/Financing%20Capital%20Investment.pdf

Kleibergen, F., & Paap, R. (2006). Generalized reduced rank tests using the singular value decomposition. *Journal of Econometrics*, *133*(1), 97–126. doi:10.1016/j.jeconom.2005.02.011

Klepper, S., & Nagin, D. (1989). Tax Compliance and Perceptions of the Risks of Detection and Criminal Prosecution. *Law & Society Review*, *23*(2), 209–240. doi:10.2307/3053715

Klovland, J. T. (1980). In Search of the Hidden Economy: Tax Evasion and the Demand for Currency in Norway and Sweden. Norwegian School of Economics and Business Administration, Mimeo.

Knack, S. (2001). Aid Dependence and the Quality of Governance. *Southern Economic Journal*, *68*(2), 310–329. doi:10.2307/1061596

Knowledge@Warton. (2012). *Europe's Financial Crisis and Its Impact on the Arab World.*

Kogler, C., Muehlbacher, S., & Kirchler, E. (2013). Trust, Power, and Tax Compliance: Testing the 'Slippery Slope Framework' Among Self-Employed Taxpayers. *WU International Taxation Research Paper Series*, No. 2013-05.

Kogler, C., Batrancea, L., Nichita, A., Pantya, J., Belianin, A., & Kirchler, E. (2013). Trust and Power as Determinants of Tax Compliance: Testing the Assumptions of the Slippery Slope Framework in Austria, Hungary, Romania and Russia. *Journal of Economic Psychology*, *34*(1), 169–180. doi:10.1016/j.joep.2012.09.010

Kolko, P. (2011). *Rethinking the State-Local Relationship: Local Economic Development*. San Francisco, CA: Public Policy Institute of California.

Konrad, K. A., & Qari, S. (2012). The Last Refuge of a Scoundrel? Patriotism and Tax Compliance. *Economica*, *79*(315), 516–533. doi:10.1111/j.1468-0335.2011.00900.x

Kontonikas, A., & Ioannidis, C. (2005, December). Should Monetary Policy Respond to Asset Price Misalignments? *Economic Modelling*, *22*(6), 1105–1121. doi:10.1016/j.econmod.2005.07.004

Krippner, G. (2005). The Financialization of American Economy. *Socio-economic Review*, *3*(2), 173–208. doi:10.1093/SER/mwi008

Krueger, A. O. (1974). The Political Economy of the Rent-Seeking Society. *The American Economic Review*, *64*(3), 291–303.

Krugman, P. (1987). The narrow moving band, the Dutch disease, and the competitive consequences of Mrs. Thatcher. *Journal of Development Economics*, *27*(1-2), 41–55. doi:10.1016/0304-3878(87)90005-8

Kudrle, R. T. (2008). The OECD's Harmful Tax Competition Initiative and Tax Havens: From Bomshell to Domp Squib. Global Economy Journal, 8(1).

Kunicova, J., & Rose-Ackerman, S. (2005). Electoral Rules and Constitutional Structures as Constraints on Corruption. *British Journal of Political Science*, *35*(04), 573–606. doi:10.1017/S0007123405000311

Kydland, F. E., & Prescott, E. C. (1982, November). Time to Build and Aggregate Fluctuations. *Econometrica*, *50*(6), 1345–1370. doi:10.2307/1913386

La Porta, R., & Scleifer, A. (2008). The unofficial economy and economic development. *Brookings Papers on Economic Activity*, *47*(1), 275–363.

Laffer, A. (1979). Statement Prepared for the Joint Economic Committee. In A. Laffer & J. Seymour (Eds.), *The Economics of the Tax Revolt: A Reader* (pp. 75–79). New York: Harcourt Brace Jovanovich.

Langfeldt, E. (1982, April). The Unobserved Economy in the Federal Republic of Germany: A Preliminary Assessment (Mimeo), University of Kiel.

Laury, S., & Wallace, S. (2005). Confidentiality and Taxpayer Compliance. *National Tax Journal*, *58*(3), 427–438. doi:10.17310/ntj.2005.3.08

Le, T. M., Moreno-Dodson, B., & Rojchaichaninthorn, J. (2008, March). Expanding Taxable Capacity and Reaching Revenue Potential: Cross-Country Analysis. *World Bank Policy Research Working Paper. No: 4559.*

LeBlanc, P. (2014, July). Tax Expenditures: An OECD-Wide Perspective. In L. Bauger (Eds.), *The Use of Tax Expenditures in Times of Fiscal Consolidation* (pp. 17-18). European Commission Economic Papers 523. Retrieved May 27, 2015, from http://ec.europa.eu/economy_finance/publications/economic_paper/2014/pdf/ecp523_en.pdf

Lechmanova, N. (2011, July 18). Macro-prudential regulation – Lessons from Asia. Special Report, Standard Chartered, London.

Lederman, D., Loayza, N. V., & Soares, R. R. (2005). Accountability and Corruption: Political Institutions Matter. *Economics and Politics*, *17*(1), 1–35. doi:10.1111/j.1468-0343.2005.00145.x

Ledyard, J. O. (1995). Public goods: A Survey of Experimental Research. In J. H. Kagel & A. E. Roth (Eds.), *The Handbook of Experimental Economics* (pp. 111–194). Princeton: Princeton University Press.

Lee, D. (2013). How does social capital reduce the size of the shadow economy? *Global Economic Review: Perspectives on East Asian Economies and Industries*, *42*(3), 251–268. doi:10.1080/1226508X.2013.833846

Leeper, E. (1991). Equilibria under 'Active' and 'Passive' Monetary Policies. *Journal of Monetary Economics*, *27*(1), 129–147. doi:10.1016/0304-3932(91)90007-B

Leibfritz, W. (2009, June). Reducing Undeclared Work in Turkey - The Role of Tax Policy and Administration. *Background Paper prepared for the World Bank Country Economic Memorandum on Informality: Causes, Consequences, Policies*. Retrieved from http://siteresources.worldbank.org/TURKEYEXTN/Resources/361711-1277211666558/bpg_ReducingUndeclaredWork.pdf

Leite, C., & Weidmann, J. (1999). Does mother nature corrupt? natural resources, corruption, and economic growth (Working Paper WP/99/85). *International Monetary Fund*.

Leuthold, J. H. (1991). Tax Shares in developing countries: A panel study. *Journal of Development Economics*, *35*(1), 173–185. doi:10.1016/0304-3878(91)90072-4

Levi, M. (1988). *Of Rule and Revenue*. Berkeley, CA: University of California Press.

Levin, A., Lin, C. F., & Chu, C. (2002). Unit root tests in panel data: Asymptotic and finite-sample properties. *Journal of Econometrics*, *108*(1), 1–24. doi:10.1016/S0304-4076(01)00098-7

Levy, D. M. (2002). *How the Dismal Science Got Its Name: Classical Economics and the Ur-Text of Racial Politics*. Ann Arbor: The Michigan University Press.

Lewin, K. (1951). *Field Theory in Social Science*. New York: Harper.

Lewis, A. (1982). *The Psychology of Taxation*. Oxford: Blackwell.

Liberati, P. (2007). Trade Openness, Financial Openness and Government Size. *Journal of Public Policy*, *27*(02), 215–247. doi:10.1017/S0143814X07000670

Lim, C., Columba, F., Costa, A., Kongsamut, P., Otani, A., Saiyid, M., . . . Wu, X. (2011, October). Macroprudential Policy: What Instruments and How to Use Them? Lessons from Country Experiences. *IMF Working Paper No. 11/238*. Retrieved from http://www.imf.org/external/pubs/ft/wp/2011/wp11238.pdf

Lindbeck, A. (1976). Stabilization Policy in Open Economics with Endogenous Politicans. *The American Economic Review*, *66*(2), 1–19.

Lindert, P. H. (1994). The Rise of Social Spending? *Explorations in Economic History*, *33*(1), 1–34. doi:10.1006/exeh.1996.0001

Lipsey, R. G. (1997). Reflections on the General Theory of Second Best at its Golden Jubilee. *International Tax and Public Finance*, *14*(4), 349–364. doi:10.1007/s10797-007-9036-x

Lipsey, R. G., & Lancaster, K. (1956). The General Theory of the Second Best. *The Review of Economic Studies*, *24*(1), 11–32. doi:10.2307/2296233

Lisi, G. (2012). Testing the Slippery Slope Framework. *Economic Bulletin*, *32*(2), 1369–1377.

Lledo, V. D., Yackovlev, I., & Gadenne, L. (2011). A Tale of Cyclicality, Aid Flows and Debt: Government Spending in Sub-Sharan Africa. *Journal of African Economies*, *20*(5), 823–849. doi:10.1093/jae/ejr022

Loayza, N. V. (1996). The economics of the informal sector: A simple model and some empirical evidence from Latin America. *Carnegie-Rochester Conference Series on Public Policy*, *45*, 129–162. doi:10.1016/S0167-2231(96)00021-8

Loretz, S. (2008). Corporate taxation in the OECD in a wider context. *Oxford Review of Economic Policy*, *24*(4), 639–660. doi:10.1093/oxrep/grn035

Lotz, J. R., & Morss, E. R. (1967). Measuring "Tax Effort" in Developing Countries (Evaluation de l'effort fiscal dans les pays en voie de developpement) (Medicion del "esfuerzo tributario" de los paises en desarrollo). *Staff Papers - International Monetary Fund. International Monetary Fund, 14*(3), 478–499. doi:10.2307/3866266

Lotz, J. R., & Morss, E. R. (1970). A Theory of Tax Level Determinants for Developing Countries. *Economic Development and Cultural Change, 18*(3), 328–341. doi:10.1086/450436

Love, I., & Zicchino, L. (2006). Financial development and dynamic investment behavior: Evidence from panel VAR. *The Quarterly Review of Economics and Finance, 46*(2), 190–210. doi:10.1016/j.qref.2005.11.007

Lozza, E., Kastlunger, B., Tagliabue, S., & Kirchler, E. (2013). The Relationship between Political Ideology and Attitudes toward Tax Compliance: The Case of Italian Taxpayers. *Journal of Social and Political Psychology, 1*(1), 51–73. doi:10.5964/jspp.v1i1.108

Lucas, R. E. Jr, & Stokey, N. L. (1983). Optimal Fiscal and Monetary Policy in an Economy without Capital. *Journal of Monetary Economics, 12*(1), 55–93. doi:10.1016/0304-3932(83)90049-1

Lucas, R. Jr. (1972). Expectations and the Neutrality of Money. *Journal of Economic Theory, 4*(2), 103–124. doi:10.1016/0022-0531(72)90142-1

Lucas, R. Jr, & Rapping, L. A. (1969, September-October). Real Wages, Employment and Inflation. *Journal of Political Economy, 77*(5), 721–754. doi:10.1086/259559

Luitel, H. S. (2014). *Is Tax Amnesty a Good Tax Policy?: Evidence from State Tax Amnesty Programs in the United States*. London: Lexington Books.

Luitel, H. S., & Sobel, R. S. (2007). The Revenue Impact of Repeated Tax Amnesties. *Public Budgeting & Finance, 27*(3), 19–38. doi:10.1111/j.1540-5850.2007.00881.x

Lutkepohl, H. (2007). *New introduction to multiple time series analysis*. Berlin: Springer-Verlag.

MacGill, I., Outhred, H., & Nolles, K. (2006). Some Design Lessons from Market-Based Greenhouse Regulation in the Restructured Australian Electricity Industry. *Energy Policy, 34*(1), 11–25. doi:10.1016/j.enpol.2004.05.009

MacKenzie, D., & Millo, Y. (2003). Constructing a Market, Performing Theory: The Historical Sociology of a Financial Derivatives Exchange. *American Journal of Sociology, 109*(1), 107–145. doi:10.1086/374404

MacKenzie, G. A. (1992). Estimating the Base of the Value-Added Tax in Developing Countries: The Problem of Exemption. *Public Finance, 47*(2), 257–270.

Macroprudential Policy: An Organizing Framework. (2011IMF. Washington: International Monetary Fund.

Mahdavi, S. (2008). The Level and Composition of Tax Revenue in Developing Countries: Evidence from Unbalanced Panel Data. *International Review of Economics & Finance, 17*(4), 607–617. doi:10.1016/j.iref.2008.01.001

Mair, V. H. (2009). *How a Misunderstanding about Chinese Characters Has Led Many Astray*. Retrieved from http://www.pinyin.info/chinese/crisis.html

Makdisi, S., Fattah, Z., & Limam, I. (2006). Determinants of Growth in the MENA Countries. In J. B. Nugent & M. H. Pesaran (Eds.), *Explaining Growth in the Middle East, Contributions to Economic Analysis* (Vol. 278, pp. 31–60). Amsterdam: Elsevier. doi:10.1016/S0573-8555(06)78002-6

Mankiw, N. G., Rotemberg, J. J., & Summers, L. H. (1985). Intertemporal Substitution in Macro Economics. *The Quarterly Journal of Economics, 100*(1), 225–251. doi:10.2307/1885743

Mankiw, N. G., Weinzierl, M., & Yagan, D. (2009). Optimal Taxation in Theory and Practice. *The Journal of Economic Perspectives*, *23*(4), 147–174. doi:10.1257/jep.23.4.147

Marcinkevičiūtė, L., & Petrauskienė, R. (2007). Performance Improvement of Public Administration Institutions: The Case of Lithuanian District Municipalities` Administrations. *Viešoji Politika Ir Administravimas*, *19*, 69–80.

Marples, D. J. (2015, April 30). *Tax Expenditures: Overview and Analysis*. Congressional Research Service Report. Retrieved May 29, 2015, from http://fas.org/sgp/crs/misc/R44012.pdf

Martinez-Vazquez, J. Vulovic, V., & Dodson, B. M. (2012). The Impact of Tax and Expenditure Policies on Income Distribution: Evidence from a Large Panel of Countries. *Hacienda Pública Española, 200*(4), 95-130.

Martinez-Vazquez, J., & McNab, R. (2000). Tax Reform in The Tax Reform Experiment in Transitional Countries. International Center for Public Policy Working Paper Series, at AYSPS, GSU paper, International Center for Public Policy, Andrew Young School of Policy Studies, Georgia State University.

Martinez-Vazquez, J. (1993). The Incidence of Tax Evasion: A Review of the Issues. *Andrew Young School of Policy Studies, Policy Research Program Archived Papers*. Atlanta, GA: Georgia State University.

Martinez-Vazquez, J. (2007). The Impact of Budgets on the Poor: Tax and Expenditure Benefit Incidence Analysis. In B. Moreno-Dodson & Q. Wodon (Eds.), *Public Finance for Poverty Reduction*. Washington, D.C.: The World Bank.

Martinez-Vazquez, J., & McNab, R. (2000). The Tax Reform Experiment in Transitional Countries. *National Tax Journal*, *53*(2), 273–298. doi:10.17310/ntj.2000.2.06

Martinez-Vazquez, J., Vulovic, V., & Liu, Y. (2011). Direct versus Indirect Taxation: Trends, Theory, And Economic Significance. In E. Albi & J. Martinez-Vazquez (Eds.), *The Elgar Guide to Tax Systems* (pp. 37–92). Cheltenham, UK: Edward Elgar. doi:10.4337/9780857933898.00009

Martin, I. W., Mehrotra, A. K., & Prasad, M. (2009). The Thunder of History: The Origins and Development of the New Fiscal Sociology. In I. W. Martin, A. K. Mehrotra, & M. Prasad (Eds.), *The New Fiscal Sociology: Taxation in Comparative and Historical Perspective* (pp. 1–28). New York: Cambridge University Press. doi:10.1017/CBO9780511627071.002

Mauro, P. (1996). The Effects of Corruption on Growth, Investment and Government Expenditure. *IMF Working Paper* WP/96/98.

Mauro, P. (1997). Why Worry About Corruption ? *International Monetary Fund (IMF) Economic Issues* (6).

Mauro, P. (1995). Corruption and Growth. *The Quarterly Journal of Economics*, *110*(3), 681–712. doi:10.2307/2946696

Mauro, P. (1998). Corruption and the composition of government expenditure. *Journal of Public Economics*, *69*(2), 263–279. doi:10.1016/S0047-2727(98)00025-5

McCallum, B. (1999b, October). Theoretical Issues Pertaining to Monetary Unions. *NBER Working Paper* 7393.

McCallum, B. (1999a). *Issues in the Design of Monetary Policy Rules*. In J. Taylor & M. Woodford (Eds.). Handbook of Macroeconomics.London: North-Holland Pub. Co.

McCallum, B. (2001). Indeterminacy, Bubbles, and the Fiscal Theory of Price Level Determination. *Journal of Monetary Economics*, *47*(1), 19–30. doi:10.1016/S0304-3932(00)00048-9

McGee, R. W. (2012). Christian Views on the Ethics of Tax Evasion. The Ethics of Tax Evasion: Perspectives in Theory and Practice (pp. 201-210), New York: Springer.

McGee, R. W. (1999). Why People Evade Taxes in Armenia: A Look at an Ethical Issue Based on a Summary of Interviews. *Journal of Accounting, Ethics & Public Policy*, *2*(2), 408–416.

McGee, R. W. (2000). Taxation in the Republic of Armenia: An Overview and Discussion from the Perspectives of Law, Economics and Ethics. *ILSA Journal of International & Comparative Law*, *7*(1), 97–109.

McGee, R. W. (2006). A Survey of International Business Academics on the Ethics of Tax Evasion. *Journal of Accounting, Ethics & Public Policy*, *6*(3), 301–352.

McGee, R. W. (2012b). Christian Views on the Ethics of Tax Evasion. In R. W. McGee (Ed.), *The Ethics of Tax Evasion: Perspectives in Theory and Practice* (pp. 201–210). New York: Springer. doi:10.1007/978-1-4614-1287-8_12

McGee, R. W. (2012c). Attitudes on the Ethics of Tax Evasion: A Survey of Philosophy Professors. In R. W. McGee (Ed.), *The Ethics of Tax Evasion: Perspectives in Theory and Practice* (pp. 125–132). New York: Springer. doi:10.1007/978-1-4614-1287-8_7

McGee, R. W. (2012d). Gender and the Ethics of Tax Evasion: An Empirical Study of 82 Countries. In R. W. McGee (Ed.), *The Ethics of Tax Evasion: Perspectives in Theory and Practice* (pp. 415–439). New York: Springer. doi:10.1007/978-1-4614-1287-8_26

McGee, R. W. (2012e). Age and the Ethics of Tax Evasion. In R. W. McGee (Ed.), *The Ethics of Tax Evasion: Perspectives in Theory and Practice* (pp. 441–449). New York: Springer. doi:10.1007/978-1-4614-1287-8_27

McGee, R. W. (2012f). Education Level and the Ethics of Tax Evasion. In R. W. McGee (Ed.), *The Ethics of Tax Evasion: Perspectives in Theory and Practice* (pp. 451–457). New York: Springer. doi:10.1007/978-1-4614-1287-8_28

McGee, R. W. (2012g). Marital Status and the Ethics of Tax Evasion. In R. W. McGee (Ed.), *The Ethics of Tax Evasion: Perspectives in Theory and Practice* (pp. 475–484). New York: Springer. doi:10.1007/978-1-4614-1287-8_31

McGee, R. W. (2012h). Income Level and the Ethics of Tax Evasion. In R. W. McGee (Ed.), *The Ethics of Tax Evasion: Perspectives in Theory and Practice* (pp. 485–495). New York: Springer. doi:10.1007/978-1-4614-1287-8_32

McGee, R. W. (Ed.). (2012a). *The Ethics of Tax Evasion: Perspectives in Theory and Practice*. New York: Springer. doi:10.1007/978-1-4614-1287-8

McGee, R. W., & Benk, S. (2016). Attitudes toward Tax Evasion in Turkey: An Empirical Study using the Latest World Values Survey Data. In M. M. Erdoğdu & B. Christiansen (Eds.), *Handbook of Research on Public Finance Perspectives on Europe and the MENA Region*. Hershey, PA: IGI Global.

McGee, R. W., & Benk, S.McGee. (2011). The Ethics of Tax Evasion: A Study of Turkish Opinion. *Journal of Balkan and Near Eastern Studies*, *13*(2), 249–262. doi:10.1080/19448953.2011.578869

McGee, R. W., Benk, S., Yıldırım, H., & Kayıkçı, M. (2011). The Ethics of Tax Evasion: A Study of Turkish Tax Practitioner Opinion. *European Journal of Soil Science*, *18*(3), 468–480.

McGee, R. W., & Gordon, M. Cohn. (2008). Jewish Perspectives on the Ethics of Tax Evasion. *Journal of Legal. Ethical and Regulatory Issues*, *11*(2), 1–32.

McGee, R. W., & Maranjyan, T. B. (2012). Attitudes toward Tax Evasion: An Empirical Study of Florida Accounting Practitioners. In R. W. McGee (Ed.), *The Ethics of Tax Evasion: Perspectives in Theory and Practice* (pp. 247–265). New York: Springer. doi:10.1007/978-1-4614-1287-8_15

McGee, R. W., Petrides, Y., & Ross, A. M. (2012). How Serious Is Tax Evasion: A Survey of Mexican Opinion. In R. W. McGee (Ed.), *The Ethics of Tax Evasion: Perspectives in Theory and Practice* (pp. 405–411). New York: Springer. doi:10.1007/978-1-4614-1287-8_25

McGee, R. W., & Smith, S. R. (2012). Ethics, Tax Evasion and Religion: A Survey of Opinion of Members of the Church of Jesus Christ of Latter-Day Saints. In R. W. McGee (Ed.), *The Ethics of Tax Evasion: Perspectives in Theory and Practice* (pp. 211–226). New York: Springer. doi:10.1007/978-1-4614-1287-8_13

McGrattan, E. R., & Prescott, E. C. (2003, August). Taxes, Regulations, and the Value of US Corporations: A General Equilibrium Analysis. *Research Department Staff Report 309, Federal Reserve Bank of Minneapolis.*

McGrattan, E. R., & Prescott, E. C. (2003, May). Average Debt and Equity Returns: Puzzling? *The American Economic Review*, *93*(2), 392–397. doi:10.1257/000282803321947407

McGuirk, E. F. (2013). The Illusory leader: Natural resources, taxation and accountability. *Public Choice*, *154*(3-4), 285–313. doi:10.1007/s11127-011-9820-0

Mehlum, H., Moene, K., & Torvik, R. (2006). Institutions and the resource curse. *The Economic Journal*, *116*(508), 1–20. doi:10.1111/j.1468-0297.2006.01045.x

Mélitz, J. (2000). Some Cross-Country Evidence about Fiscal Policy Behaviour and Consequences for EMU, European Economy. *Reports and Studies*, *2*, 3–21.

MENA-OECD Investment Programme: Recommendations on Frameworks to Support Development of National Tax Policy Reform Agendas. (2005). *OECD*. Retrieved from http://www.oecd.org/mena/investment/36086830.pdf

Mendel, J., & Bevacqua, J. (2014). *International Tax Administration: Building Bridges*. Sydney: CCH Australia.

Meon, P.-G., & Sekkat, K. (2004). Does the quality of institutions limit the MENA's integration in the world economy? *World Economy*, *27*(9), 1475–1498. doi:10.1111/j.0378-5920.2004.00661.x

Messere, K. (2000). 20th Century Taxes and Their Future (Bulletin). *International Bureau of Fiscal Documentation.*

Metin, K. (1998). The Relationship Between Inflation and Budget Deficit in Turkey. *Journal of Business & Economic Statistics*, *16*(4), 412–422.

Middle East and North African governments have high risks of defence-related corruption. (2013). Transparency International. Retrieved from http://www.transparency.org/news/pressrelease/20120206_middle_east_and_north_african_governments_have_high_risks_of_defen

Middle East Tax handbook 2014. (2014). *Deloitte*. Retrieved from www.deloitte.com

Mikesell, J. L. (2003). International Experiences with Administration of Local Taxes: A Review of Practices and Issues. Retrieved from http://citeseerx.ist.psu.edu/viewdoc/download?doi=10.1.1.199.304&rep=rep1&type=pdf

Mikesell, J. L., & Ross, J. M. (2012). Fast money? The contribution of state tax amnesties to public revenue systems. *National Tax Journal*, *65*(3), 529–562. doi:10.17310/ntj.2012.3.02

Mill, J. S. (1900). Principles of Political Economy (A. Haley, Ed.). (Vols. 1–2). New York: The Colonial Press. (Original work published 1848)

Milne, A. (2009). Macroprudential policy: What can it achieve? *Oxford Review of Economic Policy*, *25*(4), 608–629. doi:10.1093/oxrep/grp036

Mintzberg, H. (2004). *Managers not MBAs: A Hard Look at the Soft Practice of Managing and Management Development, San Fransisco: Berret-Koehler*. Publishers.

Mirrlees, S. J. (Chair), (2010). Dimensions of Tax Design: The Mirrlees Review. Oxford: Oxford University Press.

Mirrlees, S. J. (Chair), (2011). Tax by Design: The Mirrlees Review. Oxford: Oxford University Press.

Mirrlees, J., Adam, S., Besley, T., Blundell, R., Bond, S., Chote, R., & Poterba, J. et al. (2011). *Tax by Design: The Mirrlees Review*. Oxford, UK: Oxford University Press.

Mishkin, F. S. (2011). Monetary Policy Strategy: Lessons from the Crisis. *NBER Working Paper 16755*, National Bureau of Economic Research, Cambridge, MA.

Mishkin, F. S. (2009, May). Is Monetary Policy Effective during Financial Crises? *The American Economic Review*, *99*(2), 573–577. doi:10.1257/aer.99.2.573

Mitchell, D. J. (2000, September 18). An OECD Proposal To Eliminate Tax Competition Would Mean Higher Taxes And Less Privacy. *The Heritage Foundation, 1395*.

Mkandawire, T. (2010). On Tax Efforts and Colonial Heritage in Africa. *The Journal of Development Studies*, *46*(10), 1647–1669. doi:10.1080/00220388.2010.500660

Modugu, P. K., Eragbhe, E., & Izedonmi, F. (2012). Government Accountability and Voluntary Tax Compliance in Nigeria. *Research Journal of Finance and Accounting*, *3*(5), 69–77.

MOF. (2007, October). *Tax Expenditure Report*. General Directorate of the Revenue Policies, Ministry of Finance, No: B.07.0.GEP.10.10-2007.

MOF. (2015). *Public Accounts Bulletins*. General Directorate of Public Accounts, Ankara. Retrieved April 20, 2015, from https://portal.muhasebat.gov.tr/mgmportal/faces/khbDetail?birimDizini=General+Government&_afrLoop=1017212479336060&_afrWindowMode=0&_adf.ctrl-state=692ozugmw_4

Mogensen, G. V., Kvist, H. K., Kormendi, E., & Pedersen, S. (1995). *The Shadow Economy in Denmark 1994: Measurement and Results*. Copenhagen: Rockwool Foundation Research Unit.

Monterrey Consensus. (2002). United Nations (Draft Outcome of the International Conference on Financing for Development, Doc. A/AC.257/L.13).

Moore, M. (2007). How does taxation affect the quality of governance (Working Paper 280). *IDS*, Brighton, UK.

Moore, M. (2008). How does Taxation Affect the Quality of Governance? *IDS working paper*. Brighton: IDS.

Moore, M. (2013). Obstacles to increasing tax revenue in low income countries (Working Paper 15). *ICTD*.

Moore, M. (1998). Death without taxes: democracy, state capacity and aid dependence in the fourth world. In M. Robinson & G. White (Eds.), *The democratic development state*. Oxford: Oxford University Press.

Moore, M. (2004). The development of political underdevelopment. In G. Harrison (Ed.), *Global encounters: IPE, development and global governance*. London: Palgrave Macmillan.

Moore, M. (2008). Between coercion and contact: competing narratives on taxation and governance. In D. Brautigam, O. Fjeldstad, & M. Moore (Eds.), *Taxation and State-Building in Developing Countries* (pp. 34–63). Cambridge: Cambridge University Press. doi:10.1017/CBO9780511490897.002

Moore, M. (2014). Revenue Reform and Statebuilding in Anglophone Africa. *World Development*, *60*(8), 99–112. doi:10.1016/j.worlddev.2014.03.020

Morag, A. (1965). *On Taxes and Inflation*. New York: Random House.

Moreno, R. (2011, January). Policymaking from a 'Macroprudential' Perspective in Emerging Market Economies. *BIS Working Paper* No. 336. Retrieved from: http://ssrn.com/abstract=1858690

Morris, R., Rodrigues Braz, C., de Castro, F., Jonk, S., Kremer, J., Linehan, S., . . . Tkacevs, O. (2009, November). Explaining Government Revenue Windfalls and Shortfalls an Analysis for Selected EU Countries. *ECB Working Paper No: 1114*.

Morris, A., & Moberg, L. (2012). Cartelizing Taxes: Understanding the OECD's Campaign against "Harmful Tax Competition." *Colum. J. Tax L*, *1*, 1–64.

Mpatswe, G. K., Tapsoba, S. J.-A., & York, R. C. (2011). The Cyclicality of Fiscal Policies in the CEMAC Region. *IMF Working Paper* WP/11/205. Retrieved from https://www.imf.org/external/pubs/ft/wp/2011/wp11205.pdf

Muehlbacher, S., Kirchler, E., & Schwarzenberger, H. (2011). Voluntary versus Enforced Tax Compliance: Empirical Evidence for the "Slippery Slope" Framework. *European Journal of Law and Economics*, *32*(1), 89–97. doi:10.1007/s10657-011-9236-9

Mueller, D. C. (1987). The Growth of Government: A Public Choice Perspective. *International Monetary Fund Staff Chapters*, *34*(1), 115–149. doi:10.2307/3867026

Mueller, D. C. (2003). The reason for collective choice – redistribution. *Public Choice III* (Ch. 3, 3rd ed.). Cambridge: Cambridge University Press.

Musgrave, R. (1987). Tax Reform in Developing Countries. In D. Newbery & N. Stern (Eds.), *The Theory of Taxation for Developing Countries* (pp. 242–263). Oxford: Oxford University Press.

Musgrave, R. A. (1959). *The Theory of Public Finance*. New York: McGraw-Hill.

Musgrave, R. A. (1959). *The Theory of Public Finance: A Study in Political Economy*. New York: McGraw-Hill.

Musgrave, R. A. (1992). Schumpeter's crisis of the tax state. *Journal of Evolutionary Economics*, *2*(2), 89–113. doi:10.1007/BF01193535

Musgrave, R. A. (2008). Public Finance and the Three Branch Model. *Journal of Economics and Finance*, *32*(4), 334–339. doi:10.1007/s12197-008-9044-4

Nagayama, H. (2009). Electric Power Sector Reform Liberalization Models and Electric Power Prices in Developing Countries: An Empirical Analysis Using International Panel Data. *Energy Economics*, *31*(3), 463–472. doi:10.1016/j.eneco.2008.12.004

Narayan, P. K. (2005). The Saving and Investment Nexus For China: Evidence from Cointegration Tests. *Applied Economics*, *37*(17), 1979–1990. doi:10.1080/00036840500278103

Nawaz, M., Iqbal, M., Ali, A., & Zaman, K. (2012). Fiscal Theory of Price Level: A Panel Data Analysis for Selected SAARC Countries. *Romanian Journal of Economic Forecasting*, *3*, 152–170.

Ndikumana, L., & Kaouther, A. (2010). Revenue Mobilization in African Countries: Does Natural Resource Endowment Matter? *African Development Review*, *22*(3), 351–365. doi:10.1111/j.1467-8268.2010.00250.x

Nerre, B. (2008). Tax Culture: A Basic Concept for Tax Politics. *Economic Analysis and Policy*, *38*, 153–167.

Newbery, D. M. (2002). Problems of Liberalising the Electricity Industry. *European Economic Review*, *46*(4–5), 919–927. doi:10.1016/S0014-2921(01)00225-2

Neyaptı, B. (2003). Budget Deficits and Inflation: The Roles of Central Bank Independence and Financial Market Development. *Contemporary Economic Policy*, *21*(4), 458–475. doi:10.1093/cep/byg025

Nickell, S. (2003, December). Employment and Taxes, *CESIFO* Working Paper No.1109.

Nicodème, G. (2012, October 26-28). Discussion: The Tax Treatment of Housing Gayer. In C. Gayer & G. Mourre (Eds.), Property Taxation and Enhanced Tax Administration in Challenging Times. European Economy Economic Papers 463.

Nier E. W., Osiński J., Jácome, J. I., & Madrid, P. (2011). Institutional Models for Macroprudential Policy, *IMF Staff Discussion Note 11/18.*

Noland, M., & Pack, H. (2007). *The Arab Economies in a Changing World.* Washington, DC: Peterson Institute for International Economics.

Norregaard, J. (2013). Taxing Immovable Property: Revenue Potential and Implementation Challenges. *IMF Working Paper*, WP/13/129. Retrieved from http://www.imf.org/external/pubs/ft/wp/2013/wp13129.pdf

Norregaard, J., & Khan, T. S. (2007, December 2007). Tax Policy: Recent Trends and Coming Challenges. *IMF Working Paper, No: WP/07/274.*

O'Connor, J. (1973). *The Fiscal Crisis of the State.* New York: St. Martin's Press.

Oates, W. (1972). *Fiscal Federalism.* New York: Harcourt, Brace and Jovanovich.

Oates, W. (1985). Searching for Leviathan: An Empirical Study. *The American Economic Review*, *75*, 748–757.

Oates, W. (1989). Searching for Leviathan: A Reply and Some Further Reflections. *The American Economic Review*, *79*, 578–583.

Oates, W. E. (2005). Toward A Second-Generation Theory of Fiscal Federalism. *International Tax and Public Finance*, *12*(4), 349–373. doi:10.1007/s10797-005-1619-9

Oats, L., & Pemberton, L. (2012 *, October*). Key Principles for Efficient Tax Administration and Main Reform Challenges. In C. Gayer & G. Mourre (Eds.), *Property Taxation and Enhanced Tax Administration in Challenging Times, Economic Papers 463*(pp. 51–61). Brussels: European Union.

OECD. (1964). *Turkey Economic Survey.* Paris.

OECD. (1979). *OECD Report on Transfer Pricing and Multinational Enterprises.* Paris.

OECD. (1997, May 22). Recommendation of the council on the use of tax identification numbers in an international context. (Adopted by the Council at its 894th session on 13 March 1997 [C/M(97)5/PROV]), C*(97)29/FINAL.*

OECD. (1998). *Harmful Tax Competition: An Emerging Global Issue.* Paris.

OECD. (1998). *Harmful Tax Competition: An Emerging Global Issue.* Paris: OECD Publications.

OECD. (2000a). Towards Global Tax Co-Operation: Progress in Identifying and Eliminating Harmful Tax Practices. Report To The 2000 Ministerial Council Meeting And Recommendations By The Committee on Fiscal Affairs, Paris.

OECD. (2000b). *Improving Access to Bank Information for Tax Purposes.* Paris.

OECD. (2000c). 2006 Update On Progress In Member Countries. Paris.

OECD. (2000d). Tax Burdens Alternative Measures OECD Tax Policy Studies (No. 2). Paris.

OECD. (2001). *Guidance in Applying the 1998 Report to Preferential Tax Regimes.* Paris.

OECD. (2001b). Paris: Taxation and Electronic Commerce – Implementing the Ottawa Taxation Framework Conditions.

OECD. (2002). *Measuring the non-observed economy: A handbook*. Paris: OECD Publications Service.

OECD. (2002). *Measuring the Non-Observed Economy: A Handbook*. Retrieved from http://www.oecd.org/std/na/1963116.pdf

OECD. (2003). *Improving Access to Bank Information for Tax Purposes the 2003 Progress Report*. Paris.

OECD. (2004). Electronic Commerce Facilitating cross-border tax collection.

OECD. (2004b). Tax Administration in OECD Countries: Comparative Information Series, Paris.

OECD. (2006a). *OECD' Project on Harmful Tax Practices: 2006 Update on Progress in Member Countries*. Paris.

OECD. (2006b). Fundamental Reform of Personal Income Tax. Tax Policy Studies No.13. Paris.

OECD. (2009). *Experiences and Practices of Eight OECD Countries*. Forum on Tax Administration: Compliance Management of Large Business Task Group. Guidance Note. Retrieved from http://www.oecd.org/tax/administration/43241144.pdf

OECD. (2010). Choosing a Broad Base- Low Rate Approach to Taxation. Tax Policy Studies No.19. Paris.

OECD. (2010). *Tax Expenditures in OECD Countries*. Paris: OECD Publishing; doi:10.1787/9789264076907-en

OECD. (2012). *Income Inequality and Growth: The Role of Taxes and Transfers*. OECD Economics Department Policy Notes, No. 9. January. Retrieved May 29, 2015, from http://www.oecd.org/eco/public-finance/49417295.pdf

OECD. (2012). *Taxing Wages, 2011*. Paris, France: Organisation for Economic Co-operation and Development Publishing.

OECD. (2013). *Revenue Statistics 2013*. Paris: OECD Publishing; doi:10.1787/rev_stats-2013-en-fr

OECD. (2013a). *A Step Change in Tax Transparency. OECD report for the G8 summit*. June, Lough Erne, Enniskillen.

OECD. (2013a). *Co-Operative Compliance: A Framework – From Enhanced Relationship to Co-Operative Compliance*. OECD Publishing.

OECD. (2013a). *Tax Transparency 2013 Report on Progress*. Paris.

OECD. (2013b). Tax Administration. Paris.

OECD. (2013b). *Together for Better Outcomes: Engaging and Involving SME Taxpayers and Stakeholders*. OECD Publishing.

OECD. (2013b).*Tax Administration 2013: Comparative Information on OECD and Other Advanced Emerging*. Paris.

OECD. (2013c). *Addressing Base Erosion and Profit Shifting*. Paris.

OECD. (2013c). *Building Tax Culture, Compliance and Citizenship: A Global Source Book on Taxpayer Education*. OECD Publishing.

OECD. (2014a). *Practices to Strengthen Business Integrity in the MENA Region*. Retrieved from http://www.oecd.org/mena/investment/PracticesBusinessIntegrity.pdf

OECD. (2014b). *MENA-OECD Investment Programme: Fostering Investment, Growth and Employment in the Middle East and North Africa (MENA)*. OECD Publishing.

Official Gazette (2008). 5811 Sayılı Bazı Varlıkların Milli Ekonomiye Kazandırılması Hakkında Kanun, 22.11.2008 tarihli 27062 sayılı RG ve 5811 Sayılı Bazı Varlıkların Milli Ekonomiye Kazandırılması Hakkında Kanuna İlişkin Genel Tebliğ.

Official Gazette (2011). Maliye Bakanlığı, 5811 Sayılı Bazı Varlıkların Milli Ekonomiye Kazandırılması Hakkında Kanuna İlişkin Genel Tebliğ (seri no. 4), 07 Nisan 2011 Tarihli Resmi Gazete, Sayı: 27898.

Official Gazette (2013). 6486 sayılı Sosyal Sigortalar ve Genel Sağlık Sigortası Kanunu ile Bazı Kanunlarda Değişiklik Yapılmasına Dair Kanun ile 193 sayılı Gelir Vergisi Kanununa eklenen geçici 85'inci madde 29.05.2013 tarihli ve Sayı: 28661.

Oğuz, F., Akkemik, K. A., & Göksal, K. (2014). Can Law Impose Competition? A Critical Discussion and Evidence from the Turkish Electricity Generation Market. *Renewable & Sustainable Energy Reviews*, *30*, 381–387. doi:10.1016/j.rser.2013.10.024

Olovsson, C. (2009). Why Do Europeans Work So Little. *International Economic Review*, *50*(1), 39–61. doi:10.1111/j.1468-2354.2008.00523.x

Olsen, P. (2008, February 26). Tax Evaders, Beware The Liechten-sting. *Forbes*. Retrieved from http://www.forbes.com/2008/02/26/liechtenstein-tax-haven-markets-equity-cx_po_0226markets26.html

Öncel, M., Kumrulu, A., & Çağan, N. (2008). *Vergi Hukuku*. İstanbul: Turhan Kitabevi.

Önder, İ., Türel, O., Somel, C., & Ekinci, N. (1993). *Türkiye'de Kamu Maliyesi, Finansal Yapı ve Politikalar*. İstanbul: Tarih Vakfı Yurt Yayınları.

Oner, E. (2011). Tax Expenditures and the Situation in Turkey. *International Journal of Business and Social Science*, *2*(23), 165–170.

Önis, Z. (1998). Political Economy of Turkey in the 1980s, Anatomy of Unorthodox Liberalizm. In Z. Öniş (Ed.), *State and Market* (pp. 183–196). İstanbul: Boğaziçi University Press.

Orhangazi, Ö. (2008). Financialization and Capital Accumulation in the Non-Financial Corporate Sector: A Theoretical and Empirical Investigation of the US Economy: 1973-2004, *MPRA Paper No.7724*.

Orsi, R., Raggi, D., & Turino, F. (2014). Size, trend, and policy implications of the underground economy. *Review of Economic Dynamics*, *17*(3), 417–436. doi:10.1016/j.red.2013.11.001

Orta Vadeli Program 2013-2015. (2012). Retrieved from http://www.goc.gov.tr/files/files/orta-vadeli-program%20(2013-2015).pdf

Ortega, D., Ronconi, L., & Sanguinetti, P. (2013). Reciprocity and Willingness to Pay Taxes: Evidence from a Survey Experiment in Latin America. *CIAS Working Paper 2*. Buenos Aires, Argentina: Centro de Investigación y Acción Social. Retrieved from http://www.fcias.org.ar/wp-content/uploads/2013/04/CIAS-Reciprocity_and_taxes_April-2013.pdf

Ossowski, R., & Gonzales, A. (2012). Manna from heaven: the impact of nonrenewable resource revenues on other revenues of resource exporters in Latin America and the Caribbean (Working Paper 337). *Inter-American Development Bank*, Washington, DC.

Owens, J. (2000, October 19). Towards world tax co-operation. *OECD Observer.* Retrieved from http://www.oecdobserver.org/news/printpage.php/aid/271/Towards_world_tax_co-operation.html

Owens, J., & Hamilton, S. (2004). Experience and Innovations in Other Countries. In H. J. Aaron & J. Slemrod (Eds.), *The Crisis in Tax Administration* (pp. 347–388). Washington, DC: Brookings Institution Press.

Özatay, F. (1996). The Lessons From the 1994 Crisis in Turkey: Public Debt (Mis)management and Confidence Crisis. *Yapı Kredi Economic Review*, *7*(1), 21–37.

Özatay, F. (1997). Sustainability of Fiscal Deficits, Monetary Policy and Inflation Stabilization: The Case of Turkey. *Journal of Policy Modeling*, *19*(6), 661–681. doi:10.1016/S0161-8938(97)00015-X

Özatay, F. (2007). Monetary policy challenges for Turkey in the European Union Accession Process. In E. Başçı, J. V. Hagen, & S. Togan (Eds.), *Macroeconomic Policies for EU Accession* (pp. 130–165). London: Edward Elgar Publishing. doi:10.4337/9781847205230.00014

Özdemir, A. R. (2002). *Essays on the Determinants of the Level and Structure of Government Expenditures and Taxation.* (PhD Dissertation). University of Connecticut, Economics Department.

Öz, N. S. (2005). *Uluslararası Vergi Rekabeti ve Vergi Cennetleri.* Ankara: Maliye ve Hukuk Yayınları.

Öz, N. S. (2012). Controlled foreign company regime in Turkey and its valuation. *Intertax*, *40*(11).

Özülkü, H. (2006). Türkiye'de Elektriğin Tarihsel Gelişimine Özet Bakış (1900'den 2006'a Yılına Kadar), 10. *Enerji Kongresi Tebliği, Dünya Enerji Konseyi Türk Milli Komitesi*, 1-11. Retrieved from http://www.oocities.org/hasanozulku/melektriktarih.pdf

Packard, T., Koettl, J., & Montenegro, C. E. (2012). *From the Shadow: Integrating Europe's Informal Labor. The World Bank Report on Shadow Economy in the Central and Eastern Europe*. Washington, DC: The World Bank. doi:10.1596/978-0-8213-9549-3

Palley, T. (2015). The Federal Reserve and Shared Prosperity: A Guide to the Policy Issues and Institutional Challenges. Real-World Economics Review no. 70, Washington DC.

Park, C.-G., & Hyun, J. K. (2003). Examining the Determinants of Tax Compliance by Experimental Data: A Case of Korea. *Journal of Policy Modeling*, *25*(8), 673–684. doi:10.1016/S0161-8938(03)00075-9

Pashev, K. V. (2008). Monitoring of Tax Corruption in Transition Economies: Evidence from Bulgaria. In R. W. McGee (Ed.), *Taxation and Public Finance in Transition and Developing Economies* (pp. 321–362). New York: Springer. doi:10.1007/978-0-387-25712-9_18

Pechman, J. A. (1987). *Federal Tax Policy* (5th ed.). Washington, DC: The Brookings Institution.

Peltzman, S. (1980). The Growth of Government. *The Journal of Law & Economics*, *23*(2), 209–288. doi:10.1086/466962

Pennock, R. T. (1998). Death and Taxes: On the Justice of Conscientious War Tax Resistance. Journal of Accounting, Ethics & Public Policy, 1(1), 58-76. Reprinted in R. W. McGee (Ed.) (1998), The Ethics of Tax Evasion (pp. 124-142). Dumont, NJ: The Dumont Institute for Public Policy Research.

Perron, P. (1989, November). The Great Crash, the Oil-Price Shock, and the Unit-Root Hypothesis. *Econometrica*, *57*(6), 1361–401.

Persoud, B. (2002). The OECD Harmful Tax Competition Policy: A Major Issue for Small States, International Tax Competition: Globalisation and Fiscal Sovereignty. Commonwealth Secretariat.

Persson, T., & Tabellini, G. (1992). The Politics of 1992: Fiscal Policy and European Integration. *The Review of Economic Studies*, *59*(4), 689–701. doi:10.2307/2297993

Persson, T., & Tabellini, G. (1998). The Size and Scope of Government: Comparative Politics with Rational Politicians. *European Economic Review*, *43*(4-6), 699–735. doi:10.1016/S0014-2921(98)00131-7

Pesaran, M. H., Shin, Y., & Smith, R. J. (2001). Bounds Testing Approaches to the Analysis of Level Relationships. *Journal of Applied Econometrics*, *16*(3), 289–326. doi:10.1002/jae.616

Pessino, C. & Fenochietto, R. (2012). Determining Countries' Tax Effort. *Hacienda Publica Española / Revista de Economía, 195*(4), 65-87.

Petersen, H. G., Thiessen, U., & Wohlleben, P. (2010). Shadow Economy, Tax Evasion, and Transfer Fraud- Definition, Measurement, and Data Problems. *International Economic Journal, 24*(4), 421–441. doi:10.1080/10168737.2010.525973

Piancastelli, M. (2001, September 2001). Measuring the Tax Effort of Developed and Developing Countries: Cross Country Panel data Analysis – 1985/95. *Texto Para Discussao No: 818*.

Piciotto, S. (1999, November 4-5). The End Offshore? Regaining Public Control of Finance and Taxation in the Era of Globalization. *Paper for Conference on Governing the Public Domain beyond the Era of Washington Consensus? Redrawing the Line between the State and The Market*, Toronto.

Pickhardt, M., & Prinz, A. (2014). Behavioral Dynamics of Tax Evasion – A Survey. *Journal of Economic Psychology, 40*(1), 1–19. doi:10.1016/j.joep.2013.08.006

Pierce, D. W. (1992). *The MIT Dictionary Of Modern Economics* (4th ed.). New York: Macmillan Press. doi:10.1007/978-1-349-22136-3

Pigou, A. C. (1947). *A Study in Public Finance* (3rd ed.). New York: Macmillan.

Piketty, T. (2014). *Capital in the Twenty-First Century* (A. Goldhammer, Trans.). Cambridge, UK: Harvard University Press. doi:10.4159/9780674369542

Pitt, M. M., & Lee, L.-F. (1981). The Measurement and Sources of Technical Inefficiency in the Indonesian Weaving Industry. *Journal of Development Economics, 9*(1), 43–64. doi:10.1016/0304-3878(81)90004-3

Planning and Budgeting Committee Report on the Government Budget Bill for the year 2010/2011. (2010). The Planning and Budgeting Committee.

Pollitt, M. (2009). Evaluating the Evidence on Electricity Reform: Lessons for the South East Europe (SEE) market. *Journal of Regulatory Economics, 33*(2), 159–172.

Posner, E. A. (2000). Law and Social Norms: The Case of Tax Compliance. *Virginia Law Review, 86*(8), 1781–1819. doi:10.2307/1073829

Potrafke, N. (2010). Does Government Ideology Influence Deregulation of Product Markets? Empirical Evidence from OECD countries. *Public Choice, 143*(1-2), 135–155. doi:10.1007/s11127-009-9494-z

Prakash, K., & Pau, R. (2012). Monetary and Macroprudential Policy Rules in a Model with House Price Booms. *The BE Journal of Macroeconomics, 12*(1), 1–4.

Prates, D. M. (2012). How to Evaluate Financial Regulation in Brazil? *Paper prepared to the workshop "Growth with Financial Stability and New Developmentalism in Brazil"*, Sao Paulo: FGV-SP, March.

Prescott, E. C. (2004). Why Do Americans Work So Much More Than Europeans? *Federal Reserve Bank of Minneapolis Quarterly Review, 28*(1), 2–3.

Prest, A. R. (1979). The Taxable Capacity of a Country. In J. F. Toye (Ed.), *Taxation and Economic Development*. London, UK: Frank Cass.

Prud'homme, R. (1995). The Dangers of Decentralization. *The World Bank Research Observer, 10*(2), 201–220. doi:10.1093/wbro/10.2.201

Public Accounts Bulletins. (2015). *Ministry of Finance,General Directorate of Public Accounts*, Ankara. Retrieved from https://portal.muhasebat.gov.tr/mgmportal/faces/khbDetail?birimDizini=General+Government&_afrLoop=1017212479336060&_afrWindowMode=0&_adf.ctrl-state=692ozugmw_4

PwC Middle East Tax and Legal Update. (2013, January). PricewaterhouseCoopers.

Rabushka, A. (2008). *Taxation in Colonial America*. Princeton, NJ: Princeton University Press.

Ragan, K. S. (2006). *Taxes, Transfers, and Time Use: Fiscal Policy in a Household Production Model* [PhD Thesis]. University of Chicago.

Rajemison, H., Haggblade, S., & Younger, S. D. (2003, September). Indirect Tax Incidence in Madagascar: Updated Estimates Using the Input-Output Table. *Cornell Food and Nutrition Policy Program Working Paper No. 147*.

Ram, R. (2009). Openness, Country Size, and Government Size: Additional Evidence from a Large Cross-Country Panel. *Journal of Public Economics*, *93*(1-2), 213–218. doi:10.1016/j.jpubeco.2008.04.009

Ramsey, J. B. (1969). Tests for Specification Errors in Classical Linear Least Squares Regression Analysis. *Journal of the Royal Statistical Society. Series B. Methodological*, *31*(2), 350–371.

Rao, G. M. (1999). India: Intergovernmental Fiscal Relations in a Planned Economy. In R. M. Bird & F. Vaillancourt (Eds.), *Fiscal Decentralization in Developing Countries* (pp. 78–114). Cambridge: Cambridge University Press. doi:10.1017/CBO9780511559815.004

Rauscher, M. (1998). Leviathan and Competition Among Jurisdictions: The Case of Benefit Taxation. *Journal of Urban Economics*, *44*(1), 59–67. doi:10.1006/juec.1997.2060

Regulation (EC) No 713/2009 of the European Parliament and of the Council of 13 July 2009 Establishing an Agency for the Cooperation of Energy Regulators. (2009). *Official Journal of European Union*, 2009, 1-14. Retrieved from http://eur-lex.europa.eu/LexUriServ/LexUriServ.do?uri=OJ:L:2009:211:0001:0014:EN:PDF

Regulation (EU) No. 232/2014 of the European Parliament and of the Council. (2014). *Official Journal of the European Union, L*, *77*, 27–43.

Report of the International Conference on Financing for Development. (2002, March 18-22). *The United Nations*, Monterrey, Mexico. Retrieved from http://www.unmillenniumproject.org/documents/aconf198-11.pdf

Revenue Statistics. Organization for Economic Co-operation and Development. (2014). OECD. Retrieved from http://www.oecd.org/ctp/tax-policy/revenue-statistics-tax-structures.htm

Review, H. (2010). Australia's Future Tax System: Final Report to the Treasurer, Part One Overview, Commonwealth of Australia, Canberra. Retrieved from http://www.taxreview.treasury.gov.au/content/downloads/final_report_part_1/00_AFTS_final_report_consolidated.pdf

Ribeiro, M. (2014). E-fisco: The Conflict between Revenue Collection Efficiency and the Fundamental Right to Privacy: The Experience of Brazil. *Tax Administration Review*, *37*, 70–86.

Richardson, M., & Sawyer, A. (2001). A Taxonomy of Tax Compliance Literature: Further Findings, Problems and Prospects. *Australian Tax Forum, 16*(2), 137-320.

Risk Management Guide for Tax Administrations. (2006). *European Commission*. Retrieved from http://ec.europa.eu/taxation_customs/resources/documents/taxation/tax_cooperation/gen_overview/risk_management_guide_for_tax_administrations_en.pdf

Rixen, T. (2010). From double tax avoidance to tax competition: Explaining the institutional trajectory of international tax governance. *Review of International Political Economy*, 2010, 197–227. doi: doi:10.1080/09692290.2010.481921

Robinson, J. A., Torvik, R., & Verdier, T. (2006). Political foundations of the resource curse. *Journal of Development Economics*, *79*(2), 447–468. doi:10.1016/j.jdeveco.2006.01.008

Rocha, F., & Silva, E. (2004). Teoria fiscal do Nível de Preços: Um Teste Para a Economia Brasileira No Período 1966/2000. *Pesquisa e Planejamento Economico*, *34*(3), 419–435.

Rochjadi, A., & Leuthold, J. H. (1994). The Effect of Taxation on Labor Supply in a Developing Country: Evidence from Cross-Sectional Data. *Economic Development and Cultural Change*, *42*(2), 333–350. doi:10.1086/452083

Rodrik, D. (1990). Premature Liberalization and Incomplete Stabilization: The Özal Decade in Turkey. *NBER Working Paper Series* No. 3300. Massachusetts: National Bureau of Economic Research.

Rodrik, D. (1999, Winter). How Far Will International Economic Integration Go?. *Journal of Economic Perspectives*.

Rodrik, D. (1998). Why Do More Open Economies Have Bigger Governments? *Journal of Political Economy*, *106*(5), 997–1032. doi:10.1086/250038

Roger, S., & Vlček, J. (2011). Macroeconomic Costs of Higher Bank Capital and Liquidity Requirements. *IMF Working Paper, WP/11/103*. Retrieved from http://www.imf.org/external/pubs/ft/wp/2011/wp11103.pdf

Rogerson, R. (2007). Taxation and Market Work: Is Scandinavia an Outlier? *Economic Theory*, *32*(1), 59–85. doi:10.1007/s00199-006-0164-9

Roodman, D. (2009). How to Do xtabond2: An Introduction to "Difference" and "System" GMM in Stata. *The Stata Journal*, *9*(1), 86–136.

Rood, S. (2000). Decentralization, Democracy, and Development. In D. G. Timberman (Ed.), *The Philippines: New Directions in Domestic Policy and Foreign Relations* (pp. 11–135). New York: Asia Society.

Rosen, H. S., & Gayer, T. (2008). *Public Finance* (8th ed.). Singapore: McGraw-Hill. doi:10.1007/978-0-387-75870-1_22

Rosenweig, A.H. (2010). 52 *Wm. & Mary L. Rev. 923 2010-2011* (pp. 923- 996).

Rose, R., & Karran, T. (1987). *Taxation by Political Inertia*. London: Allen & Unwin.

Ross, A. M., & McGee, R. W. (2011). Attitudes toward Tax Evasion: A Demographic Study of Switzerland. *Business Studies Journal*, *3*(2), 1–47.

Rostow, W. W. (1960). *The stages of economic growth*. Cambridge: Cambridge University Press.

Rutkowski, J. J., & Scarpetta, S. (2005). *Enhancing Job Opportunities*. Washington, DC: The World Bank Group. doi:10.1596/978-0-8213-6195-5

Sabirianova Peter, K., Buttrick, S., & Duncan, D. (2010). Global reform of personal income taxation, 1981-2005: Evidence from 189 countries. *National Tax Journal*, *63*(3), 447–478. doi:10.17310/ntj.2010.3.03

Sachs, J. D., & Warner, A. M. (1995). Natural resource abundance and economic growth (Working Paper 5398). *NBER*.

Sachs, J. D., & Warner, A. M. 1997. Natural Resource Abundance and Economic Growth (Working Paper). *Center for International Development and Harvard Institute for International Development*, Harvard University.

Safadi, R. (Ed.). (2003). *MENA Trade & Investment in the New Economy: The Fourth Mediterranean Development Forum MDF4*. Cairo: The American University in Cairo Press.

Sahn, D. E., & Younger, S. D. (2003). Estimating the Incidence of Indirect Taxes in Developing Countries. In F. Bourguignon & L. A. P. DaSilva (Eds.), *The Impact of Economic Policies on Poverty and Income Distribution Evaluation Techniques and Tools*. Washington, D.C.: The World Bank and Oxford Press.

Sala-i-Martin, X., & Subramanian, A. (2003). Addressing the natural resource curse: an illustration from Nigeria (Working Paper 9804). *NBER*.

Sam, C. Y. (2010). Exploring the Link between Tax Evasion and the Underground Economy. *Pakistan Economic and Social Review*, *48*(2), 167–182.

Sancak, C., Velloso, R., & Xing, J. (2010, March). Tax Revenue Response to the Business Cycle. *IMF Working Paper No: 10/71*.

Sandford, C. T., Godwin, M., & Hardwick, P. (1989). *Administrative and Compliance Costs of Taxation*. Bath: Fiscal Publications.

Sandmo, A. (2003). Three Decades of Tax Evasion: A Perspective on the Literature. Paper Presented at the Skatteforum (The Research Forum on Taxation), Rosendal, Norway.

Sandmo, A. (2012). An evasive topic: Theorizing about the hidden economy. *International Tax and Public Finance*, *19*(1), 5–24. doi:10.1007/s10797-011-9185-9

Sargent, T. J., & Wallace, N. (1981). Some Unpleasant Monetarist Arithmetic. *Federal Reserve Bank of Minneapolis Quarterly Review*, *5*(3), 1–17.

Sausgruber, R., & Tyran, J. (2008, October). Tax Salience, Voting, and Deliberation (Discussion Paper No. 08-31). Department of Economics, University of Copenhagen.

Savaşan, F. (2006). Vergi Afları: Teori ve Türkiye Uygulamaları ("Vergi Barışı" Uygulama Sonuçları). *Afyon Kocatepe Üniversitesi İİBF Dergisi*, *8*(1), 41–65.

Sawyer, A. J. (2004). Is an International Tax Organisation an Appropriate Forum for Administering Binding Rulings and APAS? *eJournal of Tax Research, 2*(1), 8-70.

Schaffer, M. E. (2010). xtivreg2: Stata module to perform extended IV/2SLS, GMM and AC/HAC, LIML and k-class regression for panel data models. Retrieved from http://ideas.repec.org/c/boc/bocode/s456501.html

Schaltegger, C. A., & Torgler, B. (2007). Government Accountability and Fiscal Discipline: A Panel Analysis Using Swiss Data. *Journal of Public Economics*, *91*(1-2), 117–140. doi:10.1016/j.jpubeco.2006.07.003

Schansberg, D. E. (1998). The Ethics of Tax Evasion within Biblical Christianity: Are There Limits to "Rendering Unto Caesar"? Journal of Accounting, Ethics & Public Policy, 1(1), 77-90. Reprinted in R. W. McGee (Ed.) (1998), The Ethics of Tax Evasion (pp. 144-157). The Dumont Institute for Public Policy Research, Dumont, NJ.

Schmölders, G. (1959). Fiscal Psychology: A New Branch of Public Finance. *National Tax Journal*, *15*, 184–193.

Schmölders, G. (1960). *Das Irrationale in der öffentlichen Finanzwirtschaft*. Frankfurt am Main: Suhrkamp.

Schmölders, G. (1970). Survey Research in Public Finance: A Behavioural Approach to Fiscal Theory. *Public Finance*, *25*, 300–306.

Schneider, F. (2005). Shadow Economies of 145 Countries All Over the World: Estimation Results over the Period 1999 to 2003. Paper presented at the Annual Meeting of the European Public Choice Society, Durham, UK. Retrieved from http://www.businessenvironment.org/dyn/be/docs/48/Shadow%20Economy%20in%20145%20countries%201999-2003.pdf

Schneider, F. (2007, July) Shadow Economies and Corruption All Over the World: New Estimates for 145 Countries. *Economics*.

Schneider, F. (2012). The Shadow Economy and Work in the Shadow: What Do We (Not) Know? *IZA Discussion Paper*, No. 6423.

Schneider, F. (2013). *Shadow Economy, Tax Evasion and Corruption in Portugal and in Other OECD Countries: What Can Be Done?* Retrieved from www.nipe.eeg.uminho.pt/Uploads/ShadPortugal_2013_Schneider.pdf

Schneider, F. (2013). *Size and development of the shadow economy of 31 European and 5 other OECD countries from 2003 to 2013: A further decline* [Unpublished manuscript]. Johannes Kepler University of Linz, Department of Economics. Retrieved from http://www.econ.jku.at/members/schneider/files/publications/2013/shadeceurope31_jan2013.pdf

Schneider, F. (2014). The Shadow Economy and Shadow Labor Force: A Survey of Recent Developments. *Institute for the Study of Labor IZA Discussion Paper*, No. 8278.

Schneider, F., Buehn, A., & Montenegro, C. E. (2010, July). Shadow Economies All over the World: New Estimates for 162 Countries from 1999 to 2007. *World Bank Policy Research Working Paper No: 5356.*

Schneider, F. (1986). Estimating the Size of the Danish Shadow Economy Using the Currency Demand Approach: An Attempt. *The Scandinavian Journal of Economics*, *88*(4), 643–668. doi:10.2307/3440435

Schneider, F. (1997). The Shadow Economies of Western Europe. *Journal of the Institute of Economic Affairs*, *17*(3), 42–48. doi:10.1111/1468-0270.00041

Schneider, F. (2005). Shadow economies around the world: What do we really know? *European Journal of Political Economy*, *21*(3), 598–642. doi:10.1016/j.ejpoleco.2004.10.002

Schneider, F. (2014). In the shadow of the state-the informal economy and informal economy labor force. *Law and Economics Review*, *5*(4), 227–248. doi: 10.2478/danb-2014-0013

Schneider, F., Buehn, A., & Montenegro, C. E. (2010). New Estimates for the Shadow Economies All Over the World. *International Economic Journal*, *24*(4), 443–461.

Schneider, F., Buehn, A., & Montenegro, C. E. (2010). New estimates for the shadow economies all over the world. *International Economic Journal*, *24*(4), 443–461. doi:10.1080/10168737.2010.525974

Schneider, F., & Enste, D. (2000). Shadow Economies: Size, Causes, and Consequences. *Journal of Economic Literature*, *38*(1), 77–114. doi:10.1257/jel.38.1.77

Schneider, F., & Enste, D. H. (2002). *The Shadow Economy: An International Survey*. Cambridge: Cambridge University Press.

Schneider, F., & Williams, C. C. (2013). *The shadow economy*. London: Profile Books Ltd. doi:10.1017/CBO9781139542289

Schneider, M. (1989). Inter-municipal Competition, Budget-Maximizing Bureaucrats, and the Level of Suburban Competition. *American Journal of Political Science*, *33*(3), 612–628. doi:10.2307/2111065

Schultze, L. C. (1992). Is There a Bias Toward Excess in U.S. Government Budgets or Deficits? *The Journal of Economic Perspectives*, *6*(2), 25–43. doi:10.1257/jep.6.2.25

Schumpeter, J. A. [1918] (1954). The Crisis of the Tax State. In A. T. Peacock, W. F. Stolper, R. Turvey & E. Henderson (Eds.), International Economic Papers (pp. 5-38). New York: Macmillan.

Schuyler, M. (2014, January 13). *Baked In the Cake: Why the Progressivity of the Income Tax Isn't Visible in the Distribution of Tax Expenditures.* Tax Foundation. Retrieved May 29, 2015, from http://taxfoundation.org/article/baked-cake-why-progressivity-income-tax-isn-t-visible-distribution-tax-expenditures

Seater, J. J. (1982). Marginal Federal Personal and Cooperate Income Tax rates in the U.S., 1909 – 1975. *Journal of Monetary Economics*, *10*(3), 361–381. doi:10.1016/0304-3932(82)90033-2

SGI. (2009). *Economy and Employment: Taxes Report, Sustainable Governance Indicators 2009: Bertelsmann Stiftung.* Retrieved September 9, 2014, from http://www.sgi-network.org/pdf/SGI09_EconomyAndEmployment_Taxes.pdf

Shah, A. (2013). Tax Avoidance and Tax Havens; Undermining Democracy. *Global Issues*, January. Retrieved from http://www.globalissues.org/print/article/54

Shah, A. (2001). *Whalley.* The Redistributive Impact of Taxation in Developing Countries.

Sharman, J. C. (2012). Seeing Like the OECD on Tax. *New Political Economy*, *17*(1), 17–33. doi:10.1080/13563467.2011.569022

Sheffrin, S. M. (1993). What Does the Public Believe about Tax Fairness? *National Tax Journal*, *46*(3), 301–308.

Sheffrin, S. M. (2010). Fairness and Market Value Property Taxation. In *R. Bahl, J. Martinez-Vazquez, & J. M. Youngmand (Eds.), Challenging the Conventional Wisdom on the Property Tax* (pp. 241–262). Cambridge, Mass.: Lincoln Institute of Land Policy.

Shimer, R. (2009, January). Convergence in Macroeconomics: The Labor Wedge. *American Economic Journal. Macroeconomics*, *1*(1), 280–297. doi:10.1257/mac.1.1.280

Shirakawa, M. (2009, June 26). Some Thoughts on Incentives at Micro- and Macro-level for Crisis Prevention. *Remarks at the Eighth Bank of International Settlements Annual Conference*, Basel, Switzerland. Retrieved from http://www.bis.org/review/r090703a.pdf

Shleifer, A., & Vishny, R. W. (1993). Corruption. *The Quarterly Journal of Economics*, *108*(3), 599–617. doi:10.2307/2118402

Shoup, C. (1969). *Public finance*. Chicago: Aldine Publishing.

Sigala, M., Burgoyne, C. B., & Webley, P. (1999). Tax Communication and Social Influence: Evidence from a British Sample. *Journal of Community & Applied Social Psychology*, *9*(3), 237–241. doi:10.1002/(SICI)1099-1298(199905/06)9:3<237::AID-CASP516>3.0.CO;2-7

Silvani, C., & Baer, K. (1997). Designing a Tax Administration Reform: Experience and Guidelines. *IMF Working Paper*, Fiscal Affairs Department, WP/97/30. Washington DC: International Monetary Fund.

Simple, fair and pro-growth: proposals to fix America's tax system. (2005). President's Advisory Panel for Federal Tax Reform. Retrieved from http://govinfo.library.unt.edu/taxreformpanel/final-report/

Sims, C. (1997). *Fiscal Foundations of Price Stability in Open Economies, Mimeo*. Department of Economics, Princeton University.

Sims, C. A. (1994). A Simple Model for Study of the Determination of the Price Level and the Interaction of Monetary and Fiscal Policy. *Economic Theory*, *4*(3), 381–399. doi:10.1007/BF01215378

Sinn, S. (1992). The Taming of Leviathan: Competition Among Governments. *Constitutional Political Economy*, *3*(2), 177–195. doi:10.1007/BF02393119

Şiriner, İ. (2013). *Political Economy of Macroprudential Policies: Case of the Central Bank of the Republic of Turkey*. Torino: IRES Publication.

Slack, E. (2010). The Property Tax … in Theory and Practice. *IMFG Working Paper 02*. Institute on Municipal Finance and Governance Munk School of Global Affairs University of Toronto. Retrieved from http://www.munkschool.utoronto.ca/imfg/uploads/72/property_tax_paperwithlogos.pdf

Slemrod, J. (2003). Trust in public finance. In S. Crossen & H. W. Sinn (Eds.), *Public Finance and Public Policy in the New Century* (pp. 49–88). Cambridge: MIT Press.

Slemrod, J., & Gillitzer, C. (2014). *Tax systems*. Cambridge, MA: MIT Press. doi:10.7551/mitpress/9780262026727.001.0001

Slemrod, J., & Yitzhaki, S. (2002). Tax Avoidance, Evasion, and Administration. In A. Auerbach & M. Feldstein (Eds.), *Handbook of Public Economics* (Vol. 3). Elsevier Science.

Small states: meeting challenges in the global economy. (2000). *World Bank*, Washington, DC.

Smatrakalev, G. (1998). Walking on the Edge: Bulgaria and the Transition to a Market Economy. In R. W. McGee (Ed.), *The Ethics of Tax Evasion* (pp. 316–329). Dumont, NJ: The Dumont Institute for Public Policy Research.

Smatrakalev, G. (2012). Is Tax Evasion Our National Sport? The Bulgarian Case. In R. W. McGee (Ed.), *The Ethics of Tax Evasion: Perspectives in Theory and Practice* (pp. 371–385). New York: Springer. doi:10.1007/978-1-4614-1287-8_23

Smith, S. R., & Kimball, K. C. (1998). Tax Evasion and Ethics: A Perspective from Members of the Church of Jesus Christ of Latter-Day Saints. In R. W. McGee (Ed.), The Ethics of Tax Evasion (pp. 220-229). Dumont, NJ: The Dumont Institute for Public Policy Research.

Solow, R., & Wan, F. Y. (1976). Extraction Costs in the Theory of Exhaustible Resources. *The Bell Journal of Economics*, *7*(2), 359–370. doi:10.2307/3003261

Sossin, L. (1992a). Squeezing Blood from Stones: The Income Tax Industry in Canada. *Journal of Law and Social Policy*, *8*, 178–203.

Sossin, L. (1992b). Welfare State Crime: The Politics of Tax Evasion in the 1980s. *Windsor Yearbook of Access to Justice*, *12*, 98–127.

Spiro, P. S. (2005). Tax Policy and the Underground Economy. In C. Bajada & F. Schneider (Eds.), *Size, Causes and Consequences of the Underground Economy* (pp. 179–201). Aldershot, UK: Ashgate Publishing.

Srinivasan, T. N. (1973). Tax Evasion: A Model. *Journal of Public Economics*, *2*(4), 339–346. doi:10.1016/0047-2727(73)90024-8

Staff Report on Common Policies for Member Countries. (2012). *International Monetary Fund*. Retrieved from http://www.imf.org/external/pubs/ft/scr/2012/cr1259.pdf

Stein, E., Talvi, E., & Gristani, A. (1999). Institutional Arrangements and Fiscal Performance: The Latin American Experience. In J. M. Poterba & J. von Hagen (Eds.), *Fiscal Institutions and Fiscal Performance* (pp. 103–134). Chicago, IL: University of Chicago Press.

Steinmo, S. (2002, September). Globalization And Taxatıon Challenges to the Swedish Welfare State. *Comparative Political Studies*, *35*(7), 839–862. doi:10.1177/0010414002035007004

Stephenson, E. F. (1998). Average marginal tax Rates Revisited. *Journal of Monetary Economics*, *41*(2), 389–409. doi:10.1016/S0304-3932(97)00081-0

Stigler, G. J. (1957). The Tenable Range of Functions of Local Government. In US Congress Joint Economic Committee (Ed.), Federal Expenditure Policy for Economic Growth and Stability (pp. 213-219). Washington, DC: Government Printing Office.

Stigler, G. J., & Friedland, C. (1962). What Can Regulators Regulate? The Case of Electricity. *The Journal of Law & Economics*, *5*, 1–16. doi:10.1086/466579

Stiglitz, J. (2010). Government Failure vs. Market Failure: Principles of Regulation. In E. J. Balleisen & D. A. Moss (Eds.), Government and Markets, *Toward a New Theory of Regulation* (pp. 13-51). Cambridge: Cambridge University Press.

Stiglitz, J. (1974). Growth with Exhaustible Natural Resources: Efficient and Optimal Growth Paths. *The Review of Economic Studies*, *41*, 123–137. doi:10.2307/2296377

Stiglitz, J. E. (2012). *The Price of Inequality: How Today's Divided Society Endangers Our Future*. New York: W. W. Norton & Company.

Stockhammer, E. (2010). Neoliberalism, Income Distribution and the Causes of the Crisis. *Research on Money and Finance*, Discussion Paper no.19, June 2010

Stone, M. R., Roger, S., Nordstrom, A., Shimizu, S., Kisinbay, T., & Restrepo, J. (2009). The Role of the Exchange Rate in Inflation-Targeting Emerging Economies. *International Monetary Fund Occasional Paper No. 267.*

Stotsky, J. G., & WoldeMariam, A. (1997, September). Tax effort in Sub-Saharan Africa. *IMF Working Paper No: WP/97/107.*

Strümpel, B. (1969). The Contribution of Survey Research to Public Finance. In A. T. Peacock (Ed.), *Quantitative Analysis in Public Finance* (pp. 13–32). New York: Praeger.

Sturm, M., Gurtner, F., & Alegre, J.-G. (2009). Fiscal policy challenges in oil-exporting countries a review of key issues (Working Paper 104). *European Central Bank Occasional Paper Series.*

Surrey, S. S. (1977). The Concept of Tax Reliefs Its Relation to Tax Policy and Budget Policy. In *Subsidies, Tax Reliefs and Prices,Proceedings of 33rd Congress of IIPF*. Academic Press.

Surrey, S. S., & Sunley, E. M., Jr. (1976). General Report. In Tax Incentives as an Instrument for Achievement of Governmental Goals (Vol. LXla, pp. 15-63). Cahiers de Droit Fiscal International.

Surrey, S. (1969). Complexity and the Internal Revenue Code: The Problem of the Management of Tax Detail. *Law and Contemporary Problems*, *34*(4), 673–710. doi:10.2307/1190905

Surrey, S. S. (1958). Tax Administration in Underdeveloped Countries. *University of Miami Law Review*, *12*(2), 158–188.

Surrey, S. S. (1973). *Pathways to Tax Reform*. Cambridge, MA: Harvard University Press. doi:10.4159/harvard.9780674436503

Svensson, L. E. O. (2012). The Relation between Monetary Policy and Financial Stability Policy. *International Journal of Central Banking*, *8*(Suppl. 1), 293–295.

Swank, D. (1988). The Political Economy of Government Domestic Expenditure in the Affluent Democracies, 1960-1980. *American Journal of Political Science*, *32*(4), 1120–1150. doi:10.2307/2111203

Swank, D. (1998). Funding the Welfare State Revisited: Globalization and Taxation in Advanced Market Economies. *Political Studies*, *46*(4), 671–692. doi:10.1111/1467-9248.00161

Swank, D., & Steinmo, S. (2002). The New Political Economy of Taxation in Advanced Capitalist Democracies. *American Journal of Political Science*, *46*(3), 642–655. doi:10.2307/3088405

Swift, Z. L., Brixi, H. P., & Valenduc, C. (2004). Tax Expenditures: General Concept, Measurement, and Overview of Country Practices. In H. P. Brixi, C. M. A. Valenduc, & Z. L. Swift (Eds.), *Tax Expenditures – Shedding Light on Government Spending through the Tax System: Lessons from Developed and Transition Economies* (pp. 1–18). Washington, DC: The World Bank.

Tait, A. A., Grätz, W. L. M., & Eichengreen, B. J. (1979). International Comparisons of Taxation for Selected Developing Countries, 1972-76. *IMF Staff Papers*, *26*(1), 123–156. doi:10.2307/3866567

Talpoş, I., & Crâşneac, A. O. (2010).. . *The Effects of Tax Competition, Theoretical and Applied Economics Volume XVII, No.*, *8*(549), 39–52.

Talvi, E., & Vegh, C. (2000). Tax base variability and procyclical fiscal policy. *NBER Working Paper* # 7499.

Tamari, M. (1998). Ethical Issues in Tax Evasion: A Jewish Perspective. In R. W. McGee (Ed.), The Ethics of Tax Evasion (pp. 168-178). Dumont, NJ: The Dumont Institute for Public Policy Research.

Tankard, M. E., & Paluck, E. L. (2015). Norm Perception as a Vehicle for Social Change. Princeton University January, *Social Issues and Policy Review (in press)*. Retrieved from http://static1.squarespace.com/static/5186d08fe4b065e39b45b91e/t/550a18b8e4b0d34e8f584d3d/1426725048339/Tankard_Paluck_2015_SIPR.pdf

Tanner, E., & Ramos, A. (2002). Fiscal Sustainability and Monetary and Versus Fiscal Dominance: Evidence from Brazil, 1999-2000. *IMF Working Paper* WP/ 02/5.

Tanzi, V. (1972, Summer). *Fiscal Reform in Colombia: The Report of the Musgrave Mission*. Inter-American Economic Affairs.

Tanzi, V. (1983). The Underground Economy in United States: Annual Estimates. 1930-1980. *Staff Papers-International Monetary Fund, 30*(2).

Tanzi, V. (1996). Globalization, Tax Competition and the Future of Tax Systems. *IMF Working* Paper No. 96/141. Retrieved from http://papers.ssrn.com/sol3/papers.cfm?abstract_id=883038

Tanzi, V. (1996). Taxation in an Integrating World. Washington, DC: Brookings.

Tanzi, V. (1998). Corruption around the World: Causes, Consequences, Scope, and Cures. *International Monetary Fund (IMF) Working Paper 63.*

Tanzi, V. (2000, November 20-21). On Fiscal Federalism: Issues to Worry About. *Paper presented in the Conference of Fiscal Decentralization*, Washington, DC: IMF Headquarters.

Tanzi, V., & Davoodi, H. (1997). Corruption, Public Investment, and Growth. *International Monetary Fund (IMF) Working Paper 139.*

Tanzi, V., & Davoodi, H. R. (2000). Corruption, Growth and Public Finances. *IMF Working Paper* WP/00/182.

Tanzi, V. (1970). International Tax Burdens: A Study of Tax Ratios in the OECD Countries. In *Taxation: A Radical Approach*. London: Institute for Economic Affairs.

Tanzi, V. (1974). Redistributing Income through the Budget in Latin America. *Quarterly Review. Indexes - Banca Nazionale del Lavoro*, *27*(108), 65–87.

Tanzi, V. (1978). Inflation, Real Tax Revenue, and the Case for Inflationary Finance: Theory with an Application to Argentina. *IMF Staff Papers*, *25*(3), 417–451. doi:10.2307/3866679

Tanzi, V. (1980). The Underground Economy in the United States: Estimations and Implications. *Quarterly Review. Indexes - Banca Nazionale del Lavoro*, *135*(4), 427–453.

Tanzi, V. (1987). Quantitative Characteristics of the Tax Systems of Developing Countries. In D. Newberry & N. H. Stern (Eds.), *The Theory of Taxation for Developing Countries* (pp. 205–241). New York: Oxford University Press for the World Bank.

Tanzi, V. (1992). Structural Factors and Tax Revenue in Developing Countries: A Decade of Evidence. In I. Goldin & L. A. Winters (Eds.), *Open Economies: Structural Adjustment and Agriculture* (pp. 267–281). Cambridge: Cambridge University Press. doi:10.1017/CBO9780511628559.023

Tanzi, V. (2008). The Role of the State and Public Finance in the Next Generation. *OECD Journal for Budgeting*, *8*(2), 1–27. doi:10.1787/budget-v8-art6-en

Tanzi, V. (2014). Globalization and Taxation: A Brief Historical Survey. *Rivista di Diritto Finanziario e Scienza delle Finanze*, *73*(1), 3–20.

Tanzi, V. (2015). Public Finance in Developing Countries: An Introduction. In M. M. Erdoğdu & B. Christiansen (Eds.), *Handbook of Research on Public Finance in Europe and the MENA Region*. Hershey, PA, USA: IGI Global.

Tanzi, V. (2016). Public Finance in Developing Countries: An Introduction. In M. M. Erdoğdu & B. Christiansen (Eds.), *Handbook of Research on Public Finance Perspectives on Europe and the MENA Region*. Hershey, PA: IGI Global.

Tanzi, V., & Davoodi, H. (1997). *Corruption, Public Investment, and Growth*. Washington, DC: IMF.

TARC. (2014, June). *The Definition, Measurement, and Evaluation of Tax Expenditures and Tax Reliefs*. Technical Paper Prepared for the National Audit Office, Tax Administration Research Centre. Retrieved July 30, 2015, from http://www.nao.org.uk/wp-content/uploads/2014/03/TARC-Tax-Expenditures-and-tax-reliefs-technical-paper.pdf

Tax Incentives for Investment: A Global Perspective Experiences in MENA and Non-MENA Countries. (2008). In *Making Reforms Succeed: Moving Forward with the MENA Investment Policy Agenda*OECD. Paris: OECD Publishing. Doi: doi:10.1787/9789264052826-11-en

Taylor, J. B., & Woodford, M. (Eds.), (1999). Handbook of Macroeconomics. Elsevier: Amsterdam.

TEDAŞ. (2014). Dağıtım Şirketleri. Retrieved from http://www.tedas.gov.tr/Sirketler/Sayfalar/Anasayfa.aspx

TEİAŞ. (2012). *Elektrik İstatistikleri 2012*.

Tekin-Koru, A., & Özmen, E. (2003). Budget Deficits, Money Growth and Inflation: The Turkish Evidence. *Applied Economics*, *35*(5), 591–596. doi:10.1080/0003684022000025440

Teobaldelli, D. (2011). Federalism and the shadow economy. *Public Choice*, *146*(3-4), 269–289. doi:10.1007/s11127-009-9590-0

Ter-Minassian, T. (2007). Fiscal Rules for Subnational Governments: Can They Promote Fiscal Discipline? *OECD Journal on Budgeting*, *6*(3), 1-12. Retrieved May 27, 2015, from http://www.oecd.org/gov/budgeting/43469443.pdf

Ter-Minassian, T. (2009). *Challenges in Tax Reform for Turkey, in an International Perspective*. The Ministry of Finance-UNDP Seminar on Tax Policy Options on the Way to EU Accession, Ankara, Turkey.

Ter-Minassian, T., & Craig, J. (1997). Control of Subnational Government Borrowing. In T. Ter-Minassian (Ed.), *Fiscal Federalism in Theory and Practice* (pp. 156–172). Washington, DC: IMF.

The Action Plan of Struggling Against Shadow Economy. (2011). *The Republic of Turkey Ministry of Finance,* Ankara. Retrieved from http://www.gib.gov.tr/index.php?id=1366

The EuroMed Partnership. (2014). EuroMed. Retrieved from http://www.enpi-info.eu/medportal/content/340/About%20 the%20EuroMed%20Partnership

The Financial Statement for the Government Budget Plan for the year 2014-2015. (2014). The Ministry of Finance.

The Global Forum on Transparency and Exchange of Information for Tax Purposes. (2011, December 15). *Information Brief, OECD.*

The Interaction of Monetary and Macroprudential Policies: Executive Summary. (2013, January). *International Monetary Fund.* Retrieved from http://www.imf.org/external/np/pp/eng/2013/012913.pdf

The Interaction of Monetary and Macroprudential Policies-Background Paper. (2012, December). *IMF.* Washington: International Monetary Fund. Retrieved from http://www.imf.org/external/np/pp/eng/2013/012713.pdf

The World Bank Group, & PricewaterhouseCoopers (2013). *Paying Taxes 2014: The Global Picture: A Comparison of Tax Systems in 189 Economies Worldwide.* Retrieved from http://www.pwc.com/gx/en/paying-taxes/assets/pwc-paying-taxes-2014.pdf

The World Bank. (2005). *World Development Report.* Washington, D.C.: The World Bank.

Thirsk, W. (1991). Jamaican Tax Incentives. In R. Bahl (Ed.), *The Jamaican Tax Reform* (pp. 701–725). Cambridge, MA: Lincoln Institute of Land Policy.

Thomas, A., & Treviño, J. (2013). Resource dependence and fiscal effort in Sub-Saharan Africa (Working Paper 13/188). *International Monetary Fund.*

Thornton, J. (2008). Explaining Procyclical Fiscal Policy in African Countries. *Journal of African Economies, 17*(93), 451–464.

Tiebout, C. (1956). A Pure Theory of Local Expenditure. *Journal of Political Economy, 64*(5), 416–424. doi:10.1086/257839

Timofeev, A., & Wallace, S. (2013, October 4). Tax Incidence Report: Jordan, Jordan Fiscal Reform II, DAI, Inc. /USAID Washington, D.C. Retrieved from http://frp2.org/English/Portals/0/PDFs/Technical%20Reports/Tax%20Incidence%20 Report.pdf

Timofeev, A., & Wallace, S. (2016). The Incidence of Taxes in Jordan. In M. M. Erdoğdu & B. Christiansen (Eds.), Handbook of Research on Public Finance in Europe and the MENA Region. Hershey, PA: IGI Global.

Toder, E., & Baneman, D. (2012). *Distributional Effects of Individual Income Tax Expenditures: An Update. Urban-Brookings Tax Policy Center.* Paper presented at the National Tax Association Meetings, New Orleans, LA. Retrieved July 20, 2014, from http://www.taxpolicycenter.org/UploadedPDF/412495-Distribution-of-Tax-Expenditures.pdf

Toker, Ç. (2014) Torba Kamulaştırma Dönemi. *Cumhuriyet.* Retrieved from http://www.cumhuriyet.com.tr/koseya-zisi/139637/Torba_Kamulastirma_Donemi.html

Torgler, B., & Schneider, F. (2007). The Impact of Tax Morale and Institutional Quality on the Shadow Economy. *IZA discussion paper* n. 2541. Retrieved from http://ftp.iza.org/dp2541.pdf

Torgler, B., & Schneider, F. (2007a). The Impact of Tax Morale and Institutional Quality on the Shadow Economy, *CESIFO Working Paper*, No. 1899.

Torgler, B., & Schneider, F. (2007b). Shadow Economy, Tax Morale, Governance and Institutional Quality: A Panel Analysis, *Department of Economics, Johannes Kepler University, Economic Working Paper Series*, No.1.

Torgler, B. (2001). Is Tax Evasion Never Justifiable? *Journal of Public Finance and Public Choice*, *19*, 143–168.

Torgler, B. (2003a). Tax Morale, Rule-Governed Behaviour and Trust. *Constitutional Political Economy*, *14*(2), 119–140. doi:10.1023/A:1023643622283

Torgler, B. (2003b). To Evade Taxes or Not to Evade: That Is the Question. *Journal of Socio-Economics*, *32*(3), 283–302. doi:10.1016/S1053-5357(03)00040-4

Torgler, B. (2005). Tax Morale and Direct Democracy. *European Journal of Political Economy*, *21*(2), 525–531. doi:10.1016/j.ejpoleco.2004.08.002

Torgler, B. (2007). *Tax Compliance and Tax Morale: A Theoretical and Empirical Analysis*. Cheltenham, UK: Edward Elgar. doi:10.4337/9781847207203

Torgler, B. (2010). Serious Tax noncompliance: Motivation and Guardianship. *Criminology & Public Policy*, *9*(3), 535–542. doi:10.1111/j.1745-9133.2010.00648.x

Torgler, B., Schneider, F., & Schaltegger, C. A. (2010). Local autonomy, tax morale, and the shadow economy. *Public Choice*, *144*(1-2), 293–321. doi:10.1007/s11127-009-9520-1

Torre, A., Ize, A., & Schmukler, S. L. (2012). Financial Development in Latin America and the Caribbean: The Road Ahead. *World Bank Publications*. Retrieved from http://siteresources.worldbank.org/LACINSPANISHEXT/Resources/FLAGSHIP_eng.pdf

Torvik, R. (2002). Natural resources, rent seeking and welfare. *Journal of Development Economics*, *67*(2), 455–470. doi:10.1016/S0304-3878(01)00195-X

Tosun, M. S. (2006). Explaining the variation in tax structures in the MENA region (Working Paper 06-0018). *University of Nevada Economics Working Paper Series*.

Tosun, M. S. (2010). *Middle East and Western Asia. In United Cities and Local Governments (UCLG) Second Global Report on Decentralization and Local Democracy - Local Government Finance: The Challenges of the 21st Century* (pp. 233–253). Northampton, MA: Edward Elgar Publishing.

Tosun, M. S., & Yılmaz, S. (2010). Decentralization, Economic Development, and Growth in Turkish Provinces. *Emerging Markets Finance and Trade*, *46*(4), 23–44. doi:10.2753/REE1540-496X460405

Towards Global Tax Cooperation: Progress in Identifying and Eliminating Harmful Tax Practices. (2000OECD. Paris: OECD.

Traxler, C., & Winter, J. (2012). Survey Evidence on Conditional Norm Enforcement. *European Journal of Political Economy*, *28*(3), 390–398. doi:10.1016/j.ejpoleco.2012.03.001

Trivedi, V. U., Shehata, M., & Mestelman, S. (2005). Attitudes, Incentives, and Tax Compliance. *Canadian Tax Journal*, *53*(1), 29–61.

Tucker P. (2011, February 28). National Balance Sheets and Macro Policy: Lessons from the Past. *Speech by the Deputy Governor of the Bank of England at the Society of Business Economists' Annual Dinner*, London.

Türkiye Elektrik Dağıtım Sektörü Özelleştirmesi. (2010). Republic of Turkey Prime Ministry Privatization Administration. Retrieved from http://www.oib.gov.tr/2010/dosyalar/TEDAS%20Teaser%20T%C3%BCrk%C3%A7e%20v05-comments%20removed.pdf

Türkiye Elektrik Enerjisi 10 Yıllık Üretim Kapasite Projeksiyonu (2012 – 2021). (2012). EPDK. Retrieved from http://www.epdk.org.tr/documents/elektrik/rapor_yayin/Elk_Yayin_Uretim_Kapasite_Projeksiyonu_2012_2021.pdf

TURKSTAT. (2014). *Labour Force Statistics Database 2014*. Retrieved from http://tuikapp.tuik.gov.tr/medas/?kn=72&locale=tr

U.S. Joint Committee on Taxation. (2011, February 28). *Background Information on Tax Expenditure Analysis and Historical Survey of Tax Expenditure Estimates* (JCX-15-11). Retrieved August 13, 2014, from https://www.jct.gov/publications.html?func=startdown&id=3740

U.S. Joint Committee on Taxation. (2013, February 1). *Estimates of Federal Tax Expenditures for Fiscal Years 2012-2017*. Retrieved August 13, 2014, from https://www.jct.gov/publications.html?func=startdown&id=4503

UN. (2001, September 10-14). Transfer Pricing, History C C State of the Art C Perspectives. *Ad Hoc Group of Experts on International Cooperation in Tax Matters Tenth meeting Geneva.*

UN. (2003a, December 15-19). The interaction of tax, trade and investment, Ad Hoc Group of Experts on International. Cooperation in Tax Matters Eleventh meeting Geneva

UN. (2003b). *Manual for the Negotiation of Bilateral Tax Treaties between Developed and Developing Countries.*

UNCTAD. (2014). *World Investment Report 2014*. United Nation Publication.

UNDP. (2013, January 28). *Jordan Poverty Reduction Strategy – Final Report*. Retrieved from http://www.undp.org/content/dam/jordan/docs/Poverty/Jordanpovertyreductionstrategy.pdf

United Nations Development Programme. (2013). *Human Development Report 2013. The Rise of the South: Human Progress in a Diverse World. Explanatory Note on 2013 HDR Composite Indices.* Retrieved from http://hdr.undp.org/sites/default/files/Country-Profiles/IND.pdf

United Nations. (2009, October 19-23). Note by the Secretariat: Proposed Code of Conduct on Cooperation in Combating International Tax Evasion. *Committee of Experts on International Cooperation in Tax Matters, fifth session*, Geneva.

US Joint Committee on Taxation. (2014, August 5). *Estimates of Federal Tax Expenditures for Fiscal Years 2014-2018.* Retrieved December 12, 2014, from https://www.jct.gov/publications.html?func=startdown&id=4663

USA Department of Treasury (2000). The Deferral of Income Earned Through U.S. Controlled Foreign Corporations.

Vaguine, V. V. (1998). The "Shadow Economy" and Tax Evasion in Russia. In R. W. McGee (Ed.), *The Ethics of Tax Evasion* (pp. 306–314). Dumont, NJ: The Dumont Institute for Public Policy Research.

Valenduc, C. (2004). From Tax Expenditure Reporting to Tax Policy Analysis: Some Experience from Belgium. In H. P. Brixi, C. M. A. Valenduc, & Z. L. Swift (Eds.), *Tax Expenditures – Shedding Light on Government Spending through the Tax System: Lessons from Developed and Transition Economies* (pp. 69–96). Washington, DC: The World Bank.

Van Brederode, R. (Ed.). (2012). *Science, Technology and Taxation*. Kluwer Law International.

Vazquez-Caro, J., & Bird, R. (2011). Benchmarking Tax Administrations in Developing Countries: A Systemic Approach. *eJournal of Tax Research, 9*(1), 5-37.

VDK. (2014). *Vergi Denetim Kurulu Başkanlığı Faaliyet Raporu 2014*. Ankara: Vergi Denetim Kurulu Başkanlığı.

Velasquez, M., Andre, C., Shanks, T. S. J., & Meyer, M. J. (1990). Justice and Fairness. *Issues in Ethics*, 3(2). Retrieved from http://www.scu.edu/ethics/practicing/decision/justice.html

Verboon, P., & Goslinga, S. (2009). The role of fairness in tax compliance. *Netherlands Journal of Psychology*, *65*(4), 136–145. doi:10.1007/BF03080136

Vlachaki, M. (2015). The impact of the shadow economy on indirect tax revenues. *Economics and Politics*, *27*(2), 234–265. doi:10.1111/ecpo.12054

von Mises, L. (1966). *Human Action: A Treatise on Economics* (*3rd* Revised ed.). Washington, DC: Henry Regnery Company.

Wadhawan, S. C., & Gray, C. (1998). Enhancing Transparency in Tax Administration: A Survey. *EAGER Discussion Paper*, No. 5. Retrieved from http://pdf.usaid.gov/pdf_docs/pnadw512.pdf

Wahid, U., & Wallace, S. (2008). The Incidence of Taxes in Pakistan: Primer and Estimates (International Studies Program Working Paper). *Andrew Young School of Policy Studies*, Georgia State University, Atlanta, GA.

Wahl, I., Kastlunger, B., & Kirchler, E. (2010). Trust in Authorities and Power to Enforce Tax Compliance: An Empirical Analysis of the "Slippery Slope Framework." *Law & Policy*, *32*(4), 383–406. doi:10.1111/j.1467-9930.2010.00327.x

Wall, H. J. (2009). Journal Rankings in Economics: "Handle with Care, Federal Reserve Bank of St. Louis", April, Working Paper 2009-014A. Retrieved from. http://research.stlouisfed.org/wp/2009/2009-014.pdf

Wallace, S. (2007). Tax Incidence. Encyclopedia of Social Sciences.

Wallace, S., Wang, D., & Xu, Y. (2006). On the Equivalence of an Ad Valorem Tax (International Studies Program Working Paper). *Andrew Young School of Policy Studies*, Georgia State University, Atlanta, GA.

Walsh, C. E. (2009). Inflation Targeting: What Have We Learned. *International Finance*, *12*(2), 195–233. doi:10.1111/j.1468-2362.2009.01236.x

Warde, I. (2007). The war on terror, crime and the shadow economy in the MENA countries. *Mediterranean Politics*, *12*(2), 233–248. doi:10.1080/13629390701398033

Webber, C., & Wildavsky, A. (1983). *History of Taxation and Expenditure in the Western World.* New York: Simon and Schuster.

Webley, P. (2004). Tax Compliance by Businesses. In H. Sjögren & G. Skogh (Eds.), *New Perspectives on Economic Crime* (pp. 95–126). Cheltenham: Edward Elgar. doi:10.4337/9781843769835.00012

Webley, P., Cole, M., & Eidjar, O.-P. (2001). The Prediction of Self-Reported and Hypothetical Tax-Evasion: Evidence from England, France and Norway. *Journal of Economic Psychology*, *22*(2), 141–155. doi:10.1016/S0167-4870(01)00026-5

Wenzel, M. (2003). Tax Compliance and the Psychology of Justice: Mapping the Field. In V. Braithwaite (Ed.), *Taxing Democracy. Understanding Tax Avoidance and Tax Evasion* (pp. 41–69). Aldershot: Ashgate.

Wenzel, M. (2005). Motivation or Rationalisation? Causal Relations between Ethics, Norms and Tax Compliance. *Journal of Economic Psychology*, *26*(4), 491–508. doi:10.1016/j.joep.2004.03.003

West, E. G. (1991). Secular cost changes and the size of government: Towards a Generalized Theory. *Journal of Public Economics*, *45*(3), 363–381. doi:10.1016/0047-2727(91)90032-W

WGI - WB (World Governance Indicators - World Bank). (2014). Retrieved from http://info.worldbank.org/governance/wgi/index.aspx#home

Whistleblower Office First Report to Congress. (2008). *Internal Revenue Service*. Retrieved from http://www.irs.gov/uac/Whistleblower-Office-Annual-Reports

Whistleblowing in Europe: Legal Protections for Whistleblowers in the EU. (2013). Transparency International. Retrieved from http://www.transparency.org/whatwedo/pub/whistleblowing_in_europe_legal_protections_for_whistleblowers_in_the_eu

Wibless, E., & Arce, M. (2003, Winter). Globalization, Taxation, and Burden-Shifting in Latin America. *International Organization*, *57*(1), 111–136.

Wildasin, D. E. (1989). Inter-jurisdictional Capital Mobility: Fiscal Externality and a Corrective Subsidy. *Journal of Urban Economics*, *25*(2), 193–212. doi:10.1016/0094-1190(89)90034-X

Williams, J. H., & Ghanadan, R. (2006). Electricity reform in developing and transition countries: A reappraisal. *Energy*, *31*(6–7), 815–844. doi:10.1016/j.energy.2005.02.008

Wilson, J. D. (1986). A Theory of Interregional Tax Competition. *Journal of Urban Economics*, *19*(3), 356–370. doi:10.1016/0094-1190(86)90045-8

Wilson, J. D. (1999). Theories of Tax Competition. *National Tax Journal*, *52*(2), 269–304.

Woodford, M. (2010). Financial Intermediation and Macroeconomic Analysis. The Journal of Economic Perspectives, 24(4), 21–44. doi:10.1257/jep.24.4.21 doi:10.1257/jep.24.4.21

Woodford, M. (1994). Monetary Policy and Price Level Determinacy in a Cash-In-Advance Economy. *Economic Theory*, *4*(3), 345–380. doi:10.1007/BF01215377

Woodford, M. (1995). Price Level Determinacy Without Control of a Monetary Aggregate. *Carnegie-Rochester Conference Series on Public Policy*, *43*(Dec), 1–46. doi:10.1016/0167-2231(95)90033-0

Woodford, M. (1998). Doing Without Money: Controlling Inflation in a Post-Monetary World. *Review of Economic Dynamics*, *1*(1), 173–219. doi:10.1006/redy.1997.0006

Woodford, M. (2001). Fiscal Requirement for Price Stability. *Journal of Money, Credit and Banking*, *33*(3), 669–728. doi:10.2307/2673890

World Bank Doing Business Database. (2011).

World Bank. (2013). *World Governance Indicators*. Retrieved from http://data.worldbank.org/data-catalog/world-governance-indicators

World Bank. (2014). *World Development Indicators*. Retrieved from http://data.worldbank.org/data-catalog/world-development-indicators

World Bank. (2014, May 20). Turkey in Transition: Time for a Fiscal Policy Pivot? Report No. 85104-TR. *Turkey Public Finance Review*, Poverty Reduction and Economic Management Unit Europe and Central Asia Region. Retrieved from http://www.worldbank.org/content/dam/Worldbank/Feature%20Story/ECA/Turkey/turkey-pfr-report-21-may-2014.pdf

World Bank. (2014, May 20). Turkey in Transition: Time for a Fiscal Policy Pivot? Report No. 85104-TR. *Turkey Public Finance Review*. Retrieved November 11, 2014, from http://www.worldbank.org/content/dam/Worldbank/Feature%20Story/ECA/Turkey/turkey-pfr-report-21-may-2014.pdf

World Development Indicators Data Bank. (2014). International Bank for Reconstruction and Development-International Development Association World Bank. Retrieved from http://data.worldbank.org/indicator/MS.MIL.XPND.GD.ZS

World Development Indicators. (2014World Bank. Washington, DC: The World Bank Group.

World Development Report 1997: The State in Changing World. (1997World Bank. Washington, DC: The World Bank Group.

World Development Report 1999/2000: Entering the 21st Century. (1999World Bank. New York: Oxford University Press.

Yackley, A.J. (2009, September 8). UPDATE 3-Turkey Gov't Hits Media Group Dogan with Tax Fine. *Reuters*. Retrieved from http://uk.reuters.com/article/2009/09/08/turkey-dogan-idUKL815352620090908

Yaraşır, S. (2013). Vergi Afları ve Türkiye'deki Vergi Aflarının Değerlendirilmesi. *Vergi Dünyası*, *379*, 175–187.

Yavaşlar, F. B. (2008). Türk Vergi Hukuku'nda Uzlaşma. *Marmara Üniversitesi İ.İ.B.F. Dergisi*, *25*(2), 309–337.

Yeldan, E. (2001). *Küreselleşme Sürecinde Türkiye Ekonomisi: Bölüşüm, Birikim ve Büyüme*. İstanbul: Iletişim Yayınları.

Yi-Chong, X. (2006). The Myth of the Single Solution: Electricity Reforms. *World Bank Energy* (31), 802-814.

Yitzhaki, S. (1974). A Note on Income Tax Evasion: A Theoretical Analysis. *Journal of Public Economics*, *3*(2), 201–202. doi:10.1016/0047-2727(74)90037-1

Younger, S. D. (1996). Estimating Tax Incidence in Ghana: An Exercise Using Household Data. In D. E. Sahn (Ed.), *Economic Reform and the Poor in Africa*. Oxford: Clarendon Press.

Younger, S. D. (1999). The Relative Progressivity of Social Services in Ecuador. *Public Finance Review*, *27*(3), 310–352. doi:10.1177/109114219902700304

Younger, S. D., Sahn, D. E., Haggblade, S., & Dorosh, P. A. (1999). Tax Incidence in Madagascar: An Analysis Using Household Data. *The World Bank Economic Review*, *13*(2), 303–331. doi:10.1093/wber/13.2.303

Yusuf, S. M. (1971). *Economic Justice in Islam*. Lahore: Sh. Muhammad Ashraf.

Zaklan, G., Lima, F. W. S., & Westerhoff, F. (2008). Controlling Tax Evasion Fluctuations. *Physica A. Statistical Mechanics and Its Applications*, *387*(23), 5857–5861. doi:10.1016/j.physa.2008.06.036

Zaklan, G., Westerhoff, F., & Stauffer, D. (2009). Analysing Tax Evasion Dynamics via the Ising Model. *Journal of Economic Interaction and Coordination*, *4*(1), 1–14. doi:10.1007/s11403-008-0043-5

Zax, S. J. (1989). Is There a Leviathan in Your Neighborhood? *The American Economic Review*, *79*(3), 560–567.

Zhang, Y., Parker, F., & Kirkpatrick, C. (2008). Electricity Sector Reform in Developing Countries: An Econometric Assessment of the Effects of Privatization, Competition and Regulation. *Journal of Regulatory Economics*, *33*(2), 159–178. doi:10.1007/s11149-007-9039-7

Zivot, E., & Andrews, D. W. K. (1992). Further Evidence on the Great Crash, the Oil-Price Shock, and the Unit-Root Hypothesis. *Journal of Business & Economic Statistics*, *10*(3), 251–270.

Zodrow, R. G., & Mieszkowski, P. (1986). Pigou, Tiebout, Property Taxation, and the Under-provision of Local Public Goods. *Journal of Urban Economics*, *19*(3), 356–370. doi:10.1016/0094-1190(86)90048-3

Zodrow, R. G., & Mieszkowski, P. (1989). Taxation and Tiebout Model: The Differential Effects of Head Taxes, Taxes on Land Rents, and Property Taxes. *Journal of Economic Literature*, *17*(September), 356–370.

Zoli, E. (2005, April). How Does Fiscal Policy Affect Monetary Policy in Emerging Market Countries? *Bank of International Settlements Working Papers*, No. 174.

About the Contributors

M. Mustafa Erdoğdu is a professor of economics at Marmara University in Istanbul, Turkey, where he is the head of Financial Economics. He received his MA and PhD in developmental economics from Manchester University, UK. He is an associate editor of the International Journal of Applied Behavioral Economics and the International Journal of Productivity Management and Assessment Technologies, an international advisory board member of the International Journal of Sustainable Economies Management, and an editorial board member of several other journals including the Turkish Studies Journal. He has published articles on a wide range of issues, a book on social budgets, and has co-edited several books on economic development and public finance. His major research areas are international political economy and development, sustainable development, renewable energies, global commons and public goods, behavioral public finance, tax compliance, developmental states, industrial policy, technological capability building, employment policy, and financial crises.

Bryan Christiansen Since 2004, Bryan Christiansen has progressively held the positions of President, CEO, and then Chairman in PryMarke, LLC, a Michigan, USA-based Business Analytics and Management Consultancy. Bryan has also been an Adjunct Business Professor at Capella University, DeVry University, and Ellis University (formerly Ellis College of New York Institute of Technology) in the USA, and a Senior Business Lecturer at Gumushane University in Turkey. Born in Washington, DC and raised in Asia, Bryan is fluent in Chinese, Japanese, Spanish, and Turkish, and has traveled to 40 countries during his 28-year business career involving Global 1000 firms. Bryan holds a Bachelor's degree in Marketing from the University of the State of New York and an MBA degree from Capella University. Bryan will complete his Doctor of Business Administration degree (DBA) from Middlesex University in London, England in 2020.

***

Hale Akbulut is the post-doctoral research assistant in the Department of Public Finance at Hacettepe University, Turkey. She received her B.S. degree (2006) in Economics from Hacettepe University. And, she received her M.S. degree (2009) in Economics from Hacettepe University. She received her Ph.D. degree (2013) in Public Finance from Hacettepe University. She has been the TUBITAK (The Scientific and Technological Research Council of Turkey) scholar in the Department of Economics, Faculty of Business, Economics and Statistics at the University of Vienna, Austria. Her research interest include public economics, public finance, fiscal policies, development and economic growth. She has published in national and international journals.

James Alm is a Professor and Chair of the Department of Economics at Tulane University. Previously, he was Regents Professor in the Department of Economics at the Andrew Young School of Policy Studies at Georgia State University in Atlanta, Georgia, where he served as Chair of the Department and Dean of the School. He has also taught at Syracuse University and at the University of Colorado at Boulder. He earned his master's degree in economics at the University of Chicago and his doctorate at the University of Wisconsin-Madison. His teaching and research are in the area of public economics. He has also worked extensively on fiscal and decentralization reforms overseas. He is currently the Editor of the Public Finance Review, and is on the editorial board of several other economics journals.

Murat Aydın, Ph.D, is an Associate Professor at the Department of Economics in Biga Faculty of Economics and Administrative Sciences of Canakkale Onsekiz Mart University, Turkey. Previously, he worked for Economics and Administrative Faculty of Kocaeli University. He completed his BA and MA degrees in Anadolu University in Turkey. He got his PhD degree in finance from Marmara University. He gives lectures at bachelor's degree and graduate studies degrees. His subject field is financial economics. His research activities are focused on economic crises, externality, tax policy, income distribution and poverty. He has written articles, papers and a book about his subject fields. He has also contributed to inter-disciplinary studies particularly social politics.

Ömer Faruk Batırel is a Professor of Public Finance born in Gaziantep in 1944. Batırel graduated from the İstanbul Academy of Economics & Administrative Sciences (currently Marmara University) in 1967. He joined the faculty staff in 1970 and received all degrees (Ph. D, associate & full professorship) in the field of Public Finance at the same institution. He completed his post-doctoral studies at University of York, U.K. (1973-1974). He served as Dean and President of Marmara University, a member of the Higher Education Council and after retirement in 2007, became a faculty member of the İstanbul Commerce University. He has, since then, taught public finance and tax law courses. Batırel participated in several tax reform groups and has published numerous books and articles in the field of public finance, public economics, tax systems, tax law and governmental budgeting. He is a member of the International Institute of Public Finance since 1974. He currently serves as a faculty member of the Istanbul Ticaret University.

Ioan Batrancea is currently a Professor of Finance at the Babes-Bolyai University, Cluj-Napoca, Romania, where he has been an academic since 1979. He received his Ph.D. in political economy from Babes-Bolyai University in 1992 and completed advanced programs in economics at the University of Oslo (Norway - 1991), in management at the Wharton School, University of Pennsylvania (Philadelphia, USA - 1993) and in marketing at Kellogg School of Management, Northwestern University (Chicago, USA - 1993). In 2000, he became the chair of economic and financial analysis at the Babes-Bolyai University. He benefited from 11 international and national research grants financed by the World Bank, the Romanian government and various Romanian companies, either as principal investigator or as a member. He has published 48 books and course handbooks as well as around 150 scientific articles on the topics of economic and financial analysis, financial and managerial accounting, auditing, public finance and informatics.

Larissa Batrancea is an Assistant Professor at the Babes-Bolyai University, Cluj-Napoca, Romania, where she has been an academic since 2003. She received her Ph.D. in economics from Babes-Bolyai University in 2009, after graduating from two BA and two MSc programs (economics – class valedictorian; mathematics) at the same institution. From 2011-2013, she was a postdoctoral researcher within a program coordinated by the Romanian Academy and completed it with the highest GPA. She was invited to be a lecturer at the University of Brescia, Italy (2008-2011) and a visiting researcher at the University of Vienna, Austria (2011-2014) and the University of Brescia (2007-2008). She specialized in economics and neuroeconomics at the University of Amsterdam, the University of Bologna, Colorado State University, the University of Copenhagen, Heidelberg University, the Humboldt University of Berlin, the National Research University - Higher School of Economics, Moscow, the Pompeu Fabra University, and the University of Economics, Bratislava. Her research interests are centered on cross-cultural tax behavior, experimental economics, neuroeconomics and financial analysis. Her publication record is comprised of 23 books and over 75 scientific articles covering topics from the aforementioned fields. She translated the book "The Economic Psychology of Tax Behaviour" (Cambridge University Press, 2007) into Romanian, authored by Erich Kirchler and released in 2013 under the title "Psihologia Economica a Comportamentului Fiscal" (Risoprint Publishing). She activated as a principal investigator and a member in 6 national and international research grant teams. She was awarded 10 national prizes for excellence in research.

Nihal Bayraktar got her Ph.D. degree in economics at the University of Maryland, College Park. She joined Pennsylvania State University, Harrisburg, in the fall of 2003 as an assistant professor. Her basic research interest is on macroeconomics and development macroeconomics. She works on problems related to fixed investment, inflation, poverty, banking sector, public finance, and financial markets in developed and developing countries.

Serkan Benk is an Associate Professor in the Department of Public Finance at Inonu University in Turkey, where he has been a faculty member since 2012. He received a B.S. degree in Public Finance (1999) and an M.S. degree in Public Finance from Karadeniz Technical University (2002). Benk completed his Ph.D. at Uludag University (2007). His research interests in public finance are the theory of taxation, public economics, tax compliance and taxpayer behavior. In recent years, he has focused on the ethics of tax evasion. He has collaborated actively with researchers in several other disciplines of social science, particularly psychology, business and law.

Richard M. Bird is Professor Emeritus of Economics, Rotman School of Management, and an Adjunct Professor and Senior Fellow of the Institute for Municipal Governance and Finance, Munk School of Global Affairs, University of Toronto. He is also a Distinguished Visiting Professor at the Andrew Young School of Public Policy at Georgia State University in Atlanta, and an Adjunct Professor of the Australian School of Taxation and Business Law of the University of New South Wales, Australia. He has served with the Fiscal Affairs Department of the IMF, and has been a visiting professor in the United States, the Netherlands, Australia, Japan, and India, as well as a frequent consultant to the World Bank and other national and international organizations.

Salvatore Capasso is a full professor of Economics at University of Naples, "Parthenope." He obtained his PhD in 2001 from the University of Manchester, UK, where he also has been a Research Fellow. He has been a research fellow at IDEGA University of Santiago de Compostela, Spain (2004-2006) and a visiting professor at University of Wisconsin, Milwaukee (2006/07). Capasso is currently affiliated to the Centre for Studies in Economics and Finance of the University of Naples Federico II and to the Center for Research on International Economics of University of Wisconsin, Milwaukee. He is also a fellow of the Institute for Studies on Mediterranean Societies of the Italian National Research Council. His fields of interest are economic growth, contract theory, monetary economics and the theory of financial intermediation. His latest research focuses on the interrelationship between criminal activity, corruption and growth and on the role of the underground economy in economic development.

Tarkan Çavuşoğlu is an Associate Professor of Macroeconomics in the Department of Public Finance at Hacettepe University in Ankara, Turkey. He received his B.S., M.S. and Ph.D. degrees in Economics from Middle East Technical University in Ankara, Turkey. His research interests are macroeconomics, public finance and econometrics. He is teaching Macroeconomics and Econometrics in the graduate and undergraduate programs at Hacettepe University. He has been the TUBITAK visiting scholar at Groningen University in 2005 and the Fulbright visiting scholar at Illinois State University in 2011-2012. He has publications in national and international journals.

Savaş Çevik earned his bachelor's degree from Selcuk University in 1996. He received his master's degree in 2000 and his doctorate degree in public finance in 2005 from Marmara University. He has been a visiting scholar at the University of Texas at Dallas. He is currently a full time faculty member in the Department of Economics at Selcuk University in Turkey. He teaches public finance, public economics and taxation economics, while his research interests are in public economics, politics and economics of taxation and behavioral economics. He has recently published papers and books on tax morale, tax compliance, international taxation and tax structure and growth.

Simon James is an Associate Professor in Economics in the Department of Organisation Studies at the University of Exeter Business School, an Honorable Member of the Society for the Advancement of Behavioral Economics, a Fellow of the Chartered Institute of Taxation, a Fellow of the Higher Education Academy and a Fellow of the College of Teachers. He has also held visiting positions at six universities overseas including the Australian National University and the most recent was a Visiting Erskine Fellowship at the University of Canterbury, New Zealand in 2013. He holds a MBA as well as Masters degrees in Economics, Law, Education and Educational Management, and the subject of his PhD was 'Taxation and Economic Decisionss' He has published over 60 research papers and 15 books. Simon James' current teaching includes Public Finance and he has taught at a number of universities including the London School of Economics, part-time at the Australian National University for ten years and the University of Canterbury, New Zealand. He also gave two day sessions on tax economics on the Tax Development Programme at HM Treasury in London from 2008 to 2010.

Mustafa Kahveci is a Research Assistant of Public Finance in the Department of Public Administration, Faculty of Political Sciences, Istanbul University. He received his B.A. (2010) and his M.A. (2012) in Economics, from the Faculty of Economics at Istanbul University. He is a PHD student in the Istanbul University Social Sciences Institute Economics PHD programme. His current research areas are in the labor market and the economic analysis of the public procurement process.

Erich Kirchler graduated in 1979 in psychology and human anthropology from the University of Vienna, Austria, and received his habilitation in psychology in 1989 from the University of Linz, Austria. Since 1992, he has been a professor of applied psychology (economic psychology) part of the Faculty of Psychology, University of Vienna, Austria. He was invited as a guest professor at various European universities (e.g., France, Germany, Italy, Switzerland) and has visited as a scholar at the University of Illinois, Urbana-Champaign, USA, and ANU, Canberra, Australia. He received a call for C4-professorship from the University of Erlangen-Nuremberg, Germany, and a call for C4-professorship from the University of Cologne, Germany. His research focuses on money management in the household, expenditures and credit use, tax behavior, and the well-being of working people. Most of his 400 scientific publications are dedicated to these research fields. Some relevant books are: "Wirtschaftspsychologie: Individuen, Gruppen, Märkte, Staat" (Economic Psychology: Individuals, Groups, Markets, Nation-State) (2011; 4th edition) published by Hogrefe, Germany; "Arbeits- und Organisationspsychologie" (Work and Organisational Psychology) (2011, 3rd edition) published by Facultas, Austria; "Conflict and Decision Making in Close Relationships," (2001) published by Psychology Press, UK, and "The Economic Psychology of Tax Behaviour," (2007) published by Cambridge University Press, UK.

Hülya Kirmanoğlu a Professor of Public Finance at Istanbul University. From 1982 to 2012 she worked at the Faculty of Economics and she has been working at the Faculty of Political Science from 2012 on. She lectures in the fields of public finance, social policies, political economy of public enterprises and privatisation. She has published severel articles and a book on public sector economics, social policies in Turkey, local governments and decentralisation.

Debi Konukçu Önal is an Assistant Professor in the Department of Public Finance at Hacettepe University, Ankara, Turkey. She received her B.S. and M.S. degrees in Public Finance from Hacettepe University, and her Ph.D. degree in Public Finance from Gazi University in Ankara. Her research interests are taxation, tax psychology and fiscal policy. She is teaching Monetary Theory and Policy, Environmental Economics, Economics of Public Debt and the fiscal structure of the Turkish economy at Hacettepe University. She has been a visiting researcher at the University of Illinois and at the University of Texas at Austin, School of Law. She has publications in national and international journals.

Belkacem Laabas is an Algerian National working as an Economic Consultant at the Arab Planning Institute in Kuwait. He holds a PhD from the University of Bradford, England. He also worked as Associate Professor at Algiers University and as an Associate Researcher at the Center of Applied Economics and Development in Algeria. His research interests cover the issues of labor market policies, competitiveness and trade in Arab countries, unemployment and poverty, as well as economic growth.

Tuan Minh Le is a Senior Economist at the World Bank. Prior to joining the World Bank, he worked at the Public Finance Group, Harvard Institute for International Development, Harvard University, and was Assistant Professor of Economics at Suffolk University. He has engaged in a broad range of teaching, research, policy consulting and operations on public finance in Asia, Eastern Europe, the Middle East, and Sub-Saharan Africa. His publication focuses on tax policy design, revenue forecasting, tax administration, appraisal of development expenditures and public investment management. He obtained his Ph.D. degree in Public Policy from Harvard University.

Sarah Mansour is an Assistant Lecturer in the Department of Economics-Faculty of Economics and Political Science, Cairo University, Egypt. She is currently a PhD candidate in Economics at Warwick University, UK. She has obtained her Master's degree in Economics from Warwick University (UK).

Sarah is interested in using experimental methods to address issues related to the political economy of the Egyptian transition. She has conducted three lab experiments on undergraduate students at Cairo University. She has travelled to Atlanta in January 2013 to pilot her first experiment at the Experimental Economics Center at the Andrew Young School for Policy Studies. On her return, she prepared the lab at FEPS with both software and computer dividers for her real experiments that started to take place at Cairo University in March 2013. Her academic work in progress includes: a. An Economic Laboratory Experiment on: "Tax Compliance and Trust in Post-revolutionary Egypt: An Experimental Approach". This study is jointly conducted with Prof. Sally Wallace and Dr Vjollca Sadiraj (Georgia State University, USA) and includes a laboratory-experiment on 270 Egyptian students. This project is considered the first known economic laboratory experiment in Egypt. Its main purpose is to examine the significance of a number of factors assumed to affect levels of tax compliance in Egypt using a laboratory based tax compliance experiment. It tests several assumptions based on the context of post-revolutionary Egypt. It aims at assisting policy-makers, in this transitional period, better understand the behavioral aspects of taxpayers' decisions to comply with the tax system- something critical to the country's fiscal sustainability. Thus, the course on the evaluation of public policies is highly important to enhancing her research skills. b. "Political Polarization and Support for Reform: Experimental Evidence from Egypt". This study is jointly conducted with Prof. Rebecca Morton (New York University, USA) and Dr Mazen Hassan (Cairo University, Egypt). We examine whether political polarization in elections is an obstacle to reform in an incentivized laboratory experiment using natural ideological differences in Egypt. Specifically, we create political societies which subjects join based on ideological preferences. Then, voters choose between enacting a reform, which will lead to higher payoffs for all (but has a differential benefit for supporters of one of the political societies) versus not enacting the reform and everyone facing the same lower payoffs. Finding that when voters are provided with information that support for the reform varies across ideological societies in previous sessions, they are significantly more likely to report that their vote choices are influenced by their society membership to a greater extent than when such information is not provided. We also find some evidence that the information influences voter choices in the election. Results suggest that ideological polarization can impede reform in elections.

Blanca Moreno-Dodson is an experienced development economist with 21 years of World Bank service worldwide, especially in Africa and Latin America. She is accomplished in macroeconomics and fiscal policy for developing countries, with a focus on growth, inequality and poverty reduction. She is skilled in public expenditure analysis, fiscal sustainability, tax reforms, and transfer pricing, among others. Previously, she worked as junior economist at the European Union (European Commission and European Parliament). She is the editor of three World Bank books: "Reducing Poverty on a Global Scale", 2005, "Public Finance for Poverty Reduction", 2007, and "Is Fiscal Policy the Answer? A Developing Country Perspective", 2012. She has also published on macroeconomics, public finance, growth, and poverty issues at the National Tax Association Journal, Banca d'Italia Fiscal Policy Annual Volume, Hacienda Pública Española Journal, and the Bulletin of Economic Research, as well as several World Bank Working Papers. She holds a PhD and a Masters in International Economics and Finance from the Aix-Marseille II University, France, as well as a Masters in Economics from the Madrid Autonomous University, Spain. She is fluent in Spanish, French, English and Portuguese. She has been currently working as a Lead Economist in the World Bank (Global Lead for Tax Policy, Macroeconomics and Fiscal Management).

Anca Nichita received her Ph.D. in finance with honors (summa cum laude) from Babes-Bolyai University, Cluj-Napoca, Romania, after graduating with a BA (class valedictorian) and a MSc in economics from the same university. She was a visiting researcher during the years 2011-2014 at the University of Vienna, Austria. She pursued research training at various universities from Denmark, Germany, Italy, The Netherlands and Russia. Currently, she is a postdoctoral researcher in the realm of tax behavior, within a program coordinated by the Romanian Academy. Her research interests stem from over 25 published articles and books revolving around public finance, experimental economics, neuroeconomics and financial analysis.

Asuman Oktayer is an associate professor in the Department of Economics at Yıldız Technical University, in İstanbul, Turkey. She received her Bachelor's degree in 1998 and Master's degree in 2001 both in Economics and both from İstanbul University, Turkey. She went on to earn a doctoral degree in 2007 in Economics from Yıldız Technical University. After attending the doctoral program, she started her professional career as a research assistant at the same University. She has taught courses in monetary theory, financial markets, derivative markets and macroeconomics. Her research focuses on monetary and fiscal policy interactions, financial markets, growth, inequality and globalization.

Nagihan Oktayer is a Professor of Economics at Istanbul University, Turkey. She received her Bachelor's degree in 1993, Master's degree in 1996 and Doctoral degree in 2002 in Economics from the same University. In 2005, she was awarded a scholarship by the Turkish Academy of Sciences to study on the European Union budget. For the purpose of making deep researches in European Union economics, she went to Sussex, UK. During this period, she received a second Master's degree from the University of Sussex in Contemporary European Studies in 2006. Her research interests are Public Finance, Borrowing, Taxation, European Union Budget, European Union Regional Policy, and Tax Harmonization in the European Union.

Semih N. Öz was born in Istanbul in 1963. He graduated from the Faculty of Political Science of Istanbul University in 1984. He started working as a revenue controller at the Ministry of Finance in 1985. He completed his master's degree in economics at Northeastern University, Boston, between 1992 and 1994. He worked as the head of the department at the General Directorate of Revenues between 1997 and 2005. He received his PhD from Ankara University. Presently, he is professor in the Faculty of Political Science of Ankara University. His teaching and research interests involve the study of international taxation.

Ali Rıza Özdemir is a tenured Professor of Economics in the Faculty of Economic and Administrative Sciences at Gazi University, Ankara. He is also the chair of the Public Finance Department at the same university. Prior to that, he was Associate Professor of Economics at Balıkesir University and assistant professor at Eastern Connecticut State University. He received higher education training at Ankara University, receiving his bachelor's degree in Public Finance, and at the University of Connecticut, receiving his M.A. and Ph.D. degrees in Economics. He became a faculty member at Gazi University, Ankara in August 2013, having served at Turkey's Science and Technology Council after 5 years of service. He also thought courses at Economy and Technology University (TOBB ETU). His research interests span public economics, macroeconomics, taxation theory and policy, public choice, urban economics and applied microeconomic theory. He has authored of more than 20 professional journal articles. He has presented papers at professional conferences, universities, and other venues on more than 30 occasions. He has been serving as an editorial board member on professional journals and reviewing submissions of research papers for about 10 years.

W. A. Razzak has a PhD in economics (1994). He has been an economic adviser for various departments of the New Zealand government (The Reserve Bank of New Zealand; the Labor Market Policy Group and the Labor Market Dynamics at the Department of Labor, and the New Zealand Treasury). He was also an Adviser at the Arab Planning Institute (2007-2012). He was a research fellow at the Hong Kong Institute for Monetary Research at the Hong Kong Monetary Authority, IGIER - Bocconi University, Milan. Research Inter at the IMF and the World Bank. He was the president of the New Zealand Association of Economists (2003-2004). He has been published in a number of refereed journals. The topics include monetary economics, international finance, business cycles, growth, and labor.

Lodovico Santoro is an Italian researcher in economic sciences. Santoro obtained his Ph.D in Economics from University of Naples Parthenope where he worked as a research fellow. His main fields of interest are public finance, corruption and the evaluation of public policies. Actually, he works as a research fellow at Institute for Research on Innovation and Services for Development (IRISS) - CNR, Italy. The latest research regarding the economic evaluation of non market goods and the innovation models especially in the agro-food chains.

Keremet Shaiymbetova, is currently an executive director at Vanilla Handmade Coffee LLC and has recently completed her master's degree in Economic Policy at Kocaeli University in Turkey. She holds B.A. in Finance and Banking System (International Ataturk Alatoo University, Kyrgyzstan). Her research interest includes public economics, public finance and economic development.

İsmail Şiriner, Ph.D, is a Professor in the Department of Economics at Batman University Faculty of Economics and Administrative Sciences. After receiving his Ph.D. in Economic Policy (Effectiveness of Demand-Side Policies in Turkish Economy: 1989-98) in 1999, he was a postdoctoral researcher at the Wageningen University in Nederland for 3 months, then continued his research in the United Kingdom from 2002 to 2003. Siriner was a visiting lecturer at the University of Westminster in the UK for one year and a visiting professor at the Silesian University in Opava, Czech Republic, for one year. He has worked extensively in monetary and fiscal policies, globalization, political economies, growth, and economic policy. He is the author of five books and a number of research articles. He is also an editor of Turkish Journal of Political Economy, and the International Journal of Politics and Economics and an organizing chair of the annual International Conference of Political Economy Series.

Vito Tanzi is a former Professor and Chairman of the Economics Department, American University, Washington D.C. He also served as Head of the Tax Policy Division and later as Director of the Fiscal Affairs Department at the IMF. From 1990-1994 he served as President of the International Institute of Public Finance (IIPF). Since 2000, he has been active as a Senior Associate, Carnegie Endowment for International Peace; State Secretary for Economy and Finance in the Italian Government; and a senior consultant to the Inter-American Development Bank. He received many awards, including Honorary

President of the IIPF and Honorary degrees from the University of Cordoba (Argentina), the University of Liege (Belgium), the University of Torino (Italy), the University of Lisbon (Portugal), and the University of Bari (Italy). An economic effect, the Tanzi effect, is named after him.

Andrey Timofeev is a Research Associate with the International Center for Public Policy and a Research Assistant Professor at the Department of Economics, both at the Andrew Young School of Policy Studies, Georgia State University. In this capacity, he has contributed to numerous reports on tax policy, intergovernmental fiscal relations, and budget transparency. In particular, he was engaged in the development of tax incidence models for the Ministry of Finance for the Government of Jordan and tax simulation models for the Federal Board of Revenue (FBR) for the Government of Islamic Republic of Pakistan. He has worked on fiscal reform projects in over a dozen countries since he was first recruited by Georgia State University in 1999 for the USAID Fiscal Reform Project in the Russian Federation. He holds a B.S. in Mathematics from Novosibirsk State University (Russia) and Ph.D. in Economics from Charles University (Czech Republic).

Mehmet Serkan Tosun is the Barbara S. Campbell Distinguished Professor of Nevada Tax Policy at the University of Nevada, Reno. He is also an Associate Professor of Economics and Chairman of the Department of Economics. He is a research fellow at the Institute for the Study of Labor (IZA) in Bonn, Germany, an affiliate research fellow at the Oxford Institute of Population Ageing at the University of Oxford, and a research fellow at the Economic Research Forum (ERF) for Arab Countries, Iran and Turkey. Dr. Tosun received his Ph.D. in Economics from the Maxwell School of Citizenship and Public Affairs at Syracuse University. His research interests and expertise include public finance, economics of population and demographic change, international political economy, regional economics and economic growth. He has been a consultant for the International Monetary Fund, the World Bank, the United Cities and Local Governments (UCLG), the United Nations Development Fund for Women (UNIFEM), and the United Nations Economic and Social Commission for Western Asia (UNESCWA). Dr. Tosun has received Dean's Research Professorship Award from the UNR College of Business in 2013. He was recognized as the Best Researcher of the Year in 2009 by the Nevada Alpha Chapter of Beta Gamma Sigma, an international honor society for business studies. He was the recipient of the Middle East Economic Association's Ibn Khaldun Prize in 2005.

Sally Wallace is a Professor of Economics and Chair in the Andrew Young School of Policy Studies and Director of the Fiscal Research Center at Georgia State University. She is also an Extraordinary Professor of the African Tax Institute at the University of Pretoria. Previously, she was a Financial Economist at the U.S. Treasury Department, Office of Tax Analysis specializing in the analysis of legislation of individual income tax and savings issues, pension plans, long term health care financing, and employee benefits and compensation. Currently, she is pursuing a research agenda in the field of public finance, specifically state, federal and international taxation, and fiscal federalism. She is interested in behavioral aspects of taxation, the interdependence of federal, state and local governments, and the behavioral aspects of public spending and taxation. She has served as an advisor on issues of public finance for the states of Georgia, Ohio and Nebraska and abroad in Jamaica, India, Pakistan, Guyana, Egypt, Jordan, Guatemala, Russia, Philippines, Uzbekistan, Ukraine, Kazakhstan, and China.

Binhan Elif Yılmaz is a Professor of Economics at Istanbul University, Turkey. She received her Msc degree in Theory of Public Finance from Istanbul University Social Sciences Institute at 1994 and her Phd degree on Public Finance at 2001, from the same institute. She was selected as a research assistant for Public Finance Department of Faculty of Economy in Istanbul University when she was a MS student. She became an associate professor at 2008 and professor at 2014 in Public Finance. The areas which are she is interested in and tutoring are Public Debts, Public Finance, Political Economy and Fiscal Sociology. She has written numerous articles in national and international and presented papers in various conferences. She is the author of four books which are named as, The Debt Predicament from Ottomans to Our Today (2008-2014-2015), The Transformation of Global Crisis into the Debt Predicament in Europe (2013), The Economics of Social Security System in Turkey (2014) and Public Finance (2015). Beside the several administrative duties, she is the vice president of the Department of Public Finance.

Serdar Yılmaz is an international development specialist with expertise in public finance, regional development and local government finance. He has extensive experience in developing and transition countries around the world. Working in the various departments of the World Bank, Dr. Yilmaz has contributed to policy reforms in over fifteen developing and transition countries around the world, including Bosnia, Bulgaria, Burkina Faso, Cabo Verde, Egypt, Ethiopia, Republic of Georgia, Ghana, Iran, Jordan, Kyrgyz Republic, Tanzania, Turkey and Yemen. Dr. Yilmaz has authored and contributed to numerous books, book chapters, articles, and reports on intergovernmental finance (fiscal decentralization), public expenditure management, and poverty reduction. In addition to his academic research and expertise in the management and provision of technical assistance, Dr. Yilmaz has considerable experience in the development and delivery of academic courses and professional training programs in the areas of economic development, municipal finance and fiscal federalism. As a scholar-practitioner, Dr. Yilmaz uses quantitative and qualitative analytical techniques in order to inform evidence-based policy advice and policy recommendations. Dr. Yilmaz is an inspiring leader with proven ability to motivate his team. As a cluster leader in the Africa region of the World Bank, he oversees three hundred millions dollars portfolio of investment projects across twelve countries managed by a team of six people. In his capacity as a cluster leader, he manages the team's work program, ensures quality and advises senior management team on strategic decisions. Dr. Yilmaz has a PhD in public policy from the School of Public Policy at George Mason University (2000). He is a member of the American Economic Association (AEA), the National Tax Association (NTA), the American Society for Public Administration (ASPA), and the Association for Budgeting and Financial Management (ABFM).

Index

G

H

I

J

K

L

M

N

O

P

R

S

T

U

V

W

www.ingramcontent.com/pod-product-compliance
Lightning Source LLC
LaVergne TN
LVHW080402011026
849161LV00009B/2335
* 9 7 8 1 5 2 2 5 0 0 5 3 7 *